会話作文 英語表現辞典

JAPANESE-ENGLISH SENTENCE EQUIVALENTS 3rd EDITION

第三版
増補・改訂版

ドナルド・キーン／羽鳥博愛＝監修　山田晴子／伊良部祥子＝編集

朝日出版社

まえがき

　昨今世に出ている和英辞典には，その内容，形式の面で多種多様のものがあり，それぞれ優れた特色を誇っている。その中にあって，この度敢えて新たに和英辞典を上梓するのは，従来にも増して現実に用いられている英語を聞きとり，話し，書き綴る力を蓄えていきたいという英語学習者の要請に応えるためである。

　言うまでもなく言葉の持つ世界は広い。詩歌の中にみられるような典雅，幽艶な言葉や，公の場にふさわしい格式ばった表現など，とりあげていけば際限ないであろう。また言葉は時代と共に変化し，かつてはなじみ深かった言葉が，今では古色蒼然としているということもよくみられる現象である。本辞典はこの言葉の海の中から最大多数の人間が最もよく用いる言葉，即ち，今ここで，我々が常用する言葉をとり出して扱うことを主眼に編集された。在来の辞典が網羅的に語を収録している傾向を持つのに対し，この態度は画期的なものと自負するものである。

　見出しの日本語は数種の国語辞典，および国立国語研究所の基本語彙比較対照表を参照し，基本語彙，多頻度語彙を選び出した。また使用頻度とは別に，文化的背景の影響で一般に表現し難いとされている感情・感覚表現に特に紙数をさいている。この様にして精選された見出し語は，総数2,500語余りにのぼる。配列は使用者の便宜を考え，あいうえお順にした。

　英語は，現在日本で最も一般的であるアメリカ英語を主体とし，その口語的表現を採用した。
　英語学習者にとって，一つの母国語に対応して示される数々の英語から，その時その場に合った語句や表現を知ることは非常に難しい。ある時は堅苦しすぎ，ある時は逆にくだけすぎる言いまわしをする恐れが，ともすればつきまとう。また現代ではあまり耳にしない古風な表現が他の部分と不釣合に現れて，滑稽な結果を生ずることもままあるのである。既成の和英辞典は残念ながらこの弊を免れるのに必ずしも有効であるとは言い難い。本辞典の特色は，表現の適不適に対する学習者の懸念を払拭し，少なくとも日常生活の場ではためらわずに使用できる英語を収録したところにある。

　更に本辞典の特色として，相対応する和・英の表現が，すべて文章の形で示されていることを挙げることができる。
　語句というものはそれ自体単独に存在することはなく，すべて文脈の中で生きてくるものである。学習者にとっては，同じ様な意味を持つ語句が数あるうち，どれがその時の状況に一番ふさわしいかはなかなかつかみ難い。また文章の中で英語の慣用句がどの様に用いられるかも判断がつき難く，極端な場合には，主格と目的格が転倒したりすることさえ起こり得るのである。

本辞典は，我々が日常よく用いる典型的な和文を作り，それに対応する英文を示した。従って学習者がニュアンスをとり違えたり，活用の形を誤ったりすることはまずあり得ない。また英文は和文の単なる説明的な訳にとどまらず，和文の内容に最も近い慣用的表現がとられている。またその際，大学受験者の便宜を考え，過去五年間の大学入試に出題された英作文問題の中から頻出語句，重要語句を可能な限りとり入れるよう心がけた。

　この様な文例を選ぶにあたり，個人の恣意的な表現に偏らないよう和文，英文ともに複数の人間が厳しくチェックした。またこれも和文，英文ともに，例文を基礎として他の状況にも応用できるものを採用するように努力している。

　日本語と英語という，構造，語彙，文化的背景等あらゆる面で異質な言語を結びつけるのであるから，両国語の表現の間にニュアンスの相違や誤解を生じる恐れが十分ある。これを避けるため，それぞれ他方の国語にかなり通暁している両国人の間で徹底した議論が交わされた。

　この様にして創り出された本辞典が，英作文，英会話の習熟に大いに役立つと信じ，年齢，性別を超えたすべての学習者に実生活の場で活用していただけることを願ってやまない。

　もとより言葉は生き物であり常に変化する。また紙数の関係で収録される語にも限りがある。さまざまの不備な点に関し，大方の今後の御叱正，御批判を待ち，改善を重ねていくつもりである。

　本辞典の作成にあたり，次の方々にひとかたならぬ御助力を賜った。

　　薗田　美和子　　　　　　　James J. Nelson
　　寺田　百合子　　　　　　　Charles Quinn, Jr.
　　Cecilia M. Hamagami　　　　Terry Sherwin
　　Robert Hiroshige　　　　　 David F. Thompson
　　Robert A. Mintzer　　　　　Edith M. Yamanoha

　また朝日出版社の小栗氏をはじめ，編集の諸氏の御尽力は言葉に尽くせないものがある。終わりにあたり，こういう方々に深く謝意を捧げる次第である。

　　1982年10月

　　　　　　　　　　　　　　　　　　　　　　　ドナルド・キーン
　　　　　　　　　　　　　　　　　　　　　　　羽鳥　博愛

新訂にあたって

　本辞典を上梓してから3年半になる。学校の授業の場だけでなく、職場や家庭においても、英語で文章を書いたり話さなければならない機会はますます増えている。このような場合、一応の英文は書いたり話したりできても、伝えたい事柄や情報、喜びや悲しみなどの感情が、日本語を書き話す場合と同じく正しく表現できたかということに不安を感じるものである。このような不安感を少しでも解消せんがため、本辞典が企画された。

　本辞典では、まず日本語の例文をあげ、その例文の持つ内容を正確に伝えるのはもちろん、微妙な感情までも表現した英文を容易に検索・利用できるように配慮した。また、本辞典を利用することにより、くだけた英語からていねいな英語、ビジネス英語まで、場面や立場に応じた生きた英語をだれもが操ることができるようにと願ってきた。
　幸い従来の辞典にはない本辞典の特色が理解され、学生、ビジネスマン、技術者、教師、医者、主婦等の幅広い層、幅広い年代に渡って、多くの人々の支持を得ることができた。

　今回、本辞典をより一層充実させ、使いやすいものとするべく改訂にふみきった。改訂に当たっては、本文の英語2万例文のすべてをチェックし、より自然でより正確な表現となることを期した。同時に、本辞典をより効率よく利用できるように、巻末に索引を兼ねた和英単語集を完備した。これは本文中に出てくる表現の索引に、一般に必要性が高いと思われる単語・熟語を加えたものである。これにより、本辞典は表現辞典としてだけでなく、1万1千語の網羅的和英辞典として利用することが可能となり、大方の英会話、英作文が本辞典のみで間に合うようになった。旧版にも増してこの新訂版が読者の皆様のお役に立てれば、これ以上の喜びはない。

　今回の改訂には、多くの読者の方々の御要望、御指摘が生かされている。また、David F. Thompson 氏には英文チェックで大きな御助力をいただいた。これらの方々に深く謝意を表するものである。

　今後もお気づきの点を御教示いただければ幸いである。

1986年2月

編　者

第三版にあたって

　1982年の初版以来好評をいただいてきた本辞典は、新訂版刊行後はや20年近くが経過した。その間、冷戦の終結、EUの誕生など、世界的に大きな構造変化がおきた。また、インターネットなどのインフォメーションテクノロジー（情報技術）は深く私達の生活に浸透し、生活形態が大きく変わってきている。このような社会の変化にともない数多くの新語が生まれている。既存の語の中には新たな意味やニュアンスが付加されたものや使われなくなった語も出てきた。

　本辞典の目指すところは、日本語で表現された内容が話し言葉であれ書き言葉であれ、使われる状況にふさわしく、話し手と聞き手あるいは書き手と読み手の関係を適切に維持し、その言葉に込められた気持ちや意図を時代に合った英語に表現するための道具として役立つことにあり、常に、時代の変化に対応した辞典であることである。

　したがって、今回の第三版においては、21世紀の新しい時代に相応した、更にパワーアップした会話作文辞典にすべく、本文項目、巻末の和英単語集ともにすべて見直し、以下のような全面改訂を行った。

　本文項目増補——新見出し220項目を増補した。日本語の微妙なニュアンスを伝えたい語やよく使う会話表現、原語との意味のずれに注意を要するカタカナ語、ビジネスシーンに役立つ言葉などである。情報化社会に生きる現代人が避けて通れないIT関係の用語も31項目含まれる。

　既存項目の全面改訂——日本語のニュアンスに、より忠実に過不足のない自然な英文になるように、日本人著者と英語インフォーマントの間で一文一文について徹底的な話し合いが行われた。その文は会話文か文書に書く文か、特定のことに対する言及かそれとも一般論か、その文が使われる状況はどうか、話し手と聞き手の関係は親子か、友達か、他人か、同僚か、上司と部下の関係かなど様々な場面を想定し、検討を行った。また、日本語、英語ともに古めかしい言葉は現在最もよく使われる言葉に修正した。性差別などにつながるような表現は破棄し、新しい文に差し替えた。日本語独特の謙譲表現、部下に対する叱責の仕方の違い、「うそ」に対する認識の違いなど、日本と欧米の文化の違いによる表現の差異については、適宜、注を入れたり、対訳英文を複数例挙げたりした。

　巻末和英単語集の大幅増補——日常生活において使用頻度の高い語句をはじめ、「携帯電話」「電子マネー」「表計算ソフト」等のIT用語、「クローン」「遺伝子組み換え食品」等の先端科学用語、「構造改革」「民営化」等の時事用語、「介護」「在宅看護」など高齢化社会で必要な用語、「アルツハイマー病」「アトピー性皮膚炎」「花粉症」等の病名、新しい省庁名、国の枠組の変化を反映さ

せた主要国名、主要都市名など、約3,000語を加えた。本文項目も含めて約16,500項目になる。

　以上のような増補、改訂を行った結果、読者の方々が利用しやすい、新しい時代にふさわしい会話作文表現辞典になったと自負している。読者の皆様が英語を実践する様々な場面において本辞典がお役にたてば、これ以上の喜びはない。

　最後に、Jane Nishi Goldstone 氏に心からお礼を申し上げたい。氏の緻密さと忍耐強さは今回の改訂に必要かつ欠かせないものであった。村上直哉氏はじめ朝日出版社編集部の方々に厚くお礼を申し上げたい。特に、渡辺洋氏、佐藤久代氏、谷岡美佐子氏には言葉に尽くせないほど多くのご尽力をいただいた、心から感謝の意を表したい。

　　　　　2003年12月

　　　　　　　　　　　　　　　　　　　　　　　　　　　　　　編　者

本書の使い方

1．見出し

(1) 見出し語は基本語句，頻出語句の観点から選択し，2,700余語を収録している。なお，英語の用例を挙げるまでもない，ごく基本的な名詞等は割愛し，巻末の和英単語集で扱った。
(2) 見出し語表記は仮名（平仮名および片仮名）である。
(3) 見出し語に相当する漢字を，見出し語の右に（ ）に入れて示した。
   【例】 **しげき**（刺激）
(4) 接頭語，接尾語，助詞，助動詞などは，語の前または後に「～」を付けた。
   【例】 **～から**
(5) 見出し語の配列は五十音（あいうえお）順とした。細則は次のとおりである。
   (a) 清音・濁音の順に配列する。
       【例】 **いし**（意思・意志）
             いじ（意地）
   (b) 促音「っ」，拗音「ゃ」「ゅ」「ょ」はそれぞれ「つ」「や」「ゆ」「よ」のあとに配列する。
       【例】 **りよう**（利用）
             りょう（量）
   (c) 片仮名の長音（ー）は，その直前の音を伸ばしたときの母音として配列する。下の例の「ユーモア」は「ユウモア」と考えるわけである。
       【例】 **ゆうめい**（有名）
             ユーモア
             ゆうゆう（悠々）
   (d) 「～」の部分を除く仮名表記が同じ場合，「～」の付く語は付かない語のあとに配列する。
       【例】 **から**（空）
             ～から

2．小見出し

　見出し語の意味，用法がいくつかに分かれる場合，検索の便宜を図るべく，小見出しを【 】に入れて付けた。例文の数が少ない場合は，容易に検索できるものとして小見出しを省略したものもある。小見出しの語は，同意・説明・用法の語などである。

3．例文

　日本語の例文と，それにあたる英語の例文を対応させている。一つの日本

語例文に対して英語の例文が二つ以上考えられる場合，並列させて間に／（スラッシュ）を置くか，あるいは改行した。

英文中のイタリック書体（斜体）は，書名・映画名など，文中で強調したい語句，英語として一般的でない外国語に用いた。

【例】 Let's go see *The Invisible Man.*
【例】 I may sound like I'm repeating myself, but this door is *not* to be opened.
【例】 *Pasokon* in Japanese is short for personal computer.

4．注・説明

英語例文だけでは使い分け，ニュアンス等の理解が不十分であると思われるものには番号を付し，項目の最後に枠囲みの説明を付けた。

5．＊ ＊＊印と英語のレベル

本書の英語のレベルは「書い」ても「話し」てもおかしくないという範囲内（スタンダードな表現および，ごく一般的な口語表現）で選択するよう努めた。しかし，見出し語あるいは例文によっては，書き言葉的な表現や俗語表現が要求される場合もある。また，日本語に対して意味的にぴたりと合致する英語が，書き言葉や俗語表現である場合もある。それらの場合，前者に＊印，後者に＊＊印を付して学習者の便宜を図るようにした。

＊印……親しい友人同士や家族の間で使うと堅苦しく感じられる改まった表現
＊＊印……あまり親しくない人に対して，あるいは改まった席で使うことは避けるべきだと思われる俗語表現

これらの印の付していない大半の表現は，日常英語として，書くときにも話すときにも安心して使えるものである。

6．その他の記号

( )　① 見出しにおいては，見出し語に相当する漢字表記を表す。
　　　【例】　へんけん（偏見）
　　　② 例文においては，省略することができることを表す。
　　　【例】　就職はあちこちに口をかけるより的を（一つに）絞って狙ったほうがいいよ．　When you're looking for a job, rather than trying here, there and everywhere, it's better to narrow it down (to one).
　　　③ 日本語例文においては意味の補足的説明を表すこともある。
　　　【例】　寒さで指の感覚がなくなってしまった（まひした）．
　　　④ 日本語例文においてはまた難読漢字および読みの紛らわしい漢字の読みを表す。

【例】　まずは下手(へた)に出たほうがいい．
[　]　直前の語句をかっこ内の語句と置き換えても意味がほとんど変わらないことを表す．
　　　【例】　I get along [on] well with him.
〔　〕　直前の語句をかっこ内の語句と置き換えられるが，意味的には異なることを表す．日本語例文と英語例文の〔　〕内は意味的に対応する．
　　　【例】　ふろは日本式　I prefer a Japanese 〔Western〕 style
　　　　　　〔洋式〕のほうがいい．　bath.
†　　上記二種の置き換え可能かっこを使用している例文で，かっこ内の語句が†印の次の語句から置き換えられることを表す．ただし，置き換えられる語が一語対一語で対応する場合，および文頭から置き換えられる場合，あるいは数字（および単位記号）の読み方を示す場合は，†印を省略した．
　　　【例】　The bill was †rejected [voted down].
　　　【例】　I thought it was hot today, and sure enough it was
　　　　　　　32℃ [thirty-two degrees centigrade].
／　　訳例が二つ以上あり，並列させる場合，間に置いた．
　　　【例】　おあいにくさま．　(That's) Too bad.／(I'm) Sorry.

JAPANESE-ENGLISH SENTENCE EQUIVALENTS
3rd EDITION

あ

あい (愛)
彼女は両親の愛を一身に受けて育った.	Her parents showered her with love when she was growing up.
彼は奥さんを深く愛している.	He really loves his wife.
彼女への愛は冷めてしまった.	My love for her has cooled.
彼は愛すべき男だ.	He's a lovable man.
彼は愛のない家庭に育った.	He was brought up in a loveless home.
彼女〔彼〕は母性愛〔父性愛〕が強い.	She's [He's] a very loving mother [father].

あいかわらず (相変わらず)
彼女は相変わらず忙しそうだ.	She seems to be as busy as ever.
日曜日は相変わらずゴルフ？	Do you still play golf on Sundays?
この番組は相変わらず馬鹿なことをやっているな.	They're still doing the same old silly things on this TV show.
「最近, どう？」「相変わらずさ」	"What's new?" "Nothing much." "How are you doing?" "Same as ever."

あいきょう (愛敬)
彼女は愛敬たっぷりだ.	She's really cute[1] [charming, nice].
彼女は目に愛敬がある.	She has cute [charming, nice] eyes.
あの娘は愛敬がない.	She isn't very friendly.
ウェートレスが客に愛敬を振りまいている.	The waitress is going out of her way to be nice to the customers.
こんな失敗はご愛敬だよ. 気にするな.	That's OK. [Don't worry about it.] Anybody could've made a mistake like this.

> 1) cute は否定文で使うと「(容貌が) かわいくない」という意味になる.

あいさつ (挨拶)
小さな女の子が頭を下げて私に挨拶した.	The little girl greeted me with a bow.
彼とは以前に挨拶を交わしたことがある.	We've †said hello [spoken] to each other before.

「おはよう」と彼女に挨拶した.	I said good morning to her.
彼は道で会っても挨拶もしない.	He doesn't acknowledge my existence even when we pass each other on the street.
堅苦しい挨拶は抜きにしよう.	Let's do away with stiff formalities.
隣に引っ越して来た人が挨拶回りにやって来た.	The people who moved in next door came over to introduce themselves.
彼女は何の挨拶もせずに引っ越してしまった.	She moved away without even saying good-bye.
毎年, 新年にはアメリカの友人と季節の挨拶状を交わしている.	My American friend and I exchange greeting cards every New Year's.
【公式の挨拶】大統領は就任の挨拶を述べた.	The President gave his inaugural address [speech].
彼は開会の挨拶をした.	He gave the opening speech [address].
一言ご挨拶申し上げます.	Please allow me to say a few words (of greeting) to you.

あいじょう (愛情)

日本人は一般に愛情表現が下手だ.	Japanese are generally poor at showing [expressing] affection [love].
母親は愛情を込めて幼い我が子に話しかけた.	The mother spoke to her little child †affectionately [with deep affection].

あいず (合図)

私が合図したのに彼は気づかなかった.	He didn't notice even though I †gave the signal [signaled].
彼に部屋を出るように目で合図した.	I †made a sign to [signaled] him with my eyes to leave the room.
1時の鐘を合図に行列が繰り出した.	At the sound of the one o'clock bell the parade began.

あいそう (愛想)

【人当たり】彼女はだれに対しても愛想がいい.	She's friendly [nice, amiable] to everybody.
ここの店員は愛想が悪い.	The salesclerks here are not very friendly.
彼女は社長の言葉に愛想笑いをした.	She smiled diplomatically at what her boss said.
	She forced herself to smile at her boss's remark.
彼はまた課長にお愛想を言っている.	He's trying to flatter the boss again.
彼は愛想ばかり言って信用できない.	He's such a smooth talker that I can't trust him.
【好意】息子には愛想が尽きた.	I've given up on my son.

彼は借金ばかりしているので皆から愛想を尽かされていた.	They've all had it with him because he's always borrowing money.

あいだ

【時間】留守のあいだに電話があったよ.	There was a phone call for you while you were out.
そのあいだずっと私は黙っていた.	I kept silent the whole time.
しばらくのあいだここでお待ちください.	Please wait here for a while.
彼とはもう長いあいだ会っていない.	I haven't seen him for a long time.
夏休みのあいだ中別荘にいた.	I stayed at our cottage during my whole summer vacation.
休暇のあいだ中天気が悪かった.	The weather was bad throughout my vacation.
彼は講義のあいだ中眠っていた.	He slept †all through [throughout] the lecture.
体が丈夫なあいだは働くつもりだ.	I intend to work as long as I am physically able to.
4時と5時のあいだに来てください.	Please come between four and five.
食事と食事のあいだをもっと空けなさい.	Take more time between meals.
【空間】行と行のあいだを空けなさい.	Leave a space between the lines.
前の列とのあいだをもっと詰めなさい.	Move [Step] up closer to the row in front of you.
電柱が一定のあいだをおいて立っている.	The utility poles are spaced at regular intervals.
名古屋は東京と大阪のあいだにある.	Nagoya †lies [is situated] between Tokyo and Osaka.
雲のあいだから日が差して来た.	The sun came shining through the clouds.
【人間関係】学者のあいだではそれは常識となっている.	Among scholars that's taken for granted.
この問題は家族のあいだで解決しよう.	Let's settle this matter within the family.
我々は互いに遠慮のない間柄だ.	We're very informal with each other.

あいちゃく (愛着)

この古いテディベアには愛着がある.	I'm very attached to this old teddy bear.
このソファは長いこと使っている	I've had this sofa for so long that I've

あいて (相手)

【仲間】老人には話し相手が必要だ.	Elderly people need companionship.
ダンスの相手に不足したことはない.	I've never had trouble finding a dance partner.
もうだれも私を相手にしてくれない.	Nobody †pays any attention to me [takes me seriously] anymore.
子どもの相手は苦手だ.	I'm not very good with children.
しばらくのあいだお客さんの相手をしてくださいませんか.	Would you mind keeping the guests company for a while?
【相手方】我々は高校時代いい競争相手だった.	We were †friendly rivals [good competition for each other] in high school.
けんかの相手はだれだ.	Who were you fighting with?
あのチームが相手じゃ勝ち目はない.	We don't have a chance of winning against that team.
囲碁ではとても君の相手にはなれない.	I'm no match for you at *go*.
彼なら相手に取って不足はない.	He's a good match for me.
住民は国を相手取って訴訟を起こした.	The residents filed a suit against the government.
【対象】相手を見て物を言え.	You have to know who you're talking to.
借金の相談なら相手が違うよ.	If you want to borrow money, you came to the wrong person.
彼らは学生相手の商売をしている.	They cater to the student trade.

アイデア

会議でいいアイデアが出た.	Good ideas came out of the meeting./The meeting generated some good ideas.
いいアイデアが浮かばない.	I can't seem to think of any good ideas.
君たちには斬新なアイデアを期待している.	I'm counting on you to come up with some great new ideas.
彼女のとっぴなアイデアにはいつも驚かされる.	I'm always shocked by her wild ideas.
彼の企画はアイデア倒れのものばかりだ.	None of his ideas turn out to be any good./His ideas never turn out.
彼はなかなかのアイデアマンだ.	He's a real idea man./He's full of ideas.
このプレゼントはアイデア商品の店で買った.	I bought this present at a novelty shop.

あいにく

あいにくその日は忙しくて彼女の見送りに行けなかった.	Unfortunately I was busy that day and couldn't go to see her off.

あいにく父は今出かけています.	I'm sorry but my father is not in right now.
あいにくの天気だね.	It's too bad the weather is like this.
	What a pity we're having such bad weather!
おあいにくさま.	(That's) Too bad.／(I'm) Sorry.

あいまい

犯人の動機はあいまいだ.	The criminal's motive is vague [unclear].
彼女はあいまいな返事をした.	She gave †an ambiguous [a vague, a noncommittal] answer.
	She replied ambiguously [vaguely, noncommittally].
自信がなかったのであいまいな態度をとった.	I wasn't very confident, so I took a noncommittal stance.
日本語のルーツはいろいろな説はあるが，まだあいまいだ.	Despite a number of theories, the origin of the Japanese language remains obscure.

あう¹ (合う)

【適合】この服は私にぴったり合う.	This suit fits[1] me perfectly.
かぎが錠に合わない.	The key doesn't fit the lock.
ここの気候は私には合わない.	The climate here doesn't agree with me.
カキはどうも私に合わない．いつも胃の調子がおかしくなる.	Oysters disagree with me. They always give me an upset stomach.
このネクタイは背広によく合う.	This tie †matches [goes well with][2] this suit.
肉には赤ワインが合う.	Red wine goes (well) with[3] meat.
【一致】何度計算しても合計が合わない.	The figures don't †add up [agree] no matter how many times I go over them.
私たちは初めて意見が合った.	For the first time our opinions agreed.
父とは考え方が合わない.	I don't see things the same way my father does.
	My father and I don't think the same way.
【正確】答えが合っているかどうか確かめたい.	I want to check whether this answer is right [correct] or not.
この時計は合っていますか？	Is this clock right [correct]?
【引き合う】これは割に合わない仕事だ.	This work (just) doesn't pay.
	This work (just) isn't worth it.

---

1) fit は「大きさが合う」こと．2) 服装や色などが合うのは match または go well with．3) 飲食物の場合は match は使わない．

あう² (会・遭う)

【人に】

彼女にはその時初めて会った.	I met her then for the first time.
彼にはしばらく会っていない.	I haven't seen him for a while.
今度いつ会える?	When can I see [meet] you again?
いつ会いましょうか?	When shall we †get together [meet]?
昨日ばったり彼に会った.	I ran [bumped**] into him yesterday.
今日5時に鈴木教授に会う.	I'm going to meet (with) Prof. Suzuki at five today.
彼には会わないようにしたほうがいい.	You'd be better off not seeing him.

【物事に】

ひどい目にあった.	I had a terrible time.
帰宅途中で雨にあった.	On the way home I †was caught in [ran into] some rain.
彼は交通事故にあった.	He was in a traffic accident.

あおい (青い)

今日の空は本当に青い.	The sky is really blue today.
草木が青々と茂っている.	The vegetation is thick and green.
それはまだ青くて食べられない.	It's still too green to eat.
	It isn't ripe enough to eat yet.
顔が青いよ. 大丈夫?	You look pale. Do you feel OK?
その知らせを聞いて彼はさっと青ざめた.	He went pale at the news.
君はまだまだ青い (青臭い) ね.	You're still pretty green.
	You're still pretty wet behind the ears.

あかい (赤い)

木々が赤く色づいてきた.	The trees began to turn red.
鉄が赤く焼けている.	The iron is red hot.
彼は真っ赤になって怒った.	He turned bright red with anger.
彼の言葉に彼女は顔を赤らめた.	She †blushed [turned red] at what he said.

あかじ (赤字)

今月も赤字を出してしまった.	We went into the red[1] this month, too.
わが家の家計は今月も赤字になりそうだ.	It looks like our household budget is going to be in the red[2] again this month.
大手百貨店が軒並み赤字を出した.	All the big department stores †lost money [showed a deficit].
電子事業部は赤字続きだ.	The electronics department is continuing to show a deficit.
定期預金を取り崩して赤字を埋めている.	We're covering our losses[3] by cashing in our term deposits.

	We're cashing in our term deposits to keep up with [on] our household expenses.
政府は毎年，赤字国債を発行し続けている．	Every year, the government issues bonds to cover the budget deficit.

> 1) go into the red, 2) be in the red, 3) cover *one's* loss はいずれも会社の場合にも使える．

あかぬける（あか抜ける）

都会で暮らすうちに彼女はすっかりあか抜けてきた．	Living in the city has given her a new refinement.
彼女は女優をしていただけあってさすがにあか抜けている．	She has all the style you'd expect from a former actress.

あがる（上・挙・揚がる）

【上方へ動く】7時に幕が上がる．	The curtain †goes up [rises] at seven.
あっ！ 花火が上がった．	Oh! There go the fireworks.
ダムの水位が上がった．	The water level of the dam rose.
壁の絵は右側が少し上がっている．	The picture on the wall is a little too high on the right.
【登る】屋上に上がろうよ．	Let's go up on the roof.
3階まで上がってください．	Please go up to the third floor.
彼女なら今しがた階段を上がって行きましたよ．	Oh, she just went upstairs.
【出る】風呂〔プール〕からあがったばかりだ．	I've just gotten [come] out of the bath [pool].
【入る】どうぞお上がりください．	Please come (on) in.
娘は今年中学校に上がった．	My daughter entered junior high school this year.
【程度・価値が上昇する】午後になって気温が上がってきた．	The temperature rose in the afternoon.
列車のスピードが上がった．	The train (has) picked up speed.
物価が上がった．	Prices have gone up.
たばこの値段が30円上がった．	Cigarette prices went up 30 yen.
家賃が月4万円に上がった．	My rent has been raised to 40,000 [forty thousand] yen a month.
給料が上がった．	I got a raise.
土地の値段の上がり方が著しい．	The way the price of land has been going up is remarkable.
満点が多かったのでクラスの平均点が上がった．	There were a lot of perfect test scores, so the class average went up. The large number of perfect scores on the test brought the class average up.

最近，漫画家の社会的地位は上がってきた．	It's becoming more socially acceptable to be a comic-book writer these days.
技術の水準が上がった．	The level of technology has risen.
【のぼせる】試験のあいだ中あがりっぱなしだった．	I was nervous all through the exam.
人前に出るとあがってしまう．	I get self-conscious in front of people.
【起こる】その発表に歓声が上がった．	The announcement drew cheers.
【終了する】原稿は月末までに上がるはずだ．	The manuscript ought to be done [ready] by the end of this month.
やっと雨が上がった．	The rain has finally stopped.
トランプで彼女が一番に上がった．	She went out first and won the card game.
【食べる・飲む】どうぞケーキをおあがりください．	Please go ahead and have some cake.
夕食には何をおあがりになりますか．	What would you like for dinner?
【見つかる】殺人犯はまだあがらない．	The murder suspect is still at large.
【掲揚する】旗が揚がっている所が裁判所です．	The place flying the flag is the courthouse.
【慣用】風采の上がらない男だ．	What an unimpressive looking guy!

あかるい (明るい)

外はまだ明るい．	It's still light outside.
今は5時頃明るくなる(夜が明ける)．	It gets light at about five now.
明るい部屋のほうが好きだ．	I prefer a bright room.
月が明るい．	The moon is bright.
照明は昼のように明るかった．	The lighting was as bright as day.
空がだいぶ明るくなってきた．	The sky has brightened up.
明るい色が好きだ．	I like bright [light] colors.[1]
【陽気・明朗】彼女は明るい性格だ．	She has a cheerful personality.
この頃彼女の表情が明るくなってきた．	Her face has brightened up recently.
合格の知らせを聞いて彼女の顔は明るくなった．	When she heard she had passed the examination, her face brightened [lit] up.
彼女の歌は人の心を明るくする．	Her songs lift people's hearts.
【前途が】君の将来は明るい．	You have a bright future (ahead of you).
【詳しい】彼は出版界の事情に明るい．	He's †very familiar with [well acquainted with] the publishing world.

---

1) bright colors は鮮やかな色，light colors は明度の高い色を指す．

あき (空き)

【空間】私の本棚にはもう空きがない． — There's no more space [room] on my bookshelf.

ここの空きには電話台を置こう． — Let's put the phone in this space.

【未活用の施設】希望していたマンションにやっと空きが出た． — There's finally a vacancy in the apartment building that we've been wanting to move into.

裏の空き地にマンションが建つんだって． — I hear they're going to build an apartment on the vacant lot behind us.

わが家の隣はここ3年ほどずっと空き家だ． — The house next door to us has been vacant for the last three years.

この商店街は空き店舗が目立つ． — This shopping street has a lot of vacant stores.

小学校の空き教室がほかの用途に活用され始めている． — Empty classrooms in elementary schools are starting to be used for other purposes.

「空き」（会議室・トイレの表示） — Not Occupied／Unoccupied

【空席など】金曜日の福岡便にまだ少し空きがある． — There's still a little room [There are still a few seats] left on Friday's flights to Fukuoka.

今のところ企画部にはポストの空きがありません． — There are no openings in the planning department at this time.

この仕事はちょっとした空き時間に家でできます． — You can do this job at home during your spare time.

【空の容器】空瓶をリサイクルに出した． — I put my †empty bottles [empties][1] out to recycle.

> 1) empties は通例，複数形で「空瓶」について使う．「空缶」の場合は普通，empty をつけずに cans のみでよい．

あきらか (明らか)

事故の原因が明らかになった． — The cause of the accident became clear.

明らかにそれは間違いだ． — That's clearly [obviously] a mistake.

それは自ずから明らかだ． — That's self-evident* [obvious].

火を見るよりも明らかだ． — It's plain [clear] as day.
It's (as) plain as the nose on your face.

あきらめる

【断念する】彼は家庭の事情で大学進学をあきらめた． — He †abandoned [gave up] his plans to go on to college because of his family.

あきらめるのはまだ早い． — It's too early to give up.

もうあきらめて君の言うとおりにするよ． — I give up. I'll do it the way you told me.

あきる

あの娘のことはあきらめろよ.	Forget about her.
【観念する】すべて運命とあきらめた.	I've written it all off to fate.
息子はもう死んだものとあきらめている.	I've given my son up for dead.

あきる (飽きる)

勉強に飽きた.	I'm tired of studying.
この絵は見飽きない.	I never get tired of looking at this picture.
彼女の愚痴は聞き飽きた.	I'm sick of hearing her complaints.
彼の長話には飽き飽きした.	I'm sick and tired of his endless chatter.
彼は何に対しても飽きっぽい.	He easily gets tired of everything.
	He never sticks to anything.
	He has no stick-to-itiveness.**
アイスクリームを飽きるほど食べた.	I filled (myself) up on ice cream.

あきれる

彼の愚かさにはあきれる.	His stupidity amazes me.
	I'm amazed at his foolishness.
あきれるほどの食欲だ.	What an amazing appetite!
君がそんなことをするなんてあきれたよ.	I'm shocked that you would do something like that.
大学を辞めたいと彼が言い出したときは, あきれて物も言えなかった.	When he told me he wanted to quit college, I was †too shocked to speak [speechless].
あきれた人だ.	You're unbelievable!
自分の頑固さには我ながらあきれた.	My stubbornness amazed even me.

あく¹ (空く)

【からになる】「この席は空いていますか」「はい, 空いています」	"Is this seat taken?" "No, it's not."
2階の部屋が空いている.	The room on the second floor is vacant.
この部屋は月末には空く.	This room will be vacated at the end of the month.
彼が退職したので助手のポストが空いている.	His retirement has left the position of assistant open.
駐車場はどこも空いていない.	There are no empty spaces in the parking lot.
【用がなくなる】コンピュータが空いたら貸してください.	Please let me use the computer when you are done [finished, through] with it.
火曜日の午後は空いている.	I'm free on Tuesday afternoon.

あく² (開く)

このドアは外に〔内に〕開く.	This door opens outward [inward].
その店は朝10時に開く.	The store opens at 10 a.m.
午後7時半に幕が開く.	The curtain rises at 7:30 p.m.
ワインの栓が開いている.	The wine bottle is uncorked [open].
彼の言葉に開いた口がふさがらなかった.	His remark left me staring open-mouthed.

あくじゅんかん (悪循環)

このままでは悪循環が続くだけだ.	It'll be just a vicious circle unless we do something about it.
テロとの戦いで，世界は暴力の悪循環に陥った.	With the war on terrorism, the world spun into a vicious cycle of violence.
この悪循環を断ち切らなくてはならない.	We have to break this vicious cycle.

> a vicious circle と a vicious cycle は置き換え可能.

あくせく

あくせく働いても暮らしは楽にならない.	I work and slave but I can't seem to make ends meet.
小さなことにあくせくするなよ.	Don't worry about trifles.

アクセス

新しい国際空港は交通のアクセスがよい〔悪い〕.	Access by car [train] to the new international airport is good [poor].
【コンピュータ】お気に入りのサイトに毎日アクセスしている.	I access my favorite sites every day.
ハッカーの不正アクセスを防ぐには，強力なファイアウォールが必要だ.	You need a well-managed firewall to †keep out hackers [keep hackers from accessing your computer].

あくまで(も)

【最後まで】原告側はあくまでも国と戦うつもりだ.	The plaintiff intends to fight the government to the very end.
彼女はあくまで口を割らなかった.	To the very end, she never did let on (that she knew).
【全く】これはあくまで僕の個人的な意見だ.	This is purely my own personal opinion.
これはあくまで仮定の話だけど，どう思う?	This is just an idea but what do you think?
彼女はあくまでも純粋な人だ.	She is an absolutely pure individual.
あくまでも青い空が広がっていた.	There was nothing but blue skies as far as

the eye could see.

あける¹ (空ける)

砂糖を砂糖入れに空けてください.	Please empty the sugar into the sugar canister.
一気にグラスを空けてくれ.	Empty the glass in one gulp.
通れるように道を空けてください.	Please clear the way for us.
1行〔2行〕ずつ空けて書きなさい.	Write on every other [third] line.
月末までに部屋を空けてください.	Please be out by the end of the month.
明日は家を空けています.	I won't be (at) home tomorrow.
家は長いあいだ空けておくと早く傷む.	A house ages more quickly if it's not lived in.
君のために一日空けてあるよ.	I'm keeping the whole day open for you.

あける² (明ける)

1時間もすれば夜が明ける.	The sun will be up in another hour.
梅雨が明けた.	The rainy season is over.
明けましておめでとう.	Happy New Year!

あける³ (開ける)

窓を開けましょうか.	Shall I open the window?
50ページを開けなさい.	Open to page fifty.
贈り物の包みを開けた.	I unwrapped the present.
ドアは開けたままにしておいて.	Leave the door open.
栓抜きがないのでビールが開けられない.	I can't open the beer because I don't have a bottle-opener.

あげる (上・挙・揚げる)

【上方へ動かす】ブラインドを上げてください.	Please raise the blinds.
荷物が重くて持ち上げられなかった.	The package was so heavy that I couldn't lift [raise] it.
この本を棚に上げてください.	Please put this book up on the shelf.
恥ずかしくて顔を上げられなかった.	I was so embarrassed that I couldn't †look up [lift my eyes].
【入れる】彼女を訪ねて行ったが,家へ上げてもらえなかった.	I went to see her but she wouldn't let me in.
彼女は女手一つで息子を大学に上げた.	She single-handedly put her son through college.
【程度・価値を高める】部屋の温度をもう少し上げてください.	Please raise the room temperature a little more.
パトカーが急に速度を上げた.	The police car suddenly speeded up.

もっと車のスピードを上げて！	Make the car go faster!／Speed up!
テレビの音量を上げると近所の人からきっと苦情を言われるよ．	The neighbors are bound to complain if you turn up the television.
家主は部屋代を5,000円上げた．	The landlord raised [increased] the rent 5,000 yen.
給料を上げて欲しいと社長に頼んだ．	I asked the boss for a raise.
【声を出す】彼は大声を上げた．	He raised his voice.
彼は大声を上げて泣いた．	He cried loudly.
生徒たちは歓声を上げた．	The students cheered.
彼女は泥棒を見て悲鳴を上げた．	She screamed when she saw the burglar.
【与える】これを君にあげる．	This is for you.／I'll give this to you.
【示す】例をあげて説明しなさい．	Explain it by giving [citing] an example.
なぜこのほうがいいのか理由をあげなさい．	Give me a reason why this (way) is better.
彼は欠席者の名前をあげた．	He announced the names of those who were absent.
彼は収賄の容疑であげられた．	He was arrested on suspicion of accepting a bribe.
【挙式】彼らは教会で結婚式をあげた．	They had a church wedding.
【全部で】学校をあげて非行問題に取り組んだ．	The entire school tackled the delinquency problem.
国をあげて大統領を歓迎した．	The whole nation welcomed the president.
全力をあげて間に合わせます．	We'll do †all we can [everything in our power] to get it done in time.
【高く上げる】花火を上げよう．	Let's set off some fireworks.
子どもたちが原っぱでたこを揚げている．	Children are flying kites in the field.
【揚げ物を作る】夕食には魚を揚げよう．	I'll make deep-fried fish for supper.
【慣用】彼は新薬を開発して名をあげた．	He developed a new medicine and †made a name for himself [became famous].
彼は一旗揚げようと20年前に東京にやって来た．	He came to Tokyo twenty years ago to make it big.

あこがれる

あこがれのパリに着いた．	I arrived in the Paris of my dreams.
彼は名声にあこがれている．	He's attracted by fame.
彼女は心ひそかに彼にあこがれていた．	She was secretly attracted to him.
彼女はスチュワーデス[客室乗務員]にあこがれている．	Her dream is to become a flight attendant.

あさい (浅い)
【深さが】浅い所で泳ぎなさい.	Swim in the shallow part.
この箱は浅い.	This is a shallow box.
【程度が】彼の考えは浅い.	His thinking is shallow.
私は眠りが浅い.	I'm a light sleeper.
彼女とはまだつきあいが浅い.	I haven't had much of a chance to get to know her yet.
あの歯科医は経験が浅い.	That dentist hasn't had much experience.
【日数が】春はまだ浅い.	It's still early in spring.
【色が】この布地は思っていたより色が浅い.	The color of this material is lighter than I thought.

あさはか
そんなあさはかなことはするな.	Don't do such a silly thing.
そんなあさはかな考え方ではだめだ.	We have to [Let's] get beyond this kind of shallow thinking.
あさはかにも彼女は言うべきでないことを言ってしまった.	She foolishly said exactly what she shouldn't have.

あさましい
何てあさましい (情けない) 世の中だ.	What a wretched [miserable] world we live in!
困っている人から絞り取るなんて何とあさましいことだ.	How deplorable (it is) to exploit people in distress!
金のために結婚するなんて彼女はあさましい.	How shameless of her to marry for money!
あんなことをしてしまってあさましいと思う.	I'm ashamed of having done such a thing.
何てあさましい (卑しい) 考えなんだろう.	What a base [mean] idea!

あざやか (鮮やか)
彼女の服は鮮やかなピンクだ.	Her dress is bright pink.
このテレビの画像は鮮やかだ.	This TV has a bright image.
彼女は鮮やかな印象を残した.	She left a vivid impression.
彼は難局を鮮やかに乗り切った.	He overcame the difficulty brilliantly.
そのテニス選手は鮮やかなサーブで知られている.	That tennis player is known for his brilliant serve.
我がチームは鮮やかな勝利を収めた.	Our team won a brilliant victory.

あし (足・脚)
【足】だれかに足を踏まれた.	Somebody stepped on my foot.

左足から踏み出せ.	Step out with your left foot.
足を引っこめろ.	Pull your foot [feet] in.
足の裏〔甲〕が痛い.	The sole [instep] of my foot hurts.
【脚】足を折った.	I broke my leg.
足が棒になるまで歩いた.	I walked my legs off.
	I walked till my legs got stiff.
足の向くままに歩いた.	I just went where my feet led me.
彼は足の向くままふらりと旅に出た.	He †took off for [went off traveling to] wherever he felt like going.
テーブルの脚が壊れた.	The table leg broke.
この3本脚のテーブルは不安定だ.	This three-legged table is unstable.
【歩行】私は足が達者だ〔弱い〕.	I'm a good [poor] walker.
彼は足が速い〔遅い〕.	He walks [runs] fast [slowly].
	He's a fast [slow] walker [runner].
彼女は足を速めた.	She quickened her pace.
足取りも重く歯医者に行った.	I practically dragged myself to the dentist's.
玄関に足音が聞こえた.	I heard the footsteps at the door.
【往来】何度足を運んでもむだだよ.	I don't care how many times you come. You're wasting your time.
実家から足が遠のいてきた.	I don't get back to my parents' place much any more.
あの事件以来この店は客足が途絶えた.	Since that incident almost no one sets foot in this store.
東京まで来たのだから足を延ばして日光まで行こうよ.	We're already in Tokyo. We might as well go on to Nikko.
一足違いで彼に会えなかった.	I just missed meeting him.
鉄道のストライキで足が奪われた.	The railway strike immobilized the city.
彼らは電車事故のために足止めを食い,コンサートに遅れてしまった.	They were held up by the train accident and ended up being late for the concert.
【慣用】盗品から泥棒の足がついた.	The robber was traced by stolen goods.
他人の足を引っ張るようなことはするな.	Try not to get in people's way.
彼はその仕事から足を洗った.	He has made a clean break with that kind of work.
宴会の予算に足が出ないようにいろいろ工夫した.	We did all kinds of things to keep the dinner party from going over (the) budget.

あじ (味)

【食物】塩を入れると味が良く〔悪く〕なる.	Salt will improve [spoil, ruin] the taste [flavor[1)]].
冷蔵庫に入れたら味が悪くなった	When I put it in the refrigerator, it †lost

[落ちた].	its flavor [got stale].
シチューの味が薄い.	This stew doesn't have much taste [flavor].
このスープは味がない.	This soup has no taste [flavor].
	This soup is tasteless [flavorless].
どんな味がするの？	What does it taste like?
これはレモンの味がする.	This tastes like [of] lemon.
塩とこしょうで味つけしなさい.	Season[2] it with salt and pepper.
これは砂糖で味つけして(甘くして)ある.	This is sweetened[3] with sugar.
しょうが味〔コーヒー味〕のクッキーが好きだ.	I like ginger-flavored[4] 〔coffee-flavored〕 cookies.
塩味が足りない.	It isn't salty enough.
【経験】ぜいたくの味が忘れられない.	I can't forget the taste of luxury.
彼は味を占めて何度でもやって来る.	Encouraged by his first success [Having got a taste of success], he keeps coming back.
【趣き】彼はつきあえばつきあうほど味の出る人だ.	The better you know him, the more interesting he seems.
この文章は味がある.	This is a beautiful [lovely] †passage [piece of writing].

> 1) flavor には香り，風味の意味合いが入る．2)3)4)「味つけする」は season または flavor. ただし砂糖で味つけする場合は sweeten を使う．

あじけない (味気ない)

仕事に追われて味気ない生活をしている.	I have to work so hard that it takes all the fun out of life.
一人で食事をするのは味気ない.	Eating by yourself is dull [uninteresting, dreary].
都会の生活は味気ない.	City life is insipid.
味気ないなあ！	How boring [insipid*]！

あしらう

彼女は私を冷たくあしらった.	She treated me coldly.
君は客あしらいがうまいね.	You handle (the) customers well.
	You are good with (the) customers.
体よくあしらわれた.	I was given a polite brush-off.
	I was politely brushed off.
彼は私の提案を鼻であしらった.	He turned his nose up at my proposal.
【取り合わせ】料理のあしらいにこれを使いたい.	I want to use this to garnish the dish.

あじわう (味わう)

よく味わって食べてください．	Please savor the taste.
味わい深い随筆だ．	This is an essay to be savored.
この詩を深く味わうために何度も読んだ．	I read this poem a number of times in order to appreciate it fully.
フランス映画を見てパリにいる気分を味わった．	I saw a French movie and it almost made me feel as if I was [were] in Paris.
彼は息子の死で深い悲しみを味わった．	His son's death plunged him into sadness.

あずかる (預かる)

この荷物を預かっていただけますか．	Could you hold [keep] this baggage for me?
君への預かり物があるよ．	I have something I'm holding for you.
お金は私が預かっている．	I'm taking care of the money.
そんな高価な物を預かるのは嫌だ．	I don't want to be left in charge of such a valuable thing.
1年間兄の家を預かることになった．	I'm going to look after my brother's house for one year.
子どもを預かって（面倒を見て）くださる？	Would you mind taking care of my children?

あずける (預ける)

クロークにかばんを預けた．	I checked my bag in the cloakroom.
この金は銀行に預けなさい．	Deposit [Put] this money in the bank.
銀行に1万ドル預けてあります．	I have $10,000 [ten thousand dollars] in the bank.
彼には金は預けられない．	I can't trust him to keep [hold] my money.
カメラは彼に預けたほうがいいよ．	You'd better leave your camera with him.
子どもは彼女に預けました．	I left my children in her care.
この件は君に預けておくよ．	I'm leaving you in charge of this matter.
宿題が終わるまでこのケーキはお預けよ．	You can have this piece of cake after you finish your homework.
雨のため勝負はお預けになった．	The game was postponed because of rain.

あせ (汗)

汗をかいた．	I was sweating [perspiring].
	I got sweaty.
テニスをやって汗を流した．	I played tennis and worked up a good sweat.
力士の体から汗が滝のように流れている．	The *sumo* wrestler is sweating like a horse.
ずっと走ってきたので汗びっしょ	I ran all the way here, so †I'm all sweaty

りだ.	[I'm dripping with sweat].
汗でシャツがびっしょりだ.	My undershirt is soaked with sweat.
彼の額に玉のような汗が出ていた.	Beads of sweat †stood [came out] on his brow.
このTシャツは汗臭い.	This T-shirt smells of sweat.
彼女はちょっと汗ばんでいた.	She was perspiring a little.
怖くて冷や汗が出た.	I was so scared I broke out in a cold sweat.
これは父が額に汗して得たお金です.	This is money earned by the sweat of my father's brow.

あせる (焦る)

焦らなくてもいいよ.	You don't have to hurry. There's no hurry. You don't need to be in a hurry.
焦って結論を出すことはない.	You don't have to make up your mind in a hurry.
彼は成功を焦り過ぎた.	He was too eager for success.
気ばかり焦ってもしかたないよ.	It's useless to get so worked up.
締め切りまで2週間になって焦りを感じ始めた.	I'm really anxious now that the deadline is only two weeks off.
彼は自分の失敗をカバーしようと焦っていた.	He was struggling to make up for his mistake.

あそび (遊び)

今度の旅行は仕事じゃなくて遊びだ.	This trip is for pleasure, not work.
遊びなんだからそうむきになるなよ.	We're only doing it for fun. Don't get so uptight.
彼女とのつきあいは最初は遊びだった.	At first, I went out with her just for the fun of it.
遊び半分でしてはいけない.	Don't do it unless you're sincere.

あそぶ (遊ぶ)

子どもたちは公園に遊びに行った.	The children went to play in the park.
鬼ごっこをして遊ぼうよ.	Let's play tag.
弟は積み木で遊んでいる.	My little brother is playing with building blocks.
彼らは楽しそうに遊んでいる.	They seem to be having a good time. They seem to be enjoying themselves.
今度の日曜日に遊びにおいでよ.	Come over next Sunday.
近いうちに遊びに行きます.	I'll come over soon.
日曜日に伊豆に遊びに行きます.	We are going on a trip to Izu this Sunday.

遊んでばかりいてはだめだ.	You can't just †be idle [goof off**] all the time.
丸一日遊んでしまった.	I †idled away [goofed off,** loafed about] the whole day.
彼は働きもしないで遊んで暮らしている.	He's not even trying to work. He's just fooling around.
お金を遊ばせておくわけにはいかない.	I don't want to let my money just sit in the bank.
	I want to have my money working for me.

あたえる (与える)

彼女はめいに小遣いを与えた.	She gave her niece some spending money.
彼にチャンスを与えよう.	Let's give him a chance.
彼女は赤ん坊にミルクを与えた.	She gave her baby its bottle.
動物にえさを与えないでください.	Please don't feed the animals.
彼の作品に金賞が与えられた.	His work was awarded first prize.
彼は生徒にたくさんの宿題を与えた.	He gave [assigned] his students a lot of homework.
彼女は与えられた仕事を一生懸命やっている.	She's applying herself diligently to the work assigned to her.
彼の失敗は会社に大打撃を与えた.	His blunder dealt a heavy blow to* his company.

あたたかい (暖・温かい)

【温度】最近暖かい日が続いている.	It has been warm recently.
暖かくしていなさい.	Keep yourself warm.
今年の冬は暖かい.	We are having a mild winter.
温かいうちに食べなさい.	Eat it while it's hot.
【気持ち】あの人は心の温かい人だ.	He is a warm-hearted man.
彼はおいに温かく接したことがなかった.	He never had a warm relationship with his nephew.
彼を温かく迎えよう.	Let's give him a warm welcome.
彼女の態度には何の温かみも感じられなかった.	I felt no warmth in her attitude.
【慣用】今日は懐が温かい.	I'm rich today.

あたためる (温める)

冷めたスープを温めた.	I heated [warmed] up the cold soup.
旧交を温めた.	We renewed our old friendship.
その考えは私が長年温めてきたものだ.	I've cherished that idea for many years.

あたま (頭)

頭を上げなさい.	Lift your head up. ／Raise your head.
頭が痛い.	I have a headache.
風邪をひいて頭が重い.	I caught a cold and my head †feels heavy [is all stuffed up].
頭がくらくらする.	I feel dizzy.
頭がぼーっとしている.	I can't think straight.
頭がはっきりしてきた.	I can think more clearly now.
彼は頭が良い〔悪い〕.	He's smart [stupid].
仕事が多過ぎて頭が変になりそうだ.	I'm about to go crazy from too much work.
やつは頭が変だ.	That guy is crazy.／He's off his rocker.**
彼は少し頭が足りない.	He's a little dense [slow]. He's missing †something [a few marbles**].
彼女のことで頭がいっぱいだ.	She's all I think about. I'm preoccupied with her.
そのことが頭から離れない.	I can't get that out of my head [mind].
彼は頭が古い.	He's an old fogy.**
父は頭が固い.	My father is rigid [inflexible] in his thinking.
【慣用】彼女には頭が上がらない.	I can't compete with her.
彼の努力には頭が下がる.	I take off my hat to his effort.
人に頭を下げるのは大嫌いだ.	I hate having to play up to[1] people.
彼はその問題に頭を抱えている.	That problem is giving him a headache.
彼は資金不足に頭を痛めている.	The shortage of funds is giving him a headache.
私の提案は頭から否定された.	My proposal wasn't even considered.
この本の売り上げは頭打ちだ.	Sales of this book have peaked.
彼は頭でっかちで商売が下手だ.	He's an armchair theorist and bad at business.
彼に母の悪口を言われて頭に来た.	It really got to me when he insulted my mother.
時間に遅れても言い逃れのうまい彼のやり方は頭に来る.	The way he always gets away with being late just burns me up.
頭を冷やせよ.	Cool off!

1) play up to は「〜にこびへつらう」の意味.

あたらしい (新しい)

新しい靴だね.	Those are new shoes, aren't they?
見るもの聞くものすべてが新しかった.	Everything I saw and heard was new to me.

その出来事は我々の記憶に新しい.	That incident is fresh in our memories.
これはいちばん新しいニュースだ.	This is the latest news.
これは新しい傾向です.	This is a recent trend.

あたり¹（辺り）

【場所】辺りを見回した.	I looked around.
辺りには人影一つなかった.	There wasn't a soul to be seen. There was no one about.
彼らはたぶん今ごろ郡山辺りを運転しているよ.	They're probably driving around Koriyama just about now.
僕の眼鏡を見なかった？ この辺りに置いておいたんだけど.	Have you seen my glasses? I left them around here someplace.
この辺りにスーパーはありますか.	Is there a supermarket in this neighborhood?
辺り一面, 花が咲いていた.	Flowers were blooming everywhere I looked.
彼は辺り構わずどなり散らした.	He ranted and raved, oblivious to his surroundings.
【時】明日あたり〔あさってあたり〕から雪になりそうだ.	It looks as though it's going to snow †sometime tomorrow 〔the day after tomorrow or so〕.
来週あたり田舎へ帰ろうかと思っている.	I'm thinking of going home sometime next week.
【人・物】次期会長には彼あたりが適任だろう.	I think he 〔Someone like him〕 would be suitable as the next president.

あたり²（当たり）

【殴打】「痛快な当たりでしたね」「これで巨人は勢いづいたね」	"That was a great hit, wasn't it?" "The Giants have pulled ahead with this one."
【くじ・選択】当たりが出る確率は10パーセントだ.	There's a ten percent chance of †winning 〔getting a hit〕.
大当たりが出ると１万円分の商品券がもらえる.	You can get a ten thousand-yen gift certificate if you hit the jackpot.
当たりくじをなくしてしまった.	I lost a winning lottery ticket.
中古車は当たり外れが激しい.	You can (either) get really lucky or lose big time buying a used car.
引越し業者をあそこにしたのは当たりだったね.	We made the right decision hiring that moving company.
「このごはん, カリフォルニア米でしょ」「当たり！ よく分かったわね」	"This is California rice, isn't it?" "Right on! How did you guess?"
【成功】あの新製品は大当たりした.	That new product was a big hit.
サロメはあの女優の当たり役だ.	The actress's hit role was Salome.

あたりまえ

【見当】推理小説を半分読んだところで犯人の当たりがついた. — Half way through the mystery novel, I figured out who was guilty.

送別会の場所, 2, 3, 当たりをつけておいてくれ. — Could you check out two or three possible places for the farewell party?

【人に接する態度】彼女は当たりの柔らかい人だ. — She has good social skills.

【〜につき】原価は1個あたり75円です. — The cost price is ¥75 †apiece [each, per piece].

会社から1人あたり1,000円の補助が出る. — The company pays a subsidy of ¥1,000 per person.

あたりまえ (当たり前)

【当然】そんなことを言ったら彼女が怒るのは当たり前だよ. — Of course [It's natural] she got angry when you said something like that.

約束を守るのは当たり前のことだ. — It's only proper to keep promises.

彼女が首になるのは当たり前だ. — She deserved to be fired.

「怒ってるの?」「当たり前だよ」 — "You're not angry, are you?" "You bet I am."

当たり前のことをしただけです. — I only did what was right.

【普通】当たり前の人ならそんなことはしない. — A normal person would never do such a thing.

当たり前の方法じゃだめだよ. — Doing it the obvious way won't work.

あたる (当たる)

【ぶつかる】右肩にボールが当たった. — A ball hit [struck] me on the right shoulder.

込んだ電車で学生のスポーツバッグが背中に当たって居心地が悪かった. — The student's sports bag was sticking uncomfortably into my back on the crowded train.

矢は的に当たらなかった. — The arrow missed the target.

【相当する】今度の祭日は日曜日に当たる. — The next national holiday falls on Sunday.

1フィートは30.48センチに当たる. — One foot is equivalent to 30.48 [thirty point four eight] centimeters.

君は彼の何に当たるの? — How are you related to him?

【的中する】彼の予言が当たった. — His prophecy came true.

あの占師はよく当たるそうだ. — That fortuneteller often seems to be right.

当たらずといえども遠からずだ. — You're on the right track.

福引で指輪が当たった. — I won a ring in the lottery.

【成功する】あの会社は新製品が当たって景気がいい. — That company has been doing well ever since the success of its new product.

【中毒する】昼に食べた物にあたったようだ. — Something I ate at lunch seems to have disagreed with me.

暑さにあたった.	I got sick from the heat.
【試す】ほかを当たってごらん.	Try someone [somewhere] else.
当たって砕けろ.	Take a [your] chance.
【従事する】今年からクラブの後輩の指導に当たる.	Starting this year, I am to lead the younger members of the club.
彼女はその雑誌の編集に当たっている.	She's involved in editing that magazine.

あつい¹ (厚い)

この板はかなり厚い.	This is a pretty thick board.
この辞書は7センチの厚みがある.	This dictionary is seven centimeters thick.
彼は情の厚い男だ.	He is a very caring man.
厚くお礼申し上げます.	I am deeply grateful.

あつい² (暑い)

暑くならないうちに出かけよう.	Let's go before it gets too hot.
今日も暑くなりそうだ.	We're going to have another hot day.
うだるように暑い.	It's sweltering [scorching].
私は暑さに弱い.	I'm sensitive to (the) heat.

あつい³ (熱い)

紅茶は熱いのが好きだ.	I like my tea hot.
彼女の親切に胸が熱くなった.	I was deeply moved [touched] by her kindness.
二人はお熱い仲だ.	They are in love.

あつかう (扱う)

【人を】彼を家族の一員として扱おう.	We'll treat him as [like] a member of the family.
子どもの扱い方を知らないね.	You need to learn how to handle children.
彼は扱いにくい人だ.	He's hard to deal with.
【物を】そういう商品は当店では扱っていません.	We don't carry that product.
この箱は丁寧に扱ってくれ.	Handle this package with care.
この機械は扱い方に注意してください.	Be careful in operating [using] this machine.
その事件は日本のマスコミで大きく扱われた.	The incident was widely reported in the Japanese media.

あつかましい (厚かましい)

厚かましいやつだ.	He's (really) pushy.
厚かましくも彼は1ヵ月もここに滞在した.	He had the nerve to stay here for a whole month.

厚かましい願いだが, 金を貸してもらえないだろうか.	I realize I'm asking a big favor, but could you lend me some money?

あっけない

物語の幕切れはあっけないものだった.	The story ended too abruptly. The story just kind of** ended.
大騒ぎした割にはあっけなく事が解決した.	In spite of all the fuss the problem was easily solved.
あんなにあっけなく試合が終わるなんて夢にも思わなかった.	I never dreamed the game would end so soon [quickly].
彼はあっけなく死んでしまった.	He died suddenly./He up and**1) died.

> 1) up (and *do*) は「突然行動を起こす」という意味の動詞で, 原形のまま用いられることが多い.

あっさり

君はあっさりしたデザインの服が似合うよ.	You look good in simple clothes.
あっさりした食事にしてね.	Make it a light1) meal, OK?
彼はあっさりしたやつだ.	He's an easygoing (kind of) guy.
随分あっさりと承知したね.	You sure were quick to agree, weren't you?
あっさり断られた.	I got turned down †flat [just like that].

> 1)「淡白な」の意味で, rich (こってりした) の反対. simple and light (簡単であっさりした) という言い方もできる.

あっとう (圧倒)

彼女の気迫に圧倒されて何も言えなかった.	I was so overcome by her energy that I couldn't say anything.
彼は強烈なパフォーマンスで観客を圧倒した.	The audience was overwhelmed by his powerful performance.
S高校が圧倒的な強さで優勝した.	S High School won because of its overwhelming strength.
客層は年配の女性が圧倒的に多い.	The clientele is made up overwhelmingly of older women.
議案は圧倒的多数で可決された.	The legislation (was) passed by an overwhelming majority.

あつまる (集まる)

週に1回集まって英語の勉強をしています.	We get together once a week and study English.
人々は彼の周りに集まった.	People gathered around him.

ここは学生の集まる場所だ.	This is a meeting [gathering] place for students.
バザーで多額の金が集まった.	A large sum of money was collected at the bazaar.

あつめる (集める)

もっと人を集めてください.	Get more people (together).
切手を集めています.	I collect stamps.
新事業の資金を集めなければならない.	We have to raise money for our new project.
この芝居は以前ほど客を集めない.	This play doesn't attract as many people as it used to.

あて (当て)

【目的】別に使う当てもないが,安いので買った.	I don't know what I'll use it for, but it was too cheap to pass up.
家を飛び出したものの,どこにも行く当てはなかった.	I ran away from home without having given any thought to where I would go.
彼らは当てもなく新宿をさまよい歩いた.	They wandered around Shinjuku aimlessly.
【信頼・期待】当てにしてくれていいよ.	You can count [depend] on me.
彼は値上がりを当てにしてかなり金を買い込んだ.	He bought a sizable amount of gold in anticipation of a rise in price.
ボーナスを当てにして新型のスポーツカーを買った.	In anticipation of my bonus I bought the latest-model sports car.
当てが外れてがっかりした.	I was really disappointed when it fell through.

あてはまる (当てはまる)

今度の減税はわが家には当てはまらない.	The new tax cut doesn't apply to us.
その条件は僕の場合,当てはまらない.	Those conditions don't apply to me.
私の希望条件に当てはまるのはこの会社だけだ.	This is the only company that meets my criteria.
もちろん,それが全てにおいて当てはまるとは限らない.	Of course, it is not always applicable.
ある社会の規範がほかの社会にも当てはまるとは限らない.	What works for one society does not necessarily work for another.
空欄に当てはまる語を選択肢から一つ選んで記入しなさい.	Choose the appropriate [correct] word from the list and fill in the blank.

あてる (当・充てる)

【触れさせる】
貝に耳を当てて海の音を聞いてごらん. — Put the shell up to your ear and listen to the sound of the ocean.
子どもの額に手を当てると熱かった. — When I put my hand to the child's forehead it felt warm.
日に当てて乾かした. — I dried it †in [by exposing it to] the sun.

【的中させる】
くじで1等を当てた. — I won first prize in the lottery.
株で当てた. — I made a killing on the stock market.
女性の年齢を当てるのは難しい. — It's hard to tell [guess] a woman's age.
何を考えているか当ててごらん. — Guess what I'm thinking about.

【指名する】
英語の時間に当てられた. — I was called on during English class.

【充当する】
夏の休暇は自分の研究に充てるつもりだ. — I plan to devote my summer vacation to my research.
給料の一部を借金の返済に充てている. — I put part of my salary aside to repay a loan.

あと¹ (後)

【うしろ】
あとについて来なさい. — Follow me.
子どもがあとを追って来た. — My child ran after me.
一番あとから彼女が入って来た. — She came in last.
私があとに残ります. — I'll stay behind.
東京をあとにパリに旅立った. — Bidding farewell to Tokyo, I set off for Paris.
彼は妻をあとに残して死んだ. — He died, leaving his wife to live on after him.
その子は怖くてあとずさりした. — The child †drew back [stepped backward] in fear.
200メートルほどあと戻りしたところで落とした財布を見つけた. — After backtracking 200 meters, I found the wallet I had dropped.

【のち】
またあとでね. — See you later.
あとで教えてあげるよ. — I'll †tell [explain it to] you later.
あと払いでいいですか. — May I pay later?
あとから悔やんでもしょうがないよ. — There's no point in worrying about it after it's done.
パーティーのあとどこへ行ったの. — Where did you go after the party?
君が出かけたすぐあとに電話があった. — There was a call for you soon after you left.
あとは君に任せたよ. — I'm leaving the rest up to you.
 — Can you take care of the rest?
あとのことも考えてよ. — Think of the consequences.
その話はあとに回して, まず簡単なものから片づけよう. — Let's skip that topic till later and get the easier stuff out of the way first.

あと先も考えずに家を飛び出してしまった.	I ran away from home without thinking of the consequences.
【残り】あと5分で6時だ.	Five more minutes and it's six o'clock.
頂上まであと一歩だ.	One more push and we'll be at the top.
あと3人しか座れない.	There's only room for three more people to sit.
【慣用】もうあとには引けない.	There's no turning back now.
今度は負けられないよ. うちのチームにはもうあとがない.	We can't lose this one. Our team has its back to the wall.
こんなことはあとにも先にも一回切りだ.	This sort of thing can happen only once.
そんなことをするとあとが怖いよ.	I hate to think what will happen if you do something like that.
あと腐れのないようにしよう.	Let's make sure this isn't going to come back and haunt us.
あとは野となれ山となれ.	What happens afterward is of no concern to me.
あとの祭りだ.	The damage is done.

あと² (跡)

消しゴムで落書きを消したが, 跡が残ってしまった.	I tried to erase the scribbling, but it wouldn't all come off.
種痘をすると(傷)跡が残ることがある.	Vaccinations sometimes leave a permanent scar.
犬に彼の跡を付けさせよう.	Let's put dogs on his trail.
ここは宮殿の跡です.	These are the remains [ruins] of a palace.
その家の跡地には美術館が建っている.	There's an art museum now where that house once stood.
今では城の跡形もない.	Nothing remains of the castle now.
建物は跡形もなく壊された.	The building was completely destroyed.
長男に跡を継いで欲しい.	I want my eldest son to †succeed me [take over (for me)].

あとかたづけ (あと片づけ)

遊び終わったら, きちんとあと片づけしなさい.	Clean up after you've finished playing.
彼女はいつもあと片づけを人まかせにする.	She always leaves the cleaning up to someone else.
料理をするのは楽しいが, あと片づけが面倒だ.	I like cooking but doing dishes[1] is a real chore.

> 1) do (the) dishes でテーブルを片づけることから皿を洗うことまで, 料理・食事のあと片づけ全般を指す.

あどけない

そのいたずらっ子の寝顔は実にあどけなかった． As he slept, the naughty child's face was the picture of innocence.

彼女にはまだあどけなさが残っている． There's still something innocent about her.

あな (穴)

壁に穴をあけるな． Don't make any holes in the wall.

この毛布は穴だらけだ． This blanket is full of holes.

この針の穴は小さい． This needle has a small eye.

【慣用】彼は私を穴のあくほどじっと見つめた． His eyes bored (right) into me.

弟が会社の帳簿に穴をあけたので穴埋めしてやった． I made up the difference for my brother after he created a deficit for the company.

彼の論旨は穴だらけだ． His argument is full of holes.

穴があったら入りたい． I'm so ashamed I wish I could disappear. I wish I could sink into [through] the floor.

彼は今日の競馬で大穴を当てた． He won on a dark horse in today's horse race.

この店はフランス料理の穴場です． This is a good, little-known French restaurant.

あなどる (侮る)

人を侮るものではない． You shouldn't †underestimate* [look down on] people.

簡単な問題だと侮ってはいけない． Don't be fooled into thinking it's a small problem.

あのチームの力は侮れない． That team is stronger than you think.

彼を侮ったのは私の誤りだった． My mistake was to have treated him lightly.

アナログ

アナログの時計のほうが時間の感覚が分かる． You can get a better sense of the time with analog(ue) watches [clocks].

アナログのレコードの音にはCDにはない味わいがある． Analog(ue) records have a special quality that you don't find in CDs.

あばれる (暴れる)

乗っていた馬が突然暴れだした． The horse I was riding [on] suddenly †went crazy [ran amok*].

あの子は暴れだすと手がつけられ There's nothing anyone can do when that

ない.
酔っ払いが路上で暴れている.
明日の夜はライブハウスで大いに暴れるつもりよ.

child gets rowdy.
There's a drunk making a scene outside.
I'm going to go wild at the club tomorrow night.

アピール

彼の歌はまさに平和へのアピールそのものだ.
この化粧品シリーズは若い女性にアピールする.
店長が新製品の特長を客にアピールしている.
彼は常に自己アピールを欠かさない.
男の人の大きな手にセックスアピールを感じる.

His song is truly an appeal for peace.
This makeup line appeals to younger women.
The manager is selling the customer on the special features of the new product.
He's always promoting himself.
I find big hands sexually appealing in men.

あびる (浴びる)

【水・湯を】夏はよく近くの川で水を浴びた.
サッとひと風呂浴びて来よう.
夕食後シャワーを浴びた.
【光線などを】富士山が朝日を浴びて輝いていた.
作業員たちは埃を浴びた.
彼らは放射能を浴びた.
【質問・非難などを】教授は次々に質問を浴びた.
彼の演説は多くの非難〔拍手, やじ〕を浴びた.
【慣用】彼は毎晩浴びるように酒を飲む.

I used to splash [bathe] in the river near my house in summer.
I'll take a quick bath.
I took a shower after dinner.
Mt. Fuji was glowing in the morning sun.

The workers got covered with dust.
They were exposed to radioactivity.
The professor was showered with questions one after another.
His speech got [received] a lot of criticism [applause, boos].
He drinks like a fish every evening.

あぶない (危ない)

【危険】夜, 無灯火で自転車に乗るのは危ない.
彼にその金を預けるのは危ない (冒険だ).
危ないことはしないほうがいい.
危ない目にあった.
危ない思いをした.
危ない! 下がって!
危ないところだった.

It's dangerous [unsafe] to ride a bicycle without a light at night.
It's risky [dangerous] to trust him with that money.
It's better not to take the risk.
I had a close call.
I had a †scare [close call].
Watch [Look] out! Step back!
That was close.

	I had a narrow escape.
あの会社はもう危ない．	That company is on the verge of bankruptcy.
彼の命が危ない．	His life is in danger.
彼女の病気は重く，今日明日にも危ない．	She is seriously [critically, dangerously] ill and she could go at any time.
危ない橋は渡らないほうがいい．	It's better not to walk on thin ice.
【不安・不確か】彼の商売のやり方は危なくて見ていられない．	His way of doing business is so precarious that I can't stand to watch. He has such a risky way of doing business.
期日までにこの仕事ができるかどうか危ないものだ．	It's doubtful whether we can get this job done on time.
息子の歩き方はまだ危なげだ．	My son is still unsteady on his feet.
危なげのない演技だ．	It's a sure performance.

あぶら （油・脂）

【油】タマネギをしんなりするまで（油で）いためなさい．	Sauté onions (in oil[1]) till tender.
鳥肉を少量の油で焼きなさい．	Brown the chicken in a small amount of cooking oil.
機械に油をさした．	I lubricated [oiled, greased[2]] the machine.
この機械は油が切れている．	This machine needs lubrication [lubricating, oiling].
パイ皿に油を塗りなさい．	Grease the pie plate.
手が油でべとべとだ．	My hands are greasy.
【脂】この肉は脂身が多い．	This meat has a lot of fat[3] on it.
中華料理は脂っこい．	Chinese food tends to be oily.
日本人は脂が乗っている魚や肉をおいしいと思う．	Most Japanese prefer fish and meat that contain a little fat.
【慣用】彼はまた油を売っている．	He's shooting the breeze again.
また授業に遅れて先生に油を搾られた．	I got †raked over the coals by [a severe dressing down from] my teacher for being late again.
そんなことを言うと，かえって火に油を注ぐことになる．	Saying something like that will only add fuel to the fire.
あの作家は脂が乗っていて3年で五つのベストセラーを書いた．	That novelist is going great guns** and has produced five bestsellers in three years.

---

1) oil は液状の植物油および鉱物油． 2) 名詞形の grease は固形油．
3) fat は動物の脂肪．

あふれる
【液体が】湯船から水があふれた.	The bathtub overflowed.
風呂場の水が廊下まであふれてきた.	Water from the bathroom overflowed into the hall.
【物・人が】店頭はどこも品物があふれている.	All the stores are overflowing with merchandise.
週末の街は人であふれかえっている.	The streets are congested [overflowing] with people on the weekends.
【感情・雰囲気が】彼は喜びにあふれていた.	He was brimming with joy.
	He was full of joy.
彼女の声には自信があふれていた.	Her voice was full of confidence.
彼はエネルギーにあふれている.	He has energy to spare.
京都の街は独特の情緒にあふれている.	The streets in Kyoto have a special atmosphere.

あまい (甘い)
【味・香りが】これは甘過ぎる.	This is [tastes] too sweet.
紅茶は甘くしてください.	Please sweeten my tea.
	Please make my tea sweet.
甘いものが好きだ.	I like sweets.
このバラは甘い香りがする.	These roses smell sweet.
私は甘党です.	I have a sweet tooth.
このサケは塩が甘い(薄い).	This salmon is not salty enough.
【言葉が】甘い言葉に誘われた.	I was enticed by his sweet talk.
彼は若い女と見ると甘い言葉をかける.	He flirts with every young woman he meets.
【態度・考えが】彼は子どもに甘い.	He is indulgent with his children.
彼は甘い父親〔夫〕だ.	He's †an indulgent [a permissive, a doting] father [husband].
彼は女に甘い.	He's nice to women.
加藤先生は点が甘い.	Mr. Kato is generous in giving grades.
勉強しないで合格すると思っているのなら考えが甘いよ.	If you think you can pass the examination without studying, you're kidding yourself.
君は物事を甘く考え過ぎだ.	You don't take things seriously enough.
私を甘く見るな.	Don't underestimate me.

あまえる (甘える)
子どもが母親に甘えている.	The child is demanding his mother's attention.
	The child is clinging to his mother.
彼女は随分君に甘えているね.	She really depends on you for everything, doesn't she?

甘えるんじゃない. — Stop expecting everyone to do everything for you.[1]
You shouldn't take everything for granted.[2]

彼女は男の人には甘えた口調で話す. — She always talks like a little girl around men.

いつまでも他人の好意に甘えるわけにはいかない. — I can't take advantage of people's kindness forever.

お言葉に甘えてそうさせていただきます. — I'll accept your kind offer.

> 1) いつも人に頼ってばかりいる人に言う. 2) 自分の境遇について不平ばかり並べて自助努力しない人に言う.

あまやかす (甘やかす)

彼女は子どもを甘やかして育てた. — She brought up her child †indulgently [with indulgence].
She pampered her child.

親に甘やかされたので,彼女はわがままになった. — Her parents are overindulgent and she's become spoiled.

学生を甘やかしてはいけない. — Don't be too †lenient on [permissive with] the students.

あまり (余り)

【余剰・残り】あめをみんなに均等に配ったら余りが出た. — There was some candy left after distributing it equally to everyone.

会は思ったより安く上がって余りが出た. — We had some money left over because the reception didn't cost as much as expected.

【〜以上】クラス会には30人あまり集まった. — There were over 30 people at the class reunion.

寄付金が4万円あまり集まった. — The donations came to over ¥40,000.

【〜すぎる・ひどい】あまりの痛さに声をあげた. — I cried out in pain.
I cried out because it was so painful.

彼女があまり主張するので,最後には皆折れた. — She was so insistent that everyone finally gave in.

あまりに腰が痛かったので起き上がれなかった. — My back was so painful that I couldn't get up.
My back was too painful to get up.

それはあまりな要求だ. — That's asking too much.

彼の言うことは,あまりに理不尽だ. — What he has to say is outrageous.

【〜のあまり】彼女はショックのあ — She was so shocked that she had to go to

まり寝込んでしまった.	bed.
私は驚きのあまり, しばらく口がきけなかった.	I was so surprised that I couldn't say anything for a while.
彼は熱心さのあまり時々やりすぎる.	He's so eager that he sometimes goes overboard.
	In his enthusiasm he sometimes goes too far.
【～して余りある】彼の成功は今までの失敗を補って余りある.	His success more than[1] makes up for past failures.
彼女の悲しみは察するに余りある.	I can really understand her sorrow.
【それほど(～ない)】うちはあまり外食しません.	We don't often eat out.
	We don't eat out much.
あまり時間がない. 急ごう.	There isn't much time. Let's hurry.
現実的な選択肢はあまりない.	There aren't very many realistic choices.
彼女といても, もうあまり楽しくはなかった.	It wasn't very enjoyable being with her anymore.
「英語はしゃべれるんでしょう？」「いえ, あまり…」	"Can you speak English?" "Not really."
【割り算の】5割る3は1余り2.	Five divided by three equals one with a remainder of two.

> 1) この more than は, 動詞句 makes up for にかかる副詞句.

あまる (余る)

「鉛筆は何本余っていますか」「3本余っています」	"How many †pencils are left [extra pencils are there]?" "There're three left."
旅費が1万円ほど余った.	About 10,000 [ten thousand] yen of the money for the trip was left over.
3から2を引けば1余る.	Two from three leaves one.
人手が余っている.	We have more than enough people [hands].

あやうく (危うく)

危うく車にひかれるところだった.	I was almost [nearly] hit by a car.
	I †narrowly escaped [came close to] being hit.
危うく飛行機に乗り遅れるところだった.	I almost [nearly] missed †the plane [my flight].

あやしい (怪しい)

【うさんくさい】怪しい素振りの男がこの辺りをうろついている.	A questionable looking man is hanging around the neighborhood.
彼は怪しげな商売をしている.	He's doing a shady business.

あやしむ

【気味の悪い】隣の部屋で怪しい物音がした.	There was a strange [funny, weird] sound in the next room.
部屋の中は赤や青のライトで照らされ, 怪しい雰囲気だった.	The red and blue lighting in the room created an sleazy atmosphere.
【疑わしい】彼の話は本当かどうか怪しいものだ.	I really wonder whether his story is true or not.
	His story is doubtful [suspicious].
	I have my doubts about his story.
この減量法は効果があるかどうか怪しい.	I have my doubts about whether this diet really works or not.
彼のアリバイは怪しい.	His alibi sounds fishy.
怪しい空模様だ.	The weather looks a little threatening.
雲行き(事態)が怪しくなってきた.	The situation has taken a dark turn.
あの二人の仲はどうも怪しい.	Those two seem to be having some kind of affair.
【まずい・下手】随分怪しげな英語を使っているけど, あの人は本当に英語の先生かしら?	The English he uses is awfully unconvincing. Is he really an English teacher?
彼女は怪しい手つきで魚をおろし始めた.	She awkwardly [ineptly] began to cut the fish.

あやしむ (怪しむ)

事件の張本人ではないかと怪しまれた.	I was suspected of being behind it all.
みんなその大金の出どころを怪しんでいる.	Everybody is skeptical about where all that money came from.

あやまる (謝る)

彼は書類の提出が大幅に遅れたことを謝った.	He apologized for the long delay in sending in the papers.

あらい[1] (荒い)

今日は波が荒い.	The sea is rough today.
彼は言葉は荒っぽいが実際は優しい人だ.	He uses rough language but actually he's a very nice person.
彼女は金遣いが荒い.	She's too free with money.
	She's a spendthrift.
	She spends money carelessly [extravagantly].
彼は気が荒くてすぐ子どもに手を上げる.	He's so violent that he often hits his children.
走ったあと, 息遣いが荒くなった.	I was gasping for air after jogging.
病人の息遣いが荒くなってきた.	The patient is having difficulty breathing.

彼は鼻息が荒い.	He's assertive.
うちの上司は人使いが荒い.	Our boss pushes us too hard.

あらい² (粗い)

この網は目が粗い.	This net has a coarse mesh.
編み目の粗いセーターを見せてください.	Please show me a loosely knit sweater.
この画像は目が粗い.	This picture is grainy.
このパーコレーターには粗くひいたコーヒーを使いなさい.	Use coarsely ground coffee in this percolator.

あらう (洗う)

彼女は夕食の前に子どもたちに手を洗わせた.	She made her children wash their hands before dinner.
プールからあがったらよく目を洗いなさい.	Rinse your eyes out thoroughly when you're through swimming in the pool.
コックはサラダを作る前に, まず野菜を全部洗った.	The cook washed off all the vegetables before preparing the salad.
傷口をよく洗って薬を塗った.	I cleansed the wound and put medicine on it.
僕が食器を洗うよ.	I'll do the dishes.
床をごしごし洗った.	I scrubbed the floor.
この布地は普通の洗剤で洗ってもいいですか.	Is it †OK [all right] to wash this material with an ordinary detergent?
すすぎ洗いは済みましたか.	Have you rinsed these yet?
	Have these [Has it] been rinsed off yet?
この染みは洗っても落ちない.	This stain won't wash [come] out.
波がデッキを洗っていた.	The waves were sweeping up onto the deck.
【調べる】警察は容疑者を洗っている.	The police are making a thorough investigation of the suspect.
やつの素性を洗え.	Check into that guy's past.

あらそう (争う)

金のことで争うのは愚かだ.	It's stupid to fight over money.
法廷で争おうじゃないか.	I'll †see you in [contest it in, take you to] court.
先を争って入ろうとするな.	Don't try to fight your way in first.
バスの中で席を争ってはだめだ.	Don't fight over seats on the bus.
人と争うのは好きじゃない.	I don't like fighting with people.
これは一刻を争う問題だ.	There's no time to lose with this problem.
患者の状態は一刻を争う.	The patient requires immediate attention.
血は争えないね. 彼の作風は亡	It must run in the family. His style is very

なった彼の父親によく似ている. | similar to his late father's.

あらたまる (改まる)
【新しくなる】年が改まったら引っ越す予定だ. | I plan to move early next year.
【形式ばる】そんなに改まることはないよ. | You don't need to be so formal.
彼が急に改まった口調で話し出したので驚いた. | It surprised me that he suddenly started talking in a formal tone.
改まって一体何の話ですか. | Why are you being so stiff [formal]?

あらためて (改めて)
その件は改めて連絡します. | I'll get back to you on this later.
それは改めて話し合いましょう. | We'll talk it over again.
日を改めてお伺いします. | I'll come †another day [some other day].
改めて言うまでもないだろう. | I'm not going to repeat myself.
改めて言うまでもないが, 旅行中は体に気をつけなさい. | I know I'm repeating myself, but you do have to look after yourself when you're traveling.
その事故は雪山の恐ろしさを改めて思い知らせた. | That accident reminded us anew of[1] the dangers of snow-covered mountains.
ゴミの分別の徹底を改めてお願いします. | Please be reminded that the garbage must be separated for recycling.
 | Reminder: garbage must be separated for recycling.[2]

> 1) reminded us of (私たちに〜を思い出させた) に副詞 anew が挿入された形. 2) 掲示板などの貼り紙に書く注意文.

あらためる (改める)
今年になって交通法規が改められた. | The traffic regulations have been revised this year.
その悪習は改めなくてはいけない. | You have to †get over [get rid of] that bad habit.
お釣りを改めてください. | Please check your change.

あらゆる
この動物園にはあらゆる種類の動物がいる. | This zoo has all kinds of animals.
私たちはあらゆる手段を尽くしたが患者を助けることはできなかった. | We tried †every means available [every possible means], but we couldn't help the patient.
彼女はあらゆる機会をとらえて布 | She makes use of every opportunity for

教している. preaching.

あらわす¹ (表す)
今度の失敗は彼の愚かさを表している. This blunder is a perfect example of his stupidity.
言葉に表せないほど夕焼けが美しかった. The beauty of the sunset was beyond all description.
この気持ちをどう言葉に表したらいいのだろう? How can I express my feelings in words?
"V.S.O.P." は何を表していますか? What does "V.S.O.P." stand for?
この抽象画は人間の苦悩を表している. This abstract picture expresses human agony.

あらわす² (現す)
彼はパーティーの終わりになって姿を現した. He showed up just as the party was ending.
彼は紳士を装っていたが遂に正体を現した. He pretended to be a gentleman but in the end he showed himself up for what he really was.

あらわす³ (著す)
その本は10年前に先生が著したものだ. That book was written by my teacher 10 years ago.

あらわれる¹ (表れる)
彼は何も言わなかったが, 苦悩がその顔に表れていた. He didn't say a word, but you could see the suffering in his face.
これは彼女の愛情の表れだ. This is an expression of her love.

あらわれる² (現れる)
霧の中から山々が現れた. The mountains appeared through the mist.
5分たっても現れないなら彼抜きで出発しましょう. If he doesn't show up in five minutes, let's go without him.
明日の朝になっても彼女が現れない場合は捜索隊を組んで彼女を捜さなければならないだろう. If she doesn't turn up by tomorrow morning, we will have to organize a search party to look for her.

ありがたい
【感謝】ご親切にありがとう. Thank you for your kindness.
それはありがたい. That's great./That'll really help.
そうしてくれるとありがたい. I would appreciate it.
それはありがた迷惑です. Don't bother!/Stop meddling.

	Thanks but no thanks.
【喜ばしい】ありがたいことに雨がやんだ.	Fortunately, it stopped raining.
彼はどこの家でもありがたくない客だ.	He's an unwelcome guest at any house.
【尊い】教会でありがたいお説教を聴いた.	I listened to an edifying* sermon at church.
彼は病気になって初めて健康のありがたさが分かった.	Only after experiencing illness did he feel grateful for his (good) health.

ありふれた

彼はありふれた(特別どうということはない)家庭に育った.	He was raised in an ordinary home.
ありふれた名前だったので覚えていない.	It was such a common name that it's slipped my mind.
ありふれた話だね.	It's an old story.
その映画はありふれた恋愛物語だった.	The movie was †a run-of-the-mill [just another] love story.
ありふれた宣伝文句(きまり文句)では買い手の心をとらえられない.	You can't get people to buy things with clichéd [run-of-the-mill] advertising.

ある (有・在る)

【存在する】机の上に本がある.	There's a book on the desk.
ここにいい辞書がある.	Here is a good dictionary.
私のはどこにあるの?	Where's mine?
部屋には大きな窓がある.	The room has a big window.
時間は十分ある.	There's plenty of time.
【位置する】そのホテルは市の中央部にある.	That hotel is (located, situated) downtown.
駅は家から歩いて10分の所にある.	The station is a ten-minute walk from my house.
教会は丘の上にある.	The church stands on the hill.
その島は中国の東にある.	That island is to the east of China.
【持っている】お金はいくらかある.	I have a little money.
彼には妻子がある.	He has a wife and children.
【起こる】今朝地震があった.	There was an earthquake this morning.
昨夜近所で火事があった.	There was a fire [A fire broke out] in my neighborhood last night.
この横断歩道ではよく事故がある.	Traffic accidents often occur [happen] at this pedestrian crossing.
そんなことがあるものか.	That's impossible.
彼女はあることないことを言いふ	She spread around stories †with no founda-

らした.	tion [she had just made up].
【行われる】日曜日にクラス会があった.	We had [There was] a class reunion last Sunday.
試験はいつあるの？	When is the test?
【経験がある】パリに行ったことがありますか？	Have you ever been to Paris?
彼には会ったことがある.	I've met him before.
【数量がある】駅から家まで1キロある.	It's one kilometer from the station to my house.
あの人は背が170センチある.	He's 170 centimeters tall.
私は体重が60キロ以上ある.	I weigh over 60 kilograms.
【売っている】(この店には) 牛乳はありますか？	Do you have milk (at this store)?
その本ならどこの本屋にでもある.	Any bookstore has that book.
【時には〜する】土曜日は本来休みだが，仕事に行くこともある.	I'm supposed to have Saturdays off but there are times when I have to work.
彼女に会うことはあってもなかなか話をしない.	Even when I see her we scarcely talk.

ある〜

ある日見知らぬ人が訪れた.	One day a stranger came to my house.
昨日ある喫茶店で彼女を見かけた.	Yesterday I saw her at a coffee shop.
ある書評ではこの本は絶賛されている.	One of the reviews praised this book highly.
ある人が君のことを褒めていたよ.	Someone [A certain person] was saying nice things about you.
ある人は正しいと言い，ある人は間違っていると言う.	Some say it's right while others say it's wrong.

あるいは

この夏はドイツかあるいはフランスに行きたいと思う.	I'd like to go to Germany or else [maybe] France this summer.
あるいはそうかもしれません.	It just may be so.

あるく (歩く)

車に乗るより歩くほうが好きだ.	I prefer walking to going by car.
疲れてもう一歩も歩けない.	I'm so tired I can't take [walk] another step.
家から駅まで歩いて5分です.	It's a five-minute walk [It takes five minutes to walk] from my house to the station.

アルバイト

明日は午後アルバイトがある.	I'll be at my part-time job tomorrow afternoon.
彼の奥さんは小遣い稼ぎにコンビニでアルバイトをしている.	His wife works part-time at a convenience store to earn spending money.
彼は会社に勤めるかたわら,住所入力のアルバイトをしている.	Besides his full-time job at the company, he moonlights inputting address lists.
夏休みは海の家でアルバイトに精を出す毎日だった.	I worked hard every day at my summer job at the beach house.
うちの部は正社員よりアルバイトのほうが多い.	There are more part-timers than regular employees in our department.
あの新入社員はまだアルバイト気分が抜けない.	That new employee is still acting like a part-timer.

あれる (荒れる)

今日外は荒れ模様だ.	We're having quite a storm out today.
今朝から海が荒れてきた.	The sea has become rough since this morning.
庭が荒れている.	The garden is overgrown.
畑が荒れている.	The field lies in waste.
一家が去って家は荒れていた.	After the family moved out the house became run-down [dilapidated].
水仕事をたくさんすると手が荒れる.	When you do a lot of scrubbing and washing, your hands get rough and dry.
彼は今日荒れてるよ.	He's in a really bad mood today.

アレルギー

アレルギーのある方は事前に申し出てください.	Please let us know ahead of time if you have any allergies.[1]
	Those with allergies should inform us in advance.[2]
彼はアレルギー体質だ.	He has allergies.
彼女は重度の猫アレルギーだ.	She has severe allergic reactions to cats.
私は慢性のアレルギー性鼻炎だ.	I have chronic nasal inflammation from allergies.
【毛嫌い】私は高校時代から数学アレルギーなの.	Ever since high school I've been allergic to math.

> 1) の文はどちらかと言えば口語的,2) の文は書き言葉的.

あわせる (合わせる)

【一つにする】力を合わせて頑張ろう.	Let's work together and hang in there.

全部合わせて(金額)いくらですか.	How much is it all together?
	How much does it all come to?
私の高校には全学年合わせて900人の生徒がいます.	My high school has a total enrollment of 900 students.
声を合わせて歌った.	We sang in chorus.
【適合・照合させる】じゅうたんに合わせてカーテンの色を選んだ.	We picked out the color of the drapes to match the carpet.
型紙に合わせて裁断しなさい.	Cut it †to fit [according to] the pattern.
そのスカートにこのブラウスを合わせるとすてきですよ.	This blouse would be stunning with that skirt.
お父さんの仕事の都合に合わせて出発の日取りを決めよう.	Let's arrange the date of departure to fit Father's work schedule.
原文と合わせてみると誤訳がたくさんあった.	I found a lot of mistranslations when I compared it with the original.
答案を先生の解答と合わせた.	I checked my answers against the teacher's answer sheet.
目覚まし時計を6時に合わせた.	I set the alarm clock for six o'clock.
私たちは音楽に合わせて踊った.	We danced to the music.

あわただしい (慌ただしい)

かなり慌ただしい旅行だった.	It was a rather hectic trip.
彼女は慌ただしく会社から出て行った.	She left work in a hurry [rush].

あわてる (慌てる)

慌てるな.	Don't be so hasty.
	Don't be in such a hurry [rush].
彼は慌てて列車に飛び乗った.	He hastily jumped on the train.
慌てて,財布を忘れてきた.	In my haste I forgot my wallet.
彼女はどんなときにも慌てない.	She never loses her cool.
彼の失敗は皆を慌てさせた.	His mistakes threw everyone into confusion.
彼女は慌て者だ.	She's a scatterbrain.

あわれ (哀れ)

哀れな話を聞いた.	I heard a pathetic story.
彼は彼女の哀れな生活を知っても何の手助けもしなかった.	He made no effort to help her even after he found out what a wretched [miserable] life she was living.
哀れにも子どもたちは両親を交通事故で一度に失った.	Tragically, the children lost both their parents in the same traffic accident.

あわれむ (哀れむ)

彼らを哀れむのはよそう.	Let's not pity them.
人に哀れまれるのは嫌いだ.	I don't like being pitied by others.
彼に哀れみは請いたくない.	I don't want (to ask for) his pity.
哀れみ深い婦人に助けられた.	I was helped by a compassionate lady.

あん (案)

いい案が浮かんだよ.	I have a good idea.
彼の案は会議で審議された.	His plan [proposal] was deliberated at the meeting.
議案は否決された.	The bill was †rejected [voted down].
案に相違して彼女はパーティーに着物姿で現れた.	She surprised everyone by coming to the party dressed in a *kimono*.

あんい (安易)

君は物事を安易に考え過ぎる.	You take things †lightly [too easily].
安易な方法ばかり探していては良くない.	It's not good to just look for easy ways out.
最近は皆, 安易に離婚するようになった.	Recently people divorce so casually.

あんがい (案外)

彼女は案外若いんだよ.	She's younger than you'd think.
彼は案外親切なのかもしれない.	He may be kind for all I know.
列車は案外すいていた.	The train was not as crowded as we had expected.
	Contrary to expectations,* the train was not so crowded.

あんじる (案じる)

【心配】母親は外国に一人住む娘の身を案じている.	She frets constantly about her daughter who lives by herself overseas.
案ずるより生むが易し.	It's easier than you think.
【考え出す】彼の鼻をあかそうと一計を案じた.	I've come up with a way to show him who's who.

あんしん (安心)

それを聞いて安心した.	I'm relieved to hear that.
どうぞご安心ください.	Please put your mind at ease.
安心するのはまだ早い.	It's too early yet to †rest easy [put your mind at ease].
ここまで来ればもう安心だ.	Now that we've come this far, we can relax.

病人はもう安心です.	The patient is out of danger.
彼は安心できる（信頼できる）人だ.	He's a reliable man.
子どもが立派に成人したのでいつでも安心して死ねる.	Knowing that my children are grown up and doing well on their own, I can die in peace.

あんぜん（安全）

ここにいれば安全だ.	We're safe if we stay here.
安全運転をしなさい.	Drive safely.
国家は国民の生命，財産の安全を保障すべきだ.	The government should guarantee the safety of its citizens' lives and property.

あんてい（安定）

政局はかなり安定してきた.	The political situation has become relatively stable.
経済の安定は政府の責務だ.	Economic stability is the duty [responsibility] of government.
中年になってやっと生活の安定を得た.	I finally secured a stable life when I became middle-aged.
このテーブルは不安定だ.	This table is unstable.

あんな

あんなやつを信用するな.	Don't trust a guy like him.
あんな小説のどこがいいの？	What do you see in a novel like that?
あんなうそつきは相手にしない.	I won't have anything to do with such a liar.
あんなに心配しなくてもよかったのに.	You shouldn't have worried so much.

あんない（案内）

家まで案内します.	I'll show you the way to my house.
この方を席に案内してください.	Please show him to his seat.
町をご案内しましょうか.	Shall I show you around the town?
	Would you like me to show you the town?
案内所は駅の構内にある.	The information counter [center] is inside the station.
私は東京は不案内です.	I don't know my way around Tokyo very well.

あんのじょう（案の定）

案の定，彼は遅れて来た.	Sure enough, he showed up late.
案の定，彼は失敗した.	As I had feared, he failed.

あんらく (安楽)

安楽な生活が好きだ.	I like a comfortable life.
老後は安楽に暮らしたい.	I want to lead an easy life when I grow old.
安楽死が社会問題になってきた.	Mercy killing [Euthanasia] has become a social problem.

い

いい

【良い】あの人はいい人だ.	He's a good [nice] person.
彼は人がいい.	He's too easygoing for his own good.
彼女は歴史の試験でいい成績を取った.	She got good marks on the history test.
このかばんは品物がいい.	This bag is of high quality.
この花瓶は形がいいですね.	This vase has a nice shape, doesn't it?
とてもいい話でみんな感動した.	That story was so good that it moved everyone.
いい天気ですね.	It's nice [clear, sunny] out, isn't it?
	It's a nice day, isn't it?
彼女はいい女だ.	She's quite a woman.
	She's beautiful [good-looking].
彼はいい男だ.	He's †all man [a handsome hunk**].
	He's handsome [good-looking].
何かいいことがあったの？	(Did) Something good happen?
【効力がある】この薬はぜんそくにいい.	This medicine is good for asthma.
【かなりの】いい値段だね.	This is rather expensive.
【十分】もういいよ. おなかがいっぱいだ.	I've had enough. I'm full.
手伝いはもういいから勉強なさい.	I'll do the rest. Go (and) study.
古くても使えればいい.	If I can use it, it doesn't matter how old it is.
「君も一緒に来るかい」「僕はいいよ」	"Do you want to come, too?" "No thanks."
【望ましい・好ましい】明日晴れるといいね.	I hope it's nice tomorrow.
こんなとき彼がいたらいいのに.	I wish he were around at times like this.

その人に会えればいいですね.	I hope you'll be able to meet him.
コーヒーと紅茶とどちらがいいですか.	Which would you prefer [like], coffee or tea?
僕はロックよりジャズのほうがいい.	I prefer jazz to rock.
早く出発したほうがいい.	You'd better †hurry up and leave [get going].
【かまわない】「いいかい」「いいよ」	"OK?" "OK."
「これでいいですか」「いいですよ」	"Is this all right?" "Yes, that's fine."
「入ってもいいですか」「いいですよ」	"May I come in? [Is it all right if I come in?]" "Sure."
「たばこを吸ってもいいですか」「いいですよ」	"Do you mind if I smoke?" "No, go ahead."
明日は来なくてもいいよ.	You don't have to come tomorrow.
試験〔あいつ〕なんかどうなってもいい.	I couldn't care less about †the test [that guy].
この文章は省いてもいい.	This sentence can be omitted.
ちょっといいですか. 質問があります.	Do you have a minute? I have a question to ask you.
【適当な】君のいいようにしてくれ.	Do as you like.
もう彼が来てもいい頃だ.	It's about time he got here.
いいところへ来た.	You've come at just the right time.

いいかげん

【でたらめ】彼の言うことはいいかげんだ.	What he says is unreliable.
	You can't rely on what he says.
いいかげんなことを言うな.	Don't give me that.
いいかげんに答えておいた.	I put him off with a vague answer.
彼の法律の知識はいいかげんなものだ.	His knowledge of law isn't very reliable.
私はいいかげんな仕事はしない.	I never do sloppy [slipshod] work.
いいかげんな気持ちではこの仕事はできない.	You can't do this job if you're halfhearted about it.
【ほどほど】いいかげんにしろ.	That's enough./Enough's enough.
おしゃべりもいいかげんにしろ.	That's about enough of your chattering.
もういいかげんにしておいたら？	Haven't you had enough?
もう勉強もいいかげんにしたら？	Haven't you studied just about enough?
【この辺で】いいかげんに寝たら？	Isn't it about time you went to bed?
いいかげんにあきらめなさい.	Why don't you just give up?
彼もいいかげん分かりそうなものだ.	He should have gotten the message by now.

この仕事にもいいかげん飽きてきた.	I've had just about all of this work I can take.
	I'm starting to get fed up with this work.

いいきみ (いい気味)

あいつが失敗するとはいい気味だ.	That guy blew it. (It) Serves him right.
彼は私が落第したのをいい気味だと思っているようだ.	He seems to think †I deserve [it serves me right] to have failed a grade.

いいすぎる (言い過ぎる)

君は彼女にちょっと言い過ぎたようだ.	I think you gave it to her a bit too strong.
それはちょっと彼に対して言い過ぎじゃないか.	Wasn't that too strong a thing to say to him?
昨日は僕も言い過ぎた. 許してくれ.	I really overdid it yesterday. Forgive me.
彼に文句を言うのもいいけれど言い過ぎるなよ.	You can complain to him, but don't overdo it.

いいわけ (言いわけ)

そんなことは言いわけにすぎない.	That's nothing but an excuse.
夫はいつも言いわけばかりする.	My husband is always †full of excuses [making excuses].
遅刻の言いわけを考えながら待ち合わせ場所へ向かった.	I headed for our meeting place trying to think of an excuse for being late.
私はいっさい言いわけするつもりはない.	I have absolutely no intention of making excuses for myself.
そいつは苦しい言いわけだな.	That's a pretty poor [lame, sorry] excuse.
言いわけするんじゃない！	I don't want to hear any excuses!
	Don't give me that!
言いわけがましい男は嫌いだ.	I can't stand men who make up excuses.

いいん (委員)

委員は全員会議室に集合してください.	Will all committee members please gather in the conference room?
その議案は委員会にかけられ通過した.	That bill was presented [sent] to the committee and passed.
彼は生徒会の委員〔市の教育委員〕だ.	He's a member of †the student council [the city's school board].
彼女はクラス委員長だ.	She's (the) president of her class.

いう (言う)

【口に出す】彼は君に何と言った？	What did he say to you?

あなたはそう言い切れるか？	Are you positive?
私の口からは言いかねる．	It's hard for me to broach the subject.
そのことを言いそびれた．	I just couldn't bring myself to talk about that.
私の言うことを聞きなさい．	Listen to †me [what I say].
彼はそう言い捨てて出て行った．	He said that over his shoulder as he went out.
言うことはそれだけか．	Is that all you have to say?
ほかに何か言うことはありませんか．	Do you have anything else to say?
	Is there anything you'd like to add?
もうあなたには何も言うことはない．	I don't have anything to say to you.
彼は世界で十指に入る芸術家と言ってよいだろう．	You could probably say that he's one of the 10 best artists in the world.
私は人前でものを言うのは苦手だ．	I'm not good at speaking in front of people.
彼のあの言い方は許せない．	I won't stand for the way he talked to me.
あなたの言うことが分からない．	I don't understand what you mean.
	I can't follow you.
彼が有能な若者だということは言うまでもない．	He's obviously a capable young man.
彼は勉強など言うに及ばず，外で遊ぶことさえ面倒臭がる怠け者だ．	He's so lazy that he doesn't even bother to go out and have a good time, †let alone [much less] study.
彼はよく独り言を言う．	He talks to himself a lot.
【うわさする】市民は皆市長のことを良く〔悪く〕言っている．	All the townspeople speak well [ill] of the mayor.
みんなそう言っていますよ．	That's what everybody's saying.
【告げる】人に言うなよ．	Don't tell anyone.
彼に来るように言いなさい．	Tell him to come.
だから言ったじゃないか．	I told you, didn't I?
	What did I tell you?
そんなこといちいち言われなくとも分かっている．	I can understand something like that without it being spelled out to me.
【表現する】言葉では言い尽くせない．	It's beyond description.
	I can't fully express myself with words.
「セミ」は英語で何と言いますか．	How do you say "semi" in English?
彼の仕事ぶりは良く言えば丁寧，悪く言えばのろい．	Putting it nicely I'd say he does his work conscientiously, otherwise I'd say he's just slow.
彼女は言いしれぬ不安を覚えた．	She sensed an inexpressible uneasiness.
【称する】山本さんという人が来た．	A man named Yamamoto came by.
彼は子どもの頃神童と言われた．	As a child, he was called a prodigy.

彼は先生というより友達みたいだ.	He is more like a friend than a teacher.
【伝え聞く】彼は入院しているということだ.	They say [I hear] he's in the hospital.
彼はなかなかの金持ちだと言われている.	He's said to be quite wealthy.
鈴木氏が次期社長だろうと言われている.	Everyone's saying that Mr. Suzuki will probably be the next president.
好景気は当分続くだろうと言われている.	It is said that favorable economic conditions will continue for quite some time.
【～という】近々引っ越すという手紙を彼女からもらった.	I got a letter from her saying that she's going to be moving soon.
息子から金を送ってくれという電話を受けた.	I got a phone call from my son asking me to send some money.
【～と言えば】ジョンと言えば,今彼はどこに住んでいるの?	Speaking of John, where's he living now?
そう言えば,彼はどうしているかな.	That reminds me. How is he?
【慣用】この世界では金〔実力〕がものを言う.	In this world, †money talks [ability counts].

いか (以下)

【～から下】59点以下は不合格だ.	Fifty-nine points or less[1] is a fail.
机の幅が1.5メートル以下ならそのドアから入る.	If the width of the desk is less than 1.5 [one point five] meters, it will make it through the door.
外の気温は10°C以下だ.	It's †below [less than] ten degrees centigrade outside.
彼は自分の生活水準を平均以下と考えている.	He thinks his standard of living is below the average.
3歳以下の子どもは入場無料です.	Children three years of age and under[2] are admitted free of charge.
中学生以下は親の許可がいる.	Those of middle school age and under require parental consent.
そのビルの7階以下は店舗になっている.	Stores occupy the first seven floors of that building.
あいつは動物以下だ.	He's lower than an animal.
【あと】時間がないので以下は略す.	I'll omit the rest for lack of time.
以下の事は内密に願います.	Please keep the following a secret.
【始めとして】団長の考古学者以下10名の発掘隊が中国を訪れた.	Ten excavators including the chief archaeologist went to China.

> 1) 数量を厳密に言う必要があるときはこのように ... or less を使う.
> 2) 年齢を厳密に言う場合は ... and under とする.

いがい¹ (以外)

私以外にそのことを知る人はいない.	Nobody knows about that but [except, besides] me.
彼はそれ以外にスペイン語も話す.	He speaks Spanish †as well [too].
彼は詩以外に多くの小説も書いた.	He's written many novels †as well as [besides] poems.
職員以外は立ち入りを禁ずる.	Employees only.

いがい² (意外)

意外な結果に終わった.	It turned out unexpectedly.
コンサートで意外な人に会った.	I ran into someone at the concert I never expected to see.
意外に早く病気が治った.	My recovery was surprisingly rapid.
意外なことに彼が (選挙に) 当選した.	He surprised everyone by winning the election.
	He won the election to our surprise.
彼が猫好きとは意外だ.	It's surprising that he's a cat-lover.
	I didn't expect [I wouldn't have expected] him to be a cat-lover.
彼が犯人とは意外だ.	I never would have thought that he would turn out to be the criminal.
	He's the criminal? Who would have expected it?

いかが

ご機嫌いかが.	How are you?
いかがお過ごしですか.	How are you getting along?
ご商売はいかがですか.	How's business?
(お味は) いかがですか.	How do you like it?／How is it?
パーティーはいかがでしたか.	How did you enjoy the party?
	How was the party?
いかがお考えですか.	What do you think about it?
この古いいすはいかがいたしましょうか.	What shall I do with this old chair?
紅茶を一杯いかがですか.	Would you †like [care for] a cup of tea?
月曜の6時はいかがですか.	How is six o'clock next Monday?

いかす (生・活かす)

【生かす】この魚は殺さずにしばら	I want to keep this fish alive for a while.

【活用する】今の会社では彼の才能はいかされていない.	His talent is not being put to use [They don't make use of his talent] at his present company.
才能を最大限にいかす道に進みなさい.	Pursue that which makes the most of your talent.
彼女は経験をいかして料理教室を開いた.	Putting her experience to good use [Using her experience] she started a cooking school.
いい辞書なんだからいかして使いなさい.	It's such a good dictionary that you should put it to good use.

いかり (怒り)

その言葉が彼の怒りを買った.	That statement angered him.
彼は私に怒りをぶちまけた.	He took his anger out on me.
	He vented his anger on me.
彼は激しい怒りに燃えた.	He was burning with rage.
彼女はそれを見て怒りを爆発させた.	She blew up when she saw it.

いき¹ (息)

走るとすぐ息が切れる.	I start gasping for air as soon as I start running.
少年は息を切らして走った.	The boy ran gasping for breath.
吐く息が白く見えた.	(It was so cold that) I could see my breath.
息が苦しい.	I can hardly breathe.
まだ息はあるか.	Is he still breathing?
虫の息だ.	His breathing is faint.
彼はたった今, 息を引き取った.	He breathed his last just now.
	He just stopped breathing.
彼は息もつかずにしゃべった.	He talked breathlessly.
息つく暇もないほど忙しい.	I'm too busy to even take a breather.
彼女のあまりの美しさに私たちは息をのんだ.	She was so beautiful that †it took our breath away [we held our breath].
たばこの煙で息が詰まりそうだ.	The tobacco [cigarette] smoke is suffocating.
彼といると息が詰まる.	I find it oppressive to be with him.
私は物陰から息を詰めてその光景を見守った.	Holding my breath, I watched the scene from the shadows.
彼らは息を殺して敵の現れるのを待った.	They held their breath and waited for the enemy to appear.
我々はぴったり息が合っている.	We are in perfect harmony.
焦らずに息の長い仕事をしていき	I don't want to rush into anything. I want

たい. | to commit (myself) to something long-term.
息の長い女優になりたい. | I want to have a long career as an actress.

いき² (意気)
我がチームの意気が上がった. | Our team's morale has soared.
私たちは試合に勝って意気揚々と帰って来た. | We won the game and †returned in high spirits [came back in a great mood].
彼は意気消沈している. | He's downhearted.
彼は意気込んで仕事に取りかかった. | He enthusiastically buckled down to the task.
最初の意気込みもうせた. | I lost my initial enthusiasm.
二人はすっかり意気投合した. | They really hit it off.

いきいき (生き生き)
彼女はいつも生き生きしている. | She's always lively.
生き生きとした描写だ. | This is a vivid [lively] description.
彼は生き生きと様子を語った. | He described the scene vividly.
この絵は生き生きしている. | This picture is full of life.

いきおい (勢い)
彼は勢いをつけて跳び上がった. | Mustering his energy, he leaped.
あのヒットでうちのチームは勢いづいた. | That hit gave our team a new burst of energy.
あの会社の勢いも衰えてきた. | That company's growth has slowed down.
その場の勢いでスト決行が決まった. | The momentum built up then and there and we decided to strike.
酒の勢いで彼は上司に不満をぶつけた. | Emboldened by alcohol, he finally expressed his dissatisfaction to his boss.
彼も時の勢いには逆らえなかった. | He wasn't able to go against the tide of the times.
いくら放水しても火の勢いは衰えなかった. | No matter how much water was poured on it, the fire kept on burning as fiercely as ever.
川が勢いよく流れている. | The river is flowing swiftly.
水道の水が勢いよく出た. | The water gushed out.
彼らは勢いよく目的地に進んで行った. | They made their way energetically to their destination.
彼が勢いよく部屋に飛び込んで来た. | He burst into the room.

いきぐるしい (息苦しい)
たばこの煙で部屋が息苦しくなった. | The smoke made the room very stuffy.

た.
満員電車の中は暑く息苦しかった. / It was hot and suffocating on the packed train.
絶望的な状況に部屋の中には息苦しい沈黙が流れた. / In that hopeless situation a heavy silence filled the room.

いきさつ
ここへいたるまでには様々ないきさつがあった. / So many things happened before getting to this point.
離婚までのいきさつを友人に打ち明けた. / I confided to my friend about the circumstances leading to my divorce. / I told my friend all [everything] about my divorce.
今までのいきさつから見ても解決するのは難しそうだ. / Given the complexity of the situation †to date [until now], it would seem very difficult to resolve.
どういういきさつで地球の反対側に住むようになったのですか？ / How did you come to live on the opposite side of the world?

いきづまる¹ (行き詰まる)
賃上げを巡る労使の交渉は行き詰まっている. / Negotiations between labor and management over raising wages have come to a standstill.
仕事で行き詰まったときはいつも彼に相談する. / I always consult him when I get stuck at work.
手を使い果たし, 次の一手に行き詰まった. / After trying everything, I just couldn't figure out what to do next.[1]
このようなやり方ではすぐに行き詰まってしまうだろう. / If we keep doing this, we'll probably soon †find ourselves at a dead end [reach a dead end].
これが行き詰まりを打開する唯一の方法だ. / This is the only way †out of the deadlock [to break the deadlock].

1) 実際のゲームの場合にも比喩的な意味にも使う.

いきづまる² (息詰まる)
テニスコートでは二人の息詰まる熱戦が繰り広げられた. / A breathtaking match between the two of them unfolded on the tennis court.
彼女はその場の息詰まるような緊張に耐え切れず外に出た. / Unable to bear the pressure, she went outside.
その戦争映画は息詰まるような場面の連続だった. / That war film was cram-packed with thrilling scenes.

いきる (生きる)

【生存】
この亀は生きているの？	Is this turtle really alive?
生きて帰れるとは思わなかった．	I never thought I would return alive.
父は80歳まで生きた．	My father lived to be eighty.
彼らは20日間パンと水だけで生きた．	They lived on only bread and water for 20 days.
彼は生きるか死ぬかの瀬戸際にいる．	He's hovering between life and death.
それは私にとって生きるか死ぬかの問題だ．	That is a question of life or death for me.
彼女は生き返った．	She †came back [returned] to life.
ただ生きているというだけだ．	I'm just [merely] existing.
生きているうちに世界中の人々の暮らしを見たい．	I want to see the way people live around the world before I die.
人類は氷河期を生き延びた．	The human race survived the ice age.
その料理屋では目の前で生きた魚を料理する．	They prepare live fish for serving right before your eyes at that restaurant.
草だって生きている．	Even a blade of grass has life.[1]
生き物をかわいがりなさい．	Be kind to all creatures (great and small). Be nice to all living things.

【生活】
生きるために働いた．	I worked in order to live.
生きるとは辛いことだ．	Life is hard.
生きるだけでやっとだ．	It's all I can do to keep body and soul together.
彼の生き方は理想的だ．	His way of life seems ideal.
彼は芸一筋に生きた．	He lived his life for his art. Art was his life.

【効果・価値を持つ】
この一語で文全体が生きる．	This one word brings the whole sentence to life.
先生のその時の言葉は今なお私たちの心の中に生きている．	The teacher's words spoken at the time still remain fresh in our minds today.
彼の思想は今日なお生きている．	His thought lives on today.
彼は死すともその理想は生き続けるだろう．	His ideals will live on after his death.
これで彼の残した金も生きるだろう．	This means the money he left will be put to good use.
生きた英語を学ぶためにアメリカに渡った．	I went to America to learn †living English [English as it's really spoken].

> 1) live は「生きて動いている」ニュアンスなのでここでは使えない．

いく (行く)

今度はいつアメリカに行くの．	When will you go to America next?

彼は今パリに行っている.	He's in Paris now. / He's gone to Paris.
ハワイに行ったことがありますか.	Have you ever been to Hawaii?
どこへ行ってたの？	Where have you been?
銀行へ行ってきたところだ.	I've just been to the bank.
「ちょっと来てくれないか」「今行きます」	"Can you come here a minute?" "I'm coming. [I'll be right there.]"
お隣に行って，金づちを借りてきなさい.	Go next door and ask if you can borrow a hammer.
娘は短大へ行っています.	My daughter †is going [goes] to a junior college.
日曜日には教会に行きます.	I go to church every Sunday.
旅行〔遠足〕に行った.	I went on †a trip [an excursion].
ハイキングに行った.	I went †hiking [on a hike].
釣り〔買い物, スキー〕に行った.	I went fishing [shopping, skiing].
散歩〔ドライブ〕に行った.	I went for a walk [drive].
彼女は病院と家を行ったり来たりしている.	She goes back and forth from her house to the hospital.
どんな母親でも自分の息子が戦場に行くことはないようにと願うものだ.	Every mother hopes her son will never have to go off to war.
考え事をしていて彼の家を行き過ぎてしまった.	I was so absorbed in thought that I walked right past his house.
彼は往来を行く人々を眺めていた.	He was watching the people coming and going.
この電車は渋谷へ行きますか.	Does this train go to Shibuya?
【行われる】うまくいったか.	Did it †go [turn out] well?
計画は思いどおりにいっている.	The project is going as †planned [we want it to].
【～ていく】おばあさんは足もとに気をつけながら階段を下りていった.	Watching her step, the old woman walked down the stairs.
食事していったら？	Why don't you stay and eat?
だんだん暖かくなっていく.	It's gradually getting warmer.

いく～ (幾～)

そこに集まったのはみんなで幾人ですか？	How many people in all were gathered there?
ブラジルから日本まで船で来ると幾日かかりますか.	How many days does it take to get to Japan from Brazil by ship?
幾度となく彼女に電話したが留守だった.	I kept calling her but she never answered the phone.
彼ほど優秀な成績を収めた者はこ	Only a handful of people have ever gotten

れまでに幾人もいない. | grades as good as his. / Only a few people have been able to obtain such good grades as he.
今年もあと幾日もない. | There are only a few days left in the year.

いくつ
【数】いくつあめが欲しいの？ | How many candies do you want?
問題がいくつかある. | There are [We have] some problems.
桃はいくつか残っていますか. | Are there any peaches left?
(桃は) もういくつもない. | There're hardly any (peaches) left.
イチゴをいくつも食べた. | I ate a lot of strawberries.
ミカンならいくつでも食べられる. | There's no limit to the number of tangerines I can eat.
いくつでも好きなだけお持ちください. | Take as many as you want.
お砂糖はいくつ？ | How many cubes [spoonfuls] of sugar would you like?

【年齢】坊や, 年はいくつ？ | How old are you, boy?
いくつからピアノを始めたの？ | How old were you when you started piano lessons?

いくら
【どのくらい】これはいくらですか. | How much is this?
米5キロでいくら (値段) ですか. | How much is it for five kilograms of rice?
いくらで買ったんですか. | How much [What] did you pay for it? / How much did you buy it for?
この指輪をお金にするといくらぐらいになりますか. | About how much (money) †is this ring worth [can I get for this ring]?
小麦粉はいくら買いましたか. | How much flour did you buy?
いくら (値段) でもいい, 買うよ. | I'll pay whatever you ask for it.
金はいくらでも出しましょう. | I'm willing to pay any amount of money.
米ならいくらでもある. | There's plenty of rice.
まだいくらでも方法はある. | There are still quite a few ways left.
米ならいくらでも持って行きなさい. | Take as much rice as you want.

【少し】金はいくらも持っていない. | I don't have much money with me.
面白い本はいくらもない. | There aren't many interesting books.
コーヒーはいくらも残っていない. | There's not much coffee left.
時間はもういくらもない. | There's hardly any time left.
私がいくらか払うよ. | I'll pay for †some [a part] of it.
いくらかお金を貸してくれませんか. | Would you mind lending me †some [a little] money?
「米はいくらか残っていますか」 | "Is there any rice left?" "Yes, there is

「はい,（いくらか）残っています」	(some)."
【どんなに～しても】いくらお金を出してもらってもこの絵は売りません.	I won't sell this painting, no matter how much money you offer me.
いくら時間がかかってもよいからいいものを作りなさい.	You can have as much time as you like, so please make something nice [good].
いくら水を飲んでものどが渇く.	No matter how much water I drink, I'm still thirsty.
いくら遅く〔少なく〕てもかまわない.	It doesn't matter [I don't care] how late [little] it is.
いくら働いてもお金がたまらない.	No matter how much I work, I can't save any money.
いくら彼が頭が良くてもこの問題は解けないだろう.	No matter how smart he is, he probably won't be able to solve this problem.
いくらあなたの頼みでも私にはできません.	I (simply) can't do it, even for you.
いくら早く来ても早過ぎるということはない.	You can't come too early.
いくら厳重に警戒してもし過ぎるということはない.	You can't make security too tight. The security can't be made too tight.
いくら何でもその言い方はひど過ぎる.	No matter how you look at it, that's a terrible way to put it.

いけない

【悪い】風邪をひいたの？ それはいけないね.	You have a cold? That's too bad.
いけない子ね. また散らかしたままにして.	Bad boy [girl]—leaving your things scattered about like that again.
いけないのは君だ.	It's your fault. You're the one to blame.
君のいけないところは人の話をよく聞かない点だ.	The trouble with you is that you don't listen to what others are saying.
この計算のしかたではいけない.	You shouldn't calculate like this. This way of calculating is wrong.
【必要】朝御飯を食べなければいけないよ.	You †have to [should] eat breakfast.
友達を迎えに空港まで行かなければいけないんだ.	I've got to go to the airport to meet my friend.
【禁止】ここでたばこを吸ってはいけません.	You †can't [shouldn't, must not] smoke here.
【不都合】雨が降るといけないから傘を持って行きなさい.	Take an umbrella in case it rains.

彼に怒られるといけないからやめておこうよ.	We'd better not get him mad at us, so let's not do it.

いけん (意見)

【考え】これについてあなたの意見はどうですか.	What's your opinion about this? What do you think about this?
彼の意見ではその値段は高過ぎる.	In his opinion that price is too high.
何か意見はありませんか.	Does anybody have any comments?
私は特に意見はない.	I don't have any †comments [particular opinion].
この問題についてはあなたと同意見です.	I agree with your opinion on this problem.
この点では意見が合う〔合わない〕.	We agree [disagree] on this point.
我々は意見の一致をみた.	We were of the same opinion.
我々は意見の相違をみた.	We had a difference of opinion.
結局意見がまとまらなかった.	In the end nobody saw eye to eye.
意見が分かれた.	Opinion was divided.
【説教】父は息子に意見した.	The father gave his son a talking-to. The father admonished his son.*

いげん (威厳)

彼は威厳がある〔に欠ける〕.	He has [lacks] dignity.
彼はどこかしら威厳がある.	There's something dignified about him.
それは彼の威厳にかかわるのでやらないだろう.	It's beneath his dignity so he won't do it.

いご (以後)

あの事件以後彼はどうなった？	What happened to him after that incident?
それ以後彼からの便りはない.	That was the last I ever heard from him.
10日以後なら家にいます.	I'll be at home from the 10th on.
以後注意しなさい.	Be more careful in the future.

いざ

いざ自分がやってみると難しいものだと分かった.	I realized how difficult it was when I actually tried it myself.
彼はいざというときになっておじけづいた.	When it really came down to it, he lost his nerve.
彼はいざというときに頼りになる.	You can rely on him in a crunch. He'll come through for you (in a crunch).
彼女はいざというときのために貯金している.	She's saving money †against the unexpected [for when it's necessary, for a rainy day].

いさましい (勇ましい)

彼は勇ましい軍人だった.	He was a gallant officer.
兵士たちは勇ましく戦った.	The soldiers fought gallantly.
一人で敵方に乗り込んでいくとは勇ましい.	Venturing into enemy territory alone is a courageous act.
消防士たちは勇ましい格好をしていた.	The firemen looked courageous in their uniforms.
勇ましい音楽が流れてきた.	Stirring music began to flow.

いし (意思・意志)

【考え】あなたの意思に沿えるよう努力しましょう.	I'll do my best to arrange things according to your wishes.
彼には父親の商売を継ぐ意志がない.	He has no intention of taking over his father's business.
彼らはお互い意思の疎通を欠いている.	There's a lack of understanding between them.
君は彼に対して何らかの意思表示をすべきだ.	You'd better let him know what your intentions are.
【強い気持ち】私は自分の意志でそうした.	I did it of my own free will.
彼女は意志の強い〔弱い〕人だ.	She is a person of strong [weak] will.
	She †has a lot of [lacks] willpower.

いじ (意地)

彼女は意地を通した.	She got [had] her own way.
彼は意地になって拒んだ.	He obstinately [stubbornly] refused.
私は意地でも同時通訳の資格を取ってみせる.	I'm bound and determined to become certified as a simultaneous interpreter.
意地を張るのもいいかげんにしろ.	Stop being so stubborn.
私にも意地がある.	I have my pride.
彼は意地っ張りだ.	He's obstinate [stubborn].
彼に意地悪をされた.	He was really mean to me.
彼は意地汚い.	He's greedy.

いしき (意識)

彼の意識はまだあるか?	Is he still conscious?
山は空気が非常に薄く, ハイカーの中には意識を失う者も出た.	The air was so thin in the mountains that some of the hikers †passed out [lost consciousness].
気を失った婦人は, 意識を取り戻したとき自分がどこにいるのか分からなかった.	The woman who had fainted didn't realize where she was when she †came to [regained consciousness].
彼女は濡れたタオルを額に当てて	She put a wet towel on his forehead to

彼の意識を戻そうとした.	bring him †to [back to consciousness].
彼は意識不明で倒れていた.	He lay unconscious.
意識がもうろうとしてきた.	My mind has become clouded.
彼には罪の意識がない.	He has no sense of guilt (about it).
彼は被害者意識が強い.	He has a strong sense of being †victimized [a victim].
彼は階級意識が強い.	He's very class-conscious.
彼女は彼の存在を意識している.	She's got him on her mind.
あなたは自意識過剰だ.	You're too self-conscious.
私は意識して〔無意識に〕やったんだ.	I acted consciously [unconsciously].
	I was [wasn't] aware of what I was doing.
彼女は政治に対する意識が高い〔低い〕.	She has a strong [weak] political consciousness.
	She's [She's not] very politically aware.
これについて高校生はどういう意識を持っているのだろう.	I wonder how high school students feel about this.
サラリーマンの意識調査が行われた.	A public opinion survey of company employees was conducted.

いじめる

子どもの頃よく彼にいじめられた.	He used to †pick on [bully, tease]¹⁾ me a lot when we were kids.
会社で上司にいじめられた.	One of my superiors at work picked on me.
彼女は学校で同級生にいじめられているようだ.	Her classmates seem to †be hard on²⁾ [pick on] her at school.
彼は近所でも有名ないじめっ子だった.	He was a well-known bully in the neighborhood.

> 1) pick on が最も一般的. bully は子どもの場合のみに使い「弱い者いじめをする」ニュアンス. 軽く「ちょっといじめてみる」程度なら tease (からかう) を使う. 2) 行為というよりは日常の態度をいう場合は be hard on (〜につらくあたる) で表す.

いじょう¹ (以上)

【〜から上】3個以上買うとおまけが付きます.	Buy three or more and you get a special gift.
この棒は2メートル以上ある.	This stick is at least two meters long.
20歳以上の女性を募集している.	We're seeking applications from women 20 years of age and older [over].
高校生以上は大人料金です.	Those of high school age and older [over] pay full fare.
それ以上言うな.	Don't say any more.

これ以上は知らない.	That's all I know. / I don't know any more (than that).
あなたにはこれ以上話せない.	I can't tell you anything further.
もうこれ以上待てない.	I can't wait any longer.
彼女の成績は平均以上だ.	Her grades are above average.
7年以上たつと無効になる.	It becomes invalid after seven years.
このビルの8階以上は事務所になっている.	This building has offices from the 8th floor up.
必要以上に要求するな.	Don't ask for more than necessary.
【上述】以上で終わります.	That's all.
以上のように決定しました.	We decided as stated above.
以上がこれまでの経過です.	What we have seen [The above] is the way things have developed until now.
【~からには】やりかけた以上は最後までやりなさい.	Now that you've begun, keep at it †to the end [till you finish].
俳優である以上プライバシーはある程度侵害される.	Being an actor involves some invasion of privacy.

いじょう² (異状)

【機械などの】ランプが点滅して異状を知らせた.	The flashing light †signaled [warned of] †a malfunction [an emergency, a breakdown].
電気系統に異状が生じて電車が止まった.	The train stopped when the electrical system malfunctioned.
定期点検の結果すべて異状なかった.	Regular inspections showed that everything was in order.
【心身の】健康診断の結果どこも異状はなかった.	A physical (checkup) determined that there were no problems.
生まれてきた子供の心臓に異状が見つかった.	An abnormality was discovered in the baby's heart.
娘の死後,彼女は精神に異状をきたした.	She started suffering from a psychological disorder after her daughter's death.

いじょう³ (異常)

彼の最近の行動は異常だ.	He's been acting abnormally lately.
株主総会は異常な緊張感がみなぎっていた.	The stockholders' general meeting was unusually tense.
空港で異常事態が発生した.	There was a crisis at the airport.
異常に暑い日が続いている.	We've been having a run of unusually hot weather.
日本全体が異常寒波に見舞われた.	An unusually severe cold snap hit the whole of Japan.
異常乾燥注意報が出ているので火	There are reports warning of extremely

事に注意してください. | dry weather. Take precautions against fire.
近年, 世界のあちこちで異常気象が起きている. | In recent years, weather conditions have been abnormal in different parts of the world.

いせい (威勢)
威勢のいい魚屋の店員たちが生きのいい魚を売っていた. | Spirited fish mongers were selling fresh fish.
彼らは威勢よく競技場へと向かった. | They headed for the stadium in high spirits.

いぜん (以前)
私は以前彼に会ったことがある. | I've met him before [previously].
彼女は以前ほど歌がうまくない. | She doesn't sing as well as she used to. Her singing isn't what it used to be.
以前からあなたにお会いしたいと思っていました. | I've always wanted to meet you.
明治以前の日本は自給自足社会だった. | Society in pre-Meiji Japan was self-contained.

いそがしい (忙しい)
来週は仕事で忙しい. | I'll be busy with my work next week.
注文をこなすのに忙しい. | We're busy filling orders.
お忙しいところをすみません. | I'm sorry to bother you when you're so busy.
お忙しい中をいらしていただきありがとうございました. | Thank you for taking the time to come.

いそぐ (急ぐ)
急がないとバスに乗り遅れるよ. | Hurry up, or you'll be late for the bus.
彼女はデートに急いだ. | She hurried to meet her date.
急ぐことはないよ. | There's no (need to) hurry.
急いでいて手紙を出すのを忘れてしまった. | I was in such a hurry [rush] that I forgot to mail the letter.
急がされるのは嫌だ. | I don't like to be rushed.
運転手に急がせてくれ. | Tell the driver to †go faster [hurry].
急ぎの手紙だから速達にしてくれ. | This is an urgent letter, so send it (by) special delivery.
【慣用】急がば回れ. | Haste makes waste.
善は急げ. | Once you've made up your mind (to do something), do it. Let's get on with it.

いたい (痛い)

痛い！	Ouch!／Ow!
どこが痛いの．	Where does it hurt?
背中のこの辺が痛い．	My back hurts right around here.
ほかに痛いところは？	Do you have pain anywhere else?
頭〔歯，腹〕が痛い．	I have a headache [toothache, stomachache].
	My head [tooth, stomach] aches [hurts].
足〔腰，のど〕が痛い．	My foot [back,[1]] throat] hurts.
	I have a sore foot [back, throat].
目が痛い．	My eyes †hurt [are sore].
擦り傷がひりひりと痛い．	It smarts where I scraped myself.
煙〔太陽の光〕で目が痛かった．	The smoke [sun] hurt my eyes.
子どもが痛がっている．	My child is complaining of pain.
痛みがだんだん増して〔和らいで〕きた．	The pain has gotten †worse and worse [better].
【慣用】彼の質問はいつも私の痛い所を突いてくる．	His questions always strike at my weak points.
そんな中傷は痛くもかゆくもないよ．	I couldn't care less about the gossip.
	The gossip doesn't affect me at all.

> 1) back は「背中」を指すこともあるので，「腰」を明確に表したい場合は I have lower-back pain. という．

いだい (偉大)

彼は偉大な芸術家だった．	He was a great artist.
彼の偉大な業績は忘れ去られることはないだろう．	His great achievement will never be forgotten.

いたずら

うちの息子はいたずらばかりして困る．	We're having trouble with our son who is always getting into mischief.
私はいたずらっ子が好きだ．	I like mischievous children.
彼はクラスの子によくいたずらをする．	He often plays pranks [tricks] on the kids in the class.
いたずらして彼の机の中にゴムの蛇を入れた．	I put a rubber snake in his desk as a †prank [practical joke].
私はいたずら半分にしただけだ．	I meant it just as a joke.
彼はいたずら好きだ．	He's a real prankster.
いたずら電話で起こされた．	I was awakened by a prank call.
悪質ないたずらだ．	That's a vicious [nasty] prank.
【むだに】彼女は仕事を辞めて以来いたずらに時を過ごしている．	She's been idling her time away ever since she quit her job.

いたむ (痛・傷む)

【痛む】運動した翌日体じゅうが痛んだ. — The day after I exercised I ached [hurt] all over.

彼女はその話を聞いて心が痛んだ. — It broke her heart to hear that.

【傷む】箱を開いてみると品物は傷んでいた. — I discovered that the goods were damaged when I opened the box.

夏は野菜が早く傷む. — Vegetables †go bad [spoil] quickly in summer.

桃は傷みやすい. — Peaches †don't keep long [are perishable*].

いち (位置)

絵はいい位置に掛かっていた. — The picture was hanging in the right place.

私の位置からはよく見えなかった. — I couldn't see it very well from where I was.

みんな所定の位置についた. — Everybody took his place [position].

机の位置はこれでいいかい. — Is the desk OK here?

その城は町の中央に位置している. — The castle is located [situated] in the center of town.

地図でその町の位置を示してくれませんか? — Could you please show me where that town is located on the map?

その事件が歴史の中で位置づけられるのはずっと先のことだ. — It's up to future generations of historians to determine the significance of that event.

彼は美術界でどういう位置を占めているのですか. — Where does he stand in the art world?

位置について, 用意, ドン! — On your marks! Get set! Go!

いちおう (一応)

あなたのおっしゃることは一応納得しました. しかし…. — You've almost convinced me. Nevertheless....

一応先生に話を聞いてもらおう. — In any case [At any rate], I am going to talk it over with my teacher.

辞表は一応預かっておく. — I'll keep your letter of resignation for the time being.

私も一応は学者だ. — I guess you could call me a scholar of †sorts [a sort].

私も一応調べてみます. — I'll see what I can do to find out about it.

いちど (一度)

彼には一度会ったことがある. — I met him once.

彼が嫌な顔をするのを一度も見たことがない. — I've never seen him frown. / Not one time have I seen him frown.

もう一度計算してみなさい.	Calculate it once more.
もう一度言ってください.	I beg your pardon? / Pardon me?
彼は年〔月，週〕に一度しか家に帰らない.	He comes home only once a year [month, week].
彼は一度言い出したら聞かない.	Once he says he's going to do something he won't listen to anybody.
一度に二つのことはできない.	I can't do two things at once.
彼は競馬で一度に20万円損をした.	He lost 200,000 [two hundred thousand] yen on one bet at the race track.
一度にやって来ないで一人ずつ来なさい.	Don't all of you come at once. Come one at a time.
一度彼に会いたいと思っている.	I'd like to meet him some time.

いちにんまえ (一人前)

寿司を一人前注文したところだ.	I've got an order of *sushi* coming.
早く一人前になって両親を楽にさせてあげなさい.	Hurry up and get yourself established so you can make life easier for your parents.
彼も一人前の大工になった.	He became a full-fledged carpenter.
彼も一人前の口をきくようになった.	He can now speak his own mind.

いちぶ (一部)

【一つ】コピーを一部ずつ取って.	Please make one copy each.
【部分】この本は一部落丁している.	A part of this book is missing.
ビルは一部完成した.	One section of the building has been completed.
一部の人だけがそれに気づいている.	Only certain people are aware of that.

いちりゅう (一流)

【一級】結婚記念日に一流レストランで食事をした.	We had dinner at a first-class restaurant for our anniversary.
そのシンクタンクの研究員は一流大学の出身者ばかりだ.	That think tank is made up completely of graduates from prestigious universities.
彼は某一流企業の役員だ.	He is an executive at a certain top-flight company.
不正で起訴された大物政治家は一流の弁護士を雇った.	The powerful politician charged with wrongdoing hired a first-rate lawyer.
あの美容師のスタイリングの腕は超一流だ.	That beautician's styling skills are outstanding.
【独特の癖のある】それは彼一流の皮肉だ.	That's just his own (particular) brand of sarcasm.

のらりくらりと相手をかわすのが彼一流のやり方だ.	He's incredibly good at being elusive.

いつ

アメリカへはいつおたちになりますか?	When do you leave for America?
夏休みはいつから始まるのですか.	When does summer vacation begin?
私たちはいつからともなく親しくつきあうようになっていた.	At a certain point in our relationship we found ourselves intimately involved.
あの店はいつ行ってもすいている.	That store is never crowded.
彼はいつでもにこにこしている.	He's always cheerful.
	He always has a smile on his face.
いつでもいいですから一度うちへ遊びに来てください.	I'd really like to have you over sometime.
	Please stop by whenever!
あなたはそのことをいつ頃知ったのですか.	How long have you known about that?
	When did you find out about that?
ご主人のお帰りはいつ頃になりますか.	When [What time] do you expect your husband home?
いつの間に来たの.	Where did *you* come from?
	When did *you* show up?
この本はいつまで借りられますか.	How long may I †keep this book [borrow this book for]?
彼は一体いつまで寝ている気だろう.	I wonder just how long he intends to sleep.

いつか

いつかどこかでお会いしましたね.	We've met before, haven't we?
	I'm sure we've met before.
彼とはいつかの夜, 銀座でばったり会った.	I ran into him one night on the Ginza.
あなたの努力はいつかきっと報われるだろう.	I'm sure all of your hard work will pay off someday.

いっさい (一切)

その件に関する質問には一切お答えできません.	I can't answer any questions concerning that matter.
彼は酒は一切口にしない.	He doesn't drink at all.
	He never touches alcohol.
そのことは彼に一切任せてある.	That is being left entirely up to him.
その火事で彼は財産を一切無くしてしまった.	He lost all he had in that fire.
その件に関して一切の責任は彼にあります.	He has full responsibility for that.

| 今度の旅行には，交通費，食費その他一切で5万円かかった． | Travel, food and all other expenses for this past trip came to 50,000 [fifty thousand] yen (in) total. |

いっしょ (一緒)

我々は一緒に事業をやっていた．	We were in business together.
彼と一緒にいると楽しい．	It's fun to be with him.
ご一緒させてください．	Let me †accompany you [go with you].
ご一緒に食事しませんか．	Will you join me for dinner?
彼が書いた本が2冊一緒に刊行された．	Two books that he wrote were published †at the same time [together].
彼と一緒にされては (同じに見られては) 困る．	I don't want to be put in the same class as him.
父は私をジムと一緒にさせるつもりだ．	My father intends to make me marry Jim.

いっしょう (一生)

彼女はテニスに一生をかけている．	She's devoting her life to tennis.
その失敗で彼は一生を棒に振った．	That mistake ruined his life.
彼女は一生独身で通した．	She remained single all her life.
これは一生に一度のチャンスだ．	This is the chance of a lifetime.
あなたの親切は一生忘れない．	I won't forget your kindness as long as I live.

いっしょうけんめい (一生懸命)

彼はいつも一生懸命やる．	He always works as hard as he can.
彼は何をするにも一生懸命だ．	He always puts his heart into what he does.
私は一生懸命彼女を看病した．	I put all my energy into nursing her back to health.
彼女は一生懸命ケーキを焼いた．	She eagerly [earnestly] baked cakes. She put her heart and soul into baking cakes.

いっせん (一線)

【横並び】上位3頭がゴール直前で一線に並んだ．	The three top horses were running neck and neck at the finish line.
【境界・限度】いくら友人同士でも超えてはならない一線がある．	No matter how close you may be, there comes a point where you have to draw a line. No matter how close you are, there are certain boundaries you have to respect.
彼女は酒量がある一線を超えると	After a certain amount of alcohol, she'll

誰彼かまわずからみ始める.	start picking a fight with anyone.
会社の顧客データを他社の人間に見せたとき, 彼は最後の一線を超えた.	He crossed the line when he showed client data from his company to another company.
法律違反だと言う人もいるかもしれないが, 最後の一線は守っている.	Some may consider this illegal but I'm still toeing the line.
当社は他社とは一線を画するサービスを提供します.	Our company offers services clearly superior to others.
その夜二人は最後の一線を超えた.	They finally went all the way that night.
【現役・最前線】彼は経営の一線から退いている.	He's no longer involved in the day-to-day running of the company.
彼は政治の一線で活躍している.	He's (active) in the front lines of government.
彼女は一線の報道記者だ.	She's a field reporter.

いっそう (一層)

一層努力してください.	Please make even [still] greater efforts.
彼は叱られれば一層やる気の出てくるタイプだ.	He's the type of person who gets all the more motivated when criticized.
一層のご協力をお願いします.	We request your continued cooperation.

いったい (一体)

【強調】こんな遅い時間にドアをノックするのは一体だれだろう.	I wonder who in the world would come knocking at this late hour.
一体どうしてそんな大切な本を無くしてしまったのですか.	Would you please tell me how [why] anyone could [would] misplace [lose] such a valuable book?
この楽器は一体どうやって演奏するのですか.	How the devil is this instrument played?
【一つ】選手が一体となって戦ったことが今日の勝因です.	The players owe their victory today to teamwork.
彼らは子どもたちのために夫婦一体となって働いた.	That couple worked undividedly for their children.
【おしなべて】日本人は西洋人に比べて一体に背が低い.	Generally speaking, Japanese are shorter than Westerners.

いっち (一致)

彼とは意見がぴったり一致している.	I completely agree with him. I am in complete agreement with him.
一致した意見は次のとおりです.	The consensus is as follows.
我々は全員一致で値上げを決議した.	We decided unanimously to raise the prices.

彼の言行は一致しない.	He doesn't practice what he preaches.
大国は一致した行動をとった.	The world powers took concerted action.
我々は一致協力して事態に臨まねばならない.	We must make a united effort to face the situation.
彼らは理想が一致している.	They have the same ideals.
偶然の一致だね.	What a coincidence!
二つの暗号はぴたりと一致した.	The two codes matched perfectly.

いっぱい (一杯)

【一杯】水〔ミルク, ビール, ワイン〕を一杯いただけますか.	Could I have a glass of water [milk, beer, wine], please?
コーヒー〔紅茶〕を一杯彼女に出してあげてください.	Please bring her a cup of coffee [tea].
カップ一杯の水に茶さじ一杯の塩を加えなさい.	Add one teaspoon of salt to a cup of water.
仕事が済んだら一杯やろうよ.	Let's have a drink after work.
【満ちる】事務所は人でいっぱいだ.	The office is filled with people.
風呂桶の水がいっぱいになる前に水道を止めてね.	Turn off the faucet before the bathtub is [gets] full.
彼女は目に涙をいっぱいためて私を見つめた.	She looked at me intently with her eyes full of tears.
腹いっぱい食べた.	I ate my fill.
おなかがいっぱいだ.	I'm full.
その計画で頭がいっぱいだった.	I couldn't take my mind off that plan.
【ずっと】今月いっぱい滞在する予定だ.	I'm planning to stay until the end of the month.
この仕事は今年いっぱいかかりそうだ.	This work will probably take the rest of the year.

いっぱん (一般)

保守化が一般の傾向である.	The general tendency is towards conservatism.
背広にネクタイというのが会社員の一般的な服装だ.	Corporate employees generally wear suits and ties.
一般的に言って女性は男性より長生きだ.	Generally speaking [In general], women live longer than men.
それは一般に知られていない.	It's not generally known. It's unknown to the public.
広く一般にわたって討議した.	We discussed a broad range of topics.
それが世間一般の考えだ.	That's the prevalent view of society.
この品は一般の店には置いていない.	This product is not found in ordinary stores.
一般の立ち入りを禁止する.	Not open to the general public.

一般大衆の意見をもっと政治に反映させるべきだ.	Public opinion should be reflected more in politics.
招待者はこちら, 一般の方はあちらです.	By special invitation, this way; general admission, that way.
この商品は一般向きです.	This product is aimed to suit †popular taste [the general public].
この国宝は年に2回しか一般公開されない.	This national treasure is shown to the public only twice a year.

いっぽう (一方)

【一方向】この道は一方通行だ.	This is a one-way street.
彼はぼんやりと一方を見ていた.	He absent-mindedly stared off into space.
【片方】彼は一方の耳が聞こえない.	He can't hear out of one of his ears.
	He's deaf in one ear.
その双子の一方は学者で, もう一方は詩人だ.	One of the twins is a scholar and the other is a poet.
一方の肩ばかり持つのは良くないよ.	It's not good to always be sticking up for one side.
一方の言い分を聞いただけでは判断をくだせない.	You can't pass judgment after hearing only one side of the story.
一方からだけ見れば, それは正しいのだろう.	I guess that would be correct if looked at from only one party's point of view.
【その傾向のみ】彼はまじめ一方の教師だ.	He's a thoroughly conscientious teacher.
いくらダイエットに励んでも, 体重は増える一方だ.	No matter how much I diet, I just keep gaining weight.
試合はジャイアンツの一方的な勝利に終わった.	It was a one-sided victory for the Giants.
試合はチャンピオンの一方的な勝利に終わった.	It was the champion's fight from start to end.
【その反面】夫はステーキが好きだ. 一方, 私はサラダが好きだ.	My husband loves steak. On the other hand, I prefer salad.
怒る人がいる一方で, 笑って許してくれる人もいた.	While there were those who got angry at me, there were also those who laughed it off and forgave me.
その宗教家は清貧を説く一方で, 自分は美食に明け暮れている.	Even as he preaches the virtues of poverty, that religious leader †eats high on the hog [always eats well].
【相手を無視した】そんな一方的な条件はのめない.	I can't accept such one-sided conditions.
先方は一方的に期日の変更を通告してきた.	The other party notified us of the change of date without any consultation.
彼女は捨て台詞を吐き, 一方的に	She hung up on him after a final parting

電話を切った. shot.

いつまでも

あなたのご好意はいつまでも忘れません. — I'll never forget your kindness.

いつまでも親のすねをかじってはいられない. — I just can't sponge off my parents forever!

いつまでも精神だけは若くありたいものだ. — I hope to remain young in spirit forever.

いつも

彼はいつも6時半に起きてジョギングする. — He always gets up at 6:30 and goes jogging.

私は買い物に出かけるといつも衝動買いをしてしまう. — I buy something on impulse every time I go shopping.

彼が遅刻するのはいつものことだ. — It's just like him to be late.

彼はいつものように〔いつもより早く〕散歩に出かけた. — He went out for his walk †as usual [earlier than usual].

それは彼のいつもの言いぐさだ. — That's what he always says.

それは彼のいつもの言いわけだ. — That's his usual excuse.

いと (意図)

彼の意図が測りかねる. — I can't figure out his intentions.

彼は政界に進出する意図があってその役を引き受けた. — He accepted the post, thinking it would help him launch a career in politics.

私は意図的に彼に厳しくした. — I was intentionally strict with him.

いない (以内)

5分以内に戻って来るよ. — I'll be back within five minutes.

2,000円以内なら何か買ってあげるよ. — I'll buy you something if it's †under [not more than, less than] 2,000 yen.

駅から歩いて5分以内の所に家を持ちたい. — I want to have a house that's not more than a five-minute walk from the station.

いなか (田舎)

退職後は田舎に引っ込んで田舎の景色を味わいたい. — When I retire I want to move out to the country and savor the rural scenery.

私は田舎育ちだ. — I was raised [bred] in the country. / I'm a country boy [girl].

あんな田舎臭いやつ[田舎者]のどこがいいの. — What do you see in a country hick like him?

田舎はどちらですか. — What part of the country are you from?

いのち (命)

彼は命の恩人だ.	I owe him my life.
	He saved my life.
胃がんが彼の命取りになった.	Stomach cancer took his life.
彼はあと3ヵ月の命だ.	He has three months left to live.
命拾いをした. 命綱がなかったら今頃は….	It was †a narrow escape [a close call]. If there hadn't been a life line....
命にかけて誓います.	I swear on [upon] my life.
彼は山で遭難し, わずかな食料だけで命をつないだ.	After the mountain accident, he managed to stay alive on a very small amount of food.
昨日, 交通事故を起こしそうになり命の縮む思いをした.	Yesterday I came so close to getting into a traffic accident. I felt like it had taken years off my life. [I nearly had a heart attack.]
彼は命懸けで刑事をやっている.	He risks his life working as a police detective.
彼は全く命知らずだ.	He's a real daredevil.
命あっての物種だ.	Where there is life, there is hope.

いのる (祈る)

病気全快を神に祈った.	I prayed to God for complete recovery.
成功〔幸運〕を祈る.	I wish you †success [the best of luck].
	Good luck!
私の祈りが通じたようだ.	My prayers seem to have been answered.

いばる (威張る)

彼は威張っている.	He really thinks he's something (big).
	He thinks he's better than others.
	He likes to throw his weight around.
	He acts conceited [haughty].
彼は同輩に対して威張っている.	He acts big in front of his peers.
彼女は満点を取ったと言って友達に威張った.	She boasted [bragged] to her friends that she got a perfect score.
勝者は威張って出て行った.	The winner left arrogantly [haughtily].
あの先生はいつも威張った歩き方をする.	That teacher always walks around with †an arrogant [a haughty] air.

いはん (違反)

今後, 違反行為を厳重に処罰します.	Hereafter, all violations will be strictly punished.
それは明らかに法律違反だ.	That is clearly in violation of the law.
	That is clearly illegal.

彼の秘書が選挙違反で捕まった.	His secretary was caught breaking election laws.
他社と取引するのは契約違反だ.	It is a breach of contract to do business with other companies.
タバコのポイ捨てはマナー違反であるばかりでなく，条例違反になる町もある.	It's not only bad manners to throw your cigarette stubs on the ground but in some places it's against city ordinances.
うちの学校ではピアスをつけるのは校則違反だ.	Wearing pierced earrings is against †our school rules [school rules here].
駐車違反で切符を切られた.	I got a parking ticket.
駐車違反で罰金をとられた.	I was fined for a parking violation.
彼はしょっちゅうスピード違反で捕まっている.	He's always getting caught for speeding.

いま (今)

今すぐ行きます.	I'll come [go] right away.
	I'll be right there.
たった今彼は出て行った.	You just missed him.
今から始めれば間に合うよ.	If you start now you'll †make it [finish] in time.
今から3年前に彼は死んだ.	He died three years ago.
今頃彼は帰り着いているだろう.	He should be home by now.
来年の今頃は私はインドにいる.	About this time next year I'll be in India.
今さらあとへ引けない.	There's no turning back now.
	We can't back out †now [at this point].
今どきそんな考えははやらない.	That kind of thinking isn't popular †nowadays [these days].
今に後悔するよ.	You'll be sorry †one of these days [someday].
	You'll regret it one day.
今にも女の子は泣き出しそうだった.	The little girl looked ready to burst into tears at any moment.
今まで一体何をしていたの.	What have you been doing †till now [all this time]?
今までに何冊の本を読んだ?	How many books have you read †up to now [so far]?

いみ (意味)

「取る」は多くの意味を持つ言葉だ.	"Toru" is a word with many meanings.
この文はどういう意味ですか.	What does this sentence mean?
この略語は何を意味するの.	What does this abbreviation stand for?
契約を更新したいという意味の手紙が届いた.	We've just received a letter to the effect that they want to renew the contract.

そんな意味のことを言ったかもしれない.	I may have said something to that effect.
「どういう意味でその言葉を使っているの?」「一般的な意味で〔あらゆる意味を込めて〕です」	"In what sense are you using the word?" "In the general sense. [In every sense of the word.]"
彼の言葉を反対の意味に取ったかもしれない.	I may have taken what he said in the opposite sense of what he meant.
ある意味で君のしたことは正しい.	In a sense what you did was right.
言葉の真の意味において彼は比類のない指導者だった.	He was an incomparable leader in the true sense of the word.
悪い意味で言ったのではない.	I didn't mean anything bad.
人生の意味を知っているか?	Do you know the meaning of life?
そんなことをしても意味がない.	It's meaningless to do something like that.
彼は意味ありげに笑った.	He gave a meaningful smile.
	He smiled meaningfully.
彼らは意味ありげに顔を見交わした.	They exchanged meaningful glances.

イメージ

雲を見ていると様々なイメージがわいてくる.	All kinds of images come to mind when you gaze up at clouds.
彼女は大学生活に華やかなイメージを思い描いている.	She's imagining a †wonderful life [great time] on campus.
ポスターはイメージ通りの仕上がりだった.	The poster turned out just as I imagined.
このワンピースは君のイメージにぴったりだね.	This dress is *you*!
	This dress is perfect for you.
彼女, イメージが変わったね.	She has a new image./She looks different.
質屋に対するイメージは昔ほど暗くない.	Pawn shops don't have the same bad [negative] image they used to.
彼女は髪を切ってイメージチェンジを図った.	She went for a change of image by cutting her hair.
スキャンダルで, その会社のイメージダウンは避けられない.	There's no way the scandal won't affect that company's image.

いや (嫌・否)

嫌な天気が続くね.	We're sure having a lot of unpleasant weather.
	This unpleasant weather won't go away.
人のあら捜しばかりして本当に嫌なやつだ.	He's really awful, finding fault with everybody.
彼女は嫌な顔一つせずに頼みを聞いてくれた.	She did me the favor without the slightest look of annoyance.

今日嫌なことがあった.	Something unpleasant happened today.
今の仕事が嫌になった.	I'm tired [sick] of my present job.
彼は時間に追われる生活がつくづく嫌になった.	He got fed up with constantly being pressed for time.
嫌なら断りなさい.	If you don't want to (do it), say so.
甘いものは見るのも嫌だ.	I hate even the sight of sweets.
私は嫌がる彼を無理に連れ出した.	I took him out against his will.
嫌な予感がする.	I have forebodings* about that.
嫌な世の中になってきた.	It's turned into a rotten world.
いやがおうでも彼を仲間に入れよう.	He's with us whether he likes it or not.

いやしい (卑しい)

「卑しい」身分の人とか「卑しい」身なりの人とかいう言い方は死語になりつつある.	Expressions like a person of "lowly" origins or of "lowly" appearance are becoming obsolete.
あんな品性の卑しい人はだれにも紹介できない.	I couldn't introduce a vulgar person like him to anyone.
そんな卑しい (がつがつした) ことはやめなさい.	Don't be so greedy. Don't make such a pig of yourself.

いやらしい

いやらしいことを言うのはやめろ.	Stop saying such vulgar things.
その男はいやらしい (みだらな) ことをしたと訴えられた.	Complaints were brought against that man for indecent behavior.
あの男はいやらしい目つきで私を見た.	That guy leered at me.
いやらしい (見下げた) やつだ. 社長におべっかばかり使って.	What a despicable* guy—flattering the boss all the time.
抜き打ちテストなんかしてあの先生はいやらしい.	That teacher's unfair—springing a surprise test like that.
この問題はいやらしい. 思わぬ落とし穴がある.	This is a nasty problem. There are unexpected pitfalls.

いよいよ

【ますます】辺りはいよいよ暗くなってきた.	The surroundings [area] grew darker and darker.
いよいよ面白くなってきた.	It's getting more and more interesting.
【とうとう】いよいよ試合当日だ.	The day of the game has arrived at last.
いよいよというときになって彼女は病気になってしまった.	She got sick at the worst possible time.

いよく (意欲)

彼は勉強したいという意欲は人一倍ある. — He has an extraordinarily strong drive to study.

彼は意欲的に仕事に取り組んだ. — He buckled down to work enthusiastically.

彼は意欲満々だ. — He's full of drive.

いらい (以来)

それ以来彼女は寝込んでいる. — She's been ill in bed since then.

彼女が結婚して以来, 彼女とは会っていない. — I haven't seen her since she got married.

彼はこの劇団始まって以来の名優と言われている. — They say he's the best actor they've had since the theater troupe was formed.

いらいら

彼にはいらいらさせられる. — He irritates me./He gets me irritated.

彼のおしゃべりにはいらいらさせられる. — His chatter gets on my nerves.

約束の時間に遅れているので, いらいらしながら電車を待った. — I waited for the train impatiently because I was already late for my appointment.

いる¹ (居る)

【存在する】見てごらん. アリが1匹〔たくさん〕いるよ. — Look! There's an ant. 〔There're lots of ants.〕

神様は本当にいるのかしら. — I wonder if God really exists./I wonder if there really is a God.

昔はこの山にも鹿がいた. — A long time ago there used to be deer on this mountain, too.

解答用紙がない人はいますか? — Is there anyone without an answer sheet?

彼ほど滑稽な人はいない. — He's the zaniest guy.

【在宅・居住・滞在する】彼女は今台所にいる. — She's in the kitchen now.

次郎君はいますか? — Is Jiro in?

日曜日なら(家に)います. — I'm home on Sunday.

彼は今どこに (住んで) いるの? — Where is he (living) now?

このアパートにジョン・スミスさんという人はいますか. — Does John Smith live in this apartment?

ドイツに2ヵ月ほどいました. — I was in Germany for two months.

もう2, 3日ここにいます. — I'll be here for two or three more days.

【居合わせる】あの時は彼がいたので助かった. — I sure was lucky to have him around that time.

彼女がいる前でこの話はするなよ. — Don't talk about this in front of her.

彼らはおしゃべりに夢中で先生がいるのにも気づかない. — They're so wrapped up in talking to each other that they haven't even noticed the

【所有する】うちには犬が1匹いる. We have a dog.
私には子どもはいない. I have no children.
【すわる】彼女は息子の無事な姿を見るまではいても立ってもいられないようだ. I don't think she'll be able to calm down until she sees that her son is safe and sound.

いる² (要る)

この企画のためには1千万円〔優秀な人材〕が要る. We're going to need †¥10 million 〔some highly capable people〕 for this project.
要らない物が多過ぎるので少し処分しよう. We've got too many things we don't need, so let's get rid of some of them.
私たちの家は山のほうにあるので8月でもクーラーは要らない. Our house is up in the mountains, so we don't need air-conditioning even in August.

いれる (入れる)

【中へ】封筒の中に写真を入れた. I put the photographs in the envelope.
花瓶に水を入れてください. Please put some water in the vase.
この缶にお茶の葉を入れてもいいですか. Can I put the tea in this can?
この箱に何を入れているの. What do you keep [have] in this box?
夜は気温が下がるのでベランダの植木を家の中へ入れておかなければならない. It gets so cold at night that I have to bring the plants on the porch inside the house.
風を少し入れよう. Let's let a little air in.
【加入させる】私も仲間に入れて. Include me./Count me in.
娘は私立の女子校に入れました. We put our daughter in a private girls' school.
【導入する】うちの事務所では今度新しいコンピュータを入れた. We've †put in [installed] new computers at the office.
【含める】リストに私の名前も入れて. Put [Include] me on the list.
一行は団長を入れて15人だった. The party, including its leader, consisted of 15 persons.
【茶・コーヒーを】コーヒーを入れてくれない? Will you make me some coffee, please?

いろいろ

私はいろいろなことに興味がある. I'm interested in †a lot of [many, various] things.
彼はカメラをいろいろ持っている. He owns all kinds [sorts] of cameras.
アパート住まいをするために机や I have to buy a desk, chair and a lot of

いすなど，いろいろと買い揃えなければならない．	other things that I'll need to set up an apartment.
いろいろ考えたがよく理解できなかった．	I thought and thought but still didn't understand it very well.
いろいろと試行錯誤を重ねたあげく答えを見つけ出した．	I finally found the answer after much trial and error.
役所へ行くなどいろいろしなければならない．	I've got to do a lot of things, including going to the government office.
人の心はいろいろだ．	So many men, so many minds.
いろいろとありがとう．	Thank you for everything.

いわい (祝い)

誕生日のお祝い〔合格祝い〕に彼女に時計を贈った．	I gave her a watch †for her birthday [to celebrate her passing the exam].
今度彼に会ったら私の分もお祝いを言ってくれ．	Congratulate him for me the next time you see him.
心からお祝いを申し上げます．	Congratulations.

いわう (祝う)

家族みんなで彼女の合格を祝った．	The entire family celebrated her passing the exam.
彼の昇進を祝ってみんなで乾杯した．	Everyone toasted his promotion.

いんき (陰気)

あの人は陰気な人だ．	That guy's gloomy.
何だか陰気な音楽だ．	This music is kind of gloomy.
この家は日が当たらないので陰気くさい．	This house seems gloomy because it doesn't get any direct sunlight.

いんけん (陰険)

あの教授は陰険だ．	That professor is treacherous.
	That professor can be tricky.
あの会社は陰険なやり方をする．	That company operates in an underhanded manner.

いんしょう (印象)

彼の第一印象はどうでした？	What's your first impression of him?
とてもいい印象を受けました．	He left me with a very good impression.
彼女の印象が深く心に残った．	Her image made a deep impression on my mind.
	She left a deep impression on me.
彼女の印象が薄れてきた．	My memory of her is fading.

それは私には非常に印象的な出来事だった.	That (event) left a very strong impression on me.

インストール

CD-ROMを使って新しいソフトをインストールした.	I installed my new software from a CD-ROM.
何度やってもインストールがうまくいかなかった.	I couldn't get it to install, no matter how many times I tried.

インターネット

インターネットで劇場の場所を調べた.	I looked up the location of the theater on the Internet.
インターネットを使えばたいていのことは調べられる.	You can look up almost anything on the Internet.
彼はインターネットでチェスを楽しむ.	He enjoys playing chess online.
僕のパソコンはインターネットにつながっていない.	My computer isn't connected to the Internet.
うちの会社もインターネットでの販売を始めた.	Our company has also started †doing business online [selling on the Internet].

う

ウィルス

新型ウィルスの治療法はまだ確立されていない.	A cure has not yet been found for the new virus.
【コンピュータ】たちの悪いウィルスにやられてしまった.	My computer has been attacked by a nasty virus.
うちの会社はウィルス対策をほとんどしていない.	Our company has done almost nothing about protecting its computers from viruses.

うえ (上)

【上部・上方】飛行機は雲の上を飛んでいる.	The airplane's flying above[1] the clouds.
彼女は左の目の上にほくろがある.	She has a mole over[2] her left eye.
窓の上に棚を付けよう.	Let's build a shelf above [over] the window.

彼の事務所はこの上の階です.	His office is on the next floor up.
上から5行目に間違いがある.	There's a mistake in the fifth line from the top.
階段のいちばん上から転げ落ちた.	I fell all the way down the stairs.
彼が身につけているものは上から下まで英国製だ.	Everything he has on is made in England.
山の上はとても寒かった.	It was very cold on the mountain (top).
1段上に上がってください.	Move up another step.
上を向いてごらん.	Look up.
	Take a look †above you [overhead].
あのビルは上半分がホテルです.	The upper half of that building is a hotel.
【表面】彼は帽子を机の上に置いた.	He put the hat on[3] the desk.
屋根の上に猫がいる.	There's a cat up on the roof.
上に浮いているのは脂だ.	That's fat floating on top.
【年長】彼は私より二つ上です.	He's two years older than I am.
いちばん上の子は中学生です.	The oldest child is in junior high school.
いちばん上の兄がアメリカに住んでいる.	My eldest brother lives in America.
【優れている・上位】テニスの腕は私のほうが上だ.	I'm the better tennis player.
上のクラスに入るためには試験を受けなければならない.	I have to take a test to get into the higher class.
会社の上のほうからの命令だ.	It's an order from my superiors at work.
彼の成績は学年でも上のほうだ.	His grades are among the best in his entire grade.
彼は人の上に立つ器ではない.	He doesn't have what it takes to be a leader.
【〜に加えて】彼は頭がいい上に運動もできる.	He's smart, and on top of that, good at sports.
そのレストランはおいしい上に安いので学生たちに人気がある.	That restaurant is very popular with the students because in addition to having good food it is inexpensive.
その家は駅から遠い上に家賃が高いので,だれも借りる人がいない.	Nobody will rent that house because in addition to being far from the station it is expensive.
この上は何も言うことはない.	I have nothing further to say.
【〜の結果】欠陥が明らかになった上は修正しなければならない.	The defects must be corrected now that they have become apparent.
実際に見た上でそれを買うかどうか決めます.	I'll decide whether or not to buy it once I've actually seen it.
あれは酒の上での冗談だよ.	That was just a joke said over drinks.

1)2)3) on は表面に接している場合. 表面から離れると above を用

いる. over は「真上に」の意味になる.

うえる (植える)
彼は松の苗木を庭に植えた. He planted a pine seedling in the garden.
花壇に植えたチューリップの花が咲いた. The tulips I planted in the flower bed have bloomed.
親の言動が子どもの心に偏見を植え付けることがある. What parents say and do can sometimes implant prejudice in children.

うかがう (伺う)
【訪問する】明日お宅にお伺いしてもよろしいでしょうか. Would it be all right if I called on you tomorrow?[1]
【尋ねる】教授の明日のご予定を伺ってみます. I'll ask the professor what his schedule is for tomorrow.
ちょっと伺いますが, バス停はどこでしょうか. Excuse me, but could you tell me where the bus stop is?
社長に伺いを立てたほうがいい. You'd better consult the president.
【聞く】おうわさは伺っております. I've heard so much about you.
あなたの考えを伺いたいのです. I'd like to hear what you think.
お話を伺いましょう. What is it you wanted to talk about?

1) 英語には「伺う」のような敬語はないが, 尋ねるときや頼むときに would や could を用いることにより, 丁寧な響きが出る.

うかつ
妻の病気に気づかなかったとは私もうかつだった. It was very negligent of me not to notice my wife's illness.
My thoughtlessness kept me from noticing that my wife was sick.
うかつに彼を非難すると反対にやり込められることになる. You should be careful if you're going to take him on because he'll put you down.
相手が子どもであればこそ, うかつなことを言ってはいけない. Especially with children you should be careful about what you say.
すみません. 私がうかつでした. I'm sorry. It was thoughtless [careless] of me.
I'd like to apologize for my carelessness.
そんな大事な約束を忘れるなんて彼もうかつなやつだ. It certainly was careless of him to have forgotten such an important appointment.

うかぶ (浮かぶ)
【水・空に】空に雲が浮かんでいる. There are some clouds floating in the sky.

沖には船が浮かんでいた.	There was a boat offshore.
【心に】ある考えが浮かんだ.	An idea occurred to me.
	An idea crossed my mind.
一日中考えたけれどいい案は浮かばなかった.	I thought about it all day long but couldn't come up with a good idea.
そのとき父の言葉が心に浮かんだ.	Father's words came to my mind then.
	I thought of my father's words then.
こんなとき英語で何と言えばいいのか言葉が浮かばない.	The appropriate English for this kind of situation doesn't come to mind.
【現れる】彼の名が容疑者として浮かび上がってきた.	He began to be mentioned as a suspect.
彼女の顔にほほえみが浮かんだ.	A smile came to her lips.
霧の中から人影が浮かび上がってきた.	A figure loomed out of the fog.
【慣用】今度そんな失敗をしたら彼はもう浮かび上がれないだろう.	He'll be sunk if he makes another mistake like that.
彼が自堕落に暮らしていては死んだ母親も浮かばれまい.	The dissolute life he leads must make his mother turn in her grave.

うかれる (浮かれる)

祭りの日は皆浮かれている.	A festival puts everyone in high spirits.
昇進が決まったので彼は浮かれて私に花を買って来た.	When he got his promotion, he was so overjoyed he bought me some flowers.
自分たちの野球チームが優勝したので学生たちは浮かれて騒いだ.	The students celebrated noisily when their school team won the baseball game.

うきうき (浮き浮き)

彼はうきうきとデートに出かけた.	He left for his date in a great mood.
彼はあこがれの人に声を掛けられてうきうきしている.	He's on cloud nine since the woman of his dreams spoke to him.
彼女は旅行に出かける1週間も前からうきうきしていた.	She started getting really excited about her trip a whole week before she left.

うく (浮く)

油は水に浮く.	Oil floats on water.
彼の案は宙に浮いた形になっている.	His proposal has been left †pending [up in the air].
この赤い花瓶はバックの青にくっきり浮き出て見えるだろう.	This red vase will really stand out against a blue background.
歩いてバス代を浮かせよう.	Let's walk and save the bus fare.
どうしたの, 浮かない顔して.	Why so glum?
	What's with the glum face?

うけつけ (受付)

受付をすませてから試験会場に入ってください.	Please check in at the reception desk before proceeding to the examination room.
結婚式の受付を手伝った.	I helped out at the reception desk for the wedding.
受付時間は午前10時から午後6時までです.	We are [The reception desk is] open from 10 in the morning to 6 in the evening.
受付の人に書類を渡した.	I gave the documents to the receptionist.
彼女は予約受付係だ.	She's in charge of reservations.

うけつける (受け付ける)

願書は郵送でのみ受け付けます.	Applications must be mailed in.
チケットの予約は6月10日の正午から受け付けます.	We will be taking seat reservations from June 10th at noon.
彼は今,他人の忠告を受け付けられる状態ではない.	He's too upset now [He's not in any mood] to listen to advice.
胃が弱くて油っこいものは受け付けない.	I have a sensitive stomach and can't eat greasy foods.
彼のことは生理的に受け付けない.	There's something about him that puts me off.

うけとる (受け取る)

【受領する】書類は受け取りました.	I received the papers.
今日その手紙を受け取りました.	I received [got] that letter today.
郵便局まで小包を受け取りに行かなければならない.	I have to go to the post office to pick up a package.
彼は釣り銭を受け取らずに店を出た.	He left the store without †taking [picking up] his change.
感謝のしるしとしてこれを受け取ってください.	Please accept this as a token of my gratitude.
【解釈する】彼は賛成だと私は受け取っている.	I understand him to be in favor of it.
	I take it that he is in favor of it.
人によって言葉の受け取り方が違う.	Different people will interpret the same statement in different ways.

うける (受ける)

【受け止める】彼はボールを素手で受けた.	He caught the ball with his bare hands.
一塁手は送球を受け損ねた.	The first baseman missed the throw.
雨漏りを受けるバケツが必要だ.	We need a bucket to catch the leaking rainwater.
風を帆に受けて船はぐんぐん進ん	The sail caught the wind and the boat

	moved ahead quickly.
だ.	
【授業・試験などを】その大学を受けようと思っている.	I'm going to take the entrance exam for that university.
彼女は高名な音楽家からバイオリンのレッスンを受けている.	She's taking violin lessons from a famous musician.
祖父はまともな教育を受けていない.	My grandfather never had much formal education.
【検査・手術などを】視力検査を受けなければならない.	I have to take an eye test.
医者の診察を受けるべきだ.	You should have a doctor look at you.
父は胃の手術を受けた.	My father had a stomach operation.
【受け付ける】電話を受けたのはだれですか.	Who took the (telephone) call?
質問は最後に受けます.	I'll take questions at the end.
【受け入れる】彼の申し出を受けることにした.	I've decided to accept his offer.
彼らの挑戦を受けようじゃないか.	Let's accept their challenge.
【得る・与えられる】知らせを受けて彼は急いで出て行った.	He rushed out when he got the news.
彼は奨学金を受けていた.	He was on a scholarship.
その俳優は昨年賞を受けた.	That actor won an award last year.
【解する】彼の言葉を真に受けるな.	Don't take what he says seriously.
【好評を得る】そういう記事はインテリに受ける.	That kind of article goes over well with intellectuals.
彼の冗談はとても受けた.	His joke went over very well.

うごかす (動かす)

【物を】ロボットを動かしてみせてください.	Please make the robot move for me.
車を5メートル動かしてくれ.	Move the car five meters.
無断で機械を動かさないでください.	Don't operate the machine without permission.
健康のために少しは体を動かしたほうがいい.	You should get some exercise for your health.
【人を】思いどおりに人を動かすのは難しいことだ.	It's hard to get people to do things the way you want them to.
彼は会社で大勢の人を動かしている.	He has a lot of people working under him at the company.
【心を】彼の話は人々の心を動かした.	His story †moved [touched the hearts of] the people.
彼の情熱に動かされて私はその仕事を引き受けた.	His enthusiasm inspired me to take the job.

うごく (動く)

【体・物が】
彼は左足が動かない.	His left leg doesn't [won't] move.
疲れて一歩も動けない.	I'm so tired I can't move another step.
彼女は先月足を折って、今は動き回るのがとても大変だ.	She broke her leg last month and it's very difficult for her to get around.
この車は電気で動く.	This car moves [runs, works, functions] on electricity.
プリンターが動かない.	The printer doesn't work.
工場の機械は夜も動いている.	The machines in the factory run at night, too.
選挙のとき大金が動いた.	Big money moved at election time.

【人が】
皆忙しくて今動ける人間がいない.	We're too busy to spare anyone for that now.
彼のような実力者が動けばどんな問題でも解決するだろう.	When an influential person like him acts, just about any problem can be solved.
彼は金で動くような人ではない.	He's not the kind of person who's moved by money.

【状態が】
彼の昇進は動かないだろう.	His promotion is fairly firm.
金の相場は常に動いている.	The price of gold fluctuates constantly.
これが動かぬ証拠だ.	This is incontrovertible evidence.

うしなう (失う)

彼らは戦争で家を失った.	They lost their houses in the war.
リーダーを失ってまもなくグループは解散した.	The group disbanded soon after losing its leader.
彼女は地震のときも冷静さを失わなかった.	She didn't lose her composure [cool] even during the earthquake.
彼に謝る機会を永久に失ってしまった.	Now I'll never be able to apologize to him.
得たものも大きいが失ったものも大きい.	I gained a lot but I also lost a lot.
彼女は三つのときに父親を失ったそうだ.	I understand that she lost her father when she was three.

うしろ (後ろ)

あの山の後ろは絶壁だ.	The other side of that mountain is a sheer cliff.
子どもがいすの後ろに隠れた.	The child hid behind the chair.
もう少し後ろに下がってくれ.	Please move back a little more.
試験問題を後ろのほうにも回してください.	Please pass the tests to the back.
後ろにもたれると楽ですよ.	You'll be more comfortable if you lean

	back.
後ろから押してください.	Please give me a push from behind.
後ろからだれかついて来た.	Someone came following after us.
決して後ろを振り向くな.	Don't look back under any circumstances.
後ろ向きに飛び込んでごらん.	Try diving in backward(s).
彼はこの列の後ろのほうにいる.	He's in the back [rear] of this line.
後ろの列は上級生だ.	The back rows [The rows at the rear] are upperclassmen.
その人の後ろ姿しか見えなかった.	I could only see his back.
彼女はセーターを後ろ前に着た.	She put her sweater on backward(s).

うしろめたい (後ろめたい)

後ろめたかったが, そのことは黙っているしかなかった.	I felt guilty, but I had no choice but to keep quiet about it.
君がそのことで後ろめたく思う必要はない.	There's no reason for you to feel guilty about it.

うすい (薄い)

【厚さ】薄い布地の服が欲しい.	I want a dress made of thin material.
肉を薄く切ってください.	Slice [Cut] the meat thin, please.
上着のひじの所が薄くなった.	The elbows of my jacket have worn thin. My jacket has worn thin at the elbows.
【濃度・密度】薄い牛乳はまずい.	Thin milk doesn't taste good.
高い山の上は空気が薄い.	At the top of a high mountain the air is thin.
髪が薄くなってきた.	My hair has gotten thin.
スープの味が薄い.	This soup tastes bland.
コーヒーは薄くしてください.	Please make the coffee weak.
【色・光など】壁を薄い青に塗った.	We painted the wall a light blue.
デッサンに薄く色を付けた.	I colored in the sketch lightly.
印刷が薄くて読みにくい.	The print is almost too faint to read.
窓に薄日がさしてきた.	Faint sunlight shone through the window.
彼女は口紅を薄く付けて出かけた.	She put on a little lipstick and went out.
【度合い・程度】彼のアメリカへの留学は望み薄だ.	There is little hope that he can go to America to study.
彼の商売は儲けが薄い.	His profit margin is slim.

うそ

彼は見え透いたうそをつく.	He tells †the most blatant [transparent] lies.
彼は私のうそを見抜いていた.	He saw through my lie.
うそがばれて母にひどく叱られた.	My mother really yelled at me when she found out I had been lying.

うそも方便ということもある. | There are times when it is †better to hide the truth [advisable not to reveal the whole truth].
彼の言ったことは真っ赤なうそだった. | What he told me was †an outright [an out-and-out, a bald-faced] lie.
彼がアメリカの大学を出たというのはうそだと分かった. | It turned out to be †false [a lie] that he had graduated from a university in America.
彼女にうその住所を教えられた. | She gave me a false address.
うその報告をしたところで何の解決にもならないよ. | Falsifying reports isn't going to solve anything.
うそのようだが本当の話だ. | It's an incredible story, but it's true.
うそをつけ！ | Don't talk nonsense!
　　 | I'm not falling for that.
彼もうそつきだなあ. 会議には必ず出席すると言っていたのに. | He said he'd attend the meeting. You just can't believe anything that guy says.
うそつきは泥棒の始まり. | Show me a liar and I'll show you a thief.
彼が大統領の親戚だというのもまんざらうそではないらしい. | There seems to be an element of truth in his claiming to be a relative of the president.
「今日, テストをやるんだってさ」「うそ！」 | "Did you hear we're having a test today?" "You're kidding!"

うたう (歌・謳う)

【歌う】僕はギターに合わせてフォークソングを歌った. | I sang a folk song to the accompaniment of a guitar.
みんなで声を揃えて歌おう. | Let's all sing together.
木々のあいだから鳥の歌う声が聞こえてくる. | I can hear a bird singing in the trees.
これは, ある詩人が子どもを失った深い悲しみを歌った詩です. | This is a poem that recounts the deep sadness of a poet who lost his child.
【謳う】戦争放棄は憲法の条文にうたってある. | The renunciation of war is declared in the provisions of the constitution.
広告ではその団地は駅から近いとうたっていました. | The advertisement said the apartment complex was close to the station.

うたがい (疑い)

【疑惑】彼の疑いがようやく晴れた. | He has finally been cleared of suspicion.
彼のその日の行動が疑いを招いた. | His activities that day raised [aroused] some suspicion.
その金は賄賂の疑いが濃い. | It's strongly suspected [There's a strong suspicion] that that money was a bribe.
彼はコレラの疑いで病院に送られ | Cholera was suspected, and he was sent to

た.	the hospital.
疑いのまなざしで僕を見るなよ.	Don't look at me with such †an unbelieving [a doubting] look.
【疑問】彼は教育制度それ自体に疑いを抱いている.	He has doubts about the educational system itself.
彼女の実力は疑いを挟む余地がない.	There's no doubting her ability.
それは疑いようのない事実だ.	That's an unquestionable [undeniable] fact.
本当だよ. 疑い深い人だなあ.	It's true, I tell you! What a doubter! [You're so doubting!]

うたがう (疑う)

【嫌疑をかける】君を疑うわけではない.	It's not that I suspect you of anything.
彼は彼女が秘密を漏らしたのではないかと疑っている.	He suspects that she leaked the secret.
疑われるようなことはするな.	Don't do anything that would arouse suspicion.
【疑問視する】彼は定説を疑っている.	He doubts [questions] the accepted theory.
彼の優勝を疑う者はだれもいない.	Nobody doubts that he will win.
そんなことをしたら君は良識を疑われるよ.	Do something like that and of course people will question your judgment.

うたがわしい (疑わしい)

今度の選挙での彼の当選は疑わしい.	It's doubtful whether he will win the next election.
この記事の内容はどうも疑わしい.	I can't help †being suspicious of [having my doubts about] this article.
警察は彼の疑わしい点を徹底的に洗っている.	The police are investigating all his suspicious points.
疑わしきは罰せず.	You should always give people the benefit of the doubt.

うち (内)

【内部・内面】部屋の内と外との温度差が激しい.	The temperatures inside and outside the room are quite different.
窓の内側に水滴が付いている.	There are drops of water on the inner side of the window.
内からかぎが掛かっている.	It's locked from the inside.
彼の内に秘めた情熱は人一倍だ.	He has far more passion in him than the average man.

【自宅・身内】明日はうちにいる.	Tomorrow I'll be (at) home.
うちに電話してきます.	Excuse me while I call home.
うちにお寄りください.	Please drop in on us.
おうちの方に連絡しましょう.	I'll contact someone at your home.
うち中で旅行に出かけた.	Our whole family went on a trip.
主人はうちのことは私に任せっきりです.	My husband leaves me in complete charge of running the house.
うちはたった5人だけの会社です.	There are only five employees in our company.
【あいだ】一晩のうちに桜が散ってしまった.	All the cherry blossoms fell in a single night.
2, 3日のうちに返事します.	I'll answer within the next two or three days.
朝の涼しいうちに勉強を済ませておこう.	Let's get our studying done while the morning is still cool.
雨が降らないうちに帰ろう.	Let's go home before it starts raining.
若いうちは何でもできる.	You can do anything while you're young.
手紙を書いているうちに無性に彼女に会いたくなってきた.	An overwhelming desire to see her came over me as I wrote the letter.
【～の中】君たちのうち, どちらか手伝って.	One of you, give me a hand, please.
彼の小説のうちで処女作がいちばん好きだ.	Of all his novels, I like his first one best.
彼女など美人のうちに入らない.	I wouldn't say she's beautiful. I wouldn't call her a beauty.
彼は不正事件の内幕を知っている.	He knows the facts behind that scandal.
これは内々だけの話だ.	This is just between us.
内輪もめはよせよ.	Let's not have any infighting.

うちき (内気)

彼は内気なので自分から人に話しかけることができない.	His shyness prevents him from striking up conversations with people.
君は内気を克服するように努力すべきだ.	You should make an effort to overcome your shyness.

うちとける (打ち解ける)

彼は最初は緊張していたが, しばらく話をするうちに打ち解けてきた.	He was tense at first, but after talking with him for a while he gradually loosened up.
彼も最近ようやく私たちに打ち解けてきた.	Recently he's finally begun to relax with us.
彼らとなら打ち解けられそうな気がする.	I think I can †be myself with [feel comfortable around] them.

| なぜか彼とは打ち解けられない. | Somehow I never feel relaxed around him. |
| 彼はどこか打ち解けない. | He's a little reserved. |

うちょうてん (有頂天)

| 彼は大学に合格して有頂天だ. | He made it into college and is beside himself with joy. |
| 一度満点を取ったぐらいで有頂天になるな. | Don't get carried away just because you got a perfect score once. |

うつ (打・撃つ)

【たたく・ぶつける】転んで頭を強く打った.	I fell and hit [struck, banged] my head hard.
今度こそホームランを打ちたい.	I'm going to hit a home run this time or else.
彼は力一杯太鼓を打ち鳴らした.	He beat the drum with all his might.
今6時を打ったところです.	It just struck six.
彼女がタイプを打ってくれるそうだ.	I understand she'll type for us.
壁にくぎを打ってもいいですか.	Is it OK to drive nails into the wall?
彼女に平手打ちを食わされた.	She slapped me across the face.
【感動する】その話に心打たれた.	I was deeply touched [moved] by that story.
先生の熱意に打たれて私もまじめに勉強するようになった.	My teacher's enthusiasm inspired me to start studying more seriously.
【電報を】彼は家へ電報を打った.	He sent a telegram home.
【番号を】学校の備品には番号が打ってある.	Numbers are printed on all school equipment.
【慣用】打てば響くような生徒は教えがいがある.	Responsive students make teaching worthwhile.
彼は老体に鞭打って組織のために奔走している.	The old man has whipped himself into action on behalf of the organization.
【撃つ】彼の撃った弾は木に当たった.	The bullet he shot hit a tree.
今日12時に空砲を撃ちます.	They're going to fire the cannons in salute at 12 o'clock today.

うっかり

うっかり秘密を話してしまった.	I let the secret slip.
うっかり塩を砂糖と間違って入れてしまった.	I added salt instead of sugar by mistake.[1]
今日が約束の日だということをうっかり忘れていた.	It slipped my mind that today was the day we'd agreed on.

> 1) by mistake の代わりに, before I knew it, without realizing it, absent-mindedly などを用いることもできる.

うつくしい (美しい)

彼女の部屋から美しい山並みが見える.	A beautiful range of mountains can be seen from her room.
美しい歌声が聞こえた.	I heard a beautiful [sweet[1]] voice singing.
月が美しく輝いていた.	The moon was shining beautifully.
彼女の美しい心にだれもが胸を打たれた.	Everyone was moved by her †beautiful soul [noble mind,[2] pure heart].
彼女は心の美しい人だ.	She's a beautiful person.[3]
女性は皆美しくなりたいと思っている.	All women want to be beautiful.
彼女は美しく着飾って現れた.	She showed up dressed in a stunning outfit.

> 1) sweet は若い女性の声について言う. 2) noble mind は「気高い心」の意. 3) a beautiful woman とすると「美人」の意.

うつす¹ (写す)

彼は熱心に参考書のリストを書き写した.	He diligently copied the list of reference books.
薄い紙の上からなぞって, その図を写した.	I copied the diagram by tracing it onto a thin piece of paper.
この見取り図の写しが欲しい.	I want a copy of this sketch.
彼のレポートは本の丸写しだ.	His paper is copied right out of the book.
3人で一緒に写真を写そう.	Let's take a picture of the three of us together.

うつす² (映す)

山が湖に影を映している.	The mountains are reflected in the lake.
白い壁にスライドを映そう.	Let's project the slides onto the white wall.
鏡に映してよく見てごらん.	Take a good look in the mirror.

うつす³ (移す)

【動かす】事務所を市内に移した.	We moved the office into the city.
木を移したら部屋が明るくなった.	The room became brighter when we transplanted [moved] the tree.
彼は支店へ移された.	He was transferred to the branch office.
私はまだ住民票を東京に移していない.	I haven't transferred my official residence to Tokyo yet.
シチューを別のなべに移して.	Put the stew in another pot.

このファイルを資料室に移してくれませんか.	Could you transfer these files to the archives?
【感染させる】子どもに風邪をうつさないでね.	Don't give your cold to the children.
彼に風邪をうつされた.	I got [caught] my cold from him.

うったえる (訴える)

【告訴する・告げる】遺族は病院を訴えた.	The family of the deceased †sued the hospital [took the hospital to court].
今度来たら警察に訴えるぞ.	I'll call the police if you ever come here again.
彼女は以前から仕事の辛さを友達に訴えていた.	She had been complaining to her friend for quite some time about how rough her work was.
生徒全員が腹痛を訴えた.	All of the students complained of stomach pains.
彼は街頭に立ち，難民問題の深刻さを通行人たちに訴えていた.	He stood in the street making appeals to passers-by about the seriousness of the refugee problem.
【手段を用いる】暴力に訴えてはいけない.	Don't resort to violence.
裁判に訴えても彼に私の正当性を認めさせなければならない.	I must make him recognize that I was in the right, even if it means going to court.
【働きかける】彼の淡々とした口調がなぜか私の心に訴える.	His low-keyed way of speaking somehow appeals to my emotions.
看板は視覚に訴えるように大きなものを作ってください.	Please make a big sign that will appeal to the eye.

うっとうしい

どんよりとしたうっとうしい天気が続いている.	The weather continues to be overcast [gray] and depressing [gloomy].
前髪が伸びてうっとうしい.	My hair has grown annoyingly long in front.

うっとり

彼女はダイヤモンドの美しさにうっとりした.	She was spellbound by the beauty of the diamond.
彼女の優しい歌声にうっとりと聞き入った.	I was captivated [enchanted] by her gentle singing.
花の香りにうっとりした.	I was †carried away [enraptured] by the fragrance of the flowers.

うつる¹ (写る)

この写真はよく写っている.	This picture came out well.
どの写真にも私は写っていない.	I'm not in any of these pictures.
このコピーは細かい所まではっきり写る.	These photocopies are clear right down to the fine details.

うつる² (映る)

湖面に月が映っている.	The moon is reflected on (the surface of) the lake.
窓に映った自分の姿に驚いた.	I was surprised at my own reflection in the window.
この鏡は大きく映る.	This mirror magnifies whatever is reflected in it.
私の家が今日テレビに映った.	My house appeared on TV today.

うつる³ (移る)

【移動・異動する】窓際の席が空いたから移ろうよ.	The window seats are empty now, so let's move over there.
別の会社に移ることにした.	I decided to switch to a different company.
彼は経済学部から移って来た.	He came to us from the Economics Department.
【変化する】私たちは町の移り変わりを記録した.	We've recorded the changes the town has †seen [been through].
人の心は移ろい易い.	People are fickle [capricious].
【感染する】そばに寄ると病気がうつるよ.	Don't get too close. The disease is contagious.
あくびがうつるって本当?	Is it true that yawning is catching?
父の口癖がうつってしまった.	I've picked up my father's speech habits.

うで (腕)

彼は腕が長い.	He has long arms.
彼は腕を組んで考えた.	He folded his arms and thought.
彼らは腕を組んで歩いた.	They walked arm in arm.
【腕力】腕ずくでも彼をここへ連れて来い.	Bring him here even if you have to use force.
【腕前】あのレストランには腕のいいコックがいる.	The cook at that restaurant is †very good [excellent].
君のゴルフの腕を拝見しよう.	Let's see how good [skillful] you are at golf.
君と今度腕比べをしよう.	Next time let's compare [see] who's better.
そのコンテストで全国の美容師たちが腕を競った.	Hair stylists from all over the country put their talents to the test in that competition.

スキーなら腕に覚えがある.	Skiing? That's something I'm confident in.
さあ，ここからが君の腕の見せどころだ.	Well, †this is [here's] your chance to show your skill.
彼は随分テニスの腕を上げた.	He's made great progress in his tennis skills.
	His tennis game has improved quite a bit.
彼は最近碁の腕を上げた.	He's improved at playing *go* recently.
あの弁護士は腕が立つ.	He's a crackerjack lawyer.
彼は料理が得意なのだが，腕を振るう機会があまりない.	He's an excellent cook, but he seldom gets the chance to show off his talent.
今日のパーティーのごちそうは妻が腕によりをかけて作った.	My wife went all out to prepare the food for tonight's party.
彼は友人が堕落していくのを腕をこまねいて見ているだけだった.	He just stood by and watched as his friend fell into a life of depravity.
もうすぐ囲碁大会だ．腕が鳴る.	The *go* tournament is almost here. I can hardly wait for the chance to put my skill to the test.

うとい (疎い)

彼は世事に疎い.	He's out of touch with the world.
彼は海外の事情に疎い.	He knows very little about (the situation in) other countries.
彼は疎いのでガールフレンドが髪型を変えたことに気がつかない.	He's dense about such things and hasn't noticed that his girlfriend changed her hairstyle.
去る者，日々に疎し.	Out of sight, out of mind.

うなる

高熱のために彼はうんうんうなって寝ていた.	He lay in bed, moaning from the high fever.
彼はうなり声をあげて倒れた.	He groaned and fell to the floor.
犬がこちらを見てうなっている.	The dog's looking this way and growling.
エンジンをうならせて暴走族が駆け抜けていった.	The motorcycle gang gunned their engines and sped past.
彼の演技は批評家たちをうならせた.	His performance really made a hit with the critics.
	He greatly impressed the critics with his performance.

うぬぼれる

彼女は美人だとうぬぼれている.	She's stuck-up about her looks.
私は自分には才能があるとうぬぼれていた.	I was flattering myself to think that I had any talent.

ちょっと褒められたぐらいでうぬぼれるな.	Don't let a little praise go to your head.
彼はうぬぼれの強い人だ.	He's really in love with himself.
	He's really stuck on himself.
うぬぼれるのもいいかげんにしなさい.	I've had just about enough of your conceitedness.

うばう (奪う)

【強奪する】その男は車を奪って逃げた.	He got away in a car he stole.
	He got away in a stolen car.
満員電車で財布を奪われた.	I had my wallet stolen on a crowded train.
すれ違いざまに男にバッグを奪われた.	A man snatched my bag as he was walking past me.
【取り上げる】戦争で多くの生命が奪われた.	Many lives were lost in the war.
彼らは私たち学生の発言権を奪おうとしている.	They're trying to rob [deprive] us students of our right to speak.
彼は陰謀によってその地位を奪われた.	The conspiracy robbed [deprived] him of his position.
空き地に工場が出来て子どもたちの遊び場が奪われた.	Putting up a factory in the vacant lot has robbed the children of a place to play.
汗が蒸発するとき体温を奪う.	As it evaporates, perspiration lowers the body temperature.

うまい

【上手・いい】彼は英語は話せるがうまくはない.	He can speak English, but not very well.
練習すればうまくなれるよ.	If you practice, you'll get better.
彼は車の運転がうまい.	He's a good driver.
彼はギターがとてもうまい.	He's really good at playing the guitar.
それはうまい考えだ.	That's a great idea!
なかなかうまいことを言うね.	You really put things well.
【おいしい】このステーキはうまい.	This steak really tastes good.
今日はたばこがうまい.	Cigarettes really taste good to me today.
【得する】うまい話には気をつけろ.	Beware of offers that sound too good to be true.
彼が一人でうまい汁を吸った.	He took the best for himself.

うまく

実験はうまくいった.	The experiment went well.
たぶん私の計画はうまくいかないと思う.	I'm afraid that my plan won't work out.
彼の今度の金儲け計画は絶対うま	I'm certain that his latest moneymaking

くいかないと思う.	scheme won't pan out.[1]
うまくいけば彼に会えるかもしれない.	If everything goes well I may be able to meet him.
この頃, あの二人はうまくいっていない.	Those two haven't been getting along very well recently.

> 1) pan out は特に規模の大きな計画や, リスクの大きい仕事が成功する場合に使う.

うまれる (生まれる)

私は1972年8月17日に生まれた.	I was born on August 17, 1972.
これがチャーチルの生まれた家です.	This is the house where Churchill was born.
これまでのものとは全く異なった新しいカメラが生まれた.	A new camera which is completely different from all previous ones has been invented.
このテニスクラブが生まれてから今年でちょうど10年です.	This year is the 10th anniversary of the founding of this tennis club.

うむ (産・生む)

彼女は男の子を産んだ.	She gave birth to a baby boy.
妻は春に子どもを産みたいと言っている.	My wife †is saying [says] she'd like to have a baby in the spring.
この鶏はよく卵を産む.	This hen lays a lot of eggs.
そのニュースは数々の風評を生んだ.	That news has given rise to various rumors.
彼の思慮深さが良い結果を生んだ.	His discretion paid off.
その作家は次々に名作を生み出す.	That writer produces one masterpiece after another.
彼はこの制度の生みの親だ.	He's the originator of this system.

うめる (埋める)

ここが古代人が宝物を埋めた場所だ.	This is the place where the ancients buried the treasure.
水道管を埋める工事をしている.	They're laying water pipes.
適当と思われる単語や語句で空欄を埋めなさい.	Fill in the blanks with the appropriate word or phrase.
欠員の穴を埋めなければならない.	We've got to fill this vacant post.
デモ隊が公園をほぼ埋め尽くした.	The demonstrators filled up most of the park.
この辺りは埋め立て地だ.	This is all reclaimed land around here.
【償う】今日遅れた分の時間はきっと埋め合わせをします.	I'll be sure to make up for the time I was late today.

うやまう (敬う)

| 目上の人を敬いなさい. | Respect your superiors. |
| 老人を敬う心をいつも忘れるな. | You should always treat older people with respect. |

うら (裏)

教会はあのビルの裏です.	The church is behind that building.
車を裏に回してください.	Bring the car around back.
その写真の裏には撮影地と日付が書かれていた.	The place and the date the photograph was taken were written on the back.
靴の裏を張り替えてください.	I'd like these shoes resoled.
裏地の色が気に入らない.	I don't like the color of this lining.
彼は8回の裏に三塁打を放った.	He hit a triple in the bottom of the eighth.
(硬貨の)表か裏か?	Heads or tails?
靴下を裏返しにはいた.	I put my socks on inside out.
書類を裏返しに置いた.	I left the papers face down.
本を裏返して値段を見た.	I turned the book over to look at the price.
【隠れた面】物事には裏と表がある.	There's a hidden side to everything.
言葉の裏を読み取れなければ一人前の記者ではない.	You can't call yourself a full-fledged reporter if you always take what you hear at face value.
私は裏の社会をあまり知らない.	I don't know much about the seamy side of life.

うらぎる (裏切る)

仲間を裏切ってはいけない.	Never betray a friend.
親の期待を裏切ってしまった.	I disappointed my parents badly. / I let my parents down.
彼の裏切り行為は許しがたい.	I can't bring myself to forgive his treachery.
先生に告げ口をした裏切り者がいるに違いない.	Somebody must have turned on us and †told [squealed to**] the teacher.
あの裏切り者をこのまま許してはおけない.	We can't just let that traitor go scot-free.

うらみ (恨み)

| 彼のきまじめさが時に人の恨みを買うのを彼は知らない. | He doesn't realize that his earnestness sometimes makes people resent him. |
| 彼は恨みを晴らそうと企んでいる. | He's planning [scheming] to take revenge. |

うらむ (恨む)

| 私はしかたなく彼を首にしたが, | I had no choice but to fire him, but I'm |

彼は私のことを恨んでいるに違いない.	sure he holds a grudge against me.
人を恨んでも始まらない.	Bearing a grudge won't get you anywhere.

うらめしい (恨めしい)

彼女は背が低いのを恨めしく思っている.	She resents the fact that she's short.
学生時代に勉強しなかったことが恨めしい.	I regret that I didn't study when I was in school.
彼が本当のことを言ってくれなかったのが恨めしい.	It's a pity that he didn't tell me the truth.

うらやましい

君がうらやましい.	I wish I were †you [in your shoes]. How I envy you![1]
家族で海外旅行とはうらやましい.	Isn't it great that you can take the whole family on a trip abroad!
だれもが彼の頭の良さをうらやましく思っている.	Everyone envies his intelligence.
その女の子はうらやましそうに私のお菓子を見ていた.	The little girl was looking longingly at my candy.

> 1) この表現は軽く使えないこともないが,口調によっては「ねたましい」「嫉妬している」というネガティブな感情と相手に受けとられかねないので注意.

うらやむ

人の成功をうらやむより自分で努力しろ.	Forget about envying other people's success, and work on your own.
彼らは人がうらやむほど仲の良い家族だった.	They were such a happy family that everyone envied them.

うる (売る)

これをいくらで売ってくれますか.	How much will you sell this for? How much will you take for this? How much do you want for this?
100ドル以下では売れない.	I can't †sell it [let it go] for less than $100.
あの店ではその品物を2,000円で売っている.	That store is selling that product for ¥2,000.
卵はダースで売っている.	Eggs are sold by the dozen.
売り惜しんでかえって損をした.	I held out on selling it too long and ended up taking a loss.
早く行かないと売り切れるよ.	If you don't go soon, they'll be sold out.

それは見かけは悪いが耐久性が売り物だ.	It doesn't look too good, but its durability is its selling point.

うるさい

車の音がうるさくて眠れない.	The traffic is so noisy I can't sleep.
ハエがうるさくてゆっくり食事することもできなかった.	We couldn't enjoy our meal because of the flies.
彼は金〔時間〕にうるさい.	He's fussy [particular] about money [time].
うちの親はうるさい.	My parents are always bugging** me.
世間とかくうるさいものだ.	People †will [tend to] talk.

うれしい

君にここで会えてうれしい.	It's nice to meet you here.
君の出世〔昇進〕をうれしく思っている.	I'm happy to hear of your success [promotion].
涙が出るほどうれしかった.	I nearly wept for joy.
こんなにうれしいことはない.	Nothing †could make [makes] me happier!
うれしい！	Great!／I'm so happy!
犬がうれしそうに尾を振った.	The dog wagged its tail happily.

うれる（売れる）

彼女の本はよく売れる.	Her books sell well.
飛ぶように売れている.	They just can't keep enough of them in stock.
	They're selling like hot cakes.
彼女は売れっ子作家だ.	She's quite a popular writer.

うろたえる

何があってもうろたえるな.	No matter what happens, don't †get flustered [lose your cool].
電話の声を聞いてうろたえた.	When I heard the voice on the phone, I got flustered.
彼はうろたえることなく落ち着いて行動した.	He acted calmly, without getting flustered.

うわき〔浮気〕

ほんの出来心で浮気してしまった.	What started out as just having a little fun turned into an affair.
妻に携帯電話のメールをチェックされ，浮気がばれた.	My wife discovered the affair after checking the e-mail on my cell phone.
彼は妻に悪いと思いつつ浮気を重ねた.	He continued to have affairs, all the while feeling bad for his wife.
彼は浮気性の奥さんを持って苦労	His flirtatious wife is causing him a lot of

している.	pain.
テレビの視聴者は浮気っぽい.	TV viewers are fickle.

うわさ

彼女が結婚するといううわさは前からあった.	There were already rumors that she was going to get married.
この辺に高速道路が走るといううわさが立った.	A rumor started that an expressway is to be built around here.
変なうわさを立てたのはあなたでしょう.	I bet it was you who started that ugly rumor.
その男について黒いうわさが流れている.	Dark rumors are circulating about that man.
良きにつけ悪しきにつけ,とかく彼はうわさに上る人だ.	His name often comes up in gossip, whether it's good or bad.
そんなうわさ,どこから出ているんですか.	Where did that rumor come from?
それは根も葉もないうわさだ.	That's a completely unfounded rumor.
町のうわさでは,ただの事故ではなかったらしい.	Rumor has it that it wasn't just an accident.
おうわさは彼から聞いております.	I've heard †a lot [all] about you from him.
うわさで知っているだけだ.	I know it only by hearsay.
会社はそのうわさでもちきりだ.	It's all anybody talks about at the office.
近所の人がうちの息子のうわさをしているのを聞いた.	I heard (one of) the neighbors gossiping about our son.
人のうわさも七十五日.	Rumors don't go on forever.
うわさをすれば影.	(Well,) Speak of the devil....

うん (運)

あなたは運のいい〔悪い〕人だ.	You're †a lucky [an unlucky] person.
運良く彼は家にいた.	Luckily [Fortunately] he was home.
彼にもやっと運が向いてきた.	Luck finally turned his way.
最近運が向いてきた.	Things have been going my way lately.
運が尽きてからでは遅い.	After your luck runs out it will be too late.
彼に出会ったのが運の尽きだった.	My luck ran out when I met him.
やるだけのことはやった. あとは運を天に任せよう.	I did all I could. Now I'll just leave everything to fate [luck].
運試しに宝くじを買った.	I bought some lottery tickets to try my luck.
今月のあなたの運勢はあまり良くない.	The stars aren't in your favor this month.
彼は悪運が強い.	He has the devil's own luck.
彼はまたも悪運に見舞われた.	Bad luck paid him yet another visit.

うんざり

彼の説教はもううんざりだ.	I've had enough [I'm sick] of his sermons.
勉強なんてうんざりだ.	I'm sick of studying.
スパゲティにはうんざりだ.	I'm sick of spaghetti.
ケーキをうんざりするほど食べた.	I had enough cake to make me sick.
そのパーティーではうんざりするほどのごちそうが出た.	There was enough food at that party to make you sick.

うんどう (運動)

得意な運動は何ですか.	What sports are you good at?
毎日軽い運動をしたほうがいい.	You ought to get [do] †some [a little] exercise every day.
日本では運動会は10月に行われることが多い.	Athletic festivals are often held in October in Japan.
彼は運動神経が発達している〔鈍い〕.	He has good 〔poor〕 coordination. He's 〔He's not〕 well coordinated.
近年, 反核運動が盛んになってきた.	In recent years the anti-nuclear [ban-the-bomb] movement has become quite strong.
彼女の留任を求める運動を起こさなければならない.	We should start a movement to keep her in office.

うんめい (運命)

運命はだれにも分からない.	Nobody knows his own destiny.
それも運命とあきらめた.	We chalked it up to fate.
彼らと運命をともにするつもりだ.	I'll take my chances with them.
運命の日が来た.	The day arrived that was to determine my future.
運命のいたずらで彼女と結婚できなかった.	A quirk of fate prevented me from marrying her.
運命は自分で切り開くものだ.	What you amount to in this life is (entirely) up to you.
我々は皆同じ運命にある.	We're all in the same boat.
運命の女神がほほえんでくれるかもしれない.	The Fates may smile upon us.
その悲しい事故以来, 彼は運命論者になった.	That tragic accident turned him into a confirmed fatalist.

え

えいきょう (影響)
吉田松陰は当時の若者に大きな影響を与えた. — Yoshida Shoin exerted a strong influence on the younger generation of his day.
彼は父親の影響を受けて同じ電子工学を専攻した. — Influenced by his father, he too majored in electronic engineering.
仲間の影響で彼はたばこを吸うようになった. — He picked up the habit of smoking from being around his friends.
台風の影響で今日は風が強い. — There's a strong wind today because of the typhoon.
彼女は人に影響され易いタイプだ. — She's easily influenced. / She's the type who's easily swayed.

えいぎょう (営業)
【販売・売り込み】彼はこのところ新製品の営業にまわっている. — He's making the rounds these days, promoting a new product.
営業成績上位者の名前が毎月, 壁に貼り出される. — The names of the top sales persons are posted on the wall every month.
レンタル事業部は営業不振だ. — Business in the rentals department is slow.
営業部はいつも活気にあふれている. — The sales department is always full of activity.
彼は営業部員です. — He's in the sales department.
仙台営業所に転勤になった. — I was transferred to the Sendai office.
【開店・業務】営業時間は午前10時から午後8時までです. — Business hours are [We are open] between 10 in the morning and 8 at night.
まだ営業中ですか? — Are you still open (for business)?
あの店は食中毒で3日間の営業停止処分を受けた. — That restaurant was shut down for three days because of food poisoning.

えいせい (衛生)
夏場は衛生に気をつけよう. — We have to be careful about sanitation in the summer.
熱湯で食器を洗うのはとても衛生的だ. — It's very hygienic to wash dishes in hot water.
これは衛生的な台所だ. — This is a sanitary kitchen.
ゴミを放置しておくのは不衛生だ. — Leaving garbage around isn't sanitary.

えいよう

あのキャンプ場の衛生設備は良くない.	That campsite has inadequate facilities for good hygiene.
その国ではまだ人々の衛生観念が低い.	The people in that country still really aren't aware of the importance of sanitation.
保健所は公衆衛生の向上に大きな役割を演じてきた.	Public health centers have played an important role in the improvement of public health.

えいよう (栄養)

君はもっと栄養を取る必要がある.	You need to take more nourishment.
栄養のある食事を取って安静にしていれば風邪は治るよ.	You'll get over your cold if you eat nutritious food and get plenty of rest.
この食物はあまり栄養がない.	This food isn't very nutritious.
チーズは非常に栄養価が高い.	Cheese has a very high nutritional value. Cheese is very nutritious.
その子どもは栄養不良だった.	The child was suffering from malnutrition.

えがく (描く)

【絵にかく】この絵は農村の風景を描いたものだ.	This is a painting of a rural scene.
その洞くつの壁には動物の絵が描かれている.	There are drawings of animals on the walls of that cave.
彼は見事なシュプールを描いて滑って行った.	He cut a splendid figure as he skied.
【描写する】彼はその小説で現代の若者を生き生きと描いた.	He vividly depicted today's young people in his novel.
この小説はその島の昔の生活を描いている.	This novel portrays how the people of that island lived long ago.
【思い描く】30年後の自分の姿を思い描いてみた.	I tried to picture [imagine, visualize] what I would look like thirty years from now.
彼らは勝利を胸に描いて厳しい練習に耐えた.	The thought of victory kept them training hard.

えらい (偉い)

ヘレン・ケラーは偉い人だった.	Helen Keller was †an exceptional [a great] human being.
彼は医者として偉かった.	He was a distinguished doctor.
そこが彼の偉いところだ.	That's what's admirable about him.
彼は自分が偉い人間だと思っている.	He really thinks he's something.
彼は偉い役人だ.	He's an official of high rank. He's †a high ranking [an important] offi-

	cial.
彼の息子は会社でだいぶ偉くなった.	His son has risen to a rather high position in the company.
彼は偉そうな顔をしている.	He puts on airs./He acts big.
偉そうなことを言うな.	Don't talk so big.
父はいつも家で偉そうにしていた.	My father always acted big around the house.
偉い！よくやった.	Great! You did a good job!
【大変な】吹雪でえらい目にあった.	I had a terrible time in the blizzard.
これはえらいことになったぞ.	Now we're in a mess.
君もえらいことをしでかしたな.	Now you've really done it.

えらぶ（選ぶ）

五つの中から一つ選びなさい.	Choose [Select] one †out of [from] the five.
上手に選んだね.	You made a good choice.
	You chose well.
私に最初に選ばせて.	Let me have the first choice.
どれを選ぶ？	Which one do you choose?
君のほうで日を選んでください.	*You* pick [choose] the day.
彼女はその賞〔主役〕に選ばれた.	She was selected [chosen] for †that prize [the leading role].
彼は議長に選ばれた.	He was †elected [chosen to be] chairman.

える（得る）

私は主に外国の本から知識を得ている.	I get [obtain, acquire] most of my knowledge from foreign books.
彼は慶応大学で教授の職を得た.	He got [obtained] a professorship at Keio University.
彼女はその小説で名声を得た.	She got [attained, achieved*] fame as a result of that novel.
練習の成果があってその試合で勝利を得た.	Our practice really paid off—we won the match.
彼は得がたい友人です.	He's a friend who would be hard to replace.

えん（縁）

その仕事とは縁が切れた.	I'm finished with that job.
芸術とは全く縁がなかった彼が画商を始めた.	Despite a complete lack of background, he started up his own art dealership.
彼は母の縁続きだ.	He's on my mother's side of the family.
親子の縁は切っても切れない.	The parent-child relationship can never be broken.
	The bond between parent and child is

	eternal.
私は彼女と縁もゆかりもない.	She's no friend or relative of mine.
彼はその会社とは縁もゆかりもない.	He has nothing to do with that company.
不思議な縁で彼と再び巡り合った.	By curious coincidence I ran into him again.
ここであなたに会ったのも何かの縁でしょう.	It must be fate, meeting you here.

えんき (延期)

決勝戦は雨のため明日に延期された.	The final game has been postponed until tomorrow on account of rain.
試験は1週間後に延期します.	I'm postponing the examination until a week from now.
天候が回復するまで出発は延期しよう.	Let's †postpone [put off] leaving until the weather clears up.

えんぎ (縁起)

母はよく縁起をかつぎます.	My mother is very superstitious.
虹を見るのは縁起がいい.	Seeing a rainbow is supposed to bring good luck.
黒猫は縁起が悪いとされています.	Black cats are said to be bad luck [omens].
そんな縁起の悪いことを言うな.	Don't say that. It'll [It might] bring bad luck.
そんなことを言うなんて縁起でもない.	You'd better knock on wood after saying something like that.
縁起直しに一杯飲もうよ.	Let's have a drink. Maybe it'll change our luck.

えんきょく (婉曲)

彼女は婉曲に彼のプロポーズを断った.	She turned down his proposal (of marriage) in a roundabout way.
「トイレの婉曲表現はありますか」「レディズルーム,またはメンズルームと言います」	"Is there a more polite word for toilet?" "Well, you can say the ladies' room or men's room."
「リストラ」はしばしば「人員削減」の婉曲表現として使われる.	"Restructuring" is often used as a euphemism for cutting staff.

えんそう (演奏)

その交響楽団の演奏は素晴らしかった.	The orchestra gave a wonderful performance.
彼女は初めて大勢の聴衆の前でピ	She played the piano before a large audi-

アノを演奏した. ence for the first time.
10月に演奏会を開きます. I'm giving a concert in October.

えんりょ（遠慮）

彼女はいつも遠慮がちだ. She always tends to be reserved.
彼女は遠慮がちにドアを開けた. She opened the door hesitantly.
遠慮して彼らの話には口を挟まなかった. Feeling it was not my place to speak, I stayed out of the conversation.
彼らに遠慮して席を外した. I got up and left out of respect for their privacy.
彼は私に遠慮するところがある. He maintains a somewhat reserved attitude toward me.
ビールをたくさん飲んで彼はすっかり遠慮が無くなった. Drinking a lot of beer †loosened his tongue [made him lose his restraint].
用があれば遠慮なく言ってください. If there's something I can do, don't hesitate to ask.
遠慮なくお召し上がりください. Please help yourself.
この件について遠慮のない意見を聞かせてください. Please give me your candid [frank] opinion about this.
遠慮のない批評がいちばんためになる. Honest criticism is most helpful.
私たちはお互いに全く遠慮がない. We're perfectly †at home [open] with each other.
【やめる】たばこはご遠慮ください. Please refrain from smoking.
この招待は遠慮したい. I'd rather not accept this invitation.
【席を外す】二人だけで話したいのでしばらく遠慮してくれる？ The two of us would like to talk, so could you leave us alone for a while, please?

お

おいかえす（追い返す）

彼がまた来たら追い返せ. If he comes again, send him away [packing].
寄付を頼みに行ったら玄関先で追い返された. I got the door slammed in my face when I went to ask for a donation.

おいかける（追いかける）

追いかけろ. After him!

すりを追いかけたが見失った.	I ran after the pickpocket but lost (sight of) him.
犬に追いかけられた.	I was chased by a dog.

おいこす (追い越す)

前の車を追い越そう.	Let's pass the car in front.
ここは追い越し禁止だ.	This is a no-passing zone.
彼らは電子工学の分野でアメリカを追い越そうと努力している.	They're trying to overtake America in the field of electronics.
弟の背は彼を追い越した.	His younger brother's gotten taller than he is.

おいこむ (追い込む)

羊を囲いの中に追い込め.	Drive the sheep into the pen.
長引く不景気で彼の会社は倒産に追い込まれた.	The long recession pushed his company into bankruptcy.
受験勉強は最後の追い込みに入っている.	I'm making a final push studying for my entrance exams.
そろそろ追い込みをかけないと間に合わない.	We won't make it (in time) if we don't give it a final push now.

おいしい

このシチューはおいしい.	This stew †tastes good [is good, is tasty].
おいしいパンが食べたい.	I feel like eating some tasty [fresh] bread.
ステーキのおいしい店がある.	I know †a good steakhouse [a place that serves really tasty steak].
その店はあまりおいしくない.	The food there isn't †so good [that great].
ああ, おいしかった.	Umm, that was good.
ごちそうさま, とてもおいしくいただきました.	Thank you. That was really delicious.
今朝は食事がおいしかった.	Breakfast today was delicious.
山の空気はおいしい.	The mountain air is delicious.

おいだす (追い出す)

彼を追い出せ.	Get him out of here!
父親は息子を家から追い出した.	He threw his own son out of the house.
家賃を半年もためてしまったのでアパートから追い出された.	I hadn't paid my rent for six months, and got kicked out of my apartment.
出て行かないなら追い出すぞ.	If you don't leave on your own, I'll throw you out.

おいつく (追いつく)

走れば彼に追いつくだろう.	If you run, you can probably catch up

	with him.
ああ，やっと追いついた．	Whew! I finally caught up.
当時の人々は西洋に追いつこうとしていた．	People at that time were trying to catch up with the West.
彼に追いつき追い越せと自分に言い聞かせている．	I keep telling myself to catch up with him and pass him.

おう（追う）

【追いかける】犯人を追え．	Go after the culprit!
家事に追われて本を読む暇がない．	I'm so pressed with housework that I don't have time to read.
【追い払う】その子犬はいくら私が追ってもついてきた．	That puppy followed me no matter how much I tried to shoo him away.
彼は部下の汚職で地位を追われることになった．	He ended up being driven from his post because of a corrupt subordinate.

おうじる（応じる）

【受けて立つ】彼はチャンピオンだからだれの挑戦にも応じる．	He's the champion so he takes on all comers.
彼は講演のあと，聴衆の質問に応じた．	He took questions from the audience after his lecture.
【要望に答える】たくさんの人々が献血の呼びかけに応じた．	There was a tremendous public response to the call for blood donations.
人々の需要に応じて商品は製造される．	Products are manufactured in response to public demand.
【見合う】景気の変動に応じた柔軟な対策が必要とされている．	A flexible policy that responds to economic fluctuations is necessary.
彼のところでは収入に応じた生活をしている．	He and his family live within their income [means].
彼らは能力に応じて仕事を配分された．	The work was allotted to them according to their (respective) abilities.
賃金は出来高に応じて支払われた．	Wages were paid in proportion to output.

おうちゃく（横着）

彼は横着だから自分の部屋の掃除などしない．	He's too lazy to do anything like cleaning his room.
横着をせずに自分で辞書を引きなさい．	Stop being lazy and look up the words in the dictionary yourself.
横着を決めこんで旅行の段取りは全部人任せにした．	I was negligent in leaving all our travel plans up to the others in the group.

おうふく（往復）

往復で50キロある．	It's fifty kilometers †round trip [there and

	back].
私は通学に往復1時間かかる.	It takes me one hour to commute to and from school.
駅までの往復時間はどのくらいですか.	How long does it take to (get to) the station and back?
シアトルまでの往復運賃はいくらですか.	How much is [What's] the round-trip fare to Seattle?
彼らの間には月に1度手紙の往復がある.	They exchange letters once a month.

おうへい（横柄）

彼は態度が横柄なので友達が出来ない.	His arrogant attitude keeps him from winning friends.
彼は賞を取ってから横柄になった.	Winning the prize went to his head.

おうぼう（横暴）

彼はおとなしそうに見えるが，家ではひどく横暴だそうだ.	He looks mild-mannered, but I hear he's quite †the tyrant [tyrannical] at home.
政府の横暴なやり方には腹が立つ.	The government's arbitrary way of doing things makes me angry.
彼の発言は横暴だ.	His statements are high-handed.

おうよう¹（応用）

てこの原理を応用しよう.	Let's use some leverage.[1]
彼の理論は広く応用できる.	His theory has wide application.
	His theory is widely applicable.
実際に応用して，その理論が正しいことを証明しよう.	Let's demonstrate the theory's validity by †applying it to reality [putting it into practical use].
実地に応用できる知識を身につけておいたほうがいい.	You should learn something that you can †apply in the real world [actually put to use].

1) この文は「有力者を利用しよう」という比喩的な意味で使われることもある.

おうよう²（鷹揚）

彼のおうような人柄はみんなに好かれている.	Everyone likes him for his liberal character.
彼は金におうようだ.	He's generous with his money.
試験前だというのに彼はおうように構えている.	Even though there's a test coming up, he's as relaxed [laid-back**] as can be.
彼女はおうような育ち方をしたの	She must have been brought up in a care-

だろう.　　　　　　　　　　　free environment.
　　　　　　　　　　　　　　　She must have had a carefree childhood.

おえる（終える）
　彼は一日の仕事を終えてほっと一息ついたところだ.　　He's just catching his breath after finishing a hard day's work.
　掃除を終えたら牛乳を買いに行ってください.　　Please go buy some milk when you're finished [through] with the cleaning.
　私は学業を終えるとすぐ自分で事業を始めた.　　I started my own business as soon as I finished [completed] my studies.

おおい（多い）
　このクラスは人数が多い.　　There are †a lot of [many] people in this class.
　この辺は車の事故が多い.　　There are †a lot of [many] car accidents around here.
　この国は湖が多い.　　This country has many lakes.
　この地方は雪が多い.　　There's a lot of snow [It snows a lot] in this area.
　その川は水かさがあまり多くない.　　There's not much water in the river.
　　　　　　　　　　　　　　　The water level of the river isn't very high.
　緑の多い町だ.　　It's a town with a lot of greenery.
　多ければ多いほどいい.　　The more, the better.
　彼は休みが多い.　　He has [takes] a lot of time off.
　彼女はいつも一言多い.　　She always says one word too many.
　この問題を全部解ける生徒は多くて2, 3人だろう.　　At (the) most there're only two or three students who can solve all of these problems.

おおいに（大いに）
　お祭りは大いに楽しもう.　　Let's really enjoy ourselves at the festival.
　彼を大いに見習いなさい.　　You should do your best to follow his example.
　あなたの意見は大いに参考になりました.　　Your opinion proved to be of great use.

おおう（覆う）
　私の部屋の家具は白い布で覆ってある.　　The furniture in my room is covered with white cloth.
　春が来て牧場は一面緑で覆われた.　　When spring came, the pasture became covered with green.
　村は一晩ですっぽりと雪に覆われた.　　The village was entirely blanketed [covered] with snow overnight.

干ばつと飢きんが国じゅうを覆った.	Drought and famine descended on the entire country.
スタンドは熱気に覆われた.	Excitement swept through the bleachers.
事故現場は目を覆うばかりの惨状だった.	The scene of the accident was horrible enough to make people cover their eyes.
彼は私に耳を覆いたくなるような悪口を浴びせた.	He rained such abuses on me that I wanted to cover my ears.
政策の失敗は覆うべからざる事実だ.	The failure of government policy is an unconcealable fact.
市当局は助役の収賄を覆い隠そうとした.	The city officials tried to cover up the deputy mayor's acceptance of a bribe.

おおきい (大きい)

彼は大きな家に住んでいる.	He lives in a big [large] house.
スティーブは兄さんより大きい.	Steve is bigger than his older brother.
大きな火事があったそうだ.	I hear there was a big fire.
年に1度の大きな集会だ.	It's a large annual meeting.
彼の思想は若者たちに大きな影響を与えた.	His ideas influenced young people greatly.
新聞に出てから問題は更に大きくなった.	The problem became even bigger after it came out in the papers.
大きな失敗がなければ彼の優勝は間違いない.	He's assured of victory provided he doesn't make any serious errors.
設計に大きなミスがある.	There's a serious error [flaw] in the design.
娘も随分大きくなった.	Our daughter has really grown.
もっと大きい声で言ってください.	Please speak †a little louder [up].
彼は大きなことを言っているが当てにならない.	He's talking big, but you can't take him at his word.

おおく (多く)

その国では多くの人々が飢えに苦しんでいる.	Many [A lot of] people are starving in that country.
会社はその製品の開発に多くの金と人材をつぎ込んだ.	The company poured †a great deal of [a lot of] money and human energy into the development of that product.
国民の多くは現行憲法を支持している.	Most of †the nation supports [the people support] the existing constitution.
彼はその件について多くを語ろうとしなかった.	He didn't attempt to relate †a great deal [much] about the affair.
経験が浅いので彼には多くは望めまい.	Not much can be expected from him since he has little experience.

おおげさ (大げさ)
彼の話はいつも大げさだ. — He always exaggerates.
彼女は大げさな身振りで話す. — She speaks with exaggerated gestures.
週刊誌はそれを大げさに書きたてた. — The weeklies sensationalized that story.
救急車を呼ぶなんて大げさだ. — Calling an ambulance is overdoing it.
披露宴はあまり大げさにしたくない. — We don't want to have an extravagant wedding reception.

おおざっぱ (大ざっぱ)
大ざっぱに見積もって修理にいくらぐらいかかりますか. — Can you give me a rough estimate on the repairs?
大ざっぱなやり方ではこの仕事はうまくいかないよ. — This job mustn't be done in a haphazard way.
大ざっぱだが一応の趣旨は彼に伝えておいた. — I didn't go into specifics [details] but I did convey the main idea to him.
大ざっぱなことを言うやつだ. — He speaks in broad generalizations. He's never very specific.

おおぜい (大勢)
広場には人が大勢いた. — Many people were in the square.
キャンプには大勢で行った. — We went to camp in a large group.
私はあがってしまうので,大勢の人の前では話すことがなかなかできない. — I get so self-conscious that it's almost impossible for me to speak in front of a large group of people.
このクラスには成績のいい生徒が大勢いる. — There are †many [quite a few] students with good grades in this class.

オーバー
【超過】彼女にねだられた指輪は予算オーバーだった. — The ring she talked me into buying was †beyond my means [over my budget].
博多行きの新幹線は定員オーバーで発車した. — The bullet train to Hakata departed with a passenger overload.
【大げさ】今世紀最高傑作だって? ずいぶんオーバーな表現だな. — The masterpiece of the century, you say? That's an exaggeration, to say the least.
彼のオーバーなリアクションは人を疲れさせる. — His excessive behavior tires people out.

おおめ (多め・大目)
【少し多く】コーヒーに砂糖を多めに入れて飲んだ. — I drank my coffee with a little extra sugar in it.
あの店では肉をいつも多めに計ってくれる. — That shop always weighs meat on the heavy side.

おおらか

【寛大】今度の失敗だけは大目に見てやろう.	I'll overlook your slip-up, but just this once.
こんなに門限破りがたび重なってはもう大目に見るわけにはいかない.	You've broken curfew so many times now that I can no longer †overlook it [let it pass].
今まで君のことを大目に見てきたが,もう許すわけにはいかない.	So far I've been patient with you, but now I've had it.

おおらか

彼はおおらかな心の持ち主だ.	He has a generous heart.[1]
彼女は恵まれた家庭でおおらかに育った.	She had a carefree childhood in a privileged family.

> 1) He's generous. とすると「他人に対してお金を使うのを惜しまない」「気前がいい」の意味になる.

おかげ (お陰)

私が今日あるのもみんな母のお陰です.	Everything I am [have] today, I owe to Mother.
毎日何不自由なく暮らしていけるのもみんな一生懸命働いてくれる父のお陰です.	We owe our comfortable lifestyle in all respects to my father's hard work.
君が協力してくれたお陰でこの研究を完成できた.	This research was completed thanks to your cooperation.
うんと勉強したお陰で目指す大学に入ることができた.	I was able to enter the college of my choice because I studied really hard.
君があんなことを言ったお陰で彼女に嫌われてしまった.	She hates me now, and it's all thanks to your big mouth.
彼のエラーのお陰で試合に負けてしまった.	His error lost us the game.
お陰様で病気は全快しました.	Fortunately,[1] I've completely recovered.

> 1)「お陰様で」に相当するような英語はないが,こういう場合,英語では習慣的に fortunately を使う.

おかしい

【こっけいだ】おかしくてたまらない.	That's too much. ／That's a scream!** I can't help laughing.
何がそんなにおかしいの?	What's so funny?
彼は自分がハンサムだと思っているからおかしい.	It's too much [It just kills me] that he thinks he's handsome.
彼女は彼のしぐさがおかしいと言って笑った.	She laughed at his gestures.

【変だ】車の調子がおかしい.	Something's wrong with the car.
おなかの具合がおかしい.	My stomach feels funny.
彼は頭がおかしいんじゃないか？	He's a little off, don't you think?
彼が遅れるなんておかしい.	It's strange that he'd be late.
議長を責めるのはおかしい.	It's not right to blame the chairman.
その服にその靴はおかしい.	Those shoes look funny with that suit.
最初は君のことをおかしなやつだと思ったよ.	I thought you were a strange guy at first.
最近, おかしな男が公園で目撃されている.	A strange man has been seen in the park recently.
おかしいな, ここに置いた時計はどこにいったんだろう.	That's strange. Where's the watch I put here?

～おき (～置き)

6時間置きに体温を測った.	I took my temperature every six hours.
1時間置きに電話を入れてくれ.	Call me †once an hour [once every hour, every hour].
1日置きにこの薬を飲みなさい.	Take this medicine every other day.
彼は三日置きに訪ねてくる.	He comes to visit every four[1] days.
会議は1週置きに開かれる.	Meetings are held every other week.
レポートは1行置きに (ダブルスペースで) 書きなさい.	Double-space[2] this report when you write it.
試験のときは一つ置きに席に座らされた.	We were seated every other chair when we took the test.
5メートル置きに杉の苗を植えた.	I planted the cedar saplings †five meters apart [every five meters].

> 1)2) 英語の数は日本語の数より一つ大きいことに注意.

おぎなう (補う)

市会議員の欠員を補うための選挙が行われた.	An election was held in order to fill the vacant post on the city council.
その国はほとんどの食糧を輸入で補っている.	Almost all of that country's food is supplied by imports.
あの会社は事業の損失を補うために, 無理な操業を余儀なくされている.	That company has been forced to push its operations to the limit in order to †compensate [make up] for business losses.
この地方の農家は出稼ぎで収入を補っている.	The farmers in this region supplement their incomes with jobs away from their farms.
彼女の優しさはほかの欠点のすべてを補って余りある.	Her kindness more than makes up for all her other faults.

おきる (起きる)

もう起きる時間だ.	It's (already) time to get up.
今朝は目覚ましが鳴らず，起きた(目が覚めた)のは10時過ぎだった.	My alarm clock didn't go off this morning, so I didn't wake up until after ten o'clock.
彼ならもう起きているだろう.	He †should [ought to] be up by now.
仕事で遅くまで起きていた.	I stayed [was, sat] up late working.
ベッドに入ってからもしばらくは起きていた.	I lay awake for a while after getting into bed.
起き上がって本を読むことは医者から許されている.	The doctor has said I can sit up and read.

おく¹ (置く)

いすをどこに置きますか.	Where should I put the chair?
食卓がいっぱいでパンを置く所がない.	There's no room †on the table for the bread [to put the bread on the table].
これは日陰に置いたほうがいい.	We'd better keep this out of the sun. We'd better put this in the shade.
あのフロアランプは隅に置いたらどうでしょう.	Why don't you stand that floor lamp up in the corner?
【残す】子どもは家に置いてきた.	We left the children at home.
彼は書き置きを置いて家出してしまった.	He left a note and abandoned his family.
出かける前に少しお金を置いていってください.	Would you leave (me) some money before you go out?
【保存する】このとうもろこしは明日まで置くと味が落ちるよ.	If you let this corn sit till tomorrow, it won't taste so good.
この肉だんごは何日くらい置けますか.	How many days will these meatballs keep?
【扱う】「この店は靴下を置いていますか」「あいにく置いてないんです」	"Do you have [sell] socks in this store?" "No, I'm sorry we don't."
カルバン・クラインの服を置いていますか.	Do you carry¹⁾ Calvin Klein?
【住まわせる】彼の家は下宿人を二人置いている.	He has two boarders at his house.
私の家は昔お手伝いさんを置いていた.	A long time ago we had a live-in maid.
【駐在させる】パリに駐在員を置くことにした.	We're going to station [have] a representative in Paris.
【差し置く】彼を置いて私が議長に選ばれるなんておこがましい.	It would be presumptuous of me to accept the chairmanship over him.
彼を置いて私がこんな大切な決定	It would be impossible for me to leave him

を下すなんてできない.	out of making such an important decision.
【除く】この役ができるのは彼女を置いてほかにない.	There's no one besides her who can play this role.
【隔てる】三日置いてからまた来てください.	Please come again four[2] days from now.
私の家の一軒置いて隣が彼女の家だ.	Her house is two[3] doors down [away] from mine.
【そのままにする】気持ちが落ち着くまでそっとしておいてやろう.	Let's leave him alone till he calms down.
窓は(閉めないで)開けておいてください.	Please leave the window open.
【前もって〜する】前もって断っておけば叱られずに済んだと思う.	I think I would have gotten by without getting scolded if I had asked (for permission) beforehand.
見ておいて損はない.	There's no harm in having [taking] a look at it.

> 1) carry はあるブランドの品物が置いてあるかどうかという場合に使うことが多い. 2)3) 英語の数は日本語の数より一つ大きくなることに注意.

おく² (奥)

預金通帳は引き出しの奥だ.	The bankbook is in the back of the drawer.
奥の方にある建物は全部理学部の建物だ.	The buildings in the back are all the science department's.
これより奥には行けない.	You can't go in any further than here.
私は山奥の小さな村で育った.	I grew up in a small village deep in the mountains.
表通りから一歩奥まった所においしいレストランがある.	There's a good restaurant just a little †off [back from] the main street.
彼は心の奥では何を考えているのか分からない.	I don't know what he's thinking deep down [inside].
こうなったら奥の手を使うしかない.	We have no choice at this point but to play our ace in the hole.

おくびょう (臆病)

彼は慎重というより臆病だ.	I'd say that he's †a coward [chicken-hearted**] rather than cautious.
彼は昔は臆病者と言われていたそうだ.	I hear he used to be called a coward.
レースの前日になって急に臆病風	The day before the race, I †lost my nerve

に吹かれて棄権した.	[chickened out, got cold feet] and defaulted.

おくる¹ (送る)

アメリカの友人にビデオテープを送った.	I sent a video tape to a friend in America.
代金は為替で送ることにした.	I decided to send the payment by money order.
帰りがけに彼女を家まで送って行くよ.	I'll see her home on my way (home).
昨夜, 友人が車でうちまで送ってくれた.	My friend drove me back home last night.
朝, 子どもと夫を送り出すまではとにかく忙しい.	I'm really busy till I get my husband and the children out in the morning.
彼は病院のベッドで退屈な日々を送っているらしい.	I hear he's spending his days bored in a hospital bed.

おくる² (贈る)

彼に何を贈ろうか.	What should we give him for [as] a present?
寄付を募って母校に時計台を贈った.	We collected donations and presented our alma mater with a clock tower.
優勝チームに賞金が贈られた.	The winning team was awarded †a cash prize [prize money].
これはあなたへの贈り物です.	This is a present for you.
誕生日の贈り物には何がいいですか.	What would you like for your birthday?

おくれる (遅れる)

学校に遅れそうだ.	It looks like I'm going to be late for school.
約束の時刻に1時間遅れた.	I was an hour late for the appointment.
期日より三日遅れて宿題を提出した.	I handed in my homework three days after the due date.
夕食に遅れないように戻れ.	Get back in time for dinner.
列車に乗り遅れたら大変だ.	It'll be terrible if we miss the train.
列車は雪で遅れている.	The trains are running behind schedule because of the snow.
山道をさほど行かないうちに, 小さい子どもたちは遅れてしまった.	The younger children had fallen behind before we got very far up the mountain.
病気のため勉強が遅れた.	I fell behind in my schoolwork because I was sick.

この時計は5分遅れている.	This watch [clock] is five minutes slow.

おこす (起こす)

明日6時に起こして.	Wake me [Get me up] at six tomorrow.
転んだ子どもを起こした.	I helped the child who fell down stand up.
病人をベッドの上に起こした.	I made [helped] the patient sit up on the bed.
倒れた看板を起こしてください.	Would you put the sign back up?
彼女はどこへ行ってもいざこざを起こす.	She causes [makes] trouble wherever she goes.
ダムの水力を利用して電気を起こしている.	Water power from the dam is used to generate electricity.

おごそか (厳か)

裁判官は厳かに判決文を読み上げた.	The judge solemnly read out the verdict.
戴冠式は厳かに行われた.	The coronation was performed with great stateliness [majesty, dignity].

おこない (行い)

彼は日頃の行いが悪いから，いざというときに助けてくれる人がいない.	His everyday conduct [behavior] is so bad that no one will help him if he gets in a bind.
あの人は常に正しい行いをしている.	He always conducts himself properly.

おこなう (行う)

卒業式は3月10日に行われる.	The graduation ceremony will be held on March 10.
これから英語の試験を行います.	We will now start the English exam.
公園で野球の試合が行われている.	There's a baseball game going on in the park.
会議は毎月上旬に行われる.	A meeting is held early every month.
定期的に車の点検を行っている.	Car inspections are †carried out [performed] at fixed intervals.
保健所は市内の飲食店に抜き打ちで立ち入り検査を行う.	The public health center conducts unannounced inspections of the city's bars and restaurants.
臨時委員会で意見の調整が行われた.	An attempt to reach a consensus was made at a meeting of the provisional committee.

おこる¹ (怒る)

何をそんなに怒っているの.	What are you so angry [mad] about?
つまらないことで怒るなよ.	Don't get angry [mad] over trifles.
彼は怒って出て行った.	He left in anger.
彼はとても怒りっぽい人だ.	He loses his temper easily.
腹が減ればだれでも怒りっぽくなるものだ.	People tend to get touchy when they're hungry.
先生に怒られても知らないよ.	Don't come to me if the teacher gets angry [mad] with you.
	It's not my fault if †the teacher gets mad at you [you catch it from the teacher].

おこる² (起こる・興る)

【生じる】彼の身に何か起こったに違いない.	Something must have happened to him.
昨夜この町で殺人事件が起こった.	There was a murder in this town last night.
クーデターが起こり，軍部が政権を握った.	The military seized power in a coup d'état.
中近東で戦争が起こった.	War broke out in the Middle East.
貿易問題で両国間に摩擦が起こった.	Trade problems †brought about [caused] friction between the two countries.
大雨でがけ崩れが起こった.	Heavy rains triggered a land slide.
【始まる】オスマン帝国は13世紀末に興った.	The Ottoman Empire came into being late in the thirteenth century.
戦後，その地方に化学工業が興った.	After the war, the chemical industry rose up in that area.
【燃える】炭火が真っ赤におこっている.	The charcoal fire is blazing bright red.

おごる

【驕慢】過去の成功におごることなく努力を続けなさい.	Don't let past successes make you proud. Just keep on working hard.
彼のおごりたかぶった態度には嫌気がさす.	His arrogance puts me off.
【ごちそうする】先生が食事をおごってくれた.	One of my professors invited me out for a meal.
昼は部長のおごりで寿司を食べた.	Our boss treated us to *sushi* for lunch.
今日は僕がおごるよ.	It's my treat today./It's on me today.
	Let me pay today.
一杯おごるよ．つきあわない？	Come on. Let me buy you a drink.

おさえる (押さえる・抑える)

【押さえつける】荷物を運び込むまでドアを押さえておいてください.
Please hold the door open until I've brought (all) the packages in.

のりで貼った紙が乾くまで指で押さえていた.
I held down the paper I had glued until it set.

子どもは痛みでおなかを押さえた.
The child held his stomach in pain.

彼女は強い風に吹かれるスカートを押さえた.
She held down her skirt to keep it from being blown by the strong wind.

彼はハンカチで傷口を押さえて出血を止めた.
He pressed a handkerchief to the wound and stopped the bleeding.

彼女は口を押さえて笑いをかみ殺した.
She covered her mouth to stifle a laugh.

【抑止・抑制する】彼女は客に吠えかかる犬を抑えた.
She restrained her dog from barking at her guests.

物価上昇を抑える有効な手段はないだろうか.
Isn't there any effective way to †restrain [hold down] escalating prices?

もっと生産コストを抑えないと収益が上がらない.
If we can't bring production costs down, we won't be able to increase profits.

彼は怒りを抑えて穏やかに話した.
He restrained his anger and spoke softly.

エースは敵のチームを無得点に抑えた.
Our ace pitcher held the opposing team scoreless.

【捕える】彼の報告は要点を押さえてむだがなかった.
His report was concise and to the point.

犯人は現場で押さえられた.
The culprit was apprehended [arrested] at the scene of the crime.
The culprit was caught red-handed.

おさない (幼い)

彼は幼い頃から並々ならぬ音楽の才能を見せていた.
He had already begun to show an uncommon talent for music in early childhood.

彼女の考え方は幼い.
She's childish.

僕と彼とは幼なじみだ.
He and I are childhood friends.

おさまる¹ (収・納まる)

あれだけの荷物がよくこのスーツケースに収まったね.
You really fit all those things into that one suitcase, didn't you?

この記事はどうしても１ページに収まらない.
I just can't get this article down to one page.

その二人はまた元のさやに納まったらしい.
It appears as if those two have really gotten back together again.

がき大将だったあいつが今では大
As a child he was a bully and now he

会社の社長に納まっている.	holds down the presidency of a large company.
彼は官庁を退職後，ある会社の役員として閑職に納まった.	After retiring from a government position, he settled into a comfortable spot as a company executive.

おさまる² (治まる)

戦乱が治まり，再び平和が訪れた.	With the cessation of hostilities, peace came again.
機動隊の出動で暴動はやっと治まった.	The riot was finally brought under control when the riot squad went into action.
消防隊の迅速な活動で火事は治まった.	The swift response of the fire brigade brought the fire under control.
注射をしたら痛みが治まった.	The pain subsided after I got †a shot [an injection].
強風は夜になって治まった.	The gale subsided when night fell.
彼が謝ったので夫婦げんかは丸く治まった.	The argument he had with his wife ended peacefully when he apologized.

おさめる¹ (収・納める)

【しまう】この建物には国宝が収められている.	National treasures are housed in this building.
彼は書類をかばんに収めた.	He put the documents into his briefcase.
これらの書簡は彼の全集に収められている.	These letters [correspondences] are included in his collected works.
【得る】今年のサッカーのワールドカップは，イタリアが勝利を収めた.	Italy †won [pulled down] the championship in this year's world cup soccer tournament.
【納入する】税金を納めるのは国民の義務である.	Paying taxes is a citizen's obligation.
ピアノの月謝をまだ納めていない.	I haven't paid my piano tuition yet.
その品物は今月中に納めてください.	Please deliver these goods by the end of this month.
あの店は学校に事務用品を納めている.	That store supplies office supplies to the school.

おさめる² (治・修める)

【統治する】その国は国王によって治められた.	That country was ruled by a monarch.
【鎮静する】彼は両国間の紛争を治めるために活躍した.	He played an active role in settling the conflict between the two countries.
警官があいだに入って騒ぎを治めた.	The police officer stepped in and brought the disturbance under control.

【修得する】彼女は大学〔大学院〕で経済学を修めた.	She got a bachelor's [master's, doctor's] degree in economics.

おし (押し)

彼は押しが強いので交渉の代表者には適役だ.	His aggressiveness makes him the perfect man to represent us in the negotiations.
彼は最後の押しがいつも足りない.	He never gives it his all when it comes to the final push.

おしい (惜しい)

まだ食べられるのに捨てるのは惜しい.	It's a shame to¹⁾ throw it out when [while] we can still eat it.
彼の才能をこのままうずもれさせるのは惜しい.	It's a shame to²⁾ let his talent go down the drain.
命が惜しければおれの言うことを聞け.	If you value your life, listen good**³⁾ to what I say.
彼は競馬で儲けた金を惜し気もなく使い果たした.	He †went through [used up] the money he won at the track without the least regret.
文壇は惜しい人をなくした.	The literary world has lost a dear friend.

> 1)2) What a waste to...! と言ってもよい. 3)「脅し」などの場合によく使う表現.

おしえる (教える)

私は高校で数学を教えている.	I teach mathematics at a high school. I'm a high school math teacher.
彼は犬にいろいろな芸を教えた.	He taught his dogs all kinds of tricks.
小さい弟に悪いことを教えてはいけません.	You shouldn't teach your little brother such bad things.
父は人生いかに生きるべきかを身をもって教えてくれた.	My father's example taught me how to live my life.
やり方を教えてください.	Please tell [show, teach] me how to do it.
市役所へ行く道を教えてください.	Could you please tell me how to get to city hall?

おす (押す)

彼はドアを押して開けた.	He pushed the door open.
彼らは車を押してぬかるみから出した.	They pushed the car out of the mud.
彼は雑踏の中を人を押し分けながら進んだ.	He pushed his way through the crowd.
彼女は契約書に判を押した.	She placed her seal on the contract.

彼女は病を押して勤めに出た.	She forced herself to go to work despite her illness.
彼は自分の目的を達するまでは, どこまでも強気で押し通す.	He'll stubbornly go to any length to attain his ends.
【慣用】彼は裏切り者のらく印を押された.	He was branded a traitor.

おせじ (お世辞)

あの人は心にもないお世辞を言う.	He pays insincere compliments.
彼はお世辞がうまい.	He knows how to flatter people.
私はお世辞が言えない性分だ.	It's not my nature to †flatter people [pay compliments].
お世辞を言っても何も出ないよ.	Flattery will get you nowhere!
彼女の料理はお世辞にもうまいと言えない.	You couldn't call her a good cook by any stretch of the imagination.
	It would be flattery to say she's a good cook.

おせっかい

彼はおせっかいな人だ.	He's a busybody. ／He's meddlesome.
彼女はすぐにおせっかいをやく.	She's always ready to †meddle in [poke her nose into] what's none of her business.
余計なおせっかいをやかないでくれ.	Don't do me any unnecessary favors.

おそい (遅い)

【時刻・時機が】今夜はもう遅いからお休みなさい.	It's already late tonight. Good night [Go to bed].
	It's about time for bed.
彼はこの頃帰りが遅い.	He's been getting home late recently.
もう遅いので, そろそろ失礼します.	It's getting late, so I think I'd better be leaving before long.
あまり遅くならないうちに帰りなさい.	Get home before it gets too late.
遅くとも10時までには帰って来なさい.	Return [Be] home by ten at the latest.
昨日は遅くまで残業した.	I worked overtime until late last night.
彼は約束の時間より遅く来た.	He was late for the appointment.
悔やんでも今からではもう遅い.	It's too late now for regret.
駅に着くのが一足遅く, 電車は出たあとだった.	I got to the station seconds after the train had pulled out.
遅かれ早かれ, このうわさは彼の耳に入るでしょう.	Sooner or later he'll probably hear this rumor.

【速さが】彼女は仕事が遅い.	She's a slow worker.
彼女は歩くのが遅い.	She walks †slowly [at a slow pace].
この曲はテンポが遅い.	This tune has a slow tempo.
渋滞で車の速度は自転車よりも遅いぐらいだった.	In the traffic jam, cars were traveling almost slower than bicycles.

おそらく (恐らく)

| もう遅いから恐らく彼はやって来ないだろう. | He probably [I'm afraid he] won't show up since it's already late. |
| この分では明日も恐らく雨でしょう. | At this rate, it will probably rain tomorrow as well. |

おそれ (恐・畏れ)

【恐怖・畏怖】犬の鳴き声に恐れをなして泥棒は逃げて行った.	Scared by the dog's barking, the thief ran away.
神への畏れと科学的な探究心とは矛盾するものではない.	Fear of God and the spirit of scientific inquiry don't contradict each other.
【危険性】堤防が決壊するおそれがある.	There's a danger of the levee giving way.
1週間雨が続いて水不足になるおそれはなくなった.	A week of rain (has) eliminated the danger of a water shortage.
今から寝ると寝坊するおそれがある.	I'm afraid we might oversleep if we go to bed now.

おそれる (恐・畏れる)

失敗を恐れてはいけない.	You can't be afraid of †failure [making mistakes].
彼らは死をも恐れず戦いに挑んだ.	They rose to the challenge of battle, not fearing even death.
クビになるのを恐れて,だれも社長を批判できなかった.	Afraid of getting fired, no one would criticize the president.
彼のテニスの天才的な腕前はプロからも恐れられている.	Even the pros fear his prowess on the tennis court.
山を畏れて昔の人がここに神社を建てた.	In awe of the mountain, the people of old built a shrine here.

おそろしい (恐ろしい)

高層ビルの火事は恐ろしい.	Fires in skyscrapers are terrifying.
恐ろしい事件が続いている.	There has been one terrible incident after another.
旅先で恐ろしい目にあった.	I had a †dreadful time [terrible experience] when I went on my trip.
つららも時に恐ろしい武器になる.	An icicle can make a formidable [fear-

	some] weapon.
彼は金のためなら何でもできる恐ろしい人だ.	He's a dreadful person who would do anything for money.
飛び込み台から下を見たら急に恐ろしくなった.	When I looked down from the diving platform, I was seized with fear.
彼は恐ろしいほど頭が切れる.	He's so sharp it's frightening [scary].
東京は恐ろしく物価が高い.	In Tokyo, prices are awfully [terribly] high.

おだてる

そんなにおだてないで.	Don't butter me up like that!
彼は女性をおだてるのがうまい.	He's good at flattering women.
おだてに乗せられて会議の司会を引き受けてしまった.	I was cajoled [flattered, coaxed] into chairing the meeting.
社長はおだてに乗るような人ではない.	The president is not one to be flattered [coaxed] into anything.

おだやか (穏やか)

穏やかな天気が続いている.	We're having a spell of mild weather.
今日は穏やかな日だった.	Today was a nice quiet day.
皆は彼女の穏やかな物腰を好いている.	She's loved by everyone for her mild manner.
彼は年とともに考え方が穏やかになってきた.	His way of seeing things has mellowed as he's grown older.
彼の話を黙って聞いたが心中は穏やかではなかった.	I listened silently to what he said, but inside I was anything but calm.
交渉は穏やかに行われた.	The negotiations were conducted in a peaceful atmosphere.

おちつき (落ち着き)

彼は若いのに似合わず落ち着きがある.	He has an uncommon self-assuredness for his age.
彼女は飽きっぽくて落ち着きがない.	She's restless and gets tired of things quickly.
落ち着きのない態度に警官は彼が怪しいと睨んだ.	His lack of composure made the policeman suspicious of him.
このいすは落ち着きが悪い.	This chair is wobbly.

おちつく (落ち着く)

【安定する】落ち着いたら便りをくれ.	Write (to) me when you're settled.
何度も転職したが今度の会社に落ち着きそうだ.	I've tried a lot of different jobs but I feel as if I've found my place here.

三日間も討議した末，結局は現状維持の線に落ち着いた．	After three days of debate, we finally settled on keeping things as they are.
【静まる】慌てるな．落ち着け．	Don't get rattled. Calm down.
非常のときに落ち着いて行動するには訓練が必要だ．	Training is necessary in order to function [act] calmly in an emergency.
心を落ち着けて自分のしたことをよく考えてみなさい．	Calm down and think carefully about what you did.
部屋が広過ぎて落ち着かない．	The room's so big I don't feel at ease.
じゅうたんは落ち着いた色にしたい．	I'd like a nice quiet color for the carpet.
落ち着いて本を読む暇がない．	I don't have any time to relax and read (books).

おちる (落ちる)

【落下する】リンゴが落ちるのを見てニュートンは引力を発見した．	Newton discovered (the law of) gravity when he saw an apple fall.
大工が屋根から落ちてけがをした．	The carpenter fell off the roof and hurt himself.
地震で橋が落ちた．	The bridge collapsed in the earthquake.
道にお金が落ちていた．	There was some money lying in the street.
【とれる】強力な漂白剤を使ってもインクのしみは落ちなかった．	The ink stain didn't wash [come] out even when I used strong bleach.
洗ったら色が落ちてしまった．	When I washed it, the color †faded [came out].
索引に落ちがないか調べてくれ．	Check and see if there are any omissions in the index.
【劣る】最初の作品の素晴らしさに比べると，彼の次作はやや落ちる．	Compared to the magnificence of his first work, his next was a bit of a comedown.
【不合格になる】試験に落ちたらどうしよう．	What'll I do if I fail [flunk] the test?
【堕落する】賄賂を贈るとは彼も落ちたものだ．	He really lowered himself to have offered a bribe.

おっくう

体の具合が悪いので動くのがおっくうだ．	I feel so awful that it's a pain just to move.
一度休むと次に仕事に取りかかるのがおっくうだ．	It's a chore to go back to work after taking a rest.
彼はものぐさで何をするにもおっくうがる．	He's so lazy that it pains him to do the least thing.
彼女は手紙を書くのをちっともおっくうがらない．	Writing letters is never a chore for her.

おとす（落とす）

【落下させる】
彼女はお皿を落として割ってしまった． — She dropped the dish and it broke.

広島に世界で初めて原爆が落とされた． — Hiroshima was the first city in the world to have an atomic bomb dropped on it.

【無くす】
財布を落としてしまった． — I lost my wallet.

彼は交通事故で命を落とした． — He was killed in a traffic accident.

彼女は単位を落として進級できなくなった． — She failed a course and couldn't advance to the next year.

ぜい肉を落とすために運動することにした． — I've decided to start exercising in order to get rid of extra weight.

油汚れを落とすにはどの洗剤がいいですか． — Which detergent is good for cutting grease?

名簿から転入生の名前を落としてしまった． — The names of the (new) transfer students got omitted from the register.

【低くする・下げる】
品質を落とすより価格を上げたほうがよい． — It's better to raise the price than lower the quality.

だれかが部屋に入ってきたので彼は慌てて声を落とした． — He abruptly dropped [lowered] his voice because someone entered the room.

カーブにさしかかり，列車はスピードを落とした． — As the train entered the curve, it slowed down.
The train lowered its speed as it entered the curve.

【～し逃す】
うっかりして薬の注意書きを見落として服用してしまった． — I inadvertently took the medicine without noticing the warning.

書き落としのないよう，もう一度答案を見直しなさい． — Look over the answer sheets again to make sure you haven't left any blanks.

パーティーの開催時間を聞き落してしまった． — I †failed to hear [missed hearing] the time the party's to be held.

【経理処理】
この費用は必要経費で落とそう． — Let's write this off as a necessary expense.

おどす（脅す）

ナイフで脅されて金を渡した． — I was threatened with a knife into handing over my money.

そんな脅しに乗るものか． — You think that sort of threat scares me?

ただの脅し文句と思って本気にしていなかった． — I thought it was just an empty threat and didn't take it seriously.

脅かすなよ．冗談にも程がある． — Come on. That's not even funny.

おとなしい

彼女はおとなしいが意志の強い人 — She's mild-mannered but has a strong will.

だ.	
今日はやけにおとなしいね.	You're really quiet today, aren't you?
小さな子が一人でおとなしく遊んでいる.	The little child is playing quietly by himself.
おばあさんの家に行ったらおとなしくするんですよ.	When you go to †grandma's [your grandmother's] house, you behave yourself!
おとなしく医者の言うことを聞いたほうがいいよ.	You'd better just listen to what the doctor tells you.
彼女はいつもおとなしい服を着ている.	She always wears quiet colors.
うちの犬はおとなしい.	Our dog is †really tame [docile].
おとなし過ぎて退屈な絵だ.	This painting is so subdued it's dull.

おとる (劣る)

彼のほうが兄よりも音楽家として有名だが, 才能では劣る.	He's a more famous musician than his brother but he's not as talented.
手料理は決して一流の店の料理に劣るものではない.	Home cooking is by no means inferior to the cooking in a good restaurant.
書くことでは, 彼はだれにも劣らない.	In writing, he is second to none.

おどる (踊る)

見てばかりいないで踊れよ.	Don't just (sit [stand] there and) watch. Dance!
これはインドの踊りです.	This is a dance from India.
警察は誤報に踊らされた.	That false report had the police jumping [hopping].

おとろえる (衰える)

このところ, めっきり体力が衰えてきた.	I'm really going downhill lately. I don't have any stamina at all these days.
祖父は足腰が衰えてきた.	My grandfather is not as steady on his feet as he used to be.
50を過ぎてから記憶力の衰えを実感するようになった.	I became more conscious of memory loss after turning 50.

おどろく (驚く)

彼の突然の来訪に驚いた.	I was surprised at his sudden visit.
彼が知っていたとは驚いた.	It's surprising that he knew. I never thought he would know.
君が優勝したって? これは驚いた.	You won? What a surprise!
驚いたことに彼女には夫も子ども	Astonishingly enough, she's married and

もあるんだそうだ. | has children.
本当に彼が犯人だとしても驚くに当たらない. | I wouldn't be surprised if he does turn out to be the criminal.
彼女の美しさには皆驚く. | Everyone is taken aback by her beauty.
患者は驚くべき精神力で痛みをこらえている. | The patient is bearing (up under) the pain, thanks to his incredible inner strength.

おなじ (同じ)

これは前聞いたのと同じ話だ. | This is the same story I heard before.
私もあなたと同じ意見だ. | I see it the same (way) as you (do).
君と同じペンを買った. | I bought a pen just like yours.
結局は同じことだ. | It really makes no difference.
だれが頼んでも答えは同じだ. | No matter who may ask, the answer's the same.
君なんかいてもいなくても同じだ. | It's all the same [It doesn't matter, It makes no difference] whether you're here or not.
仕事は終わったも同じだ. | The job is as good as finished.
彼の絵は皆同じように見える. | His pictures all look †the same [alike].
その問題もさっきのと同じようにやればいいんだよ. | Just do that problem the way you did the one before.
彼のやり方と同じようにやってみなさい. | Do it the same way he does it.

おのおの (各々)

人間はおのおの長所も短所も持っている. | Each person [Every individual] has his own †strong and weak points [strengths and weaknesses].
子どもたちは公園でおのおの好きなことをして遊んだ. | The children played in the park—each one doing whatever he wanted to.
この仕事はおのおのが持っている力を全部出して協力し合わなければとうていできない. | Unless each and every one of us cooperates by pitching in and giving one hundred percent, this work will never get done.

おびえる

彼は裏口入学がばれるのではないかとおびえている. | He's scared stiff that it'll get out that he bought his way into school.
彼は動物嫌いで猫にさえおびえて逃げ出してしまう. | He can't stand animals. He even gets scared and runs away from cats.

おぼえ (覚え)

【学習】彼女は仕事の覚えが早い. | She learns her work quickly.

あの子は物覚えが悪い.	That child is a poor learner.
【記憶】そんなことを言った覚えはない.	I †don't remember [have no recollection of] saying anything like that.
子どもの頃彼女に会った覚えがある.	I remember [recollect] having met her when I was a child.
それは身に覚えのない話だ.	I have no memory of having done so.

おぼえる（覚える）

【記憶する】この電話番号は覚え易い.	This telephone number is easy to remember.
彼の顔をはっきり憶えている.	I remember his face clearly.
【習い覚える】こんなにたくさんの単語を一度に覚えられるわけがない.	There's no way you can (expect to) learn this much vocabulary all at once.
新しい機械の使い方を覚えるのに3ヵ月かかった.	It took three months to learn how to use this machine.
【感じる】娘の結婚の話には寂しさを覚えずにはいられない.	I can't help feeling lonely at (the idea of) my daughter's getting married.
立ち上がったときに軽いめまいを覚えた.	When I stood up, I felt †some dizziness [a little dizzy].

おぼれる（溺れる）

海で溺れそうになった.	I almost drowned at the beach.
溺れるところを彼が助けてくれた.	He saved me from drowning.
溺れる者はわらをもつかむ.	A drowning man will grasp [grab, clutch, catch] at a straw.
君は恋に溺れて一生を台無しにしてもかまわないのか.	You mean you don't care if you ruin your whole life by giving yourself up to love?
麻薬に溺れるとなかなか立ち直れない.	Once you get hooked on drugs it's almost impossible to get off them.

おめでとう

おめでとう.	Congratulations!
ご卒業〔ご栄転〕おめでとうございます.	Congratulations on your graduation [promotion]!
就職おめでとう.	Congratulations on your new job!

おも（主）

肺がんの主な原因はたばこだ.	The principal [major] cause of lung cancer is smoking cigarettes.
あの小説家の主な作品は大体読んだ.	I've read just about all of that author's main works.
コンサートの聴衆は若い女性が主	The audience at the concert was made up

だった.	mostly of young women.
あの店は主に食料品を扱っている.	That store handles mostly groceries.
日曜日は主に読書をして過ごします.	I spend most of my time reading on Sundays.
学生時代, 休暇は主にアルバイトをした.	When I was a student, most of my vacation time was spent working.

おもい¹ (重い)

本を入れたのでかばんが重い.	My bag [briefcase] is heavy because I put the books into it.
私は生まれたとき体重が重かった.	I weighed a lot when I was born.
彼はクラスの中でいちばん体重が重い.	He weighs more than anyone else in the class.
爆弾を作った活動家は今重い刑に服している.	The activist who made the bombs is now serving a heavy sentence.
【コンピュータ】画像データは重すぎて受信に時間がかかることがある.	Picture data is so heavy that it can take a long time to download.

おもい² (思い)

【思考・思索】半年も前からもう思いはパリへ飛んでいる.	My thoughts have been on nothing but Paris for half a year now.
彼は部屋にこもって思いにふけって〔沈んで〕いる.	He's shut up in his room, deep [sunk] in thought.
頭の中は逃げ出したいという思いでいっぱいだった.	All I could think about was how I wanted to run away.
【気持ち】パーティーで皮肉を言われ嫌な思いをした.	A sarcastic comment someone made to me at the party made me feel unpleasant.
卒論がなかなかまとまらなくて泣きたい思いだ.	I feel like I could cry because I just can't get my graduation thesis into shape.
やっとの思いで原稿を締め切りに間に合わせた.	I got the manuscript in just barely on time.
【想像・予想】彼がそんな間違いをするとは思いもよらなかった.	It never entered my mind that he could make a mistake like that.
思いもよらない場所で先生とばったり出会った.	I happened to come face to face with my teacher in the last place I ever expected to meet him.
試験は思いのほかよくできた.	I did unexpectedly well on the test.
【願望】思いがかなって彼は留学する.	He's going to study abroad, just as †he'd hoped [he wanted].
【愛情】彼への思いは日ごとに募る.	My feelings for him grow day by day.
彼女に思いを寄せているのは君だけではない.	You're not the only (one) who's interested in her.

| 【好き好きの】ハイキングの目的地に着き，みんな思い思いのことをして遊んだ． | After we hiked to our destination, we all did whatever we liked. |
| 仮装パーティーには思い思いのふん装をして行った． | We all went to the masquerade party dressed up in different costumes. |

おもいがけない (思いがけない)

思いがけない事故が起こった．	An unforeseen accident happened.
思いがけない人に会った．	I ran into someone unexpectedly.
思いがけないときに思いがけないことが起こった．	At an unexpected time, the unexpected happened.
思いがけなくも私の作品が最優秀賞に選ばれた．	Quite unexpectedly, my work was chosen for first prize.

おもいきって (思い切って)

思い切って彼女に胸の内を打ち明けた．	I got up my courage and opened up my heart to her.
思い切って10万円のデジタルカメラを買った．	I took the plunge and bought a ¥100,000 [one hundred thousand yen] digital camera.
思い切って会社を辞めることにした．	I finally decided to go ahead and quit the company.
あんな女とは思い切って別れてしまえよ．	You should break it off with that woman once and for all.

おもいきり (思い切り)

【決断】長年勤めていた会社を辞めるとは思い切りのいいやつだ．	He's very decisive. He went through with quitting the company he had worked at for so long.
彼は思い切りよく会社を辞めた．	He just made up his mind and quit the company.
彼女は思い切りが悪く，生まれた町をなかなか離れることができない．	She can never make up her mind and just do something, so she'll probably never be able to tear herself away from the town where she was born.
【あきらめ】彼は思い切りのいい人で，自分に歌手の才能がないと分かるとすぐ田舎に引っ込んだ．	Knowing when to quit, he moved back to the country as soon as he realized he didn't have the talent to become a singer.
よくも思い切りよくこれだけのむだづかいをしたものだ．	How could you †throw away [waste] this much money?
もう済んでしまったことをいつまでも考えているなんて思い切り	You just don't know when to give up, thinking forever about something that's

が悪いね.	finished and done with.
【存分に】ここなら思い切り騒いでもだれも文句を言わないだろう.	Here we can let loose and raise all the hell** we want (to) and no one should mind.
宿題を済ませて思い切り遊ぼう.	Let's finish our homework, and then play all we want to.

おもいこむ (思い込む)

彼は一度思い込んだら人の言うことなど聞き入れない.	Once †he's convinced of something [he gets an idea into his head], he won't listen to what anyone says.
彼は自分の病気は治らないと思い込んでいる.	He's convinced [He talked himself into thinking] that his illness is incurable.
君は数学ができないと思い込んでいるだけだ.	You've just talked yourself into thinking [believing] you aren't good at mathematics. That's all.

おもいすごし (思い過ごし)

彼の機嫌を損ねたかと心配したが私の思い過ごしだった.	I was afraid that I had offended him, but I realized it was all in my mind.
僕が隠し事をしているなんて君の思い過ごしだよ.	Me? Trying to conceal things from you? It's all in your imagination. [You're just imagining things.／You're letting your imagination run too far.]

おもいだす (思い出す)

その歌を聞くと母を思い出す.	Hearing that song reminds me of my mother.
その話で以前読んだ小説を思い出した.	That story reminded me of a novel I once read.
写真を見ながらあれこれ思い出していた.	As I looked at the pictures, I †thought of [thought back on, recalled] this and that.
彼の顔は知っているんだが名前が思い出せない.	I know the face, but I can't remember his name.
彼は時々思い出したように仕事をする.	He works when the spirit moves him.

おもいつき (思いつき)

両親を招待するというのはいい思いつきだね.	Inviting your parents is a good idea.
私はただの思いつきで提案しているのではありません.	My proposal isn't just something off the top of my head.

おもいつく（思いつく）
いいことを思いついた． I just had a good idea.
新しい拡販計画を思いついた． I hit on a new program to expand sales.
子どもは時々とんでもなくおかしなことを思いつくものだ． Children sometimes come up with the funniest ideas.
どうやって小説家はあんなにいろいろな筋を思いつくのだろうか． I wonder how writers †think up [come up with] all the different plots for their stories and novels.
どうしてもっと早く思いつかなかったのか不思議だ． It amazes me that I didn't think of it sooner.
適当な表現を思いつかない． I can't †think of [come up with] the right expression.

おもいつめる（思い詰める）
彼は仕事がうまくいかなくて思い詰めている． He's obsessed with how badly his work has been going.
彼は彼女のことを思い詰めている． He is obsessed with her.

おもいで（思い出）
この歌には悲しい思い出がある． This song brings back sad memories.
思い出にふけりながら窓の景色を眺めていた． Lost in my memories, I gazed at the scenery outside the window.
祖父が懐かしい昔の思い出を話してくれた． My grandfather told me his fond memories of the good old days.
久しぶりの同窓会で思い出話に花が咲いた． It was the first reunion in a long time and the reminiscing made for lively conversation.

おもいどおり（思いどおり）
すべて思いどおりに事が運んだ． Everything went as I had hoped.
　 Everything went well [smoothly].
思いどおりの結果が得られた． We were able to get the results we had wanted.
何でもあなたの思いどおりというわけにはいきません． You can't expect everything to go as you want it to.
　 You can't have everything your own way.
あなたの思いどおりに仕事をしていい． You can do the work †as you see fit [in your own way, just the way you want].

おもいやり（思いやり）
彼はとても思いやりがある． He's very considerate [thoughtful].
彼女のお年寄りに対する思いやりは人一倍だ． She shows far more consideration for elderly people than the average person.

先生の思いやりの深い言葉には，どの生徒も皆感動した．	Each and every one of the students was moved [touched] by the teacher's †deeply sympathetic [thoughtful] words.
そんな思いやりのないことを言ってはいけない．	You shouldn't make such unsympathetic [inconsiderate, thoughtless] remarks.

おもう (思う)

【考える】私はそう思わない．	I don't think so. / I don't see it that way.
試験のことを思うと気が重くなる．	I get depressed just thinking about the exam.
君が僕のことをどんなふうに思おうと，僕は何とも思わない．	I couldn't care less what you think of me.
彼は何を思ったのか，突然熱心に勉強するようになった．	I don't know what got into him, but suddenly he started studying hard.
【信じる】彼は雪男は実在すると思っている．	He believes that †yeti [the abominable snowman] really exists.
【感じる】どことなく彼の態度がおかしいと思った．	I felt there was something funny about his attitude.
【想像・予想する】今，私が何を考えていると思う？	What do you suppose [Can you guess what] I'm thinking about now?
彼女は今25歳くらいだと思う．	I'd say she's about twenty-five.
明日は雨だと思う．	I think[1] it may rain tomorrow.
思ったほど怖くはなかった．	It wasn't as frightening as I †thought it'd be [expected].
まさかこんなことになろうとは，夢にも思わなかった．	I never even dreamed it would turn out like this.
【つもりである】1年間イギリスに留学しようと思っている．	I intend to go to Britain to study for a year.
週末にハイキングに行こうと思っている．	I'm planning to go hiking over the weekend.
【望む・願う】仕事が思うように進まない．	The work [job] isn't going as well as I'd like.
彼女もパーティーに来るといいと思う．	I hope she comes to the party, too.
そのカメラを買いたいと思ったがお金が足りなかった．	I wanted to buy that camera, but I didn't have enough money.
今日は思う存分運動した．	Today I worked out to my heart's content.
私のおごりだ．思う存分食べてくれ．	This is on me. Eat as much as you like.
今怒っては彼らの思うつぼだ．	Getting angry now is just †what they want [playing right into their hands].
【怪しむ】そのつぼは偽物だと思う．	I think [suspect] that pot is a fake.
彼があの事件の犯人ではないかと	I think [suspect] he may be the one who

思う.	committed that crime.
【懸念する】彼にだまされたのではないかと思う.	I think [I'm afraid] he may [must] have tricked me.
【愛する】彼は心ひそかに彼女のことを思っている.	He secretly loves her.
彼女の子どもを思う気持ちに皆, 心を打たれた.	Everyone was touched by her maternal devotion.

1) 懸念している場合は I'm afraid... となる.

おもしろい (面白い)

この漫画は面白かった.	This comic book was funny.
彼の冗談は面白くない.	His jokes are not funny.
学校は面白い？	Is school fun [interesting]?
数学の面白さが分かってきた.	Math has become more interesting to me.
この小説のどこが面白いのか分からない.	I don't understand what's so interesting about this novel.
彼女は一風変わっていて面白い.	She's interesting in a different way.
面白半分に言っただけだ.	I was only kidding.
この試合は面白い勝負になりそうだ.	This game looks like it's going to be a good one [contest].
彼のようなおべっか使いが昇進するのは面白くない.	What a drag to see a brownnose like him get promoted.**

おもて (表)

この紙はどっちが表ですか.	Which is the front side of this paper?
表の戸締まりは大丈夫？	Did you close the front (door)?
表へ出ろ.	Step outside.
表を飾るばかりではいけない.	Just dressing it up on the surface won't do any good.
彼女は感情を表に出さない.	She doesn't let her feelings show.
彼は小説も書くが新聞記者が表看板だ.	He writes novels, too, but he's primarily a newspaper reporter.
党内のいざこざを表ざたにしたくない.	We don't want any leaks about the disagreement within the party.
彼は表向きは老齢のために引退したことになっている.	The official story is that he retired because of his age.
9回の表に逆転した.	They turned the game around in the top of the ninth.

おもわく (思惑)

【意図】各人各様の思惑があって意見の調整が難航している.	The diversity of private interests is making it difficult to reach a consensus.

彼は何か思惑があるのか，しきりに私にお世辞を言う．	He wouldn't be playing up to me like this unless he had an ulterior motive.
この慈善事業には政治的な思惑はないと思う．	I don't think this charity has any political motives.
すべて私の思惑どおりに事が運んだ．	Everything went off exactly as I had intended.
【予想】彼が失敗するだろうと考えたのはとんだ思惑違いだった．	Assuming he would fail was a terrible miscalculation.
彼は思惑が外れて相場で大変な損をした．	He made a bad investment and lost a fortune on the stock market.
【評判】彼は人の思惑ばかり気にしている．	He's obsessed by what others think of him.
世間の思惑を気にするな．	Don't worry about †what people think [public opinion].

おもわず (思わず)

思わず秘密を漏らしてしまった．	I let the secret slip †without meaning to [unintentionally].
無事な子どもの姿を見ると母親は思わず駆け寄った．	The mother rushed towards her child, relieved to see him unharmed.
先生の話し方がおかしいので思わず笑ってしまった．	The teacher's funny way of speaking made me laugh in spite of myself.
衣装の美しさに思わずため息をついた．	The beauty of the costume made me gasp in spite of myself.

およそ

この町の人口はおよそ5万人です．	The population of this town is roughly [about, around] 50,000 [fifty thousand].
それに関する資料はおよそ集まった．	We've collected just about all of the materials related to that.
彼の考えていることはおよその見当がつく．	I can †just about [pretty much] guess what he must be thinking.
彼がその試験で100点を取るようなことはおよそありえない．	There's almost [practically] no way he can score 100 points on that exam.
彼にそんなことを聞いてもおよそむだなことだ．	It's virtually useless asking him about something like that.
およそ商売では信用ほど大切なものはない．	In business, there's virtually nothing more important than trust.

およぶ (及ぶ)

負債総額は10億円に及ぶ．	The deficit comes [amounts] to a billion yen.
捜査は全職員に及んだ．	The investigation covered [included] all

	the employees.
大気汚染は郊外にまで及んだ.	The air pollution has spread out to the suburbs.
会議は深夜に及んだ.	The conference lasted deep into the night.
この期に及んで何を言うか.	What do you mean by saying something like that at this stage of the game?
読書量で彼女に及ぶ者はない.	Nobody can match her for the amount she reads.
若い俳優の演技はベテランの俳優に及ばなかった.	The young actor's performance didn't come up to that of the veteran actor.
及ばずながら力になろう.	I'll †be of what help [do what little] I can.
このままで十分. 書き直すには及ばない.	This is OK as is. There's no need to rewrite it.

おりる (下・降りる)

【上から下へ】母が階段を下りてきた.	My mother came down the stairs.
歌手が客席に下りて歌った.	The singer came down into the audience and sang.
明るいうちに山から下りよう.	Let's get down the mountain while it's still light.
エレベーターが下りてきた.	The elevator came down.
幕が下りても拍手は続いた.	The applause continued even after the curtain came down.
【乗り物から】私はそこで電車〔バス〕から降りた.	I got off the train [bus] there.
【やめる】彼は今回限りで議長を降りる.	He's stepping down †as chairman [from the chairmanship] after this meeting.
彼は自ら正選手を降りた.	He decided to quit playing as a regular.
この勝負は降りるよ.	Count me out of this one [bet, game].
【許可になる】銀行の融資が下りた日に私は新しい車を買った.	I bought my new car the same day the bank loan came through.
エジプトへのビザがやっと下りた.	I was finally granted an Egyptian visa.
【霜が】明日は霜が降りると思う.	I think we'll have some frost tomorrow.

おる (折る)

書類を折らないでください.	Please don't fold the papers.
毛布を二つ折りにした.	I folded the blanket in half.
目印にページの端を折っておいてください.	Fold the corner of the page down to mark the place.
針金を折り曲げた.	I bent the wire.
いたずら坊主が花を折った.	Some mischief-maker broke off some flowers.

桜の枝を折ってはいけない.	Don't break any branches off the cherry tree.
彼はスキーで左足を折った.	He broke his left leg skiing.
出口の付近で人々が折り重なるように倒れた.	People fell down on top of each other by the exit.
【慣用】彼は決して我を折らない人だ.	He's a person who never gives in.

おれる (折れる)

この鉛筆はしんが折れ易い.	The lead in this pencil breaks easily.
嵐で木の枝が折れた.	The storm snapped tree limbs.
【曲がる】その角を左に折れるとすぐ駅です.	If you turn left at that corner, the station is right there.
【妥協する】私が先に折れて謝ったので, けんかは治まった.	Our argument got settled when I gave in and apologized first.

おろす (下・降ろす)

2階から荷物を下ろした.	I brought the luggage down from the second floor.
彼女はアップにしていた髪を下ろした.	She undid her hair and let it down.
トラックから積み荷を下ろした.	We unloaded the packages from the truck.
バスは客を降ろして走り去った.	The bus let off its passengers and drove off.
運転手さん, ここで降ろして.	Let me out here, driver.
【初めて使う】今日新しい靴を下ろした.	I wore my new shoes today for the first time.
彼女は下ろしたての洋服を着てパーティーに行った.	She went to the party wearing brand new clothes.
【預金を】銀行で5万円下ろした.	I withdrew ¥50,000 [fifty thousand yen] from the bank.
【いかりを】その船は横浜港にいかりを下ろしている.	That ship †is anchored [has dropped anchor] in Yokohama harbor.
【魚を】彼は魚を下ろすのがうまい.	He's really good at filleting fish.
【すりおろす】大根をおろし, 焼魚に添えて食べた.	I grated the radish and ate it with grilled fish.

おわり (終わり)

その映画は終わりが物足りなかった.	The ending [conclusion] of that movie left something to be desired.
この番組を終わりまで見せて.	Let me watch this show to the end.
終わりまで読んだら貸してください.	When you've †read it through [finished reading it], lend it to me.

終わりまで聞きなさい.	Hear me out.
長い教員生活に終わりを告げる日も近い.	The day is near when I'll finish up my long career as a teacher.
今日はこれで終わりです.	That's all for today.
ここで失敗したらこの計画も一巻の終わりだ.	If we slip up now, †this project is done for [it'll be the end of this project].
終わりよければすべてよし.	All's well that ends well.

おわる (終わる)

仕事は5時に終わる.	Work †is over [ends] at five.
試験が終わるまで漫画は読めない.	I can't read any comics till the test is over.
講演が終わる頃に目が覚めた.	I woke up as the lecture was ending.
受付は終わっていた.	The reception desk was closed.
さあ終わったぞ. さっさと帰ろう.	We're done [finished]. Let's go right home.
今日の仕事はこれで終わった.	That does it for †today [today's work]. I'm through for the day.
宿題は一日では終わらない.	You can't finish the assignment in just a day.
交渉は失敗に終わった.	The negotiations ended in failure.
劇は成功のうちに終わった.	The play ended a great success.

おん (恩)

このご恩は決して忘れません.	I'll never forget this favor [kindness].
あなたには一生かかってもこのご恩はお返しするつもりです.	I'll repay this favor even if it takes a lifetime.
彼は何でも恩に着せる.	He always lets people know how big a favor he's done them.
君のした行為は恩をあだで返すようなものだ.	Despite his kindness, you did him a disservice.
彼は恩知らずなやつだ.	That guy's an ingrate.
親の恩は子どもを持って初めて分かるものだ.	You never realize how much you owe your parents until you have children of your own.

か

かい¹（甲斐）

長年の努力のかいがあって彼はいい成績で卒業した. — His years of hard work paid off when he graduated with honors.

必死の看護のかいもなく彼女は死んでしまった. — She died even though everything possible was done.

こんなことをしても何のかいもない. — It's meaningless [pointless] to do something like this.

親身になって彼の相談に乗ってあげたのに, そのかいがなかった. — I did everything I could to advise him but it didn't do much good.

彼女が死んでしまい生きがいを失った. — Her death took away my reason for living.

もう少し働きがいのある仕事をしたい. — I'd like to find a more rewarding job.

彼は甲斐性のある男だ. — He's a man of substance.

それが男の甲斐性というものだ. — Now, that's what being a man is all about.

かい²（回）

うちの会社は年に1回〔2回, 3回〕ボーナスが出る. — My company gives out bonuses †once〔twice, three times〕a year.

彼女は同じ曲を何回も練習した. — She practiced the same piece again and again.

彼女は懸垂が1回もできないけどあなたは何回できる？ — She can't do a single chin-up, but then how many can you do?

父親に何百回となく小言を言われたが, 彼は全く気にしていない. — His father has lectured him hundreds of times, but he always just lets it go in one ear and out the other.

次回も同じ場所で会議をします. — Next time we will hold the meeting at the same place.

そのテレビドラマは回を重ねるごとに面白くなる. — That TV show gets more interesting with each episode.

9回の裏, そのピンチヒッターは逆転サヨナラホームランを放った. — In the bottom of the ninth (inning) the pinch hitter hit a come-from-behind game-ending home run.

かい³ (会)

運動会が楽しみだ.	I'm really looking forward to the athletic meet.
同窓会幹部の尽力で同窓会には多くの人が集まった.	The alumni association's efforts resulted in a large turnout for the class reunion.
彼の歓迎〔送別〕会は盛大に催そう.	Let's have a big welcome [farewell] party for him.
生徒会長が突然病気になり,生徒総会は中止になった.	The president of the student council suddenly got [became] sick and the general assembly meeting was called off.
環境委員会が召集された.	A meeting of the Environmental Commission was called.
「野鳥を見る会」に入会したい〔から脱会したい〕.	I want to †join [withdraw from] the bird-watching society.

かい⁴ (階)

彼の家は3階建てだ.	His house has three stories.
	He has a three-storied house.
ロンドンでは2階建てのバスが走っている.	In London there are double-decker buses.
そのビルは何階建てですか.	How many stories tall is that building?
2階に風呂があるので,階下に下りる必要はありません.	There's a bath on the second floor so there's no need to go downstairs.
紳士服売り場は何階ですか.	What floor is men's clothing on?
そのマンションの1階にはいろいろな店が入っている.	There are a lot of stores on the first floor of that apartment building.
地下1階は食品売り場です.	Groceries are sold on the first basement level.

がい (害)

薬は飲み過ぎると害になる.	Taking too much medicine is bad for you.
たばこは百害あって一利なし.	Smoking does much harm but no good.
この薬品が有害か無害かを今調べている.	This drug is currently being tested for toxicity.

かいがい (海外)

3週間の海外旅行は夢のようだった.	Our three-week trip abroad was like a dream.
我が社では毎年多くの人を海外に派遣する.	Our company sends a large number of employees overseas every year.
海外市場でもこの製品は売れるだろう.	This product would also sell well in overseas markets.
このラジオは海外放送がよく入る.	This radio can really pick up overseas

かいぎ 142

[international] broadcasting.

海外事情に詳しい人を探している. We're looking for someone who's really up on †the situation in other countries [the international scene].

かいぎ（会議）

今日は会社で会議があるから夕食には遅れるよ. There's a meeting [conference] at work today so I'll be late for dinner.

部長はただいま会議中です. The department head is in conference just now.

その問題に関して今会議中だ. They are †in conference [conferring] now over that question.

うちはよく家族会議を開く. We often hold family councils.

かいけつ（解決）

両国間の紛争は解決しそうもない. It doesn't look as though the conflict between the two nations will be resolved.

証人が現れて事件はついに解決した. A witness appeared and the case was finally solved.

労使間の紛争が円満に解決した. The dispute between management and labor was settled amicably.

何かいい解決策はないものか. Isn't there some way to resolve this?

未解決の問題が山積している. Unsolved problems are piling up.

これは金で解決がつくような問題ではない. This is not a problem which can be solved with money.

がいこく（外国）

外国を旅行しているときに交通事故にあった. I was in a traffic accident while traveling †in a foreign country [abroad].

日本語のうまい外国人を知りませんか. Do you know any foreigners who speak Japanese fluently?

彼は外国生まれです. He was born in a foreign country.
He was born overseas.

外国製品には関税がかかる. We have to pay duties on foreign products.

外国に電報を打ちたいのですが. I'd like to send an overseas telegram.

外国郵便はこちらの箱です. Overseas mail goes in this box.

今日の外国為替相場を見てみよう. Let's check today's foreign exchange rate.

父は外国航路の船長だ. My father is captain of an ocean liner.

かいしゃ（会社）

この会社はいつ設立されたのですか. When was this company established [founded]?

会社が倒産した．	The company went bankrupt.
私は商事会社に勤めている．	I work for a trading company.
彼は会社ではまじめ人間だ．	He's a serious person at work.
彼女は会社に傘を置いてきてしまった．	She left her umbrella at the office.
彼はいつも6時頃，会社を出る．	He always leaves the office at about six p.m.
会社組織にしたほうがいい．	You should incorporate.

かいしゃく (解釈)

この文をどう解釈しますか．	How would you interpret this sentence?
解釈しだいでどちらとも取れる．	It can be taken [interpreted] either way.
私の解釈はあなたとは違う．	My interpretation [understanding] (of this) differs from yours.

かいしん (会心)

それは彼の会心の作だ．	That's (a piece of) work he can be proud of.
会心の一打に，彼は思わず一塁コーチと握手を交わした．	He was so pleased with his hit that he spontaneously shook hands with the first-base coach.
思いどおりの試合運びに，監督は会心の笑みを漏らした．	Watching the game unfold according to his strategy, the manager grinned with satisfaction.

かいせい (改正)

道路交通法が改正された．	The traffic laws have been revised [changed, amended[1]].
彼は憲法改正に反対している．	He's opposed to revision [amendment[2]] of the constitution.
4月からJRの時刻表が改正された．	The JR timetable [schedule] was revised in April.

1)2) amend, amendment は「一部だけを改正する」場合に使う．

かいだん (階段)

彼は2段ずつ階段を下りた．	He went down the stairs two steps at a time.
階段の上で待っているよ．	I'll be waiting at the head [top] of the stairs.
階段の下で待っているよ．	I'll be waiting at the foot [bottom] of the stairs.
階段の途中で彼と擦れ違った．	I passed him on the stairs.

32段の階段を一気に上った.	I climbed the flight of 32 steps without stopping once.

かいちょう (快調)

エンジンはすこぶる快調だ.	The engine's in excellent condition.
ここまで快調に車を飛ばしてきた.	We've been speeding along smoothly so far.
仕事は快調に進んでいる.	The work is going †smoothly [without a hitch].
	The work is making good headway.
	The work is progressing well.
この頃あの作家は快調に作品を出している.	That author has been publishing regularly recently.
その横綱は快調に勝ち進んでいる.	That *yokozuna* has been winning regularly.

かいてき (快適)

とても快適な住まいだ.	It's a very comfortable house.
ここは湿度が低くて快適だ.	The low humidity here makes it comfortable.
エアコンを取り付けたので今年の夏は快適に過ごせる.	We installed an air conditioner, so this should be a comfortable [pleasant] summer.
彼は引退した後,ハワイで快適な生活を送っている.	He's been living a comfortable life since he retired to Hawaii.
快適な旅行をするには何を持って行ったらいいかな.	What should I take along to make it a pleasant trip?

かいもく (皆目)

彼女がどこへ行ってしまったのか皆目判らない.	I don't have the slightest idea where she could have gone.
世界情勢の行方は皆目見当がつかない.	I have no idea what's going to happen to the world situation.
どこに書類をしまったのか皆目思い出せない.	I can't remember †at all [for the life of me] where I put those papers.

かいわ (会話)

旧友と久しぶりに会い,楽しい会話が弾んだ.	I met an old friend whom I hadn't seen for a long time and we had a great talk [conversation].
子どもたちの会話を聞いていると面白いよ.	It's interesting to listen to children's conversations.
学生たちの会話の中には流行語が	A lot of trendy words come up in stu-

たくさん出てくる.	dents' conversations.
英語は読めるが会話ができないという日本人が多い.	There are many Japanese who can read English but can't converse in it.
彼はドイツ語会話を習っている.	He's studying conversational German.

かう¹ (買う)

それはあの店で安く買った.	I bought it cheap at that store.
彼女から絵を2万円で買った.	I bought a picture from her for 20,000 [twenty thousand] yen.
その会社の株を買うつもりだ.	I'm going to buy some stock in that company.
指輪を高い値段で買った.	I paid a lot for the ring.
帰りにパンを買って来てください.	Please pick up some bread on your way home.
彼女から絵を買い戻した.	I bought back the picture from her.
山へ行くので缶詰をたくさん買い込んだ.	We stocked up on canned goods because we're going up to the mountains.
彼がこの辺の土地を買い占めた.	He bought up the land in this area.
彼は二人の共同経営者の株を買い取った.	He bought out his two partners.
【慣用】僕は彼の手腕を買っている.	I appreciate his ability.
彼が両社の仲裁を買って出た.	He offered his services as mediator between the two companies.

かう² (飼う)

カナリアを飼っています.	I have [keep] a canary.
田舎の家では豚と鶏を飼っています.	We raise pigs and chickens at our home in the country.
彼はイノシシを飼い慣らすのに成功した.	He succeeded in taming a wild boar.

かえす¹ (返す)

先週貸した本を返してください.	Please †return [give me back] the book I lent you last week.
本は元の所に返しなさい.	Please put the book back in its place.
贈り物が気に入らなかったら私に返してください.	If you don't like the gift, then please give it back to me.
このコートが気に入らないなら, 返して別なのを選びなさい.	If you don't like this coat, take it back and choose another.
やっと借金を返し終わった.	I finally paid off [back] †my debt [the loan].

かえす² (帰す)

台風が来そうなので学校は子どもたちを早く帰した.	The school sent the children home early on account of an approaching typhoon.
彼はその晩はそこに泊まることにしたので運転手を帰した.	He decided to stay there overnight, so he sent the chauffeur home.
パーティーで主人がなかなか帰してくれず, 家に着くのが遅くなった.	The host kept insisting we stay longer at the party, so we didn't get home until late.

かえって

そんなことをすると彼はかえって怒ると思うよ.	I think doing something like that would make him mad instead.
私は教師をしているが, かえって子どもに教えられることが多い.	I'm a teacher, but as it turns out I learn a great deal from my students.
道路が込んでいるときは車に乗るより歩いたほうがかえって早い.	When the traffic is bad it's actually faster to walk than to drive.
こちらの安いカーテンのほうがかえって私の部屋に合いそうだ.	I think these less expensive curtains will actually go better in my room.
私は学生時代より今のほうがかえって本を多く読んでいる.	I actually read more books now than when I was in college.
軽い運動をしたらかえって気分が良くなった.	I felt surprisingly better [I actually felt better] having gotten a little exercise.

かえり (帰り)

帰りは何時になるか分からない.	I don't know what time I'll be back.
帰りはタクシーにしよう.	Let's go back by taxi.
みんな帰り支度を始めた.	Everybody started getting ready to go [leave].
会社からの帰りに友達に出会った.	I ran into my friend on my way home from the office.
帰り道はひとりでも分かります.	I can find my way home by myself.
お帰り.	Welcome home.[1]

> 1) 旅行などでしばらく家を空けていた人に対して言う. 日常的には Hi! などと挨拶を交わす.

かえる¹ (返る)

手紙が宛先不明で返ってきた.	The letter †came back [was returned] stamped "address unknown."
貸し出していた本がやっと返ってきた.	The book which was checked out has finally been returned.
落とした財布が返ってくるのはもうあきらめた.	I have given up on ever †having that lost wallet returned [getting back the wallet

	I lost].
歳月は返らない．	You can't turn back the clock.
初心に返れ．	Get back the spirit you had when you began.
彼女は心配のあまり泣き叫んだが，子どもの姿を見て我に返った．	Beside herself with worry she cried and screamed, but the sight of her child brought her back to her senses.
彼女は考えごとをしていたが，ハッと我に返ると時間は5時を過ぎていた．	She was lost in thought and when she became aware of her surroundings it was past five o'clock.

かえる² (帰る)

父は月曜日には帰って来ます．	Father will †come back [return] on Monday.
彼女はふるさとに帰った．	She †went back [returned] to her hometown.
20分もあれば歩いて帰れます．	I can walk home in 20 minutes.
車で真っすぐうちに帰った．	I drove straight home.
激しい嵐の中を飛行機で帰った．	I flew back through a heavy storm.

かえる³ (変える)

彼は決心を変えた．	He changed his mind. He reversed his decision.
彼は始終意見を変える．	He's constantly changing his mind.
今日は道を変えて行こう．	Let's take a different way today.
今さら彼を自覚ある社会人に変えるのは無理だと思う．	I don't think there's any way to make him more civic-minded.

かえる⁴ (換・替える)

電池が切れてきた．換えなくては．	The battery is running low. We have to change it.
この指輪をお金に換えたい．	I want money for this ring. I want to exchange this ring for money.
僕のラケットと君のを換えよう．	Let's trade rackets.
100円玉を10円玉10枚に替えてください．	Would you change this 100-yen coin for ten 10-yen coins, please?

かお (顔)

彼は私の顔を覗き込んだ．	He looked into my face.
彼女は顔が自慢だ．	She's proud of her good looks.
彼なら顔は知っている．	I know him by sight.
窓から顔を出すな．	Don't stick your head out the window.
彼女は顔を上げた〔背けた〕．	She looked up [aside].

二人は顔を見合わせた.	They looked at †each other [one another].
私がそう言うと彼は顔をしかめた.	When I said that, he †frowned [showed displeasure*].
【表情】その悲報に彼女の顔は曇った.	Her face clouded over at the sad news.
私は感情を顔に出すまいとした.	I tried not to show my emotions.
母はほっとした顔をしていた.	Mother looked relieved.
彼女は今にも泣き出しそうな顔をしていた.	She looked as if she would start crying at any moment.
そしらぬ顔で彼は黙っていた.	He remained silent with a blank look on his face.
彼は会っても知らん顔をする.	Even if he sees me, he ignores me.
【慣用】彼はあちこちに顔がきく.	He's very influential.
	He's very well connected.
彼は顔が広い.	He has contacts everywhere.
	He knows a lot of people.
	He has a wide circle of acquaintances.
彼は顔が売れている.	He's well-known.
あの新人歌手も顔が売れてきた.	That new singer is starting to become a real star.
政治家になるつもりなら顔を売っておかなくてはならない.	If you intend to become a politician, you have to get people to know what you look like.
彼は遅れて会議に顔を出した.	He showed up late for the meeting.
彼の顔を立ててまず彼のところに行った.	First of all I visited him at his place to show my respect for him.
彼は,就職で世話になった先生の顔をつぶさないように一生懸命働いた.	He worked hard in order not to reflect badly on his teacher who had helped him find the job.
私の推した学生が試験でカンニングをしたので私の顔はつぶれてしまった.	I lost face when the student I recommended was found cheating during the exam.
親の顔に泥を塗るようなことをしてはいけない.	Don't do anything to disgrace your parents.
彼に合わす顔がない.	I'm ashamed [embarrassed] to face him.
彼が大きな顔ができるのも今のうちだ.	He won't be able to act the big shot much longer.
彼の手品はプロ顔負けだ.	He puts (even) professional magicians to shame.

かおいろ (顔色)

【顔の血色】どうしたの? 顔色が悪いよ.	What happened? You look so pale.

さっきよりだいぶ顔色がよくなったね.	You look much better now.
【表情・機嫌】彼は何でも顔色に出す.	His expression always gives him away.
	He can't hide a thing. It's always written all over his face.
相手の顔色を見て話題を選ぶようにしている.	I always try to see how a person is feeling before talking to him about something.
彼はいつも上司の顔色ばかり伺っている.	He's always †looking out to see [aware of] what his boss might be thinking.
両親の話に触れた途端に彼の顔色が変わった.	His expression changed [He tensed up] as soon as the conversation turned to his parents.
大口顧客を失ったことを聞くと社長は顔色を変えた.	The president's face fell [The president turned pale] when he heard that they had lost a big client.
独裁者は顔色ひとつ変えずに謀反者の死刑を言い渡した.	The dictator's face was impassive as he condemned the rebel to death.

かかえる (抱える)

彼女は手に大きな荷物を抱えていた.	She carried a large package in her arms.
彼は本を小わきに抱えて立っていた.	He stood there holding [with] his book under his arm.
セントバーナード犬は抱えきれないほど大きくなる.	A St. Bernard grows so big you can't put your arms around it.
彼は急ぎの仕事を抱えて今動きがとれない.	He has urgent work and can't do anything else.
あの会社は多くの負債〔問題〕を抱えている.	That company has a lot of debts [problems].
夫に死なれ,彼女は3人の子どもを抱えて生きていかなければならない.	Her husband died and she has to go on living with three children to support.
その会社は従業員をたくさん抱えている.	That company has a lot of employees.
	That company employs a great number of people.

かがやかしい (輝かしい)

彼はこの分野で輝かしい業績をあげた.	He's made brilliant accomplishments in this field.
彼の輝かしい栄光の時代は終わった.	His days of shining glory are over.

かがやく (輝く)

シャンデリアがまぶしいほど輝いていた.	The chandelier gave off a dazzling brilliance.
宝石が七色に輝いた.	The jewel sparkled with all the colors of the rainbow.
星の輝く夜だった.	The stars were shining that night.
良い知らせに彼の顔は輝いた.	His face †brightened [lit up] at the good news.
喜びに輝く目をして彼女は私を見た.	She looked at me, her eyes sparkling [shining] with joy.
彼は柔道で金メダルに輝いた.	He basked in glory after winning the gold medal in *judo*.

かかり (係)

係の人を呼んでください.	I want to speak to the person in charge.
私は連絡〔受付〕係だ.	I'm in charge of †communications [the reception desk].
彼女は係長になった.	She became a supervisor.

かかる¹ (罹る)

彼女はよく病気にかかる.	She gets sick a lot. ／She often gets sick.
風邪にかかったときは暖かくして寝るのがいちばんです.	When you catch (a) cold, the best thing to do is keep warm and stay in bed.
娘ははしかにかかって1週間寝ていた.	My daughter came down with the measles and was sick in bed for a week.

かかる² (掛・架・懸かる)

壁に絵が掛かっている.	A picture is hanging on the wall.
あなたのオーバーはハンガーに掛かっています.	Your overcoat is on the hanger.
窓にレースのカーテンがかかっている.	The window is hung with lace curtains.
はしごが塀に掛かっている.	There's a ladder leaning against the fence.
ストーブにやかんがかかっている.	There's a kettle on the heater.
川に鉄橋が架かっている.	There's a railroad bridge over the river.／A railroad bridge spans the river.
虹がきれいにかかっている.	There's a beautiful rainbow.
ズボンに跳ねがかかるから注意して歩きなさい.	Walk carefully so that the mud doesn't splash on your pants.
服に雨がかからないよう真っすぐに傘を差した.	I held my umbrella straight so my clothes wouldn't get rained on.
このエンジンはなかなかかからない.	This engine is hard to start.

かかわる

さあ，かかってこい．	Come on. Give it to me.
弟は私にかかってきた．	My little brother attacked me.
彼はこの仕事にかかりきりだ．	He's tied up with this work.
今日はそれにかかれない．	I can't get to it today.
しぶしぶ仕事にかかった．	I turned to my work reluctantly.
この機械を借りるかどうかは君にかかっている．	It's up to you to decide whether or not we rent this machine.
ゴルフクラブを外国から持ち込むと税金がかかる．	You have to pay duty if you bring in golf clubs from abroad.
修理代は3,000円かかった．	It cost ￥3,000 to fix it. The repair bill was ￥3,000.
塀のペンキ塗りに丸一日かかった．	It took me †a whole [an entire] day to paint the fence.
医者にかかったほうがいい．	You should go see a doctor.
ウサギが罠にかかった．	A rabbit got caught in the trap.

(〜にも)かかわらず

悪天候にもかかわらず大勢の人が集まった．	A lot of people came in spite of the bad weather.
彼は老齢にもかかわらず若者と一緒に富士登山をした．	Despite his advanced age, he climbed Mt. Fuji with the young people.
一生懸命勉強したにもかかわらず試験の結果はさんざんだった．	Even though I studied very hard, I scored terribly on the exam.

かかわる (関・係・拘る)

【関連する】将来は医療に関わる仕事につきたい．	In the future, I would like to work in the healthcare field.
これはアジア全体に関わる問題だ．	This problem concerns all of Asia.
【携わる】こんなことにかかわってはいられない．	I can't afford to be involved in this kind of thing.
お隣さんに誘われて住民運動に関わるようになった．	I became involved in a citizen's movement after being asked by my neighbor.
今関わっている仕事は3ヵ月後に終わる予定だ．	My present job will end in three months.
【相手にする】子ども〔動物〕と関われる職につきたい．	I'd like to work with children [animals].
あの人とはできるだけ関わりたくない．	I'd rather stay away from him as much as possible.
【左右する】雪山ではちょっとしたミスが命に関わる．	In the snow-covered mountains, even the smallest error can turn life-threatening.
会社のイメージに関わるから，そんな仕事は引き受けられない．	We can't do that kind of work because it would affect our company's reputation.

かぎ (鍵)

かぎがやっとかかった.	The lock finally caught.
かぎはかかっていない. お入り.	Come in. It's not locked.
かぎを開けて中に入った.	We unlocked the door and went in.
親かぎですべてのドアが開く.	The †master key [passkey] opens all doors.
これの合いかぎを作ってくれ.	Make a duplicate of this key.
このクイズのかぎを教えて.	What's the key to this puzzle?

かぎり (限り)

私の我慢にも限りがある.	There's a limit to my patience.
彼のアイデアには限りがない.	There's no end to his ideas.
人間の欲望には限りがない.	There's no limit [end] to human desires.
限りある資源を大切に使おう.	Let's use our limited natural resources wisely.
彼は病気で限りある命だ.	He has a terminal illness.

～かぎり (～限り)

彼が謝らない限り許さない.	I won't forgive him unless he apologizes.
生きている限りあなたを忘れない.	I won't forget you as long as I live.
できる限り協力するよ.	I'll help as much as I can.
見渡す限り白一色だった.	It was white with snow as far as the eye could see.
力の限り引っ張った.	I pulled with all my might.

かぎる (限る)

時間は限られている. 急ごう.	We don't have much time. Let's hurry.
その会社は今年の採用人数を10人に限るつもりだ.	The company plans to limit the number of employees it hires to ten this year.
入場は大学院生に限ります.	Graduate students only. Only graduate students †are [will be] admitted.
おいしいスパゲティならあの店に限る.	If you want good spaghetti, that's the only place to go.
日曜はごろ寝しているに限る.	Sundays are days for lying around.
彼に限ってそんなことはしない.	He'd be the last person (in the world) to do such a thing.
今日に限り5割引で売ります.	This is being sold at a 50% discount today only.

かく¹ (掻く)

背中がかゆい. かいてよ.	My back itches. Could you scratch it for me, please?
彼はいらいらして髪をかきむしっ	He pulled at his hair in frustration.

た.
彼は落葉を熊手でかき集めた. | He raked (the fallen) leaves.

かく² (書・描く)

【書く】名前を書いてください. | Will you write down your name, please?
それはちょっと書いておかなくては. | I must make a note of that.
 | I'll just jot that down.
彼女はお得意のチョコレートケーキの作り方を詳しく書いた. | She wrote out the recipe for her famous chocolate cake.
私が買い物に行くまでに必要な物を忘れずに全部書いておいて. | Be sure to write down everything you need before I leave to go shopping.
彼は小説を数冊書いた. | He's written several novels.
新聞にはそう書いてある. | That's what it says in the newspaper.
手紙には何て書いてあった? | What did the letter say?
 | What was in the letter?

【描く】絵をかくのが好きです. | I like to draw [paint].
この絵は私をかいたものです. | This is a picture of me.

かく³ (角)

この角の大きさは40度だ. | This angle measures 40 degrees.
三角形の三つの角の和は常に180度である. | The three angles of any triangle always add up to 180 degrees.
90度の角のことを直角と言う. | A 90 degree angle is called a right angle.
ひし形は四角形の一つである. | The diamond shape is one kind of quadrilateral.
アメリカ国防総省は建物が五角形なので通称「ペンタゴン」と呼ばれる. | The U.S. Department of Defense is referred to as the "Pentagon" because the building in which it is located has five sides.
彼の顔は角張っている. | He has a square face.
彼はコーヒーに角砂糖を二つ入れた. | He put two cubes of sugar in his coffee.
あらゆる角度から検討した結果この案を採用することにした. | We considered it from every conceivable angle and decided to adopt this plan.

かく〜 (各〜)

各家庭から1,000円ずつ寄付を集めた. | We collected a donation of ¥1,000 from each family.
各地で値上げ反対運動が起こった. | Demonstrations against a price increase were held throughout the country.
世界各国の若者がこの競技場に集まった. | Young people from all over the world assembled at this sports arena.

かぐ (嗅ぐ)

このバラの香りをかいでみて.	Smell this rose.
肉が腐っていないかどうかかいでみた.	I smelled the meat to see whether it was rotten.
犬は私の足をくんくんかいだ.	The dog sniffed my foot.
どこでそんな話をかぎつけてきたの.	Where did you get wind of something like that?

かくご (覚悟)

彼は死を覚悟していた.	He was resigned to dying.
	He was prepared to die.
非難を浴びるのは覚悟のうえで私はそう言った.	I said what I said, fully aware that I was inviting a storm of criticism.
彼は部下に首を覚悟させた.	He prepared his men for dismissal.
覚悟を新たに再出発した.	He started again with new determination.
覚悟はいいか.	Are you ready?

かくじつ (確実)

彼が昇進することは確実だ.	His promotion is a sure thing.
	His promotion is certain.
我々が欲しいのは確実な情報〔確実な証拠〕だ.	What we want is †reliable information [sure proof].
確実なことは分からない.	I don't know for sure [certain].
合格するための確実な方法はこれしかない.	This is the only sure way to pass.
彼は確実に来る.	He'll definitely come.
	He'll come for sure.

がくしゅう (学習)

この百科事典は学習に役立つ.	This encyclopedia is a useful study aid.
その学校では5年生から英語を学習する.	That school begins teaching English in the fifth grade.
先生は生徒たちに家庭での学習時間をノートにつけさせた.	The teacher had his students keep a record of how much time they spent studying at home.

かくす (隠す)

それを早くここに隠して.	Quick! Hide it here.
真実を隠そうとしてもだめだ.	You cannot [It's useless to] hide [conceal] the truth.
その政治家は汚職を隠そうとした.	The politician tried to †hide [cover up] the bribery.

かくにん (確認)

忘れ物がないか確認しなさい.	Are you sure you've got everything?
念のために開始時刻を確認しておいたほうがいいよ.	It would be a good idea to confirm the starting time, just in case.
もう一度確認するけど，本当にこれでいいんだね.	I'd like to check to make sure that this is really all right with you.
先方の担当者に確認しておいてくれ.	Check with the person responsible in that company.
この件については先方の確認を得ています.	I have gained the approval of the other party concerning this matter.
会合の出欠確認を求めるメールが届いた.	We've received an e-mail asking us to confirm our attendance at the meeting.
家族のきずなを再確認した旅だった.	The trip strengthened family bonds.
失礼ですが，かばんの中身を確認させてください.	Excuse me. I'd like to check your bag.
未確認情報だが，南米で大きな地震が起こったようだ.	It's still unconfirmed but there seems to have been a big earthquake in South America.
遭難に巻き込まれた妹の安否確認がいまだに取れない.	We still haven't been able to confirm the safety of my younger sister who was caught in the disaster.

がくねん (学年)

学年は何年ですか.	What year[1] are you in (at school)?
	What grade[2] are you in?
学生は1学年に300人います.	There are 300 students in each grade.
春の遠足は学年ごとに違う場所に行った.	Each grade went to a different place for its spring outing.
学年末試験の勉強をしている.	I'm studying [preparing] for final exams.

> 1)2) 大学の学年には year を用いる．高校でも year を用いる場合もあるが，6-3-3制や8-4制などを通して数える場合は grade を用いる．例：I'm in the 11th grade.

かくべつ (格別)

今年の寒さは格別だった.	It was especially cold this year.
今日は格別のサービスだね．何かいいことがあったの.	You're being especially nice today. Did something good happen?
今日の彼女は格別にきれいだ.	She's looking exceptionally pretty today.

かくれる (隠れる)

| 彼女は柱の陰に隠れた. | She hid behind the pillar. |

親に隠れてたばこを吸った.	I hid from my parents and smoked a cigarette.
彼は隠れた天才だ.	He's an undiscovered genius.
隠れん坊しよう.	Let's play hide-and-(go-)seek.

かげ¹ (影)

地面に塔の影が差している.	The tower casts a shadow on the ground.
カーテンに男の影が映った.	A man's silhouette appeared against the curtain.
銅像が水面に影を映している.	The bronze statue is reflected on the water.
暗闇の中で人影が動いた	A human figure moved in the darkness.
彼は影の薄い人だ.	He's unobtrusive. He fades into the background.
娘の病気がその家庭に暗い影を落とした.	Their daughter's illness cast a dark shadow over their home.
【姿】自転車置き場に戻ったら，私の自転車は影も形もなかった.	When I went back to the bicycle lot there was no sign of my bike.
彼女はやつれ果てて見る影もなかった.	She was so haggard that she was a mere shadow of her former self.

かげ² (陰)

日陰で休んだ.	I rested in the shade.
暑いな. 日陰に入ろう.	It's hot. Let's get out of the sun.
私の家はあの建物の陰になっている.	My house is in the shadow of that building over there.
彼の顔半分が物陰に隠れて見えなかった.	Half of his face was blocked from view.
木陰で彼を待った.	I waited for him under the tree.
ドアの陰に男が隠れていた.	There was a man lurking behind the door.
彼は陰で人の悪口を言う.	He †says bad things about [speaks ill of*] people behind their backs.
やつらは陰で何か企んでいる.	They're plotting something on the sly.
彼は陰で私を笑っているに違いない.	He must be laughing at me behind my back.
陰で糸を引いている人がいる.	There's someone pulling wires behind the scenes.
私は彼を陰ながら応援している.	I'm rooting for him on the side.
彼女は陰になりひなたになり私を支えてくれた.	She supported me both openly and behind the scenes.
彼は陰ひなたがある.	He's †double-dealing [a double dealer].
彼は過去に暗い陰のある人だ.	He has a dark past.
犯罪の陰に女あり.	Cherchez la femme.[1]

> 1) Look for the woman. の意味のフランス語で，諺的に使われる．

(〜に)かけて(は)
【〜に向けて】渋谷から六本木にかけて道が渋滞している． Traffic is tied up between Shibuya and Roppongi.
今夜半から明朝にかけて大雨が降るでしょう． There will probably be heavy rains between late tonight and tomorrow morning.
夜にかけて天気がくずれるらしいよ． I hear that we're in for some bad weather tonight.
週末にかけて台風がくるらしいよ． It looks like there's a typhoon coming this weekend.
週末にかけて温泉に一泊してきた． I spent a night at the hot springs over the weekend.
20代後半から30代にかけてドイツに住んでいた． I lived in Germany from my late 20's and into my 30's.
30代から50代にかけては，いちばん仕事に脂が乗るときだ． The 30's to the 50's are †your [a person's] prime working years.
【〜に関しては】彼女は場をなごませることにかけては天才的だ． She's a genius when it comes to creating a relaxing atmosphere.
セールストークにかけては彼の右に出る者はいない． There's no one who can match him when it comes to sales talk.

かける¹ (掛・架・懸ける)
上着を洋服掛けに掛けた． I hung my jacket on the hook.
母はあの絵を自分の部屋に掛けた． My mother hung up that painting in her room.
母はエプロンを掛けてから料理を始めた． My mother put on an apron before she started cooking.
彼女は眼鏡を掛けている． She's wearing glasses.
フライパンをガスに掛けた． I put the skillet on the burner.
テーブル掛けを掛けてください． Please spread the tablecloth.
毛布を掛けて寝た． I covered myself with a blanket and went to sleep.
橋を架ければ便利になるだろう． It'd be really convenient if they built a bridge across the river.
屋根にはしごを掛けた I leaned the ladder against the roof.
ソースを掛けたほうがいいよ． You'd better put some sauce on it.
子どもに水を掛けられた． I had water thrown on me by the kids.
車のエンジンをかけておいて． Will you start the car for me, please?
1ヵ月もかけてこの本を読んだ． I spent a whole month reading this book.
彼は今度の旅行に10万円かけた． He spent 100,000 [a hundred thousand]

	yen on that trip.
どうぞお掛けください.	Please have a seat.
彼女はお気に入りのCDをかけた.	She put on her favorite CD.
彼は家に保険をかけた.	He took out insurance on his house.
3掛ける6は18.	Three times six is eighteen.

かける² (欠ける)

茶わんが欠けた.	The rice bowl got chipped.
彼の演説はいまひとつ説得力に欠けていた.	His speech wasn't quite persuasive [convincing] enough.
今度の決定は小数意見への配慮に欠けている.	That decision doesn't give enough consideration to minority opinion.
あなたが欠けたら我々のチームは負けてしまう.	Without you our team would lose.

かげん (加減)

【具合・程度】今日はお加減はいかがですか.	How are you feeling today? How do you feel today?
湯加減はどうですか.	How's the water temperature?
塩加減をみてくれ.	See if this needs more salt.
君の馬鹿さ加減にはあきれた.	I've had just about enough of your stupidity.
彼女は首を傾き加減にして私の話をじっと聞いていた.	Her head slightly tilted, she listened intently as I spoke.
【調節】冷房が利きすぎる. 少し加減しよう.	The air-conditioning is too strong. Let's adjust it a little.
塩を入れて味を加減しなさい.	Season to taste with salt.

かこ (過去)

過去には戻れない.	We can't go back to the past.
過去2年間というもの服を1着も新調していない.	I haven't had any new clothes made for the past [last] two years.
彼は過去の人だ.	He belongs to the past. He's a has-been.**
彼女は(暗い)過去のある女らしい.	She seems to be a woman with a (dark) past.
過去のことは水に流そう.	Let's let bygones be bygones.

かこむ (囲む)

四方を敵に囲まれた.	The enemy surrounded us.
おじいちゃんは孫たちに囲まれてとても幸せそうだ.	Surrounded by his grandchildren, the old man seemed very happy.
生け垣で家を囲んである.	The house is surrounded by a hedge.

テーブルを囲んで楽しく食事をした.	We all sat around the table and enjoyed a pleasant meal.
正解の番号を丸で囲め.	Circle the number of the correct answer.

がさつ

彼女のようながさつな女とは結婚したくない.	I don't want to marry a coarse [vulgar, crude] woman like her.
彼はがさつな男なので客商売には向かない.	He's too coarse [vulgar, crude] for work dealing (directly) with customers.
彼は根は優しいが, がさつなところがあるので誤解され易い.	He's actually quite gentle, but his coarse side tends to make people take him the wrong way.

かさなる (重なる)

テーブルに皿が重なっていた.	The dishes were stacked neatly on the table.
紙が2枚重なっている.	The two pieces of paper are on top of each other.
本が机の上に山のように重なっている.	There's a pile [stack] of books on my desk a mile high.
	There's a mountain of books piled [stacked] on my desk.
乗客は重なり合って倒れた.	The passengers fell down one on top of †another [the other].
仕事が重なって休む暇もない.	Work is piled up and I can't take any time off.
彼は喜びが二重に重なった.	He was doubly blessed.
彼は失敗が重なって降格された.	He was demoted because he made one mistake after another.
彼の研究と私の研究は一部重なり合っている.	Part of my research overlaps[1] with his.
今度の祭日は日曜日と重なる.	The coming national holiday falls on a Sunday.

---

1) overlap は紙などが重なり合う場合にも使える.

かさねる (重ねる)

本を2冊重ねて置いた.	I stacked the two books.
	I put two books one on top of the other.
彼はそれを一つ一つ重ねていった.	He stacked [piled] them one on top of the other.
セーターを2枚重ねて着た.	I wore two sweaters one on top of the other.

封筒を2枚重ねてその中に写真を入れた.	I inserted one envelope into another and then put in the photos.
新聞がたくさん重ねてある.	A lot of newspapers are piled [stacked] up.
彼は多くの悪事を重ねてきた.	He's committed †one crime after another [a string of crimes].
彼は苦労に苦労を重ねてきた.	He's suffered one hardship after another.
その本はロングセラーで版を多く重ねてきた.	That book is a steady seller that's gone through one printing after another.
重ねて言うが彼は無実だ.	How many times do I have to tell you? He's innocent!

かざり (飾り)

クリスマス・ツリーの飾りがとてもきれいだった.	The Christmas tree ornaments were very lovely.
クリスマスの飾りつけをした店内は, 楽しげな気分にあふれていた.	The Christmas decorations filled the store with a wonderful atmosphere.
彼女は今日かわいい髪飾りをつけている.	She's wearing a pretty hair accessory today.
飾り気のない部屋だ.	It's a simple room.
彼は飾り気のない人だ.	There's nothing pretentious [affected] about him.
彼は飾り気のない文章を書く.	He writes plain, unadorned sentences.
彼の飾り気のない言葉に心を動かされた.	I was moved by the artlessness of his words.

かざる (飾る)

誕生パーティーのために部屋を飾った.	We decorated the room for the birthday party.
おひな様を飾った.	We set [put] up the dolls for the Doll Festival.
身を飾るための金はない.	I can't afford extravagant clothes and accessories.
あの飾ってある手袋を見せて.	Let me see the gloves on display.
店のウインドーを飾った.	I dressed the shop window.
うわべを飾っても本質は変わらない.	A fancy veneer doesn't [won't] change what you really are.

かしこい (賢い)

あの子は賢い子だ.	That child is clever [bright].
イルカは賢い動物です.	Dolphins are intelligent animals.
彼はいつも賢く立ち回る.	He's always maneuvering in a clever way [fashion].

かじる
- このリンゴはおいしいよ．一口かじってごらん．ー This apple is good. Have a bite.
- 少年はパンにかじりついた．ー The boy bit into a piece of bread.
- ネズミがチーズをかじってしまった．ー A mouse has been nibbling at the cheese.
- 学生時代ちょっとドイツ語をかじった．ー I dabbled in German when I was a student.

かす (貸す)
- 金を貸してもらえないか．ー Will you lend me some money?
- 傘を貸していただけますか．ー May I borrow an umbrella? / Would you lend me an umbrella?
- これをかたにいくら貸してくれますか．ー How much can I borrow on this? / How much will you lend me with this as security [collateral]?
- 私は月2,000ドルで家を貸しています．ー I rent [let] the house (out) for 2,000 dollars a month.
- 電話を貸してください．ー Please let me use your phone.
- 火を貸してください．ー May I have a light?

かず (数)
- 娘はまだ10以上の数は数えられない．ー Our little daughter still can't count past ten.
- これまでに出版された本は数知れない．ー The number of books published up to now is countless [uncountable].
- 数あるイタリア料理店の中でもこの店が最高だ．ー This is the best of all the many Italian restaurants in town.
- 彼女は数々の小説を発表した．ー She published numerous novels.
- 彼に比べれば私なんかものの数に入らない．ー Compared to him, I'm nothing.

かすか
- かすかに声が聞こえる．ー I hear a faint voice.
- 遠くにかすかな光が見える．ー I see a glimmer of light in the distance.
- 遠くでかすかな影が動いた．ー A dim [faint] figure moved in the distance.
- 彼が良くなる希望はかすかながらある．ー There's a chance, however dim, that he may recover.
- 彼にナイトクラブで会ったことはかすかに覚えている．ー I dimly [faintly] remember meeting him at the nightclub.

かすむ
- 遠くがかすんでいる．ー It's hazy [misty, foggy] in the distance.

| 雨の日は山がかすんでよく見えない. | It's so misty on rainy days that you can't see the mountains. |
| 目がかすんでよく見えない. | My vision is blurred. |

かぜ¹ (風)

北風が吹いている.	The wind is blowing from the north.
	The north wind is blowing.
風が出てきた.	It's getting windy.
夕方になって風が出てきた.	As night fell, the wind began to blow.
風がやんだ.	The wind has †stopped [died down].
今日は風がひどい.	It's really windy today.
少しも風がない.	There's not one little bit of wind.
風のある〔ない〕日に外へ出た.	I went out on a windy [windless] day.
風の向きが西に変わった.	The wind has shifted westward.
	The wind is now blowing to the west.
その日は大風が吹いた.	There was a strong wind that day.
心地よいそよ風が入ってきた.	A nice breeze blew in.
隙間風がどこかから入る.	There's a draft from somewhere.
周りに何もないので私の家は風当たりが強い.	The wind blows hard against my house since there's nothing around it.
伝統的な日本の家屋は風通しが良い.	Traditional Japanese houses are well ventilated.
ちょっと風に当たってくるよ.	I'm going out to get †some [a breath of] air.
明日は明日の風が吹く.	Tomorrow's another day.
	Tomorrow will take care of itself.
世間の風当たりは強かった.	There was severe criticism [It came under intense criticism] from the public.
	There was a lot of flak.**

かぜ² (風邪)

今風邪をひいている.	I have a cold now.
窓を開けて寝たら風邪をひいてしまった.	I left the window open when I went to bed and caught a cold.
風邪気味だ.	I have a touch of a cold.
風邪声だね.	You sound like you have a cold.
彼は風邪で寝ている.	He's in bed with a cold.
風邪はもうだいぶ良くなった.	My cold is much better now.
鼻風邪をひいているだけだ.	I just have †a runny nose [a head cold].

かせぐ (稼ぐ)

| 【お金を】毎月30万円稼いでいる. | I earn ¥300,000 a month. |
| 彼は稼ぐ先から使ってしまう. | He spends money as fast as he earns it. |

稼ぐに追いつく貧乏なし.	Hard work never sent anyone to the poorhouse.[1]
	Work hard and you'll never have to worry about being poor.
【点数・時間などを】彼は得意科目の理科で点数を稼いだ.	His high marks in science, his favorite subject, brought up his average.
義母の好物を送って点数を稼いだ.	I sent my mother-in-law her favorite food and scored.
彼は上司に対して点数稼ぎに余念がない.	He's really into scoring points with his boss.
世間話をして時間を稼げ. その間にぼくが調べて教えてやるから.	Keep him busy with some small talk. In the meantime, I'll check into it and let you know.

1) 「勤勉は救貧院に人を送らず→勤勉に働けば赤貧状態になることはない」という諺.

かぞえる (数える)

一つ一つ数えなさい.	Count them one by one.
人数を数えなさい.	Count how many people there are.
彼女は指を折って数えた.	She counted on her fingers.
村に残った若者は数えるほどしかいなかった.	Only a handful of young people had stayed on in the village.
彼が来た回数を数え上げた.	I counted up the number of times he came.
私の数え違いでした.	I counted it wrong.
私が去る理由は数えきれない.	There are innumerable [countless] reasons for my leaving.
数えきれないほど人がいた.	There were countless [innumerable] people.
彼は日本で十指に数えられる彫刻家だ.	He's counted among the top ten sculptors in Japan.

かた[1] (型)

こんな型の財布は便利だ.	This kind [type] of wallet is convenient.
この型のコートは流行遅れだ.	This style of coat has gone out of fashion.
こんな型の庭園を造りたいのですが.	I'd like to model my garden after this kind [type].
これは最新型だ.	This is the latest model.
型紙に沿って布地を裁った.	I cut the cloth following the outline of the pattern.
石こうで型を取った.	I made a plaster cast of it.
私たちは型どおりの結婚式をあげ	We had a conventional wedding.

毎日の型にはまった仕事のあとは一杯やりたくなる.	I always want a drink after my daily routine at the office.
型にはまった教師になるな.	Don't become just another ordinary [stereotyped] teacher.
祖父は型破りの人間だった.	My grandfather was †unconventional [a man who broke with convention].

かた² (方)

あの方はどなたですか.	Who is that person?
あの方は私の学校の1年先輩です.	He's [She's] a year ahead of me at school.
平和のために努力している立派な方々がいます.	There are many outstanding individuals working for peace.
この夏は父方〔母方〕の親戚を訪ねます.	I'm going to visit relatives on my father's [mother's] side (of the family) this summer.
彼のしゃべり方〔歩き方〕は父親によく似ている.	The way he talks [walks] is very similar to the way his father does.
この道具の使い方を教えて.	Please tell me how to use this tool.
同じことでも言い表し方によって随分印象が変わるものだ.	An idea can have a very different impact depending on how it is expressed.

かた³ (肩)

彼はかばんを肩に掛けている.	He's carrying his bag slung over his shoulder.
あの人は肩幅が広い〔狭い〕.	He has broad [narrow] shoulders.
彼女はなで肩だ.	She has sloping shoulders.
肩を貸してください. 頭がくらくらするんです.	May [Can] I put my head on your shoulder? I feel dizzy.
彼女は肩越しに私を見た.	She looked over her shoulder at me.
彼は肩を怒らして怒鳴った.	He drew up his shoulders and shouted.
彼は肩をすくめて笑った.	He shrugged his shoulders and smiled.
彼は肩で風を切って歩く.	He walks with a swagger.
その女の子は肩で息をしながら話した.	The girl spoke with her shoulders heaving from heavy breathing.
肩が凝った.	My shoulders are stiff.
【慣用】肩の凝る話はこれくらいにしよう.	Let's end this serious talk here.
何か肩の凝らない読み物が欲しいな.	I'd like some light reading.
末っ子が大学を卒業して肩の荷がおりた.	It took [was] a load off our minds when our youngest child graduated from college.

君はあいつの肩を持つのか.	Are you siding with him?
	Are you taking his side?
彼と肩を並べる者はいない.	No one's on a par with him.
	He's head and shoulders above the rest.
彼はS候補に肩入れしている.	He's backing candidate S.

かたい (固・堅・硬い)

堅いいすに座らされた.	They had me sit on a hard chair.
かたいパンのほうが好きだ.	I prefer bread with a firmer texture.
この肉はかたい.	This meat is tough.
硬い岩だ.	This is a hard rock.
彼は硬い鉛筆を使っている.	He uses pencils with hard lead.
結び目が固くてほどけない.	This knot is so tight I can't †get it undone [untie it].
彼女と固い約束をした.	I made a firm promise with her.
食料品店は堅い商売だ.	A grocery store is a sound business.
この成績なら合格は堅い.	With these grades you're sure to pass.
	You'll definitely make it with these grades.
彼は終始硬い表情を崩さなかった.	He maintained [kept] a stone-like [firm] expression from beginning to end.
彼の書く文章は硬い.	His writing style is formal.
	He has a formal writing style.

かたくるしい (堅苦しい)

堅苦しい人と話すと疲れる.	It's tiring to speak [talk] with a stiff and formal person.
堅苦しい挨拶は抜きにしよう.	Let's do away with stiff and formal greetings.
堅苦しいことはやめよう.	Let's be informal.
	Let's do away with formalities.
あまり堅苦しく考えないで.	You don't have to think of it in such strict [rigid] terms.

かたち (形)

それはどういう形をしていますか.	What shape is it?
	What does it look like?
形は丸く色は赤です.	It's round and red.
	The shape is round and the color is red.
魚の形をした文鎮を買った.	I bought a paperweight shaped like a fish.
私の学校の建物は変わった形をしている.	My school has a strange design.
欲望は種々の形をとって表れる.	Desire expresses [shows] itself in various forms.

形にとらわれることなくその本質を見なさい.	Don't be misled by form. Look at the substance.
彼の研究の成果は本の形にまとめられた.	The results of his study were put together in book form.
感謝を何かの形に表すことが必要です.	It's necessary to express your gratitude in some form.
彼らは形ばかりの結婚式をあげた.	They had a very small wedding.
姿かたちの良い人は得だ.	It's advantageous to be good-looking.

かたづける (片づける)

自分の部屋を片づけなさい.	Clean [Straighten] up your room.
テーブルの上を片づけよう.	Let's clear off the table.
今度買った新車を置くためガレージの中を片づけた.	We cleared out the garage to make room for the new car we bought.
散らばっている本を片づけて場所を空けなさい.	Straighten up the scattered books and make space.
この仕事を片づけてしまわねば帰れない.	We can't leave until we get this work finished.
やっと難問を片づけた.	I finally solved the difficult problem.

かたまり (固まり・塊)

蟻が砂糖の固まりを運んでいる.	Ants are carrying clumps of sugar.
彼は氷〔雪, 土〕の塊を投げた.	He threw †pieces of ice [lumps of snow, clods of dirt].
肉屋で大きな豚肉の塊を買って来た.	At the butcher's I bought a big piece of pork.
女学生がひとかたまりになって歩いて来る.	The women students are walking toward us in a group.
彼は欲〔エゴイズム〕の塊のような人間だ.	He is the very personification of greed [egotism].

かたまる (固まる)

のりが固まってしまった.	The paste has dried out.
服についた泥が固まった.	The mud on the clothes has dried up.
ゼリーはもう固まったの？	Has the gelatin set yet?
【集まる・まとまる】学生たちはリーダーの周りに固まり始めた.	The students began to gather [group, cluster] around the leader.
人々があちこちで固まっているのが見える.	We can see groups of people here and there.
隅に固まらず前に出なさい.	Get out in front instead of huddling in the corner.
やっと会社を辞める決心が固まった.	My resolve to quit the company finally hardened.

委員会としての意見が固まった. The committee's opinion solidified.

かたむく (傾く)
柱が少し傾いている. The pillar leans a little.
木が南の方に傾いている. The tree tilts to the south.
この床は少し傾いている. The floor isn't level.
机の傾きを直さなくてはならない. I have to make this desk level.
その船は一方に大きく傾いた. The ship listed heavily to one side.
お盆が傾かないようにしっかり持っていてください. Hold the tray firmly so it doesn't tip.
太陽が西に傾いた. The sun is in the west.
彼女は彼の意見に傾いている. She leans toward his opinion.
身代が傾きかけている. My fortune is on the decline.

かたむける (傾ける)
水槽を傾けて中の水を流した. I dumped the water out of the tank.
彼女は話を聞くときいつも首を傾ける. She always listens with her head tilted to one side.
その計画の失敗が会社を傾けることになった. The plan's failure threw the company off balance.

かためる (固める)
この板は木くずを固めて作ったものです. This board was made by compressing sawdust.
セメントで土台を固めた. We used cement to strengthen the foundation.
彼女は手作りキャンディを固めるために冷蔵庫に入れた. She put the home-made candy in the fridge to harden.
プリンを固めるのにコーンスターチが使える. You can use cornstarch to thicken the pudding.
忘れ物をしないように荷物は一か所に固めておきなさい. Keep your things together in one place so you won't forget them.
彼は怒ってこぶしを固めた. He clenched his fists in anger.
彼は社長となって会社の基礎を固めた. He became president and whipped the company into shape.
敵の攻撃に備えて守りを固めねばならない. We have to fortify our defenses in preparation for the enemy attack.

かち (価値)
彼の絵の価値はその死後認められるようになった. People began to recognize the value of his paintings after his death.
この皿には全く美術的価値がない. This plate is of no artistic value.
これは1万ドルの価値がある. This is worth $10,000 [ten thousand dol-

一見の価値がある.	It's worth a look.
物事の価値判断の基準は人によってさまざまだ.	Everyone has different standards for judging a thing's worth.

〜がち

彼はすぐあきらめがちだ.	He tends to give up easily.
彼は遅れがちだ.	He tends to be late.
彼は飲み過ぎになりがちだ.	He has a tendency to drink too much.
君は借金しがちだね.	You have a tendency to borrow money.
	You're always running up debts.
母は病気がちです.	My mother gets sick easily.
あの家は留守がちだ.	They're often out.
	They're not at home much.

かちき (勝気)

彼女は勝気な人だ.	She's a strong-minded individual.
彼は勝気な性格で人に負けるのが嫌いだ.	His unyielding spirit makes him hate losing.
彼は勝気な性格だから自分の非をなかなか認めようとしない.	He has such an unyielding personality that it blinds him to his own faults.

かつ (勝つ)

今回は君に勝たせてあげよう.	I'll let you win this time.
我々のチームが試合に勝った.	Our team won the game.
この問題についての議論で彼に勝った.	I won the argument with him over this matter.
今のところ10点勝っている.	They're ten points ahead right now.
君にはどうしても勝てない.	I just can't seem to beat you.
彼が相手じゃ勝ち目はない.	There's no way I could win against him.
あまり勝ち誇った態度をとるなよ.	Don't gloat so much about winning.
彼女は努力して困難に打ち勝った.	She overcame her troubles through hard work.

がっかり

仕事がうまくいっていないと聞いてがっかりした.	I was disappointed to hear that business was not going well.
彼女の返事にがっかりした.	Her response disappointed me.
がっかりするな.	Don't let it get you down.
がっかりしたことにパーティーはお流れになった.	To my disappointment, the party was †canceled [called off].
彼には全くがっかりだった.	He was an utter disappointment.

かっき (活気)

活気のない顔をしているね.	You look so lifeless.
すべてが活気に満ちあふれている.	Everything is so full of life.
その職場は活気に満ちている.	People in that office are so energetic.
彼女の言葉に皆活気づいた.	Her words aroused everyone's enthusiasm.

かつぐ (担ぐ)

一人で全部担げますか.	Can you carry it all by yourself?
彼は病院へ担ぎ込まれた.	He was carried into the hospital.
彼を会長に担ぎ出すつもりだ.	We intend to get him to be our chairman.
【だます】まんまとかつがれた.	I was completely taken in.
彼は人をかついでばかりいる.	He's always playing jokes on people.
最初は彼の話を信じたが、やがてかつがれているのが分かった.	At first I believed his story, but then I realized he was †putting me on [pulling my leg].

かっこう (格好)

彼女は格好がいいね.	She looks good, doesn't she?
彼女は格好のいい靴を履いている.	She's wearing great-looking shoes.
彼はいつもいきな格好をしている.	He's always dressed elegantly.
何て格好なの.	What's that getup?
彼はいつも変わった格好をしている.	He always wears strange clothes.
彼は歩く格好が父親にそっくりだ.	He walks exactly [just] like his father.
この計画もやっと格好がつき始めた.	This project is finally beginning to take shape.
彼もやっと先生としての格好がついてきた.	He's finally begun to look like a teacher.
そんなことをしては親戚に格好が悪い.	If we do something like that, it won't sit well with our relatives.
【ちょうどいい】格好な大きさのテーブルが見つかりました.	I found a table of just the right size.
ここは子どもたちに格好の遊び場です.	This is a perfect playground for children.

かつて

彼にはかつて会ったことがある.	I've met him once before.
彼もかつてはぜいたくな暮らしをしていた.	He used to lead a life of luxury.
彼はかつての様に元気ではない.	He is not as energetic as he used to be.
そんな話はいまだかつて聞いたことがない.	I've never heard such a story.

かって (勝手)

君は勝手な言い分ばかり並べるね.	You only tell your side of things.
勝手なことばかり言ってごめんなさい.	I'm sorry for sounding so selfish.
彼女は勝手なことばかりする.	She does everything her own way.
勝手にしろ!	See if I care!／Suit yourself!
勝手にやっていいよ.	You can do as you please.
それは君の勝手だ.	It's up to you.
何をしようと私の勝手だ.	Nobody tells me what to do.
ここにある本は勝手に持ち出さないでください.	Please don't take these books out without permission.
それは彼女が勝手に決めたことで私たちは知りません.	She made that decision on her own authority. We don't know anything about it.
【様子】東京は初めてなので勝手がわからない.	It's my first time in Tokyo, so I'm not very familiar with it yet.
新しいミシンを買ったのだが, 勝手が違って使いにくい.	I bought a new sewing machine, but it's hard to use because of all the unfamiliar functions.

かっと

かっとなって部下を怒鳴り飛ばした.	I lost my temper and really chewed out my staff.
彼に馬鹿にされたので, かっとなって殴ってしまった.	I lost my temper when he made fun of me and I hit him.
彼の話を聞いてかっと頭に血がのぼった.	I was infuriated by what I heard him say.

かつどう (活動)

祖父は町内でいろいろな活動をしている.	My grandfather is quite active in the community.
火山には活動しているものと, していないものがある.	There are active volcanoes and dormant volcanoes.
フクロウは夜になると活動する.	Owls are active at night.
私たちのグループはなかなか活動的です.	Our group is quite dynamic.
着物は活動的でない.	It's hard to be active in a *kimono*.
小学校の5, 6年になるとクラブ活動の時間がある.	When children get to the fifth and sixth grades there's a period for club activities.
彼は学生時代に政治活動をしていた.	He was active in politics when he was in college.

かっぱつ (活発)

彼は活発な少年だ.	He's a lively boy.
彼女は動作が活発だ.	Her movements are brisk [lively].
市況は活発だ.	The market is active.
我々は活発な議論をした.	We had an animated discussion.
もっと活発に意見を出してください.	Express your opinions more vigorously.

かつやく (活躍)

我が校の卒業生は様々な分野で活躍している.	Our graduates are playing an active role in many fields.
最近の芸能人には作家として活躍する人も多い.	These days many entertainers are also successful writers.
今シーズンは彼の活躍が目立つ.	He's doing a great job this season. He's been playing a fantastic game this season.
このプロジェクトにおける彼の活躍ぶりには目を見張るものがあった.	It was amazing to watch him contribute to this project.
今年の文化祭では生徒会副会長が大活躍した.	The vice-president of the student council was very active in this year's †open house [school festival].
新天地での活躍を期待しています.	I wish you the best of luck in your new †endeavor [overseas post].

かてい (家庭)

彼女は裕福な〔貧乏な〕家庭に育った.	She grew up in †an affluent [a poor] home.
彼は家庭では妻のしりに敷かれている.	At home his wife has him wrapped around her finger. His wife wears the pants in his family.
彼は仕事にかまけて家庭のことは少しも顧みない.	He's busy with work to the utter neglect of his family.
結婚した二人には幸福な家庭を築いてほしい.	I hope the new couple will establish a happy home.
彼女は大変家庭的な女性だ.	She's a very domestic type.
彼は会社では有能なビジネスマンだが, 家では大変家庭的な男だ.	He's a capable businessman at work, but he is a real homebody in private.
そこは非常に家庭的な雰囲気のレストランだ.	That restaurant has a very homey atmosphere.
明日は家庭科の時間がある.	I have home ec [economics] tomorrow.
私は高校生の男の子の家庭教師をしている.	I'm a private tutor for a high school boy.

かど (角)

転んだ拍子に机の角に頭をぶつけてしまった.	I struck [bumped] my head on the corner of the desk as I fell.
この岩は角がごつごつしている.	This rock has jagged edges.
次の角を右に曲がりなさい.	Turn right at the next corner.
角から2軒目の家が私の家だ.	My house is the second one from the corner.
角でばったり彼女と会った.	I ran into her on the corner.
その四つ角に今度信号機がついた.	There's a traffic light at that intersection now.
【慣用】それでは角が立つよ.	That would only create bitter feelings.
彼も年のせいで角が取れてきた.	He's mellowed with age.

かなう

【匹敵する】英語では君にかなわない.	There's no way I can measure up to you when it comes to English.
テニスで彼にかなう者はいない.	No one can match him in tennis.
この暑さにはかなわないよ.	I'm no match for this heat.
彼のへ理屈にはかなわないよ.	I can't stand his quibbling.
彼女はおせっかいでかなわない.	Her meddling annoys me.
【実現する】長年の望みがやっとかなった.	What I had been wishing for all these years finally came true.
流れ星に願い事をすると夢がかなう.	Dreams come true when you wish upon a shooting [falling] star.
彼が私の夢をかなえてくれた.	He made my dreams come true.
彼女はかなわぬ恋をしている.	Her love is in vain.
【適合する】それではこちらの目的にかなっていない.	That won't serve our purpose.
彼のしたことは礼儀にかなっていない.	What he did was inconsistent with common courtesy.

かなしい (悲しい)

そんな事言われると悲しくなるよ.	Being told that makes me sad.
悲しいことに友人が先日病気で死んでしまった.	I'm sad to say that my friend died from an illness the other day.

かなしみ (悲しみ)

両親を失った私の悲しみはだれにも分からない.	Nobody understands the sorrow I felt when I lost my parents.
母は悲しみに沈んでいます.	My mother has sunk into grief.

かなしむ (悲しむ)

彼女は友人の不幸を悲しんでいる.	She feels sad about her friend's misfortune.

悲しんでいる時ではない.	This is no time to be sad.
いつまでも悲しんでばかりはいられない.	You can't go on grieving forever.
入試に失敗したことをいくら悲しんでも始まらない.	Feeling depressed about failing the entrance exam won't get you anywhere.

かならず (必ず)

必ず彼女を連れて来いよ.	Make sure [certain] you bring her along.
必ず時間どおりに行きます.	I'll be sure [certain] to be there on time.
必ず手紙を投函しなさい.	Make certain [sure] you mail the letter.
夕食の前には必ず手を洗うようにしなさい.	Be sure to wash your hands before dinner.
私たちが留守のあいだ忘れずに必ず猫にえさをやってください.	Make sure the cat's fed every day while we're gone.
あの二人は会えば必ずけんかをする.	Those two can't get together without quarreling.
この方法が必ずしもベストだとは言えない.	This method is not necessarily the best. I can't be positive that this is the best method.
金持ちが必ずしも幸福とは限らない.	Money doesn't necessarily bring happiness.

かなり

かなり遅くなると思う.	I'll probably be pretty late.
かなり長いあいだ待っていた.	I waited for a fairly long time.
彼はかなり英語が話せる.	He can speak English fairly [rather] well.
かなり疲れているようですね.	You look really tired.
駅まではかなりの距離がある.	It's a good distance from here to the station.
電話代はかなりの額になっていると思う.	I think we've built up a pretty big phone bill.
寄付金はかなり集まった.	The donations amounted to a considerable sum.
彼らはかなりの暮らしをしている.	They are pretty well off.

かね (金)

なけなしの金をはたいて新車を買った.	I bought a new car with what little money I had.
そんなことに金をかけるな.	Don't spend [waste] your money on that.
君は最近金に困っているらしいね.	I've heard that you're pressed for money lately.
人の命は金に換えられない.	Human life is priceless.
万事金の世の中だ.	Money makes the world go round.

先立つものは金だ.	Money is the first consideration.
この絵を売って金にしてくれ.	Sell off this painting for the money.
この小切手を金に換えてくれ.	Cash this check.
この仕事は金にならない.	This job doesn't pay.
彼はおいしいものには金を惜しまない.	He's willing to pay for a good meal.
彼は金に糸目をつけずに絵を買った.	He bought paintings as if price were no object.
彼は金に目がくらんで仲間たちを裏切った.	Blinded by greed, he sold out his friends.
彼の家には金がうなっている.	His family is rolling in †dough** [the money].
彼女は急に金回りがよくなった.	Suddenly she had a lot of money on her hands.
彼は金離れのいい人だ.	He's generous with his money.
金の切れ目が縁の切れ目.	When poverty comes in at the door, love flies out at the window.

～かねない

彼女なら本当にやりかねない.	Knowing her, she could very well get it done.
彼はまじめ一方だから冗談も本気にしかねない.	He's so over-conscientious that he could take you seriously even when you're joking around.
ここでは小さなミスが大事故につながりかねない.	A small error here can lead to serious consequences later.

かねもち (金持ち)

彼女は金持ちの家に生まれた.	She was born into a rich family.
彼は町いちばんの金持ちだ.	He's the richest man in town.
事業がうまくいって彼は大金持ちになった.	His success in business made him a very rich man.

かねる (兼ねる)

そのチームでは監督がコーチを兼ねている.	The manager doubles as the coach on that team.
その部屋は食堂と居間を兼ねている.	That room serves as both dining room and living room.
仕事も兼ねて旅行に出ます.	I'm going on a trip but I plan to get a little work done too.
大は小を兼ねる.	The bigger, the better.
	Too big is better than too small.

かのう (可能)

そんなことが可能だと思う？	Do you think such a thing is possible?
電車が遅れる可能性は十分ある．	It's quite possible that the train will be late.
彼の成功の可能性はないと思う．	I don't think there's any chance [possibility] of his success.
あなたはまだ若いからどんなことでも可能だ．	You're so young and you can do anything you choose. Anything is possible for you because you're still young.

カバー

【覆い】しばらく使わないので，エアコンにカバーをかけた．	I put a cover on the air conditioner because we won't be using it for a while yet.
この本のカバーが気に入っている．	I really like this book cover [jacket].
枕カバーに染みがついてしまった．	The †pillow slip [pillowcase] got stained.
【補う・援護する】課長はいつも私のミスをカバーしてくれる．	My †section chief [boss] always covers for me.
私ができる限りカバーするから，思い切ってプロジェクトリーダーに挑戦してみなさい．	Go ahead and take over as project leader. I'll back you up.
今年度の赤字をカバーするには大幅なコストダウンが必要だ．	We'll really have to bring down costs in order to †cover [make up for] our losses this fiscal year.
【曲の】最近はカバー曲がよくはやっている．	Cover versions of pop songs are very popular these days.

かぶる

彼女は外出するときはいつも帽子をかぶる．	She †puts on [wears] a hat whenever she goes out.
この帽子をかぶってごらん．	Try this hat on.
工場内では頭に何かかぶっていないと危険だ．	It's dangerous to be in the factory without anything on your head.
毛布を頭からかぶって寝た．	I slept with a blanket over my head.
このブラウスは頭からかぶって着ます．	You put this blouse on by pulling (it) over your head.
富士山の頂上が雪をかぶっている．	The top of Mt. Fuji is covered with snow.

かべ (壁)

壁に耳あり．	The walls have ears.
我々の計画は壁に突き当たった．	Our plans have run up against a wall.
人種の壁はまだまだ厚い．	Racial barriers are still strong.

100メートル10秒の壁がついに破られた.	The 100-meter 10-second barrier was finally broken.

かまう (構う)

【気にする】人が何と言おうと構わない.	I don't care (about) what others might say.
彼女は人の迷惑などお構いなしだ.	It doesn't bother her to inconvenience others.
彼女は身なりを構わない.	She doesn't care much [She is not particular] about her appearance.
私のことはお構いなく.	Don't worry about me.
【気をつかう・世話する】そんなことに構っていられない.	I can't be bothered with something like that.
忙しくて自分のことを構っている暇もない.	I'm too busy to look after personal matters.
赤ちゃんが生まれても,上の子もちゃんと構ってあげなくちゃね.	You should remember to pay (special) attention to your older child after the baby comes.
彼女は一人息子を構い過ぎる.	She makes a fuss over her only son.
どうぞお構いなく.	Please don't go to any trouble. Please don't trouble yourself.
何のお構いもいたしませんで.	I hope you had a nice time.[1]
【かまわない】「窓を開けてもかまいませんか」「かまいませんよ,どうぞ」	"Do you mind if I open the window?" "No, not at all. Go ahead."
明日のパーティーはノーネクタイでもかまわない.	It's all right if you don't [You don't need to] wear a tie to the party tomorrow.
この料理では牛肉の代わりに豚肉を使ってもかまいません.	It doesn't matter if you use pork instead of beef in this recipe.
何でもかまわないから不用な物をバザーに持ってきてください.	Just bring anything you don't need anymore to the bazaar.
クレジットカードでかまいませんか.	Do you mind if I use a credit card?
休みたければ休んでもかまわない.	Go ahead and take some time off if you want to.
私はいつでもかまいませんよ.	Any time is fine with me.

1) 意味は違うが,客が帰るときによく言う決まり文句.

がまん (我慢)

その痛みは我慢できた.	I could take [stand, handle] the pain.
その痛みは我慢できなかった.	I couldn't stand the pain. The pain was unbearable.

彼のわがままにはもうこれ以上我慢できない.	I can't bear [endure] his selfishness anymore.
	I lost patience with his selfishness.
嫌でも我慢しなさい.	You're just going to have to put up with it whether you like it or not.
泣き〔笑い〕たいのをじっと我慢した.	I forced myself not to cry [laugh].
ジュースがないので水で我慢しよう.	There's no juice so let's make do with just water.
彼に秘書なしで我慢するように頼んだ.	I asked him to try to do without a secretary.
トイレに行きたいのを我慢するのは良くない.	It's not good to force yourself to wait to go to the bathroom.
ここが我慢のしどころだ.	Now's when we're going to find out just how much we can take.
彼女は非常に我慢強い人だ.	She is extremely patient.
	She can put up with a lot.

かむ

子どもによくかんで食べるように教えるべきだ.	Children must be taught to chew their food well.
肉がかたくてかみ切れない.	The meat is so tough I can't bite into it.
それ以上犬に近づくとかみつかれるよ.	If you get any closer to the dog, you'll get bitten.
彼女は悔しくてくちびるをかんだ.	She bit her lip in frustration.
氷をかみ砕いた.	I crunched the ice in my mouth.
【比喩】分からない生徒にはよくかみ砕いて(かんで含めるように)教えてやりなさい.	Teach the students who don't understand in plain language.
	Spell it out (in black and white) for the students who don't understand.

～かもしれない

そうかもしれない.	That might [may] be the case.
	That [It] might [may] be so.
君の言うとおりかもしれない.	You may well be right.
そう言ったかもしれないが, はっきり覚えていない.	I might [may] have said so but I don't remember very clearly.
彼は来るかもしれないし, 来ないかもしれない.	He might come, and then again he might not.

かゆい (痒い)

背中がかゆい.	My back itches.
この新しいウールのセーターを着るとかゆくなる.	This new wool sweater is itchy [scratchy].

彼女はかゆい所に手が届くように世話をしてくれた.	She was extremely attentive in looking after me.

かよう (通う)

【人が】彼は図書館へよく通っている.	He goes to the library regularly.
娘は毎日学校に通っている.	My daughter goes to school every day.
会社へ通うのに往復2時間以上かかる.	It takes me more than two hours to commute to and from work.
これは子どもの頃よく通った道です.	I often took this street when I was a child.
運よく通いの家政婦が見つかった.	I was lucky enough to find a maid to come in and clean the house regularly.
【乗り物が】冬のあいだその山奥の村にはバスが通わなくなる.	There's no bus service to that remote mountain village during the winter.
嵐のためその島へは4日間も連絡船が通っていない.	Ferry service to that island has been canceled [The ferry hasn't been making runs to that island] for the past four days due to the storm.
【心が】私たちはもう気持ちが通い合わなくなってしまった.	We no longer feel the same about each other.[1]
	We no longer see eye to eye.[2]

[1] 恋人同士の場合の言い方. [2] 友達同士や親子の場合の言い方.

から (空)

この瓶は空だ.	This bottle is empty.
この部屋は彼が借りるまで何ヵ月も空だった.	This room was vacant for months before he rented it.
やつは頭が空っぽだ.	He's empty-headed. / He's spacy.
彼はいつも空約束をするので信用できない.	He can't be trusted. He always makes promises he doesn't keep.
彼女のは空元気だよ. 本当はすごく落ち込んでいるんだ.	She's put on a good front but she's actually feeling quite depressed.
先生は自信のなさを隠そうとして空威張りしていた.	The teacher was putting up a front to hide his lack of confidence.
彼らは空騒ぎした.	They made a fuss about nothing.
チェーンが外れて車輪が空回りした.	The chain became disengaged and the wheel was spinning free.
空くじを引いてしまった.	I drew a blank in the lottery.

〜から

【場所の起点】私の家は駅から歩い	My house is a five-minute walk from the

て5分です.	station.
向こうから来るのはだれですか.	Who's that coming from over there?
私の部屋の窓から海が見える.	I can see the ocean from the window in my room.
窓から物を捨てないでください.	Please don't throw anything out (of) the window.
こちらの戸口から入ってください.	Please come in through this door.
太陽は東から昇る.	The sun rises in the east.
【時間の起点】朝早くから夜遅くまで働いた.	I worked from early in the morning until late at night.
会議は午前10時から始まる.	The meeting begins at 10 a.m.
二学期は9月から始まる.	The second semester starts in September.
夏休みは7月21日から始まる.	Summer vacation starts (on) July 21st.
母が死んでから3ヵ月たつ.	It's been [It's] three months since my mother died.
【範囲の起点】今日は40歳から60歳までの方のがん検診をします.	There will be a checkup for cancer today for those between the ages of 40 and 60.
次の授業までにテキストの12ページから28ページまでを読んできなさい.	Have pages 12 to 28 in the text read[1] before the next class. Read pages 12 to 28 in the text by the next class.
この本は子どもから大人まで楽しめる.	This book may be enjoyed by people of all ages.
このレストランの夕食のコースは3,000円からある.	Full-course dinners at this restaurant start at 3,000 yen.
ここからが大切なところです.	The important part begins here.
今日は15ページから始めます.	Today we'll start at page 15.
何から始めましょうか.	What should [shall*] I begin with?
食事はスープから始まった.	The meal began with soup.
【出所】ジムから電話があった.	There was a phone call from Jim.
君のことは父から聞いていた.	I've heard about you from my father.
そのクラブから君の住所を聞いた.	I got your address through the club.
彼は親切心〔好奇心〕からその男に声をかけた.	He spoke to that man out of kindness 〔curiosity〕.
【判断の基準】若い人から見れば君も時代遅れに見えるだろう.	From a young person's standpoint, you'd probably be considered behind the times.
書評から判断すると, その本はかなりいい本のようだ.	Judging by [from] the reviews, it seems to be a pretty good book.
【原材料】ワインはブドウから作られる.	Wine is made from[2] grapes.
【〜あと】彼と相談してから連絡します.	I'll contact you after I discuss it with him.

しばらく考えてから返事をします.	I'll give you an answer after I've thought about it for a while.
彼女は大学を卒業してから，経済の勉強を始めた.	She began to study economics after she graduated from college.
【原因・理由】疲れたから帰ります.	I'm tired, so I'm going back home.
悲しいから泣いているんだ.	I'm crying because I'm sad.
君は私の友人だから社長に紹介しよう.	You're my friend. Let me introduce you to the president of my company.
彼女は今日忙しいから君には会えないだろう.	She'll probably be too busy to see you today.
謝ったからそれで済むという問題ではない.	This isn't the kind of problem that can be cleared up with (just) an apology.
彼女が怒るからにはそれだけの理由があるのだろう.	She wouldn't be this angry without a good reason.
一度決心したからには途中でやめるつもりはない.	Now that I've made up my mind, I have no intention of quitting along the way.

---

1) この read は過去分詞で [réd] と発音する. 2) 原料は from, 材料は of を使う.

からい (辛い)

このカレーはとても辛い.	This curry is very spicy [hot].
海の水は塩辛い.	Sea water tastes salty.
辛口のワインはありますか.	Do you have any dry wine?
あの先生は点が辛い.	That teacher is a strict grader.

からかう

彼は子どもをからかって喜んでいる.	He's getting a kick out of teasing the children.
子どもたちは彼がバレエを習っているのをいつもからかった.	The kids always teased him about his ballet lessons.
	The kids always †made fun of [poked fun at] his ballet lessons.
昨日言ったことはうそだよ．ちょっとからかった (かついだ) だけなんだ.	What I told you yesterday was just a white lie. I was only pulling your leg.
彼女は約束の場所で何時間も待たされ，からかわれていたことを知った.	She waited at the pre-arranged spot for hours before she realized that she had been †made fun of [fooled].
からかい半分に彼を誘ったらついて来た.	I was only half-serious when I invited him but he came along anyway.
からかい半分にその講義に出てみたら随分面白かった.	I thought I'd sit in on that lecture just for †the fun of it [a lark], but it actually

turned out to be quite interesting.

からだ（体）

【体格】彼は体が大きい． — He has a big build [frame].

日本人は西洋人に比べて一般に体が小さい． — Japanese are generally smaller than Westerners.

この背広は君の体に合っていない． — This suit doesn't fit you.

彼はボクサーのような体つきをしている． — He's built like a boxer. / He has a boxer's build.

【身体・肉体】私は心も体も健康だ． — I'm healthy in mind and body.

彼は強健な体をしている． — He has a strong body.

若いうちに体を鍛えなさい． — Get your body in shape while you're still young.

体じゅうが痛い． — I'm sore [I ache] all over.

今日は体が空いている． — I'm free today.

【健康】海草は体にいい． — Seaweed is good for you.

息子は生まれつき体が弱い． — Our son has †been sickly from birth [not been blessed with good health].

こう忙しくては体がもたない． — I'll end up ruining my health if I stay this busy.

勉強しすぎて体をこわさないように． — Don't ruin your health from studying too hard.

お体をお大事に． — Take care of yourself.

からむ（絡む）

【物がからまる】ロープが足に絡んで転びそうになった． — I almost tripped when my foot got tangled up in the rope.

詰まりの原因は排水溝に絡んだ髪の毛だった． — The water wouldn't drain because there was hair clogging up the pipe.

最近，たんがのどに絡む． — I get phlegm caught in my throat these days.

【関わる】この事件には女が絡んでいる． — There's a woman involved in this incident.

この事件にはやくざが絡んでいる． — There are gangsters †mixed up [involved] in this.

彼女の失踪には政治家が絡んでいる． — There's a politician behind her disappearance.

金の問題が絡んでくるのなら弁護士に頼んだほうがいい． — You'd better get a lawyer if there's money involved.

3社の利害が絡み合い，なかなか話が進展しない． — With the interests of three different companies involved, it's difficult to move ahead.

彼は贈収賄事件に絡んで辞職し — He resigned after being implicated in the

	corruption scandal.
この1ヵ月間で医療ミスに絡んだニュースが8件もあった.	There were as many as eight news reports this past month referring to incidents of medical error.
【難癖をつける】彼は酒が入るといつもだれかに絡む.	He always †gets nasty [picks a fight] when he's drunk.
やくざに絡まれて怖い思いをした.	I had a terrifying experience when I was accosted by gangsters.

かり¹ (仮)

仮に君の言い分が正しいとしよう.	For the sake of argument, let's say you're right.
仮にそれをXと呼んでおこう.	Let's just call it X for now.
新しい机は仮にここに置いておこう.	Let's put the new desk here †for the time being [for now].
彼女は昨日, 仮採用になった.	She was hired yesterday on a trial basis.
昨日, 自動車の仮免許を取った.	I got a temporary driver's permit yesterday.
この世は仮の宿である.	This world is a temporary abode.
仮に(もし)今出発すれば6時までには着くだろう.	We should arrive by six, provided we leave now.
仮に(たとえ)雨が降ったとしても予定どおり出かけます.	We're leaving according to schedule even if it's raining.
仮にもそんなことは言うべきでない.	God forbid! Perish the thought!
仮にも教授ともあろう人がこんな間違いを犯すなんて.	A professor, of all people, shouldn't make a mistake like that!

かり² (借り)

君に借りがあったね. いくらだったっけ? 返すよ.	Don't I owe you some money? How much was it? I want to pay you back.
あの人には大きな借りがある.	I'm truly indebted to him. I owe him big time.
これで君に借りができたね.	I guess I owe you one.
この借りは倍にして返すよ.	I'll pay you back double.
これで貸し借りなしだ.	Now we're even.

> owe, be indebted to, pay back, be even のいずれも,「借金」と「恩義」の両方の場合に使える.

かりる (借りる)

彼から1万円借りた.	I borrowed 10,000 [ten thousand] yen from him.

このペンを借りるよ.	I'm borrowing this pen.
友達の車を借りてきた.	I borrowed my friend's car.
電話を借りたいんですが.	I'd like to use your phone.
この家を借りたいんですが.	I'd like to rent this house.
その湖ではボートが借りられる.	You can rent a boat [There are boat rental facilities] at that lake.
身元保証人として名前をお借りしたいんですが.	I'd like to use your name as a guarantor.
父の力は絶対に借りたくない.	I don't want help from my father under any circumstances.
教授に知恵を借りるといいよ.	You ought to take advantage of your professor's expertise.
この本を借り出したい.	I'd like to †check out this book [check this book out].

かる (刈る)

髪を短く刈ってくれ.	Cut my hair short.
庭の芝生を刈らなくてはならない.	I've got to †mow the lawn [cut the grass].

かるい (軽い)

この机は軽い.	This desk is light.
彼女は体重が軽い.	She doesn't weigh much.
何か軽い読み物を貸してくれ.	Please lend me something light to read.
彼女は病気で軽い食事しかできなかった.	She could only eat light food because of her illness.
幸い彼の刑は軽くて済んだ.	Fortunately, he got off with a light sentence.
手伝って彼女の仕事の分担を軽くしてやってくれ.	Please lend her a hand to make her work load lighter.
あなたの病気が軽くて安心した.	It's a relief to know that your illness isn't serious.
風邪を軽く見るな.	Don't take your cold lightly.
彼ならそれを軽くやってのけるよ.	He'll get it done easily.
軽い気持ちで引き受けたが, 実は大変な仕事だった.	I took the job on casually but it turned out to be really rough.
軽々しい行動をするな.	Don't act thoughtlessly.
そんなことを軽々しく口に出してはいけない.	That is not something to mention lightly.

かるはずみ (軽はずみ)

軽はずみなことをするな.	Don't be so rash!
軽はずみなことを言って彼を傷つ	I inadvertently hurt his feelings with my

けてしまった. / off-handed remark.
一人で山へ入るなんて軽はずみだったと思う. / It was reckless of me to go up that mountain by myself.

かれる¹ (枯れる)

日照りが続いて木々が枯れ始めた. / The trees began to wither under the constant blaze of the sun.
よく枯れた枝を集めてたき火をしよう. / Let's gather some dead branches and make a fire.
枯れ葉が庭の隅に積もっていた. / There was a pile of dead leaves in the corner of the garden.

かれる² (涸れる)

井戸がかれてしまった. / The well has †dried up [run dry].
日照り続きで池の水がかれてしまった. / The pond has dried up after all these days of blistering heat.

かろうじて

かろうじてバスに間に合った. / I just barely made the bus.
スキーヤーたちはかろうじて雪崩から逃れた. / The skiers †just barely [narrowly] escaped the avalanche.

かろやか (軽やか)

うれしい知らせに彼女は足取りも軽やかに帰って行った. / She skipped home, elated by the good news.
彼女の軽やかに舞う姿に見とれていた. / The gracefulness of her dance held me †spellbound [in rapture].
素晴らしい天気に恵まれ,みんな軽やかな気分で旅行に出かけた. / Being blessed with fine weather, everyone left on the trip in a buoyant mood.
街を行く人々の服装も軽やかになり,初夏の訪れを感じさせる. / The light and cheery clothes that people are wearing on the streets make you feel that summer has come.

〜がわ (〜側)

道の両側に家が並んでいる. / Houses line both sides of the street.
通りの向こう側にポストがある. / There's a mailbox on the other side of the street.
彼女は私の左側に座っていた. / She was sitting on [to] my left.
日本の家は大抵南側に大きな窓がある. / Most Japanese houses have large windows (on the side of the house) facing south.
彼は経営者側についた. / He sided with management.

かわいい
彼女はかわいい顔をしている.	She has a cute face.
彼らは小さなかわいい家に住んでいる.	They live in a cute little house.
彼には少しもかわいいところがない.	There's nothing likable about him.
かわいい子には旅をさせよ.	If you really love your child, you've got to send him out into the world on his own.

かわいがる
彼女は子どもをとてもかわいがっている.	She's very fond of her child.
彼は子どもをかわいがり過ぎる.	He's too soft on [He makes too much of] his child.
娘は子犬をかわいがっている.	My daughter loves her puppy.
彼は社長にかわいがられている.	The president has taken him under his wing.

かわいそう
かわいそうに.	Poor ...![1]／Poor thing.
そんなに責めては彼女がかわいそうだ.	I feel sorry for her, the way you keep blaming her like that.
かわいそうなやつだ.	I feel sorry for that guy.
それはかわいそうな孤児の物語だ.	It is the story of a pathetic orphan.
かわいそうだと思って助けてくれ.	Have a little sympathy and help me.
動物にそんなかわいそうなことをするんじゃない.	Don't be (so) cruel to animals.

> 1)「...」の部分に人の名前などがくる.

かわかす（乾かす）
洗濯物を日に当てて乾かした.	I dried the laundry in the sun.
火のそばで服を乾かしなさい.	Dry the clothes by the fire.

かわく（乾・渇く）
夏は洗濯物がすぐ乾く.	(The) Laundry dries fast in summer.
ペンキが乾くまで触るな.	Don't touch the paint until it dries.
長い日照りで田畑が乾ききっている.	The long drought completely dried [parched] the fields.
のどが渇いた. 何か飲もう.	I'm thirsty. Let's get something to drink.

かわった (変わった)

あの人は変わった人だ.	He's different.
彼女は変わった名前だ.	She has †a rare [an uncommon] name.
彼はいつも変わった格好をしている.	He always has an odd appearance.
	He's always dressed in strange clothes.
変わった趣味をお持ちですね.	You have an unusual hobby, don't you?
変わった建物だ.	That's a distinctive building.
たまには変わったものが食べたい.	I'd like to eat something different for a change.
いつもジーパンにTシャツばかりだけど, 時には変わった格好もしてみれば.	You always wear jeans and T-shirts. Why don't you try wearing something different for a change?
こちらでは特に変わったことはありません.	Nothing worth mentioning has happened here.

かわり (代わり)

君の代わりに私が行こう.	I'll go for you.
代わりにこれを使いなさい.	Use this instead.
レモンの代わりに酢でもよい.	It's all right to use vinegar instead of lemon.
	You can substitute vinegar for lemon.
これはいすの代わりになるよ.	This can serve as a chair.
	You can use this as a chair.
秘書が辞めたので代わりを探している.	My secretary quit so I'm looking for †someone to take her place [a replacement].
数学を教えてもらった代わりに彼に英語を教えてあげた.	I taught him English in exchange for his teaching me mathematics.
代わりに (お返しに) 何をあげようか.	What shall I give you in return?
お代わりはいかがですか.	Won't you have [How about] another helping?
お代わりはできますか.	Can [May] I have seconds?

かわる¹ (変わる)

【変化する】気が変わった.	I've changed my mind.
天気が変わるまで待とう.	Let's wait until the weather changes.
秋になると木の葉が赤や黄色に変わる.	In autumn the leaves on the trees turn red and yellow.
風が南風に変わった.	The wind shifted to the south.
山の天気は変わり易い.	The weather is changeable in the mountains.
彼は気の変わり易いやつだ.	He's always changing his mind.

	He changes his mind a lot.
お変わりありませんか.	How are you doing?
【移動する】あちらの席に変わりたいのですが.	I'd like to move to that seat [table].
彼はパリ支店に変わった.	He's been transferred to the Paris branch.
彼は所属が変わった.	He's changed positions.
明日から別の会社に変わる.	I start working for another company tomorrow.
【異なる】所変われば品変わる.	Every country has its own way of life.[1]
	Every country has its own resources and products.[2]

1) 風俗習慣全般について言ったもの. 2) 資源や産物に焦点を当てた言い方.

かわる[2]（代わる）

ちょっと代わってくれないか.	Will you take over for me for a moment?
彼に代わって私が議長になろう.	I'll †replace him [take his place] as chairman.
席を代わろう.	Let's change seats.
鈴木さんに（電話を）代わります.	Let me connect you to Mr. Suzuki.[1]
	Here's Mr. Suzuki.[2]
子どもたちが代わる代わる子犬を見に来た.	Group after group of children came to look at the puppies.

1) 電話を切り換えて代わる場合. 2) すぐそばにいる人に受話器を渡して代わる場合.

かん（勘）

なんで分かったの？ 勘がいいな.	How did you know? You're really intuitive.
あの子はなかなか勘が鋭いから用心したほうがいい.	You'd better be careful. That child is extremely intuitive.
あれで気がつかないなんて, 君は勘が鈍すぎるよ.	You're really †slow [out of it] if you didn't get [catch] that.
君は妙なところで勘が働くね.	You have the strangest hunches.
私の勘は当たるんです.	I can always †trust [count on] my sixth sense.
	My hunches are always on [right].
勘が外れた.	My instincts [hunches] were off.
勘に頼ってばかりではいけない.	You can't always trust your instincts.
選択肢問題をすべて勘で答えた.	I guessed at all the multiple-choice questions.

僕の勘では彼は来ないね.	I have a gut feeling that he's not going to come.
2年間住んでいたので，長崎には土地勘がある.	Having lived in Nagasaki for two years I have a feel for the place.

かんがえ (考え)

いい考えが浮かんだ.	I've got a good idea.
君の考えを言ってくれ.	Tell me what you think.
彼の考えは進歩的だ.	His thinking is progressive.
その件については自分でも考えが足りなかったと思う.	I admit that I didn't give that matter sufficient thought.
彼がそう言ったのは深い考えがあってのことだ.	He had good reasons for saying that.
そういう場合も考えに入れておきなさい.	Be sure to take that (kind of case) into consideration [account].
そういう場合は考えに入れていなかった.	We left that (kind of case) out of consideration.
私には考えも及ばぬことだ.	It's something that would never occur to me.

かんがえる (考える)

彼はアメリカに留学しようと考えている.	He's thinking of going to America to study.
試験は考えていたより難しかった.	The exam was harder than I thought it would be.
君のことしか考えられない.	I can't think of anything but you.
あんな田舎に引っ越すなんて考えるのも嫌だ.	Moving out to the country like that—I don't even want to think about it.
よく考えて返事をしてくれ.	Think it over well and give me an answer.
よく考えてみると私が間違っていた.	Thinking it over [On second thought], I was wrong.
私に聞かないで自分でよく考え（て答えを出し）なさい.	Don't ask me. Make up your own mind.
とくと考えた上で書かなければならない.	I have to think this through before I can write it up.
倒産の可能性も十分考えられる.	Bankruptcy is quite conceivable.
彼女がそんなことをするなんて考えられない.	I can hardly imagine she'd do such a thing.
考え直してくれないか.	Won't you reconsider?
随分考え込んでいるね.	You sure are deep in thought.
これは彼が考え出した計画だ.	He thought up this project.
考えごとをしていて玄関のベルが鳴ったのに気がつかなかった.	I was lost in thought and didn't hear the doorbell.

父と私は考え方が違う.	My father and I think differently.
それは考えものだなあ.	Well, I don't know.
	Well, I'm not so sure about that.
ものは考え様だ.	It all depends on how you look at it.

かんかく¹ (感覚)

人間には五つの感覚がある.	Human beings have five senses.
寒さで指の感覚がなくなってしまった(まひした).	My fingers got [became] numb from the cold.
彼女は数学に対する感覚が優れている.	She has a good feeling [flair] for mathematics.
彼女は音楽に対する感覚が優れている.	She has a good ear for music.
彼は感覚的な人間だ.	He goes by his feelings.

かんかく² (間隔)

【距離】高速道路では前の車との間隔を50メートル以上あけないと危険だ.	It's dangerous to drive on an expressway unless you keep at least a 50-meter interval between your car and the one in front of you.
10メートル〔一定の〕間隔で道路に電柱が立っている.	Utility poles stand at 10-meter 〔regular〕 intervals along the street.
もう少し間隔をあけて並んでください.	Please line up farther apart from each other.
【時間】どのくらいの間隔でバスの便がありますか.	How often does the bus run?
バスは5分間隔で出ている.	A bus leaves every five minutes.

かんぐる (勘ぐる)

どうしてそんなにものごとを勘ぐるんだ?	Why do you have to read so much into things?
	Why are you so suspicious?
下司の勘ぐりはやめろ.	You're just imagining things.[1]

> 1) この英文は心配し過ぎの人に対して「思い過ごしだよ, 考え過ぎだよ」という意味でも使う.

かんけい (関係)

その二つの関係が分からない.	I don't understand the relation(ship) [association, connection] between the two.
彼とはどんな関係にあたるの.	How are you †related to [connected with] him?
これとそれとは大いに関係がある.	This has a great deal to do with that.

これとそれとは全く関係がない.	This has nothing to do with that. This is totally unrelated to that.
彼女が何をしようと私には関係がない.	What she does has nothing to do with me.
作物の出来は天候と関係がある.	Weather affects crop yields.
彼らは収賄事件に関係していた.	They had something to do with the bribery case.
あんな女に関係するな.	Don't get involved with a woman like that.
我々のあいだには愛情関係なんかない.	There's no romantic involvement between us.
日本と米国は関係が深い.	Japan and the U.S. have strong ties.
その二つの国は外交関係を断絶した.	Those two countries broke off diplomatic relations [ties].
息子の意思に関係なく（を無視して）母親が入学願書を取り下げた.	She withdrew the college application in complete disregard of her son's wishes.
私に関係なくパーティーを始めてください.	Don't worry about me. Go ahead and start the party.

かんげい (歓迎)

心から歓迎します.	A most cordial welcome to you.
ぜひ来てください，歓迎します.	Do come. You'll be most welcome.
その処置は一般から歓迎された.	The measure was well received by the public.
その世界的女優は久しぶりの帰国で大歓迎を受けた.	That world-famous actress received a big welcome when she came back to her home country after a long absence.
彼はどこでも歓迎されない客だ.	He is an unwelcome guest anywhere he goes.

かんさつ (観察)

子どもを観察していると飽きない.	I never get tired of observing [watching] children.
生徒たちはウサギを飼育して観察している.	The schoolchildren are raising rabbits and observing them.
彼女は観察が鋭い.	She makes sharp observations.

かんじ (感じ)

留守中にだれかが私の部屋に入ったような感じがした.	I had a feeling that someone had been in my room while I was out.
初めて飛行機に乗ったときはどんな感じがしましたか.	How did it feel the first time you flew in an airplane?

あなたのお父さんはどういった感じの方ですか.	What kind of person is your father? What is your father like?
彼はいかにも弁護士といった感じの人だ.	He really has the presence of a lawyer.
彼は感じのいい〔悪い〕人だ.	He's †a pleasant [an unpleasant] person.

かんしゃ (感謝)

心からあなたに感謝します.	I'm deeply grateful (to you). I thank you from the bottom of my heart.
ご協力いただいた皆様には感謝の念に耐えません.	I am extremely grateful to those who cooperated with us.
何と言って感謝してよいか分かりません.	I don't know how to thank you enough.
彼女は感謝の気持ちを贈り物で表した.	She expressed her gratitude with a gift.

かんしょう (干渉)

子どものやることに干渉しすぎるのは良くない.	It's not good to interfere too much with what your children are doing.
お隣さんは何かと干渉してくる.	Our neighbor is always sticking his nose into our business.
これ以上, 私のことに干渉するのはやめて.	Stop meddling in my affairs.
あの国のやっていることは内政干渉だ.	What that country is doing amounts to state intervention.

かんじょう¹ (勘定)

売り上げを勘定しなさい.	Add up [Figure up, Total] the sales receipts.
勘定を済ませてホテルを出た.	We paid the bill and left the hotel.
お勘定をお願いします.	(Could I have the) Check, please.
そんなことまで勘定に入れていなかった.	I hadn't taken that into account.
彼女はすべてに勘定高い.	She's self-serving [self-seeking] in everything she does.

かんじょう² (感情)

人間は機械ではない, 感情を持っている.	Human beings are not machines. They have emotions.
彼はあまり感情を表さない.	He rarely lets his feelings show.
一体何を言って秘書の感情を害したんだい.	What on earth did you say to the secretary that †hurt her feelings [upset her so]?
彼はすぐ感情的になるから議論し	It's hard to have a discussion with him

にくい. | because he gets †emotional [upset, up in arms] right away.

かんじる (感じる)

足がしびれて何も感じなかった.	My legs went completely numb.
彼はまだ眼鏡の必要を感じない.	He doesn't feel that he needs glasses yet.
田舎に住んでいろいろの不便を感じた.	I experienced a lot of inconvenience living in the country.
この絵を見て何も感じないの?	Doesn't this picture make you feel anything?
体に感じない程度の地震は毎日何回も起こっている.	There are many earthquakes that can't be felt every day.
あの子は感じ易い子だから言葉に気をつけなさい.	That child is very sensitive, so be careful what you say to him.

かんしん¹ (感心)

彼女の絵はあまりに素晴らしくて感心した.	I was impressed by how marvelous her painting was.
感心して彼の論文を読んだ.	I read his thesis with admiration.
感心にも彼女は1週間ずっと禁煙している.	I'm really impressed that she's gone without a cigarette for a whole week. I'm really impressed by [with] her going for a whole week without a cigarette.
感心, 感心!	Well done!／Good for you!／Excellent!
授業中にガムをかむのはあまり感心しない.	You won't impress anyone by chewing gum in class. I don't particularly think you should chew gum in class.
その案にはあまり感心しない.	That idea really doesn't appeal to me. I'm not very impressed with that idea.

かんしん² (関心)

多くの女性はダイエットに関心がある.	Many women are interested in dieting.
彼女は君に関心があるようだよ.	She seems to be interested in you.
私は環境問題に関心を抱いている.	I'm concerned about environmental issues.
彼は最近アフリカ音楽に関心を寄せている.	He has recently taken interest in African music.
この問題に関しては高年齢層の関心が高い.	The older population is very concerned about this problem.
彼は芸術に対する関心が薄い.	He has little interest in art.
市長選に対する市民の関心は低	There is little public interest in the elec-

い．	tion for mayor.
保険の加入には全く関心がありません．	I have no interest at all in buying insurance.
株の話になった途端，彼女は急に関心を示しだした．	As soon as the conversation turned to stocks she immediately became interested.
彼の一挙一動に皆の関心が集まる．	Everyone is curious about his every move.
事件は人々の関心を集めた．	The affair attracted public attention.
彼の関心事といえば，もっぱら賭けごとだ．	What he is preoccupied with is gambling.

かんじん（肝心）

どんな球技においても球から目を離さないことが肝心だ．	In any ball game, it is critical to keep your eye on the ball.
何事も最初が肝心だ．	No matter what the undertaking, the beginning is crucial.
ここが肝心な点だから，よく聞きなさい．	Listen carefully. This is the key.
彼は肝心なところでいつもミスをする．	He always makes a mistake at the most important point.
部長は肝心なことは何も言ってくれない．	The manager doesn't tell me anything important.
肝心なことを忘れていたよ．彼から預かったお金を君に渡さなくちゃ．	I forgot the most important thing! I have to give you the money he gave me for you.

かんする（関する）

私は仏教に関する本を集めている．	I'm collecting books on Buddhism.
彼女の私生活に関して調査報告書を出してほしい．	I'd like you to make a report about [on] her private life.
この問題に関して何か質問がありますか．	Are there any questions regarding [relating to] this problem?
彼に関する限りそんな心配はない．	There's no need to worry about that in his case.

かんせい（完成）

彼の作品はもうすぐ完成する．	His work is nearly completed [finished, done].
ビルは8月に完成の予定だ．	The building is to be completed [finished, done] in August.
その仏像には完成された美がある．	That Buddhist statue has the look of perfect beauty.

かんせつ (間接)
間接的な情報を信じるものではない.	Indirect information is not to be trusted.
その話は間接的に彼に伝わった.	That story got to him indirectly.

かんぜん (完全)
彼は完全な答案を書いた.	All of the answers he wrote were perfect.
君は自分で完全無欠な人間だと思っているのか.	Do you actually think you have no faults?
完全に君が間違っているよ.	You're a hundred percent wrong.
もう完全に遅刻だ.	I'm late for sure.
彼は完全主義者だ.	He's a perfectionist.

かんそう (感想)
その本を読んだ感想を書きなさい.	Write your impressions of that book.
あの映画を見た感想を聞きたい.	I'd like to hear what you think of that movie.
作家はリポーターたちにその事件についての感想を述べた.	The writer gave the reporters his †impressions of [thoughts about] the incident.

かんたん (簡単)
その問題を解く簡単な方法を教えてあげよう.	Let me show you †an easy way to solve [a short cut to solving] that problem.
先生は難しい内容を簡単な例をあげて説明した.	Our teacher explained the difficult material with a simple example.
それについて簡単な報告書を書いてくれ.	Give me a brief written account of it.
彼は簡単にその問題を解いた.	He solved that problem with ease.
簡単に言ってください.	Please make it short [brief].
簡単に言えばどういうことですか.	Quite simply, what's it all about?
簡単に言えばそれはほとんど不可能だ.	To put it simply [Briefly speaking, In a word, In short], it's almost impossible.
その辺で簡単に食事しよう.	Let's have something light over there. Let's grab a bite (to eat) over there.
君は結婚というものを簡単に考えすぎている.	You're thinking about marriage too simplistically.

かんちがい (勘違い)
それは単なる勘違いが原因だ.	That was only because of a misunderstanding.
ぼくがセクハラしただなんて, ひどい勘違いだ.	That I should be thought guilty of sexual harassment is a gross misunderstanding.
勘違いしないで, 深い意味はない	Don't misunderstand me. I don't mean any-

から.
友人に手を振ったら, 隣にいた女性が勘違いしてウィンクを返した.
When I waved to my friend, the woman next to him misunderstood and winked back.

勘違いしてはいけない. この業績は君一人のものじゃないんだよ.
It's important that you understand. You didn't do this all by yourself.

勘違いしていたよ. 彼は君の兄弟じゃないんだね.
My mistake. So he's not your brother?

校長先生を用務の人と勘違いして話しかけた.
I started talking to the principal mistaking him for the custodian.

かんづく (感づく)

彼女のためにパーティーをこっそり計画していたのに感づかれた.
She somehow sensed that we had been planning a surprise party for her.

私たちの計画を彼女に感づかれないようにするのは大変だった.
Trying to keep her from catching on to our plan was really tough.

かんとく (監督)

彼はそのプロジェクトを監督している.
He's the supervisor on that project. He supervises that project.

そのプロジェクトは彼の監督の下に行われた.
That project was carried out under his supervision.

彼は部下に対する監督が不行き届きだったことを反省している.
He regrets not having given his workers enough supervision.

彼が監督したその映画は好評だ.
The movie he directed was well received.

私はバスケットボール・チームの監督をしている.
I manage [I'm a manager of] a basketball team.

彼はその野球チームの監督を首になった.
He was fired as manager of that baseball team.

試験の監督をしなければならない.
I've got to monitor the exam.

今日の試験の監督はW先生です.
The monitor for today's exam is Mr. W.

戦時中, 出版は政府の監督下に置かれた.
During the war, publishing was placed under government control.

かんねん (観念)

【概念】彼は時間の観念がない.
He has no sense of time.

そのことについて君は誤った観念を抱いているよ.
You have the wrong idea [conception] about that.

彼は観念的な話ばかりする.
He talks only in theoretical terms.

【あきらめる】もう飛行機に間に合わないと観念した.
I resigned myself to the fact that it was too late to make my plane.

いいかげんに観念しろ.
You might as well give up.

がんばる(頑張る)

【やり通す】どんなに人生が苦しくなろうと家族のために頑張り通さねばならない.
I must continue to hold on for the sake of my family, no matter how hard life becomes.

頑張って締め切りまでに論文を書き終えた.
I worked as hard as I could and finished writing my paper by the deadline.

ゴールまであと100メートルだ.頑張れ!
Only 100 meters to the finish line! Hang in there!

彼女は頑張り屋だ.
She really hangs in there.[1]
She's a hard worker.[2]

【主張する】彼は旅行に犬を連れて行くと頑張った.
He insisted on taking his dog with him on the trip.

彼は私がそこに行くべきだと頑張った.
He insisted that I go there.

> 1)「粘り強い人」を言う. 2)「一生懸命に働く[勉強する]人」を言う.

がんぼう(願望)

業界一の会社になるのが社長の願望だ.
The president's ambition is to see his company lead the industry.

彼はアメリカへ留学したいという願望が強い.
He has a strong desire to go to America to study.

かんり(管理)

私がクラブのお金を管理している.
I manage the club's money.

その公園は国が管理している.
The state administers that park.

戦時中,産業は国家の管理下にあった.
During the war, industry was under state control.

このアパートは管理が行き届いている.
This apartment building is well managed.

ニューヨークではアパートの管理人を「スーパー」と呼ぶ.
In the New York area, an apartment manager [caretaker] is called a "super."

かんれん(関連)

胃潰瘍はストレスと関連の深い病気だ.
Stomach ulcers are closely related to stress.

この病気は喫煙との関連性は薄い.
There's little connection between this disease and smoking.

二つの事件の間には何の関連もない.
There is no relationship between the two incidents.

この法案は私たちの日常生活と密接に関連してくる.
This bill is going to have a direct impact on our daily lives.

それに関連して一言つけ加えさせてください.	I have a comment †to add to that [concerning that].
宝塚関連の記事は全部スクラップしている.	I'm putting all the articles about [concerning] the Takarazuka Theatre Troupe into scrapbooks.
「環境問題のレポートを書かなければならないんだ」「今日の新聞に関連記事が出ていたよ」	"I have to write a report on environmental problems." "There was an article about that in today's paper."
コンピュータ関連の会社に勤めています.	I'm working for a company dealing in computers.[1]
取引先の関連会社を紹介してもらった.	I was introduced to a company affiliated to a firm we do business with.

> 1) 日本語同様あいまいな言い方. 英語圏では社名・職業名などを具体的に言うのが普通.

き

き（気）

こんなに宿題をためて一体どうする気なんだい.	Just what do you intend to do, letting so much homework pile up?
やる気がないのなら引き受けるな.	If you don't feel like doing it, don't take it on.
働く気があるのなら私の会社で雇ってあげよう.	If you want a job, I'll hire you at my company.
【気が】彼とはよく気が合う.	I get along [on] well with him.
この種類の犬は気が荒いので番犬にもってこいだ.	The aggressiveness of this breed of dog makes it perfect as a watchdog.
彼は彼女に気があるようだ.	He seems to be interested in her.
彼は気がいいので頼まれると断らない.	He's so good-natured that if you ask him to do you a favor he won't turn you down.
ボーナスが出て気が大きくなった.	I got my bonus, and I feel like †I can really let myself go [I'm on top of the world, a million dollars**].
歯医者に行くことを考えると気が重くなる.	Whenever I think about going to the dentist, I get depressed.
弟が入試に合格したと聞いて急に	When I heard that my brother passed his

気が軽くなった.	entrance exams I suddenly felt relieved [unburdened].
彼はよく気が変わる.	He changes his mind a lot.
彼女はよく気が利く.	She's on the ball.
	She's considerate [thoughtful].
母が入院したので気が気ではない.	I've been †beside myself [uneasy] since my mother was hospitalized.
あんなにいい会社を辞めるなんて彼の気が知れない.	I just can't understand why he would go and quit such a good company.
彼の招待ではあまり気が進まない.	Since *he* invited me, I don't really feel †like going [inclined to go].
社長は今日は気が立っているから逆らわないほうがいいよ.	The boss is touchy today so don't contradict him.
暗い所が怖いなんて気が小さいんだね.	You're really †timid [a chicken**]—scared of dark places!
テレビがついていると気が散って勉強ができない.	I get distracted and can't study when the television is on.
彼の奥さんはよく気がつく人だ.	His wife is very attentive.
彼女は気が強い.	She has a mind of her own.
	She's strong-minded.
宿題がこんなにあるのかと思うと気が遠くなってくる.	I feel overwhelmed when I think about how much homework I have.
試験が延期になって気が抜けてしまった.	I lost my steam when the exam was postponed.
瓶のふたを開けたままにしておいたので,コーラの気が抜けてしまった.	I left the cap off the bottle of coke and it went flat.
この仕事にはあまり気が乗らない.	I can't get very enthusiastic about this work.
もう夏の旅行の計画を立てるなんて気が早いね.	Aren't you a little bit ahead of yourself, making plans for summer vacation already?
彼に頼むなんて気がひける.	I don't have the nerve to ask him.
彼は受験に失敗してから気がふさいでいる.	He's been †down in the dumps [moping around] since he failed the exam.
彼女は何事にもよく気が回る.	She's always on the ball.
	She's quick on the uptake.
彼は気が短い.	He's quick-tempered.
	He has a short temper.
	He loses his temper easily.
気が向いたら遊びに来いよ.	Come over any time you'd like.
	If you're so inclined, please stop by.
最近なぜか気がめいってしかたが	For some reason I've been so depressed

彼は気が弱い．	He's not very assertive.
【気が済む】気が済むまでやってみろよ．	Do it to your heart's content.
これでは私の気が済まない．	I can't let it go at this.
一体どう謝ったら気が済むのか？	How can I apologize to your satisfaction?
【気がする】彼は来ないような気がする．	I have a feeling he won't come.
ベルが鳴ったような気がした．	I had a feeling the bell rang.
今日飲みに行きたい気がする．	I feel like going out drinking today.
【気がつく】⇒きづく（気づく）	
【気が緩む】気が緩んだ隙に大事な書類をとられた．	I was off guard for just a second when I had some important papers stolen.
こんなミスをするなんて，気が緩んでいるぞ．	It's careless of you to make such a mistake.
試験が終わって，学生はみな気が緩んでいる．	The students are relaxed now that the test is over.
【気に】君の就職口は気にかけておくよ．	I'll keep an eye out for a job for you.
気にくわないやつだ．	That guy rubs me the wrong way.
彼のすることは何から何まで気にさわる．	Absolutely everything he does gets on my nerves.
彼は回りの声を気にも留めず，我が道を行く．	He goes his own way, paying no heed to what others say.
過ぎたことを気に病んでもしかたがない．	There's no point in letting the past weigh on your mind.
【気に入る】この部屋が気に入った．	I like this room.
彼のどこが気に入ったの．	What do you see in him?
どうすれば君の気に入るんだい．	What can I do to please you?
彼の態度が気に入らなかった．	I didn't care for his attitude.
ここは私の気に入りの店だ．	This is one of my favorite stores.
【気にする】過ぎたことをいつまで気にしてもしかたがないよ．	There's no point in dwelling on the past.
彼女は人の評価を気にしない．	She's indifferent to what others think of her.
父親がもう学資を送らないと言っても彼女は気にしなかった．	Even when her father said he wouldn't send any more money for school, she didn't let it bother her.
気にするなよ．	Take it easy. Don't let it bother [upset] you. Never mind.／Don't worry about it.
何をそんなに気にしているの？	What are you so concerned [worried] about?

【気になる】息子からずっと便りがなくて気になっている.	I'm worried because I haven't heard from my son for a long time.
ちょっと気になるうわさを聞いた.	I heard a rumor that bothered me a little.
彼女は方言混じりで話すが、気になるほどではない.	She mixes in a little dialect when she speaks, but it's not that noticeable.
【気の】彼は気のおけない友人だ.	He's a friend I can feel †relaxed [at ease] around.
気のせいか彼女は最近太ったみたいだ.	It may just be my imagination, but she seems to have put on weight recently.
彼は気のない返事をした.	He answered half-heartedly.
彼は気の向くままふらりと旅に出る.	He goes off traveling whenever he feels like it.
緊張の連続で気の休まるときがなかった.	The unbroken tension didn't allow for a moment's relaxation.
【気の利く】気の利いた事を言うね.	You make such witty remarks.
気の利いた贈り物だね.	This is a well-chosen gift, isn't it?
彼女はいつも気の利いた服を着ている.	She's always smartly dressed.
気の利かないやつだ.	What an insensitive lout!
もう少し気の利いたことができないのか.	Can't you do anything more clever than that?
【気は】何でもいいと思うよ. 気は心なんだから.	Anything will do, I think. It's the thought that counts.
(そんなことをするなんて) 気は確かか?	Are you insane [crazy, mad]?
	Have you lost your senses [mind]?
	Have you taken leave of your senses?
【気も】彼とのデートの日, 彼女は仕事中, 気もそぞろだった.	She couldn't keep her mind on her work the day she was to have a date with him.
【気を】もっと気を入れて仕事をしてくれよ.	Put more effort into your work.
彼女は気を失って倒れた.	She fainted and collapsed.
どうしたら彼の気を静められるだろうか.	How can I get him to calm down?
一度失敗したくらいで気を落とすなよ.	Don't get discouraged just because you made one mistake.
彼女の恋人が来たので, 私は気をきかせて帰ってきた.	When her boyfriend showed up I thought I should make myself scarce, so I came home.
パーティーの客にはよく気を配っておいてくれ.	Please be attentive to the guests at the party.
気を確かに持ちなさい.	Keep hold of yourself.
	Keep your composure.

	Pull yourself together.
気を散らさないで勉強しなさい.	Keep your mind on your studies.
そんなに気を使わないで.	Don't go to so much trouble on my account.
彼女は試験の失敗のあとやっと気を取り直し,勉強を始めた.	She finally pulled herself together after failing the examination and returned to her studies.
今,気を抜いちゃいけないよ.	You can't let up now.
彼女の気を引いてみようとしたがだめだった.	I tried to get her interested in me, but it didn't work out.
映画でも見て気を紛らわそうよ.	Let's go see a movie to get our minds off things.
気を回すなよ.僕と彼女は何でもないよ.	Don't get the wrong idea. [Don't read too much into our relationship, please.] There's really nothing between her and me.
気を持たせるような返事をしておいた.	I gave them a (somewhat) encouraging answer.
母親は子どもたちの帰りが遅いので気をもんだ.	The kids' mother was anxious because they were late coming home.
息子の受験に母親が気をもんでもしかたがない.	There's no point in a mother getting all worked up over her son's exam.
彼には気を許せない.	I always have to be on my guard with [around] him.
低い山だからといって気を緩めてはいけません.	Just because it's a small mountain, don't get caught off guard.
彼女の態度があまりひどいので彼は気を悪くした.	He was offended by her terrible attitude.
【気をつける】道を渡るときは自動車に気をつけなさい.	Watch out [Be careful to look out] for cars when crossing the street.
階段が急だから足元に気をつけなさい.	Watch your step. The stairs are very steep.
数値に間違いがないかどうか気をつけながら書類を読み直した.	I reread the documents, checking for mistakes in the figures.
私がこれから言うことを気をつけて聞いてください.	Please listen carefully to what I'm going to say.
今後遅刻しないように気をつけます.	I'll be careful not to be late from now on.

きえる (消える)

突然電気が消えた.	All of a sudden the lights went out.
山のキャンプでは寝ているあいだに火が消えてしまわないよう注	When camping in the mountains, you must make sure that your fire does not

きおく

意しなければならない.	go out while you are sleeping.
明かりが消えているから彼は留守だと思う.	I don't think he's in since all the lights are out.
暖炉の火が消えかけている.	The fire in the fireplace is dying down.
夜になってやっと火事が消えた.	The fire was finally †put out [extinguished] after nightfall.
ろうそくの火が風で消えた.	The wind blew out the candle.
うるさいラジオの音が消えた.	The noisy sound of the radio stopped.
サイレンの音は遠くへ消えていった.	The sound of the siren died away into the distance.
香辛料を使うと肉の臭みが消える.	You can get rid of the smell of meat with spices.
午後になると道に残っていた雪も消えてしまった.	The snow left on the street melted away in the afternoon.
看板の文字が消えかかっている.	The lettering on the sign is fading.
この辞書の背表紙の文字が消えかかっている.	The lettering on the spine of this dictionary has begun to rub off.
このパスポートはよく使ったので表紙の文字が消えてしまった.	I've used this passport so much that the letters on the cover have worn off.
この町から彼の姿が消えた.	He has disappeared [vanished] from this town.
水質汚染で川から魚の姿が消えてしまった.	Fish have disappeared from the river because of water pollution.
強烈な印象はなかなか消えない.	Strong impressions don't †just fade away [fade away easily].
あのうわさもいつの間にか消えてしまった.	That rumor just kind of died out.
【慣用】娘が嫁に行ってから家の中は火が消えたようだ.	Ever since our daughter got married, the house seems empty [deserted].

きおく (記憶)

そんなことを言った記憶はない.	I †don't remember [don't recall, have no memory of] saying such a thing.
内容をよく記憶しておきなさい.	Commit it to memory.
私の記憶に間違いがなければ, 彼はその日は出張で東京にいなかった.	If †I remember right [I'm not mistaken, memory serves me right], he was away on a business trip and wasn't in Tokyo that day.
すみません. 私の記憶違いでした.	I'm sorry. My memory must be faulty.
記憶力が年とともに衰えてきた.	My memory has failed with age.
君の記憶も当てにならないね.	Your memory isn't very reliable either.
彼女は私の記憶の中に生きている.	She still lives in my memory.
ふるさとの景色は私の記憶に鮮や	I still have vivid memories of scenes from

かに残っている. my hometown.
その事件は記憶に新しい. The incident is still fresh in our minds.

きおくれ (気後れ)

大勢のお偉方の前で話すのは気後れがした. I felt small [timid] when I made a speech in the presence of so many important people.

答えは分かったが気後れがして手を上げることができなかった. I knew the answer, but I felt too self-conscious to raise my hand.

皆があまり仲が良いので気後れがして仲間に入ることができなかった. Everyone got along so well with each other that I felt self-conscious and couldn't mix in.

きかい (機会)

彼女に会う機会があればよろしく伝えておいてください. Please give her my best regards if you get the chance to see her.

海外旅行に行く機会を失った. I lost a chance to go on a trip overseas.

彼が金儲けの機会を見逃すはずがない. He'd never pass up a chance to make a fast buck.

こんな機会は二度とないよ. This is a once-in-a-lifetime opportunity.

絶好の機会だ. It's a golden [great] opportunity.

いい機会だから彼に紹介してあげましょう. This would be a great opportunity for me to introduce you to him.

その話なら次の機会にしてください. If that's what you want to talk about, please save it for the next time.

きがね (気兼ね)

伯父の家に泊まったが気兼ねしてくつろげなかった. When I stayed at my uncle's, I felt too constrained to relax.

隣の人に気兼ねしてステレオの音を小さくして聞いた. Afraid I might disturb the neighbors, I listened to the stereo with the volume turned down.

病気の父に気兼ねして最近あまり遊びに出かけていない. Since I don't feel right about leaving my father sick in bed, I haven't been going out much recently.

気兼ねせずに何でも言ってくれ. Don't hesitate to tell me anything.
私に気兼ねしないでくれ. Don't mind me.

きがる (気軽)

気軽な集まりだから友達をたくさん連れておいでよ. It'll be †an informal [a casual] gathering, so bring a lot of friends.

いつでも気軽に遊びに来いよ. Feel free to come over anytime.

彼はだれにでも気軽に話しかける. He readily †speaks to [strikes up a conver-

この本は気軽に読める.	This book is very light reading.
もっと気軽に考えなさい.	Don't take it too seriously.
気軽に引き受けたが,なかなか大変な仕事だ.	I accepted the job casually but it turned out to be really difficult.

きかん (機関)

彼は政府の機関で働いている.	He works for a government agency.
図書館は重要な教育機関だ.	Libraries are important educational facilities.
蒸気機関はジェームズ・ワットによって発明された.	The steam engine was invented by James Watt.
彼は政党の機関紙を編集している.	He's an editor for the party's official publication.

きく¹ (効・利く)

すぐに効いてくると思うよ.	I think it'll take effect right away.
この薬を飲みなさい.よく効くはずだ.	Take this medicine. It should be very effective.
息子にお説教したが,だいぶ効いたらしい.	I gave my son a good lecture and it seems to have been very effective.
けがをして右手が利かなくなってしまった.	I injured my right hand and can't use it.
この生地は洗濯がよく利く.	This material washes well.
この靴は修理が利かない.	These shoes are beyond repair.
この料理はよく塩が利いている.	This dish is salted just right.

きく² (聞・聴く)

その名前は聞いたことがある.	I've heard that name before.
誕生日の贈り物を断る人なんて聞いたことがない.	I have never heard of anyone refusing to accept a birthday gift.
どのレコードが聴きたい?	Which record do you want to listen to?
人の悪口は聞き苦しいよ.	I hate to hear nasty things being said about people.
彼女は聞きしに勝る美人だった.	She was even more beautiful than I had heard.
それは聞き捨てならない.	I'm not going to let it pass.
一体どうやって彼からその話を聞き出したんだい?	Just how did you get him to tell you that?
君の聞き違いだよ.	You heard (it) wrong.
ここからがこの曲の聴きどころだ.	This is where the best part of this tune begins.
彼が早口なので聞き取れなかった.	He talked so fast (that) I couldn't catch

	what he said.
彼の言ったことなんか聞き流せばいいんだよ.	You should just let what he said go in one ear and out the other.
聞き慣れない地名だ.	It's an unfamiliar place name.
いちばんいいところを聞き逃した.	I †missed hearing [didn't hear] the best part of it.
彼女の美声にうっとりと聴きほれてしまった.	I was enraptured by her beautiful voice.
私は二人の会話に聞き耳を立てた.	I eavesdropped on their conversation.
講義を一言も聞き漏らすまいとした.	I tried not to miss a single word of the lecture.
その話は耳にたこができるほど聞かされた.	I'm sick and tired of hearing that story.
【聞き入れる】息子は最近ちっとも言うことを聞かない.	My son doesn't obey [mind] me at all recently.
先生の言うことを聞きなさい.	Mind your teacher.
友人の忠告は素直に聞くものだ.	You should be grateful for advice from a friend.
会社側はついに組合の要求を聞き入れた.	The company finally accepted the union's demands.
彼女は私の意見など聞き入れようとしなかった.	She turned a deaf ear to my opinion.
【たずねる】あの店で道を聞いてこよう.	I'll go ask for directions at that store.
彼に何度聞き返しても同じことしか教えてくれなかった.	I asked him over and over again but the answer was always the same.

きけん (危険)

夜道の独り歩きは危険だ.	It's dangerous to walk alone late at night.
高い柵があるから,そこから落ちる危険はない.	There's no danger of falling from there because there's a high fence.
彼は危険が迫っているのに気づかなかった.	He wasn't aware of the danger threatening him.
この仕事は危険を伴う.	This work carries a lot of risk.
暴動の危険は遠のいている.	The risk of riots is receding.
母親は身の危険を冒して子どもを助けようとした.	She risked her life to try to save her child.

きげん[1] (期限)

論文の提出期限は明日だ.	Tomorrow is the deadline for handing [turning] in the paper.
これは期限付きの仕事だよ.	This job has a †time limit [deadline].

この本は返却期限を過ぎている.	This book is overdue.
契約の期限が切れてしまった.	The contract has expired.
この定期券は有効期限が切れている.	This commuter pass has expired.

きげん² (機嫌)

ご機嫌いかが.	How are you?
今日は父の機嫌がいい.	My father's †in a good mood [in good humor] today.
彼は今日はなぜか機嫌が悪い[ご機嫌斜めだ].	For some reason he's in a bad mood today.
	He got up on the wrong side of the bed.
彼の機嫌ももうすぐ直るだろう.	He should be back to normal before long.
彼はやっと機嫌を直して,いつものように私たちの話に加わった.	He finally got over being miffed and joined our conversation the way he used to.
彼は機嫌の取りにくい人だ.	He's hard to please.
彼に頼むなら機嫌を取ってからにしろ.	Humor [Play up to] him before you ask him.
彼女は夫の機嫌を取って新しいドレスを買ってもらった.	She cajoled her husband into buying her a new dress.
彼女の機嫌を損なってしまった.	I offended her.
ご機嫌伺いに彼の所に寄ってみよう.	I'll drop in at his place to see how he is.

きこえる (聞こえる)

私の言うことが聞こえますか.	Can you hear what I'm saying?
変な物音が聞こえてきた.	I heard a strange noise.
電話の声が聞こえなくなった.	The voice on the telephone †died away [faded out].
うぬぼれに聞こえるかもしれないが,それは私にしかできないと思う.	It may sound conceited of me to say so, but I think I'm the only one who can do that.
彼らは私の悪口を聞こえよがしに言っていた.	They were saying awful things about me almost as if they wanted me to overhear them.

ぎこちない

彼女といると,ついぎこちなくなってしまう.	I can't help feeling clumsy [awkward] around her.
彼の文章はぎこちない.	His writing is clumsy [awkward].
彼女のスキーはまだぎこちない.	Her skiing is still clumsy [awkward].

きさく (気さく)

叔父は気さくな人だ．	My uncle is easy to get along with.
この大学の学長は気さくな人柄で学生に親しまれている．	The president of this university is †an amiable [a friendly] person and is well liked by the students.
彼はあまり親しくない人にも気さくに話しかける．	He strikes up a friendly conversation even with people he doesn't know very well.

きざむ (刻む)

タマネギをできるだけ細かく刻んでください．	Please chop the onion as fine as possible.
サラダ用のキャベツを刻んだ．	I shredded cabbage for a salad.
山の木に名前を刻む登山者が多くなってきた．	The number of mountain climbers who carve their names on mountain trees has increased.

ぎじゅつ (技術)

何か技術を身につけておくといいよ．	It's good to acquire some kind of skill.
あのピアニストは技術的にはうまいが，それ以上のものはない．	That pianist has a fine technique, but that's about all.
彼は文学者というより技術者に向いている．	He has more aptitude for engineering than literature.
科学技術は日に日に進歩している．	Progress is made in science and technology day by day.

きしょう (気性)

彼の気性は私がいちばんよく知っている．	I know his temperament best.
彼は気性は激しいが優しい面もある．	He has a violent temper but he also has his gentle side.
彼は真っすぐな気性なので，その不正を見逃せなかった．	He has such a righteous disposition that he couldn't overlook that injustice.

きず (傷)

【けが】彼は自動車事故で脚に軽い傷を負っただけで済んだ．	He got away with just a slight leg injury in the car accident.
このひっかき傷はどうしてついたの？	How did you get this scratch?
彼は傷口を6針も縫ったらしいよ．	I heard he had six stitches.
傷跡が残りそうだ．	It'll probably leave a scar.
【傷んだところ】このオレンジを傷のないのと取り換えて．	Please exchange this orange for one without any blemishes.

傷のある商品をバーゲンセールに出した.	They put the damaged merchandise on sale at a special low price.
【汚点・欠点】その事件で彼は家名に傷をつけてしまった.	His involvement in that affair damaged his family's reputation.
彼女はいい先生だが,厳しすぎるのが玉に傷だ.	She's a good teacher. Her only flaw is that she's too strict.

きずく (築く)

中世にこの城を築くのは大変な難事業だったろう.	Building this castle in the Middle Ages must have been an extremely difficult undertaking.
彼は自分一人の力でこれほどの財産を築き上げた.	He built up this entire fortune all by himself.
彼女はピアニストとしての名声を20代で築き上げた.	She established her name [fame] as a pianist in her twenties.
新婚の二人には幸せな家庭を築いてほしい.	I hope the newlyweds will create a happy home.

きずつく (傷つく)

不良品が出てブランドイメージが大きく傷ついた.	The defective product really hurt the brand's image.
彼女は友人に裏切られて深く傷ついている.	She's deeply hurt by her friend's betrayal.
ぼくのこと,そんなふうに見ていたんだ.傷つくなぁ.	I didn't realize that you thought of me like that. I really feel hurt.
人前で恥をかかされ,彼女のプライドは傷ついた.	Her pride was hurt when she was humiliated in front of others.
彼の傷ついた心が癒えるのに長い時間がかかった.	It took him a long time to get over †it [the hurt].
ああ見えて,彼は傷つきやすいんだよ.	You would never know it but he's actually a very sensitive person.

きずつける (傷つける)

漆の箱を傷つけないように指輪を外してから触った.	I took off my ring so that I wouldn't scratch the lacquer box when I handled it.
この桃,傷つけないようにそっと扱ってね.	Handle this peach carefully so that it doesn't †get bruised [bruise].
不用意な言葉で彼女を傷つけてしまった.	My careless remark hurt her feelings. Her feelings were hurt by my careless remark.
社員の自尊心を傷つけないような叱り方をしなさい.	When you reprimand employees, do it in such a way that it doesn't damage their

	self-esteem.
一社員の不正が会社全体の信用を傷つけた.	One employee's dishonesty [wrongdoing] damaged the reputation of the whole company.

ぎせい (犠牲)

会社は汚職事件で彼を犠牲にして社の名誉を保とうとした.	The company tried to preserve its honor by making him a scapegoat in the corruption scandal.
彼は公共のために自分の利益を犠牲にした.	He sacrificed his personal interest for [to] the public good.
彼女は自分の恋を犠牲にして病気の母親の世話を続けた.	She sacrificed her romance to continue taking care of her sick mother.
彼は多くの犠牲を払ってその地位を手に入れた.	He got that position by making many sacrifices.
列車事故で多くの犠牲者が出た.	The train accident resulted in many victims.

きせる (着せる)

彼は妻にコートを着せた.	He helped his wife on with her coat.
母親は娘に着物を着せるのが楽しみらしい.	The mother seems to enjoy dressing her daughter up in *kimono*.

きそ (基礎)

ビルの基礎工事が始まった.	They have started laying of the building's foundation.
彼の父がこの会社の基礎を作った.	His father established (the base for) this company.
先生は英文法の基礎を生徒に厳しく教えた.	The teacher was very strict in teaching the fundamentals of English grammar to his students.
数学を基礎から勉強し直しなさい.	Study mathematics over again from the basics.

きそく (規則)

この寮は規則づくめで, うんざりだ.	I'm fed up with all the rules and regulations at this dorm.
学校の規則に従いなさい.	Obey the school rules [regulations, codes].
彼は交通規則を破って罰金を取られた.	He violated a traffic rule [regulation] and was fined.
規則正しい生活をしなさい.	Try to lead a well-regulated life.
何事も規則どおりにはゆかない.	Things don't always go by the rules.
一日3回, 規則的に食事をしなさい.	Try to eat three meals a day regularly.

彼からは週に1回規則的に手紙が届く.	I get a letter from him regularly once a week.

きたい (期待)

ご期待に添えず,申しわけありません.	I'm very sorry that I didn't [couldn't] †come up to [meet] your expectations.
両親は私に大きな期待をかけ過ぎている.	My parents expect too much of me.
いつかまた君に会うことを期待している.	I'm looking forward to seeing you again.
君が来てくれるものと期待していたのに,がっかりしたよ.	I was so looking forward to your coming. What a letdown!
早くから大雪が降り,スキー場の経営者たちはいいシーズンになりそうだと期待している.	With the heavy and early snowfall, the ski resort operators are anticipating[1] a good season.
チームはその新人選手に期待を寄せた.	The team was counting on the new player [member].
被告人は減刑を期待して罪を白状した.	In hopes of getting a lighter sentence, the defendant confessed to the crime.
彼は親の期待を裏切って船乗りになった.	He disappointed his parents by becoming a sailor.
彼の成績は全くの期待外れだった.	His performance turned out to be quite a letdown.

---

1) anticipate, anticipation は期待するものが目前に迫っている場合に言う.

きたえる (鍛える)

この高校の野球部はよく鍛えられている.	This high school baseball team has been trained into top condition.
若いうちに体を鍛えなさい.	You should get in shape while you're still young.

きたない (汚い)

彼の部屋はとても汚い.	His room is very dirty.
汚いシャツは着替えなさい.	Change (out of) that dirty shirt.
汚らしい身なりの男が家の前に立っている.	There's a shabby character standing in front of the house.
彼は汚い手を使ってその土地を手に入れた.	He used a dirty trick to get that land.
食事中にそんな汚い話をしてはいけない.	You shouldn't talk about such filthy things at the table.
彼は金に汚い.	He's mean about money.

きちょう (貴重)

博物館から貴重なつぼが盗まれた.	A precious [valuable] urn was stolen from the museum.
私は貴重な時間をむだに過ごしてしまって後悔している.	I really regret having wasted all that precious [valuable] time.
人の命は何にも増して貴重だ.	There is nothing more precious than human life.
彼は社の貴重な人材だ.	He's an invaluable asset to our company.
貴重品はクロークに預けてください.	Please check your valuables at the cloakroom.

きちょうめん (几帳面)

彼は几帳面だからこの仕事に向いていると思う.	I think he's suited for this work because he's †good with details [meticulous, methodical].
彼女は几帳面で約束の時間に遅れたことがない.	She's always quite punctual and has never been late for an appointment.
彼は几帳面に自分の分の宿代を払った.	He paid his fair share of the hotel bill.

きちんと

彼女の部屋はいつもきちんとしている.	Her room is always neat.
彼はいつもきちんとした身なりをしている.	His appearance is always neat.
部屋代はきちんと払ってください.	Please pay your rent promptly.
彼は仕事をきちんとする人だ.	He's a conscientious worker.
きちんと座りなさい.	Sit up straight.
彼女はきちんと時間どおりにやって来た.	She came along right on time.

きつい

包帯をきつく巻いてくれ.	Wrap the bandage tight.
荷物にはきつくひもがかけてあった.	The package was bound tightly with twine.
この瓶のふたはきつくて開けられない.	I can't get the lid off this bottle, it's on so tight.
靴がきつくて痛い.	These shoes pinch.
【厳しい】仕事があまりきついので彼女は体をこわしてしまった.	Her job was so demanding that it ruined her health.
彼をそんなにきつく叱らないで.	Don't be so stern with him.
気が立っていたので子どもにまできついことを言ってしまった.	I was so worked up that I even said harsh things to the kids.

彼女はきつい女だ.	She's a strong-minded woman.

きっかけ

きっかけは些細な出来事だった.	It started with an insignificant incident.
ふとしたことがきっかけで彼らは知り合った.	A chance meeting brought them together.
コンサートで隣同士に座ったことがきっかけで二人は仲良くなった.	They became good friends after they happened to sit next to each other at a concert.
彼女のその一言がきっかけとなり,激しい口論が始まった.	Her comment set off a terrible argument.
その出来事が彼が立ち直るきっかけとなった	It was that incident that got him back on his feet.
きっかけさえつかめば,まだ逆転は可能だ.	We can still win if we seize the opportunity.[1]
	We can still come (up) from behind if we grab that chance.[2]
どんなきっかけで二人は知り合ったの?	How did you two meet?
フラメンコを習い始めたきっかけは?	What made you take up flamenco dancing?

> 1) は win を使っているので試合やコンテストなどの場合の言い方.
> 2) の come (up) from behind は試合などのほか比喩的にも使える.

きづく (気づく)

擦れ違ったのに彼は私に気づかなかった.	He walked right past me without noticing me.
彼は部下の背信に気づかなかった.	He †didn't notice [didn't catch on to, wasn't aware of] the betrayal of his subordinates.
自分の誤りにやっと気づいた.	I finally realized my (own) mistake.
ふと気づくと彼が私の前に立っていた.	I suddenly †realized [became aware] that he was standing in front of me.
だれにも気づかれずに家を脱け出した.	I slipped out of the house unnoticed.

きっと

明日はきっと晴れるだろう.	I'm sure it'll be clear tomorrow.
この知らせを聞けば彼もきっと喜ぶことだろう.	I'm sure he'll be happy to hear this news.
彼女はきっといい先生になると思う.	I just know she'll make a good teacher.

彼女は小さいときはきっとかわいかったに違いない.	She (certainly) must have been cute when she was a child.

きてい (規定)

契約には両社の権利義務が規定されている.	The contract †stipulates [spells out] the rights and obligations of both companies.
憲法には国民の権利と義務が規定されている.	Citizens' rights and duties are stipulated in the constitution.
規定の書式に従って契約書を作成した.	I drew up the contract according to the standard format.
この小包は規定の大きさを超えています.	This package is over the size limit.
彼は不正乗車が見つかって規定の料金の3倍を取られた.	He got caught trying to ride for free on the train and was fined three times the regular fare.

きてん (機転)

新しい秘書は大変機転が利く.	The new secretary is very quick-witted.
彼は機転を利かせてその場の気まずい雰囲気を和らげた.	He used his wits to break the awkward atmosphere.
彼は機転を利かせて車掌を呼びに行ってくれた.	He was quick-witted enough to go for the train conductor.

きどう (軌道)

【天体の】我が国で打ち上げた人工衛星が地球を回る軌道に乗った.	The satellite our country launched has gone into orbit around the earth.
人工衛星は軌道を外れた.	The satellite went out of orbit.
ロケットの軌道を修正する必要がある.	The rocket has to get back into orbit.
【仕事・計画の】新規事業は軌道に乗せるまでが一苦労だ.	It's a struggle getting a new business off the ground.
新店舗の経営が軌道に乗り始めた.	The new store is †taking off [getting into gear].
早いうちに軌道修正しないと大変なことになるよ.	If we don't †fix this [make an adjustment] now we'll be in big trouble. There'll be big trouble if we don't make some changes now.
プロジェクトは当初の計画から大きく軌道をそれていった.	The project has diverged greatly from its original plan.* Judging from the original proposal, the project seems to have gone off track.

きどる (気取る)

彼女は気取った歩き方をする.	She has an affected way of walking.
彼女は気取らない人柄で皆に好かれている.	She's well liked because of her unaffected manner.
そんなに気取るなよ.	Don't put on such airs.
彼はすっかり芸術家気取りだ.	He behaves as if he were an artist.
	He comes on like** an artist.
彼らは夫婦気取りで生活していた.	They carried on as if they were married.
	They lived like a married couple.

きなが (気長)

彼女のことは気長に待ったほうがよさそうだ.	It's probably best to give it a little time in her case.
気長に構えていなくては, のんびり屋の彼とはつきあえない.	You've got to put yourself in a patient frame of mind if you want to be friends with a happy-go-lucky guy like him.
焦らず気長にやってくれ.	Take your time. There's no need to get excited.

きねん (記念)

その作家を記念して賞を設けた.	They established a prize to commemorate that writer.
卒業の日に記念植樹をした.	We planted a commemorative tree on our graduation day.
記念に皆で一緒に写真を撮った.	We took a group picture to remember the occasion.
今日は10回目の結婚記念日だ.	Today is our tenth wedding anniversary.
記念品としてこの時計をもらった.	I got this watch as a remembrance.
これがその詩人の記念碑です.	This is a monument to that poet.

きのどく (気の毒)

ご両親が亡くなられたそうでお気の毒です.	I'm so [I was] sorry to hear that your parents passed away.
日曜日も働かなくてはいけないなんて気の毒だね.	I really feel sorry for you that you have to work on Sunday.
なんて気の毒な境遇だろう.	What an unfortunate situation!

きはく (気迫)

彼は気迫に満ちている.	He is full of vigor [spirit].
気迫がなければこの相手には勝てない.	You'll never beat this opponent unless you've got spirit.
技より気迫で彼に負けてしまった.	I was beaten more by his spirit than by his skill.

きばつ (奇抜)

奇抜な柄のシャツを着ているね.	The shirt you're wearing has †an unusual [a novel] pattern, doesn't it?
彼はいつも奇抜なことをして人を驚かせる人だ.	He's always surprising people with the bizarre [weird] things he does.
奇抜なアイデアですね.	That's a novel idea, isn't it?

きばらし (気晴らし)

気晴らしに映画でも見よう.	Let's go see a movie for a change of pace.
彼とおしゃべりして気晴らしになった.	It was refreshing to have a chat with him.
勉強ばかりしてないでたまには気晴らしに出かけろよ.	Go out and have a good time once in a while instead of just studying all the time.

きびしい (厳しい)

我が家はしつけが厳しかった.	We were brought up †strictly [with strict discipline].
父は時間に厳しい.	My father is strict [particular] about punctuality.
あまり厳し過ぎても子どもは反抗するものだ.	If you're too strict, children will rebel.
彼は厳しい上司〔先生〕だ.	He's a demanding boss [teacher].
競技スポーツは厳しい修練を要する.	Competitive sports demand rigorous discipline.
学校の規則が厳しくなった.	The school tightened up its regulations.
見張りが厳しくて逃げられそうもない.	We're under such strict surveillance that there's little hope of escape.
彼は友人から厳しく批判された.	His friends roundly criticized him.
君もだんだんと世の中の厳しさを知るだろう.	You'll find out bit by bit just how harsh the world really is.
物価が上がって生活が厳しくなっている.	Life is getting harder with prices going up.
砂漠の気候は厳しい.	The desert has a harsh climate.
こちらは厳しい暑さが続いています.	We're having a relentless heat wave here.

きびん (機敏)

彼は動作が機敏だ.	He's quick and agile.
彼はその問題を機敏に処理した.	He handled that problem promptly.
彼は機敏に機会を捕えて成功してきた.	He has become successful by being prompt in seizing opportunities.

きぶん (気分)

【具合】
気分はどうですか. — How do you feel?
少し気分が良くなった. — I'm feeling a little better.
気分が悪い[優れない]ので先に帰ります. — I feel ill. [I don't feel so well.] I'm going home early.

【気持ち】
今日はパーティーに行く気分ではない. — I'm not in the mood to go to the party today.
彼は皆にちやほやされてスターになったような気分だった. — They all made such a fuss over him that he felt as if he were a star.
彼女はその日の気分で髪型を変える. — She changes her hair style to suit her mood each day.
ケーキがあったほうが誕生日パーティーの気分が出るよ. — Having a cake will †make it more like a birthday party [create the proper birthday party mood].
水着にならないと海に来た気分が出ない. — If you don't change into a bathing suit, you won't feel like you're really at the beach.
彼は気分を害して出て行った. — His feelings got hurt and he left.
気分転換に旅行でもしたら? — I think you need a vacation [trip].
彼は気分屋の秘書に悩まされている. — His moody secretary is giving him headaches.
町じゅうお祭り気分だ. — The whole town is in a festive mood.

きぼ (規模)

君の計画は規模が大き過ぎて, 我が社では実現不可能だ. — The scale of your plan is too big for our company to handle.
新聞社が大規模な世論調査を行った. — The newspaper conducted a large-scale opinion poll.
東海地方で大規模な地震が起きた. — A large earthquake occurred in the Tokai region.
あの国で大規模な反乱が起きた. — A widespread rebellion occurred in that country.
最初は大規模な〔小規模な〕集会だった. — In the beginning, it was a big [small] meeting.
最初は小規模で低予算の事業だった. — We started off on a small scale with a modest budget.
不景気のため経営規模を縮小した. — The business was scaled back [down] because of the recession.
うちは全国規模の組織です. — Our organization is nationwide.
原因不明の熱病が世界的規模で流行している. — A mysterious fever is spreading throughout the world.

きぼう (希望)

どんなときにも希望を失ってはいけない.	No matter what, you mustn't †lose hope [despair].
パリで絵を学びたいという彼の長年の希望がやっとかなった.	His long-cherished hope [dream] of studying painting in Paris finally came true.
彼女の言葉が私に希望を与えた.	Her words gave me hope.
彼女は何の希望もない生活を送っていた.	She led a life devoid of hope.
彼女は, 息子が生きているかもしれないというはかない希望を頼りに日々を送った.	The faint hope that her son might still be alive kept her going from one day to the next.
彼は希望どおり医学部に入学できた.	He got into medical school as he had hoped.
彼は父親の希望に添って医者になった.	He became a doctor †in keeping with his father's wishes [in order to live up to his father's expectations].
ご希望に添えなくて申しわけありません.	I'm sorry I couldn't fulfill your wishes.
クラス全員の希望で先生は試験を延期してくれた.	The teacher postponed the test at the request of the entire class.
それは君の希望的観測にすぎない.	That's just wishful thinking (on your part).

きほん (基本)

基本を忘れるな.	Never forget the basics.
彼は英語を基本からやり直した.	He studied English again starting from the basics.
基本的には彼は正しい.	He is fundamentally [basically] correct.
基本的人権は尊重されなければならない.	Fundamental human rights must be respected.
僕の基本給は大したことはない.	My base pay isn't much.

きまえ (気前)

こんなにチップをくれるなんて気前のいい客だ.	What a generous person [customer] to give me such a big tip!
伯父は気前がよくて, 欲しいものは何でも買ってくれる.	My uncle is very generous and buys me whatever I want.
彼は教会に気前よく多額の寄付をした.	He made a handsome donation to the church.

きまぐれ (気まぐれ)

彼は気まぐれで当てにならない.	He's too fickle to be depended upon.
彼は気まぐれだから, 来ると言っ	He's whimsical. Even if he says he'll come,

ていてもどうだか分からない. / you just can't tell.

一時の気まぐれでそんな重大なことを決めてはいけない. / You shouldn't decide such an important matter on just a passing whim.

山の天気は気まぐれだから気をつけたほうがいい. / You should be careful since the weather up in the mountains is changeable.

さっきまでは晴れていたのに気まぐれな天気だ. / It was clear just a moment ago. What fickle weather!

きまずい (気まずい)

その席に出て大変気まずい思いをした. / I felt extremely awkward being there.

あの事件以来彼女とは気まずくなってしまった. / My relationship with her has been strained ever since that happened.

その言葉に彼は一瞬気まずく黙り込んでしまった. / He fell awkwardly silent for a moment when he heard that.

きまま (気まま)

彼女は気ままな性格でつきあいにくい. / She has such a tendency to do as she pleases that it's hard to do things with her.

あの作家のような気ままな人生も悪くない. / Living a carefree life like that writer wouldn't be bad, would it?

父は勝手気ままな人生を送った. / My father led a self-indulgent life.

きまり (決まり)

【規則】彼は学校の決まりを破って教室の隅に立たされた. / He broke a school rule and was made to stand in the corner of the classroom.

その書類の書き方には別に決まりはありません. / There are no particular rules for writing that kind of document.

共同生活をするためには、めいめいが決まりを守る必要がある. / When living together everybody must obey the rules.

月に一度皆で集まるのが決まりになっている. / We have a rule that we all meet together once a month.

彼の仕事のやり方には一定の決まりがない. / He has no set way of doing his work.

【決着】この問題にできるだけ早く決まりをつけたい. / I want to settle this matter as quickly as possible.

遺産相続問題もやっと決まりがついた. / The inheritance has finally been worked out.

【習慣】また彼のお決まりのお説教が始まったよ. / He started in on his usual sermon again.

食事のあとこの店で一杯やるのが彼らのお決まりのコースだ. / They usually come here for a few drinks after dinner.

それは何か失敗したときの彼の決まり文句だ.	That's what he always says when he's made a mistake.
君の決まり文句は聞き飽きた.	I'm tired of hearing the same clichés from you.
日本語の決まり文句は英語に訳しにくい.	Japanese idioms are difficult to translate into English.

きまりがわるい (きまりが悪い)

だれの助けも借りないと言った手前, きまりが悪くて助けてくれとは言えない.	Since I said I wouldn't need anybody's help, it'd be too embarrassing to ask for help now.
仮病を使っていたのが判ってきまりの悪い思いをした.	I felt embarrassed [awkward] when they found out I had pretended to be sick.
彼はきまり悪そうに借金を申し込んできた.	Looking embarrassed, he asked me for a loan.

きまる (決まる)

【決定】会合の場所はまだ決まらない.	The meeting place has not been decided on yet.
彼女の結婚相手はもう決まっている.	She's already engaged.
	She already has a fiancé.
試験日は3月1日と決まった.	The examination date has been set for March 1st.
彼の転勤が急に決まった.	His transfer was decided quite suddenly.
それで話は決まったね.	It's (all) settled then.
すでに決まったことを蒸し返すな.	Don't drag up again what has already been decided.
【一定】彼には毎月決まった収入がない.	He doesn't have a fixed monthly income.
このテレビ番組にはいつも決まった顔ぶればかり登場する.	The same people always appear [They always have the same people] on this TV show.
【当然】彼は来ないに決まっている.	Of course he won't come.
そんなのうそに決まっている.	That's got to be a lie.
彼だっていつも失敗するとは決まっていない.	Even in his case, it doesn't necessarily follow that he'll make a mistake every time.
【慣用】今日のスーツ, きまってるね.	You look very sharp in that suit today.
彼の強烈なシュートがゴールの右隅に決まった.	His powerful shot made the right-hand corner of the goal.

～ぎみ (～気味)

彼は少しあがり気味だった.	He was a little nervous.
彼女は最近太り気味だ.	She seems to be putting on a little weight lately.
風邪気味なので休みます.	I have a touch of a cold, so I'm taking the day off.

きみがわるい (気味が悪い)

ここは何だか気味が悪い.	Somehow this place gives me the creeps.
気味の悪い話はよせよ.	Stop such creepy talk.
父の大切な釣りざおを折ったのに叱られないなんて気味が悪い.	It felt weird not getting scolded even though I broke my father's favorite fishing rod.
薄気味の悪い笑い方をするやつだ.	That guy has sort of a weird smile.

きみょう (奇妙)

あの建物は奇妙な格好をしている.	That building has a weird shape.
奇妙な帽子をかぶっているね.	That sure is a weird hat you have on.
この村には奇妙な風習がある.	This village has strange customs.
奇妙なことに，戦死したはずの息子からの手紙が届いた.	Strange as it seems, we received a letter from our son who was supposed to have been killed in action.

ぎむ (義務)

彼には両親を養う義務がある.	He is obliged to support his parents.
	He has the duty of supporting his parents.
私たちには彼を助ける義務がある.	We have an obligation to help him.
私たちは国民としての義務を果さなければならない.	We must fulfill our duties as citizens.
彼は生徒を監督するという義務を怠った.	He neglected his duty of overseeing his students.
彼女は2年間，ただ義務的に働いた.	She worked for two years merely out of a sense of duty.

きむずかしい (気難しい)

あの老人は気難しい.	That old man is †difficult [hard to please].
その話をすると父は急に気難しい顔つきになった.	When I spoke to him about it, my father's face suddenly took on a hard expression.

きめる (決める)

私たちは5時に駅前で会うことに決めた.	We decided to meet in front of the station at five (o'clock).

行くのか行かないのか,早く決めろ.	Hurry up and †decide [make up your mind] whether you're going or not.
彼は大学院に進むことに決めた.	He decided to go on to graduate school.
パーティーは次の日曜日に決めましょう.	Let's set the party for next Sunday.
分担を決めて仕事をしよう.	Let's do the work by assigning tasks.
私は毎朝散歩することに決めている.	I make it a rule to take a walk every morning.
彼は私がうそをついているものと決めてかかっている.	He has just assumed that I'm lying.

きもち (気持ち)

彼は人の気持ちが分からない.	He doesn't understand the feelings of others.
君の本当の気持ちを聞かせてくれ.	Tell me your true feelings.
一等賞をとったときは,どんな気持ちでしたか.	How did you feel when you won first prize?
朝からなぜか不安な気持ちがして落ち着かない.	For some reason I've felt uneasy since this morning and haven't been able to settle down.
彼の態度には感謝の気持ちなんて全く見えなかった.	His attitude completely lacked any feeling of gratitude.
彼女は私の気持ちを傷つけても平気な顔をしている.	She hurt my feelings and now acts as if nothing had happened.
もう少し彼女の気持ちになって考えてあげたら?	Why don't you try a little harder to imagine how she feels?
水でも飲んで気持ちを落ち着けてから話してくれ.	Have a glass of water, calm down, and then tell me what happened.
私が素直に謝ると彼は少し気持ちを和らげてくれたようだった.	When I offered him my sincere apology, he seemed to soften a little.
食べ過ぎて気持ちが悪い.	I ate too much and feel unpleasant.
彼が女装した姿を想像するだけで気持ちが悪い.	It's revolting [disgusting] just to imagine what he would look like dressed in women's clothes.
かなり気持ちがよくなってきた.	I feel much better now.
暑いときに冷たいシャワーを浴びるのは気持ちがよい.	It feels good to take a cold shower when it's hot.
あの人は気持ちのいい人だね.	He's a pleasant person, isn't he?
彼は気持ちよくその仕事を引き受けてくれた.	He took on the job quite willingly.

ぎもん (疑問)

彼が我々の話に乗ってくれるかど	It's doubtful whether he'll take us up on

うか疑問だ.	our offer.
彼の誠実さには疑問を抱いている.	I have doubts about his sincerity.
この件について疑問があれば遠慮なく質問してください.	If you have any doubts about this, please feel free to ask questions.
それには疑問の余地がない.	There's no doubt about it.
	That leaves no room for doubt.

ぎゃく (逆)

列車は逆の方向に進みだした.	The train started to move in the opposite direction.
そんなことを言ったら逆効果だよ.	If you say something like that, it will have the opposite effect.
我々の予想とは逆の結果が出た.	The outcome was completely contrary to our expectations.
順序が逆だよ.	They're in reverse order.
今年は彼が優勝し,二人の立場は逆になった.	This year he won the championship and reversed their positions.
アルファベットを逆から言える？	Can you recite the alphabet backwards?
壁に絵を逆に掛けてしまった.	I hung the painting on the wall upside-down by mistake.
靴を逆にはいているよ.	You're wearing your shoes on the wrong feet.
巨額の遺産の相続は逆に彼に不幸を招いただけだった.	Contrary to what one might have expected, the enormous inheritance he came into brought only unhappiness.
彼を喜ばせるつもりが逆に怒らせてしまった.	My intentions were to please him but †instead [on the contrary] I ended up angering him.
道が行き止まりだったので逆戻りした.	I had to backtrack when the road I was on came to a dead end.
逆は必ずしも真ならず.	The converse does not always hold true.

ぎゃくじょう (逆上)

話を聞いて彼は逆上した.	He went wild when he heard that.
逆上のあまり我を忘れて彼を殴ってしまった.	In my rage, I lost control of myself and punched him.
かわいがっていた小鳥を猫に殺されて彼女は逆上した.	She was beside herself when the bird she loved so much was killed by a cat.

きやすい (気安い)

彼は知らない人にも気安く話しかける.	He has no qualms about going up and speaking to a stranger.
気安く借金の保証人などになって	You should not readily volunteer to be a

はいけない.
簡単な仕事だと思って気安く引き受けてしまったのを今では後悔している. | guarantor for loans.
Thinking that it was an easy job [task] I took it on without hesitation and now I regret it.

きやすめ (気休め)

気休めを言わないでくれ. | Don't say things just to try to make me feel better.
口先だけの気休めなら欲しくない. | Nothing you can say will make me feel better.
気休めに新しい薬も試してみたら? | Why don't you try some new medicine just to ease your mind?

きゅう (急)

【急ぎ】それは急を要する問題だ. | It's an urgent problem.
 | It's a problem which demands your immediate attention.
【突然】急な気温の変化で風邪をひいてしまった. | I caught a cold from the sudden change in temperature.
電話で急に社長室に呼び出された. | I was suddenly summoned by phone to the president's office.
部屋を出てくれと家主に急に言われた. | I was suddenly told by my landlord to move out.
彼は急に笑い出した. | All of a sudden he burst out laughing.
【角・坂・流れなど】その先のカーブは急で事故が多い. | The curve up ahead is very sharp and has been the scene of many accidents.
彼らは急な坂道を登っていった. | They were climbing up the steep slope.
あの川の流れは急だ. | The current of that river is very fast [swift].

きゅうか (休暇)

忙しくて当分休暇はとれない. | I'm so busy that I won't be able to take time off for a while.
一週間の休暇をとって旅行に出た. | I took a week off from work and went on a trip.
彼は今週休暇でいない. | He's away on vacation this week.
学校は夏期休暇に入った. | School went on summer vacation.

きゅうくつ (窮屈)

このコートは窮屈になってきた. | This coat has gotten too small [tight] for me.
車の中は窮屈でほとんど身動きできなかった. | The inside of the car was so cramped I could barely move.

こんな窮屈な規則はやめて欲しい.	I wish they would get rid of such restrictive regulations.
そんなに窮屈に考えないで.	Don't take things in such a rigid way.
ずっと伯父と一緒で窮屈な思いをした.	I felt uncomfortable since I was with my uncle the whole time.

きゅうけい (休憩)

歩き疲れたので少し休憩した.	Walking had made me tired, so I took a short rest.
10分間の休憩にしましょう.	Let's take a ten-minute break.
この会社の休憩時間は短過ぎる.	Work breaks are too short at this company.
この芝居は休憩がない.	This play has no intermission.
美術館の休憩室で彼に会った.	I met him in the lounge of the art museum.

きゅうじつ (休日)

日本では春分の日は休日です.	In Japan the vernal equinox is a holiday.
休日には, この商店街は買物客で混雑します.	On Sundays and holidays this shopping mall is crowded with customers.
久しぶりの休日に家族そろって海水浴に行った.	On my first day off in a long time, our whole family went to the beach.

きよう (器用)

彼は手先が器用で何でも自分で作る.	He's good with his hands and makes everything by himself.
彼は大工道具を持たせればとても器用だ.	He's handy with carpenter's tools.
彼女は随分器用に編物をする.	She's very good at knitting things.
彼のような人を器用貧乏というんだろうな.	He's the kind of person you could call a jack-of-all-trades and master of none.

きょうい (驚異)

大自然の驚異に打たれた.	I was struck by the marvels [wonders] of nature.
彼の見事な作品に人々は驚異の目を見張った.	Everyone †gazed on in wonder [marveled] at his magnificent work.
日本経済は戦後驚異的に成長した.	The Japanese economy achieved spectacular growth after the war.

きょういく (教育)

彼は教育という仕事に情熱を持っている.	He takes a passionate interest in his work in education.

彼女は十分な教育を受けることができなかった.	She wasn't able to receive an adequate education.
彼女は子どもたちを厳しく教育した.	She was strict in the education of her children.
この番組は教育的だ.	This program is educational in nature.

きょうかん（共感）

彼の思想に共感する.	I sympathize with his way of thinking.
父の意見には全く共感できなかった.	I couldn't go along with my father's opinion at all.
彼の演説は人々の共感を呼び起こした.	His speech struck a responsive chord in everyone.

きょうぎ（競技）

彼は陸上競技の選手です.	He's a track and field athlete.
彼らは体操の競技会に向けて猛練習を続けている.	They've been training vigorously for the upcoming gymnastics meet.
年に1回のダンスの競技会が開催された.	The annual dance contest was held.

ぎょうぎ（行儀）

彼女の息子は行儀の良い子だ.	Her son is well-behaved.
なんて行儀が悪い子だろう.	What a rude brat!
お行儀良くなさい.	Behave yourself.
母に厳しく行儀作法を教えられた.	My mother was very strict about teaching me manners.
他人行儀はやめろよ.	Stop standing on ceremony.
	Stop acting like a stranger.

きょうきゅう（供給）

この地方の電力の供給はまだ不十分だ.	This region still does not get an adequate supply of electric power.
原油の供給不足は重大問題だ.	The inadequate supply of crude oil is a serious problem.
うちはその会社から部品を供給してもらっている.	We're having that company supply us with parts.
自衛隊は災害地に人力を供給した.	The Self-Defense Forces provided manpower to the area hit by disaster.

きょうこう（強硬）

彼は私の意見に強硬に反対した.	He was completely [adamantly, strongly] opposed to my opinion.
会社側は強硬な態度をとった.	The company assumed an uncompromis-

	ing attitude.
人質救出のために警察は強硬手段をとった.	The police took drastic measures to rescue the hostages.

きょうしゅく (恐縮)

彼の助力には恐縮しました.	I felt obliged to him for his help.
わざわざおいでいただいて恐縮です.	I'm very grateful for your taking the time to come.
褒められるとかえって恐縮します.	I really don't deserve your praise.

きょうそう (競争)

奨学金を受けるために多数の学生が競争した.	Many students competed for the scholarships.
親友との競争が励みになってよく勉強した.	Rivalry with my best friend motivated me to study harder.
日本の一流大学の入学競争は激しい.	Competition to enter top Japanese universities is intense.
彼は成績に関しては競争心が強い.	He's very competitive when it comes to grades.
彼が競争相手じゃ, とても勝ち目はない.	There's no chance of winning with him as my opponent.
消費者はメーカーの値下げ競争を歓迎している.	The consumers are welcoming the price war being waged by the manufacturers.

きょうつう (共通)

彼らには共通点がない.	They have nothing in common.
学者の彼とは共通の話題がない.	He's a scholar. We wouldn't have anything in common to talk about.
インフレ〔デフレ〕は多くの国に共通の問題だ.	Inflation [Deflation] is a problem common to many countries.
子どもの幸福はどの親にも共通の願いだ.	All parents share the desire to see their children happy.

きょうどう (共同)

この寮では台所は共同です.	The kitchen in this dorm is †shared by everyone [communal].
公園は住民の共同の憩いの場所だ.	Parks are recreation areas for all citizens to use.
彼は利己的で共同生活には向かない.	He's too self-centered to live with others.
この製品は両社が共同で開発したものです.	This product was jointly developed by the two companies.
彼と共同して事業を始めた.	I went into business with him.

きょうふ (恐怖)

突然，恐怖に襲われた．	I was suddenly seized with fear.
彼女は恐怖に足がすくんだ．	She froze in her steps with fear.
彼女はそのむごたらしい光景を見て恐怖にかられた．	She was horrified by the brutal spectacle.
恐怖映画は嫌いだ．	I hate horror movies.
彼は高所恐怖症だ．	He's afraid of heights./He's acrophobic.

きょうみ (興味)

私は歴史に興味がある．	I'm interested in history.
登山の話をすると彼は興味を示した．	He expressed [showed] interest when we were talking about mountain climbing.
授業がつまらないので勉強に興味を失ってしまった．	The classes were so boring that I lost interest in studying.
新聞の批評を読んだらあの映画への興味がそがれてしまった．	Reading the newspaper review dampened my interest in that movie.
隣近所の人たちはその外国人一家に対して興味津々だった．	The neighbors were all extremely curious about the foreign family.
興味本位で他人の私生活について聞くな．	Don't ask about people's private lives just out of curiosity.

きょうめい (共鳴)

二つの楽器が共鳴した．	The two instruments resonated in harmony.
私は彼の考え方に共鳴してこのグループに加わった．	His way of thinking moved me to join this group.
彼らの運動にはだれも共鳴しなかった．	No one was moved to action by their campaign.

きょうよう (教養)

彼は教養のある人だ．	He's a very cultured person.
その商売人は教養はないが世渡りはうまい．	He may not be culturally refined but that businessman knows how to get ahead.
彼の言葉の端々に教養が顔をのぞかせた．	Here and there, some of the things he said revealed a highly cultivated mind.
父は年をとってからも教養を高める努力を怠らなかった．	Even in his later years my father never ceased trying to improve his mind.
この教養番組はためになるよ．	This educational program has a lot to offer.

きょうりょく (協力)

君の協力を感謝している．	I appreciate your cooperation.
彼は喜んで仕事に協力してくれた．	He was happy to cooperate with the work.

事件の解決に協力してくれ. Help us solve this case.
彼だけがこの計画に非協力的だった. He was the only one who would not cooperate with this plan.
He was the only uncooperative person in this plan.

きょうれつ (強烈)
その映画は強烈な印象を残した. That film made a strong impression on me.
彼のパンチは強烈だった. His punch was devastating.
強烈な光に目がくらんだ. I was dazzled by the intense light.
あの画家は強烈な色彩を用いるので有名だ. That painter is famous for his use of intense colors.

ぎょうれつ (行列)
切符売り場の前に行列ができた. A line formed in front of the ticket window.
仮装行列が通りを練り歩いた. The costume parade wound its way down the avenue.
行列を乱さないでください. Please stay in line [step].[1]

1) 並んでいる列の場合には line, 行進の場合には step を用いる.

きょか (許可)
課長の許可を得てこの企画を中止した. I canceled this project with the section chief's approval.
許可なく部屋を出るな. Don't leave the room without permission.
我々は当局にデモの許可を求めた. We applied for an official permit to hold a demonstration.
屋内での撮影は許可されなかった. We weren't permitted to take photos inside.
営業許可がやっと下りた. I was finally granted a commercial license.

きょくたん (極端)
それはかなり極端な例だ. That's a rather extreme case.
彼は何事も極端に走る人だ. He tends to go to extremes in everything.
愛と憎しみは両極端のものではない. Love and hate do not rule each other out.
Love and hate are not mutually exclusive.
それは極端過ぎるよ. That's †going too far [too extreme].
極端な環境の変化が原因で彼女は体をこわした. She got sick from the radical change in environment.
極端な運動はしないようにと医者に言われた. My doctor told me not to do any strenuous exercise.

きょり (距離)

東京, 大阪間の距離はどのくらいですか?	How far apart are Tokyo and Osaka?
直線距離で500キロある.	It's 500 km as the crow flies.
駅まではちょっと距離がある.	It's quite a way(s) to the station.
家までほんの少しの距離だ.	It isn't far at all to my house.
学校までどのくらい距離がある?	How far is it to your school?
歩いて3分の距離だ.	It's a three-minute walk.
【比喩】あの事件以来, 我々のあいだには距離ができた.	We have grown distant since that incident.
彼は彼女とはまだつきあっているが少し距離をおいている.	He still sees her but is trying to keep a little distance in their relationship.

きらい (嫌い)

彼は勉強が嫌いだ.	He doesn't like to study. He hates studying.
彼女のことが嫌いになった.	I don't like her anymore.
食べず嫌いはいけないよ.	If you've never tasted it, how can you be sure you won't like it?
【傾向】年を取ると保守的になるきらいがある.	People †are apt to [tend to] become conservative as they grow older.
彼は何にでもへ理屈をこねるきらいがある.	He tends to argue about everything just for the sake of argument.

きらう (嫌う)

彼は自分の家の商売を嫌っている.	He dislikes [hates] his family business.
人に嫌われるようなことをするな.	Don't do things that will make people dislike you.
彼女に嫌われたらしい.	She seems to have taken a dislike [disliking] to me.
彼は数学を毛嫌いしている.	He hates math.／He can't stand math.

きらく (気楽)

一人暮らしは気楽だよ.	Living alone is carefree.
彼は親の遺産で気楽に暮らしている.	Since he received an inheritance from his parents, he hasn't had a care in the world.
皆さん, 気楽にしてください.	Please make yourselves †comfortable [at home].
気楽にやれよ.	Take it easy.
気楽なやつだよ.	He's †happy-go-lucky [a free spirit, easygoing, lighthearted].

きり

【区切り】きりのいいところで休憩にしようよ. — Let's take a break after this.
Let me know when you're ready to take a break.

きりがつくところまでテレビゲームをやらせてよ. — Just let me play this (video) game till I get to the good place to stop.

【際限】あの人にしゃべらせるときりがない. — He'll never stop talking once he starts.

そんなことを認めていたらきりがないよ. — If you allow that, there'll be no end to it.

上を見ればきりがない. — There's no end to it. Someone is always going to be better than you.
There's always going to be something that looks better.

【つまらないもの】バイクもピンからきりまである. — There are motorbikes and then there are motorbikes.

【だけ】机が一つあるきりの殺風景な部屋だった. — The room was bare with only one desk.

別荘番のおじいさんはシーズンオフは一人きりで過ごす. — The old caretaker at the summer villa is completely on his own during the off-season.

【～しっぱなし】彼女は北欧へ行ったきりだ. — She went off [She's gone off] to Northern Europe.

息子が3日前に出かけたきり戻ってこない. — My son left home three days ago and hasn't come back since.

ぎりぎり

面接時間にぎりぎりで間に合った. — I just made it in time for the interview.

終了時間ぎりぎりまで試験問題に取り組んだ. — I worked on the exam questions until the very last minute.

定足数ぎりぎりで会議は開かれた. — The meeting was held with barely a quorum.

これが譲歩できるぎりぎりの線です. — This is as far as we can go in our negotiations.

調査委員会の追及は厳しかったが、彼はぎりぎりのところで切り抜けた. — Just as investigating committee was getting close, he slipped away.

きりょく (気力)

病気がよくなるにつれて働く気力もでてきた. — As I recovered from my illness I was feeling energetic enough to work again.

あの生徒は勉強する気力に乏しい. — That student †lacks [doesn't have enough] drive to study.

彼は何をする気力もない.	He doesn't have the energy to do anything.
困難にもくじけない気力が必要だよ.	An unbreakable spirit is necessary in difficult times.
妻を失って以来, 彼は気力が衰えてきた.	He's lost his vitality [drive, get-up-and-go**] ever since his wife passed away.

きる¹ (切る)

ナイフで指を切ってしまった.	I cut my finger with a knife.
魚の大きなかたまりを小さく切ってから猫にやった.	I cut up the large piece of fish before I fed it to my cat.
彼女はカレーに入れる野菜を切った.	She chopped [cut] up vegetables for the curry.
彼らは駐車場を造るため木を切り倒した.	They chopped down the trees to build a parking lot.
つめを切らなくては.	I've got to trim my nails.
船は波を切って進んで行った.	The ship cut through the waves.
洗ったホウレン草をざるにあげて水を切った.	I washed the spinach and drained it in a sieve.
彼は急に言葉を切った.	He abruptly stopped speaking.
借金の返済期限を3日間と切られた.	The final extension for paying back the loan was set at three days.
原価を切って商品を売った.	The merchandise was sold below cost.
貯水池の水量が30万トンを切った.	The water volume in the reservoir has fallen below 300,000 [three hundred thousand] tons.
寝る前に暖房〔テレビ〕を切りなさい.	Turn off the heater [TV] before you go to bed.
彼は突然電話を切った.	He suddenly hung up.
彼が先頭を切ってゴールに入った.	He took the lead and crossed the finish line first.
あの二人は切っても切れない仲だ.	Those two are inseparable.

きる² (着る)

パーティーに何を着ようかな.	What shall I wear to the party?
コートを着てから外へ出なさい.	Put your coat on before you go outside.
息子はまだひとりで服が着られない.	My son can't get dressed by himself yet.
彼は着るものに構わない.	He doesn't pay attention to what he wears.
服を着たまま寝てしまった.	I fell asleep with my clothes on.
この服を着てみたら?	Why don't you try this on?
彼はきちんとした上着を着ていないので, あの高級レストランに入れない.	They won't let him into that exclusive restaurant because he isn't wearing a jacket.

だれかがチャイムを鳴らしたので慌てて服を着た.	Somebody rang the doorbell, so I threw on some clothes.
人々は着飾って劇場に来た.	The people came to the theater all dressed up.
これは私には着こなせない.	This just isn't (for) me.

きれい

【美しい】
桜の花がきれいだ.	The cherry blossoms are pretty [beautiful].
今日は空がきれいだね.	The sky is beautiful today, isn't it?
彼の恋人はきれいな人だよ.	His girlfriend is very pretty.
君の字はきれいだね.	Your handwriting is very neat.

【清潔】
手をきれいに洗いなさい.	Wash your hands clean.
彼の部屋はいつ行ってもきれいだ.	His room is neat and tidy whenever I go there.
部屋をもう少しきれいにしなさい.	Clean up your room a bit more.
机の上をきれいにしなさい.	Please clean off the desk.

【すっかり】
よほど空腹だったのか彼は料理を全部きれいに食べた.	He must have been pretty hungry because he ate his plate clean.
彼女のことはきれいさっぱりあきらめた.	I've put her completely out of my mind.
借金を全部きれいに返した.	I paid off all the loan.

【慣用】
きれいごとを言っている場合じゃない.	This is no time to put up a front.

きれる (切れる)

この包丁はよく切れる.	This knife cuts well.
糸が切れてしまった.	The string broke.
雲が切れて日がさしてきた.	The sun came shining through the clouds.
大雨で川の堤防が切れた.	The banks of the river gave way under the heavy rain.
この電球は切れているよ.	This light bulb is burned out.
契約は月末に切れる.	The contract †runs out [expires] at the end of the month.
時間切れだ.	Time's up.
話し中なのに電話が切れた.	We were cut off in the middle of our phone call.
その商品はあいにく切れています.	Unfortunately we're out of that.

【鋭い・敏腕な】
彼女は(頭が)切れる.	She has a sharp mind.
	She's extremely bright.
課長は切れ者と言われている.	The section chief is said to be sharp.

【感情が抑制できない】
普段おとなしい人がキレると恐い.	When someone who is usually quiet snaps, you better watch out.

きろく (記録)

彼は毎日の気温を記録している.	He's keeping a daily record of the temperature.
その事件は記録にはない.	There's no record of that case.
彼は走り幅跳びの世界記録保持者だ.	He holds the world broad-jump record.
関東地方に記録的な豪雨が降った.	There was a record downpour in the Kanto area.
彼は記録映画を撮影している.	He's making a documentary movie.

きわだつ (際立つ)

彼の演技は際立っていた.	His performance was outstanding.
彼女は際立って美しかった.	She was stunningly [strikingly] beautiful.
彼の論文は皆の中で際立って優れていた.	His thesis was distinctly better than everyone else's.

きわどい (際どい)

際どいところで間に合った.	I made it in the nick of time.
際どいところで交通事故を免れた.	I came within an inch of having a car accident.
際どいところで試合に勝った.	They won the match by a narrow margin.
際どい勝負になった.	It turned into a close game.
彼は際どい話をよくする.	He's always telling off-color stories. / He's always saying suggestive things.

きわめて (極めて)

それは極めて重大な問題だ.	That's an extremely serious problem.
彼は極めて困難な状況にある.	He's in an extremely [exceedingly] difficult situation.
極めて急を要する問題だ.	This is a problem of the utmost urgency.

きんし (禁止)

学校はオートバイ通学を禁止した.	The school †placed a ban on [prohibited] commuting by motorcycle.
図書館の本の無断持ち出しは禁止されている.	Removing books from the library without permission is prohibited [forbidden].
その芝居は上演禁止になった.	That play has been banned.
立ち入り禁止.	Off limits. / Keep out.
駐車禁止.	No parking.

きんじょ (近所)

家の近所に郵便局がある.	There's a post office in the neighborhood.
この近所に駅がありますか?	Is there a station nearby?

近所のスーパーマーケットに行ってきた.	I've just been to the local supermarket.
彼が近所に住んでいるとは知らなかった.	I didn't realize he was living in the area [neighborhood].
彼は近所づきあいがいい.	He gets along well with all his neighbors.
あの犬はうるさくて近所迷惑だ.	That dog is a nuisance to the neighbors [neighborhood].

きんだい (近代)

近代史を学んでいる.	I'm studying modern history.
その辺りは今, 近代的な建物が立ち並んでいる.	There's a row of modern buildings standing there now.
最近工場の設備が近代化された.	The facilities at the factory were modernized recently.
あの国は近代化が遅れている.	That country is lagging behind in modernization.

きんちょう (緊張)

試験となると緊張してしまう.	I get tense whenever I have an exam.
彼は緊張しているみたいだ.	He looks tense.
私たちは全神経を緊張させて事の成り行きを見守った.	Our nerves were on end as we watched over the course of events.
緊張した雰囲気だった.	The atmosphere was charged [tense].
彼の冗談で皆の緊張がほぐれた.	His joke broke the tension.
両国間の緊張を緩和することが必要だ.	The tension between the two countries must be eased.
両者は緊張関係にある.	They have a tense relationship. Their relations are tense.

きんぱく (緊迫)

両国の関係は緊迫している.	Relations between the two countries are strained [tense].
試合は緊迫してきた.	The match grew tense.
政局は緊迫の度を増してきた.	Political tension has increased.
緊迫感あふれる場面だった.	It was a tension-packed scene.

きんべん (勤勉)

彼は勤勉な学生だ.	He's a hard-working [diligent] student.
彼女は勤勉によく働く.	She's †a hard [an industrious, a diligent] worker.
彼の勤勉さは学校でも有名だ.	He's known for his diligence even at school.

く

ぐあい（具合）
【調子】機械の具合はどうですか. How is the machine running?[1)]
エンジンの具合が悪い. The engine isn't running well.[2)]
The engine is in bad shape [condition].
電池を換えたら時計の具合が良くなった. The clock is running fine since I changed the batteries.
今日は体の具合はいかがですか. How do you feel today?
熱があって具合が良くない. I'm not feeling well. I have a fever.
おなかの具合が良くない. I have an upset stomach.
My stomach is upset.
彼女の(病気の)具合はだいぶいい. She's in much better shape now.
She's feeling much better.
【ありさま・やり方】肉の焼け具合はこれくらいがちょうどいい. The meat is done just right.
戸の閉まり具合が悪い. The door doesn't close well [properly].
商売はどんな具合ですか. How's business?
How is your business going?
今朝の電車の込み具合はひどかった. The train was terribly [awfully] crowded this morning.
ここ2,3日天気の具合がはっきりしない. The weather has been unpredictable the past two or three days.
「どんな具合にやればいいの」「こういう具合にです」 "What's a good way to do this? [How should I do this?]" "Like this. [This way.]"
今月は懐具合が寂しい. I'm short of money this month.
【都合】今日は具合が悪いんですが,明日なら時間がとれます. Today isn't good [convenient] for me, but I'll have time tomorrow.
駅を出ると,いい具合にすぐバスが来た. The bus pulled up just as I was coming out of the station.
【体裁】会社に遅刻するのは具合が悪い. Being late for work doesn't go over very well.

---

1)2) 作動している機械またはエンジンについて言う.

くい (悔い)

彼は悔いのない充実した学生生活を送った. — He had a rich and rewarding student life with no regrets.

今日は決勝戦だから, 悔いを残さないよう精一杯やりなさい. — Today is the final match. Give it everything you've got so you don't have any regrets later.

悔い改めるのに遅すぎるということはない. — It's never too late to change your ways.

くいさがる (食い下がる)

彼はその問題で教授に執拗に食い下がった. — He harassed the professor on the question.

野党議員たちは鋭い質問を浴びせて大臣に食い下がった. — The opposition party Diet members besieged the minister with sharp questioning.

そのチームは相手にリードされても粘り強く食い下がった. — They kept fighting hard even after the other team had taken the lead away from them.

くう (食う)

【食べる】そばでも食うか. — How about some noodles or something?

そんなにがつがつ食うなよ. — Don't gobble down your food (like that).

【暮らす】食うために働かなければならない. — We have to work to eat.

私の給料だけでは食っていけない. — We can't get by on my salary alone.

家族4人どうにかこうにか食っていける. — Our family of four somehow manages to make ends meet.

彼は食うに困って大切な家宝を売ってしまった. — He was †so hard up [in such desperate financial straits] that he sold the family heirlooms.

アパートの賃貸料が毎月入るので食うに困らない. — My monthly income from apartment rents gives me enough money to live on.

彼は食うや食わずの生活だ. — He barely †gets by [makes a living].

【虫が食う】虫の食った小学校の教科書を物置で見つけた. — I found a worm-eaten elementary school textbook in the storage room.

セーターが虫に食われた. — My sweater is moth-eaten.

鼻の頭を蚊に食われた. — I got bitten on the tip of my nose by a mosquito.

【費やす】大きな車はガソリンを食って不経済だ. — Big cars are gas-guzzlers; they're uneconomical.

病院で待たされて随分時間を食ってしまった. — I lost a lot of time waiting my turn at the hospital.

【やっつける】我が校のチームは1 — Our school team beat the leading con-

回戦で優勝候補を食った.	tender (for the championship) in the first round.
この世界は食うか食われるかの競争だ.	It's a dog-eat-dog world.
【領分を侵す】大きなスーパーマーケットが進出して、この辺の小さな店は客を食われている.	Since the big supermarket moved into the neighborhood, the local retailers have lost a lot of business [customers].
その新人女優は主役を食っている.	The new actress is upstaging the lead performer.
【だまされる】今度はその手は食わないよ.	You won't fool me (with that trick) this time.
エープリル・フールに彼に一杯食わされた.	He put one over on me on April Fools' Day.
【挑む】息子は父親に食ってかかった.	He defied his father.
【慣用】父の大切にしていた茶碗を割って大目玉を食った.	I got hell** from my father after I broke his precious bowl.
殺人犯は何食わぬ顔をして葬儀に参列していたそうだ.	I heard that the murderer himself attended the funeral as if nothing had happened.
彼はいつも人を食ったことを言う.	He always has something cheeky to say.

くうき (空気)

田舎の空気はおいしい.	The air in the country †smells good [is fresh and clean].
たばこの煙で部屋の空気が汚れている.	The room is filled with tobacco [cigarette] smoke.
窓を開けて空気を入れ換えよう.	Let's open the window and let in some fresh air.
自転車のタイヤに空気を入れなければならない.	I have to put some air in my bicycle tires.
【雰囲気】彼が入社して職場の空気が一変した.	The atmosphere in the office has completely changed since he joined the firm.
ボールの判定を巡って、審判と投手のあいだに険悪な空気が流れた.	The atmosphere heated up between the pitcher and the umpire because of his call on the pitch.

ぐうぜん (偶然)

道で昔の友達と偶然会ったよ.	I †happened to run [ran] into an old friend on the street.
コピー用紙を探していたら、偶然祖母からの古い手紙を見つけた.	When I was looking for some printing paper, I ran [came] across an old letter from my grandmother.
私は偶然その事故現場に居合わせ	I just happened to be at the scene of the

二人は偶然同じ車を買った.	They both bought the same model of car by coincidence.
ここで会うなんて偶然ね.	What a coincidence meeting you here!
同じ電車に乗り合わせるとはほんとに偶然だった.	It certainly was a coincidence that we were both on the same train.
偶然の一致ですね. 私はあなたと同じ誕生日です.	What a coincidence! You and I have the same birthday.
試合に勝ったのは偶然だ.	We won the game by sheer luck.

くぎる (区・句切る)

彼はくいで土地を区切って, 菜園として貸し出した.	He staked off his property into lots to rent out as vegetable gardens.
先生は時間を区切って父母と個人面談をした.	The teacher divided up the time and met individually with the parents.
この文章を三つの段落に区切りなさい.	Divide this into three paragraphs.
長い文は, 意味が通るように句切って読みなさい.	Take pauses as you read the long parts to make the meaning clear.

くぐる (潜る)

【下を通る】このトンネルをくぐると神奈川県に入る.	You'll be in Kanagawa Prefecture after you go through this tunnel.
どこかの猫が垣根をくぐって庭に入ってきた.	Some cat got into the yard by crawling under the fence.
【すり抜ける】彼は長年, 法の網をくぐって詐欺まがいの商売をやってきた.	He has, for many years, been engaged in deceptive business practices that †border on [are on the fringes of] illegality.
税関と入国管理の厳しい監視の目をくぐって, 麻薬を日本に持ち込もうとする旅行者が少なくない.	More than a few travelers are managing to bring narcotics into Japan, passing undetected through strict customs and immigrations inspections.
すりは人目をかいくぐって逃げてしまった.	The pickpocket got away unnoticed.

くさい (臭い)

【におう】何か臭くないですか.	Don't you smell something?
この肉は臭いから食べるのはよせ.	Don't eat this meat. It smells bad [spoiled].
足が蒸れて臭い.	My feet smell sweaty [bad].
息(口)が臭いよ.	You have bad [foul] breath.
酒臭いな. どこで飲んだんだ?	You smell of alcohol. Where were you drinking?

この部屋はたばこ臭い.	This room smells of [like] tobacco [cigarette] smoke.
ガス臭いよ. 火をつけるな.	I smell gas. Don't light anything.
【怪しい】この事件では彼が最も臭い.	He's the leading suspect in this case.
【感じられる】その話はインチキ臭い.	That story sounds fishy.
一日中座ってテレビを見てるなんて年寄り臭い.	You're just like an old man [woman], sitting around watching TV all day.
【慣用】彼は5年も臭い飯を食ってきた.	He's been locked up in jail for five years.
臭いものにふたをするような学校のやり方に批判の声が上がっている.	Voices of criticism are being raised against the school for trying to cover up what happened.

くさる (腐る)

肉を冷蔵庫に入れないと腐りますよ.	If you don't put the meat in the refrigerator, it will spoil.
夏は食物が腐りやすい.	Food spoils quickly in the summer.
この肉は腐っている.	This meat is spoiled.
この牛乳は腐っている.	This milk is sour.
猫は腐った魚を食べた.	The cat ate some rotten fish.
この卵は腐りかけている.	These eggs are beginning to go bad.
腐りかけたまくら木が取り換えられた.	The rotten railroad ties have been replaced.
【堕落した】あの男はしんまで腐ったやつだ.	That man is rotten to the core.
彼は根性が腐っている.	He's corrupt at heart.
【慣用】彼は受験に失敗してくさっている.	He's in the dumps over having failed the entrance examination.
せっけんなら家に腐るほどある.	We have so much soap we hardly know what to do with all of it.
腐っても鯛.	It may not be what it once was, but it is still first-class.

くしん (苦心)

司会者はクラスの意見をまとめるのに苦心した.	The moderator took great pains to get a consensus from the class.
苦心の末, やっと卒業論文を書き上げた.	It was a lot of hard work, but I finally got my graduation thesis written.
彼のこれまでの苦心は結局むだに終わった.	All his toil up until now has been in vain.
彼は金策に苦心さんたんしたよう	He seems to have struggled hard to raise

だ.	money.
彼は当時の苦心談を語った.	He told of his sufferings at that time.

くず (屑)

部屋に紙くずを散らかすな.	Don't scatter wastepaper around the room.
彼女は毎朝パンくずをスズメにやる.	She gives [feeds] bread crumbs to the sparrows every morning.
木くずを集めて燃やした.	I gathered up the wood chips and burned them.
日本はくず鉄を輸入している.	Japan imports scrap iron.
空缶はくず入れに入れなさい.	Put (empty) cans in the †trash bin [waste basket].
あいつらは人間のくずだ.	They're the dregs of humanity.
彼らは社会のくずだ.	They're society's castoffs.

ぐずぐず

ぐずぐずしていたので, 彼らに先を越されていい席を取られてしまった.	I wasn't quick enough and they got ahead of me and took the good seats.
ぐずぐずしないで早く出かけないと学校に間に合わないよ.	If you don't get on the stick you'll be late for school.
ぐずぐずするな. 電車の出発まであまり時間がない.	Get a move on. There's no time to lose before the train leaves.
【不平を言う】彼は私の忠告が気に入らなくてぐずぐず言っている.	He's grumbling about the advice I gave him.
ぐずぐず言ってないでお使いに行ってきなさい.	Stop grumbling and go do the errand.

くすぐったい

犬が手のひらをなめるのでくすぐったい.	My palm tickles from my dog licking it.
【照れ臭い】そんなに褒められると何だかくすぐったい.	It's almost embarrassing to get so much praise.
下手な英語を褒められて, くすぐったかった.	I felt silly being told how good my awful English was.

くずす (崩す)

彼は積木〔砂山〕を弟に崩された.	His †toy blocks [sand castle] got knocked over by his little brother.
宅地にするために裏の山を崩しています.	The hill out back is being leveled for a new residential area.
人々は列を崩さないで行儀よく開場を待っている.	The people kept the line neat and orderly as they waited politely for the doors to

	open.
机に向かうときは姿勢を崩さないようにしなさい.	Sit up straight when you're at your desk.
どうぞひざを崩して，楽にしてください.	Stretch your legs out and make yourself comfortable.
この千円札を100円玉にくずしてください.	Please change this 1,000-yen bill for 100-yen coins.
彼女の字は崩してあるので読みにくい.	Her handwriting runs together so much that it's hard to read.

くすり (薬)

この薬を一日3回飲みなさい.	Take this medicine three times a day.
風邪にはこの薬が良く効く.	This medicine is really effective against colds.
薬が効いたと見えて頭痛が治まってきた.	The medicine apparently works; my headache is much better.
この薬を患部に塗りなさい.	Apply this medicine to the affected area.
【慣用】馬鹿につける薬はない.	There's no cure for a fool.
今度の失敗は彼にはいい薬になったようだ.	This failure seems to have been a good lesson [medicine] for him.
若いときに苦労するのは身の薬です.	It's good for you to have a few hardships when you're young.
彼は毒にも薬にもならない男だ.	He's rather blah**—neither a help nor a hindrance.

くずれる (崩れる)

積み上げてあった材木の山が崩れた.	The big pile [stack] of logs came tumbling down.
大雨で山が崩れた.	The heavy rain caused a landslide.
地震で壁が崩れ落ちた.	The earthquake reduced the wall to rubble.
だれかに踏まれて帽子の形が崩れてしまった.	Someone stepped on my hat and crushed it (out of shape).
選手たちは隊列が崩れないように行進した.	The athletes marched along, taking care not to fall out of step.
長時間腰掛けていると，どうしても姿勢が崩れてしまう.	When you sit for a long time, you can't help slouching after a while.
20ドル札がくずれますか.	Can you change †a twenty [a twenty-dollar bill]?
天気予報では，週末は天気が崩れるそうだ.	The weather forecast said the weather will turn bad over the weekend.

くせ (癖)

彼女は爪をかむ癖がある.	She bites her nails out of habit.
寝る前の読書が癖になった.	I've gotten into the habit of reading before I go to sleep.
食事前に手を洗う癖をつけなさい.	Get into the habit of washing your hands before meals.
彼は夜更かしの癖が抜けない.	He can't get out of the habit of staying up till all hours of the night.
彼女の忘れ物をする癖を先生が直してくれた.	Her teacher cured [broke] her of her habit of forgetting to bring things.
朝寝坊の癖を直すように努力しなさい.	Try to break yourself of the habit of †oversleeping [sleeping in].
彼はちょっと癖のある人だ.	He has certain idiosyncrasies.
彼は癖のある話し方をする.	He has a peculiar way of speaking.
彼女の文章は癖がある.	She has a very individualistic [peculiar] writing style.
彼女の文章は癖がない.	She has simple writing.
私の髪は癖がある.	My hair is curly.
賞状を丸めたら，癖がついて元に戻らなくなった.	After I rolled up the certificate, it wouldn't go back to its original condition.

ぐたい (具体)

こういう具体的な例がある.	Here's a specific example.
これまでのところ，新しい企画について具体的には何も決まっていない.	So far, nothing definite has been decided about the new plan.
もっと具体的に理由を説明してください.	Please explain the reasons in more concrete terms.
具体的な数字で示しましょう.	Let's express it in specific numbers.
具体的な形で感謝の気持ちを示しなさい.	Show your appreciation in a tangible way.
具体案〔具体例〕を一つあげます.	I'll give you a concrete proposal [example].
彼の話はいつも具体性を欠く.	He always speaks in abstract terms.
計画が具体化するまで長い時間を要した.	A long time was required before the plan took concrete shape.
計画を具体化する時が来た.	The time has come to execute the plan.

くだく (砕く)

彼女は氷を細かく砕いてコップに入れた.	She crushed the ice up and put it in a glass.
彼は難しい言葉の意味を砕いて説	He explained the meaning of the difficult

明した。 / words in simpler terms.

くだける（砕ける）

落としたコップが粉々に砕けた．	The glass I dropped shattered into tiny fragments.
大きな波が岩に当たって砕け散った．	A big wave dashed against the rocks.
【親しみ易い】酒が進むにつれて，だんだんみんなの話がくだけてきた．	The more everyone drank, the more informal their conversation became.
あの先生はくだけた人で生徒に人気がある．	That teacher is popular with his students because he's very relaxed and informal.

くだらない

この小説はくだらない．	This novel is dumb [trivial, worthless].
くだらないテレビ番組が多い．	There are a lot of silly TV programs.
くだらないことを言うな．	Don't talk nonsense.

くだる（下る）

彼らは山を下って行った．	They went down the mountain.
この坂を下って行くと花屋がある．	There's a flower shop at the bottom of this hill.
被告に対し懲役8年の刑が下った．	The defendant was sentenced to eight years in jail.
明治から下って，大正，昭和と日本の西洋化は進んだ．	Westernization of Japan started in the Meiji era and continued through Taisho and Showa.
今度の台風による死者は10名を下らない．	At least 10 persons died in the recent typhoon.

くち（口）

口を大きく開けて歌いなさい．	Sing with your mouths wide open.
お使いを頼むと息子は口を尖らせた．	When I asked my son to do an errand, he pouted.
少年は口を一文字に結んで何も答えようとしなかった．	The young boy squeezed his lips tight and refused to answer.
父はいつも口をへの字に結んでいる．	My father's lips are always drawn in a frown.
彼女は子ども部屋のあまりの散らかりように，開いた口がふさがらなかった．	She was appalled by the mess her child's room was in.
お口に合うといいんですが．	I hope †it tastes good [you'll like it].
このワインは口当たりがいい．	This is a very palatable wine.

【入口】瓶の口が小さくてこれは入らない.	The mouth of this bottle is too small for this to fit inside.
明日の朝10時に駅の北口で会いましょう.	Let's meet at ten tomorrow morning at the north entrance of the station.
この山の登山口は2ヵ所ある.	There are two approaches from which you can climb this mountain.
彼とはホームの階段の上り口〔下り口〕で1時に待ち合わせている.	I'm supposed to meet him at one at the bottom [top] of the platform stairs.
【勤め口】いい就職口を知りませんか.	Do you know about any good jobs that are available?
【しゃべること】彼は口がうまいから注意しろ.	He's †a fast talker [a slick** talker], so watch out.
彼女は口が堅い.	She can keep a secret.
	She knows how to hold her tongue.
彼は口の軽いやつだ.	He can't keep a secret.
	He doesn't know how to hold his tongue.
	He has a loose tongue.
あの人は口の重い人だ.	He's a man of few words.
彼は口は悪いが根は優しい人だ.	He always says a lot of offensive things, but he's basically a gentle person.
まったく口の減らないやつだ.	He has a comeback for everything.
つい口が滑って君と彼女のことを彼に話してしまった.	I inadvertently told him about you and her.
つい口が滑って秘密を漏らしてしまった.	I let slip the secret.
借金をするなと口が酸っぱくなるほど彼に言った.	I told him †over and over again [a thousand times] not to borrow money.
	I told him till I was blue in the face that he shouldn't borrow money.
彼女は嫌なことがあっても決して口に出さない.	Even if something unpleasant happens to her, she doesn't talk about it.
口は災いの元.	Open your mouth too often and you're likely to put your foot in it.
私が社長に口を利いてあげよう.	I'll have a word with the boss.
あの映画を見た人は口を揃えて「つまらなかった」と言います.	Everyone who saw that movie is unanimous in calling it a bore.
彼はよくもあれだけのお世辞が口をついて出てくるものだ.	It's amazing how thick he lays on the flattery.
自分の生い立ちのことになるといつも彼女は口をつぐんでしまう.	Whenever someone asks her about her upbringing she clams up.
医者は, 彼に後遺症が残るかどうかについては口を濁した.	The doctor wouldn't come out and tell him whether or not there would be any

	aftereffects.
彼女は他人の話に口を挟みたがる.	She's always trying to †butt in on [intrude on] other people's conversations.
犯人は警察の厳しい追及にやっと口を割った.	The suspect finally began to confess under harsh police interrogation.
【口裏】彼らは口裏を合わせて事実を隠そうとした.	They made sure their stories were consistent with each other and tried to hide the truth.
【口うるさい】彼は行儀には口うるさい.	He's particular about people's manners.
母は私に対して口うるさく文句を言う.	Mother's always carping at me with complaints.
【口数】今日は口数が少ないがどうかしたのか.	You sure don't have much to say today. What's wrong?
【口汚い】彼女は私を口汚くののしった.	She hurled abuse at me.
【口癖】彼女は「悪くないわね」というのが口癖だ.	She's always [She has a habit of] saying, "Not so bad."
【口答え】私に口答えする気か.	Are you trying to talk back to me?
【口ごもる】突然先生に質問されて口ごもってしまった.	I faltered [hesitated] when the teacher suddenly asked me a question.
【口先】彼は口先だけの男だ.	He's all talk.
彼女の約束は口先だけだ.	Her promises are empty.
名前が口先まで出かかっているのに出てこない.	The name is on the tip of my tongue.
口先だけのお世辞はよせ.	Enough of your empty flattery!
彼の毒舌は口先だけだから気にするな.	Don't let his sharp tongue get to you. He doesn't mean it. [It's just talk].
【口添え】先生の口添えで就職できた.	My teacher put in a good word for me and I got the job.
【口出し】横から余計な口出しをするな.	Don't interrupt us with unasked-for remarks.
彼女は何事につけ口出ししないと気が済まないたちだ.	She's just never satisfied until she gets in her two cents worth.
【口止め】そのことは口止めされているから言えないんだ.	I'm not allowed [permitted] to talk about this matter.
口止め料として彼女から1万円渡された.	She paid me 10,000 [ten thousand] yen to keep my mouth shut.

くちびる (唇)

彼のくちびるは厚い.	He's thick-lipped./He has thick lips.
彼女はくちびるをかんで涙をこらえた.	Biting her lips, she held back her tears.

くつう (苦痛)

手術後の激しい苦痛に耐えた. — I was able to endure the intense pain after the operation.

注射で少し苦痛が和らいだ. — The injection relieved the intense pain a little.

階段を上るのが苦痛だというお年寄りもいる. — It is painful for some elderly people to climb stairs.

人前で話をするのは苦痛を感じる. — It is painful for me to speak in front of people.

くつじょく (屈辱)

今は屈辱に耐えなければならない. — Now I have to live with the humiliation.

親戚から施しを受けるという屈辱的な生活が6年続いた. — The humiliation of living off my relatives went on for six years.

大勢の前で謝らされ, 屈辱を感じた. — I felt humiliated at being forced to apologize in front of the crowd.

くつろぐ

どうぞおくつろぎください. — Please make yourself at home.

やはり我が家はくつろぐ. — I can relax at home.

同窓会は先生を囲み, くつろいだ雰囲気で話し合いができた. — At the class reunion everyone gathered about the teacher and talked in a very relaxed atmosphere.

くどい

もう分かった. くどいよ. — All right already! Stop harping on it.

彼にはいくらくどく説明してもしすぎではない. — You can't be too redundant in explaining things to him.

くどいようだが, 決してこのドアは開けるな. — I may sound like I'm repeating myself, but this door is *not* to be opened.

老人はくどくどと昔話をした. — The old man went on and on with his reminiscing.

この色はちょっとくどい. — This color is a little gaudy.

中華料理はくどいのであまり好きではない. — Chinese cooking is too heavy for me.

くばる (配る)

彼は通行人一人一人にパンフレットを配った. — He †distributed [handed out] pamphlets to everyone that passed by.

一人に4個ずつ配ると1個余る. — If we †give out [distribute] four per person, there'll be one left over.

私は毎朝, 新聞を配っています. — I deliver newspapers every morning.

彼女は皆にスープを配った. — She served (up) soup to everybody.

だれか試験用紙を配ってほしいのだが.	I'd like someone to pass these tests out for me.
彼がトランプの札を配った.	He dealt (out) the cards.

くび（首）

朝起きると首が痛かった.	I had a stiff neck when I got up this morning.
もっとよく見ようと彼は首を伸ばした.	He craned his neck to get a better view.
瓶の首のところを持ってください.	Hold the bottle by the neck.
その馬は首の差で負けた.	That horse lost the race by a head.
【頭】列車の窓から首を出さないように.	Don't put [stick] your head out of the train window.
少年はうまく首をすくめてボールをよけた.	The boy ducked (his head) just in time to avoid getting hit by the ball.
参列者は首を垂れて1分間の黙とうをした.	The people [mourners] bowed their heads in silence for a (full) minute.
【慣用】私の言葉に彼は首をかしげた.	He cocked his head in skepticism at what I said.
みんな彼の発言に首をひねった.	Everyone seemed skeptical about his statement.
彼女はその話に首を縦に振るだろうか.	I wonder if she'll give her nod [assent] to that plan (or not).
私たちの要求に対して彼は首を横に振った.	He shook his head at our request.
彼女は首を長くして息子の手紙を待っている.	She's been waiting eagerly for a letter from her son.
彼は何にでも首を突っ込む.	He sticks his nose into everything.
借金で首が回らない.	I'm up to my neck in debt.
君は首だ.	You're fired.
私は首になった.	I got fired. ／ I got the sack.**

くふう（工夫）

サーブのやり方をもうちょっと工夫してごらん.	Work on your serve a little bit more.
この部分をもう少し工夫すればいい絵になる.	If you work on this part a little more, you'll have a good painting.
何事も工夫しなくてはいい結果は出せない.	No matter what you want to do, you have to be resourceful if you want it to turn out well.
英単語を覚える何かうまい工夫はないですか.	Can you come up with any good ideas for learning English vocabulary?
この自動車は乗り心地を良くする	This car incorporates a variety of features

ためにいろいろな工夫が凝らしてある. | designed to provide maximum riding comfort.

くべつ（区別）

公私の区別をはっきりさせろ. | Make a clear distinction between public and private.
燃え方で木綿と合成繊維は区別できます. | Cotton and synthetic fibers can be distinguished by how they burn.
ヒラメとカレイの区別のしかたは分かりますか. | Do you know how to †tell a turbot from a halibut [distinguish between a turbot and a halibut]?
あの双子はほとんど区別できないほどよく似ている. | Those twins look so much alike that it's nearly impossible to tell them apart.
老若男女の区別なくだれでもこの会に入会できる. | Anyone, irrespective of age or sex, can join this club.

くみ（組）

【クラス】本校は1学年が3組に分かれている. | Each grade in this school is divided into three classes.
【集まり】4人ずつ組みになりなさい. | Form groups of four.
彼女と組みになってテニスの試合に出た. | I paired off with her to play in the tennis match.
【一揃い】このカップは5個で一組になっている. | These cups come five to [in] a set.
彼にボールペンとシャープペンシルを組みにして贈った. | I gave him a pen and pencil set.

くみたてる（組み立てる）

彼はプラモデルを組み立てている. | He †puts together [builds] plastic models.
折り畳み式いすを組み立てた. | I set up the folding chairs.
盆踊りのやぐらが組み立てられている. | The scaffolding for the *Bon* festival is being set up.
あの工場では自動車を組み立てている. | That plant assembles automobiles.
テレビを組み立てるのが私の仕事だ. | My job is assembling televisions.

くむ¹（汲・酌む）

このコップに水を汲んできなさい. | Fill this glass with water (and bring it here).
池の水をバケツに汲んだ. | I scooped pond water into the bucket.
私たちは酒をくみ交わした. | We had a drink together.

【推し測る】お父さんの気持ちもくんであげなさい.	Try to consider your father's feelings.
警官は彼の事情をくんで駐車違反を見逃してやった.	The police officer took the man's situation into consideration and decided to ignore the parking violation.

くむ² (組む)

彼と組んで仕事をしている.	He and I are working as a team.
今度のテニスの試合では彼女と組む.	I'm pairing off with her in the next tennis match.
私たちは4人で組んで調査している.	We formed a group of four to conduct the survey.
我々が組めば怖いものなしだ.	If we join forces, we'll have nothing to fear.
あの会社と組んで商売をしている.	We do business in conjunction with that company.
彼らは腕を組んで歩いた.	They walked arm in arm.
彼は腕を組んで考えた.	He thought it over with his arms folded.
彼女は足を組んで座っている.	She's sitting with her legs crossed.

くもり (曇り)

昨日は曇りだった.	It was cloudy yesterday.
曇りの日はうっとうしい.	Cloudy days make me feel gloomy.
空は薄曇りだ.	The sky is slightly overcast.
彼は眼鏡の曇りを拭き取った.	He wiped the fog from his glasses.
湯気で鏡に曇りができた.	The steam fogged up the mirror.
彼の生涯には一点の曇りもなかった.	There wasn't a (single) (dark) cloud in his life.

くもる (曇る)

空が曇っている.	The sky is cloudy.
空が曇ってきた.	The sky has gotten cloudy.
朝のうちは曇るだろう.	It will be cloudy in the morning.
湯気で眼鏡が曇った.	The steam fogged up my glasses.
彼女の目は涙で曇った.	Her eyes clouded with tears.
声を曇らせて彼女は母親の病気について話した.	She choked back tears as she told me about her mother's illness.
事故の知らせに彼の顔は一瞬曇った.	His face clouded over momentarily when he was notified of the accident.
その話を聞いて彼女は表情を曇らせた.	Her expression turned gloomy when she heard that story.

くやしい (悔しい)

彼女に負けたのは本当に悔しかった.	Getting beaten by her was truly frustrating [mortifying].
彼は競馬で損をして悔しがった.	He was fit to be tied** over his losses at the track.
思わぬ失敗をして悔しくてたまらない.	I could kick myself for making such a stupid mistake.
悔しいことに彼だけが女の子にもてる.	It's really maddening how he's the only one that's popular with the girls.
悔しいことに我がチームは逆転負けした.	How frustrating! Our team blew the lead and lost the game.
選手たちは試合に負けて悔し涙を流した.	The frustration of losing brought tears to the players' eyes.
彼は悔し紛れに当たり散らした.	He took it out on them purely out of spite.

くやむ (悔やむ)

今になって悔やんでももう遅い.	It's too late for regret now.
彼は試験に落ちて,不勉強だったことを悔やんだ.	After he failed the test, he regretted not having studied more.
彼は親友の死を悔やんだ.	He grieved over the death of his friend.
お悔やみ申しあげます.	Please accept my condolences.

くよくよ

くよくよするな.	Take it easy./Don't worry.
何をくよくよしているんだ?	What's got you so upset?
くよくよしても始まらないよ.	Brooding won't get you anywhere.
今さら済んだことをくよくよするな.	Don't dwell on the past.

くらい (暗い)

森の中は昼間も暗い.	It's dark in the woods even during the day.
外は暗くなってきた.	It's getting dark outside.
暗くならないうちに帰ってくるのよ.	You have to get home before it gets dark.
彼は朝まだ暗いうちに起きて,釣りに出かけた.	He got up †while it was still dark [before daybreak] to go fishing.
この電灯は暗いから換えましょう.	This light is too dim. Let's change it.
部屋を暗くしてスライドを見た.	We †turned off [dimmed] the lights and looked at the slides.
電池が弱くなったので懐中電灯の光が暗くなった.	The batteries are running low and the flashlight's getting dim.
陰になって暗いからそこをどいて	Stand out of the light. You're casting a

よ.	shadow.
その画家は専ら暗い色を用いる.	That painter uses mainly dark colors.
【陰気】彼は性格が暗い.	He has a very somber personality.
彼女は夫に死なれて暗い顔をしている.	Ever since her husband's death, she's been gloomy.
このような暗い音楽は好きではない.	I don't like gloomy music like this.
彼には暗い過去がある.	He has a dark past.
会社が倒産し,私の前途は暗い.	With the company going under, my prospects for the future are dim.
【よく知らない】彼女は法律に暗い.	She's not very well-versed in (the) law.
この辺の地理には暗い.	I'm not familiar with this area.

～くらい

私たちは30分くらい話し合った.	We talked for about 30 minutes.
ひげぐらいはそって出かけなさい.	At least shave before you go out.
それくらいはだれにでもできる.	Anyone could do something †like that [that simple].
彼ぐらい暗算の速くできる人はめったにいない.	There are few people who are as quick at mental calculations as he is.
彼の絵は先生も驚くくらいうまかった.	His painting was good enough to amaze even his teacher.

くらし (暮らし)

豊かな暮らしがしたい.	I want the good life.
彼は最近暮らし向きがいい.	He's getting on quite well of late.
分不相応な暮らしはよせ.	Stop living beyond your means.
こんなに一生懸命働いているのに暮らしは少しも良くならない.	No matter how hard I work, life just doesn't get any easier [better].
今,職がなくて暮らしに困っている.	I'm a bit hard up now that I'm out of work.
何で暮らしを立てているの？	How do you support yourself?
私は文筆業で暮らしを立てている.	I make my living as a writer.
彼は売れない絵を描きながら細々と暮らしを立てている.	He ekes out an existence painting pictures that scarcely sell.

くらす (暮らす)

彼女は母親と暮らしている.	She lives with her mother.
いかがお暮らしですか.	How are you getting along?
家族4人で楽しく暮らしています.	Our family of four has a good time.
遊んで暮らしたいものだ.	I wish I could live a life of leisure.
こんな安月給では暮らしていけない.	We can't †get by [live] on such a low salary.

安い給料ですが、どうにか暮らしています．	My salary is low, but I manage. We manage to scrape by even on my meager wages.

くらべる（比べる）

この二つをよく比べてみなさい．	Carefully compare these two.
母は事あるごとに私を姉と比べる．	My mother is forever measuring me up against my sister.
彼と力比べをした．	I had a test of strength with him.
彼女とどちらが速く泳げるか比べてみた．	She and I had a race to see which of us could swim faster.
今年の梅雨は去年に比べ雨が少ない．	There hasn't been much rain this rainy season compared with last year's.
中国に比べると日本は小さな国だ．	Japan is a small country compared to China.
彼と私ではゴルフの腕は比べものにならない．	There is no comparison between his golf game and mine.
生の音楽は録音とは比べものにならない．	A recording cannot be compared to a live concert.

くりかえす（繰り返す）

もう一度繰り返して言ってください．	Please repeat what you said.
同じ失敗を二度と繰り返すな．	Don't repeat the same mistake.
この文を2回繰り返して読みなさい．	Read this sentence twice (in a row).
何度も繰り返し芝居の練習をした．	We rehearsed the play repeatedly.
あの火山は噴火を繰り返している．	That volcano has been erupting repeatedly.
その問題は繰り返し起こるだろう．	I'm afraid it's a recurrent problem.
歴史は繰り返す．	History repeats itself.

クリック

カーソルをファイル名〔アイコン〕に合わせてクリックしなさい．	Put the cursor on †the name of the file 〔the icon〕 and click.
ソフトを動かすときは、そのアイコンをダブルクリックする．	When you want to open up the software, double-click on the icon.

くる（来る）

彼がやって来たよ．	Here he comes [is].
やあ、また来たよ．	Here I am again!
さあ、電車が来た．	Here comes the train.
バスがなかなか来ない．	The bus is a long time coming.

うちへ来ないか.	Won't you come to my place?
もう二度とここへ来るな.	Don't ever come here again.
何の用でここへ来たの?	What brought you here?
いつでもここへ来なさい.	Drop in (here) anytime.
昨夜,友人たちが思いがけず私の家にやって来た.	Some friends came over unexpectedly last night.
この町へ来てからどのくらいですか.	How long have you been in this town?
さあ,かかって来い!	OK! Come on and try me!
ついて来い.	Come along. ／Follow me.
春が来た.	It's spring. ／Spring has come.
サーカスが町にやって来た.	The circus has come to town.
先日彼から手紙が来た.	I had a letter from him the other day.
とうとうテスト結果の発表の日が来た.	The day for the announcement of the test results has finally arrived.
多くの文化が中国から日本に来た.	Much of Japan's culture came from China.
【原因】彼女の病気は過労から来ている.	Her illness stems [comes] from overwork.
胃の痛みは精神的なものから来ることが多い.	Many stomach disorders †stem from [are caused by] nervousness.
【次第になる】雨が激しくなってきた.	It has begun to rain violently.
	The rain has begun to come down violently.
やっと仕事にも慣れてきました.	I'm finally beginning to get used to my job.
都心に近づくにつれて,電車が込んできた.	The train got more and more crowded as it approached the center of town.

くるう (狂う)

【狂気】彼は少し気が狂っているに違いない.	There's no doubt about it; he's gone a bit mad.
夫の死で彼女は悲しさのあまり気が狂った.	She went mad with grief when her husband died.
彼は事故の知らせを聞いて,狂ったように家を飛び出した.	He rushed out of the house like a madman when he heard about the accident.
彼女は突然狂ったように泣き出した〔笑い出した〕.	She †burst into tears 〔burst out laughing〕 as if she had suddenly gone mad.
彼は怒り狂った.	He flew into a rage.
東海地方では台風が荒れ狂い,大きな被害が出た.	A typhoon raged through [across] the Tokai district, causing a great deal of damage [havoc].
彼はジャズに狂っている.	He's crazy about jazz.

【正しい状態でない】この時計は狂っている.	This clock is off.
私の時計はよく狂う.	My watch isn't keeping (the right) time.
雨で旅行の計画が狂った.	The rain †upset [threw off] our travel plans.
大雪のため列車のダイヤが狂っている.	The heavy snow has thrown the trains off schedule.
人のラケットだと調子が狂う.	Using someone else's racket throws my game off.
銃の狙いが狂って鳥に逃げられてしまった.	The bird got away because it was not in the sights of the rifle.
この書類はページの順序が狂っている.	The pages in this document are †mixed up [out of order].
戸が狂ってなかなか開かない.	The door is warped and just won't open.

くるしい (苦しい)

【肉体的に】食べ過ぎて胸が苦しい.	I got heartburn from overeating.
階段を駆け上がって来たので息が苦しい.	I'm short [out] of breath from running up the stairs.
彼女はベッドで苦しそうに息をしていた.	She lay in bed breathing with difficulty.
苦しい! 押さないでくれ.	You're crushing me! Stop pushing.
【心理的に】離婚当初は彼も苦しそうだった.	He seemed to take the divorce pretty hard in the beginning.
彼は無実の罪を着せられ, 苦しい思いをしてきた.	He's been through a lot since he was framed for a crime he had nothing to do with.
彼は上司と部下のあいだに挟まれて苦しい立場にある.	He's in an awkward position, caught between his superiors and subordinates.
ずる休みが母親に知れて苦しい言いわけをした.	I made a lame excuse when my mother found out that I had played hooky.
苦しいときの神頼みでお守りを買いました.	I bought an amulet to †help me during hard times [get me through my difficulties].
【経済的に】私の収入だけでは家族5人の生活は苦しい.	It's rough for the five of us (to live) on just my salary.
家計が苦しくなってきた.	The family budget has gotten tight.
給料日前は経済的にいちばん苦しい.	The last few days before payday are the roughest financially.

くるしむ (苦しむ)

| 彼は高熱で三日間苦しんだ. | He suffered from a high fever for three days. |

犯人は罪悪感に苦しみ，自首してきた．	Tormented by a guilty conscience, the culprit turned himself in.
この町の住民は水不足に苦しんでいる．	The people in this town are suffering a water shortage.
人々は悪政に苦しんだ．	The people suffered due to misgovernment.
若い頃は借金に苦しんだ．	I had a rough time with debts when I was young.
会社が倒産して彼は生活に苦しんでいる．	He's had a hard life since the company went bankrupt.
彼のような人がどうして万引きなどしたのか理解に苦しむ．	I find it hard to understand why a person like him would stoop to shoplifting.

くれる¹（呉れる）

叔父さんが海外旅行の土産に香水をくれた．	My uncle brought me back a bottle of perfume from his trip abroad.
昨日，彼が出張先から電話をくれた．	He gave me a call yesterday from where he had gone on business.
その本を私にくれない？	Could I have that book, please?
この時計は祖父が父に残してくれたものですが，父はいつか私にくれると思います．	My grandfather handed this watch down to my father who will, I think, hand it down to me some day.
【～してくれる】よく来てくれた．	How nice of you to have come.
彼はそこへ行く地図をわざわざかいてくれた．	He even drew me a map of how to get there.
誕生日のお祝いに彼女がマフラーを編んでくれた．	She knitted me a scarf for my birthday.
明日の朝は6時に起こしてくれ．	Wake me at six tomorrow morning, please.

くれる²（暮れる）

日が暮れてきた．	It's getting dark.
日の暮れる前には帰りなさい．	Try to be home before (it gets) dark.
冬は日が暮れるのが早い．	It gets dark early in winter.
長かった一日もやっと暮れた．	It was a long day, but it's finally over now.
今年もあと二日で暮れてしまう．	There are only two days left in this year.
秋も暮れて，木々は葉を落とし始めた．	Now that autumn is ending, leaves have begun to fall off the trees.
【慣用】火事で家を焼かれ，彼は途方にくれてしまった．	He was at a loss for what to do when his house burned down.
彼をどう説得したらいいものか思案にくれている．	I've been trying to think of how to persuade him.
彼女は娘を失って，毎日涙にくれている．	She drowns herself in tears every day over her daughter's death.

父の死を聞いて彼女は悲嘆にくれた.	She was †overcome with sorrow [heartbroken] when she heard her father had died.

くろ (黒)

彼女は黒い服がよく似合う.	She looks good in black.
彼は日に焼けて色が黒い.	He has a dark (sun) tan.
彼は黒っぽい服を着ていた.	He was wearing dark clothes.
シャツの襟が黒ずんできた.	My shirt collar developed a grimy ring.
【慣用】警察は彼が黒だとは判断していない.	The police have not (yet) concluded that he's guilty.
この1年の日本の貿易収支は黒字だ.	Japan's trade balance for this year is in the black.

くろう (苦労)

彼は一生苦労のしどおしだった.	He suffered many hardships in his life.
彼女は女手一つで苦労して5人の子を育て上げた.	She worked as hard as she could to raise five children all by herself.
昔, 彼は金で随分苦労した.	He used to be extremely hard pressed financially.
私は病弱な子どもだったので, 親には苦労をかけました.	As a sickly child, I was a constant source of anxiety for my parents.
わがままな彼には随分苦労させられた.	He put me through hell because he was such a spoiled brat.
苦労をかけてすみません.	I'm sorry to have put you to so much trouble.
彼は苦労の末, やっと会社を軌道に乗せた.	With a lot of effort, he finally got the company into financial shape.
私の苦労もむだではなかった.	My †efforts were [hard work was] not wasted.
君はまだまだ苦労が足りないね.	You've still got a lot to learn.
彼女の苦労の種は尽きない.	There's no end to the hardships she suffers.
彼は苦労の無い人だ.	He's a carefree man.
今日は浮世の苦労を忘れて楽しんでください.	Why don't you go have a good time and forget the cares of the world?
彼女は子どものことで気苦労が絶えない.	Her children cause her endless worry.
彼女は苦労性だ.	She's a worrywart.
彼は苦労人だ.	He's been through a lot.
ご苦労さまでした.	Thank you./Thanks ever so much!

くわえる (加える)

【足す】
この辞書では新たに500語を加えました. — We added 500 new words to this dictionary.
6に5を加えると11です. — Five plus six is eleven.
彼も仲間に加えよう. — Let's count him in. / Let's include him.
列車は速度を加え,駅はあっという間に見えなくなった. — The train picked up speed and the station disappeared from view in no time.

【与える】
今度の台風は農作物に多大の被害を加えた. — The typhoon caused a lot of crop damage.
その猿はおとなしいので人に危害を加えることはない. — That monkey is tame and has never harmed anyone.
当時は報道機関に対して政府が圧力を加えていた. — At that time the government exerted pressure on the media.
彼はあごに一撃を加えられダウンした. — He was dealt a blow to the chin that laid him out.
この薬品は衝撃を加えると爆発する恐れがある. — This chemical can explode when subjected to a sudden jolt.

くわしい (詳しい)

彼はそのいきさつを詳しく説明した. — He gave us a detailed explanation [account] of the situation.
学校を中退した詳しい事情を話してください. — Please tell me precisely the circumstances that led to your quitting school.
現代美術についてはこの本のほうが詳しい. — This book gives more information on modern art.
京都市内の詳しい地図が欲しいんです. — I'd like a detailed map of Kyoto, please.
旅行の詳しい日程については手紙で連絡します. — I'll send you more detailed information about the travel itinerary by letter.
詳しいことは案内所で尋ねてください. — You can get more detailed information at the information service.
私はこの辺の地理には詳しい. — I know every inch of this neighborhood.
彼は中国の歴史に詳しい. — He's an authority on Chinese history.

くわだてる (企てる)

彼はヨットでの太平洋単独航海を企てている. — He's planning to cross the Pacific alone in his sailboat.
我が社は海外進出を企てている. — Our company is planning to expand its business overseas.
彼らは何か悪いことを企てているに違いない. — I'm sure they're up to no good.
彼女は若い頃,自殺を企てたことが何度かあった. — She attempted suicide several times in her youth.

くわわる (加わる)

今年から試験科目に数学が加わった.	Mathematics was added to the test subjects beginning (from) this year.
彼は先月, 会社の経営陣に加わった.	He joined the company's management team last month.
彼がチームに加わって雰囲気が明るくなった.	His joining the team has †made things more pleasant [brightened things up].
ここのところ日増しに寒さが加わっている.	It's been getting colder by the day recently.

け

け (毛)

彼女は髪の毛を染めている.	She dyes her hair.
彼は髪の毛が濃い.	He has a thick head of hair.
	He has thick hair.
髪の毛が薄くなってきた.	My hair is thinning.
彼は毛深い腕をしている.	He has hairy arms.
その動物は全身が硬い毛で覆われている.	That animal's entire body is covered with coarse hair.
このヘア・ブラシは豚の毛でできている.	This hairbrush is made with boar bristles.
彼は鶏の毛をむしって料理した.	He plucked the chicken and cooked it.
冬になると毛のシャツを着る.	I wear wool shirts in winter.

けいい (敬意)

彼らは敬意を込めて恩師をもてなした.	They entertained their former teacher in a spirit of respect and admiration.
この論文はよく資料を集めて書かれている点には敬意を払うが, 学問的な価値はあまりない.	I acknowledge that this is a well-documented thesis, but it doesn't have a great deal of scholarly value.
あなたの立派な行いに対して心から敬意を表します.	I sincerely admire your splendid deed.

けいえい (経営)

彼は銀座でレストランを経営している.	He manages [runs] a restaurant in Ginza.
あの会社は経営がうまくいっている.	Business at that company is going well.

る.	
新製品が当たったので経営が少し楽になった.	Business has picked up a little because the new product is a success.
生徒数の減少で私立学校を経営していくのは大変だ.	The decline in general enrollment has made it difficult for private schools to stay open.
彼は企業〔ホテル〕の経営者だ.	He manages [runs] a business [hotel].

けいえん (敬遠)

彼はすぐ難しい話を始めるので, みんなから敬遠されている.	Everyone †keeps him at a (respectable) distance [stays clear of him] because he always brings up difficult topics.
4番バッターは敬遠のフォアボールで歩かされた.	The cleanup hitter was walked intentionally.

けいかく (計画)

夏休みにはアメリカを旅行する計画です.	I plan to take a trip to the United States during summer vacation.
彼は夏休みの計画を立てた.	He made plans for his summer vacation.
ちゃんと計画を立てて勉強しなさい.	Set up a study schedule and stick to it.
参加人数が決まらないので旅行の計画が立たない.	Plans for the trip can't be finalized, as the number of participants still isn't known.
仕事は計画どおりに進んでいる.	Work is progressing [going] as planned.
計画は取りやめになった.	The plan was †called off [canceled].
計画は早速実行に移された.	Implementation of the plan was begun immediately.
この地域には大規模な開発計画がある.	We have a large-scale development project in this area.
この殺人事件は計画的犯行に違いない.	This murder was definitely planned.

けいき (景気)

あの会社は景気がいい.	That company is doing well.
このところ店の景気が悪い.	Recently, business has †not been going very well [been bad].
景気は上向いている.	The economy is picking up.
景気は後退している.	The economy is slowing down.
景気が回復した.	The economy has recovered.
大変な好景気が続いている.	The highly favorable business conditions are continuing.
景気はどうですか.	How's business?
【元気】魚屋さんが景気のいいかけ	The fishmonger is hawking his fish in a

| 声をかけながら魚を売っている. | spirited voice. |
| 一杯飲んで景気をつけよう. | Let's have a drink to †perk us up [lift our spirits]. |

けいけん (経験)

私はイギリス暮らしの経験がある.	I've lived in England before.
船で働いた経験がある.	I once worked on a ship.
私は株で苦い経験をした.	I had a bitter experience on the stock market.
彼女はまだ経験が浅い.	She doesn't have much experience.
この仕事は経験がものを言う.	It's experience that counts in this job.
彼は人生経験が豊かだ.	He has had a life rich in experiences.
目的は果たせなかったけれど, とてもいい経験になった.	I didn't achieve my goal, but it was still a very good experience.
彼は長年の経験を積んだ医者です.	He's a doctor with many years of experience.
彼は過去の経験を生かして商売に成功した.	He succeeded in business by putting his experience to use.
私の経験ではそんなことはありえない.	Judging from my experience, I'd say that would be impossible.

けいこ (稽古)

【習い事】
| 私は週1回踊りのけいこをしている. | I have [take] dance lessons once a week. |
| 彼はけがをして柔道のけいこを休んでいる. | He hasn't been attending *judo* practice since he got injured. |

【練習】
彼女は毎日熱心にバイオリンのけいこをする.	She enthusiastically practices the violin every day.
そんなことではまだまだけいこが足りない.	That's just not good enough. You still need a lot of practice.
今日は先生にけいこをつけてもらった.	The teacher let me practice with him today.
今日は新しい劇の舞台げいこがある.	There will be a stage rehearsal today for the new play.

けいこう (傾向)

若い人たちに活字離れの傾向がある.	The younger generation has a tendency not to read.
あの生徒には反抗的な傾向が見られる.	That student exhibits rebellious tendencies.
虫は明るい所に集まる傾向がある.	Insects tend to gather in brightly lit places.
物価は相変わらず上昇〔下降〕の傾向にある.	Prices remain on an upward [downward] trend.

世論調査では内閣の支持率は減少の傾向にある.	According to the polls, the percentage of those who support the Cabinet is on the decrease.

けいざい (経済)

【国・社会の】彼は日本の経済に明るい.	He is †an expert on [well acquainted with] Japanese economics.
あの国の経済は逼迫(ひっぱく)している.	That country's economy is on the verge of a crisis.
政府は経済の立て直しを図った.	The government attempted to put the economy back on its feet.
彼は経済界の大物だ.	He's †a prominent figure [a big shot**] in financial circles.
私は大学で経済学を勉強している.	I'm studying economics at (the) university.
【家計】彼は経済的に困っている.	He's having financial difficulties [problems].
海外旅行なんて経済が許さない.	I couldn't possibly afford to travel abroad.
共稼ぎをしないと経済が成り立たない.	We won't have enough money to live on unless we both work.
【経済的な】この車は経済的だ.	This car is economical.
世帯を二つ持つのは不経済なので両親と同居することにした.	Keeping two households is not economical, so I decided to live with my parents.
彼は経済観念のない男だ.	He's a man with (absolutely) no financial sense.

けいさん (計算)

私は計算が苦手だ.	I'm poor at math [figures, calculations].
何度やっても帳簿の計算が合わない.	No matter how many times I check, the figures in the book do not tally [balance].
計算機のお陰で計算が楽になった.	Calculators have made doing figures much easier.
コーヒー代を計算に入れて全部でいくらになりますか.	How much †is the bill [does the bill come to], including the coffee?
彼は計算高い男だ.	He's a very calculating person.
【予測】うまくいかない場合も計算に入れておかねばならない.	You must †consider [take into account] the possibility of it not working out.
物事は計算どおりに運ばないものだ.	Things never work out as planned.
それはとんだ計算違いだった.	That was an absurd miscalculation.

けいしき (型式・形式)

【型式】

この型式の蒸気機関車は日本に1台しか残っていない.	This is the only steam engine of its kind [type] left in Japan.
彼の車は型式が古い.	His car is an old model.

【形式】

この曲はソナタ形式を取っている.	This piece is in sonata form.
彼は何事をするにも形式にこだわらない.	He's not a stickler for form.
公害の調査は形式的に行われるだけで意味がない.	Pollution is being monitored in such a perfunctory way as to be meaningless.

げいじゅつ (芸術)

彼は芸術への関心が深い.	He has a deep interest in art.
歌舞伎は日本の伝統芸術です.	*Kabuki* is a traditional Japanese art form.
彼は偉大な芸術家だ.	He's a great artist.
これは芸術的な作品だ.	This work is artistic.

けいはく (軽薄)

彼は軽薄な男だ.	He's a frivolous man.
	He has no substance.
軽薄な行動は慎みなさい.	You really should refrain from acting so frivolously!
あのDJはしゃべる内容が軽薄だ.	That disc jockey says the most inane things.

けいべつ (軽蔑)

彼は貧しい人を軽蔑している.	He †looks down on [disdains*] poor people.
彼女は考え方の古い両親を軽蔑すると言いながら, 実は両親に認めて欲しくてたまらないのだ.	While she says she despises her parents for their old-fashioned thinking, she actually craves their approval.
彼がみすぼらしい服装をしているからといって軽蔑してはいけない.	You shouldn't look down on him just because he dresses shabbily.
彼女は軽蔑したように私を見た.	She looked at me contemptuously [scornfully].

けいやく (契約)

土地売却の契約を交わした.	I signed a contract for the sale of land.
彼は今日3件も保険の契約を成立させた.	He concluded three insurance contracts today.
彼はその契約を破棄した.	He †broke off [canceled] the contract.
その契約はもう無効だ.	The contract is no longer valid.

それは契約違反だ.	That violates the contract.
あの歌手はあるプロダクションと契約している.	That singer is under contract with a promotion agency.
そんな契約はした覚えがない.	I don't remember ever having signed a contract like that.
2年契約でアパートを借りている.	I'm renting my apartment on a two-year lease.

けが (怪我)

彼は交通事故でけがをした.	He was injured in a car accident.
戦争で多くの人がけがをし, 死んでいった.	Many were killed or wounded in the war.
彼は転んでけがをした.	He fell and hurt himself.
彼女はひどいけがをしている.	She has been seriously injured.
けががすっかり治った.	I have completely recovered from my injury.
	The wound has completely healed.
誤って彼にけがをさせてしまった.	I accidentally hurt him.
けが人を早く病院に運べ.	Rush the injured to the hospital.

げきれい (激励)

彼女は病気で寝ている私を毎日激励してくれた.	She †cheered me up [encouraged me] every day that I was sick in bed.
沿道の人々は, マラソン選手たちを大声で激励した.	The crowd along the way loudly cheered the marathon runners.
校長は競技会に出場する選手団に激励の言葉を送った.	The principal spoke several words of encouragement to the team participating in the tournament.

けしき (景色)

山頂から眺めた景色は素晴らしかった.	The view from the top of the mountain was magnificent.
景色のいい所でお弁当を食べよう.	Let's have lunch in a scenic place [spot].
	Let's have lunch where the scenery is nice.
窓を開けると外は一面の雪景色だった.	When I opened the window, everything outside was white with snow.

けじめ

【区切り】公私のけじめをつけなさい.	We don't take care of personal business on company time.[1]
	You'd better not use company time for your own business.
	You'd better make a distinction between

	your private and your public life.[2]
最近うちの部署では仕事と休憩時間のけじめがなくなってきている.	Lately, we've been getting a little loose about breaks in our section.
この辺でけじめをつけて、ちゃんと就職〔結婚〕しなさい.	It's time to get serious and †get a real job [get married].
僕たち, もうだらだら会うのはやめて, けじめをつけよう.	I don't want to continue this relationship. Let's call it quits here.
【責任ある決着】今回の件で, おたくはどうけじめをつけてくれるのかね?	I would expect that your firm will want to take responsibility for this slip-up?[3]
	How can we settle this matter fairly?
僕自身のけじめとして, 先方にきちんと謝りに行きます.	I'd like to take responsibility for this and go over to apologize to our client.
国会議員は再選され,「これで疑惑のけじめはついた」と語った.	The diet member declared that his re-election automatically settled any question of wrongdoing.

> 1) We don't... は直接的な You を避けて一般論で相手に柔らかくさとす言い方で, 会社などで口頭による注意としてよく使う. 2) 公人たる高級公務員・高級官僚などについて使う. 3)「この落度のけじめをつけてくれるつもりなんでしょうね」と慇懃に迫る言い方.

けす (消す)

彼は電気を消した.	He turned off the light.
暑くなってきたのでストーブを消した.	It was beginning to get hot so I turned off the heater.
テレビを消してください.	Please turn off the television.
消防隊が駆けつけて火事を消した.	The firemen rushed to the scene and †put out [extinguished] the fire.
活性炭はにおいを消す働きがある.	Activated carbon functions †as an odor eliminator [to eliminate odor].
間違った字を消しゴムで消して書き直した.	I erased the incorrect letter [character] (with an eraser) and rewrote it.
彼は町から姿を消した.	He disappeared from the city [town].
その事件は彼の経歴に消し難い汚点を残した.	That incident left a stain on his record that will be hard to remove.
邪魔者は消せ!	Eliminate anyone who gets in the way!
彼は身内のスキャンダルをもみ消そうと謀った.	He tried to cover up the family scandal.

けずる (削る)

【刃物で】彼は上手にナイフで鉛筆を削る.	He's very good at sharpening pencils with a knife.

彼はかんなで板を削った.	He planed the board.
みそ汁を作るから，かつお節を削ってね.	I'm going to make *miso* soup, so please shave off some dried bonito.
【減らす】道路拡張で土地を少し削られた.	We lost a little bit of land when the road was widened.
衣料費を削らないと家計がもたない.	If we don't cut down our spending for clothes, the household budget will go into the red.
この記事は長過ぎるから最後の部分を削ろう.	This article is too long, so let's omit the last part.

けつい (決意)

彼はブラジルへ移住しようと決意した.	He †made up his mind [resolved] to immigrate to Brazil.
彼の辞職の決意は固い.	His decision to †resign [step down] is firm.
私は弁護士になる決意を固めた.	I firmly committed myself to becoming a lawyer.
私は立候補の決意を新たにした.	I've reaffirmed my commitment to run for office.

けっか (結果)

結果が良くてもやり方が悪ければ考えものだ.	It's unwise to do something in a bad way even if the results are good.
実験の結果は全く予想と違っていた.	The results of the experiment were completely different from what had been anticipated.
努力の結果，彼は成功した.	He succeeded as a result of his effort.
彼は数々の悪事の結果，捕えられて処刑された.	As a result of his many evil deeds, he was arrested and executed.
審査の結果この作品が最優秀賞に決まった.	The judges chose this work for the grand prize.
結果的には彼の方法は間違っていなかった.	His way turned out to be right in the end.

けっきょく (結局)

結局その問題は解くことができなかった.	We were never able to solve that problem.
結局だれも私に勝てる人間はいなかった.	It turned out that nobody could beat me.
長い議論が続いたが，結局最初の案に落ち着いた.	After a long debate, they finally settled on the original proposal.
彼は結局何を言いたかったんだろう.	What was it he wanted to say after all?[1]

| 私の考えも結局のところは君と同じだ. | In the final analysis, my thoughts are the same as yours. |

> 1) after all を疑問文以外で使うと「やはり」の意味合いになる.

けっこう (結構)

【いい】結構なお住まいですね.	What a fine [lovely] home!
結構なお品をありがとうございました.	Thank you for the lovely gift.
【構わない】お支払いはいつでも結構です.	You can [may] pay whenever you like.
ご記入はペンでも鉛筆でも結構です.	You can use either pen or pencil when you fill this out.
【いらない】もう結構です. 十分いただきました.	No more, thanks. I've had more than enough.
「お手伝いしましょうか」「いえ, 結構ですよ」	"Can I help?" "No, thanks."
【かなり】この眼鏡は結構な値段だった.	These glasses were pretty expensive.
彼は数学が得意だが, 国語も結構できる.	His best subject is mathematics, but he's also pretty good at Japanese.
彼はああ見えても結構きまじめなところがあるんだよ.	Don't let his appearance fool you. He has his serious side, too.
この車は10年以上乗っているが, まだまだ結構よく動く.	I've been driving this car for more than ten years and it still runs fine.

けっこん (結婚)

僕と結婚してください.	Please marry me.
私たちは来月結婚します.	We're getting married next month.
彼は彼女と結婚した.	He married her.
彼は結婚している.	He's married.
この2月で結婚して10年になる.	We'll have been married (for) ten years this February.
私は彼女に結婚を申し込んだ.	I proposed to her.
あの二人は結婚の約束をしている.	Those two are engaged (to be married).
彼は結婚に失敗した.	His marriage failed.
彼には結婚適齢期の娘がいる.	He has a daughter of marriageable age.
結婚式はハワイであげた.	We had our wedding (ceremony) in Hawaii.
今日は両親の25回目の結婚記念日です.	Today is my parents' silver [twenty-fifth] wedding anniversary.
結婚祝いは何がいいですか.	What would you like for [as] a wedding present?

私は結婚生活に満足している． I'm happy with married life.

けっして (決して)
彼は決してうそをつかない． He would never tell a lie.
あなたの親切は決して忘れません． I'll never forget your kindness.
そんなことは決して許さないぞ． Believe me, I would never (on my life) allow you to do such a thing.
この土地は決して宅地造成業者には売らないぞ． I wouldn't sell this land to a housing developer †by any means [under any circumstances].
彼女は決して悪い人間ではありません． She's certainly not a bad (sort of) person.

けっしょう (決勝)
彼は次々に強敵を破り，決勝へ進んだ． He put down one tough opponent after another on his way to the finals.
そのチームはよく活躍し，決勝まで残った． That team played hard and made it to the finals.
彼は決勝で敗れてしまった． He was defeated in the finals.
彼の得点が決勝点になった． The point he scored turned out to be the winning point.

けっしん (決心)
彼はアメリカへ留学しようと決心した． He †decided [made up his mind, resolved] to go to America to study.
彼女は体の不自由な人たちのために一生をささげようと固く決心した． She committed her life to helping the handicapped.
彼女の会社を辞めるという決心は固かった． Her resolve [determination] to quit the company was firm.
行こうか行くまいか決心がつかない． I can't decide whether to go or not.
教師になるかどうか，彼はまだ決心がつかないでいる． He hasn't decided whether to become a teacher or not.

けっせき (欠席)
斉藤さんは風邪で欠席です． Miss Saito is absent because of a cold.
明日の会議は欠席させていただきます． I'll be absent from [I won't be able to attend] tomorrow's meeting.
私は入学以来一度も欠席していません． I haven't missed a day since entering this school.
今日は欠席が多い． There are many †people absent [absentees] today.

彼は今日も無断欠席している.	He's absent without permission again today.
欠席届けを出しなさい.	Please submit notification if you are going to be absent.

けっちゃく (決着)

明日の話し合いで決着をつけるつもりだ.	I intend to settle the matter at tomorrow's meeting.
この問題が決着するまでは次のステップに移れない.	We can't go on to the next step until this problem is settled first.
いつまでたっても紛争の決着がつかない.	There seems to be no end in sight for the dispute.
なぜ今の段階で決着を急ぐ必要があるのか?	Why do we have to rush into resolving everything at this stage?
延長1時間だが,まだ試合の決着がつかない.	An hour's overtime and we still don't know who the winner is.

けってい (決定)

千秋楽を待たず横綱の優勝が決定した.	The *sumo* grand champion clinched the championship before the final day.
秋の国体の開催日が決定した.	The dates for the fall national athletic meet have been set.
この件に関しては決定次第お知らせします.	We'll inform you about the decision as soon as it is made.
彼の勝利は決定したようなものだ.	His victory is almost a †sure thing [foregone conclusion].
決定的な解決策が浮かばない.	I just can't come up with a decisive plan to settle this.
この写真は決定的瞬間をとらえている.	This photograph captures the decisive moment.
その事件は彼に決定的な打撃を与えた.	That incident dealt †him [his career] a fatal blow.

けってん (欠点)

だれにも欠点はある.	Everyone has his faults [shortcomings].
彼は気の弱いのが欠点だ.	His main problem is that he's not assertive enough.
この論文は欠点だらけだ.	This thesis is full of flaws [defects].
このエアコンは音が大き過ぎるのが欠点だ.	The drawback [disadvantage] of this air conditioner is that it makes too much noise.

けねん (懸念)

この天候が米の出来具合に与える影響を懸念している. — I'm concerned about the effect of this weather on the rice harvest.

懸念された父の手術が無事に済んだ. — My father came through the operation that we had been so apprehensive about in fine shape.

懸念された会談〔交渉〕も無事話がまとまった. — The talks [negotiations] that we were so concerned [apprehensive] about were concluded without incident.

その件に関しては, ご懸念には及びません. — There's no cause for concern about that.

げひん (下品)

あんな下品な人とはつきあいたくない. — I have no desire to associate with such †a vulgar [an uncouth[1)]] character.

彼は下品な食べ方をする. — He's rude when he eats.

彼はすぐに下品な話をする. — He likes telling dirty stories.

> 1) 発音は [ənkúːθ]. 本来硬い表現だが, 会話で使うとかえってふざけた言い方になる.

けむたい (煙たい)

【煙い】たばこの煙が煙たいので, 向こうで吸ってください. — Could you smoke over there, please? I'm suffocating in here.

キャンプファイアの煙が煙たくて目を開けていられない. — I can't keep my eyes open because of the smoke from the campfire.

【親しみを持てない】彼は細かいところにうるさいので, みんなから煙たがられている. — He's such a stickler for detail that everyone stays away from him.

今度の先生は何となく煙たい. — Our new teacher is sort of unapproachable.

けむり (煙)

山の端から一筋の煙が立ち昇っている. — There's a trail of smoke rising from the mountain ridge.

工場の煙突から煙が出ている. — Smoke is coming out of the factory chimney.

火山が煙を吐いている. — The volcano is spewing smoke.

火事になったら煙に巻かれないように気をつけなさい. — If there's a fire, be careful not to get caught in the smoke.

その火事の犠牲者のほとんどは煙に巻かれて死んだ. — Almost all the victims of the fire died from smoke inhalation.

火事で家も財産も煙になって消え — My house and possessions all went up in

てしまった.	smoke in the fire.
バスは砂煙を上げて走り去った.	The bus drove off in a cloud of dust.
【慣用】火のない所に煙は立たない.	Where there's smoke, there's fire.
彼は一方的にしゃべりまくって相手を煙に巻いた.	He talked a blue streak and completely befuddled the person he was talking to.

ける (蹴る)

彼は思いきりボールをけった.	He kicked the ball with all his might.
人をけったりしてはいけない.	Don't kick people.
彼は怒って席をけって部屋を出て行った.	He got angry and stormed out of the room.
組合は会社側の回答をけった.	The union flatly rejected the company's counteroffer.

けれど (も)

鷗外もいいけれど, それ以上に漱石にひかれる.	Ogai is fine but I find Soseki even more appealing.
兄は秀才だけれど, 弟は落ちこぼれだ.	The older brother is bright but the younger brother is kind of slow.
熱は下がったけれど, まだせきが続いている.	My fever has gone down but I still have a cough.
英語は読めるけれど, 聞いたり話したりすることはできない.	I can read English, but I'm no good at listening and speaking.
彼はいろいろやってみたけれど, 失敗した.	He tried many different things [ways] but failed.
あなたは彼を嫌っているけれど, どうして?	I know that you hate him, but why?
先日の話だけれど, 無かったことにしてくれないか.	About the other day's conversation, please forget I ever brought it up, OK?
山田ですけれど, のぼる君はいますか.	This is Yamada. Is Noboru home [there]?
【願望】僕に翼があればいいんだけれど.	If only I had wings.
コンピュータがあればもっと仕事が楽なんだけれど.	This job sure would be easier if we had a computer.
【婉曲】ちょっとお願いがあるんですけれど.	Excuse me, but could you do me a favor?
そのことに関しては全く伺っていませんけれど.	(I'm sorry but) I haven't heard a thing about that.

けわしい (険しい)

険しい山道を登った.	I climbed up a steep mountain trail.
両国の対立はますます険しくなっ	The conflict between the two countries is

てきた.	deepening.
彼は険しい目つきで私を睨んだ.	He glared at me with a grim look in his eyes.
悪い知らせを聞き,彼の顔は険しくなった.	His face turned grim when he heard the bad news.

けんあく (険悪)

彼らの仲は険悪だ.	They have a stormy relationship.
彼は険悪な顔つきをして私を睨んだ.	He shot me a menacing look.
会議は意見の対立が続出し,険悪な雰囲気になってきた.	The meeting took on an ugly mood as one point after another was disputed.

げんいん (原因)

その火事は寝たばこが原因だった.	The cause [origin] of the fire was smoking in bed.
この病気はまだ原因が判っていない.	The cause of this illness [disease] is not yet known.
調査団がその事故の原因を追求している.	The investigating committee is looking into the cause of the accident.
あの騒ぎの原因は何だったの？	What caused [started] that commotion?

けんお (嫌悪)

彼女は狡猾で怠惰な彼のことを嫌悪している.	She detests him because he's sly and shiftless.
あの人の欺瞞的行為には嫌悪を感じる.	I loathe that person's deceitful [deceptive] actions.

けんか

けんかをしてはいけません.	Don't get into fights [arguments].[1)]
彼らは殴り合いのけんかを始めた.	They got into a fist fight.
彼はけんかっ早い.	He's always ready for a fight.
	He'll fight at the drop of a hat.
おれにけんかを売る気か.	Are you trying to †pick a fight with me [start something]?
以前は警察は夫婦げんかに介入しなかった.	Formerly, the police did not intervene in marital disputes.
夫婦げんかは犬も食わない.	There's [It's] no use interfering in marital squabbles.
彼女は口げんかなら負けない.	She never loses an argument.
そうけんか腰にならずに落ち着いて話し合おう.	Don't get excited. Let's talk about it calmly.

1) fight は「口げんか」「殴り合いのけんか」などを含め,「けんか」一般を言う. argument は「口げんか」.

げんかい (限界)

おのれの限界を知るべきだ.	You should know what your own limitations are.
この仕事は私の能力の限界を超えている.	The job is beyond my abilities.
まだ限界じゃない. 君はもっとやれるよ.	You haven't reached your limit yet. There's still a lot more that you can do.[1]
	You still haven't reached your full potential. There's so much more that you can still do.[2]
彼の才能には限界が見えない.	There seems to be no limit to his capacities.
こんな資金量じゃ, プロジェクトの限界が見えているよ.	The project is going to be limited with this kind of funding.
トライアスロンで体力の限界に挑戦するつもりだ.	I want to test my physical limits in the triathlon.
彼の体力はとうとう限界に達した.	He finally reached the limit of his physical strength [endurance].
過酷な旅が続き, 精神的にも体力的にも限界に近づいていた.	As the ordeals of the journey continued, I felt myself reaching the end of my spiritual and physical endurance.
彼は歌手としての自分の能力に限界を感じた.	He felt the limits of his own ability as a singer.
言葉でその感動を伝えるのは限界がある.	Words cannot adequately convey the excitement I felt.*
	I just can't express [describe] how moved I was.
限界だ. もう我慢できない!	That's it. I can't take it anymore!

1) は「能力的にまだやれる余裕がある」, 2) は「まだ伸びる余地がある」という言い方.

げんき (元気)

【気力】
元気を出しなさい.	Cheer up.
彼は医者から何も心配することはないと言われて元気が出てきた.	He cheered up when the doctor told him there was nothing to worry about.
あの子はいつも元気がいい.	That child is always so cheerful.
彼は最近元気がない.	He hasn't seemed very cheerful recently.

先生の言葉は彼を元気づけた.	What the teacher said †cheered him up [gave him a lift, encouraged him].
子どもたちは元気よく歌った.	The kids sang with vitality.
夜更かしして3時まで起きていたので，今朝は洗濯する元気もない.	I stayed up till three and I don't really feel up to doing the laundry this morning.
【健康】お元気ですか.	How are you?／How've you been?
お陰様で私は毎日元気に暮らしています.	I'm getting along quite well, thanks.
彼はすっかり元気になった.	He recovered completely.

けんきゅう (研究)

彼はフランス文学を研究している.	He is †doing research on [studying] French literature.
彼はこの問題について実によく研究している.	He has done a lot of research on this problem.
彼は研究に没頭した.	He threw himself into his research.
こんなことも分からないなんて研究不足もはなはだしいよ.	Not even knowing about this demonstrates a gross lack of research.
彼女は研究心が旺盛だ.	She has a passion for research.
彼は製薬会社の研究所に勤めている.	He works in the research laboratory of a pharmaceutical company.

けんきょ (謙虚)

彼は実に謙虚な人だ.	He's truly a modest person.
彼は自分の過ちを謙虚に認めた.	He humbly admitted his own error.
友達の忠告は謙虚に受け入れるもんだよ.	You should be grateful for a friend's advice.
実力のある人ほど謙虚なものだ.	The more capable one is, the more modest one tends to be.

けんこう (健康)

彼は心身ともに健康だ.	He's healthy †in body and mind [physically and mentally].
父はこの頃，健康が優れない.	My father has been in poor health recently.
適度な運動は健康に良い.	Moderate exercise is good for †your health [you].
夜更かしは健康に悪い.	It's bad for your health to stay up late at night.
祖母は健康に恵まれ，今でも元気に暮らしている.	My grandmother is blessed with good health and is full of vitality even now.
彼は健康を害して自宅で静養して	He ruined his health and is convalescing at

	home.
彼は健康を損ない,会社を辞めた.	He quit the company because of failing health.
健康にはくれぐれも注意してください.	Pay strict attention to your health.
彼女はやっと健康を取り戻した.	She finally got her health back.
健康を保つために毎朝体操をしている.	I'm doing exercises every morning to keep healthy.
定期的に健康診断を受けている.	I get †physicals [physical examinations, checkups] on a regular basis.
この近くに健康食品の店はありますか.	Is there a health-food store close by?
最近,玄米などの健康食品がはやっている.	Recently health foods like brown rice have become popular.

けんさ (検査)

この製品は出荷する前に厳しく検査されます.	This product undergoes strict inspection before it is shipped.
税関で手荷物を検査された.	My luggage was inspected [examined, searched] at customs.
川の水質検査が行われた.	The quality of the river water was tested.
機械の定期検査が済んだ.	Periodic overhaul of the machinery has been completed.
明日は学校で身体検査がある.	We're having a physical examination at school tomorrow.

げんざい (現在)

現在,私は独身です.	I'm single at present.
私は現在の生活に満足している.	I'm satisfied with my life as it is now.
現在では結核は昔ほど恐ろしい病気ではなくなった.	Today tuberculosis is no longer as terrifying a disease as it once was.
私の考えは現在でも変わらない.	My thinking remains unchanged, even now.
5月1日現在,この学校の生徒数は876人です.	As of May 1st, the pupils enrolled in this school numbered 876 [eight hundred seventy-six].
現在までの売上高を調べた.	I checked the amount sold up to the present.

けんさく (検索)

電子辞書は検索が楽だ.	It's easy looking things [words] up in an electronic dictionary.
その名前をインターネットで検索	I looked up the name on the Internet.

した.	I did a search (on the Net) for the name.
URLを知らなくても, 検索すれば簡単にサイトに行きつける.	You can easily get to a site even if you don't know the URL by using a search engine.

げんじつ (現実)

現実は君の考えているよりも厳しいものだ.	Reality is harsher than you think.
もっと現実を直視すべきだ.	You ought to face up to reality more.
現実に即して物事を考えなさい.	Think realistically.
現実の問題として,こんなに家賃が高くてはとても生活していけない.	In practical terms, I can't afford to live paying rent as high as this.
今日,信じられないようなことが現実に起こった.	A seemingly incredible thing actually happened, today.
最近の子どもは現実的過ぎて夢が無いと言われている.	It is said that today's children are too realistic [pragmatic] and lack idealism.
彼は現実主義者だ.	He is a realist.
彼の夢が現実となった.	His dream came true.
	He realized his dream.

げんしょう (減少)

村の人口は毎年減少している.	The population of the village is decreasing annually.
野生動物が減少の傾向にある.	Wild animals are †on the decrease [dwindling].

けんせつ (建設)

このコンサートホールを建設するのに35億円かかる.	It will cost ¥3.5 billion [three point five billion yen] to construct this concert hall.
学校では今,新校舎を建設中です.	A new school building is now under construction at school.
道路の建設工事が進んでいる.	The road construction is making progress.
住民は原子力発電所の建設に反対している.	The residents are opposed to construction of the nuclear power plant.
彼は建設会社で働いている.	He works at a construction company.
この問題についてもっと建設的な意見を述べてください.	Please express a more constructive suggestion about this problem.

けんとう¹ (見当)

何人くらい申し込みがありそうか, おおよその見当をつけた.	I made a rough estimate of how many people might apply.

この建物の建設費がいくらかだなんて見当もつかないよ.	I can't even guess what this building would cost to build.
犯人がだれなのか, だいたいの見当はついている.	We have some idea of who the culprit is.
どうやらぼくの見当は外れたようだ.	I guess I was wrong [off, mistaken]. I guess my estimate[1] was off.
君の言っていることは全く見当外れだ.	What you are saying is beside the point. You are completely off base.
彼を抜擢したのはとんだ見当違いだった.	Choosing him was a big mistake. It was a big mistake †to choose him [choosing him]. His choice[2] was completely off.
【目安・～ほど】彼に5千円見当の品物を贈ることにした.	We decided to give him something costing around [about] ￥5,000.
「どんな人だった？」「40見当のサラリーマンふうの男だったよ」	"What was he like?" "He looked like a company employee around [about] forty years old."

> 1) estimate は特に数字に関わる「見当, 予測」に使う. 2) His choice は文脈により「彼を選んだこと」と「彼が選択したこと」のどちらの意味にもなりうる.

けんとう² (検討)

検討させてください.	We'd like to think about it. I would like to give this a little more thought.
納期については検討させてください.	Can we get back to you about the delivery date?
これは検討に値する企画だ.	This project is worth considering.
慎重な検討の結果, 残念ながらあなたの案は不採用となりました.	I'm sorry but after careful consideration your proposal was not accepted.
十分な検討を加えたうえでお答えいたします.	I will get back to you after giving it careful consideration.
社内で検討したのち, ご連絡いたします.	May I contact you after we have had a chance to discuss it here? May I get in touch with you after our company has had a chance to discuss it (a little) further?
この件については再検討が必要です.	We have to reconsider this matter.

けんぶつ (見物)

観光バスで東京見物をした.	I took in the sights in Tokyo on a sight-

	seeing bus.
京都へ行って名所, 旧跡を見物しようと思っている.	I'm thinking about going to Kyoto to visit famous and historical places.
今日, 芝居見物に出かけた.	I went to see a play today.
ピエロは見物人に愛敬を振りまいた.	The clown charmed the spectators.

げんみつ（厳密）

製品は最後に厳密な検査を受けてから市場に出ます.	Products are marketed only after they've undergone strict inspection.
厳密に言えば, この文章は文法的に間違っている.	Strictly speaking, this sentence is not grammatically correct.
彼女の校正は厳密だ.	Her proofreading is scrupulous.

けんめい（賢明）

彼は賢明な人だ.	He's a wise man.
それは賢明な処置だ.	That's a wise move.
それは賢明なやり方ではない.	That's not a very wise [shrewd, astute] way to do it.
そういう発言は避けたほうが賢明だ.	You'd be wise to steer clear of such statement.

げんめつ（幻滅）

彼は入学してすぐ大学生活に幻滅した.	He became disillusioned with college life as soon as he entered school.
今度の件で, すっかり彼に幻滅を感じた.	This incident completely disillusioned me about him.
あの美人が整形手術を受けていたとは幻滅だ.	What a letdown to know that her good looks come from plastic surgery!

けんやく（倹約）

彼は倹約してお金をためた.	He †economized [was thrifty] and built up his savings.
むだづかいをしないで, もっと倹約しなさい.	Don't waste money. Economize. [Be thriftier.]
彼は倹約家だ.	He's thrifty.／He economizes.

けんり（権利）

人間はだれでも幸福を求める権利がある.	The pursuit of happiness is a universal human right.
私には父の遺産を受け取る法律上の権利がある.	I have the legal right to inherit my father's estate.
他人の権利を侵してはならない.	No one may infringe upon another's

彼は店の権利を人に譲った.	He turned the rights to the store over to someone else.
何の権利があって僕にそんな命令をするんだ.	What gives you the right to give me an order like that?
だれも私を非難する権利はない.	Nobody has the right to criticize me.

げんりょう（原料）

合成繊維の原料は石油，石炭などである.	Synthetic fiber is produced from materials such as petroleum and coal.
日本の工業は原料の多くを輸入に頼っている.	Japanese industry depends on imports for most of its raw materials.
パンの原料は小麦粉です.	Flour is the basic ingredient of bread.
この製品は原料費が高いので値段も高い.	This product is expensive because of the high cost of the materials used to make it.

こ

こい¹（濃い）

【濃度・密度】濃いお茶〔コーヒー〕をください.	Please give me some strong tea 〔coffee〕.
私の水割りはあまり濃くしないでください.	Please don't make my whiskey and water too strong.
このスープは濃い.	This soup is thick.
濃いめの味が好きだ.	I like full flavor.
この味は濃過ぎる.	This tastes too strong.
濃い霧が立ちこめていた.	There was a thick fog.
息子の髪が濃くなってきた.	My son's hair has started to get thick.
彼女のまつげは濃い.	She has thick eyelashes.
【色】濃い紫〔緑，オレンジ〕色だ.	It's deep 〔dark〕 purple 〔green, orange〕.
彼のスーツは濃い灰色〔茶色〕だ.	His suit is dark gray 〔brown〕.
彼女の化粧は濃過ぎる.	Her makeup is too thick.
【内容】中味の濃い授業〔話し合い〕だった.	It was a very informative lesson 〔discussion〕.
【度合い】我がチームの敗色が濃くなった.	It began to look more certain that our team would lose.
これで彼が賄賂を受け取った疑い	This has made the suspicion all the

はますます濃くなった.	stronger that he took the bribe.

こい² (恋)

僕は彼女に恋している.	I'm in love with her.／I love her.
二人は初めて会った日に恋に落ちた.	They fell in love (on) the first day they met.
彼女は今恋わずらいだ.	She's hung up on someone. She's lovesick.
それが私の初恋だった.	That was my first love.
彼〔彼女〕の恋人はだれ？	Who's †his girlfriend 〔her boyfriend〕? Who's his 〔her〕 lover?[1]
恋は盲目.	Love is blind.

> 1) lover はよく使われるが，暗に肉体関係があることを意味するので使い方に注意.

こい³ (故意)

彼は故意に私を傷つけた.	He hurt me †intentionally [on purpose, deliberately].
故意にか偶然にか，私が訪ねるといつも彼は留守だ.	I don't know whether it's intentional or just coincidence, but every time I go to see him he's out.
彼の行為がもし故意だとしたら許せない.	If what he did was †deliberate [intentional, on purpose], it's unforgivable.

こいしい (恋しい)

彼女を恋しく思う.	I miss her.／I long for* her.
彼は時々故郷が恋しくなる.	He sometimes †gets homesick [misses his hometown].
離れていると恋しさが募る.	Absence makes the heart grow fonder.

こうい¹ (行為)

彼の親切な行為に彼女は喜んだ.	She was overjoyed by his kindness.
それは大人にあるまじき行為だ.	What you did was unworthy of an adult.
それは不法行為だ.	That's †against the law [an unlawful act].
感謝の気持ちを行為で表しなさい.	Demonstrate your feelings of gratitude †by deeds [through actions].

こうい² (好意)

それは彼が好意でしたことです.	He did it with good intentions.
好意でしたことを悪意に取られた.	My good intentions were taken for bad.
あなたのご好意に感謝します.	I appreciate your kindness.
彼の好意で一晩泊めてもらった.	He kindly let me stay overnight.

彼の好意を素直に受け取りなさい.	Accept his offer (of assistance) gracefully.
彼女は彼に好意を寄せている.	She's very fond of him.
彼は我々に好意的だ.	He's friendly toward us.

ごういん (強引)

彼は強引な人だ.	He is coercive.
彼の強引さに負けた.	He was so pushy [forward] that I gave in.
	He came on so strong that I gave in.
彼は強引に彼女をデートに誘った.	He coerced [forced] her into dating him.
与党は法案を強引に通過させた.	The party in power forced †the bill through [passage of the bill].

こううん (幸運・好運)

合格できたのは幸運だった.	Fortunately [Luckily], I passed.
	It was sheer luck that I passed.
幸運にもすぐタクシーが来た.	Fortunately, a taxi came right away.
泊まっていたホテルが火事になったが, 幸運にも死なずに済んだ.	A fire broke out in the hotel where I was staying, but I was lucky enough to escape with my life.
幸運にすっかり見放されてしまった.	My luck has completely run out.
幸運を祈る.	Good luck.
	I wish you the best of luck.
彼は好運児だ.	He's a lucky guy.
	He was born under a lucky star.

こうえい (光栄)

選手に選ばれて光栄だ.	I'm honored to have been selected as a competitor.
賞をもらって大変光栄だと思う.	I feel very honored to receive the prize.
身に余る光栄です.	This is an undeserved honor.

こうか (効果)

テレビで宣伝した効果があって売り上げが増えた.	Advertising on TV was effective and sales increased.
生徒を叱っただけの効果があった.	Scolding the students proved effective.
彼には〔彼が〕何を言っても効果がない.	Nothing †I say to him [he says] has any effect.
薬の効果で熱が下がった.	The medicine brought my [the] temperature down.
薬を変えてみたら, 効果てきめんだった.	After I changed my medication, the results were almost immediate.
彼らのコンサートでは光が効果的に使われていた.	The lighting at their concert was very effective.

ごうか (豪華)

彼女は豪華なダイヤの指輪をしていた.	She wore a gorgeous diamond ring.
豪華なホテルですね.	It's really a luxurious hotel.
彼女の誕生パーティーには豪華な食事が出た.	A sumptuous meal was served at her birthday party.
私たちは豪華船で世界一周旅行をしました.	We took an around-the-world cruise on a luxury liner.
彼の豪華版の詩集が出版された.	A deluxe edition of his poetry has been published.

こうかい (後悔)

怠けたことを後悔している.	I regret having been (so) lazy.
今さら後悔してもむだだ.	It's no use regretting it now.
後悔することのないようによく考えて決めなさい.	Decide after careful consideration so you won't have any regrets later on.
後悔先に立たず.	What's done is done.
	It's no use crying over spilt milk.

こうがい (郊外)

私は(東京の)郊外に住んでいます.	I live in the suburbs (of Tokyo).
彼はよく郊外をドライブする.	He often takes a drive in the suburbs.
この町の郊外には住宅が急増している.	The number of residences †in the suburbs [on the outskirts] of this town is increasing rapidly.

ごうかく (合格)

彼はX大学に合格した.	He was accepted by X University.
彼が合格するかどうかは微妙だ.	It's hard to say whether he will †make the grade[1)] [pass] or not.
この製品は厳しい製品検査に合格したものです.	This is a product that has passed (a) strict inspection.
60点以上が合格です.	Sixty points (and above) is passing.
彼なら私の後継者として合格だ.	If it's him, he has my approval as my successor.
彼は英語が合格基準に達しなかった.	He didn't meet the qualifying standards in English.
合格者の名前が発表された.	The names of those who passed were announced.
合格通知が届いた.	I received notification that I had passed.
	I got a letter of acceptance.

> 1) make the grade は試験に限らず「合格基準に達する」という意味で使う.

こうかん¹ (交換)

私の帽子とあなたのとを交換しませんか.	Wouldn't you like to trade hats?
このカメラはレンズが交換できる.	The lens of this camera can be changed.
このテープレコーダーは部品を交換する必要があります.	This tape recorder needs to have a part replaced.
人形と交換に彼女に私のバッグをあげた.	I traded her my bag for her doll.
その会議で教師たちは, 教育上の問題について活発に意見を交換し合った.	The teachers at the conference had a lively exchange of opinions about educational problems.
おたくの会社と技術に関する情報を交換したい.	We would like to exchange technical information with your company.
大学にアメリカから交換学生〔教授〕がやって来た.	An exchange student 〔professor〕 from America has arrived at the university.
我々は相手の交換条件をのんだ.	We went along with their conditions (for the deal).

こうかん² (好感)

彼は好感の持てる人だ.	He makes a favorable impression on people.
みんなが彼に好感を持っている.	Everyone feels friendly toward him.
彼のはきはきした話し方が聴衆に好感を与えた.	His crisp way of talking made a favorable [good] impression on the audience.

こうき (好奇)

彼は好奇心が強い.	He's very curious[1]
	He has a strong sense of curiosity.
私は何にでも好奇心をそそられる.	My curiosity is aroused by anything and everything.
その話は私の好奇心をそそった.	That (story) aroused my curiosity.
好奇心から聞いてみただけです.	I only asked out of curiosity.
皆は好奇の目で私たちを見た.	Everybody stared at us with curiosity.

> 1) curious は, strange, peculiar (変な, 奇異な) の意味で使われることも多いので注意.

こうきゅう (高級)

この壺は高級そうに見えるが, 実	This may look like a high-quality vase but

は安物だ.	it's really not.
待合室には高級な雑誌が置いてあった.	There were first-class magazines in the waiting room.
彼女は高級マンションに住んでいる.	She's living in an upscale apartment.
これは高級なトマトですよ.味と香りが全く違います.	This is a high-grade tomato. There's a distinctive difference in taste and fragrance.
そんな高級車は我が家には高嶺の花だ.	A luxury car like that is simply beyond our reach.
	That kind of luxury car is beyond our household budget.
その店は高級品しか置いていない.	That store only deals in luxury goods.
彼女はいつも高級品ばかり身につけている.	She always †wears [has on] only the most expensive clothing and accessories.
芦屋は高級住宅街だ.	Ashiya is an exclusive residential area.
高級クラブで客を接待した.	We entertained our clients at an expensive nightclub.

こうきょう (公共)

平気で道にゴミを捨てたりして、彼は公共心に欠けているね.	He throws litter in the streets without giving it a second thought. He isn't very civic-minded.
その政治家は公共の利益を図ろうと努力した.	That politician strove to promote public welfare [good].
公共料金の値上げは社会的影響が大きい.	The social impact of increases in the cost of public utilities is very large.
政府は失業対策の一環として公共事業を増やそうとしている.	The government is trying to expand public works as part of its policy to reduce unemployment.

ごうけい (合計)

合計を出してください.	Please add it up.
	How much does it come to?
1週間で合計80冊売れた.	A total of 80 copies (of the book) were sold in one week.
今日の買い物の合計は6,500円になった.	Today's shopping bill came to 6,500 yen.
僕たち三人のお金の合計はいくらになる?	What is the total amount of money the three of us have?

こうげき (攻撃)

基地は突然敵の攻撃を受けた.	The base was suddenly attacked by the

	enemy.
彼の案は国会で激しく攻撃された.	His proposal was †aggressively attacked [sharply criticized] in the Diet.
突然彼は攻撃的になり，私たちを激しく非難した.	He suddenly became aggressive and reproached us sharply.
攻撃は最大の防御である.	A good offense is the best defense.

こうさい (交際)

私は彼女と交際している.	I go out with her./I'm seeing her.
彼とはあまり交際はない.	I don't see him very often.
	I don't have much to do with him.
彼女とは学校時代同級だったが，個人的交際はなかった.	I was in the same class at school with her, but we didn't see each other on a personal basis.
彼は最近，人との交際を避けている.	He's been keeping to himself lately.
	Recently he's been avoiding people.
彼女は交際が広い.	She knows a lot of people.
彼女は交際好きだ.	She's fond of company.
	She likes being around people.
彼〔会社〕の交際費が多過ぎる.	His [The company's] entertainment expenses are too high.
彼は交際家だ.	He's very sociable.

こうじ (工事)

家の前の道路を工事している.	The road in front of the house is being worked on.
鉄道の建設工事が急ピッチで進められている.	Railroad construction is moving forward at fever pitch.
そのトンネル工事には多くの年月と費用がかかった.	A large amount of time and money was spent on the construction of that tunnel.

こうしょう¹ (交渉)

そのことについては私が相手方と交渉しよう.	Let me talk to them about that.
	Let me discuss that with them.
組合は会社側と賃上げについて交渉している.	The union is negotiating a pay raise with management.
こちら側からはだれが交渉に当たりますか.	Who's going to negotiate for us?
両者は明日から交渉に入る.	They will begin negotiations tomorrow.
会社側がなかなか交渉に応じようとしない.	Management refuses to negotiate.
賃上げ交渉がまとまった.	Negotiations for a pay raise have reached

	a settlement.
交渉が決裂して組合はストライキに突入した.	The negotiations broke down and the union immediately went on strike.
店員と交渉してテレビを安く買った.	I bargained with the sales clerk and got a good deal on my TV.

こうしょう² (高尚)

随分高尚な雑誌を読んでいるね.	That's an awfully highbrow[1] [intellectual] magazine you're reading.
私には高尚な文学は分からない.	I can't understand highbrow literature.
高尚な趣味をお持ちですね.	You have very elegant taste.

1) highbrow はからかいの気持ちを込めた言い方.

ごうじょう (強情)

彼は強情な人だ.	He's †a stubborn [an obstinate] person.
強情を張らないで謝りなさい.	Don't be so obstinate. Apologize!
君みたいな強情っ張りとはもう話したくない.	I'm through talking to someone as obstinate [stubborn, pigheaded] as you.

こうせい (公正)

国民は公正な裁判を求めている.	The people want fair courts.
社長は彼の仕事を公正に評価していない.	The president hasn't evaluated his work fairly.

ごうせい (豪勢)

彼は豪勢な宴会で私たちをもてなした.	He entertained us with a sumptuous banquet.
彼らは豪勢に飲み歩いた.	They painted the town red.
	They went out on the town drinking.
彼は競馬で儲けた金を豪勢に使った.	He lavishly spent the money he had won at the horse races.
あの家は大変な金持ちで豪勢な暮らしをしている.	That family is very rich and leads a life of luxury.

こうぞう (構造)

このビルは地震に強い構造になっている.	This building has a structure resistant to earthquakes.
この長い文章の構造がどうなっているか分かりますか.	Do you understand the structure of this long sentence?
日本の社会構造は戦後大きく変わった.	The structure of Japanese society has changed greatly since the end of the war.

あの車は構造上の欠陥があって、メーカーが回収を始めた.	The manufacturer has issued a recall for that car because of a structural defect.

こうたい (交代・交替)

場所を交代しよう.	Let's trade places.
君がまず運転しろ. 100キロ走ったら交代するよ.	You drive first and we'll switch after 100 kilometers.
だれか交代してくれないか.	Will any of you take my place?
交代の人が来た.	My alternate [relief] has come to take over.
投手〔学長〕が交代した.	They've changed pitchers [presidents].
私たちは交代で運転した.	We took turns driving.
工場は昼夜3交代で操業している.	The factory operates around the clock on three shifts.
交代時間です.	It's time to change shifts.

こうちょう (好調)

その選手は今日は好調だ.	That player is in good form today.
仕事は好調に進んでいる.	The work is making good progress.
新製品は注文が好調に増えている.	Orders for our new product are showing a steady [good] increase.
あの芝居は客の出足が好調なようですね.	That play seems to be enjoying a good turnout.

こうつう (交通)

この道路は交通が激しい〔少ない〕.	Traffic is heavy [light] on this road.
吹雪で交通が途絶えている.	The snowstorm has brought traffic to a standstill.
がけ崩れで交通が遮断された.	A landslide has blocked the road.
巡査が交通整理をしている.	The policeman is directing [regulating] traffic.
ここは交通の便が良い〔悪い〕.	It's easy [difficult] to get here by public transportation.
地下鉄が出来て交通の便が良くなった.	It's become much easier to get around since the subway opened.
今朝は交通渋滞に巻き込まれた.	I got caught in a traffic jam this morning.

こうどう (行動)

最近彼の行動はおかしい.	His behavior has been odd recently. He's been acting strangely recently.
彼の行動を監視しなさい.	Keep him under close surveillance. Keep a close eye on him.

彼は動物の行動を調査している.	He's investigating animal behavior.
彼は言うばかりで行動が伴わない.	He's all talk and no action.
	He talks a lot but never carries out his ideas [plans].
思い立ったらすぐ行動を起こせ.	Once you decide to do something, don't waste any time before you do it.
例の計画を早速行動に移そう.	Let's †carry out [execute] the plan as soon as possible.
地震のときは敏速に行動しよう.	Take swift action when earthquakes occur.
勝手に行動しないで指示を待ちなさい.	Don't go off on your own. Wait for instructions.
指示を待ってばかりいないで, 時には自分で考えて行動しなさい.	You can't always wait for instructions. Sometimes you have to act on your own authority.
昨日は一日中彼と行動をともにした.	I spent the entire day with him yesterday.
旅行中はずっと団体行動をとった.	We did everything as [in] a group throughout the trip.
旅行中三日間自由行動をとった.	We had three days to do as we pleased during the trip.
彼女は行動的な人です.	She's a woman of action.
彼は理論派というより行動派だ.	He's more of an activist than a theorist.
車があると行動半径が広がる.	Having a car expands your sphere of activities.

こうふく (幸福)

彼は幸福な一生を送った.	He led a happy life.
どうぞ幸福な家庭を築いてください.	I wish you every success in creating a happy home.
彼女は幸福な結婚生活を送っている.	She is happily married.
その後彼らは幸福に暮らした.	And they lived happily ever after.
子どもたちの幸福を祈っている.	I pray for my children's happiness.
私はこの上なく幸福だ.	I couldn't be happier.

こうふん (興奮)

何をそんなに興奮しているの.	What are you so †excited [agitated, worked up] about?
そんなに興奮するな.	Don't get so excited.
その夜は興奮して眠れなかった.	That night I was so excited [agitated] I couldn't sleep.
彼女は興奮し易いたちだ.	She gets excited [agitated] easily.
患者を興奮させないように.	Don't excite the patient.

私は興奮を抑え切れなかった.	I couldn't contain my excitement.
彼女は興奮のあまり大声で叫んだ.	She shouted in a loud voice out of excitement.
やっと彼女の興奮が収まった.	She finally calmed down.
馬が興奮して暴れ出した.	The horse got excited [agitated] and started acting up.

こうへい (公平)

審判員は公平でなければならない.	An umpire must be fair [impartial].
それは公平な意見だ.	That is †a fair [an impartial] opinion.
二人の言い分を公平に聞いてやりなさい.	Listen impartially to what the two have to say.
生徒たちを公平に扱いなさい.	Treat the students fairly [impartially].
父の遺産は公平に分けられた.	My father's estate was divided fairly.
そのけんかに対する彼の処置は公平ではなかった.	The way he dealt with that fight was not fair.
公務員は公平無私であるべきだ.	Civil servants should be fair [impartial] and disinterested.

こうまん (高慢)

彼女は高慢だから嫌われている.	She's †always on her high horse [haughty] so no one likes her.
彼女は美人だが高慢なところが気に入らない.	She's beautiful, but I don't care for her arrogance.
会社では彼は高慢に振る舞っている.	At work he lords it over everyone.
そのうち彼の高慢な鼻をくじいてやりたい.	I'd like to knock him off his high horse one of these days.
彼が高慢な態度ができるのも今のうちだ.	He's not going to be able to have such a high opinion of himself much longer.

こうみょう (巧妙)

犯人は巧妙な手口で金を盗み出した.	The criminal used a clever ploy to steal the money.
彼の巧妙なうそにころりとだまされた.	I was completely taken in by his skillful lying.
実に巧妙に仕組まれた罠だ.	It's really a cleverly devised trap.
彼の巧妙な論理には納得せざるをえない.	I can't help being convinced by his clever reasoning.

こうめい (公明)

公明な選挙でなければならない.	Elections must be open and fair.
あの政治家は何をするにも公明正	That politician is fair and square in what-

大だ.	ever he does.
私は公明正大, 悪いことはしていない.	Everything I do is fair and aboveboard. I haven't done anything bad.

ごうり (合理)

彼女は合理的な考え方をする.	She has a rational mind.
それは多数決で決めるのが合理的だろうね.	The reasonable thing to do would be to settle that by majority decision.
その方法の合理性はだれもが認めている.	Everyone recognizes the rationality of that method.
彼は徹底した合理主義者だ.	He's an all-out rationalist.
組合は合理化のための人員整理に反対している.	The union is opposing any cutback in personnel for the purpose of †improving efficiency [streamlining operations].
そんな不合理なことは納得できない.	Such an irrational thing won't convince me.

こえ (声)

【人の】彼はいい声をしている.	He has a nice voice.
大きな〔小さな〕声で話しなさい.	Speak in a loud [soft] voice.
彼は声を張り上げた〔ひそめた〕.	He raised [lowered] his voice.
しっ！声を立てるな.	Shh! Keep quiet.
風邪で声が出ない.	I've lost my voice because of a cold.
彼はサッカーの応援で声がかれて〔つぶれて〕しまった.	He †got hoarse [lost his voice] from cheering at the soccer match.
声をからして叫んだが, だれも助けに来てくれなかった.	I shouted myself hoarse, but no one came to my rescue.
彼はまだ声変わりしていない.	His voice hasn't changed yet.
後ろからだれかに急に声を掛けられた.	Somebody suddenly called out to me from behind.
声の届くところで遊んでいなさい.	Play within hearing distance.
私は声を限りに助けを求めた.	I shouted for help at the top of my lungs.
彼女は涙で声を詰まらせた.	Her voice choked with tears.
彼女は声を殺して泣いた.	She cried, choking back her sobs.
私たちは人に聞かれぬよう声を殺して話した.	We kept our voices low so (that) nobody could hear us talking.
役者の好演に客席から声が掛かった.	The actor's excellent performance brought cheers from the audience.
今度集まるときは私にも声を掛けて.	The next time you get together, let me know.
彼らは声を揃えて反核を訴えた.	They spoke out unanimously against nuclear weapons.
政府の無策に非難の声が高まって	Criticism has risen in reaction to the gov-

	ernment's lack of policy.
その記事に対し多くの読者の声が寄せられた.	That article drew reactions from many readers.
社長の鶴の一声で一気に事態は収拾された.	The situation was brought under control by one word from the president.
【動物の】鳥の鳴き声で目が覚めた.	The singing of birds woke me up.
草むらから虫の声がする.	Bugs are chirping in the grass.

こえる (越・超える)

【通り越す】飛行機は赤道〔国境〕を越えた.	The airplane crossed the equator 〔border〕.
ヘリコプターで砂漠を越えた.	We crossed the desert by helicopter.
この山を越えると目的地に着く.	We'll arrive at our destination after †going over [crossing] this mountain.
山〔川〕を越えれば隣の町だ.	The next town is on the other side of the mountain 〔river〕.
今日中に三国峠を越える予定だ.	We plan to get over the Mikuni Pass today.
この塀は簡単に越えられる.	This fence is easy to climb over.
猫が塀を越えて入ってきた.	The cat got in over the fence.
彼の車はセンターラインを越えて対向車にぶつかった.	He drove over the center line and ran into a car coming from the opposite direction.
【乗り越える・克服する】いちばん苦しい時期もどうやら越えた.	Somehow I got through the roughest period.
彼は幾多の障害を越えて今日の地位を築いた.	He overcame numerous obstacles to achieve the position he has today.
【～以上になる】応募者は1,000人を超えた.	The number of applicants exceeded one thousand.
台風による被害は10億円を超える見込みだ.	It is estimated that damage caused by the typhoon will exceed one billion yen.
期末試験で彼は平均90点を超えた.	In the final exams he got an average of better than 90 points.
彼は70の坂を越えた.	He is over seventy.
今月の売り上げは目標額を超えそうだ.	Sales this month look as if they might exceed the projected goal.
車は制限速度を超えて走った.	The car was going over the speed limit.
1947年, 人間は初めて音速の壁を超えた.	In 1947 man broke the sound barrier for the first time.
【追い越す】彼の我慢も限界を超えた.	He's run out of patience.
彼の剣道の腕は師を越えた.	His skill in *kendo* surpassed that of his teacher.

【超越する】彼の行動は常識を超えている.	His actions have gone beyond the bounds of common sense.
民族の違いを超えて世界各国から選手が集まった.	Athletes from around the world gathered, transcending ethnic differences.

こおる (凍る)

水は0度で凍り始める.	Water begins to freeze at zero degrees centigrade.
魚がかちかちに凍っている.	The fish is frozen stiff.
朝方の冷え込みで水道管が凍った.	The morning drop in temperature froze the pipes.
地面が凍って滑り易くなっている.	The ground has frozen and become slippery.

ごかい (誤解)

世間は彼のことを誤解している.	People misunderstand him.
みんなの彼に対する誤解はなかなか解けなかった.	Everyone's misunderstanding of him just wouldn't go away.
違うよ，君は僕の言いたいことを誤解している.	No! You're taking what I'm trying to say the wrong way.
それは誤解だよ.	You've got it wrong.
そういう言い方は誤解を招き易い.	Putting it that way leaves it open to misunderstanding.
私が黙っていたら，彼らは私が同意したものと誤解した.	They mistook my silence for consent.

こきゅう (呼吸)

魚はえらで呼吸する.	Fish breathe with gills.
深呼吸しなさい.	Take a deep breath. ／Inhale deeply.
その子は人工呼吸で助かった.	That child was saved by artificial respiration.
全速力で走ったので呼吸が乱れた.	I ran as fast as I could and †began to pant [my breathing became labored].
腹式呼吸は深い呼吸ができる.	You can breathe deeply by breathing from your abdomen.
患者は再び呼吸困難に陥った.	The patient began to have difficulty breathing again.
【慣用】あのバッテリーは呼吸がぴったりと合っている.	That battery works in perfect harmony.
剣道の呼吸がつかめてきた.	I'm beginning to get the hang of *kendo*.

こきょう (故郷)

彼は5年前故郷をあとにした.	He left his hometown five years ago.

東京が私の第二の故郷だ.	Tokyo is my second hometown.
彼女は故郷が恋しくて泣いた.	She cried out of homesickness.
「あなたの故郷はどこですか」「岐阜です」	"Where are you from?" "I'm from Gifu."

こくさい (国際)

彼は国際的な画家だ.	He is a painter of international stature.
その女優は国際的に有名だ.	That actress is internationally famous.
彼は国際人として活躍している.	He's very active internationally.
彼女は国際結婚した.	She married a foreigner.
イギリスに国際電話をかけた.	I made an international (phone) call to England.
この町で国際会議が開かれた.	An international conference was held in this city.
日本のそのやり方は国際社会では通用しない.	The Japanese way of doing that is not acceptable to the rest of the world.
国際情勢が悪化していて,戦争の危険がある.	With the international situation worsening there is danger of war.
それは国際問題にまで発展した.	That developed into an international problem.
ここは国際色豊かな港町です.	This is a harbor town with a rich international flavor.

こくみん (国民)

私は日本国民の一人です.	I'm a citizen of Japan.
両国民は互いにもっと理解し合う必要がある.	There is a need for the people of the two nations to reach greater mutual understanding.
彼は国民的英雄だ.	He is a national hero.
それは国民性の違いというものでしょう.	That may †be due to [have to do with] a difference in national character.
首相の演説は国民感情を刺激した.	The prime minister's speech stirred up national sentiment.
国はその問題を国民投票に諮ることにした.	The country decided to put the question to a referendum.

こげる (焦げる)

魚が焦げているよ.	The fish is burning!
御飯が焦げてしまった.	The rice got burned [scorched].
	I burned the rice.
魚が真っ黒に焦げてしまった.	The fish was burnt black.
何か焦げ臭いよ.	I smell something burning.
たばこの火で畳が焦げてしまった.	The *tatami* was burned by the cigarette.

フライパンに焼きソバが焦げ付いた.	The noodles got burned and stuck to the pan.
あの会社に貸した金は焦げ付いてしまった.	The money lent to that firm was never returned.

ここち (心地)

心地よいそよ風が吹いている.	A pleasant breeze is blowing.
心地よいうたた寝だった.	I had a pleasant doze.
子どもが心地よさそうに眠っている.	The child seems to be sleeping so peacefully.
今朝は心地よく目覚めた.	This morning I woke up refreshed.
このいすはとても座り心地がよい.	This chair is very comfortable.
寝心地のよいベッドだ.	This bed is comfortable to sleep on.
乗り心地のよい車だ.	The car has a comfortable ride.
この家は住み心地がいい.	This house is comfortable to live in.
私は夢見心地だった.	I felt as if I were in a dream.
生きた心地がしなかった.	I felt more dead than alive.

こころ (心)

【心温まる】電車の中で心温まる光景に出会った.	I came across a heartwarming scene in the train.
【心ある】心ある人なら，それを黙って見過ごしはしないだろう.	A conscientious person would not keep silent and let it pass.
【心が・は】私たちは心が通い合っている.	We have an emotional rapport.
彼には花を愛する心がない.	He doesn't know how to appreciate flowers.
行こうか行くまいか，私の心は揺れている.	My heart is torn between going and not going.
【心から】心から君に感謝している.	I thank you from the bottom of my heart.
彼は心からそう信じている.	He honestly [sincerely] believes that.
彼は私の合格を心から喜んでくれた.	He sincerely rejoiced over my being accepted.
彼女に心からの賛辞を贈った.	I paid her a heartfelt compliment.
【心ない】心ないハイカーたちが次から次へとごみを捨てていく.	One after another, inconsiderate hikers throw litter in their path.
【心ならずも】私は心ならずも承諾した.	I consented but my heart wasn't in it.
【心に】素晴らしい考えが私の心に浮かんだ.	I've come up with a great idea.
彼女は自分が80歳になった姿を心に描いてみた.	She tried to picture herself at the age of eighty.
そのことが心にかかってゆうべは	That was weighing on my mind last night

こ

眠れなかった.	and I couldn't sleep.
親は子どものことをいつも心にかけている.	Parents are always concerned about their children.
私はその言葉を心に刻み込んだ.	Those words are etched in my mind.
心にしみるような彼女の歌を聞いて多くの観客が目に涙を浮かべていた.	Listening to her deeply moving song, many in the audience had tears in their eyes.
このことは心に留めておいてくれ.	Please keep this in mind.
彼の忠告をしっかりと心に留めた.	I took his warning to heart.
彼は心にもないこと(お世辞)を言った.	He said something that wasn't in his heart. He made an insincere compliment.
【心の】彼は心の温かい人だ.	He's warm-hearted.
彼女は心の優しい人だ.	She's kind-hearted.
彼は心の広い〔狭い〕人だ.	He's a broad-minded 〔narrow-minded〕 person.
彼から心のこもった贈り物をもらった.	I received a thoughtful present from him.
【心の中】彼は心の中では何を考えているか分からない.	I don't know what he's actually thinking.
私はそのとき顔では笑っていたが心の中では泣いていた.	At the time I was smiling on the outside and crying on the inside.
【心ゆくまで】心ゆくまで楽しんでください.	Please enjoy yourself to your heart's content.
【心を】彼女は息子の非行に心を痛めている.	Her son's delinquency is breaking her heart.
彼は心を入れ替えてまじめにやっている.	He †reformed completely [turned over a new leaf] and is now a serious fellow.
その悲しい話に心を動かされた.	I was moved by that sad story.
彼女の勇気ある行動に心を打たれた.	Her courageous act moved me.
私はその少女に心を奪われた.	I fell in love with that girl. That girl stole my heart.
彼は美しい幻のチョウに心を奪われていた.	He was captivated by the beauty of the rare butterfly.
その頃, 私はラテン音楽に心を奪われていた.	I was enraptured then by Latin music.
彼女は考古学に心を傾けた.	She devoted herself to the study of archaeology.
私はもう心を決めた.	My mind is already made up.
先生は私の就職のために心を砕いてくださった.	My teacher went out of his way to help me get a job.
彼女の心をくんでやってくれ.	Please take her feelings into account.
彼女は夫のために心を込めて料理	She prepared a meal for her husband with

を作った. | loving care.
ビートルズの音楽は世界の若者の心をとらえた. | The Beatles' music captured the hearts of young people all over the world.
私はその絵に心を引かれた. | I was †attracted by [drawn to] that painting.
昔の恋人が目の前に現れ, 心を乱した. | I got all upset when my ex-boyfriend suddenly appeared right there before me.
彼女はある男性に密かに心を寄せている. | She's secretly in love with a certain man.

こころあたり (心当たり)

彼の行き先に心当たりはないですか. | Do you have any idea where he might be?
だれが本を持っていったか心当たりはありませんか. | Do you have any idea who took the book?
この仕事に適任と思われる人の心当たりがあります. | I have someone in mind who is just right for the job.
心当たりの所を捜してくれ. | Look for it every place you think there's a chance it might be.

こころがける (心掛ける)

健康のため車に乗らず歩くように心掛けている. | For my health I'm trying to walk more and drive less.
君のためにいい参考書がないか心掛けておくよ. | I'll keep my eyes open for a good reference book for you.
毎月貯金するとはいい心掛けだ. | You're really smart to save money every month.
ふだんの心掛けが悪いから, こんなことになるんだ. | This is what you get for never thinking about what might happen.

こころづよい (心強い)

彼女がリーダーなら心強い. | I'll feel confident [reassured] as long as she's the leader.
彼が我がチームに入ってくれれば心強い. | It would †boost our confidence [be reassuring] if he joined our team.
君が一緒に来てくれて心強かった. | It was reassuring for you to come with me.

こころぼそい (心細い)

夜道を一人で帰るのは心細い. | I feel uneasy [It's lonesome] returning home alone at night.
旅費がこれだけでは心細い. | I feel uneasy having only this much for travel expenses.

こころみ

未経験者だけでその仕事をするなんて心細い限りだ. / Having only inexperienced people do that work makes me feel extremely uneasy.

一人教室に取り残され，心細い思いをした. / I felt lonesome being left in the classroom by myself.

こころみ (試み)

それは新しい試みだ. / That is a new attempt.
試みにやってみよう. / Let's try it (out).
その試みは失敗に終わった. / That attempt ended in failure.

こころみる (試みる)

だれもそれを試みたことはない. / No one has tried that before.
この絵では新しい技法が試みられている. / The artist has tried a new technique in this painting.
あの山には今まで何人もの登山家が登頂を試みたが，ことごとく失敗している. / A number of mountain climbers have attempted to scale that peak but all have failed.

こころよい (快い)

春の日差しが快い. / Spring sunlight is very pleasant.
快い音楽が聞こえてきた. / I began to hear the sound of pleasant music.
その言葉は耳に快い. / Those words are pleasing to the ear.
彼女は快く承諾してくれた. / She agreed quite readily.
突然の訪問だったのに，彼らは快くもてなしてくれた. / They entertained us pleasantly even though we just popped in on them.
彼は私の昇進を快く思っていないようだ. / He doesn't seem to be pleased by my promotion.

こし (腰)

彼女の髪は腰まで伸びている. / Her hair hangs [comes] down to her waist.
警官は腰にピストルを下げている. / The policeman is wearing a pistol in a holster at his waist.
座りっぱなしで腰が痛くなってきた. / Sitting all that time has given me a pain in my lower back.
中腰で作業すると腰を痛めるよ. / You get a bad back if you work bent over.
祖父は年を取って腰が曲がってきた. / My grandfather's back has gotten bent over with age.
彼は腰をかがめた. / He stooped over.
疲れたので道端に腰を下ろした. / I was tired and †sat down [squatted] on the side of the road.
腰から下を冷やさないようにしなさい. / Don't let the lower half of your body get cold.

【慣用】彼は殺人の現場を見て腰を抜かした.	He was †terrified [scared stiff] when he came upon the scene of the murder.
彼は海賊が隠した財宝の山を見つけて腰を抜かした.	He was astounded when he saw the huge piles of pirate treasure.
そろそろ腰を上げよう.	Let's get going.
うちの女房は腰が重い.	My wife is slow to †act [get down to work].
	My wife is lethargic [sluggish].
彼は腰の落ち着かないやつだ.	He never sticks to anything for very long.
私は腰を据えてその研究に取り組んだ.	I settled down to my research.
彼は腰の低い人だ.	He's very humble.
彼はすぐ人の話の腰を折る.	He always puts a damper on people's conversations.
【粘り・張り】腰の強いうどんが好きだ.	I don't like my noodles soft.
私の髪は腰がないのでパーマがかかりにくい.	My hair has so little body that it can't take a perm.

こしつ (固執)

彼は最後まで自説に固執した.	He stuck to his opinion to the end.
一つの考え方ばかりに固執していてはだめだ.	Don't limit yourself to just one way of thinking.

こしょう (故障)

途中で車が故障した.	The car broke down on the way.
電車が故障して20分止まった.	Something went wrong with the train and it stopped for 20 minutes.
うちのテレビは故障している.	Something is wrong with my TV (and it doesn't work).
この公衆電話〔自動販売機〕は故障している.	This †public phone [vending machine] is out of order.
故障車のせいで道路が渋滞した.	A disabled car caused a traffic jam.
あのピッチャーは肩に故障がある.	That pitcher is having shoulder trouble.

こじん (個人)

【各人】手続きは個人でしてください.	Please do the procedure individually.
それは個人個人の問題だ.	That's a problem for each individual.
彼らは個人個人はみんないいやつなんだが, 集まるとろくなことをしない.	Individually they're fine, but when they get together they lose all decency.
学校には個人用のロッカーがある.	There are individual lockers at school.

成長には個人差がある.	There are individual variations in the way people grow up.
アメリカは個人主義の国だ.	The United States is a nation of individualism.
【私人】それは私個人の問題です.	That's my personal problem.
私個人としては賛成だ.	As an individual, I (can) agree with you. Personally I can agree with you.
私は彼を個人的に知っている.	I know him personally.
私と彼女とは個人的なつきあいはない.	I don't see her privately.
私は彼から英語の個人教授を受けている.	I am taking private English lessons from him.

こす (越す)

【越えて行く】この山なら5時間で越せる.	We can get over this mountain in five hours.
ジープは半日がかりで砂漠を越した.	It took the jeep half a day to get across the desert.
列車は利根川を越して茨城県に入った.	The train crossed the Tone River and entered Ibaraki prefecture.
【越えて出る】川の水が堤防を越した.	The river flooded its banks.
【年月を過ごす】あの患者もこの冬を越せれば大丈夫でしょう.	If that patient gets through this winter, he will be all right.
冬を越した虫たちが活動を始めた.	The insects that survived the winter started to stir.
【大変な時期を越える】彼女の病気は峠を越した.	She got through the critical period in her illness.
【～以上になる】気温は30度を超した.	The temperature went over 30 degrees centigrade.
旅行参加希望者は定員の20名を超した.	The number of applicants for the trip has exceeded the limit of twenty.
【追い越す】彼の身長は父親を越した.	He's become taller than his father.
【勝る】早く行くに越したことはない.	It's best to go early.
遅くてもやるに越したことはない.	Better late than never.
給料は多いに越したことはない.	You can't beat a large salary.
【引っ越す】いつ越すんですか.	When are you moving?
私は昨日ここに越してきた.	I moved here yesterday.

こする (擦る)

汚い手で目をこすってはいけません.	Don't rub your eyes with dirty hands.

寒くて手をこすり合わせた.	It was so cold that I rubbed my hands together.
風呂に入って体をよくこすりなさい.	Please take a bath and scrub yourself well.
服についた泥をこすり落とした.	I rubbed the mud off my clothes.
手についた絵の具を壁にこすりつけた.	I rubbed the paint off my hands onto the wall.
机をずらすとき,床をこすって傷をつけてしまった.	I scratched the floor when I moved the desk.

こせい (個性)

人にはそれぞれ個性がある.	Each person has his own personality.
彼は強烈な個性の持ち主だ.	He has a strong personality.
その女優は個性豊かだ〔個性に欠ける〕.	That actress †has [doesn't have] a very distinctive personality.
この文章には君の個性がよく出ている.	This passage really shows your personality.
自分の個性に合った服装をしなさい.	Wear clothes which reflect your personality.
その教師は常に生徒の個性を尊重する.	That teacher always takes each student's personality into account.
三つ子のあいだにも個性の違いが現れてきた.	Differences in personality among the triplets have begun to show up.
彼女は個性の発揮できる仕事をやりたがっている.	She wants a job where she can show her originality.
彼女は個性的な顔立ちをしている.	She has a distinctive face.

～こそ

今年こそ日記をつけよう.	This year for sure I'm going to keep a diary.
今日こそ彼女をデートに誘おう.	Today for sure I'm going to ask her for a date.
彼こそ市長にふさわしい.	He's just right for mayor.
これこそ私が求めていた物だ.	This is just what I wanted.
彼を信ずればこそ,すべてを任せているのだ.	I'm leaving everything to him because I know I can trust him.
これを無くしたらそれこそ大変だ.	We'll really be in trouble if we lose *this*.
「どうもお邪魔しました」「いいえ,こちらこそ何のお構いもできなくて」	"Thanks for such a nice time." "Well, I'm afraid I wasn't much of a host."
お母さんは喜びこそすれ,怒るはずはない.	Your mother won't get angry. It will make her happy.

こたえ (答え)

あなたの答えが聞きたい.	I want to hear your answer.
明日までに答えを出してくれ.	Please give an answer by tomorrow.
それは答えになっていない.	That's no answer.
やっと正しい答えが出た.	At last, the correct answer!
ドアを叩いても答えはなかった.	I knocked on the door but there was no answer.
彼はその問題に彼なりに答えを出した.	He responded to the problem in his own way.

こたえる (答・応・堪える)

その質問には答えられない.	I can't †answer [give a reply to] that question.
私が手を振ると彼は笑ってこたえた.	I waved my arm, and he smiled back in response.
アンコールにこたえて彼は短い曲を弾いた.	In response to calls for an encore he played a short piece.
私は親の期待にこたえられない.	I can't live up to my parents' expectations.
この冬の寒さはこたえる.	I really feel the cold this winter.
母親の死が彼にはこたえた.	He took his mother's death hard.
その厳しい批評が彼には随分こたえたようだった.	He seems to have taken that severe criticism quite hard.
風呂上がりのビールはこたえられない.	There's nothing like a beer right after taking a bath.

こだわる

彼は服装にこだわらない.	He's not particular about clothes.
彼女は形式にこだわる人だ.	She is stiff and formal.
彼女は形式にこだわらない.	She doesn't stick to formalities.
何をそんなにこだわっているの?	What are you being so particular about?
つまらないことにいつまでもこだわってはいけない.	Don't let little things keep †holding you back [bothering you].
この年になって親の援助を受けるのにはこだわりを感じる.	At my age I feel a little awkward getting help from my parents.
彼らはそれまでのこだわりを捨てて仲直りした.	They cleared up the misunderstandings they had had up until then and made up with each other.

ごちそう (ご馳走)

食卓にはごちそうが並んでいた.	The table was arranged with attractive food.
今夜はごちそうだね.	We're really going to have a feast tonight.
ごちそうさま.	I really enjoyed the meal.

	That was a delicious meal.
何かおいしいものをごちそうしてあげよう.	I'll treat you to something good to eat.
夕食は友達の家でごちそうになりました.	I had dinner at a friend's house.
一杯ごちそうするよ.	I'll buy you a drink.
寒い夜には温かいお風呂が何よりのごちそうだ.	There's nothing like a hot bath on a cold night.

こちら

こちらにはよくいらっしゃるんですか.	Do you come here very often?
どうぞこちらへおいでください.	Please come over here.
お帰りはこちらからどうぞ.	This is the way out.
お会計はこちらでお願いします.	Please †make your payment [pay] here.
その品物はこちらでは扱っておりません.	(I'm sorry but) We don't carry that here.
部屋のこちら側にベッドを置こう.	Let's put the bed on this side of the room.
お探しの品物はこちらですか.	Is this what you were looking for?
こちらはみな元気です.	Everyone here is fine.
佐藤さん, こちらは井上さんです.	Mr. Sato, this is Mr. Inoue.
もしもし, こちらは高橋です〔と申します〕.	Hello, †this [my name] is Takahashi.
こちらのほうからまた電話します.	I'll phone again. ／I'll call you back.

こつ

彼とうまくやっていくこつを教えて.	How can I get along with him?
彼とうまくやっていくこつは何かにつけて彼をたてることです.	The way to get along with him is to †make him feel important [boost his ego] whenever you can.
折り紙をきれいに仕上げるこつはしっかり折り目をつけることだ.	The trick to making good *origami* is getting the creases right.
揚げ物をおいしく作るこつを教えて.	Tell me the secret for [of] making good deep-fried food.
あの課長は人をうまく使うこつを知っている.	That section chief has a real knack for managing people.
いったんこつをつかめば, そんなに難しくないよ.	It's not so difficult once you get the knack [hang] of it.
彼は何事もこつを呑み込むのが早い.	He always catches on quickly.

こっか (国家)

新しい国家が誕生した.	A new nation has come into being.
彼は国家のために尽くした.	He served his country well.
彼は国家存亡のときを救った.	He saved the nation in a time of crisis.
彼女は国家公務員です.	She works for the national [federal[1]] government.
その国では国家予算の1割が防衛費だ.	One tenth of that country's national budget is spent on defense.
医者になるには国家試験に通らなければならない.	You have to pass a national board examination to become a doctor.
1930年代には国家主義が勢力を得た.	Nationalism became a powerful force in the 1930s.

1) アメリカ, ドイツなどの場合.

こづかい (小遣い)

おじいさんに小遣いをもらった.	I got some spending money from Grandfather.
1ヵ月の小遣いはいくらですか.	How much is your monthly allowance?
夫の小遣いは1日2,000円です.	My husband's allowance is 2,000 yen a day.
お母さん, お小遣いもっと増やしてほしいんだけど.	Mom, can you increase my allowance?
月々5,000円の小遣いではとても足りない.	A monthly allowance of 5,000 yen isn't nearly enough.
小遣い帳はつけていますか.	Do you keep an account of your cash expenditures? Do you keep track of how much you spend?
彼は小遣い銭稼ぎに翻訳をしている.	He does translation work to get a little extra spending money.

こっけい (滑稽)

彼はよく滑稽なことを言って人を笑わせる.	He often makes people laugh with the jokes.
彼はよく滑稽なしぐさをする.	He often comes up with some comical gestures.
彼の踊り方はどこか滑稽だ.	There's something comical about the way he dances.
彼が教師になったとは滑稽だ.	I think it's really funny that he became a teacher.
彼はあれで一流の物書きのつもりなんだから滑稽な話だ.	He thinks he's a first-class writer. What a joke.

こっそり

彼はこっそりと教室を抜け出した.	He sneaked out of the classroom.
私にだけこっそり教えてくれ.	Can't you just let me in on it?
監督は敵チームをこっそり偵察した.	The manager secretly scouted the opposing team.
彼女は彼とこっそり会っていた.	She was meeting him on the sly.
彼女はこっそりと英会話の勉強をしている.	She is secretly studying English conversation.
彼女はだれにも気づかれないようにこっそりと電話をかけた.	She quietly made the phone call so that no one would notice.
母は父に気づかれないようにこっそりと私にお金を渡してくれた.	Mom quietly slipped me the money so that Dad wouldn't notice.

こと (事)

【出来事】今日, 学校でおかしなことがあった.	Something odd happened today at school.
どんなことがあっても遅れるなよ.	Don't be late under any circumstances.
事は重大だ.	The situation is serious.
これを無くしたら事だ.	I'm in real trouble if I lose this.
【事柄】世の中には不思議なことがあるものだね.	There really are some amazing things in this world, aren't there?
君に相談したいことがあるんだ.	There's something I want to discuss with you.
そんなことは言われなくても分かっている.	You don't have to tell me that. I already know that.
彼は家のことは妻任せだ.	He leaves his wife in charge of everything at home.
あなたの言うことはもっともだ.	I couldn't agree more with †what you're saying [you].
彼は人のことにすぐ口を出したがる.	He just can't help telling people what to do.
自分のことは自分でしなさい.	Take care of your own affairs.
【事情・場合】あいつのことだからまた寝坊したんじゃないか.	Knowing him, he's probably overslept again.
そんなことではとても大学に合格できないよ.	You'll never make it into the university that way.
肺炎で死ぬこともある.	Pneumonia can be fatal.
事によると彼女は先に行ったのかもしれない.	She might [may] have gone on ahead.
【必要】彼にわざわざ知らせることもない.	There's no need [reason] to go to the trouble of telling him. There's no need to tell him.
彼の悪口を気にすることはない.	Don't let †his bad-mouthing [him] get to

	you.
	You shouldn't let his back-biting bother you.
それなら彼に聞くことだね.	That's something you'll have to ask him about.
【事実】彼女が頭のいいことはだれでも知っている.	Everyone knows (that) she's bright.
この話は聞かなかったことにしてください.	Please forget you ever heard this.
【経験】日食を見たことがある.	I've seen a solar eclipse.
アメリカへ行ったことがありますか.	Have you ever been to America?
【伝聞】彼は死んだということだ.	He is supposed to have died.
	I hear [They say] he died.
【結果】この夏で東京には3年住んだことになる.	I will have lived in Tokyo for three years this summer.
明日も彼女が休まなかったら,今週彼女は毎日ここへ来たことになる.	She will have come here every day this week if she doesn't take tomorrow off.
【予定】彼は5時には来ることになっている.	He's supposed to come at five.
【決心】明日,大阪へ出発することにした.	I decided to leave for Osaka tomorrow.
酒もたばこもやめることにしました.	I've made up my mind to quit drinking and smoking.
【習慣】毎朝,食前にジョギングすることにしている.	As a rule I [I make it a rule to] go jogging before breakfast.
【行為】走ることは健康によい.	Running is good for your health.
恋をすることは悲しみを知ることである.	Falling in love brings sadness and grief.
【命令】午前7時,駅前広場に集合のこと.	We're meeting in the square in front of the station at 7:00 a.m.

こどく (孤独)

彼女は孤独な人だ.	She is a †solitary person [loner].
彼は晩年,孤独な生活を送った.	He led a solitary life in his last years.
私は孤独を愛する.	I love solitude.
私は時として孤独感に襲われる.	From time to time I'm overcome with feelings of loneliness.

ことづかる (言づかる)

すぐ帰って来るようにと君の奥さんから言づかった.	Your wife asked me to tell you to come home right away.

あなたのお母さんからこれを言づかりました.	Your mother left this with me.
あなたへの手紙を彼から言づかったが, 家に置いてきた.	He gave me a letter to give to you, but I left it at home.

ことづける (言づける)

彼にすぐ電話をよこすようにと, 家族の人に言づけてきました.	I left a message with his family for him to telephone me right away.
彼から何か言づけはなかったか.	Wasn't there any message from him?
	Didn't he leave a message?
田中さんに言づけをお願いしたいのですが.	I would like to leave a message for Mr. Tanaka.

ことなる (異なる)

私の意見は彼とは異なる.	My opinion †differs [is different] from his.
人それぞれ考え方は異なるものだ.	Different people have different ways of thinking.
場所が異なれば人の暮らしもまた異なる.	Ways of life differ [vary] from place to place.
音が空中を伝わる速さは気温により異なる.	The speed of sound traveling through the air varies according to the temperature.
その双子は髪の色が異なるだけであとはそっくりだ.	Those twins have different colored hair, but otherwise they look just alike.
ロンドンの街は想像していたのとは異なっていた.	London was different from what I had imagined.

ことば (言葉)

【言語】人間は1歳頃から言葉を話し始める.	Human beings start learning how to talk at about the age of one.
日本語は非論理的な言葉だと言う人もいる.	Some say that Japanese is an illogical language.
【単語・表現】うまい言葉が見つからない.	I can't find the right †words [way to put it].
別の言葉で言い換えてください.	Please paraphrase what you said.
その美しさは言葉に表せない.	Its beauty †cannot be expressed in words [is beyond description].
そのときの気持ちを言葉に表してごらん.	Try to express †verbally [in words] how you felt at that time.
	Try to tell us how you felt at the time.
彼の言葉を借りれば, 彼女は手のつけられないじゃじゃ馬だ.	To borrow his words, she's as uncontrollable as a wild horse.
彼は難しい言葉を使う.	He uses difficult language.
彼女は言葉を飾らない人だ.	She doesn't mince words.

言葉尻をとらえていては建設的な議論はできない.	Tripping someone up with his own words is not conducive to good consultation.
【言葉づかい】彼は言葉が汚い.	He uses foul language.
言葉に気をつけなさい.	Be careful what you say.
彼女は上品〔下品〕な言葉を使う.	She uses refined (vulgar) language.
そんな乱暴な言葉づかいをしてはいけない.	Don't use such coarse language.
【しゃべること】彼の言葉に甘えて夕飯をごちそうになった.	I accepted his kind offer and he treated me to dinner.
彼女は言葉に窮した.	She was at a loss for words.
彼の言葉をうのみにした.	I accepted what he said unquestioningly.
お言葉を返すようですが、問題はそれほど単純ではありません.	I don't mean to contradict you, but the problem isn't that simple.
彼のあまりに馬鹿げた発言に私は返す言葉がなかった.	I had nothing to say in answer to his ridiculous statement.
道で知らない人に言葉を掛けられた.	A stranger started talking to me on the street.
彼女とは会えば言葉を交わす仲だ.	I know her well enough to speak [talk] to her.
彼は私の言葉をさえぎって話し始めた.	He interrupted me and started speaking.
彼女は言葉を濁してはっきりと答えなかった.	She wouldn't come out with a clear answer.
私たちの話に言葉を挟まないで.	Please don't interrupt our conversation.
それが親に向かって言う言葉か!	How can you say something like that to your own parents?
甘い言葉に乗って彼の言うとおりにしたのが間違いだった.	It was a mistake to †fall for his line [listen to him] (and do as he said).
彼は言葉巧みに彼女を食事に誘った.	He smooth-talked her into going out to dinner with him.
売り言葉に買い言葉で二人は大げんかした.	Their verbal tit-for-tat escalated into a big fight.
彼は言葉数が多い.	He's talkative.
彼は言葉数が少ない.	He's a man of few words.
私は彼の受賞パーティーで祝いの言葉を述べた.	I offered some words of congratulation at a party held in honor of his winning the prize.

ことわる (断る)

【拒絶する】彼はだれに借金を頼んでも断られた.	Everyone he asked for a loan turned him down.
彼は先方の依頼を体よく断った.	He politely †refused [turned down] the other party's request.

ネクタイをしていなかったので，入場を断られた．	I was †denied entrance [turned away at the door] because I wasn't wearing a tie.
レストランは満員でほかの客は断られていた．	The other customers were turned away because the restaurant was full.
せっかくの招待だが断らなければいけないな．	It was nice of them to invite us, but we have to decline.
彼は両親の援助を断った．	He refused his parents' help.
彼はその賞を丁重に断った．	He respectfully †turned down [declined] the prize.
熱心に誘われて，断り切れなかった．	They invited me so warmly that I just couldn't say no.
またマージャンの誘いならお断りだよ．	If it's mah-jong you're asking me to again, no thanks.
【了解をとる】彼の本を借りるなら，本人に断ったほうがいいよ．	If you are borrowing his book you should ask his permission.
だれに断って入ってきたんだ？	Who gave you permission to come in here?
来月引っ越すことを大家さんに断っておいた．	I gave notice to my landlord that I would be moving out next month.
断っておくが，この話はだれにも言うなよ．	Let me warn you. Don't talk about this to anybody.
断っておきますが，私はあなたの妻であって母親ではありません．	Let's get this straight. I am your wife, not your mother.

こなす

彼は何でもそつなくこなす．	He's really clever at everything.
彼は一人でほかの人の3倍の仕事をこなしている．	He's doing the work of three people.
与えられた仕事をこなすだけの毎日だ．	I'm just doing what I'm asked to do every day.
この運動メニューをこなせば，2週間で体が変わってくるよ．	If you follow this exercise program, your body will change in two weeks.
彼女はどんなに気性の荒い馬でも楽々と乗りこなす．	She can handle any horse, no matter how wild it may be.

このあいだ

このあいだうちの猫が子を生んだ．	Our cat had kittens the other day.
このあいだの晩に停電があった．	There was a power outage the other night.
このあいだから体の具合が悪い．	I haven't been feeling well these past few days.
このあいだの話はどうなった？	What came of the talk we had the other day?
このあいだのパーティーはどうで	How was the party the other day?

した?	
ついこのあいだまで子どもだと思っていたが,彼はもう立派な大人だ.	Until quite recently I had thought of him as a child, but he's become a fine adult.

このごろ (この頃)

この頃忙しいようだね.	You've been busy recently [lately], haven't you?
この頃あまり運動していない.	I haven't been getting much exercise recently [lately].
この頃の電化製品は昔に比べて省エネになっている.	Electrical appliances today don't use as much energy as they used to.
「この頃の若いもんは…」というのが祖父の口癖だ.	"Young people †these days [nowadays]..." is the way my grandfather starts many of his sentences.

このまえ (この前)

この前あなたと一緒にいた人はだれ?	Who was that person you were with then?
この前彼に会ったのはいつだったかな.	When was the last time I saw him?
この前の日曜は海に行った.	I went to the beach last Sunday.
この前の旅行は楽しかった.	The last trip we took was fun.

このましい (好ましい)

彼は好ましい人物だ.	He's a nice [pleasant, agreeable] person.
運動をする人が増えたのは好ましい傾向です.	It's nice to see more people exercising.
今ここでその話をするのは好ましくない.	This is not the time or place to talk about that.
派手な服装はこの職場には好ましくない.	Fancy clothes are not appropriate in this office.

このみ (好み)

人の好みはさまざまだ.	Everyone (according) to his taste. To each his own.
これはあなたの好みにぴったりだ.	This suits your taste perfectly. This is you.
これなら彼の好みにかなうでしょう.	This should suit his taste.
彼は服装の好みが難しい.	He has fastidious taste in clothes.
私と彼とでは食べ物の好みが合わない.	His taste in food and mine don't match.

彼女は何でも夫の好みに合わせるようにしている.	She always accommodates herself to her husband's tastes.
どんな女性が好みのタイプですか.	What kind of woman do you like?
好みの色は何ですか.	What colors do you like?
好みの料理があったら頼みなさい.	If there's anything you'd especially like, go ahead and order it.
君にプレゼントをしたいんだけど, 何か好みはないですか.	I'd like to give you a present. Is there anything in particular you want?

コピー

【複写】この資料を人数分コピーしてください.	Please †run off [xerox] enough copies of this document for everyone.
アルバイトの仕事は主にコピー取りです.	The part-timer's job consists mainly of †making copies [photocopying documents].
このコピーは濃すぎる〔薄すぎる〕.	This copy is too dark [light].
自宅にコピー機を買い入れた.	I bought a †photocopier [Xerox machine] for home.
【複製】CDの違法コピーが出回っている.	Illegal copies of CDs are appearing on the market.
【真似】あの曲はヒット曲のコピーに過ぎない.	That song is just an imitation of a hit song.
【コンピュータ】その段落をコピーして, 別の文書に貼りつけた〔ペーストした〕.	I copied the paragraph and pasted it into another document.

イギリスやヨーロッパでは,「複写」の意味の copy の代わりに, 名詞・動詞とも photocopy をよく使う.

ごぶさた (ご無沙汰)

ごぶさたしています. お元気ですか？（手紙文)	It's been some time since we were last in touch. How are you doing?
すっかりごぶさたして申し訳ありません.	I'm sorry I haven't been in touch (with you) for †so long [such a long time].[1] Please forgive me for not writing sooner.[2]
あれほど熱中していたテレビゲームも, 今ではすっかりごぶさただ.	I've completely lost interest in the video games I was so crazy about.

1) は手紙でも会話でも使える. 2) は手紙文.

こぼす

コーヒーをテーブルにこぼした.	I spilled coffee on the table.
小さい子はよくご飯をこぼす.	Small children often spill their food.
彼女は給料のことでいつも何やらこぼしている.	She's always griping [grumbling, complaining] about her salary.

こぼれる

運んでいるうちにバケツの水がこぼれた.	Some water spilled out of the bucket while I was carrying it.
袋が破れて米が床にこぼれた.	The bag split and the rice spilled onto the floor.
包丁の刃がこぼれて使いものにならない.	The knife is useless because the edge is nicked.
彼女はこぼれんばかりの笑顔で私を出迎えた.	She was full of smiles as she came to meet me.

こまかい (細かい)

細かい雨が降っている.	It's drizzling.
ここの砂は細かい.	The sand here is fine-grained.
ニンジンを細かく切ってください.	Cut the carrot into small pieces.
字が細かすぎて読めません.	The characters [letters] are too small to read.
	The print is too fine [small] to read.[1]
このくしは目が細かい.	This is a fine-toothed comb.
目の細かいざるを使いなさい.	Use a fine strainer.
細かいお金を持っていませんか.	Do you have any change?
この100円玉を細かくしてください.	Please change this 100-yen coin.
【ささいな】細かいことに気を取られるな.	Don't get worked up over †trivial things [nothing].
【詳細な】細かいことは彼に聞きなさい.	Ask him about the details.
彼は部下に細かい指示を与えた.	He gave his subordinates detailed instructions.
この事件の原因について細かい分析が必要だ.	It's necessary to make a detailed analysis of the causes of this incident.
この作業は細かい注意を払って進める必要がある.	We must proceed with this operation paying close attention to detail.
事前に細かく打ち合わせよう.	Let's make all the detailed arrangements in advance.
二つの言語を細かく比較してみよう.	Let's make a detailed comparison of the two languages.
レポーターは事件の様子を事細か	The reporter explained the incident in

に説明した.	detail.
【神経などが】彼は神経が細かい.	He's very sensitive.
うちの上司はお金に細かい.	Our boss is particular about money.
あの役者は芸が細かい.	As an actor he pays great attention to detail.
彼女はお金に細かい人だ.	She's tight with money.
	She's a penny-pincher.

1) 印刷された文字の場合.

ごまかす

彼に理由を聞かれたが, 適当にごまかした.	I simply evaded the question when he asked me why.
ごまかさないで! ちゃんと答えてよ!	Don't be so evasive. Just give me a straight answer.
君のおかげでうまくごまかせたよ.	Thanks to you I was able to get around it.
本当のことが言えなくて, 笑ってごまかした.	I just laughed it off because I couldn't come out with the truth.
彼は年をごまかしている.	He's passing himself off as older (younger) than he really is.
あの肉屋はよく目方をごまかす.	That meat store often cheats on the weight.
タクシーの運転手にお釣をごまかされた.	The taxi driver †shortchanged me [didn't give me enough change back].
会計係は帳簿をごまかしていたのを見つかった.	The bookkeeper got caught fudging the books.

こまる (困る)

【困惑】困ったことが起きた.	There's [We have] a problem.
財布を無くしたの? それは困ったね.	You lost your wallet? That's too bad.
さあ困った. 当てにしていた彼に断わられたぞ.	Now we're in trouble. I was counting on him and he turned me down.
困ったな. 雨が降り始めたけど傘を持っていない.	Oh, no. It's started to rain and I don't have an umbrella.
雨が降ったら困るから傘を持って行きなさい.	You'll get wet if it rains, so take an umbrella.
彼は返答に困った.	He was at a loss for an answer.
いい方法が見つからず私たちは困り果てた.	Unable to come up with a good solution [method], we were at a complete loss as to what to do.
友達に200万円貸してくれと頼まれて困ってしまった.	My friend really put me on the spot when he asked me to lend him ¥2 million

	[two million yen].
【迷惑】彼は言われたとおりにしないから困るよ.	The trouble with him is he never does as he's told.
最近の若者の礼儀知らずにも困ったものだ.	It's annoying that today's young people don't have (good) manners.
公園にゴミを散らす人が多いのは困ったことだ.	It's aggravating that there are many people who throw their trash just anywhere in the park.
困ったことに店が閉まっていた.	It was †unfortunate [too bad] that the store was closed.
もう帰るんですか. それは困ります.	You're going home already? You can't do that.
明日までに仕上げてくれないと困ります.	You must have (it) finished by tomorrow.
【難儀】困ったらいつでも私のところに来なさい.	Come to me whenever you have a problem.
彼は困っている人を見捨てておけないたちだ.	It's not his nature to ignore people in trouble.
当時は皆生活に困っていた.	At that time everyone was having trouble †getting by [making ends meet].
彼は食うに困らないだけの収入は何とか得ている.	Somehow he makes just enough money to †eat [keep himself in food.]
彼は金に困って強盗を働いた.	He got hard up for money and committed robbery.
昨年は水不足で困ったよ.	The water shortage last year caused a lot of trouble.
	We had problems due to the water shortage last year.
眼鏡がなくても別に困らない.	I can get by without glasses.
	I don't have any particular problem seeing without glasses.
外国で言葉が通じないと本当に困る.	It's really inconvenient [It's a (real) pain] not knowing the language when you're in a foreign country.

ごみばこ (ごみ箱)

部屋のごみ箱〔台所のごみ箱, ガレージのごみ箱〕が一杯になった.	The †wastepaper basket in the room [garbage can in the kitchen, trash can in the garage] was full.
公園のごみ箱を子どもたちがひっくり返した.	The children knocked over the garbage can in the park.
【コンピュータ】不要なファイルをごみ箱に捨てた.	I deleted the files I didn't need anymore by putting them in the Recycle Bin.[1]

空きメモリを増やすためにごみ箱を空にした.	I emptied the Waste Basket[2] to free up some memory.

> 1) the Recycle Bin はウインドウズ系コンピュータの, 2) the Waste Basket はマッキントッシュの用語. 表現としては入れ換え可能.

こむ (込・混む)

映画館はとても込んでいた.	The movie theater was very crowded.
朝の電車は通勤通学客で込んでいる.	Trains in the morning are crowded with commuting workers and students.
道が込んでいて着くのが遅れた.	The roads were congested, so I arrived late.

こめる (込める)

彼は銃に弾を込めた.	He loaded the rifle.
彼は力を込めてくいを引き抜いた.	He mustered his strength and pulled out the stake.
作者はこの一文に多くの意味を込めている.	The author put a lot of meaning into this single sentence.
この手袋には母の愛情が込められている.	Mother made these gloves for me with tender loving care.
彼らは健康に育つようにという願いを込めて息子にこの名を付けた.	They gave their son this name in the hope that he would grow up strong and healthy.

ごめん (御免)

遅れてごめん.	Sorry to be late.
ごめんなさい. 私が悪かった.	Forgive me. I was wrong.
ちょっとごめん. そこをどいてくださいませんか.	Excuse me. Would you step out of the way?
ごめんください. ご主人はいらっしゃいますか.	Excuse me. Is your husband at home?
そんな面倒はごめんだ.	There's no way I'm going to go to that much trouble.
あんな仕事はもう二度とごめんだ.	There's no way I'd ever do that kind of work again.

こらえる (堪える)

足がしびれたけど, ずっとこらえていた.	My feet were numb, but I put up with it to the end.
私はおかしいのをこらえて彼の話を聞いていた.	I stifled my laughter as I listened to him.

私はこらえ切れずに吹き出した.	I couldn't stand it any longer and burst into laughter.
彼は涙をこらえ切れなかった.	He couldn't hold back the tears.
彼は必死に怒りをこらえていた.	He desperately tried to suppress his anger.
こらえていた悲しみが爆発して彼女は泣きだした.	The sadness she had been suppressing finally exploded and she burst into tears.
ここで腹を立ててはこちらの負けです. どうかこらえてください.	Try and control your temper because if you lose it now it will ruin everything for us.
彼女が職場を転々とするのはこらえ性がないからだ.	Her moving from one company to another shows her lack of perseverance.

こりる (懲りる)

彼も今度の失敗には懲りたでしょう.	He's probably learned a lesson from this failure [mistake].
競馬で負けてばかりなのに彼はまだ懲りない.	He loses constantly at the races but still hasn't learned his lesson.
私が何度追い返しても彼は懲りずにやって来る.	No matter how many times I send him away he just keeps coming back.

こる (凝る)

【熱中する】私は今オセロゲームに凝っている.	I'm into the Othello game now.
彼はアフリカの文学に凝っている.	He's into African literature.
彼は凝り性だ. 何か始めるとほかのことは目に入らない.	He really gets into things. Once he starts something he's oblivious to everything else.
【工夫する】彼は服装に凝るほうだ.	He tends to be particular about how he dresses.
あの家は凝った造りをしている.	That house is elaborately built.
これは随分凝った柄ですね.	This is a very fancy [intricate] pattern, isn't it?
大変凝った料理ですね.	This is very fancy [elaborate] cooking.
【筋肉が】昨夜遅くまで書き物をして, 肩が凝った.	I got a stiff neck from staying up late writing last night.

ころ (頃)

もう夕刊が来る頃だ.	It's about time for the evening paper to come.
そろそろアップルパイが焼き上がる頃だ.	The apple pie should be done about now.
そろそろ電車が着く頃だ.	The train should be arriving †any minute [about now].

午後2時頃地震があった.	There was an earthquake at around [about] two in the afternoon.
彼女は5月の半ば頃日本に来る予定だ.	She's planning to come to Japan around [about] the middle of May.
若い頃は走るのが速かった.	I was a fast runner when I was young.
時間どおりに着くように頃(合)を見計らって出かけた.	I timed my departure so (that) I would arrive on time.

ころがす (転がす)

彼はタイヤを転がして車庫まで運んだ.	He rolled a tire along to the garage.
ボールを転がすと猫がじゃれついた.	When I rolled the ball the cat playfully pounced on it.
彼らは丸太の上を転がして大きな石を運んだ.	They moved a large stone by rolling it on logs.

ころがる (転がる)

ボールが転がって川に落ちた.	The ball rolled into the river.
鉛筆が転がって机から落ちた.	The pencil rolled off the desk.
芝生の上で子どもがごろごろ転がって遊んでいる.	The children are playfully rolling around on the lawn.
宝くじに当たり,彼のところへ大金が転がり込んできた.	He had a winning lottery ticket and he was rolling in money.
家出した友人が私の家に転がり込んできた.	My friend ran away from home and wound up †crashing** [staying over] at my place.

ころす (殺す)

彼は何者かによって殺された.	He was killed by someone.
ライオンはシマウマをかみ殺した.	The lion mauled the zebra to death.
【抑える】彼は自分を殺して命令に従った.	He stifled his own feelings and followed the order.
今の仕事は彼女の才能を殺している.	That job is stifling her natural abilities.
彼の話を聞きながら私は笑い〔あくび〕をかみ殺していた.	I †stifled [held back] †my laughter (a yawn) while listening to his story.

ころぶ (転ぶ)

その男の子は石につまずいて転んだ.	The boy tripped on a stone and fell.
道路が凍っていたので滑って転んだ.	The road was covered with ice and I slipped and fell.
彼女はぬかるみに足を取られて転	She got her foot stuck in the mud and fell.

んだ.	
彼は，自転車に乗っていて転び，腕を骨折した.	He was riding (on) his bike when he fell off and broke his arm.
【慣用】転ばぬ先のつえ.	Better safe than sorry.
どっちに転んでも損はない.	I have nothing to lose either way.

こわい (怖い)

ああ，怖かった.	Gee [Boy], was I scared!
話を聞くうちに怖くなってきた.	I started to get scared as I listened to the story.
昨日の地震は本当に怖かった.	Yesterday's earthquake really scared me.
飛行機に乗るのが怖くてまだ海外旅行をしていない.	I'm afraid of flying, so I still haven't traveled overseas.
怖い目にあった.	I had a frightening experience.
怖い映画は大好きだ.	I love scary movies.
怖い夢を見たの？	Did you have a †bad dream [nightmare]?
怖いもの見たさでその映画を見に行った.	I wanted to see something scary, so I went to see that movie.
彼は怖いもの知らずだ.	He's not afraid [scared] of anything.
小さいとき私は父が怖かった.	I was afraid [scared] of my father when I was small.
怒ったときの母はとても怖い.	Mother is really frightening when she's angry.
彼は怖い先生だ.	He's an intimidating teacher.
彼は怖い顔をして私を見た.	He gave me a fierce look.
これが部長に知れたら怖いぞ.	There'll be hell to pay if the boss finds out about this.

こわがる (怖がる)

彼は手術を受けるのを怖がった.	He was afraid of having the operation.
何を怖がっているの？	What are you afraid of?
怖がらないでやってみてごらん.	Don't be afraid. Try it.

こわす (壊す)

模型飛行機を落として壊してしまった.	I dropped the model plane and broke it.
時計をいじって壊してしまった.	I tampered with the clock and broke it.
私たちはかぎを壊してドアを開けた.	We broke the lock and opened the door.
彼はギターを叩き壊した.	He smashed his guitar.
この古い家を壊して新しい家を建てよう.	Let's tear down this old house and build a new one.
観光道路が出来ると山の自然を壊	Building a road for tourists might destroy

してしまう恐れがある.	the environment on the mountain.
【計画・話をだめにする】君は私たちの計画を壊すつもりか.	Do you intend to ruin our plans?
父親が彼女の縁談を壊した.	Her father put a stop to her marriage plans.
【健康を損なう】彼は体を壊してずっと家にいる.	He ruined his health and is now confined to his house.
最近彼は体を壊している.	He's been in poor health recently.
彼女はよくおなかを壊す.	Her stomach frequently gives her trouble. She often gets upset stomachs.

こわれる (壊れる)

時計が壊れた.	My watch broke.
ズボンのファスナーが壊れた.	The zipper on this pair of pants is broken.
このいすは壊れて使えない.	This chair can't be used. It's broken.
その子は壊れたおもちゃを大切にしている.	That child still treasures his broken toy.
このテレビは壊れていて映りません.	This TV is out of order. You can't get a picture.
この家は壊れかかっている.	This house is beginning to fall apart.
壊れ易いものはこの箱に入れてください.	Put fragile items in this box.
「壊れ物注意」	"Fragile—Handle with Care"
【計画・話がだめになる】彼女の過去がばれて縁談が壊れた.	Her past was uncovered and the relationship [arrangement] was broken off.
あの話はいいところまで行って壊れてしまった.	That fell through just when it was going well.

こんがらかる

糸がこんがらかった.	The string got tangled up.
その劇は筋がこんがらかっていて分かりにくかった.	The play's plot was confusing and hard to understand.
話がこんがらかって分からなくなった.	The story was so confusing that I couldn't understand it.
こんな難しい問題は頭がこんがらかって解けない.	This difficult problem has me so confused that I can't solve it.

こんき (根気)

編物は根気の要る仕事だ.	Knitting requires patience [perseverance].
職人は概して根気がいい.	Craftsmen generally have a lot of patience [perseverance].
根気が続かないのが彼の欠点だ.	His shortcoming is that he doesn't stick with things long enough.

彼は根気よく親を説得した.	He patiently tried to persuade his parents.
今度の交渉は彼と私の根気比べだった.	The recent negotiations were a test of endurance between him and me.

こんきょ（根拠）

彼女は明確な根拠を示しながら説明した.	She gave solid grounds for her explanation as she went along.
面白い推論だが，学会で発表するには根拠に乏しい.	That's an interesting conjecture but it isn't solid enough to present at an academic conference.
何を根拠にそんなことを言うんですか？	What is your basis for saying that?
	On what grounds can you make such a claim?
	What evidence do you have for saying that?
それ相応の根拠があって主張しているんでしょうね.	I trust you have enough evidence to support your claim.[1]
根拠のない噂だ．信じるな.	It's a groundless rumor. Don't believe it.
彼は根拠のない自信の持ち主だ.	His self-confidence is unjustified.

1) 日本語同様に疑いを込めた言い方で，文末のイントネーションを上げて言う．

こんざつ（混雑）

混雑した所へ出るのはおっくうだ.	I dislike going to crowded places.
デパートは買い物客で混雑していた.	The department store was crowded [packed] with customers.
朝の駅は通勤客で大変な混雑だ.	In the morning the station is extremely crowded [congested] with commuters.
月末はいつも道路が混雑する.	The roads are always congested (with traffic) at the end of the month.
彼は朝夕の混雑を避けて通勤している.	He commutes to and from work avoiding the morning and evening rush hours.
バイパスが出来て，市内の道路の混雑が緩和された.	The bypass has helped alleviate traffic congestion in the city.

こんじょう（根性）

彼の根性が気に食わない.	I don't care for his personality.
お前のひねくれた根性を叩き直してやる.	I'm going to straighten you out.
	I'll make a new man out of you.
あいつは根性が腐っている〔曲がっている〕.	He has a rotten [perverse] character.
彼は根性がある〔ない〕.	He †has [has no] guts.

彼は根性で山の頂上まで登り切った.	By sheer determination he climbed to the top of the mountain.

こんど (今度)

今度引っ越すことになった.	We're going to move.[1]
今度彼は昇進したそうだ.	I hear he got a promotion.[2]
今度は私の番だ.	It's my turn this time.
今度はいつ来るの.	When are you coming next time?
今度から気をつけます.	I'll be careful from now on.
今度こそ君は成功するよ.	Next time you'll succeed.
今度の日曜日はどこかへ行くの.	Are you going somewhere this Sunday?
今度の選挙に彼は立候補する.	He's a candidate in †this [the upcoming] election.
彼の今度の小説は非常に面白い.	His latest novel is very interesting.
今度の先生は厳しい.	This teacher is strict.

> 1)2) このような場合,英語では特に「今度」にあたる言葉は入れないのが普通.

こんな

こんなズボンが欲しいと思っていました.	These are the kind of pants I had in mind.
犯人はこんな顔の男だった.	The criminal had a face like this.
こんな所にあったのか. 探していたんだ.	So this is where it was. I've been looking for it.
こんなにおいしいワインは初めてだ.	I've never had such good wine before.
こんなに遅くまで何をしていたのですか.	What were you doing this late?
こんなに雨が降ったのは久しぶりだ.	It's been a long while [time] since we've had this much rain.
車はパンクするし雨には降られるし,こんなことなら来るんじゃなかった.	First I had a flat tire and then I got rained on. If I knew it was going to be like this I wouldn't have come.
こんなことだろうと思ったよ.	This is just what I thought would happen.
こんなもんだよ,世の中なんて.	That's life. That's the way the ball bounces. That's the way the cookie crumbles.

こんなん (困難)

彼の前途には困難が待ち受けている.	Difficulties lie ahead for him.
彼はいくつもの困難に打ち勝って	He has overcome numerous hardships.

彼はどんな困難にあってもへこたれない男だ.	He never loses heart no matter what the difficulty.
彼女は困難をものともしなかった.	She made nothing of her difficulties.
残念ながら計画の実行は困難です.	Unfortunately, putting the plan into effect is a difficult matter.
この仕事をやり遂げるには困難な問題が多過ぎる.	There are too many difficulties in trying to do [accomplish] this job.

コンピュータ

今の時代, コンピュータが使いこなせなければ就職に不利だ.	These days, when you're looking for a job it's a disadvantage not being able to use a computer.
コンピュータの電源を入れると自動的にOSが立ち上がる.	The OS starts [boots] up automatically as soon as you turn on the computer.
彼はコンピュータを取り出して, 電車の中で報告書を書き始めた.	He took out his computer and started writing the report in the train.
スキャナを使えば, 写真もコンピュータに取り込むことができる.	If you use a scanner you can also put photos into your computer.
この工場はすべてコンピュータ制御されている.	This factory is completely computerized.
「パソコン」は「パーソナルコンピュータ」の略である.	*Pasokon* in Japanese is short for personal computer.

こんぽん (根本)

彼の思想の根本は愛である.	His philosophy is based on love.
彼女は根本から間違っている.	She's fundamentally mistaken.
彼の言うことは根本においては正しい.	What he says is basically correct.
制度の根本的な改革が必要だ.	A fundamental revision of the system is necessary.
それは根本的な解決にならない.	That doesn't go to the root of the problem.
あの計画は根本的に考え直す必要がある.	That plan needs to be completely rethought.
その国の根本問題は貧困である.	That country's fundamental problem is poverty.
自由競争は資本主義の根本原理である.	Free competition is the fundamental principle of capitalism.

さ

さ (差)

彼らの学力の差はほとんどない.	There's hardly any difference among them in scholastic ability.
砂漠では昼夜の気温の差が激しい.	The difference between daytime and night-time temperatures in the desert is extreme.
この国では貧富の差が大きい.	The gap between the rich and the poor in this country is wide.
1位は2位に大きく差をつけてゴールインした.	The winner finished with a wide margin over the runner-up.
Aチームは3点差でBチームを負かした.	Team A beat Team B by (a margin of) three points.
たった1分の差で電車に間に合わなかった.	I missed the train by just a minute.

サービス

【周りの人への気遣い】彼女はサービス精神が旺盛だ.
 She always makes sure that everyone has a good time.
 She's always the life of the party.

週末は家族サービスでディズニーランドに行った.
 I took the time to go to Disneyland on the weekend with my family.

【顧客への応対】値段が安い割にサービスのいい店だ.
 Considering their reasonable prices, the service is pretty good here.

この旅館は細かいところまでサービスが行き届いている.
 This Japanese inn †has excellent service [takes very good care of its guests].

当店はセルフサービスになっております.
 This restaurant is cafeteria-style.

当ガソリンスタンドはセルフサービスです.
 This is a self-service gas station.

サービス料込みで1泊1万6千円です.
 The room is ￥16,000 a night including service charges.

その国では労働者の約半数がサービス業に従事している.
 Approximately half of the workers in the country are employed in the service industry.

【無料・安価】今ならパソコンをお
 Right now, we are giving away a digital

買い上げの方全員にデジカメをサービスでおつけしています.	camera to everyone who purchases a computer.[1] If you buy a computer now, we'll give you a free digital camera.[2]
この券1枚につき, 生ビールを1杯サービスします.	We will serve you a free glass of draft beer with this ticket.
値段のほう, もう少しサービスしてもらえませんか.	Could you bring the price down a bit more?

1) は宣伝文, 2) は客への口頭での説明.

さいきどう (再起動)

パソコンの調子が悪いので, 再起動をかけた.	I rebooted [restarted] my computer because it wasn't working properly.
アプリケーションをすべて閉じて再起動してください.	Close all your application software and restart.

さいきん (最近)

最近私は新車を手に入れた.	I recently got a new car.
つい最近までこの道路は舗装されていなかった.	This road was not paved until just recently.
彼女が会社を辞めたのはつい最近のことだ.	She quit working at the company just recently.
最近の世界情勢は不安定だ.	International conditions have not been very stable lately[1] [recently].
最近は若い人がたくさん外国へ出かける.	Lately[2] [Recently] a lot of young people have been going abroad.
最近3年間の輸出の伸びは驚くべきものだ.	The growth of exports over the past [last] three years is quite surprising.

1)2) lately は人や世の中の「傾向, 動向」などについて使う.

さいご (最後)

各列の最後の人は立ってください.	Those at the end of each line, please stand up.
これは彼にとって最後のチャンスだ.	This is the last chance for him.
彼は最後の手段として警察に訴えた.	He went to the police as a last resort.
会社を出たのは私が最後だった.	I was the last person to leave the office.
彼女と最後に会ったのはいつですか.	When was the last time you saw her?
最後には彼女も私の言うことを分	In the end she understood what I was say-

かってくれた.	ing.
最後に笑う者が最もよく笑う.	He who laughs last laughs best.
この本は最後まで読んだ.	I read this book to the end.
最後まで希望を捨ててはいけない.	Never despair.
最後の最後まであきらめるな.	Don't give up until the very end.
毒ヘビにかまれたら最後だと思え.	If you get bitten by a poisonous snake, you can be sure that'll be the end of you.
この会社で彼に睨まれたら最後だ.	In this company, if he has it in for you, it's all over.
彼はこうと決めたら最後, 人の言うことなど聞かない.	Once he's made up his mind, he won't listen to what anyone else has to say.
彼に会ったら最後, 夜遅くまでつきあわされる.	Once you run into him, you'll end up not being able to get away from him until late at night.

さいこう (最高)

富士山は日本の最高峰だ.	Mt. Fuji is the highest peak in Japan.
最高点はだれがとりましたか.	Who scored the highest marks?
今日の気温は今年最高を記録した.	Today's temperature was the highest recorded this year.
彼は100メートル競走の最高記録を作った男だ.	He's the man who set the record for the 100-meter dash.
彼女の今度の作品は最高の出来だ.	This time her work is really top notch.
今日は釣りには最高の天気だね.	Today's weather is perfect for fishing.
今や祭りは最高潮に達した.	Now the festival has reached its peak.
彼女は最高級品しか好まない.	She only likes the best of everything.

さいさん (採算)

この店もやっと採算が合うようになった.	This store is finally starting to show a profit.
この事業は長期的に見れば十分に採算が見込める.	In the long run, this business should be very profitable.
こんな料金設定では採算が取れるはずがないよ.	There's no way †the business can be profitable [you can make a profit] at these prices.
このプロジェクトは, 宣伝費だと思って採算を度外視して行っている.	We're not worrying [worried] about making a profit from [with] this project as long as we get a lot of good publicity out of it.
	We're doing this project for the publicity, not for any profit that might come of it.
あの会社は不採算事業から撤退す	That company decided to pull out of an

ることにした.	unprofitable business.

ざいさん (財産)

彼は全財産をなげうって孤児院を設立した.	He used his entire fortune to establish an orphanage.
あの女の結婚は財産目当てに違いない.	She obviously married for money.
私は株で一財産作った.	I made a fair amount in the stock market.
彼は大した財産を持っていない.	He has few assets.
君はこの会社の大切な財産だ.	You're an important asset to this company.

さいしょ (最初)

その本は最初の1日で売り切れた.	The book sold out (on) the first day.
このゲームは最初は面白いがすぐ飽きる.	This game is fun at first, but you soon get bored with it.
最初に勉強してから遊びなさい.	You can play only after you've studied.
物事は最初が肝心だ.	A good beginning is always of the essence.
その映画は最初から最後まで観客を笑わせる.	That movie makes the audience laugh from beginning to end.

さいそく (催促)

彼は催促されるまで借金を返さない男だ.	He never pays back borrowed money until he's pressed to do so.
彼に本を返してくれるよう何度も催促したが返してくれない.	I †tried to get [pressed] him to give me the book back many times, but he wouldn't (do it).
原稿の催促の電話が鳴りっぱなしだ.	The phone is ringing off the hook with demands for the manuscript.
催促がましいことを言うなよ.	Don't be so demanding!

さいだい (最大)

世界最大のダムが完成した.	The largest dam in the world has been completed.
リオでは南米で最大の祭りが開かれる.	The biggest festival in South America is held in Rio.
彼は今世紀最大の画家だと言われる.	He is referred to as the greatest painter of this century.
当局は大統領の警備に最大の努力を払った.	The authorities made the greatest efforts possible in guarding the president.
それは彼にとって最大の侮辱だ.	That would be the most insulting thing you could do [say] to him.
太陽光線を最大限に利用すべきだ.	The sun's light should be used to the great-

最大限3日しか待てない. | I can only wait for three days at the most. / The longest I can wait is three days.

さいちゅう (最中)
車を洗っている最中に雨が降ってきた. | It started raining while I was washing the car.
食事の最中に新聞を読むのはやめたら？ | Couldn't you stop reading the paper while eating?
彼は今報告書を作っている最中です. | He's in the midst [middle] of putting the report together.
パーティーの真っ最中, 急に照明が消えた. | The lights went out right in the middle of the party.
新しい体育館は今建築の最中です. | The new gymnasium is now under construction.

さいなん (災難)
自分の身にそんな災難が降りかかったとしたらどうしますか. | What would you do if you were visited by such a misfortune?
災難だと思ってあきらめなさい. | Accept it as †a misfortune [bad luck].
病気やら火事やら, あの家は災難続きだ. | That family has suffered one misfortune after another—illnesses, fires, you name it.

さいのう (才能)
彼女には絵の才能がある. | She has a talent for drawing.
あの子は生まれながら音楽の才能を備えている. | That child possesses natural music talent.
むざむざその才能をうずもれさせたくない. | I don't want to stand by helplessly and watch your talent go down the drain.
彼はその才能を買われて編集長になった. | His talent was recognized and he became chief editor.
才能に溺れ努力を怠ってはいけないよ. | You can't just sit back and hope your talent will get you by.
君の才能はまだまだ伸びるよ. | You have a lot more ability inside you.
彼女は自分の才能の限界を知った. | She found out the limits of her own ability.
自分の才能を生かせるような仕事をしたい. | I want to do work that will let me put my abilities to good use.

ざいりょう (材料)
彼は高価な材料をふんだんに使って家を建てた. | He was lavish in the use of expensive materials in building his house.

この料理はどんな材料を使っていますか.	What ingredients does this dish use?
彼は身近なところから研究材料を見つけてくる.	He finds material for study in things which are very close to him.
材料費に5ドルほどかかります.	The materials will cost about five dollars.

さいわい (幸い)

幸い彼はまもなく回復した.	Fortunately [Luckily] he got well soon.
その交通事故では幸いだれもけがをしなかった.	Fortunately [Luckily] no one was injured in the traffic accident.
幸いにも私の誕生日は日曜日と重なります.	I'm lucky that my birthday will fall on a Sunday.
あの火事でだれも死ななかったのは不幸中の幸いだ.	It could have been worse. At least no one died in the fire.
時間に遅れたことが幸いして事故を免れた.	I luckily avoided the accident because I was late.
上役がいないのを幸いに, 彼は早く帰った.	He took advantage of his boss's absence and went home early.
私たちの研究が少しでも人類の役に立てば幸いです.	We will be happy if our research serves humanity in some way.

〜さえ

【〜でも】こんな簡単な単語は子どもでさえ知っている.	Even a child would know such a simple word.
彼の絵は金賞どころか入選さえしなかった.	Far from winning first prize, his picture didn't even place.
こんな小さな舟では海はおろか池さえ渡れないさ.	This small a boat couldn't make it across a pond, much less an ocean.
【〜だけ】人間は水さえあれば1ヵ月は生きられる.	Man can survive for a month as long as he has water.
君さえいてくれればほかに何もいらない.	As long as you're around, I don't want anything else.
時間さえあれば数学の試験で満点を取れたのに.	If only I had had more time, I could have gotten a perfect score on the math exam.
酒さえ飲み過ぎなければいい男なんだが.	He'd be a nice guy if only he didn't drink so much.
あなたさえよければこの映画を見ましょう.	Let's see this movie if it's all right with you.
【〜までも】寒くてたまらないのに雨さえ降ってきた.	It was unbearably cold to begin with, and to make things worse it started to rain.
私には病気の母がいる上に多大な借金さえある.	On top of having a sick mother I have a lot of debts as well.

強盗は男ばかりか女子どもさえ殺してしまった.	The robber didn't stop at killing just the men. He even killed women and children.

さえる (冴える)
【音・色が】バイオリンのさえた音色が会場を包んだ.	The clear notes of the violins filled the auditorium.
町に鐘の音がさえ渡った.	The sound of a bell rang clearly throughout the town.
画家はさえた赤で花を描いた.	The artist painted the flowers in vivid red.
さえ渡った月が雪山を照らしている.	The crystal clear moon is shining on the snowy mountains.
【技術が】彼の祖父は非常に腕のさえた大工だった.	His grandfather was a very skillful carpenter.
この料理を見ると料理人の腕のさえが分かる.	This dish shows the masterly [skilled] hand of the cook.
今日の彼のスマッシュはさえている.	His smashes are really on target today.
【頭・考えが】朝コーヒーを飲まないと頭がさえない.	My head isn't clear until I've had a cup of coffee in the morning.
今日の君はさえてるね.	You're really clear-headed today.
彼ならさえたアイデアを出してくれるよ.	He'll come up with a good idea for us.
【顔・姿が】さえない顔をしているね. どうかしたの?	You look glum. Something wrong?
さえない風体の男が訪ねて来た.	A shabby-looking man came to visit.

さがす (探・捜す)
【捜索する】彼女が落としたコンタクトレンズを皆で30分も探した.	We all searched for her contact lens for at least half an hour.
机の中を探してみなさい.	Try searching through the desk.
手探りで電気のスイッチを探した.	I groped for the light switch.
草の根を分けても犯人を捜し出せ.	Search high and low for the criminal.
その地名は地図の中では探し出せなかった.	I couldn't find that place (name) on the map.
その投書の主をやっと探し当てた.	We finally tracked down (the identity of) the anonymous contributor.
昔の友人の家をやっと探し当てた.	I finally located my old friend's house.
【探し求める】父は今, 職を探している.	My father is looking [hunting] for a job.
我が社では秘書を探している.	Our company is looking for a secretary.
私はこの一週間, 赤外線写真に関する本を探している.	I've been looking for a book on infrared photography for the past week.

さからう (逆らう)

【逆方向に進む】 彼は人の流れに逆らって入口から走り出た. — He ran out the entrance, against a stream of people coming in.

彼は世の潮流に逆らった生き方をしている. — His lifestyle goes against the mainstream.

【反抗する】 おれに逆らう気か? — Are you going to oppose[1] [disobey[2]] me?

10代の頃は父親の言うことにいちいち逆らっていた. — As a teenager, I often disobeyed [contradicted[3]] my father.

部長の命令には逆らうな. — Don't oppose your manager's directives.

社長命令に逆らって首になった. — I was fired for going against my boss's directives.

父の希望に逆らって歌手を目指すことにした. — I decided to become a singer against my father's wishes.

杉原千畝は政府の命令に逆らって、ヨーロッパのユダヤ人にビザを発行し続けた. — Sugihara Chiune continued to issue visas for European Jews in defiance of government orders.

> 1) oppose は積極的に反対の態度を示すこと. 2) disobey は言うこと [命令] をきかないこと. 3) contradict は相手と反対のことを言うこと.

さかり (盛り)

今頃がツツジの花の盛りです. — The azaleas are in full bloom around this time.

イチゴは今が盛りだ. — Strawberries are in season now.

夏の暑い盛りには働く気がしないよ. — I don't have much desire to work in the hottest part of summer.

あの子は今がいたずら盛りだ. — That child is at a mischievous age.

40代といえば男の働き盛りだ. — A man is at his working prime in his forties.

彼は男盛りだ. — He's in his prime as a man.

彼女は女盛りだ. — She's in her prime as a woman.

盛りのついた猫が毎晩騒いでいる. — There's a cat in heat yowling (noisily) every night.

さがる (下がる)

【下方へ動く】 山の上にあった雲が下がってきた. — The clouds that were above the mountains have come down lower.

クモが天井から下がってきた. — The spider lowered itself down from the ceiling.

気球が下がり始めた. — The balloon has begun to descend.

ベルトが緩くてズボンが下がってしまう. — My belt is so loose that my pants fall down.

【垂れ下がる】木の枝からクモが下がっている.	There's a spider hanging from the tree.
壁に下がっている服を取ってください.	Get those clothes hanging on the wall for me, please.
ビルの屋上から垂れ幕が下がっている.	A banner has been hung from the roof of the building.
【低くなる】日が沈むと急に気温が下がった.	When the sun went down, the temperature fell [dropped] rapidly.
どんな薬でも彼女の熱は下がらなかった.	Her temperature wouldn't go down no matter what medicine she took.
庶民は物価が下がることを願っている.	The average person is hoping for †lower prices [prices to go down].
豊作のお陰でオレンジの値段が下がった.	A large crop brought the price of oranges down.
人工ダイヤは天然のものより価値がぐっと下がる.	Synthetic diamonds cost much less than natural ones.
君の成績が下がったのは何が原因なんだ?	Why is it that your grades have dropped?
その仕事の失敗で会社での彼の地位は下がった.	Because of his failure at work he was demoted in the company.
彼の肩は左下がりになっている.	His shoulders slope down to the left.
【後退する】一歩後ろに下がれ.	Take a step back.
	Move back one step.
群衆は警官に押されてじりじりと後ろに下がった.	The crowds were pushed back by the policemen little by little.

さかん (盛ん)

彼の新商売はなかなか盛んのようだ.	His new business really seems to be prospering.
ブラジルではサッカーが大変盛んです.	Soccer [Football] is very popular in Brazil.
小学生のあいだでも英語を習うことが盛んになっている.	It's become very common for even grade school children to learn English.
その英雄は盛んな拍手をもって迎えられた.	The hero was greeted with enthusiastic applause.
首相は訪れる国々で盛んな歓迎を受けた.	The prime minister was warmly received in the countries he visited.
彼女は盛んに喫煙の害を説いている.	She spends a lot of time telling people how harmful smoking is.
彼は老いてますます盛んだ.	He becomes more and more vigorous with age.

さき (先)

【先端】
このはしは先が尖っている.	These chopsticks †are pointed [have sharp ends].
鉛筆の先が丸くなってきた.	My pencil's getting dull.
防波堤の先まで行ってみよう.	Let's walk out to the end of the breakwater.
ナイフで指の先を切ってしまった.	I cut †the tip of my finger [my fingertip] with a knife.
スキーの先が折れてしまった.	I broke the tip off of one of my skis.

【先方】
この荷物の届け先はどこ?	Where should I deliver this package?
彼は行先をメモに書いておいた.	He left a note that said where he was going.

【前方】
3キロ先にガソリンスタンドがありますよ.	There's a gas station three kilometers ahead.
あの交番の先を左折してください.	Turn left just past that police box.
これから先は車は通れない.	A car can't make it through from here on.
霧で1メートル先も見えなかった.	I couldn't even see a meter ahead because of the fog.
さあ, 先を急ごう.	Let's get moving.

【未来・将来】
あまり先のことを心配してもしょうがない.	There's no use worrying about something so far in the future.
10年先に君はどんな人間になっているのだろう.	I wonder what kind of person you'll be ten years from now.
これから先どうやって生きていったらいいの.	How can I go on living now?
この仕事は先が長いから今日はこのくらいにしておこう.	There's a lot of work left so let's stop here for today.
あの人も先は短いようだ.	He doesn't have long to live.
この商売も先が見えたな.	This business no longer has a future.

【続き】
その先はどうなったの.	What happened after that?
その先は言わなくても分かるよ.	I already know what lies ahead.

【先行】
先に頂上に着いたほうが勝ちだ.	The one who gets to the top first is the winner.
女子どもを先に降ろすんだ.	Women and children off first!
彼女のほうが君より先に入会を申し込んだ.	She applied for membership ahead of you.
私が遅れたら先に行ってください.	If I'm late, go on ahead.
お先にどうぞ.	Please go ahead.
皆は先を争うようにその本を読んだ.	They all wanted to be the first to have read the book.
彼女にデートを申し込もうと思っていたが, 彼に先を越された.	I was thinking of asking her for a date, but that guy got the jump on me.
子に先立たれるほど悲しいことは	There's nothing as sad as losing a child.

先立つものは金だ.	You can't get anywhere without money. Money makes the world go around.
時代を先取りしたスタイルの車ですね.	The car's style is ahead of its time.
彼女の行動がフェミニズム運動の先駆けとなった.	Her actions led the way for the feminist movement.
【前もって】代金は先に払ってください.	Please pay in advance.
先に断っておくが, 飲み代は割り勘だぞ.	I'm giving you advance notice: you pay for your own drinks.
【この前】先の話し合いで決まったことを発表します.	Now I will announce what was decided at the last meeting.

さく¹ (咲く)

この花が咲くともう春です.	When this flower blooms, you'll know it's spring.
桜の花が見事に咲き揃った.	The cherry blossoms are all in full bloom.
砂浜にはビーチパラソルの花が咲いている.	The beach umbrellas have opened like flowers on the shore.
若い娘たちで会場は花が咲いたようだった.	The meeting place seemed to be in bloom with young girls.

さく² (裂・割く)

彼は怒って手紙をずたずたに裂いてしまった.	He lost his temper and tore the letter into shreds.
干しイカを細かく裂いてください.	Please shred [tear] the dried squid into narrow strips.
稲妻が木を真っ二つに裂いた.	Lightning split the tree right in two.
大きな魚の腹を裂くと小魚が出てきた.	We found a small fish when we cut open the big fish.
二人の仲を裂いてしまったものは何だろう.	What was it that came between them?
お金が二人の仲を裂いてしまった.	Money destroyed their relationship.
彼女の一日のほとんどの時間は育児に割かれる.	Almost all of her time is taken up by caring for her children.
悲しみに胸を裂かれるような思いがした.	I was stricken with grief.

さくひん (作品)

『英雄』はベートーベンの作品です.	The "Eroica" was composed by Beethoven.
シェークスピアは優れた作品を数	Shakespeare left many magnificent works.

多く残している.
その作曲家の新しい作品は好評だ. That composer's new work is being received well.
写真展を開いて今までの作品を発表したい. I want to hold a photo exhibition to present my work up until now.

さぐる (探る)
ポケットの中を探ったが何も入っていなかった. I felt inside my pocket but there wasn't anything there.
彼の部屋を探れば何か証拠品が見つかるだろう. You'll probably find some evidence if you search his room.
潜水艇で海底の様子を探った. We explored the ocean floor in a bathyscaphe.
スパイが敵国の情勢を探っている. The spy is feeling out the situation in the enemy country.
彼女の本心を探ったがむだだった. I tried to sound out what she really felt, but it was useless.
暗闇を手探りで進んだ. I groped my way through the darkness.

さけぶ (叫ぶ)
彼は声を限りに叫んだ. He yelled at the top of his voice [lungs].
その母親は子どもの遺体の前で泣き叫んでいた. The mother screamed and cried before her child's corpse.
女の叫び声が隣の部屋から聞こえてきた. A woman's scream came from the next room.
国民は戦争反対を叫んでいる. The people are voicing their opposition to war.

さける¹ (裂ける)
缶詰を入れ過ぎて紙袋が裂けてしまった. The paper bag ripped because of all the cans inside.
地震で道路が裂けてしまった. The road was torn apart by the earthquake.
突然,耳が裂けるような音がした. Suddenly there was an ear-shattering noise.
たった一言のうそで我々の友情は裂けた. With one little lie our friendship was destroyed.

さける² (避ける)
自動車は脇道から飛び出した子どもをかろうじて避けた. The car barely avoided the child who had run out from a sideroad.
狩人は雨を避けるためにほら穴に入った. The hunter went inside a cave to avoid the rain.

ラッシュアワーを避けて30分早く家を出た.	I left home 30 minutes early to avoid the rush hour.
君はこの頃,僕を避けているね.	You seem to be avoiding me lately.
彼らは人目を避けて夜出発した.	They left at night to avoid being noticed.
むだな争いごとは避けたいものだ.	Pointless conflict is something I'd like to †avoid [steer clear of].
政府は防衛問題を避けて通ることはできない.	The government cannot get by with avoiding [evading] the defense problem.
犯人が警察の追求を避けるのは難しいだろう.	It will be hard for the criminal to evade the police search.
このままでいくと交渉決裂は避けられない.	At this rate a breakdown in the negotiations will be unavoidable.
天災は避け難いものだ.	It's hard to escape natural disasters.

さげる (下げる)

【下方へ動かす】もう手を下げていいですよ.	You can put your hands down now.
レバーを下げてください.	Pull the lever (down).
彼は私たちに頭を下げて挨拶をした.	He bowed and greeted us.
【吊る】窓にカーテンを下げた.	I hung curtains on the window.
カウボーイはいつも腰に拳銃を下げていた.	Cowboys always wore their pistols in holsters.
彼は両手に荷物を下げていた.	He was loaded [weighed] down with packages.
【低くする】タイヤの空気圧を下げた.	I reduced the air pressure in the tires.
飛行機は着陸のために高度を下げた.	The plane lowered its altitude in preparation for landing.
注射を打って熱を下げてもらった.	I was given a shot to lower my fever.
会社は休日を増やし,その代わりに給料を下げた.	The company increased the number of days off, but also decreased salaries.
これ以上値段を下げたら赤字だよ.	If we lower prices any more, we'll go into the red.
ほんの少しの傷が宝石の値段を下げてしまう.	Even a minor flaw reduces the value of a jewel.
父親が寝ているので,彼女はステレオの音量を下げた.	She turned down the stereo because her father was sleeping.
【後方に移動させる】あと1メートルほど車を下げてください.	Back the car up[1] about another meter.
お皿をお下げしてもよろしいでしょうか.	May I take your plate now?[2]

> 1) up は習慣的につけることが多い. 2) May I clean the table? もあるが，その場合は卓上のすべてを片づけてしまうことをいう.

ささえる (支える)

天井を太い柱が支えている.	The large pillars support the ceiling.
彼は, 気を失って倒れそうな女の人を支えた.	He held the fainting woman to keep her from falling.
彼女は女手一つでこの店を支えてきた.	She's managed to keep this store going by herself.
これ以上の扶養家族を支え切れない.	I couldn't support a bigger family.
この本は私にとって大きな支えとなった.	This book was a great source of inspiration.

さしず (指図)

おれは人の指図など受けないぞ.	I'm not going to take orders from anyone.
俳優は監督の指図に黙って従った.	The actor silently followed the director's commands.
指図どおりにしていればいいんだ.	All you have to do is follow directions.

さしつかえる (差し支える)

勉強に差し支えるようならアルバイトなどやめろ.	If it's going to affect your studies, you should quit your job.
彼は生活に差し支えるほど競馬に金をつぎ込んでいる.	He spends so much money on horse racing that it's affecting his life.
明日に差し支えるといけないので今日はこの辺で切り上げよう.	If we don't call it a day before long, it'll †affect [interfere with] how we do tomorrow.
差し支えなければ多数決で決めたいと思います.	If there are no objections, I'd like to settle this with a majority vote.
差し支えなければこの本を貸していただけませんか.	Do you mind if I borrow this book?
窓を開けても差し支えありませんか.	Would it bother you [Would you mind] if I opened the window?
午後お宅にお邪魔しても差し支えありませんか.	Would it inconvenience you if I came by your house in the afternoon?
署名はどなたのでも差し支えありません.	Anybody's signature will do.

さす¹ (刺す)

彼はナイフで人を刺した.	He stabbed a man with a knife.
彼女はバラのとげで指をちくりと	She pricked her finger on a rose thorn.

刺した.	
彼女は肉の焼け具合を見るために串で刺してみた.	She stuck a skewer into the meat to see if it was done.
ハチに腕を刺された.	I got stung on the arm by a bee.
蚊に刺されたところがかゆい.	I itch where I got stung by mosquitoes. My mosquito bites itch.
外は肌を刺すような寒さだ.	The cold outside is really biting.
刺すような痛みが胃に走った.	I felt a stabbing pain in my stomach.
彼の刺すような視線にぞっとした.	His piercing glance made me shudder.

さす² (指す)

【指などで示す】私は彼が指している方向を見た.	I looked in the direction he pointed.
シカゴはこの地図のどこか指してごらん.	Point out where Chicago is on this map.
時計の針が12時を指している.	The hands of the clock are pointing to twelve o'clock.
【表す】Xとは何を指しているのですか.	What are you referring to by (using) "X"?
【指名する】あの先生の授業では, いつ指されるか分からないので心配だ.	I'm uncomfortable in that teacher's class because I never know when I'm going to get called on.
【向かう】一行はその山を指して進んだ.	The group headed off for the mountain.
列車は北を指して走っている.	The train is heading north.
【将棋】昨晩は友人と将棋を指して過ごした.	I spent last night playing Japanese chess with my friend.
次の一手はどこに指そうか.	Where should I move now?

さす³ (挿・射・差・注す)

【挿し入れる】カーネーションが一輪, 花瓶に挿してある.	A single carnation has been put in the vase.
かぎを車のドアに挿しっぱなしにしておいた.	I left the key in the car door.
この板をたんすの下に挿し込んでくれ.	Slip [Stick] this board in under the wardrobe.
【日が】カーテンの隙間から朝日がさし込んでいる.	The morning sun is shining in through a gap in the curtains.
この花は日がさしているあいだだけ咲いている.	These flowers only bloom when they're exposed to sunlight.
【傘を】私は慌てて傘を差した.	I hurriedly opened up my umbrella.
彼は彼女に傘を差し掛けた.	He shared his umbrella with her.
【加える・加わる】君の自転車は油	You should oil your bicycle.

をさしたほうがいいよ.	
彼女は日に2, 3回目薬をさす.	She uses eyedrops two or three times a day.
ワインを飲んだせいか, 彼女の顔に赤味がさしてきた.	Maybe it's because she had some wine, but her face has gotten red.
【慣用】その男は私たちの話に水をさした.	He threw †a wet blanket [cold water] on our conversation.
彼が横領するとは魔がさしたとしか思えない.	All I can think is that some uncontrollable urge possessed him to commit embezzlement.

さすが

有名なバイオリニストだけあってさすがにうまい.	He plays just as well as one would expect a famous violinist like him to play.
さすが百万長者だけあって, 持っている物が豪華だ.	He is †truly [certainly, indeed, just like] a millionaire. His possessions are extravagant.
さすがにそこまではっきりとは言えなかった.	I just wasn't able to be that explicit.
世話になった人に「いや」とはさすがに言えない.	How could I say no to someone who's been so good to me?
好き嫌いはないけれど, さすがにこれは食べる気がしない.	I'm not picky about food, but when it comes to this I sure lose my appetite.
さすがの勇者も美人には弱い.	(Even) The bravest of heroes can be spellbound by a beautiful woman.
さすがのコンピューターも人間の脳にはかなわない.	Even the best computer is no match for the human mind.
さすがのアインシュタインもその問題には頭を痛めた.	That problem gave even Einstein a headache.

ざせつ (挫折)

彼の計画は思わぬ原因で挫折した.	His plans fell through for reasons he hadn't considered.
彼の医者になる志は挫折した.	His aim of becoming a doctor ended in failure.
私の人生は挫折の繰り返しだった.	My life has been one setback after another.
挫折から立ち直るには努力と勇気が必要だ.	It takes effort and courage to get back on your feet after a setback.
彼女は深い挫折感に襲われた.	She was overcome with a deep sense of futility.

～させる

彼女は無理やり結婚させられた.	She was forced to marry against her will.

母親は子どもたちに部屋の掃除をさせた.	The mother made her children clean up their room.
社長はその企画を中止させた.	The president of the company had the project canceled.
家のペンキを塗り替えさせよう.	Let's have the house painted.
妻には金のことで苦労させたくない.	I don't want my wife to have to suffer financially.
私にも味をみさせて.	Let me have a taste, too.
あいつの好きなようにさせておこう.	Let him do as he pleases.

さそう (誘う)

彼女を映画に誘ってみようと思う.	I'm thinking about asking her out[1] to see a movie.
彼を誘ってパーティーに行こうよ.	Let's ask him along[2] to the party.
3時に誘いに行くよ.	I'll come for you at three.
今の電話は友達からの釣りの誘いだよ.	It was my friend calling to ask me if I wanted to go fishing.
彼も私たちのクラブに誘おう.	Let's ask [invite] him to join our club.
あいつは金儲けの誘いにはすぐ乗ってくる.	He'll jump at a chance to make money if we ask him.
おいしそうなにおいに誘われてそのレストランに入った.	A delicious smell lured me into the restaurant.
その音楽は私の眠りを誘った.	The music lulled me to sleep.

1) ask *someone* out は「誘い出す」. 2) ask *someone* along は「一緒に連れて行く」.

さだまる (定まる)

その法律が定まるまでに長い時間がかかった.	It took a long time for that law to get passed.
集会の日時が定まりしだい連絡をください.	Please get in touch with me as soon as the time for the meeting has been settled.
会社の方針がなかなか定まらない.	The company just can't seem to arrive at a policy.
彼と結婚するかどうかまだ気持ちが定まらない.	I'm still uncertain about whether or not I should marry him.
風向きが定まったら出発だ.	Once the wind direction becomes fixed, we'll be off.
この頃,天気が定まらない.	The weather has been unstable recently.
銃の狙いが定まらない.	I can't steady the gun to get a fix (on the target).

さだめる (定める)

政府は新しい祝日を定めた.	The government established a new national holiday.
私は行先を定めないで旅に出ることが多い.	Most of the time I go off on trips with no fixed destination in mind.
その企画の予算をまず定めた.	First of all we decided on the budget for the project.
定められた規則には従うべきだ.	Rules which have been decided on should be followed.
この高速道路の制限速度は時速80キロと定められている.	The speed limit on this highway is fixed at 80 km/h [eighty kilometers per hour].
彼は狙いを定めて釣糸を投げた.	He took careful aim and cast his fishing line.
目標を定めて勉強したほうがよい.	You should study with a fixed goal in mind.
君と僕は一緒になるように定められていたんだ.	You and I were made for each other.[1]

1) 決まり文句に近い表現.「お互いのために生まれてきたんだ」.

ざつ (雑)

この家具は随分雑な作りですね.	This furniture is really shoddy.
彼女はやることが雑だ.	She does things carelessly.
彼は私の大事なカメラを雑に扱った.	He was very rough with my good camera.
このチームは雑なプレーが目立ちますね.	This team sure botches [bungles] a lot of plays.
棚に本が雑に置かれている.	The books are all jumbled up on the shelf.
あの人は雑学の大家だ.	He has a wealth of trivia.
雑談はやめてください.	Cut the chitchat.**
この2, 3日雑務に追われている.	I've been pressed with odd chores [duties] for the last two or three days.

さっかく (錯覚)

猫の鳴き声がしたと思ったが錯覚のようだった.	I thought I had heard a cat but it was just my imagination.
大きな鏡のせいで部屋が広いと錯覚した.	The big mirror created [gave] the illusion of space in the room.
	Because of the big mirror, the room looked bigger than it was.
時々私は彼がまだ生きているような錯覚を起こす.	Sometimes I fool myself into thinking that he's still alive.
あの事件が2年前というのは君の	You're imagining things if you think that

錯覚だよ.	happened two years ago.
この複雑な柄は目の錯覚を起こす.	This complicated pattern plays tricks on your eyes.
ピサの斜塔が傾いて見えるのは目の錯覚ではない.	The tower of Pisa's tilt is not an optical illusion.
彼は味方の兵士を敵と錯覚して撃ち殺してしまった.	He shot one of his fellow soldiers, mistaking him for the enemy.
あの歌手は人気を実力と錯覚している.	That singer is confusing his popularity with ability.
毎日電車で会うので, ついうっかり彼女を顔見知りだと錯覚しておじぎをしてしまった.	I see her on the train every day, so I inadvertently mistook her for an acquaintance and bowed to her.

さっき

さっきの電話はだれからだったの.	Who just called? Who was that call from?
彼はさっき出かけたばかりだからまだ追いつくでしょう.	He just left a moment ago, so you should still be able to catch him.
かばんはさっきまでここにあったのに, いつの間にかなくなっている.	My briefcase was here just a second ago and now it's gone.
彼はさっきから時計ばかり気にしている.	He's barely been able to take his eyes off the clock for the last few minutes.

さっそく (早速)

早速その計画を実行に移せ.	Put that plan into effect immediately.
早速ですが仕事の話に入りましょう.	Let's get right down to business.
彼はパリに着くと早速宿を探し始めた.	When he arrived in Paris, the first thing he did was try to find a place to stay.

さっぱり

【さわやか】風呂に入ってさっぱりしたら?	Why don't you freshen up by taking a bath?
言いたいことを言ったらさっぱりするよ.	You'll feel so relieved if you say what you want to say.
父はさっぱりした性格の持ち主だ.	My father's a very simple, forthright man.
「風邪はいかがですか」「どうも今ひとつさっぱりしません」	"How's your cold?" "I just can't seem to get rid of it completely."
彼はいつもこざっぱりした格好をしている.	He always looks nice and neat.
何かさっぱりした物が食べたい.	I want something simple to eat.
【一向に】手紙の返事がさっぱり来	I've gotten absolutely no reply to my

	letter.
哲学の授業などさっぱり分からない.	I have no idea what's going on in my philosophy class.
私は化学はさっぱりだ.	I'm at a total loss when it comes to chemistry.

さとる (悟る)

【気づく】あとをつけていることを彼女に悟られないようにしろ.	Be careful not to let her notice [know] we are following her.
私は他人に悟られないようにその計画を進めた.	Careful to keep anyone from catching on, I proceeded with the plan.
だまされたと悟ったのは金を取られたあとだった.	I realized that I had been tricked only after they had taken the money.
彼女が変装していると悟るには時間がかかった.	It took me a long time to realize that it was her in disguise.
【理解する】彼はかけ事は結局割に合わないものだと悟った.	He realized that gambling doesn't pay in the end.
病気をして初めて健康の大切さを悟るでしょう.	You'll understand how important your health is once you've been sick.
【真理を知る】あの人はまるで悟ったような口をきく.	He talks like he's seen it all before.
彼は修行の末, 悟りを開いた.	At the end of his ascetic training he achieved enlightenment.

さびしい (寂しい)

一人暮らしは寂しいものだ.	Living by yourself is lonely [lonesome].
その音楽家は寂しい晩年を送った.	The composer spent his last years in loneliness.
彼は寂しさを酒で紛らわした.	He drowned his loneliness in drink.
君がいなくなると寂しくなるなあ.	I'm going to miss you when you're gone.
男は寂しく笑った.	He gave a wistful smile.
それは月のない寂しい夜だった.	It was a lonely, moonless night.
壁に何もないと寂しいから絵でも掛けよう.	The wall looks bare, so let's hang a picture on it.
今日は懐が寂しいんだ.	I don't have much (money) on me today.

さびる (錆びる)

私の自動車はさびてきた.	My car's getting rusty.
この機械はさびついて動かない.	This machine's rusted and won't work.
長いあいだテニスをしていないので腕がさびついてしまった.	I haven't played tennis for a long time, so I'm a little rusty.

サボる

【出席しない】 授業〔仕事〕をサボってカラオケに行った. — I skipped class [work] and went to *karaoke*.

仮病を使って体育の授業をサボった. — I pretended to be sick and skipped †phys. ed. [physical education., P.E. (class.)]

しばらく練習をサボっていたので, 腕がなまってしまった. — I'm not playing as well since [because] I've been skipping practice.

一度授業を休んだらサボり癖がついてしまった. — I picked up the habit of skipping class after missing one lecture.

【怠ける】 彼はちょっと目を離すとすぐサボる. — He stops working as soon as I'm not looking.

サボってないでしっかり働け! — Stop †goofing off** [loafing around] and start working!¹⁾
Let's get back to business.²⁾

> 1) のように頭から叱りつけるより, 2) のような人格を傷つけない言い方のほうが好まれる.

さます (覚・醒ます)

赤ちゃんが目を覚ますから静かにしなさい. — Be quiet. You'll wake the baby.

だれかの足音に目を覚まされた. — The sound of somebody's footsteps woke me up.

病人は目を覚ましています. — The patient is awake.

酔いをさましてから運転しなさい. — Don't drive until you've sobered up.

冷たい風に当たって酔いをさまそう. — Let's go out in the cold wind to †get sober [sober up].

女にうつつを抜かしていないで, いい加減に目を覚ませ. — Open your eyes and smarten up. Your infatuations get you nowhere.

さまたげる (妨げる)

この木は交通の妨げとなる. — This tree obstructs traffic.

彼の出世を妨げる者はだれもいなかった. — Nobody blocked his path to success.

過保護は子どもの自立心の発達を妨げる. — An overprotective parent hinders the development of a child's independence.

彼女の美貌がかえって結婚の妨げになっている. — Her beauty actually turns out to be an obstacle in finding a husband.

さむい (寒い)

おお寒い. — I'm so cold. ／ I'm freezing.

寒くて一晩中震えていた. — It was so cold that I was shivering all night.

外は身を切るような寒さだ. It's bitterly cold outside.
今はシャツ一枚だと肌寒い. It's chilly now with only a shirt on.
この仕事をするのにこの顔ぶれではお寒い限りだ. This work will never get done with a miserable staff like this.

さめる¹ (冷める)
早く来ないとスープが冷めるわよ. If you don't come soon, your soup will get cold.
二人の仲はすっかり冷めてしまった. Relations between the two have cooled to nothing.

さめる² (覚・醒める)
目が覚めるとそこは病院のベッドだった. When I came to, I found myself in a hospital bed.
父は起こしてもなかなか目が覚めない. It's almost impossible to wake my father up.
はっとして恐ろしい夢から覚めた. I suddenly woke up from a frightening dream.
ひと眠りすれば酔いもさめるよ. You'll sober up if you take a nap.
彼女のドレスは目が覚めるような赤だった. Her dress was a startling shade of red.
お話を聞いて目が覚めました. What you told me really brought me to my senses.
最近の子どもはさめているなあ. Kids nowadays sure have a cool attitude about things.

さよう (作用)
薬の作用で一時的に痛みが治まった. The medicine was effective in controlling the pain temporarily.
この薬はよく効くが副作用が出ることがある. This medicine is very effective but it also produces some side effects.
胃液は胃の消化作用を助ける. Gastric juices work to aid digestion.
リニアモーターカーは磁気の作用で車体を浮かせて走る. The linear motor car is suspended in place by magnetism as it runs.
彼女の発作は幼い頃の出来事が心に作用しているためだ. Her attacks [fits] are brought on by the memory of traumatic events in early childhood.

ざらざら
この画用紙は表面がざらざらしている. This drawing paper has a rough surface.
口の中に砂が入ってざらざらする. I got some sand in my mouth and it feels gritty.

砂ぼこりで机の上がざらざらしている. — The desk top is gritty with sand.

さらに (更に)

夜になって風は更に強くなった. — After dark the wind started blowing even harder.

私は道に迷ったが，更に悪いことに日が暮れてきた. — First I got lost and then to make matters worse it got dark.

私はセーターの上に更にコートを着ていた. — In addition to my sweater I had a coat on.

私は箱を一度ペンキで塗って更にもう一度塗った. — I painted the box once, and then †painted it again [gave it another coat].

彼は更に講演を続けた. — He †continued [went on further] with his lecture.

さる (去る)

彼女は一人で町から去っていった. — She left town by herself.

嵐が去って太陽が顔を出した. — The storm passed and the sun appeared.

風邪が治ったと思ったら足首をねんざした. 全く一難去ってまた一難とはこのことだ. — Just when I had gotten over my cold, I went and sprained my ankle. Really, †if it's not one thing, it's another [it's been one disaster after another].

去る者は追わず. — There's no use going after someone who's made up his mind.

さわがしい (騒がしい)

私は騒がしい場所は苦手です. — I don't like noisy places.

そのスキャンダルで世の中が騒がしい. — That scandal has stirred up a lot of commotion.

こう騒がしい時代では長生きするのも考えものだ. — In turbulent times like these, you really wonder whether or not it's worth it to live a long life.

さわぐ (騒ぐ)

もう夜もふけたし，あまり騒がないほうがいい. — It's already late at night. You had better not make any noise.

あの子は教室でいつも騒いでいる. — That child is always making a fuss in class.

ことさら騒ぎ立てるほどのことではない. — It's not worth making such a fuss over.

下手な演技に客が騒ぎ出した. — The audience was in uproar over the bad performance.

殺人事件がその町を騒がせている. — The murder caused a big commotion in that town.

組合が賃上げの件で騒いでいる.	The unions are clamoring for higher wages.
今日は何だか朝から胸騒ぎがする.	For some reason I've been uneasy all day today.

さわやか（爽やか）

さわやかな風が吹いている.	There's a nice breeze blowing.
さわやかな朝ですね.	It's nice and cool this morning.
泳いだあとはさわやかな気分になる.	You feel pleasantly refreshed after swimming.
これはさわやかな飲み物だ.	This is a refreshing drink.
こんなにさわやかな青年は見たことがない.	I've never seen such a fine, healthy young man.
彼は弁舌さわやかにスピーチした.	He made an eloquent speech.

さわる[1]（触る）

だれかの手が肩に触った.	Somebody's hand touched my shoulder.
触るべからず.	Do not touch.
この布は手触りが良い.	This material has a nice texture.
触らぬ神にたたりなし.	Just let sleeping dogs lie.

さわる[2]（障る）

夜ふかしは翌日の仕事に障る.	Keeping late hours will †affect [interfere with] your work the next day.
あまり心配すると体に障るよ.	Worrying too much †will affect [is bad for] your health.
彼は人の気に障ることばかり言う.	Everything he says gets on people's nerves.
彼女にうそをつかれたことがしゃくに障ってならない.	Her lying to me was more than I could take.

さんか（参加）

オリンピックは勝つことより参加することに意義がある.	At the Olympics participation is more significant than winning.
このツアーに参加を希望する方は集まってください.	Everybody who wants to †join [participate in] this tour, please come together.
参加, 不参加にかかわらず返事をください.	Please reply regardless of whether or not you plan to participate.
参加者の名前をチェックしてください.	Please check off the names of participants.
その祭りの参加者は年々増えている.	Every year the crowds get larger in that festival.

ざんぎょう (残業)

今日は残業で遅くなるよ.	I'm going to be late tonight. I have to work overtime.
ここ1ヵ月ほど残業が続き, 疲れがたまっている.	I'm exhausted. I've been working overtime for a month.
深夜まで残業して仕事を終わらせた.	I worked late into the night and got everything done.
経費削減のため, 残業手当がカットされた.	Overtime pay was cut in order to reduce costs.
サービス残業をなくすよう通達が出た.	A notice went out to †end [stop, put an end to] unpaid overtime.

さんこう (参考)

犯人のモンタージュ写真は目撃者の証言を参考にして作られた.	The composite photo of the criminal was made up on the basis of eyewitness accounts.
この本は心理学のレポートをまとめるのにとても参考になった.	This book was a very useful reference in writing my psychology paper.
参考までにお名前を伺います.	Please tell me your name for our reference.

ざんこく (残酷)

いくら野良犬でも殺してしまうなんて残酷だ.	Even if they're stray dogs, it's still cruel to kill them.
そんな小さな子を殴るとは何て残酷な!	How cruel to hit such a little child!
人間は時には考えられないほど残酷になる.	People can be unimaginably cruel at times.

さんせい (賛成)

君の意見に全く賛成だ.	I'm in complete agreement with you. I agree completely with you.
そういうやり方には賛成できないな.	I †can't go along with [don't agree with] that way of handling things.
両親は私たちの結婚に賛成してくれた.	My parents consented to our marriage.
彼はいやいやその案に賛成した.	He reluctantly approved the idea.
賛成の方は手を上げてください.	Those who approve, please raise your hands.
賛成か反対かはっきりしろよ.	Make up your mind, for or against.
賛成60, 反対40で可決した.	It was adopted by a vote of 60 to 40.
「ここらで一休みしようか」「賛成. もうくたくただ」	"Why don't we take a break here?" "I'm for that. [I'll buy that./I'll second that.] I'm exhausted."

ざんねん (残念)

お目にかかれなくて残念です. — I'm sorry I missed you.
ここまで来て引き返すとは残念だ. — What a shame to have to go back after coming this far!
旅行に行けなくなって彼はとても残念そうだった. — He looked like he really regretted not being able to go on the trip.
残念ながら彼はあまり勤勉ではない. — Unfortunately he's not very diligent.
友人の家に行ったが残念ながら彼はいなかった. — I went to my friend's house but unfortunately he wasn't in.

さんぶつ (産物)

東北地方の産物を三つあげなさい. — Name three products from the Tohoku region.
幽霊なんて人間の想像力の産物だよ. — Ghosts are only a product of human imagination.
最近各地で発行されているタウン誌は情報化時代の産物だ. — The community magazines which are being published in many places these days are a product of the age of information.

さんぽ (散歩)

ちょっと散歩に出てきます. — I'm †going for [taking] a walk.
その作家は毎日1時間の散歩を欠かさなかった. — That author never failed to take an hour-long walk every day.
犬は毎日散歩させなくちゃ. — Dogs have to be taken for walks every day, you know.

さんまん (散漫)

彼は注意力が散漫だから, 何をやっても必ずちょっとしたミスをする. — His attention is easily distracted, so he always makes little mistakes in whatever he's doing.
この絵は構成がいい加減なので, どことなく散漫な印象を受ける. — The composition of this painting is too haphazard, so I'm left with a somewhat vague impression.

し

し (死)

夫の死は彼女の人生を変えた.	The death of her husband changed her life.
周囲の無理解が彼女を死に追いやった.	The lack of understanding of those around her drove her to her death.
過度の心労が彼の死を招いた.	Excessive worry brought about his death.
死を目前にしながら, 彼は研究をやめなかった.	Even with death approaching he didn't quit doing his research.
彼は重傷を負い, 生と死の境をさまよった.	He sustained serious injuries and hovered between life and death.
彼女は死を覚悟して手術を受けた.	She was prepared for death as she underwent the operation.
飛行機事故で, たくさんの乗客が死傷した.	Many passengers were killed or injured in the airplane crash.
	The airplane crash produced many casualties.
彼は急死した.	He died suddenly.
被害者の死因は窒息だった.	The cause of the victim's death was asphyxiation.

しあい (試合)

明日はX大学と野球の試合をする.	We have a baseball game with X University tomorrow.
今日はチェスの試合がある.	There's a chess match [game, tournament] today.
テニスの試合に勝った〔負けた〕.	I won [lost] the tennis match.
試合は引き分けだった.	The game [match] ended up in a tie [draw].
彼が試合に出たら私たちは勝てたのに.	We would have won if he had played in the game.
BチームとCチームの練習試合が行われた.	There was a practice game between teams B and C.
彼のチームに試合を申し込んだ.	We challenged his team to a match [game].

しあがる (仕上がる)

仕上がったら見せてください.	Show it to me when it's †finished [ready, all put together].
仕上がりは上々だ.	It is very well done [made].
仕上がりがよくない.	It still has a lot of loose ends.[1] It is still rough in places.

> 1) loose ends は「今一歩のところ」.

しあげる (仕上げる)

今週中にこの仕事を仕上げなくてはならない.	I have to finish up[1] this work [job] (by the end of) this week.
今最後の仕上げをしているところだ.	I'm just †giving it [adding] the finishing touches now. I'm just finishing it up now.
仕上げにニスを塗らなくてはいけない.	I have to add a coat of varnish as a final touch.[2]

> 1) finish だけでも事足りるが up をつけると「終えてしまう」という完了のニュアンスが出る. 2) touch は「少しいじること, 手を加えること」.

しあわせ (幸せ)

今とても幸せです.	I'm very happy now.
二人はいつまでも幸せに暮らした.	The two lived happily ever after.
いい仕事に恵まれて君は幸せだ.	You †are lucky [must be happy[1]] to have gotten such a good job.
彼は幸せな星の下に生まれた.	He was born under a lucky star.
お幸せに.	Good luck./Best wishes.*

> 1) happy は主観的な観念なので, You're happy... のように相手に対して断定的な言い方はしない.

～しか

この仕事は君にしかできない.	You're the only one who can do this job. Nobody can do this job except you. You alone can do this job.
彼には1度しか会ったことがない.	I've met him only once.
今日は500円しか持っていない.	I †only have [have only] 500 yen today. Five hundred yen is all I have today.
この三日間水しか飲んでいない.	I've †had nothing but [only had] water for the last three days.
私はそれだけしか知らない.	That's †all [the only thing][1] I know.

私には彼女を慰めることしかできない.	All I can do is (to) try to console her.
彼がうそをついているとしか思えない.	He must be lying. I can't help but think he's lying.
私は北は仙台までしか行ったことがない.	I've never been any farther north than Sendai. Sendai is the farthest north I've ever been.

> 1) the only thing と言うと that の内容は一つになるので、いくつかある場合には all を用いる.

しかく (資格)

彼は英語教師の資格がある.	He is certified †to teach English [as an English teacher].
私は会計士の資格を取った.	I was certified as an accountant.
その試験を受けるにはどういう資格がいるの?	What qualifications do I need to take the test?
あなたは会員になる資格がある.	You're eligible for membership.
あなたには人を叱る資格なんかない.	You have no right to scold anyone (like that).
あなたは何の資格があって私に指図するんですか.	What right do you have to give me orders?
私にその仕事をする資格があるでしょうか.	I wonder if I †have the qualifications for [am qualified to do] this job.
君には教師の資格なんかない.	You're not qualified to be a teacher.

じかく (自覚)

自分の能力不足を自覚している.	I'm aware [conscious] of my lack of ability. I realize my lack of ability.
彼は人を指導しなければならないという自覚が足りない.	He doesn't fully realize that he must lead others.
彼に指摘されて初めて自分の立場 (の重要性) を自覚した.	I first became aware of (the importance of) my position when he pointed it out to me.
海外生活をして改めて自分が日本人であることを自覚した.	When I was living overseas I gained a new awareness of being Japanese.
夏頃から自覚症状があった.	I began to notice certain symptoms last summer.

しかし

彼は優秀な学者だ. しかし優れた教育者とは言えない.	He's an excellent scholar but he's not a particularly good teacher [instructor].

うそだと思うのも無理はない．しかし本当なんだ．	I know it's hard to believe, but [yet] it really is true.
ゆうべは8時間ほど寝た．しかしまだ眠い．	I slept eight hours last night. I'm still sleepy, however [though].
彼の戯曲は面白い．しかしながら上演は困難だろう．	His play is an interesting one, although it would be difficult to stage.
君が大食漢だとは聞いていた．しかしよく食べるなあ．	I've heard that you have a big appetite, but[1] my, you certainly can put it away, can't you?

> 1)「しかし」につながる前置きを言わないときは but は不要.

しかた (仕方)

説明の仕方が悪かったので，あまりよく分からなかった．	It was explained badly, and I didn't quite understand.
彼は挨拶の仕方もろくに知らない．	He doesn't even know how to make the usual greetings.
この魚の料理の仕方を教えてください．	Please tell me how you prepare this fish.
そんな勉強の仕方では能率が上がるはずがない．	You can't expect to improve your performance if you study that way.

しかたがない

【むだだ】小さい子に怒ってもしかたがない．	It's †(of) no use getting [useless to get] angry with a little child.
今さら後悔してもしかたがない．	It won't do any good to regret it now.
彼にお金がないのなら，返せと言ったところでしかたがない．	If he doesn't have any money himself, there's no point [use] in asking him to give me back mine.
こんな議論をいつまで続けてもしかたがない．	There's no point in continuing this argument forever.
【ほかに方法がない】バスがなければ歩くよりしかたがない．	If there's no bus, there's no other way to get there but [except] (to) walk.
今となっては彼の言葉を信じるよりしかたがない．	At this point, we have no choice but [except] to believe him.
閉まっているならしかたがない．ほかの店を探そう．	If it's closed, it's closed. Let's look for another place.
それもご時勢だと思えばしかたがない．	If that's the trend, we'll just have to †go along with [put up with] it.
しかたがない．そのままにしておこう．	It can't be helped. Let's leave it as it is.
【無理もない】彼はまだ仕事に慣れていないから間違えてもしかた	He's not used to the job yet so †of course he makes mistakes [he can't help mak-

がない.	ing mistakes].
君は働き過ぎだから病気になったのもしかたがない.	You've been overworking so it's only natural that you got sick.
【たまらない】ああ,のどが渇いてしかたがない.	I'm so thirsty I can't stand it. I'm dying of thirst.
犬がうるさくてしかたがない.	The dog's barking is really annoying.
彼女はその映画が見たくてしかたがない.	She's dying to see that movie.
その映画を見て泣けてしかたがなかった.	I could not help crying when I saw that movie.

しかも

【その上】彼女は若く,しかも美人だ.	She is young, and beautiful as well.
この本は安くて,しかも内容が良い.	This is a good book, and †it's cheap as well [besides it's cheap].
彼には才能がある.しかも努力家だ.	He has talent, and works hard as well.
【それなのに】これだけ勉強して,しかも成績が上がらなければしかたがない.	I might as well give up if I study this much and still can't raise my grades.

しかる (叱る)

母親は子どもを厳しく叱った.	The mother scolded her child harshly [severely].
宿題を忘れて先生に叱られた.	I got in trouble with my teacher [My teacher scolded me] for forgetting my homework.
そんなことをすると叱られるよ.	You'll get in trouble if you do something like that.
社長は社員の職務上の怠慢を叱った.	The president reprimanded[1] the employee for being lazy on the job.
警官は信号を無視した子どもを叱った.	The policeman †yelled at[2] [scolded] the child for ignoring the traffic signal.
彼は息子を(ひどく)叱りつけた.	He gave his son a (good) scolding.
彼は何度も時間に遅れて,課長にさんざん叱られた.	His boss dressed him down for repeated tardiness.
母親は花瓶を割った男の子を叱りつけた.	The mother bawled her little boy out for breaking the flower vase.

1) reprimand は厳しく改まった感じで,叱られる側は大抵大人である. 2) yell at は「〜をどなりつける,叱りつける」.

じかん (時間)

出発まで時間がたっぷりある.	There's plenty of time before departure.
残り時間が少なくなってきた.	Time is running out.
時間があれば奈良に行くつもりだ.	If there's enough time, I intend to go to Nara.
時間があったら見に来てください.	If you have the time, please come and have a look.
時間があいたので彼のところに寄った.	Since I had some free time, I stopped by his place.
今日の試験は時間が足りなかった.	I didn't have enough time to finish the test today.
シチューは作るのに時間がかかる.	It takes a long time to cook stew.
時間をかけて両親を説得しよう.	I'm going to try to persuade my parents gradually.
私たちは時間のたつのも忘れて語り合った.	We talked and forgot all about the passage of time.
もう少し考える時間をください.	Please give me a little more time to think.
彼は私と会うために時間を割いてくれた.	He found the time to meet with me.
30分ほどお時間を割いていただけませんか.	Would you mind sparing me 30 minutes of your time?
時間の許す限りお手伝いします.	I will help you to the extent that time permits.
時間つぶしに本屋で立ち読みした.	I browsed in a bookstore to kill some time.
いつまで議論しても切りがないから時間を区切ろう.	This discussion could go on forever, so let's set a limit on the time.
毎日, 時間に追われている.	I'm pressed for time every day.
時間を計ってください.	Please time [clock[1]] me [him, her, it].
彼らの離婚も時間の問題だ.	It's a matter of time before they get a divorce.

【時刻】

時間ですよ.	It's time!
時間切れです.	Time is up.
そろそろ彼が帰って来る時間だ.	It's (just) about time for him to come back.
その飛行機が到着する時間を教えてください.	Please tell me what time that airplane will arrive.
約束の時間を1時間間違えていた.	I was off on the appointment time by an hour.
こんな時間に電話してくるなんて.	You're not going to make a telephone call at a time like this, are you!
珍しく講義が時間どおりに終わった.	His lecture ended on time for a change.
時間に遅れると彼は怒り出す.	He gets mad when people are late.

彼は時間に厳しい.	He's very strict [particular] about time.
彼は時間に正確だ.	He is very punctual.
時間を守ってください.	Please be †on time [punctual].
【時間の単位】1時間当たり800円もらっている.	I'm getting 800 yen an [per] hour.
3時間後にまた会いましょう.	Let's meet again three hours from now.
彼女を1時間も待たせてしまった.	I kept her waiting for a whole hour.
電車は1時間半に1本しかない.	There's only one train every hour and a half.
この小説は3時間もあれば読める.	This novel can easily be read in three hours.
【授業・勤務の時間】次の時間までに考えておきなさい.	Please think about this by the next class.
歴史の授業は週に4時間ある.	History class meets four hours a week.
今日は5時間目に音楽がある.	I have music in fifth period today.
時間割が変更になった.	The schedule [timetable] has been changed.
彼は勤務時間中に映画を見ていた.	He went to see a movie during working hours.
ここは時間外勤務を禁じている.	Overtime work †is forbidden [isn't allowed] here.

---

1) clock は特にスポーツの場合に言う.

しき (式)

【儀式】ノーベル賞の授賞式が行われた.	The Nobel Prize presentation ceremony was held.
結婚式の日取りが決まった.	The date was set for the wedding (ceremony).
【方式】これが英国式の手紙の書き方だ.	This is the British style of letter writing.
ふろは日本式〔洋式〕のほうがいい.	I prefer a Japanese [Western] style bath.
これは旧式〔新式〕の機械だ.	This is †an old-model [a new-model] machine.
本式のフランス料理を食べた.	We had an authentic French meal.
電動式の鉛筆削り器を買った.	I bought an electric pencil sharpener.
【数式・化学式】割合を求める式をたてなさい.	Derive the equation for obtaining the ratio.
水の分子式は何ですか.	What is the molecular formula for water?

じき (時期・時機)

【時・期間】今がその時期だ.	Now is the best time for that.

時期がくれば君にも話すよ.	I'll talk to you in due time.
今が一年中でいちばん忙しい時期だ.	This is the busiest time [period] of the year.
私にも人生に悩んだ時期があった.	I too went through a period of worrying about life.
彼のこの時期の作品は素晴らしい.	His works from this period are magnificent.
その時期に恐竜は死滅した.	Dinosaurs became extinct in that period.
一時期私は学者になろうと考えていた.	I thought about becoming a scholar †at one time [for a while].
秋は読書に良い時期だ.	Fall is a good season [time] for reading.
もう桜の咲く時期になった.	It's already cherry blossom season.
事業を始めるには時期尚早だ.	It would be premature to start a business now.
【好機】転職の時機を逃した.	I passed up an opportunity to change jobs.
彼は新作を発表する時機をうかがっていた.	He was waiting for †an opportunity [a chance] to present his new work.
時機をみてこの案を社長と話してみてください.	When you get a chance please talk this proposal over with the president.

じぎょう (事業)

どういう事業をなさっているのですか.	What kind of business[1] are you running?
彼は一人でこの事業を興した.	He †started [undertook, took on] this business [enterprise[2]] by himself.
砂漠に水を引くのは大事業だ.	Bringing water into the desert is a big undertaking.[3]
彼は財産を社会事業につぎ込んだ.	He poured his fortune into social works.
政府は公共事業に力を入れている.	The government is putting a great deal of effort into public works.

---

1) business はこの場合は広義の「商売」一般を指す. 2) enterprise はしばしば規模が大きく投機的なものを指す. 3) undertaking は「企て,大仕事」の意.

しく (敷・布く)

じゅうたんを敷くのを手伝って.	Help me lay the carpet.
居間にじゅうたんを敷き詰めた.	We laid a wall-to-wall carpet in the living room.
まず植木鉢の底に小石を敷いてください.	First, line the bottom of the flower pot with pebbles.
その町の道路にはすべてれんがが敷き詰めてあった.	The streets in that town are all paved with bricks.

席を立つまで帽子を敷いていたことに気づかなかった.	I didn't notice I had been sitting on my hat until I stood up.
花瓶の下にレースを敷いた.	I spread [laid, put] a piece of lace under the flower vase.
スカートが汚れないようこれを敷きなさい.	Spread this out first so you won't get your skirt dirty.
【鉄道を】この町に鉄道が敷かれたのはほんの2年前です.	It's been only two years since railroad tracks were laid in this town.
【法令などを】全土に戒厳令が敷かれた.	The entire country was put under martial law.
新しい教育制度が敷かれた.	A new educational system was put into effect.

しげき (刺激)

植物の中には,光の刺激に反応して花を開くものがある.	Some plants flower in response to the stimulus of light.
カエルの神経に電気で刺激を与えて,反応を調べた.	I stimulated the frog's nerve with electricity to see how it would react.
香辛料は食欲を刺激する.	Spices stimulate the appetite.
彼の神経を刺激するようなことは言うな.	Don't say anything that will †irritate him [get on his nerves].
機嫌が悪そうだからあまり彼を刺激しないほうがいい.	He's in a bad mood [He looks irritated], so you'd better not †provoke him [get him excited].
下手に強盗を刺激すると人質の生命が危ない.	Provoking the robbers will put the lives of the hostages in danger.
その議員の発言は野党を刺激した.	That representative's statement caused a stir in the opposition parties.
警察の出動に刺激されてデモ隊が暴れ出した.	Provoked by the mobilization of the police, the group of demonstrators became violent.
この薬品は刺激臭がある.	This medicine has a pungent odor.
【啓発・興奮】彼と話すと良い刺激になる.	Talking with him is stimulating.
友達の成功が刺激になって彼は本気で仕事をするようになった.	His friend's success †motivated him [gave him the impetus] to work in earnest.
田舎はのどかでいいが,刺激がない.	It's nice and peaceful in the country, but there's no stimulation.
都会の生活は刺激が多過ぎて疲れる.	Big city life provides so much stimulus that you get tired.
こんな刺激のない生活には耐えられない.	I cannot stand this monotonous [boring, uninteresting, insipid] life.
刺激のない生活を送っている.	I'm leading †a dull [an unstimulating] life.

この映画は刺激的だ． This movie is exciting.

しげる (茂る)
ポプラの木が青々と茂っている． The poplars are thick with (green) foliage.
草が庭一面に茂っている． The grass grows thick everywhere in the garden.
向こうにこんもりと茂った森が見える． I see a thick, shady grove over there.

しけん (試験)
【考査】今日数学の試験がある． There's a math examination [test] today.
あの先生はよく抜き打ち試験をする． That teacher often gives us pop quizzes.
あの大学の入学試験を受けるつもりだ． I plan to take the entrance examination for that university.
今日の試験はどうだった？ How was the exam today?
彼は資格試験に合格した〔落ちた〕． He passed [failed] the qualifying examination.
中間〔期末〕試験の成績は良くなかった． I didn't get a good grade [mark] on the midterm [final] exam.
試験問題は難しかった． The problems [questions] on the test were difficult.
試験勉強を全くしなかった． I didn't study for my examinations at all.
筆記試験のほかに面接試験がある． In addition to the written examination, you must pass an interview.
いろいろ質問されてまるで試験されているような気分だった． They asked me all kinds of questions and I felt just like I was being tested.
【実験】エンジンが動くかどうか試験してみよう． Let's test it to see if the engine runs.
自作のグライダーの試験飛行は成功だった． The test flight of the glider I made was successful.
この機械はもう試験済みです． This machine has already been tested [proven].
新しいシステムはまだ試験段階だ． The new system is still undergoing testing.
試験的にその車を使ってみた． I used that car on a trial basis.

じけん (事件)
彼がその事件のかぎを握っている． He holds the key to that affair [incident].
そんな事件はよくあるよ． Incidents of that sort often occur.
そんな大事件になろうとは思ってもみなかった． I never thought it would turn into such a big [serious] affair [matter].
爆発事件の容疑者が捕まった． A suspect in the bombing incident was arrested.

彼は収賄事件に巻き込まれた.	He got involved in a bribery affair.
近所で殺人事件が起こった.	There was a murder in the neighborhood.
大手2社の合併は産業界の大きな事件だった.	The merger of the two major companies was †quite an [a big] event in industrial circles.
父の転勤は我が家にとって大事件だった.	Father's transfer was †a big event [something big] for our family.
彼がこの事件を担当する弁護士だ.	He's the lawyer handling this case.

じこ¹ (自己)

自己を静かに見つめてごらん.	Reflect calmly on your inner self.
彼は自己の持つ力を100パーセント発揮していない.	He hasn't yet demonstrated 100 percent of his personal [own] ability.
私は自己流で絵を描いている.	I paint in my own style.
彼は自己中心的だ.	He's self-centered.
自己満足していてはだめだ.	It's no good to be self-satisfied [complacent].
私は今ひどい自己嫌悪に陥っている.	At present I am obsessed with self-hatred.
彼は自己顕示欲が強い.	He always wants to stand out.
彼女は自己暗示にかかり易い.	She talks herself into things easily.
彼は皆の前で自己批判をした.	He criticized himself in front of everyone.

じこ² (事故)

昨日ここで自動車事故が起こった.	There was a car accident here yesterday.
小さな事故は毎日たくさん起こっている.	There are lots of minor accidents every day.
彼は酔っ払い運転で事故を起こした.	He caused a traffic accident because he was drunk.
彼女は高速道路で事故にあった.	She was in an accident on the expressway.
彼は飛行機事故で死んだ.	He was killed in an airplane accident.
その故障に気づかなければ大事故になるところだった.	If I hadn't noticed the defect [trouble], it would have caused a major accident before long.
重要書類が紛失するという事故があった.	I had the misfortune to lose some important papers.

じこく (時刻)

ただ今の時刻は7時30分です.	The time is 7:30.
そろそろ彼が帰ってくる時刻だ.	It's just about time for him to return.
その列車の発車の時刻は何時何分ですか.	What is the scheduled time of departure of that train?
列車の時間は時刻表で調べます.	I'll check the times for the train in the

しごと (仕事)

【職業】お仕事は何ですか.	What kind of job do you have?
	What is your occupation?
	What do you do?
どういう仕事がしたいのですか.	What kind of job do you want?
	What kind of work do you want to do?
いい仕事が見つかった.	I found †a good job [good work].
【職務】彼は病気で仕事を休んでいる.	He's taken off work because he's sick.
日曜日なのに彼は仕事に出かけた.	He left for work even though it's Sunday.
仕事は忙しいの？	Are you busy at †work [the office]?
今は仕事中なのであとで電話します.	I'm at work now, so I'll call you later.
彼は仕事でギリシャに行っている.	He is in Greece on business.
彼は仕事は仕事と割り切っている.	To him, work is work.
仕事の割に賃金が安い.	The pay is low for the work [job].
彼は仕事の鬼だ.	He is a †work fiend [workaholic].
【任務】学生は勉強が仕事だ.	Study is a student's job.
苦情を聞くのが彼の仕事だ.	His job is listening to complaints.
部屋の掃除は1年生の仕事だ.	Cleaning the room is a freshman's duty.
【労働・作業】今日は仕事がはかどらなかった.	I didn't get very far with work today.
彼が来なければ仕事にならない.	This work won't get anywhere unless he comes.
彼は仕事がよくできる.	He's very good at his job [work].
彼女は仕事が雑〔丁寧〕だ.	Her work is sloppy [neat].
時間をかけていい仕事をしたい.	I want to take the time to do a good job.
彼を納得させるのは大仕事だ.	It will be †quite a task [a big job] to convince him.
家の中の仕事がたまっている.	Household chores [Chores around the house] have piled up.

じじつ (事実)

【実態・真実】それは事実に反する.	That contradicts the facts.
	That goes against the facts.
事実を確かめもせずに発表してはいけない.	Don't make an announcement without checking the facts.
それは動かし難い〔歴史的〕事実だ.	That's †an established [a historic] fact.
市長は収賄の事実を認めた.	The mayor admitted that he had accepted a bribe.
事実は事実として認めよう.	I will accept †the situation as it is [the

	facts as they are].
彼らは事実を隠そうとした.	They tried to hide the truth [facts].
彼の言ったのは事実と判った.	What he said turned out to be true.
それは事実無根だ.	That's †groundless [without foundation].
事実は小説よりも奇なり.	Truth is stranger than fiction.
まず既成事実を作って彼らを納得させるしかない.	The only way to persuade them is to †go ahead and do it [create a *fait accompli*[1)]].
【実際】事実私がこの目で見たんだから間違いない.	I actually saw it with my own eyes, so there's no mistake about it.
そうあるべきだし事実そうなのだ.	That's the way it should be, and that's the way it actually is.
彼女は1週間断食すると宣言し,事実そのあいだ何も食べなかった.	She declared that she would fast for a week, and in fact she didn't eat anything during that period.
これが事実上の決勝戦だ.	For all practical purposes this is the final [deciding] match.
彼は事実上の最高権力者だ.	He's virtually the ultimate authority.

1) フランス語からきた言い方で, [fɛtakɔ̄pli] と発音する. an accomplished fact でもよい.

ししゅつ (支出)

今月は10万円の支出があった.	Expenses this month †were [came to] one hundred thousand yen.
我が家の家計は収入の割に支出が多過ぎる.	Our family spends too much for the income we have.
赤字を出さないように支出を切り詰めた.	To keep from going in the red we cut expenditures.

じじょう (事情)

【状況】その時の事情を説明した.	I explained what it was like then.
こういう事情では計画を中止せざるを得ない.	Under these circumstances we'll have to cancel our plans.
事情の許す限り参加します.	I'll take part if circumstances permit.
10年前と今とでは事情が違う.	The situation now is different from what it was ten years ago.
彼は政界の事情に明るい.	He is †well-versed in [familiar with] the state of political affairs.
交通事情は年々悪化している.	Traffic conditions are †getting worse [deteriorating] every year.
彼は家庭の事情で大学進学を断念した.	He gave up the idea of going to college because of family circumstances.

【わけ・理由】何か事情があるはずだ.	There must be some reason for it.
どういう事情か, 話してごらん.	Explain the situation to me.
事情があって今回は欠席します.	Due to circumstances (beyond my control) I will not be able to attend this time.

じしん¹ (自信)

英会話には自信がある.	I'm confident [I have confidence] about speaking English.
自分に自信を持たなくてはいけない.	You have to have †confidence in yourself [self-confidence].
彼はこの作品に自信を持っている.	He has confidence in this work.
この作品で賞を取る自信がある.	I'm confident of winning the prize with this work.
自信はないが, 頼めば彼女は引き受けてくれると思う.	I'm not sure but I think if we ask her she'll accept.
練習するうちに自信がついてきた.	I began to feel †confident [sure of myself] while I was practicing.
賞をもらって自信がついた.	Winning the award boosted my confidence.
彼は才能に自信をなくしている.	He has lost confidence in his ability.
自信を持ってこの本を薦める.	I can recommend this book with confidence.
彼女は自信なさそうに答えた.	She answered without confidence.
彼は自信たっぷりに持論を語った.	He spoke about his pet theory brimming with confidence.
彼は明日の試験には自信満々の様子だった.	He seemed †to be full of confidence [very confident] about tomorrow's examination.
彼はいつも自信満々だ.	He is always full of confidence.
	He's always very †sure of himself [confident].
彼は自信家だ.	He's confident.
	He is a confident man.
彼は自信過剰だ.	He is overly confident.

じしん² (自身)

それはあなた自身の問題だ.	That's your (own)¹⁾ problem.
	That's a question you have to answer yourself.
私自身はUFOを見たことがない.	I have never seen a UFO myself.
それ自身には問題はない.	There's no problem with that in itself.

1) your を強く発音すれば own は必要ない.

しずか (静か)
家の中は静かだった. — The house was quiet.
この辺りは静かな住宅街だ. — This is a quiet residential area.
彼女は静かにドアを閉めた. — She closed the door quietly.
森の静けさが一発の銃声によって突然破られた. — The quiet [silence] of the forest was suddenly broken by the sound of a single gunshot.
静かにしなさい. — Quiet down!／Settle down.
子どもたちはやっと静かになった. — The children finally quieted [settled] down.
彼は静かな口調で話した. — He spoke in a soft voice.
彼女は静かな人だった. — She was a quiet person.
静かにしていないと熱が上がるよ. — Your temperature will go up if you don't †rest quietly [behave yourself, stay in bed].

【穏やか】今日の海は静かだ. — The ocean is calm today.
彼は静かな生活を送っている. — He lives a quiet life.
デモ隊は静かに行進した. — The demonstrators marched peacefully.
静かな日々が続いている. — Peaceful days are continuing.
世の中がやっと静かになった. — Things have finally quieted down (in the world).

しずむ (沈む)
鉄は水に沈む. — Iron sinks in water.
船は傾いて沈んでいった. — The ship listed and sank.
この辺の海底には財宝が沈んでいるらしい. — At the bottom of the ocean near here there's supposed to be sunken treasure.
日が沈みかけている. — The sun has begun to set.
月も西に沈む. — The moon sets in the west, too.
真っ赤な太陽が海に沈んだ. — The bright red sun set over the ocean.
【気分が】今日は朝から沈んでいるね. — You've been in low spirits since this morning, haven't you?
彼は悲しみ〔憂い〕に沈んでいる. — He is lost [deep] in sadness [melancholy].
彼女は近頃物思いに沈んでいる. — Recently she has been lost [deep] in thought.
彼は何だか沈んだ声だった. — Somehow he sounded glum [depressed].

しずめる¹ (沈める)
彼は銃を海に沈めた. — He sank the gun into the sea.
彼は体を湯ぶねに深く沈めた. — He sank into the hot bath.

しずめる² (静・鎮める)

【心を】もう少し心を静めてから来なさい. — Please come after you've †calmed down [composed yourself] a little.

この音楽は私の神経を静めてくれる. — This music soothes [calms] my nerves.

【痛み・騒ぎを】この注射は痛みを鎮める. — This injection will soothe the pain.

警官が来て騒ぎを鎮めた. — The policemen came and got things under control.

しせい (姿勢)

彼女は姿勢がいい〔悪い〕. — She has good [poor] posture.

先生が入ってきたので皆は姿勢を正した. — Since the teacher came in, everyone sat [stood] up straight.

こういう姿勢だと疲れ易い. — It's easy to get tired with posture like this.

彼は立った〔座った〕姿勢で詩を朗読した. — He recited a poem †standing up [sitting down].

彼はモデルにいろいろな姿勢をとらせた. — He had the model take various poses.

楽隊は直立不動[気をつけ]の姿勢で立っていた. — The brass band stood at attention.

【態度】彼らはまじめな〔いいかげんな〕姿勢で話し合いに臨んだ. — They attended the conference in a serious [half-hearted] frame of mind.

彼は高姿勢〔低姿勢〕だった. — He took a high-handed [modest, humble] attitude.

その問題に対して首相は前向きの姿勢である. — The prime minister has taken a constructive position on that problem.

これからは姿勢を正して職務に当たっていただきたい. — From now on I'd like you to straighten up and take your work more seriously.

しぜん (自然)

【自然界】自然の力は恐ろしい. — The forces of nature are frightening.

自然の法則には逆らえない. — You can't go against the laws of nature.

アラスカの自然は厳しい. — Nature in Alaska is harsh.

自然風土に合った作物を作るべきだ. — We should plant crops that suit this land and climate.

アメリカ西部の大自然は写真には納まらない. — It's hard to capture the vastness of the American West in photographs.

【天然の】彼は自然食品以外は食べない. — He doesn't eat anything but natural food.

【無理・作為がない】そう考えるのが自然だ. — It's natural to think that.

(嵐・発熱などが) 自然に収まる — The only thing to do is let nature take its

のを待つしかない.	course.
自然の成り行きに任せよう.	Let's let things take their course.
収入が増えると自然に生活はぜいたくになるものだ.	When your salary increases, you naturally become more extravagant.
7時になると自然に目が覚める.	I wake up by myself at seven o'clock.
彼は英語が自然に出てくる.	He speaks English naturally.
彼女とは自然に親しくなった.	I just naturally got to be close with her.
自然に昔の家のほうに足が向いた.	I just found myself walking toward our old house.
このぐらいのけがは自然に治る.	A little wound like this will heal by itself.
放っておいても子どもは自然に育つというのは本当かしら.	I wonder if it's true that children just grow up by themselves if you let them be.
火事は自然発火によるものだった.	The fire was due to spontaneous combustion.
【自動的に】暗くなると自然に電気がつく仕掛けになっている.	It's set up so that the lights go on automatically when it gets dark.

しそう (思想)

日本国憲法は思想の自由をうたっている.	The Japanese Constitution declares freedom of thought.
戦前は思想統制があった.	Thought was controlled before the war.
それは私の思想に反するのでできません.	I can't do that because it would be in contradiction to my way of thinking.
私は彼の思想に共鳴してこの会に入った.	I entered this society in complete agreement with his †way of thinking [ideas].
彼は危険〔過激〕思想の持ち主だ.	He has dangerous [radical] ideas.
その時代は多くの偉大な思想家が生まれた.	Many great thinkers emerged during that era. That era †produced [turned out] many great thinkers.
私はマルクス主義思想に興味がある.	I am interested in Marxist ideology [thought].

じそんしん (自尊心)

私にだって自尊心がある.	I have my self-respect [pride] too.
彼は自尊心が強いので容易に敗北を認めようとはしなかった.	He has a strong sense of pride, so he did not readily admit defeat.
彼の自尊心を傷つけてはいけない.	You must not [Don't] hurt his pride.

した¹ (下)

【下方】その本なら書類の下にある.	That book is under the papers.
このマットの下に何かある.	There's something under this mat.

彼は机の下から大きな箱を出した.	He took a big box out from under the desk.
鉄道高架の下に店が並んでいる.	There are rows of shops beneath the elevated railroad tracks.
太陽は水平線の下に沈んだ.	The sun sank beneath the horizon.
封筒ならいちばん下の引き出しです.	The envelopes are in the bottom drawer.
彼女は下を向いて話した.	She looked down as she spoke.
下の階は人に貸している.	I rent out the floor downstairs.
彼はさっき下に降りて行った.	He went downstairs a little while ago.
階段の下から彼の声がした.	His voice came from the bottom of the stairs.
坂〔がけ〕の下に彼の家がある.	His house is at the bottom of the slope 〔cliff〕.
いちばん下の引き出しを開けてごらん.	Try opening the bottom drawer.
【下部】ついたての下のほうに模様がある.	There is a design on the lower part of the screen.
地図では南は下になる.	Maps have south at the bottom.
ビルの下のほうは日がささない.	The lower part of the building doesn't get any sun.
赤ん坊の歯は下から生える.	A baby's teeth start coming in from the bottom.
【内側】下塗りに黄色を使った.	I used yellow for the undercoat.
その紙は下が透けて見える.	You can see through that paper.
このシャツの下には何も着ていない.	I'm not wearing anything under this shirt.
緑のペンキをはがすと下はオレンジ色だった.	When I peeled off the green paint, it was orange underneath.
【年・級・地位】私の下に弟が一人いる.	I have one younger brother.
彼女は私より年が二つ下だ.	She is two years younger than I am.
私は兄弟の中でいちばん下だ.	I am the youngest in my family.
下の学年 (級) の生徒を教えた.	I taught the students in the lower classes.
彼は一つ下の学年だ.	He is one year behind me at school.
彼より私のほうが地位が下だ.	My position is lower than his.
彼の下で5人働いている.	Five people work under him.
【成績・腕】ゴルフの腕は彼よりずっと下だ.	My golf is very inferior to his.
私の成績は彼女より下だった.	My grades were lower than hers.
【数量】千円より下では売らない.	I won't sell it for less than a thousand yen.
売り上げは昨年を下回った.	Sales fell below last year's.
【前もっての】下書きを書いた.	I wrote a rough draft.

会場の下見に行った.	I went to get a preliminary look at the meeting place.
明日の授業の下調べをした.	I prepared for tomorrow's class.
下調べもせずに彼を非難すると，反対に自分に火の粉が振りかかってくるよ.	If you haven't done your homework when you take him on, the whole thing will backfire on you.
【慣用】知人の家で，下にも置かないもてなしを受けた.	I was †given the red carpet treatment [treated like a king] at the home of an acquaintance.
彼は何か下心があってそうしたに違いない.	He must have had †something in the back of his mind [some ulterior motive] to do that.
まずは下手(した)に出たほうがいい.	I'd suggest starting out low-key.

した² (舌)

彼女は何かをやり損なうとすぐ舌を出す.	She sticks her tongue out whenever she makes a mistake.
彼は酔いが回って舌がもつれてきた.	He began to slur his speech when the liquor hit him.
カミツキガメのラテン名は舌をかみそうだ.	The latin name for snapping turtle is quite a mouthful.
彼女は舌足らずな話し方をする.	She speaks with a lisp./She lisps.
彼女はおしゃべりで，感心するほどよく舌が回る.	She's a real talker and it's amazing how fast her mouth moves.
その子のピアノ演奏には審査員も舌を巻いた.	Even the judges were amazed by that child's piano performance.
これからはまじめに勉強すると言った舌の根も乾かぬうちに，彼は学校をずる休みした.	He said that from now on he was going to study hard but the words were scarcely out of his mouth before he was back to skipping classes.
あの男は二枚舌を使うから用心したほうがいい.	That guy is double-dealing so be careful.

～しだい (～次第)

【～による】成功するかしないかは明日の天気しだいだ.	Whether we succeed or not depends on the weather tomorrow.
行くか行かないかは君しだいだ.	Whether or not we go is up to you.
すべては状況〔あなた〕しだいだ.	Everything depends on †the situation 〔you〕.
彼は金しだいでどうにでもなる.	He can be bought.
【すぐに】この仕事が終わりしだいそちらに行きます.	I'll come as soon as this work is finished.

| 彼が帰りしだい私に電話するように伝えてください. | Please ask him to call me as soon as he gets home. |

じだい (時代)

【年代】
父は大正時代の生まれだ.	My father was born in the Taisho era.
その時代の終わりに疫病がはやった.	Epidemics were prevalent at the end of that period.
封建時代が長く続いた.	The feudal period continued for a long time.

【時期】
学生時代は良き友人に恵まれた.	When I was a student I †had [was fortunate to have] good friends.
私たちが子どもの時代にはテレビなんかなかった.	When we were little we didn't have anything like television.
古き良き時代だった.	Those were the good old days.
その発明が新時代を画した.	That invention marked a new epoch [age].
それは宇宙時代の幕明けだった.	That marked the dawn of the space age.
時代は変わった.	The times have changed.
だれもが宇宙旅行できる時代がやがて来るだろう.	The time when anybody will be able to travel in space is probably not far off.
手動式ポンプで井戸から水を汲んだ時代もあった.	There was a time when people pumped water from wells by hand.
電話がなかった時代は人々はよく手紙を書いた.	People often wrote letters before the advent of the telephone.

【時流】
少しは若い人と接しないと時代に取り残されるよ.	You'll †fall behind [get out of step with] the times unless you have a little contact with young people.
そういう考えは時代遅れだ.	That way of thinking is †old-fashioned [out of date].
それは〔彼は〕時代錯誤もはなはだしい.	That [He] is an outrageous anachronism.
その政策は時代に逆行する.	That policy runs counter to the times.
その商品は時代の要求にかなった.	That product met the demands of the times.
彼の思想は時代を先取りしていた.	His ideas were ahead of their time.
我が社は時代とともに歩んできた.	Our company has kept pace [up] with the times.

【昔の】
この机は時代物だ.	This desk is †an antique [a period piece].
その美術館は時代がかった建物だ.	That art museum is a period building.
私は時代劇はあまり見ない.	I don't watch "*samurai*" dramas" very often.

したう (慕う)

| 彼女は彼をとても慕っていた. | She was deeply [very] attached to him. |

その若いハンサムな先生は学生に慕われている．	The handsome young teacher is adored by the students.
夫を慕って彼女はシベリアに向かった．	Longing to be with her husband, she set off for Siberia.
その教授を慕って多くの学生が集まって来た．	Because they admired that professor deeply, many students took his classes.

したがう (従う)

【応じる・沿う】もはや彼の命令に従う者はだれもいない．	No one follows his orders anymore.
判決には従わなければならない．	You have to comply with the verdict.
彼を従わせるのは容易ではない．	It's no easy task to get him to comply.
良心に従って行動しなさい．	Act in accordance with your conscience.
彼は両親の意見に従った．	He obeyed his parents.
彼は友人の忠告に従った．	He followed his friend's advice.
先生の勧めに従って留学することにした．	I followed my teacher's recommendation and decided to study abroad.
標識に従って歩けば道に迷わない．	You won't get lost if you follow the signs.
私たちは決められた日程に従って実験を行っている．	We're conducting the experiment according to a set schedule.
私は大勢に従うことにしている．	I make it a practice to follow the majority.
【倣う】従うべき前例がない．	There's no appropriate precedent to follow.
彼らは土地の風習に従って婚礼をあげた．	They held their wedding ceremony according to local customs.
フロイトの方法に従って自分の夢を分析してみた．	I tried analyzing my dreams according to Freudian methods.
彼が荷物をまとめ始めると，皆それに従った．	When he began to pack up his belongings, everyone followed suit.
【後ろに続く】私たちは彼に従って山を下りた．	We followed him down the mountain.

したがって (従って)

【それゆえ】彼はその時間にその場所へ行けるはずがない．従って彼は犯人ではない．	He couldn't have gone to that place at that time. Therefore, he cannot be the criminal.
私は大きな買い物をしたばかりだ．従って君に貸す金はない．	I just bought something expensive, so I don't have any money to lend you.
【〜につれて】年を取るに従って一般に人は頑固になる．	The older people get, the more stubborn they generally become.
情報量の増大に従って大きなメモリが必要になる．	Computers need an increasingly larger memory in proportion to the increase in the volume of information.

したく (支度)

食事の支度を大急ぎでやった.	I prepared the meal in a big hurry.
彼女は夫の旅行の支度を手伝った.	She helped make preparations for her husband's trip.
	She helped her husband prepare for his trip.
彼女は外出の支度に時間がかかる.	It takes her a long time to get ready to go out.
(出かける)支度は出来ましたか.	Are you ready to go?
帰ると夕食の支度が出来ていた.	Supper was ready when I got home.
支度はすっかり整いました.	Everything is set [ready].

したしい (親しい)

彼は私の親しい友人だ.	He is a good [close] friend of mine.
親しそうに話してたけど, あの人だれ?	It looked like you were having an intimate conversation, but who was that person?
初対面なのに彼は親しそうに話しかけてきた.	We'd never met, but he came up and spoke to me as if we were old friends.
彼は多くの有名な作家と親しいらしい.	He seems to be on friendly terms with many famous writers.
彼とは知り合いだが, 親しいというほどではない.	I do know him, but I wouldn't say we were close.
いくら親しいといってもそんなことは頼めない.	No matter how close we may be I couldn't ask him to do something like that.
彼の家族とは親しくしている.	His family and I are (very) close.
彼とは10年以上も親しくつきあっている.	I've had a close relationship with him for over 10 years.
親しき仲にも礼儀あり.	Politeness is not just for strangers.

したしみ (親しみ)

初対面のときから彼に親しみを覚えていた.	I've had friendly feelings for him since I first saw him.
	I've felt close to him ever since †our first meeting [we first met].
それは私たちの年代の人間には親しみのある名前だ.	That's a name that people of our generation are familiar with.
彼が同郷の人だと知って急に親しみが湧いてきた.	When I found out that he was from my hometown, I suddenly began to feel close to him.
彼女にはとても親しみを覚えた.	I felt a strong sense of closeness to her.
彼はいい人だがなぜか親しみが持てない.	He's a nice person, but somehow I can't feel close to him.

したしむ (親しむ)

その先生は親しみ易い〔にくい〕人柄だ.	That teacher is easy [hard] to talk to.
都会人は自然に親しむ機会がほとんどない.	City people [Urbanites] have almost no opportunity to commune with nature.
秋は芸術に親しむのにいちばんの季節だと思う.	I think that autumn is the best season for familiarizing myself with art.
英語に親しむように努めている.	I'm trying hard to get more familiar with English.
彼は若いときから俳句に親しんでいた.	He has loved *haiku* since he was young.

しつ (質)

量より質が問題だ.	Quality is more important than quantity.
ここは質のいい鉱石が採れる.	High quality ores can be mined here.
この紙は質が良くない.	The quality of this paper is not (very) high.
今年の学生は質が落ちている.	The quality of students this year is low.
あそこの商品は質が上がった〔落ちた〕.	The quality of merchandise there has improved [dropped].
私たちは品質向上に努めている.	We are striving to improve [raise] the quality of our products.

じつ (実)

【本当】彼女が私の実の母親です.	She is my real mother.
彼女は彼を実の子のようにかわいがっている.	She cares for him as though he were her own child.
実を言うと彼女のことが嫌いだ.	To tell the truth, I don't like her.
実を言えば今金に困っている.	To be quite frank, I'm having money problems now.
実のところ, どうするつもりだ？	What are your real intentions?
【実質・内容】今度の事件では名を捨てて実を取ることにしたよ.	I decided to go for substance instead of form in this affair.
【誠意】彼の態度には実がない.	There is no sincerity in his attitude.
彼はなかなか実のある人だ.	He is a very sincere person.

しっかり

【堅固】しっかりと戸締まりした.	I locked up the house securely.
くいをしっかり打ち込んだ.	I drove the stake in firmly.
ハンドルをしっかり握りなさい.	Hold the (steering) wheel tight.
少年は硬貨をしっかり握りしめた.	The young boy grasped the coin firmly.
この箱を綱でしっかり結べ.	Tie the box tightly with the string.
このいすは作りがしっかりしてい	This chair is sturdy.

【奮起】しっかり!	Fight!／Hang in there![1]
しっかりしなさい.	Cheer up.／Pull yourself together.
しっかりしろ. もうすぐ助けが来る.	Hold yourself together. Help is on the way.
しっかりしてくれよ. 昨日教えたばかりじゃないか.	Pull yourself together! Didn't I just teach you yesterday?
気をしっかり持って私の言うことを聞きなさい.	Pull yourself together and listen well to what I have to say.
【堅実】彼女はしっかりした女性だ.	She's a good [strong] woman.
彼はしっかりした人だ.	He's a reliable [steady] person.
彼女は考えがしっかりしている.	Her thinking is sound.
彼は83歳だが足取りはしっかりしている.	He is 83 but he is very steady on his legs.
彼はしっかりした声で発表した.	He made the announcement in a steady voice.
彼はしっかりした文章を書く.	He writes a sound composition.
彼は老後のためにしっかりお金をためている.	He's conscientiously saving money for his old age.
【十分に】しっかり勉強しなさい.	Study hard.
休暇をしっかりと楽しんだ.	I enjoyed my vacation to the fullest.
彼にしっかりと教わってきた.	He just explained it to me very thoroughly.
基本をしっかり身につけなさい.	Get the basics down firmly [soundly].

1)「頑張れ, 粘れ」の意味合い.

じっかん (実感)

あの教授の講義を聞いて初めて大学生になったことを実感した.	Listening to that professor's lecture, I felt like a real college student for the first time.
自分でやってみてその仕事の難しさを実感した.	I realized just how difficult that work was when I tried it myself.
アメリカに行って文化の違いを実感した.	I went to America and was struck by the cultural differences.
人を教えることは難しい, というのが私の実感だ.	I've personally experienced how difficult teaching people is.
彼女の言葉には実感がこもっていた.	She sounded as if she was speaking from experience.
百万ドルと言われても実感が湧かない.	I can't even (begin to) imagine a million dollars.
受賞の実感はまだ湧いてこない.	It still hasn't really come home to me that I've won the prize.

着いたばかりでまだパリにいるという実感がない.	I've just arrived, so I don't really feel like I'm in Paris yet.

じっけん (実験)

化学の時間に実験をした.	I conducted an experiment in chemistry class.
安全性の確認のため実験を重ねた.	We made [conducted] repeated experiments to confirm safety.
新薬開発のため動物実験をしている.	We are conducting experiments on animals for the development of a new medicine.
まだ実験段階で発表できない.	It's still in the experimental stage, so I can't make an announcement.
彼の演出は実験的だ.	His directing is experimental.
彼の催眠術の実験台になった.	I became a subject for his experiment with hypnotism.
実験室を掃除した.	I cleaned the laboratory.

じつげん (実現)

長年の夢がやっと実現した.	My long-cherished dream finally came true.
彼女は小学校の先生になりたいという幼い頃からの夢をとうとう実現させた.	She finally realized her life-long dream of becoming an elementary school teacher.
あの計画は実現不可能になったよ.	The plan fell through.
	The plan became impossible to carry out.

しつこい

【くどい・うるさい】彼のしつこい説得に負けた.	I gave in to his dogged persuasion.
しつこいなあ, だめだと言ったらだめだよ.	Enough already! When I say no I mean no.
彼のようにしつこい男は我慢がならない.	I can't stand people like him who don't know when to give up.
彼のしつこさには閉口している.	I've had it with his persistence [pushiness].
彼に家族のことをしつこく聞かれた.	He wouldn't stop asking me questions about my family.
子どもにしつこくおもちゃをせがまれた.	My child wouldn't stop pestering me for the toy.
保険の外交員はしつこく私を勧誘した.	An insurance salesman tried to pressure me into buying a policy.
彼は原稿をしつこく催促した.	He stubbornly pressed for the manuscript.
【病気・食物・色等が】彼の病気は	His illness is very stubborn and he just

しつこくてなかなか治らない.	doesn't get any better.
この料理は私にはしつこ過ぎた.	This dish was too rich [heavy, greasy] for me.
緑地に赤と青の模様ではちょっとしつこ過ぎる.	Putting a red and blue design on a green background is just a little too gaudy [loud].

じっこう (実行)

彼は言うことは立派だが実行が伴わない.	What he says is great but he doesn't put it into practice.
計画を実行に移す前に仕事の分担を確認します.	Before we put the plan into action I'll confirm who's in charge of what.
あとは実行あるのみ.	All that's left is to put †it [the plan, the idea] into effect [action].
実行できないことを約束するな.	Don't promise what you can't deliver.
その代議士は公約を実行した.	That Diet member fulfilled his campaign promises.
彼は3年以内に自分の店を持つと宣言し，そのとおり実行した.	He declared that he would own his own store within three years and he did as he said.
音楽祭の実行委員に推薦された.	I was recommended as a member of the organizing committee for the music festival.
彼には実行力がある.	He has the ability to get things done.

じっさい (実際)

【事実】理論と実際とはなかなか一致しないものだ.	Theory and practice seldom coincide.
実際のところ，彼が盗んだという証拠はどこにもない.	In actuality there's no evidence that he stole it.
実際問題として，貸してあげたくてもそれだけのお金を持っていないんだ.	However much I may be willing to lend you the money, the fact is I don't have that much.
【実に】彼は実際よくできた男だ.	He's really a fine example of a man.
こう毎日残業では実際やりきれない.	I just can't take doing overtime every day.
彼がそう言うのを実際聞いたんだ.	I actually heard him say that.

しっそ (質素)

彼女は質素だが清潔な身なりをしている.	Her clothes are very modest, but she keeps them clean.
老夫婦はわずかな年金で質素に暮らしている.	The old couple is living modestly on a pension.

彼は質素な家に住んでいる.	He lives in a simple house.

しっと (嫉妬)

彼は同僚の昇進に嫉妬した.	He was jealous of his colleague's promotion.
うちの女房の嫉妬深さには時々うんざりする.	There are times when I really get fed up with my wife's insane jealousy.
両親が妹を溺愛するので,彼女は嫉妬のあまり妹をいじめた.	She got so jealous when her parents doted on her younger sister that she used to pick on her.

じっと

【静かにする】写真を撮りますからじっとしてください.	Don't move. I'm going to take a picture.
あの子は元気で片ときもじっとしていない.	That child is so energetic that he won't keep still a minute.
【集中する】彼はじっと考え込んでいた.	He was deep in thought.
彼はじっと私を見つめた.	He stared at me.
	He looked me over intently.
【我慢する】彼は悲しみをじっとこらえた.	He bore the sadness stoically.
彼女に嫌味を言われたが,じっと我慢した.	She said terrible things to me but I bore it stoically.

しっぱい (失敗)

一度や二度の失敗はだれにでもある.	Everyone fails once or twice.
彼は事業に失敗した.	He failed in the undertaking.
その実験は失敗に終わった.	That experiment ended in failure.
今度こそ失敗は許されない.	This time I won't put up with failure.
彼はまた同じ失敗を繰り返した.	He repeated the same failure again.
あの馬にもっとかければよかった. 失敗したなあ!	If only I had bet more money on that horse. I really blew it!
失敗は成功のもとである.	You learn from your mistakes.
彼の今度の小説は失敗作だ.	His latest novel is a flop [failure].

しつぼう (失望)

努力が報いられないので彼は人生に失望した.	He became discouraged about life because his efforts were not rewarded.
もっと優秀だと思っていたのに,君には失望したよ.	I really thought you had more ability. You really †let me down [disappointed me].
まだ失望するには早過ぎる.	It's still too early to despair.

| 期待し過ぎると失望も大きい. | The greater your hopes, the greater your disappointments. |

しつもん (質問)

記者たちは首相に矢継ぎ早に質問を浴びせた.	The reporters shot questions at the prime minister in rapid succession.
何か質問はありませんか.	Are there any questions?
そんな質問には答えられません.	I can't answer a question like that.
講義が終わってから，質問を受け付けます.	I will take questions after the lecture.
テレビの人気タレントはファンの質問攻めにあった.	The TV celebrity was bombarded [peppered] with questions from his fans.

じつりょく (実力)

【実際の力量】だれもが彼女の実力を認め始めた.	Everyone began to recognize her abilities.
運も良かったが，それだけじゃない．実力あってのことだ.	It wasn't just good luck. It was competence.
彼の今の実力では合格は無理だろう.	Given his present capabilities, he probably won't make it.
彼の今の実力では優勝は無理だろう.	Given his current standing [capabilities], he will probably not win.
実力を発揮できないまま試合に負けた.	He lost the game without being able to †play his best [show his true ability, do himself justice].
皆の応援のお陰で実力以上のプレイができた.	Thanks to everybody's support, I played better than I really can.
今度の試験で実力が試される.	This examination will be a real test of my abilities.
今度の試合で実力が試される.	This game will test my strengths [abilities]. This will test my game.[1]
もう少し実力をつけてから挑戦しなさい.	Give it a try after you've had a chance to †get a little better at it [improve a bit].
明日から実力テストだ.	We have proficiency tests starting tomorrow.
この会社は実力主義です.	This company is run on a merit system.
【実際の行動】怒った住民たちは，原子力発電所建設を阻止するために，ついに実力行使に出た.	The angry residents finally took it upon themselves to stop construction on the nuclear plant.
ここまで言ってもわからないなら実力に訴えるまでだ.	If they can't understand the situation after all this, we'll just have to show them.
【強い影響力・権力】彼は政界の実力者だ.	He's †an influential man [a power broker[2]] in political circles.

彼は陰の実力者だ.	He's the power behind the throne.
あの会社の本当の実力者は，社長ではなく奥さんだ.	The real brains behind that company is not the president but his wife.

> 1) この game は「試合ぶり，試合運び（の力量）」の意味. 2) a power broker は実力者の中でも絶大な力を持っている人物を言う.

しつれい（失礼）

失礼！	Excuse me!／Sorry!
ちょっと失礼. 電話をしてきます.	Excuse me for a minute. I have to make a call.
失礼ですが，お名前を伺わせていただきたいのですが.	Excuse me, would you mind giving me your name?
	May I ask who's calling please?[1]
失礼，ちょっといいですか. お聞きしたいことがあります.	May I interrupt you for a minute? I have something to ask you.
もうそろそろ失礼します.	I should be going before long.
約束を破るなんて彼女は失礼だ.	It's rude [impolite] of her to break her promise.

> 1) は電話の場合の言い方.

(〜と, 〜に)しても

今すぐ出かけたとしても，もうその電車には間に合わないでしょう.	We probably wouldn't make that train even if we left right now.
急用が出来たにしても，ちゃんと連絡ぐらいよこしてもよかったろう.	I don't care if something urgent did come up. You could at least have gotten in touch with me.

しどう（指導）

小川先生はクラブ活動でコーラスの指導に当たっている.	Mr. Ogawa is our school club's chorus advisor.
彼女は子どもたちに水泳の指導をしている.	She gives swimming lessons to children.
家では子どもたちに規則正しい生活をするよう指導しています.	At home I'm trying to teach my children how to lead organized lives.
彼に空手の指導を受けている.	I'm getting training in *karate* from him.
彼には指導力がない.	He has no ability for leadership.
あの子は生まれ持った指導力がある.	That child is a natural leader.
彼は反戦運動で指導的役割を果たした.	He played a leading role in the antiwar movement.

政府は科学技術の指導者を海外に派遣した.	The government sent leaders from science and technology overseas.

じどう (自動)
このドアは自動的に開閉する.	This door opens and closes automatically.
電車の切符は自動販売機で買ってください.	Please buy your train ticket from the (ticket-vending) machine.

しなもの (品物)
あの店は品物が豊富だ.	That store has a rich assortment of merchandise.
このコートは品物がいい〔悪い〕.	This coat is of high [low] quality.
彼女はデパートでいろいろな品物を買った.	She bought lots of different things at the department store.
ご注文の品物はお届けしました.	I delivered the goods you ordered.

しぬ (死ぬ)
祖父は80歳で死んだ.	My grandfather died when he was eighty.
父が死んで, もう10年になる.	It has already been 10 years since my father died.
彼はがんで死んだ.	He died of cancer.
彼は交通事故で死んだ.	He †was killed [died] in a traffic accident.
彼は妻に死に別れた.	Death took his wife away from him.
生まれてから死ぬまで彼女は苦労し続けた.	From birth until death her hardships never stopped.
死んで花実が咲くものか.	You're no good to anyone (if you're) dead. While there's life there's hope.
彼は疲れきって死んだように眠った.	He was worn out and slept like a log.
彼は死ぬほど彼女に恋い焦がれた.	He was so desperately in love with her that he thought he would die.
仕事がハードスケジュールで死にそうだ.	My hard work schedule is almost killing me.
その額縁ではせっかくの絵が死んでしまう.	That's a good picture, but it doesn't look good in that frame.
町は死んだように静まりかえっていた.	The town was as quiet as a ghost town.

しはい (支配)
【統治・管理】全世界を支配できても, 自分自身を支配できなければ何にもならない.	What good would it do to be able to control the world if you couldn't control yourself?
彼が現在の日本の政治を支配している	He controls politics in Japan today.

いる.	
安土桃山時代には豊臣秀吉が日本を支配した.	Toyotomi Hideyoshi ruled [controlled] Japan in the Momoyama era.
彼がこのホテルの支配人です.	He runs this hotel.
【影響】どんなときにも感情に支配されてはいけない.	You should never let yourself be ruled [controlled] by emotions.
マスコミが常に世論を支配する.	The mass media are in constant control of public opinion.
古代の人々の暮らしは自然に支配されていた.	Early man was [lived] at the mercy of †the elements [nature].

しばい（芝居）

祖母は芝居を見るのが大好きです.	My grandmother loves to see plays.
今日の芝居の出し物は何ですか.	What play is on today?
芝居がはねた後，真っすぐ家へ帰った.	After the play was over I went straight home.
彼は借金取りを相手に一芝居打った.	He made up a story to get the bill collector off his back.
下手な芝居はやめろ.	Stop acting.
君は全く芝居がうまい.	You're a great actor.
彼のやることは芝居がかっている.	He's very dramatic in what he does.

しばらく

【少しの時間】しばらくお待ちください.	Please wait a little.
	Just a minute, please.
あなたが出かけてしばらくして，彼から電話がありました.	He called a short while after you left.
疲れたのでしばらく休もう.	We're tired, so let's rest a while.
【少し長い時間】やあ，しばらく.	Hey, long time no see.**
	I haven't seen you for a long time.
彼とはしばらく会っていない.	I haven't seen him in quite a while.
彼は病気が治り，しばらくぶりに出勤した.	He got over his illness and returned to work after quite an absence.
このところしばらく雨が降っていない.	It hasn't rained for a while.

しばる（縛る）

彼は薪を縛って束にした.	He tied up the fire wood in bundles.
父親はいたずらをした子どもを木に縛りつけた.	The father tied the child who had misbehaved to a tree.
彼は傷口をハンカチで縛った.	He bound the wound with a handkerchief.
【束縛する】時間に縛られて彼とはゆっくり話す暇もなかった.	We were pressed for time and I couldn't speak at leisure with him.

毎日仕事に縛られて，休む暇もない．	I'm tied up with work and can't take any time off.
寄宿舎に入ったが，規則に縛られて全然楽しくなかった．	I moved into the dormitory but there were so many rules and regulations that it wasn't any fun at all.

しびれる

彼は彼女の甘い歌声にしびれた．	Her voice enchanted him.
足がしびれて立てない．	I can't stand up because my legs have gone to sleep.
だれも注文を取りに来ないので，しびれをきらして店を出てしまった．	Nobody came to take our order, so we †became impatient [got tired of waiting] and left the restaurant.

しぶい (渋い)

この柿は渋い．	This persimmon makes my mouth pucker.
彼の好みは渋い．	He has †subdued [austerely elegant] taste.
思いどおりにいかなくて彼は渋い顔をした．	He made a wry face when things didn't go as planned.

しぶしぶ

彼は娘の結婚をしぶしぶ承諾した．	He reluctantly consented to his daughter's marriage.
母親にテレビのスイッチを切られて，子どもはしぶしぶ勉強机に向かった．	The children reluctantly went off to study when their mother turned off the TV.

じぶん (自分)

もっと自分を大事にしなさい．	Take better care of yourself.
自分の行動に責任を持ちなさい．	Take responsibility for your actions.
洋服は自分で作ります．	I make my own clothes.
人に頼まないで自分でやってごらん．	Try doing it yourself without anyone's help.
彼はいつも自分だけいい子になろうとする．	He always tries to make himself look good.
彼は人に仕事を押しつけて自分では何もしない．	He dumps work on others and doesn't do anything himself.
なぜあんなことをしたのか自分でも分からない．	Even I don't understand why I did something like that.
彼女は自分勝手だ．	She thinks only of herself.／She's selfish.

しぼる (絞る)

ぞうきんを絞った．	I wrung out the wash cloth.

洗濯物をよく絞って乾かした.	I wrung out the laundry and hung it up to dry.
牛の乳を絞った.	I milked the cow.
レモンを絞ってレモネードを作った.	I squeezed lemons and made lemonade.
【無理に出す】もっと知恵を絞って考えなさい.	Use your head.
	Use your common sense and think.
彼は最後の力を振り絞ってゴールにたどり着いた.	He squeezed out his last ounce of strength and crossed the finish line.
【責める】今月の売り上げが悪くて課長にうんと絞られた.	My sales were bad this month, and the chief chewed me out.
父にたっぷり油を絞られた.	I was raked over the coals by my father.
【狭める】警察は捜査範囲をその町の周辺に絞った.	The police focused their investigation on the area around that town.
これでは議論が進まないから問題を絞ろう.	The discussion isn't getting anywhere as it is, so let's narrow down the question.
深夜なのでラジオのボリュームを絞った.	It was late at night, so I turned the volume of the radio down.

しほん (資本)

私はわずかな資本でこの事業を始めた.	I started this enterprise with just a little capital.
彼は我が社に巨額の資本を投じている.	He's invested a lot of capital in our company.
何をするにも体が資本だ.	You need your health for whatever you do.
その会社の資本金は1億円です.	That company has a capital of a hundred million yen.

しまう

【片づける】使った道具を戸棚にしまった.	I put the tools I used back on the shelf.
お金は金庫にしまってある.	The money has been put in the safe.
【取っておく】お年玉は使わずにしまっておきなさい.	Don't spend the money you got for New Year's. Save it.
このことはだれにも漏らさずに,あなたの胸だけにしまっておいてください.	Don't leak this to anybody. Keep it to yourself.
【完全に終える】宿題をやってしまいなさい.	Finish (up) your homework.
手紙を書いてしまうまで待ってください.	Wait until I finish this letter.
この本は面白くて一気に読んでし	This book was so interesting I read it in

まった.　　　　　　　　　　　　　　one sitting.

しまつ（始末）

【片づける】食品をたくさん買い込んだが，食べきれず始末に困った.
I bought more groceries than I could eat and had a hard time using them up.

あの子は始末に負えないいたずらっ子だ.
That child is unmanageable. He's always pulling pranks.

後始末をきちんとしなさい.
Make sure to put what you used in order.

あいつを始末してしまえ.
Take care of [Get rid of, Dispose of] him.

【有り様】彼の部屋はちらかっていて，足の踏み場もない始末だった.
His room was such a mess that there was no place to step.

店が不景気で従業員の給料も満足に払えない始末だ.
Business has gotten so bad the employees can't be paid in full.

【浪費を慎むこと】彼はとても始末屋だ.
He doesn't waste a penny.

しまった

しまった！
(Oh,) Darn it!／(Oh,) Damn it!
Oh, my goodness!／Good heavens!
(Oh,) I goofed!

しまる¹（締まる）

彼は筋肉が締まっている.
His muscles are firm.

彼は締まった体つきをしている.
He has a muscular [well-defined] physique.

この魚は身が締まっていて，おいしそうだ.
This fish is firm (and fresh,) and looks delicious.

しまる²（閉まる）

正門は9時に閉まります.
The front gate closes at nine.

ドアが壊れて閉まらなくなった.
The door is broken and won't close right [properly].

定休日で，店は閉まっていた.
The store was closed for its regular day off.

じまん（自慢）

新築の公民館が町の自慢の種だ.
The newly built community center is the townspeople's pride and joy.

「僕の新車を見てくれ」と彼は自慢げに言った.
"Look at my new car," he said boastfully [proudly].

彼はよく子どものことを自慢する.
He often speaks proudly of his children.

彼女は自分の英会話力を自慢して
She's proud of her ability to speak Eng-

じみ (地味)

彼女はいつも地味な色の服を着ている. She always dresses in quiet [subdued, conservative] colors.
あの画家は人柄は地味だが作品は華やかだ. That artist is a quiet [reserved] person but his paintings are colorful.

しみる

冷たい風が身にしみた. The cold wind pierced me to the bone.
The wind was bitterly cold.
煙が目にしみる. My eyes smart [burn, sting] from the smoke.
汗がシャツにしみた. The sweat stained my shirt.
薬が傷口にしみて, ひりひりする. The medicine on the wound stings.

じむ (事務)

彼は会社で事務を執っている. He does clerical work at the company.
彼女は事務の仕事を探している. She's looking for an office job.
私は新宿に事務所を持っています. I have an office in Shinjuku.
彼はあの店の事務員です. He works at that store as a clerk.
あとは事務処理を残すのみだ. Only the paperwork remains to be done.
We only have the paperwork left to do.
彼は物事を事務的に処理する傾向がある. He tends to handle things in a very perfunctory fashion.

しめす (示す)

先生が泳ぎ方の模範を示してくれた. The teacher gave a swimming demonstration.
定期券を示して改札口を出た. I showed my train pass and went out the ticket gate.
老人はステッキで駅の方向を示した. The old man pointed the way to the station with his cane.
羅針盤の針は常に北を示す. The needle of a compass always points north.
【表す】この論文は彼の思想を端的に示している. This paper expresses his thought straightforwardly.
みんなは私の提案に共感を示した. Everyone indicated support for my proposal.
彼は私の話に興味を示した. He showed interest in what I said.
彼は辞職の決意を示した. He indicated his resolve to resign.

しめる¹ (湿る)

薪が湿っていて火がなかなかつかない. — This wood is too damp to set fire to.

庭の草木が夜露に湿っている. — The plants in the garden are wet with the night dew.

クッキーが湿ってしまった. — The cookies got damp and stale.

梅雨どきは,家の中が湿りがちだ. — During the rainy season the house tends to get damp inside.

窓を開けて寝ると,湿った空気が入ってきて体に悪い. — Sleeping with the window open will let in damp air and is bad for your health.

しめる² (締める)

このねじを締めてください. — Please tighten this screw.

父は毎日背広を着, ネクタイを締めて会社へ行く. — Father goes to work every day wearing a suit and tie.

着物を着て, 帯を締めた. — I put on a *kimono* and tied the *obi*.

シートベルトを締めてください. — Fasten your seatbelt, please.

【緊張させる】最近, 部下がたるんでいるから締めてやろう. — The people under me have been lax recently, so I'm going to have to get them to shape up.

財布のひもを締めてむだづかいしないようにしよう. — Let's tighten the purse strings and cut waste.

【決算する】今日の売り上げがいくらか締めてみよう. — Let's total up today's sales.

お勘定は締めて5,000円になります. — Altogether the bill comes to 5,000 yen.

しめる³ (閉める)

風が強くなったので, 窓を閉めた. — The wind started blowing harder, so I closed the window.

ドアを静かに閉めなさい. — Close the door quietly.

そろそろ店を閉めよう. — It's about time to close the store.

商売が上がったりで, しばらくのあいだ店を閉めることにした. — Business was bad, so I decided to close the store for a while.

景気沈滞で店を閉めた自動車販売業者が多い. — Many car dealerships have closed down because of the slow economy.

しゃかい (社会)

彼は学校を卒業すると社会に出て働いた. — When he graduated from school he went out in the world and got a job.

力士の社会は番付の地位による上下関係が厳しい. — In the *sumo* wrestlers' world, the hierarchy within the ranking list is very strict.

彼女は学生生活を終え, 社会人と — She completed her life as a student and

なった. | started working.
彼は立派な社会人として活躍している. | He is active now as a full-fledged member of society.
彼の社会的地位は高い. | His social position is high.
少年の非行は大きな社会問題になっている. | Juvenile delinquency has become a major social problem.
彼は社会主義者だ. | He's a socialist.

しゃべる

彼女はよくしゃべる人（おしゃべり）だ. | She's very talkative. / She's a chatterbox.
授業中は，勝手にしゃべってはいけません. | Don't talk out of turn during class.
お姉さんは電話で30分もしゃべっている. | My sister has been talking for 30 minutes on the phone.
今言ったことはだれにもしゃべらないでくれ. | Don't breathe a word of what I just told you to anyone.
彼は何でもしゃべってしまうからうっかりしたことを言えない. | He's a blabbermouth, so you've got to watch what you say around him.

じゃま（邪魔）

お邪魔じゃありませんか. | Are you sure I won't be a bother?
お仕事中ちょっとお邪魔します. | Can I interrupt your work for a minute?
邪魔しないでください. | Don't disturb [bother] me please.
彼は私たちの仕事の邪魔をした. | He disturbed [interrupted] us in our work.
あなたの邪魔になりたくない. | I don't want to stand in your way.
若者はとかく年寄りを邪魔にする. | Young people often treat the aged as nuisances.

しゃれた

しゃれたバッグですね. | You have a nice [charming] bag.
彼は時々しゃれたことを言う. | He sometimes says witty [intelligent, clever] things.
彼らはしゃれた会話を交わしている. | They're having a sophisticated [high-toned] conversation.

じゆう（自由）

言論の自由は憲法で保証されている. | Freedom of speech is guaranteed by the constitution.
この大学には自由な雰囲気がある. | This college has a very free atmosphere.
忙しくて自由な時間が持てない. | I'm so busy I can't get any free time.
どんな仕事をしようと僕の自由だ. | I'm free to choose what kind of work I'll do.

彼は刑期を終えて自由の身になった.	He served out his sentence and became a free man.
最近, 子どもが自由に遊べる場所が少なくなった.	Recently there are fewer and fewer places where children can play freely.
どうぞ自由に意見を述べてください.	Please express your views freely.
彼は3ヵ国語を自由に話せる.	He's fluent in three languages.
ご自由にお茶をどうぞ.	Please feel free to have tea. Help yourself to some tea.

〜じゅう (〜中)

【時間】彼らは一晩じゅう飲み明かした.	They drank till dawn.
明日は一日じゅう家にいます.	I'll be home all day tomorrow.
トマトやキュウリは一年じゅう出回っている.	Tomatoes and cucumbers are available all year long.
彼は年じゅう不平を言っている.	He complains all year round. He's always complaining.
夏じゅう泳いで過ごした.	I spent the whole summer swimming.
この仕事は今日じゅうに仕上げなければならない.	This work must be finished by the end of the day.
【場所】家じゅう捜したが指輪は出てこなかった.	I searched all over the house, but I couldn't find the ring.
うわさは町じゅうに広まった.	The gossip [rumor] spread throughout the town.
彼は世界じゅうを旅した.	He traveled all over the world.

しゅうい (周囲)

日本は周囲を海に囲まれている.	Japan is surrounded by water.
その家の周囲には高い塀が巡らされている.	That house is surrounded by a high wall.
彼は周囲の様子をうかがった.	He checked out the surroundings.
キャンプ場の周囲には, ハイキングコースや牧場がある.	There are hiking paths and meadows around the camp ground.
二人は周囲の人の反対を押し切って結婚した.	The couple defied the opposition of those around them and got married.
彼は周囲から好かれている.	He's liked by everyone around him.

しゅうかく (収穫)

秋になると農家は米の収穫に忙しくなる.	In the fall farmers are busy with the rice harvest.
今年も昨年並みの農作物の収穫が見込まれている.	The crop [harvest] this year is anticipated to be on a par with last year's.

今日の釣りは大した収穫がなかった.	Today's fishing didn't bring in much of a catch.
ジョギングを続ければ,健康という大きな収穫が得られる.	If you keep up your jogging, you will reap the benefits of good health.
旅行をすると,何かと収穫があるものだ.	One benefits in various ways by traveling.

しゅうかん (習慣)

外から帰ったらうがいをする習慣をつけなさい.	Get in the habit of gargling when you come in from outside.
父は朝食前に散歩するのが習慣です.	Father makes it a rule to take a walk before breakfast in the morning.
僕は早寝早起きが習慣となっている.	I make it a habit to go to bed and get up early.
喫煙,飲酒の悪い習慣を改めないと病気になるよ.	If you don't eliminate your bad smoking and drinking habits you'll get sick.
日本には盆暮れに贈り物をする習慣がある.	In Japan it is customary to give presents in the middle of the year and at the end of the year.
この地方には古くからの習慣が数多く残されている.	In this area many ancient customs have been preserved.

しゅうごう (集合)

9時に駅前に集合してください.	Please assemble in front of the station at nine o'clock.
役員の方は本部に集合してください.	Will the officers please meet in the board room?
集合時間は必ず守りましょう.	Be sure to be at the meeting place on time.
集合場所は公園の入り口です.	We'll assemble at the entrance to the park.
消防車が広場に集合して,訓練を行っている.	The fire engines have assembled in the square and are staging a drill.

じゅうじつ (充実)

あの大学のカリキュラムは充実している.	That university has a substantial course selection.
あの図書館は子ども向けの本が充実している.	There is a good selection of children's books at that library.
このスキー場はコースが充実している.	The ski slopes at this resort are well developed.
介護制度の充実を図るべきだ.	The nursing care system must be improved.
彼女は充実した毎日を送っている.	She's living a full life.
パリ留学の2年間は,まさに充実	The two years I spent studying in Paris

した日々だった. were [was] very fulfilling.
最近の彼は気力が充実しているようだ. He seems to be full of energy lately.
国家的なプロジェクトに関わることができ, 充実感を感じる. Being able to work on a national project gives me a great sense of satisfaction.

じゅうじゅん (従順)
戦前は大抵妻は夫に従順だった. Before the war wives were generally submissive to their husbands.
彼は使用人として従順に主人に仕えた. He served his master obediently.
兄弟の中ではこの子がいちばん親に従順だ. This child †listens to [minds] his parents better than any of his brothers or sisters do.

じゅうだい (重大)
新卒者にとって職業の選択は重大な問題である. Choosing a career is †a serious [an important] matter for new graduates.
部長に昇進して, 彼は重大な責任を担うことになった. He was promoted to department chief and will be shouldering a weighty [heavy] responsibility.

しゅうだん (集団)
駅は旅行客の集団でごった返していた. The station was crowded with groups of travelers.
新入生もこの頃はすっかり集団生活に慣れたようだ. Recently even the new students seem to have gotten completely accustomed to group living.
修学旅行では集団行動をとった. We did everything as a group on the school trip.

しゅうちゃく (執着)
年寄りは旧習に執着しがちだ. Older people tend to †cling to [hold on to] old customs.
彼女は金銭に対する執着が強い. She's very money-conscious.
済んだことにいつまでも執着していてはいけません. You mustn't be forever attached to things gone by.
何かを成し遂げるには, それに執着することが必要です. If you want to succeed at [in] something, you've got to stick to it.

しゅうちゅう (集中)
精神を集中して勉強しなさい. Concentrate hard when you study.
全力を集中して事に当たれば, で If you put everything you have into some-

きないことはありません.	thing, nothing is impossible.
その問題に議論が集中した.	The discussion centered on that problem.
人口は都市に集中する傾向がある.	The population tends to concentrate in the cities.
会議でみんなは彼に集中攻撃を浴びせた.	He became the focus of an attack at the meeting.
九州地方に集中豪雨があった.	There was a torrential downpour in Kyushu.

じゅうなん (柔軟)

彼は柔軟な精神の持ち主だ.	He has flexible mind.
何事も柔軟な姿勢で取り組むことが大切だ.	It's important to approach everything with a flexible frame of mind.
彼はあの年齢にしては体が柔軟だ.	He's spry for his age.
	His body is limber considering his age.

しゅうにゅう (収入)

私の収入は月20万です.	My income is 200,000 [two hundred thousand] yen a month.
彼は収入が多い〔少ない〕.	He has a large [small] income.
彼は収入以上の生活をしている.	He lives beyond his means.
彼は年間500万円の収入を得ている.	He makes 5 million yen a year.

しゅうねん (執念)

彼はその研究に執念を燃やしている.	He is devoted to the research.
幾多の困難にもかかわらず, 彼は執念でこの仕事を完成させた.	His persistence enabled him to complete this job, despite the many difficulties.
彼は執念深いから気をつけなさい.	Be careful. He's very vindictive [spiteful].

じゅうぶん (十分)

お金〔時間, 食料〕は十分ある.	There's enough money [time, food].
十分考えた末に結論を出した.	I reached my conclusion after giving it †ample [plenty of] thought.
それは十分承知している.	I'm fully aware of that.
今日は十分楽しんだ.	I had a pretty good time today.
健康には十分注意してください.	Take good care of your health.

じゅうよう (重要)

この情報は重要である.	This information is very important.
彼は重要人物と見なされている.	He is considered (to be) an influential [important] person.

この仕事の重要さを認識してもらいたい．	I want you to be conscious of the importance of this work.
地下鉄が開通して以来，この土地は交通上重要となった．	This area has been an important transportation center ever since the subway was put through.
我が社はこの業界で重要な地位を占めている．	Our company occupies †a vital [an important] position in this industry.

じゅうらい (従来)

従来，正月は家で迎えていたが，今度の正月はハワイへ行くことにした．	In the past we've always spent New Year's at home, but this year we've decided to go to Hawaii.
従来の方法ではもう古い．	The conventional method is outdated.
卒業式は従来どおりのやり方で行います．	The graduation ceremony will be conducted as usual [always].

しゅうり (修理)

彼は大抵のものは自分で修理してしまう．	He repairs most things himself.
垣根を修理した．	I repaired [fixed, mended] the fence.
この家は修理が必要だ．	This house is in need of repair.
	This house needs some work done on it.
テレビの修理に来てくれるよう頼んだ．	I called someone to come repair the TV.
このかばん〔冷蔵庫〕は修理に出さなければならない．	I have to †take this bag in [send this refrigerator out] to be repaired.[1]
	This bag needs repairing.
車を修理に出している．	I'm having the car worked on.
公会堂は修理中で使えない．	The civic auditorium is closed for repairs.

> 1) 店に持ち込む場合は take in を，家に取りに来てもらう場合は send out を使う．

しゅかん (主観)

芸術作品は見る人の主観によって評価が分かれる．	The appraisal of an artwork varies according to the subjectivity of the viewer.
君の主観を入れずにこの問題を考えてほしい．	I want you to consider this problem as objectively as possible.
彼の意見は主観的過ぎる．	His opinion is too subjective.

しゅぎ (主義)

主義で独身でいるわけではない．	I'm not single by principle.
彼はいつも自分の主義を通そうと	He always tries to force his ideas on other

する. | people.
私の主義としてそんなことはしたくない. | I don't want to do that. It would go against my principles.
私は他人の問題にはかかわらない主義だ. | I make it a rule not to get involved in other people's problems.

しゅじゅつ (手術)

彼は胃かいようの手術を受けた. | He had †an operation [surgery] for a stomach ulcer.
彼女の病気は手術を要する. | Her illness requires surgery.
手術がうまくいって彼女は助かった. | The operation saved her life.
心臓移植の手術は成功した. | The heart transplant operation was a complete success.
けが人はすぐ手術室に運ばれた. | The injured person was immediately taken into the operating room.

しゅだん (手段)

マスコミは情報伝達の手段である. | The mass media are a means of distributing information.
体を丈夫にするための手段として僕は毎朝冷水摩擦をしている. | I rub myself down with a cold wet towel every morning as a way of keeping fit.
彼は金を儲けるためには手段を選ばない. | He'd resort to anything to make money.
どうしても言うことをきかないのなら最後の手段として体罰を加えるぞ. | If you continue to disobey, I'll have to resort to corporal punishment.

しゅちょう (主張)

彼は自分の主張を最後まで貫いた. | He stuck to his opinion to the end.
彼は主張を引っ込めた. | He backed down.
あなたの主張は正しい. | Your point is well taken.
弁護側の主張が認められた. | The defense's argument was recognized [accepted].
彼は無罪を主張し続けている. | He's still insisting that he's innocent.

しゅっせ (出世)

母は息子の出世だけを楽しみにしていた. | The mother's only joy was her son's success.
彼女は人一倍, 仕事熱心だから出世するだろう. | She'll probably get ahead in life because she works harder than anyone else.
彼は同期の出世頭だ. | He has been getting promoted more quickly than anyone else who started work-

	ing in the company at the same time.[1]
	He is the first one in his graduating class to make his mark.[2]
この映画は彼女の出世作だ.	This is the film that made her famous.
彼は出世コースを歩んでいる.	He's on the fast track.
彼は出世街道まっしぐらだ.	He's speeding along the fast track.
彼は出世コースから外れた.	He's off the career track.
出世払いでいいよ.	You can pay me after you've made it big.

1) 入社時期が同期の場合. 2) 大学の卒業が同期の場合.

しゅっせき (出席)

彼女はパーティーに出席した.	She attended the party.
私は毎日授業にきちんと出席しています.	I go to my classes every day according to schedule.
会議は10人が出席して行われた.	The meeting was held with 10 people present.
出席をとります.	I'm going to take attendance.
今日の会合は出席が悪かった.	The attendance was poor at today's meeting.

しゅっちょう (出張)

あさってからオーストラリアへ出張だ.	I'm going to Australia on business [I'm going on a business trip to Australia] the day after tomorrow.
夫はニューヨークへ出張中だ.	My husband is on a business trip to New York.
今回の北陸出張は成果があがらなかった.	My business trip to Hokuriku this time wasn't successful.
出張先から自宅へ電話をかけた.	I phoned home on my business trip.
出張費として3万円仮払いしてもらった.	I received ¥30,000 for travel [traveling] expenses before I left.

しゅっぱつ (出発)

彼らは中国旅行に出発した.	They left for their trip to China.
明朝9時に京都を出発します.	I'm leaving Kyoto at nine tomorrow morning.
彼はパリに向かって出発した.	He left for Paris.
飛行機は2時に出発する.	The plane leaves [departs] at two.
彼は船で出発する.	He's leaving by ship.
彼女は出発を延ばした.	She postponed her departure.

しゅみ (趣味)

私の趣味は切手収集です.	My hobby is †collecting stamps [stamp collecting].
私は趣味として絵を描く.	I paint [draw] (pictures) as a pastime.
彼の仕事は趣味と実益を兼ねている.	His avocation [hobby] became his work.
彼女は趣味が広いので話題が豊だ.	Her wide range of interests makes her a good conversationalist.
【好み】彼はいつも趣味のいいネクタイをしている.	He always wears attractive [tasteful] ties.
あの人は悪趣味な人だ.	He has bad taste.

じゅよう (需要)

石油の需要は年々高まる一方だ.	The demand for oil is increasing every year.
米の需要は毎年減る傾向にある.	The demand for rice is declining every year.
需要が供給を上回ると価格が上がる.	If demand exceeds supply prices †go up [increase].

しゅるい (種類)

この種類のちょうは日本では見られない.	This †species [particular kind] of butterfly is not found [seen] in Japan.
彼はいろいろな種類の人間とつきあいがある.	He †associates [hangs around, socializes] with †all sorts of people [a variety of people].
彼は何種類もの職業を経験している.	He has worked at many different kinds of jobs.
彼はあらゆる種類のスポーツをこなす.	He plays all kinds of sports fairly well.
私はこれと同じ種類の犬を飼っている.	I have a dog of the same breed as this one.
本は種類別に整理してある.	The books are arranged by subject.

じゅん (順)

左の方から順に自己紹介してください.	Starting from the left, please introduce yourselves.
では,順を追って事情を説明しましょう.	Well, I'll explain the situation in the order of events.
名簿はABC順になっている.	The directory [roster] is in alphabetical order.
申し込みは先着順50名まで受けつけます.	We'll accept the first fifty applications.

しゅんかん (瞬間)

その知らせを聞いた瞬間, 彼は真っ青になった. — He turned (deathly) pale the instant he heard the news.

次の瞬間, 車はもう走り去っていた. — The next instant [moment] the car had already zoomed by.

立ち上がった瞬間, 彼女はめまいを感じた. — She felt dizzy the moment she stood up.

彼は瞬間的に身をかわして, 飛んで来たボールを避けた. — He jumped [ducked] out of the way in a flash and avoided the ball flying toward him.

じゅんじょ (順序)

プラットホームで人々は順序よく並んで電車を待っていた. — There were people neatly lined up on the platform waiting for the train.

彼は順序立てて説明した. — He gave a well-ordered explanation.

この原稿は順序がばらばらになっている. — The pages of this manuscript are out of order.

じゅんじょう (純情)

彼は純情な男でだまされ易い. — He's easy to cheat because he's so naive.

彼の純情さには心を打たれた. — His artlessness touched my heart.

あの人はいくつになっても純情さを失わない. — No matter how old he gets, he never seems to lose his pure heart.

じゅんちょう (順調)

彼女とのつき合いは順調だ. — Our relationship is going well.

あのプロジェクトは今のところ順調に進んでいる. — That project is †going well [proceeding smoothly] so far.

「例の件はどうなってる?」「今のところ順調です」 — "And how's it going?" "So far, so good."

彼の手術後の経過は順調のようだ. — He seems to be doing well after his surgery.

じゅんばん (順番)

診察してもらうのに長いこと順番を待った. — I waited a long time for my turn to be examined.

やっと私の順番が来た. — My turn finally came.

本を順番に回し読みした. — We took turns reading the book.

じゅんび (準備)

準備は出来た. 出発しよう. — Everything's ready. Let's go.

母は食事の準備をしている. — Mother is †preparing dinner [getting dinner ready].

運動会の準備が整った.	Preparations for the athletic meet have been completed.
彼は試験の準備で忙しい.	He's very busy preparing [studying] for his examination.
何事も準備を怠ってはならない.	Whatever you do you shouldn't neglect making good preparations.
泳ぐ前に必ず準備運動をしよう.	You should always do warm-up exercises before swimming.

しよう (使用)

我が家では冬の暖房にガスストーブを使用している.	In winter, we use a gas heater at †home [our house].
ホールは改築中のため、現在使用できません.	The auditorium is under reconstruction and cannot be used at present.
節電のため、エレベーターの使用が一部制限されている.	Some elevators are not in use in order to save electricity.
この機械はまだ使用に耐える.	This machine is still usable.
会議室は現在, 使用中です.	The conference room is occupied.
「使用中」(会議室・トイレなど)	Occupied

じょう (情)

彼は息子に対しては情の薄い父親だった.	He never showed his son affection.
情が移って, その子犬を捨てることができない.	I've become so attached to that puppy that I can't just abandon it.
彼女は情の細やかな人だ.	She is a warm and considerate woman.
彼女は情の深い人だ.	She is an affectionate woman.
彼は情にもろく, 面倒見がいい.	He is tenderhearted [kindhearted] and takes good care of others.

しょうか (消化)

食べた物は胃腸で消化される.	Food is digested in the stomach and intestines.
これは消化を助ける薬です.	This medicine helps [aids] (your) digestion.
よくかんで食べないと消化不良を起こしますよ.	If you don't chew well when you eat you'll get indigestion.
【理解・吸収】日本人は外来文化を消化するのが早い.	Japanese rapidly assimilate various aspects of foreign culture.
習ったことを丸暗記するだけでなく, よく消化して自分のものにしなさい.	Don't just memorize it. Learn it so it's a part of you!
【始末・処理】勉強のスケジュールを計画どおり消化している.	I'm keeping up with my study schedule.

コンサートの日までに入場券を消化しなければならない.	I have to get all the tickets sold by the day of the concert.

しょうかい (紹介)

友人を紹介します.	Let me introduce my friend (to you).
家を建てるなら腕のいい大工を紹介しますよ.	If you're planning to build a house, let me introduce you to a very good builder [contractor].
この本はアフリカの部族の習俗を詳しく紹介している.	This book introduces the customs of African tribes in great detail.
友達が私のデートの相手を紹介してくれた.	My friend found a date for me.

しょうき (正気)

彼女は暑さで気を失ったが, まもなく正気を取り戻した.	She fainted from the heat but soon came to.
酔ってないよ. 正気だよ.	I'm not drunk. I'm sober.
あんな大会社を辞めるなんて正気の沙汰ではない.	He must have taken leave of his senses to quit a big company like that.
そんな馬鹿なことするなんて正気か.	Are you in your right mind? Why would you do such a silly thing?

しょうきょくてき (消極的)

消極的過ぎると自分を分かってもらえないよ.	If you're †not assertive enough [too passive], others won't listen to you.
彼は新企画に消極的だった.	He was negative about the new plan.
この件について, 政府は消極的な見解を示した.	The government demonstrated a negative opinion on this matter.

じょうけん (条件)

彼はもっと条件の良い仕事を探している.	He's looking for a job with better †pay and working conditions [terms of employment*].
彼は1割の利息を払うという条件で金を借りた.	He borrowed money on the condition that he pay 10% interest.
そのような条件は受け入れ難い.	It's hard for me to accept a condition like that.
僕はその仕事を引き受けるときに三つの条件をつけた.	I made three conditions when I accepted that work.
軽井沢は避暑地としての条件が揃っている.	Karuizawa is in all respects an ideal place for a summer resort.
条件が許せばすぐにでも結婚したいのだが.	If conditions permitted, I'd get married right away.

条件が整わないため，その計画は中止された．	That plan was canceled because not all of the conditions could be met.
卒業後帰って来るという条件つきで，彼は娘が東京の大学へ進学することを認めた．	He permitted his daughter to go to college in Tokyo on the condition that she must come home after graduation.

しょうこ (証拠)

犯人は現場に何も証拠を残さずに逃走した．	The criminal got away without leaving a single trace (at the scene).
証拠があがったので警察は彼を逮捕できた．	The new evidence that surfaced enabled the police to arrest him.
君は僕がお金を盗んだと言っているけど，何か証拠でもあるのかい．	You're accusing me of stealing the money but †do you have any proof [can you prove it]?
彼がやったという証拠を出せ．	Prove that he did it.
彼を愛している証拠に，彼女は彼の前ですぐ顔を赤らめる．	She blushes whenever she's in his presence. That's †a sure sign [proof] that she loves him.
論より証拠．	Example is better than precept.
	The proof †of the pudding is in the eating [is in the pudding].

しょうじき (正直)

正直なところ，辛い料理はあまり好きじゃない．	Frankly speaking [To be honest], I don't care for hot spicy food.
何があったか正直に話しなさい．	Be honest and tell me what happened.
正直者の運転手がタクシーに置き忘れた財布を警察に届けてくれた．	I left my wallet in a taxi and the driver was honest enough to turn it in to the police.
正直は最上の策である．	Honesty is the best policy.
彼は馬鹿正直だ．	He's honest to a fault.
私は馬鹿正直にも年収を教えてしまった．	I foolishly told what my income was.
私は三度目の正直で見事医学部に合格した．	I was lucky on my third time around and passed the medical school entrance exam with flying colors.

じょうしき (常識)

朝の5時に電話してくるなんて常識のない男だ．	He called me at five o'clock in the morning. He just doesn't have any common sense.[1]
日本では葬式に出るとき，黒い服を着るのは常識です．	It is proper[2] to wear black to funerals in Japan.

日本が高度な工業国というのは常識だ.	It's common knowledge[3] that Japan is a highly industrialized country.
彼に意見を求めても常識的なことしか言わない.	When I ask him his opinion, he just says †what is common knowledge to everyone [what everyone already knows].
そんな常識外れのことをするんじゃない.	Don't be rude [improper, impolite].[4] Watch your manners.[5] Use your common sense.[6]

> 1)6) common sense は主として「各自の判断力[良識]に照らし合わせた常識」について言い, 2) proper, 4) rude [improper, impolite], 5) manners は「社会的な規範に照らした常識」のあるなしを言う. 3) common knowledge は「だれもが知っている知識」について使う.

しょうたい (招待)

友達を夕食に招待しています.	I've invited a friend over for dinner.
彼は結婚式に恩師を招待した.	He invited his former teacher to his wedding.
今日のこの番組には珍しいゲストを招待しています.	We have invited a very special guest for today's program.
映画の招待券が2枚ある.	I have two complimentary tickets for the movie.

じょうたい (状態)

台風の直撃を受けた地方はひどい状態らしい.	The areas where the typhoon hit directly are apparently in a terrible condition.
その学校の教師と生徒の関係は今, とてもいい状態にある.	Relations between the teachers and students at that school now are very good.
景気は中だるみ状態だ.	The economy is in a slump.
彼の健康状態は良くない.	His health is not very good.
この頃, 彼の精神状態が不安定だ.	His psychological [mental] state has been unstable recently.

しょうち (承知)

【知っている】この件についてはあなたもよくご承知のことと思います.	I think you are well aware of this situation [issue].
無理を承知で是非お願いしたい.	I realize it's a lot for me to ask of you, but †if it's possible [if you could possibly do this for me] I'd greatly appreciate it.
そんなことは百も承知だ.	I know it only too well. I'm well aware of that.
【認める】こんな条件はとても承知	I can't possibly approve [accept] these

しょうとつ

するわけにはいかない.

お互いに承知の上でしたことなんだから.
Well, we both knew perfectly well what we were doing.

【許す】彼の悪口を言うと承知しないぞ.
If †you say anything bad [I hear any bad remarks] about him, I won't †let it pass [forgive you].

しょうてん (焦点)

【レンズ・目の】顕微鏡の焦点がなかなか合わなかった.
I had a hard time trying to focus the microscope.

このレンズの焦点距離は10センチです.
This lens has a focal length of 10 centimeters.

彼は酔って焦点の定まらない目で私を見た.
He looked at me with eyes blurred from drinking.

【注意・関心の】会議では, その問題が論議の焦点となった.
That issue became the focus of debate at the meeting.

運動会のことが, 今日の話し合いの焦点となった.
The upcoming athletic event was the focus of today's discussion.

この記事はもっと焦点を絞って書いたほうがいい.
It would be better to narrow the focus of this article.

しょうどう (衝動)

その少年はひもじさのあまり衝動的に盗みを働いた.
Hunger drove the boy to steal.

私はその場から逃げ出したいという衝動に駆られた.
I was overcome by an urge to get away.

衝動買いは損をすることが多い.
Impulse buying [Buying on impulse] is often a waste of money.

しょうどく (消毒)

化膿しないように傷口を消毒した.
I disinfected the wound to prevent an infection.

衣類は日光で消毒すると良い.
It would be a good idea to disinfect the garments in the sun.

この哺乳瓶は消毒してある.
This baby bottle has already been sterilized.

しょうとつ (衝突)

【物同士の】踏切で自動車と列車が衝突した.
A train crashed into a car at the railroad crossing.

バスとタクシーが正面衝突した.
There was a head-on collision between a bus and a taxi.

【意見の】会議で山田氏と井上氏の
Mr. Yamada and Mr. Inoue disagreed

意見が正面から衝突した.	head on at the meeting.
彼は仕事上の問題で上司と衝突した.	He had a run-in with his superior about a problem at work.
彼はすぐ人と衝突する.	He's quick to disagree with people.

じょうねつ (情熱)

彼はその研究に情熱を傾けた.	He threw himself into his research with a passion.
彼女は生涯, 自分の仕事に情熱を燃やし続けた.	Her work was her life's passion.
彼女はとても情熱的な人だ.	She is a very passionate woman.
担任の先生は情熱家です.	Our homeroom teacher is very enthusiastic.

しょうばい (商売)

【商い】今日はお客が少なくて, 全く商売にならない.	With so few customers we're not doing any business today.
お陰さまで商売が繁盛しています.	Fortunately, business is thriving.
これ以上不況が続けば商売が上がったりだ.	We're going to be put out of business if this depression [slump] continues.
こんな冷夏では商売上がったりだ.	A cold summer like this ruins business.
彼とは商売敵だ.	He's my business [trade] rival.
【職業】彼の家は酒屋を商売にしている.	His family runs [owns] a liquor store.
彼は何の商売をしているの.	What does he do?／What's his job?
彼は商売柄, 服装にうるさい.	His line of work makes him particular about clothing.

しょうひ (消費)

水や電気をむだに消費してはいけません.	You shouldn't waste water and electricity.
石油の消費量は年々増加し続けている.	Oil consumption is increasing †annually [year by year].

じょうひん (上品)

彼女の物腰はとても上品だ.	She has †an elegant [a refined] manner (about her).
その老人は白髪の上品な人だった.	The silver-haired old man was quite elegant [refined].
あの女はひどく上品ぶっている.	That woman puts on the most awful airs.
彼女は美しくはないが, 上品な雰囲気の人だ.	She may not be beautiful, but she's very refined.

しょうぶ (勝負)

今日こそは勝負をつけよう.	Today is the day I'm going to beat you.
彼では碁が弱過ぎて勝負にならない.	He's not very good at playing *go* so it's really no competition.
あの二人は頑固なことではいい勝負だ.	They're both stubborn, so it'll be a good match.
逆転ホームランが出て勝負が面白くなってきた.	The come-from-behind home run has made this an interesting contest.
この勝負は明日までお預けにしよう.	Let's drop this fight [match, contest] for now and take it up again tomorrow.

じょうぶ (丈夫)

【体が】丈夫な体を作るために, 毎日運動をしている.	I exercise every day to keep [stay] †in shape [fit].
彼は丈夫で風邪ひとつひかない.	He's so healthy that he never catches cold.
彼女は病弱だったがこの頃すっかり丈夫になった.	She used to be very sickly but now she's strong and healthy.
【物が】このいすは丈夫に作ってある.	This chair is well made.
このズボンはとても丈夫で, 長持ちしている.	These pants are very †well made [durable], so they've lasted for a long time.
箱を丈夫なひもでしっかり結わえた.	I tied the box securely with a sturdy piece of rope.

しょうめい (証明)

私が無実だと証明してください.	Please prove that I'm innocent.
裁判で彼の無実が証明された.	His innocence was proved in the trial.
彼の才能が並々でないことは, この素晴らしい彼の作品が見事に証明している.	This magnificent work admirably proves [demonstrates] that his ability is above the ordinary.
A, B二つの図形が相似であることを証明しなさい.	Prove that figures A and B are similar.
病欠届けには医者の証明書が必要です.	A doctor's certificate must accompany a notification for absence due to illness.

しょうめん (正面)

この絵はセント・パトリック大聖堂を正面から描いたものです.	This is a picture of St. Patrick's Cathedral drawn from the front.
私の部屋から真正面に富士山が見えます.	I have †an unobstructed [a perfect] view of Mt. Fuji right [directly] from my room.
舞台の正面には机が一つ置いてあるだけだった.	There was only a desk (placed) at the front of the stage.
彼に金を貸してくれと正面切って	I wasn't able to come right out and ask

しょうらい (将来)

あの夫婦は息子の将来に希望を託している.	That couple is very hopeful about their son's future.
彼は将来大物になるだろう.	He'll probably be an important figure someday.
将来に備えてしっかり勉強しなさい.	Study hard to prepare for your future.
近い将来, 宇宙旅行も夢ではなくなるだろう.	In the near future, space travel will no longer be just a dream [fantasy].
この事業は将来性がある.	This business has a future.

しょくぎょう (職業)

あなたのご職業は何ですか.	What's your occupation [job]? What do you do?
私の職業は会社員です.	I work as [I'm] a company employee.
この職業に就いて10年になります.	I've had this job for ten years.
彼はたびたび職業を変えた.	He's changed jobs a number of times.

しょくよく (食欲)

食欲がある.	I have a good appetite.
食欲がない.	I have no appetite.
この頃, 胃の調子が悪くて食欲不振だ.	My stomach's been troubling me lately and I'm suffering a lack [loss] of appetite.
毎日同じ献立では食欲が減退する.	Everyday it's the same menu. It's enough to make you lose your appetite.
彼は食欲旺盛で, いつもきれいに平らげる.	He has a keen appetite and always cleans his plate.

ショック

ショック. また英語の試験に落ちた.	What a shock! I flunked the English test again!
彼の死はクラスメートにとってすごいショックだった.	His death was a great shock to his classmates.
年寄りにはあまり大きなショックを与えてはいけない.	You shouldn't do anything to upset older people too much.
この腕時計はショックに強い.	This wristwatch is shock-resistant.
私の祖父はショック死した.	My grandfather died from shock.

しょぶん (処分)

【不要な物を】もう着ない服〔古い手紙〕をすべて処分した.	I threw out all my old clothes [letters].

残った花火の処分に困り，庭に埋めた．	Not knowing how to dispose of the leftover fireworks, I buried them in the garden.
【罰を加える】その処分は重すぎる〔軽すぎる〕と思う．	I think the punishment is too severe [light].
喫煙が発覚し，彼は2週間の停学処分を受けた．	He was suspended from school for two weeks after being caught smoking.

しょゆう (所有)

彼は北海道に広大な土地を所有している．	He owns a large piece of land in Hokkaido.
私は父の死によって，莫大な資産を所有することになった．	I came into an enormous amount of property as a result of my father's death.
この空き地は市の所有地です．	This vacant lot is owned by the city.
彼は所有欲が強く，何でも自分のものにしたがる．	He's very acquisitive and wants to get his hands on everything.

しょり (処理)

この部署の仕事は客からのクレームを処理することだ．	This department takes care of customer complaints.
支店で処理しきれなかった問題が本社に回されてきた．	Problems that couldn't be taken care of at the branch offices were sent on to the head office.
廃棄物を適切に処理しないと環境が汚染されてしまう．	The environment will be polluted if we don't dispose of our waste properly.
その国の戦後処理は国連が中心となって行われた．	It was mainly the U.N. that took care of the country's postwar rebuilding.
情報処理の資格を取得した．	I'm now a qualified data processor.

しらける

彼はパーティーに呼びたくない．座がしらけるから．	I don't want to invite him to the party. He's such a wet blanket.
彼の空威張りに周りの人はしらけた．	His empty boast made everyone feel ill-at-ease [uncomfortable].
最近の大学生はしらけている．	These days college students seem to be apathetic.
その会合には初めからしらけた雰囲気が漂っていた．	The mood at that meeting was apathetic from the very start.
私たちは「しらけ世代」と呼ばれている．	We're being called the "apathetic [unenthusiastic] generation."

じらす

彼女は結婚申し込みの返事を遅ら	She kept him hanging [dangling] by not

せて彼をじらした. | giving him an immediate reply to his marriage proposal.
じらさないで早く正解を教えてください. | Don't keep me hanging. Hurry up and give me the correct [right] answer.
あの人の決断力のなさには、全くじらされたよ. | His lack of decisiveness really kept us hanging.

しらせ (知らせ)

あなたに良い知らせがあります. | We have some good news for you.
入社試験を受けた会社から、採用するという知らせが来た. | I received a letter of acceptance from the company where I took the entrance examination.
彼からはまだ何の知らせもない. | I haven't heard anything from him. / He hasn't notified me yet.
虫の知らせがあったので友人に電話したら、今朝亡くなったところだった. | I had a †premonition [funny feeling, strange feeling] about a friend, and when I called I found out she had died this morning.

しらせる (知らせる)

彼女には病名を知らせないほうがいいでしょう. | I don't think she should be told the name of her disease.
彼は結婚したことをだれにも知らせなかった. | He didn't †tell anybody [let anybody know] that he got married.
引っ越しの日が決まりましたら知らせてください. | Please let me know †when [what day] you're moving.
そういう重要なことは早く知らせてくれなければ困る. | It makes things difficult for us if you don't †let us know [notify us] right away when important matters arise.
二人が殴り合いのけんかを始めたので警察に知らせた. | We called the police because the two started a fist fight.

しらべる (調べる)

単語の意味が分からなければ辞書で調べなさい. | If you don't know the meaning of a word, look it up in the dictionary.
この書類の数字が正確かどうか調べてほしい. | Please check to see whether the numbers on the documents are correct.
警察は地震による被害の状況を調べている. | The police are investigating the extent of the damage †from [caused by] the earthquake.
ガードマンがビルをくまなく調べたが、異状はなかった. | The guard thoroughly searched [inspected] the building but did not notice anything †strange [out of the ordinary].

警官は挙動不審の男を調べた．	The policeman searched a man who was behaving suspiciously.
警察では目下その殺人事件の犯人を調べている．	The police are presently searching for the suspected murderer.
偽札が出回り始めたので警察は印刷業者をいくつか調べた．	The police checked up on a number of printers when the counterfeit bills began to surface.
彼は音楽好きの友達を感心させようとモーツァルトのことを本で調べた．	He read up on Mozart in order to impress his friend who likes music.
この記事は彼が足で調べてまとめたものだ．	He went around in person to get all the information for this article. He did all the footwork necessary for preparing this article.
だれが欠席しているかメンバー全員のリストを調べてください．	Please run down the list of all our members to see who is not present.

しり (尻)

いたずらをした子どもは父親におしりを叩かれた．	The child's father spanked him for misbehaving.
彼女は大きいおしりをしている．	She has big hips.
このズボンはおしりのところがきつい．	These pants are too tight in the rear.
彼はしりが重いので，何事も始めるまでが大変だ．	It's a real chore getting things started because he's always dragging his feet [butt**].
彼女はしりの軽い女だ．	She's promiscuous./She's a loose woman.
彼は女房のしりに敷かれている．	He's tied to his wife's apron strings. He's henpecked.
仕事の締め切りが迫り，しりに火が付いた．	With the deadline approaching, I've got my work cut out for me.
彼はようやく今度の会社にしりを落ち着けたようだ．	It seems that he's finally come to roost at that company.
いい年をして女のしりを追い回すのはやめろ．	At your age you ought to stop chasing after women.
彼の成績順位はしりから数えたほうが早い．	It'd be faster to count from the bottom if you're trying to find his standing [ranking].
おまえの借金のしりぬぐいはごめんだ．	I'll have no part of helping you straighten out your mess of loan.
彼は妻にしりを叩かれてやっと職探しに出かけた．	His wife pestered him until he finally went out to look for work.
彼は長っちりで有名だ．	He's notorious for overstaying his wel-

come.

しりあい (知り合い)

彼は出版界に知り合いが多い.	He has many friends [acquaintances] in publishing.
彼とは仕事を通じて知り合いになった.	We [He and I] became acquainted through work.
知り合いの弁護士を紹介してあげましょう.	Let me introduce you to a lawyer I know.

じりじり

【徐々に】賃上げを要求して, 労組は会社側にじりじりと圧力をかけてきた.	Little by little the union pressured management for higher wages.
【焼けつく様】太陽がじりじりと照りつけていた.	The sun was scorching.
彼女はローソクにあまり近づき過ぎたので, 長い髪の毛が炎でじりじりと焦げた.	She got too close to the candle and her long hair got singed by the flame.
ステーキがじりじりと焼けている.	The steak is sizzling.
【いらだつ】彼は早く出かけたくてじりじりしている.	He's itching to get out of here fast.
	He's getting antsy waiting to leave.
じりじりする (じれったい) なあ.	It's [He's, She's] so exasperating.
そんなにじりじりするなよ.	Don't be so impatient.
	Don't get so exasperated.

しりょ (思慮)

あなたの取った態度は思慮に欠ける.	You got a bad attitude. You seem so thoughtless.
それはとても思慮深い発言だった.	It was a thoughtful remark.
彼女の思慮のなさにはあきれてしまう.	Her lack of consideration really amazes [disgusts] me.

しりょう (資料)

彼は英文学を研究するための資料を集めている.	He's collecting materials for a study on English literature.
彼は会議のために必要な資料を整えた.	He put [got] all the necessary material in order for the conference.
その件に関してはまだ資料が不十分なので, はっきりしたことは言えない.	Since our material concerning that issue is still inadequate, †we can't make any definite statements [we have nothing definite to state].
資料が不足しているので, 研究が	I can't †study [do the research] since I lack

できない.	sufficient materials.

しる (知る)

【情報・知識がある】彼は法律をよく知っている.	He's well-versed in law.
警察からの電話で父の死を知った.	The police called and informed me of my father's death.
母からの電話で姉に赤ちゃんが生まれたことを知った.	My mother called and told me (that) my sister had had her baby.
そんなことは知りません.	Don't ask me.
同窓会で彼の消息を知った.	I found out what he's been up to at the reunion.
彼女の消息を知っていますか.	Do you †have any idea [know] what's become of her?
あの作家は良いものを書く割には世間に知られていない.	That author isn't as well known as you might expect from the high quality of his works.
彼はすぐに知ったかぶりをする.	He thinks he's such a know-it-all.
石油の高騰はとどまるところを知らない.	The jump in oil prices knows no stopping.
彼はだまされたとも知らずに契約書にサインした.	Having no idea he was being tricked into something, he signed the contract.
彼は怖れを知らない男だ.	He's a man who knows no fear.
知らない町に行って知らない人と話を交わすのが私の楽しみだ.	I enjoy going to places I've never been to and talking to people I've never met before.
【記憶にある】彼の子どもの頃を知っている.	I remember him when he was a child.
父は昔のことをよく知っている.	My father knows a lot about things from long ago.
私は戦争を知りません.	I've never known war.
【面識・関係がある】彼のことはよく知っている.	I know him well.
	I know a lot about him.
あなたなんかもう知らない.	I've had it with you.
これはおまえの知ったことじゃない.	This is none of your business.
もうどうなっても知らないよ.	Well, it's no longer any of my business.
彼女は僕に知らん顔をした.	She pretended she didn't (even) know me.
	She gave me the cold shoulder.

しろい (白い)

野原は一面に白い雪で覆われた.	The field [plain] was covered with white snow.

紙に白いところがなくなるまで字を練習した.	I practiced writing until there were no (blank) spaces left on the paper.
彼女は色が白い.	She has a light complexion.
母は髪が白くなってきた.	My mother's hair is turning gray.
彼らは私を白い目で見た.	They gave me a cold stare.
【無実】彼は白だ.	He's innocent [clean].

しわ

母も最近, 顔に随分しわが寄ってきた.	My mother is beginning to get a lot of wrinkles on her face lately.
父の顔には深いしわが刻まれている.	My father's face is lined with deep wrinkles.
彼は額にしわを寄せて何か考えごとをしていた.	He knitted his brow, thinking about something or other.
彼はいつも眉間にしわを寄せている.	He's always frowning.
このシャツはしわだらけなので,アイロンをかけてください.	Please iron this shirt for me. It's full of wrinkles.
彼はしわくちゃのハンカチをポケットから取り出した.	He pulled a wrinkled [rumpled] handkerchief from his pocket.
赤字財政のしわ寄せで福祉予算が削られた.	The strain of deficit spending necessitated cuts in the welfare budget.

しん (心・芯)

【心】彼は奥さんをしんから愛している.	He loves his wife with all his heart.
彼は口は悪いが, しんはいい人だ.	He may be sharp-tongued but basically he's a good person.
彼女はおとなしそうだが, しんはなかなか強い.	She may seem meek but she has inner strength.
この仕事はしんが疲れる.	This work is mentally taxing.
【芯】このろうそくは芯が短いので火が付きにくい.	This candle is hard to light because the wick is short.
この鉛筆の芯は折れ易い.	The lead in this pencil breaks easily.
リンゴの皮をむき, 芯を取って食べた.	I peeled and cored the apple and (then I) ate it.
打者は球をバットの芯でとらえた.	The batter met the ball squarely with the bat.
北風に当たり体のしんまで冷えてしまった.	The cold north wind chilled me to the marrow.

じんかく (人格)

いくら小さいからといって子ども	No matter how small children may be, you

	しんけん
の人格を無視してはいけない.	shouldn't forget that they're human beings in their own right.
彼は優れた人格の持ち主だ.	He has an exceptional personality [character].
彼は学問はあるのだが、人格的に問題がある.	He's well educated but he has character flaws.
彼は人格者だ.	He's a man of character.
彼は二重人格者だ.	He has a split personality.

しんきょう（心境）

今になって婚約を破棄するとは、一体どういう心境の変化なのですか.	What in the world would make you change your mind and break off your engagement at this late date?
彼は俗世を離れて、静かな心境に達した.	He withdrew from the world and achieved a tranquil state of mind.
還暦を迎えた心境をお聞かせください.	Tell me how it feels to have reached 60.

しんけい（神経）

歯医者で神経を抜いてもらった.	I went to the dentist for a root canal.
彼は病気のために中枢神経を侵された.	The illness †affected [brought on a disorder in] his central nervous system.
彼は運動神経が抜群なので、スポーツは何をやらせても上手だ.	He has excellent reflexes and is good at whatever sport he plays.
彼は神経が太い.	He doesn't let little things †bother him [get on his nerves].
彼女は神経が細かい.	She is sensitive.
彼女は神経が細やかな女の子だ.	She is a very thoughtful girl.
今日は仕事で何人もの人に会って神経をすり減らした.	My nerves are worn out from dealing with so many people at work today.
あんなやつの言うことにいちいち神経を尖らせるなよ.	Don't get †upset [riled up] by everything he says.
彼女は神経質だ.	She's the nervous type.
彼女はこういうことには神経質だ.	She is sensitive [touchy] about this kind of thing.
あの人は神経過敏だから一緒に暮らしにくい.	He's so hypersensitive that he is hard to live with.

しんけん（真剣）

私はこの問題には真剣なんだ.	I'm serious about this issue.
真剣に考えてください.	Think it over seriously.
彼はあの娘を真剣に愛している.	He really loves her.
	He's really [seriously] in love with her.

彼の真剣な態度は，みんな見習うべきだ．	We should all try to work as seriously as he does.
この仕事は私の人生をかけた真剣勝負だ．	I have to play for keeps. I've staked my life on this work.

しんごう (信号)

その信号を右に曲がってください．	Turn right at the light.
電車は停止信号で止まった．	The train stopped for the red light.
交通信号が黄色〔赤，青〕に変わった．	The traffic light turned yellow〔red, green〕.

じんこう¹ (人口)

東京の人口は約1,200万人です．	The population of Tokyo is about twelve million.
日本は人口密度が高い．	Japan has a high population density.
この村は年々人口が減っている．	The population of this village is decreasing annually.
この町はその工場が出来てから急に人口が増えた．	The population of this town rapidly increased after the factory was built.
世界の人口は増加の一途をたどっている．	The world's population is growing steadily.
その格言は人口に膾炙(かいしゃ)している．	That proverb is familiar to everyone.

じんこう² (人工)

これは人工の湖です．	This is †a man-made [an artificial] lake.
人工的に雨を降らせる実験が行われた．	They conducted an experiment to make rainfall artificially.
この川では人工的にふ化したサケを放流している．	This river is stocked with artificially hatched salmon.
その年日本で初めて人工衛星が打ち上げられた．	The first Japanese man-made satellite was put into orbit that year.
彼は人工呼吸で息を吹き返した．	He was revived by artificial respiration.

しんこく (深刻)

あまり深刻に考えなさんな．	Don't †take [think about] it too seriously.
事態は深刻になってきた．	Things have become serious.
深刻な顔をしてどうしたの．	Why such a serious face?
	Why do you look so serious?
国境紛争は深刻の度を加えた．	The border dispute †took a turn for the worse [became more serious].
失業率の増加は深刻な問題です．	The increasing rate of unemployment is a grave problem.

| 我が社の経営難は一層深刻化してきた. | Our company's business situation has become more serious. |

しんさつ (診察)

診察は9時から始まります.	Medical examinations begin at nine.
その医師は毎日病人を50人診察する.	That doctor examines 50 patients a day.
そんなに微熱が続いているなら, 一度診察を受けたほうがいいよ.	If you've been running a slight fever that long you ought to go see a doctor.
診察の結果, 全治3週間と判った.	Results of the examination indicated that it would take about three weeks for me to recover.
彼は名前を呼ばれて診察室に入った.	His name was called and he entered the examination room.

しんじる (信じる)

彼はUFOの存在を信じている.	He believes that UFOs exist.
彼が死んだとはとても信じられない.	I simply can't believe [It's unbelievable] that he's dead.
母親は息子の無事を信じた.	The boy's mother believed that her son was still †alive [safe and sound].
私は友人を信じている.	I believe my friends.
あなたを信じてどこまでも一緒について行きます.	I trust you so much that I'd follow you anywhere.
他人の言葉を信じ過ぎてはいけない.	You shouldn't put too much faith in what other people say.
母はキリスト教を信じている.	My mother is a Christian. My mother believes in Christ.
あんないい人がこんな不幸にあうなんて神も仏も信じられない.	What an unfortunate thing to happen to such a nice person! It's enough to try [test] one's faith in God.

じんせい (人生)

彼は人生の意義を真剣に考えた.	He gave some serious thought to the meaning of life.
人生は一度しかないのだから大切に生きなさい.	You only have one life to live, so use it well.
「人生は大いに楽しまなくちゃ」と彼女は言った.	She said, "You've got to enjoy life."
この小説には作者の人生観がよく表れている.	This novel expresses the author's view of life well.
人生わずか50年と言われた時代も今ではもう夢のようだ.	Nowadays it's hard to imagine a time when people weren't expected to live

more than 50 years.

しんせつ (親切)

ご親切にありがとうございます.	Thank you for being so kind.
	Thank you for your kindness.
小さな親切で世の中を明るくしましょう.	A little kindness can make the world a better place (to live).
人の親切は素直に受けるべきです.	You should accept the kindness of others with an open heart.
こんなに親切にされたのは生まれて初めてです.	I've never been treated so well in my life.
口先だけで親切そうなことを言う人は信用されない.	If you simply say nice things without really meaning them, people aren't going to trust you.

しんせん (新鮮)

さあ,いらっしゃい! 新鮮な果物や野菜はこちらですよ.	Come and get it! Get your fresh fruit and vegetables here!
刺身は材料の新鮮さが第一だ.	The most important thing about *sashimi* is its freshness.
彼女は新しいタイプの映画スターで新鮮な感じだ.	She is a new type of movie star and a refreshing change from the usual.
山に登って新鮮な空気を思い切り吸ってきた.	I went mountain climbing and breathed my fill of fresh air.
このデザイナーはファッション界に新鮮な感覚をもたらした.	This designer has brought a fresh sense to the world of fashion.

しんぞう (心臓)

彼は心臓の病気にかかっている.	He †has [suffers from] heart disease.
彼は心臓発作で倒れた.	He suffered [had] a heart attack.
急いで走って来たので心臓が破裂しそうだ.	I ran here so quickly that my heart feels like it will burst.
【押しの強さ】彼は心臓が強い.	He really has a lot of nerve [gall].
彼は見かけによらず心臓が弱い.	Contrary to appearance, he's really [quite] timid.
彼女はなかなかの心臓だから,人前でもあがらない.	She has a lot of spunk [mettle] and doesn't †get nervous [feel self-conscious] in front of others.

しんちょう (慎重)

海外留学は慎重に計画したほうがいい.	You should be prudent when planning to study overseas.
彼は新しい計画を実行に移すのに	He is being very careful [cautious] in

は慎重だ.	putting the new plan into effect.
この機械はとても精密だから，慎重に取り扱ってください.	This is an extremely delicate device, so please handle it carefully.
社会人として常に慎重を期してもらいたい.	As a responsible member of society I expect you to use your best judgment at all times.
彼の言動には慎重さが欠けている.	He lacks discretion.
	He needs to be more careful [prudent] about his behavior and speech.
彼は何事にも慎重な態度で臨む.	He's very cautious about whatever he does.
彼は投資先を選ぶときは慎重だ.	He's circumspect about how he invests his money.

しんどう (振動・震動)

振り子の振動は規則正しい.	The pendulum's oscillation is rhythmical [methodical, regular].
モーターの震動音が聞こえてくる.	You can hear the hum [vibration] of the motor.

しんぱい (心配)

心配しないで．私は大丈夫です.	Don't worry. I'm all right.
親にあまり心配をかけるな.	Don't give your parents too much cause for worry!
彼女は心配そうな表情で辺りを見回した.	She looked around with a worried expression on her face.
彼は，何の心配もない結構な身分だ.	He's in a fine position, with nothing to worry about.
あなたのことが心配でゆうべは眠れなかった.	I was so worried about you (that) I wasn't able to sleep last night.
父の健康を心配している.	I'm worried about my father's health.
金の心配は要らないから，しっかり研究に打ち込みなさい.	You needn't worry about money. Just concentrate on your studies.
夫のがんのことを心配するあまり彼女は眠れなくなった.	Her husband's cancer caused her so much anxiety that she became unable to sleep at night.

じんぶつ (人物)

あのカメラマンは人物を撮るのがうまい.	That photographer is good at taking pictures of people.
あの小説家は歴史上の人物を題材にした小説を多く書いている.	That writer uses historical personalities as material for many of his novels.
私は人物画をかくのが好きだ.	I like to paint portraits.

彼は危険な人物だと睨まれている.	He's suspected of being a dangerous person [individual].
彼は人物が立派だ.	He's a fine person.
	He's an upstanding individual.
彼はなかなかの人物だ.	He's quite a person.
彼はひとかどの人物だ.	He's someone [somebody] of consequence.
日本の政界には傑出した人物が少ない.	There are few men of stature in Japanese politics.

しんぽ (進歩)

今世紀の科学の進歩は目覚ましいものがある.	There have been some startling advances made in science this century.
情報工学は飛躍的な進歩を遂げている.	Rapid progress is taking place in (the field of) information technology.
医学は年々進歩しつつある.	Medical science continues to make advances [progress] year by year.
やる気がなければ進歩はない.	If you don't have drive you'll never get ahead.
彼は年の割には進歩的な考えを持っている.	His thinking is very progressive for his age.

しんぼう (辛抱)

どんなに仕事が辛くとも,彼女は辛抱して働いた.	She put up with the work no matter how excruciating it was.
こんな目にあっては,もう辛抱できない.	This is the last straw.
もう少しの辛抱だから,頑張ってください.	Just a bit more perseverance [patience]. Hang in there!
辛抱に辛抱を重ねてやっと今の地位を築いた.	I've made it to where I am now by being enormously [extremely] patient.
あの人の辛抱強さには頭が下がる.	I have to hand it to him. He has a lot of patience.

しんよう (信用)

私を信用できないのですか.	Can't you trust [believe] me?
信用できる人だから,あの人に相談しなさい.	He's a person you can trust, so consult him.
銀行は信用第一です.	Trust is the most important thing for a bank.
あいつの言うことは信用ならない.	You can't take him at his word.
	That guy's words can't be trusted.
あんな政治家は信用するな.	Don't trust a politician like that.
彼は長年の努力の末,社会的な信	Many years of effort won him the trust of

用を得た.	society.
彼は得意先の信用を得ている.	He's won the client's confidence.
君のような社員がいては,我が社の信用にかかわる.	It's employees like you who give our company a bad name.
その事件で彼の信用は傷ついた.	That incident impaired his credibility.
あの会社は欠陥商品を作って信用を落とした.	That company lost credibility by manufacturing defective goods.

しんらい (信頼)

彼は信頼できる人だと思って結婚しました.	I married him because I felt [believed] he was reliable [trustworthy].
いいかげんな仕事で,上司の信頼を裏切ってはいけない.	You mustn't betray your superior's trust in you by doing slipshod work.
新しい市長には,市民の信頼に答える政治をして欲しい.	We hope the new mayor will perform his duties in keeping with the people's trust in him.
信頼すべき筋によれば,あの会社では近々社長が交代するそうだ.	We have it from a reliable source that that company will change presidents soon.

しんり¹ (真理)

彼は真理を探究するために学問の道へ進んだ.	To search for truth he pursued a life of scholarship.
彼こそは本当に真理を愛する人間だ.	He's a veritable lover of truth.
彼の言うことにも一面の真理がある.	There is a certain amount of truth to [in] what he says.

しんり² (心理)

この童話は子どもの心理をよくとらえている.	The psychology of children is well captured [expressed] in this fairy tale.
あんなことをするなんて彼はきっとそのとき異常な心理状態にあったに違いない.	He must have been under extreme psychological stress at the time to have done such a thing.
この小説の心理描写は実に見事だ.	The psychological characterization in this novel is truly superb.
彼女は大学で心理学を専攻している.	She's majoring in psychology in college.

しんるい (親類)

私と彼とは親類です.	He and I are related.
彼は私の遠い〔近い〕親類にあたる.	He's a distant (near) relative.
私には家族も親類もない.	I have no family or relations.
彼らとは親類づきあいをしている.	They're like family to me.

ず

ずいぶん (随分)
今日は随分寒いですね.	It's very cold today, isn't it?
彼女は随分わがままだね.	She is very spoiled, isn't she? She certainly is spoiled, isn't she?
随分高い本だなあ.	It sure is an expensive book.
僕だけ誘わないなんて随分じゃないか.	What nerve, inviting everyone but me!
人をペテンにかけて, 随分なやつだ.	He's too much, swindling me like that.

すう (吸う)
山のきれいな空気を胸いっぱい吸った.	I took a deep breath of the clean mountain air.
赤ん坊が母親の乳を吸っている.	The baby is nursing at its mother's breast.
蚊は動物の血を吸う.	Mosquitoes suck the blood of animals.
木は根から水を吸う.	Trees draw [absorb, take in] water through their roots.
この布はよく水を吸い取る.	This cloth soaks up water well.
掃除機がダイヤの指輪を吸い込んでしまった.	My diamond ring got sucked into the vacuum cleaner.
一服吸ってから仕事を始めよう.	Let's have a smoke and then start work.

ずうずうしい
あいつはずうずうしいやつだ.	He has †lots of nerve[1] [plenty of cheek[2]].
彼はずうずうしく借金を頼んできた.	He had the nerve to ask me for a loan.
ずうずうしいにも程がある.	There's a limit to just how nervy one can be.

> 1) アメリカでよく使われる. 2) イギリスでよく使われる.

すえ (末)
【終わり】彼に初めて会ったのは去年の末だ.	I first met him at the end of last year.

今月の末までには本を読み終えます.	I'll finish reading the book by the end of this month.
私は6人兄弟の末から2番目です.	I'm the second youngest of six brothers and sisters.
警察官が盗みをするとは世も末だ.	What's this world coming to when a policeman is caught stealing?
二人は口論の末, 殴り合いを始めた.	Their argument turned into a fistfight.
彼はよくよく考えた末, 大学を中退した.	After (giving it) a lot of thought he decided to drop out of college.
【将来】この子は頭がいいから末が楽しみだ.	This child is smart, and it'll be interesting to see what he makes of himself.
おまえは全く末恐ろしい子だ.	If you act like this as a kid, I hate to think what kind of person you're going to turn into.
末長くお幸せに.	Long life and happiness to you both.

すがた (姿)

鮎は姿の美しい魚だ.	The *ayu* is a beautiful-looking fish.
後ろ姿だけでジミーだと分かった.	Although I only saw him from behind, I knew it was Jimmy.
その女優は着物姿が素敵だ.	That actress looks good in a *kimono*.
彼女は自分の姿を鏡に映した.	She looked at herself in the mirror.
この姿を母に見せたかった.	If only my mother could see me now.
彼は最近姿を見せない.	He hasn't been around lately.
	We haven't seen him around lately.
彼は姿を隠した.	He hid [concealed] himself.
太陽が雲間から姿を現した.	The sun appeared between the clouds.
最近都会では野鳥の姿を見かけない.	You don't see wild birds in urban areas these days.
この映画は自然の恐ろしさをありのままの姿でとらえている.	This movie depicts the fury of nature just as it is.

すき¹ (好き)

彼はクラシック音楽が好きだ.	He likes classical music.
私は甘いものが大好きだ.	I †really like [love] sweets.
これは私のいちばん好きなコーヒーカップだ.	This is my favorite coffee cup.
洋食より和食のほうが好きだ.	I prefer Japanese food to Western food.
	I like Japanese food better than Western food.
チョコレートはそれほど好きではない.	I don't care much for chocolate.

ベートーベンはいいが，ブラームスはあまり好きではない．	I enjoy Beethoven, but I don't really go for Brahms.
彼は一目で彼女が好きになった．	He fell in love with her at first sight.
君の好きなように生きてごらん．	Live the way you like.
あいつの好きにさせておけ．	Let him do as he likes.
好きこそものの上手なれ．	We tend to be good at those things we like.

すき² (隙)

隙をみて彼はその家に忍び込んだ．	Waiting for his chance, he slipped into the house.
彼は部屋から抜け出す隙を狙っていた．	He was waiting for a chance to slip out of the room.
彼は決して人に隙を見せない．	He never lets himself be caught off guard.
彼はいつも一分の隙もない身なりをしている．	He's always impeccably dressed.

〜すぎ (〜過ぎ)

【時・年齢】9時過ぎまで彼女を待った．	I waited for her until after nine.
列車は7時2分過ぎに到着した．	The train arrived at 7:02 [seven-o-two, two past seven].
彼は二十過ぎになって初めて海を見た．	He was over twenty when he saw the sea for the first time.
【程度】食べ過ぎ飲み過ぎに注意しなさい．	Be careful not to eat and drink too much.
たばこの吸い過ぎだよ．	You smoke too much.

すききらい (好き嫌い)

食べ物の好き嫌いはありますか．	Is there anything in particular you like (to eat)?
	Is there anything you can't eat?
彼は何事についても好き嫌いが激しい．	He always either hates something or loves it.
好き嫌いしないで何でも食べなさい．	Don't be so fussy. Eat everything.

すきま (隙間)

猫が塀の隙間から出入りしている．	The cat goes in and out of the opening in the fence.
壁と本箱のあいだに隙間がある．	There's a space between the wall and the bookcase.
箱に本を隙間なく詰めてください．	Please pack this box tightly with books.

| 雲の隙間から太陽が覗いている. | The sun is peeking through the clouds. |

すぎる (過ぎる)

その川を過ぎると森がある.	There's a forest on the other side of the river.
列車は横浜駅を過ぎたところだ.	The train (has) just passed Yokohama Station.
彼女は50歳を過ぎてもまだ若々しい.	Even though she's over fifty, she still looks young.
借金の返済期限はとうに過ぎた.	The date for repayment of my loan has long since passed.
あっという間に10年が過ぎていた.	Before I knew it ten years had passed.
時が過ぎれば悲しいことも忘れてしまう.	Sad things are forgotten with the passage of time.
過ぎてしまったことをくよくよするな.	Don't brood over something that's over and done with.
政局の危機は政権交代もなく無事に過ぎ去った.	The political crisis blew over without a change in administrations.
【程度】泳ぐには水が冷た過ぎる.	The water is too cold to go swimming.
この本は難し過ぎる.	This book is too difficult.
彼は自分勝手過ぎる.	He wants his own way too much.
彼女は君には過ぎた奥さんだ.	She's too good a wife for you.

すく¹ (好く)

その医者はスタッフや患者たちに好かれていた.	That doctor was liked by all the staff and patients.
あいつはどうも虫が好かない.	There's something about him I don't like.

すく² (空・透く)

電車はすいていた.	The train †wasn't crowded [was empty].
道はガラガラにすいている.	The streets are (almost) deserted.

すぐ

すぐやめろ.	Stop †at once [immediately, now].
すぐ帰って来るよ.	I'll be right back.
すぐにも仕事に取りかかってくれ.	Start working †right away [immediately, at once].
彼女の家はすぐ見つかった.	I found her house right away.
彼は家に帰るとすぐ寝てしまう.	As soon as he gets home, he goes to bed.
母はもうすぐ80歳になる.	My mother is almost eighty.
妹はすぐに泣く.	My sister cries easily.
父はすぐ昔の話をしたがる.	My father always wants to talk about the old days.

私の家はここからすぐです． My house is very near here.
すぐ目の前で交通事故があった． A traffic accident occurred †right in front of me [before my very eyes].
すぐ後ろから車が1台ついてくる． There's a car following right behind me.

すくう (救う)

彼女は燃えている車の中から救い出された． She was rescued from the burning car.
どこかで救いを求める声がする． There's a voice somewhere crying out for help.
医者は人の命を救うのが仕事だ． It's a doctor's job to save people's lives.
彼は会社を破産から救おうと必死だ． He's desperately trying to save the company from bankruptcy.
あいつは救いようのない怠け者だ． That lazybones is beyond saving.

すくない (少ない)

【数】以前は大学に行く高校生は少なかった． Formerly, few high school students went on to college.
うちの学校は男子のほうが女子より10人少ない． There are 10 fewer boys than girls at our school.
ゴルフのスコアは少ないほどいい． The lower a golf score is, the better.
【量】試験の残り時間が少ない． There's only a little time left before the exam ends.
石油の埋蔵量は残り少ないと言われている． They say there aren't many petroleum deposits left.
彼の死は世界に少なからぬ影響を与えた． The effect of his death on the world was not small.
私はその事件には少なからず驚いた． I was more than a little surprised by the incident.

すくなくとも (少なくとも)

あそこまで歩いていくの？ 少なくとも1時間はかかるよ． Are we going to walk there? It'll take at least an hour.
その火事で少なくとも三人が死亡した模様だ． It seems at least three people died in the fire.
少なくとも，彼があげた成果に関しては評価するべきだ． We should at least recognize the contributions he made.
少なくとも，この程度の常識はわきまえてくれよ． I expect at least this much good sense. You should know at least this much.
私は彼女のことを理解しているつもりだ，少なくとも君よりはね． I think I understand her—at least better than you do.

すぐれる (優れる)

彼は非常に優れた数学の才能の持ち主だ.	He's exceptionally gifted at mathematics.
桂離宮は日本の最も優れた建築物の一つだ.	The Katsura Detached Palace is one of the finest architectural works in Japan.
彼は優れた成績で大学を卒業した.	He graduated from college with high marks.

すごい

「新しいベンツを買ったよ」「すごい！」	"I bought a new Mercedes." "Wow!"
あいつはすごいやつだ.	He is an amazing guy.
	He really is something.
彼はすごい選手だ.	He's really a great athlete.
彼女の歌の才能はすごい.	She has a terrific talent for singing.
彼の姉さんはすごい美人だ.	His sister is really beautiful.
1回で試験に通るとはすごいね.	Passing the test the first time is really something.
彼はすごい顔で私を睨みつけた.	He gave me a really nasty look.
犬がすごい勢いで追いかけて来た.	The dog chased after us at full speed.
それはすごい事故だった.	It was a terrible accident.
車がすごいスピードで走り去った.	The car took off at a terrific speed.
君の服はすごい汚れ方だ.	Your clothes are really filthy.
ここはすごいにおいがするな.	It smells awful in here.

すこし (少し)

オレンジを少し買った.	I bought †a few [some] oranges.
彼女は少しずつ家具を揃えていった.	Bit by bit, she got all the furniture she needed.
この薬は少しずつ飲んでください.	Take this medicine a little at a time.
少しはジュースを残しておいてくれよ.	Leave some juice for me.
少しなら泳げます.	I can swim a little.
父の容体は少しずつ良くなってきている.	My father is getting better little by little.
	My father is recovering gradually.
もう少し待ってみよう.	Let's wait a while longer.
もう少しで死ぬところだった.	I almost died.
もう少し行くと十字路がある.	There's an intersection just (up) ahead.
船はほんの少し傾いた.	The boat leaned to one side a bit.

すこしも (少しも)

この本は少しも面白くない.	This book isn't interesting at all.
彼は少しも私の話を聞いていない.	He isn't listening to a thing I say.

あの子は少しもおとなしくしていない.	That child refuses to behave himself.
彼女はよく食べるのに,少しも太らない.	Even though she eats a lot, she doesn't gain any weight at all.
私の英語は少しも上達しない.	My English isn't improving at all.
今日は少しも疲れていない.	I'm not at all tired today.
いついらっしゃっても少しもかまいません.	(Feel free to) Come whenever you like.
彼女は少しも気取ったところがない.	She isn't at all pretentious. She doesn't put on airs at all.
彼女の英語は先生と比べても少しも劣らない.	Her English is in every way as good as the teacher's.

すごす (過ごす)

この休日は何をして過ごしましたか.	How did you spend your time off?
昨日はパーティーで楽しいひとときを過ごした.	I had a pleasant time at the party yesterday.

すじ (筋)

このチョウの羽には黄色い筋が入っている.	This butterfly has yellow stripes on its wings.
足の筋を違えた.	I pulled a tendon in my leg.
父は青筋を立てて怒った.	My father was so mad he turned purple with rage.
首筋がひどく痛む.	My neck is really stiff.
この小説の筋は込み入っている.	The plot of this novel is really involved.
君の言うことは筋が通っていないよ.	What you're saying doesn't make sense.
私に怒るなんて筋違いだ.	There's no reason to get mad at me.
外交に興味があればその筋の人を紹介するよ.	If you're interested in diplomacy I'll introduce you to someone in the field.
これは確かな筋からの情報です.	This information comes from reliable sources.
彼女は踊りの筋がいい.	She has a natural flair for dancing.

すずしい (涼しい)

今日は涼しい.	It's cool today.
夜間は涼しくなってきた.	The nights have gotten cooler.
彼は上役に怒られても涼しい顔をしている.	He looks indifferent even when his boss gets angry with him.

すすむ（進む）

【前進】この道に沿って進んで行くと川があります。
If you follow along this road, you'll come to a river.

進めの号令がかかった。
The order was given to advance.

もう少し前へ進んでください。
Please move forward a little.

私の学校のチームは決勝まで進んだ。
My school's team advanced to the finals.

あの教授の授業は1日に随分進む。
That professor covers a lot in his classes in one day.

執筆中の本はまあ順調に進んでいる。
The new book I'm writing is coming along fairly well.

君は大学へ進むつもりですか。
Do you plan to go on to college?

将来は建築関係に進みたいと思っている。
I'm thinking about going into architecture in the future.

【進歩】彼女の結婚に対する考えは進んでいる。
Her ideas on marriage are very progressive.

日本製のカメラの機能は、世界で最も進んでいる。
Japanese cameras are the most technically advanced in the world.

【乗り気】今度の旅行は気が進まない。
I can't get worked up about this next trip.

君は自ら進んでその宗教の信者になったのですか。
Did you decide †on your own [by yourself] to join that religion?

夏は暑くて食が進まない。
It's too hot in summer to feel like eating much.

【悪化】患者の病状はどんどん進んでいる。
The patient's condition is steadily getting worse.

彼のがんがそれ以上進まないように祈っている。
I'm praying that his cancer doesn't get any worse than that.

すすめる¹（進める）

彼は計画を予定どおりに進めた。
He proceeded to carry out the plan as scheduled.

チェッカーの駒を一つ進めた。
I moved my checker piece one square.

母はいつも時計を10分進めておく。
My mother always keeps her watch set ten minutes fast.

すすめる²（勧・薦める）

両親は彼に大学に行くように勧めた。
His parents advised him to go to college.

彼女の家でお茶を勧められた。
I was offered tea at her house.

食前酒には何を薦めますか。
What do you recommend for an aperitif?

店員がこれを薦めてくれたんだ。
The store clerk recommended this.

医者の勧めで禁酒している。
I've stopped drinking on my doctor's

〜ずつ

リンゴをお一人1個〔半分〕ずつおあがりください.	Please help yourselves to †an 〔half an〕 apple each [apiece[1)]].
一人〔三人〕ずつ保健室に入ってください.	Please come into the nurse's office one 〔three〕 at a time.
6人ずつが一組になって理科の実験をした.	We conducted the science experiment in groups of six.
この時計は毎日2分ずつ遅れる.	This clock loses two minutes every day.
毎月5,000円ずつ貯金している.	I put away 5,000 yen in savings every month.
少しずつ日が長くなっている.	The days are gradually getting longer. The days are getting longer little by little.

> 1) この場合の apiece は「各人に」の意味.

すっかり

手紙を投かんするのをすっかり忘れてしまった.	I completely forgot to mail the letter.
辺りはすっかり暗くなった.	It became completely dark.
母もすっかり年をとった.	My mother has really gotten old.
私はすっかり疲れてしまった.	I'm dead tired.
この仕事がすっかり嫌になった.	I've come to thoroughly hate this work.
泥棒は彼女の宝石をすっかり持ち去った.	The burglar made off with all her jewels.

すっきり

ひと眠りしたら気分がすっきりした.	After taking a nap I felt much better.
今日は気分がすっきりしない.	I don't feel too [very] well today.
起きたばかりで頭がすっきりしない.	I just got up so my head isn't clear.
私は凝ったデザインよりすっきりしたもののほうが好きだ.	I prefer a simple design to a fancy one.
デンマークの現代家具はすっきりとして美しい.	Danish modern furniture is simple and beautiful.

ずっと

【続けて】この道をずっと行くと国境がある.	If you keep following this road, you'll get to the border.
少女は1時間ずっとしゃべっていた.	The little girl kept talking for a whole hour.

雪が昨夜からずっと降っている.	It's been snowing ever since last night.
昨日はずっと家にいましたよ.	I was (at) home all day yesterday.
二人はその後ずっと幸せに暮らした.	And they lived happily ever after.
【はるかに】ずっと向こうのほうに海が見える.	Way over there you can see the sea.
兄は私よりずっと背が高い.	My older brother is much taller than I am.
ずっと前にその人に会ったことがある.	I met him once a long time ago.

すっぱい (酸っぱい)

このピクルスは酸っぱくて食べられない.	These pickles are too sour to eat.
牛乳が酸っぱくなってしまった.	The milk has gone sour.

すてき (素敵)

素敵な帽子ですね.	That's a nice hat.
彼女はいつも素敵な服を着ている.	She always wears nice clothes.
何て素敵な公園なんでしょう.	What a lovely park!

すでに (既に)

彼がフランスに渡ってから既に3年がたった.	Three years have passed already since he left for France.
朝家を出て昼には既に京都に着いていた.	I left the house in the morning and was already in Kyoto by noon.
既に言ったように私は今月末で会社を辞めます.	As I have already stated, I will leave the company at the end of this month.

すてる (捨てる)

車の窓からごみを捨てるな.	Don't throw trash out the car window.
すり切れて着られなくなったので, 彼は上着を捨てた.	When the jacket became too threadbare for him to wear, he threw it away.
彼は私欲を捨てて世の中のために働いた.	Casting [Putting] aside self-interest, he worked for the good of mankind.
彼は故郷を捨てた.	He abandoned his hometown.
彼は妻子を捨ててブラジルへ行ってしまった.	He abandoned his wife and children and went to Brazil.

ストレス

現代社会はストレスが多い.	There is a great deal of stress in society today.
職場の人間関係にストレスを感じる.	I find human relations in my workplace stressful.

最近, ストレスがたまっているみたいだね.	You seem to be stressed out lately.
彼を部下にしてからストレスがたまる一方だ.	My stress level has only gone up since making him junior partner.
ストレス解消には, 気の合った仲間と飲みに行くのが一番だ.	The best way to relieve stress is to go drinking with people you get along with.

すなお (素直)

息子には素直な人間に育ってほしい.	I want my son to grow up to be good-natured.
人の言うことは素直に聞くべきだ.	You should be open [receptive] to what people say.
彼は結婚生活の破綻の原因は自分にあると素直に認めた.	He readily admitted [acknowledged] that he was at fault in the marriage breakup.
彼の文章は素直で読み易い.	His style is natural and easy to read.

すばらしい (素晴らしい)

今日は素晴らしい天気ですね.	Great[1] weather today, isn't it?
彼はマラソンで素晴らしい記録を作った.	He set a fantastic[2] record in the marathon.
山頂からの景色は素晴らしかった.	The view from the mountain top was wonderful.[3]
あのギタリストの指の動きは素晴らしく速い.	It's fantastic how quickly that guitarist moves his fingers.

[1)2)3)] great, fantastic, wonderful は同じように使うことができる.

すべて

二人の意見はすべての点で一致している.	Their opinions coincide on every point.
すべての人間は生きる権利を持っている.	All people have [Every man, woman and child has] the right to live.
彼にとっては仕事がすべてだ.	His work is everything to him.
この像はすべて銀で出来ている.	This statue is a hundred percent silver.
その件についてはすべて私に責任があります.	I have complete responsibility concerning that business [issue].

すべる (滑る)

雪道では車がよく滑る.	Cars often slide on snowy roads.
床がつるつる滑って危ないよ.	The floor is slippery, so watch out.
ゲレンデをスキーで滑り下りた.	I skied down the slope.
舟は水面を滑るように進んだ.	The boat glided over the water.

つい手が滑って花瓶を落としてしまった.	Somehow my hand slipped and I dropped the vase.
彼はまた大学をすべった.	He flunked the college entrance exam again.

すます (済ます)
【終える】食事は済まして来ました.	I've already eaten.
月賦の支払いをまだ済ましていない.	I haven't finished paying off all the installments.
時間がないので電話で用事を済ませた.	I didn't have time, so I took care of the business over the phone.
【間に合わす】朝食はパンがないので, ミルクだけで済まそう.	We don't have any bread for breakfast, so let's make do with just milk.
万年筆がなかったので取りあえず鉛筆で済ました.	Since I didn't have a pen, I made do with a pencil.

すみ (隅)
犬が部屋の隅で寝ている.	The dog is sleeping in the corner of the room.
「彼に悪いかな」と彼女は心の隅でちらっと思った.	For a brief moment, she wondered if she was †doing right by him [being entirely fair to him].
この町は隅から隅まで知っている.	I know every inch of this city.
この本は隅から隅まで読んだ.	I read every single word of this book.
おまえもなかなか隅に置けないやつだな.	There's more to you than meets the eye.

すみません
すみません.	I'm sorry./Excuse me.
仕事の邪魔をしてすみませんでした.	I'm sorry to have interrupted your work.
すみませんが塩を取ってください.	Please pass the salt.
すみませんがドアを開けてくださいますか.	Would you please open the door?
すみませんが最寄りの駅はどこですか.	Excuse me but could you please tell me where the closest station is?

すむ[1] (住・棲む)
若者は都会に住みたがるものだ.	Young people tend to want to live in the city.
住み慣れた町を出るのは辛い.	It's hard to leave the city you're used to living in.
この島にはだれも住んでいません.	No one's living on this island.

住めば都だ.	This place has grown on me.
	Once you live in a place, it grows on you.
この公園には鳥がたくさんすんでいる.	There are lots of birds living in this park.
この川は汚れがひどくて魚がすめなくなった.	This river is so polluted that there aren't any fish.

すむ² (済む)

【終わる】試験が済んだら映画を見ます.	I'm going to see a movie after the exam.
車の修理はまだ済まない.	The car isn't finished being repaired yet.
結婚式が無事に済んでみんなほっとした.	After the wedding was over everyone could finally relax.
済んだ事をくよくよするな.	Don't cry over spilled [spilt] milk.
【申し訳が立つ】人をだましてそれで済むと思うな.	Don't think you can get away with cheating me.
このままで済むと思ったら大間違いだ.	If you think this is the end of it, you're making a big mistake.
それはお金では済まない問題だ.	That's a problem that can't be solved with money.
【間に合う】ハワイは日本人が多いので英語を話さないで済む.	There are so many Japanese in Hawaii that you don't need to speak English.
今日は暖かいので暖房はつけないで済むだろう.	It's warm today, so we can probably do without turning on the heat.
もう少し早く帰れば雨に会わずに済んだのに.	If we had returned just a little earlier, we wouldn't have been caught in the rain.

すらすら

彼女はフランス語がすらすら話せる.	She can speak French fluently.
彼は数学の難問をすらすら解いてしまう.	He can solve difficult mathematical problems †easily [with ease].
私は先生の質問にすらすら答えてみせた.	I answered my teacher's question(s) †easily [with ease].
この万年筆はすらすら書ける.	This fountain pen writes smoothly.

する¹ (擦る・摺る・刷る・掏る)

【擦る】少女はマッチを1本擦った.	The little girl struck a match.
傷口にこの薬を擦り込んでください.	Rub this ointment on the wound.
階段で転び, ひざを擦りむいてしまった.	I fell down the stairs and scraped my knee.
犬が甘えて, 私の足に鼻を擦り寄	The dog rubbed his nose against my leg

せてきた.	trying to play for attention.
彼はもらったばかりの給料を競馬で全部擦ってしまった.	No sooner had he gotten paid than he blew it all at the race track.
【摺る】チーズをすりおろしてスパゲティにかけた.	I grated cheese and sprinkled it on the spaghetti.
彼はすぐ上役にごまをする.	He's always playing up to his superiors.
【刷る】その本は明日刷り上がります.	The printing of that book will be finished tomorrow.
表紙の文字は青で刷ってもらおう.	Let's have the letters on the cover printed in blue.
この名刺を今日中に100枚刷ってください.	Please print a hundred of these business cards by today.
【掏る】デパートで財布をすられた.	Someone pickpocketed my wallet at the department store.
	I had my wallet pickpocketed at the department store.

する² (為る)

【行う】今日はすることがない.	I don't have anything to do today.
そうするよりほかに方法がなかった.	There was no other way but to do that.
父は昔,本屋をしていたそうだ.	I understand that a long time ago my father used to have [run] a bookstore.
その金をどうするつもりだ.	What do you intend to do with that money?
夜は早く寝ることにしている.	I make it a point to go to bed early.
【～にする】子どもが生まれたら医者にしたい.	If we have a child I hope he or she becomes a doctor.
原油をガソリンにするのは手間がかかる.	It takes time and labor to make gasoline from crude oil.
彼は座ぶとんを枕にして昼寝をしている.	He's taking a nap using a cushion for a pillow.
【経過する】10分もすれば夫は帰ります.	My husband will be back in ten minutes.
もう1週間もすると寒くなってきますよ.	It's going to get cold in a week.
この木は2年もすれば実がなるだろう.	This tree will probably bear fruit in two years.
【～しようとする】彼は魚を捕まえようとして川に飛び込んだ.	He jumped into the river trying to catch a fish.
【値する】その傘はいくらしたの.	How much was that umbrella?
あの店のコーヒーは1杯千円もする.	A cup of coffee costs 1,000 yen at that place.

【〜としたら】もう一度生まれ変われるとしたら，男と女のどちらがいいですか． — Supposing you could be born again, which would you rather be, a man or a woman?

駅まで歩いて行くとすれば，何分くらいかかりますか． — If I were to walk to the station, about how many minutes would it take?

ずるい

宿題を親にやってもらうなんてずるいぞ． — It's not fair to have your parents do your homework.

彼はずるい手を使ってポーカーで勝った． — He won †at poker [the poker game] by cheating.

彼はずるいやつだから信用しないほうがいい． — He's sneaky, so you'd better not trust him.

彼はずる賢い． — He's cunning [devious].

え？ 会社を休んで海外旅行に行ったんだって？ ずるーい． — What? He took off work and made a trip abroad? Lucky him.

すると

私は箱を開けた．すると中に1匹のかわいい猫がいた． — I opened the box and inside was a cute little kitten.

私は寝ようとした．すると電話がかかってきた． — I was about to go to bed when the telephone rang.

容疑者は全員白だ．すると犯人はだれだ？ — All the suspects are innocent. Who then is †guilty [the guilty one]?

「するとどうなった？」とみんなは一斉に私に聞いた． — "And then what happened?" they all asked me at the same time.

するどい（鋭い）

【尖っている】死体には鋭い刃物で刺された跡があった． — The corpse had stab wounds from a sharp object.

矢の先は鋭く尖っている． — The end of the arrow is sharply pointed.

【激しい・厳しい】突然鋭い痛みが背中を走った． — A sharp pain suddenly shot through my back.

二人の意見は鋭く対立している． — Their opinions are in sharp conflict with each other.

刑事の目は鋭く光った． — The police detective's eye glinted sharply.

彼の説に鋭い批判が集まった． — His theory drew sharp criticism.

彼は教授に鋭い質問をした． — He asked the professor a pointed question.

【優れている】彼は鋭い男だ． — He's sharp.

犬は嗅覚が鋭い． — Dogs have †a keen [an acute] sense of smell.

彼は小説家だけあって，人間を観察する力が鋭い． — As may be expected from a novelist, he has the ability to make acute observations

すれちがう（擦れ違う）

今擦れ違った人は映画俳優じゃない？	Isn't that guy we just passed a movie star?
この道は狭くて車が擦れ違うことができない．	This road is so narrow that cars coming in opposite directions can't pass.
その話し合いでは双方の意見が擦れ違った．	The opinions of the two sides in that discussion were on two different planes.

ずれる

その机だけちょっと左にずれています．	Only that desk is a little out of line to the left.
この雑誌のカラー写真は印刷がずれている．	The registration of the color photographs in this magazine is out of alignment.
彼女のその絵に対する印象は僕とは随分ずれていた．	Her impression of the painting was quite different from mine.

すわる（座る・据わる）

【腰かける】いすに座りなさい．	Sit on a chair.
彼は足を組んで座っていた．	He sat with his legs crossed.
きちんと座りなさい．	Sit straight.
彼女は机に向かって座っている．	She's sitting at her desk.
私は彼と向かい合って座った．	I sat down across from him.
【動かない】社長に面と向かって文句を言うとは，君も度胸の据わった男だね．	You sure have nerve, complaining directly to the president in person.

せ

(〜の)せい

【理由】彼が集合に遅れたせいで計画が狂った．	The schedule was derailed because he was late for the meeting.
ストレスのせいで胃かいようになった．	I got a stomach ulcer from the stress.
「この頃，胃がひどく痛むんだ」「きっとストレスのせいだよ」	"I've been getting terrible stomachaches lately." "It might be stress.[1]"
年のせいか，耳が聞こえにくくな	I'm not sure if it's age[2] but I'm not hear-

った.	ing well lately.
高層マンションの上のほうに住んでいるせいか, 外出するのがおっくうだ.	Maybe it's because I live at the top of a high-rise apartment building but it's a chore for me to go out.
風邪の引きかけのせいか, 食欲がない.	I don't have much appetite. Maybe I'm †coming down with [catching] a cold.
【責任】こうなったのは君のせいじゃない.	It's not your fault that it turned out this way.
	This is not your fault.
自分のミスを人のせいにするのは良くないよ.	It's not good to blame others for your own mistakes.
	No one should blame others for his mistakes.

1)2) it's... だけで原因・理由を表す.

せいい (誠意)

彼の誠意を疑う.	I doubt his sincerity.
誠意のある人だったらそんなことをしない.	A sincere person would not do such a thing.
彼は誠意を尽くして事態の改善に努めた.	He made a genuine effort to improve the situation.
彼女の態度には誠意が見られない.	There's no sincerity evident in her attitude.
あなたは当事者として, もっと誠意を示してほしい.	I'd like you to be more serious, seeing as you're the †person involved [party concerned].

せいいっぱい (精一杯)

精一杯頑張ったのですが, できませんでした.	I tried my best, but I couldn't do it.
これが私のできる精一杯のことです.	This is the best I can do.
生きるのに精一杯です.	It is all I can do to eke out a living.

せいかく¹ (正確)

この時計は正確です.	This clock is correct.
	This watch keeps correct time.
正確な時刻を教えてください.	Please give [tell] me the exact time.
人の名前は正確に書きなさい.	Please make sure that everyone's name is spelled correctly.
彼は正確に英語を発音する.	He pronounces English properly [accurately].

日本の鉄道は時間に正確なことで有名だ.	Japanese trains are famous for running on time.
私の質問に正確に答えてください.	Please answer my questions accurately.
念には念を入れて，正確に計算した.	I †was extremely careful [took time] to calculate it correctly.

せいかく² (性格)

【人の】彼は明るい性格だ.	He has a cheerful disposition [personality].
あの兄弟は性格が正反対だ.	Those brothers' personalities are diametrically opposed.
	Those brothers have exactly opposite personalities.
彼とは性格が合わない.	He and I don't get along.
	He and I have very different personalities.
私には性格的にとてもそんなことはできない.	I'm just not the kind of person to do such a thing.
【物事の】この問題はこれまでのものとはちょっと性格が違う.	This problem is of a slightly different nature from the ones we've seen up until now.
このキャンペーンは性格があいまいだ.	This campaign is not clearly focused.

せいかつ (生活)

私はアメリカで3年間生活したことがあります.	I (once) lived in the United States for three years.
彼女は裕福な家に生まれ，恵まれた生活を送っている.	She leads a good life, having been born into an affluent family.
彼は学生時代の気楽な生活をまた送りたいと思った.	He wished that he could lead the carefree life of a student again.
年々物価が上昇し，生活が苦しくなる一方だ.	Prices rise, and life gets harder and harder every year.
私の安い給料ではとても生活していくことができない.	I can't get by on such a meager salary.
彼には生活能力がない.	He can't make a living on his own.
あの一家は貧しい生活をしている.	That family leads a poor existence.
	His family is †poor [not well off].

せいきゅう (請求)

彼は何度請求しても借金を払ってくれない.	He won't pay back what he owes me no matter how many times I ask.
酒屋がたまった支払いの請求をしてきた.	The liquor store demanded payment for the bill I had †accumulated [run up].
新聞屋に新聞代を請求された.	I was billed for my newspaper subscrip-

それに関しての詳しい案内書は葉書でご請求ください.	Please send in a postcard for a detailed guide on the subject.
大家さんに借家の明け渡しを請求された.	The landlord demanded that we vacate his house.
この買い物の請求書は父にまわしてください.	Please send the bill (for this purchase) to my father.

せいけつ (清潔)

台所は常に清潔にしておかなければならない.	The kitchen should always be sanitary.
山をトレッキングするあいだ体を清潔に保つのは難しい.	It's hard to keep yourself clean when you go trekking in the mountains.
彼女はつつましいけれど常に清潔な身なりをしている.	Her appearance is plain and simple but always neat and clean.
清潔な政治家は少ないと言われている.	They say there are few honest [clean] politicians.
社会的立場があるので, 彼は身辺をいつも清潔にしている.	He has a social position to think about, so he always keeps a clean image.

せいげん (制限)

父は血圧が高いので, 医者から塩分を制限されている.	My father has high blood pressure, so the doctor limited his intake of salt.
この道路の制限速度は40キロです.	The speed limit on this road is 40 kilometers per hour.
この試験の制限時間は50分です.	The time limit for this test is 50 minutes.
健康に悪いから, たばこをもっと制限しなさい.	Smoking is bad for your health. You should try to cut down on it.

せいこう (成功)

リンドバーグは1927年, 初の単身大西洋横断無着陸飛行に成功した.	In 1927, Lindbergh made the first successful nonstop solo flight across the Atlantic.
彼は政治家としては失敗したが, 実業家として成功した.	He was a failure as a politician, but a success as a businessman.
こんな状態では成功はおぼつかない.	Under these circumstances I have little hope of succeeding.
成功を祈ります.	Good luck.
	I wish you success.
失敗は成功のもと.	You learn from your mistakes.

せいさく¹ (政策)

政府は不況を乗り越えるための有	The government formed an effective policy

効な政策を打ち出した.	to get through the †recession [slump in the economy].
あの国の外交政策はしょっちゅう変更される.	That country's foreign policy is always changing.
W党は党大会で今後1年間の基本政策を発表した.	The W Party announced its platform for the coming year at its convention.

せいさく² (製作・制作)

【製作】あの会社は精密機械の製作にかけては日本一だ.	That firm is the leading manufacturer of precision machinery in Japan.
私の会社では自動車のエンジンを製作している.	My company makes [produces, manufactures] automobile engines.
【制作】あの彫刻家は新しい作品の制作に打ち込んでいる.	That sculptor is †caught up [immersed, involved] in creating his new work.
映画を制作するためには多くの人々の力が必要とされる.	The efforts of many people are required to make a film.

せいさん¹ (生産)

航空機を生産するためには高度な技術力が必要とされる.	Aircraft production requires a high level of technology.
あの国が世界でいちばん多く石油を生産している.	That country is the world's leading producer of oil [petroleum].
商品は大量生産されるほどコストが下がる.	Costs decline as the degree of mass production increases.
農産物の生産高は天候に左右されることが多い.	Agricultural output is frequently affected by the weather.

せいさん² (清算)

自宅を売って借金を清算した.	I paid off my debt by selling my house.
過去は清算して新天地で出直すことにした.	I decided to forget the past and make a fresh start somewhere else.
5年に及ぶ不倫関係を清算した.	I broke off an extramarital affair after five years.
本日の取締役会で子会社を清算することを決定した.	We decided to liquidate our subsidiary at today's directors' meeting.

せいさん³ (精算)

領収書を精算しなければならない.	I have to submit my receipts to get paid.
仮払いを早く精算してください.	Please calculate your expenses against your advance right away.
とりあえず僕が払っておくよ. あとで精算しよう.	I'll pay for †it [the bill] now and we can figure it out later. I'll pay for this and you can pay me later.

地下鉄の改札口で乗り越し運賃を精算した. I paid the difference on my subway fare at the ticket gate.

せいじ (政治)
国民はだれでも政治に透明性を求めている. Everyone in the country wants transparency from their government.

最近は政治に無関心な人が多くなってきた. Recently more and more people have become indifferent toward politics.

彼は立派な〔偉大な〕政治家です. He's a †fine politician 〔great statesman〕.

彼は大学で政治学を専攻しています. He's majoring in political science in college.

せいしき (正式)
就職が内定したが，正式な通知はまだ来ない. My job has been informally arranged, but a formal notification hasn't come yet.

私のピアノは独学で，正式に習ったものではない. I taught myself to play the piano. I never had any formal lessons.

学校で西洋料理の正式な食べ方を習った. We were taught Western table manners at school.

彼らはまだ正式に結婚していない. They're not officially [legally] married yet.

せいしつ (性質)
【人の】彼はおとなしい性質だ. He has a quiet nature [disposition].

あの双子は性質がまるで違う. Those twins' characters are altogether different.

生まれつきの性質はなかなか変えられないものだ. Innate [Inborn] traits aren't easily changed.

【物・事物の】羊毛と綿は同じ繊維でも性質が違う. Wool and cotton may both be fibers, but they have different qualities.

教育は短期間で成果が上がる性質のものではない. The role of education is not to bring about immediate results.

せいじつ (誠実)
あの人は誠実な人だ. He is sincere and honest.

彼は長年誠実に働いた. He worked faithfully for many years.

彼は誠実さに欠けるので人から信用されない. He is not trusted by others because he lacks integrity.

せいじょう (正常)
彼の挙動は正常とは言い難い. It would be difficult to call his behavior normal.

正常な神経の持ち主だったら，だれでもそう思うさ. Anyone in their right mind would think so.

	Anyone in full possession of their senses [faculties] would think so.
事故のため乱れていた列車のダイヤが正常に戻った.	The train schedule which had been thrown off by the accident returned to normal.

せいしん (精神)

教育の主な目的は精神と肉体の調和である.	The main purpose of education is to harmonize mind and body.
彼女への私の愛情は精神的なものだ.	My love for her is platonic [spiritual].
彼は妻の死で精神的に参ってしまった.	His wife's death †upset him psychologically [dealt him a psychological blow].
彼は肉体的には大人だが,精神的にはまだ子どもだ.	Physically he's an adult, but mentally he's still a child.
精神の病気はだれでもかかりうる.	Anyone could become mentally ill.
こんな環境に長く暮らすのは精神衛生上悪い.	Living for a long time in an environment like this is detrimental to one's mental health [well-being].
我々は憲法の精神を尊重すべきである.	We should respect the spirit of the Constitution.

せいぜい

彼が借りられるのはせいぜい100ドルまでだ.	He might be able to borrow a 100 dollars at most.
どんなに頑張ってもせいぜい入賞がいいところだ.	No matter how hard he tries, he'll be lucky if he gets an award.
まあ,せいぜいやってください.	Well, do the best you can.

せいせいどうどう (正々堂々)

我々は正々堂々と闘うことを誓います.	We pledge [swear] to compete with pride and in a spirit of fair play.
彼は正々堂々と意見を主張した.	He boldly asserted his opinion.
私は常に正々堂々と振る舞っているつもりだ.	I always try to be open and aboveboard.

せいせき (成績)

【学校の】英語の成績が良くない.	My English grades aren't good.
二学期は英語の成績が上がった.	My English grade went up in the second term.
もう少し成績が上がるよう頑張りなさい.	Work a little harder on your grades.
成績を下げないで野球を続けるのは難しい.	It's hard to continue baseball without letting my grades drop.

彼は一生懸命勉強して優秀な成績を収めた.	He studied as hard as he could and got superior grades.
彼は立派な成績で学校を卒業した.	He graduated with †fine grades [a fine record].
上位50人の試験の成績が貼り出された.	Test scores for the top 50 were posted.
アメリカにも学校の成績表はありますか.	Do you have report cards in the U.S., too?
【仕事・商売の】大変な努力の末,我が社は所期の成績を上げることができた.	With great effort our company succeeded in reaching its expected goal.
今年のこのデパートの売り上げ成績は非常に良かった.	This department store had a very good sales record this year.

せいぞう (製造)

あの工場ではオートバイを製造している.	That factory manufactures motorcycles.
この機械はスウェーデンで製造されたものです.	This machine was manufactured in Sweden.
この製品の製造過程は企業秘密である.	The manufacturing process for this product is a company secret.

せいだい (盛大)

彼の成功を祝って,盛大なパーティーが開かれた.	They held a grand party to celebrate his success.
彼は盛大に事業をやっている.	He is doing a prosperous business.
今夜は盛大にやろう.	Let's really enjoy ourselves tonight. Let's go all out tonight!

ぜいたく

随分ぜいたくな趣味をお持ちですね.	You certainly have extravagant tastes.
彼女はぜいたくな暮らしをしている.	She's living †in luxury [extravagantly].
日本人は資源がないのに,石油をぜいたくに使っている.	Even though the Japanese have few natural resources, they use oil extravagantly.
このダイヤの指輪は私にはぜいたくすぎる.	This diamond ring is too extravagant for me.
ぜいたくを言わないでこれで我慢しておけ.	Don't ask for too much. Be satisfied with this.
彼女は高価な香水をぜいたくに使っている.	She uses expensive perfume lavishly.

せいちょう (成長)

その夫婦は子どもの成長を楽しみにしている.
That couple enjoys watching their child grow up.

彼は成長するにつれてとても活発になってきた.
He's becoming very active as he grows up.

その商社はこの10年間に大きく成長した.
That trading company has grown a great deal in the last 10 years.

彼は今度の事件をきっかけにして大きく成長した.
Spurred on by this event, he grew greatly in personal stature.

せいとん (整とん)

彼女の部屋はいつもきちんと整とんされている.
Her room is always neat and organized.

机の上をきれいに整とんした.
I put everything on the desk in order.

彼女はスーツケースの中身を整とんした.
She neatly arranged the contents of the suitcase.

彼は常に身の回りの整とんを心がけている.
He always tries to keep the things in order.

せいのう (性能)

あの車は性能が良い〔良くない〕.
That car has good [poor] performance.

性能で選ぶならこれ, デザインで選ぶならあの機種だ.
If you're after performance this is it. But if it's design you're after, that's the model for you.

この電話機は性能の高さとデザインの美しさを兼ね備えている.
This telephone combines high quality and fine design.

このカメラは高性能, 高画質を誇っている.
This camera boasts high technical and picture quality.

せいめい (生命)

あの政治家はテロにより生命を奪われた.
That politician's life was taken by terrorists.

パイロットは乗客の生命を預かる厳しい職務である.
A pilot has the weighty responsibility of being entrusted with the lives of passengers.

彼は汚職事件で政治生命を失った.
The corruption scandal put an end to his life in politics.

色の美しさがこの焼物の生命だ.
This beautiful color is what gives this pottery life.

子どもが私の生命です.
My children are everything to me.

せいり (整理)

今日は一日かかって部屋を整理し
I spent the whole day putting the room in

彼のレポートはよく整理されている.	His report is well organized.
この件については問題点をよく整理してから話し合いましょう.	Let's lay out the problems to be dealt with in this matter and then have a discussion.
この辺りでは，区画整理が行われている.	This area is being rezoned.
彼女は古くなった服を整理した.	She went through her old clothes (and got rid of the ones she didn't need).
組合は会社の人員整理に反対した.	The union opposed a personnel reduction in the company.

せいりょく (勢力)

最近あの若手の政治家は政界に勢力を伸ばしてきた.	Recently that young politician has extended his power in governmental circles.
彼は財界に大きな勢力を振るっている.	He wields great power in the business world.
彼は会社でいちばん勢力がある.	He's the most powerful man in the company.
彼は学内の勢力争いに敗れた.	He lost in the power struggle at his school.
台風の勢力は依然衰えていない.	The strength of the typhoon remains undiminished.
明朝には台風の勢力は衰えているでしょう.	The typhoon should have run its course[1] by tomorrow morning.

> 1) この course は地理的な「順路」ではなく，「(発生してから消滅するまでの) 経過, プロセス」という意味. have run its course で「たどるべき経過をたどり終えた→収束した」の意味.

せかい (世界)

世界でいちばん人口の多い国は中国だ.	China is the most populous country in the world.
世界平和は人類の願いである.	All humanity longs for world peace.
彼は世界一周の旅に出発した.	He left on a trip around the world.
彼は世界的に有名な科学者だ.	He's a world-famous scientist.
【領域・分野】彼は自分の世界に引きこもりがちだ.	He tends to withdraw into his own world.
子どもの世界には子ども独自の論理がある.	Children live in their own world and exercise their own unique logic.
学問の世界は厳しいものだ.	The academic world is very rigorous.

せき (席)

空いている席に座ってください.	Please sit in an empty seat.
早く席に着いてください.	Please †take [go to] your seats quickly.
先に行って, いい席を取っておいてください.	Please go ahead and save good seats for us.
電車やバスの中ではお年寄りに席を譲りなさい.	Give your seat to old people when riding in a train or bus.
彼は今, 席を外しています.	(I'm afraid) He's away from his desk at the moment.
窓側の席に移りたいのですが.	I'd like to move to a place [table] by a window.[1]
	I'd like to move to a window seat.[2]
今日はもう満席ですので入場をお断りします.	All seats are filled today and no one else will be admitted.
新幹線の指定席が取れた.	I got a reserved seat on the Shinkansen.
【慣用】彼は憤然と席をけって議場を出て行った.	He stormed out of the conference chamber in indignation.
彼は忙しくて席の暖まる暇もない.	He's so busy he hardly has a minute to sit down.

1) レストランなどの席の場合. 2) 乗り物の席の場合.

せきにん (責任)

彼はこの会の運営に責任がある.	He is responsible for the management of the club.
なぜ君は責任をとらなかったのかね.	Why didn't you take responsibility?
野党は今度の事件における政府の責任を追及した.	The opposition party attacked the government for its responsibility in the matter.
年とった親の面倒を見るのは子どもの責任だと思う?	Do you think it is the responsibility of children to support their parents in their old age?
	Do you think children should take care of their parents in their old age?
責任の所在を明らかにしてほしい.	I'd like to have it made clear just where the responsibility lies.
最近は女性も実社会で責任ある地位に就けるようになった.	Recently it has become possible for women to find positions of responsibility in the real world.
今度の任務は責任は重いが, やりがいがある.	My new work entails heavy responsibilities but it is worthwhile.
あの人は責任感が強い.	He has a strong sense of responsibility.
責任者に会わせてください.	Let me see the person in charge.

せけん (世間)

こんな所であなたと会うなんて, 世間は狭いものですね.	It's a small world, meeting you here of all places.
彼は世間を驚かせるようなことばかりする.	He is always doing something that surprises people.
そんなことをすると世間がうるさいからやめてくれ.	Please don't do that. It will make everyone talk about us.
世間を騒がせた放火魔が捕まった.	The arsonist who had been causing panic everywhere was captured.
息子が不始末をしでかしたので, 世間に顔向けができない.	Because of my son's misconduct, I can't show my face anywhere anymore.
彼は世間知らずだ.	He's ignorant of the (real) world. He's naive.
彼女は世間知らずのお嬢さん育ちだ.	She was a sheltered daughter.
もうこうなったら世間体など構っていられない.	At this point I don't care what people think.
ぶらぶらしていると世間体が悪いから, 仕事を見つけて働きなさい.	It makes us look bad when you hang around like this. Why don't you go (and) look for a job?
彼は世間並の生活を送っている.	He leads a life no different from anyone else.
【慣用】渡る世間に鬼はない.	There's a little good in everyone you meet.

せっかく

彼がせっかく作ったのだから, 使ってみよう.	He took the trouble to make it, so let's use it. He really put himself out making it. We should use it.
せっかく行ったのに, その店は閉まっていた.	We went all the way to that store only to find it closed.
伯父さんがせっかくくれたペンを無くしてしまった.	I've lost the pen my uncle was so kind to give me.
今日はせっかくの休みだから映画でも見に行こう.	Today is one of my few days off. Let's go to the movies.
「今晩家でパーティーを開きますから, どうぞお出かけください」「せっかくですが遠慮させていただきます」	"We're having a party tonight. Please come." "Thank you for asking, but I'm afraid I can't."
せっかくのチャンスだから, 伯父のヨーロッパ旅行にお供することにした.	I have no idea when another opportunity like this will come up again, so I've decided to accompany my uncle on his trip to Europe.

せっかち
彼女はせっかちだから(私の)仕事が片づくまで待ってくれない. She's the impatient type, so I'm sure she won't wait for me to finish.
せっかちに結論を出してはだめだ. Don't draw any hasty conclusions.
あの人は全くせっかちな性格だ. What an impatient person he is!

せっきょく (積極)
彼女はボランティア活動に積極的である. She's active in volunteer work.
彼は私との契約に積極的だ. He seems quite interested in signing a contract with me.
政府はその件では積極策をとる予定だ. The government is going to adopt an aggressive policy on that.
もっと積極的に我々の活動に参加してください. Please participate more actively in our movement.
彼女は与えられた仕事はよくやるが積極性に乏しい. She does her assigned work well but she isn't very proactive [enthusiastic].

せつじつ (切実)
市長は市民の切実な訴えに答えた. The mayor responded to the citizens' fervent appeal.
水質汚染は日本の最も切実な問題の一つである. Water pollution is one of Japan's most urgent problems.
外国に行って英会話の必要性を切実に感じた. I really felt the need to speak English when I went overseas.

せつぞく (接続)
【つなぎ目】パイプの接続部分から水が漏れている. Water is leaking out of the joint in the pipe.
イヤホンが聞こえなくなった. 接続が悪いのかな. I can't hear anything through the earphones anymore. I wonder if the connection is faulty?

【交通機関の】電車の接続がよくて, 予定より早く着いた. I arrived earlier than expected because my train connections were good.
この急行は大阪で9時ちょうどの東京行き新幹線に接続します. This express connects in Osaka with the 9:00 o'clock bullet train to Tokyo.
【コンピュータ】インターネットに接続するにはモデムが必要だ. You need a modem to connect to the Internet.
今では安い料金で常時インターネットに接続できる. You can now be on line twenty-four hours a day at a low cost.

ぜったい (絶対)
絶対に口外しないと約束してくだ Promise me you'll never tell anyone.

さい.
「仲間に入れよ」「絶対に嫌だ」 "Come on and join us." "Forget it! [Not on your life!]"

絶対そう思います. I'm positive.

「あの人たちは結婚するかしら?」「絶対するよ」 "Do you think they'll get married?" "Absolutely!"

頼むから絶対に来てよね. Be sure to come, OK?
You've just got to come.

我が家では父の言うことは絶対だ. In our house, my father's word is law.

彼は独裁者の地位に就いて絶対的な権力を誇示した. Having assumed the position of dictator, he flaunted absolute power.

これはどうしても曲げられない絶対の真理だ. This is an absolute, incontrovertible truth.

せつに (切に)

彼は妻と両親がうまくいくようにと切に望んだ. He earnestly hoped that his wife would get along with his parents.

切にご自愛のほどお祈りいたします. I sincerely hope you'll take good care of yourself.

あの人が無事に帰れますようにと若い妻は切に願った. The young wife fervently prayed that her husband would return safely home.

せつび (設備)

この体育館にはいろいろな設備が整っている. This gymnasium is equipped with many facilities.

あのホテルは設備が悪くて不便だ. That hotel has poor facilities and the rooms are not comfortable.

この建物は防火の設備が不十分だ. Fire-prevention facilities in this building are inadequate.

不景気で設備投資を控える会社が多い. Because of the recession, many companies are cutting back on investments in equipment.

ぜつぼう (絶望)

あなたの場合は絶望的だ. In your case, it's hopeless.

私は絶望のどん底に突き落とされた. I was driven to the depths of despair.

最愛の息子を失った彼女は, 人生に絶望した. She had nothing to live for after she lost her dearly beloved son.
Having lost her dearly beloved son, she despaired of life.

せつめい (説明)

それでは説明が不十分でよく分かりません。
This explanation is insufficient. I don't understand it very well.

機械の仕組みと使い方を説明してもらった。
I had the design [mechanics] and use of this machine explained to me.

昨日学校を休んだ理由を説明しなさい。
Explain why you were absent from school yesterday.

この仕事の内容を説明します。
I'll explain what this work consists of.

ちゃんと筋道を立てて説明してください。
Please explain in an orderly and logical fashion.

せつやく (節約)

彼は家を建てるために節約してお金をためている。
He's economizing and saving money so that he can build a house.

水を節約して使うよう心がけなさい。
Try not to waste water.

バスよりタクシーで行けば時間の節約になる。
It will save time to take a taxi instead of a bus.

コンピューターを導入したら、かなりの事務的労力が節約できるようになった。
After installing a computer, we were able to save quite a bit of manpower in the office.

せなか (背中)

母親の背中で赤ん坊が眠っている。
The baby is sleeping on her mother's back.

私の家は彼の家と背中合わせに立っている。
My house is built right up against his house.

【慣用】人に背中を見せるとは、卑怯だぞ。
You're just a coward to turn your back and run.

ぜひ (是非)

【良し悪し】君ももう物事の是非が分かってもいい年頃だ。
It's about time you understood right from wrong.

新聞紙上で現在の大学入試制度の是非が問われている。
The validity of the present university entrance examination system is being debated in the newspapers.

【必ず】今度、是非遊びにいらしてください。
Please make sure to stop by next time.

あなたに是非うちの息子の家庭教師になってもらいたい。
I would very much like to have you give our son private lessons.

この試合は是非彼に勝たせたい。
I really want him to win this match.

今度のクラス会には是非出席したい。
I really want to attend the next class reunion.

せまい (狭い)

この道路は道幅がとても狭い.	This road is very narrow.
この家は家族6人で住むには狭すぎる.	This house is too small for a family of six.
今度の試験は出題範囲が狭いので楽だった.	That test was easy because it didn't cover very much.
父は交際範囲の狭い人でした.	Father had a narrow range of acquaintances.
彼の考え方は視野が狭い.	His thinking is very narrow.
そんな狭い了見ではうまくやっていけるはずがない.	You're not going to get anywhere with such a narrow outlook.
【慣用】1回戦で負けてしまって,肩身の狭い思いをした.	I felt like I couldn't hold my head up when I got beaten in the first round.
その学者の家には所狭しと本が積んである.	That scholar's house is cramped because of all the books piled up in it.

せまる (迫る)

【近づく】強盗がナイフを持って迫ってきた.	The robber approached, holding a knife.
火の手が目と鼻の先まで迫ってきた.	The flames came almost within reach.
彼女の身の上に危険が刻々と迫ってきた.	Her predicament grew more dangerous by the minute.
原稿の締め切りが明日に迫った.	The deadline for handing in the manuscript is only a day away.
試験が3日後に迫ってきた.	The exam is only three days away.
辺り一面に夕闇が迫ってきた.	Darkness is descending all around.
彼の晩年の絵には鬼気迫るものがある.	A certain eeriness looms [hangs] over his later paintings.
【要求する】彼は決断を迫られた.	He was pressed for a decision.
彼は仕事で重大なミスを犯し,社長から辞職を迫られた.	After he committed a grave blunder at work, the president put pressure on him to quit.

せめて

会えなくても,せめてあなたの声だけでも聞きたい.	Even if we can't meet, I'd at least like to hear your voice.
もうお帰りですか. せめてお茶ぐらい召しあがっていらして.	You're leaving so soon? At least stay for a cup of tea.
入賞はできなくても,せめて佳作にでも入れたらよかったのになあ.	Even if I couldn't win a prize, it would have been nice to at least get honorable mention.
ささやかですが,これはせめても	It's really quite modest but it's the least I

の償いです. | can do to repay you.

せめる¹（攻める）

| 彼の将棋は守るより攻めるほうがうまい. | He is better at offense than defense in Japanese chess. |
| 相手チームは，こちらの守備の乱れに乗じて果敢に攻めてきた. | The opposing team took advantage of the disarray in our defense and launched a bold attack. |

せめる²（責める）

この件に関して私だけを責めないでください.	Don't blame just me for this.
彼は彼女の裏切りを責めた.	He criticized her for her treachery.
彼はいつも他人より自分を責める性格だ.	He's the kind of person who always reproaches himself rather than blaming others.
女房に責められて，次の日曜は家庭サービスをするはめになった.	My wife really layed into me [My wife's been after me], so I'm spending next Sunday with my family.
借金取りに責められて困っている.	A loan collector is after me and I'm really in trouble.

せわ（世話）

小鳥の世話は娘にやらせている.	I've put my daughter in charge of taking care of the birds.
彼はまだ親に世話をかけている.	He still gets help from his parents.
家が見つかるまで友人のところで世話になっている.	I'm †staying with friends [staying at my friend's] until I can find my own place.
母はあれこれ人の世話をするのが好きだ.	Mother likes to do things for people.
この子は世話の焼けない子だ.	This child is no trouble to look after.
こんなことぐらい一人でできないなんて，何て世話の焼けるやつだ.	You can't even do this by yourself? You're pretty helpless, aren't you?
お世話になった方が突然亡くなってしまった.	A person who had been very kind to me suddenly died.
その節は大変お世話になりました.	You were a great help to me at that time.
子どもがいつもお世話になっています.	We always appreciate your kindness to our child.
結婚相手にいい人をお世話しましょう.	Let me find a nice man [girl] for you to marry.
彼は私の就職を世話してくれた.	He helped me get a job.
大きなお世話だ.	Mind your own business.

せん (線)

私は線の入っていない便せんを使っている.	I use unlined [plain] writing paper.
図面に細い線を真っすぐに引いた.	I drew thin, straight lines on the plan [drawing].
彼は国際線〔国内線〕のパイロットだ.	He's a pilot on the international [domestic] routes.
また一つローカル線が廃止された.	Yet another local line has been eliminated.
彼は線の細い感じの人だ.	He looks fragile.
それはいいアイデアだ. その線でいこう.	That's a good idea. Let's follow that line.
彼の演奏はいい線いってる.	His playing isn't bad.

ぜん〜 (全〜)

その案は全会一致で可決された.	That proposal was unanimously approved.
彼の病気は全快した.	He has completely recovered from his illness.
彼は借金を全額返済した.	He paid back the loan in full.
国連総会は全世界の注目を浴びて開催された.	The general assembly of the U.N. was convened with the attention of the entire world focused on it.
ゲーテの全集を手に入れたい.	I want to get the complete works of Goethe.
車は全速力で走った.	The car went at full speed.
全長30メートルの鯨が捕獲された.	A whale measuring 30 meters in length was caught.
彼は全面的に非を認めた.	He fully admitted his guilt.
その小説は今度初めて全訳された.	That novel has now been translated in full for the first time.
刑事は事件の解決に全力をあげた.	The detective put all his effort into solving the case.

ぜんこく (全国)

この地方は日本全国でいちばん米がとれる.	This region is the leading rice producing area in all of Japan.
この祭りは全国からの見物客でにぎわう.	This festival gets crowded with tourists from all over the country.
平和運動は全国的な盛り上がりを見せた.	The peace movement gained momentum throughout the country.
今年は全国的に不作が予想される.	A bad harvest is anticipated this year for the entire country.
我が校はサッカーの全国大会で優勝した.	Our school team won the championship at the national soccer tournament.

せんさい (繊細)

彼は音楽を聞き分ける繊細な耳を持っている.	He has a good ear (for music).
彼女は非常に繊細な人なので, 社会に出ると傷つくことが多い.	She's so sensitive that she's easily hurt by others.
彼の絵は繊細なタッチで有名だ.	His paintings are famous for their delicate [refined] quality.
あの女性の繊細さにひかれた.	I was attracted by her †delicacy [sense of refinement].

せんしゅ (選手)

リレーの選手に選ばれた.	I was chosen to run in the relay race.
彼はテニスの選手だ.	He's a tennis player.
彼の夢は将来プロ野球の選手になることだ.	His dream for the future is to become a professional baseball player.

センス

彼はセンスがいい〔悪い〕.	He has good [poor, bad] taste.
彼女は実にセンスのない服を着ている.	She's wearing a really tasteless dress.
あの人は秘書としてのセンスが優れている.	As a secretary, she's very [extremely] capable.
私はヨーロッパへ行ってデザイナーとしてのセンスを磨いた.	I went to Europe to refine my sense of design.

ぜんぜん (全然)

その件については全然知らない.	I don't know †a thing [anything] about that at all.
子どものときから丈夫で, これまで全然病気したことがない.	I was healthy as a child and haven't been sick a day of my life.
彼の言うことは, 全然無意味だ.	What he said has no meaning whatsoever. What he said is †utter nonsense [absolutely senseless].
君の仕事ぶりは全然なってないぞ.	Your work is just no good.

ぜんたい (全体)

この病気の特徴は体全体に発しんが見られることだ.	This disease is characterized by a rash over the entire body.
遠足ではクラス全体で行動します.	On a class trip everyone stays together.
この論文は全体としてよくまとまっている.	On the whole, this thesis is well organized.
この学校の生徒は全体的に成績が良い.	All the students in this school get good grades.

せんたく (選択)

彼は職業の選択を誤った.	He made a mistake in his choice of work.
子どもには良書を選択して与えることが大切です.	It's important to choose suitable books to give children to read.
彼女はパーティーに何を着ていくか選択に迷った.	She couldn't make up her mind what to wear to the party.
家庭科は選択科目です.	Home economics is an elective course.

せんでん (宣伝)

この車は今, 盛んにテレビで宣伝されている.	This car is being advertised a lot on TV.
その会社は新製品を鳴り物入りで宣伝している.	That company is promoting its new product vigorously.
あそこの店で, 歳末大売り出しの宣伝をしている.	That store is advertising a big year-end sale.
彼は自分の宣伝ばかりする.	He's always blowing his own horn.

ぜんぶ (全部)

小遣いを全部使ってしまった.	I used up all my spending money.
クラスの人を全部集めてください.	Please bring together everyone in the class.
あの小説家の作品は全部読んだ.	I've read all of that novelist's works.
今日の仕事は全部終わった.	Today's work is all finished.
全部でいくらですか.	How much is it altogether?
英文学のクラスの課題図書は全部で15冊ある.	There is a total of 15 books on the reading list for the English literature class.

せんもん (専門)

私の専門は経済学です.	My speciality is economics.
彼はアメリカ文学を専門に研究している.	He specializes in the study of American literature.
この会社はカメラを専門に作っている.	This company specializes in making cameras.
この書店は洋書を専門に扱っている.	This bookstore specializes in Western books and magazines.
彼は法律に関する専門的知識を持っている.	He has specialized knowledge in law. He's a legal expert [specialist].

せんれん (洗練)

大使は洗練された趣味と作法を身につけている.	The ambassador has refined tastes and manners.
彼は洗練された人物だ.	He is a cultivated [refined] person.
洗練された文体がこの作家の身上です.	A polished [refined] style is this author's strong point.

そ

そう（沿・添・副う）
- 通りに沿って杉が植えられている. — Cedar trees line the street.
- 二人は川に沿って散歩した. — The two of them took a walk along the river bank.
- 私たちは海沿いの道をドライブした. — We took a drive along the coast.
- 山沿いの地方は今夜から雪になるでしょう. — There will probably be snow this evening in the areas along the mountains.
- 会社の方針に沿って企画を立てた. — The plan was formed in line with company policy.
- 話し合いは議題に沿って進められた. — The discussion proceeded in keeping with the topic.
- 事業は最初の計画に沿って進められた. — The project was carried out along the lines of the first plan.
- 二人は寄り添ってベンチに座った. — The two sat beside each other on the bench.
- 【かなう】彼は意に添わないことがあるとすぐ怒る. — He gets angry when things don't go his way.

～そう
- 【～に見える】彼女は悲しそうだね. — She looks unhappy [sad].
- これはおいしそうなケーキだ. — This cake looks delicious.
- 雨はやみそうもない. — It doesn't look like it's going to stop raining.
- レポートは明日までに仕上がりそうもない. — It doesn't look †as if [like] the report is going to be completed by tomorrow.
- この池には魚がいそうもない. — There don't seem to be any fish in this pond at all.
- 少女は今にも泣き出しそうだ. — The little girl looks as if she's on the verge of tears.
- ろうそくの火が風で消えそうだ. — The candle flame looks like it's about to be blown out by the wind.
- 今にも雨が降り出しそうだ. — It looks as if it's about [going] to rain.
- 今日は暑くて死にそうだよ. — I'm about to die from this heat today.
- 何をそんなにうれしそうにしてい — What are you looking so happy about?

るの?
【～と聞いている】中国で雪男が見つかったそうだ. / I hear [understand] that †the abominable snowman [yeti] was found in China.

彼女の父親は警察官だそうだ. / I hear [They say] that her father is a policeman.

しばらくインフレは続くそうだ. / They say that inflation will continue for †some time [a while].

【～して当然】彼女はもう来てもよさそうなもんだ. / She should be getting here before long. It's about time she got here.

君の年ならこれくらいのことは分かりそうなものだ. / You're old enough to understand something like this.

ぞうか (増加)

去年は輸出が10%の増加を示した. / Exports last year showed a 10% increase.

人口増加は食糧危機を招く恐れがある. / Population growth threatens to bring about a food crisis.

この付近の交通量は近年著しく増加している. / In recent years the traffic in this vicinity has increased remarkably.

この町の交通事故の数は増加の一途をたどっている. / The number of traffic accidents in this city has been steadily increasing.

そうごん (荘厳)

教会で荘厳な音楽が演奏された. / Solemn music was performed in the church.

その寺には, 荘厳な雰囲気が漂っていた. / A solemn air pervaded the temple.

そうぞう (想像)

自分が大金持ちになったと想像してごらん. / Just imagine yourself with a large sum of money.

その後彼がどうなったかは, 想像がつく. / I can imagine [guess] what happened to him after that.

君のタキシード姿など想像もつかない. / I just can't imagine what you would look like in a tuxedo.

想像を絶する大平原が目の前に広がっていた. / An unimaginably vast plain lay before my eyes.

その光景は想像を絶するものがあった. / The scene was beyond imagination.

物語の結末は皆さんの想像にお任せします. / I'll leave the end [conclusion] of the story (up) to your imagination.

あなたは私が想像していたとおりの人です. / You are †exactly the kind of person [just as] I imagined you would be.

アメリカの広さは想像以上だった.	The vastness of America surpassed what I had imagined.
彼は想像力に富んでいる.	He has a rich imagination. He's very imaginative.
彼は想像力の乏しい作家だ.	He has little imagination as a writer.
人魚は想像上の動物だ.	A mermaid is an imaginary being.
彼女はすぐに想像をたくましくするので、気をつけなくてはいけない.	You'd better watch what you say to her because she lets her imagination get [run] away with her sometimes.

そうだい (壮大)

ナイアガラの滝の壮大な眺めに感激した.	I was moved by the †grand spectacle [spectacular view] of Niagara Falls.
彼はサハラ砂漠を灌漑しようという壮大な夢を持っている.	He has †an ambitious [a grand] dream of irrigating the Sahara Desert.

そうだん (相談)

私の家では何かあるとみんなで相談して決めます.	When a problem arises in our family, we all talk about it and decide what to do.
彼に仕事のことで相談を持ちかけられた.	He came to me wanting to talk about work.
ちょっと相談があるのですが.	I'd like to talk to you about something for a moment.
私に何の相談もなしに決めてしまったとはけしからん.	It's inexcusable, deciding without even consulting me.
困ったことがあればいつでも相談に乗りましょう.	Any time you have a problem, I'll be glad to talk it over with you.
先生は親身に私の相談に乗ってくれた.	My teacher warmly offered me his advice.
それはとてもできない相談だ.	You're asking the impossible.

そうとう (相当)

【かなり】彼は株で相当稼いだらしい.	He seems to have made quite a †bit of money [killing] on the stock market.
彼の心臓は相当だ.	He's got quite a lot of nerve.
彼も相当の悪人だな.	He's †a real louse** [really low], isn't he?
【当てはまる】200万円相当の指輪が盗まれた.	A ring worth 2,000,000 [two million] yen was stolen.
日本の首相は米国大統領に相当するほどの権限を持たない.	The prime minister of Japan doesn't have as much power as the president of the U.S.
この日本語に相当する英語はない.	There is no English equivalent for this Japanese.

【ふさわしい】
このポストは責任が重いから、それ相当の待遇が必要だ. — The salary for this job [post] should correspond to the heavy responsibility it entails.

彼の罪は死刑に相当する. — His crime draws [deserves] the death penalty.

そうれい (壮麗)
私たちは壮麗な宮殿を見学した. — We took a tour of the grand [imposing] palace.

朝日を受けた富士山の壮麗な姿が見えてきた. — A majestic sight of Mt. Fuji bathed in morning light came into view.

そえる (添える)
彼女からの贈り物には手紙が添えてあった. — Her present was accompanied by a letter.

本の注文は郵送料を添えて申し込んでください. — When ordering a book, please include the postage.

パーティーでは女性の振りそで姿が花を添えた. — Girls in formal *kimono* added an extra touch of beauty to the party.

ぞくする (属する)
鯨は哺乳類に属する. — The whale belongs to the mammal class.

彼はどの派にも属していない. — He doesn't belong to any faction. He's nonpartisan.

その島は日本に属している. — That island belongs to Japan.

司法権は裁判所に属する. — Judicial power lies with the court.

そこ (底)
バケツの底に穴が開いている. — There's a hole in the bottom of the bucket.

靴の底がすり減ってしまった. — The soles of my shoes are completely worn out.

潜水艦は海の底に着いた. — The submarine reached the ocean floor.

彼女は底抜けの馬鹿だ. — She's a total fool.

彼は底なしの大酒飲みだ. — He drinks like a fish.

貯えはついに底をついた. — My savings finally ran out.

彼は自分がしたことを心の底から悔やんだ. — He regretted what he had done from the bottom of his heart.

彼はどこか底の知れないところがある. — There's something about him I just can't fathom.

今朝は底冷えがする. — It's freezing this morning.

そこなう (損なう)
観光地のネオンサインや派手な看 — The neon lights and gaudy signs from the

板は，美しい景観を損なうものだ．	resort area mar the beauty of the scenery.
そんなことをすると，君の品位が損なわれるよ．	Doing such a thing will reflect poorly on you.
これをやり損なったら二度とチャンスはないぞ．	If you fail to do it this time, you'll never get another chance.
彼は交通事故で死に損なった．	He almost died in a traffic accident.
こんな出来損ないの料理なんか，食べられないよ．	I can't eat such poorly prepared food.

そしき（組織）

社会において個人は大抵何らかの組織に所属している．	Most individuals in society belong to some organization.
この会社の組織は複雑すぎる．	This company's organizational structure is too complicated.
彼が中心になって会社に労働組合を組織した．	He acted as leader in organizing a labor union at his company.
僕らは今度，サッカーチームを組織することにした．	We've decided to organize a soccer team.
彼らは組織的な活動を行っている．	They're carrying on organized activities.
この分野では更に組織的な調査研究が必要とされている．	This field requires investigative research that is more systematic.
【生物の】私は魚の神経組織について研究している．	I'm doing research on nerve tissue in fish.

そして

彼は学校から帰るとすぐ宿題を片づけた．そして遊びに行った．	As soon as he got home from school he did all his homework. Then he went out to play.
彼はこつこつとまじめに働いてきた．そして今では大金持ちだ．	He worked diligently for a long time and now he's rich.
悪いのは田中と鈴木と，そしてお前だ．	The ones at fault are Tanaka and Suzuki—and you.
彼は有能で，そして勤勉だ．	He's capable and hard-working.
彼女は美しく，そして聡明だ．	She's beautiful and intelligent as well.

そそっかしい

彼は明るい性格だが少しそそっかしい．	He is a cheerful person, but a little bit of a scatterbrain.

そそる

少量の酒は食欲をそそる．	A small amount of liquor stimulates the appetite.

将来性がありそうなので，その仕事に気をそそられた．	That job caught my interest because it seemed to have a future.

そだつ (育つ)

子どもが育つのは早いものだ．	Children grow up quickly.
彼は裕福な家庭に育った．	He grew up in a wealthy [well-to-do] family.
手入れがいいので，トマトの苗がよく育っている．	Because you take good care of them, the tomato seedlings are growing well.
彼の下から何人もの国際的な音楽家が育った．	Quite a few internationally renowned musicians were fostered under his tutelage.
ひなが育って鶏になった．	The chicks grew up into chickens.

そだてる (育てる)

その夫婦はみなしごを引き取って大事に育てた．	The couple adopted an orphan and raised him with loving care.
彼は厳格な父親に育てられた．	He was †raised [brought up] by a stern father.
美術学校へやってもっとあの子の才能を育ててやるべきです．	They should send that child to an art school to develop his artistic talent.
彼は私の育ての親です．	He's my foster father.
彼はこの会の育ての親です．	He's the principal [main] promoter of this group.
彼はたくさんの弟子を育てた．	He trained [fostered] many disciples.

そっくり

【よく似ている】
あの子は父親にそっくりだ．	He looks exactly like his father.
	He's the spitting image of his father.
本物そっくりの偽札が出回った．	Counterfeit bills that looked just like the real thing got into circulation.

【全部】
彼は父親の財産をそっくり受け継いだ．	He inherited his father's entire estate.
泥棒に入られて有り金をそっくり持っていかれた．	A thief got in and stole all the money I had.
彼は食欲がなく，出された料理をそっくり残してしまった．	He had no appetite and didn't even touch the food he'd been served.
その建物はそっくりそのまま残されることになった．	It's been decided to leave that building standing as it is.

そっちょく (率直)

率直に言って，彼はあまり好きではない．	To be frank [Frankly speaking], I don't like him very much.
彼は率直に批判する．	He is frank in his criticism.

君の率直な意見のお陰でやっと結論が出た.	Thanks to your candid opinion, we finally reached a conclusion.

そっと

【静かに】彼は家人に気づかれないようにそっと家を出た.	Careful not to be noticed by anyone in the family, he quietly slipped out of the house.
遅刻したので,そっと教室に入った.	Arriving late, I entered the classroom quietly.
隣の部屋をそっと覗いてみた.	I quietly peeked into the room next door.
【そのままに】辛い目にあってきたのだから,そっとしてやってください.	Please leave her alone. She's been through quite a hard time.
寝ている子どもをそっとしておいた.	I left the sleeping child undisturbed.
父は機嫌が直るまで,そっとしておくに限る.	The best thing to do is to wait until Dad gets over his bad mood.

ぞっと

戦争のことを考えただけでぞっとする.	I shudder at the very thought of war.
彼女のお化けの話はぞっとするほど怖かった.	Her ghost story was so scary (that) it sent chills up my spine.

そと (外)

【戸外】子どもは外で遊びなさい.	Children, go play outside.
彼女はぼんやり窓の外を眺めていた.	She was staring blankly out the window.
【よそ】日曜日には外で食事することにしている.	We always eat out on Sundays.
彼は外面はいいが,家では威張り散らしている.	He puts on a friendly face in public, but at home he acts like a tyrant.
【表面】家の中は自分たちでペンキを塗り,外は業者に頼んだ.	We painted the interior of the house ourselves and got the painters to do the outside.
このスーツケースは内も外も皮張りだ.	This suitcase is covered in leather both inside and out.

そなえる (備える)

【準備する】災害に備えて,保存食料をたくさん買い込んだ.	Just in case of disaster, I stocked up on nonperishable foods.
彼は入試に備えて勉強している.	He's studying in preparation for his entrance exams.

万一の場合に備えて貯金をしている.	I'm saving up money just in case something comes up.
【常備する】このホテルでは各部屋に冷蔵庫が備えてあります.	Every room in this hotel †has [is equipped with] a refrigerator.
これは英文学を研究する人なら必ず備えるべき辞書です.	This dictionary is a must for students of English literature.

そのうち

【いつか】そのうちお宅へお邪魔します.	I'll visit you one of these days.
そのうち彼から連絡してくるだろう.	I guess he'll be getting in touch before long.
噂話はそのうち収まった.	The rumors died down in due course.
いつまでも彼を待たせると，そのうち逃げられてしまうよ.	If you keep him waiting, he may get away.
「いつ遊園地に連れて行ってくれるの？」「そのうちね」	"When are you going to take me to the amusement park?" "Someday...."
「だれが彼女のハートを射止めたの？」「そのうち分かるよ」	"Who was it that captured her heart?" "Time will tell."
【その中で】うちのクラスは40人だったが，そのうちの7人が教師になった.	There were forty in our class, seven of whom became teachers.
今日アボカドを5個買ったが，そのうち2つが腐っていた.	Two out of the five avocados I bought today were rotten.

そのかわり (その代わり)

あなたの絵を1枚くれない？ その代わり，私の陶器のうち好きなのをあげるから.	Could I have one of your drawings? You can pick out any piece of pottery that you like in return.
(礼を言われて) その代わりに僕の方でも頼みがあるんだ.	Could I ask you a favor in return?
ヨーロッパは遠すぎる気がしたので，その代わりに韓国に行くことにした.	Europe seemed too far away, so I decided to travel to Korea instead.
彼は仕事が丁寧だが，その代わり時間がかかる.	He does a good job but it takes him a lot of time.
晩ご飯は僕が作る. その代わり，あと片づけは君がやってよ.	I'll make dinner. So, could you wash [do] the dishes afterwards?
今日は早く帰っていい. その代わり明日の朝は早く来いよ.	You can go home early today but you have to come in early tomorrow morning to make up for it.

そのへん (その辺)

【場所】
鍵はその辺に置いたはずだが. — I thought I left my keys around there somewhere.
ちょっとその辺を散歩してくる. — I'm just going for a walk around there.
その辺でご飯でも食べようか. — Shall we have dinner around here somewhere?

【内容】
お金のこと, 彼に話してないの？ その辺ははっきりさせておかないと. — Haven't you talked to him about the money? Better make that part of it clear.
その辺のことは把握していますから心配ご無用です. — Please don't worry about a thing. I understand exactly what you're talking about.

【程度】
値段は5万円かその辺だったと思う. — I think the price was about ¥50,000.
酒はもうその辺にしておけ. — I think you've had enough (to drink) now.

【並の】
年はいってるが, まだその辺の若造には負けんぞ. — I may be getting older but I'm not about to let some young kid beat me out.
うちはその辺のラーメン屋とは違います. 秘伝のスープを味わってみてください. — We're not just another *ramen* shop. You've got to taste our secret soup recipe.

そのほか (その外・他)

そのほかの意見はありませんか. — Any other opinions?
サトシは追試のために残らなければならなかった. そのほかの者はみんな帰った. — Satoshi had to stay behind for a make-up exam. Everyone else went home.
ニットの色は, ベーシックな黒, ベージュ, 白, そのほかピンク, 黄色もあります. — This knit comes in basic black, beige, and white, as well as pink and yellow.
その古いかばんには, 手紙, 写真, 鍵, 万年筆, 磁石, そのほか雑多なものが入っていた. — There were letters, photos, keys, a fountain pen, a compass and assorted other things in that old bag.

そば

私の家は駅のそばです. — My house is †by [next to] the station.
彼はうちのそばに住んでいる. — He lives †near [close to] me.
もっと私のそばにいらっしゃい. — Come closer to me.
この犬は私のそばを離れない. — This dog won't leave my side.
彼女は何にでもすぐにそばから口を出す. — She always has to put in her two cents worth.

【すぐあとで】
私は物覚えが悪く, 教わるそばから忘れてしまう. — I'm a poor learner and forget things as soon as I'm taught them.
彼はお金が入ると, すぐそばから使ってしまう. — He spends money the minute he gets it.

そびえる

うちの庭には杉の大木がそびえている.	There's a tall cedar standing in our garden.
あのひときわ高くそびえているのがエベレストだ.	That peak rising far higher than the rest is Mt. Everest.
ニューヨークの街には巨大なビルがいくつもそびえている.	New York City is filled with towering skyscrapers.
彼はそびえるような大男だ.	He's a giant in stature.

ソフト

【物が】この生地のソフトな肌ざわりをお試しあれ.	Feel how soft this fabric is!
コンタクトレンズをハードからソフトに変えた.	I switched over from hard to soft contacts.
【言葉・態度・声などが】話し合いは終始ソフトムードだった.	The talks were conducted throughout in a calm atmosphere.
彼は物腰がソフトなので接客業に向いている.	He is mild-mannered and would do well in the service industry.
彼女は傷つきやすいので, もう少しソフトな話し方のほうがいい.	It would be better to talk to her more gently because she gets hurt easily.
彼の甘くソフトな歌声は多くの女性をしびれさせた.	His mellow[1] singing voice had many women swooning.
【ソフトウェア】うちのOSは古いので最新ソフトは動作しない.	We can't use the latest software because of our old OS.
日常の業務なら統合ソフト1セットあれば十分間に合う.	One software suite is sufficient for everyday-work purposes.
表計算ソフトを使えばグラフも簡単に作れる.	Spreadsheet software makes it easy to produce graphs.

> [1] 女性の「甘くソフトな歌声」は mellow ではなく sweet を使う.

そぼく (素朴)

彼は山育ちで素朴だ.	He was raised in the mountains and is very down-to-earth [unaffected].
この生地はとても素朴な風合いがある.	This material has a very homespun [earthy] feeling.

そまつ (粗末)

留学中は粗末な食べ物で我慢した.	I made myself eat the awful food when I was studying overseas.
その粗末な身なりの男が, 私の友人だと判ってびっくりした.	I was very surprised to discover that that shabbily dressed man was a friend of mine.

粗末に扱われて憤慨した.	I became indignant at being so poorly treated.
お金を粗末にしてはいけない.	You shouldn't handle [spend] money so carelessly.

そむく (背く)

彼は親に背いて家を出た.	He rebelled against his parents and left home.
彼は社長の命令に背き,首になった.	He got fired for disobeying the president.
彼は恋人に背かれてから酒びたりになった.	He's been drinking heavily ever since his girlfriend †left him [passed him over] for someone else.
彼は親の期待に背くようなことは決してしない.	He'll never do anything to betray his parents' expectations of him.
私は自分の主義に背いてまで,そんなことをしようとは思わない.	I would never stoop to betraying my own principles to do something like that.

そめる (染める)

彼女は毛糸を青く染めた.	She dyed the wool blue.
母は白髪を染めている.	My mother dyes her hair to hide the gray.
彼女はマニュキュアで爪を赤く染めた.	She painted her nails red. She colored her nails with red nail polish.
この事業に手を染めてから,もう30年にもなる.	I've been in this business for 30 years already.
彼女は恥ずかしさのあまり頬を染めてうつむいた.	She was so embarrassed that she blushed and lowered her head.

そや (粗野)

彼は粗野だがいい男だ.	He may be rough-mannered but he's a nice guy.
彼は言葉遣いが粗野だ.	He speaks rather roughly [coarsely].

それから

買い物をして,それから伺います.	I'm going shopping, and after that I'll stop by to see you.
それから,どうしたの.	Well, what happened †next [after that, then]?
彼女とは3ヵ月前に映画を見に行って,それからずっと会っていません.	It was three months ago that I went to a movie with her and I haven't seen her since.
学校を出て就職し,それからもう10年になります.	It's already been 10 years since I finished school and started working.

それぞれ

僕の友達はそれぞれが個性的だ.	All of my friends are unique in their own way.
この仕事の完成のために, それぞれの立場を越えて協力して欲しい.	In order to accomplish this job [task], I want you to overcome your respective differences and all work together.
私の家族は夕食後それぞれ好きなことをして過ごす.	After dinner everyone in my family does whatever he likes.
青と赤の鉛筆をそれぞれ1ダースずつください.	I'd like a dozen each of both blue and red pencils.
あの二人は同じ兄弟でもそれぞれ性格がまるで違う.	They may be brothers but they have completely different personalities.

それだけ

1時間もかかって, できたのはたったそれだけですか.	It took a whole hour, and that's all you've gotten done?
それだけのことでなぜそんなに怒るの.	Why are you so angry over such a little thing?
残りはもうそれだけです.	That's all that's left.
それだけあれば十分だ.	That much should be enough.
それだけ勉強すればきっと成績が上がりますよ.	If you study that much, your grades are bound to go up.
それだけは人に任せられない.	That's one thing I refuse to leave [trust] to anyone else.

それで

彼は風邪をひいてしまいました. それで今日はお休みしています.	He caught a cold so he's taking today off.
ゆうべは徹夜をしたんだ. それで昼まで寝ていたんだよ.	I stayed up all night last night. That's why I slept till noon.
「試合は逆転また逆転の連続だったよ」「それで, どっちが勝ったの?」	"The lead in the match kept changing back and forth." "Well, who finally won?"
「会社を辞めました」「それで, これからどうするつもり?」	"I quit my job." "Well, what do you intend to do now?"

それでも

今日は雨になるそうですよ. それでも出かけますか.	It's supposed to rain today. Do you still plan to go out (anyway)?
だれも信用しないけど, それでも本当なんだ.	No one believes me, but I tell you it's true.
彼女はそんなに食べない. それでもあんなに太っている.	She doesn't eat so much. And yet look how fat she is.

彼はよく遊ぶ．それでも勉強はよくできる．	He manages to †have a good time [play around a lot] and still get good grades.

そろう (揃う)

この合唱は声が揃っていない．	The voices in this chorus are not in unison.
参道には大きさの揃った小石が敷き詰められていた．	The path to the shrine was paved with stones of uniform size.
あの家の子は，みんな揃って頭がいい．	All the children in that family are smart [bright].
揃いも揃って英語の話せない人ばかりだった．	Not a single person was able to speak English.
たまには家族揃ってレストランで食事をしよう．	How about taking the whole family and going out to eat for a change?
お二人揃ってお出かけですか．	Are you (two) going out together?
スチュワーデス[客室乗務員]たちは，揃いの制服に身を包んでいる．	The flight attendants are all dressed in matching uniforms.
あの店はスポーツ用品が何でも揃っている．	That shop has anything you might need in the way of sports equipment.
あの書店は語学関係の本がかなり揃っている．	That bookstore has a large selection of works on (foreign) languages and linguistics.
全員揃ったら出発します．	We'll leave once everyone gets here.
証拠は揃っている．	We've got all the evidence we need.
条件が揃わないので計画を中止した．	We †called off [canceled] the plan because not all the conditions could be met.
あの学校は優秀な先生が揃っている．	That school has an outstanding faculty.
あのチームには強豪が揃っている．	That team has a strong [powerful] lineup.

そろえる (揃える)

靴を脱いだらきちんと揃えなさい．	Arrange your shoes neatly after you take them off.
両足を揃えて跳んだ．	I jumped with both feet together.
紙の大きさは揃えたほうがいい．	You should make the papers all the same size.
彼らは口を揃えて反対した．	They were unanimous in declaring [stating] their opposition.
みんなで声を揃えて歌を歌った．	They all sang in unison.
必要なものは水曜日までに揃えておきます．	I'll have all the necessary items ready by Wednesday.
レポートを書くのに必要な資料を	I've gotten together all the materials I

揃えた.	need to write the report.
百科辞典を少しずつ買い足して全部揃えた.	I got a complete set of the encyclopedia by buying [adding] one or two volumes at a time.
マージャンをするなら，まずメンバーを揃えなければならない.	If we're going to play mah-jong, first we'll have to get together enough people to play.

そろそろ

【ゆっくり】バケツの水をこぼさないよう，そろそろと歩いた.	I walked slowly so that I wouldn't spill the water in the bucket.
寝ている友人を起こさないよう，そろそろと引き戸を引いた.	I slid open the door softly so as not to awaken my friend.
【ぽちぽち】そろそろ日が沈む頃だ.	It's nearly time for the sun to go down.
そろそろご飯が炊き上がる頃だ.	The rice will be ready soon.
そろそろ海開きの季節だ.	It's almost time for the beach to open for the summer.
彼がいなくなって，そろそろ1年になる.	It's been almost a year since he left.
そろそろ休憩にしませんか.	Shall we take a break (soon)?
もう遅いし，そろそろ帰ろうか.	It's getting late. It's about time we started for home. [Shall we be leaving?]
彼女もそろそろ結婚を意識し始める年齢だ.	She's about the age when a young girl starts thinking about marriage.
九州では桜がそろそろ咲き始めた.	The cherry blossoms have started to bloom in Kyushu.
母はそろそろ足元がおぼつかなくなってきた.	Mother's legs have started to give out on her.

そわそわ

子どもの入試が近づいて親のほうがそわそわしている.	It is the parents who are on pins and needles as their children's entrance examinations approach.
祭りが近づくと，町中の人々がそわそわし始める.	As the festival draws near, the townspeople all start getting excited.

そん (損)

彼は相場に手を出して100万円の損をした.	He lost 1,000,000 [one million] yen dabbling in the stock market.
安物の靴を買ったらすぐ壊れてしまい結局損をした.	Buying a cheap pair of shoes was actually a waste because they fell apart right away.
もうすぐ卒業なのに今大学をやめ	To quit school now with graduation so

たら損だよ.	close would be a real waste.
上の男の子は「年上は損だ」といつも文句を言っている.	The oldest boy is always complaining that there's no advantage in being the oldest.
ただ話を聞くだけなら損にはならないだろう.	It's not going to cost you anything to listen.
それは不可能だから、やるだけ損だ.	It's just not possible, so it would be a waste to even try.
彼は口下手で損をしている.	Not having a way with words puts him at a disadvantage.
自分の意見を積極的に言うようにしないと損だよ.	You'll only be putting yourself at a disadvantage unless you state your opinion in a positive way.

そんけい (尊敬)

私は先生を尊敬しています.	I †respect [look up to] my teacher.
私は彼の学識を深く尊敬している.	I deeply respect his erudition.
その牧師は多くの人々の尊敬を集めている.	That pastor has earned the respect of many people.

そんちょう (尊重)

私たちは他人の権利を尊重しなければなりません.	We must respect the rights of others.
今回は彼の意見を尊重しておきなさい.	This time you should respect his opinion.

そんな

そんなわけで、彼は今日は来られません.	That's why he can't come today.
そんな怖い顔をして、僕を睨まないでくれ.	Don't look at me with such an angry expression.
そんな大金は持っていません.	I don't have such a large sum of money.
そんなことはないだろう.	I doubt if that's the case.
	That can't be.
そんな無理は言わないでくれ.	Don't ask such unreasonable things of me.
そんなつもりではありません.	That's not my intention.
そんなことではこの仕事は勤まらない.	If that's the case this isn't the job for you.

た

たい（対）
空気は窒素と酸素が4対1の割合で出来ている. — Air contains nitrogen and oxygen in the proportion of four (parts) to one.

5対4で，我が野球チームが勝った. — Our baseball team won 5 to 4.

今日のバスケットボールの試合は日本対アメリカだ. — Today's basketball game is between Japan and the United States.

アメリカの対日貿易政策は厳しさを増している. — America's trade policy with respect to Japan is becoming more severe.

〜たい
コーヒーが飲みたい. — I'd like some coffee.

あなたにもう一度会いたい. — I'd like [I want] to see you again.

来たければ来なさい. — Come if you want. / If you want to come, come.

スキーに行きたくてたまらない. — I'm dying to go skiing.

だいいち（第一）
家へ帰るとまず第一に手を洗った. — The first thing I did after I got home was to wash my hands.

彼は帰省すると第一に祖父母の墓参りに行った. — The first thing he did after returning to his home town was to visit the graves of his grandparents.

行きたいけど，忙しいし，第一お金がないよ. — I'd really like to go, but I'm too busy——and besides, I don't have any money.

「なぜ漫画ばかり見るの」「第一に面白いからだよ」 — "Why do you watch cartoons all the time?" "First of all, they're funny [interesting]."

彼女の第一印象は悪かったが，すぐ気さくでいい人だと分かった. — My first impression of her was bad, but I soon realized what a nice friendly person she was.

この会の第一の目的は会員の利益を図ることです. — The foremost goal of this group is to benefit its members.

風邪には安静が第一です. — Rest is the most important thing for cur-

彼は財界の第一人者だ.	He's a leading figure in the financial world.

たいかく (体格)

そんな体格で相撲は無理だよ.	With a build like yours, *sumo* is out of the question.
この子は年の割には体格がいい.	This boy has a good build for his age.

たいぐう (待遇)

この旅館は客の待遇が良い〔悪い〕.	This inn treats its guests very well [poorly].
彼の家へ行くと,いつも親切に待遇してくれる.	He always treats his guests kindly.
あの会社は待遇が悪いから辞めた.	I quit that company because of its poor †working conditions [employment terms].
組合は会社に対して社員の待遇改善を要求した.	The union demanded that the company improve the employees' working conditions.

たいくつ (退屈)

分からない講義は退屈だ.	Lectures you cannot understand are boring.[1]
あいつは退屈な男だ.	He's boring.[2] / He's a bore.
何もすることがなくて退屈した.	We had nothing to do, so we were bored.
退屈しのぎにテレビでも見よう.	Let's watch TV to †kill time [while away the time].

---

1) dull, tiresome, tedious, monotonous でもよい. 2) dull, tiresome でもよい.

たいざい (滞在)

上京したら息子の家に滞在するつもりです.	While I'm in Tokyo, I plan to stay at my son's home.
アメリカでの滞在予定は3ヵ月です.	I plan [intend] to stay in the United States for three months.

たいさく (対策)

同じような事故を起こさないように対策を講じるべきだ.	We must take measures to prevent accidents of this kind from occurring again.
事故後,安全対策が強化された.	Safety precautions were stepped up following the accident.

万引き防止の具体的な対策はあるのか？	Do you have a concrete strategy for preventing shoplifting?
この家の防犯対策は万全です．	This house is completely burglar-proof.
当局は電話会社に対して，迷惑メールに関する抜本的対策を求めた．	The ministry asked the phone companies to take drastic measures to stop †nuisance e-mails [spam] from coming into cell phones.
政府が大胆な景気対策を打ち出した．	The government set out a bold strategy for overcoming the recession.
過去問を研究し，対策を練った．	I looked at past examination questions and came up with a study strategy [plan].

だいじ（大事）

【大切】
大事な書類を無くした．	I lost some important papers.
彼は私にとって大事な人だ．	He's very important [precious][1] to me.
この指輪は私にとって大事な物です．	This ring is very precious[2] [valuable] to me.
彼はおじいさんの代から受け継いだ金の指輪を大事にしている．	He cherishes [treasures] the gold ring handed down from his grandfather.
彼女はその着物を大事にしまっている．	She keeps that *kimono* carefully put away.
この本は人から借りた物だから大事に扱ってください．	This book is borrowed, so please take good care of it.
ご両親を大事にしなさい．	Take good care of your parents.
お体をお大事に．	Take care (of yourself).
お金は大事に使いなさい．	Don't waste money.
	Use your money wisely.

【大ごと】
大事に至らないうちに彼を病院に入れたほうがいい．	We'd better put him in the hospital before it becomes serious.
大事を取って今日は学校を休みなさい．	Just to be on the safe side, stay home from school today.

> 1)「世話になっている人」「大きな影響力を持つ人」は important,「大切に思っている人」「好きな人」には precious を使う． 2) また precious は物については宝石などの貴重品あるいは形見の品などに対して用いる．

たいした（大した）

彼は大した悪党だ．	He's a real scoundrel [baddie**].
彼女の英語は大したものだ．	Her English is really something.
今日の遊園地は大した人出だ．	The amusement park is really crowded today.
こんなもの大した宝石ではない．	This jewel is nothing special.

母は三日ばかり寝ているが大した病気ではない. — My mother's been in bed for three days, but it's nothing serious.

だいじょうぶ (大丈夫)
大丈夫ですか. — Are you all right?／Are you OK?
彼に任せておけば大丈夫だよ. — If you leave it to him it'll be all right.

たいする (対する)
米の消費量が減っているのに対して小麦の消費量は増えている. — Whereas rice consumption is declining, consumption of wheat is on the rise.
投票は賛成25に対し反対14だった. — There were 25 votes in favor versus 14 against.
横暴な上司に対して部下たちが反旗を翻した. — The workers rebelled against their tyrannical boss.
この頃の学生は政治に対する関心が薄い. — Students these days have little interest in politics.
彼の見事な演奏に対して聴衆は大きな拍手を送った. — The audience gave him a loud round of applause for his outstanding performance.
彼の今の発言に対して何か意見がありますか. — Do you have any comments on the statement he just made?
あなたは彼に対してちょっと冷た過ぎるわ. — You're a little too cold towards him.
彼女は毅然とした態度で上司に対した. — She confronted her boss with a firm attitude.

たいだ (怠惰)
彼は怠惰な生活を送っている. — He's leading †an idle [a lazy] life.
全く怠惰なやつだ. — He's such a lazy guy.

だいたい (大体)
【おおよそ】日本の人口は大体1億2千万です. — The population of Japan is about 120 [a hundred and twenty] million.
私も大体あなたと同じ意見です. — My opinion is about the same as yours.
仕事は大体片づきました. — I finished most of my work.
大体の計画を述べてください. — Give me a rough outline of your plan.
【そもそも】彼は考え方からして大体間違っている. — To begin with, his basic way of thinking is wrong.
大体私は彼に会った覚えはない. — To begin with, I don't remember ever meeting him.

だいたん (大胆)
大胆な計画だ. — That's a bold [daring] plan.

皆の前で上司を無視するなんて彼は随分大胆だ.	He has a lot of nerve[1] to ignore his boss in front of everyone.
大胆かつ細心の注意を払ってやれば成功するだろう.	If you do it boldly while paying attention to details, you will succeed.
その兵士は大胆不敵だった.	That soldier was fearless.

> 1) It is bold [daring] of him... でもよい.

たいてい (大抵)

【おおかた】日曜日は大抵家にいます.	I'm generally at home on Sundays.
父は大抵7時に会社から家に戻ってきます.	My father generally gets home from work at seven.
夕焼けがきれいな日の翌日は大抵晴れる.	After a beautiful sunset the following day is usually nice.
大抵の学生はアルバイトをしている.	Most students work part-time.
【ひととおり】彼は大抵の仕事はこなしてしまう.	He can handle just about any work he's given.
大抵のことでは驚かないがこの話はひど過ぎる.	I'm not easily surprised, but this story is too awful (to believe).
ふざけるのも大抵にしておけよ.	That's about enough clowning around. Stop clowning around (already**)!
夜更かしも大抵にしておきなさい.	Don't make a habit of staying up till all hours.

たいど (態度)

彼は仕事中の態度が悪い.	His attitude at work is really bad.
態度を改めなさい.	Improve [Straighten out] your attitude.
彼はそれまでの態度をすっかり改めた.	He completely changed the attitude he had had up till then.
最後まで責任を取った彼の態度は立派だった.	It was admirable the way he took responsibility right till the end.
どうも近頃の君の態度はおかしいぞ.	You're acting a little strangely lately.
向こうの出方によってこちらも態度を決めよう.	Let's see what they do first before we decide how to react.
あの男は態度が大きい.	That guy doesn't know his place.

だいなし (台無し)

君の不注意のせいでこの計画は台無しになった.	This project was ruined because of your carelessness.
急に嫌な客が来て, せっかくの休	An unwelcome guest popped in and

日が台無しになった.	ruined our precious day off.

だいひょう (代表)

僕は学校の代表として英語弁論大会に出た.	I represented our school in the English speech contest.
彼は日本代表として世界会議に出席した.	He attended the world conference as a representative from Japan.
電子工業は日本の代表的産業である.	Electronics is one of Japan's major industries.
この論文は構造主義の考え方を代表するものだ.	This paper is representative [typical] of the structuralist school of thought.
この小説は彼の代表作の一つである.	This novel is one of his †most famous [best-known] works.

タイプ

このタイプの容器はリサイクルできません.	We can't recycle this type of container.
今年の商品見本市で新しいタイプのコピー機が登場した.	A new type of copier was debuted at the exhibit for new products this year.
ああいうタイプの人には気をつけたほうがいいよ.	You'd better be careful when dealing with a person like that.
どういうタイプの男性が好きですか？	What kind of men [guys] do you like?
彼女はまさに僕のタイプだ.	She's just my type.
彼女はお嬢様タイプだ.	She's very ladylike.
彼は学者タイプだ.	He's an academic.／He's a scholarly type.

だいぶ

電車がだいぶ込んできた.	The train has gotten quite crowded.
この仕事はだいぶ時間がかかりそうだ.	This work looks like it will take quite a long time.
今日はだいぶ勉強がはかどった.	I made quite a bit of progress in my studying today.
風邪がだいぶ良くなった.	My cold is much better.

だいぶぶん (大部分)

この学校の大部分の学生は大学に進学する.	The majority [Most] of the students at this school go on to college.
マラソン大会の参加者の大部分は完走した.	Most of the participants in the marathon finished the race.
この小説の大部分は主人公の心理描写に充てられている.	The larger part [Most] of this novel is taken up with a psychological description of the protagonist.

| 彼は人生の大部分を外国で過ごした. | He spent †the major part [most] of his life abroad. |

たいへん (大変)

【大ごと】大変だ！ 子どもが溺れている.	Oh my God! There's a child drowning.
お父さんが病気ですって？ 大変ですね.	I heard that your father is sick. It must be hard (for you).
家が浸水して大変だった.	It was just terrible [awful] when our house was flooded.
大変な失敗をしてしまった.	I made †a terrible [an awful] mistake.
新潟は大変な雪らしい.	They're supposed to be having some terrible snow in Niigata.
これは大変な仕事だ.	This is †a big job [hard work].
野性の馬をならすのは大変だ.	It's a real job to tame a wild horse.
常にトップを守るというのは大変なことだ.	It's really hard [difficult] to stay at the top all the time.
【とても】これは大変面白い映画だ.	This is †an awfully [a terribly][1] interesting movie.
大変お世話になりました.	You've been so terribly kind to me.

1) awfully, terribly の代わりに very, really に強勢をおいて言ってもよい.

たいまん (怠慢)

| 当局の怠慢がこの事故を招いた. | Negligence (of duty) by the authorities brought on this accident. |
| 君は怠慢だ. 言われたことはすぐやりなさい. | You're †negligent of [derelict in] your duty. Do what you were told to immediately. |

タイミング

餃子をおいしく作るには水を入れるタイミングが大切だ.	The timing for adding the water is important in making good *gyoza*.
このゲームはボタンを押すタイミングが狂うと負けだ.	You can lose this game if your timing (pressing the controls) is off.
彼はいつもタイミングよくシャッターを切る.	He always presses the shutter at exactly the right moment.
波とタイミングを合わせてサーフボードに体を乗せた.	I got on the surfboard after timing myself with the waves.
彼に連絡しなくちゃと話しているところに, タイミングよく本人が現れた.	He appeared just as we were saying that we should contact him. Good timing! [His timing was perfect.]

今，賃上げを要求するのはタイミングが悪い．もう少し待とう．	This is not a good time to ask for a raise. Let's wait a bit.
こんな場面で先生と出くわすなんてタイミングが悪いな．	What bad luck to be bumping into my teacher here.
結婚はタイミングだよ．	Getting married is a matter of timing.

たいら（平ら）

山を切り崩して平らな土地にする工事が進められている．	The work to tear down the mountain and make the land flat is making progress.
ローラーででこぼこなグラウンドを平らにならした．	We flattened out the bumpy playground with a roller.

だいり（代理）

私は都合が悪いので代理の者を出席させます．	I can't make it but I'll send someone to act in my stead.
会議に参加できない方は代理（人）を立ててください．	Could those who cannot make it please send someone to represent them at the conference?
佐藤の代理でまいりました．	I've come on behalf of Mr. Sato.
彼の肩書きは部長代理〔支店長代理〕だ．	He's †an assistant manager [a branch assistant manager].
あのサッカー選手の代理人はやり手だ．	That soccer player's agent is very capable.
彼は保険代理業を営んでいる．	He manages an insurance agency.
近くの旅行代理店でタイツアーを申し込んだ．	I signed up for a tour to Thailand at a nearby travel agency.
アメリカのいくつかの州では代理母が法的に認められている．	Surrogate mothers are legally recognized in a number of American states.

ダウンロード

ダウンロードがうまくいかない．	It isn't downloading properly.
OSに合ったファイルをダウンロードしたのち解凍してください．	Download the file compatible with your OS and unpack [decompress] it.

たえず（絶えず）

その泉からは絶えず水があふれていた．	Water flowed ceaselessly from the spring.
彼女はどんな辛いことがあっても絶えず明るく振る舞った．	She was always cheerful, no matter what hardships she was going through.
彼は絶えず愚痴をこぼしている．	He complains constantly. He's constantly [always] complaining.
事務所には絶えず電話がかかってくる．	The phone in the office never stops ringing.

たえる¹ (耐・堪える)

【我慢する】
彼はじっと傷の痛みに耐えた. — He stoically endured [bore] the pain of his wound.

彼は長年の苦労に耐え, やっと画家としての名声を獲得した. — He finally made a name for himself as a painter after enduring many years of hardship.

彼女は恥ずかしさに耐えられず部屋から逃げ出した. — Unable to bear the embarrassment, she ran out of the room.

彼は彼女に聞くに堪えない悪口を言った. — He said unspeakably abusive things to her.

彼の酔っ払った姿は見るに堪えない. — I just can't bear to see him drunk.

【持ちこたえる】
この金属は1万度の高温にも耐えられます. — This metal can withstand temperatures of up to 10,000°C [ten thousand degrees centigrade].

その建物は今度の地震に耐えた. — That building withstood the recent earthquake.

ファンベルトは5万キロの走行に耐える. — The fanbelt will last for 50,000 kilometers.

彼の理論はどのような批判にも十分に耐えるものだ. — His theory is sound enough to withstand any criticism.

この美術館には鑑賞に堪える作品が少ない. — Few works in this art museum are noteworthy. There is little to admire in this art museum.

たえる² (絶える)

息子からの連絡が絶えて久しい. — It's been a long time since I stopped hearing from my son.

道楽者の夫を持って彼女は苦労の絶える時がない. — With a playboy for a husband, her hardships never end.

あの政治家には黒いうわさが絶えない. — Scandalous rumors about that politician never cease.

たおす (倒す)

慌ててコップを倒してしまった. — In my haste [rush] I knocked over the glass.

木を倒して土地を広げた. — I cut down the trees to clear the land.

彼はチャンピオンを倒した. — He overthrew the champion.

彼らは政府を倒し, 軍政を敷いた. — They overthrew [toppled] the government and set up a military regime.

たおれる (倒れる)

彼は後ろから押されて，前のめりに倒れた.	Someone pushed him from behind and he fell flat on his face.
切られた大木が大きな音を立てて倒れた.	The huge tree which had been sawed through fell with a loud crash.
地震で塀が倒れた.	The wall toppled over in the earthquake.
革命によりあの国の君主政権はついに倒れた.	The monarchy of that nation was eventually overthrown by a revolution.
スーパーの進出により付近の小売商店はばたばたと倒れてしまった.	The opening of the new supermarket put the nearby small retail stores out of business one by one.
【病気になる】母が過労で倒れてしまった.	My mother collapsed from extreme fatigue.
無理をして倒れないように気をつけてください.	Please be careful not to overdo it and get sick.
父が脳いっ血で倒れた.	My father had a stroke.
【殺される】大統領は凶弾に倒れた.	The President was struck down by an assassin's bullet.

たかい (高い)

【高さ】富士山は日本でいちばん高い山です.	Mt. Fuji is the highest mountain in Japan.
村外れに高い木があります.	There's a tall tree on the outskirts of the village.
ヒバリが高く舞い上がった.	A skylark soared skyward.
【程度】日本人の生活水準は決して高くはない.	The Japanese standard of living is by no means high.
あの教授の講義は程度が高い.	That professor's lectures are advanced.
理想は高く持つべきだ.	You should have high ideals.
彼は高い教養を身につけている.	He's very cultured.
批評家は今度の彼の作品を高く評価した.	The critics gave his most recent work very high marks.
この市民会館は設備が整っているので利用価値が高い.	This civic auditorium is well equipped and serves many functions.
この実験の成功の確率は高い.	This experiment has a high probability of success.
【温度】明日は気温が高くなるでしょう.	The temperature will be high tomorrow.
その子は高い熱を出して寝込んでいる.	That child is in bed with a high fever.
【金額】このバッグの値段は高過ぎるよ.	This bag is too expensive.
高い物が必ずしも品質が良いとは	Expensive things aren't necessarily of high

限らない.	quality.
彼女は高い月謝を払ってバイオリンを習っている.	She pays high tuition fees every month to learn the violin.
税金が年々高くなる.	Taxes get higher every year.
素人がやるとうまくいかないで，かえって高くつくことがある.	When an amateur does something by himself it usually ends up costing him more than if he had had a professional do it.
【声】彼女は声が高い.	She has a high(-pitched) voice.
【態度】彼女は美人なのを鼻にかけ，お高くとまっている.	She's very stuck up about her looks.

たがい (互い)

二人は互いにののしり合った.	They cursed at each other.
彼らはお互いに信じ合っている.	They trust †one another [each other].[1]
人はそれぞれの立場をお互いに尊重し合わなければいけない.	People should respect †each other's [one another's][2] positions.
もう二度と同じ過ちを繰り返さないようお互いに気をつけましょう.	Let's both be careful never to repeat the same mistake.
疲れているのはお互い様だ.	You're not the only one who's tired. So am I.

> 1)2) one another は主に三人以上の場合に使う. each other は二人の場合でも三人の場合でも使うが，イメージとしては一対一の二人.

たかさ (高さ)

面積に高さを掛けると体積が出る.	Multiplying the area by the height gives the volume.
このビルは世界一の高さを誇っている.	This is the tallest building in the world.

たがやす (耕す)

彼は庭の一部を耕して小さな畑を作った.	He plowed over part of his garden and made it into a small field.
最近，田畑は機械で耕すようになった.	Nowadays fields are being plowed by machines.

たから (宝)

子どもは親の宝だ.	Children are their parents' treasure.
いくら宝を積まれてもあんな人と結婚するのは嫌です.	I wouldn't marry someone like him for all the money [treasure] in the world.
この刀は我が家に伝わる宝物です.	This sword is a family heirloom [treasure].
彼みたいな人があの絵を持ってい	It's a waste for someone like him to own a

たって宝の持ち腐れだ. | painting like that.

だから
彼は強情だ. だから人とけんかばかりしているんだ. | He's stubborn. That's why he's always arguing with people.
きみは甘い物を食べ過ぎるよ. だから虫歯になるんだ. | You eat too many sweets. That's why you get cavities.
「学校に遅刻しちゃった」「だからいつも早く家を出なさいと言っているでしょう」 | "I was late for school." "That's why I always tell you to leave the house early."

〜たがる
彼はあなたに会いたがっている. | He wants to see you.
彼女は何でも知りたがる. | She always wants to know everything.
子どもは何でも自分でやりたがる. | Children always want to do everything (by) themselves.

だきょう（妥協）
私たちは結局妥協した. | In the end we compromised.
妥協点は見いだせなかった. | We could not reach a compromise.

たく（焚・炊く）
彼は枯れ木をたき, 暖をとった. | He burned some dead wood for warmth.
今日は寒いのでストーブをたいた. | I turned on the heater today because it was cold.
私の家では今でもまきで風呂をたく. | We still use wood to heat our bath.
あなたの炊く御飯はいつもおいしい. | The rice you cook is always delicious.
高い山では気圧が低いので御飯がうまく炊けない. | Rice doesn't cook well high in the mountains because the air is thin.

だく（抱く）
若い母親が赤ん坊を抱いている. | The young mother is holding her baby.
彼女を抱いて浅瀬を渡った. | I carried her across the shallow stream.
恋人たちはしっかりと抱き合った. | The lovers hugged each other tightly.
 | The lovers embraced passionately.
飛行機に乗る前に, アメリカ人の友人に抱き締められた. | My American friend gave me a big hug before I boarded the plane.
鶏が卵を抱いている. | The hen is †sitting on [hatching] her eggs.

たくさん
彼女は帽子をたくさん持っている. | She has †a lot of [many] hats.

披露宴にはお金がたくさんかかった.	The wedding reception cost †a lot of [a great deal of, much*] money.
もうたくさんいただきました.	I've had enough, thank you.¹⁾
もうたくさんだ!	Enough is enough!²⁾

> 1) 食事などを更に勧められたときの言い方. 2) 小言やお節介などでうんざりしたときの言い方. ほかに That's enough. とか I've had it! あるいは I'm fed up (with it). とも言う.

たくましい

その相撲取りはたくましい体をしている.	That *sumo* wrestler is powerfully built.
子どもにはたくましく育ってほしい.	I want my children to grow up big and strong.
母は体は小さかったがたくましい精神の持ち主だった.	My mother was physically small but she had a strong spirit.
彼は逆境にめげずたくましく生きている.	He's working with all his might under adverse conditions.
彼は商魂たくましい.	He's always out to make a buck.

たくみ (巧み)

彼女は巧みに人形を操った.	She worked the marionette skillfully.
老練な先生は巧みに生徒を扱った.	The experienced teacher managed his pupils with skill.
彼は巧みに責任を逃れた.	He cleverly [skillfully] got out of the responsibility.
私は結局, 彼に巧みに操られていたのだ.	As it turned out, he had been skillfully using me.
そのセールスマンはとても言葉巧みだった.	The salesman was very clever in his speech.
なかなか巧みな細工のブローチだ.	It really is a skillfully crafted brooch.

たくわえる (蓄える)

母は万一のためにいつも小銭を蓄えていた.	My mother always had a little money †put away [saved] for a rainy day.
彼は学生時代に蓄えた知識を仕事にいかしている.	He's putting the knowledge he gained during his student days to very good use in his job.
彼は必死に勉強して実力を蓄えた.	He studied as if his life depended on it and strengthened his ability.

～だけ

| 【同分量・同程度】お小遣いは必要 | I'll give you as much spending money as |

なだけあげます．	you need.
今年はバラがたくさん咲いたのでお好きなだけお持ちください．	Lots of roses bloomed this year, so please take as many as you'd like.
成功はおぼつかないが，とにかくやれるだけやろう．	There isn't much hope for success, but let's do the best we can, anyway.
高く上がれば上がるだけ，空気は薄くなる．	The higher you go, the thinner the air gets.
食べれば食べるだけ太りますよ．	The more you eat, the more weight you'll put on.
【〜のみ】この問題を解けたのは彼だけだった．	He was the only one who could solve the problem.
彼女は歩くだけで精一杯だった．	It was all she could do just to walk.
旅行には僕らだけで行こう．	Let's take the trip just by ourselves.
とりあえず，希望する半分だけでも貸していただけませんか．	For the time being, would you mind lending me just half of what I asked for?
せめて山口君だけでも来てくれたら助かるんだけど．	It would be fine [helpful] even if only Yamaguchi could come.

〜だけのことがある

苦労しただけのことがあって，いい作品が出来たと思う．	I think my efforts really paid off with this work.
うんと勉強しただけのことはあって試験の結果は大変良かった．	All of the hard work he put into studying showed in his test scores.
彼が自慢するだけのことはあって彼の奥さんは確かに美人だ．	His wife really is as pretty as he's boasting she is.
さすが専門家だけのことはあって彼は一目で偽物と見抜いた．	The specialist sure proved himself when he identified the fake at a glance.

たしか (確か)

【明白】確かにそれは事実だと思う．	I'm sure [positive][1] that's a fact.
彼は確かに頼りにできる人物だ．	He's definitely [certainly] someone that can be depended on.
お手紙確かに受け取りました．	I received your letter.[2]
確かな返事はもらえなかった．	I couldn't get a definite answer.
【確実】それは確かな情報ですか．	Is that information reliable [correct]?
警察は確かな証拠をつかんだ．	The police got hold of solid evidence.
あそこは身元の確かな人しか採用しない．	They employ only persons with respectable backgrounds.
あの会社の製品は確かな物ばかりだ．	All of that company's products are reliable.
そのことがあってから二人の関係は確かなものになった．	Ever since that happened the two of them have had a solid relationship.
彼女のフランス語は確かだ．	She has a solid command of French.

あの職人の腕は確かだ.	He's a very able craftsman.
【きっと】たしか彼は今仙台にいるはずだ.	I'm pretty sure he should be in Sendai now.
あれはたしか3年前のことでした.	It was three years ago, if I'm not mistaken.*

> 1) sure より positive のほうが意味が強く断定的. 2)「確かに」に当たる英語がないが，入れるとかえって不自然になる.

たしかめる (確かめる)

明日の集合時間を確かめるために友人の家に電話をした.	I called my friend at home to check what time we were all supposed to meet tomorrow.
彼女は戸締まりを確かめてから床に就いた.	She went to bed after checking to see that the doors and windows were locked.
彼の意向をもう一度確かめたほうがいい.	We should confirm his intentions once again.

だす (出す)

【内から外へ】彼女は戸棚から箱を出した.	She took a box out of the cupboard.
彼はポケットからハンカチを出した.	He took a handkerchief out of his pocket.
彼は窓から顔を出した.	He poked [stuck] his head out of the window.
彼女は掃除をするので子どもたちを部屋の外へ出した.	She got the children out of the room so she could do the cleaning.
舌を出すのはやめなさい.	Stop sticking your tongue out.
ごみは決められた日に出さなければならない.	The garbage should be put out only on set days.
茶色の背広は洗濯に出してある.	My brown suit is at the dry cleaner's.
【公表する】その日は午後から強風注意報が出された.	A strong wind warning was issued that afternoon.
掲示を出してみんなに知らせよう.	Let's post a notice [bulletin] to let everyone know.
今度の展覧会に作品を出すつもりだ.	I intend to display my works at the upcoming exhibition.
その出版社から私の2冊目の本を出します.	I'm going to have my second book published by that publishing firm.
新聞に新製品の宣伝広告を出した.	We put an advertisement in the newspaper for the new product.
記事には名前を出さないでください.	Please don't use [include] my name in the article.

【生じさせる】昨日，隣が火事を出した．	A fire broke out next door yesterday.
新建材は燃えるときに有毒ガスを出すものが多い．	There're many new building materials that give off poisonous gases when they burn.
その列車の脱線事故はたくさんのけが人を出した．	The train derailment left many people injured.
大声を出さないでください．	Please don't raise your voice(s).
映画監督は主演スターの持ち味をよく出すように努めた．	The director tried his best to bring out the leading star's special qualities.
彼は話しているうちにぼろを出した．	He gave himself away as he spoke.
【提出・提供する】彼は時間になったので答案を出した．	The time was up so he handed in his answer sheet.
明日までに書類を出してください．	Please turn in the documents by tomorrow.
手紙を出しにポストまで行った．	I went to the mailbox to mail a letter.
この事業の資金は彼が出している．	He's the one who's putting up the money for this project.
彼は酒を出して友人をもてなした．	He served his friends some drinks.
新しい先生は宿題をたくさん出します．	My new teacher assigns a lot of homework.
刑事はなかなか口を割らない容疑者に動かぬ証拠を出した．	The detective confronted the tightlipped suspect with conclusive evidence.
【卒業させる】彼女は苦労して息子を大学まで出した．	She went through a lot to put her son through college.
【〜し始める】彼女は笑い出したら止まらない．	Once she starts laughing she can't stop.
彼はゆっくり歩き出した．	He slowly began to walk.

たすう (多数)

一つの製品が消費者の手に渡るまでには多数の人手がかかわっている．	A product passes through many hands before it reaches the consumer.
国民の多数は住宅に不満を抱いていると言う．	It seems †much of the nation is [a large number of citizens are] dissatisfied with housing conditions.
決議結果は賛成が多数を占めた．	The majority approved the resolution.

たすかる (助かる)

嵐で漁船が転覆したが，乗組員は全員助かった．	The fishing boat capsized in the storm, but the entire crew was saved.
3階の窓から落ちたのにその子は	The child fell from a third-story window

奇跡的にかすり傷一つ負わずに助かった.	but miraculously survived without a scratch.
彼はもう助かる見込みがほとんどない.	There's almost no hope for his recovery.
【ありがたい】彼に手伝ってもらってとても助かった.	It really helped us out to have him lend a hand.
部屋代が安くて助かる.	The low rent †helps me out [makes things easier].
けがが軽く済んで助かった.	I was very lucky to get away with such a light injury.

たすける (助ける)

【救助する】飛行機事故の遭難者は救助隊に助けられた.	The victims of the plane crash were saved by a rescue squad.
【援助する】難民を助けるために募金に協力してください.	Please contribute to help the refugees.
彼はいつも困っている人の相談に乗って, 彼らを助けている.	He's always lending an ear to troubled people and helping them out.
【手伝う】彼は父を助けて家業に精を出した.	He helped his father out by working hard for the family business.
私は毎日家事を手伝い, 母を助けています.	Every day I help my mother out by lending a hand around the house.

たずねる¹ (尋ねる)

私はお店の人に駅までの道を尋ねた.	I asked the salesperson in the store the way to the station.
彼女は私に欠席の理由を尋ねた.	She asked me why I had been absent.
飛行機が落ちたので航空会社には肉親の安否を尋ねる電話が殺到した.	After the plane crashed, the airline was swamped with calls from relatives asking about the safety of the passengers.
母親は家出した娘の行方を必死で尋ねて回った.	The mother frantically went around trying to find the whereabouts of her runaway daughter.
彼は伝説を尋ねてその地方を訪れた.	He visited that area looking for (local) legends.

たずねる² (訪ねる)

昨日久しぶりに友人宅を訪ねた.	Yesterday I †went to [visited] my friend's house for the first time in a long while.
父が孫の顔が見たいと言って, 突然家を訪ねてきた.	My father popped in on us, saying he wanted to see his grandchild.
先日彼を訪ねたらあいにく留守だった.	I went to visit him the other day, but unfortunately he was out.

新製品の売り込みのために，取引先の会社を訪ねた．	I called at a company we deal with to try to sell our new product.

ただ

【無料】あの店で風船をただで配っていた．	They were giving away free balloons at that store.
今日は祝日なので動物園の入園料がただです．	Today is a holiday, so admission to the zoo is free.
開店記念で，ただで髪を刈ってくれた．	I got my hair cut for free because it was the shop's opening day.
彼はただ同然でその土地を手に入れた．	He acquired that land for †virtually [next to] nothing.
【普通】彼はただの人ではない．	He's no ordinary [run-of-the-mill] person.
ただでさえ暑いのに電車が満員でひどい目にあった．	It was awful. As if it weren't hot enough to begin with, the train was packed.
そんなことが父の耳に入ったらただでは済まないよ．	If Dad were to get wind of that, you'd get it for sure.
田中先生が君のことを気に入っているのは知っているけど，締め切りあとの論文提出というのはただでは済まないよ．	I know that Mr. Tanaka likes you but you will never get away with handing your essay in late.
【だけ・しか】クラスで満点を取ったのは，ただ一人だけだった．	Only one person in class got a perfect score.
あなたはただ言われたとおりにすればいいのです．	You should just do as you're told.
その子は何を聞いてもただ泣くばかりだった．	No matter what I asked that child, all he did was cry.
彼はその素晴らしい景色にただため息をつくばかりだった．	He just sighed and sighed at the spectacular scene.
この絵はただ色がきれいなだけだ．	All that can be said for this painting is that the colors are pretty.
【ただし】彼女はいい人だけど，ただお節介なのが難点だ．	She's a nice person but she's a real busybody.
デパートに連れて行ってあげましょう．ただやたらに物を欲しがってはいけませんよ．	OK, I'll take you to the department store. Just don't start asking for everything in sight.
映画を見に行ってもいいよ．ただ終わったら早く帰って来なさい．	You can go to the movie, just as long as you come right home when it's over.

ただいま (唯今)

ただいま父は外出中です．	Father is out right now.
はい，ただいま参ります．	OK, I'll be right there.
【挨拶】ただいま．	I'm home.[1]

> 1) 日本語の「ただいま」のように決まった帰宅の挨拶ではない．

たたかい (戦・闘い)
その戦いで多くの人が死んだ． Many people were killed in that battle.
ボクシングのタイトルマッチで激しい戦いが繰り広げられた． The boxers fought a pitched battle in the title match.
シェア拡大を巡る両社の闘いには激しいものがある． The struggle between the two companies to gain a larger share of the market is intense.

たたかう (戦・闘う)
【争う】彼らは自由を求めて戦った． They fought to gain their freedom.
百年戦争ではイギリスとフランスが戦った． England and France fought in the Hundred Years' War.
彼は戦争で勇敢に戦って死んだ． He died courageously †in battle [fighting in the war].
両チームは最後まで正々堂々と戦った． Both teams fought it out to the end, fair and square.
この選挙で彼は別の三つの政党の候補者を相手に戦うことになる． In this election he will be running against candidates from three other parties.
彼らはその問題で激しく議論を戦わせた． They disputed that problem fiercely with each other.
【困難や苦しみと】彼女はもう10年間も病気と闘っている． She's been battling [struggling, fighting] with illness for the past ten years.
これを実現するには多くの困難と闘わねばならない． In order to make this a reality many difficulties will have to be overcome.

たたく (叩く)
【打つ】だれかが戸を叩いている． Someone is knocking at the door.
父の肩を叩いてあげた． I massaged my father's shoulders.
彼は手を叩いてウエートレスを呼んだ． He called the waitress by clapping his hands.
父親はいたずらした子どものおしりを叩いた． The father spanked his child for misbehaving.
彼は息子の手を (ぴしゃりと) 叩いた． He slapped his son on the hand.
肩を (ポンと) 叩かれたのでだれかと思って振り返った． I turned around to see who tapped me on the shoulder.
彼は机を (ドンドンと) 叩いた． He pounded his fist on the desk.
彼は祭りで太鼓を叩いた． He beat a drum at the festival.
雨が激しく屋根を叩いている． Rain is pelting down hard on the roof.
【慣用】彼の小説は批評家にさんざ His novel was severely panned by the

ん叩かれた.	critics.
中古車を叩いて半値で買った.	I drove a hard bargain and bought the used car for half price.
彼は有名な陶芸家の門を叩いた.	He asked to apprentice under a famous potter.

ただしい (正しい)

彼の言っていることは全く正しい.	What he says is absolutely right.
何度も計算してやっと正しい答えを出した.	I calculated it many times before I finally came up with the right answer.
この文章は文法的に正しい〔正しくない〕.	This sentence is grammatically correct [incorrect].
この英文を正しく訳しなさい.	Translate this English accurately.
正しい姿勢で本を読みなさい.	Sit up straight when you read.

ただちに (直ちに)

その計画は直ちに実行に移された.	The plan was immediately put into action [practice].
負傷者は直ちに病院に運ばれた.	The injured were immediately taken to the hospital.
時間がないので直ちに出発したほうがいい.	You don't have much time, so you'd better get started immediately.

たたむ (畳む)

彼女は洗濯物を畳んで, たんすにしまった.	She folded the laundry and put it away in the chest of drawers.
布団をきちんと畳みなさい.	Fold up your bedding neatly.
紙を四つに畳みます.	Fold the (piece of) paper in quarters.
雨がやんだので, 傘を畳んだ.	It stopped raining so I closed my umbrella.
【慣用】彼は店を畳んで, よそへ移って行った.	He closed his business and moved away.

たちあげる (立ち上げる)

社長は苦労してこの会社を立ち上げた.	The president went through much hardship starting up this company.
パソコンを立ち上げ, ファイルを開いた.	I †turned on [started up] the computer and opened the file.
ついに自分のホームページを立ち上げた.	I finally †created [set up] my own website.

たちば (立場)

彼はクラスを指導する立場にある.	He occupies a position of leadership in his class.

日本はこの問題では微妙な立場に置かれている.	Japan is in a delicate situation on this question.
あなたに全部やってもらっては私の立場が無くなる.	If you do everything for me, I'll lose my standing [position].
彼はその問題に対し強硬な立場を取っている.	He's taking a firm position [stance] on that question.
お互いの立場を尊重することが大切です.	It's important for us to respect each other's positions.
私の立場も考えてください.	Please think of my position, too.

たつ¹ (絶・断・裁つ)

【やめる】私は3ヵ月前にたばこを絶った.	I stopped smoking three months ago.
両国は国交を断っている.	The two countries have †severed [cut off] diplomatic relations.
彼らは契約に関する重大な誤解をして,取引関係を絶ってしまった.	They broke off their business relationship after a serious misunderstanding about a contract.
【なくする】これで我がチームの優勝の望みは断たれた.	This puts an end to our team's hopes [chances] of winning.
犯人は逃げ道を断たれて山へ逃げ込んだ.	His escape route cut off, the criminal fled into the mountains.
彼は自ら命を絶った.	He took his own life.
【切る】スカートを作るために布を裁った.	I cut the cloth to make a skirt.

たつ² (立・発つ)

交番の前にお巡りさんが立っている.	A policeman is standing in front of the police box.
彼女は舞台に立って歌い始めた.	She came out on stage and started singing.
立ったり座ったりしないで落ち着きなさい.	Sit still and calm down.
庭に大きな桜の木が1本立っている.	There's a big cherry tree in the garden.
角にポストが立っています.	There's a mailbox on the corner.
【去る】「いつおたちですか」「明日大阪へたつ予定です」	"When are you leaving?" "I plan to leave for Osaka tomorrow."
彼女は昨日,日本をたちました.	She left Japan yesterday.
彼女は昨日,成田からたちました.	She †left [took off] from Narita yesterday.
彼は怒って席を立った.	He got angry and left his seat.
【出る・起こる】やかんから湯気が立っている.	Steam is coming out of the teakettle.
山の頂から煙が立ち昇っている.	Smoke is rising from the mountain peak.

トラックが通ったあと砂ぼこりが立った.	The passing truck raised a lot of dust.
このせっけんはよく泡が立つ.	This soap makes a lot of bubbles [suds].
【決起する】多くの人々が平和のために立ち上がった.	Many people stood up for peace.
【立場・状況にある】5回裏, ジャイアンツは優位に立った.	The Giants took the lead in the bottom of the fifth.
この電気製品は使う人の側に立って設計されている.	This appliance was designed with the user in mind.
彼は苦境に立たされた.	He was put in a difficult position.
彼は新聞記者の質問の矢面に立たされた.	He was made to bear the brunt of the questioning from the newspaper reporters.
【立候補する】今度の選挙でこの地区からは三人立った.	Three candidates are running in the coming election from this district.
【注意を引く】彼は人目に立たないように暗くなってから家を出た.	To avoid being noticed, he left home after dark.
【優れている】彼は筆が立つ.	He's a skillful writer.
彼女は大変弁が立つ.	She has a way with words. She speaks eloquently.

たつ³ (建つ)

裏の空地に家が建った.	A house has gone up on the empty lot out back.
この町にもやっと図書館が建ちました.	This town finally got its own library.
山の頂上に塔が建っている.	There's a tower on top of the mountain.
校庭には創立者の銅像が建っています.	In the schoolyard there's a bronze statue of the school's founder.

たつ⁴ (経つ)

時のたつのは早いものだ.	Time passes quickly.
時がたつにつれ水害の被害状況が判ってきた.	As time passed, the extent of the water damage became clear.
5分たったら教えてください.	Tell me when five minutes have passed.
父が死んでから5年たちました.	Five years have passed [It's been five years] since my father died.
10年たてばこの辺りにも家が立ち並ぶでしょう.	In 10 years, this area too will probably be built up with houses.
彼は入社して1週間もたたないうちに会社を辞めてしまった.	He quit the company within his first week on the job.

たっする (達する)

探検隊はついに北極点に達した.	The expedition finally reached the North

	Pole.
募金額は目標の100万円に達した.	We have reached our goal of ¥1,000,000 [one million yen] in contributions.
火災による損害は1億円に達した.	Damage from the fire †reached [amounted to] one hundred million yen.
彼の通算安打は3,000本に達した.	He has reached 3,000 career hits.
そのデモの参加者は2万人に達した.	There were 20,000 [twenty thousand] demonstrators.
その提案に賛成の者はクラスの過半数に達しなかった.	The number of people in the class agreeing with the proposal didn't reach a majority.
彼女のピアノはプロの域に達している.	Her piano playing has reached a professional level.
彼も成年に達した.	He has become an adult.

たった

この近所で小学校に通っている子はたった一人しかいない.	There is only one child in this neighborhood going to elementary school.
あの航空機事故の生存者はたった三人だった.	There were only three survivors from that airplane crash.
たった二日間では北海道旅行はできない.	You can't see Hokkaido in just two days.
彼はたった一人で海へヨットで乗り出して行った.	He set out to sea on his sailboat all alone.
僕のお小遣いは1ヵ月にたった5,000円です.	My monthly allowance is (just) a meager [measly**] ¥5,000.
彼はたった今出かけたところです.	He just left. He went out just now.

だって

「もう寝なさい」「だって, まだ8時だよ」	"Go to sleep!" "But it's only eight o'clock."
「こんないい天気にどうして傘なんか持っているの」「だって, 天気予報で今日降るって言ったんだもん」	"Why are you carrying an umbrella around on a nice day like this?" "Well, the weather forecast said it's supposed to rain today."
旅行へ行くのはやめた. だって, 仕事が忙しいんだ.	I've decided not to go on the trip. I'm just too busy with work.

〜だって

私だってそんなことをするのは嫌だ.	I wouldn't want to do something like that either.
中古車にだっていいのがあるよ.	Some used cars aren't bad either, you

	know.
このことは君にだって言えない．	I can't talk about this even with you.
彼は国語だって算数だって得意だ．	Japanese, arithmetic—he's good at everything.
お父さんは昆虫のことなら何だって知っている．	My father knows everything about insects.
そのことはだれだって知っている．	Everyone knows that.
今では世界中どこにだって行ける．	Nowadays you can go anywhere in the world.
私は1日だって会社を休んだことはない．	I've never missed a single day of work.

たて（縦）

この窓は縦が2メートル，横が1メートルあります．	This window is two meters high and one meter across [wide].
縦の線は細く，横の線は太く書いてください．	Please draw the vertical line thin and the horizontal line thick.
縦1列〔2列〕に並びなさい．	Please line up in single [double] file.
	Please make a single [double] file here.

たてる¹（立てる）

祝日には国旗を立てる家もある．	Some people raise flags at home on national holidays.
新しい映画の宣伝のために駅前に大きな看板を立てた．	A big sign has been put up in front of the station to advertize the new movie.
スキーを壁に立て掛けた．	I stood the skis against the wall.
彼は正座ができないので，ひざを立てて座る．	He can't sit with his legs under him, so he sits with his knees pulled up.
【ほこり・波を】砂ぼこりを立ててバスがやって来た．	The bus drove up raising a cloud of dust.
波を立ててモーターボートが走っている．	The motorboats are making waves.
【人を】各党とも今度の選挙に候補者を一人ずつ立てた．	Each party †is running [has put up] one candidate in this election.
息子の縁談は人をあいだに立てて進めている．	A go-between is handling my son's marriage talks.
彼女はいつも控え目にして夫を立てている．	She always keeps a low profile around her husband (and makes him look good).
【説を】あの学者は日本人の起源について新しい学説を立てた．	That scholar †formulated [put forth] a new theory on the origin of the Japanese people.
【伺いを】一応社長にお伺いを立てないと返事はできないな．	I can't give you an answer until I confer with the president.

【手柄を】この事件では警察犬が手柄を立てた.	Police dogs performed a valiant service in this case.
【生計を】あの夫婦は共稼ぎをしてどうにか暮らしを立てている.	That couple just gets by by both working.
【誓い・志を】彼は禁煙の誓いを立てた.	He has made a vow to quit smoking.
彼女は画家になろうと志を立ててフランスに渡った.	She resolved to become an artist and went to France.
【筋道を】ちゃんと筋道を立てて話してくれよ.	Please put what you have to say in logical order.
【音を】大地震でビルが音を立てて崩れた.	The building collapsed noisily in the earthquake.
赤ちゃんが静かな寝息を立てて眠っている.	The baby takes soft breaths as it sleeps.
シーッ, 声を立てるな.	Shh! Be quiet.

たてる² (建てる)

彼は念願のマイホームを建てた.	He made a dream come true by building a house of his own.
村にもう一つ学校を建てることになった.	It was decided to build another school in the village.

たとえ

たとえ両親が反対しても私はあの人と結婚します.	Even if my parents are against it, I'm going to marry that man.
たとえどんなことがあっても, 学校は続けるつもりだ.	I intend to stay in school no matter what happens.
たとえ冗談でもそんなことを言ってはいけません.	You shouldn't say such a thing, even as a joke.
たとえそれが法律には触れないとしても, 人の道に外れている.	Granting that there is [Even though there may be] no law against that, it is still immoral.
たとえ火の中, 水の中, あなたのためなら何でもします.	If it's for you I would do anything, be it going through fire or water.

たとえば (例えば)

【例をあげると】私はフランスの近代絵画, 例えばセザンヌやルノアールの絵が好きだ.	I like French modern art, for example the paintings of Cezanne and Renoir.
野草には薬になるものがあります. 例えばトリカブトがそうです.	There are wild grasses such as monkshood which can be used as medicines.
【もし】例えば核戦争が起こったとしたら, 人類は生き残れるかど	It is impossible to say whether or not the human race could survive if there were

うか分からない. / a nuclear war.
これは例えばの話だ. 気にしなくてもいい. / There's no need to be concerned. This is only hypothetical.

たとえる (例える)
この童話では人の一生を旅に例えている. / This children's story likens man's life to a journey.
彼女を花に例えると, 深紅のバラです. / If I were to compare her to a flower it would be to a crimson rose.
その風景は例えようもないほど美しかった. / The beauty of the scenery was beyond (all) description.

たどたどしい
彼のしゃべる英語はたどたどしい. / He speaks broken English.
His English is very faltering.
幼い娘がたどたどしい筆跡で手紙を書いてきた. / My little daughter wrote me a letter in her unsteady hand.
日本人の学生がたどたどしく英詩を朗読した. / The Japanese student falteringly recited the English poem.

たにん (他人)
【ほかの人】そんなことで他人の手を煩わせてはいけません. / You shouldn't cause trouble to others by doing that.
他人の話に口を挟むな. / Don't butt into other people's conversations.
【関係のない人】ここは他人の出る幕ではない. / This is no time for an outsider to get involved.
彼女と私とは赤の他人です. / She and I are complete [total] strangers.
She and I have nothing to do with each other (anymore).
他人の空似とはいえ我々はよく間違えられる. / We happen to look so much alike that we're often mistaken for each other.
もう20年のつきあいなんだから, そんな他人行儀はやめてくれ. / We've known each other for 20 years. Why don't you stop being so formal with me?

たね (種)
【種子】子どもたちは庭に朝顔の種をまいた. / The children planted morning glory seeds in the garden.
種に気をつけてスイカを食べなさい. / Be careful of the seeds when you're eating watermelon.
種なしブドウが出回り始めた. / Seedless grapes have begun to appear in the stores.

【原因・材料】彼女にはいつも苦労の種が尽きない.	There's no end to her sources of hardship.
成績の悪い息子が悩みの種です.	My son's bad grades are a source of concern [anxiety].
話の種にエスカルゴを食べてみよう.	Let's try some escargot. It'll be something to talk about later.
彼は自分の不幸も冗談の種にしてしまう.	He makes jokes even about his own misfortunes.
その殺人事件は町中のうわさの種だ.	The murder case is the talk of the town.
口論の種はささいなことだった.	Their argument was over a trivial matter.
アイデアも種切れだ.	I've run out of ideas.
【仕掛け】手品には必ず種がある.	There is always a gimmick to every magic trick.
【諺】まかぬ種は生えぬ.	Nothing ventured, nothing gained.

たのしい (楽しい)

今夜のパーティーは楽しかった.	We had †a good time [fun] at the party tonight.
	We enjoyed the party tonight.
楽しい音楽が聴きたいなあ.	I want to listen to some lively music.
狭いながらも楽しい我が家だ.	However small it may be, ours is a happy home.
学校に行くのは楽しいかい.	Do you like going to school?
どうせやらなければならないのなら楽しくやりなさい.	As long as you have to do something, you might as well †enjoy what you're doing [have fun doing it].

たのしみ (楽しみ)

読書は私の楽しみです.	Reading is a source of enjoyment for me.
	I enjoy reading.
ようやく最近になって酒の楽しみが分かってきた.	Recently I have finally learned how to enjoy drinking.
彼は定年後は庭いじりに楽しみを見いだしている.	Since retirement, he's found pleasure in gardening.
彼女はひたすら子どもの成長を楽しみに生きてきた.	She's lived solely to delight in watching her children grow up.
頭のいい息子さんで、これからが楽しみですね.	You have a lot to look forward to with such a bright son.
お目にかかれるのを〔パーティーを〕楽しみにしています.	I'm looking forward to †seeing you [the party].

たのしむ (楽しむ)

今夜は仕事を忘れて楽しもう. — Let's forget about work and enjoy ourselves tonight.

このあいだの日曜日はドライブを楽しんだ. — We went for an enjoyable drive last Sunday.
— We went for a drive and had †a good time [fun] last Sunday.

たのみ (頼み)

【依頼】今日は折り入ってあなたに頼みがあります. — I have a special favor to ask of you today.

母の頼みで, 叔母の家に行きました. — I went to my aunt's house for my mother.

【頼り】親の援助をいつまでも頼みにしてはいけません. — Don't think you can always get help from your parents.

彼はいつでも頼みになる男だ. — He is someone who can always be relied on.

アメリカ旅行では, この辞書だけが頼みの綱でした. — On my trip to the U.S., this dictionary was my one real lifesaver.

たのむ (頼む)

【お願いする】父に彼女との結婚を許してくれるように頼んだ. — I asked my father for permission to marry her.

彼女に相談に乗ってくれと頼まれた. — She asked me to talk over something with her.

この仕事は彼に頼めば安心だ. — If we ask him to do this work, †we'll have nothing to worry about [we can rest assured].

父は友人に私の就職口を頼んだ. — Father asked his friend to look for a job for me.

彼は頼まれれば嫌とは言えないたちだ. — He is the type who can't refuse when asked to do a favor.

この荷物を駅まで頼むよ. — Please take this baggage to the station.

彼女は近所の人に子どもを頼んで勤めに出た. — She entrusted her children to one of her neighbors and left for work.

昨日は夜中に子どもが熱を出し, 医者に往診を頼んだ. — Yesterday, in the middle of the night my child developed a fever and I asked the doctor if he could make a house call.

【頼りにする】彼は自分の才能を頼み過ぎて失敗した. — He relied too much on his own ability and failed.

彼は金の力を頼んで当選するつもりだ. — He intends to rely upon the power of money to win him the election.

与党は勢力を頼んで法案を強引に — The ruling party used its power to push

たのもしい (頼もしい)

あの男は頼もしいやつだ. — He's a dependable [reliable] man.

彼が仲間に加わることになり，我々は頼もしい味方を得た. — With his joining us we gained a dependable [reliable, trustworthy] ally.

あの男の子はもう一人で旅行できるなんて頼もしいね. — Isn't it great that that boy is reliable enough to travel by himself!

たば (束)

このホウレンソウは一束200円です. — This spinach is ￥200 a bunch.

田のあちこちに稲の束が干してあった. — Sheaves of rice plants had been left to dry here and there in the rice paddy.

彼女は野原で花を摘んで花束を作った. — She picked flowers in the field and made a bouquet.

彼はかばんから札束を取り出した. — He took a bundle [stack] of bills out of his briefcase.

一人二人は面倒だ. 束になってかかってこい. — I'm not going to fool around with you one or two at a time. I'll take you all on at once.

たび (度)

あの女の子は見るたびにきれいになっていくね. — That girl looks prettier every time I see her.

故郷へ帰るたびに恩師を訪ねる. — I visit my former teacher †every time [whenever] I go back to my hometown.

このたびはお世話になりありがとうございました. — Thank you very much for all that you have done for me.

何ごとも一たび始めたら最後までやり通しなさい. — Once you've started something, see it through to the end.

たび重なる不幸に彼女はうちひしがれた. — Experiencing one misfortune after another has left her crushed.

たびたび (度々)

彼はたびたび私を訪ねて来ます. — He often [frequently] comes to see [visit] me.

私は仕事でたびたび大阪へ行きます. — My work often [frequently] takes me to Osaka.

彼女は体が弱いのでたびたび学校を休みます. — She has a weak constitution and often misses school.

たびたびすみませんが，また辞書を貸してください. — I'm sorry to keep bothering you, but could I borrow your dictionary again?

たぶん

彼はたぶん来るでしょう.	He'll probably[1] come.
「明日来ますか」「たぶんね」	"Will you come tomorrow?" "Probably. [Maybe.[2] ／ Perhaps.[*3]]"

> 1) probably は可能性が高いことを表す. 2) maybe は「五分五分ぐらいの可能性」, 3) perhaps は「はっきりとは分からない」ことを表す.

たべる (食べる)

お昼を一緒に食べましょう.	Let's have lunch together.
私は好き嫌いがありませんので, 何でも食べられます.	I don't have any strong likes or dislikes; I'll eat anything.
そんなに食べるとおなかをこわしますよ.	If you eat like that you'll get an upset stomach.
彼は全くよく食べる.	He's a huge eater.
これは食べられます〔食べられません〕.	This is edible [inedible].
【生活する】私の安月給では食べていくのがやっとだ.	With my meager salary I'm just barely able to †eke out a living [keep myself fed].
彼のような安サラリーマンが家族5人を食べさせていくのは大変なことだ.	A low-paid company worker like him has a rough [hard, terrible] time †providing for [supporting] a family of five.

だます (騙す)

【うそをつく】今年のエープリルフールは彼にすっかりだまされた.	He completely put one over on me on April Fool's Day this year.
彼女は人をだますのがうまい.	She is good at deceiving [fooling] people.
セールスマンにだまされて不良品を買わされた.	I was tricked by a salesman into buying a defective product.
人にだまされないよう気をつけなさい.	Be careful not to be fooled by others.
彼はうそつきの名人で, まんまとみんなをだました.	He was such a skillful liar that he completely fooled them all.
【なだめる】泣いている赤ん坊をやっとだまして寝かしつけた.	I finally got the baby to stop crying and lulled her back to sleep.
この機械は半年もだましだまし使っている.	I've managed to keep this machine going for six months.

たまに(は)

私はたまに旅行をします.	I occasionally go on trips.
彼女はたまに面白いことを言う.	She occasionally says something funny.
たまに家を空けることもありますが, 大抵はいます.	There are times when I'm not home, but usually I am.

たまには遊びに来てください.	Please stop by every †now and then [once in a while].
同じ大学に通っているけれど,彼とはたまにしか会わない.	I hardly ever see him even though we go to the same university.
たまにしかない休日なのに,雨になってしまった.	I have so few days off, and then it had to go and rain.

たまらない

蒸し暑くてたまらない.	It's unbearably hot and humid. I can't stand this heat and humidity.
トイレに行きたくてたまらない.	I really have to go to the bathroom. I can't wait any longer.
彼女はおかしくてたまらなかった.	It was so funny she couldn't control herself.
海外旅行中は日本料理が食べたくてたまらなかった.	I was dying for Japanese food during my overseas trip.
コーヒー1杯で3時間もねばられてはたまらない.	I can't stand to have someone sit over a single cup of coffee for three hours.
彼らの演奏はたまらなくいい.	Their performance is †indescribably good [sooo[1]) good**].

> 1) so を強調して長く伸ばす.

たまる (溜る)

雨上がりの校庭に水がたまっている.	The rain has left †puddles [pools of water] in the schoolyard.
ごみがたくさんたまってしまった.	A lot of garbage has piled up.
2,3日風邪で休んだら,仕事がたまってしまった.	The work piled up when I was off work with a cold for a couple of days.
金がだいぶたまった.	I've †saved [put away] quite a bit of money.
家賃が3ヵ月もたまってしまった.	I'm three months behind in my rent.

だまる (黙る)

黙れ!	Shut up!
彼は何を聞かれても黙っている.	He †doesn't say a word [stays silent] no matter what he's asked.
彼女は授業のあいだずっと黙りこくっていた.	She remained silent throughout the entire class [period].
そんなことを言われては黙っていられない.	I can't keep quiet when someone says something like that to me.
黙って言われたとおりにしなさい.	Keep your mouth shut and do as you are told.

【無断で】黙って遊びに行ってはいけません.	You mustn't go out to play without telling me (first).
彼は親に黙って旅に出た.	He left on a trip without telling his parents.
彼は黙って会議に欠席した.	Without a word to anyone, he skipped the meeting.

ため

【目的・利益】彼は健康のためにたばこをやめた.	He quit smoking for the sake of his health.
彼は家族のために一生懸命働いた.	He worked hard for the sake of his family.
何のために勉強するの.	What are you studying for?
私はあなたのためを思って忠告しているのです.	I'm giving you this advice for your own sake.
彼はバイクを買うためにアルバイトをしている.	He's doing some part-time work in order to buy a motorcycle.
同じ過ちを繰り返さないためにはどうしたら良いだろうか.	What shoud we do in order to avoid repeating the same mistake?
この本はためになるよ.	This book †is useful [has a lot to offer].
漫画は子どものためにならないという意見がある.	Some people think that comic books are not good for children.
そんなことをしても何のためにもならない.	There's no point in doing something like that.
【原因・理由】彼は頭痛のために学校を休んだ.	He didn't go to school because he had a headache.
地震のために電車が遅れた.	The trains were delayed on account of the earthquake.
彼女がうっかり口をすべらしたため, 秘密の計画がばれてしまった.	Her careless slip of the tongue caused the secret plan to be exposed.

だめ

【良くない・役に立たない】僕はだめな男だ.	I can't do anything right. I'm †useless [good for nothing].
彼は父親としてはだめな人間だ.	As a father he's no good. He's a failure as a father.
このままでは彼女はだめになる.	If things continue as they have been, she'll be ruined.
僕はもうだめだ. 生きていく望みを失った.	It's all over (for me). I've lost all desire to go on living.
僕はゴルフはだめなんです.	I don't know how to play golf.[1] I'm terrible [bad] at golf.[2]
あの患者はもうだめらしい.	It seems there's no hope for that patient.

この靴はもうだめだ.	These shoes are no good anymore.
	These shoes have had it.
夏は野菜がすぐだめになる.	In summer vegetables †spoil [go bad] very quickly.
【失敗・むだ】彼はK大学を受けたがだめだった.	He took the entrance exam for K University but didn't get in.
私の提案はだめだった.	My proposal was †turned down [rejected].
私の計画はだめになった.	My plan †was ruined [fell through].
彼にいくら頼んでもだめだった.	No matter how many times I asked him it did no good.
その子はいくら注意してもだめだ.	No matter how many times you warn that child, it does no good.
【いけない】「これを使ってもいいですか」「いや,だめです」	"May [Can] I use it?" "No, you †may not [cannot]."
「明日までにやらなければだめですか」「はい,だめです」	"Do I have to [Must I] do it by tomorrow?" "Yes, you †have to [must]."
教室でたばこを吸ってはだめだ.	Don't smoke in the classroom.
【慣用】先方に期日についてだめを押しておいたほうがいい.	You'd better double-check the date with the other party.
彼は満塁ホームランを打ってだめを押した.	He hit a grand slam homer and put the game out of reach.
演出家はその女優に何回もだめを出した.	The director made the actress do the scene over and over until she got it right.

1) 全くできない場合. 2) よくできない場合.

ためす（試す）

彼女は買ってきた包丁の切れ味を試してみた.	She tried out the knife she bought to see how it cut.
あの車も試していいですか.	May I try out that car?
彼女は靴を20足試してみたが,どれも気に入らなかった.	She tried on 20 pairs of shoes, but couldn't find any that she liked.
この仕事は君の力を試すいい機会だ.	This job is a good opportunity for you to test your ability.
家から学校まで何分で走って行けるか試してみよう.	Let's see how many minutes it takes to run to school.

ためらう

私は彼女に本当のことを言うのをためらった.	I †hesitated[1] [was reluctant[2]] to tell her the truth.
彼はためらわずに転職した.	He changed jobs without hesitation.
彼はためらいがちに「明日休みをとってもいいですか」と言った.	He said hesitatingly, "Can I have the day off tomorrow?"

昔は知らない人に会うのをためらったものだ.	I used to shy away from meeting people I didn't know.

1)は「ためらう」行動そのものを表し、2)はその気持ちを表す.

ためる (溜・貯める)

この島では雨水をためて飲料水にしている.	Rain is collected and used for drinking water on this island.
彼女は夏休みの宿題をためてしまい、お姉さんに手伝ってもらった.	She had a lot of summer vacation homework left to do and got her older sister to help her.
母はその話を聞きながら目にいっぱい涙をためていた.	Mother's eyes filled with tears as she listened to that story.
彼女はヨーロッパ旅行のためにお金をためている.	She is saving up for a trip to Europe.

たもつ (保つ)

今度見つかった古い土器はほぼ原形を保っていた.	This ancient earthen vessel was found virtually intact.
実験室の温度を一定に保たなければならない.	We have to keep [maintain] the laboratory at an even temperature.
彼は絶対に安静を保つようにと医者に言われた.	He was told by the doctor to keep absolutely quiet.
健康を保つためには適度な運動が必要です.	The proper amount of exercise is necessary in order to maintain one's health.
彼はいつまでも若さを保っている.	He just never seems to get old.
平和を保つためには、全人類が努力しなければならない.	The entire human race must work together to maintain [preserve] peace.

たやすい

この問題を解くのはたやすいことだ.	This problem is easy to solve.
最近は日本でもいろいろなチーズがたやすく手に入る.	Recently, a wide variety of cheeses have become readily available in Japan.
土地の高い東京では家を建てるのはたやすいことではない.	It's not an easy matter to build a house in Tokyo, where land is so expensive.
何事も口で言うのはたやすいが実際に行うのは難しい.	Many things are easy to talk about but difficult to actually carry out.
手紙をポストに入れて来るくらいならたやすい御用です.	I'd be happy to go and mail a letter for you.

たより[1] (便り)

またお便りください.	Please write me again.

たより

故郷からの便りは何にもましてうれしいものだ.	Nothing makes me as happy as news from home.
最近彼から便りがありましたか.	Have you heard anything from him recently?
彼女は結婚したと風の便りに聞きました.	I heard through the grapevine that she got married.
春になると各地から花の便りが聞かれるようになる.	In spring, news of the first cherry blossoms comes from every area.

たより² (頼り)

頼りにしているよ.	I'm counting on you.
彼は頼りになる[頼りがいがある].	You can depend on him. He's dependable.
彼一人では頼りないから, 君も一緒に行きなさい.	I can't depend on him alone, so you go with him too.
彼女は頼りなさそうな返事をした.	The answer she gave me made me wonder if I could count on her.
地図を頼りに彼女の家を捜し当てた.	I found my way to her house with the help of a map.

> depend on はいずれも rely on, count on と置き換えられる.

たよる (頼る)

老後は子どもに頼るつもりはない.	I don't intend to depend [rely, count] on my children when I get old.
親類を頼って上京した.	I went to Tokyo where I could rely [depend, count] on my relatives.
悩みを解決するために多くの人は宗教に頼る.	Many people look to religion to solve their problems.

だらしない

彼がこんなにだらしないやつだとは知らなかった.	I didn't know he was so sloppy about everything.
彼はだらしない格好をしている.	He's sloppily dressed.
彼はだらしない生活をしている.	He's leading a loose life.
彼の仕事のやり方はだらしない.	He does sloppy [messy, slipshod] work.
彼女は時間にだらしない.	She's sloppy about †keeping time [being on time].
男がだらしなく床に横たわっていた.	The man was sprawled out all over the floor.
それぐらいの運動でへこたれるなんてだらしないね.	You can't even exercise that much without getting exhausted? Pretty sad [pathetic].

たりる (足りる)

【十分である】映画を見るだけならこのお金で足りる. — If we're only going to see a movie then we have enough money.

この本を買うには, 1000円で足りる. — One thousand yen is enough to buy this book.

いすが二つ足りません. — We are two chairs short.

料理をしていたら, 砂糖が足りなくなってしまった. — I ran out of sugar while cooking.

彼は何をするにも真剣さが足りない. — He's never serious enough about anything he does.

お互いに足りないところは補い合って協力していきましょう. — Let's work together to make up for each other's deficiencies.

これで事が足りたと思ったら間違いだ. — If you think this is good enough you are mistaken.

何を配達してもらうにも大抵電話一本で足りる. — A single phone call is sufficient to get almost anything delivered.

だるい

今日は何となくだるくて何もしたくない. — I feel so lethargic today. I don't want to do anything.

体がだるい. 風邪をひいたのかもしれない. — I feel run down. I think I may have caught (a) cold.

昨日はずっと庭の手入れをしていたので体がだるい. — I worked in the yard all day yesterday and I feel worn out.

一日じゅう立っていたので足がだるい. — My legs are sore because I was standing all day long.

たれる (垂れる)

【下がる・下げる】彼女の髪は肩まで垂れている. — Her hair hangs down to her shoulders.

雲が低く垂れている. — The clouds are hanging low in the sky.

橋の上で釣り人たちがのんびり釣り糸を垂れている. — Fishermen are relaxing letting their lines hang down from the top of the bridge.

【落ちる】軒先から雨のしずくがたれている. — Rain is dripping down from the edge of the eaves.

彼の額からは汗がたれている. — Sweat is dripping from his forehead.

【慣用】僕に教えを垂れて欲しくなんかないね. — I don't want you to preach down to me.

だれる

この映画は長過ぎて途中でだれてしまう. — This movie is so long that by the middle it †really drags [becomes quite tedious].

長くて退屈な講義に学生たちはだ — The lecture was so long and boring that

れてきた.	the students began to lose interest in it.
休日が続いたらすっかりだれてしまった.	I became completely listless as the vacation went on.
昼食が重いと午後だれてしまうことが多い.	I often get listless in the afternoon after eating a heavy lunch.
このところ皆ちょっとだれ気味だ.	Everyone's been seeming a little out of it recently.

～だろう

明日はきっと雨だろう.	I'm sure it's going to rain tomorrow.
5年後の私は学校の先生になっているだろう.	I'll probably be a school teacher five years from now.
彼は時間どおりに来るだろう.	He should [He'll most likely] be on time.
彼が殺人犯だというのは何かの間違いだろう.	Him a murderer?! There must be some mistake. / There must be some mistake, accusing him of murder.
彼が手を貸してくれたら、この仕事は成功していただろう.	If only he had lent us a hand, this (work) would have been a success, I'm sure.

だん (段)

彼女は階段のいちばん上の段から転げ落ちた.	She fell down the stairs from the top step.
寝台車の上〔下〕の段に寝た.	I slept on the upper [lower] berth in the sleeping car.
その本は本箱の真ん中の段にある.	That book is on the middle shelf of the bookcase.
この石段を登れば学校です.	The school is at the top of these stone steps.
【区切り】この文章は4段に分けられます.	This passage can be divided into four paragraphs.
【等級】彼は柔道三段だ.	He is at the third rank of *judo*.
【場合・程度】彼はいざという段になるといつも逃げ腰になる.	He always loses his nerve at the most critical stage.
冬のシベリアは寒いどころの段ではない.	The word "cold" doesn't begin to describe winter in Siberia.
この万年筆は私のに比べて段違いに書き易い.	This fountain pen is far and away easier to write with than mine.

たんじょう (誕生)

彼に男の子が誕生した.	His wife had a baby boy.
お誕生日おめでとう.	Happy birthday!
私たちは母の55歳の誕生日を祝っ	We celebrated our mother's fifty-fifth

た.
我がスキー同好会が誕生してから10年たった.
その年,日本で初めて女性知事が誕生した.

birthday.
Our ski club was formed 10 years ago.
That was the first year that a woman became governor in Japan.

だんだん (段々)

【段】段々になった道を登って行くと見晴らし台に出た.

Climbing the stepped path, I came to a clearing with a wide view.

【次第に】空がだんだん明るくなってきた.

The sky has gradually brightened.

暗くなって公園にいた人たちがだんだん帰り始めた.

When it became dark the people in the park gradually began to leave.

たんとう (担当)

このプロジェクトの担当者を呼んでください.

I would like to see someone †working on [connected with] this project.

この商品の仕入れ担当者はだれですか.

Who is responsible for stocking this product?

北海道地域を担当している荻原です.

My name is Ogiwara and I'm †in charge of [taking care of, responsible for] Hokkaido.

今,担当の者に代わりますので,少々お待ちください.(電話で)

Please hold the line. I will transfer you to the person in charge.

担当の者はただ今,外出して〔席を外して〕おりますが.

The person in charge is not †in the office [at his desk] at the moment.

外国人社長が会社の再建を担当することになった.

A non-Japanese president was put in charge of turning the company around.

僕の担当についたのは研修中の新人看護師だった.

A new student nurse was placed in my charge.

> in charge (of) はその仕事の「担当責任者」について使う表現.

だんどり (段取り)

彼の段取りが良かったおかげで作業は短時間で片付いた.

Thanks to his planning we were able to finish the work in good time.

だれが何を受け持つか決めてなかったの? 段取りが悪いな.

Wasn't it decided ahead of time who would do what? Pretty poor planning.

そろそろ結婚式の段取りを決めましょう.

Let's start the wedding arrangements.

段取りさえつけば,この仕事はほとんど終わったようなものだ.

Once the preparations have been taken care of, this job is as good as done.

たんねん (丹念)

我々はデータを丹念に調べた.	We painstakingly examined the data.
	We examined the data in detail.
あの職人は丹念な仕事をする.	That craftsman does elaborately crafted work.

ち

ち (血)

ハンカチに血が付いているけど, どうかしたの.	There's blood on your handkerchief. What happened?
チャンピオンの右のまぶたから血が出て〔流れて〕いた.	Blood was coming [flowing] from the champion's right eyelid.
顔中血だらけの人が救急車で運ばれて行った.	Someone whose head was covered with blood was taken away in an ambulance.
【血筋】彼は武士の血を引いていることを誇りに思っている.	He's proud of his *samurai* ancestry.
血は水よりも濃い.	Blood is thicker than water.
【慣用】国民は政府にもっと血の通った福祉行政を望んでいる.	People are hoping for a more humane welfare policy from the government.
あいつは血の気の多いやつだ.	He's a hot-blooded guy.
母親が交通事故にあったと聞いて彼女の顔から血の気が引いた.	She turned pale when she heard that her mother had been in a traffic accident.
今日の彼の成功は, 若い頃の血のにじむような努力のたまものだ.	His current success is the result of the blood, sweat and tears of his youth.
こんな簡単なことが分からないなんて, 血の巡りの悪いやつだ.	He's really slow to catch on. He should understand something as simple as this.
あの高利貸しは血も涙もない.	That loan shark is cold and heartless.
海を見ると船乗りの血が騒ぐ.	Whenever I see the ocean, the sailor in me starts to stir.

ちいさい (小さい)

彼は体は小さいが, 体力がある.	He's a small man but he has stamina.
私は小さい家に住んでいる.	I live in a small house.
小さい子には優しくしなさい.	Be gentle with little children.
小さい頃は正月によくたこ揚げをして遊んだ.	When I was little, we often flew kites at New Year's.
テレビが子どもに与える影響は決	The influence television has on children is

して小さくありません.	by no means insignificant.
小さいことにはこだわらないようにしなさい.	Don't get hung up on** trivial [insignificant] things.
あの男は人物が小さい.	He's small-minded.
彼らは何かひそひそ小さい声で話している.	They're talking about something in hushed voices.
ラジオの音をもう少し小さくしてください.	Please turn down your radio just a little (bit) more.
【慣用】彼は先生に叱られて小さくなった.	He felt really small because the teacher scolded him.
彼は上司の前ではいつも小さくなっている.	He always cowers in front of his boss.

ちえ (知恵)

あの子は小さいけれど, よく知恵が回る子だ.	He's only a child but he has his wits about him.
3歳にもなると知恵がついてきて, 怒られないようにとうそをつく子どももいる.	By the age of three, some children have learned to lie in order to stay out of trouble.
何かいい知恵があったら貸してください.	Please let me know if you have any good advice.
同じ事の繰り返しでは知恵がなさ過ぎる.	Doing the same thing over and over again shows a complete lack of resourcefulness.
無い知恵を絞って考えたが, やはり名案は浮かんでこなかった.	I racked my brain but still couldn't come up with any good ideas.
昔の人はいろいろ生活の知恵を身につけていた.	In the old days, people were very resourceful.
だれかが彼に知恵をつけたに違いない.	Somebody must have clued him in.
彼に入れ知恵したのはだれだろう.	Who planted that idea in his head?

チェック

この表の数字をチェックしてください.	Could you please check the figures [numbers] on this chart [spreadsheet]?
参加者が来たら名前をチェックしてください.	Please check off the names of the participants as they arrive.
この商品があるかどうか在庫をチェックしてください.	Could you check to see if we have this product in stock?
盗まれた物はないか引き出しの中身をチェックした.	I checked the drawers to see if anything had been stolen.
答案用紙の解答に漏れがないかチェックしなさい.	Please make sure that you have filled in all the blanks on the answer sheet.

彼の経費の使いみちをチェックしたほうがいい.	You should check (on) his expenditures.
彼は常に最新の流行をファッション誌でチェックしている.	He is always checking the latest trends in fashion magazines.
彼女は他人の服装に対するチェックが厳しい.	She's very critical about how people dress.

ちかい (近い)

【距離】
私の家は学校に近い.	My house is †close to [near] school.
駅へ行くにはこの道を行ったほうが近い.	This is a shorter way to the station.
この道は駅への近道だ.	This is a shortcut to the station.

【時間】
近いうちにまた会おう.	Let's meet again soon.
近いうちにまた会って,詳しいことを決めなければならない.	We'll have to get together again soon to work out the details.
近い将来きっと二人は結婚するだろう.	I'm sure they'll get married in the near future.
家に帰ったのは夜中の1時近かった.	I didn't get home until close to one in the morning.
お正月も近いね.	It's almost New Year's, isn't it?
学校の新しい図書館の完成は近い.	The school's new library is near completion.

【数値】
| 祭りは1万人に近い人出でにぎわった. | The festival drew crowds of almost [nearly] 10,000 [ten thousand] people. |
| 彼のお父さんはもう70に近い. | His father's already close to seventy. |

【関係】
| 猿は人間に近い動物だと言われている. | Apes are animals that are said to be close to human beings. |
| フランス語よりイタリア語のほうがラテン語に近いのですか. | Is Italian closer to Latin than French is? |

ちがい (違い)

【差異】
従来の製品と新製品との違いはこの点にあります.	This is where the new product differs from the earlier ones.
二人の語学力には格段の違いがある.	There's a marked difference in their linguistic abilities.
電車で行っても車で行っても時間的には大した違いはない.	It doesn't make much difference timewise whether you take the train or go by car.
お兄さんとはいくつ違いですか.	How many years apart are you and your older brother?

【誤り】
そのことで私を責めるのは筋違いだ.	It's unreasonable to blame me for that.
彼は何か思い違いをしている.	Somehow he's got the wrong idea.
	I think he may be mistaken.

あなたは時々計算違いをしますね. You sometimes make mistakes in your calculations, don't you?

ちがいない (違いない)

この時計は彼が無くしたものに違いない.	This †must [has to] be the watch he lost.
彼はあの時怒っていたに違いない.	He must have been mad at the time.
その犯行は彼の仕業に違いない.	He must have committed that crime. That crime has to have been his doing.
彼女は今，家にいるに違いない.	I'm sure she's at home now.

ちがう (違う)

【異なる】僕と弟では身長が10センチ違う. There's a 10-centimeter difference in height between my brother and I.
野菜の値段は日によって違う. The price of vegetables changes daily.
これは私の傘とは色が少し違う. The color of this umbrella is a little different from mine.
彼女は毎日違う服を着る. She wears different clothes every day.
新鮮な魚は味が違う. Fresh fish sure tastes better.
それじゃ話が違うじゃないか. But that's not what you said before.
彼はどこか普通の人と違ったところがある. He's got something that sets him apart from others.
姉は私と違って社交的です. Unlike me, my older sister is very outgoing.
【間違う】請求書の計算が違っています. The bill is not calculated correctly.
There's †a mistake [an error] in this bill.
電話番号が違っていますよ. You've got the wrong number.
違う道を来てしまったらしい. It seems we've taken the wrong road.

ちかく (近く)

【距離】私の家は学校の近くです. My house is near school.
家の近くで火事があった. There was a fire near my house.
私は彼の近くに座った. I sat near him.
近くまで来たのでちょっと寄ってみました. I thought I would stop by as I happened to be in the neighborhood.
【時間】1時近くに関東地方に地震があった. There was an earthquake in the Kanto region just before one o'clock.
私はこの町に10年近く住んでいる. I've been living in this town for nearly 10 years.
娘をお使いにやってから1時間近くたつのにまだ帰ってこない. It's been nearly an hour since I sent my daughter on an errand and she's not home yet.
彼は近く帰国する予定だ. He's planning to return soon.

【数値】車の修理に5万円近くかかった.	Car repairs cost me nearly ¥50,000 [fifty thousand yen].
講演会には2,000人近くの人が集まった.	Nearly 2,000 people came to the lecture.

ちかごろ (近頃)

この辺は近頃物騒だ.	It's not safe around here lately.
彼は近頃訪ねて来ない.	He's stopped coming by here lately.
近頃の若い人は体が大きくなった.	Young people are quite big nowadays.

ちかづく (近づく)

【距離】そのとき電車がホームに近づいてきた.	The train was just approaching [nearing] the station.
台風が近づき, 風雨が強くなった.	The wind and rain got stronger as the typhoon †approached [got closer].
バス停で知らない人が近づいて来て, 私に荷物を運ぶのを手伝ってくれと頼んだ.	A complete stranger came up to me at the bus stop and asked me to help him carry his luggage.
【時間】夏休みが近づいて来た.	Summer vacation is getting close.
私の入学試験が近づいて来た.	My entrance exams are coming up.
彼の絵は完成に近づいている.	He's nearing completion of his painting.
【親しくなる】ああいう連中には近づかないほうがいい.	You shouldn't get mixed up with a crowd like that.
彼は無愛想で近づきにくい.	He's gruff [cranky] and difficult to approach.
	He's so unsociable (that) it's hard to get to know him.
【似てくる】彼女の料理の腕前はだいぶプロに近づいてきた.	Her cooking skills are almost as good as a pro.

ちから (力)

【物理的な力】水車は水の力で動く.	A water wheel is moved by the force of water.
この機械は電気〔蒸気〕の力で動く.	This machine is powered by electricity [steam].
【人の力・体力】こんな大きな岩を人間の力で動かすのは無理だ.	It would be impossible to move this big rock by hand.
腹が減って力が出ない.	I'm so hungry (that) I don't have any strength left.
	I'm weak from hunger.
彼は最後まで力いっぱい走った.	He ran as hard as he could until the very end.
彼は力まかせにロープを引っ張っ	He pulled the rope with all his strength

た.	[might].
彼はクラスでいちばんの力持ちだ.	He's the strongest person in our class.
力仕事は苦手です.	I'm not very good at hard labor.
彼は落選の知らせに体中の力が抜けてしまった.	After learning of his defeat he felt totally drained of energy.
彼女は病弱でいつも力のない声で話す.	She's frail and always speaks in a weak voice.
力ずくで人を従わせるのはよくない.	You shouldn't force people to do what you want (them to).
【気力】彼は事業に失敗して力を落としている.	His failure at business has got him down.
彼の力のこもった演技は評論家のあいだで好評だ.	His dynamic performance was well received by the critics.
【能力】彼女は最近英語の力をつけてきた.	Her English has improved lately.
もっと数学の力をつけなさい.	Work harder on your math.
彼はその試合で持てる力を出し切った.	He really put all he had into that game.
あの歌手が売れているのは自分の力ではなく事務所の力だ.	That singer is popular not so much because he is talented but because he has a good agent [office].
自然の力に比べて人間の力は小さなものだ.	Man's strength is insignificant compared to the forces of nature.
【努力】彼は生涯, 植物の研究に力を注いだ.	He put a lifetime of effort into the study of plants.
彼女の力で同窓会を開くことができました.	Thanks to her efforts, we were able to hold the class reunion.
みんなの力で学校の文化祭を成功させよう.	Let's all do our best to make the school festival a success.
【財力】私にはまだ家を建てる程の力はない.	I certainly don't have the resources [means] to do anything like build a house yet.
【助力】力を貸してくれないか.	Could you help me?
	Could you give me some assistance?
力を貸してもらえると助かります.	I'd sure appreciate it if you'd lend a hand.
人の力を頼むのは男らしくない.	It's not manly to ask for help.
困ったときには力になりますよ.	If you're ever in trouble, I'll be there to help.
【効力・影響力】彼は今も政界で強い力を持っている.	He still has great influence within government circles.
警察の力で騒ぎは治まった.	Police intervention brought the commotion under control.

ちこく (遅刻)

学校に遅刻してはいけません.	Don't be late for school.
会議に30分遅刻した.	I was 30 minutes late for the meeting.
彼女とのデートにもう少しで遅刻するところだった.	I †was almost [came close to being] late for my date with her.
彼は遅刻の常習犯だ.	He's habitually late.

ちしき (知識)

博識の彼と話していると,いろいろな知識が身につく.	I learn a lot by talking to such a knowledgeable man.
私はこの本からいろいろな知識を得た.	I learned a lot from this book.
私はコンピューターに関する知識が全くない.	I don't know anything about computers.
彼女は絵画についての知識が豊富だ.	She's very knowledgeable about painting.
祖父は老いても知識欲に燃えている.	Even though my grandfather is very old, he has a genuine thirst for knowledge.
彼はいわゆる知識人だ.	You could call him an intellectual.

ちぢむ (縮む)

このブラウスは洗濯したら縮んでしまった.	The blouse shrank when I washed it.
ズボンの丈が少し縮んだようだ.	The pants seem to have shrunk in length a bit.
レールは気温により伸びたり縮んだりする.	The rails expand and contract with changes in temperature.
トップを走っている選手と2位との差が縮まってきた.	The distance has closed between the front-runner and the person in second place.
彼はヤクザ風の男に睨まれて縮み上がった.	He cowered under the stare of a man looking like a gangster.

ちぢめる (縮める)

スカートの丈を少し縮めた.	I took up the hem of my skirt a little.
2位の走者はじりじりと1位との距離を縮めた.	Little by little, the runner in second place closed the gap between himself and the leader.
酒の飲み過ぎが彼の寿命を縮めた.	Drinking too much alcohol †shortened [took several years off] his life.

ちてき (知的)

その雑誌の知的水準は高い.	The intellectual level of that magazine is high.

彼女は知的美人だ. She's smart and beautiful.
She has both brains and beauty.

ちみつ (緻密)
その研究には緻密さが要求される. That research requires a high degree of precision.

成功するには緻密な計画を立てる必要がある. We have to make up a detailed plan if we want to succeed.

優れた科学者となるためには緻密な頭脳を持っていなければならない. To be a good scientist, you must have a precise mind.

ちゃくじつ (着実)
彼は着実に仕事をするので信頼できる. We can depend on him. He is a steady worker.

彼女は着実に成績が伸びている. Her grades are steadily improving.

女性はいろいろな専門職に着実に進出している. Women are steadily advancing into specialized areas of work.

ちゃくちゃく (着々)
工事は着々と進んでいる. The construction is progressing †step by step [steadily].

労働条件は着々と改善されてきている. Working conditions are improving steadily.

チャンス
またとないチャンスだ. It's a once-in-a-lifetime opportunity.

5年待ったが, ついにチャンス到来だ. I finally got my chance after five years.

チャンスは今だ. 行け！ This is your chance. Go for it! [Do it!]

もう一度だけチャンスを与えよう. I'll give you one more [last] chance.

チャンスさえあれば映画に出演してみたい. I'd like to have a chance to be in movies.

せっかくのチャンスを生かせなかった. I couldn't take advantage of that opportunity.

彼女に声をかける絶好のチャンスをみすみす逃してしまった. I missed my best opportunity to talk to her.

バッターは三振を取られ, チームは逆転のチャンスを逸した. The batter struck out, ruling out all chances of a recovery.

今週, いて座のあなたには恋のチャンスが訪れることでしょう. Love may be in store for the Sagittarian this week.

ちゃんと

【確かに】
- 旅行の用意はちゃんと出来ている. — Everything's all set [ready] for the trip.
- 私の手紙はちゃんと届きましたか. — Did my letter arrive †all right [OK]?
- かぎはさっきまでちゃんとここにあったのに. — I'm sure the key was lying here a minute ago.
- 彼の腹の内は私にはちゃんと分かっている. — I know exactly what he's up to.

【きちんと】
- 部屋をちゃんと片づけなさい. — Get your room straightened [cleaned] up.
- 頰づえをつかないで, ちゃんと座りなさい. — Don't sit there with your chin in your hand. Sit up straight.
- 彼はいつも身なりがちゃんとしている. — He always looks well-dressed. / He always dresses neatly.

【立派な】
- ちゃんとした職業に就きなさい. — Get yourself a proper job.
- 手術を受けるなら, ちゃんとした病院を選びなさい. — If you have to have an operation, you should choose a reputable hospital.

ちゅう (中)

【平均的】
- 私の成績はクラスで中くらいです. — My grades are about average for the class.
- 彼は中くらいの背の高さです. — He's of about average height.

【期間中】
- 品物は今週中にお届けします. — I'll deliver the goods sometime within the week.
- 授業中は静かにしなさい. — Please be quiet during class.
- 今日の授業は午前中だけです. — Today, classes will be held only in the morning.
- 彼女とはアメリカ滞在中に知り合った. — I met her while I was in the United States.

【進行中】
- 彼は今, 会議中です. — He's in conference now.
- この道は工事中で通れません. — The road's under construction. You can't get through.
- 昨日の夜, 何度あなたの家に電話しても話し中だった. — Last night, your phone was busy every time I tried calling.

【〜の中】
- 我々の合唱団は, 50人中35人が女性です. — Thirty-five of the fifty members of our chorus group are women.
- 彼の合格は十中八九間違いない. — The chances are ten to one that he'll pass.

ちゅうい (注意)

【留意・注目】
- 授業中はよく注意して先生の話を聞きなさい. — During class you should pay attention and listen to what your teacher says.
- 彼女はいつも交通標識によく注意 — She always pays close attention to the

して運転する.	traffic signs when she drives.
僕は車を買うとき燃費の点に注意を払う.	When I buy a car, I make sure to check the mileage it will get.
奇抜な服装の女性がロビーに現れみんなの注意を引いた.	A woman in a bizarre outfit entered the lobby and drew everyone's attention.
この子は注意散漫だから,うっかりした間違いが多い.	This child makes a lot of careless mistakes because he gets distracted easily.
【用心】旅行中は風邪をひかないように注意しなさい.	Be careful not to catch (a) cold while you're on your trip.
道路を横断するときは車に注意しなさい.	Watch out for the traffic when you cross the street.
小さい子がいるのでストーブには十分注意しています.	I'm very careful with the heater because we have a small child.
雨で道が滑り易くなっていたので,注意して運転した.	I drove very carefully because the road was slippery from the rain.
彼は要注意人物だよ.	He's someone you've got to †watch out for [keep your eye on].
【忠告・警告】警官から注意を受けた.	He was given a warning by the policeman. He was warned by the cops.**
母から帰りが遅いと注意された.	Mother scolded me for coming home late.
先生の注意をよく守りなさい.	Mind your teacher. Do what your teacher says.
あの店の店員はあまり無作法なので,注意してやった.	The salesperson in that store was so rude that I told him off.

ちゅうおう (中央)

部屋の中央には会議用のテーブルが置かれていた.	There was a conference table set up in the middle of the room.
駅は町のほぼ中央にあります.	The station's just about in the center of town.
この町の中央郵便局はどこにありますか.	Where's the central post office in this town?
最近,中央よりも地方での就職を望む者が増えている.	Lately, more people are wanting to find jobs in outlying areas rather than in large population centers.

ちゅうし (中止)

その計画は実行に移される前に中止された.	The plan was †canceled [called off] before it could be put into action.
雨のため運動会は中止となった.	The athletic meet was †canceled[1)] [called off[2)]] on account of rain.
その車に欠陥が見つかり,製造〔販売〕が中止になった.	Production of that car was halted[3)] [That car is no longer sold] due to defects.

彼は病気のため研究を一時中止した.	He had to temporarily stop working on his research due to illness.

> 1)2)3) 予定の計画・行動が実行される前に中止する場合は cancel または call off, 実行されている最中なら halt を使う.

ちゅうじつ (忠実)

彼は上司に対してそんなに忠実ではない.	He's not very loyal to his boss.
私は忠実に言われたとおりのことをしたまでだ.	I only did exactly as I was told.
この翻訳は必ずしも原文に忠実ではない.	This translation is not always faithful to the original.
そのドラマは歴史に忠実ではない.	That drama is not †historically accurate [faithful to history].

ちゅうしょう (中傷)

彼は同僚の中傷でノイローゼのようになっている.	His colleagues' backbiting brought him close to a nervous breakdown.
彼女は中傷に悩まされた.	The malicious gossip upset her.
彼はライバルを中傷するためにそう言ったのだと思う.	I think he said it to damage[1] his rival's reputation.
政治家はその中傷記事に反論した.	The politician objected to the slanderous article about him.

> 1) hurt, harm, injure でもよい.

ちゅうしん (中心)

【真ん中】矢は的の中心に当たった.	The arrow †hit the exact center of the target [hit the bull's eye].
台風の中心は沖縄の東100キロにある.	The center of the typhoon is 100 kilometers east of Okinawa.
【要所・要点】東京は日本の政治・経済の中心である.	Tokyo is the political and economic center of Japan.
同窓会では子育てが話題の中心になった.	Conversation at the class reunion centered on how to raise children.
その会議の中心議題は, いかに学校から暴力をなくすかということだった.	The conference focused on how to create a violence-free environment in schools.
彼が中心となって新しい劇団が作られた.	He played a central role in creating the theater group.
あの人が事件の中心人物だ.	That person is the key figure [man] in the case.

ちゅうとはんぱ（中途半端）

彼の仕事はいつも中途半端だ．
He always leaves his work half done.

中途半端な気持ちでこの仕事を続けていてはらちが明かないよ．
You won't get anywhere if you continue to work halfheartedly on this project.

インフレは中途半端な方法では抑えられない．
Inflation cannot be controlled with halfway measures.

中途半端な時間に駅に着いてしまった．
Our arrival at the station was poorly timed.

話し合いは中途半端に終わってしまった．
The discussion †ended [left everything] up in the air.

ちゅうもん（注文）

【発注】注文した品物が届いた．
The things I ordered have arrived.

父は新しい背広を注文した．
My father ordered a new suit.

コーヒーをもう1杯注文した．
I ordered another cup of coffee.

昨日は大口の注文を受けた．
We got a big order yesterday.

【要求】その指揮者はオーケストラに厳しい注文をつけるので有名だ．
That conductor is famous for being hard on his orchestra.
The conductor is known to place harsh demands on his orchestra.

そんな無理な注文には応じられない．
It would be impossible to comply with such an unreasonable request.

試合は，こちらの注文どおりにうまく展開した．
The game turned out just as we had hoped.

ちょうさ（調査）

警察は列車事故の原因の調査を進めている．
The police are now investigating the cause of the train accident.

その件については，詳しく調査してから発表します．
We will issue a statement about that after making a thorough investigation.

公害問題で現地に調査団が派遣された．
An investigative group was sent to the site to look into the pollution problem.

先日，世論調査が行われた．
An opinion poll was taken [conducted] the other day.

ちょうし（調子）

【音・リズム】彼の歌は調子外れだ．
He sings out of tune.

彼は怒った調子で妻に話しかけた．
He spoke to his wife in an angry tone.

【具合】今日は体の調子がいい．
I feel better [well] today.

ピッチャーの調子はいいようだ．
The pitcher seems to be in good form.

あの俳優は今日調子がいい．
That actor is doing very well today.

車の調子が悪い．
The car isn't running very well.
The car is a little out of tune.[1]

このテレビは調子が悪い.	This TV set isn't working very well.
「仕事の調子はどうですか」「調子よくいっています」	"How is your business?" "It's going †well [all right]."
試合までに体の調子を整えておきなさい.	Try to get yourself in good shape before the game.
【勢い】その調子, その調子!	That's it! ／ Now you've got it!
その(勉強の)調子では試験に受からないよ.	If you don't change your study habits, you won't pass the examination.
この調子でやれば来月までにこの仕事が仕上がる.	If we continue at this rate, we can complete this work by next month.
今日はどうも調子が出ない.	I just can't get into it today.
そのチームは1点を上げてから, がぜん調子づいてきた.	After scoring one point, that team suddenly got into the swing of it.
【慣用】彼はだれとでも調子よくつきあう.	He can get along with anybody.
彼は調子がいいからあまり信用してはいけない.	Don't count on him. He's all talk (and no action).
社長はおだてるとすぐ調子に乗って大声で歌い出す.	The minute you butter him up, the boss gets carried away and starts singing in a loud voice.
彼はテンポがのろいので一緒に話をすると調子が狂ってしまう.	He's so slow-paced that our conversations always seem disjointed.

1) out of tune の反対は in tune (調子がいい).

ちょうせん (挑戦)

【困難への】来月, フルマラソンに挑戦する予定です.	I'm going to try a full marathon next month.
少しでも可能性があるなら挑戦してみるべきだ.	If there's even the slightest chance, you should give it a try.
あの水泳選手は世界新記録に挑戦し続けている.	That swimmer is continuing to try to set a new world record.
たまにはミニスカートに挑戦してみたら?	How about trying out a miniskirt once in a while?
【人への】彼はその挑戦を受けて立った.	He took up [on] the challenge.
	He rose to the challenge.
これは私への挑戦状と受け取っていいんだね.	I take it that you're challenging me on this.
彼の挑戦的な態度はあちこちでいざこざを引き起こした.	He's so competitive that he created problems in a number of places.
チャンピオンは4回戦で挑戦者をノックアウトした.	The champion knocked out the challenger in the fourth round.

ちょうど

この背広は私にちょうどいい.	This suit is just my size.
ちょうど夕食が終わったところに彼がやって来た.	He came when I had just finished supper.
ちょうどいいところに来た.	You came at just the right time.

ちょうわ (調和)

彼女の家のカーテンは部屋の色とうまく調和している.	The curtains go nicely with the colors of her room.
彼はいつも周囲と調和がとれるような建物を設計する.	He always designs buildings to harmonize with their surroundings.

ちょきん (貯金)

私は郵便局に貯金が50万円あります.	I have ¥500,000 [five hundred thousand yen] in savings in a post office account.
ボーナスをそっくり銀行に貯金した.	I put my entire bonus in the bank.
これからは毎月少しずつ貯金をしよう.	We'll put a little away in savings each month.
彼は毎月給料から1万円ずつ貯金している.	He takes ¥10,000 [ten thousand yen] out of his salary each month for savings.
彼は貯金を下ろしてカメラを買った.	He withdrew some of his savings and bought a camera.
僕の貯金通帳は母が持っている.	My mother keeps my savings passbook for me.

ちょくせつ (直接)

飛行機墜落の直接の原因はパイロットの操縦ミスだった.	The plane crash was directly attributable to pilot error.
彼に会って直接話を聞きたい.	I want to hear it directly from him.
私は彼女を直接知っているわけではない.	I don't really know her personally.
今日会社が終わったら直接お宅に伺います.	I'm going straight to your place (right) after work today.

ちょっかん (直感)

直感的に彼がそれをやったのだと分かった.	I intuitively knew that he had done it.
	I just knew that he had done it.
彼女は直感的に物事をとらえる.	She perceives things intuitively.
私の直感が当たった.	My hunch was right.

ちょっと

【少し】彼女はいつもちょっとしか	She never eats very much.

食べない.	
その絵はもうちょっと上に掛けたほうがいい.	Try hanging the picture a little higher.
この問題は彼にはちょっと難しいようだ.	I think this problem's a little too difficult for him to solve.
この本はもうちょっとで読み終わる.	I'm almost through with [reading] this book.
	I only have a little more to read before I finish with this book.
この絵が本物かどうかちょっと見ただけでは分からない.	At a glance, I can't tell whether the painting is the real thing or not.
ちょっと考えさせてください.	Give me a little time to think about it.
すみませんが, ちょっとお待ちください.	I'm sorry, but could you wait a minute, please?
君にちょっと話がある.	I've got something to talk to you about.
	I have to talk to you about something.
彼女のちょっとした思いやりにはいつも感心する.	I'm always impressed by her small kindnesses.
【かなり】彼にはちょっとした貯金があるそうだ.	I hear he has a fair amount in savings.
【簡単には】彼が交通事故を起こすなんてちょっと考えられない.	I find it a little hard to believe that he could cause a car accident.
あの人の名は何といったのかちょっと思い出せない.	I can't quite remember what his name is.
【呼びかけ】ちょっと, 電話が鳴っているよ.	Hey, the telephone's [phone's] ringing!

ちらかす[る] (散らかす[る])

公園にゴミを散らかしてはいけません.	Don't litter in the park.
	Don't leave your garbage in the park.
校門のところにゴミ〔たばこの吸い殻〕が散らかっていた.	There was some garbage [There were some cigarette butts] littered [scattered] around the school gate.
彼はいつも部屋を散らかしている.	His room is always a mess.

ちらす (散らす)

サラダの上に粉チーズを散らして食べた.	I sprinkled cheese on my salad before eating it.
昨夜の風が桜の花を散らしてしまった.	Last night's wind blew all the cherry blossoms off the trees.
先生の姿を見ると, 深夜の街にたむろしていた若者たちはクモの子を散らすようにいなくなった.	The youth hanging around the streets late at night scattered at the sight of their teacher.

| ラグビーの試合で両チームは火花を散らして戦った. | The two teams fought bitterly during the rugby match. |
| 彼は怒って，周りのだれかれ構わずどなり散らした. | He got angry and started yelling at everyone around him. |

ちりょう（治療）
私は病院でけがの治療を受けた.	I was treated for the injury at the hospital.
私は週に一度治療のために病院へ通っている.	I go to the hospital once a week for treatment.
歯の治療にとてもお金がかかった.	It cost me a lot of money to have my teeth fixed.

ちる（散る）
桜の花びらが音もなく散っていた.	The cherry blossoms fell silently.
風に吹かれて木の葉が散っていた.	The leaves were blown off the trees by the wind.
電車が通ると架線に火花が散った.	Sparks flew from the overhead wires as the train passed.
デモ行進が終わると，参加者は散っていった.	The demonstrators dispersed after the march.

ちんぷ（陳腐）
| 大抵のメロドラマは陳腐な筋立てである. | Most soap opera plots are banal [hackneyed]. |
| 「覆水盆に返らず」なんて陳腐なことを言うなよ. | Don't †use clichés [say trite things] like "It's no use crying over spilt milk." |

つ

つい
【うっかり】講義中つい居眠りしてしまった.	I inadvertently fell asleep during the lecture.
つい口が滑って秘密を漏らしてしまった.	I just [unintentionally] let the secret slip.
ゆうべはつい飲み過ぎた.	I drank too much last night against my better judgment.
つい不要な物を買ってしまった.	I bought something I didn't need †on an [out of] impulse.

【ほんの】彼はつい今しがた帰った.	He left just now.
大学へ入学したのもつい昨日のことのように思える.	It seems like only yesterday that I entered [started] college.

(〜に)ついて

【〜に関して】彼はコンピューターについてよく知っている.	He knows a lot about computers.
今日はこの問題について話し合いましょう.	Let's talk about this problem today.
彼らはダーウィンの進化論の真偽について議論した.	They argued over the validity of Darwin's theory of evolution.
教授は初期のビザンチン帝国について講演した.	The professor gave a lecture on the early Byzantine Empire.
【〜ごとに】私の学校では生徒40人について先生一人です.	At my school there is one teacher for every 40 students.
あのガソリンスタンドはほかの店と比べて1リットルについて10円も安い.	Gasoline is ¥10 a liter cheaper at that gas station than at other stations.
【そこで】彼は来月大阪へ転勤することになりました. ついては明日送別会を開きたいと思います.	He's being transferred to Osaka next month, and so I thought we might hold a going-away party for him tomorrow.

ついで(に)

図書館に行くの？ついでにこの本も返しておいて.	Are you going to the library? Can you return this book when you go?
テレビを買うんだったら, ついでにビデオも買っちゃおうよ.	If we're buying a TV (set) we might as well buy a video deck while we're at it.
ついでに私の分もコピーしてもらえますか.	Do you mind making a copy for me at the same time?
近くまで来たから, ついでに寄ったんだよ.	(I) Just happened to be in the neighborhood and thought I'd drop in [by].
急ぎませんから, ついでのときに持ってきてください.	I'm not in a hurry. Just bring it by when you happen to be in the area [neighborhood].
新宿に来たついでに買い物して行こうか.	Since we're in Shinjuku anyway, we might [may] as well go shopping.
この料理は辛すぎる. ついでに言うと, 見た目も良くないね.	This dish is too spicy. And it doesn't look that great either.

ついに

彼はついにその仕事を成し遂げた.	He finally[1] got that job done.
ついに彼は現れなかった.	He never showed up.

1) finally の代わりに at last, in the end, at length* をそれぞれ文頭または文末に持ってきてもよい. finally, at last, at length は否定文には用いない.

つうかい (痛快)

彼のような高慢な男が失敗するのを見るのは痛快だ. — It gives me no small satisfaction to see such an arrogant man make a mistake.

その船乗りは痛快な冒険物語をしてくれた. — The sailor told us some thrilling adventure stories.

つうかん (痛感)

体力の衰えを痛感している. — I really can feel myself getting physically weaker.

最近, 英語の必要性を痛感しています. — Recently I've become acutely [painfully] aware of the need to learn English.

事の重大さを痛感しています. — Its importance [The importance of that matter] has really come home to me.

つうじる (通じる)

【交通・通信が】この道路は東京へ通じている. — This road leads to Tokyo.

駅から村までバスが通じている. — There is a bus running from the station to the village.

この町まで地下鉄が通じ, 外出するのに大変便利になった. — Getting about has become much more convenient now that the subway runs out to this town.

電話が故障で通じなかった. — I couldn't get through because the phones were out of order.

【了解される】彼にはこの件について話が通じていないようだ. — It seems he hasn't been informed about what's happened.

子どもたちには私の気持ちが通じていないようだ. — It seems that the way I feel hasn't gotten through to the children.

私の気持ちがやっと彼に通じた. — He finally †realized [found out] how I felt about him.

アメリカ人に話しかけたが私の英語は通じなかった. — I tried to speak to an American, but he didn't understand my English.

彼は冗談が通じない人だ. — He never gets jokes.

【通暁する】彼は日本美術に通じている. — He has a thorough knowledge of Japanese art.
He's well versed in Japanese art.

彼は政界の事情に通じている. — He has a thorough knowledge of the political world.

彼女は4ヵ国語に通じている.	She can communicate in four languages.
彼はこの辺りの地理に通じている.	He is familiar with this area.
【内通する】あの男はライバル会社と通じていた.	He was in secret communication with a rival company.
【期間・範囲】この場所は一年を通じて観光客でにぎわっている.	It's full of tourists around here †all year round [throughout the year].
郵便料金は全国を通じて同じです.	Postal rates are the same for all parts of the country.
【仲介とする】彼はあらゆる機会を通じて軍縮の必要性を説いた.	He took every opportunity available to explain the need for arms reduction.
当選番号は新聞〔テレビ〕を通じて発表いたします.	Winning numbers will be †listed in the newspaper [announced on TV].
私たちは彼〔クラブ活動〕を通じて知り合った.	We got to know each other through †him [club activities].

つうしん (通信)

漁船は無線で通信する.	Fishing boats communicate by radio.
地震のため，その村との通信は途絶えている.	Due to the earthquake, all means of communication with that village have been cut off.
通信機関の発達で私たちは世界じゅうのニュースをいち早く知ることができる.	Developments in communications have made it possible to get news from anywhere in the world instantaneously.
彼は通信教育によって大学を出た.	He received his college degree by taking correspondence courses.
通信販売で食器を買った.	I bought my tableware by mail order.

つうよう (通用)

そんなやり方は今の若い社員には通用しないよ.	That way of doing things †isn't acceptable among [won't be popular with] young company employees today.
	That's not going to wash with** today's young employees.
そんなやり方がどこでも通用すると思うなよ.	Don't think that you can get away with that everywhere you go.
その古い格言は現代の社会でも通用する.	That old maxim also holds true in modern society.
ユーロはヨーロッパのほとんどの国で通用する.	The euro is accepted in almost all of the European states.
表門は閉めたので通用口から帰ってください.	The main gate is closed. Please use the side entrance.

つうれつ (痛烈)

痛烈な批評にあの高慢な作家もさすがにがっくりした. — The scathing criticism discouraged even that conceited [overconfident] writer.

彼の言葉は痛烈な一撃だった. — His words came as a crushing blow.

つかう (使う)

【物を】最近の子どもたちははしを使うのが下手だ. — Children these days aren't very good at using chopsticks.

この本は良い紙を使っている. — This book is printed on very good paper.

このストーブには灯油を使います. — This heater uses kerosene.

このトイレは詰まっていて使えません. — This toilet is clogged up (so it can't be used).

【お金を】彼は飲み食いによくお金を使う. — He spends a lot of money on food and drink.

若者はオートバイを買うためにお金を全部使ってしまった. — The young man used up all his money to buy a motorcycle.

【時間を】時間をもっと有効に使いなさい. — Use your time more effectively.

【人を】彼の店ではアルバイトを5人使っている. — He has five part-timers working for him at the store.

あの課長は人を使うのが実にうまい. — That section chief really knows how to get the most out of his people.

【言葉を】彼はだれに対しても丁寧な言葉を使う. — He speaks politely to everyone.

彼女は英語が使える. — She has a good command of English.

【頭・神経を】もっと頭を使え. — Use your head!

これはとても神経を使う仕事だ. — This job is very hard on the nerves.

【慣用】借金取りが来たので私は居留守を使った. — I pretended I wasn't in when the bill collector came.

彼は私をだしに使って姉とデートしようとしている. — He's just using me to try to get a date with my sister.

つかえる (支える)

屋根裏部屋では頭が天井につかえてしまう. — The ceiling in the attic is too low for me to stand up straight.

彼は背が高いので, 頭がかもいにつかえてしまう. — He's so tall that he has to bend over when he walks through the doorway.

おもちがのどにつかえてしまった. — Some †*mochi* [rice cake] got caught in my throat.

道路が込んで車がつかえている. — The road is congested with traffic.

急用なのに公衆電話がつかえていて, いらいらした. — I got irritated because the pay phone was being †used [tied up, busy] when I had to make an emergency call.

仕事がたくさんつかえていて，息をつく暇もなかった．	I had so much work (that) I couldn't even catch my breath.
彼は感激のあまり言葉がつかえてうまく話せなかった．	He was so deeply moved that he got choked up and couldn't say what he wanted to.

つかまえる (捕まえる)

刑事はすりを現行犯で捕まえた．	The detective caught the pickpocket †in the act [red-handed].
かごから逃げた小鳥をやっと捕まえた．	I finally caught the bird that had gotten out of its cage.
彼は大通りでタクシーを捕まえた．	He caught a taxi out on the main street.
遊びに行こうとしているところを母に捕まえられて買い物に行かされた．	Just when I was about to go out, my mother caught me and sent me out shopping.
娘が私のそでを捕まえておもちゃを買ってくれとせがんだ．	My daughter grabbed my sleeve and pestered me to buy her a toy.

つかむ

【握る】彼は私の腕をつかんで帰ろうとするのを引き止めた．	He †grabbed my [caught me by the] arm and stopped me from going home.
うなぎはなかなかつかみにくい．	Eels are really hard to get hold of.
リレーでは，バトンをしっかりつかんで走りなさい．	Make sure you have a firm grip on the baton when running in a relay.
【手に入れる】彼は事業に成功して大金をつかんだ．	His business success brought him a lot of money.
この小説は多くの読者の心をつかんでいる．	The novel has captured the hearts of many readers.
警察は事件の確実な情報をまだつかんでいない．	The police still haven't got hold of any accurate information about the incident.
彼女は良い人と結婚してやっと幸福をつかんだ．	She married the right person and finally found happiness.
【慣用】彼の話は雲をつかむようで信じられない．	His story is so vague [nebulous] that I can't believe it.

つかれ (疲れ)

最近，疲れがたまっている．	I've really been exhausted lately.
金曜日には1週間分の疲れが出る．	By the end of the week, I'm just exhausted.
サウナに入ったあとはいつも心地よい疲れを覚える．	I always feel tired after a sauna but it's a good feeling.
マッサージしてもらって疲れが取れた．	I felt refreshed after getting a massage.

祖父の看病疲れで母が倒れた.	My mother collapsed from the strain of looking after my sick grandfather.
慣れないパーティーに出席し, 気疲れしてしまった.	I felt stressed out after the party because I don't usually go to them.

つかれる (疲れる)

大仕事で本当に疲れた.	I'm very tired [exhausted] from the hard work.
	The hard work really wore me out.
彼のような堅苦しい人と話すと疲れる.	It's exhausting talking to a stiff and formal person like him.
父親は疲れて電車の中で眠ってしまった.	The father was tired and fell asleep on the train.

つぎ (次)

次の方どうぞ(お入りください).	Next (person), please.
ポストは次の角を曲がったところにあります.	The mailbox is just around the next corner.
次の文を読んで, 問いに答えなさい.	Read the next section [passage] and answer the questions.
次の日曜日にまたおいでください.	Please come again next Sunday.
上の兄は医者で, 次の兄は弁護士です.	My oldest brother is a doctor and the next oldest is a lawyer.
彼は部長の次に偉い.	He's next in rank after the department chief.

つきあい

【交際】彼女はつきあいが広い.	She knows †a lot of [a great many] people.
	She has a wide circle of friends.
彼とは仕事だけのつきあいだ.	I only know him from work.
彼女とはもう10年のつきあいになる.	I've known her for about ten years now.
つきあいが深まるにつれ, 彼をますます尊敬するようになった.	The more I got to know him, the more I respected him.
私たちは良いおつきあいをしています.	We have a good relationship.
私たちは家族ぐるみのつきあいをしている.	Our families are friends.
私の故郷では親戚づきあいがさかんだ.	Extended families are very close in my hometown.
	Where I come from, families get together all the time.
この辺りは近所づきあいがほとん	People have very little to do with one

どない.	There's very little contact between neighbors around here.
【社交・義理】昨夜は仕事上のつきあいで飲みに行った.	I had to go out drinking last night with my business contacts.
明日のゴルフは気が進まないが,つきあいだから仕方ない.	I don't really feel like golfing tomorrow but I'll go just to be sociable.
また彼らと一緒に飲みに行ったの？つきあいのいいやつだ.	You went out drinking with them again. You're very sociable.
あいつはつきあいが悪い.	He's unsociable./He's not very sociable.

つきあう

【交際する】彼とは10年近くつきあっている.	I've known him for about ten years now.
彼女はつきあいにくい人だ.	She's a hard person to get along with.
私はみんなと親しくつきあっています.	I get along pretty well with everyone.
彼は同じ女の子と5年間もつきあっている.	He has been going with the same girl for five years.
【一緒に行動する】映画に行くならつきあいます.	If you want to go to the movies, I'll go with you.
母の買い物につきあった.	I went (along) shopping with my mother.
上役につきあって会社の帰りに酒を飲んだ.	I went out with my boss and had a few drinks on the way home from work.
あまりおなかはすいていなかったが,彼女につきあってスパゲッティを食べた.	I wasn't very hungry, but I had some spaghetti just so she wouldn't have to eat by herself.

つく¹ (突く)

うっかり指先を針で突いてしまった.	I carelessly pricked my finger with a needle.
飼育係が象に牙で突かれ大けがをした.	The trainer was severely wounded from being gored by the elephant.
お寺では大みそかに百八つ鐘をつきます.	Temple bells are struck 108 times on New Year's Eve.
最近ではもちをつく家が少なくなった.	There aren't as many people who pound rice and make home-made †*mochi* [rice cake] lately.
昔はよくまりをついて遊びました.	In the past, we often used to bounce balls for fun.
【支えとする】彼は手をついて立ち上がった.	He steadied himself with his hands to stand up.
彼女は頬杖をついて何か考えごと	She was lost in thought with her head rest-

をしていた.	ing on her hands.
老人が杖をついてやってきた.	The old man came along using his cane as he walked.
【核心を】その社説は問題の核心をついている.	The editorial touches on the core of the problem.
【悪態・溜息を】彼は酔って, 上司に悪態をついた.	He got drunk and told his boss off.
彼女はショーウインドーに飾られてあった宝石の値段を見て, 思わずため息をついた.	She could only sigh as she saw the price of the jewelry in the store window.
【〜の中を】風雨をついてサッカーの試合が行われた.	The soccer game was held †in the face of [through] wind and rain.

つく² (付く)

【付着する】晴れ着に染みが付いてしまった.	I got a stain on my best set of clothes.
電柱に接触して車に傷が付いた.	The car got scratched from brushing against the light pole.
雪の上に犬の足跡が付いている.	A dog has left its tracks on the snow.
松の木に付いた虫を退治した.	We got rid of the bugs on the pine trees.
どうやらサツキの挿し木が付いたようです.	It looks like the azaleas have taken root.
【付け加わる】このキャラメルにはおまけが付いています.	There's a prize in this package of caramels.
彼女はフードの付いたジャケットを着ている.	She's wearing a jacket with a hood.
新幹線には昔食堂車が付いていた.	There used to be a dining car on the Shinkansen.
私の部屋にやっとエアコンが付いた.	I've finally got an air conditioner in my room.
当座預金には利子が付きません.	You don't earn any interest on a current account.
彼女はおなかにぜい肉が付いてきた.	She's gaining weight around her stomach.
【決着する】彼らのけんかもやっとけりがついたようだ.	It seems like they have finally settled their argument.
【値段が】安物を買うと結局高くつくことがある.	Buying something cheap can sometimes end up costing you more.
その絵はあまりいい値がつかなかった.	That picture didn't bring much.
【付き従う】先生のあとについて英語のリーダーを読んだ.	We read the English reader aloud after the teacher.
野良犬が私の家までついて来た.	A stray dog followed me home.

弟は母親について，買い物に出かけた．	My little brother went along shopping with my mother.
最近は子どもの大学入試について来る親が多い．	Recently, many parents have been coming with their children to the college entrance exams.
私たちが夫婦げんかすると，娘はいつも妻の側につく．	My daughter always takes sides with my wife whenever we fight.
彼は部長に昇格し，秘書が一人ついた．	He was given a secretary when he was promoted to department chief.
彼の意見はいつもどっちつかずではっきりしない．	His opinions are always vague and unclear.
【運がいい】彼は最近何をやってもついている．	He's lucky at whatever he does lately.
【～のため】店内改装中につき，来月10日まで休業します．	We will be closed until the tenth of next month for remodeling.
日曜につき休診です．	The clinic is closed on Sundays.
【慣用】彼女の母親ぶりもすっかり板についてきた．	She's looking like a real mother now. She's really taken to motherhood.
彼のスーツ姿も板についてきた．	He's starting to look good in a suit.

つく³ (点く)

このスイッチを入れると電気がつきます．	This switch turns the lights on.
カーテンにストーブの火がついて燃えあがった．	The flame from the heater set the curtains on fire.
火のついたタバコを投げ捨ててはいけません．	Don't throw burning cigarettes on the ground.
この部屋はストーブがついているから暖かい．	This room is warm because the heater is on.

つく⁴ (着・就く)

【到着する】さあ着いたよ．	Well, we've arrived.／Here we are.
列車は定刻に駅に着いた．	The train arrived at the station on schedule.
交通ストで，会社に着いたのはもう昼過ぎだった．	Because of the transportation strike, it was already past noon by the time I arrived at the office.
郷里から私の荷物が着いた．	My things arrived from home.
【触れる】彼は頭がかもいに着くほど背が高い．	He's so tall that his head hits the doorway.
体を曲げると手のひらが床に着く．	I can bend over and touch my palms to the floor.
このプールは，大人の足がやっと	The pool is so deep that an adult can

底に着くくらいの深さだ. | barely touch the bottom with his feet.
【身を置く】夕食は家族全員で食卓に着くことにしている. | We make it a rule for everyone in the family to have dinner together.
早く席に着きなさい. | Take your places quickly.
昨日は10時に床に就いた. | Yesterday I went to bed at ten.
彼は先月重役のポストに就いた. | He was appointed to the board of directors last month.
彼は去年教職に就いた. | He entered the teaching profession last year.
彼は一日の仕事を終え,帰途に就いた. | He finished his day's work and headed for home.
彼女は有名な先生に就いてピアノを習っている. | She's studying piano under a famous teacher.

つぐ (継・接ぐ)

【受け継ぐ】彼は父のあとを継いで医者になった. | He followed in his father's footsteps and became a doctor.
息子は家業を継ぎたがらない. | My son doesn't want to †continue [take on, take over] the family business.
私は恩師の遺志を継いで医学の研究を続けている. | I'm carrying on the medical research that my former professor wanted continued after his death.
【繕う】母親は子どものズボンの破れ目を継いだ. | She †sewed up [fixed, repaired, mended] the tear in her son's pants.
【つなぐ】短いホースを接いで使った. | He used the short hoses by connecting them together.
建設工事は夜を日に継いで行われた. | The construction work went on night and day.
【足し加える】火を絶やさないように炭を継いだ. | He added more charcoal to keep the fire from going out.

つくす (尽くす)

医者はあらゆる手段を尽くして彼女の治療に当たった. | The doctor exhausted every means at his disposal to cure her.
その男は捕まるまで悪事の限りを尽くした. | By the time they caught him he had run the gamut of evil.
私の感謝の気持ちは言葉ではとても言い尽くせません. | It's impossible for me to adequately express my gratitude in words.
母は苦労をし尽くした末死んだ. | My mother died, having lived a life of ceaseless toil.
この本には当時の様子が描き尽くされている. | This book provides a complete picture of those times.
その火事は町を焼き尽くしてしま | The fire completely destroyed the town.

| 高山植物はやがて採り尽くされてしまうかもしれない. | Alpine plants may soon be picked clean. |

つくる (作・造)

【製作・創作する】彼は本箱を作った.	He built [made] a bookcase.
この工場では自動車を作っている.	This factory manufactures [builds] cars.
あの出版社では今, 百科事典を作っている.	That publishing company is compiling an encyclopedia now.
彼らはグループで映画を作った.	They made a film [movie] as a group.
彼は余暇に詩を作っている.	He writes poetry in his spare time.
彼女はケーキを作るのが上手だ.	She's very good at making pastries.
母が昼食を作ってくれた.	Mother made lunch for me.
【建造する】今度, 町に高校が造られる.	They're going to build a high school in town.
都心とベッドタウンを結ぶ地下鉄が造られた.	A subway was built to connect the suburbs with the downtown.
【栽培する】家では庭で野菜を作っています.	We're growing vegetables in our garden.
【形成する・生み出す】新聞が世論を作ると言われる.	They say newspapers create public opinion.
彼は結婚して楽しい家庭を作った.	He got married and made [created] a happy home.
ジャズ好きな人が集まって「ジャズ愛好会」を作った.	Some people who like jazz got together and formed a "Friends of Jazz Club."
彼女はそろそろ子どもを作りたいと言っている.	She says she wants to start a family soon.
大人になってからでは友達を作るのは難しい.	It's difficult to make friends after you've grown up.
彼は株で財産を作った.	He made his money in stocks.
暇を作って私の家に遊びに来てください.	Find some time and come over to my place.
【虚構を】彼はいろんな口実を作っては仕事をサボる.	He makes all sorts of excuses to skip work.
それは彼が作った話だよ.	That's just a story he made up.
彼女は子どもたちの前では涙を抑えて笑顔を作った.	She held back her tears and forced herself to smile in front of her children.
彼女は年よりも随分若く作っている.	She makes herself look a lot younger than she really is.

つける¹ (付・着ける)

| 【くっつける】服に泥を付けて汚し | I got my clothes muddy. |

てしまった.	
パンにジャムを付けて食べた.	I put [spread] some jam on the bread and ate it.
傷口に薬を付けた.	I put some medicine on the wound.
廊下に足跡を付けたのはだれだ.	Who left the footprints in the hall?
【取り付ける・添える】彼はカメラにフィルターを付けて撮った.	He attached a filter to the camera and took some shots.
彼女は部屋にカーテンを付けた.	She hung curtains in the room.
ボタンがとれたので付けてください.	My button came off. Could you please sew it back on?
彼からのプレゼントに手紙が付けてあった.	He had attached a letter to the present.
自分の持ち物には全部名前を付けておきなさい.	Make sure your name is on all your possessions.
【乗り物を停める】車をあの建物の前に着けてください.	Park the car in front of that building over there.
彼はボートを岸に着けた.	He brought the boat to shore.
【身に】あの会社では制服を着けることになっている.	That company requires everyone to wear a uniform.
彼女は胸にきれいなブローチを着けている.	She's wearing a pretty brooch.
あの女の子は頭に赤いリボンを着けている.	She's got [wearing] a red ribbon in her hair.
彼女は香水をつけている.	She's wearing perfume.
うちの猫は首に小さな鈴を着けている.	My cat wears a little bell around its neck.
【体力を】体力をつけるために水泳を始めました.	I've started swimming to build up my strength.
【付き添わせる】病気のおじいさんに看護師を付けました.	We've hired a nurse to look after my sick grandfather.
彼は息子に英語の家庭教師を付けた.	He's hired an English tutor for his son.
【あとをつける】彼はだれかにつけられているような気がした.	He felt as if someone were following [tailing] him.
パトカーは怪しい車のあとをつけた.	The police car followed [tailed] the suspicious vehicle.
【決める】彼女は犬にスヌーピーという名前を付けた.	She named the dog Snoopy.
この本は値段が付けられないほど貴重なものです.	This book is so valuable (that) it's impossible to put a price on it.
	This is a priceless book.
【書き付ける】私は毎日日記を付けています.	I write in my diary every day.

【慣用】彼はやっと仕事の片を付けた.	He finally got his work done.
今日の勘定は付けておいてください.	Could you (please) put today's bill on my tab?

つける² (点ける)

私は部屋に入り，電灯〔テレビ〕をつけた.	I went into the room and turned on the light 〔TV〕.
彼はたばこに火をつけた.	He lit a cigarette.
ストーブをつけているときには部屋の換気に注意しなさい.	Be careful about ventilation when you have the heater on.

～つける

今日はやりつけない仕事をして疲れた.	I really got tired today from doing a job I wasn't used to.
私には行きつけのバー〔美容室〕がある.	There's a bar 〔hairdresser's〕 I always go to.
父親は子どもを叱りつけた.	The father really gave his child a good scolding.
刑事は容疑者の居所を聞きつけた.	The detective got wind of the suspect's whereabouts.

つげる (告げる)

彼は牧師にだけ真実を告げた.	He told the truth only to the pastor.
彼女は見送りの人たちに別れを告げた.	She bid farewell to all those who had come to see her off.
その人は名前も告げずに行ってしまった.	He left without even giving his name.
時計台の鐘が正午を告げた.	The clock tower bell sounded noon.

つごう (都合)

土曜日はご都合いかがですか.	Is Saturday convenient for you?
もしご都合がよろしければ明日お目にかかりたいのですが.	If it's convenient (for you), I would like to see you tomorrow.
今日はちょっと都合が悪い.	It's a little inconvenient today.
彼が都合よく現れた.	He showed up at a good [convenient] time.
都合よく，それを買うだけのお金の持ち合わせがあった.	Fortunately [Luckily], I had enough cash with me to buy it.
都合の悪いことにメンバーの一人が病気で倒れた.	Unfortunately, one of the members fell sick.
万事都合よくいっています.	Everything is going without a hitch.
彼女は家庭の〔一身上の〕都合で会社を辞めた.	She quit the company because of family 〔personal〕 circumstances.

彼は時間を都合して教え子の結婚式に出席した.	He took time from his schedule to attend his student's wedding.
明後日までにどうしても金を都合しなければならない.	I absolutely have to come up with the money by the day after tomorrow.

つたう（伝う）

泥棒は屋根を伝って侵入した.	The thief got in from the roof.
少年は2階の窓から木を伝って脱け出した.	The boy climbed out of the second-floor window and escaped down a tree.
雨水がといを伝って流れ落ちている.	Rain water flows down through the gutter.
涙が彼女の頬を伝って流れた.	Tears ran down her cheeks.

つたえる（伝える）

【知らせる】皆さんにお伝えしたいことがあります.	I have something to tell all of you.
お電話をくださるよう彼女にお伝えいただけませんか.	Would you mind asking her to call me back?
彼女に僕の本当の気持ちを伝えたい.	I want to tell her how I really feel.
彼の言づてを彼女に伝えた.	I gave her his message.
皆さんによろしくお伝えください.	Give my (best) regards to everyone.
その政治家は巨額の賄賂を受け取ったと伝えられている.	It's going around that that politician took an enormous bribe.
テレビで全国大会での我が校のチームの優勢が伝えられた.	They said on TV that our team was dominating the national championships.
【継承する】これはこの島に代々伝えられてきた行事です.	This is an event that has been held on this island for generations.
伝統工芸を伝える人が最近少なくなっている.	The number of people who can hand down the traditional arts has been decreasing lately.
【伝来する】仏教は6世紀に日本に伝えられた.	Buddhism was brought to Japan in the sixth century.
鉄砲はポルトガル人によって日本に伝えられた.	Guns were introduced into Japan by the Portuguese.
【伝導する】銅は電気をよく伝える.	Copper is an efficient conductor of electricity.
やかんやなべには熱をよく伝える金属を使う.	Teapots and pans are made of metals which conduct heat efficiently.

つたわる（伝わる）

【知られる】彼が交通事故を起こしたことは親戚の人たちにも伝わ	Even some of his relatives got word of his having caused a traffic accident.

先生の悪口を言っていたことが，当の先生に伝わってしまった．	The bad things I had said about the teacher got back to him.
そのうわさは町中に伝わった．	That rumor spread throughout town.
大統領暗殺のニュースが全世界に伝わった．	News of the president's assassination spread around the world.
その絵をじっと見ていると，作者の気持ちが伝わってくる．	As I gaze at the painting, I can feel what the artist wanted to express.
選手たちの熱気が，試合を見ている私たちにも伝わってきた．	The enthusiasm of the players spread through all of us watching the game.
【継承される】この祭りは古くからこの地方に伝わっている．	This festival has been performed in this area for a long time.
これはこの家に代々伝わる人形です．	This doll has been in my family for generations.
【伝来する】昔からいろいろな文化が中国から日本に伝わってきた．	Many aspects of culture have been transmitted from China to Japan since ancient times.
【光・音などが】光は音より速く伝わる．	Light travels faster than sound.
ガラス窓越しに外の暑さが伝わってくる．	The heat from outside †comes in [is transmitted] through the windowpane.
通りに面した家では自動車の震動が伝わってくる．	People in houses facing the street feel the vibrations from the cars driving by.

つづき (続き)

【連続した物の次】さっきの話の続きを聞かせて．	Continue what you were saying before. Let's continue where we left off.
この続きはまた来週の授業で．	I will continue with this topic next lecture.
毎日，新聞の連載小説の続きが楽しみだ．	I look forward every day to reading the next installment of the novel serialized in the newspaper.
この漫画の続きを貸してくれない？	Will you lend me the next issue in this †comic series [*manga*]?
「先週よりの続き」(連続ドラマなど)	Continued from last week.
【接続】私の家は隣と棟続きです．	I live in a semidetached house.
引き潮のとき，あの二つの島は地続きになる．	When the tide goes out, those two islands become connected.

つづく (続く)

【継続・維持する】祭りは1週間続いた．	The festival lasted [continued] for a week.
その教授の講義は6時間も続いた．	The professor's lecture †lasted [continued,

このところ，天気のいい日が続いている．	We're having a run of good weather these days.
	Recently, we've had a spell of good weather.
雨の降らない日が1ヵ月も続いている．	It hasn't rained for a month.
彼の禁煙はまだ続いているの．	Is he still off cigarettes?
母の病気は小康状態が続いている．	My mother's condition remains stable.
彼は毎朝ジョギングすると決心したが，いつまで続くことやら．	He made up his mind to jog every morning but I wonder how long he'll keep it up.
毎日外食していてはお金が続かないよ．	Your money's not going to last if you eat out every day.
彼女は根気が続かなくなってレース編みを途中で投げ出した．	She ran out of patience and gave up on her crocheting before finishing it.
二晩も徹夜をしては，体が続かない．	Working all night two nights in a row isn't good for your health.
【繰り返し起こる】秋は運動会に文化祭と，行事が続く．	In the fall with Sports Day and the Culture Festival, we have one event after another.
彼はこのところ不運が続いている．	He has recently had a run of bad luck.
彼女の家は最近，不幸が続いている．	Recently her family has experienced one tragedy after another.
あの競馬場は今週末，大穴が続いている．	This weekend that racetrack has had a string of long shots coming in first place.
【接続・後続する】この道は国道に続いている．	This road joins the national highway.
この記事は次ページの上段に続く．	This article continues at the top of the next page.
「続く」（連続ドラマなど）	To be continued.
彼のあとに続く優秀な学者はいない．	There is no scholar of his caliber who can carry on after him.
【並ぶ】駅前には商店街が続いている．	There are streets lined with stores in front of the station.
この通りはイチョウ並木が続いている．	This street is lined with ginkgo trees.
ラッシュアワーには道路に車が続く．	During rush hour, the cars are lined up on the road.
球場の開門を待つ行列が100メートルも続いていた．	The lines of people waiting to get into the baseball stadium went on for 100 meters.

つづける

【次の順位】
彼は山田君に続いて優秀な学生だ. — He's second only to Yamada in his schoolwork.
あの町では洪水に続いて伝染病が発生した. — A contagious disease broke out in that town after the flood.
続いて次の議題に移ります. — Let's move on to the next subject.

つづける (続ける)

彼女は子どもが生まれても勤めを続けるつもりだ. — She's planning to continue working after the baby (is born).
彼は毎朝ジョギングを続けている. — He's still jogging every morning.
勉強を続けなさい. — Go on [Continue] with your studying.
私たちは頂上を目指して歩き続けた. — We continued to walk toward the top of the mountain.
15分休憩して11時から会議を続けます. — We will resume the conference at 11:00 after a fifteen-minute break.
彼は1時間も続けて泳いでいる. — He's been swimming continuously for an hour.
我が校のサッカーチームは2年続けて全国大会で優勝した. — Our school soccer team has won the national championship two years †running [in a row].
2本続けて映画を見た. — I watched two movies in a row.

つつしみ (慎み)

彼女は慎み深い女性です. — She's a discreet [reserved, modest] woman.
初対面の人からお金を借りるなんて慎みがない. — How could you be so indiscreet as to borrow money from someone you've just met for the first time?

つつしむ (慎む)

身を慎みなさい. — Watch what you do./Behave yourself.
医者から酒を慎むよう言われた. — The doctor advised me to watch my drinking.
口を慎みなさい. — Watch your tongue.
Watch [Be careful] what you say.

つつみ (包み)

母は買い物の包みを抱えて帰ってきた. — Mother came home from shopping with a (big) parcel [package] in her arms.
私は誕生日のプレゼントにもらった包みを解いた. — I opened the package I had received as a birthday present.
私に小包みが届いていますか. — Is there a package [parcel] for me?
きれいな包み紙を買ってきた. — I bought some pretty wrapping paper.

つつむ（包む）

彼女はプレゼントをきれいな紙で包んで彼に渡した． — She wrapped the present in pretty paper and gave it to him.

負傷者は毛布で包まれ，病院に運ばれた． — The injured were wrapped in blankets and taken to the hospital.

彼女は黒い服に身を包んで現れた． — She appeared dressed in black.

消防車が着いたとき，家は炎に包まれていた． — The house was already engulfed in flames when the fire engines arrived.

町は夜霧に包まれていた． — The town was enveloped [veiled, enshrouded] in a night fog.

この事件は謎に包まれている． — This incident is veiled in mystery.

息子の死で遺族は深い悲しみに包まれていた． — The family was grief-stricken by the loss of their son.

【隠す】包み隠さずすべて白状しろ． — Don't try to conceal anything. Confess!

つとめ（勤・務め）

【勤務】今の勤めはとても楽です． — My work now is very easy.

お勤めはどちらですか． — Where do you work?

彼は定年で勤めを辞めた． — He retired.

彼女はいい勤め口を探している． — She's looking for a good position.

父は平凡な勤め人でした． — My father was just an ordinary office worker.

急用以外は勤め先に電話しないように． — Don't call me at the office unless there's an emergency.

【任務・義務】彼は議長の務めを立派に果たした． — He carried out his duty as chairman splendidly.

学生の務めは勉強することだ． — A student's duty is to study.

子どものしつけは親の務めだ． — A child's discipline is his parents' responsibility.

つとめて（努めて）

彼女は努めて明るく振る舞っているが，本当は夫の病気を心配しているのだ． — She forces herself to act cheerfully but in fact, she is concerned about her husband's illness.

健康維持のために毎日努めて歩くようにしている． — I try to walk as much as possible every day to stay in good health.

つとめる¹（努める）

部屋を整とんするよう努めなさい． — Try to keep your room †in order [cleaned up]. / Work at keeping [Make an effort to keep] your room neat.

従業員たちは精一杯サービスに努 — The staff worked hard to provide good

つとめる² (勤・務める)

【勤務する】息子は東京の商社に勤めている. — My son works for a trading company in Tokyo.
私はスーパーに勤めている. — I work at a supermarket.
【役目をする】私が(披露宴の)司会を務めます. — I'll be the master of ceremonies (at the wedding reception).
彼は旅行の案内役を務めた. — He served as tour guide.
この芝居の主役を務めるのは彼女です. — She'll have the leading role in this play.
父は市会議員を二期務めた. — My father served two terms as (a) city councilman.

つなぐ

犬を鎖でつないだ. — I tied up the dog. / I put the dog on a leash.
馬が木につながれている. — The horse is tied to the tree.
船頭は舟を岸につないだ. — The captain moored the boat.
ひもを2本つないで長くした. — I tied two pieces of string together to make a longer one.
母親は子どもと手をつないで歩いた. — The mother held her child by the hand as they walked.
この電話を人事課につないでください. — Please connect this call to the personnel department.

つね (常)

【習慣】彼は休日にゴルフに出かけるのを常としている. — He usually plays golf on his days off.
彼は今日も常のように散歩に出かけた. — He went off on his walk today as usual.
彼は常に健康に気を配っている. — He's always careful about his health.
【普通】易きに流れるのが人の常だ. — People tend to (want to) take the easy way out.
ままならぬのが世の常だ. — Nothing ever goes the way you want it to.
彼もやはり世の常の父親と同じで, 娘には甘い. — He's a typical father in that he spoils his daughter.

つぶす (潰す)

【崩す・壊す】ゆでたジャガイモをつぶしてください. — Could you mash the potatoes?
帽子を踏んでつぶしてしまった. — I crushed the hat when I stepped on it.
彼は畑をつぶして駐車場にした. — He plowed under his fields and turned

	them into a parking lot.
【失う】彼はギャンブルで身代をつぶしてしまった.	He blew his fortune gambling.
彼が遅れたお陰で貴重な時間をつぶされた.	His being late wasted us precious time.
電車の発車時刻まで喫茶店で時間をつぶした.	We killed time in the coffee shop until it was time for the train to leave.
【慣用】高速道路で車がスリップしたときは本当に肝をつぶしたよ.	I was scared to death when the car skidded on the expressway.

つぶれる (潰れる)

【崩れる・壊れる】家に帰って箱を開けたらケーキがつぶれていた.	When I got home and opened the box, I found the cake had been crushed.
山崩れで家がたくさんつぶれた.	Many houses were destroyed by the landslides.
【だめになる・なくなる】勤めている会社がつぶれてしまった.	The company I work for has gone bankrupt.
引っ越しの挨拶回りで一日つぶれた.	We lost a whole day just making courtesy calls to new neighbors.

つまずく

彼は石につまずいて転んだ.	He tripped [stumbled] on a rock and fell down.
暗いので,つまずかないように足元に注意しなさい.	It's dark, so watch your step and be careful not to trip over anything.
【失敗する】彼は事業につまずき,かなりの負債を抱えてしまった.	His business setback left him with considerable debts.
彼は人生につまずき,生きる気力を失ってしまった.	His setbacks in life have taken away his will to live.
入学試験は英語の問題でつまずいてしまった.	The English section on the entrance exam really tripped me up.

つまむ

彼はピーナツをはしでつまんだ.	He picked up the peanuts with chopsticks.
彼はアンモニアのにおいに思わず鼻をつまんだ.	The smell of ammonia made him hold his nose.
どうぞクッキーをつまんでください.	Please have some cookies. Help yourself to some cookies.
つまみ食いばかりしていると太るよ.	You're going to get fat if you nibble all day.
つまみ食いはいけません.食事の支度ができるまで待ちなさい.	Don't pick at the food while I'm cooking. Wait till it's ready and on the table.
家に入ってきた猫をつまみ出した.	I grabbed the cat that had gotten in the

	house and threw it out.
彼は要点をかいつまんで話した.	He discussed only the essential points.
これまでの経過をかいつまんでお話しします.	I'll explain the course of events up to now in a nutshell.
【慣用】彼の鮮やかな手品に、みんなはきつねにつままれたような顔をした.	Everybody looked quite bewildered as he deftly performed his magic tricks.

つまらない

だれも一緒に遊ぶ人がいなくてつまらない.	I'm bored because I don't have anyone to play with.
つまらない映画だった.	That was a boring movie.
彼のようなつまらない男のどこがいいのか.	I don't understand what you see in a guy like that. He's so boring.
つまらない物ですがどうぞ.	It's not all that much but I hope you like it.[1]

> 1) 日本語のような形式的な挨拶ではなく、文字どおりの気持ちを表す. ただし、実際に人に贈り物をするときにこう言うことはあまりない.

つまる (詰まる)

【ふさがる】下水が詰まって水が流れない.	The water won't drain because the pipes are clogged.
煙突が詰まって火がよく燃えない.	The fire won't burn well because the chimney's stopped up.
【いっぱいになる】箱にはミカンがいっぱい詰まっていた.	The box was packed full of mandarin oranges.
ホールには既に観客がぎっしり詰まっていた.	The auditorium was already filled to the rafters with people.
仕事が詰まっていてとても忙しい.	I'm very busy with so much work piled up.
日程が詰まっていて身動きがとれない.	My schedule is so full (that) I can't fit anything else in.
【窮する】彼は痛いところをつかれ返答に詰まった.	They got him in a sore spot and he was at a loss for an answer.
彼は金に詰まってとうとう工場を手放した.	He had to let go of the factory due to lack of money.
【縮まる】このジーパンは洗ったら丈が詰まってしまった.	These jeans shrank in length when I washed them.
【結局】つまるところ悪いのは君だ.	Put simply, it's your fault.

つみ (罪)

自殺はクリスチャンにとって恐ろ	Suicide is one of the most serious sins for

しい罪である.	Christians.
彼はついに自分の罪を認めた.	He finally admitted his guilt.
罪を犯した者が罪の意識を持つとは限らない.	Those who commit crimes do not always have a guilty conscience.
彼は友人に罪をきせて逃げた.	He fled, leaving the blame on his friend.
彼は無実の罪をきせられた.	He was framed for a crime he didn't commit.
彼女は息子の罪をかぶった.	She took the blame for her son.
彼女が使い込みをしたのは男に罪がある.	There was a man behind her embezzlement.

つむ¹ (摘む)

彼女は野原で花を摘んだ.	She picked flowers in the field.
日曜日に家族でイチゴを摘みに行った.	On Sunday, our whole family went off to pick strawberries.

つむ² (積む)

【物を重ねる】彼の部屋には本が山と積まれている.	His room is piled high with books.
いくらお金を積まれても彼は土地を手放さなかった.	No matter how much money he was offered he wouldn't give up his land.
【行為を重ねる】彼は長年修業を積んで一人前の板前になった.	After long years of study, he became an accomplished chef in his own right.
この仕事は経験を積んで覚えるしかない.	The only way to learn this job is through long experience.
【載せる】彼は荷物を車に積んだ.	He loaded the baggage into the car.
トラックは荷物をいっぱいに積んでいた.	The truck was loaded up completely with freight.

つめたい (冷たい)

【物が】スープが冷たくなった.	The soup got cold.
何か冷たいものが欲しい.	I'd like something cold.
【心・態度が】あいつは冷たい男だ.	He's a cold man.
この頃君は僕に冷たいね.	You've been cold toward me lately, haven't you?
あのときの君の, 私に対する態度は冷たかった.	Your attitude toward me at that time was very cold.
なぜか彼の挨拶は冷たかった.	For some reason he †gave me a cold greeting [greeted me coldly].
この冷たい返事こそまさに彼の心の冷たさを証明している.	This heartless answer proves just how cold he really is.
その金持ちに寄付を頼みに行ったが冷たく断られた.	I asked that rich man for a contribution, but I was coldly turned down.

犯人の家族は皆に冷たい目で見られた. / The criminal's family was looked upon with scorn by everyone.

【慣用】その恐ろしい話を聞いて背筋が冷たくなった. / Hearing that frightening story sent chills up and down my spine. / It made me shudder to hear that frightening story.

つめる (詰める)

【入れる・満たす】彼女はクッキーを箱に詰めた. / She put the cookies in the box.

箱にリンゴを詰めて送った. / I filled the box with apples and sent it off.

旅行の荷物をかばんに詰めた. / I packed what I needed for the trip into a suitcase.

小さなかばんにそんなにいっぱい物を詰め込んだら壊れてしまうよ. / A small shoulder bag will burst open if you try to stuff that many things into it.

彼は壁のひびにしっくいを詰めた. / He filled in the cracks in the wall with plaster.

席を少し詰めていただけますか. / Would you mind scooting down [over] a little bit?

去年の夏, ピクルスの瓶詰めを100個作った. / Last summer I put up one hundred jars of pickles.

【縮める】スカート〔ズボン〕の丈を1センチ詰めてもらった. / I had the †hem of the skirt 〔pants' cuff〕 taken up one centimeter.

【倹約する】借金を返すために暮らしを切り詰めなくてはならない. / In order to pay back my debts, I have to cut back on living expenses.

【議論を煮詰める】この話し合いはもっと詰める必要がある. / We have to narrow down this discussion.

【待機する】あの記者は毎日警察に詰めている. / That reporter is at the police station every day waiting for a scoop.

【逃げ場をなくす】警官は犯人を袋小路に追い詰めた. / The policeman chased the thief into a blind alley.

彼はそのことで父親に問い詰められた. / His father pressed him on that.

【継続】彼は忙しくてこの1ヵ月働き詰めだ. / He's been working nonstop for a month now with all that work.

【慣用】そんなに根を詰めて勉強すると体に悪いよ. / Chaining yourself to your studies like that is bad for your health.

つもり

今夜は外で食事をするつもりです. / I'm going [planning] to eat out tonight.

今年の夏はアメリカに行くつもりです. / I'm going [planning] to go to the United States this summer.

寝る前に宿題を済ませるつもりだ.	I intend[1] to finish my homework before I go to bed.
君を傷つけるつもりはなかった.	I didn't mean to hurt you.
案内状を送ったつもりですけれどまだ届きませんか.	I thought I sent the invitation. Haven't you received it yet?
彼は自分では偉いつもりでいる.	He thinks he's great.
この5,000円は何か買ったつもりで貯金しよう.	I'll put this 5,000 yen in my savings, making believe I bought something with it.
死んだつもりになって働けばその莫大な借金も返せるだろう.	If you work like there's no tomorrow, you may be able to repay this huge debt.

1) intend は実行しようとする強い意志を表す.

つもる (積もる)

雪がたくさん積もった.	The snow piled [drifted] up high.
棚にほこりが積もっている.	Dust has accumulated on the shelf.
彼は借金が積もってどうにも身動きがとれなくなった.	His debts have †piled up [accumulated] to the point where he has nowhere left to turn.
彼は部長に積もり積もった不満をぶちまけた.	He took out the frustration that had been building up inside him for a long time on his chief.
10年ぶりのクラス会で, みんなは積もる話に時を忘れた.	At the first class reunion in ten years, everyone had so much catching up to do that they lost track of time.

つよい (強い)

今年の野球大会ではあのチームがいちばん強い.	They're the strongest team in this year's baseball tournament.
象は力が強い.	Elephants are very strong.
強い者が勝つ世の中だ.	Only the strong make it in this world.
金の力は強い.	Money is powerful.
スポーツは体も心も強くする.	Sports develop sound minds and strong bodies.
彼は意志が強い.	He has a strong will.
彼は責任感が強い.	He's got a strong sense of responsibility.
彼女は警戒心が強い.	She's very cautious.
彼は大変酒が強い.	He can really hold his liquor.
	He has a high tolerance for alcohol.*
彼は数学に強い.	He's good at mathematics.
彼は逆境に強い.	He knows how to take adversity.
【激しい・厳しい】昨夜は一晩中強	A strong wind blew all night long last

い風が吹いていた.	night.
この酒は強過ぎてとても私には飲めない.	This liquor is too strong for me to drink.
海岸では日差しが強いのでサングラスが必要だ.	You need sunglasses at the beach because the sun is bright.
塗りたてのペンキの強いにおいで頭がくらくらしてきた.	The strong smell of fresh paint made me dizzy.
その条約は国民の強い抵抗を押し切って締結された.	That treaty was ratified in defiance of strong opposition from the people.
君は彼女に強いことを言い過ぎたよ.	The things you said to her were too harsh.
「そんな事実はない」と彼は強く言い切った.	"There's no truth to that!" he asserted firmly.
労組は社長との会見を強く望んだ.	The labor union strongly sought to have a meeting with the president.
【程度が大きい】彼は政財界に強い影響力を持っている.	He wields great influence in government and financial circles.
学校設立は実現の可能性が強い.	There is a strong possibility that the school will be established.
クラス内では体育大会を復活させるべきだという意見が強い.	Most of the class is strongly in favor of bringing back the athletic meet.
【抵抗力がある】この紙は水に強くできています.	This paper is made to hold up well when wet.

つらい (辛い)

友達との別れは辛い.	It's painful to say good-bye to my friends.
彼女が泣いているのを見るのは辛い.	I can't stand seeing her cry.
冬は朝早く起きるのが辛い.	I hate getting up early in the winter.
今日学校で辛い思いをした.	I had a hard time of it today at school.
石炭を掘るのは辛い仕事だ.	Mining coal is a tough job.
部下の不始末で彼は辛い立場にある.	He's in a difficult position because of the mismanagement of the men under him.
なぜ上司は私に辛く当たるのだろうか.	Why does the boss treat me so harshly?

つられる

華やかな看板につられて私たちはそのレストランに入った.	The colorful sign enticed us to go into the restaurant.
子どもはあめ玉につられて見知らぬ男についていってしまった.	The child was lured by candy to go with a stranger.
人々は祭りの太鼓の音につられて広場に集まってきた.	Lured by the sound of the drums at the festival, people gathered in the square.

彼は外交員の巧みな勧誘につられて保険に入った.	He fell for the insurance salesman's skillful pitch and bought a policy.
友達がCDを買ったので私もつられて1枚買った.	Seeing my friend buy some CDs made me buy one too.
みんなが笑うので彼もつられて笑い出した.	Everyone's laughter was so contagious that he started laughing too.

つりあう (釣り合う)

今月は収支が大体釣り合っている.	This month's income and expenditures pretty much balanced out.
今日の彼女の帽子と洋服はよく釣り合っている.	The hat and dress she's wearing today go together well.
君と彼女では全く釣り合わないから, 結婚してもうまくやっていけないよ.	You and she are not compatible at all, so it would never work out if you got married.

つる¹ (吊る)

私は毎日ハンモックをつって昼寝する.	I hang up a hammock and take a nap every day.
彼は部屋に棚をつった.	He †put up [suspended*] a shelf in the room.
近所の人が首をつった.	Someone in my neighborhood hanged himself.
泳いでいたら足がつってしまった.	I got a cramp in my leg while swimming.
彼の顔は怒りで引きつった.	His face grew tense with anger.
電車やバスの中にはつり皮がぶら下がっている.	Trains and buses have straps to hang on to.

つる² (釣る)

川で魚を釣った.	I caught some fish in the river.
伊豆沖でカツオを釣った.	I caught a bonito off the Izu Peninsula.
父と私はよく魚釣りに行く.	My father and I often go fishing.
子どもたちはトンボを釣りに行った.	The children went to catch dragonflies.
彼を食事で釣って買い物につきあわせた.	I got him to go shopping with me by offering to take him out to eat.
【慣用】エビでタイを釣れ.	Use small fry to catch (a) big fish.

つるす (吊るす)

風鈴を軒につるした.	I hung a wind chime from the eaves.
私の家では天井から観葉植物をつるしてある.	I have some leafy plants hanging from the ceiling in my house.
私はいつもつるしの背広で間に合	I always make do with a †suit off the rack

わせている.	[ready-made suit].
彼は生意気だと上級生につるし上げられた.	The older kids at school ganged up on him for being †cheeky [a smart-aleck].

(〜に)つれて

日がたつにつれてだんだん彼のことを忘れていった.	As †time [the days] went by, I gradually forgot about him.
夜が更けるにつれて嵐は激しくなった.	As the night wore on, the storm became more violent.
大きくなるにつれて彼女は美しくなっていった.	She became more and more beautiful as she grew up.
年を取るにつれて彼はへんくつになってきた.	As he got older, he became more obstinate.
話を聞くにつれて彼の無実を確信した.	The more he talked, the more convinced I became of his innocence.

つれる (連れる)

昨日,彼は子どもを動物園に連れて行った.	He took his children to the zoo yesterday.
僕の誕生祝いに,両親がレストランへ食事に連れて行ってくれることになっている.	My parents are taking me out to dinner for my birthday.
今度の休みには子どもを連れて旅行に行こうと思っている.	I'm thinking of taking the children on a trip this vacation.
夕方犬を連れて散歩するのが私の日課です.	Walking my dog every evening is part of my daily routine.
ちょっと山本君をここに連れて来てください.	Please bring Yamamoto here.
彼女は子どもを連れて再婚した.	She remarried, and took her children to live with her new husband.

て

て (手)

【人の】彼の手はごつごつしている.	His hands are strong and rough.
彼は手が長い.	He has long arms.
【動物の】まりを転がすと猫が手を出してきた.	When I rolled the ball, the cat reached out its paw.

うちの犬はお手をする.	Our dog knows how to shake hands.
【物の】急須の手が欠けてしまった.	The handle on the teapot broke off.
【種類】この手の仕事はもう嫌だ.	I'm sick of this kind [line] of work.
あの手の人には金が物を言う.	He's the kind of person †who'll do anything for money [who can be persuaded by money].
【方法】その手は食わない.	I won't †buy [fall for] that. That trick won't work on me.
この手でだめだったらもうあきらめよう.	Let's give up if this doesn't †work [do the trick].
彼はあの手この手を使って彼女を説得しようとした.	He used †every trick in the book [every possible means] to (try to) persuade her.
もうこれ以上, 打つ手はない.	There's nothing more that we can try.
【方向】行く手に海が見えてきた.	The sea came into view up ahead.
駅はあの高いビルの右手にあります.	The station is to the right of that tall building.
【自ら作った】私は母の手料理がいちばん好きだ.	I like my mother's home cooking best.
彼女はパーティーにお手製のドレスを着て現れた.	She came to the party in a dress she had sewn herself.
【手が】手が空いたらこっちの仕事を手伝ってくれ.	Give me a hand when †you're free [you have a minute].
いつ手が空く？	When will you be free?
手が後ろに回るようなことをしてはいけない.	Don't do anything that will get you in trouble with the law.
あの子はとても手がかかる子だ.	That child is really a handful.
この仕事にこの人数ではとても手が足りない.	This number of people isn't enough to do this work.
火事は既に手がつけられない状態だ.	The fire is already out of hand.
彼は乱暴で手がつけられない.	He's too violent to control.
あの高い枝には手が届かない.	I can't reach that high branch.
とうとう黒幕に捜査の手が伸びた.	The investigation finally caught up with the mastermind behind the crimes.
今手がふさがっているので, 明日また来てください.	I've got my hands full [I'm busy] right now. Would you please come back tomorrow?
忙しくて, とてもそこまで手が回らない.	I'm so busy that there's just no way that I can get around to that.
【手と】彼は部長の手となり足となって働いている.	He's the boss's right-hand man.
【手に】今日のナイターは手に汗を握るいい試合だった.	Tonight's baseball game †was a real spine-tingler [kept me on the edge of my seat].

この仕事は私の手に余る.	This work is †more than I can handle [too much for me to handle].
このクラスは先生の手に負えない.	This class is too much for the teacher to handle.
	The teacher can't keep this class under control.
君も何か手に職をつけておいたほうがいいよ.	You should acquire a profession or a trade.
彼は競馬で大穴を当て大金を手にした.	He bet on a long shot at the track and made a bundle.**
明日のフットボールの試合のことが気になって勉強が手につかなかった.	I was so anxious about tomorrow's football game that I couldn't get †myself to sit down and study [down to my studies].
どうぞ手に取ってご覧ください.	Feel free to pick it up and look at it.
私には彼の考えが手に取るように分かる.	I can practically read his mind.
双眼鏡を覗くとふもとの景色が手に取るようにはっきり見えた.	When I looked through the binoculars the scenery at the foot of the mountain appeared as if I could reach out and touch it.
やっと念願のものが手に入った.	I finally got what I had been wishing for so much.
あの店も今では人の手に渡ってしまった.	That store has passed into someone else's hands now.
【手の】これは相当手の込んだ細工だ.	This is quite an elaborate piece of work.
向こうの手の内は読めたぞ.	I can see through his plans.
	I'm on to his tricks.
彼の病気はもう手の施しようがないほどひどくなっている.	His illness has gotten so bad that nothing can be done.
【手も】彼と将棋をして手もなくやられてしまった.	He beat me hands down playing *shogi*.
権力者の前では手も足も出なかった.	We were completely powerless in the face of the authorities.
その試験問題には手も足も出なかった.	I was completely stumped by that exam question.
【手を】答えが分かった人は手を上げてください.	Raise your hand if you know the answer.
賛成の方は手を上げてください.	Those in favor, please raise your hands.
彼は恩師の墓前に手を合わせた.	He prayed with his hands together before the grave of his former teacher.
原稿は一応書き上がったが, もう	I've tentatively finished the manuscript but

一度手を入れるつもりだ.	I intend to †go over it once more [put some finishing touches on it later].
その問題には早急に手を打つ必要がある.	Something must be done immediately to deal with this problem.
労使は3％の賃上げで手を打った.	Management and labor struck a bargain to raise wages by three percent.
彼は彼女の気を引こうと手を変え品を変えやってみたがむだだった.	He tried every means possible to win her affections but to no avail.
彼はドアの取っ手に手をかけた.	He gripped the doorknob.
手をかけた料理はおいしい.	Food prepared with care and skill tastes good.
父が手をかけて育てた盆栽が台風でやられてしまった.	The *bonsai* tree that my father took such good care of was destroyed in the typhoon.
この仕事にはどうしても君の手を貸して欲しい.	I'd really appreciate it if you'd lend me a hand with this work.
このコートはちょっと手を加えればまだ着られる.	If I make a few alterations, I can still wear this coat.
手をこまぬいて見ていたわけではない.	I didn't just sit back with my arms folded.
彼は株に手を出して失敗した.	He dabbled in stocks and failed.
あいつのほうが先に手を出してきたんだ.	He hit me first. That guy started it.
休講だと聞くと学生たちは手を叩いて喜んだ.	The students clapped their hands (for joy) when they heard that class was canceled.
今度ばかりは手をついて謝っても許さないぞ.	I won't forgive you this time even if you beg me.
彼は手を尽くして行方不明になった息子を捜した.	He did everything in his power to try to find his missing son.
その料理にはまだ手をつけていません.	That food hasn't been touched.
問題が複雑でどこから手をつけたらいいか分からない.	This problem is so complex that I don't know where to start.
子どもたちは手をつないで学校へ行った.	The children went off to school holding hands.
彼らは手を握り合って再会を喜んだ.	They clasped hands, happy to be reunited.
彼は適当に手を抜いて仕事をする.	He doesn't do as good a job at work as he could.
彼は手を伸ばして受話器を取った.	He reached out and picked up the telephone receiver.

彼は手を(上に)伸ばして本棚のいちばん上の本を取った.	He reached up and got a book off the top bookshelf.
手を離さないでしっかりつかみなさい.	Don't let go. Hold on tight.
息子も大きくなってやっと私の手を離れた.	Now that my son is grown he's finally become independent.
母親は子どもの手を引いて道を渡った.	The mother took her child by the hand and crossed the street.
そういう危ない仕事からは手を引いたほうがいい.	You should pull out of a risky business like that.
あの事件からは一切手を引け.	Stay [Steer] clear of that affair.
今度会社は不動産部門にも手を広げることになった.	The company has now extended operations into real estate as well.
彼は列車の窓から見送りの人々に手を振った.	He waved from the window of the train to the people who had come to see him off.
彼と手を結んで仕事をすることにした.	I decided to work in cooperation with him.
あの頑固な老人を説得するのには手を焼いた.	I had a hard time trying to persuade that stubborn old man.
彼女のわがままに我々も手を焼いている.	We are having difficulty dealing with her spoiled ways.
息子のいたずらには手を焼いています.	I've about had it with my son's pranks.
彼は自分の手を汚さずに甘い汁を吸っている.	He takes his cut without †dirtying his own hands [getting his hands dirty].
【慣用】猫の手も借りたいほど忙しい.	I'm so busy it's enough to make my head spin.

であう (出会う)

今日, 町で偶然旧友に出会った.	I ran into an old friend in town today.
今日意外なところで思わぬ人に出会ったよ.	You'll never guess who I ran into today in a most unlikely place.
山道を歩いていたら突然熊に出会い, やっとの思いで逃げた.	I came across a bear as I was hiking along the mountain trail and barely managed to get away.
この本との出会いが私の人生を変えた.	My encounter with this book (has) changed my life.

てあたりしだい (手当たりしだい)

若いときは手当たりしだいに本を読むのも悪くない.	It's not a bad thing to read whatever you can lay your hands on when you're young.

彼は求人欄の仕事に手当たりしだいに応募した．

He applied for every job (he found) listed in the want ads.

てあて (手当て)
【治療】医者は私のけがの手当てをした．

The doctor treated my injury.

看護婦はてきぱきと病人の手当てをした．

The nurse quickly and efficiently treated the patient.

【報酬】超過勤務には特別な手当てが付きます．

There is special compensation for overtime (work).

私の給料には家族手当てが含まれている．

My salary includes a family allowance.

ていこう (抵抗)
社員たちは新しい社長の横暴なやり方に抵抗した．

The employees resisted the new boss's high-handed way of doing things.

銀行強盗は銀行にたてこもって警官に抵抗した．

The bank robber shut himself up in the bank and †held off [made a stand against] the police.

農民たちは国の土地買収に最後まで抵抗した．

The farmers held out to the end against the government's buying up the land.

国民は核の持ち込みに強い抵抗を示した．

The people showed strong resistance to nuclear weapons being brought in.

彼の強引さには抵抗を感じる．

His †forceful attitude [aggressiveness] puts me off.

本人のためとは言え，彼にうそをつくのは抵抗を感じる．

Even though it's for his own good, I still don't feel right about lying to him.

流線型の車体は空気の抵抗が少ない．

A streamlined body has low air resistance.

ニクロム線は抵抗が大きいので，電気を通すと発熱する．

Nichrome wire generates heat when conducting electricity because of its high resistance.

ていしゅつ (提出)
報告書を提出した．

I turned in my report.

レポートの提出が遅れたからか，Cしかもらえなかった．

Maybe I only got a C on my report because I was late handing it in.

願書は11月15日までに提出してください．

Applications must be †turned in [submitted] by November 15th.

履歴書のほかに推薦状も提出してください．

Please submit your letters of recommendation as well as your †C.V. [curriculum vitae.]

願書の提出は郵便に限ります．

Applications must be †mailed in [sent in

この書類の提出期限は金曜日です. This document is due on Friday.

ていど (程度)

その地震による被害の程度はまだ判っていない. The extent of the damage caused by the earthquake has yet to be determined.

これは中学生には程度の高過ぎる問題だ. The level (of difficulty) of this problem is too high for junior high school students.

この程度の本なら私にも理解できる. Even I can understand a book as simple as this.

子どもにどの程度厳しくすべきかという判断は難しい. It's difficult to assess just how strictly children should be brought up.

彼の言うことはある程度当っている. What he says is correct to some extent.

何にでも程度というものがある. There's a limit to everything.

そこまでしゃべってしまうなんていくら正直がいいと言っても程度があるよ. How could you say that much? You can take honesty too far, you know.

本に誤植はつきものと言ったって程度問題だ. A few misprints are inevitable, but this is ridiculous.

その頃の日本は今よりだいぶ生活程度が低かった. In Japan at that time the standard of living was considerably lower than it is now.

【～ぐらい】1,000円程度で彼に何かいい贈り物をしたい. I'd like to get him a nice gift for about ¥1,000.

パーティーの予算は、一人当たり5,000円程度で済ませたい. We'd like to keep the budget for the party to around [about] ¥5,000 per person.

ていねい (丁寧)

【礼儀正しい】彼は女性には丁寧だ. He's polite to women.

彼は丁寧な言葉づかいをする. He speaks very politely.

彼女から丁寧なお礼状が来た. She sent us a polite thank-you note.

【念入り】彼のやる仕事は丁寧だ. He does very careful work.
His work is very meticulous.

彼女は丁寧な字を書く. She writes very meticulous characters.
Her handwriting is very neat.

その旅館は客に対してとても丁寧なもてなしをする. That inn treats its guests very considerately.

この造花は丁寧に作ってある. This artificial flower has been made with great care.

このワイングラスは高価だから丁寧に扱いなさい. These wine glasses are expensive, so handle them carefully.

ていれ (手入れ)

この庭は手入れがよく行き届いている.	This garden is well taken care of.
彼女はモデルなので肌の手入れは欠かせない.	She's a model so she has to take good care of her skin.
彼は庭で植木の手入れをしている.	He's trimming the trees in the yard.
この包丁は手入れが悪いから,よく切れない.	This knife hasn't been taken good care of, so it doesn't cut well.
【警察の】昨夜,賭場に警察の手入れがあった.	There was a police raid on the gambling den last night.

デート

彼女にデートを申し込んだ.	I asked her for a date. ／I asked her out.
彼女にデートを断られた.	She said she wouldn't go out with me. I asked her out but she turned me down.
今度,デートしてください.	How about a date sometime? Would you like to go out on a date sometime? Let's go out on a date sometime.
明日は私たちの初デートだ.	We're going out on our first date tomorrow.
ここは前の彼女とよくデートした場所だ.	This is where I used to come on dates with my †old girlfriend [ex-girlfriend].
彼女の今夜のデートの相手はだれ?	Who's she going out with tonight? Who's her date tonight?
夕焼けがきれい. ここは絶好のデートスポットね.	The sunset is beautiful. Isn't this a perfect spot for a date?

てがかり (手がかり)

警察は犯人の手がかりを求めて奔走した.	The police made every effort to get a lead on the suspect.
行方不明になった弟の手がかりが見つからない.	We have no clues about my missing younger brother.
この事件を解決する手がかりをつかんだ.	We've found the key to this case.
この遺跡は弥生時代の人々の暮らしを知る手がかりになる.	These relics will probably help us understand how people lived during the Yayoi period.

でかける (出かける)

【外出する】ちょっと出かけてくる.	I'm going out for a little while.
彼女は買い物に出かけた.	She went (out) shopping.
彼は旅行に出かけた.	He left on a trip.

あいにく母は出かけています. — Unfortunately, my mother is out.
どちらへお出かけですか. — Where are you going?
彼女が出かけてからもう2時間になります. — It's been two hours since she left.
【来る】是非またお出かけください. — Please be sure to come see me again.
東京へお出かけの節は是非お寄りください. — When you come to Tokyo, please come for a visit.

でき (出来)

今年の米の出来はどうですか？ — How is the rice crop this year?
日曜大工で椅子をつくったが, 思った以上の出来栄えに満足した. — This chair turned out much better than I expected. Not too bad for a Sunday carpenter!
これらのカゴは手作りなので出来不出来がある. — Some of these baskets aren't as good as others because they're handmade.
料理の出来具合を見るために, ちょっとつまんだ. — I had a little taste of the food to see how good it was.
初めてのケーキづくりにしては上出来だよ. — This is your first cake? It's delicious!
わが子ながら出来のいい息子〔娘〕だ. — He's [She's] a pretty good kid, as kids go.[1]
出来の悪い息子を持つと苦労するよ. — Having a kid [son] who isn't doing well can be a real problem.
 — I'm having such a hard time with my no-good son.
私は出来の悪い生徒だった. — I was a poor student.
我が社の給料は出来高払いだ. — Our company's wages are based on commission.[2]
 — Our company pays its wages by the piece [job].[3]

> 1) as kids go は「子どもとしては」「世間一般の子どもと比較して」の意味合い. 2) は歩合制の場合, 3) は数量に応じて支払われる場合の言い方.

てきい (敵意)

彼らのあいだには敵意以外の何物もなかった. — There was nothing but hostility between them.
どういうわけか彼は私に敵意を抱いているようだ. — For some reason he seems †hostile toward [to harbor ill feelings against] me.

できごと (出来事)

新聞やテレビで世界中の出来事を — Newspapers and TV keep us informed of

知ることができる.	world events.
今日, 町で大変な出来事があった.	Something terrible happened in town today.
それはもう昔の出来事だ.	That happened a long time ago.
二・二六事件は1936年の出来事である.	The February 26th Incident occurred [happened] in 1936.

テキスト

【教科書】その教授は決まったテキストを使わない.	The professor does not use any particular textbook.
テキストの25ページを開いてください.	Please turn to page 25 in your textbook.
【原文】その3語は元のテキストにはない.	These three words are not in the original text.
【コンピュータ】テキスト文書と画像ではデータの重さが全く違う.	There's no comparison between the amount of memory needed for text files as opposed to picture or photo files.
原稿はテキスト形式で送ってください.	Please send the manuscript in text form.

てきする (適する)

日本の気候は稲の栽培に適している.	Japan's climate is well suited to the cultivating of rice.
製図には硬い鉛筆が適している.	A hard pencil is best for drafting.
この場合にはどの訳語がいちばん適するか, よく考えてごらんなさい.	Consider carefully what the best translation for this word would be in this context.
医者はその患者の病状に適した処置を施した.	The doctor gave the patient the proper treatment for his condition.
彼女はいい声をしているし機転が利くので司会者に適している.	Because she has a nice voice and she's quick on the uptake, she's just right to be the emcee.

てきせつ (適切)

空所に適切な語を入れなさい.	Fill in the blank with the most appropriate word.
私の気持ちを表す適切な言葉がそのとき見つからなかった.	At the time I was unable to find the appropriate words to express how I felt.
適切かつ敏速な処置で彼の命は助かった.	Swift and proper treatment saved his life.
彼の適切な助言のお陰で私の論文は立派に仕上がった.	Thanks to his pertinent advice, my paper turned out beautifully.

てきとう (適当)

何か適当な参考書はないですか.	Do you have any appropriate [suitable] reference books?
この刑事役に適当な俳優はいないか.	Isn't there an actor suitable for this detective role?
このお菓子を皆さんで適当に分けてください.	Please divide this candy among yourselves as you see fit.
適当なところで切り上げましょう.	Let's quit at †an appropriate [a suitable] †place [cutoff point].
彼はダイヤの指輪を買ってくれとうるさくせがむ妻を適当にあしらった.	He diplomatically avoided his wife's pestering for a diamond ring.
適当に答えておけばいいよ.	Just answer as you see fit.

できる (出来る)

【能力・可能】

車の運転はできる？	Can you drive?
そんな大仕事が私にできるかどうか心配です.	I'm concerned about whether or not I can handle such a big job.
その日は別の用事があるので会合に参加することはできない.	I have something else to do that day so I won't be able to attend the meeting.
今では月に行くこともできる.	It's possible to go to the moon now.
そこへは新幹線でなら日帰りすることもできる.	If you take the †Shinkansen [bullet train] you can make it there and back the same day.
お金があればもっと良い生活ができるのに.	If only I had the money, I could live a nicer life.
僕に100万円貸してくれなんて，とてもできない相談だ.	Asking me to lend you a million yen——it's out of the question.
できることならこんなことはしたくなかった.	I wouldn't have done it if I could've avoided [helped] it.
できれば今日じゅうにこれを仕上げていただきたい.	If possible I'd like to have this done by the end of the day.

【優れている】

彼はフランス語がよくできる.	He is proficient in French.
私の姉は算数がよくできる.	My sister is good with figures.
今度の試験はよくできた.	I did well on this test.
彼はこのクラスでいちばんできる学生だ.	He's the best student in this class.
彼は仕事がよくできる人だ.	He's a very competent man.
あの人は本当によくできた人だ.	He's really a good person.

【完成・完了する】

| 出発の用意が出来ました. | We're all ready to go. Preparations are complete for departure.* |
| やっと宿題が出来た. | I'm finally done with my homework |

	[assignments].
夕飯〔シチュー〕が出来ましたよ.	Dinner's (Stew's) ready.
今度, 会社の近くにレストランが出来た.	A new restaurant just opened near the office.
【生じる】急に用事が出来てしまった.	Something urgent has come up.
私たちに子どもが出来ます.	We're expecting (a child).
今年はミカンがたくさん出来た.	There's a large tangerine crop this year.
チョコレートをたくさん食べたら次の日にきびが出来た.	I ate a lot of chocolate and the next day my face broke out.
我が社とあの会社のあいだには契約が出来ている.	Our company has a contract with that company.
北海道ではトウモロコシはよく出来るが, サトウキビは出来ない.	Corn grows well in Hokkaido, but sugar cane does not.
肥料をやると, 作物がよく出来る.	Crops grow well when fertilized.
【作られる】この机は木で出来ている.	This desk is made of wood.
ワインは何から出来るの.	What is wine made from?

できるだけ

できるだけのことを君にしてあげたい.	I'd like to do as much as †I can [possible] for you.
彼はできるだけ早く事故現場に着こうとした.	He tried to get to the scene of the accident as fast [soon] as †he could [possible].
会議にはできるだけ出席してください.	Please do your best to attend the meeting.

てごろ (手頃)

やさしい英語の小説を読みたいのなら, これなんか手頃だよ.	If you want a novel that's easy to read in English, this would be about right.
あそこは手頃なハイキングコースだ.	That hiking course is easy to do.
このブランドにしては手頃な値段のワンピースだ.	Considering the brand, this dress is reasonably priced.
あの店はランチタイムなら手頃な値段で食べられる.	You can have lunch for a reasonable price at that restaurant.

デジタル

最近の家電にはデジタル機能がついている.	The latest home appliances are equipped with digital controls.
デジタルカメラで撮った写真をパソコンで編集した.	I edited my digital photos on my computer.
	I edited the photos I took with my digital

	camera on my computer.
テレビ放送のデジタル化に伴って新しいテレビを買わなくてはならなかった.	Because TV broadcasting is going digital, we had to buy a new TV.

でしゃばる (出しゃばる)

出しゃばるな.	Don't poke your nose into other people's business.
	Mind your own business.
	Butt out.**／Don't butt in.
あいつの出しゃばった態度が気に入らない.	I don't like his obtrusive manner.

てすう (手数)

これはなかなか手数のかかる仕事だ.	This work takes a lot of time and effort.
インスタント食品は手数がかからないので喜ばれる.	Instant foods are popular because they are no trouble to prepare.
お手数をおかけしますが, これをチェックしておいてください.	I'm sorry to trouble you, but would you check this, please?
これには手数料がかかります.	This requires a handling charge.

でたらめ

彼の言うことはでたらめ (全くのうそ) だ.	What he says is nonsense.
彼女はでたらめ (いいかげんなこと) を言っているだけだ.	She's just talking off the top of her head.
彼はやることなすことでたらめだ.	He does everything in a slipshod [half-assed**] manner.
彼はでたらめな人間だ.	He's very irresponsible.
この答えはまるででたらめだ.	This answer is †complete hogwash [a bunch of baloney**].
彼はでたらめな名前と住所を宿帳に書いた.	He wrote down a made-up [fictitious] name and address in the hotel register.

てつだう (手伝う)

【手助けする】彼がこの仕事を手伝ってくれた.	He helped us with †our work [this job].
娘は家事をよく手伝ってくれます.	My daughter often helps me with the housework.
机を動かすのをちょっと手伝って.	Please help me move the desk.
つっ立ってないで手伝えよ.	Don't just stand there. Give us a hand.
彼は父の店を手伝っている.	He helps out at his father's store.

あなたが手伝ってくれたお陰で，予定より早く仕事を終えることができました.	Thanks to your help, I was able to finish the work ahead of schedule.
【原因が重なる】不況も手伝って，ついに会社は倒産した.	With the recession being a contributing negative factor, the company ended up going bankrupt.
病気の上に過労が手伝って，彼は死んでしまった.	He died when his illness was compounded by overwork.

てつづき (手続き)

彼は土地を購入するのに必要な手続きを全部済ませた.	He completed all the necessary procedures to purchase the land.
裁判は法的な手続きを踏まなければいけない.	One must comply with legal processes when going to court.
役所には面倒な手続きがつきものだ.	Trying to get something done at government offices always entails red tape.
留学の手続きについては田中君が詳しい.	Tanaka is familiar with the procedures necessary for studying abroad.
入学の手続きは明日が締め切りだ.	The deadline for school registration is tomorrow.
彼らは離婚の手続きをとった.	They filed for divorce.
入会にはどんな手続きが必要ですか.	What steps are necessary to become a member?

てってい (徹底)

彼は徹底した合理主義者だ.	He's a complete rationalist.
会社の方針に彼は徹底した反対意見を持っている.	He is completely at odds with his company's policy.
刑事は事件を徹底的に調べた.	The detective made a thorough investigation of the case.
その小説は評論家に徹底的に叩かれた.	That novel was thoroughly panned by the critics.
税制の徹底的な改革が必要だ.	The tax system needs a thorough reform.
会の規則を全会員に徹底させよう.	Let's make sure that all the members know [keep] the association's rules.

てぬるい (手ぬるい)

君のやり方は手ぬる過ぎる.	You're much too easy [soft, lenient[1]].
そんな手ぬるいことでは彼には通用しない.	A soft [lax] attitude will not get you far in dealing with him.

---

1) lenient は特に「処罰」に関して用いる.

てはい (手配)

送迎の車は私が手配します.	I'll arrange for a car to meet him and take him back.
会場と司会者は手配済みです.	I've arranged for the hall and the master of ceremonies.
航空券の手配は秘書がやってくれる.	My secretary takes care of my plane tickets.
彼は全国に指名手配されている.	He is wanted throughout Japan.

てほん (手本)

習字はお手本をよく見て書きなさい.	Practice your calligraphy by looking carefully at the examples [models].
この建物は有名な宮殿を手本にして造られています.	This building was modeled after a famous palace.
兄の模型グライダーを手本にして自分のを作った.	I made my own model glider by copying my brother's.
彼は下級生のよい手本になっている.	He serves as a good model for underclassmen.

てま (手間)

この料理は簡単そうに見えて意外と手間がかかる.	This dish looks easy but it's actually quite time-consuming [complicated] to make.
手間を省くために電子レンジを使います.	I use a microwave oven to save time.
難しい数学の問題に随分と手間取った.	I spent a lot of time on a difficult math problem.
お手間を取らせてしまい, 申しわけありません.	I'm sorry for troubling you.
お使いを頼んだ男の子に手間賃を払った.	I paid the boy who did errands for me for his trouble.
彼の雑な仕事のせいで, 作業が二度手間になってしまった.	We had to do the job all over again because of his carelessness.

でむかえる (出迎える)

母はいつも父を玄関に出迎える.	My mother always meets my father at the door when he comes home.
久しぶりの帰省に母は駅まで出迎えてくれた.	When I returned to my hometown after a long absence, my mother came to meet me at the station.
有名女優の来日に, 多数の取材陣が空港に出迎えた.	When the famous actress came to Japan, a large number [contingent] of reporters met her at the airport.

でも

【～でさえも】 幼稚園へは子どもの足でも5分で行ける. — Even at a child's pace, the kindergarten is just five minutes on foot.

彼は忙しくて日曜でも休むことができない. — He's so busy that he can't even take Sundays off.

こんな立地的に悪い土地でも1平方メートルあたり100万円もする. — Even in this bad location, this property sells for one million yen per square meter.

この花は戸外でも冬を越せる. — This flower can get through the winter even if it's planted outdoors.

【～だとしても】 明日は雨でも出かけます. — We'll go tomorrow even if it rains.

書類を届けるのは明日でもかまいません. — You can deliver these papers either today or tomorrow.

【～か何〔だれ〕か】 お茶でも飲みませんか. — Won't you have some tea or something?

こんなとき, 中村君でもいてくれたらなあ. — If only we had someone like Nakamura at a time like this.

テレビでも見ようかな. — Maybe I'll watch TV.

来週にでも会いましょう. — We could meet next week.

【～であっても】 困ったときにはいつでも力になります. — I will help you whenever you get into difficulty.

こんな簡単なことはだれでも知っている. — Anybody would know such a simple thing.

気がついたことは何でも言ってください. — If you have any comments or suggestions please speak up.

あなたの行くところならどこへでもお供します. — I will go with you wherever you go.

この程度の歌手ならいくらでもいる. — There're any number of singers who sing as well as he does.

いくら何でも, これが1万円とは高過ぎる. — No matter how you look at it, ten thousand yen is too much to pay for this.

【しかし・けれども】 さんざん失敗した. でも, 僕はくじけない. — I've made many mistakes but I don't let it get me down.

でも, やっぱり君の言うことはおかしい. — But what you're saying is still funny.

てらす (照らす)

真夏の太陽が町を照らしている. — The midsummer sun is shining on the town.

月の光が湖を照らしている. — The moon is shining on the lake.

街灯が道を照らしている. — The street lights are †lighting up [illuminating] the road.

懐中電灯でここを照らしてください.	Please shine the flashlight over [right] here.
【参照する】法に照らしてみれば,彼の有罪は明らかだ.	A close look at the law will clearly establish his guilt.
彼の行為は社会的通念に照らしてみて判断されるべきだ.	His actions should be judged in light of what is socially acceptable.
過去の実績に照らして彼の表彰を決定した.	He was chosen for the award in view [light] of his past achievements.
私の経験に照らしてみれば,そのようなことはありえない.	From [In light of] my own experience, something like that would be impossible.

てる (照る)

太陽がさんさんと照っている.	The sun is shining brightly.
海岸では真夏の太陽が肌が痛いほどじりじりと照りつけていた.	The midsummer sun was so sizzling hot at the beach that my skin hurt.
満月がこうこうと照っている.	The full moon is shining brightly.

でる (出る)

【内から外へ・前へ】彼女はベランダに出て外の空気を吸った.	She went out on the veranda for a breath of air.
今日は一歩も家から外へ出ていない.	I haven't taken a single step out of the house today.
彼は今仕事で外へ出ています.	He's out now (on business).
店を出たところで友達に会った.	I met a friend as I left the store.
この線から出ないでください.	Please keep within the line.
【去る】彼は去年大学を出たばかりです.	He just †finished [graduated from] college last year.
娘は結婚して家を出ました.	My daughter got married and left home.
妻が出て行ってしまった.	My wife has (gone and) left me.
【出発する】汽車は10時に出ます.	The train leaves at 10 o'clock.
バスは駅前から出ています.	Buses leave from in front of the station.
私は毎朝9時に家を出ます.	I leave the house at nine every morning.
しばらく旅に出ることにした.	I have decided to go on a trip for a while.
【現れる】今夜は月が出ている.	The moon is out tonight.
彼は感情がすぐ顔に出るタイプだ.	He's the type who lets his feelings show on his face right away.
店にはもうサクランボが出ている.	Cherries are already on sale.
【出席・参加する】彼は10時に会社に出てきた.	He came to the office at 10 o'clock.
明日の会議には出るつもりだ.	I intend to †go to [attend] tomorrow's meeting.
彼は今度の選挙に出るらしい.	It appears he will run in the next election.

今度の劇には私も出ます.	I will also appear in this play.
ここはお前の出る幕じゃない.	This is no time for you to get involved.
【出版される】薬膳の特集号が出た.	They brought out a special (edition) about foods that heal.
彼が新しく書いた本が出た.	His new book †is out [has been published].
新しいファッション雑誌が出た.	There's a new fashion magazine out.
【載る・話題に上る】昨日の火事が新聞に出ていた.	Yesterday's fire was (written up) in the newspaper.
あなたの記事はいつ出るんですか.	When is your article coming out?
先日の同窓会であなたの話が出ました.	Your name was mentioned at the reunion the other day.
【突き出る】床にくぎが出ているから気をつけて.	Be careful. There's a nail sticking out of the floor.
彼は最近おなかが出てきた.	Recently his stomach has begun to bulge.
【生じる】この車はスピードがあまり出ない.	This car won't go very fast.
最近, 彼は仕事にやる気が出てきたようだ.	It appears that he has become more determined to work recently.
このお茶はよく出る.	You get a lot of tea from these leaves.
あの山からは銅が出る.	That mountain has large copper reserves.
昨夜の大雨で町に水が出た.	Last night's heavy rain flooded the town.
火は8階の食堂調理場から出たらしい.	The fire apparently spread from the 8th floor dining hall kitchen.
「ズボン」という語はフランス語から出ている.	The Japanese word "*zubon*" †comes [is derived] from a French word.
【見つかる】タクシーに忘れたお金が三日たって出てきた.	The money I left in a taxi turned up three days later.
部屋をいくら探しても万年筆は出てこなかった.	No matter how much I searched my room, I couldn't find my fountain pen.
【行き着く】この道を真っすぐに行けば駅に出ます.	Go straight down this road and you'll come to the station.
しばらく歩くうちに海岸に出た.	After walking for a while we came to the beach.
【売れる】うちの店ではこの本はよく出ます.	This book sells well at my store.
今はこの本がいちばんよく出ている.	This book is the number one seller right now.
【与えられる】明日ボーナスが出る.	Tomorrow bonuses will be handed out.
よく働いたので特別手当てが出た.	We got a special bonus because we did a lot of work.
彼女の誕生パーティーにはすごいごちそうが出た.	An incredible feast was served at her birthday party.
今日の試験は難しい問題が出た.	There were some difficult problems on

【超過する】その旅行の交通費は一人当たり2万円をちょっと出るくらいです.	The transportation charges for that trip will be just over twenty thousand yen per person.
【態度をとる】今度の件では彼はかなり強気に出ている.	He's taking a fairly aggressive attitude on this matter.
彼の出方しだいでは，こちらにも考えがある.	Depending on †what he wants [how he wants to do it] I know how I'm going to handle it.

てれる (照れる)

彼は照れて人前では彼女に話しかけることができない.	He's too bashful to speak to her in front of others.
彼は褒められて照れくさそうに笑った.	He smiled bashfully when he was praised.
そんなに褒められると照れるなあ.	It's embarrassing to be praised so much.

てん (点)

沖の船が点のように小さく見えた.	The ship off shore looked like a tiny dot.
漢字は点のあるなしで意味が全く違ってしまうことがある.	With Chinese characters the presence or absence of just one stroke can change the meaning completely.
この文章はここに点がないとちょっと分かりにくい.	This sentence is a little hard to understand without a comma here.
【点数】彼は試験でいい点を取った.	He †got good marks [scored well] on the test [exam].
算数のテストで100点満点中90点を取った.	I got 90 out of 100 points on the math test.
先日の英語のテストで僕は平均点以下だった.	I scored lower than the average on the English test the other day.
先生は彼の作文にいい点をつけた.	The teacher gave him a good mark [grade] on his composition.
単語のつづりを間違えて，2点引かれた.	I †lost two points [got two points taken off] for misspelling a word.
あの先生は点が辛い.	That teacher is a strict [hard] grader.
【得点】ジャイアンツは1回表にはやばやと点を取った.	The Giants scored right away in the top of the first.
我がチームは着々と点を重ねた.	Our team steadily piled up the points.
あのピッチャー相手ではそうそう点は取れないだろう.	That pitcher probably won't be too easy to score against.
【論点・観点】その点は問題ありません.	There's no question on that point.
この点では君の言い分が正しい.	Your view on this point is well taken.

この製品は品質の点で問題がある.	There's a problem with (respect to) the quality of this product.
いろいろな点から見て，この方法がいいと思う.	Viewed from various aspects, this method seems to be the best.

てんき (天気)

このところ，天気がよい.	We're having some good weather lately.
明日天気が良ければピクニックに行こう.	If the weather is nice tomorrow, let's go for a picnic.
山は天気が変わり易い.	The weather is very changeable in the mountains.
天気が悪いと，体調が悪くなる.	When the weather's bad, so is my physical condition.
旅行中は申し分のない天気が続いた.	We had perfect [ideal] weather during the entire trip.
毎朝天気予報を聞きます.	I listen to the weather forecast every morning.
東京地方の天気は今夜から下り坂になるでしょう.	The weather in the Tokyo area will take a turn for the worse tonight.
【晴天】明日は天気になるだろう.	We should have good weather tomorrow.
今日はお天気で良かったね.	I'm glad the weather's nice today.
【慣用】あの先生はお天気屋だ.	That teacher is moody.

てんそう (転送)

応募書類はすべて本社に転送してください.	Please forward all application documents to the head office.
前の住所宛ての手紙が転送されてきた.	A letter addressed to my former address was forwarded to me.
【コンピュータ】恋人からのメールを誤って上司に転送した.	I mistakenly forwarded an e-mail from my girlfriend to my boss.
転送メールに返事を出すときは，元の発信者のアドレスに送るように注意しなさい.	When answering forwarded e-mails, be careful to send back to the original e-mail address.

でんとう (伝統)

我が社は80年の伝統を誇っている.	Our company prides itself on its eighty years of tradition.
この村では伝統の行事が代々受け継がれている.	Traditional rites have been passed on in this village from generation to generation.
この高校は伝統的にサッカーが強い.	This high school has a tradition of being strong in soccer.

てんねん (天然)

このせっけんは天然の材料を使っている.	This soap is made from natural ingredients.
この地域は今度天然ガスに切り替わりました.	This area has switched to natural gas.
天然資源は無尽蔵ではない.	Natural resources are not inexhaustible.
トキは天然記念物です.	The †*toki* [Japanese crested ibis] is a protected species.
うちの娘は天然パーマだ.	Our daughter has naturally curly hair.

てんぷ (添付・貼付)

その手紙には名刺が添付されていた.	There was a business card attached to that letter.
添付書類を参考にしてください.	Please refer to the attached document(s).
履歴書には写真を貼付のこと.	Attach a photograph to your †résumé. [curriculum vitae., C.V.]
【コンピュータ】ファイルはメールに添付してください.	Please attach the file to the e-mail.
企画書を添付でお送りします.	I'll send the plan as an attachment.
添付ファイルが開けない.	I can't open the attachment.
	The attachment won't open.

でんわ (電話)

彼に電話をかけた.	I called him (up)./I telephoned him.
	I gave him a call.
あなたに電話ですよ.	You have a call.
	You're wanted on the phone.
	There's a call for you.
	The phone's [call's] for you.
前から頼んでいた電話がやっと引けた.	The telephone I ordered some time ago was finally installed.
彼女は今電話中です.	She's on the phone right now.
彼女はただ今ほかの電話に出ておりますが.	(I'm afraid) She's on another line right now.
その電話には私が出ました.	I answered that call.
公衆電話はどこにありますか.	Where can I find a public telephone?
東京の電話交換手をお願いします.	Tokyo operator, please.
電話が遠いのですが.	(I'm sorry but) †We have a bad connection [I can't hear you very well].
電話を切らないでください.	Hold the line, please.
話の途中なのに電話が切れてしまった.	We got cut off in the middle of a conversation.
電話が混線しているようですね.	It seems that the lines have gotten crossed.

彼女に何回かけても電話が通じない.	No matter how often I call her, I can't get through.
電話が嵐で不通になった.	The storm knocked out the phones.
彼に電話をかけたが話し中だった.	I called him but the line was busy.
お母さんに今夜遅くなるって電話したらどうですか.	Why don't you call your mother and tell her that you'll be home late tonight?
市内電話は3分間10円です.	Local calls [Calls within the city] are 10 yen for three minutes.
これは私への直通電話の番号です.	This number is for my direct line.
ちょっと電話を貸してください.	May I please use the phone?
この携帯電話で今すぐ飛行機の予約をしよう.	I'll make the plane reservations on [with] my cell phone right away.
長距離電話は夜間割引になる.	There's a night discount rate on long-distance calls.
電話帳で探したが,彼の番号は見当たらなかった.	I tried to look up his number in the phone book but couldn't find it.

と

ど(度)

【回数】何度やってもうまくいかない.	No matter how many times I try, I can't †get it right [do it well].
一日に何度食事をしますか.	How many times [meals] do you eat every day?
一度医者に診てもらったほうがいい.	You should see a doctor.
君の顔なんかもう二度と見たくない.	I never want to see your face again.
彼は三度続けてじゃんけんに勝った.	He won at "rock-scissors-paper" three times in a row.
【温度】今日は暑いと思ったら32度もあった.	I thought it was hot today, and sure enough it was 32°C [thirty-two degrees centigrade].
彼は風邪で39度の熱が出た.	Due to a cold he developed a fever of 39°C.
【角度】正三角形の一つの角は60度です.	In an equilateral triangle each angle is 60 degrees.
【程度・度合】最近,近眼の度が進	My nearsightedness has gotten worse

んできた.	recently.
彼は度の強い眼鏡をかけている.	He wears strong glasses.
政局は緊張の度を増している.	The degree of political tension is increasing.
彼はファッション界では知名度が高い.	He is a big name in the fashion world.
お酒も適量なら良いが, 度を越してはいけない.	It's all right to drink in moderation, but don't overdo it.
彼の冗談はいつも度が過ぎる.	He overdoes it with his jokes.
【平静】彼はいきなり証拠を突きつけられて度を失った.	When the evidence was sprung on him, he lost his cool.

とう¹ (問う)

ハイジャック事件が起こり, 空港には乗客の安否を問う電話が殺到した.	When the hijacking occurred, the airport was flooded with calls (inquiring) about the safety of the passengers.
このアルバイトの仕事は男女〔年齢〕を問わず募集しています.	Applicants are being recruited for this part-time work regardless [irrespective] of sex [age].
彼はその問題で責任を問われた.	His responsibility came into question over that matter.
彼は殺人罪に問われた.	He was charged with murder.
今, まさに首相の指導力が問われている.	Now more than ever the prime minister's leadership is in question.

とう² (等)

【等しい】ここからだと, 東京も名古屋もほぼ等距離にある.	From here, Tokyo and Nagoya are just about the same distance.
【順位・等級】彼は運動会の100メートル競走で1等賞をもらった.	He won first prize in the 100 meter dash at the athletic meet.
彼女の絵は展覧会で2等を取った.	Her picture was chosen for second place at the exhibition.
2等船室は穴蔵みたいだから1等で行きましょう.	A second-class cabin is just a hole in the wall, so let's go first class.
【など】公園内で行商等の行為を禁ず.	Activities such as peddling are prohibited inside the park.
日本は小麦, 大豆等の農産物を外国からの輸入に頼っている.	Japan is dependent on foreign imports for such agricultural products as wheat and soybeans.

どう

【どのような方法】どうしよう?	What shall we do?
このお金をどう使いますか.	How are you going to use this money?

この始末をどうしてくれる.	How do you intend to take care of this?
どう考えてもこの問題は分からない.	No matter how I look at it I can't understand this problem.
お前なんかどうなってもかまわない.	I don't care what happens to you.
おなかがすいてどうにもならない.	I'm so hungry I don't know what to do. I'm starving to death.
あの子は乱暴でどうしようもない.	That child is so wild there's nothing we can do.
彼のやり方をどう思いますか.	What do you think of the way he does things?
新しい本を出す話はどうなりましたか.	Whatever came of the talk about †putting out [publishing] a new book?
彼がこの仕事を手伝おうが手伝うまいが別にどうということもない.	It doesn't make any difference to me whether or not he helps me with this work.
君が今さら謝ってもどうなるものでもない.	Your apology doesn't mean anything at this stage.
そんないいかげんなことでどうするつもりだ.	How far do you think an attitude like that will get you?
もう, どうにでもしなさい.	I don't care. Do it your way.
【どのような様子】「この頃, どう？」「順調だよ」	"How're things going these days? [How's it going?]" "Pretty good."
ハワイ旅行はどうでしたか.	How did you like Hawaii?
こうしたらどう？	What about doing it like this?
風邪の具合はどうですか.	How is your cold?
雨がひどいので, 今夜は泊まっていったらどうですか.	It's raining very heavily, so why not stay overnight?
彼は今日来るかどうか分からない.	I don't know if he will come today or not.
それを買うかどうかまだ決めていない.	I haven't decided yet whether (or not) to buy it.
出かけるかどうかはお天気しだいです.	Whether or not we go depends on the weather.
「あの二人は結婚すると思う？」「さあ, どうでしょう」	"I wonder if those two are getting married." "Hum...it's hard to tell."

どうい (同意)

彼は僕の意見に同意した.	He agreed with me.
その提案は皆の同意を得られなかった.	Not everyone went along with the proposal.
そのご意見にはどうも同意いたしかねます.	I just can't accept your opinion [view]. I just can't go along with your idea.

どうか

【どうぞ】
- どうかご病気が早く治りますように. — I hope you get well soon.
- どうか許してください. — Please forgive me.
- どうかお願いします. — Can you do me a favor, please?

【何とか】
- みんなでどうかこうかしているうちに, やっと車のエンジンがかかった. — After trying just about everything, we finally got the engine started.
- お宅のうるさい犬, どうかなりませんか. — Can't you please do something about your barking dog?

【おかしい】
- 今日の彼は何を聞いてもうわの空でどうかしている. — Everytime I talk to him today his mind seems to be somewhere else.
- 彼のやり方に怒らないほうがどうかしている. — There's something wrong with people who don't get angry at his methods.
- 顔色が悪いようですが, どうかしましたか. — You look awfully pale. Is anything the matter?
- うるさくて頭がどうかなりそうだ. — This noise is driving me crazy. / It's so noisy I think I'm going to go nuts.**

【感心しない】
- 彼のようにまじめ過ぎるのもどうかと思う. — I really wonder about someone as serious as he is.

【時々】
- 彼はどうかすると一週間も家に帰らないことがある. — He's been known to stay away from home for a whole week at a time.
- 会社は忙しくてどうかすると昼食もとれない. — When we're really busy at the office, sometimes it's impossible even to (take a) break for lunch.

どうかん (同感)

- 同感です. — I agree with you. / I feel the same way about it.
- あなたの意見に同感です. — We share the same opinion.

どうぐ (道具)

- 人間は道具を使う動物だと言われている. — Man is sometimes called the tool-using animal.
- 本物の職人は道具を大切に扱う. — The true artisan takes good care of his tools.
- 彼女はお菓子を作る道具を揃えた. — She has a complete set of baking utensils.
- 彼のところから大工道具を一式借りてきた. — I borrowed a complete set of carpentry tools from him.
- 車を修理したくても道具がないのでできない. — Even if I wanted to fix my car, I don't have the right tools.
- 古道具屋を覗くのが私の楽しみで — I enjoy looking around antique shops.

【手段】彼は結婚を出世の道具に使った. He used marriage as a way to move up in the world.

他人を道具に使う人間は許せない. I can't stand people who use others as tools.

どうさ (動作)

彼は何をするにも動作がのろい〔素早い〕. He does everything slowly [quickly].

彼女はきびきびとした動作で掃除,洗濯をした. She quickly did the laundry and cleaning.

私は今,空手の基本動作を教わっている. I'm learning the basic moves of *karate* now.

あの役者は,あがると動作がぎこちなく,不自然になりがちだ. When that actor gets nervous, his movements [actions] tend to be stiff and unnatural.

とうし¹ (投資)

彼は有り金全部を事業に投資した. He invested all the money he had in that business.

この会社の株なら安全な投資と言える. I think this company's stock is a safe investment.

とうし² (闘志)

彼は闘志満々だ. He's all ready [set] to go [compete].

試合が近づくにつれて闘志が湧いてきた. As the match approaches, I'm really getting pumped up.**

選手たちは優勝へ向かって闘志を燃やしている. The team members are fired up to win.

とうじ (当時)

終戦当時は食糧難で苦労した. Right after the war we suffered from a severe food shortage.

当時は一世を風靡したあの俳優も今では全く売れていない. He was such a star at that time, but today he's a nobody.

今はビルが立ち並んでいるこの辺りも,私が住んでいた当時は,何もない野原だった. Buildings are crammed in here side by side today, but when I lived here, this was an open field.

その当時は,1円で米が1俵買えた. In those days a bag of rice cost one yen.

彼が当時の学長だった. He was then the president of the university.

どうじ (同時)

【同じ時】
二人が待ち合わせ場所に着いたのはほとんど同時だった. — We arrived at our meeting place at almost the same time.

私が家に着くと同時に雨が降り出した. — Just as I reached home, it began raining.

彼がホームに駆け上がると同時に列車は出てしまった. — Just as he made it up to the platform, the train pulled out.

英語の試験とフランス語の試験は同時に行います. — The English and French exams will be held †at the same time [simultaneously].

【一方】
おとなしさは彼の長所であると同時に短所でもある. — His reserve is both a strength as well as a shortcoming.

産業の発達によって生活が便利になったが, 同時に数多くの弊害も出てきている. — Industrial progress makes life easier, but at the same time it produces numerous harmful side effects.

どうして

【理由】
今日はどうして遅れたの? — Why were you late today? / How come you were late today?

君はどうしてそんなに馬鹿なんだ. — Why are you such a fool?

どうしてこんな簡単なことが分からないの. — Why can't you understand such a simple thing?

どうしてこんなひどいことになったんでしょう. — How could such an awful thing happen?

【方法】
川はどうして出来たのですか. — How were rivers formed?

父はカンカンに怒っていて私はどうしていいか分からなかった. — Father was so angry I didn't know what I should do.

この難しい問題をどうして解いたらいいんだろう. — This problem is really difficult. How do you think we should solve it?

【予想外に】
彼はどうしてなかなかの利口者だ. — As it turns out, he is quite a clever fellow.

きみはテニスは初めてだと言ったが, どうしてなかなかうまいじゃないか. — You said you were just a beginner at tennis, but actually you're quite good, aren't you?

どうしても

どうしても彼女に会わなければならない. — I've got to see her by all means. / I absolutely have to see her.

彼はどうしてもその地位を手に入れたかった. — He wanted to win the position at any cost. / He would have done anything to get that position.

私にはどうしてもそんな汚いことはできない. — There's no way I could do such a dirty thing.

彼女はどうしても帰ると言った.	She insisted on going home.
彼がだれだったかどうしても思い出せない.	I just can't remember who he was.
この問題がどうしても解けない.	I simply [just] can't solve this problem.

どうじょう (同情)

みんなその孤児に同情している.	Everyone has [feels] sympathy for that orphan.
世間の同情が彼女に集まった.	She drew the sympathy of the public.
やたらな同情は禁物だ.	Sympathy should not be doled out too easily.

どうじる (動じる)

彼はどんな脅しにも動じない.	He isn't fazed [shaken] by any threat.
昨日の大きな地震で動じなかったのは彼女だけだった.	She was the only one who wasn't shaken up by yesterday's big earthquake.
中学生はものに動じ易い年頃である.	Junior high school students are at an age when they're given to being overly sensitive.

とうすい (陶酔)

| 彼らはその素晴らしい音楽に陶酔していた. | They were enchanted [enraptured] by the magnificent music. |
| その舞踊家は自分自身に陶酔して舞っていた. | The dancer was completely absorbed in her dancing. |

どうせ

どうせ間に合わないのなら, 安全運転でゆっくり行こう.	If we're not going to make it on time anyway, let's take our time and drive safely.
私たちの願いなんか, どうせ聞き入れられっこない.	They're not going to listen to us anyway.
どうせだれもやれる人がいなくて私がやることになるに決まってる.	I'll end up doing it anyhow, since there's no one who can do it.
どうせ人は死ぬのだ.	We all have to go sometime.
どうせやるなら, きちんとやろうよ.	Since we have to do it anyway, we may as well do a good job. If it's worth doing at all it's worth doing well.[1]
「そんなことも分からないの?」「どうせ僕は頭が悪いですよ!」	"Don't you get it?" "You must think I'm really dumb."
「あの子, 家出するって言って飛び出して行ったわ」「どうせま	"That child ran out, saying he was running away from home." "He's just go-

た友達の家に1泊して帰ってくるんだろう」	ing to stay at a friend's for the night and come home anyway."
「あの子, お手伝いするって約束したのに, また三日坊主で終わったのよ」「どうせそんなところだろうと思っていたよ」	"That child promised to help out with chores but didn't keep to it." "It's just as I expected."
今度の旅行, どうせなら海外にしましょうよ.	If we're going to travel anyway, let's go abroad.
どうせなら, プレゼントは電波時計がいいな.	If you're going to get me a present anyway, I'd really like a radio-controlled watch.

> 1)「いやしくも行うに値することならきちんと行うに値する」という意味の諺.

とうぜん (当然)

それを聞いて彼が怒るのも当然だ.	It's only natural †that he'd get angry [for him to get angry] hearing that.
それは当然我々の仕事だ.	Of course that's (part of) our job.
「あの仕事, やることにしたか」「当然だよ」	"Did you accept the job?" "Of course. [Naturally.]"
彼女は当然褒められていい.	She deserves to be praised.

どうぞ

どうぞお上がりください.	Please come in.
どうぞお許しください.	Please forgive me.
「たばこを吸ってもいいですか」「どうぞ」	"Is it all right to smoke?" "Sure. [Go ahead.]"

とうちゃく (到着)

飛行機は定刻に羽田に到着した.	The plane arrived at Haneda on schedule.
このバスのサンフランシスコ〔駅〕への到着は何時ですか.	What time does this bus †arrive in San Francisco [arrive at the station]?
アメリカ政府の代表団は明日日本に到着の予定だ.	The U.S. government delegation is expected to arrive in Japan tomorrow.
ホノルル発101便の到着時刻を教えてください.	Could you tell me the arrival time of flight 101 from Honolulu?
台風のために列車の到着が大幅に遅れている.	Due to the typhoon, train arrivals are considerably behind schedule.
向こうに到着したら, すぐに連絡してくれ.	Please let me know as soon as you arrive [reach] there.
葉書の到着順に200名まで受け付けます.	We will accept the first 200 postcards.

とうとい (尊い)

人間の生命はこの世でいちばん尊いものだ. — Human life is the most precious thing in the world.

とうとう

彼はとうとう長年の研究を完成させた. — After many years he has finally completed his studies.

彼はとうとう死んでしまった. — He finally died.

彼はとうとうクラス会に来なかった. — As it turned out, he didn't show up at the class reunion.

とうとう雨になった. — Eventually it began to rain.

忙しくて,とうとうその映画は見損なった. — I have been busy, so I wasn't able to see that film at all.

山で遭難して1週間目にとうとう食糧がなくなってしまった. — One week after we got stranded in the mountains the food supply finally ran out.

彼は一文無しになり,とうとう盗みを働いてしまった. — He became penniless, and finally resorted to stealing.

どうどう (堂々)

選手たちは堂々と入場行進をした. — The players marched proudly onto the field.

学生代表が堂々と演説した. — The student representative delivered a commanding speech.

挑戦者は負けはしたものの,チャンピオンに対して堂々と戦った. — Though he lost, the challenger put up an impressive fight against the champion.

何も悪いことはしていないんだからもっと堂々と振る舞いなさい. — You haven't done anything wrong. You can hold your head up high.

彼は堂々とした体格だ. — He has a sturdy build. / He has a powerful physique.

どうにか

彼はどうにか一人でやり終えた. — He somehow managed to get it done by himself.

どうにか期日までに間に合いそうだ. — It looks like I'll make the deadline somehow.

その映画の切符を手に入れたいんだけど,どうにかならないかしら. — I'd like to get tickets to that movie. I wonder if there isn't some way you could help me.

放っておけばとにかくどうにかなるさ. — If you leave it alone it'll take care of itself.

とうばん(当番)
今日は私の当番だ.	It's my turn today.
部屋の掃除は当番ですることにしよう.	Let's take turns cleaning this room.
くじ引きで当番を決めよう.	Let's decide turns by drawing lots [straws].
当番をさぼってはいけません.	You can't skip your turn.

とうひょう(投票)
その件はクラスの投票で決められることになった.	This is to be decided by (a) class vote.
私は彼に投票しようと決めた.	I've decided to vote for him.
彼は議案に賛成〔反対〕の投票をした.	He voted for [against] the bill.
投票の結果は賛成27反対12だった.	The ballot results were 27 in favor and 12 opposed.
今回の市長選は投票率が高かった.	There was a high voter turnout (rate) for this mayoralty race.
混雑を避けるため, 早めに投票所へ行った.	I went to the polls early to avoid the crowds.

とうぶん(当分)
当分の間は安静にしてください.	Please take it easy for a while.
天気予報によると, 雨は当分降りそうにない.	According to the weather report, it's not likely to rain for a while.
この様子だと, 現政権はまだ当分続くだろう.	At this rate, the current government will go on for some time (to come).
うちの経済状態ではマイホームなんて当分先の話だ.	With our finances, it'll be some time before we can buy a house.

どうみても
どうみてもおかしい.	It's strange on all counts [accounts].
	No matter how you look at it, it's strange.
どうみても彼女は40代だ.	She †*has to* [*must*, *has got to*] be in her forties.
どうみても我々のほうが不利だ.	No matter how you look at it, †we're at a disadvantage [they have the advantage on us].

とうめい(透明)
水は無色透明だ.	Water is colorless and transparent.
その湖は透明な水をたたえていた.	The lake was filled with (crystal) clear water.
摩周湖は日本でいちばん透明度が	Lake Mashu has the clearest water of any

	lake in Japan.
高い.	
この薬品は不透明な容器に入れて保存します.	This drug is preserved in an opaque container.
『透明人間』(映画)を見に行こうよ.	Let's go see *The Invisible Man*.

どうも

【どうしても】この英文はどうもうまく訳せない.	No matter what I do, I just can't translate this English right.
彼の考えはどうもよく分からない.	I just can't comprehend his thinking.
【何となく】このところどうも体の具合が良くない.	I haven't felt up to par for a while.
どうも彼とはうまくいかない.	For some reason he and I simply can't get along.
この頃彼の様子がどうも変だ.	He doesn't seem †like himself [to be his usual self] lately.
あれはどうもうそだったらしい.	That appears to have been a lie.
【本当に】どうもありがとうございました.	Thank you very much.
どうもすみません.	I'm sorry.／My apologies.

どうよう (動揺)

彼の事業の失敗を聞いて私は動揺した.	I was upset [disturbed] by the news of his business failure.
大統領の死の知らせに国民は動揺した.	News of the President's death †caused great commotion among the people [threw the nation into a tumult].
会社が立ち入り検査を受け、さすがの社長も動揺の色を隠せなかった.	Our company was subjected to an on-the-spot investigation, and even our (normally imperturbable) president couldn't hide his consternation.

とおい (遠い)

【距離】私の家は駅から遠い.	My house is †a long way [far] from the station.
遠い所をよくおいでくださいました.	Thanks for coming such a long way.
目的地はまだまだ遠い.	We still have †a long way(s) [some distance] to go.
子どもは学校からわざと遠回りして帰ってくる.	The children take the long way home from school on purpose.
【時間】明治時代は遠い昔になってしまった.	The Meiji era has become distant history.

私たちが再び会える日は遠くない.	The day when we can meet again is not far off.
だれもが宇宙旅行に行ける日はそう遠くない.	It won't be long before anyone can travel in space.
【関係】彼女は私の遠い親せきだ.	She is a distant relative of mine.

とおく (遠く)

遠くに山が見える.	I can see a mountain in the distance.
遠くの人にも聞こえるように大きな声で話してください.	Please speak in a loud voice, so that even the people far away can hear you.
彼は遠くから引っ越してきた.	He has moved here from a great distance.
私の両親は遠くに住んでいる.	My parents live far away from here.
彼は随分遠くから学校に通って来る.	He commutes quite a long way to school.

とおす (通す)

すみませんがちょっとそこを通してください.	Excuse me, but could you please let me by?
ガラスは電気を通さない.	Glass does not conduct electricity.
祖母は眼鏡なしでは針に糸を通せない.	Grandmother can't thread a needle without her glasses.
お客様を応接室にお通ししてください.	Please show the guests to the sitting room.
父は上着のそでに腕を通した.	Father put his arms into the sleeves of his jacket.
最初から筋を通して話してみてください.	Start at the beginning and speak logically.
彼は書類にざっと目を通した.	He glanced over the documents.
【続ける】彼女は一生独身で通した.	She remained single all her life.
彼は高校時代ずっと首席で通した.	He was top of his class throughout high school.
あの子は冬でも半そでで通す.	That child wears short-sleeved shirts even in winter.
【最後まで主張する】彼はどこまでも信念を通した.	He stuck to his convictions to the end.
彼女はだれにでもわがままを通す人だ.	She insists on getting her way with everyone.
彼は自分の利益になることなら，どんな無理でも通してしまう.	He'll do anything for a profit.
【媒介にする】窓口を通して申し込んでください.	Please apply at the window.
彼は人を通して和解を申し入れてきた.	He proposed reconciliation through the good offices of a third party.

この品物は知人を通して手に入れたものです. — I got this through a friend.
【連絡をつける】その話はもう先方に通してあります. — The other party has already been informed of that.

とおり (通り)

【道路】彼の家は寂しい通りにある. — His house is on a desolate road.
そこの通りまでちょっと買い物に行ってきます. — I am going over to that street to do a little shopping.
【往来】この道は車の通りが激しい. — The traffic is very heavy on this road.
夜は人の通りが少なくなる. — At night there are fewer people (passing by).
【水・空気など】下水の通りが悪くて困っている. — We're having a lot of trouble because the sewer is clogged up.
【評判・通用】あの学者はペンネームのほうが通りがいい. — That scholar is better known by his pen name.
【同様】思ったとおり彼は来なかった. — Just as I expected, he didn't come.
言われたとおりにしなさい. — Please do just as you are told.
すべて計画どおりに進んでいます. — It is progressing exactly as planned.
部屋を元どおりに片づけなさい. — Please put the room back the way it was.
【方法】その計算には二とおりのやり方がある. — There are two ways to do that calculation.
【だいたい】所帯道具を一とおり揃えました. — I have assembled the main household furnishings.
彼は宿題を一とおり終わらせてから映画を見に出かけた. — He gave his homework a once-over, and then left for a movie.

とおる (通る)

【往来する】路地を通って表通りへ出た. — Passing through a narrow alley, I came out onto the main road.
この道は車がたくさん通る. — Many cars pass along this road.
駅まではバスが通っている. — The bus goes as far as the station.
【抜ける・経由する】この部屋は風がよく通る. — This room gets a good breeze.
彼女の声はよく通る. — Her voice carries well.
この地下鉄は池袋を通りますか. — Does this subway go to Ikebukuro?
【中へ入る】客間へ通ると彼女が先に来ていた. — Entering the guest room we found that she had already arrived.
肉に火がよく通っていないので焼き直した. — The meat wasn't done clear through, so I cooked it some more.
【認められる】彼は卒業試験に通った. — He passed the examination for graduation.

そんな言いわけは通らないぞ.	That excuse is not acceptable.
彼の腕じゃプロの宝石鑑定家として通らないよ.	His skills won't do for a professional jewelry appraiser.
【広く知られている】彼は昔から頑固者で通っている.	He has long been known for his stubbornness.
これは名の通った老舗(しにせ)のお菓子です.	This is candy from an old, well-known company [shop].
【はっきり分かる】この文章は支離滅裂でどうも意味が通らない.	These sentences are incoherent. I can't make sense of them.
彼の言っていることは筋が通っている.	What he says makes sense.
	What he is saying is very reasonable [logical].

とかす (溶・梳かす)

この子は砂糖をお湯で溶かして飲むのが好きだ.	This child likes to dissolve sugar in hot water and drink it.
氷を溶かして飲料水をつくった.	We made drinking water by melting ice.
この絵の具は水で溶かして使いなさい.	Dissolve these paints in water to use them.
髪をよくとかしなさい.	Brush [Comb] your hair well.
	Give your hair a good brushing.

とがる (尖る)

【物が】教会の屋根は尖っている.	The roof of the church comes to a point.
彼女は先が尖った靴を履いている.	She is wearing pointed shoes.
彼は鉛筆をいつもきれいに尖らせておく.	He always keeps his pencils nice and sharp.
子どもは不満そうに口を尖らせた.	The child pouted in dissatisfaction.
【気持ちが】彼はつまらないことにすぐ尖る.	He gets irritated over little things.

とき (時)

【流れる時間】この山村では時がゆっくり静かに流れていく.	Time passes so slowly and quietly in this mountain village.
時のたつのも忘れておしゃべりに興じた.	We had so much fun talking that we forgot all about the time.
彼女の心の傷は, 時がいやしてくれるのを待つしかない.	All she can do is to wait for time to heal her broken heart.
今はつらいかもしれないが, 時が解決してくれるよ.	It may be difficult now but in time it will all work out.
二人の間のいさかいも, 時が解決してくれるだろう.	Given enough time, the two of them will probably settle their differences.
【時期・時点】あの時は悪かった	I'm sorry about that.

よ.	I'm sorry about (what happened) the other day.
今が試練の時だ. 踏ん張らなくては.	This is a time of tests. We have to give it our whole effort.
彼に真実を打ち明ける時がきた.	It's time to tell him the truth.
サラリーマンを続けるか実家の仕事を継ぐか, 決断の時がきた.	The time has come to decide whether to continue as a company employee or to take over the family business.
彼女との別れの時が1週間後に近づいた.	I have to leave her in a week's time.
久しぶりの実家で楽しいひと時を過ごした.	I hadn't been home for quite a while and had a great time while I was there.
このビジネスは今が旬だから, 時を移さずに動いたほうがいい.	This is the peak time in this business so you should †act now [make the most of it].
そんなに焦らないで, 時がくるまで待ちなさい.	Don't be so impatient. Take your time.
2年前, 彼はアメリカに行った. 時を同じくして, 彼の妹はフランスへ渡った.	He went to the States two years ago. And at the same time, his younger sister went to France.
【場合・状況】「君, 飲むとどうなるの?」「その時によるけど, ちょっと愚痴っぽくなるかな」	"What are you like when you're drunk?" "It depends but I seem to complain a lot."
いい時に来たわね. ちょうどケーキが焼けたところよ.	You came just in time. I've just baked a cake.
そのことに関しては, 時を見て私から彼に話します.	I'll talk to him about it when the time is right.
彼は時を構わず社員をどなりつける.	You never know when he's going to start shouting at his employees.
時と場所をわきまえなさい.	There's a time and place for everything.
携帯電話は時と場所をわきまえて使いましょう.	Be considerate of others when you use your cell phone.
時と場合によっては妥協することも必要だ.	Sometimes [There are times when] you need [have] to compromise.
彼は時と場合に応じて口調を使い分ける.	His tone of voice changes depending on who he's talking to.
「ミスは上司に報告するべきだと思いますか」「時と場合によります」	"Do you think I should report mistakes [errors, slipups] to the boss?" "It depends."
【接続詞】彼は子どものとき引っ込み思案だった.	He was withdrawn as a child.
その女優は子どものときから目立つ子だった.	That actress stood out, even as a child.

引っ越してきたとき，初めて話しかけてくれたのは彼だった．	He was the first person to come over and talk to us when we moved here.
【時には・時として】先生は君のことを思うがゆえに，時には厳しいことも言うだろう．	Sometimes the teacher will be hard on you because he is thinking of your own good.
この漢方薬は時として劇的な効果を発揮する．	This Chinese medicine can sometimes have a dramatic effect.
【慣用】時は金なり．	Time is money.
ノーベル平和賞を受賞し，彼は一躍，時の人となった．	After receiving the Nobel Peace Prize he suddenly became a man of his times.

ときどき (時々)

彼は時々私を訪ねて来ます．	He comes to see me sometimes.
うちにも時々遊びに来てください．	Please drop by my place from time to time.
彼のことは今でも時々思い出すことがある．	Even now I still think of him occasionally.
【その時その時】私が暇なときに何をするかは，その時々の気分で違う．	How I spend my free time depends on my mood.
1ドルが何円になるかはその時々の相場で変わってくる．	The dollar-yen exchange rate fluctuates with the market conditions.
彼女には何度か会ったことがあるが，その時々で違う印象を受ける．	I've met her a number of times and each time she leaves me with a different impression.

どきどき

彼女の前に出るとどきどきする．	Whenever I'm around her, I get all nervous and excited.
1等賞を受けたとき，胸がどきどきした．	My heart started to pound with excitement when I won first prize.
	My heart †throbbed [beat rapidly] when I received first prize.
怪談を聞いている子どもたちは怖くて胸がどきどきしてきた．	The children's hearts started pounding with fear as they listened to the ghost story.

とく¹ (解く)

【ほどく】彼は靴ひもを解いて靴を脱いだ．	He untied the laces of his shoes and took them off.
母は包みを解いて買ってきた物を取り出した．	Mother opened the package and took out what she had bought.
祖母は古い着物を解いて素敵な手	Grandmother made a lovely handbag out

提げを作った.	of the old *kimono*.
【自由にする】さまざまな輸入規制が解かれてきている.	Many restrictions on imports have been lifted.
あの歌手は今度契約を解いてフリーになった.	That singer has gotten out of his contract and gone independent.
【解決する】彼がこの事件の謎を解く手がかりを持っている.	He holds the clue to solving this mystery.
彼はいとも簡単にその問題を解いて見せた.	He solved the problem very easily.
【辞めさせる】彼は部下の不始末から署長の任を解かれた.	He was relieved of his responsibilities as chief because of his subordinate's misconduct.
【解消する】彼はやっと私に対する怒りを解いてくれた.	He has finally stopped being angry with me.
彼によく事情を説明して, 誤解を解いてもらいなさい.	Please explain the situation to him carefully and clear up this misunderstanding.

とく² (得)

今株を売ったほうが得だ.	You'd be better off selling your stocks now.
貯金するなら定期にしたほうが得だ.	If you're going to save money, you'd do better to put it into a fixed deposit account.
何でも習っておいたほうが得だ.	It's to your advantage to learn †as much as [everything] you can.
今彼に手を貸しておけば, 将来得をする.	If you give him a hand now, †it will pay off later [you will benefit from it in the future].
そんなことをしても何の得にもならない.	You won't †get anything out of [gain anything from] doing that.
彼女はだれからもかわいがられる得な性分だ.	She's lucky because she's the kind of person that everyone wants to take care of.

とぐ (研ぐ)

彼はナイフを研いだ.	He sharpened the knife.
猫が爪を研いでいる.	The cat is sharpening its claws.
母は毎晩, 翌日の朝御飯のためにお米を研いでおく.	Every night mother rinses the rice for breakfast the following day.
彼女は神経を研ぎ澄まして辺りの様子をうかがった.	She sharpened her senses and looked around the area.

とくい (得意)

【よくできる】
彼は数学が得意だ。 — He's good at mathematics. / Mathematics is his forte.

得意なスポーツは何ですか。 — Which sport(s) are you best at?

【誇らしい】
少年たちにちやほやされて，彼女は得意になった。 — She was elated by all the fuss the boys made over her.

ジミーは100点を取って大得意だ。 — Jimmy's very proud of getting a 100.

彼女は得意になって身内の自慢話を始めた。 — She proudly started boasting about her family.

【好きな】
『ラブ・ミー・テンダー』は彼のお得意の歌だ。 — "Love Me Tender" is his pet song.

彼のお得意の話がまた始まった。 — He started telling his favorite story (once) again.

【顧客】
あの店はいいお得意さんをたくさんつかまえている。 — That store has won a large number of good customers.

どくだん (独断)

彼は独断で契約を破棄した。 — He broke off the contract †on his own authority [arbitrarily].

その記事は独断に満ちている。 — That article is filled with dogmatism.

彼は独断と偏見に毒されている。 — He's poisoned by dogmatism and prejudice.

とくちょう (特徴)

彼女は特徴のある笑い方をする。 — She has a distinctive smile.

この会社の特徴は徹底した能力主義です。 — This company is known for its total commitment to (the practice of) meritocracy.

際立って高い鼻が彼の顔を特徴づけている。 — His most distinctive feature is the conspicuously high bridge of his nose.

彼のしゃべり方は特徴的だ。 — He has a distinctive manner of speaking.

犯人には一つ目立つ特徴がある。左頬の長い傷あとだ。 — The criminal had one distinguishing feature: a long scar on his left cheek.

彼はこれといって特徴のない顔をしている。 — There isn't anything particularly distinctive about his face.

お捜しのお子さんに何か特徴はありますか。 — Is there anything particular about the child that would help us identify him?

とくに (特に)

今年の冬は寒いが，今日は特に寒い。 — It's been cold this winter, but today is especially cold.

彼はスポーツは万能だが，特にテニスがうまい。 — He is good at sports in general, but he is especially good at tennis.

今度の期末試験では数学が特に悪かった.	In the final exams this time, I did especially poorly in math.
契約書に目を通しましたが, 特に問題はないようです.	I looked through the contract, and it doesn't appear that there are any particular problems.

とくべつ (特別)

今日は特別暑かった.	Today was especially hot.
夏は特別健康に注意している.	I pay special attention to my health in summer.
特別いいお部屋をお取りしておきました.	I have reserved an especially good room for you.
あの人とは特別な関係はありません.	I don't have any special relationship with him.
君だけ特別扱いするわけにはいかない.	You can't be singled out for special treatment.
彼は特別だ. 何をやっても上手にできる.	He is an exceptional person. He does everything well.

どくりつ (独立)

この春, 彼は就職して親から独立した.	This spring he found employment, and moved out of his parents' to live on his own.
彼女にはまだ非常に幼いところがあるので独立してやっていくのは無理だろう.	She's still very childish in some ways so she probably couldn't live on her own.
アメリカは1776年にイギリスから独立を宣言した.	America declared independence from England in 1776.
彼は独立して商売を始めた.	He started an independent business.
彼女は独立心が強い.	She's very independent.
うちの会社は各営業所とも独立採算制だ.	Each of our company's local offices is financially independent.

とげ

バラにはとげがある.	Roses have thorns.
サボテンはとげの多い植物だ.	The cactus is a plant covered with spines.
指にとげが刺さってしまった.	I got a splinter in my finger.
彼に指のとげを抜いてもらった.	He removed the splinter from my finger.
【態度・言葉】彼女の言葉にはとげがある.	Her comments are barbed.
彼は時々変にとげとげしい言い方をする.	He has a caustic way of speaking sometimes.
今日の彼女は私に対してとげとげ	She was very curt with me today.

しかった.

とける (解・溶ける)

【ほどける】ひもの結び目がなかなか解けない.	I can't get this knot untied.
靴のひもが解けて, 危なく転びそうになった.	My shoelaces came undone and I nearly tripped.
【解決・解消する】やっと彼の怒りが解けた.	He's finally gotten over his anger.
彼の誤解が解けてほっとした.	I was relieved when his misunderstanding was cleared up.
この問題は難しくてなかなか解けない.	This problem is so difficult that I just can't solve it.
その謎は依然として解けていない.	That riddle remains unsolved.
何度か顔を合わせているうちに彼女はだんだん打ち解けてきた.	During the course of several meetings, she gradually began opening up to me.
【液体になる】春になって山の雪が解け始めた.	In spring, the snow on the mountains began to thaw.
氷が解けて水になった.	The ice melted into water.
アイスクリームが解けてしまった.	The ice cream melted.
塩は水によく溶ける.	Salt dissolves readily in water.
このせっけんは水よりもお湯によく溶ける.	This soap dissolves better in hot water than cold.
氷砂糖は溶けにくい.	Rock sugar takes a long time to dissolve.
火事で非常に高温になり, 鉄も溶けてしまった.	The temperature of the fire rose so high that even (the) iron melted.

とげる (遂げる)

【達成する】彼は事業で大成功を遂げた.	He achieved a major business success.
二人はついに思いを遂げて結ばれた.	In the end they realized their desire to get married.
【結果を得る】その戦いで彼は悲壮な最期を遂げた.	In that battle he came to his tragic final hour.
彼の英語はここ数ヵ月急速な進歩を遂げた.	He has made rapid strides in his English in the past few months.

どこ

ここはどこ?	Where am I?
えーと, どこまで話したっけ.	Ummm, where was I?
	Ummm, how far did I get?
どこまで読んだのだったかな.	Hmm, how far did I read?
	Hmm, where was I?

「宿題はどこまでやった？」「50問まで終わらせたよ」	"How far did you get with your homework?" "I did the first 50 problems."
その話のどこが面白いんですか．	What's (so) interesting about that story?
私のどこがいけないのですか．	What's wrong with me?
僕のどこが気に入らないんだ？	What have you got against me?
彼の話はどこまで本当なんだろうね．	I wonder how much of what he says is true.
この製品だったらどこへ出しても恥ずかしくない．	This product could be proudly put out anywhere.
それはどこにでもあるような話だ．	That kind of thing can happen anywhere.
どこにでもあるようなカメラです	It's just a very ordinary camera.
彼はどこを取っても立派な人〔学者〕です．	He's a fine person [scholar] in every way.
うまく化けたねえ．どこから見ても女だよ．	What a great disguise! You look just like a woman in every way.

ところが

問題は易しそうだった．ところがいざ始めてみると，なかなか厄介でてこずった．	The problem seemed easy, but once I started to work on it, I really got bogged down.
彼は絶対来ないと思っていた．ところが真っ先に現れた．	I thought that he wouldn't come, but he was the first person to arrive.

〜どころか

子どもどころか大人までもが，そのゲームにはまっている．	Some adults, not to mention children, are totally taken by that video game.
彼はあのときの失態を反省するどころか，今でも飲み歩いている．	That incident didn't teach him a thing. He still goes out drinking a lot. Far from learning his lesson from that incident, he's still going around drinking.
「1万円貸してくれない？」「1万円どころか，今日は千円も持ち合わせてないんだよ」	"Can you lend me ¥10,000?" "Sorry, I can't even scrape together ¥1,000 today, much less ¥10,000."

ところで

【それはそうとして】ところで，お父さんの具合はいかがですか．	By the way, how is your father?
ところで，そろそろ出かけましょうか．	Well then, it's about time for us to leave, isn't it?
【〜としても】君に話したところで信じてもらえないだろう．	Even if I told you about it, you probably wouldn't believe me.
母が死んだことをいくら嘆いたと	No matter how much I grieve over my

ころで，もうどうにもならない．	mother's death, there's nothing that can be done about it.

とし (年)

【歳月の年】今年も何とか無事に年を越した．	Somehow we got through the year without any trouble.
彼は毎年，ニューヨークで年を越している．	He spends every New Year's Eve in New York.
あと1分で年が明ける．	One more minute until the New Year.
年の始めには家族全員で神社にお参りにいきます．	At New Year's our whole family goes to the Shinto shrine to pray.
よいお年を（お迎えください）．	Happy New Year (everybody)![1] / Have a good New Year's.[2]
あなたとご家族にとってよい年でありますように．	Wishing you and your family all the best for the coming year.[3]
参加者数は年を追うごとに増え続けている．	Every year there are more participants.
【年齢】女性に年を聞くもんじゃない．	It's not polite to ask women how old they are.
おまえの年の頃には父さん（私）はもう自活していたよ．	At your age I was already on my own.
いとこは同い年だ．	My cousin is my age. / My cousin is the same age as me. / My cousin and I are the same age.
彼は年の割にさばけている．	He's open-minded for his age.
彼女は年の割に若い格好をしている．	She dresses younger than she is.
年を重ねるごとに面の皮が厚くなる．	The older you get the less you care about what people might think (about you).
【年配・老齢】父もずいぶん年を取った．	My father is quite old now.
お互いに年は取りたくないものだね．	Neither of us wants to get any older, do we?
もう年なんだから，あまり無理をしないようにね．	Take it easy. You're not as young as you used to be.
まだまだ若いつもりでいたが，年には勝てないね．	I've never considered myself old but lately †my age is telling on me [my age has begun to catch up with me].
いい年をして，そんな常識もないのか．	Act your age. / You should know better at your age.
クラス会で年がいもなくはしゃいでしまった．	The way we carried on at our class reunion you'd never know how old we were.

> 1)2) ともに，年末から使える挨拶．2) は「よい年始休暇を」という意味．3) the coming year (来年，新年) は，新年の早い時期（年が明けて1，2週間ほどの間）にも使える．

〜として

【資格・名目・立場】私はクラスの代表としてリレーに出場した． I ran in the school relay as the class representative.

あの子のしていることは教師として見逃せない． As a teacher, I can't ignore [overlook] what my student is doing.

彼女は日本人としてはプロポーションがいい． For a Japanese she has good proportions.

私は医者としての義務を果たしただけです． I only carried out the duties required of me as a doctor.

私が絵をかくのはあくまで趣味としてです． I draw [paint] only as a hobby.

【だれも・何も】その問題に満足に答えられる生徒は一人としていなかった． Not a single student could satisfactorily answer the question.

何一つとして最後までやり通そうとしないのが彼女の欠点だ． Her weak point is that she doesn't carry anything through to the end.

とじる¹ (閉じる)

【閉める・閉まる】幕が閉じると客席から拍手が起こった． When the curtain fell, applause came from the audience.

彼は読み終わった本を閉じた． He finished reading and shut the book.

彼女はいすにもたれて目を閉じた． She leaned back in the chair and shut [closed] her eyes.

彼の家に行ってみたが門は閉じていた． I went to his house, but the gate was shut.

【終わる】コンサート〔大会〕は盛大な拍手のうちに幕を閉じた． Amidst tremendous applause, †the curtain came down on the concert [the convention was brought to a close].

彼は店を閉じて田舎に帰った． He closed up his store and returned to the countryside.

【コンピュータ】そのファイルを閉じて別の作業にかかった． I closed the file before starting on some other work.

ファイルを保存せずに閉じようとすると警告が出る． If you try to close the file without saving, you will be reminded to save.

とじる² (綴じる)

彼女は紙をとじてノートを作った． She bound some paper together to make a notebook.

書類はばらばらにならないようにまとめてとじておいてください. / File these papers so they don't get mixed up.

とだえる (途絶える)

外国へ行った息子からの連絡が途絶えてしまった. / I stopped hearing from my son who went overseas.

森に入ると道は途絶えた. / When we entered the forest, the road came to an end.

紛争が起きて, その国からの石油の輸入は途絶えた. / When the conflict arose, oil imports from that country came to a halt.

日が暮れると人通りが途絶えた. / After dark, the streets were deserted.

とちゅう (途中)

家に帰る途中で食事を済ませた. / I had a meal on the way home.

学校から帰る途中で雨に降られた. / It started raining on my way home from school.

会社に行く途中で忘れ物に気がついた. / On my way to work I noticed I had forgotten something.

銀行なら駅へ行く途中にあります. / The bank is on the way to the station.

大阪へ行く途中, 名古屋へ寄ってきた. / On the way to Osaka, we stopped at Nagoya.

遅くなったので途中まで彼女を送った. / It was late so we saw her part of the way home.

食事の途中で遊びに行ってはいけません. / You can't leave in the middle of dinner to go off and play.

彼は会議の途中で具合が悪くなり退席した. / In the middle of the meeting he began to feel ill and left.

まだ話の途中なんだ. もうちょっと待ってくれよ. / I'm right in the middle of what I have to say, so please wait a little.

とつぜん (突然)

思いがけないことを突然聞かれたので, 何と答えていいか分からなかった. / Being asked such an unexpected question so suddenly, I didn't know how to answer.

父の死は全く突然だった. / Father's death was quite sudden.

突然, 屋根裏部屋で血も凍るような叫び声が上がった. / All of a sudden, a bloodcurdling cry was heard from the attic.

突然お邪魔してすみません. / Excuse me for barging [popping] in on you.

とっぴ (突飛)

彼は時々突飛なことをする. / He sometimes does †bizarre [unexpected and strange] things.

彼女はいつも突飛なスタイルで現れる.	She always shows up dressed in a bizarre manner.

とどく (届く)

【達する】辞書はいつも手の届くところに置いてある.	I always put [keep] my dictionary where I can reach it.
このプールは深くて背が届かない.	This pool is so deep (that) my feet don't touch bottom.
屋根まで届くはしごを持って来なさい.	Bring me a ladder high enough to reach the roof.
石を投げたが川の向こう岸まで届かなかった.	The stone I threw didn't reach the other side of the river.
薬は子どもの手の届かない所にしまっておいてください.	Please keep medicine out of the reach of children.
あの先生の声は教室の後ろまで届かない.	That teacher's voice doesn't carry to the back of the room.
父はもう60に手が届く.	My father is almost 60.
【到着する】彼から手紙が届いた.	I got a letter from him.
田舎から小包が届いた.	I received a package from home.
アメリカに行った彼から第一報が届いた.	This is the first I've heard from him since he went to the States.
【行き渡る】お宅の庭は隅々まで手入れが行き届いていますね.	You certainly are thorough in tending your garden.
彼女は細かいところまで注意が届く.	She pays close attention to even the smallest details.
生徒たちは先生の目の届かない所でたばこを吸った.	The students were smoking where the teacher couldn't find them.
【かなう】私の懸命の祈りが届いて母は危篤状態を脱した.	My fervent prayers were answered when Mother came out of critical condition.
彼にやっと私の思いが届いた.	He finally †realized [found out] how I felt about him.

とどける (届ける)

この手紙を彼女のところに届けてください.	Please deliver this letter to her (place).
ご注文の品物は明日お届けします.	The things you ordered will be delivered tomorrow.
道で財布を拾ったので交番に届けた.	I picked up a wallet on the road, and took it to a police box.
住所を変更したら必ず届けてください.	If you change your address be sure to inform us.
怪しい者を見たら至急警察に届けてください.	If you see a suspicious person, please contact the police immediately.

とどまる

【動かない】
彼はしばらくその場にとどまって考え込んでいた. — He stopped (dead) in his tracks, deep in thought.

この町が気に入ったのでしばらくとどまることにした. — I like this town, so I've decided to stay here for a while.

校長は今年も現職にとどまることになった. — The principal will remain in his present position this year.

【限られる】
彼の野心はどこまでもとどまるところを知らない. — His ambition knows no bounds.

彼の悪行はこれだけにとどまらない. — His wickedness doesn't stop here.

その学説はまだ少数意見にとどまっている. — That theory has still not been accepted by more than a few scholars.

物価はとどまるところなく上昇を続けている. — Prices continue to rise without showing any sign of leveling off.

台風による我が家の被害はかわらが数枚吹き飛んだだけにとどまった. — The damage to our house from the typhoon was limited to a few roof tiles getting blown off.

そのような傾向は日本だけにとどまらない. — Such trends are not exclusive [limited] to Japan.

となり (隣)

郵便局は中学校の隣です. — The post office is next to the junior high school.

お隣とは親しくおつきあいしている. — We're on close terms with our neighbors.

隣に座ってもいいですか. — Do you mind if I sit †beside [next to] you?

彼の左隣にいるのがお母さんです. — That's his mother on his left.

彼は私の家から2軒おいて隣に住んでいる. — He lives three doors away.

日本は隣の国と国土を接していない. — Japan doesn't share a border with any of the nearby countries.

とにかく

彼に会えるかどうか分からないがとにかく行ってみよう. — I don't know whether we'll be able to meet him or not, but let's go anyway.

ほかの科目はだめだが, とにかく数学だけは自信がある. — I may not do well in all the other subjects, but I *am* †good at [confident about] math.

彼はとにかく頭がいい. — He's just plain brilliant.

とにかくこの料理を一口食べてみてください. — At least try a bite of this.

どの〜

モーツァルトの音楽の中では，どの曲が好きですか． — Which of Mozart's works do you like?

お宅は京都市のどの辺ですか． — Where in Kyoto is your home located?

図書館で本を借りるにはどのような手続きをすればいいのですか． — What are the procedures for borrowing library books?

どの点から見ても彼には非の打ちどころがない． — He can't be criticized on any count.

どの生徒もこの問題は解けなかった． — None of the students could solve this problem.

札幌行きの飛行機はどの便も皆満席です． — All flights for Sapporo are completely booked.

どのくらい

ここから駅までどのくらい（距離が）ありますか． — How far is it to the station from here?

ここから駅までどのくらい（時間が）かかりますか． — How long does it take to get to the station from here?

このドレスをつくるのにどのくらい（お金が）かかりましたか． — How much did it cost you to make this dress?

一日にどのくらいたばこを吸いますか． — How many cigarettes do you smoke a day?

コーヒーにお砂糖はどのくらい入れましょうか． — How much sugar should I put in your coffee?

彼女はピアノはどのくらい弾けますか． — How well can she play the piano?

彼は英語をどのくらい話せますか． — How well can [does] he speak English?

とばす（飛ばす）

子どもたちは紙飛行機を飛ばして遊んだ． — The children flew paper airplanes.

風で彼女の帽子が飛ばされた． — The wind blew her hat off.

車が泥を飛ばして走っていった． — The car splashed mud as it sped along.

彼は車を飛ばして空港へ向かった． — He stepped on the gas and sped to the airport.

彼は冗談を飛ばして私たちを笑わせた． — He cracked a joke and made us all laugh.

観客はエラーをした選手に野次を飛ばした． — The spectators jeered [booed] the player who had muffed the play.

難しい問題は飛ばして先に進みなさい． — Skip the difficult problems and go ahead to the others.

彼は売り上げ不振のため地方に飛ばされた． — Because of his poor sales he was transferred to a local office.

とぶ (飛・跳ぶ)

鳥が空を飛んでいる.	The bird is soaring [flying] in the sky.
飛行機が飛んでいる.	The plane is flying in the air.
彼の打ったボールは200メートルも飛んだ.	The ball he hit sailed over 200 meters.
彼は仕事でアメリカへ飛んだ.	He flew to the United States on business.
台風で家のかわらが飛んだ.	The roof tiles were blown off in the typhoon.
この本は飛ぶように売れている.	This book is selling like hotcakes.
彼は父危篤の知らせに家へ飛んで帰った.	He rushed home when he got word that his father was in critical condition.
電話をしたら彼が飛んできた.	He rushed over as soon as I called him.
彼は軽く跳んで水たまりを越えた.	He sprang over the puddle.
彼は水たまりを跳んで避けた.	He skipped over [around] the puddles.
子どもが跳んだりはねたりしている.	The children are jumping and skipping.
彼は湖に飛び込んで泳いだ.	He jumped into the lake and swam.
転んだときに眼鏡が飛んで、レンズを割ってしまった.	When I fell, my glasses flew off and the lenses broke.
ボールがぶつかって窓ガラスが飛び散った.	The glass shattered and flew in all directions when the ball hit the window.
この本はページが飛んでいる.	There's a page missing from this book.
大地震が起こるというデマが飛んだ.	Rumors flew that a big earthquake would occur.
彼女の話はやたらにあちこちへ飛ぶから分かりにくい.	It's hard to follow her because she jumps from one topic to another.
帰省の準備をしながら彼の思いは早くも故郷に飛んでいた.	As he was preparing to return, his thoughts flew to his hometown.
ホシは香港へ飛んだらしい.	The criminal had apparently fled to Hong Kong.
この香水はにおいが飛んでしまった.	This perfume has lost its scent.
ヒューズが飛んで部屋が真っ暗になった.	A fuse blew, and the room became pitch black.

とぼける

彼はすべてを知っているのにとぼけている.	He's playing dumb even though he knows everything that's going on.
とぼけないで、ちゃんと質問に答えてください.	Don't play dumb. Please answer the question.
とぼけるな. お前のせいだぞ.	Don't play innocent. It's your fault.
あの俳優はとぼけた味がある.	That actor is humorous, unassuming and well-liked.

とぼしい (乏しい)

日本はエネルギー資源に乏しい. — Japan is poor in energy resources.

彼の話は内容が乏しくてつまらない. — His talks are boring because they lack substance.

彼は医者としての経験はまだ乏しい. — He hasn't had much experience as a doctor yet.

彼女の貯え〔持ち物, 財産〕は乏しい. — She doesn't have much in the way of savings [possessions, property].

とまどう (戸惑う)

年配の者は若者たちの行動に戸惑っている. — The older generation is bewildered [puzzled, perplexed] by the behavior of young people.

外国へ行くと習慣の違いに戸惑うことがよくある. — People are often disoriented [perplexed, confused] by the difference in customs when they go to a foreign country.

とまる¹ (止・留まる)

信号で車が止まった. — The car stopped at the light.

電車はストで止まっている. — The trains have stopped because of the strike.

この時計は止まっている. — This watch has stopped.

工事のためしばらく電気が止まった. — The electricity was cut off briefly because of the construction work.

ナイフで切った傷口の血がなかなか止まらない. — The knife cut just won't stop bleeding.

薬を飲んだら胃の痛みが止まった. — My stomachache went away after I took the medicine.

小鳥が庭の木の小枝に止まっている. — There's a bird perched on a small branch in our garden.

【固定する】この板は長いくぎでないとしっかり留まらない. — This board won't stay in place unless you use long nails.

太ってシャツのボタンが留まらなくなった. — I've put on so much weight that I can't get this shirt buttoned anymore.

とまる² (泊まる)

昨夜は彼の家に泊まった. — I stayed over at his place last night.

今夜は京都のホテルに泊まる. — I'll be staying at a hotel in Kyoto tonight.

この別荘には10人泊まれる. — This villa sleeps [accommodates] ten.

明日は泊まりがけで叔母の家へ遊びに行きます. — Tomorrow I'm going to stay over at my aunt's.

冬になるとこの辺りの旅館はどこも泊まり客が少なくなる. — The number of guests staying at the inns in this area falls off in winter.

船は三日間この港に泊まります. | The ship will be in port for three days.

とむ（富む）

彼女は富んだ家に生まれ，何不自由なく育った.	She was born into an affluent family and grew up without experiencing want.
中東諸国は石油資源に富んでいる.	Most Middle East nations are rich in oil.
彼は教師の経験に富んでいる.	He has a wealth of experience as a teacher.
日本の風景は変化に富んでいる.	The Japanese landscape is rich in variety.
彼の考え方は柔軟性に富んでいる.	He is extremely flexible and broadminded.
彼はユーモアに富んでいる.	He has a rich sense of humor.
彼は法律の知識に富んでいる.	He has a wealth of knowledge about law.

とめる¹（止・留める）

彼は車を止めて道を尋ねた.	He stopped his car to ask directions.
警官はスピード違反の車を止めた.	The policeman stopped the speeding car.
彼女はショーウインドーの前で足を止めた.	She came to a halt in front of the display window.
うるさいからラジオを止めてください.	Would you please turn your radio off? It's very irritating.
料金不払いでガスを止められてしまった.	My gas was cut off because I didn't pay my bill.
彼は注射で腰の痛みを止めた.	The shot †stopped [got rid of] the pain in his back.
「大きく息を吸って，止めてください」と，レントゲン技師は言った.	The radiologist told me to take a deep breath and hold it.
【抑止する】彼は子どもたちのけんかを止めに入った.	He intervened to stop the children's fight.
彼女は親の止めるのも聞かず，一人でアメリカへ旅立った.	Ignoring her parents' opposition, she went to the United States by herself.
彼は医者に酒とたばこを止められている.	The doctor made him give up smoking and drinking.
【固定する】私は複製名画を壁に画びょうで留めた.	I tacked a reproduction of a famous painting to the wall.
この絵は画びょうで留めてある.	This picture is stuck (to the wall) with thumbtacks.
彼女は長い髪をピンで留めている.	Her long hair is pinned with a bobby pin.
彼女は書類をクリップで留めた.	She fastened the documents together with a paper clip.
【引き止める】お忙しいところをお引き止めしてしまい，すみませんでした.	I'm sorry to have taken your time when you're so busy.
彼は昨夜泥酔して警察に留められ	He got dead drunk and had to spend last

てしまった. | night at the police station.

とめる² (泊める)

上京するのであなたの家に一晩泊めていただけますか. | I'll be going to Tokyo, and I wonder if you could put me up for one night.
アメリカ人の友人が日本にいるあいだ我が家に泊めることにした. | I'll be putting up my American friend during his stay in Japan.
あの民宿は一晩3,000円で泊めてくれる. | That guesthouse will put you up for 3,000 yen a night.
船長は嵐を避けて船を途中の港に泊めた. | To avoid the storm, the captain put the ship into (a) port part way to his destination.

とも (共)

彼は家族とともにブラジルへ渡った. | He and his family moved to Brazil.
あの夫婦は,飛行機墜落事故で運命をともにした. | Husband and wife died together in the air crash.
彼とは学生時代よく行動をともにした. | I hung around with him a lot when we were students.
彼は毎日太陽とともに起きて,仕事を始める. | He rises every day with the sun and begins work.
彼は年とともに円熟味を増してきた. | He has mellowed with age.
この馬は名実ともに日本一のサラブレッドだ. | This horse is Japan's finest thoroughbred both in name and in fact.
私の子どもは二人ともまだ小学生です. | Both of my children are still in primary school.
ズボンに共布で継ぎを当てた. | I patched the pair of pants with the same material.
この切符の有効日数は発売日とも二日です. | This ticket is good for two days from the date of purchase.

とらえる (捕らえる・捉える)

警官は殺人犯人を捕らえた. | The police arrested the murderer.
村人は三人がかりでイノシシを捕らえた. | It took three villagers to capture the wild boar.
そのうちによい機会をとらえて留学したいと思っている. | I hope I can get the chance to study abroad someday.
レーダーが台風の目をとらえた. | The radar has picked up the eye of the typhoon.
彼女はすぐ人の言葉じりをとらえて非難する. | She's quick to pounce on what people say and pick on them.

君は私の言っている意味を正しくとらえていない.	You haven't understood my meaning correctly.
警察はその事件の真相をとらえた.	The police have gotten hold of the facts of the case.

トラブル

彼は取引先とトラブルを起こしてばかりいる.	All he does is [He does nothing but] cause trouble with †our business contacts [our clients, our customers].
旅先で思わぬトラブルに巻き込まれてしまった.	I †encountered [got mixed up in] some trouble on my trip.
彼の周りでは金銭トラブルがあとを絶たない.	Wherever he goes there's always some problem with money.
まったく君はトラブルメーカーだな.	You're a trouble maker.

とりあえず

とりあえず電話で簡単に報告しました.	I phoned in a short report for the time being.
「このテーブルはどこに置きますか?」「とりあえず, そっちの壁際に寄せておいて」	"Where shall I put this table?" "Put it against that wall †for the time being [for now]."
東京に着いたらとりあえずやることをメモした.	I noted down the first things we have to do when we get to Tokyo.
とりあえず, 今晩泊まるところを探そう.	Let's find a place to stay tonight first.
とりあえず必要なものだけそろえよう.	Let's just gather up the things we need now.
詳しい事情はわからないが, とりあえず現地に向かってみよう.	I don't have any details but let's head out to the spot anyway.
知らせを聞き, 取るものもとりあえず病院に駆けつけた.	I rushed to the hospital as soon as I heard the news.
とりあえずビールで乾杯しよう.	Anyway, let's have a beer.

とりあつかう (取り扱う)

これは劇薬ですから注意して取り扱ってください.	This is a powerful drug, so please be careful with it.
このカメラは取り扱いが簡単だ.	This camera is easy to use.
お金を取り扱う仕事は気を遣う.	You tend to be especially careful when you do work that requires handling money.
あの看護師は患者の取り扱いがうまい.	That nurse is very good at handling patients.

あの先生はどんな生徒でも公平に取り扱う.	That teacher treats all students fairly.
郵便局でも電報を取り扱っています.	Post offices handle telegrams too.
うちではその商品は取り扱っていません.	We don't carry that product.
新聞によってこの事件の取り扱い方はだいぶ違います.	Various newspapers have covered this incident quite differently.

とりいれる (取り入れる)

雨が降ってきたので,洗濯物を急いで取り入れた.	I hastily took in the wash when it started raining.
修学旅行の計画には生徒の意見も取り入れられた.	The students' wishes were taken into account in planning the school excursion.
奈良時代には中国の文化が盛んに取り入れられた.	Japan absorbed much Chinese culture during the Nara period.
米は秋に取り入れる.	Rice is harvested in the fall.

とりかえる (取り替える)

あなたのお握りと私のサンドイッチを取り替えませんか.	Won't you trade your rice ball for my sandwich?
買ったCDに傷が付いていたので取り替えてもらった.	The CD I bought had a scratch, so I exchanged it.
彼女は毎日洋服を取り替える.	She changes her clothes every day.
古い蛍光灯を新しいのと取り替えた.	I replaced the old fluorescent light with a new one.

とりかかる (取りかかる)

5時までにこの仕事を終えるつもりなら,すぐに取りかかるべきだ.	If we want to finish this work by five o'clock, we had better get down to business right now.
我々は早速,仕事の話に取りかかった.	We got down to business at once.

とりくむ (取り組む)

今,難問に取り組んでいるところだ.	We're dealing with a difficult problem now.
彼女は何事にも真剣に取り組む.	She takes everything she does seriously.
国は環境問題に真剣に取り組まなければならない.	The government has to make a point of dealing with environmental problems.
これは腰をすえて取り組むべき問題だ.	This is a problem that will †take some effort to work out [take some working-

地域住民は違法駐車の一掃に一丸となって取り組んだ.	The residents were together on getting rid of illegal parking.
	The residents tackled the problem of illegal parking together.

とりけす (取り消す)

彼は服の注文を取り消した.	He canceled his order for a suit.
旅行が取りやめになったので,ホテルの予約を取り消した.	The trip fell through, so I canceled the hotel reservations.
彼女とのデートの約束を取り消した.	I called off my date with her.
今言ったことは取り消します.	I take back what I just said.

とりしまる (取り締まる)

警察は毎晩飲酒運転を厳しく取り締まっている.	The police have been cracking down on drunken drivers every night.
役人の贈収賄は厳重に取り締まらなければならない.	Strict control must be maintained over the acceptance of "gifts" by government officials.
彼は監督として,工事現場で働く人たちを取り締まっている.	He supervises the construction workers at the site.

とりひき (取り引き)

あの店とは現金で取り引きをしている.	I deal with that store on a cash basis.
会社はあの銀行と取り引きを始めた.	Our company started dealing with that bank.
彼はその商社との取り引きを中止した.	He broke off dealing with that trading company.
その法案を通すに当たって,裏で与野党間の取り引きがあったらしい.	It appears that there were some political deals made in order to pass that bill.

とりまく (取り巻く)

裁判所から出てきた被告は新聞記者たちに取り巻かれた.	Upon leaving the courthouse, the defendant was surrounded by newspaper reporters.
ファンは有名スターを取り巻いてサインをねだった.	The fans surrounded the star and clamored for autographs.
彼女は学校一の美人で,いつも男の子に取り巻かれている.	Since she is the most attractive girl in the school, she is always surrounded by boys.

あの歌手は人気が落ちて取り巻く人たちがめっきり減った.	That singer's popularity fell to the point where he didn't draw much of a crowd.

どりょく (努力)

一層努力してください.	Please try harder. Please make greater efforts.
自分の欠点を直すよう努力しなさい.	You ought to make an effort to correct your faults.
絶えざる努力で彼は富を築いた.	Through constant effort, he built up a fortune.
彼の地道な努力がついに実を結んだ.	His hard work finally †bore fruit [paid off].
せっかくの努力も水の泡となった.	All our efforts †went down the drain [were wasted].
彼はものすごい努力家だ.	He's an extremely hardworking person.

とる¹ (取・捕・撮る)

【手に取る】彼は書店で本を手に取り, ページをめくってみた.	He picked up a book in the bookstore and flipped through it.
彼女は老婦人の手を取って横断歩道を渡った.	She took the elderly lady by the hand and they crossed the street together.
書道の先生は手を取って書き方を教えてくれた.	The calligraphy instructor guided my hand through the correct stroke movements.
母は棚から鍋を取った.	Mother took the pot from the shelf.
【手渡す】ちょっとしょうゆを取ってください.	Could you please pass the soy sauce?
その大きな辞書を取ってください.	Please hand me that big dictionary.
【除く・外す】父は庭の雑草を取った.	Father weeded the garden.
彼は帽子を取って先生に挨拶した.	He took off his hat to greet his teacher.
【捕獲】ここで鳥や獣を捕ることは禁止されている.	It is prohibited to shoot game or fowl in this area.
【奪う】空巣に入られ, 金を取られた.	A prowler broke in and stole some money.
あの店は新しくできたスーパーに客を取られた.	That store has lost many (of its) customers to the new supermarket.
【購読・購入】私は新聞を2種類取っている.	I subscribe to two newspapers.
週に3回牛乳を取っている.	We get milk delivered three times a week.
酒はあの酒屋から取っている.	I have our alcoholic drinks delivered from that liquor store.
【摂取】私はいつも8時に朝食を取る.	I always have breakfast at eight o'clock.

君はもっと栄養を取らなければいけない.	You need to eat more nutritious food.
私は毎日8時間睡眠を取る.	I get eight hours of sleep every night.
どうぞお菓子をお取りください.	Please help yourself to the sweets.
【得る・手に入れる】彼は物理の試験で満点を取った.	He got a perfect score on his physics exam.
僕は運動会のパン食い競争で1等を取った.	I placed first in the bread eating contest at the sports meet.
彼は独学で弁護士の資格を取った.	He passed the bar exam by studying on his own.
運転免許を取って3年になる.	It's been three years since I got my driver's license.
息子もやっと月給を取るようになった.	My son is finally earning a salary.
今年の夏は休暇を取って山へ行くことにした.	This summer I'm taking a vacation and going to the mountains.
リンゴとミカンのどっちを取ろうかな.	Which should I take, the apple or the orange?
酒屋が注文を取りに来た.	The man from the liquor store came around to take orders.
徳川家康は関ケ原の戦いに勝って天下を取った.	After winning the battle at Sekigahara, Tokugawa Ieyasu gained [took] full control of the nation.
【料金・罰金を】彼はスピード違反で罰金を取られた.	He was fined for speeding.
最近は映画を見るのに1,800円取られる.	It costs 1,800 yen to see a movie these days.
【確保する】飛行機の切符が取れた.	I managed to get a ticket for the flight.
昨晩はあの町で宿を取った.	I took a room last night in that town.
映画館に先に行って, 席を取っておいてくれ.	Go ahead to the movie theater and save us seats.
あなたの分のケーキは取ってあります.	I've put aside some cake for you.
明日お金を持って来ますからこの本を取っておいてください.	Can you please hold this book for me? I'll come in and pay you tomorrow.
この着物は母の形見に取ってある.	I'm saving this *kimono* as a remembrance of my mother.
高速道路では車間距離を十分取って運転しなさい.	Be sure to maintain ample distance between you and the car in front of you when you're on the expressway.
博物館の見学時間は1時間取ってあります.	We've set aside an hour for touring the museum.
【占める】ベッドは場所を取るので	I don't have enough room in my room for

私の部屋には置けない.	a bed.
雑用に時間を取られて，一日じゅうまともに仕事ができなかった.	Miscellaneous chores took up all my time and I wasn't able to get any real work done all day.
【解釈する】彼女は私の忠告を悪意に取った.	She took my advice the wrong way.
【写真などを】子どもの写真を何枚も撮った.	I took lots of pictures of my child.
その曲はテープにとりました.	I recorded that song on tape.
その書類はコピーを取りますか.	Should I make copies of that document?
彼女はどの授業もノートを取っている.	She takes notes in all her classes.
【その他】新しいスーツを作るので寸法を取ってもらった.	I had my measurements taken for a new suit.
看護師は毎朝病人の脈を取る.	Every morning the nurse takes the patient's pulse.
先生は身近な例を取って，それを説明した.	The teacher illustrated his explanation with a personal example.
大臣は失言の責任を取って辞職した.	The cabinet minister resigned to atone for his slip of the tongue.
横綱は平幕との取組で思わぬ不覚を取った.	The *yokozuna* made an unexpected blunder and lost the match to the *hiramaku*.
友人が新しい取り引き先との仲介の労を取ってくれた.	My friend helped to arrange a new deal for me.
彼の意見は取るに足りない.	His opinion is not worth considering.
彼は取るに足りない人間だ.	He's a nobody.
床を取りましたからお休みください.	I've laid out the bedding, so you can go to sleep.

とる[2]（採る）

【採取する】昆虫を採って標本を作った.	I caught insects and mounted them on a board.
血液型は耳たぶから血を採って調べます.	They take a blood sample from your earlobe when testing for blood type.
警察は犯人の指紋を採って捜査の手がかりとした.	The police took the criminal's fingerprints and used them in the investigation.
【採用する】我が社では，今年は新卒を50名採ります.	This year our company will hire 50 new graduates.
今回はその方法を採ろう.	Let's †do it that way [take that method] this time.
これから決を採ります.	We'll put the matter to a vote now.

どれ

あなたの傘はどれですか.	Which umbrella is yours?
どれでもお好きなものを取ってください.	Please help yourself to whatever you like.
彼の作品はどれも好きです.	I like all of his works.

とれる (取れる)

【外れ落ちる】ワイシャツのボタンが取れた.	The button came off my shirt.
ドアの取っ手が取れてしまった.	The doorknob has come off.
本の表紙が取れてしまった.	The binding got torn off this book.
この瓶のふたは固くて取れない.	The lid of this jar is on so tight I can't get it off.
【消え去る】やっとやけどの痛みが取れた.	The burn has finally stopped hurting.
この薬を飲んだらやっと頭痛が取れた.	My headache finally went away after I took this medicine.
仕事が忙しく, 休む暇がないので疲れが取れない.	I've been too busy at work to take any time off. No wonder I can't get rid of this fatigue.
服に付いた油の染みがなかなか取れない.	The grease stains on these clothes won't come out.
【解釈できる】彼の言うことはどちらの意味にも取れる.	You can take his words either way.
【産出される】今年はミカンがたくさん取れた.	This year we had a good crop of mandarin oranges.
サケは北の海で取れます.	Salmon are caught in the northern seas.
昔は佐渡で金が取れたそうだ.	Long ago they apparently mined gold on Sado Island.
石炭からガスが取れる.	Gas can be produced from coal.

どろ (泥)

子どもが泥まみれになって遊びから帰ってきた.	The children came home from play covered with mud.
ズボンに泥が付いてしまった.	Mud got splashed on my pants.
【慣用】私の顔に泥を塗るようなことはしないでくれ.	Don't drag my name through the mud.
男はすっかり泥を吐いた.	The man owned up completely.
彼は一人で泥をかぶるはめになった.	He had to take all the blame himself.

どんかん (鈍感)

彼は人の気持ちに鈍感だ.	He's insensitive to the feelings of others.

二人の関係に気づかなかったなんて，随分鈍感だね．	It was really dense of you not to have picked up on the relationship between those two.

とんでもない

それはとんでもない考えだ．	That's an absurd idea.
彼女は時々とんでもないことを言い出す．	Sometimes she comes out with some absurd [senseless, outrageous] remarks.
とんでもない結果になってしまった．	It turned out way beyond anyone's imagination.
彼はとんでもない男だ．	He's unbelievable.
彼に金を貸すなんてとんでもない．	Lending him money is out of the question.
高校に行かないで働きたいなんてとんでもない．	You want to work instead of going to high school? That's absolutely out of the question.
彼が金持ちだなんてとんでもない．	He's the last person you could call rich.
私が社長だなんてとんでもない．ただの平社員ですよ．	Me? A company president? Don't be ridiculous. I'm just a lowly employee.
「お世話になりました」「とんでもない」	"Thank you for all your trouble." "Not at all."
「手伝おうか」「とんでもない」	"Shall I help you?" "Don't be ridiculous."
「お手伝いできなくて，どうもすみません」「とんでもない」	"I'm sorry I can't help you." "That's quite all right."
「おたくの会社，労働条件がすごくいいんですってね」「とんでもない．毎日残業ですよ」	"I hear the working conditions at your company are just great." "You must be kidding. We're always doing overtime."

どんどん

ビルの建設工事はどんどん進んでいる．	The new building is going up quickly.
バーゲンセールで，品物が良い商品はどんどん売れた．	Quality goods sold fast at the bargain sale.
会場には人がどんどん集まってきた．	More and more people gathered at the conference hall.
仕事はどんどんたまる一方だ．	Work is piling up.
会社は順調に伸び，どんどん利益を上げている．	As the company continues to grow, profits are going up.
【音】彼は太鼓をどんどんと叩いた．	He beat the drum.
だれかがドアをどんどんと叩いている．	Someone is pounding on the door.

どんな

【どのような】君の先生はどんな人	What kind of person is your teacher?

ですか.	
どんな料理が好きですか.	What kind of food do you like?
この本にはどんなことが書いてあるの?	What's this book about?
【すべて・あらゆる】どんな人でも一度や二度は失敗する.	Everyone makes a mistake or two.
彼は金のためならどんなことでもする.	He'll do anything for money.
どんなことがあってもあきらめてはいけない.	You must never give up, no matter what.
どんな犠牲を払ってもこれだけはやり遂げなければならない.	No matter what it costs me, this is one thing I want to see through to the end.
彼はどんなことでも相談に乗ってくれる.	No matter what the problem, he's always willing to listen.
どんな人でもいつかは必ず死ぬものだ.	Everyone dies someday.

どんなに

【どれほど】母が生きていたらどんなに喜んだでしょう.	How happy Mother would be if she were still alive!
英語が自由に話せたら, どんなに素晴らしいだろう.	How wonderful it would be to be able to speak English well [fluently]!
私がどんなに心配しているか, 彼は分かってくれない.	He has no idea how much I worry about him.
【いくら】彼がどんなに威張っても奥さんには頭が上がらない.	No matter how tough he may seem, he can't stand up to his wife.
どんなにお金があっても幸せになれるとは限らない.	No matter how much money you have, it doesn't guarantee happiness.
どんなに困っても, 人の助けは絶対借りないぞ.	No matter how much trouble I'm in, I never ask other people for help.

どんよく (貪欲)

彼の金に対する貪欲さは想像を絶する.	His greed for money is beyond imagination.
彼は仕事に対して貪欲だ.	He's always seeking to improve his work situation.
彼は貪欲なまでの知識欲を持っている.	He has an insatiable thirst for knowledge.

な

ない (無い)
ここには何も無い. — There's nothing here.
お金が全然無い. — I don't have any money (at all). / I have no money (at all).

彼には数学的な才能は無い. — He has no mathematical ability.
食欲が無くても何か食べたほうがいい. — You should try to eat, even if you don't have an appetite.
もうあの腕時計は無いものと思ってあきらめなさい. — You might as well †write that watch off as lost [give up on ever finding that watch].
もしあなたの協力が無かったらこの企画は成功しなかっただろう. — If it hadn't been for [Without] your cooperation, this project would never have succeeded.
祖父は眼鏡が無くても新聞が読める. — My grandfather doesn't need glasses to read a newspaper.
君の作文は良くも悪くもないよ. — Your composition may not be great but it's not bad either.

ないしょ (内緒)
この話は内緒だよ, だれにも話さないで. — This is just between you and me. Don't tell anyone else.
僕が留学することはまだ内緒にしておいてください. — Please don't tell anyone yet that I'm going to study abroad.
僕の前で内緒話はやめてくれ. — I wish you'd stop whispering in front of me like that.
私に内緒事があるなんて水くさいわ. — You don't have to keep anything from me.

ないしん (内心)
彼は平気な顔をしているけど内心怖いんだよ. — He may look calm but he's really scared deep down [inside].[1]
彼女は決して内心を見せなかった. — She never told me what she was thinking deep down [inside].[2]
She never told me her inner thoughts.

1)2) deep down inside とも言う.

なお
【いまだ】私は今もなお貧乏だ. I'm still poor. ／I'm as poor as ever.
彼は老いてなお盛んだ. He's getting old but he still gets around.
【一層】それならばなおのこと自重しなくては. In that case you'll have to watch yourself even more.
あの古い映画がカラーだったら, なお素晴らしかったのに. That old movie would have been even more spectacular if it had been in color.

なおす (直・治す)
【直す】文法の誤りを直しなさい. Please correct the grammatical errors.
カメラが壊れたので直してもらった. My camera broke, so I had it fixed [repaired].
正午の時報に合わせて時計の針を直してください. Please set the clock by the noon time announcement.
君のその悪い癖を早く直したほうがいいよ. You'd better get over that bad habit of yours fast.
【治す】その病気を治す薬は今のところ無い. At present there is no medicine to cure that disease.
私の病気を治してください. Please cure me.
Please make me well.
Help me get well, please.
【換算する】1マイルはメートル法に直すとどれだけですか. How many meters are there in a mile?
【～し直す】靴ひもを結び直した. I retied my shoelaces.
ミスがないかもう一度見直しなさい. Check it over (again) for mistakes.
彼はゆるんだネクタイを締め直して壇上に登った. He adjusted [straightened] his tie and took the platform.

なおる (直・治る)
【直る】アンテナをいじったらテレビ画面のゆがみが直った. The distorted TV picture returned to normal after I fiddled with the antenna.
この機械はもう直らないと電気屋に言われた. The electrician said this machine couldn't be repaired.
【治る】風邪がやっと治った. I finally got †over [rid of] my cold.
病気が早く治って良かったね. I'm glad you †got well [recovered] quicky.
けがの傷あとがいつの間にか治ってしまった. My scars disappeared before I knew it.
吃音(訳)が自然に治った. My stuttering went away by itself.

なか¹ (中)

その箱の中には何がありますか.	What's in that box?
家の中は外より涼しかった.	It was cooler inside the house than outside.
部屋の中に入ると異様なにおいがした.	When I †entered [stepped into] the room, I noticed a strange smell.
その湖の中には島がある.	There's an island in the middle of the lake.
三つ部屋が並んでいるうちの中の部屋を私が使っている.	Of the three rooms I'm using the one in the middle.
今月の中頃に引っ越します.	I'm going to be moving around the middle of this month.
季節の中では春がいちばん好きだ.	Spring is my favorite season.
この4冊の本の中で, どれがいちばん面白かった?	Which of these four books was the most interesting?
生徒たちの中には下宿している者もいる.	Some students live in boarding houses.

なか² (仲)

あの夫婦はおしどりのように仲が良い.	That husband and wife are like a couple of lovebirds.
学生の頃は仲の良い友人とよく旅行をしたものだ.	When I was a student I used to travel a lot with a close friend.
僕らの仲を引き裂くような, そんなひどいうそを言いふらすなよ.	Don't spread around lies like that. It's going to destroy our friendship [relationship].
あの二人は犬猿の仲だ.	Those two fight like cats and dogs.

ながい (長い)

彼女は長い髪をしている.	She has long hair.
小学生の頃は学校までの長い道のりを歩いて通ったもんだ.	When I was in elementary school, I used to walk a long distance to and from school.
戦争が終わってから長い年月がたった.	A long [Much] time has passed since the war ended.
理由を話せば長くなります.	It would take a long time to tell you why.
長い目で見れば, 今度の失敗もむだにはならないさ.	In the long run even this mistake will prove to be of some value.

ながす (流す)

蛇口をひねって水を流した.	I turned on the faucet and ran the water.
船員の遺族は海に花束を流した.	The families of the deceased sailors set adrift bouquets of flowers on the ocean.

泳いでいたら知らぬ間に沖に流されていた.	I was swimming and before I knew it the current had pulled me far from (the) shore.
かつて重罪人は佐渡ヶ島に流されていた.	In former times, †major criminals [felons] were exiled [banished] to Sado Island.
背中を流しましょうか.	Do you want your back scrubbed?
打球は強い風に流されてファウルグラウンドに落ちた.	The ball got blown off course by the strong wind and landed in foul territory.
競争相手が我が社について悪質なデマを流している.	One of our competitors is circulating vicious rumors about our company.
彼女は一時の感情に流され彼と結婚したことを後悔している.	She regrets having married him in the heat of passion.
タクシーは客を求めて街を流している.	Taxis are cruising the streets in search of passengers.
そのことはお互いに水に流そう.	Let's (just) forget about it. Let's let bygones be bygones.
友人に嫌みを言われたが聞き流した.	My friend made cutting remarks to me but I just let them go in one ear and out the other.
彼は何を言われても柳に風と受け流す.	No matter what people may say to him, he never lets it bother him.

なかなか

【かなり】なかなかいい本だ.	It's a pretty [really] good book. It's quite a good book.
君もなかなかやるじゃないか.	You're doing *so* [really] well!
彼はなかなかの学者だ.	He's quite a scholar.
【すぐには】電車はなかなか来なかった.	The train didn't come †for a long time [for quite a while].
いくら彼に手紙を書いても，なかなか返事が来ない.	No matter how many letters I write, I can't get a response [reply].
彼はなかなか仕事に取りかからなかった.	It took him forever to get down to work.
【容易には】なかなか休みが取れない.	It's pretty difficult to take time off.
数学の問題がなかなか解けない.	I just can't solve this math problem.
英単語がなかなか覚えられない.	I just can't memorize English vocabulary.
彼はなかなか勉強しようとしない.	He just won't study.

なかば (半ば)

【半分】あの建物は半ばまで出来上がっている.	That building is half [halfway] finished.

彼のホームランは半ばまぐれだ.	His home run was †half luck [a fluke].
半ば冗談で言ったことを彼はまともに受け取ったようだ.	I was half joking but he seems to have taken it seriously.
半ば無意識のうちに罪を犯してしまった.	I committed the crime without being fully aware of what I was doing.
【中央・中頃】トンネルの半ばまで行ったときに事故は起きた.	The accident occurred halfway through the tunnel.
6月半ばに渡米します.	I'm going to the States in mid-June.
【途中】反対者は会議半ばに出て行った.	The dissenters left halfway through the meeting.
兄は志半ばで死んでしまった.	My older brother died without fulfilling his life ambition.

なかま (仲間)

あの二人は飲み〔ゴルフ〕仲間だ.	Those two are drinking (golf) buddies.
仲間を集めてテニスの同好会を作った.	I got a few friends together and started a tennis club.
少しばかり変わっているからといって,彼を仲間外れにするのはよくない.	Just because he's a little different doesn't make it all right for you to exclude him from the group.
底の浅いつきあいは仲間割れを引き起こし易い.	Shallow friendships are easily broken.
いつかきっと僕も彼らのように有名な演奏家の仲間入りをするぞ.	Someday I'm going to join the ranks of famous musicians like them.

なかみ (中身)

この小包の中身は何ですか.	What's in [inside] this package?
	What are the contents of this package?
この本の題名は中身にふさわしくない.	The title of this book is not †appropriate for [suited to] its contents.
その仕事をお引き受けするかどうかは中身によって考えさせていただきます.	I'd like to decide whether or not to take on this job after I've had a chance to think about what it involves.
こんな薄っぺらな本だけど中身は豊富だ.	This may be a very slim book but it's rich in content.
この論文は短いが中身がある.	This paper is short but substantial.

ながめ (眺め)

晴れた日には東京タワーからの眺めは非常によい.	The view from Tokyo Tower is very good on a clear day.
彼の部屋からの海の眺めは素晴らしい.	The view of the sea from his room is great.
ここからの眺めは,ただ林立する	The view from here is dull. All you can see

ビルが見えるだけでつまらない.	is a forest of buildings.

ながめる (眺める)

峠から眼下に広がる景色を眺めた.	From the (mountain) pass I gazed at the vast scenery below me.
松島はここから眺めるのがいちばんよい.	The best view of Matsushima is from here.
アルバムを眺めながら亡き父をしのんだ.	Looking through the album, we reminisced about our late father.
博物館で美術品を眺めて終日過ごした.	I spent the entire day looking at works of art in a museum.

～ながら

【～つつ】僕はいつもラジオを聞きながら勉強している.	I always study listening to the radio.
新聞を読みながら食事をするのが父の癖です.	My dad has a habit of reading the paper while eating.
考えごとをしながらの運転はとても危険だ.	It's very dangerous to drive while absorbed in thought.
【～にもかかわらず】このラジオは小さいながら, よく聞こえる.	This radio may be small but the sound is excellent [good].
ぶつぶつ言いながらも, 母は小遣いをくれた.	My mother gave me spending money, all the while mumbling about this and that.
体に悪いと知りながら, なかなかたばこはやめられない.	Even though I know it's bad for my health, I just can't stop smoking.
我ながらこの絵はうまくかけたと思う.	Even if I do say so myself, I think this picture turned out well.

ながれる (流れる)

鴨川は京都の町の中を流れている.	The Kamo River runs [flows] through the city of Kyoto.
集中豪雨で橋が流れた.	The bridge was washed away by the heavy rains.
黒い雲が西から東へすごい速さで流れている.	Dark clouds are moving at a tremendous speed from west to east.
道を歩いているとバイオリンの音がどこからともなく流れてきた.	As I was walking down the street, the sound of a violin came floating through the air.
時が流れ, 時代は変わった.	Time passed and a new era began.
人間はついつい怠惰に流れてしまう.	Idleness is a common human tendency. It is easy for human beings to become idle.
今日の決勝戦は雨で流れ, 明日に	Today's final match was called off because

順延された.	of rain and postponed until tomorrow.
あの工場では車が流れ作業でどんどん生産されている.	The assembly line at that factory produces a steady output of cars.

なく¹ (泣く)

赤ん坊はおなかがすくと泣く.	Babies cry when they're hungry.
泣くのはやめなさい.	Stop crying.
子どもが歯が痛くて泣いている.	The child is crying because of a toothache.
おもちゃが欲しくて泣いているの?	Are you crying for the toy?
母は悲しい映画を見ておいおい泣き出した.	The sad movie made my mother burst into tears.
その子は母親に叱られてしくしく泣いていた.	The child was sobbing because she had been scolded by her mother.
彼女のすすり泣く声が聞こえる.	I can hear her sobbing.
子どもが注射をされてわあわあ泣いていた.	The child cried out at the top of his lungs when he was injected [vaccinated].
息子の死を知って彼女はわっと泣き出した.	She burst into tears when she learned of her son's death.
結婚式で花嫁はうれし泣きした.	The bride wept with joy at the wedding ceremony.
彼女の悲しい身の上話を聞いてついもらい泣きした.	Hearing her sad story, I found myself weeping together with her.

なく² (鳴く)

こずえでウグイスがいい声で鳴いている.	A Japanese nightingale is singing beautifully from the treetop.
屋根でハトが鳴いている.	Pigeons are cooing on the roof.
鶏が鳴いたので夜明けも近いよ.	The cock crowed. The sun will be up before long.
カラスの鳴く声がさっきからうるさい.	The crows have been making a racket (with their cawing) for a while.
子猫がミルクをねだって鳴いている.	The kitten is meowing for milk.
草むらでコオロギの鳴く声がする.	You can hear crickets chirping in that clump of grass.
たんぼでカエルが一斉に鳴き始めた.	The frogs in the rice paddy began croaking all at once.

なぐさめる (慰める)

試験に失敗した友人を慰める言葉もなかった.	My friend had failed the exam. I (just) didn't know what to say to make her feel better.

	I couldn't find the words to comfort my friend who had failed the exam.
美しい音楽は心を慰めてくれる.	Beautiful music soothes the soul [heart].
彼女は子どもたちの笑顔に慰められた.	She was consoled by* her childrens' smiling faces.

なくす¹ (無くす)

学校からの帰り道, 財布を無くした.	I lost my wallet on my way home from school.
彼は交通事故のショックで記憶を無くしてしまった.	He lost his memory from the shock of the (traffic) accident.
彼の話を聞いて, その映画を見に行く気をすっかり無くしてしまった.	After I heard what he had to say, I lost all interest in going to see that movie.
そんな非人道的な規則は無くしてしまえ.	Get rid of that inhumane regulation.

なくす² (亡くす)

昨年父をがんで亡くした.	Last year I lost my father to cancer.
飛行機事故で, 我が社にとってかけがえのない人を亡くしてしまった.	The plane crash deprived our company of an irreplaceable person.

なくなる¹ (無くなる)

彼から借りた本が無くなってしまった.	I lost the book I borrowed from him.
たばこが無くなったので, 彼はいらいらしている.	He's edgy because he ran out of cigarettes.
彼らはそろそろ水も食料も無くなる頃だ.	They're going to run out of food and water before long.
公園でゆっくりしていたら, 美術館へ行く時間が無くなってしまった.	We were relaxing in the park and ran out of time to go to the art museum.
住民運動によってこの町から公害が無くなった.	A citizens' campaign eliminated pollution from this town.

なくなる² (亡くなる)

長いこと患っていた祖母が亡くなった.	My grandmother †died [passed away] after a long illness.
彼女のお母さんが亡くなったと聞いたとき, 最初は信じられなかった.	When I first heard that her mother had †died [passed away] I couldn't believe it.

なぐる（殴る）

中学生の頃はぐれていたので時々父親に殴られた。
I was a pretty bad kid in junior high school and sometimes got hit by my father.

彼は怒って相手の男をこぶしで殴った。
He got angry and punched the other guy with his fist.

猟師はひるむことなく，襲いかかってきた熊の鼻面を棒で殴りつけた。
Without flinching, the hunter struck the attacking bear's face with a stick.

なげく（嘆く）

彼女は友人の死を嘆いた。
She grieved over* the death of her friend.

どんなに嘆いても死んだ人は生き返らない。
No amount of grieving can bring the dead back to life.

彼は仕事が忙しいと嘆いている。
He's griping [complaining] about how busy he is at work.

なげる（投げる）

石を遠くへ投げた。
I threw a rock off into the distance.

柔道の試合で彼は相手をあっという間に投げてしまった。
Before we knew it, he had thrown his opponent in the *judo* match.

人生に絶望した彼は海に身を投げた。
Having lost all hope, he threw himself into the sea.

挑戦者は途中で試合を投げてしまった。
Part way through the match, the challenger gave up on winning.

彼の病気は既に手遅れで，医者もさじを投げてしまった。
His disease is already beyond cure, and even the doctors have given up.

なごやか（和やか）

この職場の雰囲気は和やかだ。
This office has a congenial [friendly] atmosphere.

話し合いは和やかに進んだ。
The discussions proceeded amicably.

なごりおしい（名残り惜しい）

お別れするのは名残り惜しい。
It's sad [I'm sorry] to leave you.
I hate to have to leave you.
Parting is such sweet sorrow.[1]

彼は故郷を離れるのが名残り惜しかった。
It was hard for him to leave his hometown behind.

---

1) *Romeo and Juliet* に出てくるせりふで，別れるときによくふざけて言う。

なさけ（情け）

大岡忠相は公正で情け深い奉行だった. — Ooka Tadasuke was a just and compassionate magistrate.

その方は虫にも情けをかけたそうだ. — It is said that he was even compassionate towards insects.

教授たちのお情けでやっと卒業できた. — My professors were understanding enough to let me graduate.

なさけない（情けない）

寒くて腹が減っているうえへとへとで, 彼は情けない気持ちだった. — He was so cold, hungry and exhausted that he felt miserable [wretched].

私にうそをつくなんて情けない. — You should be ashamed of yourself for lying to me. / How shameful of you to lie to me!

本当のことを言いたくても言えないなんて, ああ情けない. — I feel awful not being able to tell the truth even though I want to.

なじみ

この町にはまだなじみがない. — I'm not familiar with this town yet.

彼はテレビでおなじみの司会者. — He's a familiar emcee on TV.

隣人とはなじみも薄くほとんどつきあいがない. — I hardly know my neighbors and have virtually no contact with them.

彼はだれとでもすぐなじみになる. — He makes friends with people right away.

彼はこの店のなじみ客だ. — He comes here regularly. / He's a regular here.

なじむ

彼は新しい環境になじめなかった. — He could not adapt himself to the new surroundings.

なじんだ町を離れるのは辛い. — It's hard to leave the town I'm so accustomed [used] to.

靴は履いているうちに足になじんでくる. — Shoes become more comfortable as you wear them.

なぜ

楽しい時間はなぜ早く過ぎてしまうのだろう. — Why does time always pass so quickly when you're having a good time.

彼が怒って帰ってしまったのはなぜですか. — Why did he get angry and leave?

なぜ黙っているの. 早くおっしゃい. — Why the silence? Hurry up and answer me.

「なぜ一人でインドへ行こうと思ったの」「別になぜってことは — "Why did you decide to go to India by yourself?" "No special reason."

ないよ」
彼女はなぜか彼とは気が合わない. For some reason she doesn't get along with him.

なだかい (名高い)
ここは桜の名所として名高い場所です. This place is famous for its cherry trees.

あの人はピアニストとして世界的に名高い. That person is world-famous as a pianist.

ニュートンは万有引力の発見者として歴史的に名高い物理学者である. Newton is famous in history as the physicist who discovered universal gravitation.

なつかしい (懐かしい)
懐かしいなあ, 君にまた会えるなんて. It feels just like the good old days to see you again.

外国にいると故郷が懐かしいものだ. We think longingly [wistfully] of home when we live abroad.
Everyone who lives in a foreign country †misses home [gets a little homesick].

一緒に旅行したのは懐かしい思い出だ. I feel nostalgic when I think about the trip we took together.

私は時々, 学生時代をとても懐かしく思い出す. At times I †look back on [remember] my student days with great fondness.

昨日ばったりと街で懐かしい人に出会った. Yesterday I ran into an old, familiar face on the street.

彼は懐かしそうに故郷の駅に降り立った. He seemed to be full of nostalgia as he stepped off the train in his old hometown.

なつく (懐く)
この子は私によく懐いている. This child is very attached to me.
この犬は私によく懐いている. This dog †is devoted to [just loves] me.

> be devoted to のほうが attached to より意味が強く, 何でも言うことを聞くニュアンス.

なっとく (納得)
この案には納得できない. I can't go along with this proposal.
彼女が間違っているのだと納得させるのは難しいだろう. It'll be hard to convince her that she's wrong.
もっと納得のいく説明をしてください. I'll need a more convincing explanation than that.

君の納得のいくようにしなさい. / Do as you feel best.
彼は自分の納得のいくまで何度でもやり直す. / He does things over and over again until he is completely satisfied.

なでる

母親は赤ん坊の頭を優しくなでた. / The mother gently stroked her baby's head.
犬の腹をなでてやったら, 気持ちよさそうにした. / The dog seemed to enjoy having its belly rubbed.
父は不精ひげの生えたあごをなで回した. / Father stroked his stubbly chin.

など

ライオンやトラなどがネコ科の動物です. / Animals like the lion and the tiger belong to the cat family.
百科事典や辞書, その他の参考書などは, こちらの売り場にあります. / Encyclopedias, dictionaries and other reference books are sold in this section of the store.
下宿生活を始めたので, 机やいすや食器戸棚などを買った. / I bought a desk, a chair, a kitchen cupboard and other things when I started living in a boarding house.
最近は忙しくて, 映画などを見に行く暇はない. / I've been so busy recently that I haven't been able to go to the movies or anything.
君の言うことなど, だれも信用しないよ. / Nobody believes a thing you say.
彼に比べたら, 私などまだ子どものようなものです. / I'm still just a kid compared to him.
僕は絵さえかいていれば幸せなので, 金など欲しくはありません. / As long as I'm painting, I'm so happy that I don't need any money.

ななめ (斜め)

少年は急いでいたので, 道路を斜めに横切った. / The boy was in a hurry and jaywalked across the street.
紙に斜めに線を引きなさい. / Draw diagonal lines on the paper.
不要な部分は斜めの線で消してください. / Cross out the unnecessary parts with diagonal lines.
壁の絵がちょっと斜めになっているんじゃない? / Isn't the painting on the wall a little slanted [crooked]?
あの塔は少し斜めに傾いている. / That tower is a little tilted.
コンサートで, 私は彼の斜め後ろの席に座っていた. / At the concert I sat next to the seat directly behind him.

なに (何)

そのかばんの中には何が入っているの.
What's inside that briefcase?

そこで何をしているの.
What are you doing there?

ここは何屋さんですか.
What kind of store is this?

腹痛は何科へ行けばいいのですか.
What kind of doctor should I see for a stomachache?

彼女は何不自由なく育てられた.
She grew up without wanting for anything.

あいつは何一つとしてうまくやれたためしがない.
That guy has never done anything right in his life.

おなかがすいた. 何か食べるものはありませんか.
I'm hungry. Is there anything to eat?

その箱には何か生き物が入っているらしい.
That box appears to have something alive inside it.

彼には何かにつけて世話になった.
He helped me time and again.
He was always so helpful.

私は化学については何も知りません.
I don't know †anything [a thing] about chemistry.

彼は火事で何もかも失ってしまった.
He lost everything (he had) in the fire.

私は新鮮な果物が何より好きです.
I like fresh fruit better than anything else.

健康が何より大切だ.
Health is more important than anything else.

なに? 泥棒に入られたって?
What! Your house was burglarized?

「試合に負けました」「なに, また次があるさ. 気を落とすなよ」
"I lost the match." "So what. There's always next time. Don't take it so hard."

なにげない (何気ない)

私は何気なくその本を手に取った.
I casually took the book in my hand.
I nonchalantly picked up the book.

何気なく窓の外を眺めた.
I casually gazed out the window.

何気なく言った言葉が人を傷つけることがある.
A casual remark can sometimes hurt others.

彼女の何気ない動作にも育ちの良さがうかがわれる.
Her good upbringing is evident in †her every movement [everything she does].

彼女は非常に傷ついていたはずだが, 何気ない様子でみんなと話していた.
She must have been deeply hurt but she was talking with the others as if nothing had happened.

なま (生)

大抵の野菜は生で食べられる.
Most vegetables are edible raw [uncooked].

そんな生の木を燃やすと目が痛くなるじゃないか.	When you burn fresh-cut wood like that, doesn't it hurt your eyes?
夏は生物が傷み易い.	Fresh food spoils quickly in summer.
生ゴミはこのバケツに入れなさい.	Put the garbage in this pail.
魚を切ったら包丁が生臭くなってしまった.	Cutting the fish made the knife smell fishy.
レポーターは住民の生の声を取材するためにできる限りの努力をした.	The reporter did his best to get down what the local residents really wanted to say.
事故の現場が生々しくテレビに映し出された.	Grisly details of the scene of the accident were shown on TV.
【不十分】この魚はまだ生焼けだ.	This fish is only half-cooked.
	This fish is still half-raw.
そんな生返事はよしてくれ.	I'm afraid †that's [your answer's] too vague.
	Could you be †more clear [clearer]?

なまいき (生意気)

あの娘は生意気だ.	That girl's sassy [cheeky, cocky].
	That girl's †a smart-aleck [smart-alecky].
上司に口答えするなんて生意気なやつだ.	He has a lot of nerve[1] [He's impertinent] to talk back to his boss.
近頃の子どもたちは生意気な口をきく.	Children nowadays often make impudent [smart-aleck] remarks.

> 1) have a lot of nerve は文脈によっては「勇気がある」と肯定的に使われる場合もある.

なまける (怠ける)

彼は怠け者だ.	He's lazy. ／ He is a loafer.
先週怠けたから，やらなければならないことがたくさんある.	Last week I took it easy so there are lots of things I've got to do.
仕事を怠けるな.	Don't neglect your work.
	Don't †loaf [goof off**] on the job.
学校を怠けて映画に行った.	I played hooky and went to the movies.

なまぬるい (生ぬるい)

このスープは生ぬるい.	This soup is lukewarm.
彼は生ぬるい生活に浸りきっている.	He's just drifting through life.
	He's just going from day to day.
そんな生ぬるい叱り方では，子どもは反省しないよ.	If you don't scold a child enough, he won't think about what he did wrong.

なみ（並み）

【平均・普通】

ここから島まで泳ぐなんて並みの体力では無理だ. — An average swimmer couldn't possibly make it from here to the island.

十人並みの頭があればできる仕事です. — This work can be done by anyone of average intelligence.

人並み[世間並み]の暮らしができれば十分だ. — I'm content to lead an ordinary life.

僕も人並みに結婚することになりました. — I'm getting married just like everybody else.

そう見えないかもしれないが, 彼は人並み以上の努力をしている. — He may not look like he's doing much, but he works harder than most (people).

こんな曲を作るなんて, 彼の才能は並みじゃない. — Composing a song like this shows that he has extraordinary talent.

彼は並み外れた頭脳の持ち主だ. — He is extraordinarily intelligent.

今年の夏はほぼ平年並みの暑さでしょう.（天気予報） — Temperatures this summer will not exceed seasonal averages.

「上寿司を頼みましょう」「いや, 僕は並みでいいよ」 — "Let's order the deluxe *sushi*." "I'll settle for the regular."

【～と同じくらい】

彼のカメラの腕はプロ並みだ. — He's as good as a professional photographer.

彼女はネイティブ並みの英語力がある. — Her English is as good as a native speaker. She's like a native speaker (of English).

今年の米の収穫は昨年並みと見られている. — The rice harvest this year is anticipated [expected] to be on a par with last year's.

先方の会社ではVIP並みの待遇を受けた. — We got the VIP treatment when we visited that company.

なみだ（涙）

大の男が虫歯の痛みくらいで涙を流すなよ. — A toothache shouldn't cause a grown man to cry.

母はその悲しい話を聞いて涙ぐんだ. — My mother was moved to tears by the sad story.

彼女の目に, みるみるうちに涙が浮かんできた. — Tears immediately welled up in her eyes.

彼女の目から涙があふれた. — Her eyes overflowed with tears.

あまり泣きすぎて涙もかれてしまった. — I cried so much that there were no more tears †to shed [left].

妹はハンカチで涙をぬぐった. — My little sister wiped her tears with a handkerchief.

優勝チームの選手たちはうれし涙を流した. — The (players on the) winning team shed tears of joy.

老いた父は涙もろくなった. — My father is more easily moved to tears

	now that he's older.
彼女は涙をこらえてさよならと言った.	Holding back her tears she said good-bye.
涙をのんで母の形見を手放した.	Swallowing [Choking back] my tears I parted with my mother's keepsake.
その子役の演技は観客全員の涙を誘った.	The child's performance brought tears to the eyes of everyone in the audience.
彼は涙ぐましい努力をしたにもかかわらず失敗してしまった.	He failed despite backbreaking efforts. Despite the blood, sweat and tears, his efforts ended in failure.

なめらか (滑らか)

石の表面を磨いて滑らかにした.	I polished the surface of the stone smooth.
このソースは滑らかだ.	This sauce is smooth.
事が滑らかに運んだ.	Everything went smoothly.
彼の英語は滑らかだ.	He speaks English fluently.

なめる

小さな子があめをなめている.	The young child is licking candy.
雌牛が生まれたばかりの子牛をなめてやっている.	The cow is licking her newborn calf.
海水をなめるとしょっぱい.	Sea water tastes salty.
彼は人生の辛酸をなめ続けたが,ついには目的を達した.	After repeatedly tasting life's bitterness, he finally attained his goal.
父は苦しい経験ばかりをなめてきた.	My father has seen [tasted] nothing but bad times.
彼らは冬山をなめてかかったので遭難してしまった.	They had an accident because they underestimated the danger of the mountains in winter.

なやます (悩ます)

彼女の愚痴にはいつも悩まされる.	She's always annoying[1] me with her complaints.
蚊(か)に悩まされて一晩じゅう眠れなかった.	We were †plagued with[2] [annoyed by] mosquitoes and couldn't sleep all night long.
この街道沿いの住人は騒音に悩まされている.	People living along this street suffer from[3] noise pollution.
冬になると神経痛に悩まされる.	I suffer from neuralgia in winter.

---

1)「(つまらないことで)悩ます」 2)「(ずっと)悩まされる」 3)「(苦難, 害を)被る」または「(病気で)悩まされる」

なやみ (悩み)

私の悩みを聞いてください.	Please let me tell you about my problems.
彼は何の悩みもないようだ.	He looks as if he has no problems.
それはぜいたくな悩みというものだ.	You can give me a problem like that anytime!
うちのドラ息子は悩みの種だ.	Our pleasure-loving son is a constant source of worry.
試験は学生の悩みの種だ.	Examinations are a source of pressure for students.

なやむ (悩む)

彼の会社は赤字に悩んでいる.	His company is plagued by an operating deficit.
うちの年頃の娘はにきびに悩んでいる.	Our adolescent daughter is bothered by acne.
どういう仕事に就こうかと悩んでいる.	I can't make up my mind [I'm in a quandary* over] what job I should take.
最近彼は何か悩んでいる.	Recently something's really been troubling [distressing, upsetting] him.

ならう (習う)

大人になってからピアノを習うのは大変だ.	It's difficult to learn how to play the piano after you've become an adult.
彼は世界的に有名な先生に声楽を習っている.	He's taking singing lessons from a world-famous teacher.
フランス語を習い始めた.	I've begun to †study French [take French lessons].
	I started studying French.
週1回絵を習いに行っている.	I go to painting class once a week.

ならす¹ (慣・馴らす)

新入社員は新しい職場に自分を慣らそうと苦労するものだ.	New employees have a hard time accustoming themselves to their new surroundings.
毎日英語放送を聞いて耳を慣らしなさい.	Listen to English language broadcasts every day to train your ears.
急に運動すると体のあちこちが痛むよ. 少しずつ体を慣らしなさい.	If you start exercising all at once your body will ache all over. Give your body a chance to get used to exercising gradually.
旅行に出かける前に靴を足に慣らしておきなさい.	Break in your shoes before you go on the trip.
タカ匠はタカをならして狩りをさ	A falconer tames falcons to use in hunt-

ならす² (鳴らす)

彼の家のベルを鳴らしてもだれも出て来なかった.	I rang his doorbell but there was no answer.
後ろの車がクラクションを鳴らした.	The driver behind me honked his horn.
古いSL列車が汽笛を鳴らして近づいてきた.	The old steam locomotive approached blowing its whistle.
彼も一時は速球投手として鳴らしたものだ.	At one time, he was famous for his †fast pitching [fastball].

〜ならない

【禁止】子どもはお酒を飲んではならない.	Children shouldn't[1] drink (alcoholic beverages).
そんな危ないことをしてはならない.	You mustn't[2] do such a dangerous thing.
飲酒運転をしてはならない.	You shouldn't drive under the influence of alcohol. Don't drink and drive.
【義務】どんなに遅くなっても必ず家に帰らなければならない.	I have to[3] get back home no matter how late it gets.
学校へ入ったら，学校の規則を守らなければならない.	Once you enter a school, you have to abide by its rules.
【しかたがない】寒くてならない.	I'm so cold that I can't stand it.
彼のしぐさがおかしくてならなかった.	His actions were unbearably [incredibly] funny.
彼の話に泣けてならなかった.	I couldn't help crying when I heard †his story [what he said].
病気の妹のことが心配でならない.	I'm terribly worried about my sister's illness.

---

1)2) mustn't は shouldn't より意味が強い. 3) should, have to, must の順に意味が強くなる.

ならぶ (並ぶ)

皆さん，並んでください.	Everybody, please line up.
並んで切符を買った.	We got in line and bought tickets.
新入生は2列に並んで座らされた.	The new students †were made to [had to] sit in two rows.
新郎新婦が並んで座っている.	The bride and groom are sitting side by side.
美しさではあの人には並ぶ人はい	There's no one who is as beautiful as she

彼の話術には並ぶ者がない. When it comes to having a way with words, he's second to none.

ならべる（並べる）

瓶を棚のいちばん上に並べてください. Please line up the bottles on the top shelf.

いすを横1列に並べた. I lined up the chairs (horizontally) in one row.

あの果物屋では，ミカンを店頭に並べている. That fruit store has mandarin oranges set out in front.

ボブとメリーは学校で席を並べている. Bob and Mary sit next to each other at school.

なりゆき（成り行き）

私たちは事の成り行きをじっと見守った. We kept watch over the course of events.

今しばらく事の成り行きを見守ろう. Let's wait and see.
Let's wait awhile and see how things turn out.

事の成り行き次第では弁護士に相談したほうがいいかもしれない. Perhaps we should see how things go and think about consulting a lawyer.

その場の成り行きで，やっかいな仕事を引き受けてしまった. As things turned out, I happened to take on this onerous task.*
As it happened, I got stuck with this awful job.**

二人が一緒に暮らすようになったのは自然の成り行きだった. It was just a matter of course that they should start living together.

(自然の)成り行きに任せたほうがいい. Let things †take their course [develop naturally, take care of themselves].
Let nature take its course.[1]

彼女はいつも成り行き任せだ. She always tends to let things ride.

1) 自然現象や体調・病気などについて使う言い方.

なる¹（成・為・生る）

【成立する】国会は衆議院と参議院とから成っている. The Diet †consists [is comprised] of the House of Representatives and the House of Councilors.

水は水素と酸素から成る化合物である. Water is a compound of hydrogen and oxygen.

論文は総論と本論と結論とから成る. A paper is made up of three parts: a general introduction, the main body and

	the conclusion.
【変わる】オタマジャクシがカエルになった.	The tadpole became a frog.
人間いつかは老人になる.	People eventually grow old.
彼の夢は俳優になることだ.	His dream is to become an actor.
秋は,夜になると急に寒くなります.	In the autumn it suddenly turns cold at nightfall.
彼女は新しい仕事がどうなるかとても心配していた.	She was quite worried about how her new job would work out.
【実を結ぶ】家の柿の木に初めて実がなった.	Our persimmon tree bore fruit for the first time.
今年はリンゴがたくさんなったので安くなりそうだ.	There was a good apple crop this year, so they should be cheap.

なる² (鳴る)

芝居が始まる前に開幕のベルが鳴ります.	A bell rings just before the curtain goes up at the beginning of the play.
教会の鐘が鳴ると人々は礼拝のために集まって来た.	The congregation gathered to worship when the church bells rang.
空が光ったかと思うと雷がゴロゴロと鳴った.	Just as I noticed a flash in the sky there was a loud clap of thunder.
彼のピアニストとしての名声は世界に鳴り響いています.	His fame as a pianist is resounding throughout the world.

なるべく

今日はなるべく早く帰るよ.	I'll try to get home as soon as I can today.
明日の会合には,なるべく出席してください.	Please try to make it to tomorrow's meeting if you can.
なるべく出席したいと思いますが,仕事しだいですね.	I would really like to attend but it depends on work.
なるべく古いほうから使ってください.	Please try to use up the old ones first.
なるべくなら,そんなところへは行きたくない.	I'd rather not go to a place like that if I can help it.[1]

> 1)「そうせずに済むのなら」という言い方.

なるほど

「そういうわけで彼は出席できないんです」「なるほど」	"That's why he can't attend." "Oh, I see."
彼の話は人をなるほどと思わせるものがある.	His remarks are quite convincing.
彼はなるほど頭は切れるが,ちょ	He's no doubt smart,[1] but he's also a little

っとずるいところがある.   crafty.

> 1) He *is* smart, but... のように is を強く発音し，特に「なるほど」にあたる語を入れないことも多い．

なれる (慣・馴れる)

まだ新しい仕事に慣れていない．	I'm still not used [accustomed] to the new job.
ようやくこの国の暮らしに慣れてきた．	I've †got used [become accustomed] to life in this country.
使い慣れた万年筆を無くしてしまった．	I lost the fountain pen I'd been using for years.
履き慣れた靴のほうが長く歩くときにはいいよ．	It's better to wear comfortable old shoes for long walks.
住み慣れた家を離れるのは辛いものだ．	It's hard to leave a house you've become accustomed to living in.
やっと犬が私になれてきた．	My dog has finally gotten used to me.

なん (何)

あれは何の木ですか．	What kind of tree is that?
何という町のご出身ですか．	What town do you come from?
映画は何時に始まるの？	What time does the movie start?
ピアノを始めてから何年になりますか．	How many years have you been playing the piano?
ひと冬に何度ぐらいスキーに行きますか．	How many times do you go skiing each winter?
アメリカには何度もいらっしゃったことがあるのですか．	Have you been to the States †many [a number of] times?
彼には何回か会ったことがある．	I've met him †several times [on several occasions].

なんでも (何でも)

デパートには何でもある．	Department stores have everything.
音楽なら何でも好きです．	I like all kinds of music.
言われた仕事は何でもやります．	I'll do whatever job I'm told to do.
このくらいの風邪なら何でもない．	A little cold like this is nothing.
今度の試合には何が何でも勝たなければならない．	We have to win the next match no matter what.

なんと (何と)

彼女は何と美しいんだろう．	She's so beautiful! How beautiful she is! What a beautiful girl she is!

何としてもこの仕事をやり遂げなければならない.	I have to finish this work no matter what.
何といっても母がいちばん僕のことを心配してくれる.	It's my mother, after all, who worries about me most.

なんとか (何とか)

何とかなるだろう.	It'll all work out somehow.
何とかこの仕事を終えました.	I managed to finish this work.
1ヵ月500ドルあれば何とか生活できそうだ.	I think I could get by on $500 a month.
何とかして彼女を助けてあげたい.	I want to help her one way or another.
このゴミを何とかしてください.	Please do something about this trash.
何とかいう人から電話があったよ.	There was a phone call for you from someone or other.
彼は何とかかんとか口実をつけて早く帰る.	He always comes up with some kind of excuse and leaves work early.

なんとなく (何となく)

何となくお疲れのようですね.	You look †kind of [a bit, somewhat] tired.
何となくみじめな気分だ.	I don't know why but I feel miserable.
何となく彼の家を訪ねてみるつもりになった.	I just decided to pay him a visit, for no special reason.
彼女は何となく魅力的だ.	There is something attractive about her.

に

にあう (似合う)

このネクタイの色はそのスーツに似合わない.	The color of this necktie doesn't match the suit.
あの赤いドレスはあなたによく似合いますよ.	That red dress looks good [cute] on you. That red dress is very becoming on you. You look good [cute] in that red dress.
こんなことするなんて君に似合わないね.	It's not like you to do something like that.
彼らは似合いの夫婦だ.	That couple is a perfect match.
彼はあなたにお似合いの人ね.	He's just right for you, isn't he?

におい

部屋に入るとかすかにガスのにおいがした.	There was a faint smell of gas when I entered the room.
この紙はレモンのにおいがする.	This paper smells of [like] lemon.
このチーズは嫌なにおいがする.	This cheese †smells bad [stinks].
この花のにおいをかいでごらん.	Smell this flower.
部屋の中には彼女の香水のにおいが満ちていた.	The scent [fragrance] of her perfume filled the room.
コーヒーを入れるにおいで目が覚めた.	I awoke to the aroma of coffee brewing.
彼女は全く生活のにおいを感じさせない人だ.	There's nothing domestic about her.

におう

この魚はにおう.	This fish †stinks [smells (bad)].
ライラックがにおっていた.	The lilac †were fragrant [smelled sweet].

にがい (苦い)

このお茶は濃過ぎて苦い.	This tea is so strong that it tastes bitter.
その失敗で苦い思い[経験]をした.	The failure was a bitter experience for me.
部下の失策に彼は苦い顔をした.	He frowned scornfully at his worker's failure.

にがす (逃がす)

罠に掛かっていたキツネを逃がしてやった.	I set free a fox that had been caught in a trap.
刑事さん, 僕を逃がしてくれれば, どんな情報でも教えますよ.	Let me go, officer, and I'll give you all the information you want.
うっかりしてかごの小鳥を逃がしてしまった.	I inadvertently let the bird out of its cage.
一度狙った獲物は決して逃がすな.	Once you set your sights on something, don't let it get away.
警察に通報が遅れたので, 犯人を逃がしてしまった.	They were too slow in notifying the police, and the criminal got away.
このチャンスを逃がさないように.	Try not to let this chance slip by.
逃がした魚は大きい.	The one that got away is always the biggest.

にがて (苦手)

彼は物理が苦手だ.	He's †not good at [poor at] physics.
彼女は料理が苦手だ.	She's a poor cook.
どうも子ども(を扱うの)は苦手だ.	I'm just not good with children.

彼女は何となく苦手だ.	I don't know why but I don't feel at ease with her.
うちはあのチームが苦手なんだ.	We are no match for that team. We †always lose [lose a lot] to that team.

にぎやか (賑やか)

銀座はにぎやかな街だ.	Ginza is a very busy area.
昨夜のパーティーはにぎやかだった.	Last night's party was quite a bash.
彼はにぎやかな男だ.	He's a lot of fun (to be with).
子どもが4人もいると家の中は大変にぎやかだ.	It's very lively[1] [noisy[2]] at home with four kids in the family.

1)「活気がある」 2)「騒がしい」

にぎる (握る)

電車が揺れたので, つり革をしっかり握った.	I clutched the strap when the train swayed.
老人は私の手を強く握って感謝を表した.	The old man grasped my hand tightly in thanks.
その男の子は10円玉をしっかり握って放さなかった.	The boy clutched [grasped] a ten-yen coin in his hand and wouldn't let go of it.
クーデターによって軍部が政治の実権を握った.	The military seized political power by means of a coup d'état.
私は彼が犯人だという証拠を握った.	I've got proof that he is the culprit.
その男は彼女の秘密を握って脅迫した.	He blackmailed her with the secret information he had [held] on her.
僕は妹に弱味を握られている.	My younger sister has something on me.
私の家では母が財布を握っている.	My mother holds the purse strings in our house.

にくい (憎い)

我々はあの裏切り者が憎い.	We despise [hate, detest] that traitor.
憎いやつだ.	He's a really hateful [despicable, nasty, mean] guy.

～にくい

この本は文字が小さいので読みにくい.	The print in this book is so small that it's hard to read.
こんなことは彼に言いにくい.	It's †not easy [difficult, hard] to tell him something like this.

にくむ (憎む)

彼女は彼の冷たい仕打ちを憎んだ.	She despised him for the cold way he treated her.
私にいつも辛くあたる兄を憎んでいる.	I hate my (older) brother for always being so hard on me.
私は非人間的な機械文明を憎む.	I loathe the inhumane "mechanical civilization."
父は世の不正を憎み,死んでいった.	My father died with an abhorrence of the injustices in this world.
彼は憎めない人だ.	It's impossible to hate him.

にくらしい (憎らしい)

憎らしいやつだ.	He's such a hateful guy.
彼はいつも憎らしいことを言う.	He's always saying such hateful things.

> hateful のほかに despicable, nasty, mean なども使われる.

にげる (逃げる)

泥棒は警官に追いかけられて必死に逃げた.	The thief tried desperately to get away from the policeman who was chasing him.
子どもたちはクモの子を散らすように逃げていった.	The children fled in all directions.
つないでおいた犬が逃げてしまった.	My dog was tied up but he ran away.
ヤギがさくを飛び越えて逃げてしまった.	The goat jumped over the fence and ran off.
子猫をしっかりつかまえていなさい. でないと逃げてしまうよ.	Be sure to hold onto the kitten tightly or it'll get away.
犯人はその別荘へ逃げ込んだようだ.	It appears that the criminal escaped [fled] to that summer house.
魔法瓶は熱が外に逃げないように工夫してある.	Thermos bottles are designed to prevent heat from escaping.
彼は「責任は君にある」と逃げてしまった.	He dumped it all in my lap, saying that the responsibility was completely mine.
「急にそんなことを言われてもできません」と彼はその場をうまく逃げた.	He tactfully got out of it by saying that he couldn't do something like this on such short notice.
逃げ腰では問題の解決はまず望めないよ.	You'll never solve your problems if you back away from them.
私にはもう逃げ場がない.	I have nowhere to escape [run] to.

にごる (濁る)

昨夜の雨で川の水が濁っている. — The river is muddy from last night's rain.

部屋の空気がたばこの煙で濁っている. — The air in the room is filled with cigarette smoke.

その絵は，濁った色のせいで暗い印象を与えた. — The murky colors used in that painting gave a somber impression.

～にしては

この絵は子どもにしては，とてもうまくかけている. — This picture is drawn especially well for a child.

こんな単純な間違いをするなんて彼にしては珍しい. — It's really unusual for him to make such a simple mistake.

夏にしては随分涼しい日がこのところ続いている. — We've been having quite a cool spell considering it's summer.

にじむ

インク書きのあて名が雨でにじんで読めなくなった. — Because the address was written in ink, it got smeared in the rain and was illegible.

水性のペンで書くとにじみ易い. — If you write with [in] a water-soluble pen it tends to run.

安い柄物のワンピースを洗濯したら色がにじんでしまった. — The colors in the cheap print dress ran when I washed it.

包帯を巻いたが，傷口が深く，すぐ血がにじんできた. — I dressed the wound but it was so deep that the bandage immediately got soaked with blood.

悲しみで，彼女の目には涙がにじんできた. — Her eyes blurred with tears of sadness.

一生懸命仕事に打ち込んでいる彼の額から汗がにじんでいる. — He's working so hard that he has beads of sweat on his forehead.

～にしろ

彼自身にしろ，まさか自分が1位になるとは思っていなかっただろう. — Even he himself probably never thought he would take first place.

カメラにしろ車にしろ，海外で見かける日本製品は多い. — Whether it's cars or cameras, one sees a lot of Japanese products overseas.

にせ (偽)

この骨董品は偽物だ. — This antique is a fake.

うまい手口で偽の毛皮を買わされてしまった. — I was cleverly tricked into buying a fake fur.

どうも安いと思ったら偽の宝石だ — I thought this jewelry seemed too cheap,

った. | and sure enough it turned out to be fake.
結局その男は偽の警官だった. | He turned out to be a phony cop.

にぶい (鈍い)

【刃物】この包丁は鈍くてよく切れない.	This knife is dull and doesn't cut well.
【人】彼女は動作が鈍い.	She moves sluggishly [slowly].
彼は反応が鈍い.	He's slow to respond.
	He always reacts slowly.
彼は頭が鈍い.	He's stupid.
	He's slow to †understand [catch on].
	He has a thick skull.
彼は鈍くて人の気持ちが分からない.	He's insensitive to others' feelings.
	It's hard for him to understand how others feel.
【痛み】背中に鈍い痛みを感じた.	I felt a dull pain in my back.
【光・音】塔が鈍く光っている.	The tower is faintly glimmering.
後ろのほうで鈍い音がした.	There was a dull thud somewhere in the back.

にもつ (荷物)

重い荷物を車で運んだ.	I took the heavy things [luggage] by car.
混雑した電車やバスの中での荷物は, 本当に邪魔なものだ.	Things people carry onto crowded trains and buses really get in the way.
引っ越しを控えて, 家中荷物の山だ.	The house is filled with piles of boxes in preparation for moving.
荷物は一時預かり所に預けよう.	Let's leave our things [luggage] at the checkroom.
機内持ち込みの手荷物は一個だけに制限されている.	We're allowed one carry-on each.
荷物になると思いますが, このお菓子をお子さんに持っていってください.	I hope this isn't too much to carry. This is some candy for your children.
彼はチームのお荷物になっている.	He's a burden on the team.

にゅうりょく (入力)

パスワードを入力してください.	Enter your password.
この住所録のデータをあさってまでに入力してください.	Please input the data on this address list by day after tomorrow.
僕は表計算をする場合の入力はもっぱらテンキーを使う.	I only use the numeric keypad for †inputting [punching in] spreadsheet data.

英文タイプが打てる人なら，パソコンの入力は簡単だ．	Writing on a computer is easy for anyone who can type in English.
かな入力よりローマ字入力のほうが簡単だという人が多い．	Many people say that using roman letters to write on a computer is easier than using the *kana* syllabary.
ブラインドタッチで入力できますか？	Can you touch-type?

にらむ（睨む）

【睨みつける】
| 刑事は鋭い目で容疑者を睨んだ． | The detective glared sharply at the suspect. |
| そんなに僕を睨むなよ． | Don't glare at me like that. |

【注目・監視する】
彼は経済情勢を睨みながら投資をしている．	He's making investments with a watchful eye on the economic conditions.
新聞配達員は，横目で犬を睨みながら，素早く新聞を新聞受けに入れた．	Keeping an eye on the dog, the newspaper delivery man quickly stuck the newspaper into the slot.
社長が睨みをきかせているので，社員はまじめに仕事をしている．	Everyone is working diligently because the president is keeping his eyes peeled.
毎日遅刻するので先生から睨まれている．	I'm on the teacher's blacklist because I'm late (for school) every day.

【見当をつける】
警察はその男を犯人と睨んだ．	The police suspected him of being guilty.
僕が怪しいと睨んだやつが，やっぱり犯人だった．	The guy I had suspected turned out to be guilty after all.
次はカーブだと睨んだが，ストレートが来て三振してしまった．	I was expecting a curve, but he threw me a straight ball and struck me out.

にる¹（似る）

兄は父よりも母に似ている．	My (older) brother †looks more like my mother [resembles my mother more] than my father.
トムとジムは双子なのに少しも似ていない．	Tom and Jim don't look at all alike even though they're twins.
彼女は歩き方まで母親に似ている．	She really takes after her mother, even in the way she walks.
私と弟は性格がよく似ている．	My younger brother and I have very similar personalities.
彼の考え方は僕のと似ている．	His way of thinking is very similar to mine.
彼女は母親に似て几帳面だ．	She's meticulous like her mother.
いつもの君に似ず，興奮して話していたね．	You certainly were talking excitedly. It wasn't like you.

この傘は僕のとよく似ているけれど僕のではない. / This umbrella looks just like mine but it's not.
どれもこれも似たり寄ったりだ. / They're all almost alike.
注文したものとは似ても似つかぬ品物が届いた. / What was delivered wasn't anything like what I had ordered.

にる² (煮る)

夕食に魚を煮て食べた. / I cooked some fish for dinner.
大豆を軟らかく煮ると, おいしくなる. / Soybeans taste better when they are boiled until they are soft.
彼は煮ても焼いても食えない男だ. / He's impossible to deal with. / He's a tough customer.

にんき (人気)

彼女はクラスの人気者だ. / She's one of the most popular girls in her class.
ミッキーマウスは今でも子どもたちに人気がある. / Mickey Mouse is popular with children even today.
今度出たあの作家の小説は大変な人気だ. / That writer's new novel is very popular.
日本車が海外で人気を呼んでいる. / Japanese cars enjoy popularity overseas.
あの議員は人気を取るため, 慈善事業には必ず名を連ねる. / To win popularity, that dietman always has his name associated with some form of charity work.
その歌は徐々に〔急に〕人気が出てきた. / That song gradually [suddenly] became popular.
彼の人気も衰えてきた. / His popularity is beginning to slip. / He's losing his popularity.
最近, 彼女の歌手としての人気は落ちてしまった. / Her popularity as a singer has fallen off recently.

にんしき (認識)

その代表は自分の役割の重要性を認識していた. / The delegate †was conscious of [fully realized] the importance of his own role.
彼は自分の実力に対する認識が足りない. / He doesn't realize his own limits.
災害への人々の認識が一段と高まってきた. / Public awareness of disasters has risen a great deal.
君に対する認識を新たにした. / I've come to see you in a new light.
それは君, 認識不足だよ. / You don't seem to understand.[1] / You're not well enough informed[2] (about this). / You should be better informed[3] (about

this).

1)「(内容的に) 認識が深くない」 2) 3)「知識が不足している」

ぬ

ぬう（縫う）

母は着物を縫っている.	Mother is sewing a *kimono*.
ミシンでエプロンを縫った.	I made an apron on the sewing machine.
母は私のシャツのほころびを縫ってくれた.	My mother restitched the seam of my shirt.
医者は患者の傷口を5針縫った.	The doctor sewed five stitches in the patient's wound.
祭りでにぎわう人の波を縫って歩いた.	I made my way through the crowd of revellers at the festival.
川は谷あいを縫って, 平野へと流れていく.	The river threads its way through the valley and into the plain.
彼は忙しい合間を縫ってお見舞いに来てくれた.	He took time out from his busy schedule to visit me when I was sick.
彼女は地方公演の合間を縫っては花の写真を撮っている.	In between her out-of-town concerts she takes photographs of flowers.

ぬく（抜く）

【引っ張って取る】ビールの栓を抜いた.	I took the cap off the beer bottle. I opened the beer bottle.
ワインのコルクを抜いてください.	Please †uncork [pull the cork out of] the wine bottle.
歯医者に行って虫歯を抜いてもらった.	I went to the dentist and had a decayed [bad] tooth pulled.
指に刺さったとげを抜いた.	I removed the thorn stuck in my finger.
雑草を抜いてください.	Please †pull out [remove] the weeds.
本棚から本を1冊抜いた.	I took one book off the bookshelf.
このトランプの中からどれか1枚抜いてください.	Pick a card, any card.
【除く】タイヤの空気を抜いた.	I let the air out of the tire.
講演者は, 挨拶を抜いていきなり本題に入った.	The lecturer skipped all greetings and went directly into his topic.
朝食を抜くのは体に良くない.	Skipping breakfast is unhealthy.

母は服の染みを抜くのが上手だ.	My mother is good at removing †stains from clothes [clothing stains].
【追い抜く】彼はリレーで二人抜いた.	He overtook two runners in the relay.
全力疾走したのに別の男の子が私を抜いて競走に勝った.	Although I ran as fast as I could, another boy pulled ahead of me and won the race.
【抜きん出る】彼女の美しさは群を抜いている.	She's exceptionally beautiful.
【やり抜く】彼はどんな仕事でもやり抜く男だ.	He finishes any job he starts.
彼は冬山で遭難したが,飢えと寒さに耐え抜いて,ついに救助された.	He met with disaster in the winter mountains, but he endured hunger and cold †and [until he] was finally rescued.
【徹底的に~する】社長は人手不足で弱り抜いている.	The president is really in a bind due to lack of manpower.
彼女は息子の非行に苦しみ抜いている.	She is distressed by her son's delinquent behavior.

ぬぐ (脱ぐ)

服を脱いで浴衣に着替えた.	I took off my clothes and put on my *yukata* [bathrobe].
靴下を脱いではだしで歩いた.	I took off my socks and went [walked] barefoot.
靴を脱いで部屋に入った.	I †took off [removed] my shoes and entered the room.
家の中では帽子〔コート〕を脱ぎなさい.	Take off your hat (coat) (when you're) in [inside] the house.
蛇は皮を脱ぐ.	A snake †sheds its skin [molts].

ぬけている (抜けている)

| あいつはちょっと抜けている. | He's not quite all there. He's a little silly[1] sometimes. |

1) silly の代わりに dumb, stupid, foolish などでもよい.

ぬけめない (抜け目ない)

| 彼は抜け目ない商人だ. | He's a shrewd [smart] businessman. |
| 彼は何をするにも抜け目ない. | He never misses a trick. |

ぬける (抜ける)

| 【取れる】ワインのコルクがきつくて,なかなか抜けなかった. | The cork in the wine bottle was so tight that it really took me a long time to get |

	it out.
祖父がリンゴにかぶりついたら, 歯が1本抜けてしまった.	My grandfather bit into an apple and one of his teeth came out.
髪の毛が抜けて困ると母がこぼしている.	My mother is complaining that her hair is falling out.
バケツの底が抜けてしまった.	The bottom fell out of the bucket.
人形を持ち上げたら, 首が抜けてしまった.	I picked up my doll and the head fell [came] off.
ズボンのひざが抜けてしまった.	My trousers [pants, slacks] are worn out at the knees.
【欠ける】この本は8ページも抜けている.	Eight pages are missing from this book.
僕の名前が名簿から抜けている.	My name is missing from the list.
【退く】エースがけがで抜けたので, チームは負けてしまった.	Their ace couldn't play because of an injury and the team lost.
意見が合わず, 彼は仲間から抜けた.	Due to a difference of opinion, he withdrew from the group.
【無くなる】風船の空気が抜けてしぼんでしまった.	The balloon shriveled up when the air came out of it.
油の染みは洗ってもなかなか抜けない.	Oil stains don't come out easily even if washed.
香水瓶のふたを閉め忘れたので, 香りが抜けてしまった.	I forgot to put the lid back on the perfume bottle so the perfume lost its fragrance.
喫煙癖は, なかなか抜けないものだ.	Smoking isn't an easy habit to get rid of.
田舎なまりがなかなか抜けない.	It's not easy to get rid of a rural [provincial] accent.
ようやく風邪が抜けて元気になった.	I finally got over my cold and feel better.
昨夜の酒がやっと抜けた.	I finally got over the effects of what I drank last night.
がっくりして〔安心して〕体中の力が抜けてしまった.	I was so disappointed [relieved] that I felt completely worn out.
【通り抜ける】町を抜けて野原へ出た.	We passed through the town and came to open fields.
この道は裏へ抜けられる.	This street leads through to the back.
このトンネルを抜けると隣の県です.	You'll be in the neighboring prefecture after you go through this tunnel.
涼しい風が部屋を抜けていった.	A cool breeze blew through the room.
【抜け出す】彼は, 学校を抜けて映画を見に行った.	He sneaked out of school and went to see a movie.
気分が悪くなったので, 演奏会を	I didn't feel well so I left in the middle of

途中で抜けて帰宅した.	the concert and went home.
電話が入ったので会議を途中で抜けて出た.	I left in the middle of the conference to take a phone call.

ぬすむ (盗む)

人のものを盗んではいけない.	It's wrong to steal (from others).
空巣に入られて, お金を盗まれてしまった.	A burglar broke into my house and stole some money (while I was out).
昨夜だれかに自転車を盗まれた.	I had my bicycle stolen last night.
この論文は他人の説を盗んで書いたものだ.	This paper was written with ideas stolen from other people.
あの二人は, 仕事の暇を盗んでいつもむだ話をしている.	Whenever those two can grab a free moment at work, they waste time chatting.
同僚の目を盗んでは, 二人はデートをし続けた.	The two continued to date without letting on to their co-workers.
彼らは人目を盗んで行動した.	They kept their activities secret.
	They acted †in secrecy [by stealth].

ぬらす (濡らす)

赤ん坊がおしめを濡らした.	The baby's diaper is wet.
水たまりで靴を濡らさないように気をつけなさい.	Be careful not to get your shoes wet in the puddles.
シールを水に濡らして封筒に貼り付けた.	I moistened the seal with water and put it on the envelope.

ぬる (塗る)

彼はその絵の屋根の色を赤に塗った.	He painted [colored][1] the roof in the picture red.
今日, 壁にペンキを塗った.	We painted the walls today.
木で箱を作って, 仕上げにニスを塗った.	I made a box out of wood and varnished it as a finishing touch.
彼女は口紅を薄く塗った.	She lightly put on some lipstick.
	She applied a touch of lipstick.
彼女は真っ赤な口紅を塗っていた.	She †was wearing [had on] some bright-red lipstick.
トーストにバターを塗った.	I spread butter on the toast.
	I buttered a piece of toast.
看護婦が傷口に薬を塗ってくれた.	The nurse put [applied] medicine [ointment] on my wound.

---

1) 水彩・油絵の具の場合は paint, クレヨンや色鉛筆の場合は color を使う.

ぬるい

ぬるいお茶は嫌いです. — I don't like lukewarm tea.
この服はぬるま湯で洗いなさい. — Wash these clothes in lukewarm water.
こんなぬるま湯につかったような生活には我慢できない. — I can't stand this dull [boring, monotonous] life.

ぬれる (濡れる)

夕立にあい, びっしょり濡れてしまった. — I got soaked in a sudden shower.
彼女の頬は涙で濡れていた. — Her cheeks were wet with tears.
汗で濡れた服を着替えた. — I changed out of my sweaty clothes.
若葉が露に濡れて朝日に輝いている. — The new leaves are wet with dew and shining in the morning sun.
【慣用】彼は濡れ手に粟で大儲けしている. — He's making easy money.

ね

ね (根)

この雑草の根は深くて, どんなに引っ張っても抜けない. — This weed has deep roots and won't come out no matter how hard I pull.
大根, ニンジンは根を食用にする. — Carrot and Japanese radish roots are †used for food [edible].
植え替えたバラの根が付いた. — The rosebush I transplanted has taken root.
【慣用】その岩は根が生えたように動かなかった. — It was as if the rock was rooted to the ground and wouldn't budge.
そういう悪党どもは根絶やしにしなくてはだめだ. — Criminal types like that must be †eliminated [rooted out].
民主主義は我が国に完全に根付いているとは言えない. — It cannot be said that democracy has completely taken root in our country.
彼女はいつまでも根に持つたちなので人に嫌われる. — Nobody likes her because she holds grudges forever.
私がその金を受け取ったというのは全く根も葉もない話だ. — The story that I accepted that money is totally unfounded.
【心根】彼女は無愛想だが根は優しい. — She may be a little brusque [unfriendly] but deep down she's very nice.
あいつは根が卑しくて, すぐ人に — He's so unscrupulous that he always bums

たかる.
彼は根っからの悪党だ.

things off people.
He's rotten to the core.

ねうち (値打ち)

インフレになると金(ﾈﾝ)の値打ちが見直される.
When inflation runs high, people reconsider the value of gold.

この骨董品の真の値打ちが分かる人は, そうざらにはいない.
There are not many (people) who recognize the true value of this antique.

この絵は1億円を出しても買う値打ちがある.
This painting is worth buying, even if it costs one hundred million yen.

人間の値打ちは, その人の行為によって決まる.
The worth of a man [A man's worth] is determined by his actions.

「この絵の値打ちはどのくらいでしょうか」「ちょっとお金には換算できませんね」
"How much is this painting worth?" "I'm afraid it's priceless."

ねがい (願い)

【望み】君の願いをかなえてあげよう.
I'll make your wish come true.

平和は世界の願いです.
Peace is the hope [wish, desire] of the world.

私の願いは受け入れられなかった.
My request [wish] was not accepted.

【頼み】お願いがあるのですが.
Would you do me a favor?

お願いだから私の言うとおりにしてください.
Please (just do me a favor and) do it the way I tell you to.

私から社長にお願いしてみよう.
I'll try and ask the boss for you.

ねがう (願う)

娘の幸福を願っている.
I hope my daughter will be happy.

息子の成功を願っている.
I pray for my son's success.

彼女は生まれた土地をもう一度見たいと願っている.
She wishes to see her birthplace once again.

それは願ってもないことだ.
One could ask for nothing better [more].

それは願ったりかなったりの話だ.
That's just what I was hoping for.
That sounds like a wish come true.

ねじる

私は泥棒を捕まえて, 腕をねじって押さえ込んだ.
I caught the burglar by twisting his arm and holding him down.

ドライバーでしっかりねじって留めなさい.
Screw it tight with a screwdriver.

引っ張ってもだめ. そのふたはねじれば取れるよ.
Don't pull it. That cap unscrews.

ねたむ

彼は同僚の昇進をねたんだ.	He was jealous of his colleague's promotion.
彼女は妹の才能をねたんだ.	She was jealous of her sister's talent.

ねつ (熱)

【物の】金属は熱をよく伝える.	Metal is a good conductor of heat.
この魚は生きが良くないから熱を加えて食べなさい.	This fish is not very fresh, so be sure to cook it before you eat it.
【人の】風邪をひいて熱が出た.	I caught a cold and developed a fever.
彼は熱を出して寝ている.	He's in bed with fever.
熱が39度5分もある.	I have a fever of 39.5°C.[1]
やっと熱が下がった.	My fever has finally gone down.
	I finally got over my fever.
熱をはかってごらん.	Take your temperature.
今日は何だか熱っぽい.	I feel feverish today.
【愛情・情熱】彼女は若いハンサムな先生に熱を上げている.	She's crazy about the handsome young teacher.
彼女に対する熱は冷めたのかい.	Has your passion for her cooled (off)?
彼は熱を込めて新製品の説明をした.	He explained enthusiastically how the new product worked.
親父の野球熱には困ったものだ.	My father's passion for baseball is †a real problem [really out of hand].

1) thirty-nine point five degrees centigrade と読む.

ねつい (熱意)

君の熱意には打たれた.	I was impressed with your enthusiasm [eagerness].
彼は仕事に熱意が見られない.	He doesn't appear to have any enthusiasm for his work.

ねっきょう (熱狂)

10代の女の子たちはそのロック歌手に熱狂した.	The teenage girls went crazy [wild] over the rock singer.
彼には熱狂的なファンが多い.	He has a lot of †madly devoted [wildly enthusiastic] fans.
一行(こう)は熱狂的な歓迎を受けた.	The party received a hearty welcome.

ねっしん (熱心)

君の熱心さには負けたよ.	Your enthusiasm [ardor] has convinced me.

私たちの先生は熱心に教えてくれる.	Our teacher teaches us with enthusiasm.
彼は熱心な先生だ.	He's a diligent [dedicated] teacher.
彼は熱心な生徒だ.	He's a hard-working [diligent] student.
あの国の国民のほとんどは熱心な仏教徒だ.	Most people of that country are devout [ardent, earnest] Buddhists.
彼は仕事熱心だ.	He's very dedicated to his work.
	He's work-oriented [work-minded].
子どもたちはおばあさんの話に熱心に聞き入った.	The children listened attentively as their grandmother told them a story.

ねっちゅう (熱中)

仕事に熱中していて約束を忘れた.	I was so absorbed in my work that I forgot the appointment.
彼は新しい研究に熱中している.	He has devoted himself to his new research.
少年はスポーツに熱中することが多い.	Boys often really get into sports.
	Boys are often crazy [wild] about sports.

ネット

【球技の】
ネットを張るのは1年生の仕事だ.	It's the freshmen's job to put up the net.
そのテニス選手はネットプレーが得意だ.	That tennis player's strong point is playing close to the net.
ネットインしたボールにラケットが届かなかった.	I couldn't get the ball that hit the net and fell in.

【放送網】
| この番組は全国ネットでお送りします. | We will show this program on all our local networks. |
| このニュースはCBCネット全局に配信された. | This news was distributed to all the stations on the CBC network. |

【コンピュータ】
友人はネット上で知り合った人と結婚した.	My friend married someone she met through the Internet.
古いバイクをネットオークションに出したら3万円で売れた.	My old motorbike sold for ¥30,000 on Net auction.
ネットサーフィンをしていると, つい時間を忘れてしまう.	I forget all about time when I'm surfing the Net.
ネットショッピングで散財してしまった.	I squandered my money shopping on the Net.

【正味】
ネットでいくら儲かった?	How much net profit did you make?
ネット1キロで3千円にしておくよ, どう?	We'll make it ¥3,000 per kilo net weight. How about it?
	How about ¥3,000 per kilo net weight?

ねつれつ (熱烈)

二人は熱烈な恋をして結婚した.	They fell passionately in love and got married.
彼らは熱烈な歓迎を受けた.	They received an enthusiastic welcome.
彼は熱烈な巨人ファンだ.	He's a devoted Giants fan.

ねばり (粘り)

その液体はねばりけがある.	That liquid is sticky [viscous].
彼はねばり強い男だ.	He has perseverance.*[1] He's persistent[2] [tenacious*]. He's a stubborn[3] guy.
彼はねばり強さで成功した.	He succeeded through [by] perseverance. Perseverance led to his success.
彼のねばりにとうとう負けた.	His persistence finally made us give in. We finally gave in to his persistence.

> 1) perseverance は一般に「ねばり強さ」を表し, 2) persistent, persistence は「(時には人の反対を押し切っても, または人に迷惑をかけても意志, 行為を貫く) ねばり強さ」を表す. 3) stubborn はこのように良い意味でも使う.

ねばる (粘る)

ゴムが溶けてねばりだした.	The rubber melted and became sticky.
最後までねばれ.	Stick to it to the end.
ねばってその許可を手に入れた.	We won permission through persistence.
1杯のコーヒーで長いこと喫茶店でねばった.	I sat over a single cup of coffee for a long time at the coffee shop.

ねむい (眠い)

いつも寝不足で眠い.	I never get enough rest, so I'm always sleepy.
昼食をたっぷりとったあとはよく眠くなる.	After a big lunch we often become drowsy [sleepy].

ねむる (眠る)

弟は毎日10時間眠る.	My (younger) brother sleeps ten hours every day.
最近, いろいろ心配事があってよく眠れない.	Recently I've been worried about things and can't sleep well.
ぐっすり眠っているあいだに泥棒に入られた.	A burglar broke in while I was sleeping soundly.
子どもを今眠らせたところだから, 静かにして.	I just put the baby to sleep, so be quiet.

私は眠った振りをして聞き耳を立てた.	I pretended to be asleep and pricked up my ears to listen.
昼間の疲れが出て,つい眠り込んでしまった.	The day's exhaustion got to me and I fell asleep in spite of myself.
昼食後10分ほど眠った.	I took a ten-minute nap after lunch.
私の両親は故郷の小さな墓地に眠っています.	My parents are †buried [laid to rest] in a small cemetery in the town where they were born.

ねらう (狙う)

彼は獲物を狙ってライフルを構えた.	He readied his rifle and took aim at his prey.
ミサイルが敵の軍艦を狙って発射された.	A missile was fired at the enemy warship.
ヘビがカエルを狙って近づいていった.	Preying on the frog, the snake drew closer.
彼は教授の席を狙っている.	He's after the professorship.
この企画は,何を狙ったものかよく分からない.	I don't know what you are aiming for [at] with this project.
柔道の試合で,相手の隙を狙って技を掛けた.	During the *judo* match, I waited for an opening, then attacked.
私はこの嫌な仕事から手を引く機会を狙っている.	I'm just waiting for the chance to get out of this disagreeable job.

ねる (寝る)

【床に就く】私はいつも遅く寝る.	I always †go to bed [turn in] late.
子どもは早く寝て早く起きなさい.	Children should go to bed early and get up early.
彼は風邪で寝ています.	He's in bed with a cold.
熱が下がるまで寝ていなさい.	Stay in bed till your fever goes down.
隣のおじいさんは寝たきりです.	The old man next door is bedridden.
【眠る】少なくとも8時間は寝ることにしている.	I make it a rule to get at least eight hours of sleep.
ゆうべは遅くまで寝られなかった.	I wasn't able to get to sleep till late last night.
昨夜は一晩じゅう寝ずに勉強した.	Last night I †studied all night without sleeping [stayed up all night studying].
彼は寝る間も惜しんで勉強した.	He was studying so hard he didn't want to waste (any) time sleeping.
	He studied, begrudging even the time he spent sleeping.
一晩寝れば嫌なことも忘れるものだよ.	A good night's sleep makes you forget unpleasant things.

寝ても覚めても，彼女のことが頭から離れない．	Awake or asleep, I can't get her out of my mind.
【横たわる】ソファに寝ながら本を読むのが好きだ．	I like to read lying down on the couch.
浜辺に寝て体を焼いた．	I tanned myself lying on the beach.
【資本や商品が】倉庫にいつまでも商品を寝せておくわけにはいかない．	We can't just let the goods sit in the warehouse forever.
そんな大金を銀行に寝かしておくのはもったいない．	It's a waste to let that much money just sit in the bank.
【慣用】そんな寝た子を起こすようなことは言わないでくれ．	Why did you have to go and bring that up again?

ねん (念)

念のために，ガスの元栓が締まっているかもう一度見た．	Just to be safe, I checked again to see if the gas was shut [turned] off.
	Just to be sure, I checked the gas again.
念のために，君の携帯の番号を教えといて．	Give me your cell phone number, just in case.
念のために言っておくが，ここは禁煙だからね．	Just a reminder. This is a no-smoking area.
彼に念を押しといたほうがいいよ．	You'd better remind him (again).
私はその件に関して彼にもう一度，念を押した．	I went over the matter with him one more time to be sure he understood.
「絶対にだれにも言わないでよ」と彼女は何度も念を押した．	She repeatedly asked me never to tell anyone.
客間は特に念を入れて掃除した．	I did an especially good job of cleaning the living room.
抜けがないか，念には念を入れてチェックした．	I checked to make absolutely sure there was nothing missing.
情報が漏れることのないよう，念には念を入れてデータ管理する必要がある．	You can't be too careful about managing data if you want to prevent leaks.

ねんいり (念入り)

新聞を念入りに読んだ．	I read the newspaper with great care.
彼女は念入りに化粧して出かけた．	She very carefully put on her makeup and went out.
この洋服だんすは念入りに作られている．	This wardrobe is made with meticulous care.
今度の会議は非常に重要なので，念入りな準備がなされた．	Painstaking preparations were made in anticipation of the crucial conference.

の

のうりつ（能率）

多人数でやるからといって，仕事の能率が上がるとは限らない． — Efficiency won't necessarily improve just because a lot of people are going to work on it.

長時間同じことをやっていると，能率が下がってくるものだ． — Doing the same thing over a long period of time decreases efficiency.

彼は実に能率良く仕事を片づける． — He certainly does an efficient job.

もっと能率的なやり方はないかなあ． — Isn't there a more efficient way of doing this?

だらだらと勉強していないで，能率的なやり方を工夫しなさい． — Don't study in such a sloppy way. Think of a more efficient way to get it done.

のうりょく（能力）

彼は計算能力が優れている． — He's very capable with figures.

だれもが自分の能力を生かせる職業に就けるとは限らない． — Not everyone can expect to find a job that makes the best of his ability.

君は僕の能力以上のことを要求している． — You're asking for something beyond my ability.

能力はあっても意欲のない者は成功しない． — Even people with ability won't succeed unless they have †the will to [ambition].

のこす（残す）

食欲がないので彼は食事を残した． — He †left some [didn't eat all] of his food because he had no appetite.

彼はやりかけの仕事を残して帰ってしまった． — He left his work unfinished and went home.

祖父は大変な財産を残した． — My grandfather left a large fortune [estate].

犯人は現場に証拠を残した． — The criminal left evidence at the scene of the crime.

その画家は後世に名を残した． — That painter left his name to posterity.

その出来事は彼女の心に深い傷を残した． — That event left her deeply wounded emotionally.

1,000円だけ残して貯金を下ろした． — I withdrew all but ¥1,000 of my savings.

彼女は幼子を残して死んでしまった.	She died, leaving behind a small child.
彼は国に妻子を残して働きに来ている.	He has come here to work, leaving his wife and children behind in his hometown.
客を残したまま，バスは出発してしまった.	The bus left, leaving some passengers behind.
彼は罰として放課後学校に残された.	As punishment, he was made to stay after school.

のこり (残り)

残り物を冷蔵庫にしまった.	I put the leftovers in the refrigerator.
小遣いの残りがまだ少しある.〔小遣いが残り少ない〕	I still have a little [I don't have much] spending money left (over).
あなたの仕事の残りは私がやりましょう.	I'll do what's left of your work.
貯金がどんどん残り少なくなっていく.	My savings are dwindling rapidly.
残りの宿題はいつやるんだ？	When are you going to do the †rest of the homework [homework that's left]?
残りの人たちはどこへ行ったの？	Where did the rest of the people go?

のこる (残る)

コップに水が残っている.	There's some water left in the glass.
残ったものは捨てましょうか.	Shall we throw away †the rest [what's left]?
夏休みは明日で終わりなのにまだ宿題が残っている.	Summer vacation's over tomorrow but I've still got homework left to do.
子どものときの傷あとが今でも顔に残っている.	I still have a scar (left) on my face from when I was little.
いつまでたっても祖母のことは記憶に残っている.	My grandmother has always remained in my memory.
先生のその言葉はいつまでも私の心の中に残っている.	Those words of my teacher have always remained near [close] to my heart.
その国には，厳しい身分制度がまだ残っている.	A strict caste system still exists in that country.
彼は卒業後も大学に残って研究を続けている.	He †remained [stayed on] at the university after graduation and is continuing his research.
みんなお祭りに出掛けて私一人残っています.	Everyone went to the festival, but I'm staying behind by myself.
この地方には悲しい伝説が残っている.	A sad legend still haunts this region.

のせる (乗・載せる)

【物の上に】お盆の上にコップを載せた. — I put the glasses on the tray.

不要なものは棚の上に載せなさい. — Put the things you don't need on the shelf.

【乗り物に】自転車の後ろに子どもを乗せた. — I put my child on the back of the bicycle.

タクシーは客を乗せて走り去った. — The taxi †took on [picked up] a passenger and drove off.

駅まで乗せてください. — Please give me a ride [lift] to the station.

彼女の家に寄って彼女を乗せてから君の家へ行くよ. — I'll come over after I stop and pick her up at her house.

動物を電車に乗せることはできますか. — Can you take animals on the train?

スーツケースはこのカートに載せて運ぼう. — Let's put the suitcases on this cart.

【話・おだてに】君はあの男の口車にうまく乗せられたんだよ. — You were cleverly taken in by that guy's fast-talk.

僕は彼のおだてに乗せられてしまった. — I was taken in by his flattery.

そんなにいい話なら私も一口乗せてください. — If it's that good a deal let me in on a piece of the action.

のぞく¹ (除く)

校庭に生えた雑草を皆で除いた. — We all †removed [pulled out] the weeds growing in the schoolyard.

彼の名前を名簿から除いた. — We removed his name from the †roster [name list].

この美人コンテストでは, 既婚者は除かれます. — Married women are †excluded from [ineligible for] this beauty contest.

彼の家族は彼を除いて皆左利きだ. — Except for him, everyone in his family is left-handed.

のぞく² (覗く)

かぎ穴〔ドアの隙間〕から部屋の中を覗いた. — I peeked [peeped, looked] into the room through the †keyhole [crack in the door].

変な男が窓から家の中を覗いている. — A strange man is peeking into the house through the window.

私の留守に部屋を覗かないでください. — Don't poke around my room while I'm out.

がけの上から谷底を覗き込んだ. — I peered at the bottom of the deep valley from the edge of the cliff.

彼の行きつけの店を覗いてみたが — I glanced into the place he always goes,

いなかった.	but he wasn't there.
彼は三日に一度は古本屋を覗く.	He visits a used book shop once every three days.
彼の胸のポケットから白いハンカチが覗いていた.	I could see a white handkerchief sticking out of his pocket.
向かいの家の窓に男の横顔が覗いている.	I can see the profile of a man's face in the window of the house across from us.
地質学を勉強したといっても，ちょっと覗いてみただけです.	I did study geology, but only a little.

のぞましい (望ましい)

望ましい親子関係とはどういうものでしょうか.	What is a good [desirable] relationship between parents and children?
子どもにそういう本を見せるのは望ましくない.	It's not good to let children see books of that sort.
あまり望ましくない検査結果が出た.	The results of the test weren't very good.

のぞみ (望み)

私の望みは1等賞を取ることだ.	My hope [goal] is to win first prize.
彼女は生きる望みを失った.	She lost †all desire [the will] to live.
彼の回復の望みはほとんどない.	There's almost no hope [chance] for his recovery.
これで我々の優勝の望みは断たれた.	This has killed whatever hope we had for victory.
彼の事業に成功の望みはありますか.	Is there any †prospect of [chance of, hope for] his business succeeding?
最後の一戦に望みをかけている.	We're placing [putting] our hopes on the last match.
彼女はそのことに一縷(いちる)の望みを託している.	She's pinned her last bit of hope on it.
彼女は落としたお金が戻ってくることにわずかな望みをつないでいる.	She's †still hoping [hoping against hope] that she may get back the money she lost.
望みの物は何でもあげよう.	I'll give you anything your heart desires.[1]

1) 本来大げさな言い方だが，少しふざけて日常よく使われる.

のぞむ (望む)

近頃は，会社で出世することを望まない若者も多いそうだ.	Recently it seems that there are quite a few young people who have no desire to attain positions of corporate responsibility.

子どもにそんなに多くのことを望んでも無理だ.	It's unreasonable of you to expect so much of your child.
皆さんがお望みとあれば、ここで一曲ご披露しましょう.	If you like, I'll sing a song for everyone now.
あんな大きい家に住みたいなんて、いくら望んでもむだだ.	There's no way you'll ever be able to live in a house that big, no matter how much you want to.
【眺める】私の家は、遠くに相模湾を望む丘の上にある.	My house is on top of a hill. We can see Sagami Bay in the distance.
この海岸に立つと、晴れた日には佐渡ヶ島を望むことができる.	You can see Sado Island from this beach when the weather is clear.

のち (後)

お金は品物をいただいた後にお支払いいたします.	I'll pay after †I receive [I've received] the merchandise.
仕事が済んだ後に、ゆっくり話し合いましょう.	Let's talk (it over) leisurely after work.
彼の死んだ後に真実が明らかになった.	The truth became known only after his death.
今日の天気は雨のち晴れだった.	Today it rained and then cleared up.
あの詩人の名は後の世まで残るだろう.	That poet's name will live on through the ages.
後々のことをよく考えて行動しなさい.	Give careful consideration to the consequences before you act.
後々のために貯蓄したほうがよい.	We'd better save for the future.

のっぴきならない

| のっぴきならない用事で会合に出席できなかった. | Urgent [Pressing] business prevented me from attending the meeting. |
| のっぴきならない状況に追い込まれた. | We were driven into a helpless situation. |

のどか

今日は小春日よりののどかな日だ.	It's a balmy [tranquil] Indian summer day today.
のどかな午後、一発の銃声が鳴り響いた.	A gunshot echoed through the tranquil afternoon.
ここは昔はのどかな田舎町だった.	This place used to be a tranquil country town.
私の生まれた村では、まだのどかな田園風景が残っている.	There's still a lot of peaceful[1] rustic scenery in the village where I was born.

1) peaceful の代わりに tranquil, quiet, calm などでもよい.

のばす (伸・延ばす)

【長くする】
- 爪〔髪, ひげ〕を伸ばした. — I let my nails 〔hair, beard〕 grow.
- そのドレスは短過ぎたので, 母は丈を伸ばした. — The dress was too short, so my mother let down the hem.
- 家を東のほうへ伸ばして増築した. — We added on to our house, extending it to the east.
- その鉄道を郊外まで延ばすことが決まった. — It was decided to extend that railroad to the suburbs.
- この写真を大きく伸ばしてください. — Please †enlarge [blow up] this photograph.

【まっすぐにする】
- 曲がった針金をまっすぐに伸ばした. — I stretched the bent wire straight.
- 思い切り体を伸ばしてあくびをした. — I stretched and gave a big yawn.
- 足を伸ばしてくつろいでください. — Please stretch out your legs and relax.
- 背筋を伸ばして歩きなさい. — Walk with your back straight.

【しわを】
- アイロンをかけてシャツのしわを伸ばした. — I ironed the wrinkles out of my shirt.
- 母はしわを伸ばそうと, 毎日顔のマッサージをしている. — My mother massages her face every day to get rid of her wrinkles.
- しわの寄ったお札を伸ばした. — I flattened out the wrinkled bill.

【増す】
- その店は大幅に売り上げを伸ばした. — That store increased its sales greatly.
- もっと学力を伸ばさないと, 良い学校に入れません. — If you don't do better in school, you won't get into a good school.
- この子の絵の才能を伸ばしてあげたい. — I want to help this child develop [expand] his artistic ability.

【延長・延期する】
- その町が気に入ったので滞在を三日延ばした. — I liked that town, so I †extended my stay three days [stayed three days longer than planned].
- 話し合いは予定を1時間延ばして続けられた. — The talks went on an hour beyond the scheduled time.
- レポートの提出期限を延ばして欲しいのですが. — I'd like to have an extension on my report.
- 天候が回復するまで出発を延ばします. — I'll †put off [postpone] my departure until the weather clears.

のびのび

- 彼の子どもは二人とものびのびとしている. — Both of his children are open and natural.
- 子どもはできるだけのびのびと育てなければならない. — Children should be brought up †as naturally [with as little restraint] as possible.

その体操選手はのびのびと演技した.	The gymnast's performance showed a graceful freedom of movement.
彼のフルート演奏はのびのびとしている.	His flute performances †flow easily [are relaxed].

のびる (伸・延びる)

【長くなる】暑さでレールが伸びて曲がってしまった.	The rail expanded and bent in the heat.
この輪ゴムはよく伸びる.	This rubber band really stretches.
下着のゴムが伸びてしまった.	The elastic in my underwear stretched out.
バネが伸びてしまって使いものにならない.	This spring has lost its resilience and can't be used for anything.
早く食べないとそばが伸びますよ.	The noodles will get soggy if you don't eat them up (right away).
この道路は半島の先まで延びています.	This road extends to the tip of the peninsula.
この地区まで地下鉄が延びることになった.	The subway is to be extended to this area.
その航空会社の航空路は世界中に延びている.	This airline's routes extend throughout the world.
ロッキー山脈はメキシコ北部からアラスカまで延びている.	The Rocky Mountains extend from northern Mexico to Alaska.
【成長する】タケノコは伸びるのが速い.	Bamboo shoots grow fast.
雑草は抜いても抜いてもすぐ伸びる.	No matter how often you pull them out, weeds grow right back.
息子の背が伸びて私と同じ高さになった.	My son has grown as tall as I am.
爪が伸びているね. 切りなさい.	Cut your nails. They're getting too long.
【増す】彼はこのところ, 学力が大幅に伸びた.	His academic ability has improved a great deal recently.
ここ数年, 外食産業は目覚ましく伸びている.	The restaurant industry has made remarkable growth in the past several years.
【時間が長くなる】夏になると日が延びる.	The days get [become] longer in summer.
試合時間が予定より延びてしまった.	The match continued on beyond the scheduled time.
日本人の平均寿命は年々延びている.	The average Japanese life-span is lengthening every year.
レポートの締め切り日が1週間延びた.	The deadline for the report was extended one week.
悪天候で飛行機の出発が延びている.	The airplane's departure is being †delayed [held up] by bad weather.

のべる

今度の時刻改正で電車の運転間隔が延びた.	The time between trains is now longer with the revised timetable.
【ぐったりする】そんなにたくさん一度に酒を飲んだら、伸びてしまうよ.	If you drink that much (liquor, alcohol) all at once, you'll pass out.
マラソンで5キロ走らされて生徒たちはみんな伸びてしまった.	After being made to run a five-kilometer race, the students were all dead tired.
風邪をひいて伸びてしまった.	I'm in bed with a cold.
連日の暑さでみんな伸びています.	Everyone's run down from the hot spell.
彼は、たった一発のパンチで伸びてしまった.	He got knocked out with a single punch.

のべる (述べる)

君の意見を要領よく述べてくれたまえ.	State your opinion concisely.
私の考えは先に述べたとおりです.	My thoughts are as stated previously.
私の考えを述べさせていただきます.	I would now like to offer my thoughts on the subject.
結婚式で来賓が祝辞を述べた.	The wedding guests gave congratulatory speeches.
会長が開会の辞を述べた.	The chairman addressed the opening of the meeting.
老人は、席を譲ってくれた若者に礼を述べた.	The old man thanked the young man who gave him his seat.
この論文では次のように述べています.	This thesis states the following.

のぼせる

暑さでのぼせてしまった.	I got [became] dizzy from the heat.
彼女は彼にのぼせている.	She's crazy about him.
彼女は美人コンテストに優勝して以来のぼせ上がっている.	She's had a swelled head ever since she won the beauty contest.

のほほん

皆が彼のことを心配しているのに本人はのほほんとしている.	Everybody around him is worried about him but he himself seems carefree [unconcerned].

のぼる (上・登・昇る)

【高い所へ行く】この夏は山に登ろうと思っている.	I think I'll go mountain climbing this summer.
そんな高い木に登っては危ないよ.	It's dangerous to climb up such a tall tree.
エレベーターが故障したので、5	I †climbed the stairway [went up the

階まで階段を上っていった.	stairs] to the fifth floor because the elevator was broken.
サケが川を上っていくのを見た.	I saw salmon swimming upstream.
バスが急な坂道を上っていった.	The bus drove up the steep slope.
東の空に真っ赤な朝日が昇った.	The crimson morning sun rose in the eastern sky.
【達する】会社の負債は数億円に上ると見られている.	It is estimated that the company's liabilities will rise [climb] to several hundred million yen.
列車衝突事故の死傷者は，かなりの数に上った模様だ.	The number of †dead and injured [casualties] in the train crash [collision] appears to have climbed significantly.
【取り上げられる】彼は次期社長の候補に上っている.	He's in the running to become the next president.

のまれる (飲・呑まれる)

彼は金持ちの友達の家の豪華さにのまれた.	He was overcome [overwhelmed, awed] by the grandeur of his rich friend's home.
強そうな相手にのまれて彼は実力を発揮できなかった.	He was psyched[1] out** by his strong-looking opponent and was unable to perform as well as he could have.
酒に飲まれてはいけない.	Don't become a slave to alcohol.

1) 発音は [sáikt].

のむ (飲・呑む)

【液体を】のどが渇いたので水を飲んだ.	I got thirsty so I drank some water.
赤ん坊がお乳を飲んでいる.	The baby is nursing.
父は毎晩酒を飲む.	Father drinks every night.
一杯飲みに行こうか.	Why don't we go have a drink? Let's go out for a drink.
彼は牛乳をごくごくと飲んだ.	He gulped down his milk.
ブランデーをちびりちびり飲むのが好きだ.	I like sipping brandy.
お茶でも飲みながら話しましょう.	Let's talk over a cup of tea.
【固形物を】うっかりしてキャンディーをのんでしまった.	I accidentally swallowed a piece of candy.
ヘビがツバメの卵をのんでしまった.	The snake swallowed the swallow's egg.
薬をのむ時間です.	It's time to take your medicine.
【たばこを】父はたばこを1日30本のむ.	My dad smokes 30 cigarettes a day.

たばこののみ過ぎは体に悪い.	It's bad for your health to smoke too much.
【軽く見る】議論で勝つ秘訣は,相手をのんでかかることだ.	The trick of winning an argument is to psych out** your opponent.
チャンピオンは最初から挑戦者をのんでかかっていた.	The champion had the challenger psyched out** from the beginning.
【受け入れる】そんな要求はのめない,と会社側は突っぱねた.	The company flatly refused, stating it couldn't †accept [go along with] such a demand.
しかたがない,君の条件をのもう.	Seeing (that, as) I have no choice, I'll †accept [go along with] your conditions.
【我慢する】彼の過酷な要求を,私は恨みをのんで受け入れた.	Swallowing my resentment, I accepted his harsh demands.

のりかえる (乗り換える)

家から学校まで3度乗り換えなければならない.	I have to change (trains, buses) three times to get to school from my house.
新宿へ行くなら,この駅で中央線に乗り換えます.	If you're going to Shinjuku, you change to the Chuo Line at this station.
列車から船に乗り換えて四国へ渡った.	I transferred from the train to a ship and crossed over to Shikoku.
乗り換え駅はどこですか.	What station do I change trains at?
彼女は貧しい恋人を捨てて金持ちに乗り換えた.	She threw over her poor boyfriend for a rich one.

のりき (乗り気)

彼はその提案に乗り気である.	He's very enthusiastic about the proposal. He loves the proposal. He's ready to go with the proposal. He's fired up about the proposal.

のりこえる (乗り越える)

【物を】塀を乗り越え,夜の学校に侵入した.	I snuck into the school at night by climbing over the fence.
【困難を】彼女は夫を失った悲しみを乗り越えた.	She got over (the grief of) losing her husband.
今はつらいが,頑張って乗り越えよう.	It may be hard now but we can †overcome [get over] this.
わが社は何度も倒産の危機を乗り越えてきた.	Our company successfully overcame the threat of bankruptcy many times.
【人・記録を】彼の業績はこの先,だれにも乗り越えられることは	His record will probably †never be beaten [stand unbeaten].

ないだろう.
師を乗り越えるぐらいの気持ちでやりなさい. Try to surpass your teachers.

のる (乗・載る)
【物の上に】踏み台に乗って棚の上の物を取った. I got [climbed, stepped] up on the stool and took the things off the shelf.
子どもたちがブランコに乗って遊んでいる. The children are playing on the swings.
【乗り物に】バス〔電車〕が満員で彼は乗れなかった. He couldn't get on the bus [train] because it was too full.
タクシーを見つけたので乗ろうとしたら, 回送車だと運転手が言った. I spotted a taxi and started to get in when the driver told me that he was off duty.
毎日, 自転車に乗って通学しています. I ride my bicycle [bike] to and from school every day.
I bike to school every day.
日曜日はバスに乗って美術館に行く予定だ. We're planning to take a bus to the art gallery on Sunday.
馬にはまだ一度も乗ったことがない. I've never ridden a horse.
【電波に】大統領の声明は電波に乗って全世界に流れた. The president's announcement was broadcast around the world.
【インクが】この紙はインクの乗りが良くない. This paper doesn't take ink well.
【リズムに】彼女はリズムに乗って彼と踊った. She danced with him to the rhythm of the music.
【調子に】そのチームは調子の波に乗って勝ち進んだ. Spurred on by their success the team won a series of victories.
今, その産業は好調の波に乗っている. That industry is now riding the crest of a wave.
【勧誘・依頼などに】友達の誘いに乗って宿題もせずに遊んでしまった. I gave in to my friend's urging and fooled around instead of doing my homework.
彼にその話を持ち出すとすぐに乗ってきた. No sooner did I bring the matter up than he jumped at the chance.
やつの口車に乗って嫌な仕事を引き受けてしまった. His fast-talk tricked me into taking on a job I didn't like.
父は悪徳高利貸の策略に乗って, 全財産を失ってしまった. My father †got taken in by [fell for] an unscrupulous loan shark and ended up losing everything.
【新聞・雑誌などに】ゆうべの地震のことが今朝の新聞に載ってい Last night's earthquake was written up in this morning's paper.

たよ.

私の投書が朝刊に載りました. — My letter to the editor was printed in the morning edition.

その作家の小説が載っている雑誌を全部集めている. — I've collected all the magazines that carried that novelist's stories.

のろい

彼は動作がのろい. — He's †sluggish [slow].

彼女は計算がのろい. — She's slow at †figures [making calculations].

やつは何につけてものろい. — That guy's slow [sluggish] about everything.

のんき

君はのんきだね. — You're easy-going [carefree, happy-go-lucky].
You're optimistic.
You're (too much of) an optimist.
You look on only the bright side of things.

のんびり

入試に合格したからといってのんびりしていてはだめだよ. — Just because you passed the entrance exam it doesn't mean you can afford to (just) sit back and relax.

週末はのんびり過ごしたい. — I'd like to relax and take it easy this weekend.

彼は余生をのんびり過ごした. — He spent the rest of his life free from care.

彼はのんびりした性格だ. — He's so easygoing.

は

は(歯)

牙は哺乳動物の歯が特に大きく成長したものである.	A "tusk" is a mammalian tooth which has grown especially large.
この赤ん坊は歯が生えるのが早い.	This baby is getting her teeth early.
子どもの歯は5歳くらいから永久歯に生え変わる.	At about age five baby teeth begin to be replaced by permanent teeth.
のこぎりの歯が切れなくなったので目立てをした.	The teeth of the saw wouldn't cut anymore so I sharpened them.
【慣用】この問題は難しすぎて私には歯がたたない.	This problem is way over my head.
あのチームには歯がたたない.	We're no match for that team.
彼女は歯の浮くようなお世辞を言うから嫌いだ.	I can't stand her because she makes up compliments that set my teeth on edge.
彼は歯に衣着せぬ言説で切り込んだ.	He lashed out with a verbal attack that laid it on the line.
彼は歯を食いしばって痛みをこらえた.	He gritted [clenched] his teeth in pain.
歯を食いしばって頑張ろう.	We'll just have to bite the bullet.
その男は歯の根が合わないほどおびえていた.	That man was so frightened that his teeth were chattering.
彼の人生はその事故以来,歯車が狂ってしまった.	His life's been †off the track [out of whack] ever since the accident.
今日の彼女は奥歯に物が挟まったような話し方をする.	She's not being †quite frank [very open] today.

ばあい(場合)

日本語では主語を省略する場合が多い.	In a Japanese sentence the subject is †often left out [left out in many cases].
この器具は万一の場合に役立つ.	This apparatus is useful in case of an emergency.
欠席の場合はご通知ください.	Regrets only.[1] Please advise in the event you cannot attend.
これはすべての場合に当てはまるとは限らない.	This does not necessarily apply †to all cases [under all circumstances].

彼女の場合,失恋が原因で自殺したらしい.	In her case, the suicide seems to have been caused by a broken love affair.
彼だけで大丈夫だろうが,時と場合によっては我々が乗り出さなければならない.	He shouldn't have any problems on his own, but depending on the situation we may have to go along to help him.
場合によってはコンサートは中止になることもあります.	The concert may be canceled depending on the circumstances. Circumstances may require cancellation of the concert.
ぐずぐずしている場合じゃない.	This is no time to be indecisive.

1) 招待状に書く文.

バージョン

ビートルズの曲のクラシック・バージョンを聴いた.	I heard classical arrangements of the Beatles' songs.
このソフトはウィンドウズのどのバージョンでも使えますか?	Can I use this software on any version of Windows?
バージョンの古いブラウザではエラーメッセージがよく出る.	You get a lot of error messages using an old browser.
ソフトをバージョンアップしたいときは割引価格で購入できる.	You can get a discount on your software when you upgrade.

ばい (倍)

新しい家に変わって通勤時間が倍はかかるようになった.	Since [Now that] I've moved to my new home, it takes me twice the time to commute to work.
彼は以前の倍働くようになった.	He works twice as much as he used to.
10は5の2倍である.	Ten is five times two.
日曜日にはこの辺りは平日の2倍近い人出でにぎわいます.	On Sundays there are twice as many people around here as on weekdays.

はいりょ (配慮)

いろいろご配慮ありがとうございます.	Thank you for all your kindness.
彼は人の気持ちに対する配慮が足りない.	He lacks consideration [thoughtfulness] for others.
その旅館は客に対する配慮が行き届いている.	That hotel has very good service. That hotel treats the customers †very well [with very good service].

はいる (入る)

| どうぞお入りください. | Please (do) come in. |

電車がホームに入って来た．	The train is coming into the station.
二人はレストランに入った．	The two of them †entered [went into] the restaurant (together).
古い家なので隙間風が入る．	The house is so old that the wind seeps through the cracks.
ちょっと汗をかいたので風呂に入って流そう．	I'm a little sweaty so I'm going to take a (quick) bath.
彼は野球部に入った．	He joined the baseball club.
君が入会の厳しいあのクラブに入れることは僕が保証する．	I can guarantee that you can get into that exclusive club.
労働組合はストに入った．	The labor union went on strike.
仕事は山場に入った．	Work has reached the critical point.
パソコンの普及とともにインターネット時代に入った．	We entered the Internet age when personal computers became readily available.
このバッグは物がたくさん入るので便利です．	This bag is handy because it can hold so many things.
その書類は机の引き出しに入っています．	Those papers are in the desk drawer.
アルバイトで3万入った．	I got 30,000 [thirty thousand] yen from my part-time job.
お茶が入りました．	Tea is ready.
壁にひびが入っている．	There's a crack in the wall.

はう (這う)

赤ん坊がやっとはうようになった．	The baby has finally learned how to crawl.
木の枝を虫がはっている．	A bug is crawling on the tree branch.
壁にツタをはわせた古い旅館がある．	There's an old inn with ivy †growing on [clinging to] the walls.

はえる (生える)

いつの間にか庭に雑草が生えてしまった．	In no time the garden sprang up with weeds.
お札に羽が生えて飛んでいくようにお金がなくなる．	Money disappears as if it sprouted wings and flew away.

ばか (馬鹿)

彼は馬鹿なやつだ．	He's a fool [jerk]./He's stupid.
馬鹿野郎！	You stupid jerk!
馬鹿にするな！	Don't try to make a fool out of me!
彼女を女だと思って馬鹿にしてはいけない．	You shouldn't put her down just because she's a woman.
彼は馬鹿を言っては，クラスのみんなを笑わせる．	He makes everyone in class laugh with his idiotic remarks [comments].

最近は新聞代[新聞購読料]も馬鹿にならない.	The cost of newspaper subscriptions these days is nothing to sneeze at.
	Newspapers subscriptions these days don't come cheap.
いらない物を買って馬鹿を見た.	It was ridiculous of me to have bought such a useless thing.
このねじは馬鹿になっている.	The threads on this screw are stripped.
【非常に】今日は馬鹿に暑いね.	It's ridiculously hot today.
今年はスイカが馬鹿に高い.	Watermelons are ridiculously expensive this year.
彼はつまらないことにもすぐ馬鹿笑いをする.	He laughs like a horse even at the silliest things.

はかい (破壊)

この付近にあった建物は空襲で破壊された.	The buildings that stood in this area were destroyed in air raids.
道路の建設が環境破壊につながる.	Road construction leads to destruction of the environment.

はがす

人気スターのポスターはファンがすぐはがして,持っていってしまう.	Posters of popular stars get torn off the walls right away and taken away by fans.
洋服についたガムをはがすのは大変だった.	Getting the gum off my clothes was †really awful [not easy].
息子がなかなか起きないのでふとんをはがした.	My son just wouldn't get up, so I pulled the covers [*futon*] off of him.
いつかは彼の化けの皮をはがしてやる.	Someday I'll show him up for what he really is.

はかどる

今日はだいぶ仕事〔勉強〕がはかどった.	I got a lot of work [studying] done today.
自分の家より図書館のほうが勉強がはかどる.	I can get more studying done at the library than at home.
	I study better at the library than at home.
朝から電話の応対に追われ,仕事が全くはかどらなかった.	I had so many phone calls this morning that I couldn't get any work done.
X社との交渉はなかなかはかどらない.	We're making little progress in our negotiations with X company.
名簿入力はどのくらいはかどった?	How far along are you [How are you getting along] with inputting the directory?

はかない

人生ははかないものだ. — Life is fleeting.

その映画ははかない恋の物語だ. — That movie is about a short-lived love story.

息子はまだ生きているかもしれないと, 両親ははかない望みを抱いている. — The parents hold out faint hope that their son may still be alive.

彼は世をはかなんで自殺した. — Feeling he had no reason to live, he committed suicide.

ばかばかしい

ばかばかしい. — (That's) Ridiculous!

そんな遠くまで歩くなんてばかばかしい. — It's ridiculous [absurd] to walk so far.

彼のような怠け者を雇うなんてばかばかしい. — It's foolish [stupid] to hire [employ] a lazy person like him.

そんなばかばかしい話は聞きたくない. — I don't want to hear such stupid [foolish] talk.

はがゆい（歯がゆい）

彼はいつもぐずぐずしているので歯がゆくなってくる. — I get impatient with him because he's so indecisive.
His indecisiveness irritates me.

君の子どもの叱り方は僕には歯がゆくてしかたがない. — I get impatient when I see you trying to discipline your child.

彼がいつ彼女と結婚するのか, みんな歯がゆい思いで見ている. — Everyone is waiting with bated breath to see when he's going to marry her.

ばかり

【だけ】あいつばかりが男じゃない. — He's not the only man alive.
He's not the only fish in the sea.

見渡しても見えるのは海ばかりだ. — There's nothing but ocean as far as the eye can see.

【ぐらい】コップに半分ばかりの水が入っている. — The glass is (just) about half full of water.

彼女に泣かんばかりに頼まれた. — She was on the verge of tears when she asked me to do it.

【～したところ】私も来たばかりです. — I just got here myself.

電車は駅に入るばかりのところで止まってしまった. — The train stopped before it entered the station.

【～とばかりに】えいっとばかりに水たまりを飛び越えた. — I got my strength together to jump over the puddle.

【～したために】彼は油断したばかりに事故を起こしてしまった. He caused the accident out of sheer negligence.

はかる (計・測・量・諮・図・謀る)

【計測する】身長を計ったら去年より7センチも伸びていた. When my height was measured, I found I was seven centimeters taller than last year.

しばらく安静にしてから熱を計りなさい. Take your temperature after you've rested for a while.

夏休み中, 毎日午前9時に気温を計った. I checked the air temperature every day at 9:00 a.m. during summer vacation.

目的地までの距離を測りなさい. Figure out the distance to your destination.

ストップウオッチで時間を測りなさい. Measure the time with a stopwatch.

学校では月に一度体重を量ることになっています. At school we're supposed to weigh in once a month.

小麦粉を計量カップで正確に量ってください. Please measure the flour carefully with a measuring cup.

彼は自分の意見の効果を測るようにみんなを見渡した. He looked around as if to †assess the effect [see what effect] his opinion had on the others.

【推測する】僕には彼女の真意が測りかねる. It's difficult for me to make out her true intentions.

【企てる】彼は自殺を図ったが失敗した. He attempted suicide but failed.

その会社は海外進出を図っている. That company is planning to break into foreign markets.

【努力する】政府はもっと福祉の向上を図るべきだ. The government should take more effective measures to improve public welfare.

【だます・欺く】やつにまんまと謀られた. That guy really put it over on me.

【審議する・相談する】それは会議に諮ってから決定しよう. Let's decide that after deliberating in the conference.

旅行の行き先はみんなに諮って決めたほうがよいでしょう. We should probably decide where we're going after we've checked with everyone.

はく¹ (吐く)

船に酔って吐いてしまった. I got seasick and threw up.
彼は横を向いて唾を吐いた. He turned his head to the side and spit.
彼はたばこの煙を吐いた. He †puffed out [exhaled] cigarette smoke.
SLが煙を吐きながら坂を登って Puffing smoke, the steam locomotive went

行った.	up the slope.
彼はとうとう本音を吐いた.	He finally confessed his real intentions.
やつに泥を吐かせてやる.	I'll make the guy †spit it out [come clean].
弱音を吐かないでくれよ.	Stop (your) whining.

はく² (掃く)

毎朝庭を掃いて水をまくのが日課だ.	Every morning I rake and water the garden.
ガラスのかけらをほうきで掃き集めた.	I swept up bits of broken glass with a broom.
そんな物は掃いて捨てるほどある.	That sort of thing is a dime a dozen.

はく³ (履・穿く)

遠足には履きなれた靴を履いていきましょう.	Everyone should be sure to wear well broken-in shoes on the outing.
汚れた靴下を履いてはいけません.	You mustn't wear dirty socks.
あの赤いスカートをはいた子は私のクラスメートです.	The girl in the red skirt is my classmate.

はくじょう (薄情)

私を置いてきぼりにするなんて薄情ね.	It was heartless [thoughtless] of you to leave me behind.
彼は薄情な男だ. 全く助けてくれなかった.	He's a coldhearted man. He wouldn't help me at all.
僕なら友人を裏切るような薄情なことはしない.	I wouldn't do anything as coldhearted as stabbing my friend in the back.

ばくぜん (漠然)

それは漠然とは想像できる.	I have a vague †picture of it [idea of what it's all about].
私は将来について漠然とした不安を持っています.	I feel vaguely insecure about my future.
その件については, 今はまだ漠然としたことしか言えません.	At this moment, I can only give you a very vague reply on that matter.
それは随分昔のことだから, 漠然としか思い出せない.	That was so long ago, I can only remember it vaguely.

ばくはつ (爆発)

ダイナマイトが爆発した.	The dynamite †exploded [blew up].
幸運にも爆弾は爆発しなかった.	Fortunately the bomb failed to go off.
火山が爆発した.	The volcano erupted.
みんなの不満が爆発した.	Everyone's dissatisfaction erupted.
彼は怒りを爆発させた.	He blew up in anger.

はくりょく（迫力）

迫力のある演説だった．	It was a forceful [powerful] speech.
彼の迫力のある演技は観客を魅了した．	He amazed the spectators with his impressive [powerful, overwhelming] performance.
相撲は間近で見るとやはり迫力がある．	It's definitely more impressive to watch *sumo* wrestling close up.
彼女の歌は技術的には優れているが，迫力に欠ける．	Her vocal performance is technically sound but lacks vitality [vigor].

はげしい（激しい）

昨日は雨が激しかった．	It rained hard yesterday.
激しい嵐がこの土地を襲った．	This place was hit by a violent storm.
彼は気性が激しい．	He has a fiery temperament.
激しい口調で，彼は政府の物価政策を非難した．	He bitterly criticized the government's policy on price control.
激しい議論が延々と続いた．	The heated discussion went on †and on [interminably].
激しい痛みで彼は一晩中眠れなかった．	A sharp pain kept him awake all night.
ここは盆地なので気温の変化が激しい．	Since this area is in a valley, the temperature changes dramatically [drastically].
中東紛争がだんだん激しくなってきた．	The dispute in the Middle East has gotten worse [intense, severe].
この通りは車の行き来が激しい．	The traffic is always heavy along this street.

はげます（励ます）

クラスメートがみんな我々のチームを励ましてくれた．	Our classmates all cheered our team on.
入院している彼女を励ましに行こう．	Let's go visit her in the hospital to †cheer her up [raise her spirits].
彼は自らを励ましながら42キロを完走した．	He forced himself to run the 42 kilometers to the end.
その画家は妻に励まされながら大作を描き上げた．	That artist completed his masterpiece with the support of his wife.

はげみ（励み）

もう一度チャンスを与えられたことが彼の励みになった．	Being given a second chance served as an inspiration to him.
先生が褒めてくれたことは，とても励みになりました．	The teacher's words of praise served as a source of encouragement.
彼も結婚して，働く励みができた	Getting married will probably inspire him

はげむ (励む)
彼は仕事に励んでいる.	He is working hard.
彼女は貯蓄に励んでいる.	She is doing her best to save money.
彼は食事をするのも忘れるくらいに細菌の研究に励んだ.	He was so absorbed in his research on bacteria that he practically forgot to eat.

はこぶ (運ぶ)
【持ち運ぶ】そのトランクは, 一人では運べないほど重かった.	That trunk was too heavy for one person to carry.
石油はタンカーで運ばれてきます.	Petroleum is brought by tanker.
風が春の便りを運んできた.	The wind brought us tidings of spring.
【進む】事はうまく運んでいる.	Things are progressing [moving] smoothly.
計画が簡単に運ぶとは思わない.	I don't think the plan can be carried out easily.
工事は順調に運んでいます.	Construction is †proceeding without a hitch [moving right along].

はさむ (挟む)
ドアに手を挟まれた.	My hand got caught in the door.
彼は脇の下に本を挟んで歩いている.	He's walking with a book under his arm.
二つの川に挟まれた村があった.	There was a village nestled between the two rivers.
私はビルに挟まれた狭い通りを歩いて行った.	I walked down the narrow alley sandwiched between the buildings.
彼のうわさを小耳に挟んだ.	I just happened to hear a rumor about him.

はし (端)
紙の端が破れている.	The edge of the paper is torn.
棒の端を持ってください.	Hold the stick at the end. Take the stick by the end.
彼は木の端を使って子どもにおもちゃを作ってやった.	He made a toy for the child from a piece [scrap] of wood.
町の端から端まで捜したが, その子どもは見つからなかった.	We searched the town from one end to the other but we couldn't find the child.
端のほうに座らずに真ん中に来てください.	Don't sit on the edge. Come in to the middle.

はじ (恥)
恥を知れ.	You should be ashamed (of yourself).

あの馬鹿息子は我が家の恥だ.	That stupid son of ours is a disgrace to the family.
彼は恥知らずなやつだ.	He is †shameless [without shame].
テーブルマナーを知らず,レストランで恥をかいた.	I felt humiliated at the restaurant, not knowing table manners.
恥を忍んで彼から金を借りた.	I swallowed my pride and borrowed some money from him.
彼女は恥も外聞もなく大声で息子の名前を呼んだ.	Without any inhibitions, she called out her son's name in a very loud voice.
自分の恥をさらすような事は言いたくありません.	I don't want to say anything to embarrass myself.
その化学者は,自分の新たな名声に恥じない研究をするのは大変なことだと思った.	The chemist found it quite difficult to live up to his new reputation.

はじく (弾く)

テーブルの上のパンくずを指ではじいた.	I flicked a bread crumb off the table with my finger.
自動車が小石をはじいた.	The car sent a pebble flying.
彼はそろばんをはじいた.	He used the abacus.[1]
	He was wondering whether he could benefit from this.[2]
自動車にワックスをかけると雨をはじくようになる.	Rain bounces off a car when it is waxed. A waxed car repels rain.

> 1) 文字どおりの意味. 2) 比喩的な意味.

はじまる (始まる)

公演は6時に始まる.	The performance begins at six.
原子力時代は20世紀半ばに始まった.	The age of nuclear power began in the mid-20th century.
日本での農耕は弥生時代に始まった.	Agriculture in Japan dates from the Yayoi period.
彼の口の悪いのは今に始まったことではない.	His bad language is nothing new.
決まってしまってから騒いでも始まらない.	There's no point in making a fuss after it's already been decided.

はじめ (初め)

【起源】生物の初めについてはまだよく分かっていない.	The origin [genesis] of life is still not well understood.
【最初】物事は初めが肝心だ.	Beginnings are critical.
この小説は初めは退屈だった.	The †beginning [first part] of this novel

	was boring.
何事にも「初め」がある．新しいことに挑戦するのを恐れるな．	There is a beginning to everything. [Everything has a beginning.] Don't be afraid to try something new.
初めは遊びだったが，だんだん彼女のことが本当に好きになっていった．	At first, I went out with her just for the fun of it, but then I began to get serious about her.
【代表】イギリス，フランスをはじめヨーロッパ諸国の首脳が参加して会議が行われた．	A conference was held in which the leaders of Britain, France and several other European nations participated.
人類をはじめとする霊長類の誕生はそんなに古いことではない．	The first appearance of the order of primates, which is represented by the human species, was [came] relatively late.

はじめて (初めて)

外国へ行くのはこれが初めてです．	This is my first time to go to a foreign country.
この油絵は初めてにしてはよくかけています．	For a first effort, this oil painting is good.
今，初めて芸術の素晴らしさが分かった．	I have now realized for the first time the splendor of art.
先生に指摘されて初めて間違いに気づいた．	I didn't notice my mistake until the teacher pointed it out. I first realized my mistake when the teacher pointed it out.

はじめる (始める)

今度商売を始めました．	I've started my own business.
そら，またあいつが居眠りを始めたぞ．	Look! He's started dozing off again.
始めるのは早いほうがいい．	The sooner you start [begin], the better.
一杯入ると大抵彼は歌い始める．	After he's had a little bit to drink he usually breaks into song.

はしる (走る)

彼は最初からトップを走っている．	He's been running in the lead from the outset.
最速の「のぞみ」は東京・大阪間を2時間半で走る．	The fastest "Nozomi" makes the trip [distance] between Tokyo and Osaka in two and a half hours.
海岸線を走る道路は快適そのものだ．	The road that runs along the coast is absolutely delightful.

京都の道路は碁盤の目のように走っている.	The streets of Kyoto run like the grid of a *go* board.
今日はすらすらとペンが走る.	My pen is gliding across the page today.
月末はいつも金策に走り回らなければならない.	Near the end of the month I always have to run around scrounging up money.
彼は何もかも捨てて恋人のもとに走った.	He gave up everything and abandoned himself to his lover.
人は貧困から悪事に走ることもある.	Poverty leads some people to a life of crime.
党利党略に走って本来の目的を見失ってはならない.	One must not lose sight of the original objectives in pursuit of party interests.

はず

彼なら及第するはずだ.	He should be able to pass the exam.
今日の試合は勝つはずだったのに.	We should've won today's game.
ちゃんと置いたのならなくなるはずがないだろう?	If you put it where you claim you did, it should still be there, shouldn't it?
そんな事は君だって知っているはずだ.	I would have expected you to know that.
彼は今頃は家に着いているはずだ.	He should be home by now.
彼は明日出発するはずです.	He's supposed to leave tomorrow.

はずかしい (恥ずかしい)

彼女はみすぼらしい服が恥ずかしかった.	She was ashamed of her shabby dress.
大勢の女の子の前で話すのは恥ずかしかった.	It was embarrassing to speak in front of so many girls.
彼は知らない人に会うと恥ずかしがる.	He is shy about meeting strangers.
そんなことをして恥ずかしいと思わないのか.	Don't you feel embarrassed about [Aren't you ashamed of] doing something like that?
	Shame on you, doing something like that!
挨拶もきちんとできないようでは我が社の社員として恥ずかしいよ.	It's embarrassing for an employee of this company to be unable even to greet people properly.
そんなに褒められるとかえって恥ずかしい.	It's actually embarrassing to be praised that much.

はずす (外す)

| ドアを外して直してください. | Please take the door off its hinges and fix it. |
| 彼は眼鏡を外した. | He took off his glasses. |

暑いのでボタンを外した.	I †unbuttoned (my shirt) [undid my buttons] because of the heat.
来週カーテンを外して洗濯に出すつもりです.	We plan to take down the curtains and have them cleaned next week.
しばらく席を外します.	I'll be away from my desk for a while.
【除く】日曜は予定から外しておいてください.	Please leave Sunday †out of [off] the schedule.
パーティーに招待する人のリストから彼を外すべきだ.	When you make up your list of people to invite to your party, you should leave his name off.
彼はもう役員から外したほうがいい.	It's about time to remove him from that executive position.
【つかみ損なう】ファーストがボールを外した.	The first baseman missed the ball.
この機会を外すと、次はいつ彼に会えるか分からない.	If we let this opportunity go by, I don't know when we'll have another chance to meet him.

はずれ (外れ)

【的・くじなど】3回外れが続き、4度目にようやく的に当たった.	After missing three times, I finally hit the target on my fourth try.
外れくじも捨てないで. 再抽選があるから.	Don't throw away your old lottery tickets. There's [There're][1] redraws.
外れ馬券を丸めて捨てた.	I crumpled up my losing (horse-race) ticket and threw it away.
「君, 東京生まれ?」「外れ. 北海道なんだ」	"Were you born in Tokyo?" "No,[2] …in Hokkaido."
【不良品】この物件は外れだ.	This is not a good piece of real estate.
このスイカは外れだ.	This isn't a very good watermelon.
この車〔ビデオデッキ〕は外れだ.	This †car [video deck] is a lemon.
【端】街の外れにあるラーメン屋はおいしいと評判だ.	The *ramen* shop on the outskirts of town is supposed to be really good.
この商店街の外れにさびれた映画館がある.	There's a dreary movie theater at the end of this shopping street.
【慣用】彼はいつも的外れのことを言う.	His comments are always a little off.
	He always says things that aren't quite on.
社長の葬儀は桁外れのスケールで執り行われた.	The company president's funeral was exceptionally extravagant.

1) あとにくる語が複数形の場合, There are [There're] を使うのが正式だが, 口語では There's を使うことが多い. 2) クイズなどの場合は Wrong も使える.

はずれる (外れる)

ボタンが外れてるよ.	Your button's undone.
なべの取手が外れてしまった.	The handle came off the pot.
矢は的を外れた.	The arrow missed the target.
それは道理に外れたことですよ.	That shows a complete lack of principles.
宝くじは全部外れてしまった.	All of my lottery tickets were losers.
この製品は主婦層に受けると思ったが, 狙いが外れた.	We thought that homemakers would go for this product but we were off (in our assessment).

はだか (裸)

赤ん坊が真っ裸で水遊びをしている.	The baby is splashing around in the water completely naked.
【慣用】彼は裸一貫から現在の富を築いた.	He built up his present wealth from scratch.
彼とは裸のつきあいをしている.	I have a completely open relationship with him.

はだし

彼女は砂浜をはだしで歩いた.	She walked along the beach barefoot.
【慣用】彼のカメラの腕前はくろうとはだしだ.	His photography would put a pro to shame.
彼女はくろうとはだしの素晴らしい歌を聞かせる.	Her singing is so wonderful it would put a professional to shame.

はたす (果たす)

彼は立派に責任を果たした.	He fulfilled his responsibility splendidly.
その委員会は本来の機能を果たしていない.	That committee is not fulfilling its original function.
市長は公約を果たすことなく, 病気で辞職した.	The mayor resigned due to illness, unable to fulfill his commitments to the public.
彼は一晩のうちにその金を使い果たした.	He used up all that money in one night.

はたらき (働き)

一日の働きのあとは何をする気力もない.	I don't feel like doing anything after working all day.
引力の働きで惑星はそれぞれの軌道を守っている.	Gravity works to keep the various planets in their orbits.
彼は今働き盛りだ.	He's in the prime of his life.
彼は会社で一番の働き手だ.	He's the best worker in the company.
今回の商戦で彼は抜群の働きを見せた.	In the last sales campaign he demonstrated a distinguished capability.

寝不足で今日は頭の働きが鈍い.	I'm a little slow today because I didn't get enough sleep last night.

はたらく (働く)

まじめに働けば必ず報われるものだ.	If you work seriously, you are bound to be rewarded.
だれでも働かなくては生きていけない.	Everyone must work to live.
彼女はいつもサークルの中心になって働いている.	She always takes a central role in working for the club.
彼はよく頭が働く人だ.	He has a quick mind.
パニックに陥ると群集心理が働き易い.	It is easy for mob psychology to take over in a panic.
競争心が働いて,彼は一層勉強するようになった.	Motivated by the spirit of competition, he started studying even harder.
回転している物には遠心力が働く.	Revolving objects generate centrifugal force.
彼は乱暴を働いた.	He committed an act of violence.

ばつ (罰)

この寮では門限破りの罰は窓拭きです.	The punishment for breaking curfew in this dormitory is window cleaning.
トランプで負けた罰として,歌を歌わせられた.	The penalty [price] I had to pay for losing the card game was to sing a song.
母親はいたずらの罰として坊やのおしりをぶった.	The boy's mother spanked him for his prank.
彼はあんな行いをしていると必ず罰を受けるだろう.	He will definitely get punished for doing that kind of thing.
駐車違反で罰金を取られた.	I was fined for a parking violation.

はっき (発揮)

試合本番で実力を十分に発揮できなかった.	When it came to the game, I didn't play to the best of my ability.
元俳優の彼は司会業で本領を発揮して活躍している.	As a former actor, he's in his element as emcee.
その女優はその映画で本領を発揮できなかった.	The actress' performance in the film didn't do her justice.
社会に出ても,持ち前の粘り強さを発揮して頑張ってください.	When you get out there, show them what you're made of.**
わがままぶりを発揮する孫に手を焼いている.	My grandchild is so spoiled he's †causing me a lot of distress [giving me a lot of trouble].
	I'm upset about my spoilt grandchild.

はっきり

コーヒーを飲んだら頭がはっきりした.	My head cleared after I drank some coffee.
秋空に富士山がはっきり見える.	Mt. Fuji can be seen very clearly in the fall sky.
彼は発音が不明瞭ではっきり聞き取れない.	His pronunciation is unclear and I can't make out what he's saying.
随分昔のことだが,今でもはっきり覚えている.	It happened a long time ago, but I still remember it very clearly.
彼にははっきり返事しないと誤解を生じるよ.	If you don't give him a definite [clear] answer, you'll only create a misunderstanding.
これだけははっきり言っておきます.	I want to make this point perfectly clear.
はっきりしたことはまだ言えません.	I can't say anything definite yet.
今日は天気がはっきりしない.	The weather's unstable today.

バックアップ

弁護士会がわれわれの活動をバックアップしてくれている.	The bar association is backing up our movement.
新規事業を展開するに際し,取引先が資金的にバックアップしてくれた.	One of our clients backed us up financially in developing our new business.
先生のバックアップを受けて,初の個展を開いた.	I held my first one-man show with the help [support] of my teacher.
【コンピュータ】大切なファイルは常にバックアップをとりなさい.	You should always back up your valuable files.
バックアップしなかったために数時間の努力が泡と消えた.	Hours of work were wasted because I didn't back up my file.
このソフトはバックアップファイルが自動的に作られる.	This software automatically makes a back-up file.

はっけん (発見)

ビルの工事現場から古い土器が発見された.	Some ancient pottery was discovered [unearthed] at the construction site of the building.
火災の発見がもう少し遅れたら,大惨事になったかもしれない.	If the fire had been discovered a little later, it might have turned into a terrible disaster.
効果的な治療のためにはがんの早期発見が大切だ.	Early detection of cancer is essential for effective treatment.
電気の発見は文明の発展に大きく	The discovery of electricity contributed a

寄与した.	great deal to the development of civilization.
音楽教師はその少年の素晴らしい才能を発見した.	A music instructor discovered the wonderful talent of that youth.

はっこう (発行)

この新聞は週1回発行されます.	This newspaper is published weekly.
その雑誌の発行部数は40万部です.	That magazine has a circulation of 400,000 [four hundred thousand].
4月に新しいお札が発行される.	The new bills will †be issued [start circulating] in April.
彼は身分証明書を発行してもらった.	He had an I.D. [identification] card issued to him.

はったつ (発達)

健全な心身の発達にはよい環境が必要です.	To develop a wholesome body and mind, a good environment is necessary.
台風が発達しながら近づいている.	The typhoon is developing as it approaches.
この地方には商業都市が発達した.	Commercial centers flourished in this region.
犬は嗅覚が発達している.	A dog has a highly developed sense of smell.

はってん (発展)

日本の産業は一層の海外発展を目指している.	Japanese industry is aiming at even greater overseas expansion.
その都市は戦後目覚ましい発展を遂げた.	That city achieved a striking prosperity after the war.
事件は思わぬ方向に発展した.	The affair took an unexpected turn.

はっと

地震にはっと驚いて目が覚めた.	I woke up startled by the earthquake.
財布を忘れてきたのに気づいてはっとした.	It gave me a start when I realized that I had forgotten my wallet.
はっと彼は我に返ったがもう遅すぎた.	He came to himself with a start but it was too late.

ぱっと

【瞬間的に】犬の鳴き声でぱっと眼が覚めた.	I woke up with a start to the sound of a dog barking.
めざまし時計が鳴るとぱっと飛び起きた.	I woke up as soon as my alarm went off.

蛍光灯のランプを換えたら，部屋がぱっと明るくなった．	The room got brighter as soon as I changed the fluorescent light.
銀行が倒産しそうだといううわさがぱっと広まった．	Rumors that the bank was on the verge of collapse spread like wildfire.
火はぱっと燃え広がった．	The fire spread instantly.
彼は，ぱっと見はいい人のように見える．	At first glance, he seems like a good person.
【派手に・目立って】打ち上げはぱっと豪勢にやりましょう．	Let's go all out to celebrate the end of the project.
どうせ競馬で儲けたあぶく銭だ．ぱっと使ってしまおう．	It's only money I won at the races. Let's go (out) and spend it!
彼女のぱっとした顔立ちは人目を引く．	Her striking features attract a lot of attention.
ぱっとしない男だが，あれで億万長者なんだ．	He may not look like much but he's a billionaire.
その女優は普段ぱっとしないが，舞台では存在感がある．	That actress doesn't stand out in real life but really has a stage presence.
出演者の顔触れはぱっとしないが，筋立ての面白い映画だ．	There are no stars in the movie but the plot is very interesting.

はっぴょう (発表)

入試の合格発表は明日です．	The names of those who passed the entrance examination will be announced [posted] tomorrow.
まだ意見を発表していない人はいませんか．	Is there anyone who still hasn't presented an opinion?
記者会見でその事件に対する首相の見解が発表された．	The prime minister's views about that incident were made public at the press conference.
世論調査の結果が新聞で発表された．	The results of the public opinion poll were published in the newspaper.
彼は今度の学会でその論文を発表するつもりだ．	He intends to present that paper at the next conference.
大統領が発表した声明は全国民に衝撃を与えた．	The official †statement made [position announced] by the president shocked the entire nation.

はつめい (発明)

蓄音器はトマス・エジソンによって発明された．	The phonograph was invented by Thomas Edison.
発明の才能はだれにでもあるわけではない．	Not everyone has a talent for invention.
コンピュータの発明で現代社会は	The invention of the computer has greatly

大きく変わった. | changed modern society.

はで (派手)

彼女は派手な人だ.	She has a flashy personality.
彼は万事派手好みだ.	He likes to be showy in everything.
	He has loud taste in everything.
彼女は派手な色の服をいつも着ている.	She always wears bright-colored [gaudy] clothes.
	She's always dressed in loud colors.
彼女の送別会は派手にやろうよ.	Let's have [throw] a lavish farewell party for her.
彼は最近, 金の使い方がいやに派手だね.	Recently he's really been throwing his money around in a disgusting way.

はな (鼻)

人前で鼻をほじるのは禁物だ.	It is not socially acceptable to pick one's nose in front of others.
動物は一般に人間よりも鼻が利く.	Animals generally have †a more accurate sense of smell [more sensitive noses] than humans.
このあたりは硫黄のにおいが鼻をつく.	There's a penetrating [pungent] smell of sulfur around here.
鼻が詰まっている.	My nose is stuffy.
風邪をひいたらしく, 今朝からはなが出る.	I think I may have caught a cold. I've had a runny nose since this morning.
欧米では, 人前ではなをかむのはマナー違反ではない (とされている).	In the west, it's not (considered) impolite to blow your nose in public.
【慣用】彼は絵が入賞したので鼻が高い.	His painting won a prize, so he's †proud of himself [impressed with himself].
彼はエリートを鼻にかけている.	He's stuck up about being elite.
彼は鼻持ちならないやつだ.	He stinks.
彼の大げさな話し方が鼻についてきた.	His exaggerated way of talking †gets to me [makes my skin crawl, sticks in my craw].
あの人の自慢話は, もういいかげん鼻についてきた.	I'm really getting sick of his bragging.
彼はこういうことには鼻が利くから用心したほうがいい.	He has a good nose for something like this, so you should be careful.
ひそかに碁の研究をして彼の鼻を明かしてやった.	I studied up on *go* on the sly and took the wind out of his sails.
彼にお金を借りに行ったら, 鼻であしらわれた.	He turned his nose up at me when I went to borrow money from him.

鼻をつままれても分からないような闇夜だった. — It was so dark out there at night that I couldn't see two feet in front of me.

はなし (話)

【会話】彼女は話上手だ. — She's a good conversationalist.

お話中失礼ですが, あなたにお電話です. — Excuse me for interrupting, but there's a telephone call for you.

クラス会では遅くまで話がはずんだ. — The lively conversation at the class reunion continued until late.

久しぶりに時間ができて, 友人といろいろな話をした. — For the first time in a long time I had a chance to have a good talk with my friend.

ここだけの話だが, 彼は競馬で大金をすったそうだ. — Just between us, I hear he lost a lot of money at the track.

【話題】その話はもうやめよう. — Let's stop talking about that. / Let's not talk about that anymore.

話は変わるが, 最近彼女に会ったかい. — Not to change the subject, but have you seen her recently?

僕らはよく話が合う. — We speak the same language.

適当に話を合わせておいたよ. — I backed up your story.

そんなに話を落とすなよ. — Don't be so vulgar.

【相談・約束】今日はうまい話が入ったんだ. — I had a tempting offer today.

彼も加わるなら話は別だ. — It would completely change the picture if he's included.

その条件で彼らは話をまとめた. — They agreed to those conditions.

この線で話を進めてください. — Let's go along with this. / Let's conduct the talks along this line.

私が彼の所へ行って話をつけて来よう. — I will go and †convince him [get him to agree].

新製品の価格についてようやく社内で話がついた. — The price of the new product has finally been agreed on inside the company.

うちの父はとても話が分かる人だ. — My father is very understanding.

それでは昨日と話が違うではありませんか. — That's not what you said yesterday, is it?

彼はすぐに我々の話に乗ってきた. — He went along with us right away.

彼の持ってきた条件は話がうますぎるから気をつけたほうがいい. — The conditions he offered sound too good to be true, so you should be careful.

彼の意見は現実離れしていて, 全く話にならない. — His opinion is totally unrealistic. It's not even worth talking about.

【物語】子どもは動物の出てくる話が好きだ. — Children like stories about animals.

はなす¹ (話す)

彼女は英語を話します． — She speaks English.

彼は学校教育のあり方について話した． — He spoke on the nature of education in the schools.

そのことは彼に話してある． — He has been told about that.

お母さんに話してあの服を買ってもらおう． — I'll talk to Mother and get her to buy me this dress.

彼にもう二度とあんなことはしないようによく話しておいた． — I explained very clearly to him that he was never to do something like that again.

はなす² (放す)

車のハンドルを放しては危ない． — It's dangerous to let go of the steering wheel.

迷子になるから手を放してはいけませんよ． — Don't let go of my hand or you'll get lost.

今，手が放せないので，また明日来ていただけませんか． — I'm tied up right now. Would you mind coming back tomorrow?

【解放する】オタマジャクシがカエルになったので池に放してやった． — When the tadpole turned into a frog I †turned it loose [set it free, released it] in the pond.

夕方犬を放すのはやめてください． — Please don't †turn your dog loose [let your dog run free] in the evening.

【放置する】稲は植えっ放しでは育たない． — Rice won't grow if you just plant it and leave it.

【続く】彼はこのところ勝ちっ放しだ． — He's been having a winning streak recently.

はなす³ (離す)

杉の苗のあいだを1メートル離して植えた． — I left a meter between the cedar seedlings when I planted them.

机と机のあいだをもう少し離してください． — Please move the desks a little farther apart.

もっと目を離して本を読みなさい． — Hold the book farther away from your eyes when you read.

彼は2位を5メートル引き離してゴールに入った． — He crossed the finish line five meters ahead of second place.

はなやか (華やか)

私にも若く華やかな時代があった． — There was a time when I was young and spirited too.

お祭りの華やかな行列を見物した． — We saw a grand [colorful] parade at the festival.

彼女には何となく華やかな雰囲気 — There's something glamorous about her.

	She somehow has a glamorous air about her.
華やかな芸能界にあこがれる若い人は多い.	Many young people are infatuated with the glamour of show business.
結婚式には華やかに着飾った, 新婦の友人が大勢出席した.	There were many friends of the bride dressed in beautiful bright colors at the wedding.

はなれる¹ (放れる)

矢は弓を放れ, 弧を描いて飛んで行った.	The arrow left the bow, tracing an arc as it flew.
風船が手から放れて飛んで行ってしまった.	I lost hold of the balloon and it blew away.

はなれる² (離れる)

両親は5キロほど離れた所に住んでいます.	My parents live about five kilometers away.
彼はしばらく日本を離れた.	He †left [was away from] Japan for a while.
彼女はやっと全快して床を離れた.	At last she completely recovered and could get out of bed.
彼は職を離れて, 故郷に帰った.	He left his job and returned to his hometown.
子どもが手を離れて, 自分の時間が持てるようになりました.	Now that my child can look after himself I have a lot more time to myself.
これまでのいきさつを離れてもう一度話し合おう.	Let's put aside what has happened until now and talk things over once more.
一般の人々の生活と離れた所で政治が行われている.	Politics continues to be removed from the lives of average people.

ばね

ばねの飛び出したソファがごみ捨てに捨ててあった.	There was a sofa at the garbage dump with its springs coming out.
彼はばねが強いから良いランナーになるだろう.	He has such powerful legs. I'm sure he'll be a good runner.
この出来事をばねにして彼はもっと強くなるだろう.	He'll probably spring back even stronger from this incident.
父はばね仕掛けの自動車をおみやげに買ってきた.	Father bought me a little wind-up car as a present.

はねる (跳ねる)

雨上がりにカエルがたくさん跳ねていた.	A lot of frogs were jumping around after it stopped raining.

馬が跳ねて, 危なく振り落とされるところだった.	I was nearly thrown by the horse when it jumped.
車が泥を跳ねていった.	The car splashed mud as it went by.
跳ねがかかってスカートが汚れてしまった.	My skirt got dirty from splashes of mud.
【終わる】芝居が跳ねてから楽屋を訪ねた.	I went to the dressing room after the play had finished.

はば (幅)

この機械の幅は3.5メートルあります.	This machine is 3.5 meters wide.
幅の狭い川を歩いて渡った.	We crossed the narrow river on foot.
彼は歩幅が大きくて, 一緒に歩くのが大変です.	He takes such big steps that it's very hard to walk along with him.
その航空会社は大幅な運賃値上げを行った.	That airline introduced [effected] a substantial fare hike.
【ゆとり】この問題にはもう少し幅のある解釈をすべきです.	This problem should be interpreted from a broader perspective.
【威勢】彼はこの辺ではなかなか幅をきかせている.	He's a man of great influence in this region.

はぶく (省く)

あなたのお陰でとても手間が省けました.	You saved us a lot of trouble.
むだな出費を省くよう努力しなければならない.	You must strive to eliminate unnecessary expenses.
これまでの経過は省きまして今日の議題に入ります.	I'd like to skip what's gone before and start in on today's subject.
この分は計算から省いておきました.	I omitted this part from the calculations.

はめ (羽目)

【羽目になる】どうして君が謝りに行く羽目になったの？	Why did you have to end up apologizing?
駐車料金をけちったばかりに, 高い罰金を支払う羽目になった.	I was too cheap to pay for parking and ended up paying a huge fine.
【羽目を外す】仕事の打ち上げで, みんな羽目を外して騒いだ.	Everyone let loose and had a good time at the party after [when] the job ended.
彼女が羽目を外したところを見たことがない.	I've never seen her let herself go.

はめる (嵌める)

彼はコートを着てボタンをはめた.	He put on his coat and buttoned it.

彼女はダイヤをはめたイヤリングを持っている.	She has a pair of earrings with diamond insets.
今日は寒いから手袋をはめなさい.	It's cold today, so †put on [wear] your gloves.
彼からもらった指輪をはめてみた.	I tried on the ring he gave me.
私はコンタクトレンズを14時間もはめている.	I have had my contact lenses in for 14 hours.
【陥れる】あの男に一杯はめられた.	I was really †taken in [cheated] by that guy.

はやい¹ (早い)

明日は早い出発だからもう寝たほうがいい.	We're leaving early tomorrow, so you should be getting to bed.
夏は夜が明けるのが早い.	Daybreak is early in the summer.
一刻も早く彼女の所へ行くべきだ.	You should go to her place as soon as you can.
その仕事は早ければ3月から始まります.	That job will start in March at the earliest.
出発の時期は早ければ早いほど良い.	We should leave as soon as possible.
あきらめるのはまだ早いよ.	It's still too early to give up.
あの子は19だから結婚にはまだ早い.	She's only nineteen. That's too young to get married.
早くしろよ.	Hurry (it) up.

はやい² (速い)

彼は走るのが速い.	He's a fast runner.
彼女は仕事が速いので助かる.	We're lucky because she's a fast worker.
空気が乾燥しているときは火の回りが速い.	Fire spreads quickly when the air is dry.
彼は全くのみこみが速い.	He picks up on things very quickly.
この川は流れが速い.	This river has a rapid current.
彼は熱があるのか, 呼吸が速い.	His breathing's so fast. I wonder if he's got a fever.

はやがてん (早合点)

彼はいつも早合点するので困る.	We are always bothered by his hasty judgments.
早合点しないでください.	Don't jump to conclusions.
彼女は僕の話を最後まで聞かないで早合点してしまった.	She jumped to her own conclusion before she heard me out.

はやる¹ (流行る)

ショートカットが今はやりのヘアスタイルです． — Short hair is the popular style now.

あの店はよくはやっている． — That store is very popular.

今年は帽子がはやっている． — Hats are in fashion this year.

日本では，流行が廃るのははやり出すのと同様，あっという間だ． — In Japan fads usually die out as fast as they catch on.

風邪がはやっているから気をつけなさい． — Be careful because there's a lot of colds going around.

はやる² (逸る)

彼に会えると思うと心がはやる． — When I think about meeting him, I get all excited.

彼ははやる心を抑えて試合が始まるのを待った． — He calmed himself down and waited for the game to start.

はら (腹)

彼は最近腹が出てきた． — Recently he's gotten fat in the stomach.

腹が痛い． — My stomach aches. I have a stomachache.

腹が減った，何か食べる物ない？ — I'm hungry. Don't you have anything to eat?

子どもが腹をすかして待っているから早く帰らなくては． — I really must get home. My kids are probably waiting for me with empty stomachs.

【考え】こうなった以上は彼と運命をともにすると腹を決めた． — Now that it's come to this I've decided to throw my lot in with his.

父と息子は腹を割って話した． — The father and son opened up to each other.

政治家の中には腹黒い人もいる． — Some politicians are corrupt.

あいつは腹の中では何を考えているか分からない． — I can't figure out what that guy's thinking deep down.

彼らは何とかして交渉相手の腹を探ろうとしている． — They are trying somehow to feel out the man they are negotiating with.

【気持ち】彼の自分勝手なやり方には腹が立つ． — The way he does everything to suit himself burns me up.

彼のいい加減な仕事ぶりは腹に据えかねる． — His half-hearted way of doing his job really peeves me.

彼を一度ぎゃふんと言わせてやらなければ腹の虫が治まらない． — I won't be satisfied until I get him to †admit he's wrong [say uncle] once.

【度量・度胸】社長は腹の太い人だから，そのぐらいの失策で君を首にしたりはしないだろう． — The boss doesn't let little things bother him, so a failure like this probably won't get you fired.

| あの人は腹が据わっているので、決して物事に動じない. | He's prepared himself for whatever may come, so nothing will faze him. |

はらう (払う)

【支払う】彼は部屋代を払った.	He paid the rent.
今度の給料日には借金を払ってくれよ.	Pay back the money you owe me on your next payday.
高い月謝を払っているんだからしっかりピアノのレッスンをしてちょうだい.	The tuition for your piano lessons is expensive, so please take them seriously.
二人はレストランの代金をどう払うか話がまとまらなかった.	The two men could not agree on how to settle up the bill at the restaurant.
【取り去る】彼はズボンについたほこりを払った.	He brushed the dust off his pants.
庭の木の枝を払ったら明るくなった.	Trimming the tree branches in the garden made it a lot brighter.
【傾ける】彼は敬意を払って先生に挨拶した.	He greeted his teacher out of respect.

はらだたしい (腹立たしい)

彼の答えは腹立たしいものだった.	His reply made me angry.
あの売り場の店員は愛想が悪くてとても腹立たしかった.	The unfriendly salesclerk at that store really bothered [irritated] me.
公務員の汚職など最近は腹立たしい事件が多いね.	Recently there have been quite a few maddening incidents like corruption of government officials.
チャンピオンは腹立たしいぐらいに落ち着き払い, 不敵な笑いを浮かべていた.	The champion let out a defiant laugh that was so cooly deliberate as to be provoking.

はらはら

【心配】彼の思い切ったやり方にははらはらさせられる.	His reckless way of doing things makes me nervous [uneasy].
その映画ははらはらする場面が多かった.	That movie was full of suspenseful [thrilling] scenes.
彼女はよちよち歩きの子どもをはらはらしながら見守っていた.	She was anxiously keeping an eye on her child toddling along.
観客は, はらはらしながら空中ブランコを見ていた.	The spectators were breathlessly watching the flying trapeze.
【次々に落ちる】黄色くなったイチョウの葉がはらはらと落ちている.	The ginkgo leaves that have turned gold are softly fluttering down.
彼女の目から涙がはらはらとこぼ	The tears rolled from her eyes.

ばらばら

その古い書籍は，持ち上げるとばらばらに崩れた．
That old book fell apart when I picked it up.

ばらばらに持ってこないで，班ごとにまとめて提出してください．
Please don't hand these in one by one. Gather them together by group.

父の転勤と兄の留学で，家族はばらばらになった．
Our family was scattered by my father's transfer and my brother's studies overseas.

皆の意見はばらばらだった．
The views were scattered.
Everyone had different opinions.

みんなの心がばらばらのままでは試合に勝てないぞ．
We can't win this game if we're not together.
If everyone keeps doing his own thing, we're not going to win the game.

突然，ひょうがばらばらと降ってきた
There was a sudden shower of hailstones.

バランス

【体の】平均台の上でバランスをとった．
I steadied myself on the balance beam.

自転車に乗っていてバランスを失い，転んだ．
I lost my balance on the bicycle and fell down.

【数・力の】女の子があと二，三人集まれば，男女のバランスがとれるんだけどな．
We only need two or three more girls to get the right number of girls to boys.

【調和・安定】仕事と遊びのバランスをうまく取りなさい．
You need to strike a balance between work and play.

心身のバランスを保つには，食事と睡眠が大切だ．
Adequate food and sleep are important for a healthy body and mind.

母は栄養のバランスを考えながら食事を作っている．
My mother takes †a balanced diet [nutrition] into consideration when she cooks.

ジャケットの丈が長すぎるせいで，今日の私のファッションは全体的にバランスが悪い．
My outfit looks out of proportion today because the jacket's too long.

彼が加わったことでグループのバランスが崩れた．
The group's unity was destroyed after he joined it.

夫の死により彼女は精神のバランスを崩した．
She fell apart after her husband died.
She became emotionally unbalanced following her husband's death.*

彼女はバランス感覚がいいので，
I don't have to worry about leaving things

安心して物事を任せられる. up to her because she has good judgment.

はりあい (張り合い)

夫の死後, 彼女は生きる張り合いをなくした. She lost interest in life after her husband's death.

こんな安い給料では働く張り合いがない. It's not worth working for wages this low.

相手チームがあまりにも弱すぎて選手たちは張り合いが抜けてしまった. The other team was so weak that it dampened the players' drive to win.

はりあう (張り合う)

その女たちは豪華な衣装で張り合っている. Those women are trying to outdress each other.

あの二人はライバル意識を燃やして, 勉強で張り合っている. Those two are trying to outstudy each other with a keen sense of rivalry.

彼は友人と彼女を巡って張り合った. He and his friend †fought over [competed for] the girl.

この辺りに張り合うように次々と高層ビルが建った. As if in competition, the high-rises went up one after the other in this area.

二人とも, いい加減に意地を張り合うのはよせ. Both of you, stop trying to get your own way.

はりきる (張り切る)

さあ, 張り切って働こう. Let's work hard!

彼女は新しい職場で張り切っている. She's †very much involved in [working hard at] her new job.

あまり張り切りすぎて体を壊すなよ. You shouldn't work so hard. You don't want to get sick.

決勝を明日に控え, 両チームの選手は張り切っている. Both teams are worked up for tomorrow's final game.

はる¹ (張る)

【広げる】今日はここにテントを張ろう. Let's pitch the tent here for today.

その木は根を張って大きくなった. The tree spread its roots and grew.

天井にクモの巣が張っている. There's a spider's web up on the ceiling.

【引っ張る】綱をぴんと張ってください. Stretch the rope taut.

【膨れる】今日は食べ過ぎで腹が張る. My stomach's [I'm] really full after eating so much today.

産後三日目頃から乳が張ってくる. The breasts begin to swell about three days

	after giving birth.
【満たす】水を張った洗面器を持ってきてください.	Bring a wash basin full of water, please.
【覆う】台所にはタイルが張ってある.	The kitchen is tiled.
【氷が】今日は池に氷が張るほど寒かった.	It was so cold today that ice formed on the pond.
【平手で打つ】彼は父親に横っ面を張られた.	He got slapped on the face by his father.
【かさむ】この帽子は値が張る.	This hat is too expensive.
【設ける】野党は論陣を張って政府を非難した.	The opposition parties took a firm stand and criticized the government.

はる² (貼る)

履歴書に必ず写真を貼ってください.	Make sure a photo is attached to your résumé.
アルバムにこの写真を貼ってください.	Paste these pictures in the album, please.
この手紙に切手を貼って出しておいてください.	Put stamps on this letter and send it off.
このポスターを壁に貼って.	Stick [Put] this poster on the wall.

はるか

海のはるか向こうに島が一つ見えている.	Far out in the sea you can see an island.
はるかかなたに人影が見える.	I can see a figure in the distance.
それははるか昔の話だ.	That's a very old story.
航空便のほうが船便よりもはるかに早い.	Air mail is much (much) faster than sea mail.

はれ (晴れ)

【天候】このところ晴れの日が続いている.	The weather's been clear lately.
【明るい】大きな声で歌えば気も晴れるよ.	You'll feel cheerful if you sing in a loud voice.
【無実】彼はようやく晴れの身になった.	He was finally cleared (of the charges).
彼はやっと盗みの疑いが晴れた.	He has finally been cleared of all suspicion of theft.
【晴れがましい】彼は晴れがましい気持ちで卒業式に臨んだ.	He proudly attended the graduation ceremony.
この結婚衣装の晴れ姿を, お父さんにも見せてあげたかった.	If only your father were here to see how beautiful you look in your wedding

dress.

はん (半)

物価は去年の1倍半にもなっている. Prices are one and a half times what they were last year.

ここから空港までは約1時間半かかる. It takes about an hour and a half to get to the airport from here.

このあいだ彼と会ったのは半年前のことだ. The last time I saw him was half a year ago.

彼はその話を半信半疑で聞いていた. He listened to the story, only half believing it.

半病人みたいに顔色がよくないね. You really don't look well.
You look like death warmed over.

このワイシャツは定価の半額で買ったんだ. I bought this shirt at half the regular price.

ばん (番)

【順番】僕らの番を待つあいだ, 本でも読んでいよう. We might as well read something while waiting our turn.

今度は僕の番だよ. I'm next.

新宿はここから3番目の駅です. Shinjuku is the third station from here.

【見張り】みんなが町を見物しているあいだ, 荷物の番をさせられた. While everyone was off sightseeing in the city, I had to watch the baggage.

はんい (範囲)

今回の試験は範囲が広いので準備が大変だ. The next test will cover such a broad range of material that it will be difficult to study for.

パーティーの費用は予算の範囲内で収めてください. Please keep expenses for the party within the limits of the budget.

台風は勢力範囲を広げている. The area that will be affected by the typhoon is growing.

はんかん (反感)

彼女は私に反感を抱いているようだ. She seems to bear [have] ill feelings towards me.

日本製品の海外進出は各国で反感を買っている. The spread of Japanese products on foreign markets is provoking antipathy [hostility] in various countries.

他人の反感をそそるような言動は慎みなさい. Be careful not to behave in a way that will provoke antipathy from others.

はんこう (反抗)

息子は最近，私に反抗するようになった． — Recently, my son has begun to rebel against me.

彼の息子は今反抗期だ． — His son is now going through a period of rebelliousness.

大人への若者の反抗は，大人になるための一種の通過儀礼だ． — Young people's rebellion against grown-ups is one rite of passage for becoming an adult.

彼の前では絶対反抗的な態度は取るなよ． — Don't ever take an antagonistic attitude in front of him.

はんしゃ (反射)

【はね返し】池の水が光を反射してきらきら輝いていた． — Sunlight reflecting off the water made the pond sparkle.

海の深さを測るには，音波の反射を使う方法もある． — Ocean depth can be measured by the reflection of sound waves.

【無意識の反応】バットが飛んできたとき，彼は反射的に身をかわして無事だった． — When the bat came flying at him he instinctively dodged out of the way and wasn't hurt.

パブロフの犬を使った実験は，条件反射を実証した． — Pavlov's experiments with dogs demonstrated the conditioned response [reflex].

はんする (反する)

彼女の発言は事実に反する． — What she says is contrary to the facts.

わざと足をかけるとは，スポーツマンシップに反する行為だ． — Intentionally tripping your opponent is against good sportsmanship.

そんなことは私の主義に反するのでできません． — I can't do that because it would be in contradiction to my principles.

彼の行為は国益に反する． — His actions †are contrary to [go against] the best interests of our nation.

殺人はあらゆる宗教の教えに反する． — Murder violates the spiritual teachings of all religions.

結局，両親の意向に反する道を選んでしまった． — Eventually, I chose a path that went against my parents' wishes.

期待に反して，改装オープン初日の客足はそれほど伸びなかった． — Fewer people than expected turned out for the post-renovations opening.

大方の予想に反して，我がチームは決勝戦まで勝ち進んだ． — Despite all the predictions, our team went on to the finals.

はんせい (反省)

自分のやったことを反省しなさい． — Think over what you did.

私は毎日日記をつけて，一日の反省をしています． — I write in my diary everyday and think over what I did that day.

部長は今回の件で彼に反省を求めた.	His boss asked him to think over carefully what he had done wrong in this matter.
彼には全く反省の色が見られない.	He doesn't seem to have any intention of repenting.
反省しています.	I regret what I've done.

はんたい (反対)

【逆らう】私はあなたの意見に反対です.	I'm opposed to your opinion.
僕たちのクラスではそれに対する反対意見は出なかった.	No one in our class †opposed it [gave an opposing opinion].
なぜ君はいつも僕の言うことに反対するんだ?	Why do you always oppose me?
住民は高速道路の建設に反対している.	The residents are opposed to construction of the expressway.
核兵器に反対する運動が広がっている.	The movement against nuclear weapons is spreading worldwide.
思わぬところから反対の声が上がった.	There was protest from an unexpected source [quarter].
【逆】君の言うことと彼の言うことは全く反対だ.	You are saying exactly the opposite of what he is saying.
彼の乗った自転車が反対側から来た車と危うくぶつかりそうになった.	The bicycle he was riding almost got hit by a car coming from the opposite direction.
アメリカでは日本と反対に車は右側通行だ.	In America, contrary to Japan, people drive on the right-hand side.
ねじを緩めるときは, 時計の針と反対の方向に回しなさい.	To loosen the screw, turn it counter-clockwise.

はんだん (判断)

人を見かけだけで判断してはいけません.	Don't judge people only by their appearance.
彼の山岳パーティーは山の状況判断を誤って遭難した.	His team [party] of mountaineers misjudged the weather conditions and met with disaster.
医者は彼がもう退院できると判断した.	The doctor determined that he could leave the hospital.
海へは電車で行くほうがいいという君の判断は正しかった.	You were [Your decision was] right about going to the beach by train.
その事件については裁判所の判断に委ねられた.	That case was left to the court to decide [judge] on.
この二つのうちどちらがいいかは君の判断に任せます.	I'll leave it up to you to decide between these two.

はんぶん (半分)

リンゴが1個しかないから半分ずつ食べましょう.
I only have one apple, so let's each have half.

これでこの仕事は半分終わった.
We're now half done with this job.

彼の出してくる条件は話半分に聞かなくてはいけない.
The conditions he asks for should be taken †with a grain of salt [only half seriously].

面白半分に彼女をからかっていたら本当に泣き出してしまった.
I was teasing her just for fun, but she took it seriously and started crying.

彼はいたずら半分にたばこを吸ってみたら, やみつきになってしまった.
He tried smoking just for kicks but wound up getting hooked.**

ひ

ひ (日)

【太陽・陽光】雲の合い間から日がさしてきた.
The sun peeked through the clouds.

日の当たる〔当たらない〕場所にいなさい.
Stay †in [out of] the sun.

この部屋はよく日が当たる〔ほとんど日が入らない〕.
This room gets †lots of [very little, almost no] sunlight.[1]

日当たりの良い角地に家を建てた.
We built our house on a corner lot with good sunlight.

タオルは日に当ててよく乾かしなさい.
Dry your towel well in the sun.

日差しがまぶしくて目を細めた.
I squinted in the glare of the sun.

急に日が陰り, 大粒の雨が降ってきた.
It suddenly clouded over and large raindrops began to fall.

渋滞を避けるため, まだ日の高いうちに帰途についた.
I started home early in the day[2] in order to avoid the traffic.

一日中海で泳いでいたら, すっかり日に焼けてしまった.
I got completely suntanned after swimming in the ocean all day.

そろそろ日が暮れる時間だ.
It will soon be sunset.

日が沈み, 急に肌寒くなってきた.
After the sun went down, it suddenly got chilly.

【日中・昼間】初夏を迎え, かなり日が長くなった.
The days have become much longer with the onset of summer.

冬至が近くなり，随分日が短くなってきた．	With the winter solstice drawing near, the days have gotten [grown] much shorter.
【一日・日数】禁煙を誓ってからだいぶ日がたった．	Quite a few days have passed since I vowed to give up smoking.
彼女を知ってから日が浅い．	I haven't known her very long.
この会社で働き始めてからまだ日が浅い．	I'm still a relative newcomer at this company.
小学生の弟が夏休みまでの日を指折り数えている．	My brother in elementary school is counting the days[3] until the summer holidays.
受験までもうあまり日がない．	There aren't too many more days until the entrance exams.
紅葉が日を追って色鮮やかになった．	The color of autumn leaves deepened with each passing day.
ついに開店の日を迎えた．	Opening day was finally here.
雨の日も風の日も休まずに学校に通った．	I went to school in rain and in wind. / Rain or wind never stopped me from going to school. / I never missed a day of school, even when it was rainy or windy.
今日はお忙しそうなので，また日を改めて伺います．	You seem to be busy today so I'll come back another day.
「明日は何の日？」「敬老の日だよ」	"What holiday is tomorrow?" "It's Respect-for-the-Aged Day."
結婚式の日取りを決めましょう．	Let's set the wedding date.
彼は日雇いの仕事をして生計をたてている．	He makes his living as a day laborer.
【時期】君の努力が報われる日がきっとくるよ．	Your efforts are sure to be rewarded some day.
そのことは日を見て私から上司に話すつもりだ．	I'm going to talk to the boss about that at an appropriate time.
このミスが発覚した日には減給だけではすまされまい．	When this mistake is detected it won't be just a matter of a salary cut.
【慣用】彼は日の当たる場所ばかり歩いてきた人だから，僕たちの気持ちなんか分からない．	He doesn't understand †our feelings [where we're coming from] because he's always had a good position [job].
彼は日の当たらない分野でこつこつと研究を続けている．	He's working away at research in an inconspicuous field.
彼は日の目を見ないまま亡くなった．	He died before his work saw the light of day.

---

1) この sunlight は sun でもよい． 2) early in the day はこの場合，「帰るにしては早い時間に」の意． 3) 英語でも「実際に日数を数え

る」場合と，比喩的に「楽しみにして待つ」場合の両方に使える．

ひいき (贔屓)

私はこのレストランをひいきにしている．	This is one of my favorite restaurants.
君のひいきの野球チームはどこですか．	Which is your favorite baseball team?
あの力士にはひいきが多い．	That *sumo* wrestler has many patrons.
ブラウン氏は日本びいきだ．	Mr. Brown is pro-Japan.

ひえる (冷える)

スイカが冷えています．	The watermelon is chilled.
冷えたビールはありますか．	Is there any cold beer?
6月なのに今日は冷えますね．	For June, it sure is cold today.
【関係】あの事件以来，彼らの仲は冷えてしまっている．	Ever since that incident, they've been cool toward each other.
【状態】インフレのため，個人消費は冷えきっている．	Private consumption has cooled due to inflation.

ひがい (被害)

台風で被害を受けた．	We suffered some damage from the typhoon.
昨日の竜巻で大きな被害が出た．	Yesterday's tornado caused a lot of damage.
その会社の倒産で下請け業者は大きな被害を被った．	That company's subcontractors sustained a great loss when it went bankrupt.
盗難の被害にあわないよう注意してください．	Take care not to fall victim to burglary.
その殺人事件の被害者は若い女性だった．	The murder victim was a young woman.

ひかえめ (控え目)

彼は控え目な人だ．	He's low-keyed.
彼女は控え目な話し方をする．	She speaks in a reserved manner.
太るから甘い物は控え目にしておきなさい．	You'll gain weight if you don't go easy on the sweet stuff.

ひかえる (控える)

【減らす・やめる】軽率な発言は控えるべきだ．	We should refrain from making rash comments.
その件についてのコメントは控えさせていただきます．	I would like to reserve comment on that issue.

最近はどこも物騒だから，外出を控えている．	It's so dangerous everywhere these days that I don't go out (as) much anymore.
彼は健康に気をつかって塩分〔アルコール〕を控えている．	He's cut back on salt [alcohol] because he's watching his health.
塩分控え目のメニューもございます．	We also have some low-salt dishes.
【書きとめる】彼の連絡先を手帳に控えた．	I wrote down his contact information in my diary [notebook].
【予定する】来年は引っ越しに出産と，大きな行事が控えている．	We've got some big events coming up next year——a move and a new baby.
選挙を控えて，政治家の地元参りが盛んだ．	With elections coming up, politicians are actively visiting their constituencies.
就職の面接を三日後に控えて，彼は落ち着かない様子だ．	He seems pretty nervous with his job interview coming up in three days.
【待機する】社長の後ろにはいつも秘書が控えている．	The company president is always accompanied by his secretary.[1]
	The president's secretary is always standing by.[2]
時間までこちらで控えていてください．	Please wait here until it's time.
やっと問題を一つ解決したと思ったら，その先にはさらなる問題が控えていた．	Just when I thought I had solved one problem, another one was (waiting) just ahead.

> 1) は「いつも社長に同行している」，2) は「(いつでも社長の用が足せるように) 常に近くで待機している」の意味合い．

ひかく (比較)

同じ重さの水と氷の体積を比較すると氷のほうが大きい．	When you compare the volumes of water and ice of equal weight, ice has the larger volume.
日本の戦後の復旧ぶりはよく西ドイツと比較される．	Japan's post-war recovery is often compared †with West Germany's [to that of West Germany].
東京の人口密度は他の都市とは比較にならないほど高い．	The density of Tokyo's population is so high that it can't even be compared with that of other major cities.
あの店は比較的料理がうまい．	That shop's food is relatively [comparatively] good.
アメリカと比較して，日本は閉鎖社会だと思っている人が多い．	Many people think that Japan is a closed society in comparison with America.

ひがむ (僻む)

彼も旅行に誘わないと，きっとひがむよ．	He'll take offense if we don't invite him on the trip.
息子は，私が妹ばかりをかわいがっているとひがんでいる．	My son is upset about my spending most of my time caring for his younger sister.
彼女の誕生パーティーに誘われなかったのは君だけじゃないんだから，そうひがむなよ．	You're not the only one who wasn't invited to her birthday party, so don't be so sensitive.

ひかる (光る)

稲妻が光った．	There was a flash of lightning.
小川のせせらぎがきらきら光っている．	It's a sparkling little brook.
闇の中で猫の目が光った．	The eyes of a cat flashed in the darkness.
彼女の目にきらりと光るものがあった．	Her eyes glistened with tears.
飛行機から白く光る湖が見えた．	The lake, glistening white, could be seen from the plane.
ズボンがすれて，おしりの所が光ってきた．	The seat of my pants is shiny and worn.
【目立つ】あの野球チームの中では彼がいちばん光っている．	He's the shining star of that baseball team.
あの芝居では彼の演技が特に光っていた．	His performance in that play was outstanding.
	He was the one performer who really shone in that play.

ひかん (悲観)

彼は前途を悲観して自殺した．	He became pessimistic about his future and committed suicide.
受験に失敗したぐらいで，あまり悲観するな．	Don't get so discouraged [disappointed] just because you failed the entrance examination.
彼は何事も悲観的に考えるたちだ．	He takes a pessimistic view of everything.

ひきあげる (引き上・揚げる)

沈没船が海から引き揚げられた．	The sunken ship was raised from the ocean.
穴に落ちた友人をやっとこさ引き揚げた．	We were finally able to pull our friend out of the pit he had fallen into.
クラスの平均点を引き上げるのは難しいだろう．	It will be difficult to pull up the class average.
日銀は公定歩合を引き上げた．	The Bank of Japan raised the official dis-

	count rate.
彼女は社長に目をかけられて今の地位に引き上げられたんだ.	She was promoted to her present position because the boss took her under his wing.
【帰る】さあ,そろそろ引き揚げるとしよう.	Well, it's about time we got on our way.
撮影が終わってロケ隊は引き揚げていった.	The location crew left when the filming was completed.
和平条約が成立して,外国の軍隊は引き揚げた.	The foreign army withdrew after the conditions for peace went into effect.
終戦後,外地から引き揚げてくるのは大変だったに違いない.	It must have been quite an ordeal for many Japanese to †get back to [pick up and return to] Japan after the war.

ひきうける (引き受ける)

あとのことは私が引き受けるから心配するな.	I'll take responsibility for what follows, so rest at ease.
彼がその仕事を引き受けるそうだ.	He's going to undertake the job.
お嬢さんのことは引き受けました.	We'll take care of your daughter.
あの店は自動車の改造を引き受けてくれる.	That shop accepts orders for car-customizing.
私の身元引き受け人はジョーンズ氏です.	Mr. Jones is my sponsor [guarantor].

ひきかえす (引き返す)

飛行機は悪天候のため空港に引き返した.	The plane had to turn back due to inclement weather conditions.
道に迷ったら,元の所まで引き返したほうがいい.	If you lose your way, you should retrace your steps back to where you started.
雨が激しくなったので途中で家に引き返した.	The rain got so heavy [hard] that I turned around and went back home.

ひきょう (卑怯)

卑怯者! 逃げるのか.	Coward! Are you going to run away?
今になって山へ行くのをやめるとは彼は卑怯なやつだ.	He sure is a traitor to decide not to go mountain climbing at this stage of the game.
相手の弱点につけこむのは卑怯だ.	It's pretty low to take advantage of an opponent's weakness.
彼は卑怯な手段を使って試合に勝った.	He used a dirty trick to win the game.

ひく (引く)

【引っぱる】綱引きで懸命に綱を引いた．
We pulled with all our might in the tug of war.

このドアは引いて開けます．
This door pulls open.

この和だんすの小さな扉は横に引いて開けます．
The small doors on this Japanese *tansu* slide open.

【引きつける】その格好では人目を引き過ぎるよ．
That style will draw too much attention.

ロシア文学に引かれる人は多い．
Many people are drawn to Russian literature.

彼女の喪服姿は人々の同情を引いた．
The sight of her dressed in mourning aroused everyone's sympathy.

彼は企業から引く手あまただった．
He was much sought after by the business world.

【導く】横断歩道を渡るときは子どもの手を引いてやりましょう．
You should lead your child by the hand when crossing the street.

エスキモーは犬にそりを引かせる．
The Inuit [Eskimo] have their sleds pulled by dogs.

【減ずる】10引く7は3です．
Ten minus seven is three.
Seven from ten leaves three.

10から7を引くと残りはいくつですか．
What do you get when you subtract seven from ten?

給料から税金を引かれると生活費がやっと残るだけだ．
I have just barely enough left to live on after taxes are taken out of my salary.

【選び出す】意味の分からない言葉は辞書を引きなさい．
If you don't understand the meaning of a word, look it up in the dictionary.

くじを引いても当たったためしがない．
I've never come up a winner in any lottery drawing.

【引用する】過去の例を引くまでもなく，戦争は数多くの悲劇をもたらした．
Without drawing on past examples it is clear that war has been responsible for countless tragedies.

【塗る】フライパンに油を引いてから，いためものをします．
Grease the pan first and then fry the food.

【描く】点Aと点Bを結ぶ線を引きなさい．
Draw a line connecting points A and B.

【引き入れる】携帯電話の普及により家に電話を引く人が減った．
Fewer people have phones installed in their homes now with the increased use of cell phones.

あの山間の村にもようやく電気が引かれた．
Electricity was finally run out to that remote mountain village.

【続く・受け継ぐ】あの事故はその後の彼の人生に尾を引いている．
That accident left its mark on his life.

彼はスラブ人の血を引いている．
He has a little Slavic ancestry.

彼女は父親の血を引いて絵がうまい.	She gets her talent for painting from her father.
【元に戻る】足首のはれも引いたようだ.	The swelling in my ankle seems to have gone down.

ひくい (低い)

彼の背は標準より低い.	He's shorter than average.
あの山は低いから, 私にも登れそうだ.	That mountain is low enough so even I should be able to climb it.
オランダの陸地の約4分の1は海面より低い.	About one quarter of the Netherlands is below sea level.
彼女は鼻が低いので気にしているようだ.	She seems to be upset about having a button nose.
ここは夏でも気温が低く, しのぎ易い.	The low temperatures in summer make it very comfortable here.
エンゲル係数が高いほど, 生活水準は低いと言える.	A high Engel's coefficient implies a low standard of living.
ヨーロッパに比べてアジアの文化水準が低いと思うのは偏見だ.	It's a prejudice to think that Asian culture is inferior to European.
もう少し低い声で話してください.	Please try to speak more quietly.
コントラバスの重く低い音は腹に響く.	The deep notes of the contrabass have a mellow resonance.
彼は本当に低い声が出る.	He really has a deep voice.

ひくつ (卑屈)

卑屈な態度をとるな.	Don't take †a subservient [an obsequious] attitude.
彼は上司の前では, すごく卑屈になる.	He acts so helplessly subservient in front of his superior.
いくら貧しくても, 卑屈な人間にだけはなるな.	No matter how poor you may be, just don't become a subservient person.

びくびく

彼女は秘密がばれないかと, びくびくしている.	She is afraid that her secret will be disclosed.
そんなにびくびくするなよ. 彼はいい人だよ.	Don't be so afraid [scared]. He's a nice guy.
彼は遅刻して先生に怒られはしないかとびくびくしながら, 教室に入ってきた.	He entered the classroom afraid that the teacher might get angry at him for coming late.

ひさしぶり (久しぶり)

やあ, 久しぶりだね.	Well, well! Long time no see. [It's been a

	long time.]
彼らは久しぶりの休日を楽しんだ.	They enjoyed their long-awaited day off.
息子から久しぶりに電話があった.	We had a call from our son for the first time in quite some time.

ひさん (悲惨)

あの悲惨な事故を忘れることはできない.	I can't forget that tragic accident.
難民は悲惨な状況に置かれている.	The refugees have been left in a miserable [wretched] situation.
この映画は原爆の悲惨さを伝えている.	This movie portrays the tragedy inflicted by the atomic bomb.

ひじょう (非常)

シベリアの冬は非常に寒い.	Siberian winters are extremely cold.
彼はその仕事に非常な熱意を持っている.	He has a remarkable zeal for that [his] work.
その時は持ち合わせがなくて非常に困った.	I was really at a loss that time because I didn't bring enough money with me.
非常の時を想定して避難訓練を行った.	We held an evacuation drill which assumed an emergency situation.

ひじょうしき (非常識)

そんなことをするなんて君も非常識だね.	Common sense should tell you that much! You should have more common sense than that!
暴走族の非常識な行動に, この辺りの住民は迷惑している.	The residents in this area are annoyed by the hot-rodders who have no sense of consideration.
葬式に派手な服を着ていくなんて非常識にも程がある.	It's absolutely improper to wear bright, fancy clothes to a funeral.

ひっかかる (引っ掛かる)

【止められる】スカーフが木に引っ掛かった.	My scarf got caught on the tree.
たこが電線に引っ掛かったままだ.	The kite is still caught on the electric wire.
猫ののどに魚の骨が引っ掛かったようだ.	The cat seems to have a fish bone stuck in her throat.
空港の税関で引っ掛かった.	I got stopped at airport customs.
【だまされる】彼は詐欺師にまんまと引っ掛かった.	He was completely taken in by a swindler.
悪徳商法に引っ掛かり, お金をだまし取られた.	I fell for a sales scam and was cheated out of my money.

彼女はいつも悪い男に引っ掛かる.	She always falls for †a rotten guy** [the wrong guy].
【納得できない】彼女のその一言がなぜか心に引っ掛かっている.	For some reason I can't stop thinking about that comment she made.
その差別発言は引っ掛かる. 撤回してください.	I don't like discriminatory remarks. [Discriminatory remarks bother me.] I'd like you to take that back.

びっくり

ああ, びっくりした.	What a surprise [shock]!
びっくりするなよ.	Don't be surprised.
急に知らない人に声をかけられてびっくりした.	I was taken aback when a stranger suddenly called after me.
びっくり仰天するようなニュースが入った.	There was some shocking news.
あの店にはびっくりするような高い値段の品物が並んでいる.	There is a lineup of surprisingly high priced articles in that shop.

ひっこす (引っ越す)

アパートから庭付きの家に引っ越しました.	We moved out of an apartment and into a house with a garden.
彼は引っ越して居所が分からない.	I don't know where he moved to.
引っ越し先の住所を連絡してくださいね.	Please let me know your new address.

ひっこむ (引っ込む)

【へこむ・くぼむ】そのでっぱりは押すと引っ込む.	If you press that bump [bulge], it'll go in.
運動したら少し腹が引っ込んだ.	My stomach got a little flatter after exercising.
【表に出ない】息子は昨日から自分の部屋に引っ込んだままだ.	My son has †been (up)[1] [been cooped up] in his room since yesterday.
あんたには関係ないでしょ. 引っ込んでてよ.	It's none of your business. Keep (your nose) out of this!
スキャンダル後, 彼は田舎に引っ込み, そこで生涯を終えた.	Following the scandal, he †withdrew to [moved back to] the countryside where he spent the rest of his life.
彼の家は表通りから少し引っ込んだところにある.	His house is off the main road.

---

1) up を入れるのは「2階（以上）の自室」の場合.

ひっこめる (引っ込める)

【へこませる】 彼女は鏡に向かってお腹を引っ込めた.
She looked in the mirror and pulled in her stomach.

【後ろへ下げる・しまう】 亀が頭を引っ込めた.
The turtle pulled its head in.

犬になめられて, 女の子は手を引っ込めた.
The girl pulled back her hand after the dog licked it.

(車の) 窓から手〔顔〕を出すんじゃない. 引っ込めろ!
Don't stick your hand [head] out the window! Put it inside!

生ぬるいと言われ, ウエーターはビールを引っ込めた.
The waiter took back the beer after we told him it was warm.

彼の一言で彼女は笑顔を引っ込めた.
One word from him and she stopped smiling.

【撤回する】 批判されると, 彼はすぐにその提案を引っ込めた.
He withdrew that suggestion as soon as he was criticized for it.

組合は, リストラなしを条件に要求を引っ込めた.
The union withdrew its demands on the condition there would be no restructuring.

ひっし (必死)

彼女は二人の子どものために必死に働いた.
She worked hard [desperately] for the sake of her two children.

医師の必死の手当てのかいもなく彼は亡くなった.
The doctor desperately tried to save his life but to no avail.

警察は犯人の乗った車の行方を必死で捜している.
The police are frantically searching for the suspect's car.

ぴったり

【隙間・ずれがない】 隙間風が入って寒いので, 窓はぴったり閉めてください.
There's a chilly draft coming in through the window. Could you please shut it tightly?

ジーンズは体にぴったりしているので好きではない.
I don't like jeans because they fit too tight.

彼は約束どおりぴったり6時に現れた.
He came right at six, as promised.

彼の競馬の予想はぴったり的中した.
His hunch about the horse race was right on the nose.

【似合う】 この色は君にぴったりだ.
This color fits you †perfectly [just right].
This is just the right color for you.

保母さんというのは子ども好きの彼女にはぴったりの職業だ.
Since she likes children, working as a nursery school teacher would be perfect.

ヒット

【殴打】
代打の選手がセンター前にヒットを打った. — The pinch hitter hit the ball into center field.
彼はノーヒットノーランを達成した. — He pitched a no-hit, no-run game.

【成功】
彼は次々とヒット商品を企画した. — He came up with one hit product after another.
彼女の3枚目のシングルがヒットしている. — Her third single is a hit.
カラオケで去年の大ヒット曲を歌った. — I sang last year's big hit song at a *karaoke* club.
ドラマの主題歌がヒットチャートにランクインした. — The theme song for a drama series made the charts.

【検索で】
インターネットで検索したら180件ヒットした. — I found 180 references searching the Internet.

ひっぱる (引っ張る)

【強く引く】
あまり強く引っ張ると糸が切れてしまうよ. — If you pull too hard, the string [thread] will break.
そんなに強く手を引っ張らないでくれ. — Don't tug at my hand like that.

【長くのばす】
語尾を引っ張る癖はやめたほうがいい. — You should take care not to draw out your word endings.

【引き寄せる】
彼は無理やり仲間に引っ張られたんだ. — He was forced into the group against his will.
彼を野球部に引っ張ろう. — Let's try to get him †for [to join] the baseball team.

【連れていく】
彼は万引きをして警察に引っ張られた. — He was hauled off by the police for shoplifting.

ひつよう (必要)

君が説明する必要はない. — There's no need for you to explain.
どうしてもお金が必要なんだ. — I've got to get some money.
卒論を書くのに必要な本を集めているところだ. — Right now I'm gathering the material I need to write my thesis.
あの大学に入るには高い学力が必要だ. — Entering that university requires high scholastic ability.
必要に迫られて英語の勉強をしている. — I'm studying English †out of necessity [because I absolutely have to].
旅行には必要以上の荷物は持っていくべきではない. — You shouldn't take anything unnecessary on a trip.
必要は発明の母である. — Necessity is the mother of invention.

ひどい (酷い)

【残酷】ひどい！
That's awful [terrible].

赤ん坊を置き去りにするなんてひどい親だね．
Abandoning a baby! What an awful parent!

あいつに逆らうとひどい目にあうぞ．
If you don't listen to him, you're going to be in big trouble.

傘を持たずに出かけたら，雨に降られてひどい目にあった．
I had a bad experience when I was caught in the pouring rain without an umbrella.

【激しい】僕はひどい近眼なんだ．
I'm terribly nearsighted.

彼女は風邪をひいて，ひどい熱を出している．
She caught a cold and has †a very bad [an awful] fever.

今日はひどく暑いね．
It's terribly hot today.

台風が近づいているので，風と雨がひどくなってきた．
The wind and rain have gotten much worse with the approaching typhoon.

ひとしい (等しい)

この三角形の二辺の長さは等しい．
Two sides of this triangle †have the same length [are of equal length].

二人の貢献度は等しい．
Their contributions are equivalent.

彼は三人の息子たちに等しく財産を分け与えた．
He divided his estate up evenly among his three sons.

彼の行為は泥棒に等しい．
What he did amounts to theft.

その開店したばかりの店の収入はゼロに等しかった．
That newly opened store's income amounted to practically zero.

ひなた (日なた)

公園で老人が日なたぼっこをしている．
Elderly people are relaxing in the sun in the park.

洗濯物は日なたに干さないと乾きが悪い．
If the laundry is not hung out in the sun, it won't dry properly.

ひなん (非難)

野党はその問題で与党を非難した．
The opposition parties criticized the ruling party over that problem.

公務員による税金のむだづかいが世間の非難を浴びている．
The waste of public funds by government officials is being subjected to criticism.

その大臣の軽率な発言が非難の的になっている．
That cabinet minister's rash statement has become a target of criticism.

ひにく (皮肉)

【当てこすり】それは彼一流の皮肉だからまともにとるな．
It's just his (brand of) sarcasm, so don't take it seriously.

いつも約束の時間に遅れる彼女が今日は珍しく早く来たので皮肉を言ってやった.	Everytime we promise to meet at a certain time she's late, but today she came early for a change so I made a sarcastic remark.
彼は皮肉屋だ.	He's very sarcastic.
【不運な巡り合わせ】彼女が彼を愛していると気づいたときには彼は別の女性にプロポーズしていたとは皮肉だ.	The irony was that just as she realized that she loved him, he had already proposed to someone else.
皮肉にも，試験は山をかけたところからは全く出題されなかった.	Ironically, there wasn't a single question on the exam concerning the material that I thought would be covered.

ひねくれる

彼は苦労してきたけれどひねくれていない.	He hasn't gotten bitter even though he has had some hard times.
彼は結婚に対してひねくれた見方をしている.	He takes a cynical view of marriage.

ひねる

ガスの元栓をひねってくれる？	Could you turn the gas on?
体を左右にひねりなさい.	Twist your body from side to side.
父は困ったときにはひげをひねる.	When my father is perturbed, he twirls [twists] his moustache.
テニスで足首をひねって痛めてしまった.	I twisted and injured my ankle playing tennis.
頭をひねって考えたが，いい考えが浮かばない.	I racked my brains, but couldn't come up with a good idea.
なんとしても今日中にお金をひねり出さなければならない.	I've got to scrape up the money by the end of the day.
あの問題はひねってあった.	That was a tricky problem.
彼とチェスをやったら軽くひねられた.	He made short work of me in our chess match.

ひはん (批判)

彼の意見に対して批判が集中した.	His opinion became the focus of criticism.
正当な批判なら喜んで受けます.	If it's justifiable criticism, I will gladly take it.
彼は人を批判してばかりいる.	He's always criticizing people.
それは私の専門外なので批判できない.	That's †not in [out of] my field, so I can't criticize it.
彼はその考え方に対しては批判的だ.	He is critical of that way of thinking.

ひびく（響く）

彼の声はよく響く. — His voice is resonant.

トンネルの中で大声を出すとよく響く. — Your voice will really reverberate if you shout inside a tunnel.

古時計が時を刻む音が暗闇に響いていた. — The sound of the old clock ticking away the time reverberated in the dark.

飛行機の爆音が腹に響く. — I could feel the rumble of the airplane in my stomach.

寝不足が響いて今日は体調が良くない. — The lack of sleep is affecting me. I'm not in good shape at all today.

税金が上がると家計に響くから，みんな反対している. — Everyone is opposed to a raise in taxes because of the impact it would have on household budgets.

ひひょう（批評）

月曜日の朝刊にはいつも新刊書の批評が出る. — There's a review of recently published books in the morning edition of the paper every Monday.

専門家の批評をみると，彼の新作はなかなかのもののようだ. — According to the critiques I've read, his latest work is superb.

その絵は批評家のあいだであまり評価されなかった. — That painting was not very well received by critics.

彼の批評眼は鋭い. — He has a sharp, critical eye.

ひま（暇）

【時間】遊ぶ暇があったら勉強しなさい. — There's no time to play. Study.

仕事が忙しくて寝る暇もない. — I'm so busy with work that I've no time for sleep.

彼に仕事をやらせると暇がかかる. — It would take too much time if he did the job.

【手の空いている時間】明日の夜は暇ですか. — Are you free tomorrow night?

最近，暇を見つけては友人に手紙を書いています. — Recently I've been finding some time to write to my friends.

夏休みになれば暇ができるので，少し本を読みたい. — I'll have free time during my summer vacation, so I want to read a little then.

暇つぶしにゲームでもしよう. — Let's kill some time by playing a game or something.

退職した父は暇を持て余している. — Now that my father's retired, he has too much time on his hands.

君も暇な男だね. — You sure have a lot of free time.

大学が休みなので，この辺りの店 — The university is on vacation so the stores

はどこも暇です. | around here are empty.
【休み】今度暇をもらって旅行に行こうと思っている. | I'm planning to take some time off and go on a trip.
【解雇】彼は理由も分からないまま暇を出された. | He was †let go [fired] without a word of explanation.

ひみつ (秘密)

このことは秘密にしておいてくれ. | Keep this a secret.
だれかがその秘密を漏らしたんだ. | Someone let that secret out.
彼は僕にだけ秘密を打ち明けてくれた. | He revealed [confessed] his secret only to me.
他人の秘密に深入りすべきではない. | You shouldn't get too engrossed with other people's private matters.
二人のあいだに秘密の誓約が交わされた. | The two of them pledged an oath of secrecy.
インカ帝国は今でも秘密のベールに包まれている. | There is still a veil of mystery covering the Inca Empire.
その清涼飲料水の成分は企業秘密にされている. | Ingredients for that soft drink are kept a company secret.
事は秘密に運ばれた. | It was carried out in secret.

びみょう (微妙)

【断言を許さない】彼が合格するかどうかは微妙だ. | It's a little difficult to say whether he will pass or not.
どちらを選ぶかとなると微妙なところだ. | It is a delicate point as to which one to choose.
その事件で彼は微妙な立場に立たされた. | That incident put him in a delicate position.
微妙な問題だから専門家に相談しよう. | This is a ticklish problem. Let's consult an expert.
【かすか】彼らの証言には微妙な食い違いが見られた. | There was a subtle difference in their testimonies.
結婚を目前にして気持ちが微妙に揺れ動いている. | As the marriage approaches, I'm finding myself wavering a bit.

ひやかす (冷やかす)

彼らは新婚さんを冷やかした. | They teased the newlyweds.
髪を短く切って学校へ行ったら, みんなに冷やかされた. | When I went to school, I was teased for having such a short hair cut.
彼女が働いているケーキ屋へ彼と冷やかしに行った. | He and I went to the cake shop where she works to †joke around with [tease] her.

ひやす (冷やす)

このスイカを冷蔵庫で冷やしておいてくれ. — Chill this watermelon in the refrigerator.

やけどしたときにはすぐ水で冷やすことが大切です. — If you get a burn, it's important to cool it in water right away.

ビールは冷やし過ぎるとうまくない. — Beer isn't very good if it's too chilled.

頭を冷やして出直して来い. — Come back when you've cooled off.

乗っていたタクシーがぶつかりそうになって肝を冷やした. — I had a terrible scare when the taxi I was in almost hit another car.

ひよう (費用)

彼女は毎月アメリカ旅行の費用を積み立てている. — She's putting aside some money every month for her trip to America.

この部屋の家具には相当費用がかかっているね. — The furniture in this room must have been quite expensive.

彼はこの事業に莫大な費用をつぎ込んでいる. — He's putting a tremendous amount of money into this project.

ビルの建設が長引き, 費用がかさんでいる. — Construction of that building has been delayed and expenses are piling up.

ひょうか (評価)

人を試験の点数だけで評価してはいけない. — You shouldn't judge a person only by his test marks.

彼の業績は外国で高く評価されている. — His work is viewed [rated] highly abroad.

あの作曲家は日本では過大評価されている. — That composer is †overrated [overly praised] in Japan.

この辺りの土地の評価額は日本一です. — The property value in this area is the highest in Japan.

びょうき (病気)

父は病気で寝ています. — Father is sick in bed.

彼は無理がたたってとうとう病気になってしまった. — His overwork led to his becoming ill.

彼の病気が重くなければいいのだが. — I hope his illness isn't serious.

彼女の病気はだんだん良くなってきている. — She's gradually †getting better [recovering from her illness]. She's on the mend.

やっと病気が全快しました. — I have finally completely recovered from my illness.

人間は動物にはない心の病気にか — People are subject to emotional disorders

かることがある.	that don't occur in animals.
カーマニアもあそこまで行くと病気だね.	He's †gone too far [gone overboard] with his car mania.

ひょうげん (表現)

このピアノ曲は人間の苦悩を表現している.	This piano piece expresses human sufferings.
あの時の感動は言葉では表現できません.	I can't express in words how moved I was at that time.
この一節は比喩を使った表現です.	This passage is metaphorical.
この表現はあまり適切じゃないね.	This expression isn't appropriate, is it?
彼があまりオーバーな表現をするので笑ってしまった.	He used such overblown expressions that I broke out laughing.
表現の自由について裁判で争われている.	Freedom of expression is being fought over in court.

ひょうじゅん (標準)

私の体重は標準より少し重い.	My weight is a little above †what it should be [the standard].
この本は高校生を標準として書かれている.	This book is written at a level for high school students.
試験は標準的な問題がほとんどだった.	The test had mostly standard questions.

ひょうじょう (表情)

やっと退院できた母は,晴れやかな表情をしていた.	My mother beamed as she finally left the hospital.
父は孫を見て表情をくずした.	My father's expression softened when he saw his grandchild.
辞表を出す彼の表情は硬かった.	He had a serious look on his face as he submitted his resignation.
彼女は夫のちょっとした表情の変化もすぐに読み取る.	She can read the slightest change in her husband's facial expression.
父親が自殺してから,友人は表情を失った.	Since his father committed suicide my friend's face has been expressionless.
残虐なシーンを見せられても,彼は全く無表情だった.	He remained expressionless even after being shown scenes of atrocities.
あのモデルはとても表情豊かだ〔表情に乏しい〕.	That model is †very expressive [expressionless].
彼女のバレエの演技は非常に表情豊かだ.	Her ballet performance is very expressive.
この街は季節によって表情を変える.	This city looks different depending on the season.

ひょうばん (評判)

あれが今評判の車だ.	That's the car everyone's talking about.
あの店は評判が悪い.	That shop has a bad name [reputation].
新しい先生は生徒たちに評判が良い.	The new teacher has a good reputation among the students.
その新入社員の猛烈ぶりは社内でも評判になった.	That new employee's fiery enthusiasm has become famous within the company.
二人の関係は町中の評判になっている.	The relationship between those two is becoming the talk of the town.
彼は非常な資産家だという評判が立った.	He earned a reputation of being an extremely wealthy man.
彼の奥さんはすごい美人だという評判だ.	His wife is reputed to be quite a beauty.
粗悪品を製造して, あの会社の評判は落ちた.	That company damaged its reputation by producing inferior goods.

ひょうめん (表面)

太陽の表面の温度は約6,000度である.	The temperature of the sun's surface is 6,000 degrees.
内部の対立が表面に出るのはまずい.	Internal confrontation shouldn't be allowed to surface.
表面だけを繕うような人は, 人に好かれない.	A superficial person is not well liked by others.
彼は表面はとっつきにくそうだが, 本当は気さくな人間だ.	His outward bearing gives one the impression that he is difficult to approach, but actually he is quite congenial.

ひらく (開く)

【開ける】包みを開くと, 中に指輪が入っていた.	When I opened the package, I found a ring inside.
北国では遅い春が来ると花々が一斉に開きます.	When spring finally comes to the north, all the flowers open [bloom] in unison.
彼は口を開けばぐちばかり言う.	When he opens his mouth, it's only to complain.
もっと心を開いて彼と友達付き合いをするようにしなさい.	Be more open-hearted and treat him like a friend.
【催す】明日から国会〔ピカソ展〕が開かれる.	The Diet 〔The Picasso exhibition〕 will open tomorrow.
彼の成功を祝ってパーティーが開かれた.	To celebrate his success, a party was thrown [given, held].
【始める】今度銀座に事務所を開きました.	We †opened [set up] a new office in Ginza.
遺伝子治療の発展により, 医療の	The development of gene therapy promises

新時代が開かれることになる.	to usher in a new era in medicine.
【開拓する】移住者たちは荒地を切り開いて畑を作った.	The settlers cleared the wilderness for farming.
彼には運命を自分の手で切り開こうという気概がある.	He is spirited enough to try to forge his own destiny.
【離す】点数が開きすぎてゲームがつまらなくなった.	The score was so lopsided that the game was no longer interesting.
トップランナーは2位との距離をじりじりと開いていった.	The top runner built up a lead little by little over the closest challenger.
【コンピュータ】このファイルを開くには専用のアプリケーションソフトが必要です.	You need a special application to open this file.

ひらたい (平たい)

【平ら】テントを張るために平たい場所を捜した.	We looked for a level place to pitch our tent.
この平たい石に腰をおろして少し休みましょう.	Let's sit down on this flat rock and take a breather.
これは鉄を打って平たくする機械です.	This is a machine that pounds steel flat.
【平易】素人にも分かるように平たく説明してください.	Please make your explanation simple enough so (that) even an amateur will be able to understand it.
平たく言えば彼女が好きなんだろう?	In plain [simple] English, you love her, don't you?

ひるむ

謝りに行ったが, ドアの所でひるんでしまった.	I went to apologize but †got cold feet [chickened out] at the door.
彼は挑戦者の勢いに一瞬ひるんだ.	He was momentarily intimidated by the intensity of the challenger's attack.
彼はどんな強敵を相手にしても全くひるむ気配を見せなかった.	He appeared completely undaunted even in the face of the strongest enemy.

ひろい (広い)

関東平野は日本でいちばん広い平野である.	The Kanto Plain is Japan's largest.
富士山のすそ野はとても広い.	The plain at the foot of Mt. Fuji is quite vast.
揚子江の広さに日本人は驚かされる.	Japanese are quite amazed at the breadth of the Yangtze River.
彼は歩幅が広く, 歩くのが速い.	He has a long stride so he walks swiftly.
我々はこの問題を広い角度から検	We're looking at this problem from a

討している.

彼は電子工学について広い知識をもっている. — He has an extensive background in electronic engineering.

ひろう¹ (拾う)

彼女は注意深くガラスのかけらを拾った. — She picked up the pieces of broken glass with extreme caution.

道で財布を拾いました. — I found a wallet on the street.

この通りはなかなかタクシーが拾えない. — It's really hard to get a taxi on this street.

ひろう² (疲労)

彼は疲労が重なって，病気になってしまった. — An excess of fatigue resulted in his becoming ill.

仕事のし過ぎで疲労を覚えた. — He felt worn-out from overwork.

長時間車内に閉じ込められている乗客たちは疲労の色が濃い. — The passengers who have been shut up inside the train for so long look exhausted.

ひろがる (広がる)

発疹が体中に広がってしまった. — The rash spread over my entire body.

頂上に着くと眼下に素晴らしい景色が広がっていた. — Having reached the summit, a marvelous scene spread out beneath me.

伝染病はあっという間に町中に広がった. — A contagious disease spread through the town like wildfire.

悪いうわさはすぐに広がるものだ. — Bad rumors tend to spread rapidly.

彼女はすその広がったスカートをはいている. — She's wearing a skirt with a wide hem.

反戦運動は全国的な広がりを見せている. — The anti-war movement is spreading [expanding] nationwide.

ひろげる (広げる)

先生は大きな世界地図を広げた. — The teacher †rolled out [unfolded, pulled down]¹⁾ a large map of the world.

彼は列車が動き始めると弁当を広げた. — He opened his lunch when the train began to pull out.

ラッシュの時はとても新聞を広げて読むことはできません. — It's impossible to open the paper to read during rush hour.

ハクトウワシが翼を広げると2メートルはある. — When the bald eagle spreads its wings, they span two meters in breadth.

都市計画で道路が広げられた. — The roads were enlarged as a result of city planning.

過去の多くの戦争は領土を広げる — Most past wars were fought to acquire

ために戦われた.	new territory.
近々彼は店を広げるらしい.	I hear he's planning to expand the store in the near future.

> 1) roll out は巻かれたものを，unfold は折り畳んであるものを，pull down はロールスクリーン状のものを下に広げる場合に使う．

ひろまる (広まる)

社内に変なうわさが広まっている.	A strange rumor is circulating [floating] through the company.
彼の名は日ごとに広まっている.	His fame is growing daily.
核戦争の危険性に対する認識は各国に広まっている.	Awareness of the dangers of nuclear war is spreading to every country.

ひん (品)

彼女はとても品のいい人です.	She is a very elegant woman.
彼女はいつも品のいい服を着ている.	She's always elegantly dressed.
生まれがいいだけあって，彼は言葉遣いに品がある.	His refined speech is characteristic of his noble birth.
品の悪いことばかり言っていると人に嫌われますよ.	People won't take kindly to you if you persist in using such coarse [vulgar] language.

びんかん (敏感)

彼女はファッションに敏感だ.	She's very aware of fashion. She's very fashion-conscious.
この煙探知機は煙に対して非常に敏感に反応します.	This smoke alarm is extremely sensitive to smoke.
彼は寒さにとても敏感だ.	He's very sensitive to cold weather.
動物は一般に音に対して敏感です.	Animals are generally very sensitive to sound.

ひんじゃく (貧弱)

彼に比べると僕の体格は貧弱です.	Compared with him, I look like a weakling.
華やかに着飾った彼女の前では，私の服装も貧弱に見える.	I look (pretty) shabby next to that woman dressed up in fancy clothes.
この町のスポーツ施設は貧弱だ.	The sports facilities in this city are very poor [bad, limited].
私の生物学の知識は貧弱なものです.	I have very little knowledge of biology. My knowledge of biology is poor.
あの代議士の演説は貧弱な内容の	The content of the speech given by that

ものだった. Dietman was very poor.
There was very little content in the speech given by that Dietman.

ヒント
「難しいクイズだなあ. ヒントを出してよ」「じゃあ, 一つヒントをあげるよ」 "What a hard quiz. Can you give me a hint?" "Okay, I'll give you one hint."

そのセミナーで, 苦境を脱け出すための重要なヒントを得た. I got an important hint on how to get out of this predicament at the seminar.

居酒屋でのたわいのない会話が, 新商品開発のヒントになった. I got an idea for a new product from a casual [frivolous] conversation at a bar.

ピンとくる
刑事は犯行の手口を見て, ピンとくるものがあった. Something †clicked in [came to] the detective's mind after he examined the method employed in the crime.

母の応対を聞いて, だれからの電話かピンときた. I could tell who was on the other end of the line from the way my mother spoke on the phone.

父の戦争中の話は, まだ生まれてなかった私にはどうもピンとこない. Since I was born after the war, I have a hard time relating to my father's war stories.

びんぼう (貧乏)
彼女は貧乏したことがない. She's never been poor.
彼は家が貧乏で大学へ行けなかった. His family couldn't afford to send him to college.
貧乏をしていても心までは貧しくなりたくない. Even if I'm poor, I don't want to become petty.
父は家族にだけは貧乏させたくないと懸命に働いた. My father worked as hard as he did so our family wouldn't have to live in poverty.

ふ

ぶあいそう (無愛想)
あの女の子は美人だけど無愛想だ. That girl may be pretty but she's not very friendly.

彼は一見無愛想だけど, 話してみると面白いやつだよ.	He looks unfriendly at first but when you talk to him, you'll find he's an interesting guy.
あの店の主人は無愛想だが料理の腕前はいい.	The owner of the restaurant is a little gruff but he is a good cook.
彼女を映画に誘ったけど無愛想に断られた.	I asked her out to see a movie but she turned me down cold [flat].

ファイル

ファイルを電車の中に置き忘れた.	I forgot the file in the train.
その件に関する新聞や雑誌の記事をファイルした.	I filed the newspaper clippings and magazine articles on that incident.
これらの書類を顧客別にファイルしてくれ.	Please file these documents under the client name.
【コンピュータ】ファイルには一目で分かる名前をつけなさい.	Please title these files so that they can be identified at a glance.
ウィンドウズとマックではファイル形式が違うことがある.	The file formats for Windows and Macintosh can differ.

ふあん (不安)

初めての外国旅行なので少し不安です.	I'm a little uneasy [apprehensive] since this is my first trip abroad.
彼女一人にその仕事を任せるのは少し不安だ.	I feel a little uneasy leaving the job completely up to her.
この計画には一つだけ不安な点が残っている.	There's still one point in this plan that I'm uneasy about.
集中豪雨で住民は不安な一夜を過ごした.	The residents were nervous all night because of the heavy rainfall.
彼は病弱な息子の将来を不安に思っている.	He's concerned about the future of his son who often gets ill.
彼は毎日, 不安の念にさいなまれている.	He is beset by anxiety every day.* He's always full of anxiety.
その国は政情不安で揺れている.	The political situation in that country is unstable.
彼は周囲の不安を吹き飛ばすような素晴らしいピッチングをした.	He pitched such a great game that it dispelled everyone's uneasiness.

ふい (不意)

彼女は不意の来客で慌てた.	She became flustered by an unexpected visitor.
不意に先生に当てられてとまどった.	I was caught off guard when my teacher called on me.
不意に目まいを覚えて倒れた.	I suddenly became dizzy and fell down.

彼らは相手チームの不意を突いて攻撃した.	They launched a surprise attack against the opposing team.
不意を突かれて何と言っていいのか分からなかった.	Taken by surprise, I hardly knew what to say.

ふう (風)

【具合・様子】僕にはとてもあんなふうに上手に書けない.	It's practically impossible for me to write as well as that.
こういうふうに構えるとボールがうまく打てるんだ.	If you hold your stance like this, you'll be able to meet the ball much better.
ズボンの破れに気がつかないふうなので,彼に注意してあげた.	He didn't seem to notice the tear in his pants, so I told him about it.
【接尾語】家内は西洋風の料理が得意です.	My wife excels at cooking Western style food.
やくざ風の連中が道を歩いて行った.	Some gangster [hoodlum] types were walking down the street.

ふうけい (風景)

私は雪国の風景が好きだ.	I'm fond of the scenery in the snow country.
列車は美しい田園風景の中を走った.	The train passed through a lovely rural setting.
私はその一家団らんの風景を見て心が温まった.	Seeing them together at home as a family was a heartwarming experience.
彼は風景画を多く描いている.	He has painted quite a few landscapes.
今日は外で,風景を写生しましょう.	Why don't we go outdoors and do some landscape sketches today?

ふうぞく (風俗)

地方の風俗にはとても変わったものがあります.	Some of the local customs are quite unusual.
若者たちは常に風俗の先端を行こうとする.	Young people are always trying to keep up with the latest fads [crazes, fashions].
飲み屋が増えて,この町の風俗も乱れてしまった.	An increase in the number of bars has disrupted the †morals [way of life] of this town.
祖母は男女間の風俗が乱れていると嘆いている.	Grandmother complains about the decline in sexual morality [mores].

ブーム

今,日帰り温泉旅行がブームだ.	Going to the hot springs for a day is all the rage now.
世の中のブームをつくっている仕	There are certain people who bring about

掛け人がいる.	new fads.
国じゅうがサッカーブームに沸いている.	The soccer boom has hit the whole country.
カフェブームに乗って，店を3店舗増やした.	Taking advantage of the boom in coffee shops, [With coffee shops booming,] we opened three more outlets [shops].
彼女は第2次ベビーブーム世代だ.	She belongs to the second baby-boom generation.

ふうん (不運)

彼はたび重なる不運に耐えた.	He bore up under a series of misfortunes.
不運にも彼はあの飛行機に乗り合わせていた.	By ill fortune, he just happened to take that plane.
彼の打球は不運にもショートの真正面に飛んだ.	Unluckily [Unfortunately], the ball he hit went straight at [to] the shortstop.
今年は病気にけがと不運なことが続いた.	This year was an unlucky year for me. First I was sick, and then I got injured.

ふえる (増・殖える)

世界の人口は年々増え続けている.	The world's population is steadily increasing [growing] year by year.
最近,体重が増えて困っています.	I've been concerned about gaining weight lately.
今年は飲酒運転による交通事故が増えている.	The number of car accidents due to drunk driving has increased this year.
この頃ゴキブリが増えたので,殺虫剤を買ってこなくては.	There're a lot more cockroaches lately. I've got to buy a can of insecticide.
シダ類は胞子によって殖える.	Ferns multiply by spore reproduction.

フォルダ

【コンピュータ】よく使うフォルダはデスクトップに置いている.	Frequently used folders are put on the desktop.
フォルダの中がいっぱいになってきた. 整理しなければ.	I'd better sort out my folder because I have too many files in it.
いくつかのファイルをまとめて一つのフォルダに入れた.	I put a number of files into one folder.

ふかい (深い)

この鍋は深いからたくさん入る.	This pot is deep enough to hold a lot.
いつの間にか山奥深く迷い込んでいた.	Before I knew it, I found myself lost deep in the mountains.
彼は深い眠りに落ちた.	He fell into a deep sleep.
彼女は深い悲しみに襲われた.	She was overcome with profound [deep]

	sorrow.
深い考えがあって彼はそう決めたに違いない.	I'm sure he had a very good reason for that decision.
彼は美術に対する造詣が深い.	He's well versed in art.
	He has a profound knowledge of art.
私は彼に深く感謝した.	I thanked him from the bottom of my heart.
彼は彫りの深い顔をしている.	His face is very well-defined.
ロンドンは霧が深いことで知られている.	London is known for its thick fog.
8月の森は深い緑に包まれていた.	In August, the forest was covered in a luxuriant [deep] green.
二人は深い仲になった.	They('ve) developed a deep relationship.
彼はその事件に深いかかわりを持っている.	He has a deep involvement in that incident.

ぶかっこう (不格好)

そのトマトは不格好だけど, とてもおいしいよ.	That tomato looks strange but it's delicious.
彼のテニスのフォームは不格好だ.	He looks clumsy when he plays tennis.
この背広はちょっと不格好だ.	This suit is a little funny-looking.
彼はがに股のせいか, 歩き方が不格好だ.	I don't know whether it's because he's bow-legged or not but he sure walks funny.

ふかのう (不可能)

いい引きがあれば, 出世するのも不可能ではない.	If you have pull, it is not impossible to get ahead.
この仕事を今日中に終わらせるのはほとんど不可能だ.	It's unlikely that we'll †get this job done [finish this job] by today.
もうビートルズの再結成も実現不可能となった.	Now it has become impossible for the Beatles to get back together.

ふきげん (不機嫌)

彼は今日とても不機嫌だから, 話しかけない方がいいよ.	He's in a bad mood, so you'd be better off not talking to him.
彼はいつも不機嫌そうな顔をしている.	He always looks grouchy.
	He always looks like he's in a bad mood.
彼女は自分の思うとおりにならないと不機嫌になる.	It puts her in a bad mood [Her nose gets out of joint] when she doesn't get her own way.
不機嫌で口もろくろくきかない人と食事をするのは不愉快だ.	It's unpleasant to have a meal with an ill-humored person who can't even make

decent conversation.

ふきつ (不吉)

13日の金曜日は不吉な日だと言われる.	Friday the 13th is said to be an unlucky day.
あの日は朝から何だか不吉な予感がしていたんだ.	I had sort of an ominous premonition from the morning that day.
ゆうべ, 不吉な夢を見た.	I had †an ominous [a bad] dream last night.
彼は別れ際に不吉なことを言った.	He made an ominous remark when he left.

ぶきみ (不・無気味)

森の中は昼でも暗く不気味だった.	The forest was dark and eerie even in the middle of the afternoon.
湖は不気味に静まり返っていた.	The lake was eerily silent.
台風が日本に向かって不気味な動きを示している.	The typhoon is ominously moving in the direction of Japan.

ふきゅう (普及)

パソコンは今では日本のほとんどの学校に普及している.	Personal computers are now found in almost all the schools in Japan.
彼は教育の普及に功績を残した.	He made some noted contributions to the spread of education.
テレビは標準語の普及に大きな役割を果たしてきた.	Television has played an important part in propagating the use of standard speech.
彼は種痘の普及に努力した.	He worked hard in promoting the practice of vaccination.

ぶきよう (不器用)

僕は生まれつき手先が不器用なんです.	I have never been skillful with my hands.
彼は不器用な手つきで, リンゴの皮をむいている.	He's clumsily peeling an apple.
私は不器用だから, 刺しゅうのような細かいことはできない.	I'm not very good with my hands, so I couldn't do anything as meticulous [detailed] as embroidery.

ふきん (付近)

警察は現場付近一帯を捜査した.	The police made a thorough investigation in and around the scene of the crime.
この付近に泊まる所はないでしょうか.	Isn't there any place around here where we can stay for the night?
東京付近に一戸建ての家を建てる	It's very expensive to build a house in the

には大変金がかかる.	Tokyo area.
うちの付近にはお店が一軒もない.	There's not a single store anywhere in my neighborhood.

ふく¹（吹く）

今日は全然風が吹かないので蒸し暑い.	It's certainly muggy today. There's no wind at all.
今日は強い風が吹いている.	It's quite gusty today.
彼は熱いお茶をフーフー吹きながら飲んだ.	He blew on the hot tea as he drank it.
彼はろうそくの火を吹き消した.	He blew out the candle.
彼はトランペット〔口笛〕を吹くのがうまい.	He †plays the trumpet 〔whistles〕 well.
彼は政界に新風を吹き込んだ.	He brought a breath of fresh air to politics.

ふく²（拭く）

今朝は窓をきれいに拭きました.	I wiped the windows clean this morning.
このハンカチで汗を拭きなさい.	Here, take this handkerchief and wipe off that sweat.
夕食の前にテーブルを拭きなさい.	Please wipe off the table before dinner.

ふくざつ（複雑）

複雑な計算問題を片付けてほっとした.	It was a relief to get that complicated calculation solved.
これには複雑な事情があるんだ.	There are certain complications involved in this.
人生は時として複雑なものだ.	Life can be quite complex at times.
彼の話を聞いて私は複雑な気持ちになった.	My feelings became very complicated after listening to him.

ふくしゅう（復習）

彼女は今日のバイオリンのレッスンを復習しています.	She's going over today's violin lesson.
毎日, 学校で習ったことを復習すれば成績が上がります.	If you review your school lessons daily, you'll be able to improve your grades.

ふくそう（服装）

今日の会にはどんな服装がいいかしら.	I wonder what I should wear to today's party.
服装で人の価値を判断するのはよくない.	I don't think people should be judged by their appearance.
日本人の服装はほとんど洋風化さ	Japanese clothing has been almost com-

ふくむ (含む)

女性を含む5人のパーティーが遭難した. — The party of five men and women met with a mishap.

レモンにはビタミンCがたくさん含まれている. — Lemons contain a lot of vitamin C.

この費用には交通費は含まれていません. — These costs don't include transportation.

【心にとめる】このことをよくお含みおきください. — I hope you'll †take this to heart [bear this in mind].

彼の言ったことは何か含むところがあるように思える. — It's struck me that he was trying to imply something by what he said.

ふくらむ (膨らむ)

この風船を膨らましてよ. — Blow up this balloon.

あの子はおたふく風邪で, 別人みたいに顔が膨らんじゃった. — That kid has the mumps. His cheeks are so puffed out that he looks like someone else altogether.

少年の胸は希望に膨らんだ. — The young boy was filled with hope.

春が近づき, 木の芽が膨らみ始めた. — With spring just around the corner, the buds on the trees are starting to get bigger.

なぜ君のポケットはそんなに膨らんでいるんだ? — Why are your pockets bulging so much?

ふくれる (膨れる)

パンを焼くとおいしそうに膨れ上がる. — Baking bread looks delicious as [when] it's rising.

虫に刺されたところが膨れてきた. — I'm swelling up where I got bit by the bug.

もうおなかが膨れて食べられない. — I'm so full (that) I can't take another bite.

子どもたちは動物園へ連れて行ってもらえなくなって膨れている. — The children are pouting because I didn't take them to the zoo.

そんな膨れっ面をするのはやめなさい. — Stop that [your] sulking.

借金が雪だるまのように膨れ上がっていった. — The interest on my loan snowballed.

ふけいき (不景気)

不景気のせいで, このところ注文がさっぱりだ. — With the recession [depression] we haven't had any orders lately.

不景気になると自殺者が増える. — Suicides increase as times get tougher.

今, この業界は不景気だ. — This industry is in a slump now.

	Business is bad [poor, slow, slack, off] in this industry now.
今やどこへ行っても不景気な話しか聞こえてこない.	No matter who you talk to these days all you hear about is how slow business is.
【表情が冴えない】どうした, 不景気な面して?	You look a little down. Are you OK?

ふけつ (不潔)

そんな不潔な手で目をこすってはいけません.	Don't rub your eyes with such filthy [dirty] hands.
台所を不潔にしておくとゴキブリが出ますよ.	You're going to get cockroaches if you don't keep the kitchen clean [sanitary].
そんな不潔な関係は許せない.	I cannot allow such an indecent relationship.

ふける (耽ける)

彼は賭け事にふけって身を滅ぼした.	His overindulgence in gambling was the ruin of him.
彼は瞑想〔思案〕にふけっている.	He is lost (deep) in meditation [thought].
昨日は夜遅くまで推理小説に読みふけった.	Yesterday, I was completely immersed in a detective story until late at night.

ふこう (不幸)

彼は不幸な少年時代を送った.	He had a miserable childhood.
彼女は不幸にして, 子どもの時に父を亡くした.	It was unfortunate that her father died when she was a child.
不幸にも彼の乗った飛行機が墜落した.	Tragically enough, the plane he was in crashed.
台風で家は流されたが, けが人が出なかったのは不幸中の幸いだった.	The typhoon swept the houses away but luckily there were no injuries.
親戚に不幸があったので, 明日は休みます.	A relative has died and I won't be coming in tomorrow.

ふこうへい (不公平)

同じ仕事をしているのに, 彼のほうが給料がいいのは不公平だ.	It is unfair that he is paid better, even though we do the same work.
彼にだけ知らせないのは不公平だ.	It's not fair to leave only him in the dark.
不公平税制に対する国民の不満は大きい.	The citizens are quite dissatisfied with the unfair tax system.

ふさぐ (塞ぐ)

垣根の穴を早くふさがないと野良	If that hole in the fence isn't fixed soon,

猫が入ってくる.	stray cats will get in.
故障したトラックが道をふさいでいるので通れない.	There's a disabled truck blocking the road and traffic can't get through.
彼は, 傷口がふさがったのでもう大丈夫です.	He should be all right now that his wounds have closed [mended].
【気持ちが】彼は何か心配事でもあるのか今日はふさいでいる.	He seems down in the mouth [dumps] today. I wonder if there's something troubling him.

ふざける

彼はよく授業中にふざけては, 先生に叱られていた.	The teacher often scolded him for fooling around in class.
ふざけないで私の質問にまじめに答えなさい.	Stop your nonsense, look (at) me straight in the face and answer my question!
プールでは子どもたちがふざけて遊んでいる.	The children are romping about together in the pool.
ふざけて先生の真似をしていたら本人が現れた.	The teacher appeared just as I was mimicking him for fun.
ふざけるな!	Don't be ridiculous!／Stop fooling around!

ふさわしい

彼はその地位にふさわしい人だ.	He is the right man for the position.
このたぐいの本は子どもが読むのにふさわしくない.	This kind of book is not appropriate for children to read.
この絵があの部屋にふさわしいと思う.	I think this picture is suitable for that room.
会社に行くのにそんな派手な服装はふさわしくない.	It's not appropriate to wear that gaudy outfit to work.
君にふさわしい女性を紹介してあげよう.	Let me introduce you to a girl just right for you.

ふし (節)

【継ぎ目・節目】風邪をひいて体の節々が痛む.	I have a cold and my joints ache.
竹の節をくり抜いて笛を作った.	I hollowed out the joints of the bamboo to make a whistle.
この板には節が多い.	This board is very knotty.／There are many knots in this board.
こんなことに気がつかないなんて君の目は節穴か.	You must be blind not realizing something like this.
【歌や話し方の調子】彼は変な節をつけてしゃべる癖がある.	He has a habit of speaking with [in] a peculiar intonation.
この歌の節は知っているが歌詞は	I know the melody [tune] but not the

知らない. lyrics to this song.
【箇所】彼の行為には疑わしい節がある. There are some questionable points in his actions.
彼女には何か隠している節がある. She acts like she's hiding something.

ぶじ (無事)
道中の無事をお祈りしています. I'll pray for your safe trip.
交通事故にあわれたと聞きましたがご無事で何よりでした. I heard you were in a car accident. It's a relief to see [know] that you're all right.
開会式は無事終了した. The opening ceremony ended without a hitch.
The opening ceremony was a success.
空巣に入られたけど引き出しの中のお金は無事だった. A thief broke in but the money in the drawer was safe.

ふしぎ (不思議)
彼が我々にそんな多額の金を貸してくれたのは不思議だ. It's strange that he lent us so much money.
彼が議長に選ばれたのも不思議ではない. It's only natural that he was elected chairman.
不思議にその時怒る気になれなかった. Strangely enough [Oddly enough], I didn't get mad at the time.
彼女の占いは不思議にあたるそうだ. Her readings are supposed to be amazingly accurate.
子どもたちは, 彼の手品を不思議そうに見ていた. The children were watching his tricks in amazement.

ふしぜん (不自然)
彼女は不自然な笑い方をした. She smiled awkwardly.
動作が不自然だったので我々は彼を疑いだした. We started to harbor [have] doubts about him because of his unnatural behavior.
我々二人がここにいるのは不自然だ. The two of us don't belong here.
It's not natural for the two of us to be here.
あなたのような若い人がそんな厚化粧をするのは不自然ですよ. It's unnatural for a young person like you to wear such heavy makeup.

ふじゆう (不自由)
アメリカでは車なしで生活するのは不自由だ. It is inconvenient to live without a car in the U.S.
彼はいつもお金に不自由している. He's always short of money.
視力が衰え, 本を読むのにも不自由している. My eyesight is failing and reading books has become difficult.

彼女は何不自由なく暮らしている.	She is well-off.
彼は不自由な体なのによく働く.	He works hard in spite of †being handicapped [his handicap].

ぶしょう (不精)

彼の不精は父親ゆずりだ.	He gets his laziness from his father.
彼は不精だから1週間に1度しかふろに入らない.	He's such a slob that he only takes a bath once a week.
彼は筆不精だ.	He's a poor [bad] †letter writer [correspondent].
彼はいい人だが, あの不精ひげは嫌いだ.	He's an all right guy, but I can't stand his stubbly beard.

ぶじょく (侮辱)

私の提案を無視するなんて侮辱だ.	To ignore my proposal is an insult.
彼は警官を侮辱したので逮捕されてしまった.	He was arrested because he insulted a policeman.
彼からひどい侮辱を受けた.	He insulted me terribly.
米国では法廷侮辱罪で罰金を科されることがある.	In America one can be fined for contempt of court.

ふしん (不審)

その発言には不審な点がある.	That statement contains doubtful points.
この契約条項にご不審がありましたら, お問い合わせください.	If there are any items in the contract you want to question, please (feel free to) contact me.
警察官は挙動不審の男を職務質問した.	The policeman questioned the suspicious-looking man.

ふせぐ (防ぐ)

チャンピオンは素早く身をかわして挑戦者のパンチを防いだ.	The champion quickly moved to avoid his opponent's punch.
機長の冷静な判断によって大事故は防がれた.	The captain's †cool judgment [rational decision] was responsible for preventing a serious accident.
この建物には寒さを防ぐための工夫がしてある.	This building is designed to keep out the cold.

ふせる (伏せる)

彼は読みかけの本を伏せて電話に出た.	He put the book he had begun to read face down and answered the telephone.
トランプのカードを伏せて配った.	He dealt the cards face down.
あの山はおわんを伏せたような形	The mountain is shaped like an upside

をしている.	down bowl.
彼は地面に身を伏せた.	He lay flat on the ground.
【秘密にする】このことはしばらく伏せておこう.	Let's keep this secret for a while.
私の名前は伏せておいてください.	Please keep my name out of it.

ふそく (不足)

あの国では食糧が不足している.	There is (a) shortage of food in that country.
睡眠不足で頭が重い.	My head feels heavy from a lack of sleep.
そんなことを言うとは認識不足もはなはだしい.	If you say something like that, you seriously lack understanding.
人手不足で困っている.	They're suffering from a lack of help.
彼なら相手にとって不足はない.	He'll be a good match for the opponent.
あんなにたくさんボーナスをもらったのに, 彼はまだ不足そうな顔をしている.	Even though he received quite a large bonus, he still doesn't look satisfied.

ぶたい (舞台)

【演劇などの】彼女は拍手に迎えられて舞台に出た.	She was greeted by applause as she walked onto the stage.
私が初めて舞台に立ったのは5歳の時です.	The first time I stood [was] on stage was when I was five years old.
彼は舞台度胸がいいから俳優としてうってつけだ.	He doesn't get stage fright so he'd make a great actor.
【行動の場】この物語の舞台は中世の京都です.	This story is set in medieval Kyoto.
彼は世界を舞台に活躍した.	He made the world his stage.
彼の舞台裏工作は効を奏した.	His underground activities [operations] were a success.
今日の試合は, 彼のひとり舞台だった.	He gave a one-man performance in today's game.

ふたたび (再び)

二度と再びこんなことをしてはいけません.	Don't ever do this again.
彼は再び同じ過ちを繰り返した.	He repeated the same mistake.
生きて再び故国の地を踏めるとは思わなかった.	I didn't think I'd make it back home alive.

ふたん (負担)

【負荷・重荷】スノーボードはひざに負担がかかる.	Snowboarding is hard on the knees.

それを若い人にやらせるのは負担が大きすぎる.	Asking a young man to take that on would be too much.*
初めての人と話すのは負担に感じる.	I find it hard to talk to people I meet for the first time.
彼女の僕への好意が負担になってきた.	Her interest in me has become a burden.
話を聞いてもらったおかげで,心の負担が軽くなった.	I feel better after talking about it. My heart feels lighter after being able to talk about it.
毎月2万円の月謝を払うのは家計にとって負担だ.	Paying ¥20,000 a month for tuition is a burden on our household budget.
手術することになれば経済的負担が大きい.	The financial burden would be great if †it came to an operation [I had to have an operation].
【支払う】宿泊費は当社が負担いたします.	Our company will †cover the cost of accommodations [pay for accommodations].
お客様の損害金額は我が社が負担いたします.	Our company will †compensate for [reimburse] †your [the customer's] losses.
昼食代は自己負担です.	Lunches are not included.
医療費の自己負担額は3割です.	The patient pays for thirty percent of the medical expenses.

ふだん¹ (不断)

消防署は火事に対して不断の監視を怠らない.	Firemen are constantly watching out (on the alert) for fires.
何事にも不断の努力が大切だ.	Whatever it may be, †consistent effort [working hard consistently] is important.
彼は不断の努力を積み重ねて,今日の成功を収めた.	He has achieved his present success through unrelenting effort.

ふだん² (普段)

この食器はお客様用なのでふだんは使いません.	These dishes are for company [guests], so we don't usually use them.
何事もふだんの心がけが大切だ.	Whatever it is, it's important to always look out for yourself.
ふだんから勉強していれば,試験になっても慌てることはない.	If you have been studying all along, you shouldn't have to worry about the exams.
彼はふだんはおとなしいが,一度怒りだすとものすごい.	He's usually quiet but once he gets angry, watch out!
パーティーにはふだん着でいらし	Please dress casually for the party.

ふちゅうい (不注意)

その事故は彼の不注意から起きた.	His carelessness caused the accident.
彼女は子どもの栄養に関して不注意だった.	She was careless about her children's nutrition.
私は不注意で, よく財布を落としたり傘を忘れたりします.	I'm so careless; I'm always losing my wallet or forgetting my umbrella (or something like that).
彼は不注意にも会社の秘密をしゃべってしまった.	He carelessly let slip a company secret.

ふちょう (不調)

彼は体の不調を訴えた.	He complained of feeling run-down.
この車はこの頃エンジンが不調だ.	This car's engine has been out of tune lately.
話し合いは不調に終わった.	The discussion ended in failure.
	The discussion was broken off.

ふつう (普通)

私の成績は普通です.	My grades are average.
	I have average grades.
彼は普通のサラリーマンだ.	He's †an ordinary [an average, a typical] †office worker [white-collar worker].
私は普通6時には家に帰ります.	I usually get home by six.
それは特別な用語で, 普通はそういう言い方はしない.	That's a technical term and isn't generally used.
彼女は普通はそんなことを決してしないのに, 一体どうしたんだろう.	She wouldn't normally do anything of that sort. I wonder what happened?
あの男のやることは普通じゃない.	The things he does are not normal.

ぶつかる

道で人とぶつかった.	I bumped into †someone [a person] on the street.
飛んで来たボールが頭にぶつかった.	A ball came flying (through the air) and hit me on the head.
よそ見をしていて電柱にぶつかった.	Not paying attention to where I was going, I bumped into a utility pole.
車の運転を誤って木にぶつかった.	I lost control of the car and ran into a tree.
乗用車とトラックがぶつかった.	A car and a truck ran into each other.
【出会う】彼は多くの困難にぶつか	He faced many difficulties but not once

ったが決してくじけなかった.	was he disheartened.
この種の研究ではいろいろの面倒な問題にぶつかることになる.	In this kind of research, one runs up against all kinds of sticky problems.
優勝候補チームと1回戦でぶつかった.	We ran up against the team most likely to win the championship in the first match.
【対立する】二人の意見は真正面からぶつかった.	Their opinions clashed head on.
結婚問題で父とぶつかった.	My father and I clashed over the question of my marriage.
【積極的に取り組む】この件では彼に直接ぶつかってみよう.	Let's confront him directly on this issue.
実際にぶつかってみれば解決の糸口が見つかるものだ.	When you tackle something head on, you usually end up finding a solution.
【重なる】同じ日に友人の結婚式と伯父の葬式がぶつかってしまった.	My friend's wedding is going to be on the same day as my uncle's funeral.
開校記念日と日曜日がぶつかった.	The anniversary of the founding of the school falls on a Sunday.

ぶつける

のっぽの彼はかもいに頭をぶつけた.	He was so tall (that) he bumped his head on the door lintel.
けんかして石をぶつけられた.	I was hit by a stone in the fight.
彼らはお互いに意見をぶつけ合った.	They had a heated debate.
両チームはエースをぶつけて戦った.	The aces of each team were pitted against each other.
彼は上役に仕事上の不満をぶつけた.	He vented his dissatisfaction with work to his superior.
税の不公平に対して私に怒りをぶつけてもしょうがないよ.	You may rail at the unfairness of the tax, but there's nothing I can do about it.

ぶっしつ (物質)

彼は物質欲が強い人間だ.	He's consumed with material greed.
友人に物質的な援助をしてもらった.	I got material assistance from friends.
消防士の制服は熱に強い物質で出来ている.	Firemen's uniforms are made from heat-resistant materials.
彼女は物質的に恵まれた生活をしている.	She lives a materially privileged life.
現代は物質文明の時代だといわれている.	This age is said to be the era of material civilization.

ふと

ふと旅に出たくなった.	I got an urge to take a trip.
ふと気がつくと出かける時間はとっくに過ぎていた.	I suddenly realized [It occured to me that] it was way past the time I was supposed to have left.
ふと昔の友達のことを思い出した.	The memory of a friend flashed across my mind.
ふといい考えが浮かんだ.	A good idea suddenly occurred to me.
ふとしたことで彼と知り合った.	I got acquainted with him by chance.
ふとしたことから彼とけんかをしてしまった.	He and I got into a fight over a trivial thing.
ふとした風邪がもとで彼女は帰らぬ人となった.	A mere cold brought about her death.

ふとい (太い)

この家の柱は太い.	This house has thick pillars.
彼の腕はとても太い.	His arms are very big around.
彼女は足が太い.	She has stubby [fat] legs.
書類の重要な部分を太い線で囲んだ.	I drew bold circles around the important sections of the document.
彼は太い声をしている.	He has a deep voice.
【神経などが】彼女は見かけによらず神経が太い.	She has strong nerves, contrary to the way she looks.
彼は肝っ玉の太い男だ.	He's a daring man [guy].
借金を踏み倒すとは太い野郎だ.	He has a lot of nerve, not paying his debt. What a rat [scoundrel], leaving behind all those bad debts!

ふとる (太る)

彼は太っている.	He's fat [overweight].
その赤ん坊はまるまるとよく太っている.	That baby is nice and chubby.
中年になると太りだす人が多い.	Many people get fat in middle age.
私は最近かなり太った.	I've put on a lot of weight recently.
太り過ぎは体に良くない.	Obesity is bad for your health.

ぶなん (無難)

彼が副社長に任命されたが, 無難な人選だ.	He's an acceptable choice for vice-president of the company.
その場では黙っていた方が無難だと判断した.	At that point, I decided that it was safer to remain silent.
ジャケットの色は, 赤よりベージュの方が何にでも合わせやすく	A beige jacket that goes with everything is more useful than a red one.

彼女のスケートの自由演技は無難にまとめられていた.	She didn't take any risks in her free-style skating event.
「わさび味のソフトクリームを食べてみようかな」「僕は無難なところでバニラにしておくよ」	"I think I'll try the horseradish-flavored soft ice cream." "I'm going to play it safe with the vanilla."

ふふく (不服)

彼はその決定に不服だった.	The decision left him unsatisfied.
もし不服なら, 今申し出てください.	If you have any objections, tell us now.
私がこんなに譲歩しているのに彼はまだ不服そうだ.	I've been willing to compromise this much and yet he still seems to be discontent.

ぶぶん (部分)

この植物の根の部分は食べられない.	The root[1] of this plant isn't edible.
この随筆の初めの部分は日本人の日常生活について書かれている.	The first part of this essay is about Japanese daily life.
君の意見には部分的には賛成だ.	I partially agree with your view.
彼は私有地の大部分を公園として解放した.	He permitted [allowed] most of his property to be used as a park.
まだ事件の一部分しか解決していない.	Only one part of this matter has been resolved.
部分品さえあれば, この機械はすぐ直せる.	If only I had some parts, I could fix this machine right away.

1) root のみで「根の部分」という意味を十分に表している.

ふへい (不平)

彼はいつも給料が安いと不平を言っている.	He is always complaining [griping] about his low pay.
妻は私にさんざん不平を並べた.	My wife had a laundry list of complaints to tell me.
彼はきつい仕事を, 不平も言わずに次々にこなしている.	He continues to complete one assignment after another without murmuring a word of complaint about how grueling the work is.

ふべん (不便)

彼の家は不便な所にある.	His house is located in an inconvenient place.
この辺はお店が少なくて買い物に	There aren't many stores around here so

不便だ.	shopping is inconvenient.
車が壊れてしまって不便な思いをしている.	It's been really inconvenient (for me) since my car broke down.
このバッグは小さ過ぎて不便です.	This bag is too small to be of much use.

ふほんい (不本意)

本当は承諾するのは不本意なんだ.	To tell (you) the truth I'm reluctant to give my consent.
不本意ながら彼は謝罪せざるを得なかった.	Reluctantly, he forced himself to apologize.
新しい試みが不本意な結果に終わり, 残念だ.	It's a shame [pity] that the venture ended in disappointment.

ふまじめ (不まじめ)

彼の仕事ぶりは不まじめだ.	He doesn't have a serious work attitude.
あの学生は不まじめだ.	That student doesn't work [study] hard.
あんな不まじめな男とはつきあうな.	You shouldn't associate with such an insincere man.
教会で不まじめなことをしてはいけません.	You must not do irreverent things in church.
いつも授業を不まじめに聞いているから, 試験の点数が悪いんですよ.	You score poorly on the exams because you're so inattentive in class.

ふまん (不満)

彼は今の仕事に不満を持っている.	He's dissatisfied with his present job.
話し合いの結果は双方に不満を残した.	The results of the talks [discussions] left both parties feeling dissatisfied [discontented].
彼は私に対する日頃の不満を爆発させた.	His continuing dissatisfaction towards me finally exploded.
あの国は, 我が国の外交政策に不満の意を表明した.	That country has expressed its dissatisfaction with our country's foreign policy.
国民のあいだに不公平な税制に対する不満の声が高まっている.	The public has gotten vociferous in expressing its displeasure with the unfair tax system.

ふむ (踏む)

満員電車の中で足を踏まれた.	My feet got stepped on in the packed train.
子どもがいきなり飛び出して来たので慌ててブレーキを踏んだ.	The child jumped into my path, and I slammed on the brakes.
彼女は1985年に初めてアメリカの	She set foot †in America [on American

土を踏んだ.	soil] for the first time in 1985.
息子には私と同じ轍(わだち)を踏ませたくない.	I don't want my son to make the same mistake (as) I did.
彼は場数を踏んだベテラン教師だ.	He's a veteran teacher with a lot of experience.
正規の手続きを踏んでからお申し込みください.	Please apply after you have completed the regular procedure.
この絵は, どんなに安く踏んでも500万円はする.	Even at a conservative estimate, this picture must cost at least five million yen.
【韻を】この詩は脚韻を踏んでいる.	This poem rhymes. This poem is written in rhyme.
【慣用】彼女には約束をすっぽかされ, その上雨に降られて, 全くふんだりけったりだった.	She stood me up, and to add insult to injury I got rained on.

ふやす (増やす)

会社は事業の拡張に伴って人を増やした.	As the company expanded its operations it increased its personnel.
あの大学は来年から入学定員を増やすそうだ.	I hear that the university is going to increase new student enrollment.
電車の本数をもっと増やして欲しい.	I wish they would increase the number of trains running. I wish the trains ran more often.

ふゆかい (不愉快)

この頃不愉快な事件が多い.	There are many unpleasant incidents nowadays.
彼女の手紙を読んで不愉快になった.	I found her letter disagreeable. Her letter displeased me.
彼の態度は全く不愉快だ.	His attitude is entirely disagreeable [unpleasant].
あいつは自慢話ばかりして不愉快なやつだ.	He's so disgusting. All he ever does is brag about himself.

プラス

【ゼロより上】マイナスにマイナスをかけるとプラスになる.	A minus number times another minus number equals a plus number.
「明日の昼間の気温は3度だそうだよ」「プラス3度? それともマイナス3度?」	"I hear that the daytime temperature tomorrow will be three degrees." "Do you mean three degrees above or below zero?"
毎月の収支は開店6ヵ月目でやっとプラスに転じた.	We're finally †in the black [covering our monthly expenses] six months after our

【追加・増加】毎月の小遣い, あと5,000円プラスしてくれない？ — Could you add ￥5,000 a month on to my allowance?

商品の代金に送料600円をプラスしてお振り込みください. — Please add ￥600 postage to the cost of your purchase when you pay by bank deposit.

売り上げは昨年同月比15パーセントのプラスだ. — Sales are up 15% from the same month last year.

旅行の予算は一人2万円プラスアルファーを見ておいてください. — Please budget ￥20,000 plus per person for the trip.

この企画は新鮮味に欠ける. 何かプラスアルファーがほしいな. — This plan lacks life. It needs (a little) something more.

先週は競馬に大勝ちしたけど, 今週は負け続けている. 今のところだいたいプラスマイナスゼロだ. — I won a lot at the races last week but I've been losing steadily this week. I guess I'm about even now.

人生はプラスマイナスゼロだ. — Life brings the good along with the bad.

【有益・前向き】ここで経験したことは, 君の将来にとって必ずプラスになるはずだ. — This experience will definitely work to your advantage in the future.

寮における生徒の自治はプラスに作用している. — The student-run dorm †seems to be doing well [is looking good].

何事もプラス思考でいきなさい. — Always look on the positive side of things.

ふらふら

疲れてふらふらした. — I was near faint with exhaustion.
酔っ払って足がふらふらした. — I was so drunk I couldn't walk straight.
熱気で頭がふらふらする. — The heat is making my head swim.
I feel dizzy from the heat.

あんなふらふらした男は嫌いだ. — I don't like that flighty [indecisive, irresolute] sort of man.

決めた以上ふらふらするな. — Now that you have decided, don't waver.
彼女はついふらふらと万引きしてしまった. — She lifted it in spite of herself.

ふり¹ (振り)

彼女はその件に関して全く知らない振りをした. — She pretended that she didn't know anything about it.
She feigned ignorance about the matter.

彼は内心動転していたけれど, 何でもない振りをした. — Although he was upset, he acted as if nothing was wrong.

彼女は面接の時, 純情そうな振りをして効果を狙った. — She tried to make the interview go well by acting naive [unaffected].

彼はどんな小さな不正も見て見ぬ振りができない人だ.	He's the kind of person who can't overlook †the slightest hint [any kind] of dishonesty.
彼女に挨拶したのに, 知らん振りをされた.	She ignored me even though I said hello.
女手一つで子どもを育てるために, 彼女はなり振り構わず働いた.	She had to raise the child on her own, so she took on jobs without (any) regard for appearances.
人の振り見てわが振り直せ.	You can better yourself by observing others.

ふり² (不利)

彼は不利な立場に立たされた.	He was at a disadvantage. He was in an unfavorable position.
あなたは彼に不利なことを言っている.	You are saying things that will work to his disadvantage.
彼女は彼に不利な証言をした.	She offered damaging testimony against him.
形勢は私たちに不利になってきた.	The scales have turned against us.

〜ぶり

【様子・状態】

彼の生活ぶりはつつましい.	He leads a modest [frugal] life.
彼の話しぶりは穏やかだ.	He has a gentle way of speaking.
あの梅の木は見事な枝ぶりだ.	That plum tree's branches make a beautiful pattern.
外人と身振り手振りで話をした.	I spoke to the foreigner using hand and body gestures.
彼は男っぷりがいい.	He's very manly.
彼は大ぶりのカップで3杯もコーヒーを飲んだ.	He drank three large cups of coffee.

【時間が経って】

お久しぶりですね.	It's been a long time.
彼は海外から3年ぶりに家へ帰った.	He returned home after three years abroad.
10日ぶりに雨が降った.	It rained for the first time in ten days.
誘拐された子どもは1週間ぶりに無事両親の手元に戻った.	The kidnapped child was returned safely to the arms of his parents after one week.

フリーズ

最近, パソコンがよくフリーズする.	My computer is freezing (up) a lot lately.
ちょうど乗っていたところで, パ	My computer froze (up) on me just as I

ふりかえる (振り返る)

ソコンがフリーズしてしまった.	got going.
彼女は何度も振り返って見送りの友達に手を振った.	She turned around again and again to wave at her friends seeing her off.
後ろから名前を呼ばれたので振り返って見た.	Someone called my name from behind, so I turned around to look.
この1年を振り返るといろいろなことがあった.	Looking back at this year, a lot has happened.
自分のしたことを振り返って反省しなさい.	Look back and reflect on what you've done.

ふりょう (不良)

彼は成績不良で落第した.	He had bad grades and flunked.
その子は発育不良でやせ細っている.	That child is underdeveloped and very thin.
飛行機は天候不良のため空港に引き返した.	The airplane turned back to the airport because of poor weather conditions.
新しい時計を買ったのに，不良品だった.	I bought a new watch but it was †no good [defective].
あの子は不良だからつきあってはいけない.	Stay away from that boy; he's no good.
不良にからまれて時計を取られてしまった.	I got picked on by a thug [hood] who took my watch.

ふる¹ (振る)

【振り動かす】彼はいつまでも手を振って彼女を見送った.	As she left, he continued waving good-bye for a long time.
この薬は瓶を良く振ってから飲んでください.	Shake the bottle well before you take [drink] this medicine.
私は毎日バットを100回振る.	I practice swinging the bat 100 times a day.
小犬がしっぽを振って近づいて来た.	The little dog wagged its tail and came up to me.
【振りかける】トマトに塩を振って食べた.	I salted the tomato and ate it.
肉に塩とコショウを振って焼いた.	I seasoned the meat with salt and pepper and then broiled it.
【割り当てる】彼は主役を振られて張り切っている.	He was cast as the lead and is eagerly working on the role.
レポートには忘れずにページ番号を振ってください.	Remember to put the page numbers on your paper.
この本では漢字に全部かなが振っ	All the *kanji* in this book have their read-

てある.	ings printed in *kana*.
【断る・むだにする】彼は恋人に振られてしまった.	He was jilted by his sweetheart.
私の父は戦争のために青春を棒に振った人間の一人です.	My father was one of many who lost their youth because of the war.

ふる² (降る)

朝から雨が降っている.	It's been raining since morning.
火山の噴火で灰が降った.	Ashes from the volcanic eruption fell.
昨日から雪が降り積もっている.	The snow has been piling up since yesterday.
今日は星の降るような夜だね.	The sky is filled with stars tonight.

ふるい (古い)

パンが古くなり, カビが生えた.	The bread got stale and moldy.
この肉はもう古い.	This meat has gone bad.
古い家を壊して新築した.	We had our old house torn down and a new one built.
この洋服は古くなってもう着られない.	These clothes have gotten too old to wear any longer.
私と彼とは古い友達だ.	He and I are old friends.
古い切手をたくさん持っている.	I have a lot of old stamps.
彼は古い家柄の出だ.	He comes from an old family (line).
彼女は会社で古いほうだ.	She's one of the old hands at the company.
この祭りは古い歴史を持っている.	This festival has a long history.
嫁と姑の関係は古くて新しい問題だ.	The relationship between a wife and her mother-in-law is an age-old problem.
古いしゃれだ.	That's an old joke.
こんなデザインはもう古い.	This style is already passé [out-dated, old-fashioned].
そんな古い手を使ったってダメだ.	You can't get away using that old ploy.
おじいちゃんは頭が古い.	Grandpa [Grandpa's way of thinking] is old-fashioned.
そんな古くさい考え方は, 今では通用しない.	Such old-fashioned thinking isn't acceptable these days.
彼女はいつも古めかしい着物を着ている.	She always wears such old-fashioned *kimonos*.

ふるえる (震える)

外へ出るとあまりの寒さに震えてしまった.	It was so cold when I stepped outside that I shivered.
緊張のあまり手が震えてうまく字が書けなかった.	My hand was trembling so much under the strain that I couldn't write very

彼女は恐怖のあまり震えた.	She trembled in panic.
悪寒がして体が震えた.	I †felt [got the] chills and shivered.
彼女の声は怒りで震えていた.	Her voice trembled in anger.
飛行機の爆音で窓ガラスが震えた.	The roar of the airplane shook the windows.

プレッシャー

彼は大きな仕事を任されて大変なプレッシャーがかかっている.	He's under a lot of pressure because he's been given a big job to do.
何でもできる優秀な兄がいることで，いつも目に見えないプレッシャーを感じていた.	I always felt the (unspoken) pressure of having an older brother who excelled at everything.
彼はプレッシャーに強い.	He handles pressure well.
彼女はプレッシャーに負けずによく頑張った.	She played well under the pressure.
プレッシャーに押しつぶされそうだ.	I'm about to break under the pressure.

ふれる (触れる)

この薬品が肌に触れないように注意しなさい.	Be careful not to let any of this chemical †touch [get on] your skin.
作品には手を触れないでください.	Please don't touch any of the exhibits.
春風が快く頬に触れて吹き過ぎていった.	A wisp of spring wind swept pleasantly across [past] my face.
彼女は都会で目に触れるもの耳に触れるものすべてが新鮮だった.	All the sights and sounds that greeted her in the city were a new experience.
彼の勝手な行動は上司の怒りに触れた.	His arbitrary conduct provoked his superior.
そういう行為は法に触れる.	Such actions infringe on the law.
社長は私の失敗には一言も触れなかった.	The boss didn't touch on my mistake at all.
彼の発言は問題の核心に触れるものだった.	His statement touched the (very) core of the problem.
私は折に触れて身辺の出来事を書き綴っている.	I †jot down [write about] things that happen around me whenever the chance permits.

ふんいき (雰囲気)

このレストランはいい雰囲気だ.	This restaurant has a nice atmosphere.
私はどうしても今の職場の雰囲気になじめない.	I just can't seem to adapt myself to these work surroundings.
彼の名演技に会場は熱っぽい雰囲	His fine performance generated †an intense

気に包まれた. | [a fervent] mood in the audience (in the theater [hall]).
あの人は一種独特な雰囲気を持っている. | That person has †a demeanor uniquely his own* [a unique way about him].

ふんがい (憤慨)
彼女は馬鹿にされて憤慨した. | She deeply resented being ridiculed.
彼は不当な扱いに憤慨した. | He was †indignant at [very angry about] the unfair treatment he received.

ふんべつ (分別)
彼は若いけれども分別がある. | He has good judgment in spite of his youth.
彼女はその申し出を断るだけの分別があった. | She had the (good) sense to turn down the offer.
あなたも30歳だから，もっと分別があってもいい. | For being 30 you ought to know better.
あんな分別くさい人は好きじゃない. | I don't care for self-righteous people like that.

へ

へいおん (平穏)
彼は冒険好きで，平穏な生活など望んでいない. | He is adventurous and has no desire to lead a quiet life.
今年は平穏無事な年でした. | This was an uneventful year.
会議は平穏に終わった. | The conference ended †without any trouble [uneventfully].

へいき (平気)
「そんなことをしても平気ですか」「平気ですよ」 | "Is it all right to do such a thing? [Is it cool** to do something like that?]" "Sure. [Don't worry.]"
何が起こっても平気だ. | I'll take whatever comes.
彼が怒っても平気だ. | It's all the same to me [I couldn't care less] if he gets angry.
彼女は朝から晩まで働いても平気だ. | She makes [thinks] nothing of working from morning till night.

彼はクラスメートに笑われても平気だった.	He was indifferent to the laughter of his classmates.
彼は平気で汚い手を使う.	He has no second thoughts about resorting to dirty tricks.
	He thinks nothing of resorting to dirty tricks.
彼女は平気で子犬を捨てた.	She abandoned the little puppies without batting an eye.

へいきん (平均)

彼の成績はクラスの平均よりやや高い〔低い〕.	His grades are a little bit higher 〔lower〕 than the class average.
今日の気温は平均を上回った〔下回った〕.	It was above 〔below〕 the average temperature today.
彼は1日平均5時間勉強する.	He studies an average of five hours a day.
平均すると, その本は1日10冊売れている.	On the average, 10 of those books are sold per day.
クラスの平均点は何点でしたか.	What's the average grade in this class?
彼らの平均身長は180センチです.	Their average height is 180 cm.
1日当たりの売り上げの平均を出してください.	Please figure out the average amount sold †per [in one] day.
彼は平均的な家庭の平均的な高校生だ.	He's an average high school student from an average family.
この商標の製品は品質がほぼ平均している.	For the most part, the same quality is maintained in all the products with [bearing] this label.
今日の体育の授業は平均台を使ってやった.	In today's P.E.[1] class we used the balance beam.

[1] physical education の省略形.

へいこう¹ (平行)

その通りは町の中を流れる川と平行して走っている.	That street runs parallel to the river that flows through the center of town.
話し合いは平行線のまま終わった.	The talks ended up without any progress being made toward a settlement.

へいこう² (閉口)

この暑さには閉口する.	I can't stand this heat.
つまらない講義に閉口した.	The lecture bored me to death.
彼のずうずうしさには閉口する.	I'm put off by his impudence.
彼女のおしゃべりには閉口した.	I got fed up with her constant talking.
彼は隣のピアノの音に閉口してい	He's annoyed by the sounds of the piano

この仕事の難しさには閉口している.	The difficulty of this work has stumped me.

へいせい (平静)

その恐ろしい知らせを聞いても彼は平静を保った.	He kept his composure when he heard the terrible news.
彼女は子どもがけがをしているのを見て平静を失った.	She lost her composure when she saw her injured child.
しばらくしてから私はやっと平静を取り戻した.	After a little time had elapsed, I regained my composure.

へいぜん (平然)

どんな厳しい批判にも彼は平然としている.	No matter how severely he is criticized he remains unperturbed.
彼は平然たる態度で大事な試合に臨んだ.	He faced the important match with composure.
彼女は母危篤の知らせを平然と受け止めた.	She received the news of her mother's critical condition calmly.

へいぼん (平凡)

この小説は平凡で期待外れだった.	I had hoped for more but the novel was just mediocre.
どの論文も平凡なものだった.	All of the theses were mediocre.
彼は平凡な事務員として生涯を送った.	He lived out the uneventful life of a clerk.
私たちはこの地で平凡な生活を送っています.	We're having an uneventful life here.

ペース

【速度】

そのマラソン選手のペースは最後まで落ちなかった.	The marathon runner never slackened his pace.
おじいちゃんのペースに合わせてゆっくり歩いた.	We walked at my grandfather's pace. We walked slowly, matching the pace of my grandfather.
時間がないので, もう少し作業のペースをあげてください.	Please work a little faster. We're running out of time.

【調子・やり方】

新しい職場のペースがつかめてきた.	I'm catching on to how things are done at my new workplace. I'm getting the hang of how things are done at my new job.**
いつも, いつの間にか彼のペースに巻き込まれてしまう.	I always end up going along with †his ideas [what he says].

うちのチームは後半になってやっと試合のペースに乗ってきた.	Our team finally got going in the second half of the game.
君はいつもマイペースだね.	You seem to like doing your own thing.[1]
	You always seem to go at your own pace.[2]

> 1) は「(他人のことは我関せず)自分の好きなことをする」こと, 2) は「自分のペース[速さ]によってのみ物事を行う」こと.

へた (下手)

うちの妻は料理が下手だ.	My wife is not a good cook.
私は字が下手だ.	My handwriting is bad.
彼女は歌が下手だ.	She's a terrible singer.
私は英語が下手です.	My English is poor.
私のゴルフは下手の横好きです.	I like to play golf but I'm not very good at it.
下手をするとこの仕事は予定どおりに終わらないかもしれない.	If we're not careful, this work might not get done on schedule.
お父さんは今日は機嫌が悪いから, 下手に話しかけないほうがいいよ.	Dad's in a bad mood today, so you'd better stay out of his way. Don't talk to him unless you have to.

べつ (別)

【区別】
アメリカでは最近, 男女別の寮を探すのが難しくなってきている.	It's become difficult to find †separate dormitories for men and women [dormitories separated by sex] in America recently.
本を著者別に分類してください.	Please categorize the books according to the name of the author.

【別個】
解答用紙は別になっている.	The answer sheet is separate.
この書類は明日使うから別にしておいてください.	I'll be using these documents tomorrow, so please set them aside.
両親とは別の家に住んでいます.	My parents and I live apart.
当クラブでは会費とは別に施設使用料を申し受けます.	At this club, members are asked to pay a facility (usage) fee, which is †not included in [different from] the membership fee.

【違う】
数学には自信があるが, 人に教えるとなるとまた別だ.	I'm good at math, but when it comes to teaching it, well that's †another thing [a different question].
皆さん同じ料理を注文するのですか. 僕は別のにします.	Is everyone going to order the same dish? I'll order [have] something else.
今は忙しいから別のときに相談に	I'm busy at present so let's get together on

| 乗りましょう. | it some other time. |

【除外】彼を別にすれば，同僚とはうまくいっている. — Apart from [Except for] him, I'm getting along well with everyone at work.

冗談は別にして，本当にその計画を実行するつもりなんですか. — All joking aside, are you serious about putting that plan into effect?

【特別に】別に用事がなかったら映画を見に行きませんか. — If you've nothing special planned, how about going to see a movie?

留守中，別に変わったことはなかったかい. — Did anything out of the ordinary occur while I was away?

この手紙は別に急がないので都合の良いときに出しておいてください. — There's no special rush with this letter. Please (feel free to) post it at your convenience.

今日は別に何もすることはない. — I have nothing special [particular] to do today.
I have nothing to do in particular today.

彼女の様子に別に変わったところはなかった. — There was nothing out of the ordinary about her appearance.

へつらう

彼は上司にへつらって出世しようとした. — He †played up to [curried favor with, buttered up] his superiors to get a promotion.

私にいくらへつらってもむだだ. — You can't curry favor with me (no matter how hard you try).

ベテラン

ベテラン野球選手の引退が相次いでいる. — Seasoned [Veteran[1]] baseball players are retiring one after the other.

彼はベテランパイロットだ. — He's an expert pilot.

彼はベテランドライバーだ. — He's an excellent driver.

斉藤先生はこの道30年のベテラン教師だ. — Mrs. Saito is an experienced teacher who has been teaching for 30 years.

> 1) veteran は英語では第一義として「退役軍人」を連想させる.

へらす (減らす)

市当局は福祉関係の予算を減らす方針を打ち出した. — The city administration worked out a policy which would reduce the budget for welfare (spending).

不景気のため職員〔出費〕を減らさざるを得ない. — Because of the economic recession we are forced to pare our staff [expenses].

体重を減らしたいなら，まずビールの量を減らすべきだ. — If you want to lose weight, first of all, you have to cut down on the amount of beer (you drink).

へる (減る)

若者が都会へ出て行って村の人口が減ってしまった.	With all the young people moving to the cities, the rural population has decreased.
預金額がゼロ近くまで減ると、彼はまた仕事を探す.	When his bank account gets down to almost nothing, he looks for a job.
体の具合が悪くて体重が減ってきた.	I haven't been feeling well lately and have lost weight.
晴天続きで、ダムの水量が減ってきている.	With all this fine weather, the (volume of) water in the dam is going down.
この靴はかかとがすり減るほどよく履いた.	I've practically worn the heels off these shoes.

へん (変)

変だと思いませんか.	Don't you think it's strange?
今日の彼女は様子が変だ.	She doesn't seem herself today. She's not her usual self today. There's something strange about her today.
彼は頭が変だ.	He's missing a few marbles.** He's a little bit off [crazy] (in the head).
自分の家の電話番号を思い出せないなんて変だよ.	It's odd [strange] that you don't remember your own phone number.
変な男が家の周りをうろついていた.	A suspicious man was prowling around the house.

へんか (変化)

この時期は一日の気温の変化が激しい.	Temperature variations in a single day around this time of year are often acute.
戦後の日本の社会は大きな変化を遂げた.	Japanese society underwent a major transformation after the war.
爪は皮膚の一部が変化したものです.	Nails are a part of the skin that has undergone a change.
時代に伴って風俗も変化していく.	Manners vary with the times.
日本の地形は変化に富んでいる.	Japan's topography is rich in variation.
あの子は表情の変化に乏しい.	That child's face is not very expressive.
もっと日常生活に変化が欲しい.	I'd like a bit more spice in my life.

べんきょう (勉強)

彼は司法試験に備えて勉強した.	He studied in preparation for the bar exam.

大抵の子どもは勉強が嫌いだ.	Most children dislike studying.
彼は勉強家だ.	He's diligent.
この仕事は初めてですが，とても勉強になると思います.	It's my first time at this sort of work. I'm sure I will learn a lot.
今度の事件は彼にとっていい勉強になったことだろう.	That matter probably taught him a good lesson.
こんなことが分からないなんて勉強不足だよ.	If you can't understand something like this, you're not studying hard enough.
【安く売る】これは随分勉強しましたからお買い得ですよ.	This has really been marked down. Believe me, it's a bargain.
もっと勉強してもらえませんか.	Won't you mark it down a bit more?

へんけん (偏見)

それは偏見だ.	That's a prejudice [bias].
	You're prejudiced [biased].
彼は偏見にとらわれない人だ.	He's impartial.
	He's not †biased [a biased person].
人種的偏見は捨てなければならない.	We must rid ourselves of racial prejudice.
彼に対して偏見を持つのはやめなさい.	Stop being prejudiced against him.

へんじ (返事)

【答え】彼は怒っていて，私には返事もしてくれない.	He's angry and won't answer me at all.
彼はまだはっきりした返事をしていない.	He has not given a firm answer yet.
だれかに話しかけられたら黙っていないで返事をしなさい.	If someone speaks to you, don't just stand there, make a reply.
【返信】母からの手紙がうれしかったので，すぐに返事を書いた.	I was so happy to receive a letter from my mother that I wrote her †back [a reply] immediately.
出欠のご返事は1週間以内に届くようにお願いします.	Please let us know whether you will attend or not within a week.

べんしょう (弁償)

それはお金では弁償できないほど大切なものだ.	Money will not suffice to compensate for something as precious as that.
子どもは割った窓ガラスを弁償させられた.	The children were made to pay for the window that they broke.
無くした腕時計の代わりに，お金で弁償してください.	You can reimburse me for my lost watch in cash.
弁償額は100万円だった.	The compensation was ¥1,000,000 [a mil-

べんり（便利）

この荷物を開けるのに便利な道具はないか. — Isn't there some convenient tool to open this package with?

私の家は交通が便利な所にあります. — My house is conveniently located.

このガイドブックは内容が豊富でとても便利です. — This guidebook is very helpful because it's so rich in content.

ここから渋谷へ行くには電車より地下鉄のほうが便利です. — If you're going to Shibuya from here, it's easier to take the subway than the train.

ほ

ほうけん（冒険）

夏休みの一人旅はその子にとって大冒険だった. — Traveling alone during summer vacation was a daring adventure for the child.

会社にとって冒険だが，この商品の大キャンペーンをしよう. — This is a risk for the company, but let's give this product a big campaign.

君の学力であの学校を受けるのは，ちょっと冒険だね. — With your academic ability, taking the entrance exam for that school would be a stretch.

リンドバーグは，大西洋を飛行機で渡るという冒険を1927年に成し遂げた. — Lindbergh's adventure crossing the Atlantic in an airplane took place in 1927.

ほうこう（方向）

【向き】こちらの方向に行けば，駅に出られるはずだ. — If you go this way, you should reach the station.

【目標】彼は人生の方向を誤った. — His life took a wrong turn.

物音のする方向を見た. — I looked in the direction where the noise came from.

銀行は反対の方向です. — The bank is in the opposite direction.

私は方向音痴だ. — I have no sense of direction.

ほうこく（報告）

私はその件について彼から何の報告も受けていない. — I haven't received any report from him about this.

被災地からの現地報告が入りました. — An on-the-spot report from the scene of the disaster has just come in.

現地へ着いたら，その旨，直ちに報告してください. — Please †let me know [report to me] as soon as you get there.

その遺跡の発掘調査に関する中間報告をいたします. — I will make an interim report on the findings of our excavation of the ruins.

ほうしん (方針)

政府はもっと外交方針をはっきりさせるべきだ. — The government must clarify its foreign policy.

私はあくまでこの計画を進める方針だ. — I intend to follow this plan to the very end.

我が家の教育方針は独立心を育てるということだ. — My family's philosophy in raising children is to promote an independent spirit.

ほうぜん (茫然)

その恐ろしい知らせに皆茫然とした. — The terrible news left all of us speechless [dumbfounded].
The terrible news stunned all of us.

彼はその光景に茫然として立ちつくした. — He stood and stared at the sight as if paralyzed.

事故のあと彼女は茫然としていた. — She was dazed after the accident.
The accident left her dazed.

〜ほうだい (〜放題)

あいつは自分では何もしないくせに，言いたい放題だ. — He says whatever he feels like but doesn't do anything about it.

社長の息子は，無断欠勤したり経費を使い込んだりと，やりたい放題だ. — The president's son does whatever he feels like. He doesn't bother showing up for work and wastes company funds.

あの店は今，餃子の食べ放題をやっている. — That restaurant is having an eat-all-you-can special on Chinese dumplings now.

プラス2,500円で飲み放題になります. — With an additional ¥2,500 you can have all the drinks you want.

息子の部屋は散らかし放題だ. — My son's room is a real mess.
My son leaves his room in a complete mess.

隣の家の庭は荒れ放題だ. — The neighbor's garden is completely overgrown.

ほうび (褒美)

お使いのごほうびはクッキーよ. — I'll give you a cookie if you go on this errand for me.

成績が良かったほうびに自転車を買ってもらった.	I got a bicycle as a reward for my good grades.

ほうふ (豊富)

南極大陸には豊富な天然資源が眠っている.	Abundant natural resources lie hidden in Antarctica.
あのスーパーは品物が豊富だ.	There is a wide variety of goods at that supermarket.
彼は海外旅行の経験が豊富だ.	He has extensive experience in foreign travel.
語彙を豊富にするためには、本をたくさん読みなさい.	In order to enrich your vocabulary, read lots of books.
この雑誌は内容が豊富で面白い.	It's the rich and varied content of this magazine that makes it interesting.

ほうほう (方法)

この世から核兵器を無くす方法はないだろうか.	Isn't there a way to eliminate nuclear weapons from the world?
どんな方法を使ってもいいから、彼の計画をやめさせてくれ.	Stop his plan (in) any way you can. I don't care how.
彼女は父親の言いなりになるほか方法がなかった.	There was nothing she could do but do as her father said.
このテキストに書いてある方法で実験してみよう.	Let's try the experiment using the method written in this textbook.

ほうめん (方面)

【方向】台風は発達しながら九州方面に向かっています.	The typhoon is gaining strength as it heads for Kyushu.
東京方面への電車は3番線から出ています.	Trains going in the direction of Tokyo leave from platform number three.
【分野】彼はいろいろな方面に顔が利く.	His name carries weight in many different circles.
彼は生物学でも遺伝学の方面の研究をしている.	His studies in biology are directed toward genetics.

ほうもん (訪問)

今日、先生の家を訪問した.	I †called at [visited] my teacher's home today.
アメリカを訪問中の首相は、昨日大統領と会談を行った.	In the middle of his visit to the United States, the prime minister held a discussion with the president.
彼は訪問販売のセールスマンだ.	He is a door-to-door salesman.

ほえる (吠える)

うちの犬は知らない人を見るとすぐ吠える.	Our dog barks as soon as it sees a stranger.
ライオンが吠えると, さすがに怖い.	When a lion roars, it's really frightening.
そんな事をすると, あとで吠え面をかくことになるぞ.	If you do that, you'll regret it later.

ホームページ

彼はつい最近, とても凝ったホームページを立ち上げた.	He recently set up a very sophisticated website.
いろんなホームページを見ていると, 自分も作りたくなる.	When you look at different sites you start wanting to create your own.
ホームページを毎週, 更新している.	We update our website every week.
あの会社はホームページでアルバイトを募集している.	That company recruits part-timers through its website.

> website は2語で Web site または web site とも書く. 英語で (the) home page といえば, 日本語でいう「(ホームページの) トップページ」のこと.

ほか (外・他)

【別】

この時計は高過ぎるのでほかのを見せてください.	This watch is too expensive. Could you show me some others, please?
彼は今忙しいからほかの人に頼んだら?	He's busy right now, so what about asking someone else?
今日は忙しいのでミーティングはほかの日にしてもらえませんか.	I'm busy today, so could you make our meeting (for) some other day?
財布はここにはないからほかを捜そう.	The wallet isn't here, so let's look somewhere else.
ほかに質問はありませんか.	Are there any other questions?
社内に適当な人がいなければほかから探すしかない.	If there is no one right for the job on staff, then let's search outside the company.
この商品はほかでは取り扱っていません.	Other places don't deal in this product.

【以外】

彼のほかにその問題を解ける者はいなかった.	No one besides him could solve that problem.
彼は英語のほかに中国語も話せる.	He can speak Chinese as well as English.
加藤さんのほかにはだれが来ましたか.	Who else came besides Mr. Kato?
この場合, 君は謝るほかはない.	In this situation, there is nothing for you

	to do but apologize.
今回のことは彼女にとって気の毒と言うほかない.	One can only think how pitiful this situation is for her.

ほがらか (朗らか)

彼は朗らかな人だ.	He's a cheerful man.
彼は飲むと朗らかになる.	A drink puts him in a cheerful mood.
子どもたちが朗らかに笑っている.	The children are laughing cheerfully [gleefully].

ほけん (保険)

彼は3,000万円の保険に入った.	He bought a thirty million-yen insurance policy.
彼は3,000万円の保険に入っている.	He is insured for thirty million yen.
あの絵には多額の保険が掛かっている.	That picture is insured for a lot of money.
勧誘員は, 保険料, 保険金など契約に関する説明をした.	The salesman explained premiums, benefits, and other things pertaining to the insurance policy.

ほご (保護)

子どもを保護するのは親の務めだ.	It is the parents' job to protect their children.
家出少女たちは, 警察に保護された.	The runaway girls were taken into custody by the police.
その種類の鳥は現在保護されている.	That kind of bird is now under protection.

ほこり (誇り)

彼は我が校の誇りです.	He is the pride of our school.
彼は自分の仕事に誇りを持っている.	He takes pride in his work.
彼は助けが欲しかったが, 誇りが許さなかった.	He wanted to ask for help but his pride didn't [wouldn't] let him.
彼は誇りが高すぎてそんなに易しい曲を演奏しない.	He †is too proud [has too much pride] to play such an easy piece.
彼の言葉は彼女の誇りを傷つけた.	His words wounded her pride.
彼女は5ヵ国語が話せるのを誇りに思っている.	She prides herself on her ability to speak five languages.

ほこる (誇る)

わが国の精密機械産業は世界に誇	Our country's precision machinery indus-

ほしい

る高い技術を持っている. — try is held in high repute.
その高層ビルは日本一の高さを誇っている. — That skyscraper can boast of being Japan's tallest (structure).

ほしい (欲しい)

今いちばん欲しいものは何ですか. — What would you most like to have now? / What do you want most now?
最新型のパソコンが欲しい. — I'd like to have the latest-model personal computer.
のどが渇いて飲み物が欲しいと思っていたところです. — I was just feeling thirsty and thinking that I'd like something to drink.
この手紙をすぐに投函してほしい. — I'd like you to post this letter right now.
彼にすぐ戻って来てほしい. — I'd like him to come back right now.
もっと早く来てほしかった. — I was hoping you could have come earlier.
彼にはもう少し積極性が欲しい. — I'd like him to show a bit more enterprise.

ほしゅう (募集)

【働き手を】弊社では新入社員〔アルバイト〕を募集しています. — We're hiring [recruiting] †new employees 〔part-time workers〕 at our company now.
「アルバイト募集中」(掲示文, 広告文) — Part-time help wanted.
当施設では送迎ボランティアを募集しています. — This [Our] institution is looking for volunteers who can drive the patients 〔children, handicapped〕 to and from the center.
新聞に求人募集広告を出した. — We put a classified ad in the newspaper.
募集要項はホームページをご覧ください. — Please look for †job information [employment opportunities] on our website.
【生徒を】春と秋の2回, 新入生を募集しています. — We accept new student applications in the spring and fall.
中高年を対象にして, パソコン教室の生徒の募集をかけた. — I advertised classes for people middle-aged and older interested in learning how to use the computer.
「生徒募集中」(掲示文, 公告文) — Now Accepting Student Applications / Now Accepting New Students
来年度の募集人員は200名です. — We will be accepting [We have room for] 200 applicants next year.
【会員・作品などを】コーラス部が新入部員を募集している. — The chorus is now inviting [welcoming] new members.
水族館が赤ちゃんラッコの名前を募集している. — The aquarium is inviting [asking] people to submit names for the baby sea otter.
交通安全をテーマにポスター作品 — We are inviting submissions for a poster

を募集します. | contest on traffic safety.
このツアーの募集人員は50名です. | This is a tour for 50 people. / We can accommodate 50 people on this tour.
「入居者募集中」（掲示文） | For Rent

ほしょう (保証)

この時計は保証付きです. | This watch has a guarantee.
このカメラは1年間の保証が付いている. | This camera is guaranteed for one year.
保証期間中は大抵の修理はただでしてもらえる. | During the warranty period, usual repairs are done free of charge.
彼の人柄については私が保証します. | I will vouch for his character.
私は彼の保証人になるように頼まれた. | I was asked to be his guarantor.
一人で出歩くなら身の安全は保証しない. | I'm not going to guarantee your safety if you're planning to go out alone.

ほす (干す)

今日は天気が良いので洗濯物を干した. | The weather was good today, so I hung [set] out the laundry to dry.
ウールの衣類は時々虫干しをしたほうがいい. | It is good to air out wool garments from time to time.
干した肉や魚は, 独特の風味がある. | Dried meat and fish have a distinctive flavor.

ほそい (細い)

その子は細いけれど, とても元気が良い. | That child is thin but very healthy.
ナイロンで細い丈夫な糸が作れるようになった. | A thin [fine], strong thread made from nylon has been developed.
畑の中に細い道が続いていた. | The narrow path continued through the middle of the field.
彼女は声が細い. | She has a thin voice.
食の細い子は身体も弱いようだ. | Children who are skimpy eaters tend to have weak bodies.
彼は細く長く生きる主義だ. | He wants to have a long, quiet life.

ほぞん (保存)

この書類は5年間保存しなければならない. | These documents have to be kept for five years.
この書類は捨てないで, きちんと | Please don't throw away this document.

保存しておいてください.	Keep it safe.
優れた文化遺産は大切に保存しなければならない.	Important cultural treasures must be carefully preserved.
博物館はその歴史資料を永久保存することにした.	The museum decided to preserve those historical documents permanently.
ハムやベーコンは保存が利くように加工された食品です.	Ham and bacon are specially prepared to last a long time.
(この食品は)保存が利かないのでお早めにお召し上がりください.	This (food) will not keep and should be eaten as soon as possible.
開栓したあとは冷蔵庫に保存してください.	Please refrigerate after opening.
冷蔵庫がなかった昔は干物や塩漬などの保存食をよく利用していた.	Foods were often preserved by drying and salting before refrigerators were invented.
この食品には保存料は含まれていません.	This product contains no preservatives.[1]
	No preservatives used.[2]
動物には種の保存の本能がある.	Animal behavior instinctively serves to conserve the species.
【コンピュータ】ファイルはこまめに保存しなさい.	Carefully save all your files.
せっかく保存したのに, どのフォルダに入れたか忘れてしまった.	After carefully saving and closing my file, I forgot which folder I put it in.
保存の方法には, 「上書き保存」と「名前を付けて保存」の2種類がある.	There are two commands for saving your work: "Save" and "Save As."

1) 書いても話してもよい文. 2) 表示として書く文.

ほっと

彼が無事だと聞いてほっとした.	It was a weight off my mind [It was a great relief, I was relieved] to hear that he was safe.
彼女はほっとしてため息をついた.	She breathed a sigh of relief.
彼女はほっとした顔をした.	She had a relieved look on her face.
困難な仕事が終わってほっとしている.	I can breathe easier now that I've finished that hard job.

ほっとう (没頭)

彼は読書に没頭していて, 私が呼んでも聞こえないようだった.	He was buried [absorbed] in a book and didn't seem to hear me.
彼女に対する思いを振り払おうと彼は仕事に没頭した.	He immersed himself in work to get her out of his mind.

ほど (程)

【程度】
彼は物も言えないほど疲れていた.	He was too tired to speak.
あれほど言ったのに，また遅刻しましたね.	After all I've said to you, you're late again, aren't you?
程よい運動は健康に良い.	A proper amount of exercise is good for your health.
家庭ほどくつろげる所はない.	There's no place like home to make you feel at ease.
解決しなければならない問題が山ほどある.	There is a mass of problems which have to be solved.
お値段はいかほどですか.	About how much is this?
情報は多ければ多いほどいい.	The more news we have the better.

【比較】
彼は口で言うほど忙しそうではない.	He doesn't seem to be as busy as he always says he is.
彼のけがは思ったほどひどくはなかった.	His wound was not as serious as we thought.
私は彼ほど速く走れない.	I can't run as fast as he does.
彼にそう言われたときほどうれしいことはなかった.	I was never happier than †when [the time] he told me that.

【限界】
親切も程々にしないと迷惑がられますよ.	Even kindness, taken to extremes, can be a nuisance.
彼は恥知らずにも程がある.	He has absolutely no sense of shame.

ほどく

靴のひもがほどけてしまった.	My shoelaces have become untied.
壊れ物が入っていますから，荷物をほどくときには十分注意してください.	Be careful when undoing this package because there are fragile objects inside.
この包みをほどいてもいいですか.	Can I unwrap this package?

ほとんど (殆んど)

瓶にはもうウイスキーがほとんど残っていない.	There is almost no whisky left in the bottle.
彼女が会社に遅れることはほとんどない.	She has almost never been late for work.
クラスのほとんどが日曜日のハイキングに賛成した.	Almost the entire class agreed to go hiking on Sunday.
お陰様で，病気はほとんど良くなりました.	Fortunately, I've almost recovered from my illness.
彼女の持っている服は，ほとんど高級な物ばかりだ.	Most of her clothes are of high quality.

ほね（骨）

カルシウムは骨や歯をつくる．	Calcium builds bones and teeth.
魚の骨がのどに引っ掛かった．	A fish bone got stuck in my throat.
彼はサッカーをしていて足の骨を折った．	He broke his leg while playing soccer.
【骨組み】その傘は骨が折れているのでもう使えない．	A rib of that umbrella is broken and it can't be used any longer.
論文の骨組みは出来ている．	I have (completed) the outline for the thesis.
【慣用】彼は骨のあるやつだ．	He's a man with backbone.
これは骨の折れる仕事だ．	This is backbreaking work.
彼の就職のために骨を折った．	I went to †a lot of [much] trouble to get him hired.
その医者は骨を埋める覚悟でその離島に行った．	The doctor went to that isolated island aware that he might live out the rest of his life there.
寒さが骨身にしみる．	I'm chilled [frozen] to the bone [marrow].
彼は身を削って働いた．	He worked his fingers to the bone.
彼は骨惜しみせずよく働く．	He works hard without sparing himself.
骨休めに温泉に行ってきた．	I went to a hot spring to relax.

ほねおり（骨折り）

お骨折りいただき深く感謝しています．	I am deeply grateful for all the trouble you have †taken [gone to].
彼の骨折りで，この会が開かれた．	Because of his tireless efforts, this meeting has been convened.
今度の企画は大成功だったので，骨折りがいがあった．	This enterprise was a great success. It was worth all the sweat we put into it.
私はその仕事をなんとか成功させようとしたが骨折り損に終わった．	I tried everything to make a success of that job, but it ended as a wasted effort.

ほめる（褒める）

人々は彼の勇気を褒めたたえた．	People praised his courage.
先生は皆の前で彼女を褒めた．	The teacher praised her in front of everyone.
彼はあなたの作品をとても褒めていました．	He praised your work very much.
子どもは叱るばかりではなく，褒めることも必要です．	It is important not only to scold [discipline] but to praise your child as well.

ボランティア

児童館でボランティアとして働い	I'm working at the children's center as a

ている.
海岸清掃のボランティア活動に参加した.
この程度のお金しかもらえないのでは，ほとんどボランティアみたいなものだ.
彼女はボランティア精神が旺盛だ.

volunteer.
I participated in a volunteer activity to clean the †sea coast [beaches].
With this kind of pay it's almost like being a volunteer.
She really has a wonderful volunteer spirit.

ほりゅう（保留）
先方への返事を保留にしている.
合併について二人の役員が態度を保留している.
彼の処分については当分保留にします.
玄関のチャイムが鳴ったので，電話を保留にした.

I've postponed replying to the other party.
Two board members are undecided about the merger.
We won't †do anything [make any decisions] about him for the time being.
I put the phone on hold when the doorbell rang.

ほる（掘る）
この土地は深く井戸を掘らなければ水が出ない.
あの鉱山では金を掘っている.
新しい油田が発見され，早速掘り始めた.
庭で土を掘り起こしていたら，大きなミミズが出て来た.
彼女は戦前の女性史を掘り起こしている.
この問題は，もっと掘り下げてみる必要がある.
この古本は，すごい掘り出し物だ.

If the well isn't dug deeply in this ground, no water will come up.
Gold is being dug in that mine.
A new oil field was discovered, and drilling began immediately.
A big earthworm came out when I was digging (out) in the garden.
She is bringing to light the history of women before the war.
It's necessary to dig further into this question.
This old book is a great find.

ほれる（惚れる）
彼は彼女にほれている.

彼は一目で彼女にほれてしまった.
彼の腕前にほれた.

私たちは彼女の歌声に聞きほれた.

He has fallen in love with her.
He's stuck on her.
He fell in love with her at first sight.
I was deeply impressed by his ability.
I greatly admired his ability.
We were captivated [taken] by her singing.
We're totally gone** on her singing.

ほろびる（滅びる）
核の拡大をこのまま放っておくと，人類は滅びてしまうかもし

If the proliferation of nuclear weapons is not dealt with, the human race may be

れない.	annihilated.
その民族は滅びる一歩手前だ.	That tribe is on the verge of dying out.
その鳥は滅びる寸前にある.	That species of bird is on the verge of extinction.
その風習は50年ほど前に滅びた.	That custom died out about 50 years ago.

ほろぼす (滅ぼす)

為政者の腐敗は国を滅ぼす.	The corruption among the leadership will ruin a nation.
彼はギャンブルで身を滅ぼした.	He ruined his life by gambling.

ほんかく (本格)

いよいよ本格的な夏がやってきた.	Summer is finally here. It finally feels like summer.
本格的なスキーシーズンがやってきた.	The weather is perfect for skiing now.
本格的にデザインの勉強をしたい.	I'd like to study design in earnest now.
来月からその法案の審議が本格化する.	Full-scale deliberation on that bill starts next month.
あの店では本格派インドカレーが味わえる.	You can eat authentic [real] Indian curry at that restaurant.
彼は本格派ピッチャーだ.	He's a real pitcher.

ほんき (本気)

本気ですか.	Do you really mean it? Are you serious?
「君は本気で言っているのか」「本気だとも」	"Do you really mean what you are saying?" "Yes, I mean it."
彼は本気で怒っている.	He's seriously mad [angry].
あいつはうそつきだから, あいつの言うことを本気にしてはいけない.	That guy is a liar so you can't take what he says seriously.
彼女は本気で音楽を勉強しだした.	She started to study music seriously.
彼が本気を出せば君なんか簡単に負けてしまうよ.	If he goes all out, the likes of you won't stand a chance.

ほんしん (本心)

だれも彼の本心を知らない.	Nobody knows †what he is really thinking [his real intentions].
彼に本心を打ち明ける気にならない.	I don't really feel like †telling him what's on my mind [letting him know how I really feel].
彼は気にしないと言っているが,	He says he doesn't mind but deep down

本心はそうじゃないんだ.	that's not so.
本心から彼女がかわいそうだと思う.	I pity her from the bottom of my heart.

ほんとう (本当)

本当のことを教えてください.	Tell me the truth.
本当ですか.	Really?／Is it true?
明日ニューヨークにたつというのは本当ですか.	Is it true that you are leaving for New York tomorrow?
本当はあんな人は好きじゃない.	To tell the truth, I don't †like [care for] that type of person.
彼は若く見えるが,本当はもう40歳を越えている.	He looks young but †actually [in fact] he is over forty.
本当にそう言ったんですか.	Did you really [actually] say that?
この本は本当に面白い.	This book is really interesting.
この着物は本当の絹を使っている.	This *kimono* is made of pure silk.
本当の寒さはまだこれからだ.	The real cold weather is yet to come.
この本の本当の面白さは子どもには分からないでしょうね.	A child would not be able to fully appreciate [enjoy] this book.
彼女は体がまだ本当じゃない.	She's not fully recovered yet.
本当を言うと,まだ彼には知らせていないんだ.	To tell you the truth, I still haven't told him.

ほんね (本音)

彼は決して本音を吐こうとしなかった.	He refused to reveal his true intentions.
彼はいつも本音と建前を使い分ける.	He makes a distinction between what he says and actually thinks.

ほんの

この本はほんの2,3日前に買ったばかりです.	I bought this book just a couple of days ago.
彼はほんの今しがた出かけました.	He left just a moment ago. You just missed him.
彼はほんの子どもだ.	He is a mere child.
彼女はほんの少ししか食事を取らなかった.	She hardly [barely] touched her food.

ぼんやり

彼は少しぼんやりしている.	He's a little bit †spaced (out)** [vacant]. He has a blank look.
彼はぼんやりと川の流れを見ていた.	He stared vacantly at the flow of the river.

ぼんやりしていると交通事故を起こしますよ.	Don't be careless or you'll cause a traffic accident.
ぼんやりしていて,一駅乗り越してしまった.	I was daydreaming and rode one station past my stop.
忙しいんだから,ぼんやりしていないでどんどん仕事を片づけてくれ.	There's a lot to be done, so snap out of it and get your work finished.
寝不足で頭がぼんやりしている.	My mind is foggy from lack of sleep.
私が小さい頃亡くなった祖母のことは,ぼんやりとしか覚えていない.	I can only faintly [vaguely] remember my grandmother who passed away when I was a child.
ビルの屋上から富士山がぼんやり見えた.	Mt. Fuji was vaguely [dimly, faintly] visible from the roof of the building.

ま

ま (間)
【時間】みんなが揃っているところにやって来るなんて, 僕はなんて間がいい〔悪い〕んだろう. — My showing up when everyone was together in the same place was really good (bad) timing.
この話, 父には少し間を置いて話したほうがいい. — You should wait a little while before you talk to Dad about this.
もう少し間の取り方を工夫して踊ったらもっと良くなりますよ. — If you work on your timing a little more when you dance, you'll improve.
出発までもうあまり間がない. — There's not much time left before departure.
事業を始めてまだ間がない. — It hasn't been long since I started the business.
眠る間もないほど忙しい. — I'm so busy that I don't even have time to sleep.
彼女と話すときは間がもたない. — I run out of things to say when I talk to her.
知らぬ間に居眠りをしてしまった. — I dozed off before I knew it.
【部屋】僕のアパートは二間しかない. — My apartment has only two rooms.
【慣用】学校をずる休みして町を歩いていたら, 先生と会ってしまい, 間の悪い思いをした. — I felt so awkward the time I skipped school and then ran into my teacher when I was walking around town.

まあまあ
「試験の結果はどうでしたか」「まあまあでした」 — "How did you do on the exam?" "So-so. [O.K./Fair.]"
彼女はまあまあ美人だ. — I suppose you could †say she's [call her] beautiful.
あの映画はまあまあ面白かったですよ. — I guess that movie was sort of interesting.
彼の新しい本はまあまあの売れ行きだ. — His new book is selling just so-so.
このぐらいできればまあまあだろう. — If you can do this, it's not so bad.

マイナス
【ゼロより下】 おかしいな，合計がマイナスになるなんて．
That's strange. Why would the total come to minus zero?

明日はマイナス10度まで気温が下がるそうだ．
I hear the temperature is going down to †10 below [10 degrees below zero] tomorrow.

文化祭の屋台は差し引き2万円のマイナスになった．
The food stall at the culture festival †came out with a loss of [lost] ¥20,000.

その年の経済成長率はマイナスだった．
That year, the economy had negative growth.

その年，経済成長率はマイナスに転じた．
That year, economic growth had [experienced] a downturn.

【引く・減ること】 消費税をプラスするところをマイナスしてしまった．
Instead of adding on the sales tax, I had subtracted it.

今月の売り上げは先月比15万円のマイナスになりそうだ．
Sales this month will probably fall by ¥150,000 compared to last month.

【不利益・悲観的】 会社の合併にはプラス面とマイナス面がある．
There are advantages and disadvantages to the company merger.

あんな奴とのつきあいは君にとってマイナスにしかならないよ．
Hanging out with someone like that isn't going to do you any good.
Associating with the likes of him can work against you.

父は若い女性の一人暮らしにマイナスイメージを持っている．
My father doesn't like the idea of women living alone.

マイナス思考はよくないよ．
Negative thinking is not a good thing.

まいる（参る）
【負ける】 参った！ 負けたよ．
OK! [I give up!] You win!

【困る】 参ったなあ，また雨か．
Oh no! [Darn!] Rain again?

全然できないよ．参ったなあ．
I just can't do it at all. What am I going to do?

この大事なときに彼が来ないなんて，参りましたね．
How could he not come at an important time like this! What are we going to do?

だれにも連絡は取れないし，お金もないし，あのときは本当に参りました．
I couldn't get in touch with anyone and I didn't have any money. I was really in a mess then.

取り引きが失敗して彼はだいぶ参っている．
The deal fell through and he's a wreck.

まう（舞う）
彼女は『藤娘』を見事に舞った．
She †danced [performed the dance]

	"Fujimusume" splendidly.
木の葉が風に舞っている.	The leaves are blowing around in the wind.
粉雪が音もなく舞っている.	The powdery snow is fluttering silently.
トンビが空中高く舞っている.	The kite is circling high up in the sky.

まえ (前)

【場所】前の席へ行こう.	Let's sit up front.
皆さん, 前の方へ来てください.	Everyone, please come up front.
真っすぐ前を見なさい.	Look †straight ahead [up front].
彼は教室でいちばん前の席に座っている.	He's sitting in the front row of the classroom.
前を歩いているのはトムじゃないか?	Isn't that Tom walking in front of us?
駅の前の喫茶店で2時に会おう.	Let's meet at the coffee shop in front of the station at two.
ホームの前の方で乗ったほうが電車がすいていていいよ.	You should get on at the front end of the platform because the train isn't so crowded there.
筋がよく分からなくなったので前の部分をもう一度読みなおした.	I didn't understand the plot very well so I read the first part over again.
【時】この辺りは前は田んぼだった.	This area used to be a rice paddy.
前の校長先生は厳しい人だった.	Our former principal was very strict.
前の車は売って新しいのを買った.	I sold †my old car [the car I had] and bought a new one.
この前話したことはどうなりましたか.	What happened with what we talked about last time?
誕生日にネックレスを買ってくれるって前に約束したじゃないの.	But you promised all along to buy me a necklace for my birthday.
日光へは前から一度行きたいと思っていました.	I've always wanted to go to Nikko.
私たちは3年前にこの家に引っ越して来ました.	We moved into this house three years ago.
彼は8時前に起きたためしがない.	He never gets up before eight o'clock.
約束の時間の20分前に着いた.	I got there 20 minutes earlier than the time we agreed on.
映画の前売り券を買った.	I bought advance tickets for the movie.
給料を前借りした.	I got an advance on my salary.

まかせる (任せる)

この仕事は全部君に任せたよ.	I'm leaving you in complete charge of this work.
年を取ったので店を人に任せるこ	I'm getting old so I've decided to put

とにした.	someone else in charge of the store.
彼は大事なことを安心して任せられる人だ.	He can be entrusted [He's a person you can entrust] with important matters.
ここは一つ私に任せてほしい.	I'll [Let me] take care of this.
私は子どものことは子どものするに任せている.	I let the children do what they want to do.
この場合は彼の判断に任せるしかない.	In this case we have no choice but to leave it up to his judgment.
彼は金に任せて高価な絵を買いまくった.	He bought up one expensive painting after another, sparing no expense whatsoever.

まがる (曲がる)

【線や道などが】直線を引こうと思ったが, 曲がってしまった.	I intended to draw a straight line, but it ended up crooked [curved].
ネクタイが曲がっているよ.	Your necktie's crooked.
暑さのためにレールが曲がってしまった.	The rails warped from the heat.
この道はくねくねと曲がっている.	This road twists and turns. / This is a winding road.
【体が】あのおじいさんは腰が曲がっている.	That old man is bent over.
リューマチでひざが曲がらなくなってしまった.	I can't bend my knees anymore because of rheumatism.
【根性などが】彼は根性が曲がっているのでだれからも好かれない.	Nobody likes him because he has such a twisted personality.
僕は曲がったことが大嫌いだ.	I hate anything †crooked [that isn't kosher].
【方向を変える】駅はそこを右に曲がるとすぐです.	If you turn right there, you'll be (almost) at the station.
その家の角を曲がると学校があります.	If you turn the corner at that house, there's a school.
車はカーブを曲がり切れずにガードレールにぶつかった.	The car didn't make the curve and bumped into the guardrail.

まぎらす (紛らす)

そんなに心配しないで, 散歩でもして気を紛らしたら？	Don't worry so much. Why don't you take a walk to get your mind off things?
彼は待ち時間に小説を読んで気を紛らした.	While waiting he distracted himself (by) reading a novel.
酒は心の痛みを紛らしてくれる.	Drinking distracts the mind from grief.
彼は酒で悲しみを紛らした.	He drowned his sorrows in drink.
彼女は当惑を笑いに紛らした.	She tried to hide her embarrassment with a smile.

まぎらわしい (紛らわしい)

あなたのスーツケースは私のと似ていて紛らわしい. — Your suitcase looks like mine. It's confusing. [I can't tell which is which.]

そんな紛らわしい言い方をするなよ. — Don't be so ambiguous.

まく¹ (蒔・撒く)

【種を】庭に草花の種をまいた. — I planted flower seeds in the garden.

自らまいた種は自らの手で刈らなければならない. — As you sow, so shall you reap.

【水・豆を】玄関に水をまいた. — I sprinkled water in the entry way.

日本では厄払いとして節分に豆をまく習慣がある. — In Japan there is a custom of throwing beans on the last day of winter to cast out evil spirits.

【ビラ・金・話題を】街頭でビラをまいていた. — They were handing [passing] out handbills on the street.

彼は今回の選挙でだいぶ金をまいたようだ. — It appears that he spent a lot of money on the election this time.

あの若い歌手はいつもにぎやかな話題をまいている. — That young singer always gives people a lot to talk about.

まく² (巻く)

床の間につるしてあった掛け軸を巻いて箱にしまった. — I rolled up the scroll that had been hanging in the *tokonoma* and put it away in a box.

父は昔たばこを辞書の紙で巻いてのんだことがあると言った. — My father said that he had once smoked cigarettes rolled with the pages of a dictionary.

時計のねじを巻き忘れたので止まってしまった. — I forgot to wind up the clock and it stopped.

写したフィルムを巻き戻した. — I rewound the film I shot.

彼の腕は包帯でグルグルと巻かれていた. — His arm was all †wrapped up with bandages [bandaged up].

壊れ易い物だから柔らかい紙で巻いたほうがいい. — It's fragile, so you should wrap it up in soft paper.

まく³ (幕)

その式場には紅白の幕が張り巡らされた. — Red and white curtains were hung for that ceremony.

芝居の幕が上がった. — The curtain rose on the play.

芝居はハッピーエンドで幕になった. — The curtain fell on the play with a happy ending.

【芝居の場面】次の幕がこの芝居の — The high point of this play is the next act.

見せ場だ.	
彼女は二幕目に出演する.	She performs in the second act.
この芝居は三幕五場からなる.	This play consists of five scenes in three acts.
最後の幕までゆっくりご観覧ください.	Please relax and watch until the final curtain.
【慣用】いよいよ陸上競技大会の幕が切って落とされた.	The track and field meet finally began.
その組織は自らの役目を終え，30年の活動に幕を下ろした［幕が引かれた］.	Having played its role, the institution brought to an end its thirty-year record of activities.
ここはお前の出る幕じゃない.	This is none of your business.
	This has nothing to do with you.

まける (負ける)

【敗れる】父はひいきの野球チームが負けると機嫌が悪くなる.	My father gets in a bad mood whenever his favorite baseball team loses.
僕はじゃんけんにすぐ負ける.	I always lose right away at rock, paper, scissors.
その子はけんかに負けて，泣いて帰って来た.	That child lost a fight and came home crying.
その子どもはトランプに負けて悔しがった.	That child felt frustrated because he had lost at cards.
腕相撲だけはだれにも負けないつもりだ.	At least as far as arm wrestling goes, I don't think anyone can beat me.
【屈服する】彼は時の権力に負けてしまった.	He †gave in [lost] to the powers of the time.
父はどんな困難にも負けず頑張り抜いた.	My father fought it out doggedly not giving in to any difficulty.
君の粘り強さには負けたよ.	I give in to your persistence.
禁酒していたが，誘惑に負けてまた飲み始めた.	I was abstaining from alcohol but gave into temptation and started drinking again.
【炎症を起こす】うるしに負けて湿疹が出た.	The lacquer made my skin break out.
私はかみそりに負けるたちだ.	My skin is very sensitive to razors.
【劣る】日本映画は欧米と比べても決して負けないだろう.	Japanese movies are by no means inferior to Western movies.
体力的にはもう子どもに負けてしまう.	Physically I'm not as strong as my children anymore.
【値引きする】今日はうんとまけておくよ.	I'll give you a †huge discount [big bargain] today.
もう少しまけてくれない？	Can't you make it a little cheaper?

あの店はよくまけてくれる.	That store gives good bargains.

まげる (曲げる)

ひじを曲げると痛みます.	My elbow hurts when I bend it.
ヘルニアになってしまい、腰を曲げられない.	I got a hernia and can't bend over.
針金を曲げてハンガーを作った.	I bent the wire to make a hanger.
【歪める】だれの頼みでも法を曲げることはできない.	No matter who does the asking, the law cannot be changed.
自分の主義を曲げてまでその地位に就こうとは思わない.	I won't go (as far as going) against my principles just for the sake of status.
彼は決して信念を曲げない男である.	He never compromises his conviction.
あの人はへそを曲げたらてこでも動かない.	Once he gets ornery,** he just won't budge.
僕の言ったことをそういうふうに曲げて受け取らないでくれよ.	Don't take what I said in such a distorted way.
【傾ける】彼女は首をちょっと曲げて話をする癖がある.	She has a habit of tilting her head slightly as she talks.

まこと (真・誠)

【本当】うそか真か、調べてみればすぐ判るよ.	If you check you'll find out whether it's true or false right away.
【誠意・真心】彼は何事にも誠を尽くしてやる人だ.	Whatever he does, he does with the utmost sincerity.
誠を尽くして説得したら彼も改心してくれたようだ.	After a lot of sincere persuasion it appears that he has †mended his ways [reformed].

まことに (誠に)

それは誠にお気の毒です.	I am sincerely [truly] sorry to hear that.
誠に申しわけございません.	I am sincerely [truly] sorry.
あの映画は誠に面白かった.	That movie was really [truly] interesting.
彼は誠に立派な人物です.	He is truly a splendid individual.

まさか

まさか家を出ていくつもりじゃないでしょうね？	You can't be serious about leaving home!
彼女の姿を見たような気がしたけれど、まさかこんな場所にいるはずないよね.	I thought I saw her but I can't believe she'd be caught in a place like this.
まさか自分がリストラにあうとは思ってもみなかった.	I never dreamt I'd lose my job to restructuring.

まさかとは思っていたが,犯人はやっぱり彼だったのか.	I wouldn't have believed that he was the culprit. Surely he couldn't have been the culprit!
「富士山に3時間で登ったんだ」「まさか!」	"I climbed Mt. Fuji in three hours." "No kidding!"
「彼女,先月亡くなったそうだよ」「まさか!」	"I heard she died last month." "Oh, no!"
優勝候補のチームが,まさかの1回戦敗退を喫した.	Nobody could believe that the favorite team would be cut in the first round of games.
まさかの時に備えてお金を貯めている.	I'm saving money for an emergency.

まさつ(摩擦)

寒いときに体を布で摩擦すると温かくなる.	If you rub your body with a cloth when it's cold, you'll get warm.
摩擦によって静電気を起こすことができる.	Static electricity can be produced by friction.
【紛争・不和】人とのつきあいにおいて不要な摩擦は避けたいものだ.	In relations with other people, unnecessary friction is something to be avoided.
我が国とその国とのあいだに貿易摩擦が生じている.	Trade friction has arisen between our country and that country.
あの二人のあいだには目に見えない摩擦が起きているようだ.	There seems to be some friction [conflict] between those two.

まさに(正に)

これこそ正に私の考えていたことだ.	This is just [exactly, indeed] what I expected.
そう,正にそのとおりなんですよ.	Yes, you've hit the nail on the head.

まさる(勝る)

彼は兄弟の中ですべての点において勝っている.	He is the most outstanding among his brothers and sisters in all respects.
彼女は聞きしに勝る美人だった.	She was much more of a beauty than I had heard.
子どもたちが元気に成長してくれることが何物にも勝る喜びだ.	Seeing our children growing up strong and healthy is a joy second to †none [no other].
これは外国の製品に勝るとも劣らない製品だ.	This product is just as good as one from overseas.

まし

何もないよりはましだと思う.	I think it's better than nothing.
そんな苦しい思いをするなら死んだほうがましだ.	I would rather die than suffer so much pain.
	I would (just) as soon die as suffer so much pain.
彼にお金を貸すくらいなら捨てたほうがましだ.	I'd rather throw money away than lend it to him.
	I'd (just) as soon throw money away as lend it to him.
もう少しましなアイデアはないのかね.	Can't you come up with a little better idea?

まじめ

あの人はまじめな人だ.	He's a decent guy.
	He's a person [man] of decent character.
彼のまじめな顔を見たことがない.	I've never seen him look serious.
まじめに働けば,この経済的な苦しさも乗り越えられる.	If you work hard, you'll be able to overcome this financial difficulty.
彼女は何でもまじめに取る.	She takes everything seriously.
彼はまじめな顔をして冗談を言う.	He tells jokes with a straight face.
最近は彼もギャンブルをやめて,まじめに暮らしている.	He's given up gambling and has been leading a serious life lately.

まじる (交・混じる)

雨に雪が混じり始めた.	The rain has become mixed with snow.
この御飯は白米の中に麦が混じっている.	This white rice is cooked with barley.
彼女にはアメリカ人の血が混じっているらしい.	She's supposed to be part American.
郵便物の中に他人の手紙が1通交じっていた.	A letter for somebody else was mixed in with my mail.
この生地にはナイロンが交じっている.	This cloth contains nylon.
子どものくせに,大人に交じっていつまでも起きていてはいけません.	You're a child and shouldn't stay up till all hours with grown-ups.
そのおばあさんの言葉は方言交じりで,よく分からなかった.	Since that old lady spoke partly in her dialect, I couldn't understand her very well.
その人は,年は50くらいで白髪交じりです.	He's about 50 years old and has hair streaked with gray.

まじわる (交わる)

【交差する】この道路はしばらく行くと幹線道路と交わります. — If you follow this road a ways, it †crosses [intersects with] the main road.

平行でない2直線はいつか交わる. — Two straight lines that are not parallel intersect at some point.

【交際する】私はどんな友達とも親しく交わるようにしている. — I try to be close to all my friends.

ます (増す)

【多くなる】今年は去年よりもメーデーの参加者が増した. — More people participated in May Day this year than last year.

昨夜の雨で川の水量が増した. — Last night's rain increased the level of water in the rivers.

手紙は目方が増えるとそれだけ料金も増す. — The postage increases in proportion to the weight of the letter.

列車はだんだん速度を増した. — The train gradually increased its speed.

彼はこの1年間でかなり英語の実力を増してきた. — He has increased his ability in English quite a bit in the last year.

子どもの成長とともに親の経済的負担も増してくる. — The economic burden placed on parents by their children increases as they grow up.

【ふやす】手が足りないので, もっと人手を増すことにした. — We were shorthanded, so we decided to get more people.

父は年とともに威厳を増してきた. — My father became more dignified as he grew older.

母親の病気が良くなるにつれ彼女はだんだん明るさを増してきた. — The more her mother's health improved, the more cheerful she became.

まず

【先に・とにかく】まず初めにこの件から片づけよう. — To begin with, why don't we take up this topic?

まず最初にご用件から伺いましょう. — Well, first of all let's discuss your business.

やけどをしたら, まず水で冷やしなさい. — The first thing to do if you burn yourself is to run cold water over the burn.

まずやってみます. — I'll try (it) first.

【どうやら・おそらく】この程度の成績を取っていれば, まずあの学校に入れるだろう. — With grades like this you probably don't need to worry about getting into that school.

夕焼けだからまず明日の天気は晴れだろう. — We can see the sunset, so the weather will probably be fine tomorrow.

まずは一件落着した. — Well, we've got that settled.

今日の試合にエースが登板するこ — There's almost no doubt that their ace

とはまず間違いないだろう．	pitcher will take the mound in today's game.

まずい

この料理はまずい．	This tastes [is] bad.／This is awful.
彼のまずい歌を聞くと頭が痛くなる．	His bad singing gives me a headache.
【都合が悪い】そんなことをしてはまずいよ．	You shouldn't do that.
彼女に本当のことを言ったのはまずかった．	You shouldn't have told her the truth.
まだ出来てないって？ それはまずいよ．	You haven't got it done yet? That's no good. [That just won't do.]
私がここにいるのを彼に知られるのはまずい．	It would really be awkward [bad] if he found out I was [were] here.
これはまずいことになりましたね．	This really turned out bad, didn't it?
まずい所でまずい人に会ったものだ．	I just ran into the wrong person in the wrong place.

まずしい (貧しい)

私は貧しい家庭に生まれました．	I was born into a poor family.
彼は家が貧しかったので高校にも行けなかった．	He came from a poor family so he couldn't even go to high school.
彼女は貧しい暮らしをしているが明るく豊かな心を持っている．	She doesn't have much money, but she is cheerful and bighearted.
あの小説家は表現力が貧しいのでろくな小説が書けない．	That novelist's powers of expression are so poor that he can't write satisfying novels.

ますます

彼女は最近ますますきれいになってきた．	She's gotten more and more beautiful lately.
お陰さまで商売はますます繁盛しています．	Fortunately business is getting better all the time.
このところ，ますます暮らしにくい世の中になってきた．	The world is becoming a harder and harder place to live in these days.
秋になったら，ますます食欲が出てきた．	My appetite got larger and larger when fall came.
両国の関係はますます悪くなってきている．	Relations between the two countries are becoming worse and worse.

まぜる (交・混ぜる)

ケーキを作るのに，まず卵とバタ	I mixed eggs, butter and flour first to

ーと小麦粉を混ぜた. | make some cakes.
子どもがいたずらをして，白と黒の碁石を交ぜてしまった. | Up to mischief, the children mixed up the black and white *go* stones.

また

【もう一度】また来てください. | Please come again.
いずれまたお伺いします. | I would like to come again some other time.
またとない良い機会だからそれを逃す手はない. | We're not going to get another chance [opportunity] like this again so we can't let it pass.
また始まった！ | Here we go again!
【同様に】弟もまた，兄同様にきまじめなやつだ. | He's just as serious as his older brother.
【その上】森鷗外は軍医であり，また，偉大な文豪でもあった. | Mori Ogai was a great writer as well as an army surgeon.
| Mori Ogai was not only an army surgeon but a great writer as well.
先日はお世話さまでした. また，その節は結構な物をありがとうございました. | Thank you very much for the other day. And thank you also for the lovely gift.
【別の】今日は時間がないので，またの機会にお寄りします. | I don't have enough time today so I'll come see you another time.
【間接の】本のまた貸しはいけません. | You shouldn't lend a book you borrowed to someone else.
また聞きだけど，彼は結婚するらしい. | This is secondhand information [I got it secondhand], but it seems he's going to get married.

まだ

彼の油絵はまだ素人の域を脱していない. | His oil paintings have not yet reached beyond the amateur level.
彼はまだ独身でいる. | He's still single.
彼女は年の割にはまだ若いねえ. | She still looks so young[1] for her age.
そのことについて詳しい話はまだ聞いていない. | I still haven't heard the details about it.
不景気はまだ当分続きそうだ. | The economic slump is going to continue for a while yet.
そんなに飲んでもまだ飲み足りないの？ | After all you've had to drink, you still haven't had enough?
まだ締め切りには間に合いそうだ. | We can still make the deadline.
「今何時ですか」「まだ4時です」 | "What time is it?" "It's only four."
ここに移って来てまだ半年だ. | It's only been six months since we moved

here.
We moved here only six months ago.

> 1) look young は「外見が若い」の意.「やることが若い」という場合には act young と言う.

または
明日は雨または雪が降るでしょう. It'll probably either rain or snow tomorrow.

次の日曜日にはテニスをしようか, または映画を見に行こうか迷っている. I can't decide whether to play tennis or go to the movies next Sunday.

まち (町・街)
私は田舎の小さな町で生まれた. I was born in a small country town.

麹町界わいは昔, 屋敷町だった. Kojimachi used to be an affluent residential area [neighborhood].

【都会】弟は田舎の生活は嫌だと言って町に出て行った. My brother didn't like living in the country, so he left to go to the city.

町の生活は田舎と比べるといろいろな点で便利だ. In many respects compared to the country, living in the city is more convenient.

【通り】春になり, 街行く人々の服装が急に華やいできた. Spring has come and the people you see on the street have suddenly begun to wear bright colors.

街でばったり昔の友人に出会った. I ran into an old friend in town today.

まちあわせる (待ち合わせる)
友達と新宿駅で待ち合わせた. I met my friend as planned [arranged] at Shinjuku Station.

彼とは何時に待ち合わせしているの? What time are you supposed to meet him?

彼女は友達と待ち合わせしているところをモデル事務所にスカウトされた. She was scouted by a modeling agency while she was waiting for a friend.

待ち合わせの時間まであと20分ある. There's still 20 minutes until we're supposed to meet.

待ち合わせの場所を変更したいんですが. Could we change our meeting place?

まちがい (間違い)
【誤り・過ち】次の文章の間違いを正しなさい. Correct the mistakes in the following sentences.

この論文は間違いだらけだ. This paper [article] is full of mistakes.

彼女は間違いのない人です.	She's a reliable person.
ご注文の洋服は間違いなく明日仕上がります.	The suit you ordered will definitely [certainly, surely] be ready tomorrow.
明日は間違いなく来ます.	I'll be here tomorrow †for sure [without fail].
彼は間違いを起こして会社を辞めさせられた.	He made a big mistake and was forced to resign from the company.
【事故】彼はまだ帰って来ないけど, 間違いがなければ良いが.	He hasn't come back yet. I hope nothing has happened.

まちがえる (間違える)

僕はよく計算を間違える.	I often make mistakes in calculation.
試験の答えを間違えてしまった.	I answered the question incorrectly on the exam.
医者は患者に薬の量を間違えて投与した.	The doctor administered the wrong dose of medicine.
ホテルで部屋を間違えてしまった.	At the hotel I went into the wrong room by mistake.
母はよく電話を掛け間違える.	My mother often dials the wrong number.
私は向こうから来る人を父と間違えて大声で呼んでしまった.	I mistook the person approaching me for my father and called out loudly to him.

まちがった[て] (間違った[て])

彼について君は間違った見方をしているようだ.	You seem to be mistaken about him.
あなたの考えは間違っています.	You are wrong.
間違った情報に振り回されてはいけない.	Don't be misled by wrong information.
間違って他人の傘を持って来てしまった.	I picked up someone else's umbrella by mistake.
彼は間違って車を塀にぶつけてしまった.	By accident, he banged the car into a fence.
彼女はどうしたのか一日じゅう計算を間違ってばかりいる.	I don't know what's the matter with her but she's been making nothing but mistakes in her calculations all day long.

まちどおしい (待ち遠しい)

パーティーが待ち遠しい.	I'm looking forward to the party.
	I just can't wait to go to the party.
彼女の帰国が待ち遠しい.	I just can't wait for her to get back to Japan.
日曜日が待ち遠しい.	I just can't wait for Sunday.

まつ (待つ)

私は彼女を駅で待った．	I waited for her at the station.
彼女はこの駅の入口で待っているようにと我々に言った．	She told us to wait for her at the entrance of this station.
長いこと待っているが，出前のすしがまだ届かない．	We've been waiting for a long time but the *sushi* hasn't †arrived [been delivered] yet.
彼女は首を長くして息子の帰りを待っている．	She's eagerly waiting for her son to come back.
頼むからあと10日ほど待ってくれないか．	Would you please wait another 10 days?
彼女は待ってくれと叫んだが，兄は走り続けた．	She shouted to her brother to wait up, but he just kept on running.
彼女が真夜中に帰宅すると，両親は寝ずに彼女を待っていた．	When she returned home at midnight, she found her parents waiting up for her.
オーブンの火を消すあいだ，電話を切らずに待っているようにと友達に言った．	I told my friend on the telephone to hold on while I turned off the oven.
そのことについては今後の調査を待とう．	Let's put that aside until the next investigation.

まっすぐ (真っすぐ)

【直線的】定規を当てて真っすぐな線を引きなさい．	Draw a straight line using a ruler.
この道は真っすぐ北に延びている．	This road goes directly north.
背筋を真っすぐ伸ばしなさい．	Straighten your back.
【直接】寄り道をしないで，真っすぐ家に帰って来るんですよ．	Don't stop anywhere; come straight home.
急いでいたので真っすぐ目的地に向かった．	We were in a hurry, so we headed straight for our destination.
【正直な】彼は真っすぐな人間だ．	He's a person of upstanding character.
父は何でも真っすぐに物を言う．	My father is very blunt.

まったく (全く)

彼が市長に立候補するなんて全く驚いた．	I'm really surprised that he's running for mayor.
君の話には全く同感だ．	I agree with you completely.
彼のだらしなさには全くあきれてしまった．	I was totally amazed at his sloppiness.
その話は全く信じられないよ．	I can't believe that at all.
全くの話，彼にはこの仕事は任せられない．	Believe me, you can't leave this job up to him.

| 全くのところ，彼女の扱いには頭を痛めている． | Believe me, I'm at my wit's end as to how to handle her. |
| 全くもう，しょうがないやつだ！ | Honestly, what can you do with someone like him?! |

〜まで(に)

【時】大抵の会社では正午から1時までがお昼休みです．	At most companies lunch hour is from noon to one.
4時までには必ず家に帰っていらっしゃい．	Be sure to be home by four.
明日までにレポートを提出しなければならない．	I have to hand in my report by tomorrow.
これを月曜日までにやって〔読んで〕きてください．	(Please) Have this done [read] by Monday.
昨夜は2時まで起きていた．	I stayed up till two o'clock in the morning last night.
承諾のご返事を頂けるまで待ちます．	I'll wait until I receive your consent.
【距離】ちょっと角のお店まで行って来ます．	I'm just going to the corner store. (I'll) Be right back.
彼は駅までは歩いて，あとはタクシーに乗った．	He walked as far as the station and took a taxi the rest of the way.
【〜にさえも】子どもにまで笑われてしまった．	Even the children laughed at me.
君まで僕のことを馬鹿にするのか．	Do you have to laugh at me too?
【〜だけ】気にするなよ．ちょっと言ってみたまでだ．	Don't get upset (about it). I was just [only] teasing [joking].
【までもない】言うまでもないが，この書類の扱いは慎重に．	Needless to say, these documents must be handled carefully.
わざわざご足労いただくまでもありません．	There's no need for you to go to the trouble of coming in person.

まと (的)

【標的】彼の射た矢は見事に的のど真ん中に命中した．	The arrow he shot hit the bull's eye beautifully.
的を狙って石を投げた．	I threw a rock at the target.
ピストルの弾はわずかに的を外れた．	The bullet just missed the mark.
【狙い・対象】就職はあちこちに口をかけるより的を (一つに) 絞って狙ったほうがいいよ．	When you're looking for a job, rather than trying here, there and everywhere, it's better to narrow it down (to one).
彼の勝手な行動は非難の的になっている．	His disregard for others is the object of criticism.

それはなかなか的を射た意見だ. What you say hits the nail on the head.
きみの的外れの質問には参るよ. Your question is †so wide of the mark [so out of it,** off the wall**] that it floors** me.

まとまる

【一つになる・整う】やっと卒業論文がまとまった. I finally finished my senior thesis.

この論文はよくまとまっている. This thesis [paper] is well-organized.

修学旅行では皆でまとまって行動しなさい. On the school trip everyone must travel with the group.

急いでまとまったお金を作り出さなければならなかった. I had to get quite a large sum of money fast.

【成立する・解決する】話し合いは紛糾して, いつまでたってもまとまらない. The talks have gotten complicated and are getting nowhere fast.

意見がまとまったので, 行動に移そう. Now that we've reached †an agreement [a settlement], let's start the actual work.

娘の縁談がやっとまとまりました. Our daughter's marriage plans have finally been settled.

まとめる

【統合する】私は日曜日に一週間分の食料をまとめて買う. I buy the week's groceries all at one time on Sundays.

月末にまとめてお支払いします. I'll pay (you) in full at the end of the month.

皆の意見をまとめるのに苦労した. I had difficulty getting everyone to agree.

彼女は海外での体験を1冊の本にまとめた. She collected [gathered] her experiences abroad into a book.

データをまとめて結論を出した. I came up with the result after organizing the data.

【完成させる・成立させる】彼は難しい商談をうまくまとめた. He skillfully managed to settle the difficult business negotiations.

この研究をまとめるのに3年かかった. It took me three years to compile [complete] this study.

その話を是非まとめたいものだ. I'd really like to settle that matter.

考えをまとめるのに少し時間が要る. I need some time to organize my thoughts.

まとも

彼は思ったよりまともな人だ. He's more †serious-minded [honest and sincere] than I thought.

まどわす

会議でまともな意見を述べたのは彼だけだった.	He was the only one who expressed a sensible opinion at the meeting.
彼も今ではまともな暮らしをしている.	He's leading a respectable life now.
あんなことをするなんて, 彼女はまともじゃない.	She's crazy [insane] to do such a thing.
君の考え方はまともじゃない.	Your way of thinking is abnormal.
【正面から】排気ガスがまともに顔に掛かった.	The exhaust fumes hit [got] me right in the face.
野球のボールがまともに腕に当った.	The baseball hit [got] me right in the arm.
君は私の顔をまともに見られないだろう.	I bet you can't look me straight in the face.
彼に何か頼むときはまともに頼んでもだめだよ. だれか実力者を介さなければ.	When you want him to do something, he won't do it even if you ask him point-blank. You've got to go through someone that has more influence.

まどわす (惑わす)

誇大広告はとかく消費者を惑わすことが多い.	Exaggerated advertisements often mislead consumers.
彼は彼女の魅力に惑わされた.	He was captivated by her charm.
彼は, その思想が人心を惑わすものとして迫害された.	He was persecuted as a person whose way of thinking led people astray.

まなぶ (学ぶ)

【教わる】「我々現代人は先人に学ぶところが多い」と歴史の先生は言った.	Our history teacher said that we can learn a lot from our ancestors.
日本はまだ欧米から学ぶべきところが多い.	There is still quite a lot Japan can learn from the West.
【勉学する】彼はパリで4年間フランス文学を学んだ.	He spent four years in Paris studying French literature.
	He studied French literature in Paris for four years.
「よく遊び, よく学べ」が彼の信条である.	He lives by the motto, "Study hard, play hard."

まにあう (間に合う)

いつもより遅く家を出たが, バスに間に合った.	I left the house later than usual but was still in time to catch the bus.
レポートはかろうじて提出期限に間に合った.	I barely got the report in on time.
	I got the report in just under the wire.

早くしないと芝居の始まりに間に合わないわよ.	If you don't hurry, you'll miss the beginning of the play.
【足りる・用立つ】この机は古いが子どもたちには十分間に合うよ.	This desk may be old but it †is good enough [will do] for the kids.
砂糖が少ししかないけれど, これで間に合うかしら.	There's only a little sugar left. Will this be enough?
夕食の買い物なら3千円もあれば間に合うだろう.	Three thousand yen will be more than sufficient [enough] if you're just shopping for dinner.
その辞書で十分間に合う.	That dictionary will suffice. That dictionary is more than enough [adequate].

まにあわせる (間に合わせる)

【期日に】課題を期日までにどうにか間に合わせた.	I actually got the assignment done on time.
何とか今月末までに間に合わせてください.	I would appreciate it if this could be ready by the end of the month.
【不十分なもので】新しいものは買わないで古いノートで間に合わせた.	I made do with an old notebook instead of buying a new one.
テーブルがなかったので, ダンボール箱で間に合わせた.	I made do with a cardboard box because I didn't have a table.
これだけしか予算がないんだからそれで間に合わせるしかない.	We have to make do with this budget because it's all we have.
こんな間に合わせの対策ではだめだ.	This type of makeshift [stopgap] solution is unacceptable.

まねく (招く)

【招待する】あの大学では今度アメリカの大学から, 有名な教授を招いた.	That university has invited a famous scholar from an American university (to be their visiting lecturer).
昨日, 友人の結婚式に招かれた.	I was invited to a friend's wedding yesterday.
友人を新居に招いて歓談した.	I invited a friend over to my new house where we had a nice chat.
来週お忙しくなければ, あなたとご家族の皆さんを夕食にお招きします.	If you aren't too busy, I will invite you and your family over for dinner next week.
今夜, 私たちはすぐ隣に住む人たちを家に招いている.	We are having our next-door neighbors over tonight.
【引き起こす】自信過剰が彼の災いを招いた.	His overconfidence †invited [brought about] his misfortune.

管理のずさんさが大惨事を招きかねない.	Lack of careful supervision [Slipshod management] courts disaster.
妙な隠しだてをすると疑惑を招く.	If you go out of your way to conceal things, you will invite suspicion.
僕のあいまいな態度が誤解を招いてしまった.	My indecisive [vague] attitude †invited [brought on] misunderstanding.
彼の思いやりのない言葉が人々の怒りを招いた.	His insensitive remarks [comments] incurred people's anger.

まねる (真似る)

【模倣する】彼は人の癖を真似るのが上手だ.	He's good at imitating other †people [people's quirks].
子どもが猫の鳴き声を真似てみせた.	The kids gave us their imitation of a cat meowing.
この絵はゴッホの絵を真似ている.	This painting is an imitation of van Gogh.
他人の文章を真似ないで, 自分で思ったとおり書きなさい.	Write in your own style without imitating anyone else's writings.
【見倣う】少しはあの人の勤勉さを真似たらどうだね.	Why don't you at least try to copy his diligence?

まひ (麻痺)

交通事故で彼は下半身がまひした.	The traffic accident paralyzed him from the waist down.
ストライキで工場の機能がまひした.	The strike paralyzed the factory.
ストライキに突入すれば, JRはまひ状態になるだろう.	A strike would paralyze the JR.
寒さで指の感覚がまひしている.	My fingers are numb from the cold.

まぶしい

南太平洋の太陽はまぶしかった.	The South Pacific sun was dazzling.
部屋の明かりがまぶしくて目が痛くなった.	The light in the room was so bright that my eyes began to hurt.
彼女の笑顔がまぶしい.	She has a dazzling smile.
	Her smile is dazzling.

まま

【同じ状態】大人になってもそのままでいてね.	Don't ever change.[1]
	I hope you stay just as you are no matter how old you get.
あるがままの自分を受け入れなさい.	Accept yourself as you are.
現状のままではいけない. 何とか	Things can't remain the way they are. We

打破しなければ.	have to make a change.
事故の現場はそのままにしておいてください.	Please don't touch anything at the site of the accident.
車のエンジンをかけたままにするな.	Don't leave the engine running.
冷蔵庫を開けたままにしちゃだめよ.	Don't leave the refrigerator open.
お母さんは部屋の電気をつけたままどこへ行ったのかしら.	Mom's left the light on in the house. I wonder where she went.
靴をはいたまま教室へ入って結構ですよ.	You †can come into [may enter] the classroom with your shoes on.
ひどく疲れていたので,服を着たまま眠ってしまった.	I was so tired that I fell asleep with my clothes on.
ガードレールが壊れたままになっている.	The guardrail is still broken.
彼は足が悪いので,座ったまま挨拶した.	He greeted us †without getting up [sitting down] because he has a bad leg.
彼女は頭に浮かぶままにメロディーを譜面に取っていった.	She wrote down the melody just as it came to her.
あんなひどいことを言われたままにしておいていいの?	Are you going to let him get away with that terrible remark?
料理がほとんど手つかずのまま残された.	Most of the meal was left untouched.
【意向どおり】言われるままに署名した〔判を押した〕.	I †signed it〔put my seal on it〕just as I was told to.
あいつはおれのなすがままだ.	He does as I say.
彼は意のままにならないとすぐに癇癪(かんしゃく)を起こす.	He loses his temper whenever things don't go the way he wants.
病み上がりで外出もままならない.	I wish I could go out but I still haven't completely recovered.

1) 決まった言い方.

まもなく (間もなく)

バスは間もなく終点に着きます.	The bus will be reaching the terminal in a moment.
父は間もなく帰って参ります.	My father will be home †shortly [before long].
この雨は間もなくやむでしょう.	It should stop raining soon, I think.
その人は事故のあと間もなくして息を引き取った.	He died soon after the accident.

まもる (守る)

【遵守する】交通規則はきちんと守りましょう. — You should obey all the traffic rules.

彼女は約束をちゃんと守る人だ. — She's the type of person who always keeps her promise. / She's a woman of her word.

【保護する】親は子どもを守る義務がある. — Parents are bound [obliged] to †look after [care for] their children.

「青少年を悪の手から守ろう」と街頭で呼びかけていた. — "Protect our young people from the clutches of evil," entreated a voice in the street.

【守備する】さあ最終回だ. しっかり守っていこう. — All right, it's the last inning. Let's keep up our defense.

まよう (迷う)

彼は山の中で迷った. — He lost his way in the mountain.

この大学に願書を出すときはちょっと迷った. — I hesitated a little before I sent the application form to this college.

今学期はどの講義を取ろうか迷っている. — I can't decide what course to take this semester.

行こうか行くまいか迷っている. — I can't make up my mind whether to go or not. / I'm torn between going and not going.

どっちがいいか判断に迷いますね. — It's really hard to decide which is best, isn't it?

まるい (丸い)

【円型】台所に丸い形をしたテーブルがある. — We have a round table in the kitchen.

うちの子どもは丸い顔をしている. — Our child has a round face.

彼女は目を丸くして驚いた. — Her eyes opened wide in surprise.

丸く輪になりなさい. — Form a circle.

【円満】話を丸く収めたい. — I'd like to settle this discussion amicably.

年を取って父も近頃丸くなってきた. — Getting older, my father has begun to mellow lately.

まるで

【全く】これは本物とはまるで違う. — This is completely different from the real thing.

娘はまだ, まるで子どもで困ります. — My daughter is such a child that I don't know what to do.

この問題は難しくてまるで分からない. — This is a difficult problem so I am absolutely stumped.

そんなことになっているとは，まるで知らなかった．	I hadn't the faintest idea that things had come to such a point.
彼が相手じゃ，まるで勝負にならないよ．	Him as an opponent? That's no contest at all!
女の人に英語で話しかけられたがまるで分からなかった．	A lady approached me in English and I was thoroughly lost.
【ちょうど・さながら】あの二人はまるで兄弟のように似ている．	They look so much alike they could actually pass for brothers.
彼女はまるで男の子のような振る舞いをする．	She acts just like a boy.

まわす (回す)

子どもたちはこまを回して遊んだ．	The kids amused themselves by spinning a top.
時計の針を回して，時間を合わせた．	I turned the hands on the clock to set the time.
回覧板を早く回してください．	Please pass the bulletin on as quickly as possible.
サラダは自分の分を取ったら次の人に回してください．	After you have taken some salad, please pass it on to the next person.
迎えの車をお回しします．	I'll send the car around to your house.
【慣用】彼を敵に回すと手ごわいよ．	It'll make for rough going if we make an enemy of him.

まわり (周・回り)

【周囲・周辺】先生の周りに子どもたちが集まった．	The kids gathered round the teacher.
池の周りを自転車で一周した．	I rode around the pond on my bicycle.
学校の周りに工場がいくつも建った．	Many factories were built around the school.
家の周りを見知らぬ人がうろついている．	There's a stranger hanging around outside the house.
【巡回・迂回】彼は毎日お得意先回りをする．	He calls on his clients every day.
そこへ行くには車を使うと，かえって回り道になる．	If you plan going there by car, you'll wind up taking the long way round.
彼はヨーロッパから北回りの飛行機で帰ってきた．	He flew back home from Europe †via [by way of] the northern route.
【慣用】兄と私は年齢が一回りも違う．	My brother and I are about 12 years apart.
もう一回り大きい皿をください．	Give me the next larger size plate.
火の回りが早く，そのビルはまたたく間に全焼してしまった．	The fire spread rapidly and quickly consumed the entire building.

何も食べていないので酒の回りが早い.	The alcohol is going straight to my head because I haven't eaten anything.

まわりくどい (回りくどい)

彼は回りくどい言い方をする.	He talks in a roundabout way.
回りくどい説明は省いて実際にやってみましょう.	Let's do away with the tedious explanations and actually try it.

まわる (回る)

【回転する・旋回する】地球の周りを月が回っている.	The moon goes around the earth.
水車が回っている.	The water wheel is turning.
【立ち寄る】彼は朝から一日じゅう得意先を回る.	He spends the entire day calling on his customers.
半年かけてヨーロッパの各国を回ってきた.	We spent six months traveling around Europe.
京都の神社仏閣を歩いて回った.	We toured the shrines and temples of Kyoto on foot.
友人の家に回ってから帰ります.	I'll go home after stopping by a friend's house.
【巡る】毒が既に彼の体じゅうに回っていた.	The poison had already passed into his system.
父は酒がだいぶ回ってきた.	My father has really been hitting the bottle.
【慣用】今度は私にお鉢が回ってきた.	It's my turn this time.

まんいん (満員)

ツアー旅行のお申し込みは満員になりしだい締め切ります.	Reservations for the group tour will be closed as soon as we have a full booking.
入会希望者はすぐ満員になった.	The number of applicants immediately reached the limit.
彼は毎日, 満員電車に揺られて会社に通っている.	Every day on his commute to work he is jostled about on the packed train.
いつ行ってもあの飲み屋は満員だ.	No matter when you go, that small bar is full.
そのロックコンサートは大入満員だった.	There was a tremendous turnout at that rock concert.

まんぞく (満足)

彼は現状に満足している.	He's satisfied [content] with the status quo.
彼らのもてなしには大変満足しま	I was very much pleased with their hospi-

した.	tality.
結果は満足のゆくものだった.	The result was satisfactory.
彼女は満足な教育を受けていない.	She hasn't received a very satisfactory education.

まんなか (真ん中)

列車が鉄橋の真ん中で立往生した.	The train was stalled in the middle of the bridge.
髪を真ん中で分けてください.	Please part my hair in the middle.
この写真のちょうど真ん中にいる人はだれ?	Who's that person in the center of this photo?
部屋の真ん中に大きなテーブルが置いてある.	There's a big table smack in the center of the room.
彼女は三人姉妹の真ん中だ.	She's the second eldest of three sisters.
彼は都会のど真ん中に住んでいる.	He lives right in the heart of town.

み

み¹ (身)

【身体】彼女はいつもぜいたくなアクセサリーを身につけている.	She always wears expensive accessories.
彼女は東京の伯母の家に身を寄せている.	She's living [staying] at her aunt's house in Tokyo.
父は一家のために毎日身を粉にして働いている.	My father works himself to the bone every day for the sake of our family.
彼女はもうじき身二つになる.	She's going to be a mother soon.
彼はその研究に身も心もささげている.	He has †put his body and soul into [utterly devoted himself to] that research.
彼女の身のこなしは優雅だね.	She carries herself very eleganty, doesn't she?
外は零下20度の身を切るような寒さだ.	Outside it's a piercing [bitter] 20°C below zero.
防寒着で身を固めた.	I protected myself with winter clothes.
彼は寒さに身を縮めて歩いた.	The cold made him huddle over as he walked.
私はあまりの恥ずかしさに身の縮む思いだった.	I was so embarrassed (that) I wanted to disappear.
両親は身を切られるような思いで	The parents listened to the news of their

息子の死亡の知らせを聞いた.	son's death as if cut to the heart.
バーゲン会場は身動き一つできないほどの混雑だった.	It was so crowded at the bargain sale that there was scarcely room to budge.
ハイキングには身軽な服装で来てください.	Please wear practical clothes for the hike.
それは身の毛もよだつ話だった.	That story gave me goose bumps [flesh].
身の回りのことぐらい自分でしなさい.	It's the least you can do to take care of your personal matters by yourself.
【自分】それは身から出たさびだ.	You had it coming.
	You got what you deserved.
	You asked for it.
彼は地下での火災の恐ろしさを身をもって知った.	He experienced the terror of an underground fire firsthand.
彼は何をやっても身につかない.	No matter what he does, he always does it half-baked.
そんな話を聞くと身につまされる.	That story really hits close to home.
僕の言うことを聞いたほうが身のためだよ.	You'd better listen to what I'm saying for your own good.
彼はたび重なる失敗につくづくと身の不運を嘆いた.	He bemoaned his bad luck of repeating one failure after another.
【身分・立場】将来は洋裁で身を立てたい.	In the future I want to make a living as a tailor.
彼は会社を辞めて作家として身を立てるつもりだ.	He plans to quit his company and establish himself as a writer.
そろそろ君も身を固めたらどうだい.	Don't you think it's about time you got married and settled down?
社長からじきじきにお言葉を賜るとは身に余る光栄です.	The president pays me such direct compliments that it's really more honor than I deserve.
社長の令嬢に結婚を申し込むなんて, 君は全く身の程を知らなさすぎるよ.	You just don't know your place to go and do something like asking the president's daughter to marry you.
身の程を知れ.	Know your own bounds.
	Know your place.
文句ばかり言わないで私の身にもなってください.	Don't just bombard me with criticism. Try to see my side of it. [Put yourself in my place.]
この仕事から身を引くつもりだ.	I'm going to back out of this job.
彼は汚名を受けて政界から身を引いた.	Having earned a disreputable image, he retired from the political scene.
【心】君の忠告は身にしみたよ.	Your advice really sank in.
外国では人の親切が身にしみる.	I really appreciate people's kindness when I'm abroad.

彼もやっと身を入れて仕事をするようになった.	He's finally begun to really put himself into his work.
一度は身を焦がすほどの恋をしてみたい.	Just once, I'd like to fall passionately in love.
【生き方】彼は賭け事に夢中になり身を持ち崩してしまった.	He fell into a dissolute way of life after getting hooked on gambling.
彼は酒色に溺れ，身を誤ってしまった.	He got hooked on wine and women and ruined his life.
僕もそろそろ身のふり方を考えねばならない年になってきた.	I guess I've come to the age when I'd better start making plans for the future.
彼女は女性解放運動に身を投じた.	She threw herself into the women's liberation movement.
【中身】金がすべてだと言ってしまっては身もふたもないよ.	Saying out loud that money is everything is putting it too bluntly.
【肉】この魚は骨ばかりで身が少ない.	This fish is all bones and no meat.

み² (実)

【果実】柿の木が今年もたくさん実をつけた.	The persimmon trees bore plenty of fruit again this year.
リンゴの実が初めてなった.	The apple tree bore fruit for the first time.
この栗は実が小さい.	These chestnuts are small.
桑の実を食べたことがありますか.	Have you ever eaten mulberries?
【具】このみそ汁は実が少ないね.	There's not much †stock in [substance to] this *miso* soup, is there?
実ばかり食べないでスープも飲みなさい.	Don't just pick out the stock, drink the soup too!
【内容・中身】今日の講演はあまり実がなかったね.	Today's lecture lacked substance, I'd say. There wasn't much to today's lecture, was there?
こんな実のない論文は，読むだけ時間のむだだ.	It's just a waste of time reading this thesis. It's really unsubstantial.
【事の成就】二人の恋もようやく実を結んだ.	Their love finally joined in matrimony.
彼は努力が実を結んで実業家として成功した.	His efforts bore fruit and he became a successfull businessman.

みえ (見栄)

彼は見栄を張って高い車を買った.	He bought an expensive car just †for show [for the sake of appearances].
彼女は見栄を張って毛皮のコートを買った.	In a show of pretentiousness, she bought a fur coat.
彼女は見栄でそんなうそをついた	She told that lie out of vanity.

んだ.

みえすいた (見え透いた)

そんな見え透いたうそを僕が信じるとでも思ってるの？ — You don't expect me to believe such a transparent lie, do you?

そんな見え透いた言いわけが通るとは思っていないだろうね. — You don't expect me to accept such a flimsy excuse, do you?

そんな見え透いたお世辞なんか聞きたくないね. — I don't want to hear any more fawning compliments like that.

彼の考えていることなんて見え透いている. — It's obvious to me what he's thinking.

みえる (見える)

晴れた日には，ここから富士山がよく見える. — You can see Mt. Fuji well from here on a clear day.

暗がりに人影が見えた. — A man's shadow appeared out of the darkness.

眼鏡をかけたら遠くがよく見えるようになった. — Now that I have glasses, I can see things in the distance much better.

彼女は左眼がほとんど見えない. — She can hardly see out of her left eye.

前の人の頭が邪魔になって舞台がよく見えない. — The head of the person sitting in front of me is blocking my view of the stage.

【感じとれる】彼女は年よりもずっと若く見える. — She looks much younger than she is.

彼の作品はなかなか創意工夫の跡が見える. — His work shows great signs of ingenuity.

好調だった出版業界にも，このところかげりが見えてきた. — Publishers have been doing a good business but now it looks as if there may be a downturn.

事態好転の兆しが見えてきた. — Signs have appeared indicating that the situation is improving.

【来る】お客様がお見えになりました. — There's someone to see you.

あの方はまだ見えません. — He hasn't †come [shown up] yet.

みおくる (見送る)

友人を駅まで見送った. — I accompanied my friend as far as the station.
I saw my friend off at the station.

門の所まで客を見送った. — I saw my guest to the gate.

彼女の姿が見えなくなるまで見送った. — I watched her until she was out of sight.

【差し控える】我が社では本年度は — Our company has decided not to take on

新人の採用を見送ります.	any new employees this year.
この電車は込んでいるから見送って次の電車まで待とう.	This train is too crowded. Let's skip it and wait for the next one.
健康がすぐれないので海外旅行は見送ることにした.	I decided to pass on going abroad since I wasn't in such good health.

みがく (磨く)

彼女は毎食後必ず歯を磨く.	She always brushes her teeth after every meal.
その銀器は柔らかい布で磨かないと傷がつく.	If you don't use a soft cloth to wipe the silver, you'll scratch it.
せっかく靴を磨いたのに満員電車に乗ったらすぐ汚れてしまった.	I went to all the trouble of polishing my shoes only to get them scuffed up on the crowded train.
【練磨する】彼女は洋裁の腕を磨くために渡仏した.	In order to perfect her sewing skill, she went to France.
もっと技を磨かなければ, チャンピオンにはとうてい勝てないよ.	If you don't work harder on your technique, you won't stand half a chance against the champion.

みかた (味方)

綱引きで敵, 味方に分かれて戦った.	We divided up into opposing teams for the tug of war and fought it out.
彼を味方につければ, 怖いものなしだ.	With him as an ally, we won't have to fear anyone [anything].
彼を私たちの味方につけよう.	Let's get him on our side.
君のような心強い味方が出来たからには, もう安心だ.	Knowing that I have the support of somone like you †makes me feel much more at ease [is very reassuring].
僕はいつでも君の味方だ.	I'm always on your side.
彼はいつも弱い者に味方する.	He always takes the underdog's side.
兄は母に, 私の味方ばかりすると文句を言った.	My brother complained to my mother that she's always siding with me.
たとえ彼女が間違っているということが分かっていても, 彼はいつも彼女の味方になった.	He would always stick up for her, even when he knew that she was wrong.
私が苦しかったとき, 彼はずっと私の味方をしてくれた.	He continued to stand by me through all my difficulties.

みぐるしい (見苦しい)

そんな見苦しい真似をするな.	Don't do such an embarrassing thing. Don't act so repulsive.
親子のあいだの争いは見苦しい.	A fight between parent and child is

	unbecoming.
	It's unpleasant [disagreeable] to †see [hear (about)] quarrels between parents and children.
見苦しいから髪を切ってこいと先生に言われた.	The teacher told me to go get my hair cut because it looks awful.

みごと (見事)

彼のハンドルさばきは見事だ.	He handles the wheel beautifully.
それは見事な花嫁衣装だった.	It was a beautiful bridal gown.
彼は見事な作品を仕上げた.	He did a beautiful piece of work.
桜の花が見事に咲いている.	The cherry blossoms are blooming beautifully.
彼女に見事にふられた.	She did a beautiful job of rejecting me.
我々の計画は見事に成功〔失敗〕した.	Our plan was a total success [failure].
彼に見事にだまされた.	He sure did pull the wool over my eyes.

みこみ (見込み)

今年の売り上げは1億円の見込みだ.	Sales this year are expected to reach ¥100 million [a hundred million yen].
彼は今年の3月卒業の見込みです.	He's expected to graduate this March.
私の見込み違いだった.	It was my miscalculation.
私の見込みどおり, 彼女は一流の歌手になった.	She became a top-notch singer just as I had expected.
当分, 景気回復の見込みはない.	There will be no prospect for economic recovery for some time to come.
彼女の病気はもう回復の見込みがない.	She has no chance of recovering from her illness.
彼は新入社員の頃から見込みのあるやつだと思っていた.	I (had) thought he was a promising young man from the time he started working.

みこむ (見込む)

【予測する】今年は米の豊作が見込まれる.	We expect a good crop of rice this year.
横浜の新店舗では今年5千万円の売り上げを見込んでいる.	We expect our new Yokohama branch store to do ¥50 million [fifty million yen] in sales this year.
ボーナスを見込んで車を買った.	I was counting on my bonus when I bought a car.
今年は多額のボーナスは見込めない.	There's not much chance of a big bonus this year.
15パーセントの返品を見込んで売	I projected the sales figures taking into

り上げ予測を立てた. | account that 15% of the product would come back to us.
【人に期待をかける】彼は部長に見込まれている. | The department chief expects great things from him.
さすがに私が見込んだ男だけのことはある. | He's just the man I thought he would be.
 | He's every bit as good as I thought he would be.
君を見込んで頼みがある. | You're just the person I wanted to ask.

みじかい (短い)

短いひもを2本つなぎ合わせて長くした. | I tied together two short pieces to make one long string.
暑くなったので髪の毛を短く切った. | I had my hair cut short now that it's become so hot.
人生は短いんだ. 好きなことをさせてくれ. | Life is short so let me do as I please.
この文はもう少し短くならないものかね. | Can't this sentence be made a bit shorter?
帯に短し, たすきに長し. | Too much for one and not enough for two.

みじめ (惨め)

惨めな気分だ. | I feel miserable [wretched].
彼らは一文無しで惨めな状態だ. | They're in a miserable [pitiful, wretched] state without a penny.
彼の今度の映画の評判は惨めなものだった. | He got miserable [lousy] reviews for his new movie.
昨日の野球の試合では惨めな負け方をした. | We lost the baseball game yesterday in a miserable way.

みじゅく (未熟)

未熟な技術者は雇えない. | We don't employ inexperienced engineers.
彼は人間が未熟で, なかなか周りとうまくやっていけない. | He's so immature that he can hardly get along with others.
今思えば, その頃の私の考え方は未熟でした. | When I think about it now, my thinking was immature in those days.
彼は未熟児で生まれた. | He was born prematurely.
 | He was a premature baby.

ミス

だれだってミスをすることはあるよ. | Everybody makes mistakes.
彼女は雑な性格でミスが多い. | She's careless and makes a lot of mistakes.

交渉で重大なミスを犯したことにあとで気がついた.	I later noticed that I had made a serious error in the negotiations.
私の判断ミスでみんなに迷惑をかけてしまった.	I caused everyone a lot of trouble because of my misjudgment.
そのフィギュアスケート選手は今のところノーミスだ.	So far, that figure skater hasn't made any mistakes.

みすぼらしい

彼はいつもみすぼらしい身なりをしている.	He always dresses shabbily [poorly].
	He's always dressed in shabby clothes.
私の叔父はみすぼらしい家に住んでいる.	My uncle lives in a shabby house.
15年も前に買った車なので随分みすぼらしくなりました.	I bought this car 15 years ago so it doesn't look that great anymore.

みせる (見せる)

彼女は貴重な資料を快く見せてくれた.	She graciously showed me some priceless [valuable] documents.
息子は100点を取ったとき以外は答案用紙を親に見せない.	Our son never shows us his test papers unless he has scored †100 [a perfect mark].
彼は今日の試合で鮮かなプレーを見せてくれた.	He gave a fine performance in today's game.
運転免許証を見せなさい!	Let's see your driver's license!
彼らの子どもはいつも人前でいいところを見せようとする.	Their little boy always shows off in front of company.
今度こそきっと君に勝って見せるぞ.	Next time around, I'll show you!
困難なことでもきっとやり遂げて見せる.	No matter how complex it is, I'll pull it off.
【みせかける】彼は無理に笑って見せたが顔はこわばっていた.	He tried to make a pretense of laughter, but his face betrayed his stiffness.
彼女は上品ぶって見せたが, すぐにお里が知れてしまった.	She tried to put on airs but her true [real] nature was soon revealed.

みぞ (溝)

キャッチボールをしていて溝にボールを落としてしまった.	The ball fell into the drain while we were playing catch.
家の横に小さな溝が流れている.	There's a small gully that runs beside our house.
今日, 溝の泥さらいをした.	I cleaned the mud out of the ditch today.
この付近には溝がなく, 大雨になると水はけが悪い.	There are no †drainage ditches [drains] in this area, and so it is difficult for the

water to run off when we have a lot of rain.

敷居の溝にろうを塗ったので，戸の開け閉めがうまくいくようになった．	By applying wax to the groove in the doorsill, the door now slides open (and shut) much better.
【隔たり】彼とのあいだに溝が出来てしまった．	A gulf has come between us.
二人のあいだはだんだん溝が深まった．	They gradually [slowly] grew apart.

みそこなう (見損なう)

あのテレビ番組は帰りが遅くて見損なった．	I missed (seeing) that TV program because I got home late.
君はそんなことしないと思っていた．見損なったよ．	I thought you'd be the last person to do such a thing but †I was wrong [I'm disappointed in you].
見損なうなよ．僕にだってできるよ．	Don't underestimate me. Of course I can do it.

～みたい

このリンゴの絵は本物みたいによくかけている．	This rendering of an apple looks like the real thing.
ハワイへ行けるなんて夢みたい．	I'm actually going to Hawaii! It's like a dream!
いつまでもそんな子どもみたいなことを言って人を困らせるものではありませんよ．	You can't go around forever saying childish things and creating problems (for others).
彼みたいな人がこの仕事にはふさわしい．	Someone like him is better suited for this work.
風邪をひいたみたいだ．	It looks like I've caught a cold.
教室にはもうだれもいないみたいだ．	There doesn't seem to be anyone in the classroom any longer.
あの岩は人の顔みたいだ．	That rock resembles a person's face.

みだす (乱す)

学校の秩序を乱すような行為をしてはいけません．	You shouldn't do things †that will [to] disrupt school discipline.
列を乱さないで行進しなさい．	Please proceed without falling out of line.
そんなに髪をふり乱して，一体どうしたの．	What in the world happened? Your hair is a fright.

みだれる (乱れる)

| 風が強かったので髪が乱れてしま | The strong wind messed up my hair. |

……った.	The wind was so strong that my hair got messed up.
今朝の地震の影響でJRのダイヤが乱れている.	The JR trains aren't running on schedule due to this morning's earthquake.
整然と並んでいた人の列が乱れた.	The neatly arranged line of people broke down in disorder.
長期にわたる内戦で, その国は乱れに乱れている.	That country is in total chaos because of its long-drawn-out civil war.
大学をやめてからの彼は, 職も持たず, 乱れた生活をしている.	Without a job, he's been leading a life of complete disorder since he dropped out of college.

みち (道)

初めての町で道に迷ってしまった.	I lost my way the first time I was in town.
この辺は道が入り組んでいる.	The roads get a bit confusing [tangled] around here.
どうも道を間違えたようだ.	It appears that we took the wrong way.
我々は道なき道を歩き続けた.	We continued to walk along the uncharted trail.
曲がりくねった道がしばらく続く.	The winding road goes on for a while.
道でばったり昔の友人と会った.	I ran into an old friend on the street.
あの店で道を聞いてみよう.	Let's ask the way at that store.
【途中】学校へ行く道で先生と一緒になった.	I ran into my teacher on the way to school.
【道徳】父は放蕩息子に人の道を説いて聞かせた.	The father taught his wayward son moral principles.
そんな卑劣な行為は人の道に背くものだ.	Such base actions run contrary to basic morals.
【分野】彼はその道の達人だ.	He's a great authority on that subject. He's a master of the art.
彼はこの道に入って40年のベテランだ.	He's been in this line of work for 40 years and is a real pro.
子どもには子どもの好きな道を歩ませたい.	I want to let my children choose what they want to become.

みちがえる (見違える)

きれいになったね. 見違えたよ.	You've become so pretty. I can hardly recognize you.
久しぶりに甥に会ったら, 見違えるほど大きくなっていた.	My nephew had grown so much since the last time I had seen him that I hardly recognized him.
古くて汚かった駅が改装されて見違えるようになった.	I could hardly recognize the dirty old station after it was remodeled.

みちる（満ちる）

その若者の胸は希望に満ちていた． That youngster was brimming with hope.
彼はいつも自信に満ち満ちている． He's always overflowing with confidence.
彼女は敵意に満ちたまなざしを私に向けた． She shot me a look filled with hostility.
夜になって潮が満ちてきた． The tide came in at night.
月が満ちて元気な男の子が生まれた． When her time came due, she gave birth to a bouncing baby boy.

みつかる（見つかる）

無くなった腕時計がやっと見つかった． I finally found that wristwatch I had lost.
捜していた友人の家がやっと見つかった． I finally found my friend's house after looking long and hard for it.
欲しいと思っていた文献が古本屋で見つかった． I located those volumes I had been hoping to get at a secondhand [used] bookstore.
寄り道しているところを先生に見つかってしまった． My teacher spotted me killing time when I should have been on my way home.
いたずらしているところを見つかったら大変だ． If we get caught pulling off this prank, we'll really catch it.
カンニングが見つかってしまった． I got caught cheating on the test.
見つかったらあなたの命が危ない． If you're ever found out, your life will be in danger.
彼の論文に大変な間違いが見つかった． A glaring error was discovered in his paper [thesis].

みつける（見つける）

道路にお金が落ちているのを見つけた． I found some money that had been dropped on the street.
そのハンドバッグ，どこで見つけたの． Where did you find that handbag?
この本に誤植を見つけた． I found a misprint [typo] in this book.
机の引き出しで捜しものをしているうちに，たまたま古いスナップ写真を見つけた． I came across some old snapshots when I was going through my desk drawer.
たまたま駅の近くでのみの市を見つけ，いろんなものを買ってしまった． We happened to see a flea market near the station and ended up buying a lot of things.
【見慣れる】彼の字がいくら読みにくくても，僕なら見つけているから難なく読めます． I'm used to his handwriting, so no matter how indecipherable it may seem, †I can read it with ease [for me it's a snap].

みっともない

そんな格好をしてみっともない. — Shame on you, dressed like that.

彼はいい年をして若い女を追いかけるなんて, みっともない. — Shame on him, chasing after young girls at his age.

人前でみっともないことはよしなさい. — Don't do disgraceful things in front of people.

みつめる (見つめる)

彼女は自分の荒れた手をじっと見つめた. — She †stared [looked fixedly] at her rough hands.

彼女は庭の木をぼんやり見つめていた. — She was staring [gazing] blankly at the tree in the garden.

恥ずかしいから, そんなにじっと私を見つめないでください. — Please stop staring (so) at me. It's quite embarrassing.

彼女は私の顔を穴のあくほど見つめた. — She stared fixedly at me. Her eyes bored into me.

みとおし (見通し)

【視界】こんな見通しのいい道路でどうして事故が起きたのだろう. — I wonder why there was an accident on a road with such good visibility.

霧が発生して見通しが悪かった. — Visibility was bad because of the fog.

見通しのきかないところではスピードを落としなさい. — Drop your speed when the visibility is poor.

【具体的な予測】作業の見通しがつくまでは当分残業だ. — We're going to have to put in some overtime until we know where we are.

今のところ, 工場再建の見通しは立っていない. — There are no immediate prospects for rebuilding the factory.

老後に明るい見通しが持てない. — My prospects for a comfortable old age are pretty slim.

バブル経済のときは日本中が見通しを誤った. — Economic forecasts throughout Japan were skewed during the bubble economy.

2年で借金を返し終わるだなんて見通しが甘すぎるよ. — It's unrealistic to think that you'll be able to pay off your debts in two years.

【見透かすこと】母は私が企んでいることなど全てお見通しのようだ. — It's as though my mother can tell exactly what I'm †up to [thinking of doing].

そんなことは先刻お見通しだよ. — I was already aware of that./I knew that!

みとめる (認める)

彼は自分の過ちを認めた. — He admitted [recognized] that he had made mistakes.

自分の欠点を認めるのは難しい. — It's difficult to face up to one's own faults.

彼はその件での努力を認められた.	He gained recognition for his efforts in the matter.
あなたの胃には何の異状も認められません.	I found nothing abnormal with your stomach.
そんな計画は絶対に認められない.	I absolutely cannot approve a plan like that.
私たちの会社では一日1時間の休みが認められている.	Our company allows one hour of free time per day.
その詩人の作品は，彼の死後やっと真価を認められた.	The true value of that poet's works was finally recognized after his death.
彼の研究はやっと世の中に認められてきた.	His research has finally begun to achieve general recognition.

みとれる (見とれる)

彼はその美しい女性に見とれた.	He looked [stared, gazed] in fascination at the beautiful girl.
	He gazed in rapture at the beautiful girl.
その美しい風景にしばし見とれてしまった.	I was entranced by the beautiful scene for a few moments.

みな (皆)

彼は出されたものを皆平らげてしまった.	He †ate up [put away] everything that was set before him.
今日の数学の問題は皆解けた.	I solved all of today's math problems.
火事で何もかも皆焼けてしまった.	Everything I had went up in flames.
皆が行くなら私も行く.	If everyone's going, then I'll go too.
クラスの皆があなたの病気を心配しているわよ.	The whole class is concerned about your being ill.
皆さん，ここにお集まりください.	Attention everyone! Would you come together please?
代金は皆まとめていくらになりますか.	How much does the entire bill come to?

みなおす (見直す)

君を見直したよ.	I think better of you now than I did before.
今度の事件で彼を見直した.	After the incident I came to have a higher [better] opinion of him.
この計画は実行に移す前に見直しが必要だ.	We have to review this plan before putting it into effect.
この事件は見直しが必要だ.	It's necessary to reinvestigate the case.

みにくい (醜い)

何て醜い犬だ.	What an ugly dog!
あそこまでお金に執着するのは醜いですね.	It's repugnant to be so attached to money.
あの家では遺産を巡って醜い争いが起こっている.	That family is having an ugly struggle over an inheritance.

みのがす (見逃す)

【見損なう】連続ドラマの最終回を見逃してしまった.	I missed the last installment of the TV drama series.
その小さな記事は見逃していた.	I overlooked that small article.
打者は絶好の球を見逃した.	The batter let by a perfect pitch.
この秋は見逃せない映画が目白押しだ.	There's a flood of movies this fall that I have to see.
	There are so many must-see movies this fall.
【捕らえ損なう】このチャンスを見逃すな.	Don't miss this chance.
彼女はどんなタイプミスも見逃さない.	She doesn't miss a single †typing error [typo].
子供の心の叫びを見逃すな.	Don't overlook a child's cry for help (from the heart).
【大目に見る】今回だけは見逃してやる.	I'll overlook it just this time.
どうか見逃してください.	Please give me another chance.

みのる (実る)

今年はたくさんブドウが実った.	There was a good grape harvest this year.
秋に実る果物は多い.	Many fruits †ripen [get ripe] in autumn.
稲は秋に実る.	Rice ripens in autumn.
その柿の木は1年置きに実る.	That persimmon tree bears fruit every other year.
【成果を得る】彼の長年の努力が実った.	His long years of hard work finally bore fruit.
二人の恋が実って, このたび, めでたく結婚した.	Their love blossomed into a happy marriage.

みぶり (身振り)

あの人は話をするときの身振りが面白い.	The way he gestures when he talks is amusing.
彼女は大げさな身振りをして驚いて見せた.	She showed her surprise by exaggerating her gestures.
アメリカへ行ったが英語がまるで	When I went to America, I could hardly

分からなかったので，身振り手振りで話をした． / understand a word of English, so I communicated †with signs and gestures [nonverbally].

みぶん (身分)

地位や身分で人を判断するのは良くない． / It's not fair to judge a person by his social status.
/ Social status is not a fair measure of a person.

父は今度，会社での身分が変わった． / My father's position at the company has changed.

彼は身分の低い家に生まれたが，努力して出世した． / He was born into a lower-class family but he achieved success after great efforts.

彼は学生のくせに身分不相応な暮らしをしている． / For a student, he certainly lives well!
/ For a student, he tends to live beyond his means.

遊んで暮らせるなんて結構なご身分ですね． / What an enviable life you lead: all play and no work!

身分証明書を見せてください． / Please show me [Let me see] your identification [ID] card.

みほん (見本)

これは見本ですので，一つお試しください． / They're (free) samples. Please take [try] one.

運ばれて来た料理は見本とはだいぶ違っていた． / The food that was laid before us was quite different from the model in the shop window.

彼は怠け者の見本だ． / He's the perfect example of an idler.

靴の見本市が開催されている． / The shoe fair is open.

みまい (見舞い)

友人が病気で入院したので，見舞いに行った． / One of my friends is in (the) hospital, so I went to see him.

病人はたくさんの見舞い客の応対に疲れてしまった． / After having had quite a number of well-wishers the patient became exhausted.

叔父が病気になったと聞いたので，お見舞いの手紙〔お見舞い状〕を出した． / I heard that my uncle was ill, so I sent him a get-well letter [card].

昨夜，近所で火事があったので，お見舞いに行って来た． / One of our neighbors had a fire last night, so I visited them to express my sympathy.

みまう (見舞う)

花を持って，病気で入院中の友人を見舞って来た．	I got some flowers and visited my friend who's in (the) hospital.
水害をうけた遠方の友人を電話で見舞った．	I called my friend living in the distant flood-stricken area to see if he was O.K.
【被る】あの地方は毎年洪水に見舞われる．	That area gets hit by floods every year.
台風に見舞われ，家が倒れてしまった．	My house toppled over when we were hit by the typhoon.
けんかをして相手に一発見舞われてしまった．	I had a fight and got punched a good one.

みまわる (見回る)

警官は一日に何回か町の中を見回って歩く．	The police walk their beats several times every day.
警備員は夜，建物の中を異状がないかどうか見回った．	The security guard checked out the building at night to see if anything was amiss.
私が放課後に校内を見回る番だった．	It was my turn to †make the rounds of [patrol] the campus after classes were over.

みまん (未満)

当店は18歳未満はお断りです．	Nobody under 18 years old is allowed [permitted] on these premises.
	We don't allow anyone under eighteen (to come in).
2万円未満の支払いなら特別税はかからない．	There's no special tax on payments under ¥20,000.
1,000円未満は切り捨ててください．	Round it down to the nearest thousand yen.

みみ (耳)

雷が鳴ったので思わず耳をふさいだ．	I reflexively covered my ears when the thunder crashed.
彼は彼女の耳元で何かささやいた．	He whispered something into her ear.
彼から，耳にたこができるほど自慢話を聞かされた．	I'm sick and tired of hearing him brag about himself.
彼には何を言っても馬の耳に念仏さ．	Talking to him is like talking to a wall.
耳をつんざくジェット機の爆音で何も聞こえない．	I can't hear anything because of the earsplitting noise of the jet.
耳をすますと小鳥の鳴き声が聞こ	When I pricked [perked] up my ears, I

えてきた.	could hear the birds chirping.
たまには僕の言うことにも耳を傾けたらどうだい.	How about giving a listen to what I have to say once in a while?
それは彼の耳にも入れておこう.	Let's let him know about that, too.
彼女が結婚するって耳にしたんだけど, 本当ですか.	I heard that she's going to get married, but is it really true?
ちょっと耳を貸してくれないか.	Can I have a few words with you?
そんな話には耳を貸せないよ.	I won't listen to something like that.
あの映画のラストシーンのせりふが今も耳について離れない.	The dialogue from the last scene of the movie still lingers in my mind.
あのときの母の怒った声は今でも耳に残っている.	I can still hear the way my mother sounded when she got angry that time.
一瞬, 我が耳を疑った.	For a second, I couldn't believe my ears.
彼女は耳がいいので英語〔ピアノ〕が上達するだろう.	She has a good ear so she'll †do well [make good progress] in studying English [piano].
母はこの頃, 耳が遠くなってきた.	Mother's hearing has gotten worse recently.
祖父は耳が遠いので補聴器をつけている.	My grandfather is hard of hearing so he wears a hearing aid.
その音楽は耳障りなだけだ.	That music only grates on my ears.
それは耳寄りな話だ.	Well, that's welcome news.
それは耳の痛いお話だ.	That story makes my ears burn.
【端】弟はパンの耳が好物だ.	My younger brother loves eating the heel (of the bread).
【慣用】お借りした100万円, 耳を揃えてお返しします.	I'll pay back the 1,000,000 [one million] yen I borrowed †in full [in one lump sum].

みゃく (脈)

医者は病人の脈を見た.	The doctor checked the patient's pulse.
走ったあとは脈が速くなる.	Your pulse goes up after you've run.
時々脈が乱れることがあるので心配だ.	I'm a bit concerned about my pulse being irregular at times.
【見込み】依頼した件はまだ脈がありそうですか.	Is there still a ray of hope (open) concerning our request?
それはもう脈がなさそうだから, あきらめなさい.	You'd best forget it; it's †a lost cause [all but hopeless].

みょう (妙)

このソースは妙な味がする.	This sauce tastes strange.
妙な話だが, 彼はまだ生きていたんだ.	It may sound strange [bizarre], but he was still alive.

あなたの来る日は妙に雨が降りますね.	It sure is weird how it rains on the days you come.
彼の話が妙に気になる.	I don't know why [It's strange] but what he said sticks in my mind.
彼は今日, 妙におとなしい.	He's strangely quiet today.
妙案が浮かんだ.	A good idea hit me.
	I hit on a good idea.

みらい (未来)

未来を予見できたらいいのになあ.	I wish I could foresee the future!
未来の車はこういう形になるでしょう.	A future car will be like this.
大学を出たばかりの彼の行く手には豊かな未来が開かれている.	He's fresh out of college and his options for the future are broad and plentiful.
彼は未来のある若者だったのに, 不慮の事故で死んでしまった.	That lad had a great future before him but died in †an untimely [a sudden] accident.

みりょく (魅力)

彼女は魅力的な女性だ.	She's †an attractive [a charming] girl.
ああいうタイプの男性には何の魅力も感じない.	I don't feel the slightest attraction for that kind of man.
ロックは特に若者にとって魅力がある.	Rock music appeals especially to young people.
	Young people especially are attracted to rock music.
彼の小説の何が魅力なんですか.	What do you find appealing about his novels?

みる (見・診る)

何をぼんやりと見ているの.	What are you dreamily gazing at?
挨拶をしたら, 彼女は僕をちらっと見た.	When I said hello, she gave me a quick glance.
彼はその写真をじっと見ていた.	He kept his eyes fixed on the photograph.
人の顔をじろじろ見るのはやめなさい.	Don't stare at people like that.
人と話すときには相手の目を見て話しなさい.	When you talk to people, (you should) look them in the eye.
テレビで野球を見た.	I watched the baseball game on TV.
最近, 何か映画見た?	Have you gone to see any movies recently?
最近, 子どものときの夢をよく見る.	I've had many dreams about my childhood lately.
ここから見る富士山は日本一だ.	The view of Mt. Fuji from this location is

	the best in Japan.
その料理は見た目ほど悪くない.	That dish doesn't taste as bad as it looks.
見れば見るほど不思議な絵だ.	The longer you look at this painting, the more amazing it becomes.
見ると聞くとは大違いだ.	There's a big difference between hearing and actually seeing.
彼は, 私のあまりの貧しさを見るに見かねて金を貸してくれた.	He couldn't bear to see me so poor, so he lent me some money.
みるみるうちに川の水量が増えた.	The water level of the river increased before my very eyes.
【読む・調べる】その記事なら週刊誌でちょっと見た.	I took a look at that article in one of the weeklies.
分からない言葉は辞書を見なさい.	Look up the words you don't know in the dictionary.
今日じゅうにこの答案を見なければならない.	I have to finish grading these tests by today.
【判断・評価する】どう見てもこの記事は間違っている.	This article is wrong no matter how you look at it.
どう見ても彼女はまだ10代だ.	She looks like she's still in her teens in every way [respect].
彼を進歩主義者だと見る人は多いが, 実は違う.	Quite a few people †think he's progressive [regard him as a progressionist] but actually he's not.
警察ではこの事件を彼の犯行と見ている.	The police consider him to be the culprit in this case.
彼の表情から見て, 仕事はうまくいっているらしい.	(Judging) From his expression, the work seems to be going well.
僕の見たところでは, 彼はハイキングにはあまり気が乗らないようだ.	From what I can see, he doesn't seem very enthusiastic about the hiking trip.
私の見たところでは, 彼はその仕事に向いている.	From my point of view, I think he's cut out for that job.
彼女は見たところ普通の人と変わらない.	She doesn't look any different from anybody else.
湯加減を見てちょうだい.	Check the temperature of the bath water.
彼は人を見る目がある.	He's a good judge of character.
易者に手相を見てもらった.	I had the fortune-teller read my palm.
医者は急病の子どもをすぐに診てくれた.	The doctor soon examined our child who had suddenly become ill.
【世話する】毎晩子どもの勉強を見てやっている.	Every night I help my child with his homework.
兄夫婦が休暇をとっているあいだ子どもを見てやった.	While my brother and his wife were on vacation I looked after their children.

【経験する】親切にしてやってだまされるとは馬鹿を見たもんだ.	I felt like a fool when I ended up being cheated in return for my kindness.

みれん (未練)

彼はまだ彼女に未練がある.	He still has some feelings for her. He's still attached to her.
別れた女房にそんなふうに毎日電話するなんて未練がましいよ.	If you're phoning your ex-wife every day like this, you still haven't let go.
あんな仕事に未練はない.	I have no regrets about quitting a job like that.

む

むいしき (無意識)

考え事をしながら歩いていたら, 無意識のうちに駅に向かっていた.	While I was walking along lost in thought, I found that I had unconsciously started heading for the station.
勉強していて, 無意識に爪をかんでいることがある.	Sometimes when I'm studying, I unconsciously bite my fingernails.
君は無意識のうちにその感情を抑えているんだよ.	You have unconsciously suppressed that emotion.

むかう (向かう)

【面する】2軒並んでいる建物の向かって左側の家が私の家です.	Facing the two houses standing side by side, the one on the left is my house.
姉は暇さえあれば鏡に向かってお化粧を直している.	My sister looks in the mirror every chance she gets to check her makeup.
父は机に向かって書きものをしています.	My father's writing at the desk.
バスを降り, 進行方向に向かって最初の道を左に曲がると僕の家です.	Get off the bus. Then walk in the same direction the bus is headed. Turn left at the first street and there's my house.
【向き合う・対する】先生に向かって何ということを言うんだ.	What kind of thing is that to say to a teacher?
言いたいことがあるなら面と向かって言いなさい.	If you have something to say, face me and speak up.
病人に向かってあまり刺激的なことは言わないでください.	Please do not say anything that may upset the patients.

その男は大群衆に向かってアジ演説を始めた.	The man faced the large crowd and began to speak, inciting them to action.
【その方向に行く】タクシーですぐそちらに向かいます.	I'll be right over (there) in a taxi.
彼はニューヨークへ向かった.	He left [headed] for New York.
彼は今, 東京へ向かっています.	He's on the way to Tokyo now.
彼はゴールに向かってまっしぐらに走った.	He headed straight for the goal at full speed.
お陰さまで父の病気は快方に向かっています.	Fortunately, my father is †getting better [taking a turn for the better].
寒さに向かって風邪をひかぬようお気をつけください.	It's getting colder, so take care not to catch cold.
【逆らう】彼は向かって来る敵を皆なぎ倒した.	He mowed down the advancing enemy.
ヨットは風に向かって進んだ.	The yacht made headway against the wind.

むかえる (迎える)

隣の奥さんはご主人の帰りをいつも笑顔で迎える.	The wife next door always greets her husband with a smile.
友人が家まで自動車で迎えに来てくれた.	My friend came all the way to my house to †pick me up [give me a ride].
ちょっと幼稚園まで子どもを迎えに行ってきます.	I'm just going to the nursery school to pick up my child [kid].
フランスからのお客を迎えに飛行場まで行った.	We went to the airport to †meet [pick up] our guest from France.
彼を我がチームの監督に迎えた.	He was called on to become our team's manager.
あの病院では心臓外科の権威を病院長に迎えることになった.	A top cardiologist was engaged as the (new) director at that hospital.
新しい母親を迎える子どもたちの心境は複雑だった.	The children had mixed feelings about taking to a new mother.
【迎合する】重役会議では社長の意を迎えて反対意見は一つも出なかった.	The president's opinions didn't meet with a single objection at the executive meeting.
【敵を待ち受ける】敵を迎え撃つ準備は万端整った.	We are fully prepared to engage the enemy.
【臨む】気分も新たに新年を迎えた.	I greeted the new year with a renewed spirit.
私たち夫婦も今年, 銀婚式を迎えることになった.	This year we'll be seeing our silver wedding anniversary.

むかし (昔)

私は昔ピアノを習っていた.	I took piano lessons a long time ago. / I used to take piano lessons.
僕は昔，北海道に住んでいたことがある.	I once lived in Hokkaido.
ここには昔，薬品工場があった.	There used to be a pharmaceutical plant here.
この辺は大昔は海だった.	This area was all ocean a long time ago.
昔は電気も水道もなかった.	In the old days, there was no electricity or running water.
この山から金が採れたのは昔の話だ.	It's been a long time since gold was extracted from these mountains.
彼がサッカー選手をしていたのは30年も昔の話だ.	It's been thirty long years since he was a soccer player.
昔の人は我慢強かった.	People had a lot of endurance in the old days.
彼は昔から運動神経がよかった.	He's always been athletic.
川畑さんなら昔から知っています.	Mr. Kawabata is an old acquaintance.
昔の恋人にばったり会った.	I bumped into my former boyfriend [girlfriend].
昔はよかったなあ.	Those were the (good old) days.
昔が懐かしい.	I long for the good old days.
同級生にばったり会って昔話に花が咲いた.	I bumped into an old school friend and we had a good time talking about the good old days.
この定食屋では昔ながらの味を楽しめる.	You can enjoy the traditional taste of Japanese food in this restaurant.
昔ながらのやり方ではもうやっていけない.	We just can't run †it [our business] like we used to.
20年ぶりに会った幼なじみには，昔の面影がまるでなかった.	When I met my childhood friend for the first time in twenty years, I could hardly recognize him.
ここは江戸時代に宿場町としてにぎわったが，今では昔の面影はない.	You wouldn't know that this was once a lively post-station town in the Edo period.
彼はいつもひと昔前にはやったような服を着ている.	His clothing is always out of style.
十年ひと昔，ちょっと行かないうちにすっかり街並みが変わってしまった.	Ten years is a long time. The city had changed completely since I was last there.
父は頑固で昔かたぎな人だ.	Father is stubborn and †very traditional [of the old school].
おばあちゃん，昔話をして.	Grandma, can you tell [read] me a story?

昔, 昔, あるところにおじいさんとおばあさんが住んでいました.	Once upon a time, there was an old man and an old woman.
「おばあちゃん, ダンスができるの？」「昔取った杵柄(きねづか)でね」	"Grandma, can you dance?" "I can still teach you a thing [step] or two."

むかんしん (無関心)

政治に無関心な若者が多い.	Many young people †are indifferent to [are apathetic about, show no interest in, are unconcerned with] politics.
こっちが一生懸命新しい映画のことを話しているのに, 彼女は全く無関心だった.	I was really trying to tell her about this new movie, but she couldn't have cared less.
この問題には, 君も無関心ではいられないはずだ.	How can you remain indifferent to this problem?
彼女は僕たちの会話に無関心を装っていたけど本当は興味津々なんだよ.	She feigned indifference to our conversation, but she's really dying of curiosity.

むき (向き)

【方向】風の向きが東に変わった.	The wind shifted to an easterly direction.
北向きの部屋は夏は涼しくてよい.	A room †facing the north [with a northern exposure] is nice and cool in the summer.
横向きの顔を一枚写真に撮ってもらった.	I had a photograph taken in profile.
よく映るようにテレビのアンテナの向きを変えた.	I changed [adjusted] the direction of the antenna to get better TV reception.
【適合】だれにでも向き不向きというものがある.	Everyone is well-suited to certain things and not to others.
子ども向きの本を探している.	I'm looking for a †children's book [book for children].
これは万人向きの書物である.	This book is of general interest. This book can be read by everyone.
彼は俳優向きではない.	He's not cut out to be an actor.
このハイキングコースは健脚向きです.	This hiking course is for people with strong legs.
この家は夏向きに出来ている.	This house is designed for summer.
【傾向】私は物事を深刻に考えすぎる向きがある.	I †tend [have a tendency] to think about things too seriously.
彼女は何事でも悲観的に見る向きがある.	She †tends [has a tendency] to look at everything pessimistically.
【人】ご希望の向きにはこのパンフレットを無料でお分けします.	This pamphlet is available free of charge to anyone interested.

この意見には反対の向きもあるようだ.	It appears that there are those who take issue with this opinion.
【趣旨】ご用の向きによっては, ご一報くだされればすぐに参上いたします.	Provided we can meet your specifications, we will assist you as soon as we receive your reply [order].
【むきになる】彼女はすぐむきになる.	She gets uptight** easily. She's easily upset. She gets ticked off easily.**

むく¹ (剝く)

母はリンゴの皮をむいた.	Mother peeled the apple.
ポテトサラダを作るから, ジャガイモの皮をむいてちょうだい.	I'm going to make some potato salad. Could you peel the potatoes?
猛犬は牙をむいて子どもに襲いかかった.	With teeth bared, the vicious dog attacked the child.

むく² (向く)

写真を撮りますからこちらを向いてください.	I'm going to take a picture. Look this way, please.
右向け, 右!	Right face, right!
おしゃべりを注意されて彼女は腹を立て, プイと横を向いた.	When cautioned about talking too much, she turned her face in anger.
後ろを向かないで正面を向きなさい.	Turn your head around and face the front.
このホテルでは海に向いた部屋の料金が高い.	Rooms that face the sea at this hotel are expensive.
足が自然に公園のほうに向いていた.	I found myself walking towards the park.
テーブルをあいだに向き合って座った.	We sat facing each other with the table between us.
【適する】僕に向いた職業は何だろう.	I wonder what kind of work I'm cut out for.
この服は年輩の人に向いている.	This clothing is for older people.
このテーブルは小人数に向いています.	This table is suitable for a small number of people.

むくち (無口)

彼は無口なたちだ.	He doesn't talk much. He's not much of a talker. He's the quiet type. He †never [hardly ever] opens his mouth. He's a man of few words.
私は初対面の人には特に無口にな	I become particularly quiet when I meet

話題が家族のことになると彼は急に無口になった. | He suddenly clammed up when the conversation turned to his family.

むける (向ける)

カメラを向けたら彼女はとても嫌がった. | She didn't like having the camera pointed at her at all.
飛行機は機首を左に向けた. | The plane veered its nose (to the) left.
父は床の間に背を向けて座った. | Father sat down with his back to the *tokonoma*.
【振り向ける】毎月, 収入の1割を貯蓄に向けている. | I put †10 percent [one tenth] of my wages into savings every month.
【つかわす】お迎えに車を差し向けましょうか. | Shall I send a car around for you?
新聞社では記者をすぐさま事故現場に向けた. | The newspaper (company) immediately sent a reporter to the scene of the accident.
【慣用】彼からその情報を得ようとして水を向けてみたが, いっこうにしゃべろうとしなかった. | I tried to pump him for the information but he wouldn't say a word.

むこう¹ (向こう)

【反対側】海の向こうでまた戦争が始まった. | War has broken out again overseas.
ドアの向こうにだれかいる気配がした. | I sensed someone's presence on the other side of the door.
【あちら】向こうからやって来るのは君のお父さんじゃないか. | Isn't that your father coming from over there?
向こうへ着いたらすぐ手紙をください. | Please write as soon as you get there.
【それから先】4月から向こう半年間は既に予約でいっぱいです. | We're booked up for six months past April.
向こう1週間は良い天気が続く, と天気予報で言っていた. | The forecast said the nice weather would continue for another week.
【相手】向こうの言い分も聞いてみなければ公平な判断はできない. | You can't make a fair judgment unless you hear what the other side has to say.
彼は大男を5人も向こうに回してけんかした. | He faced off with five big bruisers.

むこう² (無効)

無記名投票は無効になります. | Unsigned ballots are invalid.
この券は期限が切れているので無効です. | This coupon is no longer valid.
| This coupon is outdated.
相手方が条項を守らなかったので | The contract is no longer binding [valid]

その契約は無効となった.	because the other party did not abide by the terms.

むし (無視)

彼は先生の指示を無視して教室を出て行った.	He ignored [disregarded] the teacher's instructions and left the classroom.
若いドライバーは交通法規を無視することが多いようだ.	It seems (that) young drivers often ignore traffic regulations.
彼は自分の意見が無視されて腹を立てた.	He got angry when his own opinion was ignored.
政府は世論を無視して選挙制度を改革した.	The government revised the election regulations †ignoring [with no regard to] public opinion.
その分野を語るとき，彼の研究は無視できない.	His research cannot be ignored when discussing that field.

むしあつい (蒸し暑い)

日本の夏は蒸し暑い.	Summer in Japan is †hot and humid [muggy].
蒸し暑い夜は寝苦しい.	It's hard to sleep on muggy nights.

むじゃき (無邪気)

寝ている子どもの無邪気な顔ほどかわいいものはない.	There's nothing so sweet [adorable] as the innocent face of a sleeping child.
彼女があまり無邪気なので怒る気もなくなってしまった.	She seemed so innocent that I just couldn't get angry with her.
彼は新しいDVDプレーヤーを買って大はしゃぎだ．本当に無邪気なやつだね.	He bought a new DVD player and is just like a big kid the way he plays with it all the time.

むじゅん (矛盾)

君の言うことは矛盾している.	You're contradicting yourself.
そんな矛盾した論理では通用しないよ.	Such an inconsistent theory won't hold water.
彼は私の論理の矛盾を突いてきた.	He started questioning a contradiction in my logic.

むしろ

辱めを受けるくらいなら，むしろ死んだほうがましだ.	I'd rather die than have to face such an embarrassing situation.
あなたはむしろ男に生まれたほうがよかったかもしれない.	You might have been better off if you had been born a man.
この時計は修理するよりもむしろ	It would probably be cheaper to replace

買い換えたほうが安くあがるだろう.	this watch than to have it repaired.
彼は天才というよりむしろ狂人に近い.	I'd say he's more a madman than a genius.

むしんけい (無神経)

彼の無神経な言葉に彼女はひどく傷ついた.	His thoughtless [callous] words hurt her deeply.
彼は無神経だから君の言ったことなんか気にしないよ.	He's thick-skinned [insensitive] and couldn't care less what you say.
こんな時間に来るなんて，何て無神経なやつだ.	How could he be so insensitive as to come at a time like this?
無神経な人ね！ 彼女が悩んでいるのが分からないの？	How can you be so unfeeling [insensitive]? Don't you realize she's suffering?
彼は会社の無神経なやり方に腹を立てている.	He's furious about the company's insensitive way of doing things.

むす (蒸す)

赤飯を蒸して食べた.	We steamed the red-bean rice before we ate it.
蒸したてのトウモロコシはおいしい.	Piping [Steaming] hot sweet corn is delicious.
父は毎朝ひげをそる前に，蒸したタオルを顔に当てる.	Every morning my father presses a steamed towel against his face before he shaves.
今日はとても蒸す.	It's very humid [muggy] today.

むずかしい (難しい)

この機械を操作するのは難しい.	It's difficult [hard] to operate this machine.
この本は中学生には難しすぎる.	This book is too difficult for junior high school students.
そんなに難しく考えるな.	It's not that hard [perplexing].
	You don't need to think too hard about it.
彼は今，難しい立場にいる.	He's in a difficult situation now.
それには難しい手続きが必要です.	That requires some complicated procedures.
	That will be complicated to handle.
そんな難しいことを言わないで首を縦に振ってくださいよ.	Please don't be so particular; say yes.
このチームでは優勝はちょっと難しいだろう.	It's going to be a little difficult to †win [expect any wins] with this team.
残念ながら，彼の病気は回復が難しいらしい.	It's too bad [It's really sad] it doesn't look like he's going to completely recover

	from his illness.
彼がどうして怒ったのか分からない。難しい人だ。	I just don't understand why he got so angry. He really is a difficult person.
父は難しい顔で何か考えていた。	My father was thinking (deeply) about something with a serious [grave] look on his face.

むすぶ (結ぶ)

【ひも・糸などを】靴のひもをしっかり結んだ。	I tied my shoelaces tight [tightly].
母に着物の帯を結んでもらった。	I had mother tie up the sash of my *kimono*.
僕の子どもはまだリボンを結べない。	My child can't tie a ribbon yet.
息子はネクタイの結び方を練習している。	My son is practicing how to knot his tie.
【点などを】A点とB点を直線で結びなさい。	Connect dots A and B with a straight line.
仙山線は仙台と山形を結んでいる。	The Senzan Line connects Sendai and [with] Yamagata.
長野新幹線は東京と長野を約1時間30分で結ぶ。	The Nagano Shinkansen †goes [runs, makes the trip] between Tokyo and Nagano in approximately an hour and a half.
【約束・契約を】両国はこの度,貿易に関する条約を結んだ。	The two countries recently signed a trade agreement.
彼は野球選手としてB球団と契約を結んだ。	He signed a contract to play baseball with team B.
二人はついに結ばれた。	They were finally joined in marriage.
【文章・話を】彼の話は諺で結ばれた。	He concluded his talk with a proverb.
この小説はゲーテの詩で最後を結んでいる。	This novel closes with a poem by Goethe.
【夢を】子どもたちは母親の子守り歌を聞きながら夢を結んだ。	The children slipped off into sleep while listening to their mother's lullabye.

むせきにん (無責任)

彼は無責任な男だ。	He has no sense of responsibility. He's irresponsible. He's an irresponsible person.
君は約束したじゃないか。今になって無責任なことを言うな。	You did promise, so don't give me any of your irresponsible excuses now.
やる気がないなら無責任なことは	Don't †make irresponsible statements [say

言わないほうがいい.	anything irresponsible] if you have no intention of following through.

むぞうさ（無造作）

彼は無造作に大金を持ち歩く.	He often carries large amounts of cash on him without thinking much about it.
彼は無造作にやっているように見えるけど，本当は難しいんだよ.	He †makes it look easy [does it artlessly], but actually what he's doing is difficult.

むだ（無駄）

彼を待つのは時間のむだだ.	It's a waste of time to wait for him. There's no point in waiting for him.
そのことを彼に尋ねてもむだだ.	It's no use [It's useless, There's no point] asking him about that.
彼女は要りもしない物を買って大金をむだにした.	She †wasted [threw away] a large amount of money on unnecessary things.
むだづかいしてはだめよ.	Don't †waste [throw away] (your) money.
我々の長い間の努力がむだになった.	Our long efforts have †come to nothing [been in vain].
彼はせっかくのチャンスをむだにした.	He threw away a precious opportunity.
むだだとは思うが，彼に頼んでみよう.	I think it's useless, but why don't we just go ahead and ask him?
そんなむだなことは，やりたくない.	I don't want to do anything as worthless as that.
そんな広い家は私たちにはむだです.	A house that spacious [Such a spacious house] would be wasted on us.
いろいろなむだを省けばもっと経費を節約できるでしょう.	If we cut down on a number of unnecessary expenses, we could save money.
むだ口を叩いていないでまじめに仕事をしろ.	Don't engage in idle chatter. Be serious about your work.

むちゃ（無茶）

彼は無茶な運転をするので怖い.	I get scared because he drives so recklessly.
あの山に一人で登るなんて無茶はよせ.	Don't do anything so rash as to go climbing that mountain all alone.
一人で5人相手に向かっていくなんて無茶だ.	To take on five guys alone is ridiculous.
これを僕一人で全部やれなんて，無茶を言わないでください.	To expect me to finish all of this by myself is asking too much. Asking me to finish all of this by myself is unreasonable.

むちゅう (夢中)

彼は古典文学の研究に夢中だ.	He's absorbed in the study of classical literature.
彼は新しい計画を立てるのに夢中になっている.	He's engrossed in planning a new project.
彼女はロックに夢中だ.	She's crazy about rock music.
彼は新しいガールフレンドに夢中だ.	He's †crazy about [completely taken with] his new girlfriend.
話に夢中で客が来たのに気づかなかった.	I was so involved in the conversation that I didn't even realize [notice] someone had come.
暗闇の中を夢中で走った.	I ran like mad through the dark.
昨日の地震は大きかったですね. 夢中で外に飛び出しました.	Yesterday's earthquake was big, wasn't it? I was so flustered that I ran outside.

むとんちゃく (無頓着)

彼は着る物にむとんちゃくだ.	He's indifferent to the clothes (he wears).
彼女は地位や名声にはむとんちゃくだ.	She's indifferent to status or fame.

むなしい (空しい)

時々私は人生の空しさを感じる.	I sometimes feel my life empty.
時が空しく過ぎてゆくだけだ.	Time goes by and I'm no further ahead.
そんな生活が空しいとは思いませんか.	Don't you think that kind of lifestyle is meaningless?
皆さんの協力も空しく, 計画は失敗に終わりました.	Everyone's efforts were in vain, as the plan resulted in failure.

むね (胸)

【胸部】胸を張って歩きなさい.	Stand up straight when you walk.[1] Walk tall.[2]
彼の胸は厚みがある.	He's thickset.
かつてはマリリン・モンローのような胸の豊かな女優がもてはやされた.	In the past, busty [large-breasted] actresses like Marilyn Monroe were very popular.
【胃】天ぷらを食べすぎて, 胸が焼けてしかたがない.	I've got terrible heartburn from eating too much *tempura*.
【肺】兄は若いときに胸の病で亡くなった.	My older brother died from lung disease when he was still young.
彼は長いこと胸を患っている.	He's been suffering from tuberculosis for a long time.
【心臓】出番を待つあいだ胸がドキドキした.	My heart pounded as I was waiting to go on.

【心・思い】感激のあまり胸がいっぱいになった.	My heart was filled with deep emotion.
事件が無事解決してほっと胸をなでおろした.	I breathed [heaved] a sigh of relief when the incident was safely resolved.
君のしたことが正しかったかどうか, 胸に手を当ててよく考えてごらん.	Do you really think what you did was right? You should think about it.
胸の内を聞かせてください.	Let me hear [Tell me] what's on your mind.
思い切って彼女に胸の内を打ち明けた.	I took the plunge and confessed my love to her.
苦労したまま死んでいった母のことを思うと胸が痛む.	It grieves me to think of my dead mother who suffered her whole life.
彼に言いたいことを全部言ってしまったら胸がすっとした.	I felt relieved after I got everything off my chest to him.
初めての彼の忠告が胸にこたえた	His first warning really cut me.
彼女の犠牲的精神に胸を打たれた.	I was moved by her sacrificing spirit.
このことは君の胸にだけ納めておいて欲しい.	I'd like you to keep this to yourself.
彼は胸を張って質問に答えた.	He answered the questions with confidence [dignity].

1) 実際に「背筋を伸ばして歩きなさい」という意味. 2) 精神的に「堂々と歩きなさい」という意味.

むやみ (無暗)

彼はいらだつと, むやみにたばこを吸う.	When he's nervous, he smokes excessively.
あの子は暗闇をむやみに怖がる.	The child has an unreasonable [irrational] fear of the dark.
むやみに子どもを叱っても効果はない.	Scolding a child †too much [excessively, unreasonably] is not effective.
むやみに人の言うことを信じてはいけない.	Don't just believe in anything anyone tells you.

むらがる (群がる)

あの広場にはいつもハトが群がっている.	Pigeons always flock[1] together in that square.
バーゲンセールの会場には人が大勢群がっていた.	The bargain sale was swarming[2] with people.
	The bargain sale was crowded with many people.
ワシントン記念塔の前には観光客	Many tourists flocked around the Washing-

が大勢群がっていた.	ton Monument.
ごみ捨て場にハエがたくさん群がっている.	There's a big swarm of flies at the garbage dump.

> 1) flock には「おとなしい」, 2) swarm には「攻撃的な」というニュアンスがある.

むり (無理)

その仕事を金曜日までに仕上げるのは無理だ.	It's impossible to [I couldn't possibly] finish the work by Friday.
3週間で英会話を完全にマスターしろなんて無理な注文だ.	Asking me to master English conversation in three weeks is unreasonable.
それは無理な注文というものだ.	You're asking the impossible!
	I'm afraid that's impossible.
この自転車は大きすぎて子どもには無理だ.	This bike is too big for a child to ride (on).
	You can't expect a child to ride a bicycle as big as this.
無理をするな.	Don't push yourself too hard.
	Take it easy.
彼は無理をして体を壊してしまった.	He pushed himself too hard and ended up ruining his health.
彼が無理を言うので困る.	The unreasonable things he says put me on the spot.
彼女は体が弱く無理が利かない.	She's weak and can't †overdo it [overexert herself].
私も年を取って無理が利かなくなった.	The years are catching up with me.
子どもを無理に勉強させるのはかわいそうです.	I feel sorry for children who are forced to study.
彼が怒るのも無理はない.	I don't blame him for getting angry.

むれ (群れ)

雁の群れが北の空へ飛んでいった.	A gaggle of wild geese flew to the north.
牧場では羊の群れが草を食べていた.	A flock of sheep were grazing in the pasture.
この広場では,いつも若者たちが群れをなしている.	Young people are always flocking together in this square.

め

め¹ (目)

彼女は目が美しい.	She has beautiful eyes.
彼は目がいい〔悪い〕.	He has good 〔bad〕 eyesight.
彼女は目が近い.	She's nearsighted.

【体験】
電車のドアが故障して, ひどい目にあった. — I had a terrible time when the doors on the train broke.

雪山登山中, 何度も恐ろしい目にあった. — I had many frightening experiences when I went climbing in the snow-covered mountains.

【織り目・網目】
このブラウスは目の粗い〔詰んだ〕生地で出来ている. — This blouse is made of coarse 〔fine〕 cloth.

目の粗い〔細かい〕ざるを使いなさい. — Use a coarse-meshed 〔fine-meshed〕 strainer.

【目が】
社長というものは人を見る目がなければならない. — The president of a company must be a good judge of character.

彼は刀剣類に目が利く. — He has †an expert [a critical] eye for swords.

彼は金〔欲〕に目がくらんで, 悪事に手を出した. — He was blinded [dazzled] by †the lure of money 〔greed〕 and couldn't hold himself back from committing a crime.

たくさんの絵を見ているうちに, 自然と目が肥えてきた. — In the process of looking at many paintings, I naturally acquired a keen eye for art.

昨夜は, なぜか目がさえて眠れなかった. — For some reason, I was wide awake and couldn't fall asleep last night.

今朝は早くに目が覚めた. — I woke up early this morning.

私はいろいろ悪事を重ねてきたが彼女のその言葉で目が覚めた. — I've done a lot of terrible things in my life but what she said woke me up.

彼女は目が覚めるような真っ赤なドレスを着て現れた. — She appeared in a dazzling [striking, stunning] red dress.

彼はだいぶ酒がまわってきたと見え, 目が据わってきた. — He was getting pretty drunk and was beginning to get a dazed [glassy] look in his eyes.

この品物を選ぶとは, さすがにあ — What a good choice! You have a good eye

なたは目が高い.	for quality (merchandise).
彼は親の目が届かないところで，いろいろと悪いことをした.	He has done a number of bad things behind his parents' back.
私はチョコレートには目がない.	I can't resist chocolate. / I love chocolate. / I have a weakness for chocolate.
小さな子どもは危なくて目が離せない.	You can never take your eyes off of small children.
今日は目が回るほど忙しかった.	I was so busy today that my head was spinning.

【目から】
壁に頭をぶつけてしまい目から火が出た.	I saw stars when I bumped my head against the wall.

【目と】
学校は私の家の目と鼻の先にある.	The school is (just) a stone's throw from my house.

【目に】
彼の傍若無人ぶりは目に余る.	His impudence is too much to tolerate.
彼のうれしそうな顔〔怒る顔〕が目に浮かぶ.	I can just see [picture] †his smiling face [him getting mad].
彼は体が大きいので目につきやすい.	He's so big that he really stands out.
その店は裏通りの, ちょっと目につきにくい所にある.	The store is in an out-of-the-way back street.
彼の絵はある画商の目に留まり, 高く買い付けられた.	His painting caught an art dealer's eye who purchased it at a high price.
新聞を開くと, よさそうな求人広告が目に留まった.	When I opened the newspaper, I spotted a job ad that I liked.
無計画なその事業が失敗することは目に見えている.	It's obvious (from the start) that a poorly planned project like that is doomed to failure.
彼女の体力は目に見えて衰えていった.	Her physical strength was declining before our very eyes.
その光景が彼の目に焼きついて離れなかった.	He couldn't get the scene out of his mind [head].

【目の】
彼は釣りの話をするときは目の色が変わる.	His eyes sparkle whenever he talks about fishing.
そのダイヤの指輪には目の玉が飛び出すような値段がついていた.	That diamond ring has an eye-popping price.
君の論文はなかなか目のつけ所がいい.	You really have hit upon some interesting ideas in your thesis.
ダイエットをしている彼女には甘いものは目の毒だ.	Because she's on a diet, the sight of sweets is too much of a temptation to her.
彼は一人娘を目の中に入れても痛くないほどかわいがっている.	Being his only daughter, she's the apple of his eye.

彼女がシースルーの服を着ていたので目のやり場に困った.	She had on a see-through blouse and I didn't know where to rest my eyes.
【目も】ガス爆発の事故現場は目もあてられない惨状だった.	The scene of the gas explosion was too horrible to look at.
子どもはおやつには目もくれず，夢中でテレビを見ている.	The kids are so wrapped up watching TV that they don't even give their snack a glance.
【目を】試験で満点をとったとき，彼は自分の目を疑った.	He couldn't believe his eyes when he saw that he got a perfect score on the test.
彼女の真っ赤なドレスは居合わせた人々の目を奪った.	Her bright red dress caught the eye of everybody there.
彼は上役に目をかけられている.	His superior favors him. He's favored by his superior.
保母さんは子どもたちに目を配りながら遊ばせていた.	The nursery school teacher kept an eye on the children while she let them play.
目を凝らしてよく見たが，その消えかかった文字は判読できなかった.	I strained my eyes to read it, but I couldn't make out the faded letters.
いいかげんに目を覚まして賭事から足を洗いなさい.	Wise up and wash your hands of gambling once and for all.
私は事故現場のあまりのむごたらしさに，思わず目をそむけた.	I couldn't keep from turning my eyes away from the horrible sight of the accident.
彼女は私と会うと，なぜかいつも目をそらす.	For some reason, she turns her eyes away whenever we run into each other.
私，あのかばんに目をつけているの.	I have my eye on that bag.
あの生徒は乱暴で，先生に目をつけられている.	The teacher keeps an eye on that student because he's rough.
今回だけは目をつぶってやるが，この次はそうはいかないぞ.	I'll overlook it just this once, but don't think I will next time.
この書類に目を通しておいてください.	Please take a look at these papers.
彼は親の目を盗んで彼女とデートを続けた.	He kept dating her without his parents' †knowledge [being aware of it].
ちょっと目を離した隙に，猫に魚をとられてしまった.	The cat got a fish when I took my eyes away for a second.
あの子はちょっと目を離すとすぐにいたずらをする.	If you take your eyes off that child for just a minute, he'll get into trouble.
彼女にはいつも親が目を光らせていて，デートにも誘えない.	Her parents always keep close tabs on her and no one can even ask her out on a date.
彼はあまりの惨状に目をふさいだ.	He covered his eyes at the terribleness of the sight.

彼女は恥ずかしそうに目を伏せた.	She shyly [bashfully] looked down.
その指輪の値段を聞いて目を回してしまった.	When I heard the price of that ring, I †almost fainted [nearly passed out].
彼はあだ名を呼ばれると目をむいて怒った.	He glared in anger when someone called him by his nickname.
大国ばかりにではなく小さな国々にも目を向けるべきだ.	We should be concerned not only with the major powers but with the smaller countries as well.
物音に気づいて窓の外に目をやった.	I noticed a noise and glanced out the window.

め² (芽)

チューリップの芽が出た.	The tulips have sprouted (up).
種をまいてから10日で芽が出てきた.	Ten days after planting the seeds, the shoots †sprouted [came up].
街路樹の柳が芽をふき始めた.	The willows along the street have started to come into leaf.
【慣用】彼は下積み生活が長かったが,ようやく芽が出てきた.	He has had many years of hardships, but at last things have begun to turn his way.
彼女はあれほど才能がありながら,とうとう芽が出ないままに終わってしまった.	Despite all the talent she had, she was unable to bring it to fruition in the end.
非行の芽は小さいうちに摘むことが重要だ.	It's important to nip delinquency in the bud.

めいめい (銘々)

その件についてはめいめいの判断に任せられた.	This matter has been left for each person to handle himself.
子どもたちはめいめい自分の好きな道に進んだ.	Each child pursued the path of his or her liking.
クラスのめいめいが勝手なことを言うので,いつまでたっても意見がまとまらなかった.	Everyone in the class expressed their own particular views, and no matter how long they talked they couldn't reach an agreement.

めいよ (名誉)

彼の受賞は我が校の名誉である.	His winning the prize is a great honor for our college.
このような事件は我が国の名誉にかかわる.	This kind of incident is a stain on our country's honor.
名誉回復のために一つ頑張ってみたらどうだ.	Why don't you try to establish your reputation all over again?

めいれい (命令)

彼は社長の命令で新商品の開発に取りかかった.   He was put to work on developing the new product †by order of the president [on the president's order].

この犬は僕の命令をよく聞く.   This dog listens well to my commands.

彼に長野への転勤命令が下った.   He was notified of a transfer to Nagano.

めいわく (迷惑)

ご迷惑を掛けてすみません.   I'm sorry to †trouble you [put you to trouble].

私が入院していたあいだ, 皆さんに大変ご迷惑をお掛けし, 申しわけありませんでした.   I'm sorry I caused you all so much trouble while I was sick in the hospital.

ご迷惑でなければ明日お邪魔したいのですが.   If it's not any trouble, I'd like to visit you tomorrow.

彼のずぼらにはいつも迷惑している.   We are always annoyed at his sloppy way of doing things.

執筆中に電話が掛かってくるのは迷惑だ.   It's a nuisance to get phone calls while I'm writing.

めうえ (目上)

何か分からないことがあったら目上の人に聞きなさい.   If there's something you don't understand, please ask your superiors.

「最近の若い人は目上の人にあまり敬語を使わなくなった」と父が言った.   Father said, "Young people nowadays don't speak very politely to their elders."

目上の人の意見は尊重しなさい.   Respect the views of your elders.

彼は目上の人にでも平気でたてつく.   He'll nonchalantly oppose even his superiors.

メール

【コンピュータ】大学時代の友人から突然メールがきた.   I got an unexpected e-mail from an old university friend.

実家の両親とメールのやりとりをしている.   My parents and I exchange e-mail.

出欠の返事はメールでお願いします.   Please inform us by e-mail whether you will be present or absent.[1)]
   Please let me know by e-mail if you will be attending or not.[2)]

携帯に届く迷惑メール〔スパムメ   I'm really fed up with all the †nuisance

ール〕が多くてうんざりだ. // mail [spam (mail)] coming in on my cell phone.

育児日記のメールマガジンを始めた. // I started up an e-mail magazine on child-rearing.

> 1) 書き言葉的な文. 2) 会話的な言い方.

めぐまれる (恵まれる)

彼女は大変家庭に恵まれている. // She †has [is blessed with] a very happy home life.

物質的に恵まれていると物のありがたみが分からなくなるものだ. // When you have everything, it's easy ††to forget what it's like to go without [not to appreciate the value of things].

彼は才能に恵まれている. // He is blessed with talent.
// He is a talented [gifted] person.

私は良い友人に恵まれて幸福です. // I'm so fortunate to be blessed with good friends.

あの子は何の心配もない恵まれた環境に育っている. // That child is blessed with a carefree environment in which to grow up.

日本は資源にはあまり恵まれていない. // Japan is not rich in natural resources.

今日のメーデーは天候に恵まれ大盛況だった. // This May Day was blessed with good weather and was very festive.

めぐむ (恵む)

飢えている人々に食べ物を恵んだ. // I donated food to the starving people.

人に恵んでもらうほど落ちぶれていません. // I haven't fallen so low that I would take charity.

やっと恵みの雨が降ってきた. // The long-awaited rain fell at last.

めざましい (目覚ましい)

彼のフランス語の進歩には目覚ましいものがあります. // His progress in French is striking.

アメリカでは小型車の売れ行きが目覚ましく伸びた. // Sales of compact cars in the U.S. have increased remarkably.

彼は物理学で目覚ましい業績を上げた. // He has made brilliant achievements in physics.

めずらしい (珍しい)

珍しい貝ですね. // That's a rare kind of shell, isn't it?

彼は珍しい型の車を持っている. // He has a rare model of car.

あの人がこんな時間に帰って来るのは珍しい. // It's unusual for him to come back at this time of (the) day.

私はその土地で珍しい経験をしました.	I had †an uncommon [an unusual, a rare] experience there.
珍しく早起きだね.	You're up so early!

めだつ (目立つ)

この掲示を目立つ所に貼ってください.	Please put up this notice †in a prominent place [where it can't be missed].
着物を着た娘がパーティーでひときわ目立っていた.	The girl in *kimono* †stood out from the other girls [was conspicuous] at the party.
白だと汚れが目立つので良くないですよ.	White is not a good color because it shows the dirt easily.
壁の汚れが目立ちますね.	The dirt on the walls †really shows up [is really noticeable].
彼の才能は若手演出家の中でも目立っている.	His talent stands out among the younger generation of directors.
学校時代の彼は目立たないほうでした.	He didn't stand out much when he was a student.
今日は欠席が目立つ.	I see a lot of vacant seats today.
この頃倒産する会社が目立って増えている.	Recently there has been a conspicuous rise in corporate bankruptcies.

めちゃくちゃ

めちゃくちゃなことを言うな.	Don't talk nonsense. Don't say unreasonable things.
彼の説明はめちゃくちゃだった.	His explanation was incoherent [nonsense].
彼のせいでパーティーはめちゃくちゃになった.	He ruined the party.
めちゃくちゃに頑張れば今夜中に宿題が終わるかもしれない.	If I work like mad, I might get my homework done tonight.
車がめちゃくちゃになって道にひっくり返っていた.	A car was completely smashed up and lying upside down on the road.
どうしてもそのつぼを譲ってくれと言ったら, 彼はめちゃくちゃな値段をふっかけてきた.	When I said I just had to have that pot, he tried to charge me an absurd price for it.

めったに (滅多に)

彼はめったに僕の家に顔を見せない.	He seldom shows up at my house.
彼女はめったに外出しない.	She seldom goes out.
父は仕事で忙しく, めったに私たちと夕食をともにすることがない.	My father is always busy with work and rarely has dinner with us.

めでたい

彼はめでたく大学に合格しました. — Happily, he passed the college entrance examination.

人にだまされてるのも分からないなんて, 君は本当におめでたいよ. — You sure are a dupe, not knowing when you've had the wool pulled over your eyes.

めど (目途・目処)

事故で電車が停まったままらしく, 復旧のめどが立ってない. — There seems to have been an accident on the tracks. It's not clear when the train can start running again.

この5年間開発してきた車の製品化のめどがやっとついた. — After spending five years developing the car, we finally have an idea when it will hit the production line.

来月末をめどに, ホームページをリニューアルする予定です. — We are rebuilding [redesigning] our website and plan to launch it at the end of next month.

メモ

スーパーで買うものをメモした. — I made a list of things to buy at the supermarket.

アイデアを思いついたらすぐにメモするようにしている. — I make a habit of jotting down ideas as they come to me.

彼女はメモを見ながら新製品の説明をした. — She looked at her notes as she explained the new product.

彼はメモ帳を自宅のいろいろなところに置いている. — He leaves a memo [scratch] pad in different places in his house.

メモ用紙を1枚もらえますか. — May I have some scratch paper?
Could you spare (me) a piece of paper? Anything will do.

メモリ

【コンピュータ】メモリの増設は専門店に任せたほうが無難だ. — It's safer to get a computer shop to increase the memory on your computer.

このソフトをインストールするには5Mb以上の空きメモリが必要だ. — You need at least 5 megabytes of memory in order to install this software.

めやす (目安)

その仕事を1週間もやれば, いつごろまでに終わるか目安がつくだろう. — I should be able to tell how long the job will take in a week's time.

発音を聞けば, 出身国のだいたい — I can usually tell a person's nationality by

の目安がつく.	his accent.
うちの給料体系は公務員を目安にしている.	Our pay scale is roughly based on †government workers' [civil servants'] salaries.
合格の目安は60点です.	Sixty is considered a passing grade. The passing grade is about 60.
選択肢が多すぎて,何を目安に選べばよいか分からない.	There's so much choice that it's hard to choose.
随分たくさん大学があるけれど,何を目安に選べばいいのだろう.	There's [There're]¹⁾ so many universities to choose from. What (factors) should I base my decision on?

> 1) 後ろに複数形がくるときは,There are [There're] が正式な言い方だが,口語では There's と言うことが多い.

めんどう (面倒)

書類を1枚1枚調べるのは面倒だ.	It's †a nuisance [too much trouble] to check the papers one by one.
事がちょっと面倒になってきた.	The matter has become a nuisance. The matter has become a little bit complicated [annoying].
彼は面倒がらずに人の世話をする.	He's always willing to †do things for other people [take the trouble to help others].
ご面倒をお掛けして申しわけありません.	I'm sorry to †be such a nuisance [cause you so much trouble].
ご面倒をお掛けいたしました.	Thank you for your trouble.
両親がいないときに彼女は子どもたちの面倒を見た.	She †looked after [took care of, cared for] the children while their parents were out.
彼はまた面倒を起こしたらしいね.	I hear he's caused some trouble again.

めんぼく (面目)

そんなことをすれば会社の面目がつぶれてしまう.	It would make our company look ridiculous if we did that.
彼がこんなことをしでかして,会社の面目は丸つぶれだ.	The reputation of the company has been completely destroyed by this mess he has made of things.
こんな不始末をしでかして面目ありません.	I've disgraced myself with this sort of carelessness [mismanagement].
女の子が集まらなかったから,合コンはお流れになっちゃったんだ.面目ない.	The mixer's been canceled because I couldn't find enough girls. I'm really sorry [I really feel bad] about that.
今日,生徒に難しい数学の問題を出されて,初めは随分手間取っ	A student popped a difficult math problem on me today. It was hard at first, but I

たけれど, どうにか解いて面目を保った. | saved face by finally coming up with the answer.

も

もう

【既に・もはや】掃除はもう済みました. | I've already finished the cleaning.
もう5時だ. 早く家に帰らなくては. | It's already five o'clock. I've got to get home.
祖父はもう80歳です. | My grandfather has already turned 80.
子どもはもう大学生になった. | My children are already in college.
今からではもう間に合わない. | It's already too late to make it in time.
もうこれ以上は待てない. | I can't wait any longer.
彼女がアメリカに行ってからもう5年になる. | It's already (been) five years since she went to America.
もう嫌だ. | I've had it.
【間もなく・今にも】いくら何でももう彼女は来るでしょう. | I know it's late but I'm sure she'll get [be] here †soon [before long].
もう行かなくては. | I must be going now.
もうじき春ですね. | Spring is just around the corner.
手術はもうすぐ終わります. | The operation will be over soon.
【この上・更に】おなかがいっぱいでもう食べられない. | I'm so full (that) I can't eat another bite.
もうしばらく待ってください. | Wait just a little bit longer.
もう一つお菓子をいかがですか. | Would you care for another (cookie)?
もう一杯コーヒーをいかがですか. | How about another cup of coffee?
もう一度言ってください. | Please say it again.
 | Please repeat †that [what you said].
もう2,3日休むつもりだ. | I intend to take off two or three more days.
卒業するにはもう2,3年かかりそうだ. | It will probably take two or three more years to graduate.

もうかる (儲かる)

【利益を得る】この仕事で30万円儲かった. | I made a profit of ¥300,000 on this contract.
あの取引でいくら儲かった？ | How much did you make on that deal?

儲かる話があるんだ．乗る？	I've got a profitable proposition for you. Are you interested?
儲かってる？（儲かりまっか？）	How's business?
【得する】送料分をまけてもらって600円儲かった．	I came out ¥600 ahead because they didn't charge me for the postage.
締切は明日だと思っていたけど，あさってだったのか．1日儲かった．	I thought the deadline was tomorrow but it was actually the day after tomorrow. I feel like †I've gained a day [I've got an extra day].

もうしこむ（申し込む）

【頼む・挑戦する】友人に借金を申し込んだが断られた．	I asked a friend for a loan but he turned me down.
僕は彼女に結婚を申し込んだ．	I asked her to marry me.
	I asked for her hand in marriage.
	I proposed to her.
手ごわい相手が試合を申し込んできた．	A formidable opponent came forth to propose a match.
【応募する】席に限りがありますので，お早目にお申し込みください．	Please apply well in advance as seating is limited.
旅行会社にツアー旅行の参加を申し込んだ．	I contacted the travel agency and †signed up for [joined] the tour.
今から申し込んでもまだ間に合います．	Even if you apply now, you should still be in time.

もうしぶんない（申し分ない）

彼女は秘書として申し分ない．	As a secretary, she couldn't be better.
	She's everything a secretary should be.
その金額だったら申し分ありません．	That's a satisfactory amount of money.
彼ならその仕事の担当者として申し分ないでしょう．	He would be just the right person to take charge of that job.

もうれつ（猛烈）

彼は猛烈に働いた．	He worked like mad [crazy].
	He worked very hard.
彼は猛烈に怒った．	He flew into a rage.
	He became furious.
その島は猛烈な嵐に襲われた．	A violent storm hit the island.
彼女は計画に猛烈に反対した．	She objected vehemently [violently] to the plan.

もえる (燃える)

【物が】この薪はよく燃える. — This wood burns well.

暖炉の火が赤々と燃えている. — The †fireplace [stone hearth] is burning brightly.

燃えるゴミと燃えないゴミに分けて出してください. — Please separate burnable from non-burnable trash when you put it out.

その家はあっという間に炎に包まれて燃えてしまった. — That house became engulfed in flames and burned down in a matter of minutes.

【気持ちが】彼は希望に燃えて大学に入った. — He entered college burning with desire.

祖父は年を取ってもなお向学心に燃えている. — Even though my grandfather is getting well on in years [No matter how old my grandfather gets], he still retains an ardent passion for learning.

彼が僕をうそつきだと言ったので僕の胸は怒りに燃えた. — I was seething with anger because he called me a liar.

【比喩】彼女は燃えるような深紅のバラが好きだ. — She adores radiant, blood-crimson roses.

山では紅葉が真っ赤に燃えている. — The mountain is ablaze with autumn leaves.

もくてき (目的)

今度の旅行の目的は取材です. — The purpose of this next trip will be to gather information.

この会の目的は親睦を図ることにある. — The purpose of this club is to promote [cultivate] friendship.

彼は目的のためには手段を選ばない男だ. — He is the kind of guy [person] who would use any trick to achieve his ends [aims].

しっかりと目的を持って行動しなさい. — You should have a definite goal before †taking action [making a move].

君の人生の目的は何ですか. — What are your goals in life?

これでやっと目的を果たすことができた. — (With this) We've finally been able to achieve our objective.

彼は所期の目的を達成した. — He attained [achieved] his desired end.

私たちの旅の目的地はデンバーです. — Our destination is Denver.

もくひょう (目標)

【目印】私の家へは教会を目標に来ると分かり易い. — If you take [use] the church as a landmark, you should be able to get to my house easily enough.

君の家の近くには何か目標になるものがありますか. — Is there anything close to your house †I can use as [that will serve as] a landmark?

【目当て】今週の我が家の目標は早寝早起きです.	My family's goal for this week is early to bed, early to rise.
1年間で50万円を目標にして毎月銀行に積み立てている.	I set a goal to save ￥500,000 [five hundred thousand yen] this year, so I've been depositing money in the bank every month.
あと3冊で今月の読書目標を達成できる.	After I've read three more books, I'll have reached my goal for the month.

もぐる (潜る)

【水中に】そこでは, 女たちは海にもぐって真珠を採り生計を立てている.	Women there make their living by diving for pearls.
彼は潜水服を着て海にもぐった.	He put on his diving suit and went deep-sea diving.
君はどのくらい水中にもぐっていられる?	How long can you stay underwater?
【物の下やあいだに】朝, 子どもたちがふとんにもぐってしまって起こすのに手間取った.	The kids buried themselves under the covers this morning and I had a tough time getting them out of bed.
プレーリードッグは土にもぐって冬を越す.	Prairie dogs spend the winter burrowed in the ground.
子どもはこたつにもぐって遊んだ.	The child crawled under the *kotatsu* to play.
ベッドの下に犬がもぐり込んでしまった.	The dog has crawled under the bed.
彼は戦争中, 地下にもぐって活動を続けた.	During the war he went underground and carried on his activities.

もし

もし人生をやり直せるなら芸術家になりたい.	If I had my life to live over again, I would become an artist.
もし借金取りがやって来たら, いないと言ってください.	If the bill collector comes around, tell him I'm out.
もしよろしければ明日お邪魔したいのですが.	If it's OK with you, I'd like to stop by tomorrow.
もし家がお分かりにならなかったら電話してください.	If you can't find my house, please call me.
もし万一試験に落ちても, 落胆してはいけないよ.	If by some †quirk of fate [chance] you don't pass the exam, you mustn't get discouraged.
もし約束の時間に間に合わなかったら先に行っていてください.	If I'm not there on time, go ahead without me.

もしくは
今日もしくは明日お伺いいたします. — I'll stop by to see you either today or tomorrow.
本人もしくは代理人が出頭しなければなりません. — Either the person (involved) or a proxy must be present.
現金書留もしくは郵便振替で送金してください. — Please remit the money by either registered mail or postal transfer.

もじばけ (文字化け)
送られてきたファイルを開いたら文字化けしていた. — When I opened the file, I found it was unreadable.
いくら調べても文字化けの原因はまったく分からなかった. — No matter how hard I tried, I couldn't figure out why the file was unreadable.

もしもし
【呼び掛け】もしもし, 財布を落としましたよ. — Excuse me but [Hey,][1) you dropped your wallet.
もしもし, 失礼ですが, あなたは伊藤さんではありませんか. — Excuse me but aren't you Mr. Ito?
もしもし, 定期券をよく見せてください. — Hey you [Sir, Ma'am,][2) let me have a good look at that pass.
【電話で】もしもし, 佐藤さんのお宅ですか. — Hello. Is this the Sato residence?

> 1)2) Hey は瞬間的に口から出やすい言葉だが, 相手に失礼に響くので, 余裕のあるときは Excuse me (but...) や Sir (男性に対して), Ma'am (女性に対して) を使いたい.

もちいる (用いる)
【使う】私は眠れないとき, 睡眠薬を用いている. — I take sleeping pills when I can't get to sleep.
その言葉は別の意味にも用いられる. — The word carries a different connotation as well.
次の語を用いて短文を作りなさい. — Make a short sentence using this word.
【採用する】彼の意見ばかりが用いられる. — It's only his opinions that are adopted.
今度から新方式を用いて練習することになった. — From now on, we're adopting a new practice method.
【登用する】彼は会社で能力を買われて重く用いられている. — Recognition of his ability gained him an important position at the office.

もちろん
もちろん私も行きます. — Of course, I'll go with you.

「明日のパーティーには本当に来れるの？」「もちろんさ」	"Can you really come to the party tomorrow?" "Absolutely. [Of course.]"
彼は英語はもちろん，スペイン語も話せる．	He speaks Spanish, not to mention English.
その大事な話し合いにはもちろんクラス全員が出席しました．	It goes without saying that [Needless to say, Of course] the whole class attended the important meeting.

もつ（持つ）

【手に取る】父はかばんを持って会社へ行きました．	My father went to work, carrying his briefcase.
その荷物は重くて一人では持てなかった．	That package was too heavy for one person to handle [carry].
彼はおかしなはしの持ち方をする．	He holds his chopsticks strangely.
【所持する・所有する】お金をいくら持っていますか．	How much money do you have (on you)?
私は自分の家〔店〕を持っている．	I have [own] my own house [store].
その本を持っていたら貸してください．	If you have that book, would you lend it to me?
彼はいかめしい肩書を持っている．	He has an impressive title.
【心に抱く】息子は飛行機に興味を持っている．	My son is interested in airplanes.
何事にも勇気を持って立ち向かいなさい．	No matter what happens, face it courageously.
僕は将来に希望を持っている．	I'm hopeful about the future.
彼女は個展を開く夢を持っている．	She has dreams about giving an exhibition of her own.
【受け持つ】今年は5年生を受け持っている．	I'm teaching [I have] fifth graders this year.
彼は会社で重い責任を持たされている．	He's been given (a job with) heavy responsibilities in the company.
彼は外回りの仕事を受け持っている．	He's in charge of making customer calls.
【負担する】交通費は全額会社で持ってくれる．	The company †covers [pays for] all travelling expenses.
水質検査にかかった費用はそちらが持ってください．	Please take care of the cost of testing for water quality.
【保たれる】いくら何でも毎日3, 4時間の睡眠では体がもたないよ．	No matter how you look at it, you can't get by on three or four hours of sleep every day.
この靴は随分長いこともった．	These shoes have lasted (me) a long time.
この陽気ではこの魚は明日までも	With this (hot) weather, this fish probably

たないでしょう.	won't keep until tomorrow.
あの店はあの給仕長でもっているようなものだ.	That head waiter seems to be †keeping the restaurant going [the mainstay of the restaurant].
20万円あれば1ヵ月はもつよ.	If you have 200,000 [two hundred thousand] yen, it will last you for a month.
病人は春まではもたないかもしれない.	The patient may not last till spring.
世の中はお互いに持ちつ持たれつだ.	To get along in the world, we must learn to live and let live.

もったいない

彼にそんなに支払うなんてもったいない.	What a waste to pay him so much money!
まだ使えるのに捨てるなんてもったいない.	What a waste to throw it away when you can still use it!
時間がもったいないのでタクシーで行きましょう.	We don't want to waste time. Let's take a taxi.
せっかくの休みに何もしないのはもったいない.	What a waste, not doing anything at all on your day off!
こんな天気のいい日に家でテレビを見てるなんてもったいないよ.	How could you just sit indoors and watch television on such a nice day?
あんな面白い映画を君も一緒に見なかったのはもったいなかった.	It's really †too bad [a shame] you weren't with me to see that movie. It was really interesting.

もってくる (持ってくる)

【物を】紅茶を二つ持ってきてください.	Please bring us two cups of tea.
明日の遠足にはお弁当を持ってくるようにと先生がおっしゃった.	The teacher told us to be sure to bring a lunch for tomorrow's excursion.
かばんを持ってくるのを忘れてしまった.	I (completely) forgot †about bringing [to bring] the briefcase.
その荷物を持ってきてちょうだい.	Would [Could] you get that package for me?
【問題・相談を】この記事はいちばん最後のページに持ってきたほうがいい.	It would be better to put this article on the last page.
彼は忙しいときに限って相談ごとを持ってくる.	He always seems to bring his problems to me when I'm busy.
やっと話をここまで持ってきたのに,彼の余計な一言で壊れてしまった.	The talk had finally (begun to) come around and then he had to stick his two cents in and ruin everything.

His uncalled-for remark wrecked the talks [discussions] that had finally gotten off the ground.

もっと

もっと勉強しないと入試に受かりませんよ. — If you don't study more, you won't pass the entrance exam.

明日からはもっと早く起きなさい. — You'er getting up earlier starting tomorrow!

君より彼女のほうがもっと英語がうまい. — She's much better at English than you.

もっといい方法はないかなあ！ — I wish I had a better way!

もっと大きな声で話してください. — Would you speak louder please?

君ともっと話していたいけれど,時間がないんだ. — I want to talk to you longer but I don't have time now.

僕ならもっと早く正確に計算できる. — I could do those calculations much more quickly and accurately.

もっとも¹ (尤も)

【無理もない】そんなことを言えば彼が怒るのももっともだ. — It stands to reason he'd get angry if you said something like that.

あなたの言っていることはもっともです. — You're quite right to say so.

【ただし】月曜から土曜まで毎日営業しています. もっとも土曜日はお昼までです. — We're open †six days a week [Monday through Saturday], but only till noon on Saturdays.

僕は何でも食べます. もっとも牛刺しだけはだめですが. — I'm not a picky eater [I can eat (almost) anything] but I draw the line at raw beef.

もっとも² (最も)

この仕事は彼女に最も適している. — This work suits her to a tee. / She's really cut out for this work.

英語は彼にとって最も得意な科目だ. — English is his best subject.

クラシック音楽の中で, 最も好きな曲は何ですか. — What's your favorite piece of classical music?

これは彼の作品の中で最も優れたものだ. — This one stands out as his finest (piece of) work.

彼女は会社で最も美しい. — She's the prettiest (girl) at the office.

もっともらしい

彼の話がもっともらしいので, つ — His story sounded so plausible that I found

い信じてしまった.	myself †taking him seriously [believing him].
「なるほど. もっともらしい言いわけだね」「いえ, 本当なんですよ!」	"Really. It sounds plausible, but nevertheless, what you say is an attempt to excuse yourself." "No, it's true."
今日のずる休みのもっともらしい理由を考えなくちゃ.	I've got to come up with a believable excuse for skipping school today.
その本にはもっともらしいことが書いてあるけど, 事実なのかなあ.	The things written in this book sound plausible, but I wonder if they're really true.

もてなす

妻は手料理で人をもてなすのが好きだ.	She likes to entertain by cooking for †her friends [people].
彼の奥さんはもてなし上手だ.	His wife is a good hostess.
その小さな旅館では心のこもったもてなしをしてくれる.	That small hotel is warm and hospitable.
私たちは姉妹都市で温かいもてなしを受けた.	We received a hearty welcome at our sister city.
本社からのお客様を手厚くもてなすように.	Please give our visitors from the home office the royal treatment.
「ごちそうさまでした」「いいえ, 何のおもてなしもできませんで」	"Thank you (so much) for a lovely dinner." "Not at all. I'm glad you enjoyed it."[1]

1) 謙遜し過ぎずに, 肯定的な言葉を返すのが英語らしい受け答え.

もと (元・基)

【起こり・はじめ】

彼の家は元をたどると徳川家康まで行き着く.	His family can (apparently) trace their origins back to Tokugawa Ieyasu.
1万円札といったって元をただせばただの紙切れじゃないか.	A 10,000 [ten thousand] yen note is really nothing more than the paper it's printed on.
元はと言えば君が悪いんだ.	When you come right down to it, it's your fault.

【基礎】

教育は国の基である.	Education is the foundation [basis] of a nation.
何事も基がしっかりしていないとすぐ揺らいでしまう.	Without a strong foundation, all things will soon crumble.

【原因】

その人は風邪がもとで亡くなった.	That person's cold †brought on [led to, hastened] his death.
失敗は成功のもと.	You learn from your mistakes.

【資本】

これで十分元が取れた.	I've made a substantial return on this.

商売がうまくいかず元も子もなくしてしまった.	My business failed and I lost everything.
こんなにたたかれたんじゃ元が取れないよ.	People haggle over prices so much that I can't †break even [recoup my expenses].
【材料】中国で見聞きしてきた話がその小説の基になっています.	Stories taken from personal experience in China were the basis for the novel.
その小説は作者の若いときの経験を基にしている.	That novel is based on the writer's experience when he was young.
豆腐は大豆を基にして作る.	*Tofu* is made from soybeans.
【以前】父は元刑事だった.	My father †was formerly [used to be] a police detective.
彼女は鈴木さんの元の奥さんだよ.	She's Mr. Suzuki's ex-wife.
アメリカの元大統領が日本を訪問した.	The former President of the United States visited Japan.
その傘を元あった所に戻しておいてください.	Put the umbrella back in its place.
一度壊したものは元どおりにはならない.	Once something is broken, it can't go back the way it was.

もどかしい

英語では思うように話せないのがもどかしい.	I cannot express myself well in English and it's really irritating [frustrating].
彼がのろのろ仕事をしているのを見るともどかしい.	It makes me [I feel] impatient to see him working so slowly.
彼は封を切るのももどかしく,手紙を取り出し読み始めた.	He impatiently opened the envelope, took the letter out and started to read it.

もどす (戻す)

読んだ本は元の場所へ戻しなさい.	Put the book back where it was when you're done with it.
この計画は白紙に戻して,別の計画を立てよう.	Let's take this plan back to the (old) drawing board, and start over from scratch.
先生は脱線した話をすぐ元に戻した.	The teacher quickly got the rambling discussion back on the right track.
時計が進んでいるので,針を戻した.	The clock was fast, so I set it back.
使った工具は全部工具箱に戻しておいた.	I put all the tools I used back in the toolbox.
演奏会が中止になったので切符を払い戻してもらった.	The concert was †canceled [called off] so they refunded our tickets.
いったん売った骨董品を,また欲しくなって買い戻した.	I bought back that antique that I sold off the other day. I decided that I really did

	want it.
彼女は食べたものを全部戻してしまった.	She threw up everything she had eaten.

もとめる (求める)

【探す・望む】仕事を求めているがなかなか見つからない.	I've been †job-hunting [looking for a job] but just can't seem to find anything.
あの会社でプログラマーを求めているので応募した.	That company is looking for a programmer, so I applied (for the job).
彼女はいつもしなくてもいい苦労を自ら求めてしているみたいだ.	It seems that she's always going out of her way to make herself miserable.
彼は人生の真理を求め, 書物をむさぼるように読みあさった.	In search of the meaning of life, he read voraciously.
【要求する】友人に援助を求めたが断られた.	I turned to my friend for assistance [aid, help, support] but was turned away [down].
暴漢に襲われそうになったので大声で助けを求めた.	I screamed for help when it looked as though I was going to be attacked [assaulted] by some thugs.
社長に面会を求めたが断られた.	I requested an interview with the president but was turned down.
【買う】そのハンドバッグはどこでお求めになりましたか.	Where did you purchase [get] that handbag?
コンサートの切符は売り切れないうちにお早目にお求めください.	Please try to purchase your tickets well in advance before the concert is sold out.

もどる (戻る)

【元の状態に】彼はせっかく良くなった病状が不摂生のために元に戻ってしまった.	Just when he had finally gotten over his condition, he suffered a relapse from not taking proper care of himself.
捜査はまた振り出しに戻った.	The criminal investigation went back to square one.
あの二人はよりが戻ったようだ.	Those two seem to have patched things up.
【元の位置・場所に】今, 戻ったところです.	I just got back.
ご主人は何時頃お戻りですか.	What time will your husband get home? What time do you expect your husband to get home?
ただ今彼は席を外していますので戻りしだいお電話させます.	He's not here right now, but I'll have him call you back as soon as he returns.
盗まれた品が10日後に戻ってきた.	The stolen goods †were returned [came back] ten days later.

過ぎ去った日々はいくら嘆いても戻ってこない.	The past is the past, and all your moaning and groaning won't bring it back.
年末調整で税金の一部が戻ってきた.	I got back a portion of my taxes after the year-end adjustment.
忘れ物をしたので急いで家に戻った.	I hurried back home because I had forgotten something.

ものたりない (物足りない)

彼の説明では物足りない.	His explanation leaves something to be desired.
	I'm not entirely satisfied with his explanation.
まあおいしいけれど,どこか物足りないなあ.	It tastes all right, but †it leaves something to be desired [there's just something missing].
君にはそんな問題は易しすぎて物足りないだろう.	A problem like that just isn't enough of a challenge for you, is it?

もはん (模範)

彼は模範的な青年だ.	He's †a model [an exemplary] youth.
実力テストの模範解答が掲示された.	Sample [Model] answers for the proficiency test were posted.
彼女は先生の質問に対していつも模範的な答えをする.	She always gives such ideal [model] answers in reply to the teacher's questions.
彼らは模範演技〔模範試合〕を見せてくれた.	They gave us †a demonstration of the performance [an exhibition game].
僕はこれでも模範生だったんだ.	Believe it or not, I used to be quite †a good [a model, an exemplary] student.

もむ (揉む)

母の肩をもんであげた.	I massaged my mother's shoulders [back].
疲れた手足を自分でもんだ.	I massaged my tired hands and feet.
店主は手をもみながら,にこやかに客に応対した.	The shopkeeper rubbed his hands as he smilingly waited on the customer.
キュウリを塩でもんで食べた.	I rubbed the cucumber with salt †before eating it [and then ate it].
ブラウスの汚れをもみ洗いした.	I gently scrubbed the grime out of the blouse when I washed it.
満員電車でもまれて,ボタンが取れてしまった.	(Being) Jostled about on the packed train, I got my button torn off.
【鍛える】君は大勢の兄弟の中でもまれて育ってきたので,さすが	Coming from such a large family, your siblings must have put you through the

にたくましいね.	mill. It's no wonder you're so tough now.
兄は温室育ちなので少しは他人の中でもまれたほうがよい.	My (elder) brother has had such a sheltered upbringing that a little exposure to strangers would be good for him.

もよおす (催す)

【行事を】教会は恵まれない子どもたちのためにチャリティーショーを催した.	The church †put on [held] a charity show for some underprivileged children.
首相は経済界の要人を招き園遊会を催した.	The prime minister invited VIPs from the economic sector to his garden party.
	The prime minister gave [held, threw] a garden party to which he invited VIPs from the economic sector.
明日の午後(彼の)送別会を催します.	We're giving (him) a farewell party tomorrow afternoon.
【生理的現象を】夜,勉強していて眠気を催したときには,コーヒーを飲むことにしている.	When I study late at night and (begin to) feel drowsy, I always drink some coffee.
寒気を催したので温かくして寝た.	I felt so cold that I warmed myself up and went to bed.
バスに酔い,吐き気を催した.	I got [felt] carsick on the bus.

もらう

友達から手紙をもらった.	I got [received] a letter from a friend.
子どもたちはおやつにお菓子をもらった.	The children received some cookies [sweets] as a snack.
あの人は今年こそ文化勲章をもらうだろう.	He's bound to receive an Order of Cultural Merit Award this year.
この仕事にはもう少し時間をもらいたい.	I'd like a bit more time to finish this job.
兄は先月お嫁さんをもらった.	My brother got married [hitched] last month.
知人から子犬をもらった.	An acquaintance gave me a puppy.
【～してもらう】手遅れにならないうちに医者に診てもらったほうがいい.	You should let a doctor examine you while there's still †time [a chance] to do something about it.
私の代わりにその会に出席してもらいたい.	I'd like you to †take my place at the meeting [attend the meeting in my place].
この仕事を今日中にやってもらいたい.	I want [I'd like] you to finish this job (sometime) today.
このスカートは母に買ってもらった	My mother bought this skirt for me.

た.	
先生にレポートを見てもらった.	I asked the teacher to †look over [check] my paper.
パソコンが故障したので直してもらった.	My computer broke down, so I had it repaired.

もらす (漏らす)
【光・水などを】明かりを外に漏らさないようにした.	We †tried [were careful] not to let any light escape.
その子は緊張のあまり小便を漏らしてしまった.	The child got so tense that he wet his pants.
【秘密・情報などを】この秘密は決してだれにも漏らしてはいけない.	You mustn't breathe a word of this secret to anyone.
	You mustn't let this secret slip to anyone.
彼は国家機密を漏らしたかどで処罰された.	He was punished for leaking state secrets.
彼は私を信用して事業計画の一端を漏らしてくれた.	Trusting me, he confided [disclosed, divulged] a part of the plan for the project to me.
【不平・不満を】彼女はいつも仕事上の不満を漏らしている.	She's always complaining about conditions at work.
	She's always giving vent to her dissatisfaction about the job.
【事柄などを】名簿から彼の名をうっかり漏らしてしまった.	His name was omitted from the roll [roster, register] by mistake.
	I left his name off the roll by mistake.
手紙に大事なことを書き漏らして出してしまった.	I mailed the letter having failed to include something important.
要点を聞き漏らさないようにメモをとった.	I took notes so as not to miss the main points.
その事については細大漏らさず調べてあります.	We've †investigated [looked into, looked over] that matter with a fine-tooth comb.
【慣用】道には警官が立ち並び, 水も漏らさぬ警戒ぶりだった.	The police were lined up across the road, providing an airtight cordon.

もりあがる (盛り上がる)
【物が】庭に土が少し盛り上がっている所があるけど, タケノコだよ, きっと.	There's a small mound in the garden. It could be bamboo shoots.
彼の二の腕の筋肉は盛り上がっている.	His upper arms are big and muscular.
【気分が】お祭りが盛り上がってい	The festival is in full swing.

今年の学園際は予想以上の盛り上がりを見せた.	The school festival this year was livelier than expected.
知事候補討論会は盛り上がりに欠けた.	The debate featuring candidates for governor was unexciting.

もる (漏る)

雨が漏って天井から落ちてくる.	Rain seeps in through the roof.
	The roof leaks when it rains.
ホースから水が漏っている.	The hose leaks.
バケツが古くなり水が漏るようになった.	This bucket [pail] has gotten so old it's starting to leak.

もれる (漏れる)

【水・光などが】どこかでガスが漏れているようだ.	Gas seems to be leaking [escaping] from somewhere.
木々の間から日光が漏れている.	The sun is shining in through the trees.
明かりが外に漏れている.	Light is leaking out.
水筒から水が漏れている.	The water is leaking from the canteen.
【秘密・話などが】その事件はいつの間にか世間に漏れてしまった.	News of that affair [incident] seeped out and became public knowledge before we knew it.
この秘密が漏れるとまずい.	It will be pretty awkward if this secret gets out.
そのうわさは, どこから漏れてきたの?	Where did that rumor get leaked from?
	I wonder who leaked that rumor!
【選・名簿から】君の作品は残念ながら選から漏れてしまった.	I'm sorry to say that your work has been excluded from the selection.
彼女の名前が招待者名簿から漏れてしまった.	Her name was †omitted from [left off] the invitation list by mistake.

もろい (脆い)

そのコップはもろいので気をつけてください.	That glass is fragile, so be careful with it.
この石は硬いけれどもろい.	This stone is hard but brittle.
床板が腐ってもろくなっている.	The floorboard is starting to rot.
昨年の優勝チームはもろくも敗れ去った.	Last year's championship team was easily beaten.
彼は情にもろい.	He's softhearted.

もんだい (問題)

【設問】今日の試験は, 易しい問題ばかりだった.	All of the problems on today's test were †a snap [easy, simple].

この数学の問題は君にはちょっと程度が高い.	The level of this math problem is a little beyond you.
試験に出た問題は全部出来た.	I answered all of the questions on the exam.
【解決すべき事柄】大した問題ではない.	It's no big problem [deal]. It's no problem at all.
どこの国でも青少年の非行化が深刻な問題となっている.	The trend in juvenile delinquency has become a serious problem everywhere in the world.
市議会では大気汚染問題を取り上げて討議した.	The question of air pollution [The air-pollution problem] was brought up and deliberated at the city council meeting.
この計画には問題点が多い.	There are many problems in this plan.
【事件】彼は得意先と問題を起こしてばかりいるので会社を辞めさせられた.	The company let him go because he was always †in trouble [causing trouble] with the clients.
彼女はいつも厄介な問題ばかり引き起こす.	She's always causing such awkward [difficult, complicated] problems.
【注目の】彼が問題の人物だよ.	He's the person in question.
これが今問題になっている本だ.	This is the book that's causing such a stir.

やがて

夜が明けると、やがて小鳥たちがさえずり始めた.	Shortly after daybreak the birds began to chirp.
彼はやがて来るだろう.	He should come before long.
醜い芋虫は、やがて美しいアゲハチョウになる.	The ugly caterpillar will in time turn into a beautiful swallowtail butterfly.
僕はやがて独立して店を持ちたいと思っている.	In time I would like to have my own store.
私たちの結婚生活もやがて20年になります.	Before long, we will have been married for 20 years.
野球の試合が始まってやがて3時間になるが、まだ5回の裏だ.	The baseball game started almost three hours ago, but it's still only the bottom of the fifth.

やかましい

【騒々しい】道路工事の音がやかましい.	The road construction is very noisy.
空地から一日じゅうやかましい子どもたちの声が聞こえてくる.	I can hear the noisy voices of children from the empty lot all day long.
【細かい・厳しい】私の学校は規則がとてもやかましい.	The regulations at my school are very strict.
彼女はやかましい義母をよく世話している.	She takes good care of her nagging mother-in-law.
どんなにやかましく注意しても、彼は姿勢の悪さを直そうとしない.	No matter how much I nag at him he refuses to correct his posture.
彼女は着る物にやかましい.	She's very particular about clothes.
彼は食べ物にやかましい.	He's fussy about food.
【評判】教科書問題が新聞でやかましく取り上げられている.	The school textbook issue is being given a lot of coverage in the papers.

やく¹ (役)

【役目】彼女は幼い弟たちの母親の役を果たした.	She fulfilled the role of mother for her little brothers.
私にはいつも損な役ばかり回って	I always get the lousy jobs.

くる.
彼はその大役を引き受けた. He accepted the leading role.
今度の計画では君に是非一役買ってもらいたい. We would really like to have you take part in this plan.
【芝居の役割】この芝居で，彼は老人の役を演じる. He plays the role of an old man in this play.
【有益】馬は役に立つ動物です. The horse is a useful animal.
私は社会の役に立つ人間になりたい. I want to be a useful member of society.
救命具はいつ役に立つか分からない. You never know when lifesaving devices will be needed.
アメリカでは私の英語はあまり役に立たなかった. My English wasn't of much use to me in the United States.
彼は何をやらせても役に立たない. He would be of no use even if we asked him to do anything.
お役に立てれば幸いです. I would be happy to be of service.
学校の勉強が社会ですぐ役立つとは限らない. What's learned at school isn't always immediately useful in society.

やく²(約)
東京から札幌まで飛行機で約1時間半かかります. It takes about an hour and a half to fly from Tokyo to Sapporo.
家から学校まで約800メートルあります. It's about 800 meters from my house to school.
講演会には約2,000人の聴衆が集まった. There was an audience of about 2,000 people at the lecture.

やく³(焼く)
彼は庭で落ち葉を焼いた. He burned the fallen leaves in the garden.
僕は不要になった手紙や書類を焼いた. I burned the letters and documents that I no longer needed.
彼は火事で家も財産も焼いてしまった. His house and property went up in flames.
昔の写真は空襲で焼いてしまいました. The old photographs got burned up in an air raid.
彼女はケーキを焼くのがとてもうまい. She is very good at baking cakes.
パンを焼いて食べた. I toasted the bread and ate it.
「ステーキはどのくらいの焼きかげんにしましょうか」「よく焼いてください」 "How would you like your steak?" "I'd like it well-done."
サツマイモをたき火で焼いて食べました. I cooked a sweet potato over a wood fire and ate it.

今では炭を焼く人は少なくなった.	Nowadays few people make charcoal.
写真を自分で焼くのは,割合簡単です.	Printing your own pictures is relatively simple.
私の趣味は陶器を焼くことです.	My hobby is making [firing] pottery.
今年の夏は海へ行って体を焼こう.	This summer I'll go to the beach and get a tan.
彼女の肌は小麦色に焼けている.	She has a golden brown tan.
医者に扁桃腺を焼いてもらった.	The doctor swabbed medicine on my tonsils.
彼の遺体は故郷で焼かれた.	His remains were [His body was] cremated in his hometown.
彼女はすぐ焼きもちを焼く.	She gets jealous right away.

やくす (訳す)

この本はうまく日本語に訳してある.	This book has been skillfully translated into Japanese.
この日本語を英語に訳しなさい.	Translate [Put] this Japanese into English.
『源氏物語』は英語に訳されている.	*Genji Monogatari* has been translated into English.
彼の訳した詩には味がある.	The poems he translated †have charm [are fresh].
この文章を分かり易く訳し直してください.	Please retranslate this so that it's easier to understand.

やくそく (約束)

彼はいつも約束を守る.	He always keeps his promises [word].
彼女は約束を破った.	She broke her promise [word].
勝手に約束を取り消さないでください.	You can't just go back on your word (any time you feel like it).[1]
	Please don't make arbitrary changes without consulting us.[2]
	You can't just cancel on me.[3]
代金は月末に支払う約束になっている.	I've promised to pay for it at the end of the month.
10時に弁護士に会う約束です.	I have an appointment with my lawyer at ten.
彼女と映画に行く約束をした.	I promised I would go to a movie with her.
彼は約束どおり6時に現れた.	He appeared at six as promised.
二人は先月結婚の約束をした.	They became engaged last month.
それでは約束が違う.	That's not what you said.
彼には社長のいすが約束されている.	He has been promised the presidency of the company.

どんなゲームも約束を守ってこそ面白い.	Any game is interesting only if you follow the rules.

> 1) 個人的な約束の場合. 2) ビジネス上の合意事項の場合. 3) 会う約束の場合.

やくめ (役目)

議長の役目は会議を円滑に進めることです.	The role [function, duty] of the chairperson is to assure the smooth running of conferences.
彼は指導者としての役目を立派に果たした.	He splendidly fulfilled his role as leader.
子どものしつけは親の役目です.	It is parents' place [responsibility] to discipline their own children.

やける (焼ける)

昨夜, アパートが火事で焼けた.	Last night my apartment was gutted in a fire.[1]
	Last night my apartment building was burned to the ground.[2]
空襲で町はほとんど焼けてしまった.	The town was almost entirely destroyed by fire in the air raid.
そろそろアップルパイが焼ける頃です.	The apple pie will †be done baking [be ready] soon.
肉がおいしく焼けました.	The meat was deliciously cooked.
この魚はすぐには焼けません.	This fish cannot be cooked quickly.
鉄が真っ赤に焼けている.	The iron is red hot.
真夏の日差しは焼けるように熱い.	The mid-summer sun is scorching hot.
彼は焼けたアスファルトの上を歩き続けた.	He continued walking on the hot asphalt.
海岸の砂は焼けて熱かった.	The sand on the beach was hot from the sun.
彼は日に焼けて真っ黒だ.	He has a very dark suntan.
本の背が日に焼けて色あせた.	The spine of the book was faded from the sun.

> 1) アパートの部屋の内部が焼けた場合. 2) アパートの建物が焼け落ちた場合.

やさしい[1] (易しい)

この機械は操作が易しい.	This machine is easy to operate.
この本は易しい英語で書かれている.	This book is written in easy English.

試験問題は思ったより易しかった.	The problems on the test were easier than I thought they would be.
もっと易しく説明してください.	Please explain it more simply.

やさしい² (優しい)

母は優しい人です.	My mother is a very gentle person.
彼は自分に厳しく人に優しい.	He's strict with himself but gentle with others.
彼は優しい目をしている.	He has gentle [tender] eyes.
先生はいつも私たちに優しい言葉を掛けてくださる.	Our teacher always speaks to us in a gentle [kind] manner.
母親は優しい声で子守歌を歌った.	The mother sang a lullaby in a gentle [tender] voice.
あの少女は花や生き物に対して優しい心を持っている.	That little girl is very gentle with flowers and other living things.
私は彼女の心の優しさに打たれた.	I was really touched by her tender-heartedness [gentle-heartedness].

やしなう (養う)

【扶養】彼は家族5人を養っている.	He supports a family of five.
【養育】両親のいない彼女は,叔母に養われている.	She has no parents and is being raised by an aunt.
【療養】彼は田舎で病気の身を養っている.	He is recuperating from his illness in the country.
【養成】私は英気を養うために旅行に出かけた.	I went on a trip to restore my spirit.
早起きの習慣を養うのはよいことだ.	It's a good idea to foster the habit of getting up early.
想像力を養うのはよいことだ.	It's good to foster [cultivate] the imagination.
若いうちに体力を養っておきなさい.	Develop physical strength while you're still young.

やしん (野心)

彼には自分の会社を一流企業に発展させようという野心がある.	One of his ambitions is to develop his company into a first-rate enterprise.
彼は作家として有名になりたいという野心を抱いている.	His ambition is to become a famous author.
彼は仕事に対して野心満々だ.	He's very ambitious about his work [career].
あの男は野心家だ.	He's very ambitious.
この小説は彼の野心作だ.	This is considered (to be) his most ambitious novel.

やすい¹ (安い)

この靴は丈夫で安い.	These shoes are durable and cheap.
安い服はすぐ型崩れする.	Cheap clothes quickly lose their shape.
あのスーパーの品物は安い.	Prices at that supermarket are low.
この中古車は安い買い物だった.	This used car was cheap.
フランス製のハンドバッグをだいぶ安く買った.	I bought a French handbag quite inexpensively.
4人で駅へ行くなら,バスよりタクシーのほうが安くつく.	If four people are going to the station, it's cheaper to go by taxi than by bus.

やすい² (易い)

言うは易く,行うは難し.	Easier said than done.
そんなことならお易いご用だ.	No problem.
冬は空気が乾燥して火事が起こり易い.	The dry air in winter makes it easy for fires to start.
彼は感じ易い少年だった.	He was a very sensitive boy.
この文章はとても読み易い.	These sentences are very easy to read.
この品物は値段が手頃で買い易い.	This article is easy to buy because it's †reasonably priced [not expensive].

やすみ (休み)

【休息】疲れたからひと休みしましょう.	I'm tired. Let's take a break. [Shall we take a break?]
窓口は12時から1時まで休みです.	The wicket [counter] is closed from twelve to one.
【休暇】日曜は学校は休みです.	There's no school on Sundays.
この講座はしばらく休みにします.	This class will not meet for a while.
彼は仕事が忙しくてちっとも休みがとれない.	He's busy with work and can't take any time off.
夏の休みには多くの日本人が海外へ出かける.	Many Japanese go abroad during summer vacation.
【欠席】今日お休みの人はいませんか.	Is anyone absent today?
今日課長は風邪でお休みです.	Today the section chief is absent with a cold.
【中断】朝から休みなく雪が降り続いている.	The snow has been falling continually [ceaselessly] since morning.
工場は一日じゅう休みなく動いている.	The factory is running continuously day and night.
【就寝】まだお休みでしたか.	Were you still sleeping?
お休み中のところを起こしてすみません.	I'm sorry for waking you (from your sleep).

やすむ (休む)

【休息】
2, 3時間休めば疲れがとれるでしょう. — If you rest for a couple of hours you'll feel refreshed.

今日は忙しくて, 一日じゅう休む暇もなかった. — I was so busy today (that) I had no time to rest all day long.

【欠席】
風邪で〔病気で〕1週間学校を休みました. — I was away from school for a week †with a cold 〔because I was sick〕.

今日は頭が痛いので会社を休みたいのですが. — I have a headache. I'd like to take off work today.

【中断】
あの店は年じゅう休まず営業している. — That store is open all year (round).

この機械は一日じゅう休まず動いています. — This machine runs 24 hours a day.

【就寝】
もう遅いから休みましょう. — It's getting late. Let's go to bed.

昨夜はよくお休みになれましたか. — Did you sleep well last night?

【休み休み】
彼らは休み休み階段を上った. — They climbed the stairs, stopping to rest many times.

馬鹿も休み休み言いなさい. — I've heard about enough ridiculous talk from you.

やすらか (安らか)

赤ん坊は母親に抱かれて安らかな眠りについた. — The baby fell into a peaceful sleep in its mother's arms.

私は毎日安らかな日々を送っている. — I'm living a quiet, peaceful life.

彼は老後を(心)安らかに暮らしている. — He's peacefully living out his retirement years.

彼は故郷の墓で安らかに眠っている. — He's been laid to rest in his hometown cemetery.

やすらぐ (安らぐ)

あの人のそばにいると不思議に気持ちが安らぐ. — I feel strangely at ease when I'm around him.

都会を離れ自然に接していると, 安らいだ気分になる. — It's relaxing to be in nature, away from the city.

彼は逃亡中, 一瞬も心の安らぐときはなかった. — He didn't know a moment's peace while he was on the run.

やせる

【体が】 今年は少しやせたいと思う. — I'd like to lose a little weight this year.

彼女は病気ですっかりやせました. — Her illness made her lose a lot of weight.

彼はやせて背の高い人でした. — He was tall and thin.

【土地が】 化学肥料を使っていると — The use of chemical fertilizers impover-

土地がやせてくる.	ishes the soil.
やせた土地には農作物はよく育たない.	Crops do not grow well in impoverished soil.

やっかい（厄介）

【面倒】これはなかなか厄介な仕事だ.	This job is a real pain.
厄介な問題に巻き込まれて困っている.	I'm involved in a real problem[1] and I don't know what to do.
彼に厄介な頼み事を持ってこられて閉口した.	I was at a loss as to how to respond to his troublesome [awkward[2]] request.
彼は何に対しても異議を唱えなければ気の済まない厄介な男だ.	He's never satisfied until he's †taken exception to something [objected]. He's really a pain.
彼が町を去ると，人々はやっと厄介払いができたと喜んだ.	Everyone was glad to be rid of him when he left town.
【世話】私はだれの厄介にもなりたくない.	I don't want to †put anyone to [give anyone] any trouble.
先日は大変ご厄介になりました.	I'm sorry to have put you to so much trouble the other day.
私は学生時代，伯父の所に厄介になっていた.	When I was a student, I stayed at my uncle's place.
警察のご厄介になるようなことは何もしていません.	I haven't done anything to bother the police.
祖父はとても丈夫で，今まで医者の厄介になったことがない.	My grandfather is very healthy and has never †been under the care of a doctor [needed a doctor].

> 1)「厄介な」に当たる言葉としては，troublesome や bothersome があるが，「厄介な問題」と言うときは，problem（あるいは trouble）自体に既に troublesome や bothersome の意味合いが含まれるので重ねて用いずに real などで強調する．そのほか，difficult, complicated, awkward なども使える．2) この場合の awkward は「立場的にやりにくい」の意．

やっと

【かろうじて】彼は疲労困憊し，やっと歩いている状態だった.	He was so exhausted (that) he could barely walk.
タクシーを飛ばしてやっと飛行機に間に合った.	I just made the plane by rushing (to the airport) in a taxi.
私の収入では家族5人が暮らしていくのがやっとだ.	On my income, it's all I can do just to feed my family of five.
彼はやっとの思いで，その少女に自分の気持ちを打ち明けた.	He finally got up the courage to reveal his feelings to the girl.

やとう

【ようやく】やっと仕事が終わった. — I finally finished my work.
彼女は1時間も遅れてやっと現れた. — She finally showed up, a whole hour late.
子どもたちが大きくなり, やっと自分の時間が持てるようになった. — Now that my children are grown up, I can finally get some time to myself.

やとう（雇う）

【人を】システムエンジニアを一人雇わなくてはならない. — We have to hire a systems engineer.
彼は運転手としてその会社に雇われた. — He was hired [employed] by that company as a driver.
息子のために家庭教師を雇った. — We hired a tutor for my son.
【車・船を】私たちはバスを雇って旅行に出かけた. — We chartered a bus and went on a trip.
彼らは船を雇って釣りをした. — They chartered a boat and went fishing.

やはり

【以前と同様】今でもやはりあの会社にお勤めですか. — Are you still working for that same company?
今年の夏休みもやはり田舎に帰るつもりです. — I'm planning to go back home this summer, too.
【他と同様】僕もやはり彼女が好きだ. — Well, I like her too.
私もやはり君の意見に反対だ. — I'm also opposed to your view.
父親と同様, 彼もやはり医者をしている. — He too is a doctor just like his father.
彼の会社もやはり不景気だ. — His company too is having a hard time.
【予期どおり】その電話はやはり彼女からだった. — I thought that call might be (from) her.
彼はやはりうそをついていた. — So it wasn't true. I might have known he was lying.
あの二人はやはり結婚した. — They got married after all.
【結論として】走ったけれどやはり乗り遅れた. — I ran but still I ended up missing the train.
やはりあの人を好きになれない. — Even so, I just can't bring myself to like that person.
利口そうでもやはり彼は子どもだ. — He seems smart, but after all he is still a child.
やはり秋がいちばん過ごし易い. — Fall is the most comfortable season after all.
私はやはり和食がいちばん好きだ. — I guess I like Japanese food the best after all.

やぶる (破る)

- 【裂く】子どもはよく障子を破ります. — Children often tear holes in *shoji*.
- くぎに引っ掛けて, シャツを破ってしまった. — I caught my shirt on a nail and tore it.
- 【壊す】金庫が破られて金が盗まれた. — The safe was broken into, and the money stolen.
- トラックが家の壁を破って飛び込んだ. — The truck drove through the wall.
- 大人は子どもの夢を破らないようにしたいものです. — Adults shouldn't shatter children's dreams.
- それを許すと前例を破ることになる. — If you allow that, it will break with precedent.
- 核兵器の生産は世界の平和を破るものだ. — The production of nuclear weapons destroys world peace.
- ナイチンゲールの鳴き声が時々辺りの静けさを破った. — The song of a nightingale would sometimes break the surrounding stillness.
- 【負かす】彼は決勝戦で強敵を破った. — He defeated a strong opponent in the final match.
- 今日の暑さは記録破りだった. — The temperature today was a record high.
- 彼の持つ日本記録はまだ破られていない. — He still holds the Japanese record for that event.
- 【違反】彼は約束を破るような人間ではない. — He isn't the type who would break a promise.
- 法律を破ると罰せられる. — You will be punished if you break the law.

やぶれる (破・敗れる)

- 買物袋が破れてしまった. — My shopping bag is torn.
- シャツのそでが破れて着られなくなった. — The sleeve on my shirt has split a seam and I can't wear it anymore.
- ズボンのひざが擦れて破れかかっている. — My pants are †worn out [torn] at the knee.
- 水道管が凍って破れてしまった. — The water pipe froze up and burst.
- 【壊れる】音楽家になろうという彼女の夢ははかなく破れた. — Her dreams of becoming a musician were dashed.
- 【負ける】我がチームは予選で敗れてしまった. — Our team was beaten in a preliminary game.

やま (山)

- 日本は山が多い. — Japan has many mountains.
- 【慣用】あいつは海のものとも山のものとも判らない. — I have no idea how that guy's going to turn out.
- 【堆積】僕は君に質問が山ほどあ — I have a bunch [pile, mountain] of

	questions to ask you.
彼は山ほど仕事を抱えている.	He is really piled up with work.
一山500円のリンゴを買った.	I bought a small basket of apples for 500 yen.
あの空地はごみの山だ.	That vacant lot is full of garbage.
【投機】彼は株で一山当てた.	He made a killing [pile] on the stock market.
試験の山が外れて全然できなかった.	I guessed wrong about what would be on the test, and did very badly.
彼は山を張るのがうまい.	He's good at acting on his hunches.
【山場】苦しさも今が山だ.	This is the hardest [worst] part.
ここがこの映画の山だ.	This is the climax of the movie.
父の病気は山を越したようです.	Father has gone through a critical point in his illness.
	Father has survived a crisis (in his illness).
私の仕事も山を越えました.	I'm over the hump in my work.
	I'm through with the hardest part of my work.
この工事もやっと山が見えてきた.	This construction work will soon be all downhill.
この勝負の山はこれからだ.	We're now getting to the decisive moment in the game.
【鉱山】彼の家は一家揃って山で働いていた.	His whole family worked in the mines.

やむ (止む)

雨がやっとやんだ.	The rain has finally stopped.
風がどうやらやんだらしい.	The wind seems to have finally died down.
朝から雪がなかなかやまない.	The snow has not stopped since this morning.
ピアノの音がやんだ.	The sound of the piano has stopped.
腰の痛みがようやくやんだ.	My lower-back pain is finally gone.
彼は理想を求めてやまない.	He relentlessly pursues his ideal.
彼にはやむにやまれぬ事情がある.	He is caught in unavoidable circumstances.

やむをえない (やむを得ない)

この暴風雨では試合の中止もやむを得ない.	We had to cancel the game because of the rainstorm.
彼女は昨日やむを得ない用事で会を欠席した.	An unavoidable engagement kept her from attending the meeting yesterday.
やむを得ない事情により出席できない場合はご一報ください.	Please inform us if unavoidable circumstances should prevent you from attend-

	ing.*
	Please let us know if it's impossible for you to attend.
身内の不幸で，やむを得ず結婚式を延期した．	The wedding had to be postponed because there was a death in the family.
ほかにだれも適任者がいなかったので，やむを得ず僕がその役を引き受けることになった．	I reluctantly took on the job because there was no other suitable candidate.

やめる（止・辞める）

私はたばこをやめました．	I quit smoking.
おしゃべりをやめなさい．	Quit your chattering.
私はいつも5時に仕事をやめて帰宅する．	I always stop working and go home at five.
今日の練習はこれでやめます．	That's enough practice for today.
金がないから旅行はやめた．	I decided not to go on a trip because I didn't have any money.
天気が悪いから出かけるのはやめましょう．	The weather's bad, so let's not go out.
彼は家業を継ぐために学校〔会社〕をやめた．	He quit †school [the company] to take over the family business.
彼は医者をやめて作家になった．	He quit practicing medicine and became a writer.
彼は定年で会社を辞めた．	He retired from his company.
彼は健康を理由に学長を辞めた．	He resigned his position as president of the university for health reasons.
市長は任期が切れるので来月辞めます．	The mayor will leave office when his term expires next month.

ややこしい

この小説は筋がとてもややこしい．	The plot of this novel is very involved [complex, intricate, complicated].
友達からコンピュータの操作の説明を聞いたが，ややこしくてよく分からなかった．	My friend showed me how to operate a computer, but it was so complicated (that) I couldn't really understand.
ややこしい問題が起こって困っている．	I'm having difficulty with a complex problem.
彼はややこしい事件に巻き込まれてしまった．	He ended up getting himself in a real mess.
私はその件に関してややこしい立場に置かれている．	I've been placed in a very awkward position with regard to that affair.

やりかた (やり方)

佐川さんにそのやり方を教わった.	I learned how to do that from Mr. Sagawa.
そんなやり方では効率が悪すぎる.	That way [method] is too inefficient.
会社のひどいやり方に多くの社員が憤った.	Many employees were angered by the terrible way the company handled the situation.
責任を子会社になすりつけるなんて、やり方が汚ない.	Shifting the blame on to a subsidiary company is a dirty thing to do.
	It's unethical to shift the blame on to a subsidiary.
彼らには彼らのやり方がある. 外から口を出すな.	They have their own way of doing things. Don't interfere. [I wouldn't interfere if I were you.[1]]
私のやり方に口を出さないでよ.	Don't tell me what to do.
この商売はやり方次第で大もうけできる.	You can make big profits in this business depending on how you run it.

> 1)「自分なら〜しない」という柔らかい忠告.

やりくり

夫は月3万円の小遣いの範囲内でやりくりしている.	My husband makes do on ¥30,000 a month.
毎月, 家計のやりくりに苦労している.	I'm having a hard time every month making ends meet.
君の奥さんはやりくり上手だね.	Your wife's really good at managing the household expenses, isn't she?
どうにかやりくりして店の開業資金を貯めた.	I somehow managed to save enough money to open the store.
時間をやりくりしてボランティアをしている.	I manage to make time for volunteer work.
この部署は少ない人手でやりくりしている.	This department is getting by with few staff members.

やる (遣る)

【行う】彼は英語の勉強をやっている.	He's studying English.
来月クラス会をやる予定です.	We're scheduled to have a class reunion next month.
「元気でやってますか」「どうにかやっています」	"How are you getting along?" "I'm managing somehow."
今何か面白い映画をやっていますか.	Are there any good movies on now?
君はピアノを何年やっているんだ	How long have you been playing the

い？	piano?
彼は大学で心理学をやるらしい．	I hear he's going to †study [major in] psychology at college.
物書きとしてやっていくのは大変なことだ．	Making a living by writing is tremendously difficult.
彼は故郷で高校の教師をやっている．	He's a high school teacher in his hometown.
こんな安い給料ではやっていけないよ．	I can't make it on such a low salary.
【与える】あの時計は友達にやったよ．	I gave that watch away to a friend.
花に水をやるのを忘れないでね．	Don't forget to water the flowers, OK?
娘は毎日文鳥にえさをやっている．	My daughter feeds her Java sparrow every day.
【〜してやる】君が困ったときにはおれが何とかしてやる．	When you're in trouble I'll do anything I can for you.
この本を君に貸してやろう．	I'll lend you this book.
彼女はよく娘に絵本を読んでやる．	She often reads picture books to her daughter.
彼も旅行に誘ってやろうよ．	Let's invite him on the trip too.
僕はあの男を殴ってやりたい．	I want to give that guy a good beating. I want to beat that guy up.
よし，今度の試験は100点をとってやる．	OK, I'm going to get 100 on this test.
【行かせる】彼は息子二人を大学にやった．	He put his two sons through college.
荷物を受け取りに娘を駅にやった．	I sent my daughter to get the baggage at the station.
娘を一人で外国にやるのは心配だ．	I'm worried about sending my daughter overseas by herself.
彼は一人娘を嫁にやった．	He married off his only daughter.
【持っていく】ここに置いてあった本をどこへやったの？	Where did you put the book I had set down here?
財布をどこへやったかな？	Where did my purse go?
【飲む】一杯やってから帰りましょう．	Let's have a drink before going home.
私はたばこはやらないんです．	I don't smoke.

やわらかい (柔・軟らかい)

彼女はやわらかですべすべした肌をしている．	She has soft, smooth skin.
祖母は歯が悪いのでやわらかい物しか食べられない．	My grandmother can only eat soft food because of her bad teeth.

この布は肌触りがやわらかい.	This material has a soft texture [touch].
彼女の髪はやわらかい.	She has soft hair.
彼は体がやわらかい.	He has a flexible body.
春のやわらかい日差しを浴びて,小川がきらきらと輝いて流れている.	The stream is sparkling in the soft spring sunlight.
父は年の割には頭がやわらかい.	For his age my father is open-minded.
私はかたい本よりもやわらかい本を読むのが好きです.	I prefer light reading to serious books.

やわらぐ (和らぐ)

3月に入り，寒さが和らいだ.	The cold eased with the arrival of March.
夕方になってやっと暑さが和らいだ.	It's finally become a little cooler in the evening.
注射を打ったら傷の痛みが和らいだ.	The pain from the wound subsided when I received an injection.
事情を詳しく説明したら彼の怒りもやっと和らいできた.	He was very angry but when I explained the situation in detail, he finally cooled off.
最近，我が国に対するあの国の態度が和らいできている.	That country's attitude toward our country has softened recently.

ゆ

ゆういぎ (有意義)

君たちに有意義な学生生活を送ってもらいたい.	I hope your school years will be full of accomplishment.
彼はこの分野では有意義な研究をしている.	He has done significant research in this field.
海外での経験は私にとってとても有意義だった.	My experiences abroad were very meaningful for me.
我々はここにいるあいだの時間を有意義に使いたい.	We want to make good use of our time spent here.
	We want to make our time spent here worthwhile.

ゆううつ (憂うつ)

彼はいつも憂うつそうだ.	He always looks †depressed [gloomy, down

	in the dumps].
来週から期末試験で憂うつだ.	I'm in low spirits because final exams start next week.
明日から仕事に戻らなければならないと思うと憂うつになる.	I get depressed whenever I think about having to go back to work tomorrow.
このところ憂うつな天気が続いている.	We've been having some pretty gloomy weather for some time now.
	We've had some depressing weather for a while now.

ゆうえき (有益)

これはとても有益な本です.	This is a really rewarding book.
夏休みは有益に過ごしましょう.	Let's put our summer vacation to good use.

ゆうえつかん (優越感)

優越感は劣等感の裏返しであることもある.	A superiority complex is sometimes the result of overcompensation for an inferiority complex.
彼女はここにいるだれよりも美しいという優越感を感じた.	She felt there was none here who was superior to her in looks.

ゆうが (優雅)

彼女の物腰は優雅だ.	Her manner is graceful.
女王は国民に優雅に手を振った.	The queen gracefully waved to her countrymen.
彼女は大金持ちと結婚して優雅に暮らしている.	She married a rich man and is living a life of luxury.

ゆうかん (勇敢)

その勇敢な消防士は子どもを救うために燃え盛る火の中に飛び込んだ.	The brave [courageous] fireman dashed into the raging fire to save the child.
乗客は船長の勇敢な行動のお陰で生命が助かった.	The passengers owed their lives to the captain's bravery [courageousness].
彼女は勇敢に困難に立ち向かった.	She faced the difficulties †with courage [bravely].

ゆうき (勇気)

彼にはこの試練に耐えるだけの勇気があるだろうか.	I wonder if †he's courageous enough [he has enough courage] to endure this trial.
彼は勇気を奮い起こして結婚を申	He got up his courage and proposed to

し込んだ．
彼はクラスのみんなの前で先生の間違いを指摘する勇気がなかった． He didn't have the nerve to point out the teacher's error in front of the class.

ゆうこう (有効)
【効果的な・充実して】初めての給料だから有効に使いたい． It's my first paycheck and I want to make good use of it.
日曜日は早起きして一日を有効に過ごします． I get up early on Sundays to make the most of my day.
インターネットは情報収集において極めて有効な手段だ． The Internet is a very efficient means of gathering information.
この錠剤はお茶の有効成分を含む． This pill contains the active ingredient found in green tea.
【効力がある】この回数券は3ヵ月間有効です． This ticket book is valid for three months.
応募は1月31日の消印まで有効です． Applications must be postmarked no later than January 31st.
あなたの定期券は有効期限を過ぎています． Your train [bus] pass has expired.

ゆうしゅう (優秀)
彼女は優秀な学生だ． She is an excellent student.
彼はその分野で優秀な業績をあげた． He did superior work in that field.
絵画コンクールで優秀な作品には賞金が贈られた． Prize money was awarded to the best work(s) entered in the painting competition.
スイスは精密機器の優秀な技術で知られている． Switzerland is known for precision instruments with superior technology.

ゆうじゅうふだん (優柔不断)
彼のような優柔不断な男はこのポストには向かない． An indecisive [A wishy-washy] person like him isn't fit for this post.
彼は優柔不断な男だ． He's never able to make up his mind.

ゆうしょう (優勝)
我がチームは初優勝を飾った． Our team clinched its first championship.
優勝を目指してみんな頑張った． They gave it their all as they aimed for victory.
彼は弁論大会で優勝した． He won the speech contest.

ゆうじょう（友情）

彼とのあいだに深い友情が培(つちか)れた．
A deep (sense of) friendship has grown between him and me.

彼女と私は変わらぬ友情を誓い合った．
She and I promised to be friends forever.

彼の温かい友情に感激した．
I was moved by his warm show [gesture] of friendship.

ゆうずう（融通）

彼は融通が利く人だから6時以降でも部屋を使わせてくれる．
He's rather flexible; he'll let us use the room even after six.

役人はとかく法の運用において融通が利かない．
Officials often lack flexibility in applying laws.

100ドルほど融通していただけませんか．
Could you please lend me about 100 dollars?

ゆうせい（優勢）

目下我々のチームが優勢だ．
Our team is †ahead [leading, in the lead] now.

資金力ではX社のほうが優勢だが，企画力ではY社のほうが優勢だ．
X Company exceeds Y Company in capital but Y Company has †a superior capacity for planning [superior planning ability].

ゆうせん（優先）

どれを優先させればよいですか？
Which one should I give priority to?

これからやるべきことに優先順位をつけた．
I've prioritized the work that has to be done.
I've organized the work to be done in order of priority.

彼女は何よりも仕事を最優先させる．
She gives her work top priority.

経済発展より環境を優先させるべきだ．
The environment should have priority over economic development.

個人の権利より公共の福祉が優先される場合がある．
There are times when public welfare takes precedence over individual rights.

ファンクラブの会員の方にはチケットを優先的に販売します．
When the tickets are available for sale we give priority to fan club members.

お年寄りや体の不自由な方たちの優先席に元気な若者が堂々と座っている．
That healthy young person is not at all hesitant about sitting in a seat reserved for the old and the infirm.

ゆうだい (雄大)

ホテルの窓から雄大な山脈が見える. — I can see magnificent [majestic] mountains from my hotel window.

それは雄大な計画だ. — That's a grand [colossal, huge] project.

ゆうのう (有能)

彼は有能な医者だ. — He's †an able [a capable, a competent] doctor.

彼女みたいに有能な秘書に辞められると困るよ. — It would be [It's] a real problem to lose a competent secretary like her.

ゆうぼう (有望)

彼の事業は有望だ. — His business is very promising.

その若い学者は前途有望である. — That young scholar †has a bright future [shows great promise, is very promising].

ゆうめい (有名)

彼女は世界的に有名なピアニストだ. — She is a world-famous pianist.

この町はテレビドラマで有名になった. — A TV drama series made this town famous.

あの人は映画好きで有名だ. — Everyone knows that he loves movies. His love for movies is well known.

その法律は有名無実になっている. — It's a law in name only.

ユーモア

彼はユーモアのある人だ. — He has a good sense of humor.

彼にはユーモアが通じない. — He has no sense of humor.

これは日本には珍しい高度なユーモア小説だ. — For a Japanese novel, this has an exceptionally highly developed sense of humor.

ゆうゆう (悠々)

彼はどんな忙しいときでもゆうゆうとしている. — No matter how busy he may be, he's always so composed.

彼は非難の怒号を浴びながらもゆうゆうと演壇に立った. — He calmly made his way to the platform amid a barrage of censure.

仕事ははかどっており, 締め切りにはゆうゆう間に合う. — The work is making good progress, so we should be able to make the deadline comfortably.

あなたの成績ならゆうゆう合格できます. — With your grades, you should easily pass the exams.

彼は会社を退職してゆうゆうと暮らしている. / Having retired from work [Since retiring from work] he's been living †the easy life [comfortably].

ゆうり (有利)

彼はいつも話を自分に有利なように導く. / He always directs a discussion to his own advantage.
この取り引きは我々に有利だ. / This business deal is to our advantage.
事態は我々に有利に展開している. / The situation is turning in our favor.
我々は今度の試合で有利な立場にある. / We'll have the upper hand in the coming match.
彼は我々にとって有利な条件を打ち出してきた. / He came up with conditions which were in our favor.

ゆうりょく (有力)

秋には景気が回復に向かうとの見方が有力だ. / It is most likely that business will pick up in the fall.
それが彼の有罪を確定する有力な証拠となった. / That was a convincing piece of evidence establishing his guilt.
有力候補も泡沫候補も平等に報道するべきだ. / All candidates, strong and weak alike, should get equal media coverage.
彼は次期大統領の最有力候補だ. / He's the strongest candidate for the next president.
彼の父親は政界の有力者だ. / His father is an influential figure in politics.
His father is a leading politician.
その提携話は地元の有力紙に載った. / A story about the partnership appeared in a leading local newspaper.

ゆうわく (誘惑)

都会は様々な誘惑に満ちている. / Cities abound in a variety of temptations.
見知らぬ人の甘い言葉に誘惑されてはいけません. / Don't be tempted by sweet talk from strangers.
彼は悪い仲間の誘惑に負けて非行に走ってしまった. / He was led into delinquency by some bad friends.

ゆかい (愉快)

彼は愉快な人だ. / He's a lot of fun.
ゆうべは古い友達と飲んで愉快だった. / I had a good [pleasant, nice] time drinking with an old friend last night.
あの威張ったやつがそんな馬鹿なへまをしたなんて愉快な話だ. / It's amusing to hear that such an arrogant jerk made such a stupid [foolish] mistake.

ゆがむ (歪む)

君が引いた線〔描いた円〕はゆがんでいるよ.	The line [circle] you drew is crooked.
彼はいつもネクタイがゆがんでいるけど一向に気にしない.	His tie is always askew [crooked] but he doesn't care at all.
彼女は注射があまり痛くて顔をゆがめた.	The intense pain of the injection caused her to grimace.
彼は動かぬ証拠を突きつけられ口をゆがませた.	He grimaced when confronted [presented] with irrefutable facts.
彼は苦労し過ぎて性格がちょっとゆがんでいる.	Too much hardship has twisted his personality.
週刊誌では事実がゆがめられていた.	The facts were distorted in a weekly magazine.

ゆく (行く)

彼女は町へ買い物に行きました.	She went to town to do some shopping.
明日は映画を見に行こう.	Let's go see a movie tomorrow.
今度の日曜日は家族でピクニックに行く予定です.	Next Sunday we plan to go on a family picnic.
私は毎日歩いて学校に行きます.	I walk to school every day.
彼の息子は来年から学校に行きます.	His son will start school next year.
【進行する】面接試験はうまく行きましたか.	Did your interview go well?
何でも自分の思うようには行かないものだ.	Everything doesn't always go the way you want them to.

ゆずる (譲る)

【与える】彼は財産を息子に譲った.	He handed his estate over to his son.
子猫を譲ってください.	Please let me have a kitten.
老人に席を譲りましょう.	Give your seat to the elderly.
彼は車を安く友人に譲った.	He sold the car to his friend †cheap [at a low price].
彼は自転車に道を譲った.	He made way [room] for the bicycle.
【譲歩する】二人とも自分の主張を一歩も譲らなかった.	Neither of them would give an inch in his assertion.

ゆたか (豊か)

彼女は豊かな家庭に育った.	She was born into a rich family.
あの国は天然資源が豊かである.	That country †is rich in [has abundant] natural resources.
10ドルもらってその少年は豊かな気分になった.	The boy felt rich when he received 10 dollars.

彼女はピアノのコンテストで豊かな才能を発揮した.	She displayed a wealth of talent in the piano competition [contest].
彼とその家族は苦境にあっても豊かな心を失わなかった.	He and his family never lost their generosity [richness] of spirit, no matter how difficult their circumstances became.
出品された絵はどれも個性豊かなものばかりだった.	All of the paintings put on exhibit revealed an abundance of originality.

ゆだん (油断)

油断するな. 一つ間違えばおしまいだぞ.	Stay alert! One slipup and you could blow everything.
地下鉄にはどの車両にもスリがいるようなものだから, 油断は禁物だ.	Don't be caught off guard! They say there are pickpockets in practically every subway car.
彼女はちょっと油断している隙に財布をとられた.	She was caught off guard for a second and had her wallet stolen.
あいつは油断がならない.	You always have to be on guard with [around] him.

ゆっくり

もっとゆっくりしゃべってください.	Please speak more slowly.
もっとゆっくりやろう.	Let's slow down.
慌てるな. もっとゆっくりでいいよ.	Don't get so flustered. Take your time.
彼はうちへ来るといつもゆっくりしていく.	Whenever he comes for a visit, he stays for a long time.
どうぞごゆっくりなさってください.	Please make yourself at home.
日曜日の朝はいつもゆっくり起きます.	I always sleep in on Sundays.
	I always take my time getting up on Sundays.

ゆでる

| 卵はゆでて食べるのが好きです. | I like my eggs boiled. |
| めんはゆで過ぎないように. | Don't overboil the noodles. |

ゆとり

【空間的】居住空間にゆとりがないと, 人はいらだってくる.	People get irritated unless there is ample [enough] living space.
【経済的】子供たちが独立し, 経済的に少しゆとりができた.	We're a little better off financially now that the children have grown up.
それだけ貯蓄があれば, ゆとりの	You should be comfortable in your old

ある老後が送れるだろう. age with that much in savings.
【時間的】正社員からパートに変わり，時間のゆとりができた. I'm not as rushed for time [I have more time for myself] since I went from full-time to part-time.
放課後は毎日，塾や習い事で，子どもたちはゆとりのない生活を送っている. Children are kept too busy with cram schools and lessons every day after school.
彼はゆとりのない毎日を送るうちに，うつ病になった. He suffered from depression because his work left him with no time for himself.
【精神的・全般的】豊かな自然は私たちの心にゆとりをもたらす. The abundance of nature gives life to our souls.
We are enriched by the bounties of nature.
当喫茶店はゆとりの空間をお客様に提供します. This coffee shop offers its customers a relaxing atmosphere.
両親はオーストラリアに移住し，ゆとりのある暮らしをしている. My parents have been enjoying life after moving to Australia.
ゆとり教育で学力が低下すると心配する親がいる. Some parents are worried that †"education free of pressure" ["education with latitude"] might lower the scholastic ability [level] of students.

ゆび (指)

彼はナイフで指を切った. He cut his finger with a knife.
息子はお正月が来るのを指折り数えて待っている. My son is counting the days until New Year's.
人に後ろ指を指されるようなことはするな. Don't do anything that will make people talk.
息子は隣の子のプラモデルを指をくわえて見ていた. My son looked enviously at the other child's plastic model.
彼は世界でも指折りの指揮者だ. He's one of the world's leading conductors.
子どもの頃よく友達と指切りをしたものだ. When I was little I used to make promises with my friends by linking our baby fingers.
この証拠物件には指一本触れてはいけません. This is material evidence. Don't (you dare) touch it. [Don't lay a finger on it.]
うちの娘に指一本触れるな. Don't you dare †lay a finger on [touch] my daughter.
彼は並んでいる車の一つを指さして「それを買いたい」と言った. He pointed to one car out of the lineup and said, "I want to buy that one."

ゆめ (夢)

【睡眠中に見る夢】ディズニーラン I dreamed [dreamt] I went to Disneyland.

ドへ行った夢を見た.	
夢の中で死んだおばあちゃんに会った.	I dreamed about my dead grandmother.
怖い夢から覚めて, ほっとした.	I was so relieved after I woke up from a bad [frightening, scary] dream.
宝くじに当たった夢が正夢になった.	I dreamed I won the lottery and it came true.
夢かと思ってほっぺたをつねった.	I pinched my cheeks to make sure I wasn't dreaming.
【願望】宇宙飛行士になるのが小さい頃からの夢だった.	I've dreamed of being an astronaut since I was a child.
今年はハワイで年を越すという夢がかないそうだ.	It looks as though my dream of celebrating New Year's in Hawaii will come true this year.
肩の故障でプロ野球選手になる夢が絶たれた.	His dreams of becoming a professional baseball player ended after a shoulder injury.
彼女は夢破れて故郷へ帰った.	She went back to her hometown after her dreams were shattered.
彼は息子に自分の夢を託した.	He's living (his dreams) through his son. He wants his son to do what he's always wanted to do.
私が社長になるなどとは夢にも思わなかった.	I never dreamed I would become a [the] company president.
サラリーマンになりたいだって? 今の子は夢がないなあ.	You want to become a whitecollar worker? What happened to the big [great, ambitious] dreams kids used to have?
【甘美な想い】彼とデートしているなんて, まるで夢のようだ.	Dating him [Going out with him] is like a dream come true.
教師生活は夢に描いていたのとは違った.	A teacher's life wasn't all that I thought [dreamed] it would be.
移住先では夢のある生活が待っていると思っていた.	I moved away thinking that a wonderful life awaited me.
入社当時は夢と希望にあふれていた.	I was full of hopes and dreams when I entered the firm.
私にも夢見る少女のころがあった.	I was once a young girl full of dreams, too.
彼からのプロポーズの言葉を夢心地で聞いた.	I listened dreamily to his proposal of marriage.
新幹線は開業当時, 夢の超特急と称された.	When it first started running, the bullet train was called the super express train of our dreams.
【空想・非現実的】夢を追ってばか	It's time to stop dreaming and face reality.

りいないで現実を見なさい.

彼が有名な小説家になるなんて, しょせん夢に過ぎない. | He's just fantasizing about becoming a famous novelist.

ブロードウェイの舞台に立つなんて夢のまた夢だ. | Being on Broadway is nothing but a dream [fantasy].

永遠の若さは人類の見果てぬ夢だ. | Mankind's quest for eternal youth will never be realized.

1回戦で敗退し, 優勝は夢物語に終わった. | All hopes of victory were dashed after being eliminated in the first round.

やっと夢から覚めた. これからは地道に働くよ. | I finally woke up. From now on, I'm going to work at a steady job.

ゆるい (緩い)

最近やせてベルトが緩くなった. | I've lost weight recently and my belt is (getting) loose.

この指輪は緩い. | This ring is loose.

ゆるす (許す)

【容赦】上司は私の失敗を許してくれた. | My boss forgave my mistake.

うそをつくなんて許せないよ. | I can't forgive you for lying.

風邪をひいているので, 今日の練習は許してください. | I've caught a cold. Could I be excused from practice today?

【許可】父は大学進学を許してくれた. | My father's letting me go on to college.

両親は私たちの結婚を許してくれない. | My parents won't consent to †us getting married [our marriage].

事情が許せばすぐフランスへ出発します. | If circumstances permitted, I would leave for France right away.

【慣用】君には心を許せる友人がいますか. | Do you have friends you can talk to? Do you have friends you can be completely open [honest] with?

この交渉は最後まで気を許せない. | I have to be on my toes until these negotiations are finished [concluded].

事態は予断を許さない. | Given this situation, we can't draw any premature conclusions.

父の病状は楽観を許さない. | We can't be optimistic about my father's illness.

彼は自他ともに許す経済界の第一人者だ. | His preeminence as a business leader is universally recognized.

ゆるむ (緩む)

靴のひもが緩んでいますよ. | Your shoelaces are coming undone.

このいすはねじが緩んでいる.	There's a screw loose in this chair.
やっと寒さが緩んできた.	The cold (weather) has finally let up.
私は旅に出ると財布のひもが緩む.	I tend to spend more than usual when I'm traveling.
大雨で地盤が緩み,崖崩れが起きる恐れがある.	The heavy rains have softened the earth giving rise to the danger of landslides.

ゆるめる (緩める)

もう少しロープを緩めてください.	Please slacken the rope a little.
彼は町なかに入ると車のスピードを緩めた.	He slowed down as he entered town.
取り締まりの手を緩めるとスピード違反が増える.	Once law enforcement is relaxed, more people start †speeding [breaking the speed limits].
政府は輸入規制を緩める方針だ.	Government policy is easing restrictions on imports.

ゆるやか (緩やか)

ここから緩やかな下り坂が駅まで続いている.	A gentle slope runs from here down to the station.
この道は左へ緩やかにカーブしている.	This road curves gently [slowly] to the left.
この曲はテンポが緩やかだ.	This tune has †a slow [an easygoing] tempo [beat].
この頃かなり規制が緩やかになった.	The rules have been relaxed [eased] lately.
春風が緩やかに頬をなでた.	The gentle spring breeze caressed [brushed] my cheek.

ゆれる (揺れる)

地震で我が家はかなり揺れた.	Our house shook badly during the earthquake.
山道ではバスがよく揺れる.	The bus sways a lot on mountain roads.
船は揺れるので嫌いです.	I don't like boats because they rock back and forth.
そのスキャンダルに政界は揺れ動いた.	The scandal shook government circles.
この小説は微妙に揺れる女性の心理を描いたものです.	This novel depicts the subtle changes [fluctuations] in feminine psychology.
プロ野球への誘いに彼の心は揺れた.	He was torn between accepting the offer to play pro baseball or not.

よい (良・善・好い)

日頃善い行いをしていれば必ず報われるものだ.	People are always rewarded for their good deeds.
それは善いことをしましたね.	What a fine deed!
	You (really) have done a good deed.
約束の時間に間に合って良かった.	I'm glad I was able to make it for the appointed time.
こんなつまらないパーティーなら来なければ良かった.	I'd have been better off not coming to such a boring party.
あの映画はとても良かった.	That was a very good movie.
よかったら明日うちに来ないか.	Would you like to come over to my house tomorrow?
彼はもう来てもよさそうなものだが.	He really should be coming soon!
このボールペンはとても書きよい.	This (ball-point) pen really writes well.

よう¹ (用)

今日は用があるので先に帰ります.	I have to leave †now [early today]. I have some things to take care of.
彼があなたに何か用があるそうです.	He has something (he wants) to talk to you about.
	He wants to see you about something.
何かご用ですか.	May I help you?
	What can I do for you?
何か私にご用でしょうか.	Do you need me for something?
あんな男に用はない.	I don't want to have anything to do with that person [guy, man].
けがが治って松葉杖には用がなくなった.	I no longer need to use crutches because my leg is better.
彼に会わないことには用が足りない.	I can't take care of my business †without talking to him [if I don't talk to him].
私の話は電話で用が足ります.	My business can be taken care of with a phone call.
二, 三用を足してから家に帰ります.	I'll go home after I run two or three errands.

こんなに進むのでは時計の用をなさない.	This watch is (of) no use if it keeps running fast like this.

よう² (酔う)

【酒に】昨日はすっかり酔ってしまって,何を言ったか全く覚えていない.	I got so drunk last night that I can't remember anything I said.
彼は酔うほどにおしゃべりになる.	The more he drinks, the more talkative he gets.
彼は酔って上司に絡んだ.	He got drunk and got into a hassle with his superior.
【乗り物に】私は船にも飛行機にも酔うので,まだ一度も外国へ行ったことがない.	Since I get †sick [motion sickness] whether I'm on a ship or a plane, I have not once traveled abroad.
彼女は車に酔うので,できるだけ電車を利用している.	She gets carsick when she rides in a car, so she takes the train as often as she can.
【人に】人に酔うので,なるべく人込みは避けたい.	Crowded places make me sick so I want to stay away as much as I can.
【陶酔する】聴衆は美しい音楽に酔いしれた.	The audience was enraptured by the beautiful music.
選手だけでなく応援団も一様に勝利に酔った.	Not only the players but the cheering section was also intoxicated with the victory.

～よう

【推量・判断】彼はもう出かけたようだ.	He seems to have already left.
私は彼に厳し過ぎたようだ.	I seem to have been [I think I was] too strict with him.
雨はもうすぐ上がるようだ.	It seems like [It looks as though] it might stop raining pretty soon.
【類似・例示】今日の暑さはまるで夏のようだ.	The hot weather today feels almost like summer.
こんな所で君に会うなんてまるで夢のようだ.	I can't believe I'm meeting you here.
彼は氷のように冷たい人間だ.	He's as cold as ice.
彼は全く信じられないというような顔つきだった.	His expression was one of complete disbelief.
彼はいつものように早く起きた.	He woke up early as usual.
彼女は何があっても自殺するようなことはしない.	Under no circumstances is she the kind of person to commit suicide.
北海道のような広いところに住みたい.	I would like to live where there are wide-open spaces, like in Hokkaido.

彼は約束を破るような人じゃない.	He's not the kind of person who would break promises.
【目的】彼は列車に遅れないように早目に家を出た.	He left his house a little early to make sure he wouldn't be late for the train.
この本は宇宙について子どもにもよく分かるように説明してある.	This book explains the universe in such a way that even children can easily understand.
彼女は夫に垣根を直してくれるように頼んだ.	She asked her husband to fix the fence.
風邪をひかないように気をつけなさい.	Take care not to catch a cold.

ようい (用意)

【準備】今日は雨具の用意をして学校に行ったほうがいいですよ.	You'd better take your rain gear with you to school today.
母は夕食の用意で忙しい.	Mother is busy †preparing dinner [getting dinner ready].
旅行の用意はできましたか.	Are you ready for your [the] trip?
あなたの好きなお菓子を用意しました.	I prepared [made] your favorite dessert.
彼は何の用意もしないで試験を受けた.	He took the examination without studying for it.
私には質問に答える用意がある.	I'm ready [prepared] to answer the questions.
【貯蓄】少しばかり用意してあったので入院費は間に合いました.	I managed to pay the hospital charges [bills] from money I have saved.

ようき (陽気)

【快活】彼女はとても陽気な人だ.	She's a very cheerful [lively] person.
彼女どうしたの. 随分陽気だね.	What happened to her? She seems so lively [cheerful, happy].
陽気な音楽を聞いていると踊りたくなる.	When I listen to lively music, it makes me want to dance.
学生たちがコンパで陽気に騒いでいた.	The students were making a lot of noise and having a good time at the class party.
【時候】今日は陽気がいいですね.	It's a beautiful day today, isn't it?
陽気に誘われて散歩に出た.	I decided to take a walk because it was such a beautiful day.
私の病気は陽気の加減で良くなったり悪くなったりです.	With this illness, how I feel is affected by the weather.

ようきゅう (要求)

組合は20%の賃上げを要求した.	The union demanded a 20% raise.
この仕事には強い忍耐力が要求される.	This job demands a lot of patience.
欲しい物は何でも要求してください.	If there's anything you'd like, please don't hesitate to ask.
よろしい,君の要求に応じよう.	Very well, I'll comply with your demands. OK, I'll †agree with [go along with] your terms.

ようじ (用事)

彼は大事な用事を思い出した.	He just remembered something very important.
あなたに頼みたい用事がある.	I'd like to ask you †to do something for me [for a favor].
彼は用事があって出かけています.	He's out running errands.
買い物に行きますけど,何か用事はありませんか.	I'm going shopping. Do you need anything?

ようじん (用心)

用心して運転しなさい.	Drive carefully.
人込みの中ではすりに用心しなさい.	Look [Watch] out for pickpockets in crowds.
入試の前なので,風邪をひかないように用心している.	Because the entrance examination is coming up soon, I've been careful not to catch a cold.
外国へ行ったとき,用心のために生水を飲まないようにした.	When I went abroad, I didn't drink †the water [unboiled water] just as a precaution.
彼女はとても用心深い人なので,電話で絶対に自分から名乗らない.	She's very cautious. She never gives her name over the phone.

ようす (様子)

【状態】東京はどんな様子ですか.	What's it like in Tokyo?
昨夜からあの病人の様子がおかしい.	There's been something wrong with that patient since last night. That patient's condition has not been good since last night.
大雨で川はすっかり様子が変わった.	The heavy rain drastically changed conditions on the river.
もう少し雨の様子を見てから出かけよう.	Let's wait and see if it stops raining before going out.

この様子では彼は当選しそうもない.	Under the circumstances, it seems unlikely (that) he'll be elected.
猫が辺りの様子をうかがっている.	The cat's checking out its surroundings.
【態度・外観】彼はあまり困った様子でもない.	He doesn't seem to be worried [concerned].
あの様子では彼は試験に落ちたようだ.	It looks †as though [as if, like¹⁾] he's failed the examination.
【兆候】夕立が来そうな様子だ.	It looks †like [as though, as if] we're going to have a shower.
彼は今夜は帰って来る様子もない.	It doesn't look †as though [as if, like] he's coming home tonight.

> 1) look like のあとに節（主語＋述部）がくる構文は米会話でよく使われるが，非文法的で間違いであるとする人もいる．

ようち (幼稚)

彼は大学生と思えないほど幼稚な人間だ.	He's so immature (that) it's hard to believe he's a college student.
君のそんな幼稚な考えにはついていけないよ.	I can't go along with your immature [childish] ideas.
この文章は幼稚だが心打たれる.	I was touched [moved] when I read this story, even though it was †childishly written [not well written].

ようやく (漸く)

ようやく春らしくなってきました.	It finally feels [seems] like spring.
彼も今年はようやく大学に合格した.	He finally made it into a university this year.
私もようやく英語が少し話せるようになった.	I can finally speak a little English. I am finally able to speak a little English.

ようりょう (要領)

【まとまり】彼は要領良く自分の意見を述べた.	He clearly stated his opinion.
あの人の答えはいつも要領を得ない.	I can never understand what he wants to say when he answers a question. His answers are always unclear.
【うまいやり方】3回失敗してやっと要領が分かった.	I finally got the knack [hang] of it after three tries.
彼は要領良く仕事をこなす.	He carries out his work efficiently.
彼は何をやらせても要領が良い.	He can figure out how to do anything you ask [want] him to.
彼は何をやらせても要領が悪い.	He can't do anything right.

彼が毎日残業しているのは要領が悪いからだ.	He works overtime everyday because he's inefficient.
【ずる賢い】あいつは全く要領のいいやつだ.	He's too clever for his own good.
この授業は要領さえ良ければあまり出席しなくても単位が取れる.	If you do it right, you can get credits for this course without going to all the classes.

よかん (予感)

今度こそ宝くじに当たりそうな予感がする.	I have a strong feeling [premonition] that I'm going to win the lottery this time.
何だか嫌な予感がしたので,今日は出かけなかった.	I didn't go out today because I had the feeling that something bad was going to happen.
予感が見事に適中した〔外れた〕.	I guessed [My guess was] right (completely off).

よき (予期)

予期していたとおりに,彼は私の援助の申し出を断った.	Just as I had expected, he turned down my request for assistance [support].
予期に反して田中君が生徒会長に当選した.	Contrary to expectations, Tanaka was elected president of the student council.
最初から失敗を予期して事業を始める人などいないものだ.	No one starts a business expecting it to fail.

よく¹

【しばしば】小さい子どもはよくはしゃぐものだ.	Small children often jump around and play.
それは世間によくあることだ.	That happens all the time.
私は若い頃はよく山に登った.	When I was young, I would often go mountain climbing.
【十分に】よく見ると,この1万円札は偽物だ.	You can tell this ¥10,000 [ten thousand yen] bill is counterfeit [fake] if you look at it carefully.
昨夜はよく眠れました.	I slept very well last night.
文字に間違いがないかよく調べてください.	Please check carefully to make sure there are no mistakes [errors] in the writing.
【感嘆】よくおいでくださいました.	How nice of you to come!
この嵐の中をよく無事で帰って来たね.	It's amazing how you made it back safely through this storm.
よくここが分かりましたね.	It's amazing how you found this place.
彼女は女手一つでよく5人の子どもを育てたものだ.	It's a wonder how she raised five children [kids] by herself.

よく，あんなひどいことが言えたものだ. / I can't believe he had the nerve [audacity] to say something as rude as that.
よくも僕の頭をぶったな. / How dare you hit me on the head!
よくしたもので，私が病気になると妻は元気になる. / When I'm ill my wife is in good health. It's a wonder how everything seems to work out.

よく² (欲)

彼は欲の深い人だ. / He's †an avaricious [a greedy] person.
彼は欲が張りすぎている. / His desires know no bounds. / His greed knows no bounds.
彼は本当に欲のない人だ. / He doesn't have a selfish bone in his body.
暑さのせいか食欲がない. / It may be the heat, but I've no appetite.
彼女は知識欲が旺盛だ. / She has an insatiable appetite [desire] for knowledge.
欲を出したばかりに詐欺師に大金を巻き上げられた. / My greed got the best of me and I got taken by that swindler for a lot of money.
彼は欲に目がくらんで，ライバル会社に買収された. / He was blinded by greed and sold out to the rival company. / Blinded by avarice, he allowed himself to be corrupted by the rival company.
どんなことでも欲を言えば切りがない. / If we let ourselves go, there'd be no end to the things we'd like to have.
あの人はいい人だが，欲を言えばもう少し積極性が欲しい. / He's a good person but †I wouldn't mind seeing a little more assertiveness [I wish he were more assertive].

よく〜 (翌〜)

彼女は7月5日に成田を飛び立ち，翌6日にロンドンに着いた. / She left Narita Airport on July 5th and arrived in London a day later on the 6th.
残業をした翌日，彼は遅くまで寝ていた. / The day after he worked overtime, he slept †in [until late].
翌朝は雨も上がり上天気でした. / It stopped raining the following morning and †the weather was fine [we had very good weather].
二人が結婚した翌年，女の子が生まれた. / The year after they were married, †a baby girl was born [they had a baby girl].

よくばる (欲張る)

彼は欲張りだ. / He's greedy.
バイキング料理を欲張って食べ過 / My eyes were bigger than my stomach and

ぎてしまった.	I wound up eating (way) too much at the smorgasbord.
	I stuffed my face** at the smorgasbord.
たった3日間で北海道を全部まわろうとは随分欲張った旅行計画を立てたものだね.	You're going to cover all of Hokkaido in just three days!? What an ambitious plan!

よけい (余計)

果物屋の主人はバナナを1本余計にくれた.	The owner of the fruit shop gave me an extra banana.
親に余計な心配をかけたくない.	I don't want to worry my parents unnecessarily.
余計な物は捨てたらどうだ.	Why don't you try throwing away things you don't need?
彼には余計な口出しをしないほうがいい.	You'd be better off not saying too much to him.
今月は少し余計にお金が入る.	I'll be getting a little extra money this month.
彼は人より余計に働く.	He works harder than (the) others.
見るなと言われると余計見たくなるものだ.	Being told not to look just makes you want to look even more.

よける (避ける)

私は水たまりをよけながら歩いた.	I avoided the puddles as I walked.
彼は自動車を危うくよけた.	He quickly moved out of the way of the car.
船は嵐をよけて港に入った.	The ship came into port to avoid the storm.
霜をよけるためにイチゴ畑にわらをかぶせなさい.	Cover the strawberry fields with straw to prevent frost.

よこ (横)

この板は横幅が2メートルある.	This board is two meters wide.
線を横に引きなさい.	Draw a †horizontal line [line horizontally].
横1列に並びなさい.	Please stand side by side in a row.
彼はベッドに横になった.	He lay down on the bed.
彼は私の要求に対して首を横に振った.	He shook his head in disapproval at my request.
この会社では横のつながりを大切にしている.	Everyone at this company places importance on maintaining [keeping] good relations between employees.
あの細い道は横から子どもが飛び出して来るので危ない.	It's really dangerous how children dart out into that narrow street.

横を向かないで正面を向きなさい.	Stop looking to the side and look straight ahead.
あなたの横に座ってもいいですか.	May I sit next to you?
	Do you mind if I sit beside you?
駅に行くにはパン屋の横を左に曲がるとすぐです.	To go to the station, make a left (turn) at the bakery and you're right there.
彼はいつも帽子を横にかぶっている.	He always wears his hat to the side.
横から口を挟まないでください.	Please don't †interrupt [butt into] our conversation.
話が横にそれてしまったが, 本題へ戻そう.	We went off on a tangent but let's get back †on topic [to the topic].
主人は縦の物を横にもしない人です.	My husband won't lift a finger around the house.

よこぎる (横切る)

道路を横切るときは横断歩道を渡りましょう.	When you cross the street, make sure you use the crosswalk.
線路を横切ったところに僕の家がある.	My house is right after you've crossed the railroad tracks.
眼の前を一匹の犬が横切った.	A dog cut across right in front of me.

よごす (汚す)

子どもはすぐ服を汚す.	Children dirty their clothes in no time.
ぬかるみを歩いたので靴が汚れてしまった.	My shoes got dirty from trudging [walking] through the mud.
車の排気ガスが空気を汚している.	Automobile exhaust pollutes the air.

よごれる (汚れる)

泥で手が汚れてしまった.	My hands got soiled from the dirt.
汚れたシャツを着替えなさい.	Why don't you change out of your dirty shirt?
この川は工場排水で汚れている.	This river's polluted with industrial waste.

よさん (予算)

彼は旅行の予算を立てている.	He's figuring out the budget for his trip.
まだ文化祭の予算が立っていない.	The budget for the cultural festival still hasn't been set.
予算がついてその計画はやっと着手された.	With this budget we were finally able to †start [go ahead with] the project.
予算がないのでこの車を買うのはやめることにした.	I've decided I can't afford to buy this car.
新空港の工事は予算をはるかにオ	Construction costs on the new airport

ーバーしている.	have far exceeded the original budget.
この予算で忘年会を開くのは無理だ.	It's impossible to hold a year-end party on this budget.

よしゅう (予習)

予習は学力をつける上でとても効果的です.	Preparation before classes is a very effective way of improving academic achievement.
彼女は英語の予習をしています.	She's preparing for her English class.
明日の授業の予習をまだしていなかった.	I haven't prepared for tomorrow's class [lesson] yet.

よす

よせよ!	Cut it out!／Stop it!
空模様が良くないから今日は出かけるのをよしましょう.	The weather doesn't look very promising [good] so let's not go out today.
悪い冗談はよしてくれ.	No more bad jokes!
犬をいじめるのはよせ.	Stop teasing the dog!
たばこ〔お酒〕はもうよしたら?	Why don't you quit [stop] smoking [drinking]?
	Isn't it about time you quit smoking [drinking]?
体の具合が悪いのでクラブ活動をするのはよしました.	I gave up my extracurricular activities (at school) because I haven't been feeling well.
よせばいいのに, 彼は調子に乗って酒を飲み過ぎた.	He should have stopped but he got carried away and drank more than he could hold.

よせる (寄せる)

彼はかばんを手元に寄せて本を取り出した.	He brought his school bag closer to him and took out a book.
車をもっと端に寄せてください.	Please pull your car over more to the edge.
【集める】あのお店では客を寄せるためにいろいろな宣伝をしている.	That store has a number of ads aimed at †bringing in [attracting] customers.
交通事故で両親を失った少女に多くの人から同情の声が寄せられた.	Many people sympathized with the girl who had lost her parents in a car accident.
【送る】その雑誌のクイズにはたくさんの回答が寄せられた.	They received many replies to the quiz in the magazine.
この番組に対するご意見をお寄せください.	Please send [mail] in your comments concerning this program.

【訪問する】今日はお忙しそうですのでまた後日寄せていただきます.	Since you're busy today, I'll come by sometime later.
【近づく】波が海岸に寄せては返している.	Waves are lapping against the shore.
敵が突然押し寄せて来た.	The enemy suddenly forced their way through.

よそ

よその人に迷惑をかけてはいけません.	Don't trouble others.
君はよそのことに口を出し過ぎる.	You poke your nose into other people's business too much.
よそではこんな値段では買えませんよ.	You won't find a better price anywhere.
昨日はよそで夕飯を食べた.	I ate dinner out last night.
彼は授業中よそ見ばかりしている.	He's always glancing around during class needlessly.
卒業式ともなると, みんなよそ行きの顔ですましている.	At the graduation ceremony everyone looked serious for once.
彼はよそ行きとふだん着の区別を全然していない.	He doesn't distinguish at all between dressy clothes and everyday clothes.

よそう (予想)

現代のような目まぐるしい世の中では, 将来を予想することは難しい.	It's hard to predict what will happen in the future when the world is in such confusion.
今年は更に物価の上昇が予想される.	Bigger increases in prices are anticipated for this year.
彼が次にすることぐらい僕にも予想がつく.	Even I can guess what he'll do next.
試験の結果は予想以上に良かった.	The test turned out better than I had expected.
	The results of the test were better than I had expected.
あの芝居は予想を上回る観客を集めた.	That play attracted larger audiences than expected.
あの二人はみんなの予想どおり結婚した.	Those two got married, just as everyone expected.
予想に反して彼は落選した.	Contrary to expectations, he lost the election.
我がチームは予想外の好成績を収めた.	Our team compiled a better record than expected.

彼は競馬の予想がうまい.	He's good at picking winners at the horse races.

よっきゅう（欲求）

人の欲求には限りがないものだ.	There is no end to things you can want.
子どもの非行は親に対する欲求不満から生じることが多い.	Juvenile delinquency is often the result of the child's frustrations toward the parents.

よてい（予定）

来年は家の新築を予定している.	I'm planning to build a house next year.
今月の仕事の予定を立てておいてください.	Please make up the work schedule for this month.
今度の日曜日は何か予定がありますか.	Do you have any plans for this Sunday?
彼は予定の飛行機に乗り遅れた.	He was late for his scheduled flight.
会議は予定より30分遅れて始められた.	The meeting was thirty minutes late starting.
ビル工事は予定どおりに進んでいる.	Construction on [of] the building is proceeding as scheduled.
結婚式は予定を繰り上げて3月に行われた.	The day of the wedding was moved up to March.
予定した講師が来られなくなった.	The teacher who was scheduled to come couldn't make it.
予定はもう動かせない.	We can't change the schedule now.

よのなか（世の中）

【世間】世の中はままならないものだ.	Things don't always go the way you want them to in life.
世の中はそんなものさ.	That's life./This is the real world.
君もなかなか世の中というものが分かってきたじゃないか.	Welcome to the real world! You're getting a taste of what it's really like out there.
今度のことで、つくづく世の中が嫌になった.	After this, I'm completely disgusted with the world.
【時代】実力がものを言う世の中になってきた.	Nowadays it's performance [ability] that counts.

よび（予備）

予備の食料を三日分持って登山しなさい.	Take along an extra three days' supply of food when you go mountain climbing.
会議に机といすの予備を少し用意しておいてください.	Please have the extra tables and chairs ready for the meeting.

万一に備えて予備のお金を貯金してあります.	I have savings for emergencies.
彼らは予備知識を持たずにその芝居を見に行った.	They went to see that play not knowing anything about it beforehand.
その交渉では予備工作が効を奏した.	The groundwork for the negotiations proved effective.
彼は予備校に通っている.	He goes to prep school.

よぶ (呼ぶ)

【声をかける】知らない人にいきなり名前を呼ばれたので驚いた.	I was surprised when a stranger suddenly called my name.
僕の名前は健一郎ですが, 長いのでケンと呼んでください.	My name is Kenichiro, but †you can [please] call me Ken for short.
助けを呼ぶ声が聞こえた.	I heard someone call "Help!"
【呼び寄せる・招く】彼はボーイを呼んで, コーヒーを注文した.	He called a waiter and ordered coffee.
「食事ですよ」と母親が外で遊んでいた子どもを呼んだ.	The mother called out "Time to eat!" to the children playing outside.
すぐ医者を呼んだほうがいい.	You'd better call a doctor fast.
彼は職員室に呼ばれた.	He was called to the teachers' room.
電話で救急車を呼んでください.	Please phone an ambulance.
彼を明日の夕食に呼びましょう.	Let's invite him to dinner tomorrow.
今度の日曜日は友達の結婚式に呼ばれている.	I've been invited to a friend's wedding this Sunday.
そのパイロットはいつでも呼び出しに応じられるようにしている.	The pilot is always on standby.
その外科医はいつでも呼び出しに応じられるようにしている.	The surgeon is always on call [standby].
【称する】東京は昔, 江戸と呼ばれていた.	Tokyo used to be called Edo.
【呼び起こす】彼の論文は医学界に大きな反響を呼んだ.	His paper caused a sensation in the medical world.
あの映画は感動を呼ぶ名作だ.	That film is a moving piece of art.
塩は湿気を呼びやすい.	Salt easily absorbs moisture.

よほう (予報)

天気予報によると今日は午後から雨が降るそうだ.	According to the weather forecast, it will rain this afternoon.
今日は天気予報が外れた.	The weather forecast for today was off.
JRはこの夏の列車の込み具合の予報を出した.	The JR issued a forecast on the number of passengers expected to use its trains this summer.

よぼう (予防)

虫歯の予防には歯磨きがいちばんです. — The best way to prevent tooth decay is to brush your teeth.

今, 村では水害を予防するための工事を進めている. — Construction to prevent flood damage is now being done in the village.

うちの子はインフルエンザ〔はしか〕の予防注射を受けてあります. — My child has received a flue [measles] shot.

彼は予想される非難に対して予防線を張った. — He anticipated the criticism and took measures to head it off.

よほど

こんなすごい車を10台も持っているとは, 彼はよほどの大金持ちに違いない. — He must really be rich to have ten such great cars.

凍傷にかかるなんて山はよほど寒かったんだね. — It must have been freezing up in the mountains for you to get frostbite.

よほどのことがなければ彼がそんなに怒るはずはない. — It must have been really bad, or else he wouldn't have gotten so mad.

彼女の今度の作品は前のよりよほどいいよ. — This work of hers is much better than her former ones.

よほど彼に本当のことを言ってやろうと思ったが, おじけづいてしまった. — I came very close to telling him the truth, but I got cold feet.

よむ (読む)

この本は読むに値する本だ. — This book is worthwhile reading.

彼女は暇をみては子どもたちに本を読んでやる. — She reads (books) to her children whenever she can.

今日の新聞は読むところが少ない. — There's not much worth reading in today's paper.

このグラフを読むといろいろなことが分かってくる. — You'll see many things by studying this graph.

将棋は相手の手が読めないといけません. — In *shogi* you must be able to read your opponent's intentions.

相手チームの作戦が読めるといいんだがく. — I'd like to be able to †read [figure out] the opposing team's strategy.

彼は選挙に当たり自分の票を読んでみた. — He made a projection of the votes he would get in the election.

彼はすっかり私の心を読んでいた. — He read my thoughts perfectly.

よゆう (余裕)

【空間的】このアパートは狭くて, — This apartment is so small (that) there

これ以上家具を増やす余裕はない.	isn't room for another piece of furniture.
このテントは3人が寝られるだけの余裕がある.	This tent †is big enough [has enough room, has ample room] for three persons.
	This tent can easily sleep three persons.
【時間的】この頃忙しくてスポーツをするだけの余裕がない.	I've been so busy lately that I haven't had any time to spare for sports.
【経済的】最近家族全員で海外旅行をする経済的余裕のある家庭が多くなった.	Recently, more people have extra money to travel overseas with the whole family.
我が家ではまだ新車を買う余裕はない.	We still can't afford a new car.
給料が安いので余裕のない生活をしている.	My meager salary is just barely enough to get by on.
【精神的】仕事に追われて自分自身を振り返る余裕すらない.	I'm so pressed with work that I can't even take time out for myself.
どんなときでも気持ちの余裕を失ってはいけない.	You should never let yourself get stressed out.
	You should always cut yourself some slack.**
彼はいつも余裕しゃくしゃくだ.	He's always calm and composed.

より

今年の冬は去年より寒い.	Winter this year is colder than last year.
私は飲むより食べるほうが好きだ.	I'd rather eat than drink.
白線より内側に下がってください.	Please stay behind the white line.
交通ストで会社まで歩くよりしかたがなかった.	The buses and trains were on strike, so I had to walk to work.
あの場合, 僕は黙っているよりなかった.	In that situation there was nothing for me to do but †keep my mouth shut [remain silent].
【もっと】より多くの人にこの本を読んでもらいたい.	I'd like more people to read this book.
より楽しい学校生活が送れるようみんなで話し合いましょう.	Let's †talk about [discuss] how we can make student life more fun [enjoyable].

よる¹ (因る)

【基づく】違反者は規則により罰せられる.	The offenders are punished according to regulations.
聞くところによるとその火事は放火だそうだ.	According to what I've heard, that fire was a case of arson.
ラジオによると高速道路は込んで	According to the radio, the highways are

いるようだ.	jammed.
彼の生活費のほとんどは親からの仕送りによるものだ.	Almost all his living expenses are paid for by his allowance from his parents.
【起因する】今回の成功は彼の働きによるところが大きい.	Our success this time is due largely to his work.
たばこの火の不始末による火事は相変わらず多い.	The number of fires caused by careless smokers is as high as ever.
【〜しだい】君の努力いかんによってはあの大学に合格する可能性もある.	There may be a chance for you to be accepted by that college, depending on how much effort you make.
この計画は今後の成り行きによって変わることもある.	This plan may change depending on how things develop in the future.
ことによると彼女はもう日本にはいないかもしれない.	She may not be in Japan anymore; I don't know.
何事によらず全力を尽くそう.	Let's put our all into whatever we do.
【手段】話し合いによって問題は解決した.	The problem was resolved through discussion.

よる² (寄る)

カメラに入らないのでもう少し左へ寄ってください.	You're not in the picture—more to the left, please.
男が隣にぴったりくっついて座ったので彼女は脇に寄った.	She moved over because a man sat down too close beside her.
駅から少し右へ寄ったところに交番があります.	The police box is a little to the right of the station.
【集まる】彼女たちは寄るとさわると人のうわさをしている.	They gossip whenever they get together.
みんなで寄ってたかって彼をいじめている.	They all gang up (on him) and tease [bully] him.
【重なる】体力には自信があるが,寄る年波には勝てない.	I have confidence in my strength, but I can't fight the advancing years.
【立ち寄る】買い物の帰りに本屋へ寄った.	On the way home from shopping I stopped at a book store.
近くへおいでの節はうちへお寄りください.	Stop by when you're in the neighborhood.

よろこび (喜び)

彼の手紙は喜びにあふれていた.	His letter was filled with joy.
彼は息子誕生の知らせに,顔に喜びの色を浮かべた.	He beamed with joy when he was told that he was the father of a baby boy.
彼女は喜びのあまり泣きだした.	She was so happy that she started to cry.
この喜びはとても表現できない.	I can't express how happy [overjoyed] I am.

| | I can't put my joy into words. |
| このたびのご出産のお喜びを申し上げます. | Joyous greetings on the birth of your new baby. |

よろこぶ (喜ぶ)

息子の成績がクラスで一番になったので母親は喜んだ.	She was very happy because her son got the best grades in the class.
子どもは父親に肩車してもらうと喜ぶものだ.	Children love to ride on their father's shoulders.
彼女はこんな安っぽい贈り物など喜ばないだろうなあ.	She probably won't be very happy with a cheap souvenir like this.
彼は私の頼みを喜んで聞いてくれた.	He accepted my request wholeheartedly.
	He was happy to accept my request.
喜んでお供させていただきます.	I'd be more than happy to join you.

よろしい

今日はもう帰ってよろしい.	You can go home now.
こちらでよろしいですか.	Is this all right?
都合のよろしい時においでください.	Please come when it's suitable for you.
コーヒーと紅茶とどちらがよろしいですか.	Which would you like [prefer], coffee or tea?
よろしい, 引き受けましょう.	OK, I'll see to it.

よわい (弱い)

ナイロンは熱に弱い.	Nylon can't stand up to heat.
この木造家屋は古いので地震には弱いだろう.	This wooden house is old and probably won't be able to stand [handle] an earthquake.
あのチームは私たちのチームより弱い.	That team is weaker than our team.
このカクテルは(アルコールが)弱い.	This cocktail doesn't have much alcohol in it.
	This cocktail isn't very strong.
【体や気が】妹は体が弱い.	My younger sister is physically weak [delicate].
彼は胃腸が弱いのでよく消化剤を飲む.	He has a weak stomach, so he often takes medicine for his digestion.
この頃祖母は足が弱くなって, なかなか散歩に出かけない.	My grandmother's legs have gotten weak recently, so she rarely goes out for a walk.
彼は意志が弱い人間だ.	He's weak-willed.
	He †lacks [doesn't have any] willpower.

彼は気が弱くて，思ったことも人に言えない．	He's so timid that he can't tell other people what he is thinking.
あの娘は少し頭が弱い．	She's not very smart [bright].
【苦手】私はメカに弱い．	I can't deal with [I'm not good with] †mechanical things [machines].
母は乗り物に弱い．	My mother gets sick on rides.
僕はあの先生には弱いんだよ．	I can't stand up to that teacher.
私は暑さに弱いので夏は嫌いだ．	I can't tolerate [take] hot weather, so I don't like summer.
この頃酒が弱くなった．	I haven't been able to handle liquor lately.
【甘い】彼は若い女の子に弱い．	He has a weakness for young women. He's a sucker for young girls.
彼は孫に弱く，甘やかしてばかりいる．	He's so fond of his grandson that he †spoils him [does anything to please him].
【弱める】暖房〔冷房〕を弱くしてください．	Please turn down the †heater [air conditioner].
ガスの火をもっと弱くしないと，シチューが焦げてしまいますよ．	You'll burn the stew if you don't †turn down [lower] the gas.

よわる（弱る）

【弱くなる】度重なる手術で彼は体が弱っている．	He's still very weak from a series of operations.
この家の土台もだいぶ弱ってきた．	The foundation of this house is †starting to go [not in good condition].
【困る・がっかりする】やつには全く弱ったよ．	That guy's really causing me a lot of trouble.
彼女をあてにして来たのに，留守とは弱ったなあ．	I don't know what I'm going to do! I came counting on her to be home and she's not here!
彼からはっきりした返事がもらえなくて弱っている．	I'm in a real bind. I can't get a clear answer from him.

ら

ライバル

彼と私は高校時代からのライバルだ.	We've been rivals[1] since high school. We've been competing against each other since high school.
私の前に強力なライバルが現れた.	I came up against a strong competitor.
企画のプレゼンテーションでライバル会社にせり勝った.	I won out over a competing company with my presentation (of the plan).
彼にはなぜかライバル意識を燃やしてしまう.	For some reason, I become very competitive when I see him.

> 1) 英語の rival は基本的に敵対関係にある人を表すので,使い方に注意.

らく（楽）

【安らか】どうぞお楽に（なさってください）. Please make yourself comfortable.

しばらく横になったら,楽になった. I felt better after lying down for a while.

彼の話を聞いて少し気が楽になった. My mind rested a little easier after I heard what he had to say.

【ゆとりを持ってできる】給料が上がったので多少生活が楽になった. I got a raise and it's made life a little easier.

彼の家は子どもが多いので,暮らしが楽ではない. Life is not easy for him with so many children to look after.

いつになれば楽に暮らせるようになるのだろうか. When am I ever going to be able to take life easy?

台所の電化が進み家事も楽になってきた. With more and more kitchen appliances, housework has gotten a lot easier.

荷物があるときは,電車より車のほうが楽だ. It's easier to drive than to go by train when you have things to carry.

彼は楽な仕事だけしかやりたがらない. All he wants to do is the easy work.

私は100メートルは楽に泳げる. I have no trouble swimming 100 meters.

君なら楽にその試験に受かるよ. You'll have no trouble passing that exam.

らくたん (落胆)

彼は入試に不合格と判り，落胆した．	He really got discouraged when he found out that he had failed the entrance examination.
一度や二度の失敗でそんなに落胆するなよ．	I wouldn't let a couple of †bad experiences [failures] get you down.

～らしい

【伝聞・推定】彼は来月結婚するらしい．	I understand he's getting married next month.
彼は学校をやめたらしい．	I understand he [he's] quit school.
あの人は偉い人らしい．	I understand he's pretty important.
午後から雨になるらしい．	It's supposed to rain in the afternoon.
彼女が言っていたことはどうも本当らしい．	What she said really appears [seems] to be the truth.
【相応】彼は男らしい人だ．	He's indeed manly. ／ He's very masculine.
彼女はあまり女らしくない．	She's not very feminine.
子どもには子どもらしい服が似合う．	Children look best in clothes meant [designed] for children.
彼女は仕事らしい仕事をしたことがない．	She's never worked at anything you could call a real job.
学生時代に，勉強らしいことは何一つしなかった．	When I was a student I didn't do anything that even resembled studying.
彼はいかにも先生らしく振る舞った．	He really acted like a teacher.
彼は役人らしくない．	He doesn't act like a public official.

らっかん (楽観)

彼は楽観的な人間だ．	He always looks on the bright side of things.
彼女は何をするにも楽観的だ．	She †is optimistic [has a positive attitude] about whatever she does.
私はこの計画が必ず実現すると楽観している．	I'm optimistic that this plan will definitely be carried out.
彼の手術は一応成功したが，まだ楽観は許されない．	His surgery was a success, but it's still too early to be optimistic.

らんぼう (乱暴)

そんな乱暴をするのはやめたまえ．	Stop acting so rowdy [wild]!
彼は酒を飲むと奥さんに乱暴を働く．	He beats his wife when he drinks.
カメラをそんなに乱暴に扱ってはだめだ．	Don't be so rough with the camera.

彼は怒ってコップを乱暴に置いた.	He got angry and slammed down his glass.
そんなに乱暴に運転しないでよ.	Don't drive so recklessly [carelessly].
そんな装備で冬山に登るなんて，乱暴な話だ.	It's reckless to go mountain climbing in winter with that type of gear.
彼は言葉遣いは乱暴だが，気はいい男だ.	He may say things in an unrefined way but he's really not a bad guy [person].

り

リード
【先導】先頭走者は2位集団を200メートルリードしている. — The lead runner is 200 meters ahead of the second-place contenders.

彼の革新的なデザインはファッション界をリードし続けている. — His revolutionary designs continue to lead the fashion industry.

彼はデートでいつも上手に女性をリードする. — He knows how to give his date a good time.

【優位】前半戦は韓国チームの2点リードで終了した. — The first half ended with the Korean team leading by two points.

打者が満塁ホームランを打ち，リードを6点差に広げた. — They increased their lead to six points when the batter hit a home run with bases loaded.

りえき (利益)
【儲け】彼は新しい商売で大きな利益を上げた. — He made big profits from his new business.

その会社は東南アジアに進出して莫大な利益を納めている. — That company is realizing [reaping] huge profits by expanding into the Southeast Asian market.

バザーで10万円の利益がありました. — The bazaar made a 100,000 [hundred thousand] yen profit.

金鉱が発見されたことによって村には大きな利益がもたらされた. — The discovery of gold brought the village great wealth [benefits].

この投資はきっと利益を生むよ. — This will definitely be a profitable investment.

利益の配分は平等になされるべきだ. — The profits should be divided up evenly.

公演の純利益金は障害児の施設に寄付されます. — The net profit from the performance will be donated to an institution for disabled

	children.
【役立つ】この条約は両国の利益となるものだ.	Both countries will benefit from this treaty.
そんなことをしても何の利益にもならないよ.	You won't get anything out of doing something like that.

りかい (理解)

あなたの言っていることは難しくてよく理解できない.	What you're saying is difficult. I can't quite grasp [understand] the details.
この論文は易しく書かれているので門外漢にも理解し易い.	This thesis is written in an easy style, so even a nonspecialist [layman] can easily understand [comprehend] it.
内容をよく理解していないと正確に翻訳できない.	If you don't understand the content very well, you can't translate it correctly.
彼がなぜあんな行為をしたのか,全く理解に苦しむ.	I can't figure out [I haven't the slightest idea, I have absolutely no idea] why he acted the way he did.
理解のあるご両親ですね.	Your parents are very understanding, aren't they?

りくつ (理屈)

その話は理屈に合わない.	That story defies logic.
物事は理屈どおりには行かないものだ.	Things don't always work out †the way you think they would [logically].
理屈を言っているだけではだめだ. 実行しなさい.	There's no use just †talking about it [theorizing]. You've got to do it.
私が悪いことは理屈では分かっているが,詫びる気にはならない.	Intellectually I know I'm in the wrong but I just can't bring myself to apologize.
この映画は理屈抜きに面白い.	There's no need to convince anyone about how great this movie is.
彼は理屈っぽい人間だ.	He's argumentative./He loves to argue.
君はいつもへ理屈ばかり言う.	Your arguments never make any sense. Your arguments are always so far-fetched.

りこ (利己)

彼女は利己的な人だ.	She's a very self-centered person.
彼は利己主義者だ.	He's completely self-centered [egotistical].
君のように利己的な態度では,チームワークの要る仕事はできないよ.	With your selfish attitude, you couldn't work at anything that requires [takes] teamwork.

りこう (利口)

この子は利口な子どもだ.	This child is clever [bright, smart].

彼女は利口そうだ.	She seems bright.
君の話を聞いてまた一つ利口になった気がする.	Listening to you, I feel like I've learned something (new).
こんな場合は黙っているほうが利口だ.	At times like this, you'd be wise [smart] to keep your mouth shut.
彼はいつも利口に立ち回るので人から煙たがられている.	People keep him at a distance because he's very good at making himself look good.

りせい (理性)

彼はどんなときでも決して理性を失わない.	He's always rational, no matter what the situation.
私は常に理性に従って行動している.	I always act †rationally [according to reason].
彼は理性的な人だ.	He's a rational person.

りそう (理想)

理想と現実との差は大きいものだ.	There's a big difference between the ideal and †the real [reality].
彼は理想を追っている.	He's working towards (realizing) his ideals.
彼女は人生に高い理想を抱いている.	She has high ideals in life.
彼は私の理想の男性です.	He's my ideal man.
彼女は理想的なプロポーションをしている.	She has an ideal figure.
彼は理想主義者だ.	He's an idealist.

りっぱ (立派)

彼の行いは立派だった.	His act was commendable.
彼女は立派な家に住んでいる.	She lives in a splendid [marvelous, wonderful] house.
とても立派なひげですね.	You have a very fine beard.
彼は立派な先生になるだろう.	He'll probably become †an excellent [a superb, a highly respected] teacher.
彼は困難と思われた仕事をひるまず立派にやってのけた.	He took on a job that was thought to be difficult and carried it out splendidly.
外見だけ立派でも中身がない人は嫌われる.	A superficial person is going to be disliked, even if he is good-looking.

りゆう (理由)

彼はいろいろな理由をあげてその計画には現実性がないことを説明した.	He gave a number of reasons why the plan [project] would be impractical.
学校を休んだ理由をはっきり言い	Tell me [Explain] why you were absent

	from school.
理由はともかく，こんなことになったのは君のせいだ.	No matter how it †happened [got this way], it's your fault.
理由もなく子どもを叱ってはいけない.	You shouldn't scold a child for no reason at all.
彼はそれに対して理由のない非難だと反論した.	He objected, saying that there was no justification for the criticism.
彼は風邪を理由に会議に欠席した.	His excuse for not attending the meeting was that he had a cold.
彼女はいろいろな理由をつけてデートを断るんだ.	She always has some kind of excuse when I ask her †for a date [out].
彼は何かと理由をでっちあげて会議をサボることが多い.	He often makes up some story to get out of meetings.

りゅうこう (流行)

彼女はその時々の流行に敏感だ.	She's very attuned to what's fashionable. She's good at knowing what's in.**
最近の若い人は流行にとらわれず，自由な服装を楽しんでいる.	Young people today can dress in any way they want, without having to conform to fashion.
ひところ洋服を着た猫の写真が流行した.	Photographs of kittens dressed in clothes were popular for a time.
今，流行している歌は何ですか.	What songs are popular now?
流行を追うのもいいが，ほどほどにしなさい.	Keeping up with the latest fashions is fine, but don't overdo it.
彼女はいつも流行遅れの服装をしている.	She always wears clothes that are out of fashion.
この冬は悪性のインフルエンザが大流行している.	A virulent strain of flu is going around this winter.

りよう (利用)

もっと太陽エネルギーを利用すべきだ.	We should make more use of solar energy.
彼は廃材を利用して物置を作った.	He used scrap wood to make a storage shed.
私は勉強するのに，よく図書館を利用します.	I often †make use of [take advantage of] the library to study.
もっと時間をうまく利用すれば，そのぐらいのことはすぐできる.	If you make better use of your time, you can finish something like that in no time.
あの男は他人の肩書を利用して人をだましている.	He is deceiving people by using other people's credentials.
その不動産屋は住民の無知を利用	That real estate company made excessive

して暴利をむさぼった. — [exorbitant] profits by taking advantage of the residents' ignorance.

りょう (量)

日照り続きでダムの水の量が減っている.	The dry spell has lowered the water level in the reservoir.
やせるためにはもう少し食事の量を減らさなければ.	I've got to cut down a little on the amount of food I eat in order to lose some weight.
あの店は品物の量をごまかして売る.	That store gives you less than what you pay for.
彼女は量より質の主義だ.	She believes in quality rather than quantity.

りょうかい (了解)

君の話は了解しました.	I understand what you're talking about.
この仕事は私に全面的に任されたものと了解していたのですが.	It was my understanding that this job was to be left entirely up to me.
社長の了解を得ないことには契約はできません.	We cannot sign [make] any contracts without the president's approval [consent].
工事の変更について先方の了解を取り付けた.	We have obtained the other party's consent for the construction changes.

りょうしん (良心)

君に良心があれば，彼女にそんなひどいことはできなかったはずだ.	Anyone with a conscience couldn't have done such a terrible thing to her.
君には良心というものがないのか.	Don't you have a conscience?
盗みをするなんて良心が許さない.	My conscience won't allow me to steal.
自分の良心に従って行動しただけだ.	I just acted on my conscience.
友達にうそを言ったあとは良心が咎めた.	My conscience bothered me after I lied to my friend.
自分の良心に恥じない行動をとりなさい.	Act on your conscience.
あの店はとても良心的だ.	They're very conscientious at that store.
彼は良心的な人だ.	He's a very conscientious person.

りょこう (旅行)

僕は夏休みに北海道を旅行した.	I traveled around Hokkaido during my summer vacation.
彼は昨日から旅行に出かけた.	He left on his trip yesterday.
父は旅行嫌いです.	My father †doesn't like [hates] to travel.

修学旅行で京都に行った.	We went to Kyoto for our school excursion.
新婚旅行はハワイに決めた.	We decided †to go to [on] Hawaii for our honeymoon.
旅行シーズンを迎え，どの列車も混雑が予想されます.	With the travel [vacation, tourist] season approaching, we can expect all trains to be crowded.

りろん (理論)

彼の理論は正しい.	His theory is right [correct].
彼の理論は間違っていると思う.	I think his theory is wrong.
理論と実際とが違うことはよくある.	Theory and reality are often different.
物事は理論どおりには運ばないものだ.	Things don't always †happen [turn out] the way they would in theory.
理論的に考えると，彼が言っていることはおかしい.	In theory [Theoretically], what he's saying doesn't make sense.
彼はなかなかの理論家だ.	He's quite a theoretician.

りんきおうへん (臨機応変)

彼は続出する難問に臨機応変に対処した.	He dealt appropriately with each of the difficult problems as they arose.
彼女は臨機応変に物事を処理できない.	She can't deal appropriately with different situations.
	She can't adapt her approach to fit the situation.

リンク

【コンピュータ】そのサイトはリンクをたどっていて見つけた.	I found that site by checking out the links.
リンクを張る作業は思いのほか簡単にできる.	Creating links is much easier than you would expect.
リンクを張るのはフリーですが，事後に必ずお知らせください.	The link is free but please make sure to inform me if you use it for your site.

りんじ (臨時)

今月は臨時の収入があった.	I had some extra income this month.
年末で忙しいので臨時に人を雇うことにした.	I was so busy at year-end that I decided to hire some temporary help.
受け持ちの先生が病気になったので，臨時の先生が来た.	A substitute came because the regular teacher was ill.
今日，臨時総会が開かれた.	A special session [An ad hoc meeting] was convened today.

ただいま臨時ニュースが入りました. A news bulletin has just come in.

る

るい (類)
この小説の面白さは, ほかに類がない. There's no novel to compare with this (one).
東大寺は世界に類を見ない壮大な木造建造物だ. There is no wooden structure as magnificent as the Todaiji anywhere in the world.
僕は果物類なら何でも好きです. I like †any kind of [all] fruit.
鯨は哺乳類である. The whale belongs to the mammal class.
【慣用】類は友を呼ぶ. Birds of a feather flock together.

るす (留守)
友人の家を訪ねて行ったが, 留守だった. I went to visit a friend but he wasn't home.
出張しますので, しばらく留守にします. I'll be gone for a while on a business trip.
僕の留守中に何かあったら, 母に相談してください. If anything happens during my absence, please talk to my mother.
お留守番をお願いね. Can you take care of things while I'm gone?
旅行に行くので弟に留守番を頼んだ. I asked my brother to look after the house while I'm on vacation.
この頃クラブ活動に忙しくて勉強がお留守になってしまった. Lately I've been so busy with club activities that I've been neglecting my studies.

れ

れい¹（礼）
- 父は礼を尽くして恩師をもてなした. — My father entertained his former teacher with the utmost courtesy.
- 最近の若者は目上の人に対する礼を知らないとよく祖父は言っている. — My grandfather often says young people nowadays don't know how to behave toward their superiors [elders].
- その生徒は軽く礼をして、職員室に入って来た. — The student came into the teachers' lounge, bowing slightly.
- 彼女は私に丁寧にプレゼントのお礼を言った. — She thanked me politely for the present.
- この仕事のお礼としていくらお支払いすればよいでしょうか. — How much should I pay you for this job? How much remuneration would you require for this job?

れい²（例）
- 【実例】何か具体的な例を示してください. — Please give (us) a concrete example.
- 僕らの先生はいつもジョージ・ワシントンを例に引いてお説教する. — Our teacher's always lecturing to us about George Washington as †the perfect model [an exemplary person].
- この事件は最近の犯罪傾向を端的に表すよい例です. — This case clearly exemplifies the recent trend in crime.
- 【いつもの】また例によってあいつの自慢話が始まったよ. — There he goes bragging again. He's blowing his own horn again.
- じゃあ、明日の5時に例の場所で会おう. — OK, I'll meet you tomorrow at five at the usual place.
- 例の話だけど、お母さんは許してくれましたか. — Has your mother given you permission to do what we were talking about the other day?
- 例年どおり、今年も修学旅行は九州へ行くことに決まった. — As usual, we'll be going to Kyushu again for our school excursion this year.
- 【先例】こんな大きな列車事故は今までに例がない. — There's never been a train accident as serious as this one until now. Such a serious train accident is unprecedented.

れいぎ (礼儀)

| 手紙をもらったら返事を出すのが礼儀です． | Answering a letter is common courtesy. |
| If you receive a letter, it's only polite to answer it. |
| あの子はいつも礼儀正しく挨拶する． | That child is always very polite when she †greets you [says hello]. |
| あなたは礼儀をわきまえなければいけません． | You have to learn good manners. |
| You have to become well-mannered. |
| 彼は礼儀知らずな男だ． | That man has no manners. |
| That man is rude [uncouth]. |

れいこく (冷酷)

あいつは血も涙もない冷酷な男だ．
He's a cold-blooded man.

その母親は冷酷にも我が子に水も食べ物も与えず，置き去りにした．
That mother was so coldhearted that she abandoned her child without leaving him any food or water.

彼はどんなに（経済的に）困っている人からでも，冷酷に借金を取り立てる．
He callously collects debts from people no matter how financially strapped they may be.

ネズミを水につけて殺すなんて，よくそんな冷酷なことができるね．
How could you be so coldhearted as to drown mice?

れいせい (冷静)

もっと冷静になりなさい．
Pull yourself together.

火事のときは，なかなか冷静に行動できないものだ．
It's not easy to †stay cool-headed [act without panicking] in a fire.

冷静に考えれば，私にも悪いところがあったと思う．
When I think about it calmly, I admit [know] I was partly to blame.

彼は何が起こっても冷静さを失わない人だ．
He †remains level-headed [keeps his cool] no matter what happens.

そのときの客室乗務員［スチュワーデス］の態度は実に冷静だった．
The cabin attendant showed admirable †presence of mind [composure] at that time.

れいたん (冷淡)

彼女はこの頃僕に冷淡だ．
She's been cool to me †these days [lately].

彼は友人が助けを求めてきたのに冷淡に突き放した．
He coldly turned down his friend who had come to ask for help.

随分冷淡な返事だなあ．
What a callous reply!

お役所というものは大抵，福祉事業には冷淡なものだ．
Public officials are generally indifferent to welfare projects.

れつ（列）

彼の葬儀には会葬者の長い列が続いた．	There was a long line[1] of mourners at his funeral.
みだりに列を離れてはいけません．	Don't get out of line.
宝くじ売り場に，人々が列を作って並んでいる．	People are lined up in front of the lottery ticket booth.
客は列を作ってデパートの開店を待った．	The customers lined up waiting for the department store to open.
2列に並びなさい．	Please †line up in [make a] double file.[2] Please †make [stand in] two rows.[3]
そのコンサートの前売り券を買うために，若者たちは長蛇の列を作った．	Young people made a long line waiting to buy advance tickets for that concert.

1)2) 縦列の場合の言い方．3) 横列の場合の言い方．

れっとう（劣等）

私は小学生の頃は劣等生だった．	I was a poor student in elementary school.
私は彼に対して劣等感など持っていない．	I don't feel inferior to him.

レベル

当英語学校はレベル別のクラスに分かれてレッスンを行います．	This English language school offers classes for students at different levels.
日本とイタリアとではサッカー選手のレベルが違いすぎる．	There is too big a difference in ability between Japanese and Italian soccer players.
今年の映画祭はレベルの高い作品が揃った．	There are some outstanding works in this year's film festival.
ずいぶんレベルの低い会話になっちゃったね．	We've hit a new low with this conversation.
師のレベルに達するまでは，まだまだ修練が必要だ．	You need a lot more training before you can †equal [be as good as] your teacher.
まずは基礎学力を身につけないとレベルアップは図れない．	You have to master the fundamentals before you can improve.
続編は一作目にくらべて大幅にレベルダウンしている．	The sequel isn't nearly as good as the original.

れんあい（恋愛）

あの二人は恋愛中だ．	Those two are [They're] in love.
彼らは熱烈な恋愛の末結婚した．	They fell madly in love and got married.

れんしゅう (練習)

彼女は毎日ピアノの練習をします. — She practices (the) piano every day.

練習不足のせいで, 思うような記録が出なかった. — I couldn't get the score [time, mark] I wanted because I didn't train enough.

ボクシングのチャンピオンになるために, 彼は毎日猛練習をした. — He trained hard every day in the hopes of becoming a boxing champion.

この高校の野球部は毎日6時間みっちり練習をする. — This high school baseball team practices for six grueling hours every day.

れんそう (連想)

豊臣秀吉というと猿を連想する. — Hearing the name Toyotomi Hideyoshi makes me think of a monkey.

冬という言葉を聞くと, すぐ大好きなスキーやスケートを連想してしまう. — When I hear the word "winter," I immediately associate it with skiing and skating—two of my favorite sports.

れんぞく (連続)

このところ毎日連続の雨だ. — It's rained continuously for the last few days.

今日で一週間も連続して雨が降り続いている. — Today it will have rained for a solid week.

近ごろ関東地方に連続して地震があった. — Recently there has been a series of earthquakes in the Kanto area.

彼は3打席連続してホームランを打った. — He hit three home runs in three consecutive at-bats.

最近この付近で連続放火事件があった. — There has been a series of arson cases in this neighborhood recently.

れんらく (連絡)

【交通】このバスはあの駅で特急に連絡します. — This bus connects with the limited express train at that station.

【通信】支店から本社へ連絡が入りました. — The branch store contacted the main office.

至急会社の父と連絡をとってください. — Get in touch with my father at work as soon as possible.

船は昨夜から連絡を絶ち, 乗客の安否が気づかわれている. — Contact was lost with the ship [Contact with the ship was cut off] last night and there is concern for the safety of the passengers.

この辺りで不審な男を見かけたら警察に連絡してください. — If you spot a suspicious-looking man around here, contact the police.

ろ

ろく (な, に)
ここ1週間, ろくな物を食べていない. — I haven't eaten properly for a week.

この町にはろくな本屋がない. — There isn't a decent bookstore in this town.

あいつが参加すると, いつもろくなことがない. — Anything he's involved in never turns out well.

彼に相談したって, ろくなことにならないよ. — There's no use talking to him.

時間がなくて彼女とろくに話もできなかった. — There wasn't enough time to have a decent conversation with her.

ろくに勉強しないまま大学を卒業した. — I graduated from university without having studied much at all.

ろくに考えもせずにその仕事を引き受けた. — I accepted the job without giving it much thought.

あの営業部員はろくに挨拶もできない. — That salesman isn't very well-mannered.

彼はいつもろくでもない話を持ち込む. — He's always coming up with †useful ideas [worthless propositions].

女性を殴るなんて, ろくでもない奴だ. — He beats up women? What a jerk [rat]!

ログイン
ログインの方法がよく分からない. — I'm not sure how to log in.

有料サイトにログインするときは料金をチェックしたほうがいい. — You'd better check the prices before logging in to a pay site.

ろこつ (露骨)
彼の表情は敵意を露骨に表していた. — His hostility was clear from his expression.

この小説には露骨な描写〔表現〕が多い. — There are many suggestive descriptions [expressions] in this novel.

そんなに人の悪口を露骨に言うものではありませんよ. — You shouldn't criticize anyone so bluntly.

わ

わかい (若い)
僕の会社には若い人が多い. — There are a lot of young people at my company.

父の若いときの写真を見つけた. — I found a picture of my father when he was young.

彼女は若いうちに結婚した. — She married when she was still young.

外国語の勉強は, 若いうちに始めたほうがいい. — It's a good idea to start studying foreign languages while you are still young.

春は, 木々の若葉が美しい. — In the spring the fresh green leaves on the trees are beautiful.

【年下】彼女は私より二つ若い. — She's two years younger than I am.

どう見ても君のほうが弟さんより若く見えるね. — You really do look younger than your younger brother.

彼は年よりずっと若く見える. — He looks a lot younger than he actually is.

【未熟】上司とけんかして会社を辞めてしまうなんて, 君も若いね. — Isn't it a bit immature to quit your job just because you had a fight with the boss?

【小さい】整理券の番号が若い順に並んでください. — Please line up according to the number on your ticket.

わかす (沸かす)
【沸騰させる】お湯を沸かしてください. — Please boil some water.

【興奮させる】世界的なロックグループが日本中の若者を沸かせた. — The world-famous rock group caused excitement among young people all over Japan.

彼は素晴らしい演奏で聴衆を沸かせた. — He excited the audience with his brilliant performance.

わがまま
彼女は甘やかされて育ったので, わがままだ. — She's selfish because she was spoiled as a child.

彼のわがままな性格は大人になってからも直らなかった. — He remained selfish, even †after he grew up [as an adult].

こんな忙しいときに自分だけ休み — I think it's selfish [thoughtless] of you to

を取りたいなんて，わがままだと思う．	want to take time off when there's so much work to be done.

わかる（分かる・判る）

【知る】10年先に私が何をしているかなんて分かるはずがない．	How could I possibly know what I'll be doing ten years from now?
台風が近づいているので，明日ハイキングに行けるかどうか分からない．	With the typhoon approaching, I don't know whether we'll be able to go hiking or not.
この数学の問題は難しすぎて，解き方が全く分からない．	This math problem is so difficult that I don't have any idea how to solve it.
私の家は白いビルの隣です．すぐ分かります．	My house is next to the white building. You'll have no problem finding it.
彼女があまりに変身していたので私はすぐには彼女だと分からなかった．	She had changed so much (that) I didn't [couldn't] recognize her at first.
【理解する】この本を読めば，表計算ソフトの使い方が一とおり分かるようになります．	If you read this book you'll get the basics [rudiments] of using spreadsheet software.
英語が分かりますか．	Do you understand English?
私の言うことが分かりますか．	Do you understand what I'm saying? Do you follow me?
彼の文章はひどく分かりにくい．	It's extremely difficult to understand his writing.
分からないことがあったら何でも聞いてください．	If there's something you don't understand, don't hesitate to ask.
私は抽象画というものは，どうも分からない．	I just don't understand abstract paintings.
彼はユーモアの分からない人だ．	He has no sense of humor. He doesn't know how to take a joke.
君が何を言いたいのか，さっぱり分からない．	I don't have the slightest idea what you're trying to say.
【了解する】彼女は自分が間違っていたと分かった．	She realized that she had been wrong.
「この書類を2通ずつコピーしてください」「分かりました」	"Please make two copies each of these documents." "OK."
【判明する】その宝石は模造品だと判った．	That jewelry turned out to be fake.
検査の結果は来週判ります．	We will know the results of the investigation next week.
火事の原因はまだ判っていない．	The cause of the fire has not yet been determined.
だれも彼の言うことを信用しなか	Nobody believed what he said, but in the

ったが，結局，本当のことを言っていたのだと判った．	end it proved to be the truth.
果物の味の良し悪しは大きさでは判らない．	You can't tell how fruit will taste by its size.

わかれ (別れ)

別れは辛いものだ．	Parting is painful [hard].
卒業の日，生徒たちは先生に別れの言葉を述べた．	On graduation day the students offered words of farewell to their teachers.
もうお別れの時間になりました．	I'm afraid it's time for me to go [leave].
戦争は数多くの生き別れの悲劇を生み出した．	The war caused many tragic separations.
私は戦争で家族と別れ別れになってしまった．	I became separated from my family during the war.
祖父のひつぎに最後の別れを告げた．	I paid my final respects before my grandfather's casket.

わかれる (別れる・分かれる)

【離別】私たちは駅で別れた．	We †parted [said good-bye] at the station.
両親と別れたのは12歳のときでした．	I was separated from my parents when I was 12.
彼女は夫の転勤で別れて暮らしている．	She and her husband are living separately because he was transferred.
彼は奥さんとうまくいかなくて別れて暮らしている．	He didn't get along with his wife very well and now they're separated.
あの夫婦は性格の不一致で別れてしまった．	That couple †split up [divorced] because they were incompatible.
別れた彼には会いたくない．	I don't want to see him now that I've split up with him.
【分岐】東北線と奥羽線は福島で分かれる．	The Tohoku and Ou Lines split at Fukushima.
その川は町の中央で二つに分かれている．	That river divides into two in the middle of the city.
ここが勝負の分かれ目だから頑張れよ．	This will decide the outcome, so give it all you've got.
【分離】日本の国会は衆議院と参議院に分かれている．	The Japanese Diet is divided into the House of Representatives and the House of Councilors.
交響曲は普通四つの楽章に分かれている．	Symphonies are usually divided into four movements.
【対立】原子力発電所の設置を巡って町は二つに分かれた．	The city is split in two over the question of whether to construct a nuclear power plant.

| 憲法第9条に対する解釈は政党によって大きく分かれている. | The political parties are widely split over the interpretation of Article 9 of the Constitution. |

わき (脇)
【体】体温計を脇の下に挟んで体温を測った.	I put a thermometer under my armpit to take my temperature.
彼は荷物を脇に抱えてやって来た.	He came holding a package under his arm.
【そば・横】家のすぐ脇に小川が流れています.	A brook flows right near my house.
私はスーツケースを脇に置いてバスを待った.	I put the suitcase down next to me and waited for the bus.
車が来たので道路の脇に寄ってやり過ごした.	When a car came, I moved to the side of the road and let it pass.
彼らは本題を脇において、雑談に熱中した.	They put aside the main topic of discussion and were absorbed in idle talk.

わきまえる
| お前たちも中学生になれば、やって良いことと悪いことのわきまえはつくはずだ. | You're junior high school students now. You should be able to tell the difference between things you should and should not do. |
| 場所柄をわきまえなさい. お葬式の席でそんな大声で笑うものではありません. | Think about †where you are [the occasion]. A funeral is no place for laughing in such a loud voice. |

わく¹ (沸く)
ストーブの上でやかんのお湯が沸いている.	The teakettle is boiling on the heater.
おふろが沸いています.	The bath water is hot. / The bath is ready.
彼の演説が終わると拍手が沸いた.	As he concluded his speech there was a burst of applause.
1964年は日本じゅうがオリンピックブームに沸いた.	In 1964, all Japan was caught up in the Olympic Games.
その問題の是非を巡って議論が沸いた.	The pros and cons of that problem were hotly debated.

わく² (枠)
窓の枠が歪んでいるのできちんと閉まらない.	The window won't close properly because the frame is warped.
メガネの枠が壊れてしまった.	The frames to my glasses broke.
レポートの中の大切な箇所を枠で	I boxed off the important passages in the

囲んだ.	report.
【限度】今年の賃上げも一桁の枠内に留まった.	This year's pay raise is also within the 10 percent range.
彼の行動は常識の枠を越えている.	His behavior †goes beyond [falls outside] the bounds of propriety.
宴会の費用は予算の枠内で収めなければならない.	Expenses for the reception must be kept within the budget.

わくわく

彼女は胸をわくわくさせて, クリスマスプレゼントの包みを開けた.	Her heart pounding with excitement, she unwrapped the Christmas present.
あこがれの映画スターと直接話ができると思うと, 彼女は胸がわくわくした.	The thought that she could actually talk to her favorite movie star made her heart pound with excitement.

わけ (訳)

【道理】そんなわけの分からないことを言うんじゃない.	You shouldn't make such unreasonable demands.
彼はもう少しわけの分かる男だと思っていた.	I had thought he'd be a little more perceptive.
【意味・内容】外国人に話しかけられたが, 何を言っているのかわけが分からなかった.	I was spoken to by a foreigner, but I had no idea what he was saying.
この小説は読んでも何が何だかわけが分からなかった.	I read this novel, but couldn't understand any of it.
【理由・事情】それとこれとではわけが違うよ.	That is quite different from this.
昨日学校を休んだわけを説明しなさい.	Tell me why you were absent from school yesterday.
彼がそんなことをするなんて, きっとわけがあるに違いない.	There has to be a reason for what he did.
わけあって今度会社を辞めることになりました.	I have decided to quit work for personal reasons.
【意図】弁解するわけではありませんが, 急用ができて遅れてしまったのです.	I don't mean to make excuses, but I was late because of an emergency.
【慣用】仕事が終わるまで帰るわけにはいかない.	I can't go home until the work is finished.
そのようなお金を受け取るわけにはいきません.	I can't accept that kind of money.
彼がそんな悪いことをするわけがない.	He would never do such a terrible thing.

| こんなパズルを解くのはわけない． | This puzzle is a cinch. |

わける (分ける)
【分割する】父は髪を七三に分けている．	Father parts his hair on the side.
先生はクラスを五つの班に分けた．	The teacher divided the class into five groups.
車の代金を5回に分けて払った．	I paid for the car in five installments.
【分配する】彼は財産を子どもたちに分けた．	He divided his property among his children.
利益はみんなで分けた．	We divided the profits among us.
ケーキを4人で分けました．	We cut the cake into four servings [portions].
	We divided up the cake among the four of us.
ダブルヘッダーで両チームは仲良く星を分けた．	The two teams split the doubleheader.
【区分する】生物は大きく動物と植物の二つに分けることができる．	Living things are broadly divided into animals and plants.
収穫されたリンゴは大きさによって分けられます．	The harvested apples are separated according to size.
町の人口変化を年度別に分けてみた．	We traced changes in the population of the town by the year.
	We recorded annual changes in the town's population.
【かき分ける】彼は人込みを分けて進んだ．	He elbowed through the crowd as he went.
草の根を分けても犯人を捜し出すつもりだ．	I intend to search every nook and cranny until I find the culprit.
	I'll leave no stone unturned looking for the culprit.

わざと
彼だって，わざとあなたの人形を壊したわけじゃないんだから，もう許してあげなさい．	You should forgive him. After all, he didn't †break your doll on purpose [mean to break your doll].
その小さい子は，母親の気を引こうとして，わざと大声をあげて泣いた．	The little child deliberately cried in a loud voice to try to get his mother's attention.
彼はわざと規則を破ったに違いない．	There's no doubt that he deliberately broke the rules.
そんなわざとらしいお世辞を言うな．	Stop making such obvious compliments.

わざわざ

彼は空港までわざわざ見送りに来てくれた. — He went out of his way to see me off at the airport.

あの店のケーキが食べたくて, わざわざ買いに行ったのに, 店は閉まっていた. — I really wanted to eat cake sold at that shop so I went all the way there, but it was closed.

わずか

【少し】目的地まであとわずかです. — It's only †a little further [a short way] to our destination. We're almost there.

彼は山で遭難し, わずかな食料で命をつないだ. — He was in an accident on the mountain and barely survived with very little food to sustain him.

4歳頃までのことはわずかに覚えている程度だ. — I hardly remember anything until I was four.

【ささいな】兄弟というものはわずかなことで言い争うことがある. — Siblings argue with each other over †the smallest thing [nothing].

海や山ではわずかな不注意がもとで命を落とすことがある. — In the mountains or on the sea, †any carelessness [the slightest negligence] can mean your life.

【やっと】その家は長男の稼ぎだけでわずかに生計を立てていた. — That family was barely getting by with only the eldest son's income.

転落現場で発見されたとき, 彼はわずかに息をしているだけだった. — He was barely breathing when he was discovered at the place where he fell.

わずらう (煩・患う)

祖母は長年リューマチを患っている. — My grandmother has suffered from rheumatism for many years.

つまらないことで思い煩わないほうがいい. — You shouldn't †worry yourself [agonize] over †unimportant things [nothing].

わずらわしい (煩わしい)

外国に留学するには煩わしい手続きが必要だ. — If you want to study overseas, you have to go through a lot of red tape.

こんなに暑いと, 食事の支度をするのも煩わしい. — Cooking is a bother [chore] when it's this hot.

わずらわす (煩わす)

彼女は小さいときから, 親の手を煩わせたことがない. — Ever since she was small, she's never given her parents any trouble.

彼は息子が交通事故を起こしたこ — He's been worrying himself sick ever since

とで, ずっと心を煩わせている.	his son caused a traffic accident.

わすれる (忘れる)

その本の著者の名前を忘れてしまって, 思い出せない.	I've completely forgotten who the author of that book is.
彼は私の顔をすっかり忘れてしまっていた.	He had completely forgotten what I looked like.
学生時代の北海道旅行は, 忘れられない楽しい思い出だ.	I will never forget the fun I had on my trip to Hokkaido when I was a student.
忘れずにバターを買ってきてね.	Don't forget to pick up some butter.
明日, 彼に電話をするのを忘れないでください.	Please †don't forget [remember] to call him tomorrow.
ご親切は決して忘れません.	I'll never forget your kindness.
本があまりに面白かったので, 彼は時がたつのも忘れて読みふけった.	The book was so interesting that he forgot the (passage of) time and kept on reading.
嫌なことは早く忘れてしまいなさい.	The sooner you forget about all those horrible [unpleasant] things, the better.
	Just put all that behind you.
彼は寝食を忘れて研究に打ち込んだ.	He forgot all about sleeping and eating and threw himself into his research.
【置いてきてしまう】カメラをどこかに忘れてきてしまった.	I left my camera somewhere.
雨が上がると, 電車に傘を忘れる人が増える.	More people leave their umbrellas on the train when it stops raining.
英語の教科書を忘れてきてしまった.	I forgot my English textbook.

わだい (話題)

彼は話題の豊富な人だ.	He always has something to talk about.
	He's always full of good conversation.
最近, あの小説が話題を呼んでいる.	That novel has stirred up a lot of discussion recently.
今日隣に越してきた人たちのことが夕食の話題に上った.	The people who moved in next door today came up in the conversation at dinner.
あなたのことは私の家でよく話題に上るんですよ.	You are often a topic of conversation at my house.
その出来事は町の話題となった.	The event was the talk of the town.

わたす (渡す)

【手渡す】彼は給料を全部奥さんに渡している.	He hands his whole salary over to his wife.
私は駅員に切符を渡して改札を出	I gave my ticket to the station attendant

た.	and passed through the wicket.
校長自ら卒業証書を全員に渡した.	The principal presented a graduation certificate to each student.
【譲渡する】彼は家を人手に渡した.	The house passed out of his hands to someone else.
与党はついに政権を野党に渡した.	The party in power finally handed the administration over to the opposition.
【架ける】水たまりに板を渡して通った.	I got across the puddle by putting a board over it.

わたる (渡る)

【越える・行く・来る】彼は川〔橋〕を渡って向こう岸まで行った.	He crossed the river [bridge] to the opposite bank.
湖面を渡って来る風が心地よい.	The wind blowing over the lake feels good.
仏教は朝鮮から渡って来た.	Buddhism was transmitted from Korea.
彼はいつも危ない橋を渡って金を稼ぐ.	He walks a fine line when it comes to earning money.
雁が北国へ渡って行く.	The geese are migrating north.
【～の手に渡る】倒産して彼の会社は人手に渡ってしまった.	His company went bankrupt and passed to other hands.
機密書類がライバル会社に渡ってしまった.	The secret papers were given to a rival company.
プリントは数が少ないので全員に渡らないかもしれません.	There aren't many copies, so not everyone will get one.
【生きていく】そんな考えでは世の中を渡っていけないよ.	That kind of thinking won't get you far in the world.
渡る世間に鬼はなし.	There is some good in everyone you meet.
【範囲が及ぶ】今日は空が晴れ渡っている.	The sky is completely clear today.
先生の怒る声が教室中に響き渡った.	The teacher's angry voice resounded throughout the classroom.
この商品は全国に行き渡っている.	This product is sold throughout the country.
10年にわたる彼の苦労がやっと実を結んだ.	His painstaking effort, spanning 10 years, finally bore fruit.
会談は6時間にわたって行われた.	The meeting took [lasted] over six hours.

わびしい (侘しい)

駅から2時間ほど歩くと, わびしい山村に着く.	About two hours from the station, you will come to a desolate [dreary] mountain village.
冬の寒さが厳しい日には, 一人暮らしのわびしさを感じる.	Harsh, cold winter days intensify the feelings of solitude when living alone.

父親の失業で，一家はわびしい生活を余儀なくされた．	The father's unemployment meant a miserable existence for the whole family.

わびる（詫びる）

彼は小さな声で自分の不注意を詫びた．	He quietly apologized for his carelessness.
彼に無礼な態度をとったことを心から詫びた．	I sincerely apologized for being rude to him.
私の間違いでした．お詫びします．	It was my mistake. I apologize. [I'm very sorry.]

わらう（笑う）

何を笑っているの？	What are you laughing [smiling] about [at, for]?
彼はにこにこ笑いながらやって来た．	He showed up with a big smile on his face.
彼女は漫画を読みながらくすくす笑っている．	She's reading a comic book and giggling [chuckling] away.
彼の一言にクラスのみんなはどっと笑った．	Everyone in the class burst out laughing at his remark.
彼のスーツ姿に思わず笑ってしまった．	The sight of him dressed up in a suit made me laugh in spite of myself.
あの映画を見たら，きっとだれでも笑わずにいられないよ．	Anyone who sees that movie can't help but laugh.
彼が笑った顔を見たことがない．	I've never seen him smile.
笑ってごまかすなよ．	Don't try to laugh it off.
彼女は必死に笑いをこらえている．	She's desperately trying to keep from laughing.
笑いごとじゃないよ．	It's not a laughing matter.
隣の部屋から笑い声が聞こえる．	I can hear laughter from the room next door.
店が大繁盛して彼は笑いが止まらない．	Business is so good that he's full of smiles.
【あざける】人の失敗を笑ってはいけません．	You shouldn't laugh at other people's failures.
こんな所で泣いていると人に笑われるよ．	You'll get laughed at if you cry in a place like this.
人に笑われても，僕は自分の思いどおりにやる．	I'll do it my way even if people laugh at me.
あいつが今度の選挙に出るんだって？ 笑わせるね．	That guy's going to run in the next election? Don't make me laugh.

わり (割)

【比率】このカメラは定価より2割安く買った. — I bought this camera at 20 percent below list [retail] price.

【割合】この仕事はきついばかりで割に合わない. — Considering all the trouble involved, it just doesn't pay to do this work. / This job just isn't worth it!

そんなことをして僕だけが割を食うのはごめんだ. — I don't know why I have to be the one to pay the price for doing this.

君は勉強した割に成果が上がらなかったようだね. — I guess your grades didn't go up much considering how much you studied.

わりあい (割合)

【比率】がんは死亡原因の中で大きな割合を占めている. — Cancer is the cause of a large proportion of deaths.

この試験の合格率は10人のうちたった2人の割合だ. — Only two people out of every ten pass this test.

【比較的】この魚は割合においしい. — This fish is quite good.

入学試験は割合簡単だった. — The entrance examination was relatively easy.

わりきる (割り切る)

これも仕事だと思って割り切ってください. — Just think of this as part of your job and do it.

君は随分割り切った考え方をする人だね. — Everything's cut and dried for you, isn't it?

その判決に対して, 彼女は何か割り切れないものがあった. — That court decision left her somewhat unconvinced.

親と子のあいだには理屈で割り切れないものがある. — Parent-child relationships can't always be explained rationally.

わりびき (割引)

あの店は学生証を見せると割引してくれる. — You can get a discount at that store if you show your student I.D.

このブランドもののバッグは3割引で買った. — I bought this name-brand bag at 30% off.

美容院の割引券をもらった. — I got a discount coupon for the beauty salon.

団体割引は何名から(適用されるの)ですか? — How many people do you need (to qualify) for a group discount?

わりびく (割り引く)

夕方5時以降は10パーセント割り引きます. — We give 10% discounts after five in the evening.

彼女の言うことは割り引いて聞いたほうがいいよ.	You'd better take what she says with a grain of salt.

わる (割る)

【砕く】彼は歯でクルミを割った.	He cracked the walnuts with his teeth.
窓ガラスを割ったのはだれだ.	Who broke the window?
彼女は手を滑らせてコップを割ってしまった.	Her hand slipped and she broke the glass.
【下回る】総会は出席者が定足数を割って不成立に終わった.	The general meeting wasn't held because it didn't have a quorum.
市長選挙の投票率は50パーセントを割った.	The total vote for the mayoral election fell below 50 percent.
【薄める】彼はウイスキーを水で割って飲んだ.	He added water to his whiskey and drank it.
【割り算をする】8を2で割ると4になる.	Eight divided by two equals [is] four.
宴会の費用は頭数で割って, それぞれが分担した.	The cost of the reception was †divided up equally among [borne by] all those attending.

わるい (悪い)

【不正】彼は悪いやつだ.	He's no good./He's a rat./He's evil.
人をだますとは, あいつは悪いやつだ.	He's despicable, deceiving people the way he does.
	He's a real lowlife taking people in like that.
もうばれたのか. 悪いことはできないものだ.	It's already gotten out? We can't get away with much (around here).
悪い仲間と悪い遊びをしちゃいけないよ.	You shouldn't †hang out [get mixed up] with the bad kids.
【責任がある】私が悪かった.	I was wrong.
悪いのは君だ.	It's your fault./You're in the wrong.
【意地悪】私の言うことを悪く取らないで欲しい.	I hope you won't take what I say the wrong way.
【不良】これは安いけど品質は悪くないよ.	It's cheap but the quality is not bad.
この豆腐は悪くなっている.	This *tofu* has gone bad.
テレビの調子が悪いけど, どこが悪いんだろう.	I wonder what's wrong with the TV.
英語のテストは悪かった.	I did poorly on the English test.
僕は頭も悪いし, 顔も悪い.	I'm stupid and ugly.
うちの息子は出来が悪い.	My son's not very bright.
私の作文にどこか悪いところはあ	Are there any rough spots in my composi-

りませんか.	tion [essay]?
私の家は日当たりが悪い.	My house doesn't get much sunlight.
お前，最近評判悪いよ.	You're getting a bad reputation lately. Your reputation is suffering lately.
【体が】彼は肝臓が悪い.	He has a bad [weak] liver.
最近目が悪くなった.	My eyesight has been †getting bad [deteriorating] lately.
彼は入院したそうですが，どこが悪いんですか.	I heard he was hospitalized. What's wrong with him? [What happened to him?]
【有害】たばこは体に悪い.	Cigarettes are bad for you.
暗い所で読書するのは目に悪い.	Reading in poorly lit places is bad for your eyes.
【申しわけない】朝早く起こして悪かった.	I'm sorry to have gotten you up so early.
悪いけど先に帰るよ.	Sorry, but I have to go home now.
約束をすっぽかしたら彼に悪いよ.	Standing him up is wrong.
何のお礼も言わないで，彼には悪いことをした.	It was wrong of me not to thank him.
言っちゃ悪いが，君の小説はつまらない.	I hate to say it but I found your novel boring.
【不快】デートを断ったら彼は気を悪くした.	He took offense at being turned down for a date.
彼女に好きと言われて悪い気はしなかった.	I wasn't displeased when I was told that she liked me.
【慣用】僕が彼女をいじめたなんて，人聞きの悪いことを言わないでください.	Don't go around saying I was mean to her. It makes me sound bad.
一緒にこの仕事をやってみないか. 悪いようにはしないから.	Would you like to try working together on this job? You can trust me.

わるぎ (悪気)

悪気があってやったのではありません.	I didn't mean any harm.
悪気がなくても，こんなことは許せない.	It may not have been done †in spite [maliciously], but something like this, I find hard to forgive.

われる (割れる)

【砕ける】ボールが当たって窓ガラスが割れた.	The ball hit the window and it broke.
花瓶が倒れて割れてしまった.	The vase fell and broke.
今日は頭が割れるように痛む.	I have a splitting headache today.
【分かれる】その問題を巡って党が	The (political) party split in two over that

二つに割れてしまった.	issue.
今後の会社の方針について社内の意見が割れた.	The company was split over future policy decisions.
【判明する】その殺人事件はついにホシが割れて解決した.	The murder case has finally been cracked and put to rest.
彼はすぐ底が割れるようなうそをつく.	His lies are transparent.
	You can see right through his lies.
【割り切れる】8は4で割れる.	Eight is divisible by four.
【音・声が】ラジオの音が割れて聞きにくい.	The radio's sound is distorted and hard to make out.
演奏が終わると割れるような拍手が起こった.	When the performance ended the applause was deafening.

わんぱく (腕白)

彼は子どもの頃, 大変な腕白だった.	He was really naughty as a child.
	He was a bit of a brat as a kid.
うちの息子は今, 腕白盛りだ.	Our son is at his most mischievous stage now.
うちの腕白小僧には手を焼いている.	Our little rascal gives us a lot of trouble.

索引
[和英単語集]

本「索引・和英単語集」は、本文中に出てくる表現の索引に、一般に必要性が高いと思われる単語・熟語を和英単語集の形で加え、五十音（あいうえお）順に並べたものである。総数は約16,500語句に上る。

凡　　例

1) ゴシック体（太字）の語句は本文中に見出し項目として取り上げられていることを表す。その見出し語を使った主な合成語や熟語、および活用変化形もその項目に含まれる。
　　【例】**げいじゅつ**　芸術
　　　　　▶「芸術家」や「芸術的な」などの用例も『げいじゅつ』の項目の中に含まれる。

2) 行末の [　] 内は参照先項目を表し、その項目の例文中にその日本語に対応する英訳例が出てくることを表す。英訳が長すぎる場合、あるいは単語・熟語レベルでは対応しにくいもの以外は英訳も併記した。
　　【例】やりすごす　やり過ごす　let *something* pass ……………[わき]
　　　　　▶『わき』という見出し項目の例文の中に「やり過ごす」の訳として let *something* pass を使った用例が出ている。
　　【例】わりかん　割り勘…………………………………………………[さき]
　　　　　▶『さき』という見出し項目の例文の中に「割り勘」の用例が出ている。

3) そのほか、一般に日常的な英作文に必要と思われる語句を和英単語集の形で取り上げた。
　　【例】きりつ　規律　order, discipline, a rule

4) 合成語や熟語、および活用変化形を出す必要がある場合は、親見出しの部分を繰り返さず、「〜」で表した。
　　【例】**いてん**　移転する　move, remove
　　　　　〜先　*one's* new address
　　　　　▶「〜先」はこの場合「移転先」を表す。

5) 同じ日本語に対応する参照見出しが二つ以上あって英訳が異なる場合、および見出し項目で取り上げている訳例と異なる訳例が他の項目に出てくる場合、二番目以降の日本語は省略した。
　　【例】うでまえ　腕前　skills ………………………………………[ちかづく]
　　　　　・*one's* ability ………………………………………………[ほれる]
　　　　　▶「腕前」の訳例として skills を使った用例が『ちかづく』の項目中に、今一つの訳例として *one's* ability を使った用例が『ほれる』の項目中に出てくる。

【例】**あこがれる**
 ・be infatuated with …………………………………[はなやか]
 ▶『あこがれる』の見出し項目で取り上げている英語表現以外にも『はなやか』の項目に be infatuated with という訳例が出ている。

【例】**あんしん 安心**
 〜して relieved ……………………………………[ぬける]
 〜だ have nothing to worry about ………………[たのむ]
 ▶「安心して」の一つの訳例として relieved が『ぬける』の項目中に出てくるが、『あんしん』の見出し項目中にも別の訳例が出ていることもあるので、あわせて参照されたい。「安心だ」についても同様。

ア

ああいう such
　〜連中 a crowd like that　[ちかづく]
アーケード an arcade
アーチ an arch
アーモンド an almond
あい 愛
あいいろ 藍色 indigo blue
あいかぎ 合鍵 a duplicate key, a spare key; (親鍵) a master key
あいかわらず 相変わらず
あいきょう 愛敬
あいこ 〜だ be even
あいこうか 愛好家 a lover, a fan, an amateur
あいこく 愛国者 a patriot
　〜心 patriotism
アイコン 《コンピュータ》an icon
あいさつ 挨拶
　〜回りをする make courtesy calls
　　　　　　　　　　　　　　　[つぶれる]
あいしょう 相性がいい get along with
あいしょう 愛称 a pet name
あいじょう 愛情
あいず 合図
アイスクリーム (an) ice cream
あいすべき 愛すべき lovable, cute
アイスホッケー ice hockey
あいする 愛する love　………[あい]
あいそう 愛想
　〜の悪い unfriendly …[はらだたしい]
あいた 空いた empty, vacant, unoccupied
あいた 開いた open
あいだ
　〜に入る step in　………[おさめる²]
あいちゃく 愛着
あいづち 相づちをうつ nod at what *someone* is saying
あいて 相手
　〜にしない not have anything to do with　………………………[あんな]
　〜の手を読む read *one's* opponent's intentions　………………[よむ]
アイデア
あいどく 愛読する like to read *something*

　〜書 *one's* favorite book
アイドル an idol
あいにく
あいま 合い間 an interval
　〜を縫う take time out from　[ぬう]
あいまい
あいよう 愛用の favorite
　〜する use *something* regularly
あいらしい 愛らしい pretty, lovely, cute, charming
アイルランド Ireland
　〜の Irish
　〜人 (男) an Irishman; (女) an Irishwoman; (全体) the Irish
アイロン an iron
　〜をかける iron
あう 会・遭う
　・pass　………………[あいさつ]
あう 合う
アウト 《野球》out
　〜になる be (put) out
アウトドア 〜の outdoor
アウトレット 〜ストア a factory outlet (store)
　〜モール an outlet mall
あえぐ pant, gasp
あえて〜する dare (to) *do*, take the trouble to *do*
あおい 青い
あおぐ 仰ぐ (見上げる) look up; (尊敬する) look up to, respect
あおぐ 扇ぐ fan
あおざめる 青ざめる turn pale
あおじゃしん 青写真 a blueprint
あおじろい 青白い pale
あおすじ 青筋を立てて ………[すじ]
あおむけ あお向けに on *one's* back
あおる (風を起こす) fan; (扇動する) stir up, fan; (刺激する) arouse
あか 垢 (目に見えるような) dirt
　耳〜 earwax
あかい 赤い
あかじ 赤字
あかす 明かす (過ごす) spend, pass; (打ち明ける) confess, tell
あかちゃん 赤ちゃん a baby
あかぬける あか抜ける
あからさま 〜な open, downright,

out-and-out
あかり 明かり a light, a lamp
あがる 上・挙・揚がる
あかるい 明るい
　…に明るい be an expert on, be acquainted with ……………[けいざい]
　・be well-versed in, be familiar with ……………………………………[じじょう]
　明るく振る舞う act cheerfully ……………………………………[つとめて]
　雰囲気が明るくなる make things more pleasant, brighten things up ……………………………………[くわわる]
あかんぼう 赤ん坊 a baby
あき 空き
あき 秋 autumn, 《米》fall
あきす 空巣 a sneak thief
　～が入る a burglar breaks into a house ……………………………………[ぬすむ]
あきっぽい 飽きっぽい get tired of things quickly ……………[おちつき]
あきらか 明らか
　～にする make clear ………[せきにん]
　～になる become known ………[のち]
あきらめる
　・put out of *one's* mind ………[きれい]
　災難だと思って～ accept *something* as †a misfortune [bad luck] ……………………………………[さいなん]
　無いものと～ write *something* off as lost, give up on ever finding *something* ……………………………[ない]
あきる 飽きる
　・have just about all of *something one* can take, get fed up with ……………………………………[いいかげん]
アキレスけん アキレス腱 an Achilles' tendon; (唯一の弱点) an Achilles' heel
あきれる
　・have had enough of ………[かげん]
あく 空く
あく 開く
あく 悪 wickedness, (an) evil, (a) vice
あくい 悪意 ill will
あくうん 悪運 the devil's own luck, bad luck ……………………………[うん]
あくじ 悪事 a crime ………[かさねる]

　～をはたらく commit a crime
あくしつ 悪質な vicious, nasty ……………………………………[いたずら]
あくしゅ 握手 a handshake
　～する shake hands (with)
あくしゅう 悪臭 a bad smell
あくしゅう 悪習 (悪い慣習) a bad custom
　(悪い癖) a bad habit ………[あらためる]
あくしゅみ 悪趣味だ have bad taste ……………………………………[しゅみ]
あくじゅんかん 悪循環
あくせい 悪政 misgovernment ……………………………………[くるしむ]
あくせい 悪性の bad, malignant
　・virulent ………………[りゅうこう]
あくせく
アクセサリー an accessory
アクセス
アクセント (強勢) a stress, an accent; (発音の癖) an accent
あくてんこう 悪天候 bad [rough] weather
　～のため due to inclement weather conditions ……[ひきかえす]
あくとう 悪党 a villain
　・a scoundrel, a baddie ……[たいした]
あくとく 悪徳高利貸 an unscrupulous loan shark ……………………………[のる]
あくにん 悪人 a bad man
　・a louse ……………………………[そうとう]
あくび a yawn
　～をする yawn
　・give a yawn ………………[のばす]
あくま 悪魔 a devil, a demon
あくまで(も)
あくみょうだかい 悪名高い notorious, infamous
あくむ 悪夢 a nightmare, a bad dream
あくゆう 悪友 an old crony; (悪友グループ) an old gang
あくよう 悪用する misuse
あぐら ～をかく sit cross-legged
あくりょく 握力が強い〔弱い〕 have a strong 〔weak〕 grip
アクリル (an) acrylic fiber
アクロバット acrobatics
あげあし 揚げ足をとる pick *someone*

up, find fault with *someone*

あけがた 明け方　dawn, daybreak

あげく　(結局) finally, ultimately; (…のあとで) after...

あけすけ　～に　openly, frankly, straightforwardly, unreservedly, candidly

あけっぱなし 開けっ放しにする　leave *something* open

アゲハチョウ　a swallowtail butterfly ················[やがて]

あける 明ける

あける 空ける

(場所を) make space ······[かたづける]

あける 開ける

あげる 上・挙・揚げる

あご (上あごまたは下あご) a jaw; (下あご, あご先) the chin

アコーディオン　an accordion

あこがれ　～の　of *one's* dreams ·····························[うきうき]

あこがれる
・be infatuated with ········[はなやか]

あさ 朝 《名詞》morning; 《副詞的》in the morning

～から晩まで from morning till night ·······························[へいき]

あさ 麻　hemp

あざ a bruise; (目のまわりの) a black eye; (生まれつきの) a birthmark

あさい 浅い

アサガオ 朝顔　a morning glory [たね]

あざける laugh at, sneer (at), ridicule, jeer

あさせ 浅瀬　a ford
・a shallow stream ···············[だく]

あさって the day after tomorrow

あさね 朝寝する　†get up [rise] late

あさねぼう 朝寝坊する oversleep, sleep in ·································[くせ]

あさはか

あさひ 朝日　the morning sun, the rising sun

あさましい

あざむく 欺く　deceive, cheat

あさめしまえ 朝飯前だ　be a cinch

あざやか 鮮やか

あざわらう あざ笑う　ridicule, scoff at

あし 足・脚

～がすくむ freeze in *one's* steps ·····························[きょうふ]

～で調べる··············[しらべる]

～の踏み場もない there is no place to step ·······················[しまう]

～を洗う wash *one's* hands of [め¹]

～を組んで with *one's* legs crossed ·······························[すわる]

子どもの～で at a child's pace [でも]

あじ 味

～がある have charm, be fresh ·······························[やくす]

アジ 鯵　a horse mackerel

アジ ～演説　an agitative speech
・·································[むかう]

アジア　Asia

～の Asian, Asiatic

～人 an Asian, an Asiatic; (全体) Asian people

～大陸 the Asiatic Continent, the Continent of Asia

あしあと 足跡　a footstep
・a track ·····························[つく²]
・a footprint ····················[つける¹]

あしおと 足音　footsteps

あしくび 足首　an ankle

あじけない 味気ない

アジサイ 紫陽花　a hydrangea

あした 明日　tomorrow

あしどり 足どり　(a) step, (a) trace

あしぶみ 足踏みする　mark time

あしもと 足もとに気をつける watch *one's* step ·······················[いく]

あしらう

あじわう 味わう

あずかる 預かる

アズキ 小豆　an adzuki bean

あずける 預ける

アスパラガス　asparagus

アスピリン　aspirin

アスファルト　asphalt

アスレチック　～クラブ a fitness center [club], a health club

あせ 汗

あせも　～ができる　have prickly heat

あせる 焦る
・rush ·······························[いき¹]

・get excited ······················[きなが]
あせる 褪せる fade
あそこ there, that place
　～に[の] there, over there
あそび 遊び
　～場 a playground ··········[かっこう]
あそぶ 遊ぶ
　・have a good time, play around
　································[それでも]
あたい 価する be worth, be worthy of, deserve
あたえる 与える
　与えられた仕事 *one's* assigned work
　································[せっきょく]
あたたかい 暖・温かい
あたたまる 暖・温まる get warm, warm *oneself*
あたためる 温める
アタック （バレーボール）a spike; （挑戦）a try
　～する （挑戦する）try and [to] *do*, have a go at
あだな あだ名 a nickname
あたま 頭
　～が上がらない can't stand up to
　································[どんなに]
　～がいい brilliant ············[とにかく]
　・smart, bright ···················[そろう]
　～が痛い have a headache ·····[やすむ]
　～がいっぱい can't take *one's* mind off
　································[いっぱい]
　～がおかしい be a little off
　································[おかしい]
　～が切れる sharp ·········[おそろしい]
　・smart ························[なるほど]
　～が下がる (have to) hand it to *someone* ·······················[しんぼう]
　～が鈍い stupid ···············[にぶい]
　～が古い old-fashioned ········[ふるい]
　～がやわらかい open-minded
　································[やわらかい]
　～が弱い not smart [bright] [よわい]
　～に血がのぼる be infuriated by
　································[かっと]
　～を痛めている be at *one's* wit's end
　································[まったく]
　～を痛める give *someone* a headache
　································[さすが]

　～を下げて with a bow ·····[あいさつ]
　～を下げる bow ···············[さげる]
　～をひねって考える rack *one's* brains ·······························[ひねる]
あたらしい 新しい
あたり 辺り
　・the surroundings, the area
　································[いよいよ]
あたり 当たり
あたりさわり 当たり障りのない （安全な）safe, harmless; （言質を取られないような）noncommittal
あたりまえ 当たり前
あたる 当たる
　（くじに）come up a winner ·····[ひく]
　（占いが）be accurate ··········[ふしぎ]
　（成功する）be a success ······[けいえい]
　当たっている correct ··········[ていど]
あちこち here and there, from place to place; （行ったり来たり）up and down
あちら there, the other
あつい 厚い
あつい 暑い
　～盛り the hottest part of summer
　································[さかり]
あつい 熱い
あっか 悪化する become [get] worse
　・worsen ························[こくさい]
あつかう 扱う
あつかましい 厚かましい
あつがみ 厚紙 thick paper; （ボール紙）cardboard
あつくるしい 暑苦しい sultry, close, hot and dump
あっけない
あつさ 厚さ thickness
あつさ 暑さ hot weather
　・heat ····························[あたる]
　～のために from the heat ·····[まがる]
　連日の～で from the hot spell
　································[のびる]
あっさり
あっしゅく 圧縮 compression; （コンピュータデータの）compression
　～する compress; （コンピュータデータを）compress
　～ファイル a compressed file

あっせん （〜の）斡旋で through the good offices of
あっち there, the other
あっというま あっという間に in no time ……………………[くわえる]
・before *one* knows it ………[なげる]
・in a matter of minutes ……[もえる]
あっとう 圧倒
アットマーク （＠） "at" character, at sign, ＠
あっぱれ 〜だ well done, bravo
  〜な praiseworthy, admirable
アップ （上昇）rise；（写真）a close-up；（髪型）an upsweep
  〜する （上昇する）rise；（完了する）be finished, be completed
あつまり 集まり a meeting, a party
あつまる 集まる
  ・come together ……………[みな]
あつめる 集める
  ・bring together …………[ぜんぶ]
あつらえる order
あつりょく 圧力 pressure
  〜をかける pressure ………[じりじり]
あて 当て
  〜になる reliable ……………[きおく]
  ・be depended upon ………[きまぐれ]
  〜にならない（言うことが）can't take *someone* at *his* word ……[おおきい]
…あて …宛て addressed to, directed to, for
あてこすり 当てこすり a snide remark, a dig
あてこむ 当て込む expect, count on
  …を当て込んで in expectation [anticipation, hopes] of
あてさき 宛先不明 address unknown ……………………………[かえる¹]
あてずっぽう guesswork, a wild guess, a shot in the dark
あてつける 当てつける put on an act
  …に当てつけられたものだ be aimed at, be meant [intended] for
あてな 宛て名 an address ……[にじむ]
アテネ Athens
あてはまる 当てはまる
あてる 当て・充てる
あと 後

あと 跡
  〜を継ぐ follow in *someone's* footsteps …………………………[つぐ]
あとあじ あと味 an aftertaste
  〜が悪い leave *someone* with a bad aftertaste
あとかたづけ あと片づけ
あとくされ あと腐れのないようにする avoid [prevent] future trouble
あどけない
あとしまつ あと始末………[あとかたづけ]
アドバイス an advice
  〜する advise
アドバルーン an advertising balloon
アトピー 〜性皮膚炎 atopic dermatitis
あとまわし あと回しにする put off, leave *something* until later
あともどり あと戻り go back, turn back；（過去の状態に戻る）relive the past
アトランタ Atlanta
アトリエ an atelier
アドリブ an ad lib
アドレス *one's* address；（インターネット）*one's* e-mail address
あな 穴
  〜を埋める fill ……………[うめる]
アナウンサー an announcer；（ニュース番組）a newscaster
あなた you；（あなたの）your；（あなたを、あなたに）you；（あなたのもの）yours；（あなた自身）yourself；（呼びかけ）《男性に》sir；《婦人に》madam, ma'am；《若い婦人に》miss；《夫婦間で》dear, my dear
あなどる 侮る
アナログ
あに 兄 a [*one's*] brother, an [*one's*] older [《英》elder] brother
アニメ a cartoon, an animated cartoon
あね 姉 a [*one's*] sister, an [*one's*] older [《英》elder] sister
あねったい 亜熱帯 the subtropical zone
あの that, the
あのよ あの世 the other [next] world；（天国）Heaven

アパート（建物）《米》an apartment house, 《英》flats, a block of flats;（1家族分の区画）an apartment, 《英》a flat
　〜の管理人　an apartment manager ……………………………[かんり]
あばく　暴く　disclose, reveal, expose
あばらぼね　あばら骨　a rib
あばらや　あばら屋　a shabby hut
あばれる　暴れる
あばれんぼう　暴れん坊　rowdy
アピール
あびせる　浴びせる　（水などを）pour, shower;（質問を）shoot, fire
アヒル　a duck
あびる　浴びる
アフガニスタン　Afghanistan
　〜の　Afghan
　〜人　an Afghan;（全体）the Afghans
アフターサービス　(repair) service, aftersale(s) service
アブダビ　Abu Dhabi
あぶない　危ない
あぶなく　危なく ………………[あやうく]
あぶら　油・脂
　〜を絞る　rake someone over the coals ……………………………[しぼる]
あぶらえ　油絵　an oil painting
アフリカ　Africa
　〜の　African
　〜人　an African
　〜大陸　the African Continent
アプリケーション　《コンピュータ》an application, applications software
あぶる　crisp [warm] something over a fire
あふれる
あぶれる　（仕事に）be out of †work [a job], be without jobs, be jobless
あべこべ（の）opposite, contrary
アベック　a couple
アボカド　an avocado
あま尼　a nun, a sister
あまい　甘い
　〜物　sweet stuff ……………[ひかえめ]
　自分の手を汚さずに〜汁を吸う　take one's cut without dirtying one's own hands ……………………………[て]
あまえる　甘える
あまえんぼう　甘えん坊（お母さん子）(a) mama's boy
あまぐ　雨具　rain gear …………[ようい]
あまざらし　雨ざらしの　weather-beaten
アマゾン　〜川　the Amazon
あまだれ　雨だれ　a raindrop
アマチュア　an amateur
あまど　雨戸　a (sliding) shutter
あまのがわ　天の川　the Milky Way
あまのじゃく　a perverse person, a cross-grained person
あまもり　雨漏り　leaking rainwater ……………………………[うける]
あまやかす　甘やかす
　・spoil ……………………………[よわい]
　甘やかされて育つ　be spoiled ……………………………[わがまま]
あまやどり　雨宿りする　take shelter from the rain, shelter oneself from the rain
あまり　余り
あまる　余る
あみ　網　a net, a mesh
あみだな　網棚　a rack
アミノさん　アミノ酸　an amino acid
あみもの　編物をする　knit things ……………………………[きよう]
あむ　編む　knit;（髪を）braid, plait;（かごを）weave
アムステルダム　Amsterdam
あめ　雨　rain;（にわか雨）a shower
　〜が降る　it rains
　〜が上がる　it stops raining ……………………………[わすれる]
　〜のため　on account of rain ……………………………[ちゅうし]
あめ　飴　《米》a candy, 《英》sweets
アメーバ　an amoeba
アメリカ　America;（アメリカ合衆国）the United States (of America)（略 the U.S.A., the U.S.)
　〜の　American
　〜人　an American;（全体）the Americans
　北〔南, 中央〕〜　North〔South, Central〕America

あやうく 危うく
あやしい 怪しい
あやしむ 怪しむ
あやつりにんぎょう 操り人形　a puppet, a marionette
あやつる 操る　handle, manage
あやとり あや取りをする　play cat's cradle
あやふや 〜な　uncertain, vague, ambiguous
あやまち 過ち　a fault, an error, a mistake
　〜を犯す　commit a fault, make a mistake
あやまった 誤った　wrong ……[かんねん]
あやまって 誤って　by mistake, by accident
　・accidentally ………………………[けが]
あやまり 誤り　a mistake
　・an error ………………………[なおす]
あやまる 誤る………………………[まちがえる]
あやまる 謝る
あらあらしい 荒々しい　rough, rude
あらい 荒い
あらい 粗い
あらう 洗う
あらかじめ　beforehand, in advance
あらかせぎ 荒稼ぎする　make some quick money
あらさがし あら捜しする　find fault with ………………………………[いや]
あらし 嵐　a storm
あらす 荒らす　harm, damage, do damage (to), lay waste (to)
アラスカ　Alaska (略 Alas., AK)
あらすじ あら筋　an outline, a plot, a summary
あらそい 争い　(論争) a dispute; (口論) a quarrel; (競争) competition
あらそう 争う
あらたまる 改まる
あらためて 改めて
あらためる 改める
　・improve, straighten out ……[たいど]
あらっぽい 荒っぽい　rough, gruff, unrefined
アラビア　Arabia
　〜の　Arabian, Arabic
　〜語　Arabic
　〜海　the Arabian Sea
　〜半島　the Arabian Peninsula
　〜数字　Arabic numerals
アラブ　Arab
　〜の　Arab
　〜人　an Arab; (全体) the Arabs
　〜諸国　the Arab nations
　〜首長国連邦　the United Arab Emirates (略 UAE)
あらまし　(概略) an outline, the gist, the main points; (大体) almost, nearly, roughly
あらゆる
あられ 霰　hail, (一粒の) a hailstone
あらわす 表す
　・exemplify ………………………[れい²]
あらわす 現す
あらわす 著す
あらわれる 表れる
あらわれる 現れる
アリ 蟻　an ant
ありあまる あり余るほどの　more than enough
ありえない　there is no way ……[およそ]
　・be impossible ………………[けいけん]
ありがたい
ありがたみ　value
ありがた迷惑　an unwanted [unwelcome] favor
ありがとう　Thank you.／Thanks.
ありきたり 〜の　ordinary, common, commonplace, run-of-the-mill; conventional
ありさま　(a) state, a scene
ありそうな　probable, likely
ありのまま　the truth, the fact
　〜の姿で　just as it is …………[すがた]
　〜に　as it is, frankly
アリバイ　an alibi
ありふれた
ある 有・在る
　(位置する) lie, be situated ……[あいだ]
ある〜
あるいは
アルカリ 〜性の　alkaline
あるく 歩く
　歩いて回る　tour ………………[まわる]

アルコール alcohol
 ～中毒 alcoholism
 ～中毒の alcoholic
 ～中毒者 an alcoholic
アルジェリア Algeria
アルゼンチン Argentina
 ～の Argentine
 ～人 an Argentine; (全体) the Argentines
アルツハイマー ～病 Alzheimer's (disease)
アルバイト
アルバム an album
アルファベット the alphabet
 ～順に alphabetically
アルプス ～山脈 the Alps
 ～の Alpine
あるまじき (…に)あるまじき行為 be unworthy of *someone* ……[こうい¹]
アルミニウム 《米》aluminum, 《英》aluminium
あれ that
あれこれ one thing or another
 ・this and that …………[おもいだす]
あれち 荒地 wilderness ………[ひらく]
あれほど ～言ったのに after all *one* has said to *someone* ……[ほど]
あれる 荒れる
アレルギー
アレンジ ～する arrange
アロマテラピー aromatherapy
あわ 泡 foam
 ・bubbles, suds …………[たつ²]
 ～だつ bubble, foam
 ～だらけの foamy
 ～を食う be flurried
あわい 淡い (色が) light; (かすかな) faint
あわせて (…に)合わせて to the accompaniment of ………[うたう]
あわせる 合わせる
あわただしい 慌ただしい
 あわただしく in a hurry, hastily
あわてもの 慌て者だ be hasty, be careless, be a scatterbrain
あわてる 慌てる
 ・get rattled …………[おちつく]
 ・worry about …………[ふだん²]
 ・become flustered by …………[ふい]
 慌てて hurriedly …………[さす³]
 ・in *one's* haste …………[たおす]
あわれ 哀れ
あわれむ 哀れむ
あん 案
あんい 安易
あんがい 案外
アンカラ Ankara
アンカレッジ Anchorage
あんき 暗記する learn *something* by heart, memorize
アンケート a questionnaire
あんごう 暗号 a cipher, a code
 ～文 a code message
アンコール an encore …………[こたえる]
あんさつ 暗殺 an assassination
 …………[つたわる]
 ～する assassinate
あんざん 暗算 a mental calculation
 …………[～くらい]
 ～する do mental arithmetic, calculate mentally
あんじ 暗示 a hint, a suggestion
 ～する hint, give a hint, suggest
あんしょう 暗証番号 *one's* PIN (number) (PIN=personal identification number)
あんしょう 暗礁に乗り上げる †run on [strike] a rock, run aground
あんしょう 暗唱する recite
あんじる 案じる
あんしん 安心
 ～して relieved …………[ぬける]
 ～だ have nothing to worry about
 …………[たのむ]
 ・feel at ease …………[みかた]
あんせい 安静 rest …………[だいいち]
 ～にする get plenty of rest
 …………[えいよう]
あんぜん 安全
アンダーシャツ an undershirt
アンダーライン an underline
あんてい 安定
アンデス ～山脈 the Andes (Mountains)
アンテナ 《米》an antenna, 《英》an aerial

あんな
　～ふうに　like that, (in) that way
あんない 案内
　～書　a guide ················[せいきゅう]
　～所　an information service
　　·····································[くわしい]
　～状　an invitation, a notice
　～状を送る　send the invitation
　　·····································[つもり]
　～役　a guide ················[つとめる²]
あんのじょう 案の定
アンパイア　an umpire
あんぴ　安否が気づかわれる　there is concern for the safety of [れんらく]
アンプ　an amplifier
アンペア　an ampere
あんまり······························[あまり]
　～だ　be unreasonable, be (just) too much, be going too far; (あんまりな要求だ) be asking too much
アンマン　Amman
あんみん　安眠　a good sleep
あんもくの　暗黙の　tacit, implicit
アンモニア　ammonia ············[つまむ]
あんらく 安楽

イ

い　胃　a stomach
いあわせる　居合わせる　happen to be, be present
いい
　～ところまで行く ················[こわれる]
いいあてる　言い当てる　guess *something* correctly
いいあらそい　言い争い　an argument, a quarrel
いいあらわす　言い表す　express
いいえ　no; (否定疑問文のあとで) yes
いいかえす　言い返す　talk back, answer back, retort
いいかえる　言い換える　say [express] in other words
　・paraphrase ·····················[ことば]
　言い換えれば　in other words, that is to say, that is
いいかげん
　～な　haphazard ···············[さんまん]
　～にしなさい　I've had just about

enough of ·····················[うぬぼれる]
いいかた　言い方　a way of speaking, how to speak
　・an expression ·················[いやしい]
　そういう～　putting it that way
　　·····································[ごかい]
いいき　いい気な　(のんきな) happy-go-lucky, nonchalant
　～になる　(うぬぼれる) be (self-)conceited, be self-assured
いいきかせる　言い聞かせる　persuade [tell] *someone* (to do)
いいきみ　いい気味
いいこ　いい子になる　make *oneself* look good ·····················[じぶん]
いいすぎる　言い過ぎる
いいそびれる　言いそびれる　fail to tell, miss the chance to tell
いいだす　言い出す　(話題などを持ち出す) bring up *something*; (提案する) suggest, propose; (意見・意向を表明する) come out and say, express *one's* opinion
いいつけ　言いつけ　(命令) an order; (指図) a direction
いいつける　言いつける　(命令する) tell, order; (告げ口する) tell on
いいつたえ　言い伝え　a legend, tradition
いいなり　(…の)言いなりだ　do just as *someone* tells *one*, be at *someone's* beck and call
いいのがれる　言い逃れる　get away with ·····························[あたま]
いいはる　言い張る　insist (on, upon), persist (in)
いいふらす　言いふらす　spread around
　···[ある]
いいぶん　言い分　*someone's* story, what *someone* has to say
e メール　e-mail ·····················[メール]
いいわけ　言いわけ
いいん　医院　a doctor's office; (内科医院) a physician's office
いいん　委員
いう　言う
　・make a remark ············[おもいやり]
　～は易く, 行うは難し　Easier said

than done. ……………………[やすい²]
言われたとおりに as *one* is told
…………………………………[だまる]
いうまでもない[く] 言うまでもない[く]
to say nothing of
・needless to say ………………[〜まで(に)]
いえ 家 (家屋) a house; (家庭) a
home; (家系) a family
〜へ上げる let *someone* in …[あげる]
〜を空ける not be (at) home
……………………………………[あける¹]
いえがら 古い家柄の出 come from an
old family (line) ……………[ふるい]
いえき 胃液 gastric juice(s) ……[さよう]
いえで 家出する run away from home
…………………………………[ころがる]
・abandon *one's* family ………[おく¹]
〜少女 a runaway girl …………[ほご]
イエメン Yemen
イエローカード a yellow card
いえん 胃炎 《医学用語》gastritis
いおう 硫黄 sulfur ………………[はな]
イカ 烏賊 a squid
いか 以下
いがい 以外
いがい 意外
いかが
いがく 医学 medical science, medicine
東洋〜 oriental medicine
〜博士 Doctor of Medicine, (略
M.D.)
〜部 the medical department, a
medical school
いかす 生・活かす
いかすい 胃下垂 a downward
displacement of the stomach,
《医学用語》gastroptosis
いかだ a raft
いかにも really ……………………[〜らしい]
いかめしい stern, dignified
いかり 〜を下ろす be anchored, drop
anchor ……………………………[おろす]
いかり 怒り
〜を爆発させる blow up in anger
……………………………………[ばくはつ]
いかる 怒る ………………………[おこる¹]
いき 生きのいい fresh ……………[いせい]
いき 息

〜をつく暇もない can't even catch
one's breath ………………[つかえる]
〜を引き取る die ……………[まもなく]
いき 意気
いき 粋な chic, stylish, elegant, smart,
tasteful
〜な格好をしている be dressed
elegantly ………………………[かっこう]
いぎ 異議をとなえる object
〜なし No objection!
いぎ 意義 meaning, sense
〜がある significant ……………[さんか]
いきあたりばったり 行きあたりばったり
の (無計画の) haphazard,
hit-or-miss, without any plans
いきいき 生き生き
いきうつし 生き写しだ look exactly
like *someone*
いきおい 勢い
いきがい 生きがい *one's* reason for
living ……………………………[かい¹]
いきかえる 生き返る revive, come
[return] to life
生き返らせる bring *someone* back to
life ………………………………[なげく]
いきかた 生き方 a way of living, a life
style
いきぎれ 息切れする get out of breath
・gasp for air ……………………[いき¹]
いきぐるしい 息苦しい
いきごみ 意気込み enthusiasm,
eagerness
いきごむ 意気込む be eager to *do*, be
all fired up
いきさつ
いきすぎる 行き過ぎる (やり過ぎる) go
too far, be excessive
いきた 生きた live, living
いきちがい 行き違い (考え方の) a
misunderstanding
いきづかい 息遣いが荒い gasp for air
……………………………………[あらい¹]
いきつけ 行きつけの店 the place *one*
always goes ……………………[のぞく²]
〜の favorite
いきづまる 行き詰まる
いきづまる 息詰まる
いきどまり 行き止まり a dead end

....[ぎゃく]
いきなり　suddenly, all of a sudden
いきぬき　息抜きする　take a break, take a breather, take a rest
　～に　for a breather
いきのこる　生き残る　outlive
　・survive ....[たとえば]
いきもの　生き物　a living thing, a creature;《集合的に》life
　・something alive ....[なに]
イギリス　Great Britain, the United Kingdom (略 U.K.); England
　～の　British, English
　～人　a Briton;（男）an Englishman,（女）an Englishwoman;（総称）the British, the English, the English people
いきる　生きる
　生きていく　go on living ....[さき]
いく　行く
いく～　幾～
いくじ　育児　child care
　～休暇　child-care leave, maternity leave
いくじなし　意気地なし　a coward
いくた　幾多の　numerous ....[こえる]
いくつ
いくぶん　幾分　(程度) somewhat, a little; (多少) more or less
いくら
いけ　池　a pond
いけがき　生け垣　a hedge ....[かこむ]
いけどり　生け捕りにする　catch *something* alive
いけない
　・not do any good ....[おもて]
いけばな　生け花　a flower arrangement, flower arranging
いけん　意見
　・a view ....[ぶぶん]
　～が合う　opinions agree ....[あう¹]
　～を出す　express *one's* opinions
....[かっぱつ]
　～を調整する　reach a consensus
....[おもわく]
　～を述べる　express a suggestion
....[けんせつ]
　・express *one's* views ....[じゆう]

　～を発表する　present an opinion
....[はっぴょう]
　～をぶつける　have a heated debate
....[ぶつける]
　～をまとめる　get a consensus from
....[くしん]
いけん　威厳
　～を増す　become more dignified
....[ます]
いご　以後
いこい　憩いの場所　a recreation area
....[きょうどう]
いこう　意向　an intention　[たしかめる]
イコール　(～に等しい)《動詞》equal
いごこち　居心地がよい　《人を主語にして》be [feel] comfortable;《部屋について》snug, cozy
　～が悪い　《人を主語にして》be [feel] uncomfortable
いこつ　遺骨　*someone's* ashes, bones
いざ
　～というとき(に)　if *one* gets in a bind ....[おこない]
　～という段になると　at the most critical stage ....[だん]
いさかい　differences ....[とき]
いざこざ　trouble ....[おこす]
　・disagreement ....[おもて]
いささか　somewhat, a little
いさましい　勇ましい
いさん　遺産　an inheritance　[みにくい]
　・*someone's* estate ....[こうへい]
　～を相続する　inherit, receive a legacy of
いし　石　(石材) stone; (石ころ) a stone,《米》a rock; (丸い小石) a pebble
いし　意思・意志
　～が弱い　weak-willed ....[よわい]
いじ　意地
いじ　維持する　maintain, keep up
いしがき　石垣　a stonewall
いしき　意識
いじける　be negative; mope
いしだん　石段　a stone step ....[だん]
いじめる
　・be mean to ....[わるい]
いしゃ　医者　a doctor; (内科の) a physician; (外科の) a surgeon

~に診てもらう see a doctor ……[ど]
いじゅう 移住する move (to)
　・immigrate to ……………[けつい]
　~者 (他国への) an emigrant; (他国から の) an immigrant
　・a settler ……………………[ひらく]
いしょう 衣装 clothes, dress
　・(a) costume …………………[おもわず]
いじょう 以上
いじょう 異状
いじょう 異常
いしょく 移植 transplant [しゅじゅつ]
　心臓~ heart transplant
いしょくじゅう 衣食住 food, clothing and shelter
いじる (指で) finger; (もてあそぶ) play with
　・fiddle with ……………………[なおる]
　・tamper with ………………[こわす]
いじわる 意地悪な mean, spiteful
いす a chair; (長いす) a sofa; (寝いす) a couch
イスタンブール Istanbul
いずみ 泉 a spring, a fountain
イスラエル Israel
　~の Israeli
　~人 an Israeli; (全体) the Israelite
イスラマバード Islamabad
いずれ (いつか) some other time
　……………………………………[また]
いせい 威勢
いせい 異性 the other sex, the opposite sex
いせいしゃ 為政者 the leadership
　……………………………………[ほろぼす]
いせき 遺跡 remains
　・ruins …………………………[ほうこく]
いぜん 以前
　・once …………………………[おもいだす]
　~から for quite some time
　……………………………………[うったえる]
いぜん 依然として still
いそ 磯 a rocky beach
いそいそ ~と cheerfully, in a cheerful mood
いそがしい 忙しい
いそぐ 急ぐ
いぞく 遺族 the family of the deceased ………………………[ながす]
いた 板 a board; (金属板) a plate
いたい 痛い
　~ところをつく get *someone* in a sore spot ……………………[つまる]
いたい 遺体 a corpse ………[さけぶ]
　・remains, a body ……………[やく³]
いだい 偉大
いだく 抱く (心の中に) hold, bear
いたさ 痛さ a pain
いたずら
　~をする misbehave ………[たたく]
　~をして up to mischief ……[まぜる]
　~盛り at a mischievous age [さかり]
　~半分に just for kicks …[はんぶん]
　~坊主 a mischief-maker ……[おる]
いただき 頂 a mountain peak [たつ²]
いたばさみ 板ばさみだ be sandwiched [caught, torn] between A and B, suffer from a dilemma
いたみ 痛み (a) pain, (an) ache
　・a disorder ……………………[くる]
いたむ 痛・傷む
　(家が) age ……………………[あける¹]
いたむ 悼む mourn over *someone's* death, lament
いためる 痛・傷める (物を) hurt, injure, damage; (心を) worry
いためる (油で) fry, stir-fry
　・sauté …………………………[あぶら]
イタリア Italy
　~の, ~語 Italian
　~人 an Italian; (全体) the Italians
いたるところ 至る所に everywhere, wherever *one* goes
いたれりつくせり 至れり尽くせりの be perfect (in every respect), leave nothing to be desired, be more than satisfactory
いたわる be kind (to)
いち 一 one
　第1(の) the first (略 1st)
いち 市 (市場) a market; (縁日・見本市) a fair
いち 位置
いちいち one by one, every
　~言う spell out …………………[いう]
いちおう 一応

・tentatively ·····························[て]
いちがいに 一概に…ない not altogether, not necessarily
  〜言えない can't generalize about *something*
いちがつ 一月 January (略 Jan.)
イチゴ a strawberry
いちじ 一次 the first
いちじ 一時 (時刻) one o'clock; (かつて) once, at one time, (しばらく) for a time, for a while
  (当座) temporarily ··········[ちゅうし]
  〜は at one time ·············[ならず²]
  〜的な (その場限りの) momentary, passing
  〜預り所 the checkroom ·····[にもつ]
イチジク a fig
いちじるしい 著しい remarkable ·····························[あがる]
  著しく remarkably ············[ぞうか]
いちだい 一代 (一生) *one's* lifetime; (一世代) a generation
いちだいじ 一大事 a serious affair, a matter of serious concern
いちだんと 一段と a great deal ·····························[にんしき]
いちだんらく 一段落する(させる) be over the hump, get it done
いちど 一度
いちなん 一難去ってまた一難 ·······[さる]
いちにち 一日 one [a] day
  (丸一日) the whole day ········[あける¹]
  1日(につき)2,000円 2,000 yen a day ·····························[こづかい]
  〜じゅう the whole day
  ・all day long ··········[まちがった[て]]
  ・the entire day ·············[こうどう]
  ・24 hours a day ················[やすむ]
いちにんまえ 一人前
いちねん 一年 one [a] year
いちば 市場 a market
いちはやく いち早く instantaneously ·····························[つうしん]
いちばん 一番 (第1番)the first; (最も) the most
いちぶ 一部
いちぶ 一分の隙もない impeccably ·····························[すき²]

いちまい 一枚 (紙などの) a sheet, a piece; (本などの) a leaf
いちみ 一味 a gang
いちめん 一面 (一つの側面) one aspect, one side; (新聞の) the front page
  〜に all over
  〜の真理 a certain amount of truth ·····························[しんり¹]
いちもくさん 一目散に for *one's* life
いちもんなし 一文無しの penniless ·····························[とうとう]
いちやく 一躍 suddenly, overnight
いちゃつく neck (with), flirt (with), touch and carry on
イチョウ a gingko [ginkgo]
いちょう 胃腸 the stomach and intestines ···················[しょうか]
  〜が弱い have a weak stomach ·····························[よわい]
いちらん 一覧表 a list, a table
いちりゅう 一流
  ・top-notch ····················[みこみ]
いちる 一縷の望みを託す pin *one's* last bit of hope on ··············[のぞみ]
いちるい 一塁 (野球) (the) first base
  〜手 the first baseman
いつ
  〜でも anytime ················[きがる]
いつか
  ・eventually ··················[なる¹]
いっか 一家 *one's* family
  グリーンさん〜 the Greens
いっかい 一回 once; (野球)the first inning
いっかいせん 1回戦 the first round ·····························[せまい]
  ・the first match ··········[ぶつかる]
いっかん 一巻の終わり be done for, it is the end of ············[おわり]
いっかん (…の)一環として as part of ·····························[こうきょう]
いっき 一気に without stopping once ·····························[かいだん]
  〜に(飲む) in one gulp ·····[あける¹]
  〜に読む read *something* in one sitting ···················[しまう]
いっけい 一計を案じる come up with a way ··················[あんじる]

いっけん 一見 at first sight, at a glance
・at first …………………[ぶあいそう]
いっけん 一件落着…………………[まず]
いっこ 一個 one, a piece
いっこう 一行 (団体) a party [いれる]
いっこう 一向に…ない not ... at all, not ... a bit
いっこく 一刻を争う there is no time to lose …………………[あらそう]
いっさい 一切
いっさくじつ 一昨日 the day before yesterday
いっさくねん 一昨年 the year before last
いっしゅ 一種 a kind, a sort
〜の a kind [sort] of *something*, *something* of a kind [sort]
いっしゅう 一周する go around [round], circle
(車で) ride around …………………[まわり]
いっしゅうかん 一週間 a week
いっしゅん 一瞬 《名詞》an instant, a moment; 《副詞的》for an instant
・for a moment …………………[きまずい]
・momentarily …………………[ひるむ]
〜にして in an instant, in a moment
いっしょ 一緒
いっしょう 一生
〜かかっても if it takes a lifetime
……………………………………[おん]
いっしょうけんめい 一生懸命
・diligently …………………[あたえる]
いっしん 一心に with *one's* whole heart, with all *one's* heart
いっせい 一斉に all together; (口をそろえて) in chorus
・all at once …………………[なく²]
・at the same time …………………[すると]
・in unison …………………[ひらく]
いっせつ 一節 a passage …[ひょうげん]
いっせん 一線
いっそ rather
いっそう 一層
いっそく 一足 a pair of
いったい 一体
いったん once

いっち 一致
〜する coincide …………………[すべて]
いっちゃく 一着 (1等) (the) first place; (服の) a suit (of clothes)
いっちょういったん 一長一短 advantages and disadvantages, merits and demerits
いっちょくせん 一直線に straight, in a straight line
いってい 一定の fixed, constant
・regular …………………[あいだ]
いってき 一滴 a drop
いつでも (いつも) always, all the time; (どんなときでも) (at) any time (you like), whenever you like; (…するときはいつでも) whenever...
いっとう 一等賞 the first prize
いつになく unusually
いつのまにか いつの間にか before *one* is aware
・before *one* knows it …………[なおる]
・in no time …………………[はえる]
いっぱい 一杯
(場所が) there is no room ……[おく¹]
いっぱく 一泊する stay overnight
いっぱん 一般
いっぷう 一風変わっていて in a different way …………………[おもしろい]
いっぷく 一服する (喫煙) have a smoke; (休憩) take [have] a rest, take [have] a break
いっぺん 一変する change completely ……………………………………[くうき]
いっぽ 一歩 a step
〜一歩 step by step
〜手前 be on the verge of [ほろびる]
いっぽう 一方
いっぽん 一本 (の) a [an], one
牛乳〜 a bottle of milk
チョーク〜 a piece of chalk
いつまでも
・always …………………[のこる]
いつも
〜のように the way *one* used to
……………………………………[きげん²]
いつわる 偽る lie, tell a lie
いてん 移転する move, remove
〜先 *one's* new address

いでん 遺伝する inherit (genetically)
　～性の hereditary
　～学 genetics ……………[ほうめん]
いでんし 遺伝子 a gene
　～工学 genetic engineering
　～操作 gene manipulation
　～組み換え食品 a genetically altered [modified, engineered] food
いと 糸 a thread; (細ひも) a string; (釣り糸) a line
いと 意図
いど 井戸 a well ……………[ほる]
いど 緯度 latitude
いどう 移動する move
いどう 異動 (人事の) a personnel change, staff reorganization
いとこ a cousin
いどころ 居所 one's whereabouts
　　……………………[～つける]
いとめる 射止める shoot; (獲得する) win
いない 以内
いない (不在だ) be away ……[きゅうか]
いなか 田舎
　～へ home ……………[あたり¹]
　～なまり a rural [provincial] accent
　　……………………[ぬける]
イナゴ a locust
いなずま 稲妻 lightning ………[ひかる]
(～するや)いなや as soon as
イニシアチブ (the) initiative
イニシャル an initial, one's initials
いにん 委任状 a letter [power] of attorney
イヌ 犬 a dog
　～小屋 a doghouse, a kennel
　子～ a puppy
イネ 稲 a rice plant
いねむり 居眠り a nap, a doze
　～する take a nap, nap, doze
　・doze off ……………………[ま]
イノシシ 猪 a wild boar ……[とらえる]
いのち 命
　～が惜しい value one's life　[おしい]
　～を落とす be killed ………[おとす]
　～をつなぐ survive ………[わずか]
いのり 祈り a prayer; (食前の) grace
いのる 祈る

いばる 威張る
　威張った arrogant …………[ゆかい]
　威張って tough …………[どんなに]
　威張り散らす act like a tyrant [そと]
いはん 違反
　～者 an offender ……………[よる¹]
いびき a snore
　～をかく snore
いま 今
　～の present ………………[ふまん]
　～は at present …………………[べつ]
　～のところ (現在) at present; (当分) for the present
　～までに until now ………[れい²]
　～しがた just ………………[あがる]
　(…できるのも)～のうち won't be able to do much longer ………[かお]
　～に始まったことではない be nothing new ……………[はじまる]
　～さら at this stage ………[どう]
いま 居間 a living room, 《英》a sitting room
いみ 意味
イミテーション an imitation, a fake
いみん 移民 (他国からの) an immigrant; (他国への) an emigrant
イメージ
イモ (ジャガイモ) a potato; (サツマイモ) a sweet potato
いもうと 妹 a [one's] sister, a [one's] younger [little] sister
いもむし 芋虫 a caterpillar ……[やがて]
いや 嫌・否
　～な disagreeable ……………[ねらう]
　～な客 an unwelcome guest
　　……………………[だいなし]
　～になる come to hate ……[すっかり]
　・become disgusted with …[よのなか]
いやいや against one's will, unwillingly
　・reluctantly ………………[さんせい]
いやがらせ 嫌がらせをする annoy, harass, give someone a hard time
いやがる 嫌がる not like to do, hate to do, be unwilling to do, be reluctant to do, avoid doing
いやけ (…に)嫌気がさす get tired of, get sick of, get fed up with

いやし 癒し healing
いやしい 卑しい
　・base, mean ……………[あさましい]
いやす 癒す (けが・心を) heal; (病気を) cure
いやに awfully, terribly, extraordinarily, exceedingly
イヤホン an earphone
いやみ 嫌み a cutting remark [ながす]
いやらしい
イヤリング earrings
いよいよ
いよう 異様な strange ……………[なか¹]
いよく 意欲
　・the will to *do*, ambition
　………………………………[のうりょく]
いらい 以来
いらい 依頼 a request
　～する ask, request
いらいら ～して edgy ……[なくなる¹]
　・in frustration ……………[かく¹]
イラク Iraq
　～の Iraqi
　～人 an Iraqi; (全体) the Iraqis
イラスト an illustration
イラストレーター an illustrator
いらっしゃい (こちらへ) Come this way, please./Come here, please.; (ようこそ) Welcome!/I'm glad to see you.
(…せずに)いられない cannot help *doing*
イラン Iran
　～の Iranian
　～人 an Iranian; (全体) the Iranians
いりぐち 入り口 an entrance; (戸口) a door, a doorway
いりくむ 入り組んでいる complicated, intricate
　・confusing, tangled …………[みち]
いりょう 衣料品 articles of clothing
いりょう 医療費 medical expenses
　～ミス malpractice, a mistake in treatment
いりょく 威力 power
いる 居る
いる 要る
いるい 衣類 clothes

　・garments ……………………[ほす]
イルカ a dolphin ……………[かしこい]
いるす 居留守を使う pretend to be out
いれかえる 入れ替える replace
いれかわる 入れ替わる be replaced, change places
いれずみ 入れ墨 a tattoo
いれば 入れ歯 false teeth
いれもの 入れ物 a case, a container
いれる 入れる
　(挿入する) insert ……………[かさねる]
いろ 色 a color
　～合い a tone of color
　～鉛筆 a colored pencil
　～紙 colored paper
　～をつける、～づく color
いろいろ
　・a number of ……………[りゆう]
いろけ 色気がある be sexy, have sex appeal; (関心) be (much) interested in, be ambitious of [for]
いろっぽい 色っぽい sexy, sensual
いろり *irori*, a Japanese-style sunken hearth
いわ 岩 (a) rock
　～の多い rocky
　～登り rock-climbing
いわい 祝い
いわう 祝う
イワシ 鰯 a sardine
いわば 言わば so to speak, what is called, as it were
いわゆる so-called
　・you could call … ……………[ちしき]
いん (脚)韻を踏む rhyme ………[ふむ]
いんき 陰気
インク ink
いんけん 陰険
インコ a parakeet
インサイダー ～取引 insider trading
いんさつ 印刷 print, printing
　～する print
　～所 a printing house
　～物 printed matter
いんし 印紙 a revenue stamp
いんしゅ 飲酒運転をする drive under the influence of alcohol, drink and drive ……………………[～ならない]

いんしょう 印象
いんしょく 飲食店 bars and restaurants ……………[おこなう]
インスタント ～食品 instant foods ……………[てすう]
インストール
インスピレーション (an) inspiration
いんそつ 引率する lead
　～者 a leader
インターネット
インターホン an intercom
いんたい 引退する retire ……[かいてき]
インタビュー an interview
インチ an inch
いんちき (偽物) a fake; (詐欺) a fraud
　～の bogus, shady
インディアン an (American) Indian, a native American
インテリ an intellectual
インド India
　～の Indian
　～人 an Indian; (全体) the Indians
　～洋 the Indian Ocean
インドネシア Indonesia
　～の Indonesian
　～人 an Indonesian; (全体) the Indonesians
イントラネット intranet, an intranet setup
いんねん 因縁 karma, fate
　～をつける invent a pretext for a fight [quarrel]
インフォームド・コンセント informed consent
インフラ infrastructure
インフルエンザ influenza, the flu
インフレ inflation ……[ちゅうとはんぱ]
いんぼう 陰謀 a plot
　・conspiracy ………………[うばう]
いんよう 引用 quotation; (引用文) a quotation
　～する quote (from)
　～符 quotation marks
いんりょう 飲料水 drinking water
　……………[ためる]
いんりょく 引力 gravitation
　・gravity ……………[おちる]

ウ

ウィーン Vienna
ウイスキー whisk(e)y
ウィルス
ウインク a wink
　～する wink (at)
ウール wool
　～の woolen
うえ 上
うえ 飢え hunger
ウエイター a waiter
ウエイトレス a waitress
うえかえる 植え替える transplant [ね]
うえき 植木 a tree, a plant; (庭木) a garden plant
　～鉢 a flowerpot
　～屋 (庭師) a gardener; (苗木商人) a nurseryman
ウエスト the waist
うえた 飢えた hungry
ウェリントン Wellington
うえる 飢える starve, get hungry
　飢え死にする die of hunger, starve to death
うえる 植える
うおうさおう 右往左往する move around in confusion
ウォーミングアップ ～する warm up
うがい ～する gargle ………[しゅうかん]
うかうか ～する (無為に過ごす) be idle, idle one's time away; (油断する) be careless, be inattentive, let one's guard down
うかがう 伺う
　・stop by ………………………[もしくは]
うかがわれる be evident …[なにげない]
うかつ
うかぶ 浮かぶ
うかべる 浮かべる float
うかる 受かる pass the exam(ination)
うかれる 浮かれる
ウガンダ Uganda
うき 雨季・雨期 the rainy [wet] season
うき 浮き (釣りの) a float; (ブイ) a buoy
うきうき 浮き浮き

うきぶくろ 浮き袋　a swimming float
うきよ 浮世　the world ……… [くろう]
うく 浮く
ウグイス 鶯　a (Japanese) bush warbler
　・a Japanese nightingale ……[なく²]
ウクライナ　Ukraine
うけ 受けがよい　be well received, be popular with [among]
うけいれる 受け入れる　receive
うけうり 受け売り　a rehash (of *something*), secondhand information
　〜をする　repeat *someone*, pass on secondhand information
うけつぐ 受け継ぐ　(位・人のあとを) succeed (to); (仕事を) take over
　・inherit …………………… [そっくり]
うけつけ 受付
うけつける 受け付ける
うけとめる 受け止める　(物を) catch; (考えなどを) take
　深刻に〜　take *something* seriously
うけとり 受け取り　a receipt
うけとる 受け取る
うけながす 受け流す　not let *something* bother *one* ………………… [ながす]
うけみ 受け身の　passive
うけもち 受け持ちの先生　a regular teacher …………………………… [りんじ]
うけもつ 受け持つ　be in charge of
うける 受ける
うごかす 動かす
うごき 動き　movement
　〜がとれない　can't do anything else
　………………………………… [かかえる]
うごく 動く
ウサギ　(飼いウサギ) a rabbit; (野ウサギ) a hare
ウシ 牛　(総称) cattle; (雌牛) a cow; (雄牛) a bull; (去勢した牛) an ox (複数 oxen)
うしなう 失う
うしろ 後ろ
　〜姿 ………………………………… [すがた]
うしろまえ 後ろ前に　back to front, backward
うしろめたい 後ろめたい

うすい 薄い
うすうす 〜気づく　be vaguely aware of, have a faint [vague] idea of, have a vague feeling that...
うずく　feel a piercing [throbbing] pain, smart
うずくまる　crouch (down), squat (down)
うすぐらい 薄暗い　dim, gloomy
うずまき うず巻き　a whirlpool; (小さな) an eddy; (大きな) maelstrom
うずまく うず巻く　whirl
うすめる 薄める　thin, dilute, water down
うずめる ………………………………… [うめる]
うずもれさせる　go down the drain ………………………………… [おしい]
うすれる 薄れる　fade ……… [いんしょう]
うそ
　〜つきの名人　a skillful liar　[だます]
うた 歌　a song
うたう 歌・謳う
うたがい 疑い
うたがう 疑う
うたがわしい 疑わしい
うたたね うたた寝　a doze …… [ここち]
うだる 〜ように暑い　sweltering, scorching ………………………… [あつい²]
うたれる 打たれる　(感動する) be struck by ………………………… [きょうい]
　・be impressed ……………… [ねつい]
うち 内
うち 家
うちあける 打ち明ける　confide, confess, tell
　・open up *one's* heart to
　………………………………… [おもいきって]
うちあげる 打ち上げる　(花火を) set off, shoot up; (人工衛星・ロケットを) launch, send up; (フライを) hit (a fly)
　(人工衛星を) put a satellite into orbit
　………………………………… [じんこう²]
うちあわせる 打ち合わせる　arrange, make arrangements
うちおとす 打ち落とす　shoot down
うちかつ 打ち勝つ　conquer
　・overcome ……………………… [こんなん]

うちがわ 内側　the inside
　～の　inside, inner
　～に[で]　inside, within
うちき 内気
うちきる うち切る　cut off, break off, put an end to
うちけす 打ち消す　(うわさなどを) deny; (声明などを) negate
うちこむ 打ち込む　drive *something* in ················[しっかり]
　・throw *oneself* into ········[わすれる]
　打ち込んでいる　be †caught up [immersed, involved] in [せいさく²]
うちとける 打ち解ける
　(…する)うちに　while ········[こぼれる]
うちひしがれた　crushed ············[たび]
うちゅう 宇宙　the universe; (大気圏外) space
　～の　space, cosmic
　～旅行　space travel
　～飛行士　a spaceman, an astronaut
　～船　a spaceship, a spacecraft
　～ステーション　a space station
うちょうてん 有頂天
うちよせる 打ち寄せる　(波が) break upon, beat upon (the shore), dash against (the shore)
うちわ　*uchiwa*, a fan, a Japanese (round) fan
　～であおぐ　fan
うちわ 内輪　the family circle, family (and close friends)
　～の　private, between ourselves [themselves]
うちわもめ 内輪もめ　internal squabbling
　～する　squabble between ourselves [themselves]
うつ ～になる　get depressed
　～病　(psychotic) depression
うつ 打・撃つ
うっかり
　・carelessly ··················[つく¹]
　・inadvertently ············[さっかく]
　・accidentally ···············[のむ]
　～した間違い　a careless mistake
　·······························[ちゅうい]
うつくしい 美しい

うつくしさ 美しさ　beauty
うっけつ うっ血　congestion
うつす 写す
うつす 映す
うつす 移す
うったえる 訴える
うってつけ ～の　perfect
　～の人だ　be just the man [woman] for *something*, be right man [woman] for *something*, be made to be *something*, be cut out †for [to be] *something*
　～のものだ　be just the thing, be (just) the right *something* for *someone*, be an ideal *something* for *someone*
うっとうしい
うっとり
うつぶせ ～になる　lie on *one's* face, lie face down
うつむく　look down, bend [drop] *one's* head
　・lower *one's* head ·········[そめる]
うつりかわり 移り変わり　change
うつる 写る
うつる 映る
　(テレビが) get a picture ·····[こわれる]
うつる 移る
うつわ 器　(入れ物) a container; (食卓用) a dish
うで 腕
　(技) skill ·····················[こえる]
　～を磨く　perfect *one's* skill [みがく]
うでずもう 腕ずもう　arm wrestling
うでたてふせ 腕立て伏せ　a push-up
うでどけい 腕時計　a wrist watch
うでまえ 腕前　skills ·········[ちかづく]
　・*one's* ability ··············[ほれる]
うとい 疎い
うとうと ～する　doze off, nods off, fall [drop] into a doze
ウナギ 鰻　an eel ··············[つかむ]
うなじ　the back [nape] of the neck
うなずく　nod
うなだれる　hang *one's* head, droop
うなる
うぬぼれる
　うぬぼれて　conceited ·······[きこえる]

うねる (道・川などが) wind; (波が) roll, swell
うのみ ～にする swallow
うばう 奪う
うぶ ～な innocent, naive, be just a kid
ウマ 馬 a horse
　雌～ a mare
　子～ (雄の) a colt; (雌の) a filly
　小～ a pony
　～の耳に念仏 ……………………[みみ]
うまい
　・right ………………………………[ことば]
うまく
　・tactfully ……………………………[にげる]
　・cleverly ……………………………[のせる]
　・skillfully ……………………………[やくす]
　～いく go well, turn out well [いく]
　・work out ……………………………[けいさん]
　(人と) get along with *someone* well
　………………………………………[わかれる]
　～運ぶ progress [move] smoothly
　………………………………………[はこぶ]
　～やる do *something* right ……[なに]
うまる 埋まる (物が) be buried; (場所が) be filled (up) with *something* [*someone*]; (席が) be occupied; (席が全体的に) be filled (up); (欠員・ポストが) be filled (up)
うまれ 生まれ birth
　～は by birth
うまれかわる 生まれ変わる be born again ………………………………[する²]
うまれつき 生まれつき by nature, naturally
　～の natural, born
　・innate, inborn ……………………[せいしつ]
うまれる 生まれる
　(出現する) emerge ………………[しそう]
　生まれた土地 one's birthplace
　………………………………………[ねがう]
　生まれたばかりの newborn [なめる]
うみ 海 a sea; (大洋, 大海) an ocean
うみのひ 海の日 Marine Day
うみべ 海辺 a beach, a seashore
うむ 産・生む
ウメ 梅(の木) a Japanese apricot (tree)

～の木 a plum tree …………[～ぶり]
うめあわせ 埋め合わせをする make up for
うめく groan, moan
うめたて 埋め立て地 reclaimed land
…………………………………………[うめる]
うめる 埋める
うやまう 敬う
うやむや ～な obscure, vague; (どっちつかずの) noncommittal; (未決定の) undecided, up in the air
　～にする leave *something*
　†undecided [up in the air]
　～になる end in obscurity
うよく 右翼 (政治の) the Right, the right wing; (人) a right-winger
うら 裏
　～の空地 the empty lot out back
　…………………………………………[たつ³]
うらおもて 裏表のある (性格が) double-faced, two-faced; (人) a double-dealer
　～のない honest, straight, straightforward
うらがえし 裏返しに inside out; (表側を下に向けて) face down
うらがえす 裏返す turn over
うらぎり 裏切り treachery ……[せめる²]
うらぎる 裏切る
　・sell out ……………………………[かね]
　・stab *someone* in the back
　…………………………………………[はくじょう]
うらぐち 裏口入学する buy *one's* way into school …………………[おびえる]
ウラジオストック Vladivostok
うらづける 裏付ける support, prove
うらどおり 裏通り a back street [め¹]
うらない 占い fortunetelling
　・a reading …………………………[ふしぎ]
　～師 a fortuneteller
うらなう 占う tell *someone's* fortune
うらはら (…とは)裏腹だ (be) contrary to
　(…とは)裏腹に in spite of
うらみ 恨み
　～をのむ swallow *one's* resentment
　…………………………………………[のむ]
うらむ 恨む

うらめしい 恨めしい
うらやましい
うらやむ
うららか 〜な bright, fine, beautiful
　〜に bright(ly), finely, beautifully
うりあげ 売上(高) sales, the proceeds
　・the amount sold ············[げんざい]
　〜が増える sales increase ·····[こうか]
　〜を伸ばす increase *one's* sales
　································[のばす]
うりきれる 売り切れる be sold out, be
　[go] out of stock
うりこむ 売り込む （商品を）sell, push
　(*one's* products), promote; (アピー
　ルする) sell, promote, advertise,
　publicize, appeal to *someone*
うりだし 売り出し （安売り）a bargain
　sale
うりば 売り場 a counter
　・a section of the store ············[など]
うりもの 売り物 an article for sale;
　（掲示の文句）For Sale.
うる 売る
うるうどし うるう年 a leap year
うるおい 潤い （湿り気）moisture
うるおう 潤う （利益を得る）profit,
　make a profit (on)
ウルグアイ Uruguay
うるさい
　・irritating ·····················[とめる¹]
　・annoying ·················[しかたがない]
　・make a racket ··················[なく²]
　・be a nuisance ·····················[きんじょ]
　（こだわる）be particular about
　································[しょうばい]
うるし lacquer ·····················[まける]
うれしい
　・smiling ·····························[め¹]
うれしがる be glad, be happy, be
　pleased
うれしさ (a) joy, (a) delight
うれしなき うれし泣きする weep with
　joy ································[なく¹]
うれしなみだ うれし涙 tears of joy
　································[なみだ]
うれっこ 売れっ子の very popular,
　sought-after, hot-selling,
　successful, in the limelight

うれゆき 売れ行き sale;
　（需要）demand
うれる 売れる
うろうろ 〜する walk around, loiter
　around, hang around
うろおぼえ うろ覚えだ not remember
　something clearly, *one's* memory is
　vague (on *something*)
うろこ a scale
うろたえる
うろつく wander about, loiter
　・hang around ··················[あやしい]
うわがき 上書き （表書き）a cover page
　[letter], a memo, a memorandum;
　（コンピュータデータの）overwriting
　〜する （コンピュータデータを）
　overwrite
　〜保存する （コンピュータデータを）
　save
うわき 浮気
うわぎ 上着 a coat, a jacket
うわさ
　・the talk ···························[たね]
うわて （…より）上手だ be better than
　someone, be above *someone*, be
　ahead of *someone*
うわのそら 上の空で absentmindedly,
　someone's mind is somewhere else
うわばき 上ばき indoor sneakers,
　slippers
うわべ 上辺 the surface, an
　appearance, show
　〜だけの (only) superficial
　〜を飾る keep up appearances
　〜を繕う (manage to) save
　appearances
うわまわる 上回る （越す）exceed; （より
　多い）be more than
うわやく 上役 *one's* superior ········[め¹]
うん 運
うんえい 運営 management [せきにん]
　〜する run, administer, manage
　〜委員会 a steering committee
うんが 運河 a canal
うんざり
　〜だ be fed up with ············[きそく]
うんそう 運送する transport
　〜会社 a transport company

うんちん 運賃 (貨物の)freight; (旅客の)a (passenger) fare
～値上げ a fare hike ……………[はば]

うんてん 運転する (車を)drive; (機械を)operate, work
～間隔 the time between trains ……………[のびる]
～を誤る lose control of the car ……………[ぶつかる]
～手 (自動車の)a driver; (電車の)a motorman, a driver; (列車の)an engine driver, 《米》an engineer; (機械・バスの)an operator; (お抱えの)a chauffeur

うんどう 運動
～する work out ……………[おもう]
～神経 reflexes ……………[しんけい]

うんめい 運命
～を切り開く forge *one's* own destiny ……………[ひらく]
～をともにする throw *one's* lot in with *someone's* ……………[はら]
～とあきらめる write it off to fate ……………[あきらめる]

エ

え 柄 (道具の)handle; (機械の)a grip; (刀・やりなどの)a haft

え 絵 a picture; (彩色画)a painting; (単彩画)a drawing

エアコン an air conditioner
～付きの air-conditioned

エアロビクス aerobics

えいえん 永遠 eternity
～に eternally, forever
～の eternal

えいが 映画 a movie, a film; (総称)the movies
～監督 a director ……………[だす]
～を作る make a film [movie] ……………[つくる]
～館 a movie house [theater]

えいかいわ 英会話 English conversation

えいき 英気を養う restore *one's* spirit ……………[やしなう]

えいきゅうし 永久歯 a permanent tooth ……………[は]

えいきょう 影響
(…の)影響で due to ……………[みだれる]
社会的～ a social impact ……………[こうきょう]

えいぎょう 営業

えいご 英語 English

えいこう 栄光 glory ……[かがやかしい]

えいじゅう 永住する settle down, reside permanently (in)

エイズ AIDS (=Acquired Immune Deficiency Syndrome)

えいせい 衛生

えいせい 衛星 a satellite
～放送 satellite broadcasting; (番組)satellite broadcasts
～中継される be transmitted by [via] satellite

えいぶん 英文 English, an English sentence

えいやく 英訳 English translation
～する translate [put] into English

えいゆう 英雄 a hero

えいよう 栄養
・nutrition ……………[ふちゅうい]
～を取る eat nutritious food [とる¹]

えいわ 英和辞典 an English-Japanese dictionary

エース an ace pitcher ……………[おさえる]

エープリルフール an April fool
・April Fool's Day ……………[だます]

エール a cheer, a yell

えがお 笑顔 a smile

えがく 描く

えき 液 liquid; (液汁)juice

えき 駅 a (railroad) station
～前で in front of the station ……………[きめる]
～前から from in front of the station ……………[でる]
～の北口 the north entrance of a station ……………[くち]
～員 a station employee
・a station attendant ……………[わたす]
～長 a stationmaster

えきしゃ 易者 a fortune-teller [みる]

エキス extract

エキスパート an expert

エキゾチック ～な exotic

えきたい 液体(の) liquid
えきでん 駅伝 *ekiden*, a long-distance relay race
エクアドル Ecuador
えくぼ a dimple
えげつない obnoxious, mean, unscrupulous
エゴイスト an egoist, an egotist, a self-centered person
エゴイズム egotism ………… [かたまり]
えこひいき 〜する be partial to, favor, give preference to, be unfair
エコロジー ecology
えさ 〜を与える feed ……… [あたえる]
えじき a prey, a victim
エジプト Egypt
　〜の Egyptian
　〜人 an Egyptian; (全体) the Egyptians
えしゃく 会釈する make a (slight) bow (to *someone*), give *someone* a (slight) bow, nod (to *someone*) (slightly), give *someone* a nod
エスカルゴ (an) escargot ……… [たね]
エスカレーター an escalator
えだ 枝 a branch; (小枝) a twig; (大枝) a bough
　〜を払う trim tree branches [はらう]
えたい 得体の知れない mysterious, dubious, strange
えだぶり 見事な枝ぶり branches make a beautiful pattern ……… [〜ぶり]
エチオピア Ethiopia
　〜の Ethiopian
　〜人 an Ethiopian; (全体) the Ethiopians
エチケット etiquette
エッセイ an essay
エッチ 〜な dirty, dirty-minded
エヌジーオー (NGO) an NGO, a nongovernmental organization
エヌピーオー (NPO) an NPO, a nonprofit organization
エネルギー energy
えのぐ 絵の具 paints, colors
　油〜 oils, oil colors
　水彩〜 water colors
えはがき 絵葉書 a (picture) post card

エビ (イセエビなど大型の) a lobster; (クルマエビなど中型の) a prawn; (小エビ) a shrimp
エピソード an episode, an anecdote
エプロン an apron
エベレスト Mt. Everest, Chomolungma
えほん 絵本 a picture book
えもの 獲物 (狩猟の)《集合的に》game; (1回の漁〔猟〕の) a catch
　・a prey
えら a gill ……………… [こきゅう]
エラー an error
えらい 偉い
えらぶ 選ぶ
　・pick out ………………… [あわせる]
えり 襟 a collar
　〜元 the neck
　〜足 the nape of the neck
エリート elite ………………… [はな]
えりごのみ えり好みする be particular [fussy] about, be choosy about
えりまき 襟巻き a muffler, a scarf
える 得る
エルサレム Jerusalem
エルニーニョ El Niño
エレベーター《米》an elevator,《英》a lift
えん 円 (円形) a circle; (貨幣単位) yen (略 ¥)
　〜高 the strong yen
　〜安 the weak yen
えん 縁
えんえん 延々と(続く) (go) on and on, for ages
えんか 演歌 a Japanese ballad
えんかい 宴会 a dinner party, a banquet
　・a reception ……………… [わく²]
　〜を開く hold [give] a dinner party
えんかつ 円滑な smooth ……… [やくめ]
えんがわ 縁側 a veranda(h)
えんがん 沿岸 the coast
えんき 延期
えんぎ 演技 a performance
 ……………………………… [はくりょく]
えんぎ 縁起
えんきょく 婉曲

えんげい 園芸 gardening; (学問としての) horticulture
えんげい 演芸 entertainments
えんげき 演劇 a play, (the) drama
エンゲルけいすう エンゲル係数 Engel's coefficient ……[ひくい]
えんし 遠視の long-sighted, far-sighted
エンジニア an engineer
えんしゅう 円周 a circumference
えんじゅく 円熟
〜した mature
〜味を増す become mellow [mature]
・mellow ……[とも]
えんしゅつ 演出する produce, direct
〜家 《米》a producer, 《英》a director
えんじょ 援助 help
・assistance, aid, support [もとめる]
〜する help, assist, aid
えんしょう 炎症 inflammation
えんじる 演じる play, act, perform
エンジン an engine
えんしんりょく 遠心力 centrifugal force ……[はたらく]
エンスト 〜を起こす stall
えんせい 遠征 an expedition; (スポーツなどの) a tour
えんぜつ 演説 an address
・a speech ……[わく¹]
〜する speak, make a speech, give an address
えんせん 沿線に[の] along, on
えんそう 演奏
えんそく 遠足 an excursion
・outing ……[がくねん]
・a class trip ……[ぜんたい]
〜に行く go on an excursion [いく]
えんだん 演壇 a platform ……[ゆうゆう]
えんだん 縁談 (申し入れ) an offer of marriage; (縁組) a match
・marriage plans ……[こわす]
・a marriage talk ……[たてる¹]
えんちょう 延長する extend, lengthen, prolong
〜戦 《野球》extra-inning game
エンドウ 〜豆 a pea

えんどう 沿道の人々 the crowd along the way ……[げきれい]
えんとつ 煙突 a chimney
エントリー (an) entry
えんばん 円盤 a disk, a disc
空飛ぶ〜 a flying saucer, a UFO
〜投げ the discus (throw)
えんぴつ 鉛筆 a pencil
〜削り a pencil sharpener
えんぽう 遠方 a distant place, distance
えんまん 円満
〜な happy; (仲の良い) harmonious; (性格が) amiable; (取り決め・関係などが) amicable
〜に解決する be settled amicably ……[かいけつ]
えんゆうかい 園遊会 a garden party ……[もよおす]
えんりょ 遠慮
〜させていただきます……[せっかく]
〜のない informal ……[あいだ]
〜なく(…する) feel free to *do* ……[ぎもん]

オ

お 尾 a tail
〜を振る wag *one's* tail ……[うれしい]
〜を引く (影響が残る) have a long-lasting effect (on)
・leave *one's* mark on ……[ひく]
おあいこ 〜だ be even
おあいにくさま (That's) Too bad./(I'm) Sorry.
おあがりください お上がりください Please come (on) in. ……[あがる]
オアシス an oasis
おあずけ お預け……[あずける]
〜にする……[しょうぶ]
おい 甥 a nephew
おい! (呼びかけ) Hey!
おいおい 〜泣き出す burst into tears ……[なく¹]
おいかえす 追い返す
おいかける 追いかける
おいこす 追い越す
おいこまれる 追い込まれる be cornered

- be driven into ……[のっぴきならない]
おいこみ 追い込みに入る put on a spurt
- make a final push ………[おいこむ]

おいこむ 追い込む
おいしい
　おいしく deliciously …………[やける]
　おいしくなる taste better ……[にる²]
おいそれと 〜(でき)ない not come right and *do*, not up and *do*
おいだす 追い出す
おいたち 生い立ち *one's* background, *one's* early history
- *one's* upbringing ………[くち]

おいつく 追いつく
おいつめる 追い詰める drive *someone* into a corner
おいてきぼり 置いてきぼりにする leave *someone* behind ………[はくじょう]
おいぬく 追い抜く pass; (しのぐ) outdo, get ahead of
おいはらう 追い払う drive away, disperse
おいる 老いてなお盛ん be getting old but still up and around ……[なお]
おう 王 a king
おう 負う (背負う) bear, carry on *one's* back; (恩を被る) owe; (責任・義務を) take *something* on *oneself*, assume
おう 追う
おうい 王位 the throne, the crown
おうえん 応援 (声援) cheering …[こえ]
　〜する (声援する) cheer; (助力する) help, aid, assist
- root for ………[かげ²]
　〜団 a cheering section
　〜団員 a cheerleader
おうかん 王冠 a crown
おうぎ 扇 a folding fan
　〜形の fan-shaped
おうきゅう 応急 first-aid, temporary, make-shift
おうこく 王国 a kingdom
おうごん 黄金 gold
　〜の golden, gold
おうじ 王子 a prince
おうじょ 王女 a princess

おうじる 応じる
おうしん 往診 a house call
おうせい 旺盛だ (食欲が) have a keen appetite ………………[しょくよく]
　(知識欲が) have a passion for ……………………[けんきゅう]
おうせつ 応接
　〜間 a drawing room, a reception room; 《米》 a parlor
　〜室 (会社の) a reception room
おうたい 応対する receive, handle
- wait on ………………[もむ]
おうだん 横断する cross, go across
　〜歩道 a pedestrian crossing
- a crosswalk ………………[よこぎる]

おうちゃく 横着
おうと 嘔吐する vomit
おうひ 王妃 a queen, an empress
おうふく 往復
おうへい 横柄
おうべい 欧米 Europe and America, the West
おうぼ 応募する apply for
　〜者 an applicant ………[こえる]
おうほう 横暴
オウム a parrot
おうよう 応用
おうよう 鷹揚
おうりょう 横領する embezzle
おえらがた お偉方 a big name, a dignitary
- important people ………[きおくれ]

おえる 終える
おおあな 大穴 a dark horse ……[あな]
　〜を当てる win on a †dark horse [long shot]
- bet on a long shot ………………[て]

おおあめ 大雨 a heavy rain
おおい 多い
おおい 覆い a cover; (光をさえぎる) a shade
おおいそぎ 大急ぎで in a great hurry, in great haste
- in a big hurry ………………[したく]

おおいに 大いに
おおいり 大入り a full house
　〜満員 a tremendous turnout
　………………………[まんいん]

おおう 覆う
オーエル (OL) a female office worker
おおがた 大型の large-scale
オオカミ 狼 a wolf
おおきい 大きい
おおきく 大きく greatly ……[こうぞう]
　〜扱う report widely ……[あつかう]
　〜分かれる (意見などが) be widely split (over) …………[わかれる]
おおきさ 大きさ size
おおく 多く
オークランド (ニュージ) Auckland
オーケー OK, okay, all right
　〜する (承諾する) approve, okay
おおげさ 大げさ
　〜な exaggerating ……………[みぶり]
オーケストラ an orchestra
おおごえ 大声で in a loud voice, loudly
おおざっぱ 大ざっぱ
おおさわぎ 大騒ぎ a fuss [あっけない]
おおしごと 大仕事 hard work
　…………………………[つかれる]
オーストラリア Australia
　〜の Australian
　〜人 an Australian; (全体) the Australians
オーストリア Austria
　〜の Austrian
　〜人 an Austrian; (全体) the Austrians
おおぜい 大勢
　〜の前 in front of the crowd
　…………………………[くつじょく]
おおちがい 大違いだ be quite different from, be far from, be a far cry from
おおて 大手の big, large, major
オーディション an audition
おおどおり 大通り a main street
　…………………………[つかまえる]
オートバイ a motorcycle, a motorbike
オードブル hors d'oeuvres
オートメーション automation
オーナー the owner
オーバー (服)《米》an overcoat, a coat;《英》a greatcoat
オーバー

〜な表現 an overblown expression
　…………………………[ひょうげん]
〜する exceed ……………[よさん]
おおはば 大幅な great, sharp
　・substantial ……………[はば]
　〜に substantially, sharply
　・greatly ……………[のばす]
　・a great deal ……………[のびる]
オービー (OB) (卒業生) a graduate, an alumnus
おおぶりの 大ぶりの large ……[〜ぶり]
オーブン an oven
おおみそか 大晦日 New Year's Eve, the last day of the year
オオムギ 大麦 barley
おおめ 多め・大目
おおもじ 大文字 a capital letter
おおもの 大物 a VIP
　・a prominent figure, a big shot
　…………………………[けいざい]
　・an important figure ……[しょうらい]
おおや 大家 one's landlord [ことわる]
おおやけ 公の public; (公式の) official
　〜にする make something public [known]
　〜になる be made public, come to light
おおゆき 大雪 a heavy snow, a heavy snowfall
おおらか
オール (かい) an oar
おか 丘 a hill; (高台) heights
おかあさん お母さん mother; (子ども用語) mamma, mom, mum
おかえし お返しする (お礼) give something in return; (仕返し) pay someone back, get back at someone
おかげ お陰
　…のお陰で thanks to ……[てつだう]
　お陰様で thanks ……………[げんき]
おかしい
　・odd ……………………[こうどう]
　・not make sense ……………[りろん]
おかす 犯す (罪を) commit; (規則を) break, violate
おかす 侵す (領土を) invade; (権利などを) violate
　(権利などを) infringe upon …[けんり]

おかす 冒す （危険を）risk, face (a danger)
おかず a (side) dish
おかっぱ a bob
おかどちがい お門違いだ bark up the wrong tree
おがむ 拝む worship, pray
オカルト (the) occult
おがわ 小川 a brook, a stream
おかわり お代わり another helping ……………………………………[かわり]
おかん 悪寒がする feel [get the] chills ……………………………………[ふるえる]
おき 沖の off shore ……………[てん]
〜に offshore ……………[うかぶ]
・far from (the) shore ……[ながす]
〜おき 〜置き
おきあがる 起き上がる get up, rise; （上半身で）sit up
おきざり 置き去りにする leave *something* behind
・abandon ……………[れいこく]
おきている 起きている be up, sit up
おきどけい 置き時計 a table clock
おぎなう 補う
おきにいり お気に入り(の) favorite, pet; （人・物）one's favorite, （人）one's pet
おきる 起きる
おきわすれる 置き忘れる leave *something* behind, forget
おく 置く
おく 奥
おく 億 one [a] hundred million
おくがい 屋外の outdoor, open-air
〜で outdoors, in the open air
おくさん 奥さん （妻）a wife; （呼びかけ）ma'am
おくじょう 屋上 the roof
ビルの〜 the roof of a building
……………………………………[ぼんやり]
おくて 奥手だ be slow, be a late bloomer
おくない 屋内の indoor
〜で indoors, inside
おくば 奥歯に物が挟まったような話し方をする be not quite frank ……[は]
おくびょう 臆病

おくまった 奥まった secluded, inmost
・off, back from …………[おく²]
おくやみ お悔やみ (a) condolence
〜に行く pay a visit of condolences
おくゆき 奥行き depth
おくらせる 遅らせる delay; （延期する）put off
おくりかえす 送り返す send back, return
おくりさき 送り先 an address, a destination; （受取人）an addressee, a receiver
おくりもの 贈り物 a present, a gift
おくる 送る
おくる 贈る
おくれ 大幅な遅れ long delay
……………………………………[あやまる]
おくれて 遅れて late
・behind schedule ……[とうちゃく]
おくれる 遅れる
・lag behind ……………[きんだい]
（時計が）lose ……………[〜ずつ]
おけ 桶 a tub; （手桶）a pail, a bucket
おこがましい 厚かましい, impertinent
・presumptuous ……………[おく¹]
おこす 起こす
おごそか 厳か
おこたる 怠る neglect
おこない 行い
おこなう 行う
おごり ……………………………[おごる]
おこりっぽい 怒りっぽい irritable, temperamental, quick-tempered, get offended easily
おこる 怒る
真っ赤になって〜 turn bright red with anger ……………[あかい]
怒られる get *someone* mad at
……………………………………[いけない]
怒って angrily
・in anger ……………[かためる]
怒りっぽい quick-tempered
おこる 起こる・興る
おごる
おさえる 押さえる・抑える
・suppress ……………[むいしき]
（気持ちを）抑え切れない can not contain ……………[こうふん]

おさがり お下がり a hand-me-down
おさと お里が知れる……………[みせる]
おさない 幼い
おさなご 幼子 a small child ….[のこす]
おさななじみ 幼なじみ a childhood friend, a friend from *one's* childhood
おざなり 〜の perfunctory, shoddy
おさまる 収・納まる
おさまる 治まる
　(けんかが) get settled …………[おれる]
おさめる 収・納める
おさめる 治・修める
おさらい (a) review; (復習) an exercise
　〜する review, exercise
おさん お産 (a) childbirth, (a) delivery
おし 押し
おじ 伯父・叔父 an [*one's*] uncle
おしあう 押し合う push one another
おしい 惜しい
おじいさん (自分の) *one's* grandfather; (老人) an old man
おしいれ 押し入れ a closet
おしえ 教え a teaching, teachings, a lesson; (教義) a doctrine
　〜子 *one's* pupil, *one's* student
おしえる 教える
おしかける 押しかける (群衆が) throng, mob, crowd into *somewhere*; (断りなく) barge in, invite [force] *oneself* to *somewhere*
おじぎ お辞儀する bow (to), make a bow (to)
おじけづく lose *one's* nerve ……[いざ]
・get cold feet ……………………[よほど]
おしこむ 押し込む push in, thrust in
おしだす 押し出す push out (of)
おしつける 押しつける (力ずくで) press [push] against; (強制する) force *something* (on)
　人に仕事を〜 dump work on others
　……………………………………[じぶん]
おしつぶす 押しつぶす crush, squash
おしどりふうふ おしどり夫婦 a couple of lovebirds ……………[なか²]
おしのける 押しのける push away, push aside
おしまい the end
　もう〜だ be finished／It's all over (for *someone*).
おしむ 惜しむ (時間・金などを)《ふつう否定文で》spare; (残念に思う) regret, be sorry
おしめ a diaper ……………………[ぬらす]
おしゃべり chatter ……………[いらいら]
・chattering ………………[いいかげん]
・constant talking …………[へいこう²]
(人) a chatterbox ……………[しゃべる]
・a real talker ……………………[した²]
〜な talkative ……………………[よう²]
〜する chatter, talk idly; (楽しく) chat
have a chat with …………[きばらし]
おしゃれ 〜な refined, chic, fashionable; (凝った) fancy(-looking)
〜だ (女性) dress smartly, be a good [smart] dresser; (男性) be a dandy
〜する dress *oneself* up, be (all) dressed up
おじゃん 〜だ fall through, come to nothing, go up in smoke／That's that.／It's all over (with *someone*).
おじょうさん お嬢さん (若い女性) a young lady; (娘) a daughter; (呼びかけ) Miss
〜育ち a sheltered daughter [せけん]
おしょく 汚職 corruption
　…………………………………[はらだたしい]
・bribery ……………………………[かくす]
〜の corrupt ………………………[おう]
〜事件 a corruption scandal
　……………………………………[ぎせい]
おしろい (face) powder
〜をつける powder
おす 押す
おす 雄 a male, a he
〜の male, he-〜
オスロ Oslo
オセアニア Oceania
〜の Oceanic
おせじ お世辞
・flattery ……………………………[くち]
口先だけの〜 empty flattery …[くち]

～を言う　play up to ………[おもわく]
おせっかい
　・meddling …………………[かなう]
オセロゲーム　the Othello game　[こる]
おせん　汚染　pollution, contamination
　環境～　environmental pollution
　～されている　be contaminated
おそい　遅い
おそう　襲う　attack
おそかれはやかれ　遅かれ早かれ　sooner or later
おそく　遅く　(時間が) late; (速度が) slow, slowly
　～とも　at (the) latest
おそなえ　お供え　an offering
　～する　make an offering
おそらく　恐らく
おそるおそる　恐る恐る　fearfully, timidly, cautiously, nervously, hesitatingly
おそるべき　恐るべき　fearful, terrible, dreadful
おそれ　恐・畏れ
おそれる　恐・畏れる
おそろしい　恐ろしい
　恐ろしさ　terror ………………[み¹]
　・fury ………………………[すがた]
おそわる　教わる　be taught, learn, take lessons from *someone*
おそわれる　襲われる　be overcome with ……………………………[こどく]
オゾン　ozone
　～層　the ozone layer
　～層破壊　the depletion of the ozone layer, ozone depletion
おたがい　お互い ………………[たがい]
オタク　a (*something*) geek, a nerd
おたくの　your …………[こうかん¹]
おだて　～に乗せられる　be taken in by *someone's* flattery ………[のせる]
おだてる
　・butter *someone* up ………[ちょうし]
おたふくかぜ　おたふく風邪にかかる　have the mumps …………[ふくらむ]
オタマジャクシ　a tadpole ………[なる¹]
おだやか　穏やか
　～な　gentle ………………[～ぶり]
　～に　softly ………………[おさえる]

オタワ　Ottawa
おちこむ　落ち込む　(落胆する) be depressed, be down, be (down) in the dumps
おちつき　落ち着き
おちつく　落ち着く
　(決める) settle on …………[けっきょく]
おちど　落ち度　a fault, an error
おちば　落ち葉　fallen leaves ……[やく³]
おちぶれる　落ちぶれる　come down in the world
　・fall low ……………………[めぐむ]
おちめ　落ち目だ　(勢力) be on the decline [wane], be down on *one's* luck; (人気) be losing *one's* popularity
おちる　落ちる
　・land ………………………[ながす]
　(飛行機が) crash …………[たずねる¹]
おつかい　お使いに行く　go on an errand ……………………[ほうび]
　～にやる　send *someone* on an errand ……………………[ちかく]
おっくう
おっちょこちょい　a scatterbrain
おっと　夫　a husband
おっと！　Oops!
おてあげ　お手上げだ　give up (on *something* [*someone*]), throw *one's* hands, can't do a thing against *something* [*someone*], be completely at a loss
おでき　a boil
おでこ　a forehead, a brow
おてつだい　お手伝いさん　a maid ……………………………[おく¹]
おてのもの　お手のものだ　be (right) up [down] *one's* alley, be (in) *one's* line, be *one's* specialty [forte]
おてん　汚点　a blot
　・a stain ……………………[けす]
おてんば　お転婆　a tomboy
おと　音　a sound; (雑音) a noise
　大きな～を立てて　with a loud crash ……………………………[たおれる]
おとうさん　お父さん　a father; (子ども用語) papa, dad, daddy
おとうと　弟　a [*one's*] brother, a

[one's] younger [little] brother
おどかす 脅かす scare, startle
おとぎばなし おとぎ話 a fairy tale, a nursery tale
おとこ 男 a man, a male, a fellow
・a guy ································[たいど]
いい〜 a nice guy ················[〜さえ]
〜の male
〜友だち a (male) friend
〜らしい manly, masculine ···[〜らしい]
〜ざかりで in the prime of his life
・in his prime as a man ········[さかり]
〜っぷりがいい manly ··········[〜ぶり]
おとしあな 落とし穴 a pit
・a pitfall ·····················[いやらしい]
おとしいれる 陥れる trap, frame
おとしだま お年玉 a New Year's present (of) money
おとしもの 落とし物 a lost article
おとす 落とす
おどす 脅す
おとずれる 訪れる visit, call on, call at
おととい the day before yesterday
おととし the year before last
おとな 大人 (男の) a man; (女の) a woman; an adult, a grown-up
〜になる grow up
おとなしい
・meek ······································[しん]
・quiet ································[せいしつ]
(動物が) tame ···················[くわえる]
おとなしさ reserve ···············[どうじ]
おとも お供する accompany [せっかく]
・join *someone* ·················[よろこぶ]
おどり 踊り dancing, a dance
おとる 劣る
劣らない be as good as ····[すこしも]
おどる 踊る
おとろえる 衰える
・slow down ·······················[いきおい]
衰えていない remain undiminished ···[せいりょく]
・as fiercely as ever ···········[いきおい]
おどろかす 驚かす surprise
おどろき 驚き (a) surprise
おどろく 驚く

・be quite amazed ················[ひろい]
〜べき surprising ············[さいきん]
おなか 〜がいっぱい be full ·······[いい]
〜をこわす get an upset stomach ···[たべる]
おながれ お流れになる be canceled, be called off ·····················[がっかり]
おなじ 同じ
おなじみ 〜の familiar ···········[なじみ]
おなら 〜をする pass gas, break wind, 《卑語》 fart
おに 鬼 a demon; (鬼ごっこの) it
〜ごっこをする play tag ······[あそぶ]
おにあい お似合い ·····················[にあう]
おにぎり お握り a rice ball ···[とりかえる]
おにもつ お荷物 a burden ······[にもつ]
おねしょ bed-wetting
〜する wet the [one's] bed
おのおの 各々
おのずから 自ずから明らか self-evident, obvious ·····[あきらか]
おば 伯母・叔母 an [one's] aunt
おばあさん (自分の) one's grandmother; (老婦人) an old woman, an elderly lady
おばけ お化け (ゆうれい) a ghost; (怪物) a monster
〜屋敷 a haunted house, a spook house
おはち お鉢が回る····················[まわる]
おび 帯 a sash, *obi*
〜に短し, たすきに長し·······[みじかい]
おびえる
おひとよし お人好し a pushover, an easy mark
〜だ be too nice for *one's* own good
おべっか 〜を使う flatter [いやらしい]
〜使い a brownnose ······[おもしろい]
オペラ an opera
おぼえ 覚え
おぼえがき 覚書を交わす sign an official memorandum with
おぼえる 覚える
オホーツク 〜海 the Sea of Okhotsk
おぼつかない (可能性) doubtful, vague; (動き) unsteady, awkward
おぼれる 溺れる

おぼろげ 〜な vague, hazy
オマーン Oman
　〜の Omani
　〜人 an Omani; (全体) the Omanis
おまいり お参りする visit (to worship at) a temple [shrine]
おまけ (割引) (a) discount
　(景品) a special gift ………[いじょう¹]
　・a prize ……………………[つく²]
おまけに (and) what's more, to boot, what is more, besides
おまもり お守り an amulet …[くるしい]
おまわりさん お巡りさん a police officer, a policeman
おみまい お見舞いに行く visit someone to express one's sympathy [みまい]
　〜の手紙 a get-well letter …[みまい]
おみやげ a present, a souvenir
　〜に買ってくる buy someone something as a present ………[ばね]
おむつ a diaper
　紙〜 a disposal diaper
オムレツ an omelet
おめい 汚名を受ける earn a disreputable image ………[み¹]
おめでとう
おも 主
おもい 重い
おもい 思い
おもいあがる 思い上がる get conceited, get too big for one's britches
おもいうかぶ 思い浮かぶ come to mind
おもいうかべる 思い浮かべる remember, picture (to oneself)
おもいがけず 思いがけず unexpectedly …………………………[くる]
おもいがけない 思いがけない
おもいきって 思い切って
　思い切った reckless ………[はらはら]
おもいきり 思い切り
　・with all one's might ………[ける]
　〜吸う breathe one's fill of …………………………[しんせん]
おもいこむ 思い込む
おもいすごし 思い過ごし
おもいだす 思い出す

　・look back on, remember
　　…………………………[なつかしい]
おもいたつ 思い立ったら once one decides to do something [こうどう]
おもいちがい 思い違い a misunderstanding
　〜をする misunderstand, take A for B, get it wrong, be mistaken
おもいつき 思いつき
おもいつく 思いつく
おもいつめる 思い詰める
おもいで 思い出
おもいどおり 思いどおり
　〜に as planned ……………[しぶい]
　〜にいく go as planned, go as we want it to ……………………[いく]
　〜にならない not get one's way
　　…………………………[ふきげん]
おもいとどまる 思いとどまる give up the idea (of doing); (自制する) check oneself, hold oneself back
おもいやり 思いやり
　・kindnesses ………………[ちょっと]
　〜のない言葉 insensitive remarks
　　…………………………[まねく]
おもいわずらう 思い煩う worry oneself (over), agonize (over) …[わずらう]
おもう 思う
　〜ように行く go the way one wants something to ……………………[ゆく]
　思ったより not as much as expected
　　…………………………[あまり]
　・than one thought …………[まとも]
おもかげ 面影 (a) trace
おもさ 重さ weight
　〜をはかる weigh
おもしろい 面白い
　面白半分 just for fun ……[はんぶん]
おもちゃ a toy
おもて 表 (表側) the face, the front, the right side; (戸外) outdoors
　(硬貨の) head ………………[うら]
　〜通り a main street …………[おく²]
　1回の〜に in the top of the first
　　…………………………[てん]
おもな[に] 主な[に] ……………[おも]
おもに 重荷 a burden, a load
おもむき 趣のある tasteful, attractive

おもわく 思惑
おもわず 思わず
おもわぬ 思わぬ unexpected [はってん]
おや 親 a parent; (両親) parents
おやしらず 親知らず a wisdom tooth
おやすみなさい お休みなさい Good night!
おやつ snack ·········[め¹]
おやゆび 親指 (手の) the thumb; (足の) the big toe
およぐ 泳ぐ swim
およそ
および 及ぶ
オランダ Holland, the Netherlands
　～の Dutch
　～人 (男) a Dutchman; (女) a Dutchwoman; (全体) the Dutch
おり 折り (機会) a chance, an occasion
　(…の)折りには when...
　～に触れて on occasion(s)
　・whenever the chance permits
　·········[ふれる]
　～よく luckily
　～あしく unluckily
オリーブ an olive
オリエンテーション (an) orientation
おりかえし 折り返し
　～地点 the turning point, the turn
おりがみ 折り紙 *origami*, paper folding
おりたたむ 折り畳む fold (up), close
　折り畳みいす a folding chair
　·········[くみたてる]
おりる 下・降りる
オリンピック the Olympic Games, the Olympics, the Olympiad
おる 折る
おる 織る weave
オルガン an organ
オルゴール a music box
おれる 折れる
オレンジ an orange
おろか 愚かな foolish, stupid
　愚かさ stupidity, foolishness
　·········[あきれる]
おろす 下・降ろす
おろそか ～にする neglect
おわび お詫び (an) apology

　～する apologize (for) ·········[わびる]
おわり 終わり
おわる 終わる
おん 恩
おんがく 音楽 music
おんきょう 音響効果 sound effects
おんけん 穏健な sound, moderate
おんこう 温厚な mild, gentle
おんし 恩師 one's former professor
　·········[つぐ]
　・one's former teacher ·········[けいい]
おんしつ 温室 a greenhouse
　～効果 the greenhouse effect
　～育ちだ have a sheltered upbringing ·········[もむ]
おんせん 温泉 a spa
　・a hot spring ·········[ほね]
おんそく 音速の壁 the sound barrier
　·········[こえる]
おんたい 温帯 a temperate zone
おんだん 温暖な mild, warm
　地球～化 global warming
おんち 音痴の tone-deaf
おんど 温度 temperature
　～をはかる take the temperature
　～計 a thermometer
おんな 女 a woman, a lady, a female, a girl
　～の female
　～らしい feminine ·········[～らしい]
　～ざかりで in the prime of her life
　・in her prime as a woman [さかり]
おんなで 女手一つで single-handedly
　·········[あげる]
　・on her own ·········[ふり¹]
　・by herself ·········[ささえる]
　・all by herself ·········[くろう]
オンブズマン (制度) an ombudsman (system)
おんぼろ ～な (荒廃した) run-down; (擦り切れた) worn-out; (おんぼろ車) a jalopy
オンライン ～の[で] online
おんりょう 音量を上げる turn up
　·········[あげる]
　～を下げる turn down ·········[さげる]
おんわ 温和な (気候が) mild; (性質が) gentle

カ

か 科 （大学・病院の）a department
（生物の）the family ……………[など]
か 課 （教材の）a lesson; （組織の）a section
カ 蚊 a mosquito
ガ 蛾 a moth
が 我を折る give in ……………[おる]
ガーゼ gauze
カーソル 《コンピュータ》the cursor
　〜をアイコンに合わせる put the cursor on the icon ………[クリック]
ガーデニング gardening
カーテン a curtain
　（厚地の）drape ……………[あわせる]
カード a card
　キャッシュ〜 a bank card
　クレジット〜 a credit card
ガードマン （護衛）a (security) guard; （ビルなどの）a watchman
ガーナ Ghana
　〜の Ghanaian
　〜人 a Ghanaian （全体）the Ghanaians
カーナビ（ゲーション） a car navigation system, a satellite-based (car) navigation system, car navigation software
カーネーション a carnation
カーブ a curve
　急〜 a sharp bend
カーマニア car mania ………[びょうき]
カール a curl
ガールフレンド a girl friend, a (female) friend
かい 甲斐
　〜がある worthwhile ……………[うつ]
かい 回
かい 会
かい 貝 a shellfish; （貝がら）a shell
かい 階
がい 害
かいいん 会員 a member
かいおうせい 海王星 Neptune
かいか 階下で［に］ downstairs
かいが 絵画コンクール a painting competition ……………[ゆうしゅう]

かいかい 開会する open
　〜式 an opening ceremony
　〜の挨拶 an opening speech [address] ……………[あいさつ]
　〜の辞を述べる address the opening of the meeting ……………[のべる]
かいがい 海外
　〜旅行をする travel overseas
　　……………[こわい、よゆう]
　〜進出を図る plan to break into foreign markets ……………[はかる]
　〜での経験 *one's* experiences abroad
　　……………[ゆういぎ]
かいかく 改革 (a) reform
　・a revision ……………[こんぽん]
　〜する reform
かいかつ 快活な cheerful
かいかぶる 買いかぶる overestimate, overrate
かいがん 海岸 the seashore, the coast, the beach, the seaside
がいかん 外観 appearance
かいぎ 会議
　〜室 a conference room ……[いいん]
かいきゅう 階級 a class; （職業上の地位）(a) rank
　上流〔中流、下層〕〜 the upper [middle, lower] class
　〜意識のある class-conscious
　　……………[いしき]
かいきょう 回教 Islam
　〜徒 a Muslim
かいきょう 海峡 a strait, a channel
かいぐん 海軍 the navy
かいけい 会計 accounting
　〜士 an accountant ……………[しかく]
　〜する （勘定を払う）pay the bill
　お〜はこちらでお願いします Please †make your payment [pay] here.
　　……………[こちら]
かいけいけんさいん 会計検査院 the Board of Audit of Japan
かいけつ 解決
　〜する （事件が）be cracked [われる]
かいけん 会見 an interview, a meeting
　記者〜 a press conference
がいけん 外見 (an) appearance, looks
　〜が立派だ be good-looking

................................[りっぱ]
かいげんれい 戒厳令　martial law
................................[しく]
～を敷く　proclaim martial law
かいこ 解雇する　discharge, dismiss, 《米》fire
かいご 介護　care
　～する　care for
　～休暇(制度)　(a) family-care leave (system)
　～保険　long-term care insurance, nursing care insurance
かいこう 開校記念日　the anniversary of the founding of the school
................................[ぶつかる]
かいごう 会合　a meeting
　～に参加する　attend a meeting
................................[できる]
がいこう 外交　diplomacy
　～の　diplomatic
　～官　a diplomat
　～政策　(a) foreign policy [せいさく¹]
　～辞令　diplomatic language
がいこく 外国
　～人　a foreigner
がいこつ 骸骨　a skeleton
かいさい 開催される　be held [きょうぎ]
　～されている　be open ……[みほん]
かいさつ 改札(口)　a wicket ……[わたす]
　・a ticket gate ………………[しめす]
かいさん 解散する　(集まりが)break up, (国会などが)be dissolved (グループが)disband ………[うしなう]
がいして 概して　generally, in general, as a rule
かいしめる 買い占める　buy up [out], corner
かいしゃ 会社
　・a firm ………………………[こげる]
　～側　management ………[こうしょう¹]
　～の帰りに　on the way home from work ………………………[つきあう]
　～を退職する　retire from work
................................[ゆうゆう]
　～を辞める　quit one's company [み¹]
　・quit work ……………………[わけ]
かいしゃく 解釈
かいしゅう 回収　a recall (for)
................................[こうぞう]
　～する　(アンケートなどを)collect; (欠陥商品などを)recall, take back
かいじゅう 怪獣　a monster
がいしゅつ 外出する　go out
　～中だ　be out ……………[ただいま]
かいしょう 甲斐性のある　dependable, reliable
　・of substance ………………[かい¹]
かいじょう 会場　a meeting place, a place of meeting
かいじょう 開場する　(何時に)doors open (at)
　～を待つ　wait for the door(s) to open ………………………[くずす]
かいじょうほあんちょう 海上保安庁　the Japan Coast Guard
かいしょく 会食　a dinner party
がいしょく 外食する　eat out …[つづく]
　～産業　the restaurant industry
................................[のびる]
かいしん 会心
かいしん 改心する　mend one's ways, reform ……………………[まこと]
かいすい 海水　sea water, seawater
　～着　a bathing suit
　～パンツ　bathing trunks
かいすいよく 海水浴　sea bathing, bathing in the sea
　～をする　bathe in the sea
　～場　a bathing [swimming] beach, a seaside resort
かいする 介する　go through someone
................................[まとも]
がいする 害する　ruin ………[けんこう]
かいせい 改正
かいせい 快晴の　very fine, fair, clear, bright and sunny
かいせつ 解説する　explain, comment (on)
かいぜん 改善する　improve, make better
かいそう 改装　remodeling ………[つく²]
　～する　remodel ………[みちがえる]
かいそう 海草　(a) seaweed
かいそう 改造する　reconstruct, remodel
　自動車の～　car customizing

·················[ひきうける]
かいそうしゃ 会葬者 a mourner [れつ]
かいぞく 海賊 a pirate
かいたく 開拓する（荒地を）reclaim;（市場などを）open up
〜者 a pioneer
かいだん 会談 a talk, a conference
〜する talk with
〜を行う hold a discussion with
·················[ほうもん]
かいだん 怪談 a ghost story [どきどき]
かいだん 階段
〜を上る climb stairs ········[くつう]
かいちく 改築する remodel
かいちく 改築中 be under reconstruction ·················[しょう]
かいちゅう 懐中電灯 a flashlight
·················[てらす]
かいちょう 会長 the chairman
かいちょう 快調
かいつう 開通する（トンネル・道路などが）open
（鉄道などが）be put through
·················[じゅうよう]
かいて 買い手 a buyer
かいてい 改訂する revise
かいてい 海底 the bottom of the sea
・the ocean floor ·················[さぐる]
〜の submarine, undersea
かいてき 快適
かいてん 回転 a turn, (a) rotation
かいてん 開店する open
〜している be open
〜したばかりの店 a newly opened store ·················[ひとしい]
ガイド a guide
かいとう 回答 an answer, a reply
会社側の〜 the company's counteroffer ·················[ける]
かいとう 解答 an answer, (a) solution
〜用紙 an answer sheet ········[べつ]
かいとう 解凍（凍った物の）thawing, defrosting;（コンピュータの圧縮データの）decompression
〜する（凍った物を）thaw (out), defrost;（コンピュータの圧縮データを）decompress, unpack, expand
がいとう 街燈 a street lamp [light]

がいとう 街頭で in the street
·················[うったえる]
かいどく お買い得 a good buy
・a bargain ·················[べんきょう]
かいぬし 飼い主 an owner, a master
がいねん 概念 a general idea, a concept
がいはく 外泊する stay out overnight
かいはつ 開発 development
〜する develop ·················[きょうどう]
かいばつ 海抜 above sea level
かいひ 会費 a membership fee
かいふく 回復 (a) recovery
〜する recover, get well
かいぶつ 怪物 a monster
かいほう 解放する liberate, set free
かいほう 介抱する look after, care fore
がいむしょう 外務省 the Ministry of Foreign Affairs (of Japan)
かいめい 解明する solve, make *something* clear
かいもく 皆目
かいもの 買い物 shopping
（買ったもの）a purchase [せいきゅう]
〜をする do (*one's*) shopping
〜に行く go shopping ·········[いく]
〜に出かける go along shopping
·················[つく²]
〜客 a customer ·········[こんざつ]
がいや 外野 the outfield
〜手 an outfielder
〜席 the outfield bleachers
かいよう an ulcer
胃〜 a gastric ulcer
がいらいご 外来語 a loan word
かいらん 回覧する pass *something* around
〜板 a bulletin ·················[まわす]
がいりゃく 概略 an outline
かいりょう 改良する improve
カイロ Cairo
かいわ 会話
かう 買う
かう 飼う
カウボーイ a cowboy
カウンター a counter
かえす 返す

かえす 帰す
かえって
カエデ 楓 a maple tree
かえり 帰り
かえりがけ 帰りがけに on *one's* way (home) ……………[おくる¹]
かえりみち 帰り道に on *one's* way home (from) …………[なくす¹]
カエル 蛙 a frog
かえる 返る
かえる 帰る
かえる 変える
かえる 換・替える
かえる 孵る hatch, be hatched
かお 顔
〜が青い look pale ……………[あおい]
〜が利く *one's* name carries weight in ……………………[ほうめん]
〜で笑って心で泣く smile on the outside and cry on the inside ………………………[こころ]
〜を赤らめる blush, turn red ……………………[あかい]
〜を上げる look up, lift *one's* eyes ……………………[あげる]
〜を見交わす exchange glances ………………………[いみ]
かおいろ 顔色
かおつき 顔つき an expression ………………………[〜よう]
かおなじみ 顔なじみ a familiar face, an acquaintance
かおぶれ 顔ぶれ the lineup, a member
かおみしり 顔見知り a casual acquaintance
かおむけ 顔向けできない can't face
かおり 香り (a) smell, a fragrance, an aroma
〜がする smell (like, of) ……[あまい]
がか 画家 a painter, an artist
かがい 課外の extracurricular
かかえて 抱えて with *something* in *one's* arms ……………[つつみ]
かかえる 抱える
かがく 化学 chemistry
〜的 chemical
〜者 a chemist
〜工業 the chemical industry ………………………[おこる²]
〜肥料 chemical fertilizers [やせる]
かがく 科学 science
〜的 scientific
〜者 a scientist
かかさない 欠かさない never fail to ………………………[さんぽ]
かかし a scarecrow
かかと a heel
かがみ 鏡 a mirror; (姿見) a looking glass
かがむ stoop down, bend forward, bend over
かがやかしい 輝かしい
かがやく 輝く
かかり 係
かかる 罹る
かかる 掛・架・懸かる
(〜にも)**かかわらず**
かかわる 関・係・拘わる
カキ 牡蛎 《貝》an oyster
かき 柿 a persimmon ……………[なる¹]
かき 下記の the following
かぎ 鍵
〜穴 a keyhole ……………[のぞく²]
事件の〜を握る hold the key to an affair ……………………[じけん]
かきうつす 書き写す copy ……[うつす¹]
かきおき 書き置き a note ………[おく¹]
かきかえる 書き換える (書き直す) rewrite; (免許などを更新する) renew
かきことば 書き言葉 written language
がきだいしょう がき大将 the strong kid on the block・a bully ………………………[おさまる¹]
かきたてる 書きたてる sensationalize ………………………[おおげさ]
かきとめ 書留の registered
〜郵便 registered mail
かきとめる 書き留める write down, make †a note [notes] of
かきとり 書き取り (a) dictation
かきね 垣根 a fence, a wall, a hedge
かきまぜる かき混ぜる mix up
かきまわす かき回す stir
かきゅうせい 下級生 an underclassman ……………[てほん]

かぎょう 家業 a family business
　〜を継ぐ continue [take on, take over] the family business ……………………[つぐ, やめる¹]
かぎり 限り
〜かぎり 〜限り
かぎる 限る
　(…とは)限らない not necessarily ……………………[のうりつ]
かく 欠く lack, be lacking (in)
　・there's a lack of ……………[いし]
かく 掻く
かく 書・描く
かく 角
かく 核 a nucleus
　〜の nuclear
　〜の持ち込み nuclear weapons being brought in ……………[ていこう]
　〜エネルギー nuclear energy
　〜戦争 a nuclear war ………[たとえば]
　〜兵器 a nuclear weapon
かく〜 各〜
かぐ 家具 (a piece of) furniture
かぐ 嗅ぐ
がくい 学位 a degree
かくう 架空の unreal, fictitious, imaginary
かくえき 各駅停車の local
かくげん 格言 a maxim
かくご 覚悟
　〜する be prepared for ……………[し]
がくし 学資 money for school ……[き]
がくしき 学識 erudition ……[そんけい]
かくしごと 隠し事をする keep *something* secret
　・conceal things from ［おもいすごし］
かくじつ 確実
　〜な accurate ………………[つかむ]
がくしゃ 学者 a scholar, a learned man
かくしゅ 各種の many [various] kinds of
　〜学校 a vocational school
かくしゅう 隔週の biweekly
　〜に biweekly, every other week
がくしゅう 学習
かくしん 確信 (a) conviction, a firm belief; (自信) confidence
　〜している be convinced [confident] (of, that)
かくしん 核心 a core …………[つく¹]
　〜に触れる touch the (very) core of the problem ………………[ふれる]
かくしん 革新的な innovative, progressive
かくす 隠す
がくせい 学生 a student
がくせつ 学説 a theory ……[とどまる]
かくだい 拡大する magnify; (写真などを) enlarge
かくだん 格段の違い a marked difference …………………[ちがい]
かくちょう 拡張する expand, enlarge
がくちょう 学長 a president of the university ……………[やめる²]
かくづけ 格付け a (credit) rating
かくてい 確定的な definite
　〜している be decided on, be settled (on), be confirmed
かくていしんこく 確定申告 a (final) income tax return
　〜をする file a [one's] tax return
カクテル a cocktail
かくど 角度 an angle
かくとく 獲得する get, win, acquire, gain
かくにん 確認
がくねん 学年
がくひ 学費 school expenses; (授業料) tuition
がくふ 楽譜 music, a score
がくぶ 学部 a college, a school, a department
　教養〜 a college of liberal arts
かくべつ 格別
かくほ 確保する secure, obtain
かくまく 角膜 a cornea
　〜の corneal
　〜炎 《医学用語》keratitis
かくめい 革命 a revolution
がくもん 学問 learning
　〜がある be well educated [じんかく]
がくや 楽屋 a dressing room [はねる]
かくりつ 確率 probability
がくりょく 学力 academic ability ……………………[のびる]

・scholastic ability ……………[さ]
がくれき 学歴 a school career, (an) educational background
かくれる 隠れる
かくれんぼう 隠れんぼう (をする) (play) hide-and-seek
がくわり 学割 a special discount for students
かけ 賭 a bet, a wager
かげ 影
かげ 陰
がけ 崖 a cliff; (絶壁) a precipice
　〜崩れ a landslide ……………[こうつう]
かけあし 駆け足する run; (ゆっくり走る) jog
かけい 家計 (予算) the (household) budget, a family budget; (生活費) living expenses
かけいぼ 家計簿をつける keep household accounts
かけがえのない irreplaceable [なくす²]
かげき 過激な radical, extreme
かげぐち 陰口 backbiting
　〜をきく backbite, speak ill of
かけごえ 掛け声 a shout of encouragement
かけざん 掛け算 multiplication
かけじく 掛け軸 a scroll …………[まく²]
かけつ 可決する pass, carry
　・approve ……………………[ぜん〜]
　〜される be adopted ………[さんせい]
かけつける 駆けつける rush to [けす]
(〜に)かけて(は)
かけひき 駆け引き (売買) bargaining; (策略) tactics
かけまわる 駆け回る run about [around]
かけよる 駆け寄る run towards ………………………………[おもわず]
かけら a fragment, a broken piece
かげり a downturn ……………[みえる]
かける 掛・架・懸ける
　・multiply ……………………[たかさ]
かける 欠ける
　・lack ………………………[せいじつ]
かける 駆ける ………………[はしる]
かける 賭ける bet (on), make a bet, wager (on)

かげん 加減
かこ 過去
かご a basket; (鳥かご) a cage
かこい 囲い (さく) a fence; (塀) a wall
かこう 囲う enclose, fence (in)
かこう 加工する (食品などを) process; (製造する) manufacture
かごうぶつ 化合物 a compound [なる¹]
かこく 過酷な harsh ……………[のむ]
かこつける …にかこつけて…する do on the pretext of *something*, use *something* as an excuse to do
かこむ 囲む
かさ 傘 an umbrella
　〜をさす put up an umbrella
　〜をつぼめる †fold up [shut] an umbrella
かさい 火災報知機 a fire alarm
かざかみ 風上の windward
かさく 佳作に入る get honorable mention ……………………[せめて]
かざしも 風下の leeward
がさつ
かさなる 重なる
かさねる 重ねる
かさばる be bulky, take up much space
カサブランカ Casablanca
かさむ pile up, mount up
かざむき 風向き the direction of the wind; (形勢) a situation
かざり 飾り
かざりけ 飾り気のない unaffected, frank, simple
かざる 飾る
　・dress *something* up …………[おもて]
かざん 火山 a volcano
　〜の噴火 a volcanic eruption [ふる²]
　活〜 an active volcano
　休〜 a dormant volcano
　死〜 an extinct volcano
かし 菓子 (ケーキ) (a) cake; (糖菓) 《米》candy, 《英》sweets
かし 貸し a loan
　貸し… *something* for rent
　〜家 《米》a house †for rent [《英》to let]
　〜衣装 clothes for rent

～ビデオ屋　a video rental shop
～金庫　a safety-deposit box
かし　歌詞　the words (of song), lyrics
かし　華氏　Fahrenheit（略 F）
かじ　火事　a fire
　～になる　a fire breaks out［こううん］
かじ　家事　household chores
　・housework ……………［てつだう］
　～を手伝う　lend a hand around the
　　house ……………………［たすける］
がし　餓死する　die of hunger, starve to
　death
かじかむ　be numb with cold
かしきり　貸し切りの　chartered,
　reserved
かしこい　賢い
かしつ　過失　(a) mistake, (an) error,
　(a) fault
かしゅ　歌手　a singer
かじゅ　果樹　a fruit
　～園　a fruit garden, an orchard
がしょう　画商　（人）an art dealer　［め¹］
　（仕事）art dealership ………［えん］
かじょうがき　箇条書きにする　itemize
かしょく　過食症　bulimia, overeating
～かしら　I wonder...
かしらもじ　頭文字　an initial, the first
　letter (of a word)
かじる
かす　貸す
かず　数
ガス　gas
　～こんろ　a gas range
かずおおく　数多くの　countless …［ひく］
かすか
カスタネット　《複数形で》castanets
カスタマイズ　customization
　～する　customize
カステラ　sponge cake
カスピかい　カスピ海　the Caspian Sea
かすみそう　かすみ草　baby's breath
かすむ
かぜ　風
　～が強い　gusty ………………［ふく¹］
かぜ　風邪
かぜあたり　風当たり　（世間の）public
　criticism, opposition
かせい　火星　Mars

かせき　化石　a fossil
かせぎ　稼ぎ　earnings
かせぐ　稼ぐ
かせつ　仮説　a hypothesis
カセット　a(n) (audio) cassette tape
かせん　下線　an underline
　～を引く　underline
がぜん　suddenly ………………［ちょうし］
かそ　過疎の　depopulated
かそう　仮装　a fancy dress, a costume
　～行列　a fancy-dress [costume]
　　parade
　～パーティー　a masquerade party
　　………………………………［おもい²］
がぞう　画像　an image ………［あざやか］
かぞえる　数える
かそく　加速する　accelerate
かぞく　家族　a family
　5人～　a family of five
　～そろって　*one's* whole family
　　………………………………［きゅうじつ］
　～サービス…………………［サービス］
ガソリン　《米》gasoline, gas;《英》
　petrol
　～スタンド　a gas [filling] station
かた　型
かた　方
かた　肩
かた（抵当）（…を)かたに　on
　something, with *something* as
　security [collateral] ……………［かす］
～かた　～方　（気付）care of（略 c/o)
カタール　Qatar
かたい　固・堅・硬い
　（毛が）coarse …………………［け］
　～本　（内容が）a serious book
　　………………………………［やわらかい］
かだい　課題　a problem, a subject;（宿
　題）homework, an assignment
かだい　過大評価する　overestimate
　・overrate, overly praise ……［ひょうか］
がたおち　がた落ちする　（値段・価値など
　が）take a nosedive;（信用をがた落
　ちさせる）destroy *someone's*
　credibility
かたがき　肩書き　a title ………［もつ］
かたく　固・堅・硬く　hard;（しっかり)
　fast, tightly;（堅固に）firmly,

かたくずれ 型崩れする lose *one's* shape ……………………………[やすい¹]
かたくるしい 堅苦しい
　～挨拶　formal greetings
　・stiff formalities …………[あいさつ]
　堅苦しく考える　take *something* seriously [strictly]
かたち 形
かたづける 片づける
　カタツムリ　a snail
かたな 刀　a sword
かたまり 固まり・塊
かたまる 固まる
かたみ 形見 a remembrance ……[とる¹]
　・a keepsake ……………………[なみだ]
かたみち 片道 one-way
　～切符 《米》a one-way ticket, 《英》a single ticket
かたむく 傾く
　・list ………………………………[しずむ]
　傾いている　be tilted …………[ななめ]
かたむける 傾ける
かためる 固める
かたやぶり 型破りの unusual, unconventional
かたよる 偏る (傾く) lean; (考えが) be biased
カタログ a catalog
かだん 花壇 a flower bed
かち 価値
～がち
かちあう かち合う clash
かちき 勝気
かちく 家畜 a domestic animal, cattle
かちぬく 勝ち抜く win *one's* way
かちめ 勝ち目はない there is no chance of winning ……[きょうそう]
かちょう 課長 a section chief [manager]
ガチョウ a goose (複数 geese)
かつ 勝つ
カツ(レツ) a (breaded and deep-fat fried) cutlet
カツオ a bonito ………………………[つる²]
かつおぶし かつお節 dried bonito ……………………………[けずる]
かっか ～する get (all) worked up, get excited, get upset, get mad
がっか 学科 (科目) a subject; (専攻の) a department
がつがつする be greedy, make a pig of *oneself* ……………………………[いやしい]
がっかり
　～した What a letdown! ……[きたい]
かっき 活気
がっき 学期 a (school) term, 《米》a semester
　1学期 the first term
がっき 楽器 a musical instrument
　管～ a wind instrument
　弦～ a string(ed) instrument
　けん盤～ a keyboard, a keyed instrument
　打～ a percussion instrument
かっきてき 画期的な epoch-making
がっきゅう 学級 a (school) class
かつぐ 担ぐ
がっくりして disappointed ……[ぬける]
かっけ 脚気 beriberi
かっこ (丸かっこ) parentheses; (角かっこ) square brackets
カッコウ a cuckoo
かっこう 格好
　・an appearance ……………[かわった]
　・a style ……………………………[ひく]
がっこう 学校 a school
　小～ an elementary school
　中～ a junior high school
　高等～ a (senior) high school
　公立～ 《米》a public school
　私立～ a private school
　美術～ an art school ………[そだてる]
　～教育 school education
　～生活 *one's* school life
　～を休む stay home from school ……………………………[だいじ]
　～をやめる quit school ……[～らしい]
がっしょう 合唱 (a) chorus
　～する sing in chorus
　～団 a chorus group …………[ちゅう]
がっしり ～した (人の体格が) muscular; (物が堅固な) firm
かっせいたん 活性炭 activated carbon ……………………………[けす]
かつて

・in former times ·················[ながす]
かって 勝手
　〜な　arbitrary ·················[ふれる]
かっと
かつどう 活動
　〜を行う　carry on activities [そしき]
かっぱつ 活発
カップ　a cup
がっぺい 合併　a merger ·········[じけん]
かつやく 活躍
かつよう 活用する　make (good) use of
　最大限に〜　make the most of
かつら　a wig, a hair piece
かつりょく 活力　vitality, energy
かてい 仮定する　assume, suppose
かてい 家庭
　〜の事情で　because of *one's* family
　·················[あきらめる]
　・for family reason
　〜サービスをする··················[せめる²]
かてい 課程　a course
かていか 家庭科　home economics
　·················[せんたく]
かていきょうし 家庭教師　a (home)
　tutor ················[やとう]
　〜をする　give *someone* private
　lessons ·················[ぜひ]
かど 角
かとう 下等な　low, mean
カトマンズ　Katmandu
かな 仮名　*kana*, the Japanese
　syllabary
　〜が振ってある ·····················[ふる¹]
かなう
　・suit ·················[このみ]
かなしい 悲しい
かなしみ 悲しみ
かなしむ 悲しむ
カナダ　Canada
　〜の　Canadian
　〜人　a Canadian; (全体) the
　Canadians
かなものや 金物屋　(人) a hardware
　man; (店) a hardware store
かならず 必ず
　・be bound to *do* ·············[はたらく]
かなり
カナリヤ　a canary

かなわない （勝てない）be no match for
　someone, can't beat [touch]
　someone, not stand a chance
　against *someone*
　・not measure up to *someone*, can't
　match *someone* ·················[かなう]
かなわない （参ってしまう）be no
　match for *something*, can't stand
　something ·················[かなう]
カニ　a crab
がにまた がに股　がに股の　bow-legged
　·················[ぶかっこう]
かにゅう 加入する　join, enter, become
　a member (of)
かね 金
　〜を稼ぐ　earn money ·········[わたる]
　〜に困っている　be pressed for
　money ·················[かね]
　・have money problems ·········[じつ]
　〜がものを言う　Money talks. [いう]
かね 鐘　a bell
かねづかい 金遣いが荒い　be too free
　with money, be a spendthrift,
　spend money carelessly
　[extravagantly] ·················[あらい¹]
〜かねない
かねもうけ 金儲けの　moneymaking
　·················[うまく]
かねもち 金持ち
かねる 兼ねる
かのう 化膿　an infection　[しょうどく]
かのう 可能
かのじょ 彼女　she; (彼女の) her; (彼女
　を、彼女に) her; (彼女のもの) hers;
　(彼女自身) herself; (恋人) a [*one's*]
　girlfriend
カバ　a hippopotamus
カバー
かばう 庇う　stand up for, protect
かばん 鞄　a bag, a briefcase
かはんしん 下半身　the lower half of
　the body
　・from the waist down ·········[まひ]
かはんすう 過半数　the greater part
　(of), the majority
　〜に達する　reach a majority
　·················[たっする]
カビ　(青かび) mold; (白カビ) mildew

〜の生えた moldy
〜が生える get moldy ………[ふるい]
がびょう 画鋲 a thumbtack;《英》a drawing pin
かびん 花瓶 a vase
かぶ 株 (切り株) a stump; (株式) a stock,《英》a share
カブ 蕪 a turnip
カブール Kabul
かぶしき 株式会社 an incorporated company, ... Inc.
カプセル a capsule
かぶと a helmet
カブトムシ a beetle
かぶぬし 株主 a shareholder, a stockholder
〜総会 a shareholders' [stockholders'] (general) meeting
かぶりつく bite into ………[ぬける]
かぶる
かぶれる (皮膚が) get a rash; (夢中になる) be influenced by
かふん 花粉 pollen
〜症 hay fever
かべ 壁
かべん 花弁 a petal
かほう 家宝 a family heirloom 〔くう〕
かほご 過保護の overprotective
………………[さまたげる]
カボチャ a pumpkin
かまう 構う
かまえる 構える ready ………[ねらう]
・hold *one's* stance ………[ふう]
カマキリ a mantis
(…に)かまける be busy with 〔かてい〕
がまん 我慢
〜する be satisfied with …[ぜいたく]
かみ 神 a god; (キリスト教の) God
〜を信じる believe in God
かみ 紙 paper
かみ 髪 hair ………[け]
〜をとく[すく] comb *one's* hair
〜にブラシをかける brush *one's* hair
〜を切って[刈って]もらう have *one's* hair cut
かみがた 髪型 *one's* hairstyle 〔うとい〕
かみくず 紙くず wastepaper ……[くず]
かみそり a razor

かみつく bite at, snap at
かみなり 雷 thunder; (いなづま) lightning
〜が鳴る thunder
・the thunder crashes ………[みみ]
かむ
ガム chewing gum
カムバック 〜する make a comeback
カメ 亀 (陸上の) a tortoise; (海ガメ) a turtle
かめい 家名に傷をつける damage *one's* family's reputation ………[きず]
カメラ a camera
〜マン (写真家) a photographer; (映画・テレビの) a cameraman
カメルーン Cameroon
〜の Cameroonian
〜人 a Cameroonian; (全体) the Cameroonians
がめん 画面 (画像) a picture; (スクリーン) screen
カモ 鴨 a (wild) duck
かもい 鴨居 a door lintel ……[ぶつける]
〜に着く hit the doorway ……[つく⁴]
かもく 科目 a subject
カモシカ (レイヨウ) an antelope; (日本カモシカ) a Japanese serow
〜かもしれない
かもつ 貨物《米》freight,《英》goods; (船荷) cargo
カモフラージュ (a) camouflage
カモメ a (sea) gull
かやく 火薬 gunpowder
かゆい 痒い
かよう 通う
かようきょく 歌謡曲 a Japanese popular song
がようし 画用紙 drawing paper
………………[ざらざら]
かようび 火曜日 Tuesday (略 Tues., Tue.)
から 空
から 殻 (穀物の) husks; (果実・貝・卵の) a shell
〜から
今年〜 beginning (from) this year
………………[くわわる]
がら 柄 a pattern ………[きばつ]

カラー color
　～テレビ color television; (受像機) a color television set
　～フィルム color film
からい 辛い
　からいばり 空威張り an empty boast ………………………………[しらける]
カラオケ *karaoke, karioki*
　～ボックス a *karaoke* [*karioki*] room
からかう
　からし 辛し mustard
カラス 烏 a crow
ガラス glass
　窓～ a window pane
　～張りの (透明性のある) transparent
からだ 体
　～が弱い have a weak constitution ………………………………[たびたび]
　・be physically weak [delicate] ………………………………[よわい]
　～つき a physique ………[しまる¹]
　～に気をつける look after *oneself* ………………………………[あらためて]
　～に障る affect *one's* health [さわる²]
　～に良くない unhealthy ………[ぬく]
　～に悪い be bad for *one's* health ………………………………[つめる]
　～の具合が悪い not feel well …[よす]
　～をこわす ruin *one's* health ………………………………[きつい]
　～を慣らす …………………[ならす¹]
　～を曲げる bend over ………[つく⁴]
　～を焼く get a tan …………[やく³]
カラチ Karachi
からて 空手 karate
からまる (もつれる) get tangled; (引っかかる) catch in
からむ 絡む
　・get into a hassle with ………[よう²]
がらもの 柄物 print ………[にじむ]
カリ 雁 a wild goose (複数 geese)
かり 狩り hunting, a hunt, shooting
　潮干～ shellfish gathering
　もみじ～ maple leaf viewing
かり 仮
かり 借り
カリキュラム a curriculum

カリスマ ～の charismatic
かりとる 刈り取る (芝) mow; (取り入れる) reap, harvest, gather in
カリブ ～海 the Caribbean (Sea)
カリフォルニア California (略 Cal., Calif., CA)
カリフラワー (a) cauliflower
かりょく 火力 heating power
　～発電所 a thermal power plant
かりる 借りる
かる 刈る
かるい 軽い
　～運動 some [a little] exercise ………………………………[うんどう]
カルカッタ Calcutta
カルシウム calcium ………[ほね]
カルタ cards; (遊び) a card game
カルテ a medical record
カルト ～教団 a cult
かるはずみ 軽はずみ
かれ 彼 he; (彼の) his; (彼を, 彼に) him; (彼のもの) his; (彼自身) himself; (恋人) a [*one's*] boyfriend
カレイ a flatfish, a flounder
　・a halibut ………………………[くべつ]
カレー curry
　～ライス curry and rice, curried rice
ガレージ a garage
かれき 枯れ木 dead wood ………[たく]
かれは 枯れ葉 a dead leaf
かれら 彼ら they; (彼らの) their; (彼らを, 彼らに) them; (彼らのもの) theirs; (彼ら自身) themselves
かれる 枯れる
かれる 涸れる
かれる 嗄れる (声が) get hoarse [こえ]
カレンダー a calendar
かろう 過労 overwork ………[くる]
　・extreme fatigue ………[たおれる]
　～死 death from overwork
　～死する die from overwork
がろう 画廊 a picture gallery
かろうじて
　・barely, under the wire ……[まにあう]
かろやか 軽やか
カロリー a calorie
　～の多い[高い] rich in calories,

high-calorie
かろんじる 軽んじる　make light of
かわ 川　a river; (小川) a stream
かわ 皮・革　(なめし皮) leather; (皮膚) the skin; (木の) a bark; (果物の) a peel
　〜張り　covered in leather ……[そと]
　〜を脱ぐ　shed *one's* skin, molt ……[ぬぐ]
　〜をむく　peel ……[ぶきよう]
〜がわ 〜側
かわいい
　・sweet, adorable ……[むじゃき]
かわいがる
　・be kind to, be nice to ……[いきる]
　・care for ……[じつ]
かわいそう
かわかす 乾かす
かわく 乾・渇く
かわす 交わす　exchange
かわせ 為替で　by money order ……[おくる¹]
　〜レート　exchange rate
かわった 変わった
かわって 変わっている　different ……[なかま]
かわら 瓦　a (roof) tile ……[とぶ]
かわり 代わり
　(…の)代わりに ……[もらう]
かわりめ 変わり目　the turn, a turning point
かわりもの 変わり者　an odd person
かわる 変わる
　変わらぬ友情 ……[ゆうじょう]
かわる 代わる
かん 缶　a can;《英》a tin
かん 巻　a volume
かん 棺　a casket,《英》a coffin
かん 勘
かん 管　a pipe, a tube
ガン 雁　a wild goose (複数 geese)
がん 癌　cancer
　〜検診　a checkup for cancer ……[〜から]
かんえん 肝炎　《医学用語》hepatitis
かんおけ 棺おけ　a casket,《英》a coffin
かんか 感化する　influence

がんか 眼科　ophthalmology
　〜医　an oculist, an eye doctor
がんか 眼下に　below *one* ……[ながめる]
かんがい 灌漑する　irrigate …[そうだい]
かんがえ 考え
　・mind ……[て]
　〜が浅い　*one's* thinking is shallow ……[あさい]
　〜が甘い　kid *oneself* ……[あまい]
かんがえかた 考え方　*one's* way of thinking; (見方) *one's* point of view
　・*one's* way of seeing things ……[おだやか]
　〜が合う　see things the same way ……[あう¹]
かんがえごと 考え事をする　think about something
かんがえこむ 考え込む　think hard
　考え込んでいる　be deep in thought ……[じっと]
かんがえなおす 考え直す　reconsider, think over
　・rethink ……[こんぽん]
かんがえもの 考えものだ　be doubtful, be debatable
　・unwise ……[けっか]
　・really wonder whether or not it's worth it to *do* ……[さわがしい]
かんがえる 考える
　よく〜　give careful consideration to ……[のち]
かんかく 感覚
かんかく 間隔
カンガルー　a kangaroo
かんき 換気　ventilation ……[つける²]
　〜する　ventilate
　〜扇　a ventilating fan
かんきゃく 観客　(演劇などの)《集合的に》the audience; (スポーツの) a spectator
かんきょう 環境　(an) environment, surroundings
　〜の変化　a change in environment ……[きょくたん]
　〜破壊　destruction of the environment ……[はかい]
　〜ホルモン　endocrine disrupters,

hormone-disrupting chemicals, an "environmental hormone"
かんきょうしょう 環境省　the Ministry of the Environment
かんきり 缶切り　a can opener, 《英》a tin opener
かんぐる 勘ぐる
かんけい 関係
かんげい 歓迎
　～を受ける　be warmly received ……………………………[さかん]
　・receive a welcome ……[ねっきょう]
かんげき 感激する　be moved by ……………………………[ゆうじょう]
　～のあまり　so deeply moved that ……………………………[つかえる]
かんけつ 完結する　conclude, complete
かんけつ 簡潔な　brief, concise
　～に　briefly, concisely
がんこ 頑固な　obstinate, stubborn
　～さ　stubbornness …………[あきれる]
かんこう 観光　sightseeing
　～する　see the sights
　～に行く　go sightseeing
　～客　a sightseer, a tourist
　～地　a resort area …………[そこなう]
　～バス　a sightseeing bus　[けんぶつ]
　～道路　a road for tourists …[こわす]
かんこうへん 肝硬変 《医学用語》 cirrhosis (of the liver), hepatocirrhosis
かんこく 韓国　the Republic of Korea, South Korea
　～の　(South) Korean
　～語　Korean
　～人　a (South) Korean; (全体) the (South) Koreans
かんごし 看護師　a nurse
　訪問～　a home-care nurse
かんさつ 観察
かんし 監視する　keep (a) watch on
　・keep someone under close surveillance, keep a close eye on ……………………………[こうどう]
かんじ 感じ
かんじ 漢字　a Chinese character
ガンジス ～川　the Ganges (River)
がんじつ 元日　New Year's Day

かんしゃ 感謝
　～する　appreciate ……[きょうりょく]
　～の気持ち　a feeling of gratitude ……………………………[こうい¹]
　～の気持ちを示す　show one's appreciation ……………………[ぐたい]
かんじゃ 患者　a patient ……[こうふん]
かんしゃく　～を起こす　lose one's temper
かんじやすい 感じ易い　vulnerable
　・sensitive ……………………[やすい²]
かんしゅう 慣習　(a) custom, (a) convention
がんしょ 願書　an application
かんしょう 干渉
かんしょう 感傷的な　sentimental
かんしょう 鑑賞　appreciation
　～する　appreciate
かんじょう 勘定
かんじょう 感情
　～に支配される　be ruled [controlled] by emotions　[しはい]
がんじょう 頑丈な　strong, tough
かんしょく 間食する　eat between meals
かんじる 感じる
かんしん 感心
　～させる　impress ………[しらべる]
かんしん 関心
　～が深い　have a deep interest in ……………………………[げいじゅつ]
かんじん 肝心
　～だ　be of the essence ……[さいしょ]
かんする 関する
　(…に)関する　pertaining to　[ほけん]
　(…に)関しては　concerning, regarding, as for
　・when it comes to ………[きょうそう]
かんせい 完成
　・completion …………………[ちかい]
かんせい 歓声　a cheer, a shout of joy
　～を上げる　cheer ……………[あげる]
かんぜい 関税　customs, a (customs) duty, a tariff
かんせつ 間接
　～的な　indirect
　～的に　indirectly
かんせつ 関節　a joint

～炎　arthritis
かんせん　幹線　(鉄道の) a main line, 《米》 a trunk line; (道路の) an arterial road, 《米》 a trunk road
かんせん　感染　infection, contagion
～症　infection
かんぜん　完全
かんそ　簡素な　simple, plain
かんそう　乾燥して　dry
～器　a drier, a dryer
かんそう　感想
かんぞう　肝臓　a liver
かんそく　観測する　observe
かんたい　寒帯　the frigid zone
かんだい　寛大な　generous, tolerant
かんたん　感嘆　admiration, wonder
～する　admire, wonder (at)
かんたん　簡単
かんだん　歓談する　have a nice chat ………………………………[まねく]
がんたん　元旦　New Year's Day
かんだんけい　寒暖計　a thermometer
かんちがい　勘違い
かんちょう　干潮　ebb tide, low tide
かんちょう　官庁　a government office
かんづく　感づく
かんづめ　缶詰　《米》 canned [《英》 tinned] food
かんてん　観点　a point of view, a viewpoint
かんでん　感電する　get shocked (by electricity)
かんでんち　乾電池　a dry cell, a dry battery
かんとう　関東地方　the Kanto region ………………………………[ちかく]
かんどう　感動する　be moved [touched] by ……………[おもいやり]
～的な　impressive, touching
かんとく　監督
カンニング　～をする　cheat in an examination
～ペーパー　a crib sheet
カンヌ　Cannes
かんねん　観念　(概念) an idea, sense
カンパ　(a) contribution, (a) donation
かんぱい　乾杯　a toast; (かけ声) Cheers!
～する　toast ………………………[いわう]
カンバス　a canvas
かんばつ　干ばつ　drought ………[おおう]
がんばる　頑張る
・give one's all ………………[ゆうしょう]
頑張り抜く　fight it out doggedly ………………………………[まける]
かんばん　看板　a signboard, a sign
～の文字　the lettering on the sign ………………………………[きえる]
かんぱん　甲板　a deck
かんびょう　看病する　nurse, take care of
かんぺき　完璧な　perfect
がんぺき　岸壁　a quay, a pier
かんべん　勘弁する　(許す) forgive; (大目に見る) overlook; (免ずる) excuse someone from
がんぼう　願望
かんぽうやく　漢方薬　Chinese medicine, herbal medicine
カンボジア　Cambodia
～の　Cambodian
～人　a Cambodian; (全体) the Cambodians
かんむり　冠　a crown
かんゆう　勧誘　a pitch ………[つられる]
～する　solicit, ask (to do)
・pressure someone into ……[しつこい]
かんり　管理
～職　(a member of) the management
かんりょう　官僚　a bureaucrat
～的な　bureaucratic
かんれい　慣例　(a) custom, (a) convention
かんれき　還暦を迎える　reach 60 ………………………………[しんきょう]
かんれん　関連
かんろく　貫禄がある　have a certain presence, have dignity, be a man of presence [dignity]
かんわ　緩和する　ease, relax
・alleviate ……………………[こんざつ]

キ

き　木　a tree; (かん木) a bush; (材木) (a) wood, lumber

~でできた wooden, made of wood
き 気
　~が荒い violent …………[あらい¹]
　~が合わない not get along with
　　…………………………[なぜ]
　~が進む get worked up (about)
　　…………………………[すすむ]
　(…しなければ)~が済まない never
　　be satisfied until …………[やっかい]
　~が立っている be worked up
　　…………………………[きつい]
　~に入らない not like …………[うら]
　~にしない not care at all …[ゆがむ]
　・couldn't care less ………[むしんけい]
　~にする be upset about …[ひくい]
　(…ばかり)~にする be obsessed by
　　…………………………[おもわく]
　~になる stick in *one's* mind
　　…………………………[みょう]
　~を落とすな Don't take it so hard.
　　…………………………[なに]
　~をしっかり持つ pull *oneself*
　　together ………………[しっかり]
　~をそそる catch *someone's* interest
　　…………………………[そそる]
　~を取られる get worked up over
　　…………………………[こまかい]
　~を引く win *someone's* affections
　　…………………………[て]
　~を悪くする take offense ….[わるい]
ギア (a) gear
きあい 気合いが入っている be showing
　a lot of fight, be full of fight
きあつ 気圧 atmospheric pressure
ぎあん 議案 a bill ……………[あん]
　~を通過させる pass a bill
キーボード (コンピュータなどの) a
　keyboard; (楽器) the keyboards
　~を見ないで入力する touch-type
きいろ 黄色(の) yellow
ぎいん 議員 a member (of an
　assembly)
　国会~ (日本の) a member of the
　　Diet, a Dietman; (英国の) a
　　member of Parliament (略 M.P.);
　　(米国の) a Congressman; (米国など
　　の上院の) a Senator
キウイ a kiwi fruit

きえる 消える
　(火が風で) be blown out ……[~そう]
　消えかかった faded ………………[め¹]
きおく 記憶
　~に新しい fresh in *one's* memory
　　…………………………[あたらしい]
　~に残る remain in *one's* memory
　　…………………………[のこる]
きおくれ 気後れ
きおん 気温 (atmospheric)
　temperature
　最高[最低]~ the maximum
　　[minimum] temperature
きか 帰化 naturalization
　~する be naturalized
　~種[動物, 植物] a naturalized
　　species [animal, plant], a species
　　[an animal, a plant] from outside
きか 幾何 geometry
きかい 機械 a machine; (総称)
　machinery
　~化する mechanize
　~的な mechanical, automatic
　~的に mechanically, automatically
　~文明 mechanical civilization
　　…………………………[にくむ]
きかい 機会
　~を外す let an opportunity go by
　　…………………………[はずす]
きがい 危害 harm
　~を加える harm, do harm (to)
きがい 気概がある be spirited enough
　　…………………………[ひらく]
ぎかい 議会 an assembly; (国会)(日本
　の) the Diet; (米国の) the
　Congress; (英国・カナダの) the
　Parliament
きがえ 着替え †a change of [spare]
　clothes
きがえる 着替える change *one's*
　clothes
　(…を)着替える change (out of)
　　…………………………[よごれる]
きがかり 気がかり (a) concern, a
　worry
きかく 企画 a plan, a project; (計画を
　立てること) planning
　~を立てる plan

- form a plan ･･････････････････････[そう]
きかく 規格 a standard
きかざる 着飾る dress up
　華やかに〜 be dressed up in fancy clothes ･････････････････････[ひんじゃく]
きがね 気兼ね
きがる 気軽
きかん 期間 a term, a period
きかん 器官 an organ
きかん 機関
きかんし 気管支 bronchus
　〜炎 bronchitis
　〜ぜんそく asthma
きき 危機 a crisis, a critical moment
　エネルギー〜 an energy crisis
　食糧〜 a food crisis
　〜管理 crisis management
　〜管理する manage a crisis
ききいれる 聞き入れる (願いを) grant; (忠告などを) take, follow
ききおとす 聞き落とす fail to hear, miss hearing ･････････････[おとす]
ききかえす 聞き返す ask again
ききしにまさる 聞きしに勝る more than I have heard ･････[まさる]
ききとる 聞き取る catch
ききながす 聞き流す let *something* go in one ear and out the other ･･････････････････････････[ながす]
ききほれる 聞きほれる be captivated [taken] by, be gone on ･･････[ほれる]
ききみみ 聞き耳を立てる strain to hear
・prick up *one's* ears to listen ･･･････････････････････[ねむる]
ききめ 効きめ (an) effect
　〜のある effective
ききゅう 気球 a balloon
きぎょう 企業 an enterprise, a business
　大〜 a large company [corporation, enterprise], big business
　中小〜 a minor enterprise
　民間〔公営〕〜 a private [public] enterprise
　外資系〜 a foreign affiliated firm
　多国籍〜 a multinational corporation
　〜秘密 a company secret [せいぞう]
きぎょう 起業家 an entrepreneur
ききん 飢饉 (a) famine
ききん 基金 (資金) a fund; (財団) a foundation
キク 菊 a chrysanthemum
きく 効・利く
きく 聞・聴く
きぐ 器具 an instrument, an appliance, an apparatus
きくず 木くず a wood chip ･･････[くず]
きくばり 気配りする pay careful attention to, be sensitive to, be considerate of [toward]
きぐらい 気位の高い proud
きげき 喜劇 a comedy
　〜的 comic
きけん 危険
　〜が迫る ･･･････････････････････[せまる]
きけん 棄権する (競技を) default ･･････････････････････････[おくびょう]
　(投票を) abstain from voting
きげん 起源 origin, beginning
きげん 期限
きげん 機嫌
　〜が直る get over *one's* bad mood ･･････････････････････････[そっと]
　〜が悪くなる get in a bad mood ･･････････････････････････[まける]
きこう 気候 climate
きごう 記号 a mark, a sign, a symbol
きこえる 聞こえる
きこく 帰国する go [come] home, return to *one's* country
　〜子女 a child [student] who has returned from overseas, a returnee student
ぎこちない
・stiff ･････････････････････････[どうさ]
きこん 既婚者 a married man [woman] ･･･････････････････[のぞく¹]
きざ 〜な affected, pretentious
ぎざぎざ notches
きさく 気さく
　〜な amiable, friendly
・congenial ･････････････････[ひょうめん]
きざし 兆し a sign ･･･････････････[みえる]
きざむ 刻む

きし 岸 (川の) the bank; (海・湖・大河の) the shore
キジ a pheasant
きじ 生地 (布地) cloth, fabric
(服の材料) (a) material ……[そぼく]
きじ 記事 an article; (新聞の) a news item, a (news) story
ぎし 技師 an engineer
ぎしき 儀式 a ceremony
きしつ 気質 disposition, temper, nature
きじつ 期日 a (fixed) date, an appointed day; (最終期日) a time limit
・the due date ……[おくれる]
・a deadline ……[どうにか]
きしゃ 記者 a journalist, a pressman, a newsman
～会見 a press interview [conference]
～クラブ the press club
きしゅ 機首 a nose ……[むける]
きしゅくしゃ 寄宿舎 a dormitory
きじゅつ 奇術 magic, jugglery
～師 a juggler, a magician
ぎじゅつ 技術
きじゅん 基準 a standard
きしょう 気性
きしょう 気象 weather (conditions)
異常～ aberrant weather
異常～が起きている Weather conditions are abnormal.
……[いじょう[3]]
～予報士 a (certified) weather forecaster, a weatherman
きしょうちょう 気象庁 the (Japan) Meteorological Agency, the weather bureau
キシリトール xylitol
キス a kiss
～する kiss
きず 傷
・a wound ……[たえる[1]]
きずあと 傷あと a scar ……[のこる]
きすう 奇数 an odd number
きずく 築く
きずぐち 傷口 wound ……[つける[1]]
～がふさがる a wound closes

[mends] ……[ふさぐ]
きずつく 傷つく
きずつける 傷つける
きずな bonds, ties
きせい 既製の ready-made
きせい 帰省する return home
・return to *one's* home ……[だいいち]
きせい 規制する (規制による) regulate; (統制する) control; (制限する) restrict
～緩和 deregulation
自主～ a self-imposed control
交通～ traffic control
ぎせい 犠牲
きせいじじつ 既成事実 a *fait accompli* ……[じじつ]
きせき 奇跡 a miracle
～的な miraculous
きせつ 季節 a season
～の seasonal
～の挨拶状 a greeting card
……[あいさつ]
～外れの unseasonable, out of season
きぜつ 気絶する faint, swoon, lose *one's* senses
きせる 着せる
きぜん 毅然とした態度で with a firm attitude ……[たいする]
ぎぜん 偽善的な hypocritical
きそ 基礎
きそく 規則
～正しい rhythmical, methodical, regular ……[しんどう]
・organized ……[しどう]
～により according to regulations
……[よる[1]]
～を破る break a rule ……[わざと]
きぞく 貴族 (総称) the nobility, aristocracy; (個人) a noble, a nobleman, an aristocrat, a peer
きた 北 the north
～の north, northern
～へ north, northward, to [toward] the north
～回り via [by way of] the northern route ……[まわり]
～向きの with a northern exposure,

facing the north ……………[むき]
ギター　a guitar
きたい　気体　gas
きたい　期待
　〜を裏切る　disappoint, let *someone* down ………………………………[うらぎる]
ぎだい　議題　a subject [topic] for discussion
　・a subject …………………………[つづく]
　・a topic ……………………………[そう]
　(全事項) agenda
きたえる　鍛える
きたく　帰宅する　go home ……[やめる¹]
　〜途中　on the way home ……[あう²]
きたちょうせん　北朝鮮　North Korea
きたない　汚い
　〜手を使う　resort to dirty tricks
　………………………………………[へいき]
ギタリスト　a guitarist ……[すばらしい]
きち　基地　a base
きち　機知　wit
きちがい　気違いの　mad, crazy
きちょう　貴重
きちょう　機長　a captain ………[ふせぐ]
ぎちょう　議長　a chairman ………[かわる²]
きちょうめん　几帳面
きちんと
　・properly ………………………[はずかしい]
きつい
　・grueling ………………………[ふへい]
　〜仕事……………………………………[わり]
きつえん　喫煙　smoking
　〜席　the smoking section, a smoking seat
きっかけ
　…をきっかけに　spurred on by
　………………………………………[せいちょう]
きづく　気づく
ぎっくりごし　ぎっくり腰　strained back
きっさてん　喫茶店　a tearoom, a coffee shop
ぎっしり　〜だ　(空間が) be packed with, be full of, be filled; (日程が) *one's* schedule is tight
きっすい　生粋
　〜の　trueborn, pure
きって　切手　a postage stamp, a stamp
　〜収集　collecting stamps, stamp collecting ……………………………[しゅみ]
　記念〜　a commemorative stamp
きっと
キツネ　a fox
きっぱり　きっぱりと　flatly, decisively
きっぷ　切符　a ticket
　〜自動販売器　a ticket vending machine
　往復〜　《米》a round-trip ticket, 《英》a return ticket
　片道〜　《米》a one-way ticket, 《英》a single ticket
　〜売場　(駅の) a ticket office; (劇場の) a box office
きてい　規定
　〜の書式　the standard format
　………………………………………[きてい]
きてき　汽笛を鳴らす　blow a whistle
　………………………………………[ならす²]
きてん　機転
　〜がきく　quick-witted
　・quick on the uptake ………[てきする]
きどう　起動する　(コンピュータを) activate, invoke, launch, startup
　再〜する　restart, reboot [さいきどう]
きどう　軌道
　〜に乗せる　(財政的に) get *something* into financial shape ………[くろう]
きどうたい　機動隊　the riot squad
　………………………………………[おさまる²]
きどうりょく　機動力　mobility
きとく　危篤　critical condition
　………………………………………[へいぜん]
　〜状態を脱する　come out of critical condition ……………………………[とどく]
　〜で　in critical condition
きどる　気取る
　・be pretentious, put on airs
　………………………………………[すこしも]
きなが　気長
きにゅう　記入する　enter, write (in), fill (in)
きぬ　絹 (の)　silk
きねん　記念
　〜植樹をする　plant a commemorative tree ………………[きねん]
きのう　昨日　yesterday
きのう　機能　a function …………[はたす]

ぎのう 技能 skill, ability
キノコ a mushroom
きのどく 気の毒
　〜な pitiful ························[ほか]
きば 牙 (ゾウ・イノシシなどの) a tusk;
　(犬・オオカミ・ヘビなどの) a fang
　〜をむき出して with teeth bared
　·································[むく¹]
　〜をむく bare *one's* fangs
きはく 気迫
きばつ 奇抜
きばらし 気晴らし
きびしい 厳しい
　・hard, harsh ················[ちゅうもん]
　・rigorous ························[せかい]
　厳しくする (人に) be strict with
　····································[いと]
　厳しさを増す become more severe
　····································[たい]
きひん 気品のある graceful, noble,
　elegant
きびん 機敏
きふ 寄付
　・a contribution
　・a donation ·····················[かく〜]
　〜金 a donation ···············[かなり]
　〜する contribute (to), donate (to)
　・make a donation ············[きまえ]
　〜を募る collect donations [おくる²]
ぎふ 義父 (継父) a stepfather; (夫また
　は妻の父) a father-in-law
きふく 起伏 ups and downs
キプロス Cyprus
　〜の Cyprian, Cypriot
　〜人 a Cypriot; (全体) the Cypriots
きぶん 気分
　(雰囲気) an atmosphere ·······[かざり]
　〜も新たに with a renewed spirit
　··································[むかえる]
　〜を味わう feel as if ········[あじわう]
　みじめな〜だ feel miserable
　·································[なんとなく]
きぼ 規模
ぎぼ 義母 (継母) a stepmother; (夫ま
　たは妻の母) a mother-in-law
きぼう 希望
　〜に満ちている be brimming with
　hope ····························[みちる]
　〜に胸を膨らませる be filled with
　hope ····························[ふくらむ]
　〜に燃えて burning with desire
　··································[もえる]
ぎほう 技法 a technique ···[こころみる]
きほん 基本
きまえ 気前
きまぐれ 気まぐれ
きまじめ 〜な serious ············[また]
　〜さ earnestness ···············[うらみ]
きまずい 気まずい
きまつ 期末試験 final exams ···[こえる]
　・final exams ···················[ゆううつ]
きまった 決まった regular, fixed
きまま 気まま
きまり 決まり
きまりがわるい きまりが悪い
きまる 決まる
ぎまん 欺瞞的行為 a deceitful
　[deceptive] action ···········[けんお]
〜ぎみ 〜気味
きみがわるい 気味が悪い
きみじか 気短か short-tempered,
　quick-tempered
きみつ 機密書類 a secret paper
　··································[わたる]
きみょう 奇妙
ぎむ 義務
　〜がある be bound [obliged] to
　··································[まもる]
きむずかしい 気難しい
きめる 決める
　決められた日に on set days ····[だす]
きも 肝を冷やす be scared to death
　・have a terrible scare ·········[ひやす]
きもち 気持ち
　〜がいい enjoy ·················[なでる]
　〜を打ち明ける reveal *one's* feelings
　to ·································[やっと]
きもったま 肝っ玉の太い daring
　··································[ふとい]
きもの 着物 clothes; (総称) clothing,
　dress; (和服) a *kimono*
ぎもん 疑問
キャーンペーン 〜する give a
　campaign ·························[ぼうけん]
きゃく 客 a visitor, a caller; (招待客)
　a guest; (商店の) a customer
　・a guest ···························[たいぐう]

～あしらいがうまい handle (the) customers well, be good with (the) customers ……………[あしらう]
　～商売 work dealing (directly) with customers ……………[がさつ]
　～間 a guest room ……………[とおる]
ぎゃく 逆
ぎゃくじょう 逆上
ぎゃくたい 虐待する ill-treat, treat cruelly [badly], abuse
　児童～ child abuse
ぎゃくてん 逆転する turn the game around ……………[おもて]
　～負けする blow the lead and lose the game ……………[くやしい]
　～また逆転 ……………[それで]
きゃくほん 脚本 a drama, a script; (映画の) a scenario
ぎゃくりゅう 逆流する flow backward
きゃしゃ きゃしゃな slight, fragile
きやすい 気安い
きやすめ 気休め
きゃっかん 客観
　～的な objective
　～的に objectively
ぎゃっきょう 逆境 adversity, adverse circumstances
　・adverse condition ……[たくましい]
　～に強い handle adversity well
　・know how to take adversity ……………[つよい]
ぎゃっこう 逆行する run counter to ……………[じだい]
キャッシュカード an ATM card, a bank card
キャッチボール ～をする play catch
キャッチホン call waiting
キャッチャー a catcher
ギャップ a gap, (a) difference
キャビネット a cabinet
キャプテン a captain
ぎゃふん ～と言わせる get *someone* to †admit *he* is wrong [say uncle] ……………[はら]
キャベツ cabbage
ギャラ a (guaranteed) fee, payment
キャリア a career, career experience
　～組 an elite bureaucrat, a career bureaucrat
　ノン～組 a non-elite bureaucrat
　～ウーマン a career woman
キャンセル (a) cancellation
　～する cancel
　～料 a cancellation charge
　～待ちする go standby, be on the waiting list
キャンデー candy
キャンプ a camp
　～に行く go camping
キャンペーン キャンペーンする campaign, carry on a campaign
キャンベラ Canberra
きゅう 急
　～に on such short notice …[にげる]
きゅう 九 nine
　第9(の) the ninth (略 9th)
　9分の1 a [one] ninth
きゅうか 休暇
きゅうかく 嗅覚 a sense of smell ……………[はったつ]
きゅうがく 休学 (a) temporary absence from school
きゅうきゅう 救急の first-aid, emergency
　～救命士 a paramedic
　～車 an ambulance
　～車で運ばれる be taken away in an ambulance ……………[ち]
きゅうきょく 究極の ultimate
きゅうくつ 窮屈
きゅうけい 休憩
きゅうこう 旧交を温める renew an old friendship ……………[あたためる]
きゅうこう 休校になる school is closed
きゅうこう 休講になる class is canceled ……………[て]
きゅうこう 急行 an express (train)
きゅうし 急死する die suddenly ……[し]
きゅうしき 旧式の old-fashioned, out-of-date
　・old-model ……………[しき]
きゅうじつ 休日
きゅうしゅう 吸収する absorb, take in
きゅうじゅう 九十 ninety
　第90(の) the ninetieth (略 90th)
きゅうじょ 救助 rescue, help, aid

～する rescue, save
～隊 a rescue squad ………[たすける]
きゅうじょう 球場 a baseball ground, a ball park, a stadium
・a baseball stadium …………[つづく]
きゅうじん 求人欄 want ads
…………………………[てあたりしだい]
きゅうす 急須 a teapot ……………[て]
きゅうせい 旧姓 *one's* former name; (女性の) *one's* maiden name
きゅうせい 急性の acute
きゅうせん 休戦 (a) truce, armistice
きゅうぞう 急増する increase rapidly
………………………………[こうがい]
きゅうそく 急速な rapid, quick, swift
きゅうだい 及第する pass ………[はず]
きゅうでん 宮殿 a palace
ぎゅうにく 牛肉 beef
ぎゅうにゅう 牛乳 milk
キューバ Cuba
～の Cuban
～人 a Cuban; (全体) the Cubans
きゅうびょう 急病 a sudden illness
～人 an emergency case
きゅうめい 救命具 a life-saving device
……………………………………[やく¹]
きゅうゆう 旧友 an old friend [かいわ]
きゅうよう 休養 (a) rest
～する rest, take a rest
きゅうよう 急用 an emergency
……………………………………[つとめ]
～ができて because of an emergency
………………………………[わけ]
～で on urgent business
キュウリ a cucumber
きゅうりょう 給料 pay, wages, salary
～が上がる get a raise [あがる, らく]
～日 (a) payday …[くるしい, はらう]
きよ 寄与する contribute to [はっけん]
きよう 器用
ぎょう 行 a line
きょう 今日 today, this day
～明日にも at any time ……[あぶない]
～じゅうに by the end of the day
………………………………[できる]
～の午後 this afternoon
きょうい 驚異
～を与える threaten, menace

きょういく 教育
～委員会 the school board [いいん]
～制度 the educational system
………………………………[うたがい]
～的な educational
～方針 a philosophy in raising children ………………[ほうしん]
きょうか 教科 a subject
きょうか 強化する strengthen, reinforce
きょうかい 協会 an association, a society
きょうかい 教会 a church
きょうかい 境界 a boundary, a border
ぎょうかい 業界 industry; (実業界) the business world
この～で in this industry
………………………………[じゅうよう]
～用語 (a) jargon
きょうがく 共学 《米》coeducation, 《英》mixed education
～の 《米》coeducational, 《英》mixed
きょうかしょ 教科書 a text, a textbook
～問題 the school textbook issue
………………………………[やかましい]
きょうかん 共感
きょうぎ 協議する confer (with), consult (with), talk (over) (with), discuss (with)
きょうぎ 競技
～場 a stadium
・a sports arena ……………[かく～]
ぎょうぎ 行儀
きょうきゅう 供給
きょうぐう 境遇 《複数形で》 circumstances
・a situation ………………[きのどく]
きょうくん 教訓 a lesson
きょうこう 強硬
～な firm ………………………[たちば]
きょうさん 共産主義 communism
反～主義 anti-communism
～主義者 a communist
～党 (日本共産党) Japan Communist Party
きょうし 教師 a teacher, an instructor; (教授) a professor

ぎょうじ 行事　an event ………[つづく]
きょうしつ 教室　a classroom
きょうじゅ 教授　(大学の先生) a professor (略 Prof.)
〜の職　a professorship ………[える]
助〜　an assistant professor, an associate professor
名誉〜　a professor emeritus
きょうしゅく 恐縮
ぎょうしょう 行商　peddling ……[とう²]
〜人　peddler
きょうしょく 教職　the teaching profession ………………[つく⁴]
きょうせい 強制する　force (to *do*), compel (to *do*)
〜終了する(コンピュータを)　kill
きょうせい 矯正する　correct
ぎょうせい 行政　administration
ぎょうせき 業績　an achievement
………………………………[いだい]
・an accomplishment　[かがやかしい]
・*one's* work ………………[ひょうか]
きょうそう 競走　a race
100メートル〜　the 100-meter dash
………………………………[さいこう]
きょうそう 競争
〜相手　a rival, competitus [あいて]
・a competitor ………………[ながす]
〜心　a spirit of competition
………………………………[はたらく]
きょうぞん 共存する　coexist
きょうだい 兄弟　(男の) a brother; (女の) a sister
・a sibling ……………………[わずか]
異母〜〔姉妹〕　a half-brother 〔half-sister〕
きょうだい 鏡台　a dressing table, a dresser
きょうだん 凶弾に倒れる　be struck down by an assassin's bullet
………………………………[たおれる]
きょうだん 教壇　a platform
きょうちょう 強調する　emphasize, stress, lay stress (on)
きょうつう 共通
きょうてい 協定　(an) agreement, a pact
きょうてき 強敵　a strong opponent
………………………………[やぶる]
きょうど 郷土　*one's* native place, *one's* native country, *one's* hometown
きょうとう 教頭　a head teacher; (副校長) a vice principal
きょうどう 共同
〜の　(合同の) joint; (共同社会の) communal
〜事業　a joint enterprise
〜生活する　live together ……[きまり]
〜体　community
きょうはく 脅迫　a threat
〜する　threaten
・blackmail ………………[にぎる]
〜状　a threatening letter
きょうはん 共犯　complicity
〜者　an accomplice
きょうふ 恐怖　(a) fear, (a) terror, horror
〜にかられる　be terrified
〜のあまり　in panic ………[ふるえる]
〜映画　a horror movie
高所〜症　acrophobia
きょうふう 強風注意報　a strong wind warning ……………………[だす]
きょうみ 興味
〜津々で　be dying of curiosity
………………………………[むかんしん]
〜深い　interesting
〜本位で　out of curiosity
きょうめい 共鳴
…に共鳴して　in complete agreement with ………………………[しそう]
きょうゆう 共有する　hold *something* in common, own *something* jointly
〜財産　common property
きょうよう 教養
きょうりゅう 恐竜　a dinosaur …[じき]
きょうりょく 協力
〜する　work together ……[それぞれ]
きょうりょく 強力な　powerful, mighty
・strong ………………………[おちる]
きょうれつ 強烈
〜な　powerful ………………[きまる]
ぎょうれつ 行列
きょえいしん 虚栄心　vanity
〜の強い　vain
ギョーザ　a Chinese meat dumpling

きょか 許可
　親の〜　parental consent ……[いか]
きょがく 巨額の　enormous
　……………………[ぎゃく, つたえる]
ぎょぎょう 漁業　the fishing industry
きょく 曲　a tune, music
　・a piece ………………………[けいしき]
　ピアノ〜　a piano piece　[ひょうげん]
きょくせん 曲線　a curve, a curved line
きょくたん 極端
きょくとう 極東　the Far East
　〜の　Far Eastern
ぎょこう 漁港　a fishing port
きょしょう 巨匠　a (great) master
きょしょくしょう 拒食症　anorexia
きょぜつ 拒絶する　refuse, reject
ぎょせん 漁船　a fishing boat
　…………………………………[つうしん]
きょだい 巨大な　huge, gigantic
　・towering ……………………[そびえる]
きょどう 挙動　one's behavior
　………………………………[せいじょう]
　〜不審　……………………[しらべる]
　〜不審の男　a suspicious-looking
　　man ………………………[ふしん]
きょねん 去年　last year
　〜の今日　this day last year
きょひ 拒否する　refuse, deny
きよめる 清める　purify
きょり 距離
きょろきょろ 〜する　look around
きらい 嫌い
きらう 嫌う
きらきら 〜する　glitter, sparkle; (星な
　どが) twinkle
きらく 気楽
きり 霧　mist, fog
きり
ぎり 義理の　〜-in-law
きりあげる 切り上げる　(やめる) leave
　off, quit; (端数を) raise
　・quit ………………………[てきとう]
きりかわる 切り替わる　switch
　………………………………[てんねん]
ぎりぎり
キリギリス　a grasshopper
きりさめ 霧雨　(a) misty rain, (a)
　drizzle

ギリシャ　Greece
　〜の, 〜語　Greek
　〜人　a Greek; (全体) the Greeks
きりすてる 切り捨てる　cut away; (端数
　を) omit
キリスト　Jesus Christ
　〜教　Christianity
　〜教徒　a Christian
きりつ 規律　order, discipline, a rule
きりつ 起立する　stand up
きりつめる 切りつめる　cut down,
　reduce
　支出を〜　cut expenditures [ししゅつ]
　暮らしを〜　cut back on living
　　expenses ……………………[つめる]
きりぬき 切り抜き　a clipping
きりぬく 切り抜く　clip (out), cut out
きりぬける 切り抜ける　get over, find
　one's way out of
きりひらく 切り開く　(新分野を) open
　up; (道・土地などを) clear
キリマンジャロ　(Mt.) Kilimanjaro
きりゅう 気流　an air current
きりょく 気力
キリン　a giraffe
きる 切る
きる 着る
きれ 切れ　(布) cloth; (小片) a piece, a
　bit
きれい
　・lovely ……………………[かざり]
きれる 切れる
　(電池が) run low ……………[かえる⁴]
きろく 記録
　〜破り(暑さが)　a record high
　……………………………………[やぶる]
　〜を作る　set a record ……[すばらしい]
キログラム　a kilogram (略 kg, k)
キロメートル　a kilometer (略 km)
キロリットル　a kiloliter (略 kl)
キロワット　a kilowatt (略 KW, kw)
ぎろん 議論　an argument, a
　discussion, a dispute
　〜する　discuss, argue (about), talk
　(of, about)
ぎわく 疑惑　(a) suspicion, (a) doubt
きわだつ 際立つ
　際立って　conspicuously [とくちょう]

きわどい 際どい
きわめて 極めて
きん 金 (の) gold; (金のような) golden
　〜メダル a gold medal
　〜メッキ gold plate, gilt
ぎん 銀 (の) silver
　〜メダル a silver medal
きんえん 禁煙 (掲示の文句) No Smoking／Smoking Prohibited
　〜する †give up [stop] smoking
　・go without a cigarette …[かんしん1]
　〜席 the nonsmoking section, a nonsmoking seat
　〜車 a nonsmoking car
　〜の誓い a vow to quit smoking ………………………………[たてる1]
ぎんが 銀河 the Milky Way, the Galaxy
きんがく 金額 an amount of money, a sum of money
きんがん 近眼の nearsighted, shortsighted
きんきゅう 緊急の urgent, pressing, emergent
きんぎょ 金魚 a goldfish
　〜鉢 a goldfish bowl
きんこ 金庫 a safe ………[やぶる]
きんこう 近郊 a suburb, outskirts
ぎんこう 銀行 a bank
　〜員 a bank clerk
　〜強盗 (事件) a bank robbery (人) a bank robber …………[ていこう]
きんこんしき 金婚式 *one's* golden wedding anniversary
ぎんこんしき 銀婚式 *one's* silver wedding anniversary ……[むかえる]
きんさく 金策する scrounge up money, search for funds
　・raise money ………………[くしん]
　〜に走り回る run around scrounging up money ………[はしる]
きんし 近視の nearsighted, shortsighted
きんし 禁止
きんジストロフィー 筋ジストロフィー症 muscular dystrophy
きんしゅ 禁酒する give up drinking
　・abstain from alcohol ………[まける]
きんじょ 近所
きんしょう 金賞 (the) first prize ………………………………[あたえる]
きんじる 禁じる forbid
　・prohibit ……………………[とう2]
きんせい 均整のとれた well-proportioned
きんせい 金星 Venus
きんぞく 金属 a metal
　〜製品 metal goods
　〜(性)の metallic
きんだい 近代
　〜絵画 modern art …………[たとえば]
きんちょう 緊張
　〜のあまり under the strain ………………………………[ふるえる]
　〜の連続 unbroken tension ……[き]
きんとう 均等に equally, uniformly
きんにく 筋肉 (a) muscle
　〜の発達した muscular
きんねん 近年に in recent years
きんぱく 緊迫
きんべん 勤勉
きんむ 勤務 service, duty, work
　〜時間 business [office] hours
　・working hours ……………[じかん]
　〜する serve, work
きんゆう 金融機関 a financial institution
きんゆうちょう 金融庁 the Financial Services Agency
きんようび 金曜日 Friday (略 Fri.)
きんろうかんしゃのひ 勤労感謝の日 Labor Thanksgiving Day

ク

く 九 nine
く 区 (市の) a ward; (区画) a division; (区域) a district
　〜役所 a ward office
く 苦 (苦痛) pain; (心配) anxiety, worry; (困難) difficulty
　〜にする worry (about *someone* [*something*])
　〜もなく with ease, easily, without difficulty
ぐあい 具合

(体の)〜が悪い　not feel well …………………………[このあいだ]
〜が悪くなる　feel ill ………[とちゅう]
グアテマラ　Guatemala
　〜の　Guatemalan
　〜人　a Guatemalan; (全体) the Guatemalans
グアム　Guam
クアラルンプール　Kuala Lumpur
くい 悔い
くい 杭　a stake, a pole, a post
くいき 区域　a zone, a district, an area
くいこむ 食い込む　(ひも・時間などが) cut into; (順位などに) make it into
くいさがる 食い下がる
クイズ　a quiz
　・a puzzle …………………………[かぎ]
くいとめる 食い止める　check, stop, keep [hold] in check
くいる 悔いる　regret, repent (of)
くう 食う
クウェート　Kuwait
　〜の　Kuwaiti
　〜人　a Kuwaiti; (全体) the Kuwaitis
くうかん 空間　space; (余地) room
くうき 空気
　〜圧　air pressure …………[さげる]
くうぐん 空軍　the air force
くうこう 空港　an airport
くうしゅう 空襲　an air raid ……[はかい]
くうしょ 空所　a blank ………[てきせつ]
ぐうすう 偶数　an even number
くうせき 空席　a vacant seat, a vacancy
ぐうぜん 偶然
くうそう 空想　fancy; a day-dream
　〜する　fancy, imagine
　〜的　fanciful, imaginary
くうちゅう 空中の　in the air, aerial
　〜ブランコ　a flying trapeze …………………………[はらはら]
クーデター　a coup d'état ……[おこる²]
くうはく 空白　a blank, a vacuum
くうふく 空腹　hunger
　〜な　hungry
クーラー　(飲食物冷却器) a (picnic) cooler; (エアコン) an air conditioner

くうらん 空欄　a blank …………[うめる]
クーリングオフ (期間)　a cooling-off (period)
くがつ 九月　September (略 Sept., Sep.)
くき 茎　a stem, a stalk
くぎ 釘　a nail; (木のくぎ) a peg
　〜でとめる　nail
　〜を打つ　drive a nail …………[うつ]
　〜を抜く　†pull out [remove] a nail
くきょう 苦境　a difficult position …………………………[たつ²]
くぎり 区切り・句切り　(間) a pause; (文章の切れめ) punctuation; (終わり) an end
　〜をつける　(終わらせる) put an end to; (文章などを) punctuate
くぎる 区切る・句切る
くくる　bind, tie up
くぐる 潜る
くさ 草　grass; (雑草) a weed; (牧草) pasture; (干し草) hay
　〜刈り機　a mower
　〜木　vegetation ………………[あおい]
　〜取りをする　weed
　〜の根を分けて捜す　search high and low …………………………[さがす]
　〜むら　a clump of grass ……[なく²]
　・grass …………………………[こえ]
　〜を食べる　graze ………………[むれ]
くさい 臭い
くさみ 臭み　smell ………………[きえる]
くさり 鎖　a chain
くさる 腐る
くし 串　a spit
　・a skewer …………………………[さす¹]
くし 櫛　a comb
　〜で髪をとかす　comb one's hair
くじ　a lot, lottery
　〜に当たる[はずれる]　draw a prize [blank]
　〜を引く　draw lots
くじく (手足を)　sprain; (勇気を) discourage
くじける (気持ちが)　be discouraged
　・be disheartened …………[ぶつかる]
クジャク (雄)　a peacock; (雌) a peahen

くしゃくしゃ 〜な (紙) crumpled, wrinkled; (髪) rumpled, disheveled
くしゃみ sneezing, a sneeze
　〜をする　sneeze
くじょ 駆除する　exterminate, get rid of
くしょう 苦笑する　smile wryly [bitterly]
くじょう 苦情　a complaint
　〜を言う　complain ……………[あげる]
クジラ 鯨　a whale
くしん 苦心
くず 屑
くすくす 〜笑う　giggle
ぐずぐず
　〜する　be indecisive ………[はがゆい]
くすぐったい
くすぐる　tickle
くずす 崩す
くすぶる (けむる) smoke; (いぶる) smolder
くすり 薬
　〜の量　a dose of medicine
　……………………………………[まちがえる]
くすりゆび 薬指　the third finger
くずれる 崩れる
　・collapse ……………………[たてる¹]
くせ 癖
　・a quirk ………………………[まねる]
(…の)くせに　though, although
　・for something ………………[みぶん]
くせん 苦戦　a hard fight, a close game
くだ 管　(細い) a tube; (太い) a pipe
ぐたい 具体
くだく 砕く
くたくた 〜で　be exhausted [さんせい]
くだける 砕ける
(…して)ください　Will you...? / Would you...?
くたばる　(疲労) be zonked out; (死去) kick the bucket
くたびれた　(使い古された) worn-out
くたびれる……………………[つかれる]
くだもの 果物　(a) fruit
　〜屋(店)　a fruit store [shop]; (売店) a fruit stand
くだらない
くだり 下りの　down

くだりざか 下り坂の　downhill
　〜になる　take a turn for the worse
　……………………………………[てんき]
くだる 下る
くち 口
　〜が悪い　be sharp-tongued ……[しん]
　〜癖　one's speech habits ……[うつる³]
　〜に出す　mention ……………[かるい]
　〜下手　not have a way with words
　……………………………………[そん]
　〜を出す　put in one's two cents' worth ……………………………[そば]
　・poke one's nose into …………[よそ]
　〜を挟む　interrupt [butt into] a conversation ……………………[よこ]
　〜を挟まない　stay out of the conversation ……………………[えんりょ]
　〜を割らない　tightlipped ……[だす]
ぐち 愚痴　(a) complaint, a grumble
　・complaints ……………………[なやます]
　〜をこぼす　grumble
　・complain ……………………[たえず]
くちかず 口数
　〜が多い　talkative
　〜が少ない　quiet, taciturn
くちぐせ 口癖　a pet phrase
くちぐるま 口車に乗せられる　be taken in by someone's fast-talk …[のせる]
　(…の)口車に乗る……………[のる]
くちげんか 口げんか　a quarrel
　・an argument …………………[けんか]
くちごたえ 口答えする　talk back to
　……………………………………[なまいき]
くちコミ 口コミで　by word of mouth
くちごもる 口ごもる　falter, mumble
くちさき 口先だけで　without really meaning something ………[しんせつ]
　〜だけの　empty
くちずさむ 口ずさむ　sing to oneself
くちだし 口出しする　meddle in something, stick one's nose into something, bother someone
くちばし (アヒル・ハトなどの) a bill; (ワシ・タカなどの) a beak
くちびる 唇
くちぶえ 口笛　a whistle
　〜を吹く　blow a whistle
くちべに 口紅　(a) lipstick, rouge

くちょう 口調 a tone ………[あらたまる]
・one's way of speaking [うったえる]
くつ 靴 shoes; (長靴) boots; (運動靴) sneakers
 〜のひも a shoelace …………[ゆるむ]
 〜磨き (靴墨) shoe polish; (人) a shoeshine man
 〜屋 (人) a shoemaker; (店) a shoe store [shop]
くつう 苦痛
クッキー a cookie
くっきり clearly, distinctly
くつした 靴下 (短い) socks; (長い) stockings
くつじょく 屈辱
クッション a cushion
ぐっすり fast, sound, soundly
くつずれ 靴ずれ (水ぶくれ, 足のまめ) a blister
くっつく stick (to), cling (to)
くっつける join, stick; (のりで) paste
くつろぐ
・feel at ease ……………………[ほど]
くどい
くとうてん 句読点 a punctuation mark
くどく 口説く (女性を) make advances to; (説得する) persuade
くないちょう 宮内庁 the Imperial Household Agency
くに 国 (国家) a state, a country; (故郷) one's native place, home (故郷) hometown ………………[のこす]
 〜をあげて the whole nation ………………………………………[あげる]
くのう 苦悩 agony …………[あらわす¹]
・suffering(s) ……………[あらわれる¹]
くばる 配る
くび 首
 (…の職を)首になる be fired as ……………………………………[かんとく]
 〜を縦に振る say yes ……[むずかしい]
 〜をつる hang oneself ………[つる¹]
 〜を横に振る shake one's head in disapproval ……………………[よこ]
くびかざり 首飾り a necklace
くびすじ 首筋 (うなじ) the back [nape] of the neck

・one's neck …………………………[すじ]
くふう 工夫
くべつ 区別
くぼみ 凹み a hollow
くぼむ 凹む become hollow, become depressed [sunken]
クマ 熊 a bear
くみ 組
くみあい 組合 a union, an association
 労働〜 《米》a labor union, a union, 《英》a trade union
くみあわせ 組み合わせ
 (a) combination; (試合の) a match-up
くみあわせる 組み合わせる combine; (競技で) match (A against B)
くみたてる 組み立てる
くむ 汲・酌む
くむ 組む
 (組織する) organize ………[あらわれる²]
クモ a spider
 〜の子を散らすように in all directions ………………………[にげる]
 〜の巣 a spider's web, a cobweb
くも 雲 a cloud
くもゆき 雲行き (情勢) the situation ……………………………………[あやしい]
くもり 曇り
 〜の cloudy
 〜ガラス frosted [ground] glass
くもる 曇る
くやくしょ 区役所 a ward office
くやしい 悔しい
 悔やしがる feel frustrated …[まける]
くやむ 悔やむ
くよくよ
 〜する brood over …………[すぎる]
くらい 位 rank, grade
くらい 暗い
〜くらい
グライダー a glider
クライマックス a climax
グラウンド a ground, a field
クラクション a horn
くらくら 〜する feel dizzy ……[あたま]
クラゲ a jellyfish
くらし 暮らし
クラシック 〜音楽 classical music

クラス a class
　～委員長 (the) president of *one's* class ……………[いいん]
　～会 a class reunion ……………[ある]
くらす 暮らす
グラス a glass
グラタン (a) gratin
クラッカー a cracker
ぐらつく (物が) wobble; (決心などが) waver
クラッシュ ～する (コンピュータが) crash
グラビア (a) gravure, (a) photogravure
クラブ a club
　～活動 extracurricular activities
　・club activities ……………[つうじる]
グラフ a graph
グラブ a glove
くらべる 比べる
くらむ (目が) be dazzled, be dizzy
グラム a gram (略 g.)
くらやみ 暗やみ darkness, the dark
グランド a ground, a field
クリ 栗 a chestnut
クリーニング cleaning
　～屋 (店) a laundry; a cleaner's; (人) a cleaner, a laundryman
クリーム (a) cream
くりかえし 繰り返し repetition
くりかえす 繰り返す
クリスマス Christmas
クリック
クリップ a paper clip ……………[とめる¹]
クリニック (診療所) a clinic
くる 来る
くるう 狂う
グループ a group
　～で as a group ……………[つくる]
　～に分ける classify into groups
　～をつくる form a group
くるしい 苦しい
　～思いをする suffer much pain ……………[まし]
　～経験 a bad time ……………[なめる]
くるしみ 苦しみ suffering; (苦痛) pain; (苦労) hardships
くるしむ 苦しむ
　・be distressed by ……………[ぬく]
くるしめる 苦しめる (痛みをあたえる) pain, give pain; (困らせる) trouble, distress
くるぶし an ankle
くるま 車 (自動車) a car; (荷車) a cart, a wagon; (車輪) a wheel
くるまる be wrapped up
クルミ a walnut
くるむ wrap up
グルメ a gourmet
くれ 暮れ (年末) the year-end, the end of the year; (日暮れ) nightfall, sunset
グレープフルーツ a grapefruit
クレーム complaints
　～をつける complain [make complaints] (about)
くれぐれも ～注意する pay strict attention to ……………[けんこう]
クレジットカード a credit card ……………[かまう]
ぐれている be a bad kid ………[なぐる]
(…して)くれませんか Will you...?
クレヨン a crayon
くれる 呉れる
くれる 暮れる
クレンザー (a) cleanser
くろ 黒
くろいうわさ 黒いうわさ a scandalous rumor ……………[たえる²]
くろう 苦労
　～する have a hard time ……[ならす¹]
　・have difficulty ……………[まとめる]
　・have hardships ……………[くすり]
　・suffer from ……………[とうじ]
くろうと an expert; (専門家) a professional, a pro
　～はだし put a professional to shame ……………[はだし]
クローク a cloakroom ……………[あずける]
クローバー a clover
グローブ a glove
クロール the crawl
クローン a clone
　～人間 a human clone
くろじ 黒字 (黒字額) a surplus; (状態) in the black

クロスワードパズル　a crossword puzzle
クロッカス　a crocus
グロテスク　〜な grotesque
クワ　桑　(実)a mulberry ……………[み²]
くわ　鍬　a hoe
くわえる 加える
くわえる　(口に) have [hold] *something* in *one's* mouth
くわしい 詳しい
・be familiar with …………[てつづき]
・be up on ………………[かいがい]
〜こと　details ………………[ちかい]
くわしく　詳しく　in great detail
 ………………………[しょうかい]
〜説明する　explain *something* in detail ………………………[やわらぐ]
くわだて　企て　(計画)a plan, a plot; (こころみ)an attempt
くわだてる 企てる
クワのみ　桑の実　a mulberry ………[み²]
くわわる 加わる
ぐん　群を抜いて　exceptionally …[ぬく]
ぐんい　軍医　an army surgeon …[また]
ぐんかん　軍艦　a warship
ぐんぐん　quickly ………………[うける]
ぐんじ　軍事　military affairs
〜の　military
〜費　military expenditures
くんしゅ　君主　a monarch
ぐんしゅう　群集　a crowd (of people)
〜心理　mob psychology …[はたらく]
ぐんしゅく　軍縮　disarmament
・arms reduction ……………[つうじる]
くんしゅせいけん　君主政権
　(a) monarchy ………………[たおれる]
くんしょう　勲章　a decoration, an order, a medal
ぐんじん　軍人　(陸軍の)a soldier; (海軍の)a sailor; (空軍の)an airman; (海兵隊の)a marine
(将校)an officer ………………[いさましい]
くんせい　燻製の　smoked
ぐんせい　軍政を敷く　set up a military regime ………………………[たおす]
ぐんたい　軍隊　troops, forces, an army
ぐんび　軍備　armaments
ぐんぶ　軍部　the military ………[にぎる]

くんれん　訓練　training, an exercise
・a drill ………………………[しゅうごう]
職業〜　job training
防災〜　a fire drill
〜する　train, drill

ケ

け　毛
けい　刑　(刑罰)a punishment
(判決)a sentence ………………[かるい]
げい　芸　(技能)a skill
(芸当)a trick ………………[おしえる]
けいい 敬意
〜を払う　respect, admire
〜を払って　out of respect ……[はらう]
けいえい 経営
けいえいじん　経営陣　the management team ………………………[くわわる]
けいえん　敬遠
けいか　経過　(進展)progress, (a) development; (時の) (a) passage
・the way things have developed
 ……………………………[いじょう¹]
けいかい　警戒　guard, watch; (用心)a precaution
〜する　guard, watch (for), look out (for)
厳重に〜する　make security tight
 ………………………………[いくら]
〜心が強い　cautious ………[つよい]
けいかく　計画
〜を立てる　make up a plan　[ちみつ]
けいかん　警官　a police officer; (男)a policeman, (婦人警官)a policewoman
けいき　景気
〜回復　economic recovery …[みこみ]
〜の変動　economic fluctuations
 ………………………………[おうじる]
けいけん 経験
けいこ 稽古
けいご　敬語　an honorific
〜を使う　speak very politely [めうえ]
けいこう 傾向
・a trend (in) ………………[れい²]
けいこうとう　蛍光燈　a fluorescent light [lamp]

けいこく 警告 (a) warning
  〜する warn *someone* (of, against), give *someone* a warning
けいざい 経済
  〜学部 the Economics Department ……………………………………[うつる³]
  〜情勢 economic conditions ……………………………………[にらむ]
けいざいさんぎょうしょう 経済産業省 the Ministry of Economy, Trade and Industry
けいさつ 警察 the police
  〜犬 a police dog …………[たてる¹]
  〜署 a police station [《英》office]
  〜に訴える go to the police [さいご]
  〜に連絡する contact the police ……………………………………[れんらく]
  〜のご厄介になる bother the police ……………………………………[やっかい]
けいさつちょう 警察庁 the National Police Agency
けいさん 計算
  〜する calculate …………[ただしい]
  〜問題 calculation …………[ふくざつ]
けいじ 刑事 a detective …………[だす]
けいじ 掲示 a notice, a bulletin
  〜する put up a notice
  ・post ……………………………[もはん]
けいしき 型式・形式
けいしちょう 警視庁 the Metropolitan Police Department
けいじばん 掲示板 a notice [bulletin] board; 《インターネット》a bulletin board (system), a BBS
  〜に書き込む 《インターネット》write a new message on the BBS
けいしゃ 傾斜 (an) inclination; (坂の) a slope
  〜する incline, slope
げいじゅつ 芸術
けいしょく 軽食 a light meal; (間食) a snack
けいせい 形勢 the situation
けいぞく 継続する continue; (雑誌の予約購読) renew *one's* subscription
けいそつ 軽率 ……………………[かるはずみ]
  〜な careless, stupid, rash
  〜な発言 rash statement ……[ひなん]

けいたい 携帯用の portable
  〜電話 a cell phone, a cellular phone, a mobile phone, a portable phone
  〜品 personal effects, hand luggage, hand baggage
  〜品預り所 a cloakroom, a checkroom
けいてき 警笛 an alarm whistle; (自動車などの) a horn
  〜を鳴らす give an alarm whistle, sound a horn
けいと 毛糸 woolen yarn, wool
  〜の woolen
けいど 経度 longitude
けいとう 系統 a system
  〜的 systematic
  〜的に systematically
げいのう 芸能 entertainment, show business
  〜界 a show business, the world of show business
  〜人 an entertainer
けいば 競馬 a horse race
  〜場 a race course [track], the turf
  〜で at the track ……………………[て]
  〜で儲けた金 the money *one* has won at the horse races …[ごうせい]
けいはく 軽薄
けいひ 経費 expense(s), a cost
けいび 警備 guard; 《英》defense, 《米》defence
  〜する guard, defend
  〜員 a guard
  ・a security guard …………[みまわる]
けいひん 景品 a premium, a gift, a giveaway
けいべつ 軽蔑
けいほう 警報 a warning, an alarm
けいむしょ 刑務所 a prison, a jail, 《英》a gaol
けいやく 契約
  〜違反 a breach of contract [いはん]
  〜社員 a contracted employee
  〜書 a contract ……………………[とくに]
  〜を破棄する break off a contract ……………………………………[どくだん]
けいゆ 経由で by way of, via

けいり 経理 accounting
　～課 the accounting section
けいりょう 計量カップ a measuring cup ············[はかる]
けいりん 桂林 Guilin, Kweilin
けいれい 敬礼する salute
けいれき 経歴 a career, one's personal history
けいれん 痙攣 a convulsion, a spasm
けいろうのひ 敬老の日 Respect-for-the-Aged Day ·····[ひ]
ケーキ (a) cake
　～を焼く bake a cake ············[やく³]
ケーツー (K2) K2
ケープタウン Cape Town
ケーブルカー a cable car
ゲーム a game
　～をする play a game
　～センター a game arcade
けが 怪我
げか 外科 surgery
　～医 a surgeon
けがす 汚す (名誉などを) disgrace
けがわ 毛皮 fur
げき 劇 a drama, a play
　～的な dramatic
げきじょう 劇場 a theater
げきだん 劇団 a theater troupe ···[いらい]
　・a theater group ············[ちゅうしん]
げきど 激怒する fly into a rage [fury]
げきやく 劇薬 a powerful drug ···[とりあつかう]
げきれい 激励
けさ 今朝 this morning
ケシ a poppy
げし 夏至 the summer solstice
けしいん 消印 a postmark
けしからん inexcusable ········[そうだん]
けしき 景色
けしごむ 消しゴム an eraser
けじめ
げしゅく 下宿 one's lodgings
　～する lodge (at), board (at)
　～生活をする live in a boarding house ···[など]
　～人 a lodger, a boarder
　～屋 a lodging [boarding] house, 《米》 a rooming house
げじゅん 下旬 the latter part of a month
けしょう 化粧 (a) makeup
　～する make up one's face, put on makeup
　～品 cosmetics, makeup
　厚～をする wear heavy makeup ···[ふしぜん]
けす 消す
　・cross out ············[ななめ]
げすい 下水 sewage
　(下水管) sewer ············[とおり]
　～道 a drain; (汚水) drainage
ゲスト a guest
けずる 削る
けた 桁 a figure, a digit
げた (wooden) clogs
けだもの 獣 a beast
けち ～な stingy
　～をつける find fault (with)
　～ん坊 a miser
ケチャップ ketchup
けつあつ 血圧 blood pressure
　～が高い have high blood pressure ···[せいげん]
けつい 決意
　・one's resolve ············[しめす]
けついん 欠員 a vacancy
　・a vacant post ············[うめる]
けつえき 血液 blood
　～型 a blood type
けっか 結果
けっかい 決壊する give way ····[おそれ]
けっかく 結核(症) tuberculosis ···[げんざい]
けっかん 欠陥 a defect, a fault
　～商品 defective goods ·····[しんよう]
　～のある defective
　～のない perfect, complete, faultless
けっかん 血管 a blood vessel
げっかん 月刊の monthly
　～誌 a monthly, a monthly magazine
けつぎ 決議 a resolution, a decision
　～する resolve, decide
げっきゅう 月給 a monthly pay, a monthly salary

けっきょく 結局
・in the end ……………………[いけん]
・as it turned out ……………[たくみ]
結局…である turn out to be... [にせ]
けっきん 欠勤 (an) absence from work
無断～ absence without leave
～届 a report [notice] of absence
げっけい 月経 menstruation
けつごう 結合する combine (with), unite (with), join together
けっこう 結構
～な身分 be in a fine position ……………………………[しんぱい]
けっこう 欠航する be canceled
けっこん 結婚
～相手 (男) a fiancé; (女) a fiancée ……………………………[きまる]
～を申し込む ask someone to marry one ……………………[もうしこむ]
幸福な～をする marry happily ……………………………[こうふく]
良い人と～する marry the right person ……………………[つかむ]
けっこんしき 結婚式に出席する attend a wedding ……………[つごう]
～に呼ばれる be invited to a wedding ……………………[よぶ]
～をあげる have a wedding …[かた¹]
けっさい 決済 settlement (of account)
～する settle
～条件 financial terms
けっさく 傑作 a masterpiece
けっさん 決算する settle accounts, close the books
～期 a fiscal term
けっして 決して
・by no means ………………[たかい]
げっしゃ 月謝 a monthly tuition [fee]
～を払う pay tuition fees ……[たかい]
けっしょう 決勝
～戦 the final game ……………[えんき]
・the final match ………………[くい]
けっしょう 結晶 a crystal; (成果) fruit
けっしん 決心
けっせい 結成する form, organize
けっせき 欠席
けっせき 結石 《医学用語》calculus

けっせんしょう 血栓症 《医学用語》thrombosis
けつだん 決断 decision, determination
～する decide to do, determine to do
～力 decisiveness ………………[じらす]
～力のある decisive
けっちゃく 決着
けってい 決定
けってん 欠点
・a weak point ……………[～として]
～を直す correct one's faults ……………………………[どりょく]
けっとう 決闘 a duel
けっぱく 潔白 innocence
～な innocent
げっぷ a belch, a burp
～をする belch, burp
げっぷ 月賦で買う buy something by monthly payment
けつまつ 結末 an ending, a conclusion, an end
げつまつ 月末に at the end of the month ……………………[こんざつ]
～までに by the end of the month
げつようび 月曜日 Monday (略 Mon.)
けつれつ 決裂 a breakdown [さける²]
～する break down ……[こうしょう¹]
けつろん 結論 a conclusion
～に達する come to a conclusion
・make up one's mind ………[あせる]
・come up with a result ……[まとめる]
けとばす kick
けなす speak ill of
ケニア Kenya
～の Kenyan
～人 a Kenyan; (全体) the Kenyans
けねん 懸念
けはい 気配 a sign
けはい 気配がする sense someone's presence ……………………[むこう]
けばけばしい gaudy, showy
けびょう 仮病を使う feign sickness
・pretend to be sick [きまりがわるい]
げひん 下品
ケベック Quebec
けむし 毛虫 a caterpillar
けむたい 煙たい

けむたがる 煙たがる keep *someone* at a distance ·················[りこう]
けむり 煙
けむる 煙る smoke, be smoky
けもの 獣 a beast, a brute
けり ～をつける、～がつく settle
げり 下痢 diarrhea
ゲリラ a guer(r)illa
ける 蹴る
けれど(も)
ゲレンデ a (skiing) slope ········[すべる]
けろっと ～している be unfazed, look as if nothing happened
けわしい 険しい
けん 件 a matter ·················[あずける]
　その～に関して with regard to that affair ····················[ややこしい]
けん 券 a ticket
けん 県 a prefecture
　～知事 a prefectural governor
　～庁 a prefectural office
けん 剣 a sword; (短剣) a dagger
けんあく 険悪
けんあん 懸案 a pending problem
けんい 権威 authority
げんいん 原因
けんえんのなか 犬猿の仲 fight like cats and dogs ···················[なか²]
けんお 嫌悪
けんか
　大げんか a big fight ············[ことば]
　殴り合いの～ a fist fight ···[しらせる]
　～する quarrel ·················[かならず]
げんか 原価 (a) cost, a cost price
　～で at cost
　～計算 cost accounting
　～を切って below cost ·········[きる¹]
けんかい 見解 (an) opinion, a view
　～を示す demonstrate an opinion
　························[しょうきょくてき]
　～を述べる express *one's* opinion
げんかい 限界
けんがく 見学する visit, see (for study), go on a field trip
　・take a tour of ·················[そうれい]
げんかく 幻覚 (a) hallucination; (錯覚) (an) illusion
げんかく 厳格な strict, stern, severe

げんかん 玄関 the front door, a porch
　・the entry way ··················[まく¹]
　～先で追い返される get the door slammed in *one's* face [おいかえす]
げんき 元気
　～がよい healthy ·················[ほそい]
　～な energetic ····················[かつて]
　～な男の子 a bouncing baby boy
　·························[みちる]
　～になる feel better ·············[ぬける]
けんきゅう 研究
けんきょ 謙虚
げんきん 現金 cash, ready money
　～書留 ····························[もしくは]
げんけい 減刑 a lighter sentence
　·························[きたい]
けんげん 権限 an authority
　・a power ······················[そうとう]
げんご 言語 language, speech
けんこう 健康
　～に気を配っている be careful about *one's* health ·························[つね]
　～に育つ grow up strong and healthy ······························[こめる]
　～のため for *one's* health
　····················[こころがける]
　～を維持する stay in good health
　·························[つとめて]
げんこう 言行が一致しない One does not practice what *one* preaches.
　···························[いっち]
げんこう 原稿 a manuscript, a copy; (草稿) a draft
　～用紙 manuscript paper
げんこう 現行の present, existing, current
　～憲法 the existing constitution
　·························[おおく]
げんこうはん 現行犯で捕まえる catch *someone* †in the act [red-handed]
　·························[つかまえる]
げんこく 原告 (民事訴訟の) a plaintiff; (刑事訴訟の) an accuser
けんこくきねんのひ 建国記念の日 National Foundation Day
けんこつ 拳骨 a fist
けんさ 検査
　・an investigation ················[わかる]

げんざい 現在
けんさく 検索
げんさく 原作 the original (work)
げんし 原子 an atom
　〜の atomic
　〜爆弾 an atomic bomb, an A-bomb
げんし 原始の primitive
　〜時代 the primitive age
　〜人 a primitive man
けんじつ 堅実な steady, reliable, trustworthy
　〜に steadily, soundly
げんじつ 現実
　〜性がない impractical ……[りゆう]
　〜離れしている unrealistic [はなし]
げんしゅ 厳守する observe strictly; (時間を) be punctual
けんじゅう 拳銃 a pistol, a gun, a revolver
げんじゅう 厳重な strict, severe
　〜に strictly, severely
げんじゅうしょ 現住所 *one's* present address
げんじゅうみん 原住民 the original inhabitants, the natives; (オーストラリアの) the aborigines
けんしょう 懸賞 a prize contest; (賞) a prize
げんしょう 現象 a phenomenon, (複数) phenomena)
げんしょう 減少
げんじょう 現状 the present condition
　・the status quo …………[まんぞく]
　〜維持 keep things as they are
　　……………………………[おちつく]
　〜では under existing circumstances, under the present circumstances
けんしょうえん 腱鞘炎 《医学用語》 tenosynovitis
けんじょうしゃ 健常者 healthy people
げんしりょく 原子力 nuclear power, atomic energy
　〜発電所 a nuclear power plant
　　……………………………[けんせつ]
けんしん 献身的な devoted
　〜的に devotedly

けんすい 懸垂 a chin-up ………[かい²]
げんぜい 減税する reduce (a) tax
けんせつ 建設
けんぜん 健全な healthy, sound; (娯楽・読み物などが) wholesome
げんぞう 現像 (film) developing
　〜する develop (film)
げんそく 原則 a principle, a general rule
　〜的に in principle [general]
けんそん 謙遜な modest
げんそん 現存する existing, living
げんだい 現代 the present age, modern times, today
　〜社会 modern society ……[はつめい]
　〜的な modern, up-to-date
　〜の modern, present-day, current
けんち 見地 a point of view, a viewpoint
げんち 現地 the spot
　・the site ………………………[ちょうさ]
　・there ………………………[ほうこく]
　〜報告 an on-the-spot report
　　……………………………[ほうこく]
けんちく 建築 building, construction
　〜する build, construct
　〜中 under construction
げんてい 限定する limit, restrict
　〜された limited, restricted
　〜版 a limited edition
げんてん 減点する subtract, take off
げんど 限度 a limit
けんとう 見当
　皆目〜がつかない have no idea
　　……………………………[かいもく]
けんとう 検討
けんどう 剣道 *kendo*, Japanese-style fencing
げんどう 言動 *one's* words and deeds, *one's* speech and conduct
　・what *one* says and does ……[うえる]
　・*one's* behavior and speech
　　……………………………[しんちょう]
げんどうりょく 原動力 motive power, driving force
げんに 現に actually, really; (その証拠に) as proof of that
げんば 現場 the scene (of) ………[なま]

・the scene of the crime ……[ふきん]
〜で (犯罪の) at the scene of the crime, red-handed ………[おさえる]
事故〜 the scene of the accident ………………………………[ぐうぜん]
げんばく 原爆 an atomic bomb ………………………………[ひさん]
けんびきょう 顕微鏡 a microscope
けんぶつ 見物
・sightseeing ………………………[ばん]
げんぶん 原文 the original (text)
けんぽう 憲法 a constitution
けんぽうきねんび 憲法記念日 Constitution Memorial Day
けんぼうしょう 健忘症で forgetful
げんまい 玄米 brown rice ……[けんこう]
げんみつ 厳密
けんめい 賢明
けんめつ 幻滅
けんやく 倹約
げんゆ 原油 crude oil ……[きょうきゅう]
けんり 権利
生きる〜 the right to live ……[すべて]
げんり 原理 a principle, a theory
げんりょう 原料
げんりょう 減量する reduce *one's* weight, go on a diet
〜法 diet ………………………[あやしい]
けんりょく 権力 power
〜者 a man of power
〜のある powerful
げんろん 言論の自由 (the) freedom of speech ……………………………[じゆう]

コ

こ 子 (人間の) a child (複数 children), a kid; (動物の) the young; (クマ・キツネ・ライオン・オオカミなどの) a cub
こ… 故… the late...
ご 五 five
第5(の) the fifth
5分の1 a [one] fifth
ご 語 (単語) a word; (国語) a language
…ご …後 after; (あとで) later; (以来) since
ごあいきょう ご愛敬…………[あいきょう]

コイ 鯉 a carp
こい 濃い
こい 恋
・a romance …………………[ぎせい]
〜焦がれる be desperately in love with ……………………………[しぬ]
〜に溺れる give *oneself* up to love ……………………………[おぼれる]
こい 故意
ごい 語彙 vocabulary …………[ほうふ]
こいしい 恋しい
こいびと 恋人 (男) a boyfriend; (女) a girlfriend ……………………………[き]
コインランドリー a self-service laundry; 《商標》a Laundromat
コインロッカー a coin-operated locker
こう 効を奏する prove effective [よび]
・be a success …………………[ぶたい]
こう 請う want (to ask for) [あわれむ]
こう (このように) so, like this, thus
こうい 行為
こうい 好意
・kindness ………………………[いつまでも]
〜に甘える take advantage of *someone's* kindness ………[あまえる]
こういう such *something* as this, *something* like this
こういしょう 後遺症 an aftereffect ……………………………[くち]
こういん 工員 a (factory) worker
ごういん 強引
〜さ forceful attitude ……[ていこう]
ごうう 豪雨 a heavy [torrential] rain
・a downpour …………………[きろく]
こううん 幸運・好運
こうえい 光栄
こうえん 公園 a park
こうえん 公演 a show
・a performance ………………[はじまる]
こうえん 好演 an excellent performance ……………………[こえ]
こうえん 後援 support
〜する (支持する) support, back (up); (資金的に) sponsor
こうえん 講演 a lecture, a speech
〜会 a lecture (meeting)
〜者 a lecturer, a speaker
〜する give a lecture

こうか 効果
こうか 高価な expensive, dear; valuable
こうか 硬貨 hard money, a coin
こうが 黄河 the Yellow River, Huang He
ごうか 豪華
 ・extravagant ……………………[さすが]
 〜さ grandeur ……………[のまれる]
こうかい 公開の open, public
 〜する open to the public
こうかい 後悔
こうかい 航海 a voyage, navigation
 〜する sail (for), make a voyage
こうかい 紅海 the Red Sea
こうかい 黄海 the Yellow Sea
こうがい 公害 public nuisance; environmental pollution
 ・pollution …………………[なくなる¹]
こうがい 郊外
こうかいどう 公会堂 a public hall, a town hall
こうかく 降格される be demoted
 …………………………………[かさなる]
こうがく 工学 engineering
 〜部 the engineering department
ごうかく 合格
こうがくしん 向学心 a passion for learning ………………………[もえる]
こうかつ 狡猾な sly …………[けんお]
こうかん 交換
こうかん 好感
こうき 好奇
こうぎ 抗議 (a) protest
 〜する protest (to someone against something)
こうぎ 講義 a lecture ………[たいくつ]
 ・a course ……………………[まよう]
 〜する give a lecture (on)
こうきしん 好奇心…………………[こうき]
こうきゅう 高級
 〜レストラン an exclusive restaurant ……………………[きる²]
こうきょ 皇居 the Imperial Palace
こうきょう 公共
 〜のために for [to] the public good
 …………………………………[ぎせい]
 〜料金 public utility charges

こうぎょう 工業 industry
 〜技術 industrial technology
 〜地帯 an industrial [a manufacturing] district
 〜的に industrially
 〜の industrial
こうぎょう 鉱業 mining, the mining industry
こうきょうがく 交響楽 a symphony
 〜団 a symphony orchestra
こうきん 抗菌の antibacterial
こうくう 航空 aviation
 〜会社 an airline …………[のびる]
 〜便で by air mail
 〜郵便 《米》air mail, 《英》aerial post
 〜路 an air route
 ・a route ……………………[のびる]
こうけい 光景 a sight, a scene
ごうけい 合計
 〜が合う add up, agree ………[あう¹]
こうけいき 好景気 favorable economic conditions ……………………[いう]
こうけいしゃ 後継者 one's successor
 …………………………………[ごうかく]
こうげき 攻撃
こうけつあつ 高血圧 high blood pressure, hypertension
こうけん 貢献する contribute to
 〜度 a contribution ………[ひとしい]
こうげん 高原 heights
こうご 口語 (the) spoken [colloquial] language
こうご 交互の alternate
 〜に alternately
こうこう 〜と brightly …………[てる]
こうこう 高校 a senior high school
 〜生 a high-school student
こうごう 皇后 an empress
 〜陛下 Her Majesty the Empress
こうこがく 考古学 archaeology
 …………………………………[こころ]
 〜者 an archaeologist ………[いか]
こうこく 広告 an advertisement, an ad
 〜を出す advertise, put an ad (in)
 誇大〜 an exaggerated advertisement ………………[まどわす]

ごうコン 合コン a mixer …..[めんぼく]
こうさ 交差する cross
　〜点 a crossing, an intersection
こうざ 口座 an account
こうざ 講座 a course, a lecture
こうさい 交際
　〜範囲 a range of acquaintances
　………………………………[せまい]
こうさく 工作 handicraft
　和平〜 a peace move
こうさん 降参する surrender, give up
こうざん 鉱山 a mine ………….[ほる]
こうざん 高山植物 alpine plants
　………………………………[つくす]
こうし 公私 public and private
　………………………………[くべつ]
こうし 講師 (講演者) a speaker, a
　lecturer; (大学の) an instructor,
　a lecturer
こうじ 工事
　〜現場 construction site ［はっけん］
こうしき 公式 (数学の) a formula
　〜の formal, official
　〜に formally, officially
こうしせい 高姿勢の high-handed
　………………………………[しせい]
こうじつ 口実 an excuse
　〜をつける come up with an excuse
　………………………………[なんとか]
こうしゃ 後者 the latter
こうしゃ 校舎 a schoolhouse, a school
　building
こうしゅう 公衆 the (general) public
　〜衛生 public health ………[えいせい]
　〜電話 a public telephone; (街頭の
　ボックス) a pay phone; 《米》 a
　telephone booth; 《英》 a telephone
　kiosk, a call box
　・a pay phone ……………….[つかえる]
　〜の public
　〜便所 a (public) lavatory
こうしゅう 講習 a (short) course, a
　class
こうしょう 交渉
こうしょう 高尚
こうじょう 工場 a factory, a plant,
　a mill
こうじょう 向上 progress

　・(an) improvement ………….[えいせい]
　〜する improve, make progress (in)
ごうじょう 強情
こうじょうせん 甲状腺 thyroid gland
こうしん 行進 a march, a parade
　〜する march, parade
　・proceed ……………………….[みだす]
こうしん 更新 (契約・免許証などの)
　renewal; (情報・データなどの)
　update
　〜する (契約・免許証などの) renew;
　(情報・データなどの) update; (スポ
　ーツや売上成績などの記録を) break
こうしんりょう 香辛料 a seasoning
　・a spice ……………………….[きえる]
こうすい 香水 a scent
　・(a) perfume ……………….[つける¹]
こうずい 洪水 a flood
こうすいかくりつ 降水確率 the
　probability of rain
こうせい 公正
こうせい 後世 later [future] ages
　・posterity ……………………..[のこす]
こうせい 校正 proofreading ［げんみつ］
ごうせい 合成繊維 (a) synthetic fiber
　…………………………[くべつ、げんりょう]
　〜着色料 (an) artificial coloring
ごうせい 豪勢
こうせいとりひきいいんかい 公正取引委
　員会 the Fair Trade Commission
こうせいぶっしつ 抗生物質 an
　antibiotic
こうせいろうどうしょう 厚生労働省 the
　Ministry of Health, Labour and
　Welfare
こうせき 功績 contribution,
　achievement
　〜を残す make contributions to
　………………………………[ふきゅう]
こうせん 光線 a ray (of light), a
　beam; (光) light
こうぜん 公然の open, public
　〜と openly, publicly
こうそう 高層ビル a skyscraper
　………………………………[おそろしい]
　・a high-rise ……………….[はりあう]
こうぞう 構造
　〜改革 structural reform

こうそく 校則 school regulations
こうそく 高速で at high [full] speed
 〜道路 a superhighway, a freeway, 《英》a motorway
 ・an expressway ……………[はんたい]
こうたい 交代・交替
こうたい 後退する go back, retreat
こうだい 広大な vast, immense
 〜な土地 a large piece of land
 …………………………………[しょゆう]
こうたいし 皇太子 a Crown Prince
こうちゃ 紅茶 tea, black tea
こうちょう 好調
こうちょう 校長 (小学校の, 男性の) a head-master, (女性の) a head-mistress; (中学校の) a principal; (高等学校の) a director
こうつう 交通
 〜事故 a traffic accident ……[いのち]
 〜事故にあう be in a traffic accident ………………………………………[ち]
 〜事故を起こす cause a car accident ……………………………………[ちょっと]
 〜スト a transportation strike ……………………………………[つく⁴]
 〜費 transportation charges [でる]
 ・traveling expenses …………[もつ]
 〜法規 traffic regulations
 ……………………[あらためる, むし]
こうつごう 好都合な (事・物について) convenient, favorable
 〜に favorably
こうてい 肯定する affirm
こうてい 校庭 a schoolyard …[のぞく¹]
こうてい 皇帝 an emperor
こうていぶあい 公定歩合 the official discount rate …………[ひきあげる]
こうてき 公的な official, public
 〜資金 public funds
こうてつ 鋼鉄 steel
こうてん 好転する change for the better
こうてんてき 後天的な acquired
こうど 高度 an altitude …………[さげる]
こうど 高度な advanced
 〜な技術力 a high level of technology ………………[せいさん¹]
 〜な工業国 a highly industrialized country ………………………[じょうしき]
こうとう 口頭の oral
 〜で orally
こうとう 石油の高騰 a jump in oil prices ……………………………[しる]
こうとう 高等の high(er), advanced
こうどう 行動
 〜に移す start the actual work
 …………………………………[まとまる]
こうどう 講堂 a (lecture) hall; (学校の) an assembly hall, 《米》an auditorium
ごうとう 強盗 (人) a burglar, a robber; (行為) burglary, robbery
 〜を働く commit robbery …[こまる]
ごうどう 合同の joint
こうどく 購読する (定期的に) subscribe to
こうない (…の)構内に inside something ………………………[あんない]
こうないえん 口内炎 an inflammation of the inside of the mouth, a mouth sore, 《医学用語》stomatitis
こうにゅう 購入する purchase
 ……………………………………[てつづき]
こうにん 公認の official, authorized
こうにん 後任 a successor
こうねつ 高熱 a high fever [くるしむ]
こうねんき 更年期 the change of life; (閉経期) (the) menopause
 〜障害 menopausal disorders, climacteric suffering
こうはい 後輩 *one's* junior
こうはん 後半 the latter half
こうばん 交番 a police box ……[たつ²]
こうひょう 公表する announce, publish, make public
こうひょう 好評な popular
 〜だ be well received ……[かんとく]
こうふく 幸福
こうふく 降伏する surrender
こうぶつ 好物 *one's* favorite food [dish]
こうぶつ 鉱物 a mineral
こうふん 興奮
 〜して excitedly ………………[にる¹]
こうへい 公平
こうほ 候補 a candidate …………[かた³]

~者　a candidate ……………[たたかう]
~に上る……………………………[のぼる]
ごうほうてき　合法的な　lawful, legal
こうまん　高慢
ごうまん　ごう慢な　arrogant
こうみょう　巧妙
こうみんかん　公民館　a community center
こうむいん　公務員　a public official [servant], a public employee
 ・a civil servant ……………[こうへい]
 ・a government official [はらだたしい]
こうめい　高名な　famous ………[うける]
こうめい　公明
こうめいとう　公明党　New Komeito
コウモリ　《動物》a bat
ごうもん　拷問　torture
　~する　torture
こうや　荒野　a wilderness
こうやく　公約　a pledge
 ・*one's* campaign promise　[じっこう]
 ・commitments to the public
　…………………………………[はたす]
こうよう　紅葉　red [colored] leaves, autumn leaves
　~する　turn red
こうよう　公用で　on official business
こうらく　行楽地　a holiday resort
こうり　小売り　retail sale
　~店　a retail store [《英》shop]
 ・small retail stores …………[たおれる]
　~価格　a retail price
ごうり　合理
　~主義者　a rationalist ……[てってい]
こうりがし　高利貸し　a loan shark　[ち]
こうりつ　公立の　public
　~学校　a public school,《英》a county school
こうりゅう　交流　(an) interchange, (a) friendship
こうりょ　考慮　consideration
　~する　consider, take *something* into consideration
こうりょく　効力　effect
　~のある　effective, valid
こうれい　高齢者　a person of advanced age; (集合的に) old people, the aged, the elderly

~化社会　an aging society, a graying society
~社会　an aged society
ごうれい　号令　a command
 ・an order ……………………[すすむ]
こうろん　口論　a dispute, a quarrel
 ・an argument ………………[すえ]
　~する　quarrel (with), have a quarrel (with)
こえ　声
　~が細い　have a thin voice　[ほそい]
　~を合わせて　in chorus ……[あわせる]
　~を落とす　drop [lower] *one's* voice
　……………………………………[おとす]
　~をかける　call after ………[びっくり]
　~を揃えて　in unison ………[そろえる]
ごえい　護衛(する)　guard
こえた　肥えた　(土地が) rich, fertile; (人が) fat, stout
こえる　肥える　(土地が) grow rich [fertile]
こえる　越・超える
ゴージャス　~な　gorgeous, luxurious
コース　a course
コーチ　(人) a coach, a coacher
　~する　coach
コート　(上着・オーバー) a coat; (球技の) a court
コード　(電気の) a cord; (電信の) a code
コーナー　(角) a corner; (売り場) a department
コーヒー　coffee
　~を入れる　make coffee
コーラス　a chorus
こおり　氷　ice
　~が張る　ice forms ……………[はる¹]
こおる　凍る
　凍っている　(道路が) be covered with ice ……………………………[ころぶ]
ゴール　the goal, the finish line
ゴールイン　~する　cross the finish (line)
 ・finish (the race) ………………[さ]
ゴールデンウィーク　Golden Week
ゴールデンタイム　(the) prime time
コオロギ　a cricket ……………[なく²]
こがい　戸外　the open air

～で in the open air, outdoors
ごかい 誤解
　～が解ける　misunderstanding goes away ……………………[ごかい]
ごがく 語学　language (study)
　～力　linguistic ability ……[ちがい]
ごかくけい 五角形　a pentagon
　～の　pentagonal
こかげ 木陰　the shade of a tree
こがす 焦がす　burn
こがたの 小型の　small, compact, pocket-sized
ごがつ 五月　May
ごきげんうかがい ご機嫌伺い　see how *someone* is ……………[きげん²]
こぎって 小切手　a check,《英》a cheque
　～帳　a checkbook
ゴキブリ a cockroach ………[ふえる]
　～が出る　get cockroaches ……[ふけつ]
こきゅう 呼吸
　～困難　difficulty in breathing,《医学用語》dyspnea
こきょう 故郷
　・home ………………………[なつかしい]
　・*one's* old hometown ……[なつかしい]
　・the town where *someone* was born ………………………………[ねむる]
　～に帰る　return to *one's* hometown ………………………………[はなれる²]
こぐ　(船・ボートを) row, paddle;(自転車を) pedal
こくおう 国王　a king
　・a monarch ……………[おさめる²]
こくご 国語　(言語) a language; (自国語) *one's* mother tongue; (日本語) the Japanese language
　・Japanese ………………[～だって]
ごくごく ～と飲む　gulp down …[のむ]
こくさい 国際
　～的な　internationally renowned ……………………………………[そだつ]
　～線　an international route …[せん]
こくさい 国債(を発行する)　(issue) national [government] bonds
こくさいれんごう 国際連合　the United Nations (略 UN, U.N.)
こくさんの 国産の　homemade, domestic

　～品　home [domestic] products
こくじん 黒人　a black; (米国の) an African American, an Afro-American
こくぜいちょう 国税庁　the National Tax Agency
こくせいちょうさ 国勢調査　census
こくせき 国籍　nationality
こくそ 告訴する　sue, accuse, file a complaint
こくたい 国体　a national athletic meet ……………………………………[けってい]
こくどう 国道　a national highway [road, route] ……………[つづく]
こくどこうつうしょう 国土交通省　the Ministry of Land, Infrastructure and Transport
こくない 国内の　home, domestic
　～で[に]　at home, in the country
こくはく 告白　(a) confession
　～する　confess; make a confession
こくはつ 告発する　charge, accuse
　内部～者　an inside informant, a whistleblower
こくばん 黒板　a blackboard
　～ふき　an eraser
こくふく 克服する　overcome, get over
こくべつしき 告別式　a funeral
こくほう 国宝　a national treasure ……………………………………[いっぱん]
こくぼう 国防　national defense
こくみん 国民
　～としての　as a citizen ………[ぎむ]
こくもつ 穀物　《米》grain,《英》corn
ごくらく 極楽　a paradise
こくりつの 国立の　national
こくれん 国連　the United Nations (略 UN, U.N.)
ごくろうさま ご苦労さま ………[くろう]
コケ　moss
こけい 固形の　solid
こげる 焦げる
ここ　here, this place
　～に[で・へ]　here
ごご 午後　the afternoon
　～に　in the afternoon
　今日の～に　this afternoon
ココア　cocoa

こごえる 凍える　be frozen
ここく 故国　one's native land [country], one's home
ここだけ ～の話　just between us ·········[はなし]
** here** 心地
ここちよい 心地よい　nice ·········[かぜ¹]
・feel good ·········[わたる]
こごと 小言をいう　scold, give *someone* a scolding
・lecture ·········[かい²]
ココナッツ　a coconut
ここのところ　recently ·········[くわわる]
こころ 心
　～に ·········[のこす]
　～に浮かぶ　come to *one's* mind ·········[うかぶ]
　～に残る　make an impression on *one's* mind ·········[いんしょう]
　～にもない　insincere ·········[おせじ]
　～の温まる　heartwarming ·········[ふうけい]
　～の美しい　beautiful ·········[うつくしい]
　～の奥では　deep down [inside] ·········[おく²]
　～の底から　from the bottom of *one's* heart ·········[そこ]
　～の病気　an emotional disorder ·········[びょうき]
　～を動かす　move, touch the heart of ·········[うごかす]
　～を打たれる　be touched by [おもう]
　・be deeply touched [moved] by ·········[うつ]
　～を静める　calm down, compose oneself ·········[しずめる²]
　～を慰める　soothe the soul [heart] ·········[なぐさめる]
　～を開いて　open-hearted ·········[ひらく]
こころあたり 心当たり
こころがける 心掛ける
こころざし 志 (志望) (an) ambition; (意志) will; (目的) (an) aim
　～半ばで　without fulfilling *one's* life ambition ·········[なかば]
こころづよい 心強い
こころのこり 心残り　(a) regret
　～だ　regret
こころぼそい 心細い

こころみ 試み
　新しい～　a venture ·········[ふほんい]
こころみる 試みる
こころもち 心持ち　《副詞》somewhat, slightly, just a bit
こころもとない 心許もとない　be uneasy, be not sure
こころよい 快い
こころよく 快く　(快適に) comfortably; (喜んで) gladly, willingly
　・readily ·········[こころよい]
　・pleasantly ·········[こころよい]
　・graciously ·········[みせる]
ござ　a mat of woven rush
こざっぱり ～した　nice and neat ·········[さっぱり]
こさめ 小雨　a light rain
こし 腰
　～が曲がっている　be bent over ·········[まがる]
　～の痛み　a pain in *one's* back ·········[とめる¹]
　・a lower-back pain ·········[やむ]
　～を曲げる　bend over ·········[まげる]
こじ 孤児　an orphan ·········[かわいそう]
　～院　an orphanage ·········[ざいさん]
こじ 誇示する　show off
　・flaunt ·········[ぜったい]
こじあける こじ開ける　force open
こしかける 腰掛ける·········[すわる]
こじき　a beggar
ごしごし ～洗う　scrub ·········[あらう]
こしつ 固執
ごじつ 後日　sometime later ····[よせる]
こじつけ ～の　unnatural, distorted
ゴシップ　(a) gossip
ごじゅう 五十　fifty
　第50(の)　the fiftieth (略 50th)
こしょう 故障
　・a defect ·········[じこ²]
　～する　be broken ·········[のぼる]
コショー　pepper
　～を振る　season *something* with pepper ·········[ふる¹]
ごしょく 誤植　a misprint, a typo ·········[みつける]
こじれる (話) get complicated, get entangled; (人間関係) go [turn]

こじん　個人
　～消費　private consumption
　　……………………………………［ひえる］
こじん　故人　the deceased
こす　越す
こずえ　the treetop ……………［なく²］
コスモス　a cosmos
こする　擦る
こせい　個性
　～的な　distinctive, individual
　・unique ……………………［それぞれ］
こせき　戸籍　a family register
こぜに　小銭　(small) change
ごぜん　午前　the morning
　～中　in the morning
　明日の～に　tomorrow morning
～こそ
　(…であれば)こそ　especially ［うかつ］
こそこそ　sneakily, secretly, behind *someone's* back
こたい　固体　a solid
　～の　solid
こだい　古代　ancient times
　～人　the ancients ……………［うめる］
　～の　ancient
こたえ　答え
こたえる　答・応・堪える
　訴えに～　respond to an appeal
　　……………………………………［せつじつ］
ごたごた　(もめごと) troubles, confusion
こだま　an echo
こだわる
　・get hung up on ……………［ちいさい］
　・be a stickler for ……………［けいしき］
ごちそう　ご馳走
ごちそうさま　Thank you. ……［おいしい］
こちょう　誇張する　exaggerate
こちら
　～の方(へ, を)　this way ……［うなる］
こぢんまり　～した　(小さくて居心地のよい) cozy; (小さくて充実した) compact
こつ
こっか　国歌　a national anthem
こっか　国家　a nation, a country
　・a state ……………………………［かんり］

～機密　state secrets ……………［もらす］
　～公務員　a government employee
　～試験　a state examination
こっかい　国会　(日本の) the (National) Diet; (米国の) Congress; (英国・カナダなどの) Parliament
　・the Diet ……………………………［なる¹］
　～議事堂(日本の)　the Diet Building; (米国の) the Capitol; (英国の) the Houses of Parliament
　～を解散する　dissolve the Diet
　～を召集する　call the Diet
こっかい　黒海　the Black Sea
こづかい　小遣い
こっかこうあんいいんかい　国家公安委員会　the National Public Safety Commission
こっき　国旗　the national flag
こっきょう　国境　a border ……［こえる］
　～紛争　the border dispute ［しんこく］
コック　(料理人) a cook
こっけい　滑稽
こっこう　国交　diplomatic relations
こっこくと　刻々と　every moment, moment by moment
　・by the minute ………………［せまる］
ごつごつ　jagged …………………［かど］
　～している(手が)　strong and rough
　　……………………………………［て］
こっせつ　骨折　a break, a fracture
　脚〔腕〕を～する　break [fracture] *one's* leg 〔arm〕
こつそしょうしょう　骨粗鬆症
　《医学用語》osteoporosis
こっそり
こった　凝った　fancy ………［すっきり］
こつたこうしょう　骨多孔症
　《医学用語》osteoporosis
こづつみ　小包　《米》a package 《英》a parcel
　・a package ……………………［なかみ］
こってり　～した　(食べ物が) rich; (化粧が) thick
こっとうひん　骨董品　an antique
　　……………………………………［にせ, もどす］
コップ　a glass
こてい　固定する　fix
　～客　a regular (customer)

~給 a fixed salary
こてん 古典 (総称) the classics; (一編の) a classic
  ~の classic, classical
こてん 個展 a one-man show
  ・an exhibition of *one's* own …[もつ]
こと 事
こどう 鼓動 beat, (a) heartbeat
こどく 孤独
ことごとく every, entirely
  ・all …………………[こころみる]
ことし 今年 this year
ことづかる 言づかる
ことづける 言づける
ことづて 言づて a message [つたえる]
ことなる 異なる
ことば 言葉
  ・a remark …………………[なにげない]
  ~が荒っぽい use rough language
    ……………………………[あらい¹]
  ~巧み be clever in *one's* speech
    ……………………………[たくみ]
  ~ではとても言い尽くせない…[つくす]
  ~に表す express *something* in words
    ……………………………[あらわす¹]
  ~に表せない beyond all description
    ……………………………[あらわす¹]
  お~に甘えて accept your kind offer
    ……………………………[あまえる]
  慰める~もない not find the words
    to comfort ……………[なぐさめる]
  ~づかい wording, language
こども 子ども a child (複数 children); (男の子) a boy; (女の子) a girl; (息子) a [*one's*] son; (娘) a [*one's*] daughter
  ・a kid ……………………………[など]
  ~っぽい (悪い意味で) childish
  ~の頃 when *one* was little …[ゆび]
  ~の非行 juvenile delinquency
    ……………………………[よっきゅう]
  ~らしい (よい意味で) childlike
  ~を作る start a family ………[つくる]
こどものひ こどもの日 Children's Day
ことり 小鳥 a (little) bird
ことわざ a proverb
ことわり 断り (拒絶) a refusal; (予告) a notice; (許可) permission

ことわる 断る
こな 粉 powder; (穀物の) flour
  ~の powdery
こなす
こなゆき 粉雪 powdery snow ….[まう]
こにもつ 小荷物 a parcel
コネ ~で through connections
  あの会社に~がある have connections [contacts, influence] in [with] that company
この this
このあいだ
  ~の last ……………………[たのしむ]
このあたり この辺り this area
  ……………………………[つうじる]
このご この期に及んで at this stage of the game ……………………[および]
このごろ この頃
このさい この際 on this occasion, under the circumstances
このさき この先 ahead; (今後) in the future
このところ recently ……………[だれる]
  ・for some time now ………[ゆううつ]
  ・for the last few days ……[れんぞく]
このへん この辺に about here, near here, around here, in this neighborhood
このまえ この前
このましい 好ましい
このまま ~でいくと at this rate
  ……………………………[さける²]
このみ 好み
こばむ 拒む refuse, reject
こはるびより 小春日より a mild autumn day
  ・an Indian summer ………[のどか]
ごはん 御飯 (食事) a meal (米飯) rice …………………[こげる, まじる]
ごび 語尾 a word ending ….[ひっぱる]
コピー
コピーアンドペースト ~する 《コンピュータ》 copy and paste
コピーライター a copywriter
こびりつく stick to
こびる flatter, fawn on
こぶ a bump, a lump
こふう 古風な old-fashioned, antique

ごぶさた ご無沙汰
こぶし a fist ……………[かためる]
こぶり 小降りになる The rain is letting up.
コペンハーゲン Copenhagen
ごほう 誤報 a false report ……[おどる]
ゴボウ a burdock (root)
こぼす
こぼれる
こま a top
　～を回す spin a top …………[まわす]
ゴマ (a) sesame seed
　～をする (おべっかを使う) play up to ……………[する¹]
コマーシャル a commercial
こまかい 細かい
　～所 the fine details …………[うつる¹]
　～所にうるさい be such a stickler for detail ……………[けむたい]
こまかく 細かく (小さく) to pieces; (くわしく) in detail
　・into narrow strips ……………[さく²]
　～する (お金を) change
ごまかす
こまる 困る
　・be at a loss ……………[ひじょう]
　・have trouble with ………[いたずら]
　・have difficulty ……………[けいざい]
　・get into difficulty ……………[でも]
　・be perturbed ……………[ひねる]
　・it makes things difficult for *one* if... ……………[しらせる]
　(…されては)困る not want to *do* ……………[いっしょ]
　困ったときには ……………[ちから]
　困ったもの a problem, be out of hand ……………[ねつ]
　困って in distress ………[あさましい]
　困らせる put *someone* on the spot ……………[むり]

ごみ dust; (がらくた・紙くず) trash; (台所などの) garbage
　・garbage ……………[だす]
　・trash ……………[すてる]
　燃える[燃えない]～ burnable [unburnable] rubbish
　～捨て場 a garbage dump [むらがる]
　～を出す take out the garbage

こみいって 込み入って complicated
　(小説の筋が) involved ……………[すじ]
ごみごみ ～した (建て込んだ) built-up; (混雑した) crowded: (汚ならしい) squalid
こみち 小道 a path, a lane
ごみばこ ごみ箱
こみみ 小耳に挟む just happen to hear ……………[はさむ]
コミュニケーション communication
こむ 込む・混む
　込んでいる be jammed ………[よる¹]
ゴム rubber
　・an elastic ……………[のびる]
　輪～ a rubber band
コムギ 小麦 wheat
　～粉 (wheat) flour
　・flour ……………[はかる]
こめ 米 rice
　～屋 a rice store
こめかみ the temple
こめる 込める
　愛情を込めて with love
　願いを込めて in the hope that ...
ごめん 御免
　(…は)ごめんだ ……………[わり]
こもじ 小文字 a small letter
こもり 子守 (人) a nurse maid, a baby-sitter
　～歌 a nursery song, a cradle song
　・a lullaby ……………[やさしい²]
　～する nurse a baby, baby-sit, work as a baby-sitter
こもん 顧問 an adviser
こや 小屋 a cottage, a hut
　犬～ a doghouse
　牛～ a cowshed
　馬～ a stable
　鶏～ a chicken house, a chicken coop
　豚～ a pigsty
ごやく 誤訳 a mistranslation
こゆう 固有の peculiar (to), proper (to)
こゆび 小指 (手の) a little finger; (足の) a little toe
こよみ 暦 a calendar; (天文・気象などを記した) an almanac

こらえる 堪える
・bear (up under) ……………[おどろく]
ごらく 娯楽　an amusement, an entertainment, (a) recreation
こらしめる （罰する）punish; （教訓を与える）give *someone* a lesson
こらっ Hey!
コラム a column
こりつ 孤立した　isolated
ゴリラ a gorilla
こりる 懲りる
こる 凝る
　凝って stiff ………………[かた³]
コルク 〜を抜く　uncork, pull the cork out of ……………………[ぬく]
ゴルフ golf
　〜コンペ　a golf tournament
これ this
これから （今後は）in (the) future;（これからずっと）from now on
　これから…だ　be now getting to …………………………[やま]
コレクション a collection
コレクトコール a collect call
　〜をかける　call *someone* collect
これくらい 〜にする　end ………[かた³]
コレステロール cholesterol
これほど so, such
ころ 頃
ゴロ 《野球》a grounder
ころがす 転がす
ころがる 転がる
ころげおちる 転げ落ちる　fall down ………………………………[うえ]
ころす 殺す
コロッケ a croquette
ごろね ごろ寝する　lie around　[かぎる]
ころぶ 転ぶ
ころりと 〜だまされる　be completely taken in (by) ……………[こうみょう]
コロンビア Colombia
　〜の　Colombian
　〜人　a Colombian;（全体）the Colombians
コロンボ Colombo
こわい 怖い
　怖いものなし　have nothing to fear ………………………………[くむ²]
　怖くて　in fear ………………[あと¹]
こわがる 怖がる
　・have a fear ………………[むやみ]
こわす 壊す
こわれもの 壊れ物　a fragile object ………………………………[ほどく]
こわれる 壊れる
　・break down ………………[ふべん]
こん 根を詰めて…する　chain *oneself* to *something* ……………[つめる]
こん 紺(の)　dark blue, navy blue
こんがらかる
こんき 根気
　〜が続かなくなる　run out of patience ……………………[つづく]
　〜のよい　patient
　〜よく　patiently
こんきょ 根拠
コンクール a contest
コンクリート concrete
こんげつ 今月　this month
　〜中に　by the end of this month ………………………………[おさめる¹]
こんご 今後　after this, from now (on), in future
　〜の成り行きによっては　depending on how things develop in the future ……………………[よる¹]
コンゴ Congo
　〜の　Congolese
　〜人　a Congolese;（全体）the Congolese
コンサート a concert
こんざつ 混雑
　〜する　be crowded (with), be jammed (with)
こんしゅう 今週　this week
こんじょう 根性
　島国〜　insularity
こんすい 昏睡状態　a coma
コンセンサス a consensus
コンセント an outlet, a socket
コンタクトレンズ a contact lens
こんだて 献立　a menu
こんたん 魂胆　an underlying motive, a plot
こんちゅう 昆虫　an insect　…[〜だって]
コンディション condition

～がいい　be in good condition [shape]
コンテスト　a contest
コンテナ　a container
コンテンツ　《インターネット》the content (of a site)
こんど　今度
　～こそ　this time or else ………[うつ]
　～の　recent ………………[たえる¹]
　・coming ………………[たつ²]
こんどう　混同する　mistake *A* for *B*
こんな
　～とき　at a time like this ……[でも]
　～に　so, such
こんなん　困難
　～な　complex ……………[みせる]
　・hard ……………………[ほっと]
　～な状況　a difficult situation
　………………………………[きわめて]
こんにち　今日　today, this day; (現今) these days
　～の　current ……………………[ち]
　・present ………………[ふだん¹]
こんにちは　今日は　(午前中) Good morning.; (午後) Good afternoon.; (親しいあいだで) Hello!／Hi!
コンパ　a get-together
　・a class party ……………[ようき]
コンパス　(a pair of) compasses
こんばん　今晩　this evening; tonight
こんばんは　Good evening.; (親しい間で) Hello.／Hi.
コンビ　a pair, a duo
コンビーフ　corned beef,《米》corn beef
コンビニ　a convenience store
コンピュータ
こんぶ　昆布　a sea tangle, kelp
コンプレックス　an inferiority complex
こんぽん　根本
　～的な　basic, fundamental
　～的に　basically, fundamentally
コンマ　a comma
こんや　今夜　tonight, this evening
こんやく　婚約　engagement
　～者　(男) *one's* fiancé; (女) *one's* fiancée
　～する　get engaged (to)

こんらん　混乱する　be confused, fall into confusion

サ

さ　差
　～が激しい　quite different ……[うち]
さあ　(人をうながして) come, now; (つなぎ言葉) well; let me see; (注意をうながして) here
サーカス　a circus
サークル　a circle, a club
サーチエンジン　《インターネット》a search engine
サーバー[サーバ]　《コンピュータ》a server
サービス
サーブ　(球技) service, serve
サーフィン　surfing, surfriding
サイ　a rhinoceros, a rhino
…さい　…歳　...years old
さいあい　最愛の　dearest, beloved
　・dearly beloved ……………[ぜつぼう]
さいあく　最悪(の)　the worst
さいえん　菜園　a vegetable garden
　………………………………[くぎる]
さいがい　災害　(a) calamity
　・(a) disaster ……………[にんしき]
　～地　the area hit by disaster
　………………………………[きょうきゅう]
　～対策　disaster measures
ざいかい　財界　the financial world
　………………………………[だいいち]
　・the business world ……[せいりょく]
　～人　a financier, a businessman
ざいがく　在学する　be in school [college]; be a student
さいきどう　再起動
さいきん　細菌　a germ, bacteria (単数 bacterium)
さいきん　最近
　～の　these days ……………[つかう]
　・nowadays ……………………[れい¹]
　・today's ………………………[こまる]
さいく　細工　work; (たくらみ) tricks
サイクリング　cycling
　～に行く　go cycling
さいけつ　採決する　vote
さいげつ　歳月　years

さいけっせい 再結成する　get back together ……………………[ふかのう]
さいけん 再建する　reconstruct
さいげん 再現する　reproduce
さいげん 際限なく　limitlessly, boundlessly
さいこ 最古の　the oldest
さいご 最後
　〜まで　to the end ………[たたかう]
　・till the end ………………………[たいど]
　・until the very end …………[ちから]
ざいこ 在庫　stock
　〜がない　be out of stock
さいこう 最高
さいこうさいばんしょ 最高裁判所　the Supreme Court of Japan
さいころ　a die (複数 dice)
さいこん 再婚する　remarry ……[つれる]
さいさん 再三　again and again, many times
さいさん 採算
ざいさん 財産
　・*one's* estate …………………[ひとしい]
　・*one's* property ………………[わける]
　〜を受け継ぐ　inherit a fortune
さいじつ 祭日　a holiday; (国の) a national holiday
さいしゅう 採集　collection
さいしゅう 最終(の)　the last, the final
さいしょ 最初
　〜の　initial …………………[いき²]
さいしょくしゅぎ 菜食主義者　a vegetarian
さいしん 細心の　very careful, scrupulous
さいしん 最新の　the latest, the newest, up-to-date
サイズ　size
さいせい 再生する　(音・映像) playback, reproduce; (再利用する) recycle
　〜紙　recycled paper
ざいせい 財政　finance
さいぜん 最善(の)　the best
さいそく 催促
　〜する　press for ……………[しつこい]
　〜状　a reminder that *something* is overdue

サイダー　soda (pop)
さいだい 最大
　〜限の　maximum, full
　〜限に　fully
　〜限にいかす　make the most of ………………………………[いかす]
　〜の　the greatest, the largest, the biggest
ざいたく 在宅する　be (at) home, be in
　〜看護　in-home (nursing) care, home health care
　〜勤務　(コンピューター端末による) telecommuting
さいちゅう 最中
さいてい 最低(の)　the lowest; (最小限の) minimum; (最悪の) the worst
さいてき 最適な　the most suitable, perfect
さいてん 採点する　grade, mark
サイト (ホームページ) a site, a website
　有料〜　a pay site
さいなん 災難
さいのう 才能
　・natural abilities ……………[ころす]
　〜のある　talented, gifted
　〜を発揮する　display a talent ………………………………[ゆたか]
　絵の〜　artistic ability ………[のばす]
さいばい 栽培　growing, cultivation
　・cultivating …………………[てきする]
　〜する　grow, cultivate
さいばん 裁判　judgment, (a) trial, a suit
　〜官　a judge
　〜所　a (law) court; (建物) a courthouse
　最高〜所　the Supreme Court of Japan
　〜中で　on trial
　〜で争う　be fought over in court ………………………………[ひょうげん]
　〜に訴える　go to court　[うったえる]
　〜にかける　bring *someone* to trial
さいふ 財布　(がま口) a purse; (紙入れ) a pocketbook, a wallet
　〜のひもが緩む　spend more than usual ……………………………[ゆるむ]

～のひもを締める　tighten the purse strings ……………………[しめる²]
　～を握る　hold the purse strings ……………………………[にぎる]
さいほう　裁縫　sewing, needlework
さいぼう　細胞　a cell
さいまつ　歳末の　year-end
　～大売り出し　a big year-end sale ………………………………[せんでん]
さいみんじゅつ　催眠術　hypnotism ………………………………[じっけん]
ざいむしょう　財務省　the Ministry of Finance
ざいもく　材木　wood; (製材した)《米》lumber,《英》timber
さいゆうしゅう　最優秀賞　the grand prize ……………………………[けっか]
さいよう　採用　acceptance ……[しらせ]
　～する　(雇う)employ; (任命する)appoint; (選び取る)adopt
　・adopt ……………………………[かく³]
　～試験　an employment examination
さいりょう　最良の　the best
ざいりょう　材料
サイレン　a siren
さいわい　幸い
　～する　favor
　～にも　fortunately, luckily
サイン　(署名)a signature; (有名人の・記念としての)an autograph; (合図, 信号)a signal; (符号)a sign
　～する　sign
サウジアラビア　Saudi Arabia
　～の　Saudi Arabian
　～人　a Saudi Arabian; (全体)the Saudi Arabians
～さえ
　～さえすれば　as long as ………[など]
さえぎる　(光・音などを)shut out (話などを)interrupt …………[ことば]
さえずる　sing, twitter
　・chirp ……………………………[やがて]
さえる　冴える
さか　坂　a slope
　下り～　a downward slope
　上り～　an upward slope
さかい　境　a boundary, a border
さかさま　逆様に　upside down

さがす　探・捜す
さかずき　杯　a (sake) cup
さかだち　逆立ち　(手だけで)a handstand; (手と頭で)a headstand
　～する　stand on one's (head and) hands
さかな　魚　a fish; (魚肉)fish
　～屋　a fish shop
　・a fishmonger ………………[けいき]
　～をおろす　cut a fish ……[あやしい]
さかのぼる　(過去に)go back (to); (川を)go up
さかや　酒屋　a wine shop
　・a liquor store …………………[とる¹]
さからう　逆らう
さかり　盛り
　～である　(果実などが)be in season; (人が)be in (one's) prime
さがる　下がる
　・step back ……………………[あぶない]
　・move back ……………………[うしろ]
　・decline ………………………[せいさん¹]
さかん　盛ん
さき　先
　～に行く　go ahead to …………[とる¹]
　～を越す　get ahead of ……[ぐずぐず]
サギ　a heron; (シラサギ)an egret
さぎし　詐欺師　a swindler ………[よく²]
サキソフォン　a saxophone
さきだつもの　先立つもの　the first consideration ……………………[かね]
さきゅう　砂丘　a sand hill, a dune
さぎょう　作業　work
さく　作　a work ……………………[かいしん]
さく　策　a plan, a measure
さく　咲く
さく　裂・割く
さく　柵　a fence
さくいん　索引　an index
さくしゃ　作者　an author, a writer
さくじょ　削除する　delete, erase, remove;《コンピュータ》delete
さくせん　作戦　tactics
　・a strategy ……………………[よむ]
さくひん　作品
さくふう　作風　one's style ……[あらそう]
さくぶん　作文　(a) composition; (課題作文)a theme

英〜 English composition
さくもつ 作物 a crop, a farm product
さくや 昨夜 last night, yesterday evening
サクラ 桜 (木) a cherry tree; (花) cherry blossoms
　〜色 light pink
サクランボウ a cherry
さくりゃく 策略 a trick, a scheme, a plot
　〜に乗る get taken in by *someone*, fall for *someone* ·················[のる]
　〜を用いる use tricks
さぐる 探る
ザクロ a pomegranate
サケ 鮭 a salmon
さけ 酒 *sake*; wine; alcoholic drinks
　〜が強い hold *one's* liquor　[つよい]
　〜が弱い not be able to handle liquor ·································[よわい]
　〜で紛らわす drown *something* in drink ·································[さびしい]
　〜の勢いで emboldened by alcohol ·································[いきおい]
　〜の上での over drinks ·········[うえ]
　〜の飲み過ぎ drinking too much alcohol ··························[ちぢめる]
　〜の回り ·································[まわり]
　〜を飲む drink ·····················[のむ]
さけび 叫び a cry, a shout; (応援の) a yell
さけぶ 叫ぶ
さける 裂ける
さける 避ける
さげる 下げる
ささい 〜な trifling, insignificant
　〜なこと a trifle
　・a trivial matter ·····················[たね]
ささえ 支え a support, a prop
ささえる 支える
ささげる 捧げる (献身する) devote; (献上する) dedicate, offer
ささやか 〜な small; (控えめな) modest
　・quite modest ·····················[せめて]
ささやき 囁き a whisper
　〜声で in a whisper
ささやく 囁く whisper, talk in whispers

さじ a spoon
　〜を投げる give up ·············[なげる]
さしあたって for the present, for the moment, for the time being
さしえ 挿絵 an illustration
さしかかる 差しかかる come to
ざしき 座敷 (畳の部屋) a *tatami* room
さしこむ 差し込む insert, put *something* in
さしず 指図
　〜する give *someone* orders [しかく]
さしだしにん 差し出し人 a sender
さしだす 差し出す (手で) hold out; (物・事を) offer
さしつかえる 差し支える
さしひき 差し引き the balance, a total
さしみ 刺身 *sashimi*, slices of raw fish
さしむける 差し向ける send *something* [*someone*] around ·············[むける]
さす 刺す
さす 指す
さす 挿・射・差・注す
さすが
ざせつ 挫折
〜させる
ざぜん 座禅 Zen meditation
さそい 誘い (an) invitation
　・an offer ·································[ゆれる]
　〜に乗る give in to *someone's* urging ·································[のる]
さそう 誘う
さそり a scorpion
さだまる 定まる
さだめる 定める
ざだんかい 座談会 a round-table talk; a discussion meeting
さつ 札 a (bank) note
　・a bill ·································[よく¹]
さつ 1冊 a copy; a volume
ざつ 雑
　〜な sloppy ·······················[しごと]
さつえい 撮影する take a picture (of), photograph
　(映画を) make a movie ········[きろく]
　〜禁止 (掲示) No photographing
ざつおん 雑音 (a) noise
さっか 作家 a writer, an author; (小説

家) a novelist
サッカー soccer, 《英》football
　～くじ a soccer lottery
さっかく 錯覚
　目の～ an optical illusion [さっかく]
サツキ an azalea ....[つく²]
さっき
　～から for a while ....[なく²]
　～まで a minute ago ....[ちゃんと]
　・just a moment ago ....[きまぐれ]
さっきゅうに 早急に immediately [て]
さっきょく 作曲 composition
　～家 a composer, a songwriter
　～する compose
さっきん 殺菌する sterilize
さっさと quickly, at once, right now, briskly
ざっし 雑誌 a magazine, a journal; (週刊の) a weekly
さつじん 殺人 murder, a homicide
　～事件 a murder case
　～犯 a murder suspect ....[あがる]
　・a murderer ....[～だろう]
　～未遂 an attempted murder
さっする 察する suppose, guess read
ざつぜん 雑然と in disorder, in confusion
さっそう ～と smartly, with light steps
ざっそう 雑草 a weed ....[はえる]
　～を抜く weed
　庭の～を取る weed the garden ....[とる¹]
さっそく 早速 at once, without delay
　・as soon as possible ....[こうどう]
ざつだん 雑談 a chat
　・chitchat ....[ざつ]
　・idle talk ....[わき]
　～する chat, have a chat (with)
さっちゅう 殺虫剤 an [a can of] insecticide; (粉末) an insect powder
ざっと (大まかに) roughly, briefly; (おおよそ) about
さっとう 殺到する rush, make a rush
ざっとう 雑踏 the crowd ....[おす]
さっぱり
　～分からない not have the slightest idea ....[わかる]
さっぷうけい 殺風景
　～な bare, bleak
サツマイモ a sweet potato
ざつよう 雑用 odd jobs
　・miscellaneous chores ....[とる¹]
サトイモ a taro
さとう 砂糖 sugar
　角～ lump [cube] sugar
さどう 茶道 the tea ceremony
サトウキビ sugar cane ....[できる]
さとる 悟る
サバ 鯖 a mackerel (複数 mackerel)
さばく 砂漠 a desert
さび 錆 rust
さびしい 寂しい
　・desolate ....[とおり]
さびる 錆びる
さびれる decline
ざぶとん 座ぶとん a cushion
サプリメント a supplement
さべつ 差別 (a) discrimination
　～化する differentiate
さほう 作法 (good) manners, etiquette
　・manners ....[せんれん]
サボテン a cactus
サボる
さまざま ....[いろいろ]
さます 冷ます (冷たくする) cool, let *something* cool
さます 覚・醒ます
さまたげ 妨げ an obstacle
さまたげる 妨げる
さまよう wander
　さまよい歩く wander around [あて]
さむい 寒い
さむけ 寒気
　～がする have a chill
さむさ 寒さ the cold
サメ 鮫 a shark
さめる 冷める
さめる 覚・醒める
さゆう 左右に from side to side ....[ひねる]
　～される (影響される) be affected (by) ....[せいさん¹]
さよう 作用
さようなら good-by, goodbye

さら 皿 (深皿) a dish; (平皿) a plate; (受け皿) a saucer
ざら 〜にはいない there are not many (people) who... ……………[ねうち]
さらいげつ 再来月 the month after next
さらいしゅう 再来週 the week after next
さらいねん 再来年 the year after next
サラエボ Sarajevo
さらきん サラ金 a consumer credit company [firm]
ざらざら
さらす expose; (布を) bleach
サラダ a salad ……………………[きざむ]
さらに 更に
サラブレッド a thoroughbred ……[とも]
サラリーマン an office worker, a white-collar worker, a salaried man
  安〜 a low-paid company worker
  ……………………………………[たべる]
サル 猿 a monkey; (類人猿) an ape
さる 去る
  〜者, 日々に疎し Out of sight, out of mind. ……………………[うとい]
ざる a colander
  ・a strainer ……………………[め¹]
さわがしい 騒がしい
さわぎ 騒ぎ (騒音) (a) noise; (騒動) a riot, a trouble
  ・a disturbance ……………[おさめる²]
  ・(a) commotion ……………[ちから]
さわぐ 騒ぐ
さわやか 爽やか
  〜な fresh, refreshing
さわる 触る
さわる 障る
さん 三 three
  第3(の) the third (略 3rd)
  3倍〔回〕 three times, thrice, triple
  3分の1 a [one] third
さん 酸 an acid
さんか 参加
  〜希望者 an applicant …………[こす]
  〜者 participants ………[だいぶぶん]
  〜人数 the number of participants
  ……………………………………[けいかく]

デモの〜者 a demonstrator
  ……………………………[たっする]
さんかくけい 三角形 a triangle [かく³]
  〜の triangular, three-cornered
  正〜 an equilateral triangle ……[ど]
さんがつ 三月 March (略 Mar.)
さんかんび 参観日 (学校の) a parents' visiting day
さんぎいん 参議院 the House of Councilors ……………………[なる¹]
さんきゅう 産休 a maternity leave
さんぎょう 産業 (an) industry
  〜の industrial
  〜の発達 industrial progress
  ……………………………………[どうじ]
ざんぎょう 残業
サングラス (a pair of) sunglasses, shades
さんご 産後 after giving birth [はる¹]
サンゴ a coral
さんこう 参考
  〜書 a reference book ……[てきとう]
  〜になる be of great use [おおいに]
ざんこく 残酷
  〜な cruel, brutal, merciless
さんさん 〜と brightly …………[てる]
さんざん terribly ……[(にも)かかわらず]
さんじ 惨事 a disaster, a tragedy
  大〜 a terrible disaster ……[はっけん]
さんじ 賛辞 a compliment ……[こころ]
さんしきすみれ 三色スミレ a pansy
さんじげん 三次元 three dimensions
さんじゅう 三十 thirty
  第30(の) the thirtieth
さんじゅう 三重の triple
ざんしょ 残暑 lingering summer heat
さんしょう 参照する refer (to), compare (with), consult, see
さんじょう 惨状 terribleness ………[め¹]
  目を覆うばかりの〜 ……………[おおう]
さんしん 三振 strike-out, three strikes
  〜する be struck out
  〜にとる strike *someone* out [にらむ]
さんすう 算数 arithmetic ……[〜だって]
  〜がよくできる be good with figures
  ……………………………………[できる]
さんする 産する produce
さんせい 賛成

・in favor ....[たいする]
〜である be in favor of ....[うけとる]
〜の in favor ....[て]
さんせい 酸性の acid
 〜雨 acid rain
さんせき 山積する be piled up
 ....[かいけつ]
さんそ 酸素 oxygen ....[たい]
ざんだか 残高 the balance
サンタクロース Santa Claus
サンダル sandals
さんち 産地 a producing district
 〜直送の direct from (the) farm
サンチアゴ Santiago
さんちょう 山頂 a mountain top, the top
サンディエゴ San Diego
サンドイッチ a sandwich
さんどう 参道 the path to the shrine
 ....[そろう]
ざんねん 残念
 〜だ it's a shame [pity] that...
 ....[ふほんい]
 〜ながら it's too bad, it's really sad
 ....[むずかしい]
さんぱい 参拝する visit, pray at
サンパウロ São Paulo
さんばし 桟橋 a pier
さんぱつ 散髪 a haircut
 〜する have [get] a haircut
さんびか 賛美歌 a hymn
さんぶつ 産物
サンフランシスコ San Francisco
サンプル a sample
さんぽ 散歩
 〜する take a walk
 〜に出かける go off on one's walk
 ....[つね]
サンマ a (Pacific) saury
さんまん 散漫
さんみゃく 山脈 a mountain range, mountains
さんりゅう 三流の third-rate, third class
さんりんしゃ 三輪車 a tricycle
さんるい 三塁打 a triple ....[うら]
さんれつ 参列者 a mourner ......[くび]

シ

し 四 four
し 市 a city
 〜当局 the city officials ......[おおう]
 〜役所 the city office, the municipal office, 《米》the city hall
し 死
し 詩 a poem; (総称) poetry; (散文に対して) verse
じ 地 (本性) one's real character
 (背景) a background ....[しつこい]
じ 字 (表音文字) a letter; (表意文字) a character
 (筆跡) (one's) handwriting ...[きれい]
じ 時 (時刻) time; (〜時) o'clock
しあい 試合
 〜に臨む face a match .....[へいぜん]
 〜を投げる give up on winning (the match) ....[なげる]
 練習〜 a practice game ......[しあい]
しあがる 仕上がる be finished
 ・be completed ....[〜そう]
しあげる 仕上げる
しあさって two days after tomorrow, three days from now
シアトル Seattle
しあわせ 幸せ
しあん 思案にふける[に暮れる] be lost (deep) in thought ......[ふける]
シーアン 西安 Xian, Sian
しいく 飼育する breed
 ・raise ....[かんさつ]
 〜係 an animal trainer [keeper]
 ・a trainer ....[つく¹]
じいしき 自意識過剰 too self-conscious ....[いしき]
シーズン a season
 〜オフ an off season
 〜オフの off-season
シーソー a seesaw
しいたけ 椎茸 a (shiitake) mushroom
シーツ sheets, a (bed) sheet
シーッ (黙らせる言葉) shh ...[たてる¹]
シーディー(CD) (コンパクト・ディスク) a CD, a compact disk
ジーパン jeans ....[つまる]
しいる 強いる compel, force, press

しいれる 仕入れる lay in, buy
しいん 子音 a consonant
じいん 寺院 a temple; (主にカトリックの大寺院) a cathedral
ジーンズ jeans
しうち 仕打ち treatment
　冷たい〜……………………………[にくむ]
シェア (市場占有率) a share (of the market) ………………[たたかい]
シェアウェア (コンピュータソフトの) shareware
しえい 市営の municipal, city
　〜バス a city bus
じえい 自営
　〜の self-employed
じえいたい 自衛隊 the Japan Self-Defense Forces
シェパード a (German) shepherd
しえん 支援する support, back up
しお 塩 salt
　〜辛い salty
　〜を振る salt
　・season *something* with salt …[ふる¹]
しお 潮 the tide; (潮流) a current
しおくり 仕送り an allowance [よる¹]
しおひがり 潮干狩りをする gather clams [shellfish], dig [hunt] for clams [shellfish]
　〜に行く go clamming
しおり a bookmark
しおれる wither
シカ 鹿 a deer; (雄ジカ) a stag; (雌ジカ) a hind, a doe
〜しか
　〜しかできない have no choice other than to *do* ……[うしろめたい]
じか 〜に directly, personally
じか 時価 the current price, the market price
しかい 司会する preside at [over] (a meeting), take the chair; (パーティなどで) emcee
　〜者 a chairman; (余興の、パーティーなどの) a master of ceremonies (略 M.C., MC)
　・an emcee …………………………[なじみ]
しかい 死海 the Dead Sea
しかい 視界 sight, view

しかい 歯科医 a dentist
しかいぎいん 市会議員 a city councilman ………………[つとめる²]
しがいせん 紫外線 ultraviolet rays
しかえし 仕返しする get even (with), be revenged (on), revenge *oneself* (on), retaliate on [against]
しかく 四角 a square
　〜形 a quadrilateral; (正方形) a square
　〜形の square
しかく 資格
　〜を取る become certified as [いじ]
じかく 自覚
　〜している be conscious [aware] of [that]
しかけ 仕掛けになっている it's set up so that... …………………………[しぜん]
しかける 仕掛ける (わななどを) set
シカゴ Chicago
しかし
じかせい 自家製の homemade
しかた 仕方
しかたがない
しがつ 四月 April (略 Apr.)
じかつ 自活する support *oneself*, earn *one's* living
しがみつく cling to, stick to
しかめる (不快の念で) frown (at); (苦痛で) grimace (with)
しかも
じかよう 自家用の *one's* own
　〜車 a family car
しかる 叱る
　・criticize …………………………[いっそう]
しがん 志願する apply (for)
　〜者 an applicant
じかん 時間
　〜がない there's no time to lose
　 ………………………………[ぐずぐず]
　〜が無くなる run out of time
　 ………………………………[なくなる¹]
　〜切れだ Time's up. …………[きれる]
　〜どおりに on time ………[〜だろう]
　〜のむだ a waste of time ………[み²]
　〜を合わせる set the time …[まわす]
　〜をかける take the time …[しごと]
　自分の〜が持てるようになる have a

lot more time to *oneself* [はなれる²]
じかんわり 時間割 a timetable, 《米》a schedule

しき 式
しき 指揮 command, direction, instruction
～者(楽団の) a conductor
～する command; direct, instruct; (楽団を) conduct
じき 時期・時機
じき 食器 porcelain, china
じき 磁気 magnetism ………… [さよう]
～カード a mag-stripe card
じき(に) soon
しぎかい 市議会 a city council (meeting) ………………… [もんだい]
しきたり (a) custom, (a) tradition
しきち 敷地 a site, a lot
しきてん 式典 a ceremony
しきもの 敷物 a carpet; (床の一部をおおう) a rug
しきゅう 支給する (物を) supply (with); (給料を) pay
しきゅう 至急 as soon as possible ………………………… [れんらく]
～の urgent, pressing
しきょう 市況 the market … [かっぱつ]
じぎょう 事業
～を始める go into business ………………………… [きょうどう]
～をやる be in business … [いっしょ]
しきりに (頻繁に) often, frequently, again and again; (絶え間なく) incessantly; (熱心に) eagerly, strongly
しきん 資金 funds; (資本) capital
～不足だ shortage of funds [あたま]
～を集める raise money … [あつめる]

しく 敷く・布く
じく 軸 an axis
しぐさ a gesture ………………… [おかしい]
・*one's* actions ………… [～ならない]
しくしく ～泣く sob …………… [なく¹]
しくじる blunder, blow it, fail, make a mistake
しくはっく 四苦八苦する sweat blood, struggle (to *do*)
しくみ 仕組み a structure, a mechanism
・mechanics ………………… [せつめい]
しくむ 仕組む plot, design
しけい 死刑 (極刑) capital punishment
・the death penalty ……… [そうとう]
しげき 刺激
感情を～する stir up *someone's* sentiment ………………… [こくみん]
しげみ 茂み a thicket, bushes
しける (食物が) get damp
しけっている damp
しげる 茂る

しけん 試験
学年末～ final exams ……… [がくねん]
期末〔中間〕～ a final〔midterm〕examination
資格～ a qualifying examination
入学～ an entrance examination
入社～ an employment examination
模擬～ a trial examination
～的に on a trial basis
～に落ちる fail an examination ………………………… [ようす]
～に合格する pass an examination
～の点数が悪い score poorly on the exams ………………………… [ふまじめ]
～日 the examination date [きまる]
～問題 the problems on a test ………………………… [やさしい¹]
～を受ける take an examination
しげん 資源 resources
天然～ natural resources

じけん 事件
じげん 時限 (学校の時間割の) a period

じこ 自己
～嫌悪 self-hatred, self-hate
～紹介する introduce *oneself*
～中心的な self-centered
～の *one's* own
～満足 self-satisfaction
～流 *one's* own style

じこ 事故
～現場 the scene of the accident ………………………… [できるだけ]
しこうさくご 試行錯誤 trial and error ………………………… [いろいろ]
しごく (きたえる) put *someone* through the mill

じこく 時刻
　～改正 …………………………[のびる]
　～表　a timetable, a (time) schedule
　…………………………………[かいせい]
じごく 地獄　hell
しごと 仕事
　～が忙しい　be busy with work
　…………………………………[だって]
　～中　at work …………………[たいど]
　～で　on business ……………[とぶ]
　～にいかす　put *something* to very
　　good use in *one's* job …[たくわえる]
　～に追われる　be pressed with work
　…………………………………[よゆう]
　～に戻る　go back to work　[ゆううつ]
　～熱心だ　be dedicated to *one's*
　　work, be work-oriented, be
　　work-minded …………………[ねっしん]
じさ 時差　a time difference
　～ボケ(だ)　(suffer from) jet lag
しさつ 視察　inspection, observation
　～する　inspect
じさつ 自殺　suicide
　～する　kill *oneself*
　・commit suicide ……………[はかない]
　～を図る　attempt suicide …[はかる]
しさん 資産　property, a fortune; (個
　　人・会社などの) assets
　非常な～家　an extremely wealthy
　　man ……………………………[ひょうばん]
じさん 持参する　(持ってくる) bring;
　　(持っていく) take
　～金　a dowry
しじ 支持　support, backing
　～する　support, back
　内閣の～率　the percentage of those
　　who support the Cabinet
　…………………………………[けいこう]
しじ 指示　directions, instructions
　～する　direct, instruct
じじ 時事問題　current topics
じじつ 事実
ししゃ 支社　a branch (office)
ししゃ 死者　a dead person, the
　　deceased; (集合的に) the dead
じしゃく 磁石　a magnet; (羅針盤) a
　　compass
じしゅ 自主　independence
　～的に　(自発的に) voluntarily; (独立
　　して) independently
　～規制　self-imposed control
じしゅ 自首する　give *oneself* up (to
　　the police)
ししゅう 刺しゅう　embroidery
　…………………………………[ぶきよう]
　～をする　embroider
しじゅう 四十　forty
しじゅう 始終　always
　・constantly …………………[かえる³]
ししゅうびょう 歯周病　periodontal
　　disease
ししゅつ 支出
ししゅんき 思春期　adolescence,
　　puberty
じしょ 辞書を引く　look *something* up
　　in the dictionary ……………[ひく]
しじょう 市場　a market
じしょう 自称の　would-be
　～する　call *oneself something*
じじょう 事情
　～が許せば　if circumstances
　　permitted ……………………[ゆるす]
　～に明るい　be very familiar with, be
　　well acquainted with ……[あかるい]
　～に疎い　know little about　[うとい]
　～に通じている　have a thorough
　　knowledge of ………………[つうじる]
ししょうしゃ 死傷者　the dead and
　　injured ………………………[のぼる]
じしょく 辞職する　resign, step down
　…………………………………[けつい]
しじん 詩人　a poet
じしん 地震　an earthquake ……[ころ]
　～に強い　resistant to earthquakes
　…………………………………[こうぞう]
じしん 自信
　～に満ちている　be overflowing with
　　confidence ……………………[みちる]
　～過剰　overconfidence ………[まねく]
　～がない　not be very confident
　…………………………………[あいまい]
　～のなさ　*one's* lack of confidence
　…………………………………[から]
じしん 自身
じすい 自炊する　do *one's* own cooking
しずか 静か

しずく a drop
システム a system
しずまる 静まる become quiet, become still [calm, silent]; (嵐などが) calm down
しずむ 沈む
しずめる 沈める
しずめる 静・鎮める
しせい 姿勢
　～を正す straighten *oneself*
　低～で in a humble attitude
じせい 自制 self-control
　～する control *oneself*
じせい 時勢 the trend [signs] of the times
　・the trend ……………[しかたがない]
しせいかつ 私生活 privacy
　・*one's* private life ……………[きょうみ]
しせつ 施設 (建物) institution; (設備など) facilities
しぜん 自然
　～に支配されて at the mercy of †the elements [nature] ……………[しはい]
じぜん 事前に in advance ……[こまかい]
じぜん 慈善 charity
　～事業 a charity ……………[おもわく]
　・charity work ……………[にんき]
しそう 思想
　・philosophy ……………[こんぽん]
…しそうになる almost
じそく 時速 speed per hour
　～100キロで at a speed of 100 kilometers per hour
しそん 子孫 a descendant; (集合的に) posterity
じそんしん 自尊心
　～を傷つける hurt *one's* pride
した 下
した 舌
シダ 羊歯 a fern
じた 自他ともに許す universally recognized ……………[ゆるす]
したい 死体 a (dead) body, a corpse; (動物の) a carcass
～しだい ～次第
じたい 事態 a situation ………[ゆうり]
　～を収拾する settle the matter
　非常～ an emergency

じたい 辞退する decline, refuse
じだい 時代
　～遅れの behind the times ［～から］
　～に伴って with the times …[へんか]
　～物 an antique
しだいに 次第に gradually
したう 慕う
したうけ 下請け業者 a subcontractor
　……………………………[ひがい]
したがう 従う
したがき 下書き a draft, a rough copy; (絵) a sketch
したがって 従って
したぎ 下着 (総称) underwear; (1つ) an undershirt
したく 支度
　～する get ready to, prepare for
　～のできた ready
じたく 自宅
　～で at *one's* home
…したくてたまらない be dying to
　……………………………[～たい]
したごころ 下心 an ulterior motive
したしい 親しい
したしみ 親しみ
したしむ 親しむ
　親しまれている be well-liked
　……………………………[きさく]
したしらべ 下調べ (a) preparation, preliminary research
したづみ 下積み生活 years of hardships ……………[め²]
したて 下手に出る take a modest attitude
したて 仕立てのよい well tailored, well-made
したどり 下取りの品 a trade-in
じたばた ～する struggle, make a fuss
じだらく 自堕落な dissolute …[うかぶ]
しち 七
　7分の1 a [one] seventh
　第7(の) the seventh (略 7th)
しち 質に入れる pawn
　～屋(店) a pawnshop; (人) a pawn-broker
じち 自治 self government, home rule
しちがつ 七月 July (略 Jul.)
しちさん 七三に分ける (髪を) part

one's hair on the side ……… [わける]
しちじゅう 七十 seventy
　第70(の) the seventieth (略 70th)
シチメンチョウ 七面鳥 a turkey
しちゃく 試着 fitting
　〜する try on
　〜室 a fitting room
シチュー (a) stew
しちょう 市長 a mayor
しちょう 視聴者 a (TV) viewer, (集合的) an audience
　〜率 a (television) rating, an audience rating
じちょう 自重する be prudent
　・watch *oneself* ……………… [なお]
しつ 質
じつ 実
しっかく 失格 disqualification
　〜する be disqualified (from, for)
しっかり
　・seriously ………………… [はらう]
　〜握る clutch, grasp ……… [にぎる]
　〜結わえる tie securely …… [じょうぶ]
じっかん 実感
しっき 漆器 lacquerware, lacquerware
しつぎょう 失業 unemployment
　……………………………………… [わびしい]
　〜する lose *one's* work [job]
　〜保険 unemployment insurance
　〜率 the rate of unemployment
　……………………………………… [しんこく]
じっきょう 実況放送 a live broadcast
じつぎょう 実業家 a business person, an industrialist
　〜界 the business world
しっきん 失禁 《医学用語》(urinary) incontinence
シック 〜な chic
しっくい 漆喰 plaster ………… [つめる]
しつけ 躾 discipline …………… [つとめ]
　〜が厳しい be brought up †strictly [with strict discipline] … [きびしい]
　〜がよい well-bred, well-mannered
　〜る breed, train, drill
しっけ 湿気 moisture, dampness, humidity
　〜のある moist, damp, humid, wet

　〜を呼ぶ absorb moisture …… [よぶ]
しつげん 失言 a slip of the tongue
　……………………………………… [とる¹]
じっけん 実権 power ………… [にぎる]
じっけん 実験
　〜室 a laboratory ………… [たもつ]
　〜する experiment
　〜的に experimentally
じつげん 実現
　〜する make *something* a reality
　……………………………………… [たたかう]
　・be carried out ……………… [らっかん]
しつこい
じっこう 実行
　〜に移される implementation of *something* is begun ……… [けいかく]
じつざい 実在の real, actual
　〜する really exist ………… [おもう]
じっさい 実際
しっさく 失策 failure ………… [にがい]
じっし 十指に入る one of the ten best
　……………………………………… [いう]
じっしゃかい 実社会で in the real world ……………………………… [せきにん]
しっしん 失神する faint
しっしん 湿疹 rash
　〜が出る *one's* skin breaks out
　……………………………………… [まける]
じっせき 実績 (結果) (a) result; (業績) an achievement
　〜を上げる bring results, bear fruit
　過去の〜 *one's* past achievements
　……………………………………… [てらす]
じっせん 実践する put *something* into practice
　〜的な practical
しっそ 質素
じっち 実地の practical
　〜に in practice, practically
じっちゅうはっく 十中八九 ten to one
　……………………………………… [ちゅう]
しつど 湿度 humidity ……… [かいてき]
しっと 嫉妬
じっと
　〜聞く listen intently ……… [かげん]
　〜見る gaze at ……………… [つたわる]
しつない 室内に[で] indoors, in [inside] a room

〜の indoor
じつに 実に truly ……………[けんきょ]
じつは 実は actually, in fact, as a matter of fact, to tell the truth, The truth is...
ジッパー a zipper
しっぱい 失敗
・a blunder ………………[あたえる]
・a failure, a bad experience ……………………………[らくたん]
〜する fall through ………[まいる]
〜に終わる result in failure ……………………………[むなしい]
じっぴ 実費で at cost
じつぶつ 実物 the (real) thing, the original
〜大の full-size(d), actual-size(d); (等身大の) life-size(d)
しっぽ a tail
〜を振る wag *one's* tail ………[ふる1]
しつぼう 失望
〜する be disappointed
しつめい 失明する lose *one's* eyesight, become blind
しつもん 質問
〜に応じる take questions from ……………………………[おうじる]
しつよう 執拗に persistently, stubbornly, annoyingly
じつよう 実用的な practical
じつりょく 実力
〜のある capable …………[けんきょ]
しつれい 失礼
じつれい 実例 an example, an instance
しつれん 失恋 a broken love affair ……………………………[ばあい]
してい 指定する appoint, specify, designate
〜席 a reserved seat …………[せき]
してき 私的な private, personal
してき 指摘する point out ……[じかく]
してつ 私鉄 a private railroad
(〜と、〜に)しても
してん 支店 a branch ………[かわる1]
・a branch office ………[うつす3]
・a branch store …………[れんらく]
〜長 a branch manager

してん 視点 a viewpoint
じてん 事典 an encyclopedia
じてん 辞典 a dictionary
じでん 自伝 (an) autobiography
じてんしゃ 自転車 a bicycle, a bike
〜置き場 a bicycle lot ………[かげ1]
しどう 指導
じどう 自動
〜販売機 a vending machine ……………………………[こしょう]
じどうしゃ 自動車 a car; an automobile, 《英》 a motorcar
〜学校 a driving school
シドニー Sydney
しとやかな graceful, gentle
しな 品 a thing, an article, goods
しなぎれ 品切れ out of stock, sold out
しなびた withered, dried-up
しなびる wither
しなもの 品物
しなやかな flexible, graceful
シナリオ a scenario
しにせ 老舗 an old store, a long-established store
・an old, well-known company [shop] ……………………………[とおる]
しにん 死人 a dead person, the dead
しぬ 死ぬ
(病気で) die from an illness ……………………………[かなしい]
死んだものとあきらめる give *someone* up for dead …[あきらめる]
死んだつもりになって like there's no tomorrow …………………[つもり]
暑くて死にそうだ ……………[そう]
じぬし 地主 a landowner, a landlord; (女性の) a landlady
しのぐ (追い越す) surpass, be superior to
しのびこむ 忍び込む steal into, sneak into
・slip into ………………………[すき2]
しのぶ reminisce about ………[ながめる]
しはい 支配
しばい 芝居
じはく 自白する confess, make a confession
しばし for a few moments [みとれる]

しばしば　often, many times
しはつ　始発列車　the first train
じはつ　自発的な　voluntary, spontaneous
　～的に　voluntarily, spontaneously, of [on] *one's* own free will
しばふ　芝生　a lawn, a turf
　・lawn, grass ………………………[かる]
しはらい　支払い　payment
しばらく
　～してから　after a little time has elapsed ………………………[へいせい]
しばる　縛る
じひ　自費で　at *one's* own expense
じひょう　辞表　a letter of resignation
　………………………[いちおう]
じびょう　持病　a [*one's*] chronic disease, (*one's*) chronic illness, an [*one's*] old complaint
しびれる
　・go numb ………………………[かんじる]
しぶい　渋い
しぶき　a spray, a splash
ジプシー　a gypsy
しぶしぶ
じぶん　自分
　～勝手な　want *one's* own way ………………………[すぎる]
　～で　(by) *oneself* ………………[～たがる]
　～に厳しい　be strict with *oneself* ………………………[やさしい²]
　～の時間を持つ　get some time to *oneself* ………………………[やっと]
　～のものにする ……………[しょうか]
　一人の力で　all by *oneself* …[きずく]
しへい　紙幣　paper money;《米》a bill,《英》a (bank) note
じへいしょう　自閉症　autism
　～児　an autistic (child)
シベリア　Siberia
　～の　Siberian
しほう　四方　every side, every direction
しほう　司法権　judicial power
　………………………[ぞくする]
　～試験　the bar exam …[べんきょう]
しぼう　死亡　death
　～する　die; be killed
　～者数　the death toll

～欄　an obituary column
しぼう　志望　(望み) desire, aspiration; (選択) choice
　～する　desire, aspire, wish; choose
しぼう　脂肪　fat, grease
　～肝　a fatty liver
じほう　時報　a time announcement
　………………………[なおす]
しほうはっぽう　四方八方で[から]　in [from] all directions
しぼむ　wither
　・shrivel ………………………[ぬける]
しぼりとる　絞り取る　(搾取する) exploit
　………………………[あさましい]
しぼる　絞る
しほん　資本
　～主義　capitalism …………[こんぽん]
しま　島　an island
　～国　an island country
しまい　姉妹　sisters
　～都市　a sister city
しまう
シマウマ　a zebra
しまつ　始末
しまった
しまる　締まる
しまる　閉まる
じまん　自慢
　～する　boast ……[～だけのことがある]
　～話　bragging ………………………[はな]
　～話を聞かされる………………[みみ]
　～話をする　brag ………………[れい²]
しみ　a stain, a spot, a blot
　～のある　stained, blotted
じみ　地味
シミュレーション　simulation
しみる
しみん　市民　a citizen
　～会館　civic auditorium ……[たかい]
　～権　citizenship
じむ　事務
　～所　an office
　～的な　businesslike
　～用品　office supplies ……[おさめる¹]
しめい　氏名　a (full) name
しめい　使命　a mission, a calling
しめい　指名する　nominate, name
しめきり　締め切り　closing

・a deadline ……………[ゆうゆう]
～に間に合う　make the deadline ……………[まだ]
しめきる　締め切る（申し込みなどを）close ……………[まんいん]
しめす　示す
しめった　湿った　damp
しめる　占める　occupy, hold
しめる　湿る
しめる　締める
しめる　閉める
じめん　地面　the ground
しも　霜　frost
じもと　地元の　local
しもやけ　霜焼け　frostbite, chilblain
しもん　指紋　a fingerprint ……[とる²]
しや　視野　a view, an outlook
　～が狭い〔広い〕　have a narrow 〔broad〕 outlook
ジャー　（魔法瓶）a thermos bottle;（炊飯器）a rice cooker
ジャージー　(a) jersey
ジャーナリスト　a journalist
シャープペンシル　a mechanical pencil
しゃいん　社員　a (staff) member, an employee, a clerk;（総称的に）the staff
しゃかい　社会
　～人の　civic-minded ………[かえる³]
しゃかいほけんちょう　社会保険庁　the Social Insurance Agency
しゃかいみんしゅとう　社会民主党　Social Democratic Party（略 SDP）
ジャガイモ　a potato
しゃがむ　squat; sit down on *one's* heels
ジャカルタ　Jakarta
しゃがれた　hoarse, husky
しゃく　癪に触る　《原因を主語にして》get (to) *someone*, get on *someone's* nerves, rile *someone*;《人を主語にして》can't stand *someone* [*something*]
じゃくし　弱視　poor vision [eyesight],《医学用語》amblyopia
しやくしょ　市役所　the city office, the municipal office,《米》the city hall
じゃぐち　蛇口　《米》a faucet,《英》a tap
　～をひねる　turn on the faucet ……………[ながす]
じゃくてん　弱点　a weak point
・*one's* weakness ……………[ひきょう]
しゃくや　借家　a rented house
しゃこう　社交的な　social, sociable
・outgoing ……………[ちがう]
　～界　a social circle
　～ダンス　a (social) dance
しゃざい　謝罪　an apology
　～する　apologize, make an apology
しゃじつ　写実的な　realistic
じゃじゃうま　じゃじゃ馬　a wild horse ……………[ことば]
しゃしょう　車掌　a conductor
しゃしん　写真　a picture, a photograph, a photo
　～家　a photographer
ジャズ　jazz
しゃせい　写生　sketching
　～する　sketch, make a sketch (of)
しゃせつ　社説　an editorial ……[つく¹]
しゃだん　遮断する　block off [こうつう]
しゃちょう　社長　a [the] president, a [the] head, a [the] boss
　～のいす　the presidency of a company ……………[やくそく]
　副～　a [the] vice-president
シャツ　（ワイシャツ）a shirt,（下着）an undershirt
しゃっきん　借金　a debt, a loan
　～する　borrow money, run up debts ……………[～がち]
　～取り　a debt collector
・a bill collector ……………[つかう]
　～の保証人　a guarantor for loans ……………[きやすい]
　～を返す　pay off a loan ……[きれい]
　～を頼む　ask for a loan ……[ことわる]
　～を取り立てる　collect debts ……………[れいこく]
　～を踏み倒す ……………[ふてい]
　～を申し込む　ask *someone* for a loan ……………[きまりがわるい]
しゃっくり　a hiccup, a hiccough
　～をする　hiccup, hiccough, have (the) hiccups

シャッター　a shutter
シャットダウン　〜する《コンピュータ》shutdown
シャベル　a shovel
しゃべる
　しゃべりまくる　talk a blue streak …………………………[けむり]
シャボン　〜玉　a soap bubble
じゃま　邪魔
　〜な　get in the way …………[にもつ]
　〜になる　block *someone's* view …………………………[みえる]
　〜者　someone who gets in the way …………………………[けす]
　どうもお〜しました　Thanks for such a nice time. ………[〜こそ]
ジャマイカ　Jamaica
　〜の　Jamaican
　〜人　a Jamaican; (全体) the Jamaicans
ジャム　jam
しゃめん　斜面　a slope
じゃり　砂利　gravel
しゃりょう　車両　(乗り物) a vehicle; (鉄道の) a car
しゃりん　車輪　a wheel
しゃれ　a pun
　・a joke …………………………[ふるい]
しゃれた
じゃれつく　pounce playfully on …………………………[ころがす]
じゃれる　play with
シャワー　a shower
ジャングル　a jungle
じゃんけん　rock, paper, scissors …………………………[まける]
シャンソン　a chanson
シャンデリア　a chandelier …[かがやく]
ジャンパー　a jumper, a jacket, a windbreaker
シャンハイ　上海　Shanghai
ジャンプ　a jump
　〜する　jump, leap
シャンプー(する)　shampoo
シャンペン　champagne
しゅう　州　(米国の) a state; (英国の) a county
しゅう　週　a week
　〜一回の　weekly ……………[はっこう]
じゆう　自由
　〜競争　free competition …[こんぽん]
じゅう　十　ten
　第10(の)　the tenth (略 10th)
　10分の1　a [one] tenth
じゅう　銃　a gun; (ライフル銃) a rifle; (拳銃) a pistol; a revolver
　〜声　a gunshot ………………[のどか]
〜じゅう　〜中
　日本〜　all Japan ………………[わく¹]
しゅうい　周囲
じゅうい　獣医　a veterinarian
じゅういち　十一　eleven
　第11(の)　the eleventh (略 11th)
じゅういちがつ　十一月　November (略 Nov.)
しゅうえき　収益を上げる　increase profits ………………………[おさえる]
じゅうおく　十億　a [one] billion
しゅうかい　集会　a meeting, a gathering, an assembly, a rally
　抗議〜　a protest rally
しゅうかく　収穫
　〜する　harvest ………………[わける]
しゅうがくりょこう　修学旅行　a school excursion ……………………[りょこう]
じゅうがつ　十月　October (略 Oct.)
しゅうかん　習慣
しゅうかん　週刊の　weekly
　〜誌　a weekly magazine ……[ゆがむ]
しゅうき　周期　a period, a cycle
　〜的に　periodically, regularly
しゅうぎいん　衆議院　the House of Representatives ………………[わかれる]
しゅうきゅう　週休二日　a five-day workweek
しゅうきょう　宗教　a religion
じゅうぎょういん　従業員　an employee
しゅうきん　集金する　collect money
じゅうく　十九　nineteen
　第19(の)　the nineteenth (略 19th)
シュークリーム　a cream puff
じゅうけつ　充血した　(眼が) bloodshot
じゅうご　十五　fifteen
　第15(の)　the fifteenth (略 15th)
しゅうごう　集合
しゅうさい　秀才の　bright　[けれど(も)]

じゅうざい 重罪人 a major criminal [felon] …………………[ながす]
じゅうさん 十三 thirteen
　第13(の) the thirteenth (略 13th)
しゅうし 収支 income and expenditures …………[つりあう]
しゅうし 終始 from beginning to end …………………[かたい]
しゅうじ 習字 calligraphy
じゅうし 十四 fourteen
　第14(の) the fourteenth (略 14th)
じゅうじ 従事する engage (in)
　〜している be engaged (in)
じゅうじか 十字架 a cross
じゅうしち 十七 seventeen
　第17(の) the seventeenth (略 17th)
しゅうじつ 終日 the entire day …………………[ながめる]
じゅうじつ 充実
しゅうしゅう 収拾される be brought under control …………[こえ]
じゅうじゅん 従順
じゅうしょ 住所 one's address
　〜を変更する change one's address …………………[とどける]
じゅうしょう 重傷 a serious wound, a severe injury
　〜を負う be seriously injured
しゅうしょく 就職する find employment, get a position (in), get [find] a job
　・start working …………[それから]
しゅうじん 囚人 a prisoner
しゅうしんこよう 終身雇用(制度) the lifetime-employment (system)
ジュース (果汁) juice; (テニスの得点) deuce
しゅうせい 修正する (改正する) amend; (誤りなどを) correct
しゅうせい 習性 a habit, behavior
じゅうたい 重態・重体 a serious condition, a critical condition
　〜で in (a) serious condition, in (a) critical condition
じゅうたい 渋滞 a traffic jam ………………[こうつう, こしょう]
じゅうだい 十代 teens
　〜である be in one's teens

　〜の teenage
じゅうだい 重大
じゅうたく 住宅街 a residential area …………………[しずか]
しゅうだん 集団
じゅうたん a carpet; (床の一部に敷く) a rug
しゆうち 私有地 private land
　・one's property …………[ぶぶん]
しゅうちゃく 執着
しゅうちゅう 集中
　〜豪雨 a heavy rain ………[ながれる]
　・a heavy rainfall ……………[ふあん]
　〜講義 an intensive course
しゅうてん 終点 the last stop, the terminal (station)
しゅうでん 終電 the last train
じゅうてん 重点 an important point
しゅうと a father-in-law
じゅうどう 柔道 judo
しゅうとめ a mother-in-law
じゅうなん 柔軟
　〜性に富む flexible …………[とむ]
じゅうに 十二 twelve
　第12(の) the twelfth (略 12th)
じゅうにがつ 十二月 December (略 Dec.)
じゅうにしちょう 十二指腸 duodenum
　〜潰瘍 a duodenal ulcer
しゅうにゅう 収入
しゅうにん 就任する take office as
　〜の挨拶 an inaugural address [speech] …………………[あいさつ]
じゅうにんなみ 十人並み average …………………[なみ]
しゅうねん 執念
じゅうはち 十八 eighteen
　第18(の) the eighteenth (略 18th)
じゅうびょう 重病 a serious illness
じゅうぶん 十分
　・OK ……………………[および]
　・more than enough ………[けっこう]
　〜な adequate …………[きょういく]
しゅうぶんのひ 秋分の日 the autumnal equinox, (休日名) Autumnal Equinox Day
しゅうへん 周辺 (近隣) the [this] neighborhood; (郊外) the

outskirts; (近郊) the vicinity
…の周辺で around, in the vicinity of
～機器 a peripheral; (総合的) peripherals
じゅうまん 十万 a hundred thousand
30万 three hundred thousand
じゅうみん 住民 a (local) resident ………………[はんたい, なま]
～運動 a citizens' movement
・a citizens' campaign ……[なくなる¹]
～投票 a local referendum
～票を移す transfer *one's* official residence to ……………[うつす³]
じゆうみんしゅとう 自由民主党 Liberal Democratic Party (略LDP)
じゅうやく 重役 a director, an executive
～会 the board of directors [つく⁴]
～会議 an executive meeting
………………[むかえる]
しゅうゆうけん 周遊券 an excursion ticket
しゅうよう 収容する hold, admit, accommodate
～人員 seating capacity
じゅうよう 重要
じゅうよん 十四 fourteen
第14(の) the fourteenth (略 14th)
じゅうらい 従来 in the past
～の earlier ……………[ちがい]
しゅうり 修理
～工 a repairman
～工場 a repair shop
しゅうりょう 終了する end, close, finish, terminate; (コンピュータシステムを) terminate
じゅうりょう 重量 weight
じゅうりょうあげ 重量あげ weight lifting
じゅうりょく 重力 gravity, gravitation
しゅうれっしゃ 終列車 the last train
じゅうろうどう 重労働 hard labor
じゅうろく 十六 sixteen
第16(の) the sixteenth (略 16th)
しゅうわい 収賄 accepting a bribe
………………[あげる]
～事件 a bribery case ……[かんけい]

しゅえん 主演する star, play the leading part [role]
～スター a leading star ………[だす]
～俳優 a leading actor [actress]
しゅかん 主観
しゅぎ 主義
しゅぎょう 修行 discipline
・ascetic training ……………[さとる]
じゅきょう 儒教 Confucianism
～の Confucian
じゅぎょう 授業 a lesson, a class; school
～中である be in class
じゅく 塾 *juku*, a cram school, a private school
しゅくじ 祝辞を述べる give a congratulatory speech ……[のべる]
しゅくじつ 祝日 a national holiday
………………[さだめる]
じゅくすい 熟睡する sleep soundly, be fast [sound] asleep
じゅくする 熟する (果物が) ripen, become [grow] ripe
しゅくだい 宿題 homework, an assignment
しゅくてん 祝典 a celebration, a festival
しゅくでん 祝電 a congratulatory telegram
じゅくれん 熟練 skill
～した skilled
～する become skillful, become expert (in, at)
しゅげい 手芸 a handcraft
じゅけん 受験する take [sit for] an (entrance) examination
～科目 subjects for examination, subjects covered by the examination
～準備[～勉強]をする prepare (*oneself*) for an examination
しゅご 主語 a subject ………[ばあい]
しゅさい 主催 sponsorship
(…の)主催で under the sponsorship of *someone*
しゅざい 取材する (記者が) cover
(資料を集める) gather information
………………[もくてき]

〜陣 (a contingent of) reporters ……………………………[でむかえる]
しゅし 主旨・趣旨 the meaning, the point; (目的) an object; (ねらい) an aim
・the main idea …………[おおざっぱ]
しゅじゅ 種々の various ………[かたち]
しゅじゅつ 手術
しゅしょう 首相 the prime minister, the premier
〜の見解 the prime minister's views ……………………………[はっぴょう]
じゅしょう 受賞する win [get, receive] a prize, be awarded a prize
〜者 a (prize) winner
〜パーティ a party held in honor of *one's* winning the prize …………[ことば]
じゅしょう 授賞式 a presentation ceremony ………………………[しき]
しゅしょく 主食 a staple food
〜とする live on
しゅしょく 酒色に溺れる get hooked on wine and women …………[み¹]
しゅせき 主席である be top of *one's* class ………………………[とおす]
しゅだい 主題 the subject, the theme
しゅたいせい 主体性 independence
しゅだん 手段
あらゆる〜 every means ……[つくす]
しゅちょう 主張
しゅつえん 出演する appear (on television, on the screen); play, perform
しゅっか 出荷する ship ………[けんさ]
しゅっきん 出勤する attend *one's* office; go to work, go to the office
しゅっけつ 出欠を取る call the roll
しゅっけつ 出血する bleed …[おさえる]
しゅっこく 出国 departure (from a country)
〜する leave (a country)
〜手続き departure formalities
しゅっさん 出産する give birth (to)
しゅつじょう 出場する take part in
しゅっしん (…の)出身だ come from, be from; (学校の) be a graduate (of)
〜校 *one's* Alma Mater

〜地 *one's* home, *one's* native city [town, village]
しゅっせ 出世
しゅっせき 出席
しゅっちょう 出張
しゅつどう 出動 mobilization [しげき]
〜する go into action ……[おさまる²]
しゅっぱつ 出発
〜する be off ………………[さだまる]
しゅっぱん 出版する publish
〜界で in publishing ………[しりあい]
〜社 a publishing company
〜物 publication
しゅっぴ 出費 expenses, expenditure
しゅっぴん 出品する submit [send] *something* to an exhibition, exhibit *something*
・put *something* on exhibit …[ゆたか]
しゅと 首都 a capital
しゅとう 種痘 a vaccination ……[あと²]
しゅどう 手動(式)の manual
しゅにん 主任 a head, a chief
ジュネーブ Geneva
しゅのう 首脳 a leader, a leading member, a head
・leaders ……………………[はじめ]
しゅび 守備 defense; 《野球》fielding
〜の乱れ disarray in *one's* defense ……………………………[せめる¹]
しゅふ 主婦 a housewife
しゅみ 趣味
じゅみょう 寿命 life, the span of life, a life span
〜が長い be long-lived, enjoy a long life
〜が短い be short-lived, have a short life
平均〜 the average life-span ……………………………[のびる]
しゅやく 主役 the leading role [part], the leading actor [actress]
・the leading role ……………[えらぶ]
・the lead ……………………[ふる¹]
・the lead performer ……………[くう]
しゅよう 主要な main, chief, principal
しゅよう 腫瘍 a tumor
じゅよう 需要
しゅるい 種類

じゅわき 受話器を取る　pick up the (telephone) receiver ……………[て]
〜を置く　hang up
じゅん 順
番号〜に　in numerical order
50音〜に　in the order of the Japanese syllabary
先着〜に　on a first-come-first-served basis
じゅんい 順位　*one's* standing [ranking]……………………[しり]
じゅんえん 順延される　be postponed ………………………[ながれる]
しゅんかん 瞬間
じゅんかん 循環する　circulate
じゅんけっしょう 準決勝　a semifinal; (全体) the semifinals
じゅんじょ 順序
じゅんじょう 純情
〜な　naive, unaffected ………[ふり¹]
じゅんすい 純粋な　pure; (本物の) genuine
じゅんちょう 順調
〜に　without a hitch ……[はこぶ]
じゅんばん 順番
じゅんび 準備
しゅんぶんのひ 春分の日　the vernal equinox ……………………[きゅうじつ]
(休日名) Vernal Equinox Day
じゅんりえき 純利益金　a net profit ………………………………[りえき]
しよう 私用で　on *one's* private business
〜の　for private use
しよう 使用
〜料　the rent
しょう 賞　a prize, an award
1等〜　a [the] first prize
残念〜　a consolation prize
〜を受ける　win an award ……[うける]
〜をもらう　receive a prize [こうえい]
しょう 章　(文章の) a chapter
じょう 情
〜にもろい　be easily moved
・be softhearted ………………[もろい]
〜の厚い　very carrying ……[あつい¹]
じょう 錠　a lock ………………[あう¹]
じょうえい 上映する　show *something*, project *something*, put *something* on the screen
〜中だ　be on
じょうえん 上演する　stage ……[しかし]
しょうか 消化
〜のよい[悪い]　easy [hard] to digest
しょうか 消火する　extinguish a fire
〜器　a fire extinguisher
〜栓　a (fire) hydrant
ショウガ ginger
しょうかい 紹介
しょうかい 照会　(an) inquiry
〜する　inquire
しょうがい 生涯　a life, a lifetime; (副詞的) all *one's* life
しょうがい 障害　an obstacle, a barrier
〜者　a disabled [handicapped] person; (総合的に) the disabled, the handicapped
身体〜者　a physically handicapped person
〜児の施設　an institution for disabled children ……………[りえき]
しょうかく 昇格する　be promoted (to) ………………………………[つく²]
しょうがくきん 奨学金　a scholarship ………………………………[きょうそう]
〜を受ける　be on a scholarship ………………………………[うける]
しょうがくせい 小学生　a(n) (elementary) schoolchild [(男) schoolboy, (女) schoolgirl]
しょうがつ 正月　the New Year
〜に　at New Year's ……[ちいさい]
しょうがっこう 小学校　《米》a grade school, an elementary school; 《英》a primary school
〜に通う　go to elementary school ………………………………[たった]
しょうがない ………………[しかたがない]
・there's no point in ………[あと¹]
しょうき 正気
じょうき 蒸気　steam; vapor
〜機関　a steam engine
じょうぎ 定規　a ruler ………[まっすぐ]
じょうきゃく 乗客　a passenger
しょうきゅう 昇給する　get a raise

[《英》rise] in salary [pay]

じょうきゅう 上級
 〜生 an upperclassman, a senior student
 〜コース an advanced course

しょうぎょう 商業 commerce, trade, business
 〜都市 a commercial center ……………………………[はったつ]
 〜の commercial

じょうきょう 状況 conditions, circumstances

しょうきょくてき 消極的

しょうきん 賞金 a prize, a reward
 ・a cash prize, prize money [おくる²]

じょうげ 上下関係 (a) hierarchy ……………………………[しゃかい]

しょうげき 衝撃 a shock, an impact
 ・a jolt ……………………………[くわえる]

しょうげん 証言 (a) testimony
 〜する testify

じょうけん 条件
 〜反射 the conditioned response [reflex] ……………[はんしゃ]
 〜を打ち出す come up with conditions ……………[ゆうり]

しょうこ 証拠
 〜を握る get proof ……[にぎる]
 動かぬ〜 irrefutable facts ……[ゆがむ]
 ・conclusive evidence ……[だす]

しょうこう 小康 stable ……[つづく]

じょうこう 条項 an article, a clause; (契約などの) a stipulation
 ・an item ……………………………[ふしん]

しょうこうねつ しょう紅熱 scarlet fever

しょうこん 商魂たくましい always be out to make a buck ……[たくましい]

じょうざい 錠剤 a tablet, a pill

じょうし 上司 one's superior ……………………………[いじめる]
 ・one's boss ……………[ちゅうじつ]

しょうしか 少子化 the declining birthrate

しょうじき 正直

じょうしき 常識
 〜となっている be taken for granted ……………[あいだ]
 〜の枠を越える †go beyond [fall outside] the bounds of propriety ……………………………[わく²]

しょうしゃ 商社 a trading company ……………………………[つとめる²]

しょうしゅう 召集する call ……[かい³]

じょうしゅうはん 遅刻の常習犯 be habitually late ……………[ちこく]

じょうじゅん 上旬 the first ten days of a [the] month, the beginning of a [the] month

しょうじょ 少女 a girl, a young [little] girl

しょうじょう 症状 a sign, a symptom

しょうじょう 賞状 a certificate [くせ]

しょうしん 昇進 rise, promotion, a rise in rank
 〜する rise (in rank), be promoted
 ・get a promotion ………[こんど]

じょうず 上手な good (at), skillful (at, in)
 〜に well
 〜だ be (very) good at ……………………………[つくる, まねる]

しょうすう 小数 a decimal
 〜点 a decimal point

しょうすう 少数の a few, a small number of
 〜意見 minority opinion ……[かける²]

しょうせつ 小説 a novel, a story; (集合的に) fiction

しょうせんきょく 小選挙区制 the single-seat constituency system

じょうぞう 醸造 (ビール) brewing; (発酵) fermentation

しょうぞうが 肖像画 a portrait

しょうそく 消息 news [information] (of a person)
 ・what *someone* has been up to, what has become of *someone* [しる]

しょうたい 正体 what *one* really is, *one's* true character
 〜を現す show *oneself* up for what *one* is ……………………………[あらわす²]

しょうたい 招待

じょうたい 状態

しょうだく 承諾 consent [〜まで(に)]
 〜する consent (to), say yes, accept

- consent ················[こころ]
- agree ·················[こころよい]
- give *one's* consent ········[ふほんい]
じょうたつ 上達する　make progress, improve
しょうだん 商談　a business talk
- a business negotiation ····[まとめる]
じょうだん 冗談　a joke; fun, kidding
　～は別にして　all joking aside [べつ]
　～をいう　joke
しょうち 承知
じょうちょ 情緒　（雰囲気）(an) atmosphere; （感情）emotion
しょうちょう 小腸　the small intestine
しょうちょう 象徴　a symbol
　～する　symbolize
しょうてん 焦点
しょうてん 商店　a store, a shop
　～街　a shopping street [center, mall]
しょうどう 衝動
　～買いをする　buy *something* on impulse ················[いつも]
じょうとう 上等な　excellent, valuable, fine, superior, better
しょうどく 消毒
しょうとつ 衝突
しょうにん 証人　a witness
しょうにん 商人　a merchant; (店主) a storekeeper, a shopkeeper
じょうねつ 情熱
　～を持つ　take a passionate interest in ················[きょういく]
しょうねん 少年　a boy, a young [little] boy
　～の　juvenile
　～時代　a [*one's*] childhood　[ふこう]
　～犯罪　juvenile crime
しょうばい 商売
　～をする　do business ········[くむ²]
　家の～　*one's* family business ················[きらう]
じょうはつ 蒸発　evaporation
　～する　evaporate; （人間が）disappear (mysteriously)
じょうはんしん 上半身　the upper half of the body
しょうひ 消費

～者　a consumer ·········[たすう]
～税　a consumption tax
しょうひょう 商標　a trademark
- a label ················[へいきん]
　～登録をする　register a [*one's*] †trademark [brand's name]
しょうひん 商品　goods
- merchandise ················[きず]
　～券　a gift certificate
しょうひん 賞品　a prize
じょうひん 上品
　～ぶる　put on airs ·········[みせる]
しょうぶ 勝負
　～にならない ·············[まるで]
じょうぶ 丈夫
　～な (体が) fit ················[しゅだん]
しょうぶん 性分　*one's* nature　[おせじ]
しょうべん 小便　urine
　～を漏らす　wet *one's* pants　[もらす]
じょうほ 譲歩する　compromise ················[ふくく]
しょうぼう 消防　fire defense, fire fighting
　～訓練　a fire drill
　～士　a fireman, a fire fighter
　～自動車　a fire engine
　～署　a fire station
　～隊　the fire brigade ·······[おさまる²]
じょうほう 情報　information [たしか]
- news ················[ほど]
　～化時代　the age of information ················[さんぶつ]
　～源　a source of information
　～伝達の手段　a means of distributing information [しゅだん]
しょうぼうちょう 消防庁　the Fire and Disaster Management Agency
しょうみ 正味の　net, full
じょうみゃく 静脈　a vein
　～瘤　《医学用語》varix
しょうめい 証明
しょうめい 照明　lighting; (装飾的な) illumination
しょうめん 正面
　～衝突　a head-on collision ················[しょうとつ]
　～を向く　look straight ahead　[よこ]
しょうもう 消耗する　exhaust,

consume
～品 consumables
じょうやく 条約 a treaty
～を結ぶ sign a treaty
しょうゆ 醤油 soy, soy sauce
しょうらい 将来
～が明るい have a bright future ………………………………[あかるい]
しょうり 勝利 (a) victory, a triumph
～を得る win [gain] a victory
～を収める win [pull down] the championship ………[おさめる¹]
じょうりく 上陸する land, go ashore
しょうりゃく 省略 an omission
～する omit, leave out
じょうりゅう 上流 (川の) up stream, up the river; (社会の) the upper-class
～階級 the upper classes
じょうりゅう 蒸留する distill
～水 distilled water
しょうりょう 少量の a little
・a small amount of …………[そそる]
じょうれい 条例 an ordinance, a regulation
じょうれん 常連 a regular customer [visitor]
ショー a show
じょおう 女王 a queen
ショーウィンドウ a show window, a display window, a shop window
ショート 《野球》a shortstop
ショート 《電気》a short circuit
ショートカット 《コンピュータ》a [the] shortcut
デスクトップに～を作る put a shortcut on the desktop
ショートケーキ a shortcake
ショートステイ a short stay
ショール a shawl
ショールーム a showroom
しょか 初夏 early summer
しょかん 書簡 a letter, a correspondence …………[おさめる¹]
しょき 初期 the beginning, the early days
～の early
～化する (フロッピーディスク・コンピュータを) initialize, reinitialize
しょき 所期の expected ………[せいせき]
～の目的 a desired end …..[もくてき]
しょき 書記 a secretary
しょきゅう 初級の introductory, elementary, beginners'
じょきょうじゅ 助教授 an assistant professor
ジョギング jogging
～する jog …………………………[つづく]
しよく 私欲 self-interest ………[すてる]
しょく 食が進まない [すすむ]
～が細い be a skimpy eater [ほそい]
しょく 職がない be out of work ………………………………[くらし]
しょくいん 職員 a staff member; (職員全体) the staff
・an employee ………………[および]
～室 a teachers' room ……[よぶ]
・a teachers' lounge …………[れい¹]
しょくぎょう 職業
～に就く find a job ……[のうりょく]
～の選択 choosing a career ……………………………[じゅうだい]
しょくじ 食事 a meal, (a) dinner
～中に during the meal
・at the table ………………[きたない]
～の支度をする fix a meal
・cook ……………………[わずらわしい]
～をする have a meal, eat
しょくぜん 食前に before meal
～酒 an aperitif …………[すすめる²]
しょくたく 食卓 a dining table
しょくちゅうどく 食中毒 food poisoning
しょくどう 食堂 (家庭の) a dining room; (店) a restaurant, a cafeteria
～車 a dining car
しょくどう 食道 the gullet, 《医学用語》 the esophagus
～癌 a cancer of the esophagus, an esophageal cancer
しょくにん 職人 a craftsman ………………………………[たんねん]
・an artisan ………………[どうぐ]
しょくば 職場 an office ……[なごやか]
～結婚 an office marriage

〜を転々とする move from one company to another ……[こらえる]
しょくひ 食費 food expenses
しょくひん 食品 (a) food
冷凍〜 frozen foods
〜添加物 an additive
しょくぶつ 植物 a plant
しょくみんち 植民地 a colony
しょくむ 職務 (a) duty, a job
〜質問する question ……[ふしん]
〜上 on the job ……[しかる]
〜怠慢だ neglect *one's* duty
しょくもつ 食物 food
〜繊維 dietary fiber
しょくよう 食用の edible, eatable
〜になる be used for food, be edible ……[ね]
しょくよく 食欲
しょくりょう 食料(品) food
・groceries ……[おも, まとめる]
〜品店 a grocery store ……[かたい]
〜危機 a food crisis ……[ぞうか]
しょけい 処刑される be executed ……[けっか]
しょげる get down, be (down) in the dumps
じょげん 助言 advice, counsel
〜する advise, give advice
しょさい 書斎 a study
じょさい 如才ない (愛想のよい) sociable; (気のつく) tactful; (抜け目ない) shrewd
じょし 女子 (女の子) a girl; (婦人) a woman, a lady, a female
〜学生 a girl [woman, female] student
〜校 a girls' school
〜大学 a women's college
〜大生 (共学の)《米口語》a co-ed
じょしゅ 助手 an assistant
しょじょ 処女 a virgin
〜作 *one's* first work, *one's* maiden work
しょしん 初心 the spirit *one* had when *one* began ……[かえる¹]
〜者 a beginner
じょせい 女性 a woman, a female
〜解放運動 women's liberation movement ……[み¹]
〜的な feminine, womanly
しょせん after all, anyway, eventually; in short
じょそう 女装する be dressed in women's clothes ……[きもち]
しょぞく 所属している belong to
しょたい 所帯道具 household goods
・household furnishings ……[とおり]
しょたいめん 初対面の人 ……[つつしみ]
しょち 処置 a measure
・a move ……[けんめい]
・the way *one* deals with ……[こうへい]
〜する deal with
しょっき 食器(類) tableware ……[つうしん]
〜戸だな a cupboard
〜を洗う do the dishes ……[あらう]
ショック
しょっちゅう always, frequently, very often
しょっぱい taste salty ……[なめる]
しょてい 所定の位置 *one's* place, *one's* position ……[いち]
しょてん 書店 《米》a bookstore, 《英》a bookshop
しょどう 書道 calligraphy ……[とる¹]
しょとく 所得 income, earnings
しょひょう 書評 a (book) review ……[ある〜]
しょぶん 処分
〜する get rid of ……[いる²]
しょほ 初歩 the first step (to), the ABC's (of)
しょみん 庶民 ordinary people
・the average person ……[さがる]
しょめい 署名する sign; (記念のための) autograph
〜運動をする have a petition drive
じょやく 助役 a deputy mayor ……[おおう]
しょゆう 所有
じょゆう 女優 an actress
しょり 処理
〜する handle ……[じむ]
しょるい 書類 papers, documents
しょんぼり 〜する get down, look dejected [miserable]

〜と dejectedly, with a dejected look
しらが 白髪 gray hair, white hair
　〜の gray-haired
　〜交じり have hair streaked with gray ……………………[まじる]
しらける
しらじらしい barefaced, transparent
じらす
しらせ 知らせ
　〜を受ける get the news ……[うける]
しらせる 知らせる
しらふ 〜の sober
しらべる 調べる
　・make an investigation ……[てってい]
しらんぷり 知らん振りをする pretend not to know
　・ignore ………………………[ふり¹]
しり 尻
　〜に敷く have someone wrapped around one's finger ………[かてい]
シリア Syria
　〜の Syrian
　〜人 a Syrian; (全体) the Syrians
しりあい 知り合い
しりあう 知り合う get to know each other ……………………[つうじる]
　・get acquainted with ………[ふと]
シリーズ a series
しりごみ 尻込みする draw [shrink] back, hesitate (to)
じりじり
　〜と照りつける be sizzling hot ……………………………………[てる]
しりぞく 退く draw back, go backward; (引退する) retire
しりつ 市立の municipal, city
しりつ 私立の private
じりつしん 自立心 one's independence ……………………………[さまたげる]
しりもち 尻もちをつく fall on one's behind [bottom]
しりょ 思慮
しりょう 資料
しりょく 視力 eyesight
　〜がいい have a good eyesight
　〜が衰える one's eyesight is failing ……………………………[ふじゆう]

〜検査 an eye test ……………[うける]
しる 知る
　・be informed of ……………[できごと]
知らない not realize ……………[きんじょ]
知らない人 a stranger ……[ちかづく]
知らない振りをする feign ignorance (about) …………………………[ふり¹]
(…しても)知らないよ don't come to me if..., it's not my fault if...
　……………………………………[おこる¹]
知らぬ間に before one knows it
　……………………………………[ながす]
(…で)知られている be known for
　……………………………………[あざやか]
シルエット a silhouette
しるし 印 a mark, a sign
　(…の)印として as a token of
　……………………………………[うけとる]
　〜をつける mark
じれったい 《原因を主語にして》be frustrating, be irritating; (人を主語にして) be frustrated, be irritated
しれん 試練 a trial, a test
　〜に耐える endure a trial ……[ゆうき]
ジレンマ a dilemma
しろ 城 a castle
しろい 白い
しろうと 素人 an amateur ……[たかい]
　〜の域 the amateur level …[まだ]
シロクマ a polar [white] bear
しろくろ 白黒の black and white
シロップ syrup
しろバイ 白バイ a (white) police motorcycle
じろん 持論 one's pet theory [じしん¹]
しわ
しわくちゃ 〜の wrinkled, crumpled
しわざ someone's doing [work]
しん 心・芯
　〜まで to the core …………[くさる]
しん 芯 (鉛筆の) lead; (果物の) a core, a heart
じんいん 人員整理 a shake-up in personnel
　・(a) cutback in personnel …[ごうり]
　・a personnel reduction ……[せいり]
しんか 真価 true value ………[みとめる]
しんか 進化 evolution

～する evolve
しんがく 進学する go (on) to †college〔senior high school〕
じんかく 人格
しんがた 新型 a new model [style]
　～の latest-model ……………[あて]
シンガポール Singapore
　～の Singaporean
　～人 a Singaporean; (全体) the Singaporeans
しんかんせん 新幹線 the Shinkansen, the bullet train ……………[できる]
しんぎ 真偽 authenticity・validity ……………[ついて]
しんぎ 審議する deliberate ………[あん]
しんきいってん 心機一転する turn over a new leaf
しんきゅう 進級する (小中高) move up to the next grade
　(大学) advance to the next year
　……………[おとす]
しんきょう 心境
しんきろう 蜃気楼 a mirage
しんきろく 新記録 a new record
　世界～ a new world record
しんきんこうそく 心筋梗塞 myocardial [cardiac] infarction
しんく 深紅・真紅の crimson
　……………[たとえる]
　・blood-crimson ……………[もえる]
しんくう 真空 vacuum
ジンクス a jinx
シンクタンク a think tank
シングル ～の single
しんけい 神経
　～痛 neuralgia ……………[なやます]
　～が太い have strong nerves
　……………[ふとい]
しんけん 真剣
じんけん 人権 human rights
しんけんざい 新建材 new building materials ……………[だす]
しんこう 信仰 belief, faith
しんこう 進行 progress, advance
　～する progress, make progress, advance
　～方向……………[むかう]
　～性の (病気が) progressive

しんごう 信号
　～機 a traffic light ……………[かど]
じんこう 人口
　～増加 population growth 〔ぞうか〕
　～の多い populous ……………[せかい]
　～密度 the density of population
　……………[ひかく]
じんこう 人工
　～の synthetic ……………[さがる]
　～授精 artificial insemination
しんこきゅう 深呼吸する take a deep breath
しんこく 深刻
しんこく 申告する report, declare
しんこん 新婚さん the newlyweds
　……………[ひやかす]
　～旅行 a honeymoon ……[りょこう]
しんさ 審査する judge, examine
　～員 a judge ……………[した²]
じんざい いい人材 a talented person
　貴重な～ an invaluable asset
　……………[きちょう]
　～派遣会社 a temporary staffing agency
しんさつ 診察
　～を受ける have a doctor look at one ……………[うける]
しんさん 人生の辛酸をなめる taste life's bitterness ……………[なめる]
しんし 紳士 a gentleman
　～的な gentlemanlike, gentlemanly
じんじ 人事課 a personnel department
　……………[つなぐ]
じんじいん 人事院 the National Personnel Authority
しんしつ 寝室 a bedroom
しんじつ 真実 the truth
じんじゃ 神社 a (Shinto) shrine
　……………[おそれる]
しんじゅ 真珠 a pearl
じんしゅ 人種 a race
　～的偏見 racial prejudice 〔へんけん〕
　～の racial
しんじゅう 心中 a double suicide
　一家～ a family suicide
しんしゅつ 進出する launch a career in ……………[いと]
　・expand into ……………[りえき]

・move into ……………………[くう]
しんじょう 信条 a principle
・a motto ……………………[まなぶ]
しんじる 信じる
しんしん 心身ともに in body and mind, physically and mentally
……………………[けんこう]
しんじん 新人 (地域・組織の) a newcomer; (芸能界などの) a new face [star]; (スポーツ・野球の) a rookie
じんしん 人心を惑わす lead people astray ……………………[まどわす]
しんしんしょう 心身症 a psychosomatic disorder [disease]
しんすい 浸水する be flooded
……………………[たいへん]
しんせい 申請 (an) application
～する apply
しんせい 神聖な sacred, holy
じんせい 人生
しんせいひん 新製品 a new product
……………………[ちがい]
しんせき 親戚 a relative ………[ふこう]
しんせつ 親切
～心から out of kindness ……[～から]
しんせん 新鮮
～だ (体験が) be a new experience
……………………[ふれる]
しんぜん 親善 friendship, goodwill
しんそう 真相 the truth, a fact
事件の～ the facts of the case
……………………[とらえる]
しんぞう 心臓
～麻痺 (a) heart failure
～外科医 a cardiologist ……[むかえる]
じんぞう 人造の artificial, man-made
じんぞう 腎臓 a kidney, the kidneys
～病 kidney trouble, a kidney disease
じんそく 迅速な swift ………[おさまる²]
しんそこ 心底 truly, really, from the bottom of *one's* heart
しんそつ 新卒 a new graduate [とる²]
しんだい 身代 *one's* fortune [かたむく]
～をつぶす blow *one's* fortune
……………………[つぶす]
しんたいけんさ 身体検査 a physical examination, a medical checkup; (取り調べ) a search, a frisk
しんだいしゃ 寝台車 a sleeping car
……………………[だん]
しんたいそう 新体操 rhythmic gymnastics
しんだん 診断 medical examination
～書 a medical certificate
しんちゅう 心中は inside ……[おだやか]
しんちょう 身長 *one's* height
～を測る take *one's* height
・measure *one's* height ………[はかる]
しんちょう 慎重
しんちょう 新調の a new, newly-made
しんちんたいしゃ 新陳代謝 metabolism
じんつう 陣痛 labor (pains), birth pains; (筋肉の収縮) contractions
しんてん 進展 development, progress
～する develop, make progress
しんでんず 心電図 an electrocardiogram, a cardiogram
しんどい 《人を主語にして》 be exhausted; 《仕事などを主語にして》 exhausting, tough
しんとう 神道 Shinto, Shintoism
しんとう 浸透する penetrate, permeate
しんどう 神童 a prodigy ………[いう]
しんどう 振動・震動
しんなり tender ……………[あぶら]
しんにゅう 侵入する invade, intrude (into)
しんにゅう 新入社員 a new employee
……………………[ひょうばん]
～生 a freshman
・a new student ……………[ならぶ]
しんねん 信念 a belief
しんねん 新年 a new year
しんぱい 心配
～する be afraid that [おもいすごし]
～である be concerned about
……………………[できる]
～はない there's no need to worry
……………………[かんする]
～のあまり beside *oneself* with worry ……………………[かえる¹]
しんぱん 審判する judge; (ボクシング, フットボールなど) referee

～員 (野球などの) an umpire; (ボクシング, フットボールなどの) a referee
しんぴ 神秘 (a) mystery
 ～的な mysterious
しんぷ 神父 a priest, a father
しんぷう 新風を吹き込む bring a breath of fresh air to ……[ふく¹]
シンフォニー a symphony
しんふぜん 心不全 (a) heart failure
じんぶつ 人物
しんぶん 新聞 a newspaper
 ～記事 a newspaper article, a news story
 ～記者 a newspaper reporter [たつ²]
 ～代 a newspaper subscription ……………………[せいきゅう, ばか]
 ～に出る come out in the papers ……………………………[おおきい]
 ～配達 newspaper delivery [にらむ]
しんぽ 進歩
 急速な～を遂げる make rapid strides ……………………………[とげる]
しんぼう 辛抱
しんぼく 親睦を図る promote [cultivate] friendship ……[もくてき]
シンポジウム a symposium
シンボル a symbol
しんまい 新米の new, inexperienced
じんましん hives, (a) nettle rash
しんみ 親身になって相談に乗る do everything one can do to advise someone ……………………………[かい¹]
しんみつ 親密な close, intimate
しんや 深夜 midnight
 ～に at midnight, late at night
 ・deep into the night ………[および]
 ～放送 midnight broadcasting
しんゆう 親友 a close friend, a great friend, a true friend
しんよう 信用
しんらい 信頼
しんり 真理
しんり 心理
 ～描写 a psychological description ……………………………[だいぶぶん]
しんりゃく 侵略 invasion, aggression
 ～する invade

しんりょうじょ 診療所 a clinic
じんりょく 尽力 an effort ……[かい³]
 ～する make an effort, do one's best
しんりん 森林 (a) forest; (小さな) a wood, the woods
 ～保護 forest conservation
しんるい 親類
じんるい 人類 mankind, the human race
 ・the human species ………[はじめ]
しんろ 進路 a course, a way
しんろうしんぷ 新郎新婦 the bride and groom ……………………………[ならぶ]
しんわ 神話 a myth

ス

す 巣 a nest; (クモの) a web, a cobweb
す 酢 vinegar
ず 図 a picture; (図表) a diagram; (さし絵) a figure, an illustration
 ・a diagram ……………………[うつす¹]
すあし 素足の[で] barefoot(ed)
すいあげる 吸い上げる suck up, pump up
すいえい 水泳 swimming
スイカ a watermelon
すいがい 水害 a flood, flood [rain] damage
 ・water damage ……………………[たつ⁴]
すいがら 吸い殻 a (cigarette) butt
すいぎゅう 水牛 a water buffalo
すいぎん 水銀 mercury
 ～中毒 mercury poisoning
すいこむ 吸い込む (空気を) breathe in; (液体を) absorb
すいさいが 水彩画 a watercolor (painting)
すいじ 炊事 cooking
 ～する cook, do the cooking
すいしつおせん 水質汚染 water pollution ……………………………[せつじつ]
すいしゃ 水車 a water wheel [ちから]
すいじゃく 衰弱する become [get] weak
すいじゅん 水準 a standard
 ・a level ……………………………[あがる]
 生活～ a standard of living [ひくい]

すいしょう 水晶 (a) crystal
スイス Switzerland
　～の Swiss
　～人 a Swiss (複数同形); (全体) the Swiss
すいすい ～と (動き) swiftly; (進行) smoothly
すいせい 彗星 a comet
すいせい 水星 Mercury
スイセン 水仙 a narcissus; (ラッパズイセン) a daffodil
すいせん 推薦 recommendation
　～する recommend
すいせん 水洗トイレ a flush toilet
すいそ 水素 hydrogen
すいそう 水槽 a (water) tank ……………………………[かたむける]
すいぞう 膵臓 the pancreas
すいそく 推測 a guess
　～する guess, suppose
すいぞくかん 水族館 an aquarium
すいちゅう 水中の underwater
　～カメラ an underwater camera
　～翼船 a hydrofoil
すいちょく 垂直な[の] vertical
スイッチ a switch
すいてい 推定の estimated, presumed
すいている not be crowded [あんがい]
すいでん 水田 a rice paddy, paddy field
すいとう 水筒 a canteen ………[もれる]
すいどう 水道 city water; running water, tap water
　～管 a water pipe ………[うめる]
　～を出す[止める] turn on [off] the water
　～を止める turn off the faucet ……………………………[いっぱい]
すいばく 水爆 an H-bomb, a hydrogen bomb
すいはんき 炊飯器 a rice cooker
ずいひつ 随筆 an essay
すいぶん 水分 water; (湿り気) moisture; (果物の) (a) juice
ずいぶん 随分
　・really ……………………………[あまえる]
　・awfully ……………………………[あやしい]
　・quite ……………………………[からかう]

すいへい 水平の level, horizontal
　～線 the horizon
すいへい 水兵 a sailor, a seaman
すいみん 睡眠 sleep
　～不足 a lack of sleep ………[ふそく]
　～薬 a sleeping pill ………[もちいる]
すいようび 水曜日 Wednesday (略 Wed.)
すいり 推理する guess, reason
　～小説 a mystery
　・a detective story ………[ふける]
すいりょく 水力 waterpower
　～発電所 a hydroelectric power station
スイレン 睡蓮 a water lily
すう 吸う
スウェーデン Sweden
　～の、～語 Swedish
　～人 a Swede; (全体) the Swedish, the Swedish people, the Swedes
すうがく 数学 mathematics, 《米口語》 math
　～的な mathematical ………[ない]
すうじ 数字 a figure; a numeral
　～で示す express *something* in numbers ……………………………[ぐたい]
ずうずうしい
　ずうずうしさ impudence [へいこう²]
スーツ a suit
スーツケース a suitcase
スーパーマーケット a supermarket
すうはい 崇拝する worship, admire
スープ soup
すえ 末
　…の末 at the end of ………[さとる]
すえっこ 末っ子 the youngest child ……………………………[かた³]
スカート a skirt
スカーフ a scarf
ずがいこつ 頭蓋骨 a skull
スカウト a (talent) scout
すがお 素顔 (化粧なし) a face without makeup; (本当の姿) a true face
　～で without makeup, with no makeup (on)
すかさず at once, without a moment's delay
すがすがしい refreshing, refreshed,

すがた 姿
　〜を現す　show up …………[あらわす²]
すかれる 好かれる　be liked, be popular
ずかん 図鑑　an illustrated book
すき 好き
すき 隙
　・an opening …………………[ねらう]
スギ 杉　a cedar (tree)
〜すぎ 〜過ぎ
〜ずき 〜好き　a *something*-lover
　………………………………[いがい²]
スキー　(道具) a ski; (スポーツ) skiing
　〜場　a ski slope, a skiing ground
　・a ski resort …………………[きたい]
　〜同好会　a ski club ……[たんじょう]
　〜に行く　go skiing
すききらい 好き嫌い
　〜はない　not be picky about food
　………………………………[さすが]
すきすき 好き好きだ　be a matter of taste
スキップ 〜する　skip
すきとおった 透き通った　transparent, clear
(〜に)すぎない　nothing but..., no more than...
すきま 隙間
　・a gap …………………………[さす³]
　ドアの〜　a crack in the door
　………………………………[のぞく²]
　〜風が入る　the wind seeps through the cracks ……………………[はいる]
　〜産業　a niche industry
スキャナ　a scanner
　〜で読み取る　scan
スキャンダル　a scandal
すぎる 過ぎる
　・go by …………………………[むなしい]
　過ぎたこと　the past …………[き]
すく 好く
すく 空・透く
すぐ
　・right now ……………………[ほしい]
すくい 救い　(a) help
　〜の手　a helping hand
　〜のない　helpless

すくう 救う
すくう　(さじ・網などで) scoop; (人の足などを) trip
すぐさま immediately …………[むける]
すくない 少ない
　少なくなる　run out …………[じかん]
　少なくない　more than a few [くぐる]
すくなくとも 少なくとも
すくむ　cower
すくめる　(首を) duck (*one's* head); (肩を) shrug (*one's* shoulders)
スクラップ　(切り抜き) a clipping; (廃品) scrap
スクリーン　a screen
すぐれる 優れる
　優れた　magnificent …………[さくひん]
ずけい 図形　a figure
スケート skating
　〜場　a skating rink
　〜に行く　go skating
スケジュール　a schedule
スケッチ　a sketch
　〜する　sketch
すける 透ける　(透き通った) transparent; (衣服が) see-through
　透けて見える　can see through
　………………………………[した¹]
スコア　a score
　〜ブック　a scorebook
　〜ボード　a scoreboard
すごい
　〜速さで　at a tremendous speed
　………………………………[ながれる]
すこし 少し
すこしも 少しも
すごす 過ごす
　過ごし易い　comfortable ……[やはり]
すこぶる　excellent …………[かいちょう]
ずさん 〜な　sloppy
　・slipshod ……………………[まねく]
すじ 筋
　〜が通っている　reasonable, logical
　………………………………[とおる]
　〜を通して話す　speak logically
　………………………………[とおす]
すじがき 筋書き　(あらすじ) a synopsis; (計画) a plan
すしづめ すし詰めの　overcrowded,

すじみち 筋道を立てて in an orderly and logical fashion ……[せつめい]
すじょう 素性 birth, *one's* identity, *one's* personal history
すす soot
　すすけた sooty
すず 鈴 a bell
　〜の音 the tinkle of a bell
すすぐ wash in clean water, rinse
すずしい 涼しい
すすむ 進む
・move ahead ……[うける]
・push *one's* way through ……[おす]
・proceed ……[なごやか]
（時計が）run fast ……[よう¹]
すずむ 涼む enjoy the cool air, cool *oneself*
スズメ a sparrow
すすめる 進める
　進められている be making progress ……[たいら]
すすめる 勧・薦める
スズラン a lily of the valley
すずり an inkstone
すすりなく すすり泣く sob ……[なく¹]
すそ（衣服の）a hem ……[ひろがる]
すその（…の）すそ野 the plain at the foot of ……[ひろい]
スター a star
　映画〜 a movie star
スタイル（様式）a style;（体の）a figure
　〜がよい have a good figure
スタジアム a stadium
スタジオ a studio
ずたずた 〜に into shreds ……[さく²]
スタッフ（ひとり）a staff member;（全体）the staff
スタミナ stamina
すたれる 廃れる go out of use, go out of fashion
スタンド（観客席）a stand;（電気スタンド）a desk lamp
　（観客席）bleachers ……[おおう]
スタンプ a stamp;（消印）a postmark
スチーム steam;（暖房）steam heating
スチュワーデス a flight attendant, a stewardess
jampacked

〜ずつ
ずつう 頭痛（がする） (have) a headache
すっかり
・drastically ……[ようす]
すっきり
ずっと
・the whole time ……[あいだ]
・all the way ……[あせ]
・a lot ……[わかい]
すっぱい 酸っぱい
すっぽかす break a promise;（デートを）stand up
すっぽり 〜と entirely, completely
　〜と覆われる be entirely blanketed [covered] with ……[おおう]
すで 素手で（武器なしで）unarmed
　（手袋などなしで）with *one's* bare hands ……[うける]
ステーキ (a) steak
　〜を焼く cook a steak
すてき 素敵
　〜な stunning ……[あわせる]
ステッカー a sticker
ステッキ a walking stick, a cane
すでに 既に
すてる 捨てる
・throw over ……[のりかえる]
・rid *oneself* of ……[へんけん]
　何もかも〜 give up everything ……[はしる]
ステレオ a stereo (unit [set])
ステロイド 〜剤 a steroid
ステンレス stainless steel
ストーカー a stalker
ストーブ（暖房用の）a heater
ストッキング stockings;（パンティストッキング）panty hose
ストックホルム Stockholm
ストップウオッチ a stopwatch [はかる]
ストライキ a strike, a walkout
　〜に入る go on strike ……[こうしょう¹, はいる]
　〜をする（…を要求して[…に反対して]）strike for [against] *something*
ストライク a strike
ストレート 〜の[で] straight

ストレス
ストロー　a straw
ストロボ　a flashlight, a strobe
すな 砂　sand
　〜の(多い)　sandy
　〜ぼこり　dust …………………[たつ²]
すなお 素直
　〜に　with an open heart　[しんせつ]
　(有難く) gracefully …………[こうい²]
　〜に謝る　offer *someone one's* sincere apology
スナック　(軽食) a snack; (酒場) a bar
スナップ　〜写真　a snapshot [みつける]
スニーカー　sneakers
すね　a shank, a shin
　〜をかじる　be dependent on *one's* parents
　・sponge off *one's* parents
　　………………………………[いつまでも]
すねる　sulk
ずのう 頭脳　a head, brains
　・a mind ………………………[ちみつ]
スノーボード　〜をする　snowboard
スパイ　a spy, an agent
　〜する　spy on
スパイク　spiked shoes
スパイス　a spice
スパゲッティ　spaghetti
すばしこい　quick
ずばぬけて　outstandingly
すばやい 素早い　quick, prompt, agile
　素早く　quickly, promptly
すばらしい 素晴らしい
　・magnificent …………………[けしき]
　・brilliant ………………………[わかす]
　素晴らしさ　splendor ………[はじめて]
ずばり　〜と　(率直に) frankly, unreservedly, straightforwardly; (正確に) right
スピーカー　a loud-speaker
スピーチ　a speech
　〜をする　make a speech
スピード　speed
　〜を落とす　slow down, lower *one's* speed …………………………[おとす]
　〜違反　speeding, exceeding the speed limit

ずひょう 図表　a chart, a diagram, a graph
スプーン　a spoon
ずぶとい 図太い　bold, have nerve
ずぶぬれ　〜になる　get wet through
スプレー　a spray
スペア　〜の　spare
スペイン　Spain
　〜の、〜語　Spanish
　〜人　a Spaniard; (全体) the Spanish
すべて
すべりこむ 滑り込む　slide into; (すばやく・こっそりと) slip into
すべる 滑る
　滑り易い　slippery …………[こおる]
スポーツ　《集合的に》sport(s)
　〜施設　sports facilities　[ひんじゃく]
　〜用品　sports equipment …[そろう]
　〜マン　an athlete
ずぼら　〜な　sloppy …………[めいわく]
ズボン　trousers
　・pants …………………………[こんな]
スポンサー　a sponsor
スポンジ　a sponge
スマート　〜な　(すらりとした) slender; (洗練された) sophisticated
すまい 住まい　a house, a home, an address
すます 済ます
すみ 炭　charcoal ………………[やく³]
すみ 隅
すみ 墨　India ink, Chinese ink
すみずみ 隅々　all the corners, everywhere, every nook and cranny
すみません
スミレ　a violet
　三色〜　a pansy
すむ 住・棲む
すむ 済む
　(…で)済む　be cleared up with *something* ……………………[〜から]
　(…せずに)済む　get by without *doing* ………………………………[おく¹]
　済んでしまったこと　something that is finished and done with
　………………………………[おもいきり]
すむ 澄む　become clear [transparent]

澄んだ clear, transparent
スムーズ 〜に smoothly
ずめん 図面 a plan, a drawing [せん]
すもう 相撲 *sumo* wrestling
　〜取り a *sumo* wrestler [たくましい]
　〜をとる wrestle (with)
スモッグ smog
スモモ （実）a plum; （木）a plum tree
スライド a slide
ずらす move ························[こする]
すらすら
ずられる have *something* picked, have *one's* pocket picked
スランプ a slump
すり （人）a pickpocket; （行為）pickpocketing
すりかえる すり替える replace secretly
すりきず すり傷 a scratch
すりきれた すり切れた worn-out
　・threadbare ··················[すてる]
すりこむ すり込む rub in [into]
スリッパ slippers
スリップ 〜する slip
　・skid ···························[つぶす]
すりつぶす （硬いものを粉にする）grind; （柔らかいものを）mash
すりへる すり減る be worn out [そこ]
すりむく skin, scratch
スリラー a thriller
スリランカ Sri Lanka
　〜の Sri Lankan
　〜人 a Sri Lankan; （全体）the Sri Lankans
スリル a thrill
　〜のある thrilling
する 擦・摺・刷・掏る
する 為る
ずるい
　・crafty ·······················[なるほど]
すると
するどい 鋭い
　〜目で睨む glare sharply (at)
　································[にらむ]
ずるやすみ ずる休みする play hooky
　・skip school ······················[ま]
ずれ a difference, a gap, a lag
すれちがう 擦れ違う
　・walk past ···················[うばう]

すれる be worn ·····················[ひかる]
ずれる
スローガン a slogan
すわる 座る・据わる
　（きちんと）sit up ············[きちんと]
　座りっぱなし sit all that time [こし]
すんぜん 寸前だ just [right] before
　・be on the verge of ········[ほろびる]
すんだ 澄んだ clear, transparent
すんなり easily, smoothly
すんぽう 寸法 a measurement, the measure, (a) size
　〜を取る take the measure of

セ

せ 背 （背中）*one's* back; （背丈）height
　背が…ある be ... tall ············[ある]
　背が高い tall
せい 性 sex
　〜的な sexual
　〜教育 sex education
（〜の）せい
〜せい 〜製 （国）made in; （素材）made of
ぜい 税 a tax; （関税など）a duty
　消費〜 a consumption tax
せいい 誠意
せいいっぱい 精一杯
　〜（する）だけで精一杯だ········[〜だけ]
せいえん 声援する cheer, give a cheer (for)
せいかい 正解 a correct [right] answer
せいかい 政界 political circles
　・government circles ·······[ちから]
　・the political world ········[つうじる]
　〜入りする go into politics
せいかく 正確
せいかく 性格
　〜が不一致だ be incompatible
　··································[わかれる]
せいかつ 生活
　教員〜 a career as a teacher [おわり]
　〜水準 standard of living ····[たかい]
　〜費 living expenses ·········[よる¹]
　〜習慣病 lifestyle-related diseases, diseases associated with adult lifestyle habits

～していく　carry on ………[きどる]
～が楽になる　make life easier　[らく]
ぜいかん　税関　a custom house, (the) customs
　～を通る　go through the customs
せいき　世紀　a century
せいき　正規の　regular; (常勤の) full-time
　～手続　the regular procedure　[ふむ]
せいぎ　正義　justice, right
せいきゅう　請求
せいきょく　政局　the political situation
　………………………………[あんてい]
ぜいきん　税金　(a) tax; (関税など) (a) duty
　～のむだづかい　the waste of public funds …………………[ひなん]
せいけい　生計を立てる　make one's living ………………[もぐる]
せいけい　整形手術　(外科) orthopedic surgery
　(美容) plastic [cosmetic] surgery
　………………………………[げんめつ]
せいけつ　清潔
せいけん　政権　(政治権力) administrative power
　(政府) an administration ……[わたす]
　～交代　a change of power
　・a change in administrations
　………………………………[すぎる]
　～を握る　seize power ………[おこる²]
せいげん　制限
せいこう　成功
　～の確率　a probability of success
　………………………………[たかい]
　～はおぼつかない　there isn't much hope for success ………[～だけ]
　～を収める　achieve one's success
　………………………………[ふだん¹]
せいざ　正座する　sit on one's knees
　・sit with one's legs under one
　………………………………[たてる¹]
せいざ　星座　a constellation
せいさく　政策
せいさく　製作・制作
せいさん　生産
せいさん　清算
せいさん　精算

運賃～所　the fare adjustment office
せいじ　政治
　～生命　one's life in politics
　………………………………[せいめい]
せいしき　正式
せいしつ　性質
せいじつ　誠実
せいじゅく　成熟した　(果物などが) ripe; (体などが) mature
せいしゅん　青春　youth
　～時代に　in one's youth, in one's youthful days
せいしょ　聖書　the (Holy) Bible
　旧約～　the Old Testament
　新約～　the New Testament
せいじょう　正常
せいじょう　政情　the political situation
　………………………………[ふあん]
せいじょうき　星条旗　the Stars and Stripes
せいしょうねん　青少年の　juvenile
　～犯罪[非行]　juvenile delinquency
せいしん　精神
　～状態　one's psychological [mental] state ………………[じょうたい]
　～力　inner strength ………[おどろく]
せいじん　成人する　come of age
　・be grown up ……………[あんしん]
　～式　a coming-of-age ceremony
　～映画　an adult [X-rated] movie
　～病　adult diseases
せいじんのひ　成人の日　Coming-of-Age Day
せいず　製図　drafting ………[てきする]
せいぜい
ぜいせい　税制　the tax system
　………………………………[てってい]
　不公平～　an unfair tax system
　………………………………[ふこうへい]
せいせいどうどう　正々堂々
　～と　fair and square ………[たたかう]
せいせき　成績
　・one's performance …………[きたい]
　～が上がる　improve one's grades
　………………………………[ふくしゅう]
　～がクラス一番になる　get the best grades in the class ………[よろこぶ]
　～のいい　with good grades

..................................[おおぜい]
せいぜん 整然とした orderly, tidy, well-ordered
 〜と in good order, tidily
 ・neatly ....[みだれる]
せいそう 正装する be in full dress, be in uniform
せいぞう 製造
せいぞん 生存者 a survivor ....[たった]
せいだい 盛大
ぜいたく
 〜な暮らしをする lead a life of luxury ....[かつて]
 〜の味 the taste of luxury ......[あじ]
せいちょう 成長
せいてんかん 性転換 a sex change
 〜をする have a sex change
 〜手術を受ける have a sex change operation, have sexual reassignment surgery
せいでんき 静電気 static electricity
..................................[まさつ]
せいと 生徒 (児童)a pupil; (男生徒) a schoolboy, (女生徒) a schoolgirl; (生徒, 学生) a student
 〜を監督する oversee *one's* students
..................................[ぎむ]
せいど 制度 a system ....[うむ]
 教育〜 an educational system
せいとう 正当な just, right, proper, fair; (合法的な) lawful, legal
 ・justifiable ....[ひはん]
 〜化する justify
 〜防衛 self-defense
せいとう 政党 a political party
せいとかい 生徒会 a student council
..................................[いいん]
 〜長 the president of the student council ....[かい³, よき]
せいとん 整とん
 部屋を〜する keep *one's* room neat
..................................[つとめる¹]
ぜいにく ぜい肉が付く gain weight
..................................[つく²]
 〜を落とす get rid of extra weight
..................................[おとす]
せいねん 成年 an adult ....[たっする]
せいねん 青年 a youth; (総称) young people, the young
せいねんがっぴ 生年月日 the date of *one's* birth
せいのう 性能
せいはんたい 正反対の diametrically opposed, exactly opposite
..................................[せいかく²]
せいび 整備 maintenance, (a) repair
 〜する maintain, repair
せいひん 製品 a product, manufactured goods
せいふ 政府 a [the] government
せいぶ 西部 the west; (アメリカの) the West
 〜の west, western
 〜劇 a western
せいふく 制服 a uniform
せいふく 征服 conquest
 〜する conquer
せいぶつ 生物 a living thing, a creature
 〜学 biology
せいぶん 成分 an element
 ・an ingredient ....[ひみつ]
せいぼ 歳暮 a year-end gift
せいほうけい 正方形 a (regular) square
せいみつ 精密な precise; (詳しい) detailed; (綿密な) minute
 〜な delicate ....[しんちょう]
 〜機械 precision machinery
..................................[せいさく²]
 〜機器 precision instruments
..................................[ゆうしゅう]
せいめい 生命
せいめい 声明 an announcement
..................................[のる]
 ・a statement ....[はっぴょう]
 公式〜を出す make an official statement
せいやく 製薬会社 a pharmaceutical company ....[けんきゅう]
せいよう 西洋 Europe, the West, the Western countries, the Occident
 〜の European, Western, Occidental
 〜化 westernization ....[くだる]
せいよう 静養する rest, take a rest

・convalesce ·················[けんこう]
せいり 整理
　〜する　arrange ·············[しゅるい]
せいり　生理　(月経) a menstruation, a period
　〜休暇　a menstrual leave, a physiological leave
　〜痛　menstrual pains
ぜいりし　税理士　a licensed tax accountant
せいりつ　成立する　(法案が) be approved; (組織される) be formed; (商談などが) be arranged (条約が施行される) go into effect
　····················[ひきあげる]
せいりょう　清涼飲料水　a soft drink
　·······························[ひみつ]
せいりょく 勢力
せいりょく　精力　energy
　〜的に　energetically, vigorously
せいれつ　整列する　stand in a row [line], form a line, line up
セーター　a sweater, a jersey
セーヌ　〜川　the Seine
セーフ　《野球》safe
セーラー　〜服　a middy (blouse) and skirt; (男子用の) a sailor suit
セールスマン　a salesman
せおう　背負う　carry on *one's* back, bear, shoulder
せかい 世界
　〜一周旅行　an around-the-world cruise ···················[ごうか]
　〜情勢　the world situation
　·······························[かいもく]
　・international conditions [さいきん]
せかいいさん　世界遺産　a World Heritage site
せかす　rush, hurry (up), push
せがむ　pester ···············[つかまえる]
セカンド　《野球》(the) second baseman
　〜オピニオン　a second opinion
せき　咳　a cough
　〜をする　cough
　・have a cough ············[けれど(も)]
せき　籍　(戸籍) a family register; (会員の籍) membership
せき 席

　〜を争う　fight over seats　[あらそう]
　〜を詰める　move over
　・scoot down [over] ··········[つめる]
　〜を外す　get up and leave　[えんりょ]
せきがいせん　赤外線　infrared rays
　〜写真　infrared photography
　·······························[さがす]
せきたん　石炭　coal
　〜を掘る　mine coal ·········[つらい]
せきどう　赤道　the equator ·····[こえる]
せきにん 責任
　〜が重い····················[そうとう]
　〜を逃れる　get out of the responsibility ···············[たくみ]
　〜を果たす　fulfill *one's* responsibility ················[はたす]
せきはん　赤飯　red-bean rice ······[むす]
せきぶん　積分　integral calculus
せきめん　赤面する　blush
せきゆ　石油　petroleum; (灯油) kerosene
　〜危機　the oil crisis
せきり　赤痢　dysentery
セクハラ　(セクシャルハラスメント) sexual harassment
せけん 世間
　〜の　public ··················[おもわく]
　・of the public ············[どうじょう]
　〜一般の考え　a prevalent view of society ···················[いっぱん]
　〜並みの　ordinary ············[なみ]
せこい　(けちな) stingy, tight-fisted; (浅薄な) sleazy
せじ　世事に疎い　be out of touch with the world ···················[うとい]
せすじ　背筋が冷たくなる　send chills up and down *one's* spine [つめたい]
せだい　世代　a generation
　〜の断絶　a generation gap
せちがらい　cold, hard
せっかい　石灰　lime
せっかく
　〜の　precious ···············[むだ]
せっかち
せっき　石器時代　the Stone Age
せっきょう　説教　(小言) (a) scolding; (教会での) a sermon, preaching
　〜する　(小言を言う) give a sermon,

scold; (教会で) preach, preach a sermon
- give *someone* a good lecture [きく¹]
- lecture ················[れい²]

せっきょく 積極
~性 enterprise ···············[ほしい]
~的に in a positive way ·······[そん]

せっけい 設計 a plan, a design
~する plan, design

せっけん soap

せっこう 石こう plaster ············[かた¹]

ぜっこう 絶交する break up with

ぜっこう 絶好の機会 a golden [great] opportunity ···············[きかい]

ぜっさん 絶賛する praise *something* highly ················[ある~]

せっし 摂氏 centigrade (略 C)

せつじつ 切実

せっする 接する (隣り合う) border, adjoin; (接触する) touch; (応対する) attend to
- have a relationship with
 ·············[あたたかい]

せっせと hard, busily

せっせん 接戦 a close game

せつぞく 接続

せったい 接待 entertainment
~する entertain, receive
~費 entertainment expenses

ぜったい 絶対
~に under any circumstances
 ·············[かりる]

せっちゃくざい 接着剤 (an) adhesive, (a) glue

セット a set

せつど 節度のある moderate
~のない immoderate

せっとく 説得する persuade ·······[て]

せつに 切に

せっぱつまる 切羽詰まる be in a desperate [critical] situation, be in a fix [pinch], have *one's* back to the wall

せつび 設備
~が整っている be well equipped
 ·············[たかい]

せつぶん 節分 the last day of winter
 ·············[まく¹]

ぜっぺき 絶壁 a sheer cliff ······[うしろ]

せつぼう 切望 an earnest desire, an eager wish
~する desire earnestly, wish eagerly

ぜつぼう 絶望
~する lose all hope ···········[なげる]

せつめい 説明

ぜつめつ 絶滅する become extinct

せつやく 節約

せつりつ 設立する found, establish, set up

せとぎわ (…の)瀬戸際にいる be on the brink [verge, edge] of

せともの 瀬戸物 (陶磁器の総称) china; (陶器) pottery; (磁器) porcelain

せなか 背中
~を流す scrub *someone's* back
 ·············[ながす]

せのび 背伸びをする stand on *one's* tiptoe; 《比喩的》aim too high

ぜひ 是非
(良し悪し) the pros and cons [わく¹]

せびょうし 背表紙 the spine ···[きえる]

せびろ 背広 《米》a suit, 《英》a lounge suit

せぼね 背骨 the backbone

せまい 狭い

せまる 迫る

セミ a cicada

ゼミ a seminar

せめて

せめる 攻める

せめる 責める

セメント cement

せり 競り an auction

ゼリー jelly

せりふ (役者の) lines; (言葉) words

セルフサービス ~の self-service
 ·············[サービス]

ゼロ zero

セロテープ cellophane tape, adhesive tape; 《商標》Scotch tape

セロファン cellophane

せろん 世論 public opinion
~調査 a public opinion poll
 ·············[はっぴょう]
- the polls ···············[けいこう]

せわ 世話

お～になりました ………[とんでもない]
～になった人 ………………[さすが]
せわしい　busy;（落ち着きのない）restless
せわしく　busily, restlessly
せん　千　a [one] thousand
せん　栓　（穴や隙間をふさぐ）a plug;（瓶の栓）a stopper;（瓶のコルク）a bottle cork;（瓶のキャップ）a bottle cap
せん　線
　この～で話を進める　go along with this ………………[はなし]
ぜん　善は急げ ………………[いそぐ]
ぜん～　全～
　～人類　the entire human race ………………[たもつ]
ぜん～　前～　（以前の）ex-～, former
せんい　繊維　a fiber;（織物）textile
ぜんい　善意　goodwill, kindness
ぜんいん　全員　all the members
　～一致で　unanimously ……[いっち]
ぜんか　前科がある　have a criminal record
ぜんかい　全快　complete recovery ………………[いのる]
　～する　recover completely ………………[はなれる²]
せんきょ　選挙　an election …[こうめい]
　～権　the right to vote, suffrage
　～運動　an election campaign
　～制度　election regulations …[むし]
　～に出る　run in an election, run for *something*
　～違反する　break election laws ………………[いはん]
せんげつ　先月　last month
せんけん　先見の明　foresight
せんげん　宣言　declaration, proclamation
　～する　declare, proclaim
せんご　戦後の　postwar
ぜんご　前後に　back and forth, before and after
　…前後（およそ）about, ...or not
せんこう　専攻する　major in …[しんり²]
ぜんこく　全国
　～的な　nationwide ………[ひろがる]

せんさい　繊細
せんざい　洗剤　a detergent ……[あらう]
せんざいてき　潜在的な　potential, subconscious, latent
せんさく　詮索する　pry into
　～好きな　inquisitive
せんし　戦死する　die [be killed] in battle [war]
　・be killed in action ………[きみょう]
せんじちゅう　戦時中　during the war ………………[かんとく]
せんしつ　船室　a cabin
せんじつ　先日　the other day, a few days ago
　～の話　the other day's conversation ………………[けれど(も)]
ぜんじつ　前日　the previous day, the day before
せんしゃ　戦車　a tank
ぜんしゃ　前者　the former
せんしゅ　選手
　・an athlete ………………[くずれる]
　・a competitor ………………[こうえい]
せんしゅう　先週　last week
　～の今日　a week ago today
ぜんしゅう　全集　*one's* complete works
　・*one's* collected works ……[おさめる¹]
せんじょう　戦場　a battlefield
　～に行く　go off to war ………[いく]
ぜんしん　全身　the whole body
　～に　all over, from head to foot
ぜんしん　前進　advance
　～する　advance, move [go] forward, go ahead
センス
せんす　扇子　a Japanese fan
せんすい　潜水　diving;（1回の）a dive
　～服　a diving suit ………………[もぐる]
せんせい　先生　（教師）a teacher;（講師）an instructor;（教授）a professor;（医師）a doctor
せんせい　宣誓　an oath
　～する　take [make] an oath, swear
センセーション　a sensation
せんぜん　戦前の　prewar
ぜんぜん　全然
せんぞ　先祖　an ancestor
せんそう　戦争　a war;（戦闘）a battle, a

ぜんそく asthma ……………[いい]
ぜんそくりょく 全速力で at full speed
〜で走る run as fast as *one* can ……………[こきゅう]
センター a center;《野球》the center field;(選手) a center fielder
ぜんたい 全体
ぜんだいみもん 前代未聞の unheard-of, unprecedented
せんたく 洗濯する wash, clean
・do the laundry ……………[げんき]
〜機 a washing machine, a washer
〜物《集合的》the washing
・the laundry ……………[かわかす]
〜物を干す hang [set] out the laundry (to dry) ……………[ほす]
〜物を取り入れる take in the wash [laundry] ……………[とりいれる]
〜に出す have *something* cleaned ……………[はずす]
せんたく 選択
センチ(メートル) a centimeter (略 cm.)
センチメンタル 〜な sentimental
せんちゃく 先着順50名 the first fifty applications ……………[じゅん]
せんちょう 船長 a captain …[じこく]
ぜんちょう 前兆 an omen, a sign
せんでん 宣伝
〜文句 a catchphrase, a copy
せんてんてき 先天的な congenital, inborn
ぜんと 前途 prospects for the future ……………[くらい]
・*one's* future ……………[ひかん]
〜有望である have a bright future, show great promise, be very promising ……………[ゆうぼう]
せんとう 先頭 the head, the front, the lead
せんとう 戦闘 a battle, a fight
せんとう 銭湯 a public bath, a bathhouse
せんにゅうかん 先入観 a preconception, (a) prejudice
せんぬき 栓抜き (コルク用)a corkscrew;(キャップ用)a cap-opener
・a bottle-opener ……………[あける³]
せんぱい 先輩 ……………[かた²]
せんはん 前半 the first half
ぜんぶ 全部
・one hundred percent ……[おのおの]
せんぷうき 扇風機 an electric fan
せんべい a Japanese (rice) cracker
せんべつ 餞別 a farewell gift
せんぽう 先方 the other party ……………[りょうかい]
せんまん 千万 ten million
1億5千万 one hundred and fifty million
せんむ 専務 a (senior) managing director, an executive director
せんめい 鮮明な clear, distinct, vivid
ぜんめつ 全滅する be completely destroyed
せんめん 洗面器 a wash basin [はる¹]
ぜんめんてき 全面的に entirely, completely, fully, across the board
・entirely ……………[りょうかい]
せんもん 専門
〜家 a specialist
〜外 not in *one's* field ………[ひはん]
せんやく 先約がある have a previous engagement [appointment]
せんよう …専用である be for ... only
ぜんりつせん 前立腺 prostate
〜癌 prostate cancer
〜肥大症 hypertrophy of prostate gland
せんりょう 占領する occupy
ぜんりょく 全力を尽くす do *one's* best, do *one's* utmost, do all *one* can
〜をあげて do all *one* can, do everything in *one's* power [あげる]
〜疾走する run as fast as *one* can ……………[ぬく]
せんれい 洗礼を受ける be baptized
ぜんれい 前例 a former example, a previous example
・(a) precedent ……………[したがう]
〜を破る break with precedent ……………[やぶる]
せんれん 洗練
せんろ 線路《米》a track;《英》a line

ソ

そあく 粗悪品　inferior goods
　　　　　　　　　　　　　　[ひょうばん]
そう 沿・添・副う
そう 僧　a priest, a monk
そう 層　a layer; (石炭などの) a bed; (社会の・人々の) a class, a bracket, a group
そう (そんなに) so,《名詞の前で》such; (そのように) so, in that way, like that

～そう
　～(だ)そうである　I understand (that)... ……………………[うしなう]
ゾウ 象　an elephant
ぞう 像　an image; (立像) a statue; (胸像) a bust
そういえば そう言えば　Now that you mention it, Come to think of it, By the way
　・That reminds me. ……………[いう]
そういくふう 創意工夫　ingenuity
　　　　　　　　　　　　　　[みえる]
そううつ 躁うつ病　manic-depressive psychosis
そうおう 相応の　suitable for, fit for
そうおん 騒音　(a) noise
(公害) noise pollution ………[なやます]
ぞうか 造花　an artificial flower
　　　　　　　　　　　　　　[ていねい]
ぞうか 増加
そうかい 総会　the general meeting
　　　　　　　　　　　　　　[わる]
　～屋　a racketeer
そうがく 総額　the total (amount, sum)
　～で　in total, in all
そうがんきょう 双眼鏡　binoculars, field glasses; (観劇用の) opera glasses
ぞうかんごう 増刊号　an extra number [issue]
そうぎ 葬儀に参列する　attend the funeral ………………………[くう]
ぞうきいしょく 臓器移植　an organ transplant
　～手術(を受ける)　(undergo) a transplant operation
そうぎょう 操業する　operate [こうたい]
そうきん 送金する　send money to, remit money to
ぞうげ 象牙　ivory
ぞうけい 造詣が深い　be well versed in, have a profound knowledge of
　　　　　　　　　　　　　　[ふかい]
そうこ 倉庫　a warehouse, a storehouse
そうごう 総合的な　general, overall
　～大学　a university
そうごん 荘厳
そうさ 捜査　a search
　・an investigation …………[および]
　～する　search (for), investigate
　・make an investigation ……[ふきん]
そうさ 操作する　operate, handle, manipulate
　～が易しい　easy to operate
　　　　　　　　　　　　　　[やさしい¹]
そうさく 捜索する　search (for)
　～隊　a search party ……[あらわれる²]
　～願いを出す　request the police to search for the missing person
そうさく 創作
　～活動　creative [writing] activity
そうじ 相似の　similar ……[しょうめい]
そうじ 掃除　cleaning; (はき掃除) sweeping
　～する　clean, sweep
　・do the cleaning …………[だす]
　～人　a janitor
　電気～器　a vacuum cleaner
そうしき 葬式　a burial service
　・a funeral ………………[ぶつかる]
そうじゅう 操縦する　(機械を) operate; (飛行機を) pilot, fly
ぞうしょ 蔵書　a collection of books, a library
ぞうしょく 装飾　decoration, ornament
　～品　an ornament, (a) decoration
そうせんきょ 総選挙　a general election
そうそう 早々(に)　early, as soon as..., right after...
そうぞう 想像
そうぞう 創造　creation
　～する　create

そうぞく 相続する succeed; (財産を) inherit
～税 inheritance tax
そうたい 早退する leave *somewhere* earlier than usual
そうだい 壮大
そうだん 相談
　～ごと a problem ……[もってくる]
　～する discuss with ……[こと]
そうち 装置 an apparatus, a device
ぞうちく 増築する add on to †*one's* house [a building] ……[のばす]
そうとう 相当
そうどう 騒動 trouble, confusion
そうなん 遭難する meet with an accident; (難船する) be wrecked, be shipwrecked
　・have an accident ……[なめる]
　・meet with disaster ……[ぬく]
　・meet with a mishap ……[ふくむ]
　～者 a victim ……[たすける]
　(～し)そうになる almost ……[おぼれる]
そうにゅう 挿入する insert, put in
そうば 相場 (市場価格) a market price
　～で on the stock market [おもわく]
　～に手を出す dabble in the stock market ……[そん]
　変動～制 the floating exchange rate system
そうび 装備 equipment, fitting; (備品) equipments, fittings
　・gear ……[らんぼう]
そうべつ 送別会 a going-away party ……[ついて]
　・a farewell party ……[もよおす]
そうむしょう 総務省 the Ministry of Public Management, Home Affairs, Posts and Telecommunications
ぞうり Japanese sandals
そうりだいじん 総理大臣 the prime minister, the premier
そうりつ 創立 establishment, foundation
　～する establish, found, set up
　～記念日 the anniversary of founding

～者 a founder ……[たつ³]
そうりょう 送料 (郵送) postage; (運送) freight, carriage, freight charges
ソウル (韓国の首都) Seoul
ソウル(ミュージック) soul music
そうれい 壮麗
そうろん 総論 a general introduction
……[なる¹]
そえる 添える
　(～を)添えて along with
ソース sauce
ソーセージ (a) sausage
…そく …足 (一足) a pair of
ぞくご 俗語 slang
そくし 即死する be killed on the spot, be killed instantly
ぞくしゅつ 続出する……[りんきおうへん]
そくしん 促進する hasten, speed up; promote
ぞくする 属する
そくせき 即席の instant, impromptu
そくたつ 速達(で)《米》(by) special delivery, 《英》(by) express delivery
ぞくっぽい 俗っぽい vulgar, common
そくど 速度 speed
　最高～ maximum speed
　～を上げる speed up ……[あげる]
そくばく 束縛 restraint, restriction
　～する restrain
そくほう 速報 (ニュースの) a (news) flash
そくりょう 測量する survey
ソケット a socket
そこ 底
そこ there, that place
　～に[で，へ] there
そこく 祖国 *one's* native land
そこなう 損なう
そざい 素材 (a) material
そしき 組織
そしつ 素質 (資質) the makings; (適性) (an) aptitude; (才能) talent, a gift, (native) ability
そして
そしな 粗品 a gift, a give-away gift
そしょう 訴訟を起こす file a suit against ……[あいて]
そせん 祖先 an ancestor, forefathers

そそぐ 注ぐ　pour
そそっかしい
そそのかす　tempt, instigate, egg on
そそる
そだち 育ち
　～の良い　from a good family
　～の良さ　good upbringing
　　　　　　　　　　　　　　　[なにげない]
そだつ 育つ
　たくましく～　grow up big and strong　　　　　　　　　　　　[たくましい]
そだてる 育てる
　（気持ちを養う）promote ……[ほうしん]
そつ ～がない　touch all the bases, make no mistakes
そっき 速記　shorthand
　～する　write in shorthand
そつぎょう 卒業　graduation
　～式　a graduation ceremony, 《米》a commencement
　～生　a graduate
　～論文　a senior thesis ……[まとまる]
　・a graduation thesis ………[くしん]
　～する　graduate (from); leave school
　いい成績で～する　graduate with honors　　　　　　　　　　　[かい¹]
そっきん 即金で払う　pay in cash, buy *something* for cash
そっきん 側近　an aide
そっくり
　・be exactly [just] like ……[かっこう]
　・look just alike ………………[ことなる]
そっけない　blunt, cold
そっちょく 率直
そって （～に）沿って　along
そっと
ぞっと
そっぽ　～を向く　turn away, look the other way, ignore
そつろん 卒論　a graduation thesis
　　　　　　　　　　　　　　　[おもい²]
　・a thesis　　　　　　　　　[ひつよう]
そで　a sleeve
そと 外
　～に　outward ………………[あく²]
　～で食事をする　eat out ……[つもり]
そとがわ 外側　the outside

～の[に]　outside
そなえ 備え　preparations, equipment
そなえる 備える
その　that;（それの）its
そのうえ　besides ; moreover
そのうち
そのかわり　その代わり
そのご その後　after that, afterward;（それ以来ずっと）since (then), from that time (on)
　・ever after　　　　　　　　[こうふく]
そのころ その頃　（その時刻辺り）at that time, then;（その時代）in those days
そのさき その先の　up ahead …[きゅう]
そのすじ その筋の人　the authorities concerned
　・*someone* in the field ………[すじ]
そのとおり　～だ　That's right.／You're right.
そのとき then
　・at that time ………………[れいせい]
そのば その場で　on the spot
そのへん その辺
そのほか その外・他
そのまま　just as *one* [*it*] is
そば
そば 蕎麦　（植物）buckwheat;（麺）buckwheat noodles
　・noodles　　　　　　　　　[くう]
そびえる
そふ 祖父　a grandfather
ソファー　a sofa
ソフト
ソプラノ　soprano
そぶり 素振り　*one's* behavior, *one's* manner
そぼ 祖母　a grandmother
そぼく 素朴
そまつ 粗末
そまる 染まる　dye;（影響される）be infected (with)
そむく 背く
　・run contrary to ……………[みち]
そむける 背ける　（顔を）turn *one's* face away
そめる 染める
そもそも　in the first place, to begin

そや 粗野
そよかぜ そよ風 a breeze ……[ここち]
そら 空 the sky; (空中) the air
～模様 the weather ……[あやしい]
そらす (ゴロを) let the grounder get by [past] *one*; (目を) look away, turn *one's* eyes away; (注意を) be distracted, divert *one's* attention; (話を) change the subject [topic]; (攻撃〔非難〕を) divert *someone's* attack [criticism]
そらみみ 空耳だ be hearing things
そる 反る (板などが) warp; (からだなどが) bend backward
そる 剃る shave
ソルトレイクシティ Salt Lake City
それ it, that
それから
それぞれ
 ・each ……[こせい]
それだけ
それで
それでも
それどころか on the contrary, quite the contrary, actually, in fact, far from...
それとなく casually, indirectly, somehow
それとも or
それなら(ば) if so
 ・in that case ……[なお]
それにしても even so, still, just the same, granting that
それまで (ずっと) until then; (それまでに) by then
そろい 揃い (組) a set
～の the same, identical
そろう 揃う
そろえる 揃える
そろそろ
 ・now ……[おいこむ]
そろばん an abacus ……[はじく]
そわそわ
そん 損
～はない there's no harm in [おく¹]
そんがい 損害 damage; a loss
そんけい 尊敬

そんざい 存在 existence, presence
～する exist
ぞんざい ～な rude, rough
そんしつ 損失 loss
そんちょう 尊重
～する take *something* into account
……[こせい]
そんな
そんなに so, like that

タ

た 田 a rice field
 ・a rice paddy ……[たば]
ダーウィン ～の進化論 Darwin's theory of evolution ……[ついて]
ダース a dozen (略 doz., dz.)
～で by the dozen ……[うる]
2～の鉛筆 two dozen pencils
半～ half a dozen, a half dozen
タイ (国) Thailand
～の, ～語 Thai
～人 a Thai; (全体) the Thai(s)
タイ 鯛 (魚) a *tai*, a sea bream
たい 対
～中国外交 (Japan's) policy toward China
たい 隊 a party
～たい
だい 大は小を兼ねる The bigger, the better. ／Too big is better than too small. ……[かねる]
だい 台 a stand
だい 題 a title
～をつける entitle
たいあたり 体当たりする dash *oneself* against, charge into
たいいく 体育 (科目名) physical education (略 phys. ed., P.E.); (実技) physical training
～館 a gymnasium, a gym
たいいくのひ 体育の日 Health-Sports Day
だいいち 第一
だいいっせん 第一線で……[いっせん]
たいいん 退院する leave the hospital
……[はんだん]
ダイエット ～をしている be on a diet
……[め¹]

たいおう 対応する corresponding, be equivalent to
ダイオキシン dioxin
たいおん 体温 temperature
〜が高い〔低い〕 have a high [low] temperature
〜計 a (clinical) thermometer
・a thermometer ………………[わき]
〜を測る take *one's* temperature
………………………………[〜おき]
たいか 大家 a leading expert; (学問分野の) an authority (on)
雑学の〜だ have a wealth of trivia
………………………………[ざつ]
たいか 退化する degenerate
たいか 耐火の fireproof
たいかい 大会 a convention, a mass meeting; (総会) a general meeting
たいがい 大概 ………………[たいてい]
たいかく 体格
たいがく 退学する (自分から) leave school
〜させられる be expelled from school
だいがく 大学 (総合大学) a university; (単科大学) a college
4年制〜 a four-year university
短期〜 a junior college
〜教授 a (university) professor
〜生 a college [university] student, an undergraduate
〜1年生 a freshman
〜2年生 a sophomore
〜3年生 a junior
〜4年生 a senior
〜に合格する make it into a university ………………[ようやく]
だいがくいん 大学院 graduate school
………………………………[きめる]
〜生 a graduate student ……[かぎる]
たいき 大気 the atmosphere, the air
〜汚染 air pollution …………[および]
だいぎし 代議士 (日本の) a member of the Diet; (日本の衆議院議員) a member of the House of Representatives
だいきぼ 大規模な ………………[きぼ]
たいきゅうせい 耐久性 durability
………………………………[うる]
だいきらい 大嫌いだ hate ………[あたま]
たいきん 大金 big money ………[うごく]
・a large sum of money ………[そんな]
だいきん 代金 a [the] price, payment, the cost, the charge
だいく 大工 a carpenter
〜道具 carpenter's tools ………[きょう]
たいぐう 待遇
たいくつ 退屈
〜な dull ………………[おとなしい]
たいけい 体系 (a) system
〜的に systematically
〜づける systematize
たいけい 体形・体型 a figure
たいけつ 対決 (a) confrontation, a showdown
〜する have a showdown, confront
たいけん 体験 ………………[けいけん]
たいこ 太鼓 a drum
たいこうしゃ 対向車 a car coming from the opposite direction
………………………………[こえる]
たいこく 大国 a big power
・a world power ………………[いっち]
・a major power ………………[め¹]
経済〜 an economic power
ダイコン 大根 a (Chinese, Japanese) radish
たいさ 大差で by wide margin
〜ない there is †little [not much] difference between
たいざい 滞在
・stay ………………………………[のばす]
たいさく 大作 a masterpiece [はげます]
たいさく 対策
たいし 大使 an ambassador
〜館 an embassy
たいじ 退治する get rid of, exterminate
だいじ 大事
〜に with loving care ……[そだてる]
自分を〜にする take better care of *oneself* ………………………[じぶん]
たいした 大した
たいしつ 体質 a constitution, *one's* nature
たいして 大して…ない not very, not

much, not all that
たいして (…に)対して to, toward; (反対して) against; (〜の報いとして) for
たいしゃ 退社する (帰る) leave the office: (退職する) quit *one's* job, resign (from); (定年で) retire (from)
たいしゅう 大衆 the general public, the masses
　〜的な[向けの] popular
たいじゅう 体重 weight
　体重が〜ある weigh ……………[ある]
　〜を量る weigh ……………[はかる]
　〜が増える gain weight ……[ふえる]
たいしょ 対処する cope with
　・deal with ……………[りんきおうへん]
たいしょう 対象 an object, a target
たいしょう 対照 contrast
　〜的な be in contrast to, contrastive
たいしょう 対称 symmetry
　〜的な symmetrical
たいじょう 退場する leave, exit, walk out
だいじょうぶ 大丈夫
たいしょく 退職 (辞職) a resignation; (定年) retirement
　〜する (中途で) resign; (定年で) retire from office
　〜金 (中途で) severance pay; (定年で) a retirement allowance
たいしょくかん 大食漢 have a big appetite ……………[しかし]
だいじん 大臣 a minister (of state), a Cabinet minister;《米》a secretary
ダイズ 大豆 a soybean
だいすき 大好きだ like *something* very much, love *something*
　〜な favorite
たいする 対する
たいせい 体制 (a) system, (a) structure; (既成の権威) the establishment
　反〜の anti-establishment
たいせい 大勢 (全体の情勢) a general situation; (全体の傾向) a general trend

(支配的多数) a majority ……[したがう]
だいせいきょう 大盛況だ be very festive ……………[めぐまれる]
だいせいこう 大成功だ be a great success ……………[ほねおり]
たいせいよう 大西洋 the Atlantic (Ocean)
たいせき 体積 volume ……………[たかさ]
たいせつ 大切 ……………[だいじ]
　〜な essential ……………[はっけん]
　・favorite ……………[きみがわるい]
　・precious ……………[べんしょう]
　〜に扱う take good care of [どうぐ]
　〜にする treasure ……………[こわれる]
　・place importance on ……[よこ]
　〜に使う use *something* wisely
　　……………[かぎり]
たいそう 体操 gymnastics
　〜選手 a gymnast ……………[のびのび]
　〜をする practice gymnastics, exercise
　・do exercises ……………[けんこう]
たいだ 怠惰
　〜に流れる become idle ……[ながれる]
だいたい 大体
だいだい 代々 for generations, from generation to generation
だいたすう 大多数 the majority
　〜の most, most of, the majority of
だいたん 大胆
だいち 大地 the earth, the ground
だいち 台地 a tableland, a plateau (複数 -x, -s)
たいちょう 体調 (physical) condition
　……………[てんき]
　〜が良くない not be in good shape
　……………[ひびく]
たいちょう 隊長 a captain, a leader
だいちょう 大腸 the large intestine
タイツ tights
たいてい 大抵
　〜の usual ……………[ほしょう]
たいど 態度
　・*one's* manner ……………[でしゃばる]
たいとう 対等の equal
だいどうげい 大道芸 street performance
　〜をする perform on the streets

～人 a street entertainer
だいとうりょう 大統領 the president ……………[ほうもん]
だいどころ 台所 a kitchen
タイトルマッチ a title match ……………[たたかい]
だいなし 台無し
ダイナマイト dynamite
ダイニングキッチン a dinette
だいのおとこ 大の男 a grown man ……………[なみだ]
たいばつ 体罰 corporal punishment ……………[しゅだん]
タイピスト a typist
だいひょう 代表
 ・the delegate ……………[にんしき]
 ～団 delegation ……………[とうちゃく]
 ～番号 (電話の) the key number
ダイビング diving
タイプ
 タイプ(ライター) a typewriter
 ～を打つ type ……………[うつ]
だいぶ
 ・considerably ……………[ていど]
たいふう 台風 a typhoon
だいぶつ 大仏 a great image [statue] of Buddha
だいぶぶん 大部分
タイペイ 台北 Taipei
たいへいよう 太平洋 the Pacific (Ocean)
たいへん 大変
 ～だ be a real chore ……………[しり]
 ・be really awful, be not easy ……………[はがす]
 ・be quite an ordeal ……[ひきあげる]
 ～な difficult ……………[きがる]
 ・glaring ……………[みつかる]
たいほ 逮捕する catch, arrest
 ～状 a warrant of arrest
たいほう 大砲 a cannon, a gun
だいほん 台本 (映画の) a scenario (複数 -s); (劇・芝居の) a script; (放送の) a radio script
タイマー a timer
たいまん 怠慢
タイミング
たいめん 体面 honor, appearances, face
 ～上 for the sake of appearances, (just) to save one's honor
たいめん 対面する meet
タイヤ a tire, 《英》 a tyre
ダイヤ (運行予定) a schedule
 ～が乱れている ……………[みだれる]
たいやく 大役 the main role, an important task [role], a great mission
 ・the leading role ……………[やく¹]
ダイヤモンド (宝石の) a diamond; (野球の) the diamond
ダイヤル a dial
 ～イン direct line
たいよう 大洋 an ocean
たいよう 太陽 the sun
 ～系 the solar system
 ～熱 solar heat
 ～エネルギー solar energy …[りよう]
だいよう 代用品 a substitute
 ～する substitute (*A* for *B*)
たいら 平ら
たいらげる 平らげる eat up
 ・clean one's plate ………[しょくよく]
だいり 代理
 ～人 a proxy ……………[もしくは]
たいりく 大陸 a continent
 ～の, ～的な continental
だいりせき 大理石 marble
たいりつ 対立 a conflict ……[けわしい]
 ～している be opposed (to)
 ・be in conflict ……………[するどい]
たいりょう 大量 a large quantity (of)
 ～生産 mass production
たいりょう 大漁 a large catch
たいりょく 体力 one's physical strength ……………[め¹]
 ～的に physically ……………[まける]
 ～がある be (physically) strong
 ・have stamina ……………[ちいさい]
 ～をつける build up one's strength ……………[つける¹]
タイル a tile
ダイレクトメール direct mail (略 DM)
たいわ 対話 (a) dialogue, (a) conversation
 ～する converse with, talk to

たいわん 台湾 Taiwan
 ～の Taiwanese
 ～人 a Taiwanese(複数同形); (全体) the Taiwanese
たうえ 田植え rice planting
 ～をする plant a rice field, plant rice seedlings
タウン ～誌 a community magazine ……………………………[さんぶつ]
ダウンサイジング downsizing
ダウンロード
たえざる 絶えざる constant [どりょく]
たえず 絶えず
たえぬく 耐え抜く endure ………[ぬく]
たえま 絶え間なく continuously, continually, ceaselessly
たえる 耐え・堪える
 耐えられない cannot stand [しげき]
たえる 絶える
たおす 倒す
タオル a towel
たおれる 倒れる
 ・topple over ………………………[みまう]
タカ 鷹 a hawk
だが but, yet, though
ダカール Dakar
たかい 高い
たがい 互い
だかい 打開する break through
たかが only, just, no more than...
たがく 多額の金 a large sum of money ……………………………[あつまる]
 ～の利益 big profits ………[りえき]
たかかく 多角化 diversification
たかさ 高さ
たかだか 高々 (せいぜい) at most, only
 ～と high; (声が) loudly
たかとび 高飛び the high jump
 走り～ the running jump
 棒～ the pole jump [vault]
 ～する (逃亡する) run away
たがやす 耕す
たから 宝
だから
たからくじ 宝くじ a lottery ticket ……………………………[ころがる]
 ～売り場 a lottery ticket booth

たかる (群がる) gather, swarm
 (せびり取る) bum *something* off *someone* ………………………………[ね]
～たがる
たき 滝 a waterfall, falls
タキシード a tuxedo
だきしめる 抱きしめる hug
だきつく 抱きつく throw *one's* arm around
たきび たき火 a fire; (大がかりな) a bonfire
 ・a wood fire ………………………[やく³]
 ～をする make a fire, build (up) a fire
だきょう 妥協
たく 焚く・炊く
だく 抱く
たぐい 類 kind, sort
 この～の this kind of ……[ふさわしい]
たくさん
タクシー a taxi
 ～を飛ばす rush in a taxi ……[やっと]
たくじしょ 託児所 a day nursery, a day-care center
たくち 宅地 a housing lot
 ・a residential area ………………[くずす]
 ～造成業者 a housing developer ……………………………[けっして]
たくましい
 ・tough ……………………………………[もむ]
たくみ 巧み
たくらむ 企む plot
 ・plan, scheme ………………………[うらみ]
たくわえる 蓄える
たけ 竹 (a) bamboo ………………[ふし]
 ～細工 bamboo work
たけ 丈 (長さ) a length
 (服の)～を伸ばす let down the hem ……………………………[のばす]
～だけ
 ～だけは at least as far as *something* goes ……………………………[まける]
だげき 打撃 a blow, hit; (精神的な) a shock; (野球の) batting, hitting
たけなわ at the height of
タケノコ a bamboo shoot ……[のびる]
～だけのことがある

たこ 凧 a (paper) kite
　〜を揚げる　fly a kite …………[あげる]
タコ 蛸 an octopus
ださん 打算的な calculating
たし (…の)足しにする use *something* as a part of
だし soup stock
たしか 確か
　〜な筋 reliable sources ………[すじ]
たしかめる 確かめる
たしざん 足し算 addition
たじたじ 〜になる quail
たしなみ manners; (慎み) modesty
だしぬけ 出し抜けに out of the blue, suddenly
たじゅう 多重債務 multiple debts
　〜人格(症) multiple-personality disorder
たしょう 多少 (いくらか) some; (いくぶん) somewhat; (多かれ少なかれ) more or less
たす 足す add (to)
だす 出す
たすう 多数
たすうけつ 多数決で by a majority decision ………………[ごうり]
　・with a majority vote [さしつかえる]
たすかる 助かる
　・be saved ………………[こきゅう]
たすけ 助け (援助) help, aid, assistance; (救助) (a) rescue
　〜を求める ask for help …[れいたん]
たすける 助ける
たずねる 尋ねる
たずねる 訪ねる
　・pay *someone* a visit ……[なんとなく]
たぞうき 多臓器不全 multiple organ failure (略 MOF)
たそがれ 黄昏 dusk, twilight
ただ
　〜で free of charge ………[ほしょう]
ただいま 唯今
たたえる 讃える praise, admire
たたかい 戦・闘い
たたかう 戦・闘う
たたく 叩く
ただしい 正しい
ただす 正す correct

ただちに 直ちに
たたみ 畳 a *tatami* mat
　〜を替える renew the matting of a room
　〜を敷いた部屋 a *tatami*(-matted) room
たたむ 畳む
ただよう 漂う drift, float
たち (品質) quality; (性質) nature, character
　・a type ………………………[たのむ]
　〜の悪い mean, of bad character [nature]
たちあがる 立ち上がる (起立する) stand up, rise; (奮起する) rise (up)
たちあげる 立ち上げる
たちいり 立ち入り禁止 not open to ……………………………[いっぱん]
　(掲示の文句) Keep off [out]. ／ Off limits. ／ No admittance. ／ No trespassing.
　〜検査 an inspection ………[おこなう]
　・an on-the-spot investigation ……………………………[どうよう]
たちいる 立ち入る (干渉する) †meddle in [pry into, interfere in] *someone's* affairs [life]
たちおうじょう 立ち往生する be held up, be stalled; (行き詰まる) come to a standstill
　・be stalled ………………[まんなか]
たちぎき 立ち聞きする eavesdrop (on), overhear
たちくらみ 立ちくらみがする feel dizzy (when *one* gets to *one's* feet)
たちどまる 立ち止まる stop
たちならぶ 立ち並ぶ be crammed side by side ………………………[とうじ]
たちば 立場
たちまち at once, suddenly, in a moment
たちまわる 立ち回る (うまく) maneuver ………………[かしこい]
ダチョウ an ostrich
たちよみ 立ち読みする browse [じかん]
たちよる 立ち寄る call at (場所), drop in (at 場所, on 人)
たつ 絶・断・裁つ

たつ 立・発つ
たつ 建つ
たつ 経つ
ダッカ Dhaka, Dacca
だっかい 脱会する withdraw from ……………………[かい³]
たっきゅう 卓球 table tennis, ping-pong
だっこ 〜する hold [carry] (a young child) in *one's* arms
たっしゃ 達者 (丈夫な) well, strong; (上手に) well, fluently
たつじん 達人 an expert
・a great authority, a master …[みち]
たっする 達する
たっせい 達成する achieve, attain
だつぜい 脱税 (a) tax evasion
　〜する evade (a) tax
だっせん 脱線する (車両が) be derailed, run [get] off the track [rails]
　〜事故 a train derailment ……[だす]
だっそう 脱走する desert, escape
たった
だったい 脱退する withdraw from, leave
タッチ a touch
　〜の差で by a hair
だって
〜だって
たっぷり full, enough, good, plenty of
たつまき 竜巻 a tornado
だつらく 脱落する drop out
たて 縦
　〜の物を横にもしない won't lift a finger around the house ……[よこ]
たてかえる 立て替える pay for *someone*
たてこもる shut *oneself* up [ていこう]
たてつづけ 立て続けに in a row, in succession, without a pause
たてなおす 立て直す (組織を) reorganize
　経済を〜 put the economy back on its feet ………………[けいざい]
たてふだ 立て札 a notice, a sign
たてまえ 建て前 a principle, *one's* official stand

たてもの 建物 a building
たてる 立てる
たてる 建てる
だとう 妥当な reasonable, proper
たとえ 譬え (ことわざ) a proverb; (例) an example; (たとえ話) a fable, an allegory
たとえ
たとえば 例えば
たとえる 例える
たどたどしい
たな 棚 a shelf
たに 谷 a valley; (峡谷) a ravine
ダニ a tick, a mite
たにん 他人
タヌキ a raccoon dog
たね 種
たねまき 種まき sowing
　〜をする sow [plant] seed, sow
たのしい 楽しい
たのしませる 楽しませる delight, please, amuse
たのしみ 楽しみ
たのしむ 楽しむ
たのみ 頼み
　〜をきく do *someone* the favor ……………………………[いや]
たのむ 頼む
たのもしい 頼もしい
たば 束
たばこ (パイプたばこ・きざみたばこ) tobacco; (紙巻きたばこ) a cigarette; (葉巻き) a cigar
　〜を吸う smoke
　〜を吸ってもいいですか Is it all right to smoke? …………[どうぞ]
　〜をやめる quit smoking ……[ため]
　〜による火事 a fire caused by a careless smoker ……………[よる¹]
たばねる 束ねる bundle up
たび 度
たび 旅 ……………………[りょこう]
　〜をする travel, make a trip
　〜に出ている be away on a trip
たびかさなる たび重なる frequent
・a series of …………[ふうん, よわる]
たびさき 旅先で where *one* goes on *one's* trip ………………[おそろしい]

たびたび 度々
たびびと 旅人 a traveler; (観光客) a tourist
ダビング ～する copy
タブー (a) taboo
ダフや ダフ屋 《米》a scalper, 《英》a ticket tout
ダブリン Dublin
ダブル ～の double
ダブルクリック 《コンピュータ》a double click
　～する double-click (on) ....[クリック]
たぶん
たべすぎ 食べ過ぎ飲み過ぎ eat and drink too much ....[～すぎ]
たべすぎる 食べ過ぎる eat too much
・overeat ....[くるしい]
たべもの 食べ物 food
たべる 食べる
　何でも～ not be a picky eater ....[もっとも¹]
　食べられる edible ....[なま]
たま 玉・弾 (ボール) a ball; (弾丸) a bullet; (電球) a bulb
　～のような汗 beads of sweat [あせ]
たまご 卵 an egg
　生～ a raw egg
　ゆで～ a boiled egg
たましい 魂 a soul, a spirit
だます 騙す
・pull the wool over *someone's* eyes ....[みごと]
・cheat ....[すむ²]
ダマスカス Damascus
たまたま ～する happen to *do*
たまに(は)
タマネギ an onion
たまもの the result of ....[ち]
たまらない
たまりば たまり場 a hangout
たまる 溜る
だまる 黙る
　黙って silently ....[さしず]
ダム a dam
ため
だめ
ためいき a sigh

　～をつく sigh ....[つく¹]
・breathe a sigh ....[ほっと]
　～をついて with a sigh
ためし a trial
ためす 試す
ためらう
ためる 溜・貯める
・let *something* piled up ....[き]
たもつ 保つ
たやすい
たより 便り
たより 頼り
たよる 頼る
タラ 鱈 a cod
たらい a tub, a basin
だらく 堕落する go bad, go to the bad, be corrupted
・fall into a life of depravity ...[うで]
～だらけ be full of ....[けってん]
だらしない
　だらしなさ sloppiness ......[まったく]
～たらず ～足らず less than, no more than
だらだら ～と sluggishly, lazily
・in a sloppy way ....[のうりつ]
タラップ (飛行機の) a ramp; (船の) a gangway
ダリア a dahlia
たりない 足りない be short (of), be lacking (in), be insufficient
・not have enough ....[おもう]
　とても～ not be nearly enough ....[こづかい]
たりる 足りる
たる 樽 a barrel, a cask; (小樽) a keg
だるい
たるむ become loose, slacken
　たるんでいる be lax ......[しめる²]
だれ (だれが) who; (だれに[を]) whom; (だれか)《肯定文で》someone, somebody;《疑問文, if... の文中で》anyone; (だれでも) everyone, everybody; anyone, anybody; (だれでも～でない) no one, nobody, not ... anyone [anybody]
たれまく 垂れ幕 a banner ......[さがる]
たれる 垂れる

だれる
タレント (才能) a talent; (芸人) a (TV) personality, a performer
〜だろう
たん 痰 phlegm
だん 段
だん 壇 (踏み壇) a platform; (舞台) a stage
たんい 単位 (計量の) a unit; (学課の) a credit
　〜を落とす fail a course ……[おとす]
たんか 担架 a stretcher
タンカー a tanker
たんき 短気な short-tempered
たんき 短期の short, short-term
たんきゅう 探究心 the spirit of inquiry ……………………[おそれ]
タンク (水槽) a tank
だんけつ 団結する unite, band together
たんけん 探検 an exploration; an expedition
　〜する explore
　〜家 an explorer
　〜隊 an expedition
だんげん 断言する assert, declare, affirm
たんご 単語 a word
　(語い) vocabulary ……[なかなか]
だんご 団子 a dumpling
たんこう 炭坑 a coal mine
タンザニア Tanzania
たんさん 炭酸 carbonic acid
　〜ガス carbonic acid gas
　〜水 soda water
だんし 男子 (男の子) a boy; (男性) a man, a male
　〜学生 a boy [male] student
　〜高校 a boys' (senior) high school
だんじき 断食する fast ……[じじつ]
たんしゅく 短縮する shorten, contract, reduce
たんじゅん 単純な simple
たんしょ 短所 (弱点) a weak point; (欠点) a fault, a defect, a demerit
　・a shortcoming ……[どうじ]
だんじょ 男女別に(従って) according to sex
　〜別の (男女別に分かれた) separated by sex ……………………[べつ]
　〜問わずに regardless of sex
　〜兼用の unisex
　〜平等 sexual equality
たんじょう 誕生
　〜する come into being ……[こっか]
だんじょう 壇上に登る take the platform ……………………[なおす]
たんす a chest of drawers; (洋服だん す) a wardrobe
ダンス dancing; (一回の) a dance
たんすい 淡水 freshwater
　〜魚 a freshwater fish
たんすいかぶつ 炭水化物 (a) carbohydrate
だんせい 男性 a man, a male
　〜的な manly, masculine
たんせき 胆石 a gallstone
だんぜつ 断絶する break off relations [ties] ……………………[かんけい]
だんぜん 断然 (確かに) decidedly, absolutely; (はるかに) by far
だんたい 団体 a body; (一行) a party; (集団) a group; (組織) an organization
　〜旅行 a group tour
　〜割引 a group discount
たんたん 淡々とした low-keyed
　……………………[うったえる]
だんだん 段々
　〜と bit by bit ……[きびしい]
だんち 団地 a (housing) development
　・the apartment complex ……[うたう]
だんちがい 段違いだ be in a class in *oneself*
たんちょう 単調な monotonous, dull
だんちょう 団長 the head, the leader
たんてい 探偵 a detective
だんてい 断定する conclude
たんてき 端的に straightforwardly
　……………………[しめす]
　・clearly ……………………[れい²]
たんとう 担当
だんどり 段取り
たんなる 単なる only, mere
たんに 単に just, only, simply
たんねん 丹念

だんねん 断念する give up, abandon
・give up the idea of ……… [じじょう]
たんぱ 短波 shortwave
～放送 shortwave broadcasting
たんぱくしつ タンパク質 (a) protein
ダンピング dumping
～する dump
ダンプカー a dump truck
だんぺん 断片 a fragment
～的な fragmentary
たんぼ 田んぼ a rice paddy ……[まえ]
たんぽ 担保 (a) mortgage, (a) security
～にする mortgage
だんぼう 暖房 (room [indoor]) heating
～器具 a heater, a radiator
だんボール 段ボール(箱) a cardboard box
タンポポ a dandelion
たんまつ 端末 《コンピュータ》a terminal
だんらく 段落 a paragraph
だんりょく 弾力のある elastic
だんろ 暖炉 a fireplace, a stone hearth
……………………………………[もえる]
だんわ 談話 (a) talk; (意見) a comment

チ

ち 地 (地面) the ground; (大地) the earth; (陸地) the land
ち 血
～は争えない It must run in the family. ……………………………[あらそう]
～も凍るような bloodcurdling
……………………………………[とつぜん]
～も涙もない cold-blooded
……………………………………[れいこく]
チアノーゼ cyanosis
ちあん 治安 (law and) order, security, peace
～のよい safe
ちい 地位 a position, a post, a status; (階級) a rank
今の～ ………………………………[しんぼう]
～が上がる be promoted
～が下がる be demoted ……[さがる]
～を追われる be driven from *one's* post …………………………………[おう]
ちいき 地域 (広大な) a region ; (小さな) an area, a district
～的な local, regional
ちいさい 小さい
ちいさな 小さなこと trifles [あくせく]
～親切 a little kindness ……[しんせつ]
チーズ cheese
チーム a team
チームワーク teamwork
ちえ 知恵
(専門的) expertise ………………[かりる]
チェーン (鎖) a chain
～店 a chain (store)
チェコ the Czech Republic
～の、～語 Czech
～人 a Czech; (全体) the Czechs
チェス chess
チェック
チェック (格子縞) a check
チェロ a cello
チェンマイ Chiang Mai
ちか 地下の[で, に] underground
～街 an underground shopping center [mall, arcade]
～にもぐる go underground [もぐる]
ちかい 近い
ちかい 誓い an oath, a vow
ちかい 地階 a basement
ちがい 違い
ちがいない 違いない
・definitely ……………………[けいかく]
ちかう 誓う make an oath
・pledge, swear ……[せいせいどうどう]
ちがう 違う
・No! ……………………………………[ごかい]
ちかく 近く
ちかごろ 近頃
ちかしつ 地下室 a basement, a cellar
ちかづく 近づく
・draw closer ………………………[ねらう]
ちかてつ 地下鉄 《米》a subway, 《英》an underground (railway); (ロンドンの) a tube, the Tube
～で by subway
ちかどう 地下道 《米》an underpass, an underground passage, 《英》a subway

ちかみち 近道 a short way, a shortcut
ちから 力
　〜一杯 with all *one's* might ……[うつ]
　〜になる……………………………[および]
ちきゅう 地球 the earth
　〜儀 a globe
　〜温暖化 global warming
　〜に優しい environment-friendly, ecology-friendly
ちぎる tear
ちぎれる tear, be torn (off)
ちく 地区 a district; an area; a zone; (都市の) a quarter
　住宅〜 a residential quarter
　商業〜 a commercial [downtown] area, a business district
ちくちく 〜する prickle
ちくのう 蓄膿症 《医学用語》empyema
ちぐはぐ 〜だ (合わない) not match, not go together; (食い違う) disagree, contradict
ちけい 地形 topography ………[へんか]
ちこく 遅刻
ちじ 知事 a (prefectural) governor
ちしき 知識
ちじょう 地上 (地面) the ground; (地表) the surface
ちじん 知人 an acquaintance
ちず 地図 (1枚の) a map; (地図書) an atlas
ちせい 知性 intellect, intelligence
　〜的な intellectual; (頭がよい) intelligent
ちたい 地帯 a zone; (地域) a region; a belt
ちち 父 *one's* father
ちち 乳 milk
　〜を吸う nurse ……………………[すう]
　〜を飲む nurse ……………………[のむ]
　〜をやる nurse a baby
　〜が張る the breasts swell ……[はる¹]
ちちおや 父親ゆずり get *something* from *one's* father ………[ぶしょう]
ちちばなれ 乳離れする be weaned; (独り立ちする) be independent
ちぢむ 縮む
ちぢめる 縮める
ちちゅうかい 地中海 the Mediterranean (Sea)
ちぢれる 縮れる become wavy, get curly
　縮れ毛 wavy [curly] hair
チック(症) tic
ちつじょ 秩序 order
　・discipline ……………………[みだす]
ちっそ 窒素 nitrogen ……………[たい]
ちっそく 窒息 asphyxiation ………[し]
　〜する suffocate, be suffocated
チップ a tip
ちてき 知的
ちてん 地点 a point, a spot
ちどりあし 千鳥足で歩く stagger
ちなまぐさい 血生臭い bloody
(〜に)ちなんで after
ちのう 知能 intelligence, intellect
　〜検査 an intelligence test, a mental test, an I.Q. test
　〜指数 an intelligence quotient (略 I.Q.)
ちびりちびり 〜飲む sip ………[のむ]
ちへいせん 地平線 the horizon
チベット Xizang (西蔵), Tibet
ちほう 地方 (地域) a district; (いなか) the country; (一地方) a part (of a country); (付近) neighborhood
　・a region ……………………[ぜんこく]
　〜の local; (首都に対して) provincial
　〜色 local color
　〜なまり a local accent
　〜分権 decentralization (of power)
ちほう 痴呆症 (老人性) senile dementia
ちまなこ 血眼になって desperately, frantically
ちまめ 血豆 a blood blister
ちみつ 緻密
ちめい 地名 a place name ……[きく²]
ちめいてき 致命的な fatal
ちゃ 茶 tea
　日本〜 green tea
　抹〜 green powdered tea
　麦〜 barley tea
　ウーロン〜 oolong tea
　お〜でも飲みませんか Won't you have some tea or something?
　……………………………………[でも]

チャーハン　fried rice
ちゃいろ　茶色(の)　brown
ちゃくじつ　着実
ちゃくしゅ　着手する　start, go ahead with ……………………[よさん]
ちゃくちゃく　着々
ちゃくりく　着陸する　land, make a landing
ちゃち　〜な　cheap; shoddy
チャック　a zipper
　〜を締める　zip (up), do up the zipper
チャット　《インターネット》a chat
　〜する　chat †on line [on the Internet], talk on line
ちゃのま　茶の間　a living room
ちゃぱつ　茶髪　dyed hair
　〜にする　dye [bleach] *one's* hair brown
ちやほや　〜する　make much of, pamper
　・make a fuss over …………[きぶん]
ちゃわん　茶わん　a bowl
チャンス
ちゃんと
チャンネル　channel
チャンピオン　a champion
ちゅう　中
ちゅう　注　a note
　脚〜　a footnote, a foot note
　〜をつける　annotate
ちゅうい　注意
　〜書き　a warning …………[おとす]
チューインガム　(chewing) gum
ちゅうおう　中央
　〜集権　centralization of power
ちゅうか　中華料理　Chinese dishes
　・Chinese cooking …………[くどい]
ちゅうがく　中学生　a junior-high-school student
ちゅうがっこう　中学校　a junior high school
ちゅうかん　中間　the middle
　〜試験　a midterm examination
　〜報告　an interim report　[ほうこく]
ちゅうきゅう　中級の　intermediate
ちゅうきんとう　中近東　the Middle East ………………………[おこる²]

ちゅうけい　中継する　relay; (放送する) broadcast
ちゅうこ　中古の　secondhand, used
　〜車　a used car ……………[たたく]
ちゅうこく　忠告　advice
　〜する　advise, give advice
ちゅうごく　中国　China
　〜の, 〜語　Chinese
　〜人　a Chinese (複数 Chinese); (全体) the Chinese
ちゅうざい　駐在員　a representative ………………………………[おく¹]
ちゅうし　中止
ちゅうじえん　中耳炎　inflammation of the middle ear, 《医学用語》otitis media
ちゅうじつ　忠実
ちゅうしゃ　注射　an injection, 《口語》 a shot
　〜をする　(受ける・してもらう) get †a shot [an injection] ………[おさまる²]
　〜を打ってもらう　receive an injection ……………………[やわらぐ]
ちゅうしゃ　駐車　parking
　〜する　park (a car)
　〜場　a parking place [lot]
　〜禁止　(掲示の文句) No parking.
　〜違反　a parking violation ………………………………[いはん, くむ¹]
ちゅうじゅん　中旬に　in [about] the middle of a month
ちゅうしょう　中傷
ちゅうしょう　抽象的な　abstract
　〜画　an abstract picture　[あらわす¹]
　・abstract paintings ………[わかる]
ちゅうしょく　昼食　(a) lunch; (正式な昼食会) (a) luncheon
ちゅうしん　中心
　(活動の)〜になる　act as leader ………………………………[そしき]
ちゅうすい　虫垂炎　appendicitis
ちゅうすう　中枢神経　the central nervous system ……………[しんけい]
ちゅうせい　中世　the Middle Ages ………………………………[きずく]
　〜の　medieval ……………[ぶたい]
ちゅうせい　中性の　neutral
　〜洗剤　a neutral detergent

ちゅうせん 抽選する draw lots
ちゅうたい 中退する quit school ……[くわしい]
・drop out of ……[すえ]
ちゅうだん 中断される be interrupted
ちゅうとう 中東 the Middle East
ちゅうどく 中毒にかかる be [get] poisoned (by)
食〜 food poisoning
アルコール〜 alcoholism
ちゅうとはんぱ 中途半端
ちゅうねん 中年 middle age ……[ふとる]
〜の middle-aged ……[あんてい]
チューブ a tube
ちゅうもく 注目する pay attention (to), notice, take notice of
〜すべき remarkable
〜の的 the center [object] of attention
〜をひく attract attention
ちゅうもん 注文
〜をこなす fill orders ……[いそがしい]
ちゅうりつ 中立の neutral
チューリッヒ Zurich
チューリップ a tulip
ちゅうりゅう 中流 (川の) midstream; (階級) the middle classes
チョウ 蝶 a butterfly
ちょう 兆 《米》a trillion,《英》a billion
ちょう 腸 the bowels
ちょうおんぱ 超音波 an ultrasonic [supersonic] wave
ちょうか 超過 excess
〜する exceed
〜勤務 overtime (work) ……[てあて]
ちょうかん 朝刊 a morning paper
・a morning edition ……[のる]
ちょうき 長期の long, long-term
〜にわたる drawn-out ……[みだれる]
〜にわたって for a long time
ちょうきょり 長距離 long distance
〜電話 a long-distance call [でんわ]
ちょうこく 彫刻 (a) sculpture, (a) carving
〜する sculpture, carve
〜家 sculptor
ちょうさ 調査

〜する conduct a survey ……[くむ²]
〜団 the investigating committee ……[げんいん]
ちょうし 調子
〜がおかしい something is wrong with ……[おかしい]
〜の波に乗って spurred on by *one's* success ……[のる]
ちょうじかん 長時間 a long period of time ……[のうりつ]
ちょうじゅ 長寿 (a) long life
ちょうしゅう 聴衆 the audience
ちょうしょ 長所 a strong point, a good point, a merit, an advantage
・a strength ……[どうじ]
ちょうじょ 長女 the eldest daughter
ちょうじょう 頂上 the top, the summit; (先のとがった) the peak
ちょうしょく 朝食 breakfast
ちょうせつ 調節する adjust
ちょうせん 挑戦
ちょうせん 朝鮮 Korea
〜の、〜語 Korean
〜人 a Korean; (全体) the Koreans
〜半島 the Korean Peninsula
ちょうだ 長蛇の列 a long line ……[れつ]
ちょうちょう 町長 a mayor
ちょうちん a (paper) lantern
ちょうてん 頂点 (図形の) the apex; (絶頂) the peak, the summit
ちょうど
ちょうなん 長男 the eldest son ……[わずか]
チョウネクタイ a bow tie
ちょうはつ 挑発する provoke, arouse
〜的な provocative
ちょうふく 重複する repeat, overlap
ちょうぼ 帳簿 a book ……[けいさん]
ちょうほう 重宝な (便利な) useful, convenient; (使いやすい) handy
ちょうほうけい 長方形 a rectangle
ちょうみりょう 調味料 a seasoning, a flavoring
ちょうり 調理する cook, prepare, make
ちょうれい 朝礼 a morning assembly
ちょうわ 調和
チョーク (a piece of) chalk

ちょきん 貯金
  〜箱 a (piggy) bank, a savings box
ちょくげき 直撃する hit directly
  ....[じょうたい]
ちょくご 直後に right after
ちょくし 直視する face up to
  ....[げんじつ]
ちょくせつ 直接
ちょくせん 直線 a straight line
ちょくぜん 直前に just before
ちょくめん 直面する face, be faced with
ちょくりつ 直立の upright
チョコレート chocolate
ちょさくけん 著作権 (the) copyright
ちょしゃ 著者 a writer; an author
ちょすいち 貯水池 a reservoir　[きる¹]
ちょちく 貯蓄する save money
  ....[はげむ]
ちょっかい 〜を出す (お節介する) stick *one's* nose into *someone's* affairs [business]; (言い寄る) make a pass at *someone*
ちょっかく 直角 a right angle　[かく³]
ちょっかん 直感
ちょっけい 直径 a diameter
ちょっこう 直行する go straight to
  〜便 a direct [nonstop] flight
ちょっと
  〜寄ってみる drop by ....[ちかく]
ちらかす[る] 散らかす[る]
ちらす 散らす
チリ Chile
  〜の Chilean
  〜人 a Chilean; (全体) the Chileans
ちり 地理 geography
  〜上の geographical
ちり 塵 dust
ちりがみ ちり紙 a cleansing tissue, tissue paper
ちりとり ちり取り a dustpan
ちりょう 治療
ちる 散る
ちんあげ 賃上げ a raise ....[ようきゅう]
  ・a pay raise ....[わく²]
  〜交渉 a negotiation for a pay raise
  ....[こうしょう¹]
ちんぎん 賃金 wages

チンパンジー a chimpanzee
ちんぷ 陳腐
ちんぼつ 沈没する sink, go down
  〜船 a sunken ship ....[ひきあげる]
ちんもく 沈黙 silence
  〜する keep silent [silence]
ちんれつ 陳列する show, exhibit, display, put *something* on show [display]

ツ

ツアー 〜旅行 (団体旅行) a group [package] tour ....[まんいん]
  〜コンダクター a tour conductor
つい 対 a pair
つい
  ・in spite of *oneself* ....[ねむる]
  ・find *oneself doing* ....[なく¹]
ついか 追加 an addition
  〜する add (*A* to *B*)
  〜の additional
ついかんばん 椎間板ヘルニア herniated disc
ついきゅう 追求 pursuit
  〜する pursue, chase
ついせき 追跡 pursuit
  〜する pursue, chase
(〜に)ついて
ついで(に)
ついていく ついて行く follow; (遅れずに) keep up (with)
  ついて行けない can't go along with
  ....[ようち]
ついている be lucky
ついてくる ついて来る follow, come along
  ・come following after ....[うしろ]
ついとつ 追突する strike *something* from behind
ついに
  ・in the end ....[あらわす²]
ついほう 追放する expel, banish, exile
ついやす 費やす spend; (むだに) waste
ついらく 墜落 a fall
  〜する fall, drop; (飛行機が) crash
つうか 通貨 currency
つうか 通過する pass, pass through, go [get] through; (議案が) be

carried
～儀礼 a rite of passage …[はんこう]
つうかい 痛快
つうがく 通学する go to school, attend school, come to school
・commute to and from school
……………………………………[おうふく]
オートバイ～する commute by motorcycle ……………………[きんし]
つうかん 痛感
つうきん 通勤する go to the office, go to work; come to work
・commute ……………………[こんざつ]
～客 a commuter ……………[こんざつ]
～通学客 commuting workers and students
～時間 the time to commute to work ……………………………[ばい]
つうこう 通行する pass, go through
右側～ (掲示の文句) Keep to the right.
～止め (掲示の文句) Closed to traffic.
この先～禁止 (掲示の文句) No passage (this way).
～人 a passer-by (複数 passers-by)
つうさん 通算安打 career hits
……………………………………[たっする]
つうじる 通じる
・be answered ………………[いのる]
つうしん 通信
～社 a news agency
つうせつ 痛切に keenly
つうぞく 通俗な popular, common
つうち 通知 (a) notice, information
・a notification ………………[せいしき]
～する inform, let *someone* know, give *someone* notice
つうちょう 通帳 a bankbook, a savings passbook
つうねん 社会的通念 what is socially acceptable ……………………[てらす]
つうふう 痛風 gout
つうほう 通報する report
・notify …………………………[にがす]
つうやく 通訳 (行為) interpretation; (人) an interpreter
～する interpret

つうよう 通用
つうれつ 痛烈
つうろ 通路 a passage, a way; (乗物などの) an aisle
つえ 杖 a (walking) stick, a cane
つかい 使い・遣い (使い走りの用) an errand; (使いの人) a messenger
～に行く go do an errand [ぐずぐず]
お～を頼む ask *someone* to do an errand ……………………………[くち]
つかいかた 使い方 how to use
・a use …………………………[せつめい]
つかいこなす 使いこなす (人・機械などを) handle, manage; (言語を) have a good command of *something*
つかいこみ 使い込み embezzlement
……………………………………[つみ]
～をする embezzle
つかいこむ 使い込む・遣い込む (横領) embezzle, dip into the till
使い込んだ (長く使ってなじんだ) well-used, tried-and-true
つかいすて 使い捨ての disposable, throwaway
つかいで 使いでがある (お金が) go far, go a long way; (物が) last long
つかいはたす 使い果たす go through, use up …………………………[おしい]
つかいもの 使いものにならない can't be used for anything ………[のびる]
つかう 使う
つかえる 支える
つかえる 仕える serve; (世話) wait on
つかまえる 捕まえる
・hold onto ……………………[にげる]
つかまる (捕えられる) be caught; (すがる) hold onto
つかむ
つかる 浸・漬かる (水に) be flooded; (風呂に) soak in a hot bath; (漬物が) be well pickled
つかれ 疲れ
・fatigue ………………………[とれる]
・exhaustion …………………[ねむる]
つかれる 疲れる
疲れて with exhaustion …[ふらふら]
つき 月 (天体の) the moon; (暦の) a month

～ごとの[に] monthly
(…に)つき （理由）because; (～あたり) a [an], per, for
つぎ 次
次の次 the *something* after next
次から次へと one after another
　　　　　　　　　　　　…………[こころ]
つきあい
・a friendship …………[なかま]
～がある associate [hang around, socialize] with ………[しゅるい]
～がない have no contact with
　　　　　　　　　　　　…………[なじみ]
～にくい it's hard to do things with
　　　　　　　　　　　　…………[きまま]
つきあう
・associate with …………[げひん]
つきあわされる …………[さいご]
つきあたり 突き当たり the end
つきあたる 突き当たる run up against; （直面する）face
つきおとす 突き落とす push *something* over
つぎこむ つぎ込む （投資する）invest in （投入する）pour *something* into
　　　　　　　　　　　　…………[おおく]
つきさす 突き刺す stick, thrust, stab
つきそい 付き添い （人）an attendant; （行為）attendance
つきそう 付き添う （同行する）accompany; （世話をする）attend
つきだす 突き出す shoot out, stick out, thrust out
つぎつぎ 次々に one *something* [*someone*] after another
　　　　　　　　　　　　…………[けっしょう]
つきでる 突き出る stick out, project
つきとおす 突き通す stick (through)
つきとばす 突き飛ばす knock down, push away
つきひ 月日 time
つぎめ 継ぎ目 a joint, a seam
つきゆび 突き指する sprain *one's* finger
つきよ 月夜 a moonlit night
つきる 尽きる （なくなる）《人を主語にして》run out (of) 《物を主語にして》be used up; （終わる）come to an end
尽きない there's no end to …………[たね]
つく 突く
つく 付く
つく 点く
つく 着・就く
つぐ （…に）次ぐ be next to
つぐ 注ぐ pour
つぐ 継・接ぐ
・take over …………[いし]
つくえ 机 a desk
～の引き出し a desk drawer [はいる]
～に向かう be at *one's* desk [くずす]
つくす 尽くす
・serve …………[こっか]
つくづく completely …………[よのなか]
つぐない 償い （損害の）compensation; （罪の）atonement
つぐなう 償う make up (for), compensate for
ツグミ a thrush
つくりかた 作り方 （料理の）a recipe
　　　　　　　　　　　　…………[かく²]
つくりばなし 作り話 a lie, a fiction
つくる 作・造る
つくろう mend, patch
つけ ～で買う buy *something* on †credit [the cuff]
～にする put it on *someone's* bill [account], charge it (to *someone's* account)
～づけ ～(日)付けの dated
つげぐち 告げ口する tell (on)
つけくわえる 付け加える add
つけこむ take advantage of [ひきょう]
つけもの 漬け物 pickles
つける 付・着ける
つける 点ける
つける 漬ける （水に）dip, soak (in); （漬物を）pickle
～つける
つげる 告げる
つごう 都合
～の良いとき at *one's* convenience
　　　　　　　　　　　　…………[べつ]
～のよろしい時に when it's suitable for *someone* …………[よろしい]
つじつま ～の合う consistent

〜の合わない　inconsistent
ツタ　(an) ivy
つたう　伝う
つたえる　伝える
・convey …………………[おおざっぱ]
・portray …………………[ひさん]
つたわる　伝わる
つち　土　earth; (土壌) soil; (地面) the ground
つつ　筒　a pipe, a tube
つづき　続き
つつく　(指や棒の先で) poke; (鳥が) peck (at), pick (at)
つづく　続く
・have a spell of …………[おだやか]
つげる　続ける
つっこむ　突っ込む　thrust, stick, plunge
ツツジ　an azalea
つつしみ　慎み
つつしむ　慎む
・refrain from ……………[けいはく]
つっぱねる　突っぱねる　refuse flatly ……………………[のむ]
つつましい　modest, frugal ……[〜ぶり]
・plain and simple ………[せいけつ]
つつみ　包み
〜を開ける　unwrap ……[あける³]
つつむ　包む
つづり　spelling
〜をまちがえる　misspell a word
つづる　(単語を) spell; (文を) compose
つて　〜で　through connections [pull]
つとまらない　勤まらない ……[そんな]
つとめ　勤・務め
親の〜　a parents' job ……[ほご]
つとめて　努めて
つとめる　努める
つとめる　勤・務める
つな　網　a rope, a cord
〜を張る　stretch a rope
つながり　〜がある　be related to
つながる　connect, be connected
つなぎあわせる　つなぎ合わせる　tie together ……………………[みじかい]
つなぐ
つなひき　網引き　(a) tug of war …………………………[みかた]

つなみ　津波　a tidal wave
つね　常
〜に　all the time …………[たいへん]
つねる　pinch
つの　角　(牛・羊などの) a horn; (シカの) an antler
つのる　募る …………………[ぼしゅう]
(思いが) grow ……………[おもい²]
つば　spittle, saliva
〜を吐く　spit
ツバキ　椿　a camellia
つばさ　翼　a wing
〜を広げる　spreads *its* wings …………………………[ひろげる]
ツバメ　a swallow
つぶ　粒　a grain; (水滴) a drop
〜よりの　picked
〜ぞろいだ　be all good
つぶす　潰す
つぶやく　mutter, murmur
つぶれる　潰れる
つべこべ　〜言う　complain, grumble
つぼ　(土・金属製) a pot; (土・ガラス製) a jar
・an urn ……………………[きちょう]
つぼみ　a bud
つま　妻　*one's* wife
つまさき　つま先　tiptoe
〜で歩く　walk on tiptoe
つまずく
つまみぐい　つまみ食いする　nibble, pick at the food …………[つまむ]
つまむ
つまらない
・dull
…………………………[ながめ]
〜こと　trifles ……………[おこる¹]
・little things ……………[とがる]
・unimportant things ……[わずらう]
〜もの　a bore …………[くち]
つまり　(すなわち) that is (to say); (要するに) after all; in short, in a word
つまる　詰まる
つみ　罪
〜の意識　a sense of guilt ……[いしき]
つみかさねる　積み重ねる　pile up
つみき　積み木　building blocks [あそぶ]
・a toy block ……………[くずす]

つみたてる 積み立てる………[もくひょう]
つむ 摘む
つむ 積む
つむぐ 紡ぐ spin
つめ 爪 a nail; (動物の) a claw
　〜切り a nail clippers
　〜をかむ bite *one's* nail ………[くせ]
　〜を切る cut [clip] *one's* nails
　・trim *one's* nails ……………[きる¹]
つめあわせ 詰め合わせ an assortment
　〜の assorted
つめこむ 詰め込む cram
つめたい 冷たい
つめる 詰める
つもり
　・(an) intention ………………[そんな]
つや 通夜 a wake
つや 艶 luster; polish, shine
　〜のある glossy
　〜を出す polish, shine
つもる 積もる
つゆ 梅雨 the rainy season ……[あける²]
つゆ 露 dew
つよい 強い
　強く握る grasp ………………[にぎる]
つよき 強気で stubbornly ………[おす]
つよさ 強さ strength, the force, power
つらい 辛い
　・rough ……………………[うったえる]
　・excruciating ………………[しんぼう]
　・painful, hard ………………[わかれ]
　〜こと hardships ……………[たえず]
　〜目にあう be through a hard time
　　……………………………[そっと]
　辛くあたる be hard on ……[にくむ]
つらぬく 貫く pass through, run through, pierce
　(主張を) stick to ………………[しゅちょう]
　目的を〜 attain [accomplish] *one's* object [objective]
つらら an icicle ……………[おそろしい]
つられる
つり お釣り (支払いの) change
つり 釣り (魚釣り) fishing
　〜糸 a fishing line
　〜ざお a fishing rod
　〜針 a fishing hook

〜に行く go fishing ……………[いく]
つりあい 釣り合い balance
つりあう 釣り合う
つりかわ つり革 a strap ………[にぎる]
つりばし つり橋 a suspension bridge
ツル 鶴 a crane
つる 吊る
つる 釣る
つる 蔓 a vine
つるす 吊るす
つるつる 〜する (すべりやすい) slippery; (なめらかな) smooth
つれだす 連れ出す take [bring] *someone* out
(〜に)つれて
つれていく 連れて行く ……………[つれる]
つれてくる 連れて来る ……………[つれる]
つれる 連れる

テ

て 手
　〜が滑る *one's* hand slips ……[わる]
　〜が足りない be shorthanded [ます]
　〜に入れる win ………………[ねばる]
　〜に取る take, pick up [なにげない]
　〜を上げる hit ………………[あらい¹]
　〜を引く get out of ……………[ねらう]
　〜を振る wave *one's* arm [こたえる]
　〜を触れる touch ……………[ふれる]
　〜を焼かせる give *someone* a lot of trouble ……………………[わんぱく]
であう 出会う
てあし 手足 arms and legs, hands and feet, limbs
てあたりしだい 手当たりしだい
てあて 手当て
てあみ 手編みの hand-knitted
てあらい 手洗い (家庭のトイレ) a bathroom; (公共のトイレ) a rest room
ていあん 提案 a proposal, a suggestion
　〜する propose, make a proposal, suggest
Tシャツ a T-shirt ……………[かわった]
ディーティーピー (DTP) desktop publishing (略 DTP)
ていいん 定員 (座席の) the seating

capacity; (委員会・クラブ・クラスなどの) the fixed [regular] number of members
ティーンエイジャー a teenager
ていか 低下 a fall, a drop, a decline
　～する fall, drop
ていか 定価 a (fixed) price
ていがく 停学処分を受ける be suspended from school ［しょぶん］
ていき 定期の regular
　～的に regularly, at regular intervals [basis]
　・at fixed intervals ……………［おこなう］
　・on a regular basis ………［けんこう］
　～券 《米》 a commuter pass, 《英》 a season ticket
　・a commuter pass ……………［きげん¹］
　・a train pass ………………［しめす］
　～試験 a regular examination
　～預金 a fixed deposit (account)
　…………………………［とく²］
ていぎ 定義 a definition
　～する define, give a definition
ていきあつ 低気圧 low (atmospheric) pressure
ていきゅう 低級な low
ていきゅうび 定休日 a regular day off
　…………………………［しまる²］
ていきょう 提供する offer, provide, give; (テレビ番組などを) sponsor
ていけい 提携 cooperation, a tie-up
　技術～ a technical tie-up
　～する enter into cooperation with
ていけつ 締結する ratify ………［つよい］
ていこう 抵抗
　・opposition …………………［つよい］
ていこく 定刻 the appointed time
　～に on time
　・on schedule …………………［つく⁴］
ていこく 帝国 an empire
　～主義 imperialism
デイサービス day services
ていさい 体裁 appearance
ていさつ 偵察する reconnoiter
　・scout ……………………………［こっそり］
　～機 a reconnaissance plane
ていし 停止する stop, come to a stop, suspend

ていじせい 定時制高等学校 a part-time high school
ていしゃ 停車 a stop
　～する stop (at)
　各駅～ a local train
ていしゅく 貞淑な chaste, virtuous
ていしゅつ 提出
ていしょく 定食 a set course
ていしょく 定職 a regular occupation [job]
でいすい 泥酔する get dead drunk
　………………………………［とめる¹］
ていすう 定数 (決まった数) a fixed number
ディスカウント ～ストア a discount shop [store]
ディスコ a disco, a discotheque
ディスプレー (陳列・展示) (a) display; (コンピュータ画像) a display; (コンピュータ表示装置) a monitor
ていせい 訂正する correct
ていせつ 定説 the accepted theory
　………………………………［うたがう］
ていぞく 低俗な vulgar
ていそくすう 定足数 a quorum ［わる］
ていたい 手痛い severe, serious
ていたく 邸宅 a mansion
ていちゃく 定着する become established, take root, come to stay
ていちょう 丁重な courteous, polite
　～に politely
　・respectfully ………………［ことわる］
ティッシュペーパー a tissue, tissues; 《商標》 (a) Kleenex
ていでん 停電 a power failure [outage], blackout
　・a power outage ………［このあいだ］
ていど 程度
　～が高い be beyond someone
　…………………………………［もんだい］
ていねい 丁寧
　～に conscientiously ………［いう］
ていねん 定年 the retirement age
　～で会社を辞める(～退職する) retire (from one's company)
　…………………………［つとめ, やめる²］
　～後 since retirement ……［たのしみ］

ていひょう 定評がある have a good reputation
ていへん 底辺 a base, a bottom
ていぼう 堤防 a dike, an embankment
 ・a levee ……………………[おそれ]
 ・a bank ……………………[こす]
ていよく 体よく politely ……[ことわる]
 ～あしらう give *someone* a polite brush-off, brush *someone* off politely ……………………[あしらう]
でいり 出入りする go in and out
 ～口 (戸口) a doorway; an entrance; (門口) a gateway
ていりゅうじょ 停留所 a stop, a station
ていれ 手入れ
ディレクター a director
データ data (単数 datum)(data は本来は複数形だが単数扱いすることが多い), information
データベース a database
 ～プログラム a database management program [system]
デート
テープ a tape
 ～を切る (競技で) break the tape; (開通式で) cut the tape
テーブル a table
 ～マナー table manners ………[はじ]
テープレコーダー a tape recorder
テーマ a theme, a subject, a topic
 ～パーク a theme park
ておくれ 手遅れになる be too late, be beyond help
 ・be beyond cure ……………[なげる]
 ～にならないうちに……………[もらう]
ておしぐるま 手押し車 a cart
ておち 手落ち (過失) a fault, a mistake
てがかり 手がかり
でかける 出かける
てがた 手形 a draft, a bill; (手で押した形) a hand print
てがみ 手紙 a letter
 ～を投函する mail a letter [かならず]
 ～を航空便で出す send a letter by airmail
てがら 手柄 *one's* credit

てがる 手軽な light; (たやすい) easy; (簡単な) simple
 ～に easily; lightly; simply
てき 敵 an enemy
 ～の opposing ……………[おさえる]
 ～国 the enemy country ……[さぐる]
 ～に回す make an enemy of [まわす]
…てき …滴 (一滴) a drop
でき 出来
できあい 溺愛する dote on ……[しっと]
できあい ～の服 ready-made clothes
 ～の食品 ready-cooked food
できあがる be completed, be finished, be done
てきい 敵意
てきおう 適応する adapt *oneself* (to)
てきかく 的確な exact, right
できごころ 出来心で on (an) impulse, on the spur of the moment
てきごと 出来事
テキサス Texas
テキスト
てきする 適する
 適している suit *someone* to a tee
 ……………………[もっとも²]
てきせい 適性がある have an aptitude for
 ～テスト an aptitude test
てきせつ 適切
できそこない 出来損ないの poorly made
 ・poorly prepared …………[そこなう]
できだか 出来高 output ………[おうじる]
できたて でき立ての fresh, newly made, brand-new
てきちゅう 的中する hit (the mark), make a good hit [guess]
 ・be right on the nose ……[ぴったり]
てきど 適度な moderate
 ～な運動 moderate exercise
 ……………………[けんこう]
 ～に moderately
てきとう 適当
 ～な right ……………[おもいつく]
できない (不可能) can't; (能力の低い) be poor at [in], be weak in
てきにん 適任だ be fit (for), be suitable (for)

・be right for …………[こころあたり]
てきぱき ～した prompt, quick, businesslike
　～と promptly, in a businesslike way
　・quickly and efficiently ……[てあて]
できもの a boil
てきやく 適役 the perfect man to *do* …………………………………[おし]
てきよう 適用する apply (to)
できる 出来る
できるだけ
できれば if possible, if *one* can
てぎわ 手際 skill
　～よく efficiently, skillfully, speedily
てぐち 犯行の手口 the method employed in the crime [ピンとくる]
　うまい～にのせられる be cleverly tricked into ……………………[にせ]
でぐち 出口 a way out, an exit
てくび 手首 a wrist
てこ a lever
　(原理) leverage …………………[おうよう¹]
てこずる have a hard time with, have a lot of trouble with
てごたえ 手ごたえ (反応) a response
　～がある responsive, effective
でこぼこ ～な bumpy ………[たいら]
てごろ 手頃
てごわい 手ごわい formidable ………………………[まわす, もうしこむ]
デザート dessert
デザイナー a designer
デザイン a design
てさぐり 手探りする grope
　～で探す grope for …………[さがす]
　～で進む grope *one's* way ……[さぐる]
てざわり 手触り feel, touch
　～が良い have a nice touch [feel]
　・have a nice texture ………[さわる¹]
でし 弟子 a pupil, a follower; (徒弟) an apprentice
てした 手下 a subordinate; (悪事の) a henchman; (部下) a man
デジタル
てじな 手品 magic
　・a magic trick ……………………[たね]
　・a trick ……………………………[ふしぎ]

　～師 a magician
　～をする do a magic trick
でしゃばる 出しゃばる
てじゅん 手順 a process, (the) procedure, (the) order
　～よく smoothly, without a hitch
てじょう 手錠 handcuffs
てすう 手数
デスクトップ 《コンピュータ》the desktop
　～コンピュータ a desktop computer
　ファイルを～に置く put a file on the desktop
テスト a test
　学力～ an achievement test
　～する test, give a test
　～を受ける take [have] a test
　～に合格する pass a test
てすり 手すり a rail
てせい 手製の handmade; (自作の) of *one's* own making
てそう 手相をみる read *someone's* palm ……………………………[みる]
でたらめ
てぢか 手近の at hand; (よく知っている) familiar
てちがい 手違い a mistake, an accident
てちょう 手帳 a notebook
てつ 鉄 iron; (鋼鉄) steel
てつ 轍を踏む make the same mistake ……………………………………[ふむ]
てっかい 撤回する withdraw
てつがく 哲学 philosophy
　～者 a philosopher
デッキ (船の) the deck; (列車の) the platform
てっきょう 鉄橋 an iron bridge, a railroad [《英》railway] bridge
てっきん 鉄筋コンクリート ferroconcrete, reinforced concrete
てづくり 手作りの handmade, homemade
てっこう 鉄鋼業 steel industry
てっこうじょ 鉄工所 an ironworks
デッサン a (rough) sketch [drawing]
てつだい 手伝い (人) a help, a helper, an assistant; (事) help, assistance

てつだう 手伝う
・give *someone* a hand ………[うち]
でっちあげる frame up
・make up ………………[りゆう]
てつづき 手続き
てってい 徹底
～した all-out ……………[ごうり]
てつどう 鉄道 a railroad
てっとりばやい 手っとり早い quick and simple
手っとり早く quickly and simply
てっぱい 撤廃する abolish, do away with
てつぼう 鉄棒 (体操の) a horizontal bar, horizontal bars
てっぽう 鉄砲 a gun, a rifle
～を撃つ shoot [fire] a gun
てつや 徹夜する sit [stay] up all night
でどころ 出どころ source, origin
・where *something* comes from ………………[あやしむ]
デトロイト Detroit
でなおす 出直す (改めて来る) come again, come back; (やり直す) start again
一から～ start from scratch, make a fresh start
テニス tennis
てにもつ 手荷物 baggage, luggage
～預り所 (駅の)《米》a baggage room, 《英》a left-luggage office; (ホテル・劇場などの)《米》a checkroom, 《英》a cloakroom
機内持ち込みの～ a carry-on ………………[にもつ]
てぬるい 手ぬるい
テネシー Tennessee
てのひら a palm
デノミ(ネーション) (currency) redenomination, currency reform
では (それでは) then, now, well
デパート a department store
てはい 手配
てばなす 手放す part with; (処分する) dispose of; (なしですます) do without
てびき 手引き guidance; (入門書) a guide

デビットカード a debit card
デビュー a début
てびょうし 手拍子をとる beat time with hands
てぶくろ (1対の)手袋 (a pair of) gloves; (親指だけが別の) (a pair of) mittens
てぶら 手ぶらで with empty hands, without taking [bringing] any [a] present
テヘラン Teh(e)ran
てほん 手本
てま 手間
デマ a false rumor
・a (groundless) rumor ………[ながす]
てまえ (…の)手前 this side (of), before
でまえ 出前 (meal) delivery service
てまどる 手間取る take a long time
てまね 手まね a gesture, signs
でまわる 出回る appear in the stores ………………[たね]
・surface ………………[しらべる]
・get into circulation ………[そっくり]
てみじか 手短に briefly
でむかえる 出迎える
テムズ ～川 the Thames
デモ a demonstration ………[きょか]
～をする hold a demonstration, demonstrate
～隊 demonstrators ………[うめる]
～行進 a demonstration parade
でも
てもち 手持ちの on hand, with *one*, in *one's* possession
てもと 手元に at hand, readily available
デュッセルドルフ Düsseldorf
てら 寺 a (Buddhist) temple
テラス a terrace
てらす 照らす
デラックス ～な deluxe, gorgeous
デリー Delhi
デリケート ～な delicate; (人) sensitive
デリバティブ (金融派生商品) derivatives
てる 照る

でる 出る
テルアビブ Tel Aviv
テレクラ a telephone-dating club, a party line
テレビ television (略 TV); (受像機) a television (set), a TV (set)
　〜番組　a TV show …………[きまる]
　・a TV program …………[くだらない]
　〜ドラマ　a TV show …………[かい²]
　〜放送局　a TV station
　〜で放映する　televise, broadcast by television
　〜で見る　watch *something* on television
テレビゲーム　a video game; (機械) a video-game computer
てれる　照れる
テロ　terrorism
テロリスト　a terrorist
てわけ　手分けする　divide, share
てわたす　手渡す　hand (to), hand over, deliver
てん　天　(空) the sky, the air; (地に対して) the heavens; (天国) Heaven
てん　点
　〜が甘い　be generous in giving grades …………[あまい]
　100〜を取る　score 100 [a perfect mark] …………[みせる]
でんあつ　電圧　(a) voltage
てんい　転移　metastasis
　〜する　metastasize (to), spread (to)
てんいん　店員　《米》a clerk, a salesclerk《英》a shop assistant
　・a salesperson …………[ちゅうい]
でんえん　田園　(田舎) the country
　〜風景　rustic scenery ………[のどか]
　・a rural setting …………[ふうけい]
てんか　天下　the world; (指導権) power
てんか　添加物　an additive
でんか　電化する　electrify
てんかい　展開　development
　〜する　(移り進む) unfold; (広がる) spread; (進展する) develop
　・turn out …………[ちゅうもん]
てんかん　epilepsy
　〜の発作　an epileptic fit
てんかんき　転換期　a turning point
てんき　天気
　〜図　a weather map
　〜予報　a weather forecast
　〜しだい　depend on the weather …………[どう]
　〜に恵まれる　be blessed with fine weather …………[かろやか]
でんき　伝記　a biography; a life
でんき　電気　electricity; (電燈・電灯) an electric lamp [light]
　〜の　electric, electrical
　〜で　on electricity …………[うごく]
　〜釜　an electric rice cooker
　〜器具　(electric) appliances
　〜スタンド　(机上の) a desk lamp; (床上の) a floor lamp
　〜店　an electric(al) (appliance) store
　〜屋　an electrician …………[なおる]
テンキー　a [the] numeric keypad
でんきゅう　電球　an electric bulb
　・a light bulb …………[きれる]
てんきん　転勤　transfer …………[きまる]
　〜する　be transferred (to)
てんけい　典型　a model, a type
　〜的な　typical
てんけん　点検　a check, (an) examination
　・an inspection …………[おこなう]
でんげん　電源　(供給) a power supply; (コンセント) an outlet, a socket
てんこう　天候が回復する　the weather clears (up) …………[えんき]
　〜不良　poor weather conditions …………[ふりょう]
てんこう　転校する　change *one's* school, change from one school to another
でんこうけいじばん　電光掲示板　an electric bulletin board
てんごく　天国　Heaven; (楽園) Paradise
　〜の　heavenly
でんごん　伝言　a message
　〜板　a message board
てんさい　天才　(才能) genius; (人) a (man of) genius

〜的な　talented, gifted
〜的な腕前　prowess ………[おそれる]
てんさい　天災　a natural calamity [disaster]
てんさく　添削する　correct, look over
てんし　天使　an angel
　〜のような　angelic
てんじ　点字　braille
てんじ　展示　exhibition, display
　〜会　an exhibition
　〜する　exhibit, display
でんし　電子　an electron
　〜の　electronic
　〜工学　electronic engineering ………………………[えいきょう]
　・electronics ………………[おいこす]
　〜工業　electronics ………[だいひょう]
　〜マネー　electronic money, digital currency
　〜レンジ　a microwave oven
でんしゃ　電車　a train, an electric train; (市街電車)《米》a streetcar, 《英》a tram, a tramcar
　満員〜　a packed train
　・a crowded train ……………[みがく]
てんじょう　天井　a ceiling …[つかえる]
てんしょく　転職する　change jobs ………………………[ためらう]
でんしょばと　伝書鳩　a carrier pigeon
でんしん　電信　telegraph; (海底の) a cable
　〜で　by telegraph
　〜を打つ　telegraph, wire
てんすう　点数　a score; (試験の) a mark; (競技の) a point
てんすう　点数が開く　the score is lopsided ………………[ひらく]
でんせつ　伝説　a legend, a tradition
　〜の　legendary, traditional
てんせん　点線　a dotted line
でんせん　伝染する　be contagious, be infectious, be catching
　〜病　a contagious disease …[つづく]
　・an infectious disease
でんせん　伝線する　(ストッキングの) have a run
でんせん　電線　an electric line
てんそう　転送

てんたい　天体　a heavenly body
　〜望遠鏡　an astronomical telescope
でんち　電池　an electric cell, a battery
　乾〜　a dry cell
でんちゅう　電柱　an electric pole; (電話用の) a telephone pole
　・a utility pole ……[あいだ, かんかく²]
　・a light pole ………………[つく²]
てんてこまい　〜する　be in a flurry
てんてん　点々と　here and there, scattered
てんてん　転々と　from place to place
テント　a tent
　〜を張る　pitch a tent ……[ひらたい]
てんとう　店頭に　in front of (the store) …………………[ならべる]
でんとう　伝統
　〜工芸　traditional arts ……[つたえる]
でんとう　電燈・電灯　an electric light [lamp]
　懐中〜　a flashlight, 《英》a torch
でんどう　電動式　electric …………[しき]
てんとうむし　てんとう虫　a ladybug
てんにゅう　転入生　a transfer student ………………………[おとす]
てんねん　天然
てんねんとう　天然痘　smallpox, variola
てんのう　天皇　the Emperor
　〜陛下　His Majesty the Emperor
てんのうせい　天王星　Uranus
てんのうたんじょうび　天皇誕生日　Emperor's Birthday
でんぱ　電波　an electric wave
　〜に乗る　be broadcast ………[のる]
デンバー　Denver
でんぴょう　伝票　a slip; (勘定書き) a check, a bill
てんびん　〜にかける　weigh A against B
てんぷ　添付・貼付
てんぷく　転覆する　be overturned, be upset; (政府などを) overthrow
　・capsize ………………[たすかる]
てんぶん　天分　*one's* natural gifts, *one's* natural talents
　〜のある　gifted, talented
でんぷん　澱粉　starch
テンポ　tempo

〜がのろい slow-paced …..[ちょうし]
てんぼう 展望 a view; (見通し) a prospect, an outlook
　〜台 an observation platform
でんぽう 電報 a telegram, a wire; (海外との) a cable
　〜で by telegram [wire, cable]
　〜を打つ wire, telegram, cable
　・send a telegram …………[うつ]
デンマーク Denmark
　〜の, 〜語 Danish
　〜人 a Dane; (全体) the Danes
てんめつ 点滅する go on and off, blink
てんもん 天文(学) astronomy
　〜学者 an astronomer
　〜学の astronomical
　〜台 an astronomical observatory
てんらんかい 展覧会 an exhibition; a show
でんりゅう 電流 (an) electric current
でんりょく 電力 electricity
　・electric power ………[きょうきゅう]
でんわ 電話
　〜番号 a phone number ………[へん]
　〜代 a phone bill …………[かなり]
　〜の声 a voice on the telephone
　　…………………………[きこえる]
　〜をかける make a phone call
　　…………………………[こっそり]
　〜を受ける get a phone call …[いう]
　・take a (telephone) call ……[うける]
　〜に出る answer the telephone
　　…………………………[ふせる]
　〜がある (AからBに) there is a phone call (for B from A)
　　…………………………[なんとか]
　〜を切らずに待つ hold on ……[まつ]
　〜が殺到する be swamped with calls
　　…………………………[たずねる¹]

ト

と 戸 a door; (窓の戸) a shutter; (よろい戸) a blind
と 都 a metropolis; (東京都) Tokyo Metropolis
　〜の metropolitan
〜と (および, そして) and; (〜と一緒に) with, along with, together with; (敵対して) against, with; (ちょうどそのとき, 〜するとき) (just) as, when; on *doing*
ど 度
ドア a door
　〜を叩く knock on a door 　[こたえ]
とい 問い a question
とい 樋 a gutter …………[つたう]
といあわせる 問い合わせる inquire, ask for information
　・contact ………………[ふしん]
ドイツ Germany
　〜の, 〜語 German
　〜人 (ひとりの) a German; (全体) the Germans
トイレ (公共建造物などの)《米》a washroom,《英》a lavatory, a water closet; (ホテル・劇場などの) a rest room; (住宅の) a bathroom
　〜に行く go to the bathroom
　　…………………………[がまん]
とう 党 a (political) party …[われる]
とう 問う
とう 塔 a tower, (東洋ふうの) a pagoda
とう 等
とう 藤 (a) cane, (a) rattan
どう
　〜なってもいい couldn't care less about ……………………[いい]
どう 胴 (身体の) the torso; (着物の) the body; (楽器の) the frame
どう 銅 copper; (青銅) bronze
　〜メダル a bronze medal
とうあん 答案 an examination paper, a paper
　・an answer sheet …………[だす]
　白紙の〜 a blank paper
どうい 同意
　・consent ……………[ごかい]
どういたしまして (お礼に対して) You're (quite) welcome./Not at all./Don't mention it./No problem./My pleasure./Anytime.; (お詫びに対して) Never mind./That's all right.
とういつ 統一 unity, unification

～する　unify
どうか
とうかん　投函する　mail, post
どうかん 同感
とうき　陶器　earthenware, china, pottery
　～を焼く　make [fire] pottery［やく³］
とうぎ　討議　(話し合い) (a) discussion; (討論) a debate
　～する　discuss, debate
　・deliberate ……………………［もんだい］
どうき　同期である……………………［しゅっせ］
どうき　動機　a motive ………［あいまい］
どうき　動悸　palpitation
　～がする　*one's* heart †palpitates [beats fast]
とうきゅう　等級　a class, a grade, a rank, a degree
　～をつける　grade
とうぎゅう　闘牛　a bullfight
　～場　a bullring
どうきゅう　同級である　be in the same class ……………………………［こうさい］
　～生　a classmate
どうきょ　同居する　live with［けいざい］
とうきょく　当局　the authorities
　……………………………………［たいまん］
どうぐ　道具
どうくつ　洞窟　a cave, a cavern
とうげ　峠　a (mountain) pass
　……………………………………［ながめる］
　～を越す　(危険などの) pass the crisis; (仕事などの) finish the most difficult part; (寒さ・暑さなどが) be over
とうけい　統計　statistics
とうげい　陶芸家　a potter ………［たたく］
とうこう　登校する　go to school, attend school
とうこう　投稿する　contribute
どうこう　動向　a trend
とうごうしっちょうしょう　統合失調症　schizophrenia
とうごく　投獄される　be imprisoned
とうざ　当座　for the time being
　～の　(一時しのぎの) makeshift
　～預金　a current account …［つく²］
どうさ　動作

～が鈍い　move sluggishly [slowly]
　……………………………………［にぶい］
とうざいなんぼく　東西南北　north, south, east and west
　～から　from all directions
とうさん　倒産　bankruptcy …［おいこむ］
　～する　go bankrupt ………［かいしゃ］
　・go under ……………………［くらい］
とうし　投資
　～をする　make an investment
　……………………………………［にらむ］
とうし　闘志
とうじ　冬至　the winter solstice …［ひ］
とうじ　当時
　・of *one's* day ………………［えいきょう］
どうし　…同士の間で　among [between] themselves〔yourselves〕
どうし　同志　(仲間) a companion, a like-minded person; (政治など) a comrade
どうじ　同時
　～通訳(者)　a simultaneous interpreter ……………………［いじ］
とうじき　陶磁器　china and porcelain, pottery, chinaware
とうじしゃ　当事者　the person involved, the party concerned
　……………………………………［せいい］
とうじつ　当日　that day
　・the day ……………………［いよいよ］
どうして
どうしても
　どうしても…してしまう　can't help *doing* ……………………………［くずれる］
どうじない　動じない　not be shaken by
とうしょ　投書　a letter (to the editor)
　……………………………………［のる］
　～する　write a letter
とうしょう　凍傷　frostbite ………［よほど］
とうじょう　登場する　appear, make an appearance
　～人物　a character
とうじょう　搭乗する　board, get on
どうじょう　同情
　～を引く　arouse *someone's* sympathy ……………………［ひく］
どうじる　動じる
とうすい　陶酔

どうせ

どうせいどうめい 同姓同名である have the same family and given names

どうせき 同席する sit at the same table with *someone*, attend the same meeting

とうせん 当選する (選挙で) be elected, win the election; (懸賞・競争などで) win the prize
- win the election ……[うたがわしい]
~番号 winning numbers [つうじる]

とうぜん 当然

どうぜん …同然だ be the same as, be no better than, practically

どうぞ

とうそう 逃走する run away
- get away ……………………[しょうこ]
~中で on the run

とうそう 闘争 a fight, a struggle

どうぞう 銅像 a bronze statue [かげ¹]

どうそうかい 同窓会 (組織) a graduates' [graduate] association, an alumni association; (会合) a meeting [reunion] of graduates
- a class reunion …………[ちゅうしん]
~を開く hold a class reunion
………………………………[ちから]

どうそうせい 同窓生 a fellow student, a schoolmate

とうだい 燈台・灯台 a lighthouse

どうたい 胴体 (人間の) a body, a trunk; (彫像の) a torso; (飛行機の) a body

とうちゃく 到着

とうてい 到底 (not) possibly; (not) simply

どうてん 同点 a tie
~になる tie (with)

どうてん 動転する be upset ……[ふり¹]

とうとい 尊い

とうとう

どうどう 堂々

どうとく 道徳 morality, morals
~的な moral
~的に morally; from a moral point of view

とうなん 東南 the southeast
~アジア Southeast Asia
~の southeastern

とうなん 盗難にあう 《人を主語にして》 have *something* stolen, 《物を主語にして》 be stolen
~品 a stolen article

とうに a long time ago

どうにか

どうにも ~ならない………[ところで]

どうにゅう 導入する (なじみのなかったものを) introduce
- (機械などを) install ………[せつやく]

とうにょうびょう 糖尿病 diabetes

とうばん 当番

とうばん 登板する take the mound
………………………………[まず]

どうはん 同伴する accompany, go with

とうひょう 投票
~用紙 a ballot

とうひん 盗品 stolen goods ……[あし]

とうふ 豆腐 *tofu*, bean curd ……[もと]

とうぶ 東部 the east; (米国の) the East

どうふう 同封する enclose
~の enclosed

どうぶつ 動物 an animal
~園 a zoological garden, a zoo
~学 zoology
~学者 a zoologist
~実験 experiments on animals
………………………………[じっけん]

とうぶん 当分

とうぶん 等分する divide equally

とうぼう 逃亡する escape from, flee
~中に while *one* is on the run
………………………………[やすらぐ]

とうほく 東北 the northeast
~の northeastern

どうみても

どうみゃく 動脈 an artery
大~ the main artery
~硬化 hardening of the arteries
~瘤 《医学用語》aneurysm, aneurism

とうみん 冬眠 a winter sleep, hibernation

とうめい 透明

どうめい 同盟 an alliance, a league

～国 an ally
～する ally *oneself* (with), be allied (with), be in league (with)
どうも
どうもう どう猛な fierce, savage
トウモロコシ 《米》corn, 《英》maize
　～１本 an ear of corn [maize]
どうやら apparently, It seems to be..., It looks †as though [like]...
とうゆ 灯油 kerosene ………[つかう]
とうよ 投与する administer
　………………………[まちがえる]
とうよう 東洋 the East, the Orient
　～の Oriental
　～人 an Oriental
どうよう 動揺
どうよう 童謡 a nursery rhyme
どうよう (…と)同様………[やはり]
どうらく 道楽者 a playboy ….[たえる²]
どうり 道理 reason
　～のある reasonable, right
　～を外れる show a complete lack of principles ………[はずれる]
　～で (It's) no wonder (that)..., That's why...
どうりょう 同僚 *one's* co-worker
　………………………[ぬすむ]
　・*one's* colleague ………[ねたむ]
どうりょく 動力 (motive) power
どうろ 道路 a road, a street, a way
　～工事 road construction
　………………………[やかましい]
　～交通法 the traffic laws [かいせい]
　～標識 a traffic [road] sign
　………………………[ちゅうい]
　～を横断する cross the street
　………………………[ちゅうい]
とうろく 登録する register
とうろん 討論会 a debate, a forum
どうわ 童話 a fairy tale, a nursery tale
　・a children's story ………[たとえる]
とうわく 当惑する be confused, be puzzled, be at a loss, be embarrassed
とお 十 ten
とおい 遠い
とおく 遠く
　～へ into the distance ………[なげる]

とおざける 遠ざける keep *something* [*someone*] away, keep *someone* at a distance
とおす 通す
トースター a toaster
トースト toast
ドーナツ a doughnut
トーナメント a tournament
とおまわり 遠回りする take the long way, make a detour
とおり 通り
　～に面した家 a house facing the street ………[つたわる]
とおりがかり 通りがかりの人 a passer-by
とおりかかる 通りかかる happen to pass (by)
とおりすぎる 通り過ぎる pass, go past
とおる 通る
　・get through ………[ちゅう]
　通れない can't make it through
　………………………[さき]
とかい 都会 a city, a town
　～の urban
　～人 city people, urbanites
　………………………[したしむ]
　～へ出て行く move to the city [へる]
とかく (…するものだ) be apt to
　・will, tend to ………[うるさい]
とかげ a lizard
とかす 溶・梳かす
どかす (動かす) move; (片づける) clear, put away
とがめる blame, reproach
とがらす sharpen; (口を) pout; (神経を) get nervous
とがる 尖る
　尖っている be pointed, have a sharp end ………[さき]
トキ *toki*, Japanese crested ibis
　………………………[てんねん]
とき 時
　～として from time to time [こどく]
　・at times ………[ふくざつ]
　～の勢い the tide of the times
　………………………[いきおい]
　(…している)ときではない this is no time to *do* ………[かなしむ]

どき 土器 pottery ……………[はっけん]
・an earthen vessel ……………[たもつ]
どきっと ～する be shocked, be startled
ときどき 時々
どきどき
どきょう 度胸 guts, nerve, courage
 ～のある brave, gutsy
 ～の据わった have nerve …..[すわる]
とく 解く
とく 得
 ～だ advantageous ……………[かたち]
とく 徳 (a) virtue
 ～の高い virtuous
とぐ 研ぐ
どく 毒 poison
 ～のある人 poisonous
 ～ヘビ a poisonous snake …[さいご]
どく 退く (わきへ) step aside; (じゃまにならないように) get out of the way, make way (for)
 ・step out of the way …………[ごめん]
とくい 得意
とくい 特異体質 physical idiosyncrasy
とくいさき 得意先 a client, a customer
 ～回りをする call on *one's* clients
 ……………………………………[まわり]
どくがく 独学する study by *oneself*
 ・teach *oneself* ………………[せいしき]
とくぎ 特技 a special talent, *one's* specialty
どくしゃ 読者 a reader; (予約購読者) a subscriber
 ～欄 the readers' column
とくしゅ 特殊な special, particular
とくしゅう 特集 a feature
 ～号 a special (edition) ………[でる]
どくしょ 読書 reading (a book)
とくしょく 特色のある characteristic
どくしん 独身の unmarried, single
 ～者 (男の) a bachelor; (女の) an unmarried woman
とくせい 特製の specially made
どくぜつ 毒舌(家) a sharp tongue
 ……………………………………[くち]
 ～を吐く make barbed remarks
どくせん 独占 a monopoly, monopolization

～する monopolize
どくそう 独創的な original, creative
 ～性 originality, creativity
どくそう 独奏 a solo
とくだね 特ダネ a scoop
どくだん 独断
とくちょう 特徴
とくてい 特定の specific, particular
とくてん 得点 (試験の) marks; (運動・競技の) a score; (野球の) a run
 ～する score
とくてん 特典 a privilege
とくと ～考える think *something* through ………………[かんがえる]
どくとく 独特の peculiar (to), unique (to), *one's* own
とくに 特に
とくばい 特売 bargain sale
とくはいん 特派員 a correspondent
とくべつ 特別
 ～手当て a special bonus ……[でる]
とくめい 匿名の anonymous
とくよう 徳用の economical
どくりつ 独立
 ～心 an independent spirit
 ……………………………………[ほうしん]
とけ
とけい 時計 (懐中[腕]時計) a watch; (柱[置き]時計) a clock
 ～台 a clock tower …………[おくる²]
 ～が進んでいる the clock is fast
 ……………………………………[もどす]
 ～の針と反対に counterclockwise
 ……………………………………[はんたい]
 ～を巻く wind (up) a watch
とける 解・溶ける
とげる 遂げる
とこ 床 a bed
 ～についている be in bed
 ～につく go to bed
どこ
 ～からともなく through the air
 ……………………………………[ながれる]
どこかしら (…がある) There's something ... about *someone*.
 ……………………………………[いげん]
ととん thoroughly, to the (very) end

とこや 床屋 (人)a barber; (店)《米》a barbershop, 《英》a barber's (shop)
ところ 所 (場所)a place; (個所)a part
ところが
~どころか
ところで
どさくさ confusion, bustle
　~に紛れて take advantage of the confusion (and *do*)
ドサッと with a thud
とざん 登山 mountain climbing, mountaineering
　~する climb [go up] a mountain
　~家 a mountaineer, an alpinist
　~者 a mountain climber ……[きざむ]
とし 年
　~とともに as *one* grows older
　　…………………………[おだやか]
　・with age ……………………[きおく]
　~をとってからも even in *one's* later years ………………………[きょうよう]
とし 都市 a city
　~の urban
ドジ ~を踏む make a blunder, blow it, goof
としうえ 年上の older (than); senior (to)
とじこめる 閉じ込める shut in [up], keep *someone* indoors
　閉じこめられる be shut up
とじこもる 閉じこもる be confined (to), confine *oneself* (to)
としごろ 年ごろ (年齢)age; (婚期) marriageable age
　~の adolescent ……………[なやむ]
としした 年下の younger (than), junior (to)
~として
~としても even if, even though
としとった 年とった old, aged, 《婉曲に》elderly
とじまり 戸締まりする lock (up)
どしゃぶり 土砂降り a heavy rain, downpour
としょ 図書 books
　~館 a library
　~目録 a catalog of books
としより 年寄り an old person, an elderly person
　・elderly people ……………[おもいやり]
　・older people ………………[ショック]
　(総称)the aged ……………[じゃま]
とじる 閉じる
とじる 綴じる
としん 都心 the downtown ……[つくる]
　・the center of town ……………[くる]
どせい 土星 Saturn
とそう 塗装 painting
どそく 土足で with *one's* shoes on
どだい 土台 a foundation …[かためる]
とだえる 途絶える
　途絶えている be cut off ……[つうしん]
　交通が~ ……………………[こうつう]
とだな 戸棚 (食器の)a cupboard; (押入れ)a closet
トタン zinc
　~屋根 zinc roof
とたんに as soon as..., just after [as]..., the moment...
どたんば 土壇場で at the last moment
とち 土地 land; (一区画の土地, 敷地) a lot; (土)soil
　~の local, native
とちゅう 途中
どちら (疑問文で)which; (どこ)where
どちらか either
　~と言えば (選ぶとしたら)given a choice; (傾向がある)rather
どちらも both
とっか 特価 a special price
とっきゅう 特急 a limited express
とっきょ 特許(品) a patent
とっきょちょう 特許庁 the Japan Patent Office
とっくに a long time ago, ages ago
とっけん 特権 a privilege
どっこいどっこい ~だ (能力が)be (just about) as good as; (勝敗が) be (pretty) even
とっこうやく 特効薬 a specific medicine
とっさ ~に in an instant, instinctively
ドッジボール dodge ball
とっしん 突進 a rush, a dash
　~する rush (at), dash (at), make a

dash (at, for)
とつぜん 突然
どっちつかず ～の返事 an equivocal answer, a noncommittal answer; ～の態度をとる sit on the fence
どっちみち in any case, anyway
とっちめる (叱りつける) bawl out, give it to
とっつき ～にくい〔やすい〕 be difficult 〔easy〕 to approach
とって 取っ手 (柄) a handle; (ドアの) a knob
…(に)**とって** for, to, with
とっておきの the best, the choicest
とっておく 取っておく (保存する) keep, put aside; (予約する) reserve; (たくわえる) save ……………[せき]
とってくる 取って来る fetch, get, 《命令形で》go and get
とっぴ 突飛
トップ (the) top; (先頭) (the) lead
～を守る stay at the top …[たいへん]
～を走っている選手 the front-runner ……………[ちぢむ]
トップクラス ～の first-class, first-rate, topnotch
どて 土手 a bank, an embankment
とても quite ………………………[なる¹]
とどく 届く
(出前が) arrive, be delivered ……[まつ]
とどける 届ける
ととのう 整う (用意が) be prepared, be ready; (成立する) be settled
ととのえる 整える prepare; get 〔make〕 ready
ととのっている (設備が)整っている be equipped with ……………[せつび]
とどまる
～ところを知らない know no stopping ……………………[しる]
ドナー an organ donor, a donor
～カード an organ donor card
ドナウ ～川 the Danube
トナカイ a reindeer
となり 隣
・next door ……………………[だす]
どなる cry, shout; (応援して) yell
どなり散らす rant and rave [あたり¹]

・yell at …………………………[ちらす]
どなり飛ばす chew out ……[かっと]
～**となると** when it comes to ……[べつ]
とにかく
・really ………………………[おくる¹]
どの～
どのくらい
どのように how
とば 賭場 a gambling den ……[ていれ]
とばく 賭博 gambling
とばす 飛ばす
とばっちり ～をくう get tangled up in
とびあがる 飛び上がる jump 〔leap〕 up, spring up; (空に) fly up
とびいし 飛び石 stepping stones
～連休 several holidays separated by one or two workdays
とびおりる 飛び降りる jump 〔leap〕 down
とびきゅう 飛び級する skip a grade, skip ahead in school
とびこえる 飛び越える jump over
………………………………[にげる]
とびこみだい 飛び込み台 a diving platform 〔board〕 ……[おそろしい]
とびこむ 飛び込む jump in 〔into〕; (水中に) dive into
・dash into …………………[ゆうかん]
飛び込んで来る burst into [いきおい]
とびだす 飛び出す jump out (of)
・dart out (into) ………………[よこ]
(逃げ出す) run away from ……[あて]
とびたつ 飛び立つ (鳥などが) fly up; (離陸する) take off
とびちる 飛び散る (壊れて) fly into pieces; (液体が) splash
とびつく 飛びつく jump at
とびとび ～に at intervals
とびのる 飛び乗る jump on [あわてる]
とびら 扉 (戸) a door; (本の) a title page
とぶ 飛・跳ぶ
どぶ a ditch, a gutter
とほ 徒歩で on foot
とほう 途方にくれる be at a loss
どぼく 土木 civil engineering
～技師 a civil engineer
とぼける

とぼしい 乏しい
とぼとぼ とぼとぼ歩く　plod along
トマト　a tomato
とまどう 戸惑う
とまる 止・留まる
とまる 泊まる
どまんなか ど真ん中　right in the heart of ………………………[まんなか]
とみ 富　riches《つねに複数形》, wealth
とむ 富む
とめる 止・留める
とめる 泊める
とも 共
ともかく　anyway, in any case [event]
ともかせぎ 共稼ぎをして　by both working ………………………[たてる¹]
　〜をする　both work ………[けいざい]
ともぎれ 共布で　with the same material ………………………[とも]
ともぐい 共食いをする　prey [feed] on each other
ともだち 友だち　a friend
　私の〜　a friend of mine, one of my friends;（特定の友人）my friend
　親しい〜　a close [great] friend
　文通〜　a pen pal
　〜になる　make friends with
　〜付き合いをする　treat *someone* like a friend ………………………[ひらく]
どもる　stammer
どようび 土曜日　Saturday（略 Sat.）
トラ 虎　a tiger
トライアスロン　triathlon
ドライバー （運転手）a driver
　（ねじ回し）a screwdriver ……[ねじる]
ドライブ （車の運転）a drive;（コンピュータの）a drive
　〜に行く　take a drive, drive (a car) · go for a drive ………………[いく]
ドライヤー　a drier, a dryer
トラウマ （心的外傷）trauma;（その原因）a traumatic experience
とらえる 捕らえる・捉える
トラック （貨物自動車）a truck,《英》a lorry
トラック （競走路）a track
　〜競技　track events
ドラッグ （麻薬）a drug

ドラッグ 〜する《コンピュータ》drag
とらのまき トラの巻　a key, a crib
ドラフト 〜制度　a [the] draft system
トラブル
　〜シューティング　troubleshooting
ドラマ　a drama, a play
ドラム　a drum
ドラむすこ ドラ息子　*one's* pleasure-loving son ………[なやみ]
トランク　a trunk, a suitcase
トランプ （1組の）(a deck [pack] of) (playing) cards;（1枚の）a (playing) card
　（ゲーム）a card game …………[あがる]
　〜をする　play (at) cards
トランペット　a trumpet
とり 鳥　a bird
　〜かご　a (bird) cage
　〜小屋　a birdhouse;（ニワトリの）a henhouse
とりあえず
とりあげる 取り上げる　（手に）take up, pick up;（奪う）take away;（採用する）adopt
とりあつかい 取り扱い　（物の）handling;（人・問題の）treatment
　〜説明書　a manual
とりあつかう 取り扱う
　· deal in ………………………[ほか]
とりいれ 取り入れ　（収穫）a harvest, harvesting
とりいれる 取り入れる
とりえ 取り柄　*one's* strong points, *one's* merits
とりかえす 取り返す　（取りもどす）get [take] back, recover;（埋め合わせをする）make up for
とりかえる 取り替える
とりかかる 取りかかる
　· buckle down to …………[いき²]
トリカブト　monkshood ………[たとえば]
とりきめ 取り決め　an arrangement, an agreement
とりきめる 取り決める　（日取りなど）fix;（決定する）decide on;（合意する）agree on
とりくむ 取り組む
　· buckle down to …………[いよく]

・approach ……………………[じゅうなん]
とりけす 取り消す
とりこ a prisoner, a captive
　〜になる become a captive
とりこむ 取り込む (洗濯物を) take in, bring in
　データをファイルに〜 import data into a file
　コンピュータで写真を〜 put a photo into a computer ……[コンピュータ]
とりさげる 取り下げる withdraw ……………………………[かんけい]
とりしまる 取り締まる
とりしらべる 取り調べる (尋問する) question; (調査・捜査) investigate
とりだす 取り出す take out ……[よせる]
・pull *something* from …………[しわ]
とりたて 取りたての fresh
とりたてる 取り立てる (集める) collect; (厳しく) exact
とりちがえる 取り違える misunderstand, mistake
とりつかれる 取りつかれる be possessed [obsessed]
とりつぎ (代理人, 取り次ぎ店[人]) an agent
　〜店 an agency, an agent
とりつける 取り付ける install
とりのこされる 取り残される be left behind
とりのぞく 取り除く take away, remove
とりはずす 取り外す take off, take away
とりはだ 鳥肌が立つ get †goose bumps [《英》gooseflesh]
とりひき 取り引き
　・a business deal ………………[ゆうり]
　〜関係 business relationship [たつ¹]
　〜先の会社 a company *one* deals with ……………………[たずねる²]
とりまく 取り巻く
とりもどす 取り戻す recover, take *something* back
とりやめになる be called off, be canceled ……………………[けいかく]
とりやめる 取りやめる call off, cancel

どりょく 努力
　〜する do *one's* best ……………[いし]
　・work on *one's* own ………[うらやむ]
　・strive ………………………[こうきょう]
　〜のいかんによっては depending on how much effort *one* makes [よる¹]
　〜を怠る ……………………[さいのう]
とりよせる 取り寄せる (手に入れる) get; (注文する) order
とる 取・捕・撮る
とる 採る
ドル dollar
トルコ Turkey
　〜の, 〜語 Turkish
　〜人 a Turk; (全体) the Turks
どれ
どれい 奴隷 a slave
トレーナー (服) a sweat shirt; (人) a trainer
トレーニング training
ドレス a dress, a party dress
ドレッシング (a) dressing
どれでも any; (どれでも一つ) any one; whichever
とれる 取れる
どろ 泥
　〜を飛ばす splash mud ………[とばす]
ドロップ (菓子の) (candy) drops
トロフィー a trophy
どろぼう (こそどろ) a thief; (夜盗) a burglar; (強盗) a robber
どろんこ 〜の muddy
トロント Toronto
どわすれ 度忘れする slip *one's* mind
トン (重さの単位) a ton
とんかつ 豚カツ a pork cutlet
どんかん 鈍感
どんぐり an acorn
どんぞこ どん底 the bottom; (最悪) the worst
　・the depths ……………………[ぜつぼう]
とんだ terrible ……………………[おもわく]
　・absurd ……………………[けいさん]
とんち wit
　〜のある witty, quick-witted
とんでいる (…に)富んでいる have (a) rich *something* ………………[そうぞう]
とんでもない

とんとん ～だ be even
　～に終わる break even
どんどん
　・steadily ……………………[すすむ]
どんな
どんなに
トンネル a tunnel
トンビ a kite ……………………[まう]
どんぶり a bowl
トンボ a dragonfly ………………[つる²]
とんや 問屋 (店) a wholesale store;
　(人) a wholesale dealer
どんよく 貪欲
どんよりした gloomy, dull
　・overcast, gray ………[うっとうしい]

ナ

な 名 a name; (名声) fame, reputation
　～をあげる make a name for
　　oneself, become famous ……[あげる]
　～を連ねる have *one's* name
　　associated with ………………[にんき]
　～を残す leave *one's* name …[のこす]
ない 内 (～の中に) in; (～以内に)
　within
ない 無い
　無かったことにする forget
　　………………………………[けれど(も)]
ナイアガラ ～の滝 (the) Niagara Falls
ないか 内科 internal medicine
ないかく 内閣 the Cabinet; (米国の)
　the Administration
ないかくかんぼう 内閣官房 the
　Cabinet Secretariat
ないかくそうりだいじん 内閣総理大臣
　the Prime Minister, the Premier
ないかくふ 内閣府 the Cabinet
　Office
ないかくほうせいきょく 内閣法制局 the
　Cabinet Legislation Bureau
ナイジェリア Nigeria
ないしゅっけつ 内出血 internal
　bleeding
ないしょ 内緒
ないしょく 内職 (副業) a side job; (家
　庭での) piecework done at home
ないしん 内心
ないしんしょ 内申書 an academic
　transcript
ないせん 内線 an extension
ないそう 内装 interior decoration
ないぞう 内臓 internal organs,
　insides, intestines
　～疾患 an internal disease, an
　　intestinal disorder
ナイター a night game
　今日の～ tonight's baseball game
　　………………………………[て]
ないてい 内定する decide *something*
　unofficially
　・be informally arranged [せいしき]
ナイフ a knife
ないぶ 内部 the interior, the inside
　～の対立 internal confrontation
　　………………………………[ひょうめん]
ないみつ 内密にする keep *something* a
　secret ……………………………[いか]
ないや 内野 the infield
　～手 an infielder
　～席 the infield stands
ないよう 内容 ……………………[なかみ]
　仕事の～ what this work consists of
　　………………………………[せつめい]
　～が豊富 be rich in content [べんり]
ナイル ～川 the Nile
ナイロビ Nairobi
ナイロン nylon
なえ 苗 a seedling ………………[そだつ]
なえき 苗木 a seedling ………[うえる]
なお
なおさら all the more..., much
　more..., still more...
なおす 直・治す
なおる 直・治る
　治らない incurable ………[おもいこむ]
なか 中
なか 仲
　・a relationship ………………[けんあく]
　お熱い～ be in love …………[あつい³]
　～を裂く destroy *someone's*
　　relationship …………………[さく²]
ながい 長い
　～あいだ for a long time ……[あいだ]
ながいき 長生きする live a long life
　　………………………………[さわがしい]
ながいす 長いす a sofa; (寝いす) a

couch
ながぐつ 長靴 rain boots
ながさ 長さ length
ながし 流し (台所の) a sink
ながす 流す
なかだるみ 中だるみ a slump ....[じょうたい]
ながっちり 長っちり overstay *one's* welcome ....[しり]
なかなおり 仲直りする make friends again (with), be friends again (with), make up (with)
・make up with each other ....[こだわる]
なかなか
ながなが ～と lengthily, for a very long time
ながねん 長年の努力 years of hard work ....[かい¹]
～の希望 a long-cherished hope [dream] ....[きぼう]
なかば 半ば
ながばなし 長話 endless talk, long talk [chat]
・endless chatter ....[あきる]
ながびく 長引く be prolonged; (時間がかかる) take time
・be delayed ....[ひよう]
なかま 仲間
～意識 companionship
～に入れる include, count in ....[いれる]
～に入る mix in ....[きおくれ]
なかみ 中身
～がない superficial ....[りっぱ]
ながめ 眺め
ながめる 眺める
ながもち 長もちする keep [last] long; (衣料などが) wear long [well]
・last for a long time ....[じょうぶ]
なかゆび 中指 a middle finger
なかよし 仲よし a good [close] friend, an intimate friend, a great friend, *one's* best friend
～である be good friends, be on good terms (with), get on very well (with)
～になる make friends (with)

～ながら
ながれ 流れ a stream, a flow, a current
ながれだす 流れ出す flow out, begin to flow
ながれぼし 流れ星に願い事をする wish upon a shooting [falling] star ....[かなう]
ながれる 流れる
なき～ 亡き～ late ....[ながめる]
なきごえ 泣き声・鳴き声 (人の) a cry; (小鳥などの) a song, singing
なぎさ 渚 a beach
なぎたおす なぎ倒す mow down ....[むかう]
なきむし 泣き虫 a crybaby
なく 泣く
泣き出す burst into tears ....[くるう, こらえる]
泣かんばかりに on the verge of tears ....[ばかり]
泣きたい思いをする feel like *one* could cry ....[おもい²]
なく 鳴く
なぐさめ 慰め comfort
なぐさめる 慰める
なくす 無くす
・misplace, lose ....[いったい]
(排除する) eliminate ....[ほうほう]
なくす 亡くす
なくなる 無くなる
なくなる 亡くなる
なぐりあい 殴り合いのけんか a fist fight ....[けんか]
なぐる 殴る
なげかわしい 嘆かわしい deplorable, regrettable
なげき 嘆き grief, sorrow
なげく 嘆く
・grieve over ....[ところで]
・bemoan ....[み¹]
なげすてる 投げ捨てる throw away
・throw *something* on the ground ....[つく³]
なげつける 投げつける throw [fling] *something* (at)
なげやり ～な (仕事が) careless, sloppy; (人・態度が) apathetic

〜になる　lose *one's* drive
なげる 投げる
なこうど 仲人　a go-between, a matchmaker
なごやか 和やか
なごり 名残り　(a) trace, remains
なごりおしい 名残り惜しい
なさけ 情け
なさけない 情けない
なさけぶかい 情け深い ……………[なさけ]
ナシ 梨　a pear, a Japanese pear
なしとげる 成し遂げる　accomplish, achieve, carry out
なじみ
なじむ
ナス 茄子　an eggplant
なすりつける　rub in, smear; (責任を) put the blame on
なぜ
なぜか　somehow …………[うちとける]
・for some reason ………[つめたい]
なぜなら(ば)　because
なぞ 謎　a riddle, a puzzle; (不思議なこと) (a) mystery …[つつむ]
なぞなぞ　a riddle
なぞる　trace ………………[うつす¹]
なだかい 名高い
なだめる　soothe
なだらか　gentle
なだれ 雪崩　a snowslide, an avalanche
なつ 夏　summer
　〜じゅう　the whole summer
　　………………………[〜じゅう]
　〜休み　the summer vacation [《英》holidays]
なつかしい 懐かしい
　〜思い出　a fond memory [おもいで]
なつく 懐く
なづける 名付ける　name, give a name (to), call
なっとう 納豆　fermented soybeans
なっとく 納得
　〜する　be convinced ……[こうみょう]
なでる
など
ナトリウム　sodium
ななめ 斜め
なに 何

〜があっても　no matter what happens ……………[うろたえる]
〜から何まで　everything ………[き]
なにか 何か　something, anything, some, any
なにかと 何かと　with one thing or another, in many ways, always
なにげない 何気ない
なにごと 何事も　in everything
　………………………[きょくたん]
なにしろ 何しろ　(理由) after all; (何はともあれ) anyhow, in any case; (強調) really, simply
なにも 何も〜ない　nothing, not anything, not any
なにもの 何者かによって　by someone
　…………………………[ころす]
なにもの 何物にも勝る　second to †none [no other] ……………[まさる]
なによりも 何よりも　above all, before anything else, first of all
なのる 名乗る　give *one's* name (as), call *oneself*
なびく　(風に) blow; (草木が) bend
ナプキン　(食卓用) a napkin; (生理用) a sanitary napkin
なふだ 名札　(人の) a name plate [card]; (荷物の) a name tag
なべ　(浅い) a pan; (深い) a pot
ナポリ　Naples
なま 生
　〜の音楽　a live concert ……[くらべる]
なまいき 生意気
なまえ 名前　a name
　〜を付ける　name ………[つける¹]
　〜を伏せる　keep *someone's* name out of ……………………[ふせる]
なまぐさい 生臭い　fishy
なまけもの 怠け者　a lazy person
　…………………………[ばかばかしい]
　・an idler ………………[みほん]
　・a lazybones ………………[すくう]
なまける 怠ける
なまごみ 生ごみ　garbage
なまにえ 生煮えの　half-cooked
なまぬるい 生ぬるい
なまはんか 生半可な　(浅薄な) superficial; (身の入らない)

halfhearted
なまやけ 生焼けの half-roasted, half-baked
なまり 訛 a provincial accent, an accent, a dialect
なまり 鉛 lead
〜色の leaden
なみ 波 a wave
さざ〜 a ripple
大〜 a billow
寄せ〜 a surf
〜乗り surfing
〜に乗って …………………[のる]
好調の〜に乗る ride the crest of a wave ………………[のる]
なみ 並み
…並みの on a par with [しゅうかく]
なみかぜ 波風 wind and wave; (もめ事) (a) trouble
〜をたてる make waves, cause trouble
なみき 並木道 an avenue, a tree-lined street
なみだ 涙
なみなみ 〜と to the brim
なみなみ 並々ならぬ uncommon, unusual
〜でない above the ordinary
…………………[しょうめい]
なめくじ a slug
なめらか 滑らか
なめる
なやましい 悩ましい seductive, sexy
なやます 悩ます
・upset ………………[ちゅうしょう]
なやみ 悩み
・concern, anxiety …………[たね]
〜を解決する solve one's problems
…………………[たよる]
なやむ 悩む
ならう 習う
ならじだい 奈良時代 the Nara period
…………………[とりいれる]
ならす 慣・馴らす
ならす 鳴らす
ならす (平らにする) level
〜ならない
ならぶ 並ぶ

ならべる 並べる
なりきん 成金 a nouveau riche, a parvenu
〜なりに in one's own way ……[こたえ]
なりひびく 鳴り響く resound
・echo ………………[のどか]
なりふり なり振り構わず without (any) regard for appearances
…………………[ふり¹]
なりもの 鳴り物入りで vigorously
…………………[せんでん]
なりゆき 成り行き
なる 成・為・生る
(結果に)なる turn out ………[おもう]
なる 鳴る
(電話が)鳴りっぱなし be ringing off the hook ………………[さいそく]
なるべく
なるほど
ナレーション narration
ナレーター a narrator
なれなれしい (too) familiar, (too) friendly
なれる 慣・馴れる
なわ 縄 rope
なわとび 縄跳びをする jump rope
なん 何
〜につけても about everything
…………………[のろい]
〜にもならない ………………[しはい]
なんかい 何回 (回数を尋ねて) how often, how many times
なんかいも 何回も over and over
…………………[だめ]
なんきょく 南極 the South Pole
〜の Antarctic
〜大陸 the Antarctic Continent, Antarctica
〜探検(隊) an Antarctic expedition
なんきょく 難局 a crisis
・a difficulty ………………[あざやか]
なんこう 軟こう (an) ointment
なんじ 何時 what time
なんせい 南西 the southwest
〜の southwestern
ナンセンス nonsense
〜な nonsensical, absurd, rubbish
なんだ 何だ (驚き・失望など)

What!／Oh!; (意外) Why!
なんだか 何だか somehow
..................................[きみがわるい]
なんでも 何でも
　～いい anything will do ....[き]
　～ない It's nothing.／Forget it.
なんと 何と
なんど 何度か several times
..................................[くわだてる]
　～も many times ....[ただしい]
　・a number of times ....[あじわう]
　～でも over and over again
..................................[なっとく]
なんとう 南東 the southeast
　～の southeastern
なんとか 何とか
なんとしても 何としても......[どうしても]
なんとなく 何となく
なんとも 何ともない be all right
　～思わない couldn't care less
..................................[おもう]
なんなく 難なく with ease ...[みつける]
なんなら 何なら if you('d) like, if you wish, if necessary
なんにち 何日 what day of the month
なんぱ 難破する be shipwrecked, be wrecked
ナンバープレート 《米》a license plate, 《英》a number plate
なんぶ 南部 the south; (米国の) the South
なんべい 南米 South America
なんみん 難民 a refugee ....[ひさん]
　～問題 the refugee problem
..................................[うったえる]
なんもん 難問 a difficult problem [question]
なんようび 何曜日 what day (of the week)
なんらか 何らかの some, of some sort, some...or other

二

に 二 two
　第2(の) the second (略 2nd)
　2倍[回] twice, two times
　2分の1 a [one] half
～に (時間) at, on, in, by; (場所) at, in, into, on, to, for
にあう 似合う
ニース Nice
にえる 煮える boil, be boiled
におい
におう
にかい 2階 the second floor, 《英》 the first floor
　～建ての家 a two-story house
　～建てのバス a double-decker bus
..................................[かい⁴]
にがい 苦い
にがおえ 似顔絵 a portrait
にがす 逃がす
にがつ 二月 February (略 Feb.)
にがて 苦手
ニカラグア Nicaragua
にがわらい 苦笑いする smile bitterly
にきび a pimple
　・acne ....[なやむ]
　～が出来る one's face breaks out (in pimples) ....[できる]
にぎやか 賑やか
にぎりしめる 握りしめる grip, grasp, hold tightly
にぎりつぶす 握りつぶす crush *something* in *one's* hand(s); (提案などを棚上げする) shelve; (情報などを) hush up
にぎる 握
にく 肉 (食用の) meat; (人間などの) flesh
にくい 憎い
～にくい
にくがん 肉眼 the naked eye
にくしみ 憎しみ hatred
にくしん 肉親 one's family, one's blood relative
にくたい 肉体 the body
　～の bodily, physical
　～労働 physical labor
にくむ 憎む
にくや 肉屋 (人) a butcher; (店) a butcher's (shop)
にくらしい 憎らしい
ニクロム ～線 Nichrome wire
..................................[ていこう]
にげおくれる 逃げ遅れる fail to escape

にげだす 逃げ出す get away from
......[しょうどう]
・run out of ......[たえる¹]
にげみち 逃げ道 (逃走手段) a means of escape
(逃走路) an escape route ......[たつ¹]
にげる 逃げる
にこにこ ～する smile
にこやかに smilingly ......[もむ]
にごる 濁る
にし 西 the west
　～の west, western
　～へ west, westward, to [toward] the west
にじ 虹 a rainbow
にじ 二次 (2番目の) the second; (二次的な) secondary
　～会 the second party
～にしては
にじむ
にじゅう 二十 twenty
　第20(の) the twentieth (略 20th)
　20分の1 a [one] twentieth
にじゅう 二重の double, dual
　～人格 a split personality [じんかく]
～にしろ
ニシン a herring
ニス ～を塗る varnish ......[ぬる]
にせ 偽
　～の fake, counterfeit, sham, bogus
にせい 二世 (日系アメリカ人) nisei, a second-generation Japanese-American; (2代目) Junior
　～議員 a second-generation politician
にせさつ 偽札 a counterfeit bill
......[しらべる]
にせたい 二世帯住宅 a two-family home
にせもの 偽物 a fake ......[おもう]
　～の fake ......[～だけのことがある]
　・counterfeit, fake ......[よく¹]
にせもの 偽者 an impostor, a fraud
にちじ 日時 the date and hour, the time and date
にちじょう 日常の everyday, daily
　～生活 everyday [daily] life
　～英会話 everyday English conversation
にちぼつ 日没 sunset, 《米》sundown
にちようび 日曜日 Sunday (略 Sun.)
にちようひん 日用品 commodities, daily necessities
にっか 日課 daily routine, a daily task, one's daily work
にっかん 日刊の daily
にっき 日記 a diary
　～をつける keep a diary ......[～こそ]
　・write in one's diary ......[つける¹]
ニックネーム a nickname
にづくり 荷造り packing
にっこう 日光 sunshine; the sun
にっしゃびょう 日射病 sunstroke
にっしょく 日食 a solar eclipse [こと]
にっちゅう 日中に during the day, by day
にってい 日程 a day's program [schedule]
　(旅行の) a travel itinerary [くわしい]
　決められた～ a set schedule
......[したがう]
にている 似ている......[にる¹]
にど 二度 twice, two times, again
にとう 二等 the second prize, the second; (乗り物の) second class
　～賞 the second prize
にばい 二倍の twice as...as
にばん 二番(目の) the second; (2着の人) a runner-up
にぶ 二部 (2つの部分) two parts; (第2部) the second part; (印刷物などの数) two copies
にぶい 鈍い
にふだ 荷札 a label, a tag
にぶる 鈍る (刃物が) become dull; (決心などが) be shaken
にほん 日本 Japan
　～の Japanese
　～語 Japanese, the Japanese language
　～人 a Japanese (複数同形); (全体) the Japanese
　～海 the Sea of Japan
　～代表 a representative from Japan
......[だいひょう]

にほんきょうさんとう 日本共産党 Japan Communist Party (略 JCP)
にほんぎんこう 日本銀行 The Bank of Japan
にほんのうえん 日本脳炎 Japanese encephalitis
にまいじた 二枚舌を使う double-deal ……[した²]
にまいめ 二枚目の handsome, good-looking
〜にもかかわらず ….[(〜にも)かかわらず]
にもつ 荷物 baggage
・*one's* belongings …………[したがう]
ニュアンス a nuance, a shade of meaning
にゅういん 入院する enter (the) hospital, go to (the) hospital
・be hospitalized ……………[き]
〜している be in (the) hospital ………[みまい]
〜費 hospital charges [bills] ………[ようい]
にゅうえん 入園料 admission ….[ただ]
ニューオリンズ New Orleans
にゅうかい 入会 admission, (an) entrance
〜する join, become a member of, be admitted into
〜金 a membership fee
〜申込書 an application form
にゅうがく 入学する enter a school
〜願書 an application for admission
〜金 a(n) (school) admission fee
〜式 an entrance ceremony
〜試験 an entrance examination
〜試験に合格〔失敗〕する pass [fail (in)] an entrance examination
にゅうがん 乳癌 breast cancer
にゅうこく 入国 (an) entry, (an) entrance, immigration
〜する enter (a country)
不法〜する enter (a country) illegally
〜手続き entrance formalities, entry procedures, immigration
ニュージーランド New Zealand
〜人 a New Zealander; (全体) the New Zealanders

にゅうしゃ 入社する join a company
〜試験 an employment exam; (面接の) a job interview
にゅうしょう 入賞する get [win] a prize, place
・get an award …………[せいぜい]
にゅうじょう 入場 admission, entrance
〜無料 (掲示の文句) Admission free.
〜料 an admission fee
〜する enter
ニュース news
にゅうせん 入選する place (in a contest) ………[〜さえ]
ニューデリー New Delhi
にゅうもん 入門書 an introduction, a primer
ニューヨーク New York (略 N.Y., NY)
にゅうよく 入浴する take a bath, bathe
にゅうりょく 入力
にょう 尿 urine
〜失禁 urinary incontinence
ニラ a leek
にらみあう 睨み合う glare at each other; (反目し合う) be at odds (with)
にらむ 睨む
(敵意を抱く) have it in for …[さいご]
にりゅう 二流の second-rate
にる 似る
にる 煮る
にわ 庭 a garden
〜付きの家 a house with a garden ………[ひっこす]
〜の手入れをする work in the yard ………[だるい]
にわかあめ にわか雨 a shower
ニワトリ 鶏 (雌雄の別なく) a chicken; (おんどり) a cock, 《米》a rooster; (めんどり) a hen; (ひよこ) a chick
にんき 人気
〜が落ちる popularity falls ………[とりまく]
〜スター a popular star ……[はがす]
にんき 任期 a term ……[やめる²]
にんぎょ 人魚 a mermaid …[そうぞう]

にんぎょう 人形 a doll; (あやつり人形) a puppet, a marionette
　～を操る　work a marionette [たくみ]
にんげん 人間 (a) man, a human (being), a person
　～の　human
にんしき 認識
にんじょう 人情 (人間性) human nature
にんしん 妊娠する　become [get] pregnant
　～した　pregnant
　～中絶　an abortion
ニンジン　a carrot
にんずう 人数　the number of persons・people ……………[おおい]
　小～　a small number of people ……………………………[むく²]
にんそう 人相　looks, features
にんたい 忍耐　(我慢) patience; (粘り強さ) perseverance
　～強い　patient, persevering
にんてい 認定する　authorize, approve, qualify
ニンニク　garlic
にんむ 任務　a duty
　～を果たす　†carry out [perform] *one's* duties
　～を怠る　neglect *one's* duties
にんめい 任命する　appoint

ヌ

ぬいぐるみ　a stuffed [soft] toy animal; (着ぐるみ) an animal costume
ぬいめ 縫い目　a seam
ぬう 縫う
ヌード　a nude
ぬか 糠　rice bran
ぬかす 抜かす　leave out, skip
ぬかるみ　mud ……………………[ころぶ]
ぬきうち 抜き打ちの　unannounced, surprise
　～に　without notice
　～試験　a pop quiz …………[しけん]
　～テスト　a surprise test [いやらしい]
ぬく 抜く
ぬぐ 脱ぐ
ぬぐう　wipe ……………………[なみだ]

ぬけだす 脱け出す　slip out of …………………………[きづく, すき²]
ぬけている 抜けている
ぬけぬけ ～と　shamelessly, impudently
ぬけみち 抜け道　a byroad, a byway; (秘密の通路) a secret path; (法の) a loophole
ぬけめない 抜け目ない
ぬける 抜ける
ぬすみ 盗み　(a) theft
ぬすみぎき 盗み聞きする　eavesdrop on
ぬすむ 盗む
ぬの 布　cloth, material
　～切れ　a piece of cloth
ぬま 沼　a swamp, a marsh
ぬらす 濡らす
ぬる 塗る
ぬるい
ぬるぬる ～した　slimy, slippery; (油で) greasy; (石けんで) soapy
ぬるまゆ ぬるま湯　lukewarm water
ぬれる 濡れる

ネ

ね 値　a price
　～が張る　expensive ………[はる¹]
ね 根
　～を張る　spread *its* roots ……[はる¹]
ねあがり 値上がり　a rise in price …………………………………[あて]
ねあげ 値上げ　a price increase, a raise
ねいる 寝入る　fall asleep, go to bed
ねいろ 音色　(a) timbre, a tone
ねうち 値打ち
ネオン　a neon sign, a neon light
ネガ　a negative
ねがい 願い
ねがう 願う
ねがえり 寝返りをうつ　toss and turn, roll
ねがえる 寝返る　(敵方に移る) go over to the enemy
ねかしつける 寝かしつける　lull *someone* to sleep …………[だます]
ネギ　a Welsh onion
ねぎらう　(感謝する) thank *someone* for

ねぎる 値切る beat down the price, bargain for
ネクタイ a necktie, a tie
　〜ピン a tiepin
ネグリジェ a nightgown
ねぐるしい 寝苦しい hard to sleep ……………………………[むしあつい]
ネコ 猫 a cat
　子〜 a kitten
ねこぜ 猫背の round-shouldered
ねごと 寝言 talk in *one's* sleep; (たわごと) nonsense
　〜を言う talk in *one's* sleep
ねこむ 寝込む, 寝込んでいる be laid up
　・be ill [sick] in bed …………[いらい]
　・be in bed ………………………[たかい]
ねころぶ 寝転ぶ lie down
ねさがり 値下がり a fall [drop] in price(s)
ねさげ 値下げする reduce [cut, lower] the price
ねじ a screw; (水道などの) a stopcock
　〜まわし a screwdriver
ねじまげる ねじ曲げる twist, bend by twisting
ねじる
ねすごす 寝過ごす oversleep
ネズミ (大形の) a rat; (ハツカネズミなど小形の) a mouse (複数 mice)
　〜取り a rattrap, a mousetrap; (スピード取り締まり) a speed trap
ネズミこう ネズミ講 pyramid sales
ねぞう 寝相が悪い move about in *one's* sleep
ねそべる 寝そべる lie down
ねたきり 寝たきりの bedridden, be confined to *one's* [the] bed
ねたばこ 寝たばこ smoking in bed …………………………………[げんいん]
ねたみ 妬み jealousy, envy
ねたむ
ねだる ask, beg
ねだん 値段 a price
ねつ 熱
　〜に強い heat-resistant …[ぶっしつ]
ねつい 熱意
　〜を持つ have a zeal for [ひじょう]

ねっき 熱気 enthusiasm ……[つたわる]
ねっきょう 熱狂
ネックレス a necklace
ねっしん 熱心
　〜に diligently ………………[うつす¹]
　・enthusiastically ……………[けいこ]
ねっする 熱する heat (up)
ねっせん 熱戦 a breathtaking match …………………………………[いきづまる²]
ねったい 熱帯 the tropics
　〜の tropical
ねっちゅう 熱中
ネット
ねっとう 熱湯 boiling water
ネットワーク ……………………[ネット]
ねつびょう 熱病 a fever
ねつぼう 熱望する be eager (for), be anxious (for, to *do*), wish eagerly (for)
ねつれつ 熱烈
ねは 根は (心根は) deep down ……[ね]
　・actually …………………………[がさつ]
　・basically …………………………[くち]
ネパール Nepal
　〜の Nepalese, Nepali
　〜語 Nepali
　〜人 a Nepalese (複数同形); (全体) the Nepalese, the Nepali(s)
ねばり 粘り
ねばる 粘る
ねびき 値引きする discount, reduce a price
ねぶそく 寝不足 a lack of sleep …………………………………[ひびく]
　〜である not get enough rest …………………………………[ねむい]
ねふだ 値札 a price tag
ねぼう 寝坊する oversleep ……[おそれ]
ねぼける 寝ぼける be half asleep, be half awake
ねまき 寝巻き night clothes, a nightgown; (婦人子ども用の) a night dress; (パジャマ) pajamas, 《英》pyjamas
ねむい 眠い
ねむけ 眠気を催す feel drowsy …………………………………[もよおす]
ねむり 眠り sleep

～に落ちる fall into a sleep [ふかい]
～が浅い be a light sleeper [あさい]
～薬 a sleeping tablet [pill, drug]
ねむる 眠る
　・fall asleep ……………………[つかれる]
　眠っている（発見されない）lie hidden
　…………………………………[ほうふ]
ねらい 狙い an aim
ねらう 狙う
　・set *one's* sights (on) …………[にがす]
ねりあるく 練り歩く wind *one's* way
　…………………………………[ぎょうれつ]
ねる 寝る
　寝てしまう fall asleep …………[きる²]
　寝ずに待つ wait up for …………[まつ]
　もう寝なさい Go to sleep! …[だって]
ねる 練る (粉など) knead; (熟考する)
　ponder over, think out
ねん 年 a year; (学年) a grade
　～に一度の yearly, annual
ねん 念
ねんいり 念入り
ねんがじょう 年賀状 a New Year's
　card
ねんがん 念願のもの what *one* has
　been wishing for so much ………[て]
ねんきん 年金 a pension, an annuity
　厚生～ the Worker's Pension Plan
　国民～ the National Pension Plan
　老齢～ an old-age pension
　～で on a pension ………………[しっそ]
ねんこう 年功序列(制度) the
　seniority (system)
ねんごう 年号 an era name
ねんざ a sprain, a twist
　～する sprain, twist
ねんしゅう 年収 an annual [yearly]
　income
ねんじゅう 年じゅう all the year
　round, all year long
　・all year (round) ………………[やすむ]
ねんだい 年代 an age, (a) date, a
　generation
　～順に in chronological order
ねんど 年度 (学校の) the school year;
　(会計年度) the fiscal year
　～別に by the year ……………[わける]
ねんど 粘土 clay

ねんねん 年々 annually, year by year
　…………………………………[しょうひ]
　・every year ……………………[せいかつ]
ねんぱい 年配の elderly
　～の者 the older generation
　…………………………………[とまどう]
ねんぴ 燃費 mileage ……………[ちゅうい]
　～のいい車 a car with good gas
　mileage
ねんぴょう 年表 a chronological table
ねんぽう 年俸 *one's* annual salary
　～制 an annual-salary system
ねんまつ 年末の year-end
　～調整 the year-end (tax)
　adjustment ……………………[もどる]
ねんりょう 燃料 fuel
ねんれい 年齢 age
　あの～にしては considering *one's*
　age …………………………[じゅうなん]

ノ

の 野 a field; (平原) plains
ノイローゼ a nervous breakdown
　[wreck], neurosis
　～のようになる bring *someone* close
　to a nervous breakdown
　…………………………………[ちゅうしょう]
のう 脳 the brain
のういっけつ 脳いっ血で倒れる have a
　stroke ……………………………[たおれる]
のうえん 脳炎 encephalitis
のうえん 農園 a farm
のうか 農家 (農民) a farmer
のうぎょう 農業 agriculture, farming
　～の agricultural
のうこう 農耕 agriculture …[はじまる]
のうこうそく 脳梗塞 brain infarction
のうさくぶつ 農作物 the crops,
　agricultural products
のうさんぶつ 農産物 agricultural
　products
　～の生産高 agricultural output
　…………………………………[せいさん¹]
のうし 脳死 brain death
のうしゅく 濃縮された concentrated;
　(放射性元素が) enriched
のうそっちゅう 脳卒中 apoplexy
のうそん 農村の rural ………[えがく]

のうち 農地 farmland
のうは 脳波 brain waves
のうみん 農民 a farmer; (小規模の) a peasant; (雇われた) a farm hand [laborer]; (総称) farmers
のうやく 農薬 agricultural chemicals
のうりつ 能率
のうりょく 能力
 ～給(制度) (a) performance-based pay (system)
のうりんすいさんしょう 農林水産省 the Ministry of Agriculture, Forestry and Fisheries (of Japan)
ノート (帳面) a notebook; (注釈) a note
 ～パソコン a notebook computer, a notebook
ノーネクタイ not wear a tie …[かまう]
ノーベルしょう ノーベル賞 a Nobel prize
のがす 逃す miss
 ～手はない can't let it pass ….[また]
のがれる 逃れる escape (from), evade
のきさき 軒先 edge of the eaves ……………………………………[たれる]
のけもの のけ者にする leave *someone* out (in the cold)
のこぎり a saw
のこす 残す
のこり 残り
のこる 残る
のせる 乗・載せる
のぞきあな (ドアの)覗き穴(から覗く) (look through) a peephole
のぞきこむ 覗き込む look into [かお]
のぞく 除く
のぞく 覗く
のぞましい 望ましい
のぞみ 望み
 ～薄だ there is little hope …[うすい]
のぞむ 望む
のぞむ 臨む face ……………[いっち]
のち 後
ノック ～する knock
ノックアウト ～する knock out
のっとる 乗っ取る (飛行機などを) hijack; (会社などを) take over
のっぴきならない

のど the throat
 ～が痛い have a sore throat
 ～が渇く get thirsty ……………[のむ]
のどか
ののしる curse ……………………[たがい]
のばす 伸・延ばす
のはら 野原 a field
のび 伸び (成長・発展) (a) growth
 ～をする stretch *oneself*
のびのび
のびる 伸・延びる
のべ 延べ (合計) a total; (1人1日の作業量) a man-day
のべる 述べる
のぼせる
のほほん
のぼり 上り a rise, an ascent
 ～道 an uphill road, an ascent
 ～列車 an up train
のぼる 上・登・昇る
のまれる 飲・呑まれる
ノミ 蚤 (虫) a flea
のみ 鑿 (工具) a chisel
のみくい 飲み食い eating and drinking
 ・food and drink ……………[つかう]
のみこみ ～が速い be a quick learner
 ・pick up on things very quickly
 ……………………………………[はやい²]
のみこむ 飲み込む swallow
～のみならず not only *A* but (also) *B*, *B* as well as *A*, besides...
のみのいち のみの市 a flea market
 ……………………………………[みつける]
のみほす 飲み干す drink up
のみみず 飲み水 drinking water
のみもの 飲み物 something to drink, a drink, a beverage
のみや 飲み屋 a bar ………[ふぞく]
 ・a small bar ……………[まんいん]
のむ 飲・呑む
 (…を)飲みながら over *something*
 ……………………………………[のむ]
 飲みに行く go out drinking ……[き]
 豪勢に飲み歩く paint the town red
 ……………………………………[ごうせい]
のらいぬ 野良犬 a stray dog …[つく²]
のらねこ 野良猫 a stray cat …[ふさぐ]

ノリ 海苔 (海草) seaweed, laver; (加工した) dried seaweed
のり 糊 paste
のりあげる 乗り上げる (浅瀬に) run aground [ashore]
のりおくれる 乗り遅れる miss, be late for, fail to catch
のりかえる 乗り換える
のりき 乗り気
のりきる 乗り切る overcome ……………………[あざやか]
のりくみいん 乗組員 (ひとり) a member of the crew; (全員) the crew
のりこえる 乗り越える
・get through ……………[せいさく¹]
のりごこち 乗り心地の良さ riding comfort ……………………[くふう]
のりこす 乗り越す ride past, go beyond
・ride past *one's* stop ……[ぼんやり]
のりこむ 乗り込む get on; (進軍する) march into
乗り込んでいく venture into
……………………[いさましい]
のりだす 乗り出す (身を) lean forward; (始める) start, set about
海へ〜 set out to sea ……[たった]
のりば 乗り場 (バスの) a bus stop; (タクシーの) a taxi stand; (船の) a mooring place; (列車の) a platform
のりもの 乗り物 a vehicle
〜に弱い get sick on rides …[よわい]
のる 乗・載る
同じ電車に乗り合わせる be on the same train ……………[ぐうぜん]
ノルウェー Norway
〜の Norwegian
〜人 a Norwegian; (全体) the Norwegians
のろい
のろい 呪い a curse, a spell
のろう 呪う curse
のろける boast [rave] about *one's* partner
のろのろ slowly, at a snail's pace
のんき

のんびり
〜屋の happy-go-lucky ……[きなが]

ハ

は 刃 an edge; (替え刃) a (razor) blade
は 派 (学問・芸術などの) a school (派閥) a faction …………[ぞくする]
は 葉 a leaf; (細長い草の葉) a blade; (松葉) a needle
〜の茂った leafy
は 歯
バー a bar
ばあい 場合
(…している)場合じゃない this is no time to *do* ………………[きれい]
この〜 in this situation ………[ほか]
こんな〜 in a case like this [りこう]
はあく 把握する understand, grasp
バーゲンセール a bargain sale, a sale
バーコード a bar code
〜をスキャナで読み取る scan a bar code
バージョン
パーセンテージ percentage
パーセント percent, %
バーチャルリアリティ virtual reality
パーティー a party
ハート a heart
ハード(ウェア) hardware
パート (部分) a part
パート(タイム) (仕事) a part-time job; (人) a part-time worker, a part-timer
〜で働く work part-time
ハードコピー 《コンピュータ》 a hard copy
ハードディスク 《コンピュータ》 the hard disk
パートナー a partner
ハードル a hurdle
〜を越える clear a hurdle
ハーブ (香草) herbs
ハープ (楽器) a harp
〜奏者 a harpist
バーベキュー (a) barbecue
バーベル a barbell
パーマ a permanent wave, a perm

〜をかける have *one's* hair permed [waved]
ハーモニカ a harmonica
バーレーン Bahrain, Bahrein
はい 灰 ashes
はい 肺 the lungs
はい （応答）yes, certainly; 《米口語》okay, O.K., sure; （否定疑問文のあとで）no
…はい …杯 （一杯）a glass of, a cup of
ばい 倍
パイ （1個全体）a pie; （1片）a piece of pie
バイアグラ 《商標》Viagra
はいいろ 灰色(の) gray, 《英》grey
はいえん 肺炎 pneumonia ………[こと]
バイオリン a violin
  〜奏者 a violinist
ハイカー a hiker
バイカル 〜湖 Lake Baikal [Baykal]
はいきガス 排気ガス exhaust fumes ………………………………[まとも]
車の〜 automobile exhaust [よごす]
はいきしゅ 肺気腫 《医学用語》pulmonary emphysema
はいきぶつ 廃棄物 (a) waste
はいきゅう 配給する ration, distribute, supply
はいきょ 廃墟 ruins
はいぎょう 廃業する go out of business
ばいきん ばい菌 a germ, bacteria (単数 a bacterium)
ハイキング hiking, a hike
  〜に行く go hiking, go on a hike ………………………………………[いく]
バイキング 〜料理 buffet
  ・smorgasbord ………………[よくばる]
はいく 俳句 (a) *haiku*, a seventeen-syllable poem
バイク a motorcycle, a motor(bike)
はいけい 背景 a background; (舞台の) scenery, setting
はいざら 灰皿 an ashtray
はいし 廃止する abolish
  ・eliminate ………………………[せん]
はいしゃ 歯医者 a dentist; (歯科医院) a dentist's (office)

ハイジャック a hijack
ばいしゅう 買収する (購入) purchase, buy; (賄賂を送る) bribe, buy off
ばいしゅん 売春 prostitution
ばいしょう 賠償 compensation
はいしん 背信 betrayal ………[きづく]
はいすい 排水する drain, pump out; 《土地を主語にして》drain
  〜管 a drainpipe
はいせん 配線 wiring
  〜する wire
はいせん 敗戦 a defeat
はいた 歯痛 (a) toothache
はいたつ 配達 delivery
  〜する deliver
  〜してもらう get *something* delivered ………………………[たりる]
  〜人 a deliveryman, a carrier
  新聞〜人 a newsboy
  郵便〜人 《米》a mailman, a mail carrier, 《英》a postman
はいたてき 排他的な exclusive
ハイチ Haiti
  〜の Haitian
  〜人 a Haitian; (全体) the Haitians
はいち 配置する arrange
はいでる はい出る crawl up, creep up
ばいてん 売店 (街頭・駅などの) a stand, a stall, a kiosk
バイト ……………………………[アルバイト]
バイト 《コンピュータ》a byte
はいとうきん 配当金 a dividend
ばいどく 梅毒 《医学用語》syphilis
パイナップル a pineapple
ばいばい 売買 buying and selling
バイパス a bypass
ハイヒール high-heeled shoes, high heels
ハイビスカス hibiscus
はいひん 廃品 waste [useless] articles, junk
パイプ a pipe, a tube; (たばこの) a pipe; (巻きたばこの) a cigarette holder
はいぶつ 廃物 (a) waste
ハイブリッド 〜の hybrid
  〜車 a hybrid car [vehicle]
バイブル (聖書) the Bible; (特定分野

の) a [the] bible
はいぶん 配分する distribute
・allot ……………………[おうじる]
ハイヤー a limousine, 《口語》a limo
はいやく 配役 the cast, casting
ばいやくずみ 売約済 sold
はいゆう 俳優 (男の) an actor; (女の) an actress
ばいよう 培養する culture
ばいりつ 倍率 (光学の) (a) magnification; (試験の) competition
はいりょ 配慮
はいる 入る
はいれつ 配列する arrange, put *something* in order
パイロット a pilot
はう 這う
バウンド a bound, a bounce
～する bound, bounce
ハエ a fly
はえる 生える
はえる 映える (よく見える) look nice
はか 墓 a grave, a tomb
～場 a graveyard; (教会の) a church-yard; (共同の) a cemetery
～参りにいく visit *someone's* grave
……………………………[だいいち]
ばか 馬鹿
～にする laugh at ………[～まで(に)]
・make fun of ………………[かっと]
～を見る feel like a fool ………[みる]
はかい 破壊
はがき 葉書 a post card
絵～ a picture post card, a picture card
ばかげた 馬鹿げた ridiculous [ことば]
はがす
ばかす 化かす bewitch
ばかず 場数を踏んだ with a lot of experience ………………………[ふむ]
はかせ 博士 a doctor (略 Dr.)
はかどる
はかない
～希望 a faint hope …………[きぼう]
はがね steel
ばかばかしい
はがゆい 歯がゆい

はかり (てんびん) a balance, (a pair of) scales; (自動ばかり) a scale, a dial scale; (体重計) a weighing machine, (a) (bathroom, doctor's) scale(s)
ばかり
大学を出た～ be fresh out of college
……………………………[みらい]
(～して)ばかり constantly …[こりる]
(～して)ばかりはいられない can't go on *doing* ……………………[かなしむ]
はかる 計・測・量・諮・図・謀る
(推測する) figure out ……………[いと]
はがれる peel off, come off
はき 破棄する cancel, annul, abolish, repeal
契約を～する †break off [cancel] the contract ……………………[けいやく]
婚約を～する break off *one's* engagement ………………[しんきょう]
はきけ 吐き気 nausea
～がする feel sick, feel nauseated [nausea]
～を催させる make *someone* sick, be nauseating
はぎしり 歯ぎしりする grind *one's* teeth
パキスタン Pakistan
～の Pakistani
～人 a Pakistani, (複数 -s); (全体) the Pakistanis
はきはき ～した話し方 a crisp way of talking ……………………[こうかん²]
はきもの 履きもの footgear, footwear, shoes
はく 吐く
はく 掃く
はく 履・穿く
履き慣れた靴 comfortable old shoes
……………………………[なれる]
はぐ 剥ぐ strip, tear off
バグ 《コンピュータ》a bug
～を取り除く debug
ばくおん 爆音 (a) rumble ………[ひびく]
飛行機の～ the roar of an airplane
……………………………[ふるえる]
はくがい 迫害する persecute [まどわす]
はくがく 博学の learned

はぐき 歯ぐき gums
ばくげき 爆撃する bomb
 ～機 a bomber, a bombing plane
はくさい 白菜 a Chinese cabbage
はくし 白紙 white paper, a clean sheet of paper; (答案の) a blank paper
 ～に戻す take *something* back to the (old) drawing board ………[もどす]
はくしき 博識の knowledgeable
 …………………………………[ちしき]
はくしゃ 拍車 a spur
 ～をかける (促進する) prompt
はくしゅ 拍手 hand clapping
 ・applause ………………………[あびる]
 ～する clap (*one's* hands); applaud
 ～で迎えられる be greeted by applause ………………………[ぶたい]
 割れるような～が起る applause is deafening ………………………[われる]
はくしょ 白書 a white paper
はくじょう 白状 confession
 ～する confess ………………[つつむ]
はくじょう 薄情
はくじん 白人 a white (man), a Caucasian; (人種) the white race, white people
ばくぜん 漠然
ばくだい 莫大な vast
 ・huge …………………………[りえき]
 ・enormous amount of ……[しょゆう]
 ・tremendous amount of ……[ひよう]
バグダッド Baghdad
ばくだん 爆弾 a bomb
ばくち gambling
ハクチョウ 白鳥 a swan
バクテリア bacteria (単数 a bacterium)
はくないしょう 白内障 cataract
ばくは 爆破する blow up
はくはつ 白髪の silver-haired
 …………………………………[じょうひん]
ばくはつ 爆発
はくぶつかん 博物館 a museum
はくまい 白米 white rice, polished rice
はくらいの 舶来の foreign-made, imported
はくらんかい 博覧会 《米》an exposition, 《英》an exhibition

 万国～ a world exposition
はくりょく 迫力
はぐるま 歯車 a cogwheel, a gear wheel, a toothed wheel, a gear
ばくろ 暴露する disclose, expose
はけ a brush
はげ (部分) a bald spot; (頭) a bald head; (人) a bald(-headed) person
 ～の bald, bare
はげしい 激しい
 ・extreme ………………………[さ]
 (変化が) acute …………………[へんか]
はげしく 激しく hard, violently, heavily, severely, bitterly
 ・fiercely ……………………[たたかう]
 ・aggressively, sharply ……[こうげき]
ハゲタカ a vulture
バケツ a bucket
 ・a pail
 …………………………………[なま]
はげます 励ます
はげみ 励み
はげむ 励む
ばけもの 化け物 (幽霊) a ghost; (怪物) a monster
はげる (貼った物が) come off, fall off; (色が) fade; (頭が) become bald
ばける 化ける change [turn] *oneself* into; (変装する) disguise *oneself* as
はけん 派遣する dispatch
 ・send ………………………[かいがい]
 海外に～する send *someone* overseas
 …………………………………[しどう]
 ～社員 a temporary worker, a temp
はこ 箱 a box, a case
 ～入りの boxed
はこぶ 運ぶ
 ・take ………………………[にもつ]
バザー a bazaar ……………[かまう]
はさみ (a pair of) scissors
はさむ 挟む
はさん 破産 bankruptcy ………[すくう]
 自己～ personal bankruptcy
 ～する go bankrupt
はし 端
はし 橋 a bridge
はし 箸 chopsticks ……………[つかう]
はじ 恥
 恥知らず have no sense of shame

....[ほど]
はしか (the) measles ....[かかる¹]
　～の予防注射 a measles shot [よぼう]
はじく 弾く
はしご a ladder
はじまり 始まり the beginning, the start
はじまる 始まる
　(…しても)始まらない not get *one* anywhere ....[うらむ]
はじめ 初め
　はじめから 初めから from the very start ....[しらける]
はじめて 初めて
　(…して)初めて only after ....[ありがたい]
はじめまして 初めまして How do you do?
はじめる 始める
ばしゃ 馬車 a (horse-drawn) carriage
はしゃぐ jump around and play ....[よく¹]
パジャマ 《米》pajamas, 《英》pyjamas
ばしょ 場所 (所)a place; (空間) space, room, place
はしょうふう 破傷風 tetanus
はしら 柱 a pillar, a post
はしりがき 走り書き (書いたもの) a scribble, a jotting
　～する scribble, jot down
はしりさる 走り去る (車が) drive off ....[のせる]
はしりたかとび 走り高跳び the running high jump
はしりはばとび 走り幅跳び the (running) broad [long] jump ....[きろく]
はしりまわる 走り回る run about
はしる 走る
はじる 恥じる be [feel] ashamed (of)
ハス 蓮 a lotus
はず
バス a bus
　観光～ a sightseeing bus
　～停 a bus stop
　～に間に合う make the bus ....[かろうじて]
はずかしい 恥ずかしい

恥ずかしさ embarrassment [たえる¹]
恥ずかしそうに shyly, bashfully [め]
はずかしめ 辱めを受ける face an embarrassing situation ....[むしろ]
はずかしめる 辱める insult, disgrace, dishonor
～はずがない How could *one* possibly ...? ....[わかる]
バスケットボール basketball
はずす 外す
パスポート a passport
はずみ momentum
　～で by chance
はずむ (はねかえる) spring, bound; (調子づく) be [become] lively
パズル a puzzle ....[わけ]
　クロスワード～ a crossword puzzle
はずれ 外れ
はずれる 外れる
　・become disengaged ....[から]
　的を～ miss the mark ....[まと]
パスワード the [*one's*] password
パセリ parsley
パソコン a (personal) computer, a PC ....[コンピュータ]
はた 旗 a flag
はだ 肌 the skin
　～着 undershirts; 《集合的に》underwear
バター butter
パターン a pattern
はだか 裸
はたき a duster
　～をかける dust
はたけ 畑 a field ....[ほそい]
　～仕事 farm work
はだざむい 肌寒い chilly ....[さむい]
はだざわり 肌触りがやわらかい have a soft texture [touch] ....[やわらかい]
はだし
はたす 果たす
ばたばた ～と one by one ....[たおれる]
はたらき 働き
　～盛り at *one's* working prime ....[さかり]
はたらきかける 働きかける work on, appeal to
はたらく 働く

バタンと　with a bang
ハチ　蜂　(ミツバチ) a bee; (キバチ) a wasp
　〜の巣　a honeycomb
　〜みつ　honey
はち　八　eight
　8分の1　an [one] eighth
　第8(の)　the eighth (略 8th)
はち　鉢　(どんぶり) a bowl; (植木の) a pot
ばち　罰が当たる　get it, pay for it, ask for it, It serves *someone* right.
はちあわせ　鉢合わせする　run into
はちがつ　八月　August (略 Aug.)
バチカン　(ローマ教皇庁) the Vatican
はちじゅう　八十　eighty
　第80(の)　the eightieth (略 80th)
はちまき　鉢巻き　a headband
はちゅうるい　は虫類　a reptile
はちょう　波長　a wavelength
パチンコ　*pachinko*, a pinball game
　〜屋　a *pachinko* parlor
ばつ　罰
　〜として　as punishment ……[のこす]
はついく　発育　growth, development
はつおん　発音　pronunciation
　〜する　pronounce
ハッカー　《インターネット》a (computer) hacker, a cracker
はつがんせい　発癌性の　cancer-causing, 《医学用語》carcinogenic
　〜物質　cancer-causing substances, 《医学用語》carcinogens
はっき　発揮
　〜する　demonstrate ……………[じこ¹]
はっきょう　発狂する　go mad
はっきり
　〜させる　clarify ……………[ほうしん]
　〜した　explicit ……………[さすが]
　〜したことは言えない　can't make any definite statements, have nothing definite to state　[しりょう]
　〜した返事　a firm answer ……[へんじ]
　・a clear answer …………………[よわる]
ばっきん　罰金　a fine, a penalty
　〜を科する　fine
　〜を科される　be fined (for)
　………………………………………[ぶじょく]
　〜を取られる　be fined ………[きそく]
バック　(背景) a background ……[うく]
　〜ナンバー　(雑誌の) a back number [issue]
　〜ミラー　a rearview mirror
　〜する　back, go back
バッグ　a bag
バックアップ
はっくつ　発掘する　excavate
　〜隊　excavators ………………[いか]
　〜調査　an excavation ………[ほうこく]
バックパッカー　a backpacker
ばつぐん　抜群の　distinguished
　………………………………………[はたらき]
はっけつびょう　白血病　leukemia
はつげん　発言　a statement …[おうぼう]
　〜権　right to speak ……………[うばう]
　〜する　speak, say
はっけん　発見
はっこう　発行
はっこう　発酵する[させる]　ferment
はっさん　発散する　let off, release, relieve
バッジ　a badge, a pin
はっしゃ　発車　departure
　〜する　leave, start (from), depart (from)
はっしゃ　発射する　(銃を) discharge, fire; (ロケット・ミサイルなどを) launch
　・fire ……………………………………[ねらう]
ばっすい　抜粋　an extract, an excerpt
　〜する　extract, excerpt
ばっする　罰する　punish
はっせい　発生する　(起こる) occur, break out; (台風が) form, be born; (繁殖する) breed
はっせい　発声練習　practice in vocalization
はっそう　発想　an idea, (a way of) thinking
はっそう　発送する　send out, dispatch, mail, ship
バッタ　a grasshopper
バッター　《野球》a batter
　〜ボックス　a batter's box
　4番〜　the cleanup hitter　[けいえん]

はったつ 発達
　・development ……………[つうしん]
　〜する（台風が）gain strength
　　……………………………[ほうめん]
ばったり（音をたてて）with a thud;
　（偶然に）unexpectedly
　〜会う　run [bump] into ……[あう²]
　〜出会う　happen to come face to
　　face with …………………[おもい²]
バッティング《野球》batting
ばってき 抜てきする　select, choose;
　（昇進させる）promote
バッテリー（電池）a battery
　《野球》a battery ……………[こきゅう]
はつでん 発電　generation
　〜機　a generator
　〜所　a power plant [《英》station]
　水力〜所　a hydroelectric power
　　plant
　火力〜所　a thermal power plant
はってん 発展
はっと
バット　a bat
ぱっと
はつどうき 発動機　a motor, an engine
はつばい 発売する　sell, put *something*
　†up for [on] sale, put *something*
　on the market, release
ハッピーエンド　a happy ending [まく³]
はっぴょう 発表
　〜する　present ………………[さくひん]
　・make an announcement ……[じじつ]
はっぽうスチロール 発泡スチロール
　styrene foam;《商標》Styrofoam
はつめい 発明
はつゆうしょう 初優勝を飾る　clinch
　one's first championship
　　……………………………[ゆうしょう]
はつらつ 〜とした　lively, full of life
はで 派手
　〜な　fancy ……………………[このましい]
はてしない 果てしない　endless,
　boundless
ハト 鳩 （家鳩）a pigeon;（野鳩）a dove
　伝書〜　a carrier [homing] pigeon
パトカー　a police car …………[あげる]
ハドソン 〜川　the Hudson (River)
バドミントン　badminton

パトロール（する）patrol
　〜カー　a police car
バトン　a baton ……………………[つかむ]
　〜ガール　a baton twirler
はな 花　a flower;（果樹の）a blossom;
　（観賞用の）a bloom
　〜屋 （人）a florist;（店）a flower
　　shop, a florist's
　〜畑　a flower garden
　〜言葉　flower language
　〜が咲く　come out, bloom
　〜に水をやる　water the flowers
　　……………………………[やる]
　〜を生ける　arrange flowers
　〜を添える　add an extra touch of
　　beauty to …………………[そえる]
はな 鼻
　〜の頭　the tip of *one's* nose …[くう]
　〜をあかす　show *someone* who's
　　who …………………………[あんじる]
　〜息が荒い　assertive ………[あらい¹]
はなうた 鼻歌を歌う　hum
はなきん 花金（花の金曜日）TGIF!
　(=Thank God it's Friday!)
はなごえ 鼻声　a nasal voice
　〜だ　talk through *one's* nose
はなし 話
　（問題）a topic ………………[けいえん]
　〜がうますぎる　sound too good to
　　be true ……………………[はなし]
　〜に乗る　take *someone* up on *his*
　　offer …………………………[ぎもん]
　〜の途中で　in the middle of a
　　conversation ………………[でんわ]
　この〜は聞かなかったことにしてくださ
　　い　Please forget you ever heard
　　this. …………………………[こと]
はなしあい 話し合い　a talk ……[のばす]
　・a discussion …………………[ふちょう]
　〜によって　through discussion
　　……………………………[よる¹]
はなしあいて 話し相手　companionship
　　……………………………[あいて]
はなしあう 話し合う　have a discussion
　　……………………………[せいり]
はなしかける 話しかける　strike up
　conversations with …………[うちき]
　・speak to ……………………[きやすい]

はなしはんぶん 話半分に聞く take *something* †with a grain of salt [only half seriously] ……[はんぶん]
はなす 話す
はなす 放す
はなす 離す
はなせる 話せる (物分かりがよい) open-minded, understanding
はなたば 花束 a bouquet
・a bouquet of flowers ………[ながす]
はなぢ 鼻血 (a) nosebleed
はなづら 鼻面 one's face ……[なぐる]
バナナ a banana
はなばなしい 華々しい brilliant, splendid
はなび 花火 fireworks
　〜大会 a fireworks show
　〜を上げる set off a firework
　………………………………[あげる]
はなびら 花びら a petal
パナマ Panama
　〜の Panamanian
　〜人 a Panamanian; (全体) the Panamanians
　〜市 Panama City
　〜運河 the Panama Canal
はなみ 花見 (桜の) cherry blossom viewing
はなむこ 花婿 a bridegroom
はなやか 華やか
はなよめ 花嫁 a bride
　〜衣裳 a bridal gown ………[みごと]
はなれる 放れる
はなれる 離れる
　・tear *oneself* away from [おもいきり]
　・leave *someplace* behind
　………………………………[なごりおしい]
はなわ 花輪 a wreath; (ハワイの) a lei
はにかんだ shy, bashful
パニック (a) panic
　〜に陥る go [get, fly] into a panic, panic, be in panic
はね 羽・羽根 (羽毛) (a) feather; (翼) a wing; (プロペラ・扇風機の) a blade; (バドミントンなどの) a shuttlecock
はね 跳ねをとばす splash mud
ばね

はねかえる 跳ね返る rebound
はねまわる 跳ね回る jump about, hop about; (はしゃいで) roam about
はねる 跳ねる
ハノイ Hanoi
パノラマ a panorama
はは 母 one's mother
はば 幅
はばつ 派閥 a clique
ババロア (a) Bavarian cream
ハバロフスク Khabarovsk
パプアニューギニア Papua New Guinea
パフェ (a) parfait
はぶく 省く
　・do away with …………[まわりくどい]
ハプニング a happening, an incident
はブラシ 歯ブラシ a toothbrush
バブル 〜経済 bubble economy
　〜の崩壊 a bubble burst
はへん 破片 a piece, a fragment
はまき 葉巻 a cigar
ハマグリ a clam
はまべ 浜辺 the beach, the seashore
はまる (合う) fit; (落ちる) fall [get] into
はみがきこ 歯みがき粉 (粉の) tooth powder; (練り) tooth paste
はみだす はみ出す stick out; (人に押されて) be pushed out
ハム (食品) ham
ハム (無線の) a (radio) ham
はめ 羽目
はめつ 破滅 ruin
　〜する be ruined
はめる 嵌める
ばめん 場面 a scene
はもの 刃物 an edged tool, cutlery
はやい 早い
はやい 速い
　歩くのが〜 walk swiftly ……[ひろい]
はやおき 早起きする get up early
はやがてん 早合点
　〜する make a hasty decision [judgement]
はやく 早く early; (まもなく) soon
　・quickly ……………………[たつ⁴]
はやく 速く fast, quick, quickly

はやくち 早口でしゃべる talk fast ……[きく²]
　〜言葉 a tongue twister
はやければ 早ければ at the earliest ……[はやい¹]
はやし 林 a wood
はやす (からかって) jeer at; (かっさいを送る) cheer
はやす 生やす (ひげなどを) grow
はやねはやおき 早寝早起き early to bed, early to rise ……[もくひょう]
はやびけ 早びけする leave someplace early
はやまる 早まる (時間が) be advanced, be brought forward; (人が) be hasty
はやめ 早目に well in advance ……[もうしこむ]
はやめる 早める advance; (促進する) hasten
はやめる 速める quicken; (速度を) speed up
はやる 流行る
　・be prevalent ……[じだい]
はやる 逸る
はら 腹
　〜痛 a stomachache
　〜いっぱい食べる eat *one's* fill ……[いっぱい]
　〜が張る *one's* stomach is really full ……[はる¹]
　〜の内 what *one* is up to [ちゃんと]
バラ a rose
　〜色の rosy, rose-colored
はらいもどす 払い戻す refund [もどす]
はらう 払う
パラシュート a parachute
ばらす (ばらばらにする) take *something* apart; (暴露する) reveal, expose, let out, let *someone* in on *something*
パラソル a parasol
はらだたしい 腹立たしい
はらはら
ばらばら
ばらまく (物を) scatter, spread out; (金を) spread around a lot of cash
バランス

はり 針 (縫い針) a needle; (留め針) a pin; (釣り針) a hook; (時計の) a hand
　(手術の縫い数) a stitch ……[きず]
　〜仕事 needlework, sewing
バリ 〜島 Bali
パリ Paris
はりあい 張り合い
はりあう 張り合う
はりあげる 声を張り上げる raise *one's* voice ……[こえ]
バリアフリー 〜の barrier-free
はりがね 針金 (a) wire
はりがみ はり紙 a bill, a notice; (ラベル) a label
バリカン hair clippers
ばりき 馬力 (単位) horsepower; (精力) energy
はりきる 張り切る
はる 春(の) spring
　〜らしくなる it feels [seems] like spring ……[ようやく]
はる 張る
はる 貼る
　・put up ……[めだつ]
　(のりで) glue ……[おさえる]
はるか
バルコニー a balcony
バルセロナ Barcelona
バルト 〜海 the Baltic Sea
はるばる all the way (from)
はれ 腫れが引く the swelling goes down ……[ひく]
はれ 晴れ
バレエ (a) ballet
パレード a parade
バレーボール volleyball
はれぎ 晴れ着 *one's* best (clothes)
　・*one's* best set of clothes ……[つく²]
パレスチナ Palestine
　〜の Palestinian
　〜人 a Palestinian; (全体) the Palestinians
はれた 晴れた fine, fair
はれつ 破裂する burst, explode
パレット a palette
はればれ 〜とした[て] cheerful, in high spirits

バレリーナ　a ballerina
はれる　晴れる　clear up ……………[のち]
はれる　腫れる　swell, become swollen
ばれる　come out, come to light
・get out ………………………[おびえる]
・be uncovered ………………[こわれる]
バレンタインデー　St. Valentine's Day
パロディー　(a) parody
バロメーター　a barometer
ハワイ　Hawaii
　～の　Hawaiian
はん　半
はん　判　a seal; (事務用の) a stamp
　～を押す　seal, stamp
　・place *one's* seal on ……………[おす]
はん　班　a group
ばん　晩　an evening; (夜) a night
ばん　番
パン　bread; (ロールパン) a roll; (味つき小型ロールパン) a bun
　～1斤　a loaf of bread
　～1枚　(食パン) a slice of bread
　～食い競争　a bread eating contest
　　………………………………………[とる¹]
　～くず　a bread crumb ………[はじく]
　～の耳　the heel of the bread　[みみ]
　～屋　(人) a baker; (店) a bakery
　～を焼く　(作る) bake bread
　　　　　　(トーストにする) toast bread　[やく³]
はんい　範囲
はんえい　反映する　reflect
はんえい　繁栄する　prosper
　～して　prosperous
はんが　版画　a (woodblock) print
ハンガー　a hanger
ばんかい　ばん回する　recover, regain
はんかく　反核　against nuclear weapons ……………………………[こえ]
　～運動　the anti-nuclear [ban-the-bomb] movement
　　………………………………………[うんどう]
はんかく　半角文字　《コンピュータ》a single-byte character
はんがく　半額で　at half the price
ハンカチ　a handkerchief
ハンガリー　Hungary
　～の, ～語　Hungarian
　～人　a Hungarian; (全体) the Hungarians
バンガロー　a bungalow
はんかん　反感
はんき　反旗を翻す　rebel against
　　………………………………………[たいする]
はんきゅう　半球　a hemisphere
　北〔南〕～　the Northern〔Southern〕Hemisphere
はんきょう　反響　(音) an echo; (反応) (a) response; (大評判) a sensation
　～を呼ぶ　cause a sensation ……[よぶ]
パンク　a puncture
　～する　get a flat tire
　・have a flat tire ………………[こんな]
ハングアップ　～する　《コンピュータ》hang up
バンクーバー　Vancouver
ばんぐみ　番組　a program
バングラデシュ　Bangladesh
　～の　Bangladeshi
　～人　a Bangladeshi; (全体) the Bangladeshis
はんけい　半径　a radius
はんけつ　判決　a judgment, a sentence
　・a verdict ………………………[したがう]
　・a court decision ……………[わりきる]
　～文　a verdict ………………[おごそか]
はんげつ　半月　a half moon
ばんけん　番犬　a watchdog ………[き]
はんこう　反抗
　～する　rebel ……………………[きびしい]
はんこう　犯行　a crime ……[ちがいない]
ばんごう　番号　a number
　電話～　a telephone [phone] number
バンコク　Bangkok
ばんこく　万国の　international
　～旗　the flags of all nations
　～博覧会　a world exposition
はんざい　犯罪　a crime
　～人　a criminal
　～を犯す　commit a crime
ばんざい　万歳　cheers; hurrahs
ハンサム　～な　handsome, good-looking
ばんさん　晩餐　(正餐) a dinner
　～会　a dinner (party)
はんじ　判事　a judge
ばんじ　万事　everything ………[つごう]

はんして (…に)反して against
・contrary to ……………………[よき]
はんしゃ 反射
はんじゅく 半熟の soft-boiled, half-boiled
はんじょう 繁盛 prosperity
～して prosperous
～する prosper
・business is good ……………[わらう]
はんしょく 繁殖する breed
はんすう 半数 half (the number)
はんする 反する
思想に～ be in contradiction to *one's* way of thinking ………[しそう]
はんせい 反省
～する think about what *one* did wrong ………………………[なまぬるい]
・reflect on ……………………[ふりかえる]
はんせん 反戦運動 an anti-war movement ……………………[しどう]
ハンセンびょう ハンセン病 leprosy
ばんそう 伴奏 accompaniment
～する accompany
ばんそうこう a first-aid bandage;《商標》a Band-Aid
はんそく 反則 a foul play, a violation of the rules
～する play foul, commit a foul, violate the rules
はんそで 半そでで[の] short-sleeved
……………………………………[とおす]
パンダ a (giant) panda
はんたい 反対
～意見を持っている be at odds with
……………………………………[てってい]
～運動 a demonstration against
……………………………………[かく～]
～者 a dissenter ……………[なかば]
～する be against ……………[たとえ]
・take issue with ………………[むき]
・be opposed to ………………[けんせつ]
～を押し切る defy the opposition
……………………………………[しゅうい]
はんだん 判断
～に迷う be hard to decide [まよう]
ばんち 番地 (区域の番号) a lot number; (家の番号) a house number

パンチ a punch
～を打つ punch
パンツ (下着) underpants; (女性用の) panties; (ブリーフ) briefs; (運動用の) shorts; (ズボン) pants
ばんづけ 番付 a ranking list [しゃかい]
はんてい 判定する judge, decide, rule
ボールの～《野球》call on the pitch
……………………………………[くうき]
パンティー panties
パンティーストッキング (a pair of) panty hose
ハンディキャップ a handicap
はんてん 斑点 a spot, a speck
バント《野球》a bunt
～する bunt (the ball)
バンド (ベルト) a belt; (帽子のバンド, ゴムバンドなど) a band; (楽団) a band
はんとう 半島 a peninsula
はんどう 反動 (a) reaction
～的 reactionary
バンドエイド《商標》a Band-Aid
～を貼る put a Band-Aid on
はんとし 半年 half a year,《米》a half year
ハンドバッグ a handbag,《米》a purse
ハンドボール《球技》handball
ハンドル (柄・取っ手) a handle; (自動車の) a (steering) wheel; (自転車の) handlebars
はんにん 犯人 the culprit ………[おう]
・a criminal …………………[こうみょう]
ばんにん 万人 everybody
～向き suited to everybody's taste
・of general interest …………[むき]
ばんねん 晩年 *one's* last years
……………………………………[こどく, さびしい]
はんのう 反応 (a) reaction (to), (a) response (to)
～する react (to), respond (to)
ばんのう 万能の all-round [around], all-purpose
はんぱ 半端な (余分な) spare; (残ったもの) what's left over
ハンバーガー a hamburger
ハンバーグ(ステーキ) a hamburger steak

はんばい 販売 sale
　～する sell
　～員 a salesman
はんぱつ 反発する （はね返す）repel; （反対する）oppose
はんはん 半々 fifty-fifty
はんぴれい 反比例する be in inverse proportion (to)
パンフレット a pamphlet, a brochure, a leaflet
はんぶん 半分
ハンマー a hammer
　～投げ （競技名）the hammer throw
はんめい 判明する become clear, prove
ハンモック a hammock ……………[つる¹]
ばんゆういんりょく 万有引力 universal gravitation ………………[なだかい]
はんらん 氾濫 a flood
　～する overflow, flood
はんろん 反論する retort, argue against
　・object ……………………………[りゆう]

ヒ

ひ 日
　～がさしてくる the sun comes shining (through) …………[きれる]
ひ 比 ratio
ひ 火 (a) fire
　～に油を注ぐ add fuel to the fire
　………………………………………[あぶら]
　～のないところに煙は立たない Where there's smoke, there's fire.
　………………………………………[けむり]
　～の回り ……………………………[まわり]
ひ 灯 a light
ひ 非 a fault ………………………[かちき]
　～を認める admit *one's* guilt [fault]
　………………………………………[ぜん～]
…ひ …費 ... expense ……………[いっさい]
び 美 beauty
ピアス pierced earrings
ピアニスト a pianist
ピアノ a piano
　～を習う study piano …………[つく⁴]
ヒアリング （語学などの聞き取り） listening comprehension

ピーアール PR, P.R., public relations
　～する （宣伝する）advertise
ひいおじいさん a great-grandfather
ひいおばあさん a great-grandmother
ひいき 最贔
ヒーター a heater
ビーチパラソル a beach umbrella
　………………………………………[さく¹]
ピーティーエー（PTA）a PTA
ピーナッツ a peanut
ひいまご ひい孫 a great-grandchild （複数 great-grandchildren）；（男）a great-grandson;（女）a great-granddaughter
ピーマン a green pepper
ビール beer
　缶～ canned beer
　生～ draft beer
ひえこみ 朝方の冷え込み the morning drop in temperature ………[こおる]
ひえる 冷える
ピエロ a clown ……………………[けんぶつ]
びえん 鼻炎 《医学用語》rhinitis
　・nasal inflammation ……[アレルギー]
ひがい 被害
　・damage, havoc ………………[くろう]
　～者 a [the] sufferer(s), a victim
　～者意識 a sense of being victimized, a sense of being a victim ………………………………[いしき]
　～地 the affected area
　～の状況 the extent of the damage
　………………………………………[しらべる]
ひかえ 控え a note;（写し）a copy;（副本）a duplicate
　～室 a waiting room
ひかえめ 控え目
ひがえり 日帰りする make it there and back the same day ……[できる]
　～旅行 a day's trip
ひかえる 控える
　投資を～ cut back on investments
　………………………………………[せつび]
　（…を）控えて in preparation for
　………………………………………[にもつ]
ひかく 比較
　～する make a comparison of
　………………………………………[こまかい]

ひかげ 日陰 the shade
 〜に out of the sun, in the shade ……………[おく¹]
 〜の shady
ひがさ 日傘 a parasol, an umbrella, a sunshade
ひがし 東 the east
 〜の east, eastern
 〜へ east, to [toward] the east
ひがしシナかい 東シナ海 the East China Sea
ぴかぴか 〜の shiny, glittering, well-polished
ひがむ 僻む
ひかり 光 light, a beam; (せん光) a flash; (輝き) (a) sparkle
ひかる 光る
 ・glimmer ……………………[にぶい]
 (目が) glint ……………………[するどい]
ひかれる find someone appealing ……………………[けれど(も)]
 ・be attracted (by) ……………[せんさい]
ひかれる 車に〜 be hit by a car ……………………[あやうく]
ひかん 悲観
 〜的に pessimistically ……………[むき]
ひがん 彼岸 the equinoctial week
ひきあい 引き合い an inquiry
ひきあげる 引き上げ・揚げる
ひきいる 率いる lead
ひきうける 引き受ける
 ・take on ……………………[き]
 仕事を〜 take a job ……………[うごかす]
ひきおこす 引き起こす bring about
 ・cause ……………………[もんだい]
ひきかえ 引き換えに in exchange (for)
ひきかえす 引き返す
ひきがね 引き金 a trigger
 〜となる trigger
ひきこもる 引きこもる withdraw (into) ……………………[せかい]
ひきさがる 引き下がる back out, back down
ひきさく 引き裂く (仲を) destroy ……………………[なか²]
ひきざん 引き算 subtraction
 〜する subtract
ひきしお 引き潮 the ebb

ひきしまる 引き締まる (緊張する) become tense
ひきしめる 引き締める (気を) brace up
ひきずる 引きずる drag
ひきだし 引出し a drawer
ひきだす 引き出す pull out, extract; (預金を) draw out, take out
ひきたつ 引き立つ (表れる) be brought out; (目立つ) stand out
ひきつぐ 引き継ぐ take over
ひきつける 引きつける attract
ひきとめる 引き止める stop someone from going ……………………[つかむ]
ひきとる 引き取る (商品を) take back; (世話をする) take care of
ビキニ a bikini
ひきにく 挽肉 minced beef [pork], ground meat
ひきにげ ひき逃げ a hit-and-run case
 〜する hit and run
ひきぬく 引き抜く pull out; (人材を) pick
ひきのばす 引き伸ばす (写真を) enlarge; (延長する) extend; (延期する) put off
ひきょう 卑怯
ひきわけ 引き分け a tied game, a tie (game)
 ・a tie, a draw ……………………[しあい]
ひく 引く
ひく 弾く (楽器を) play
ひく 轢く (車が) run over
ひく (のこぎりで) saw; (うすで) grind
ひくい 低い
ひくつ 卑屈
ビクトリア 〜湖 Lake Victoria
ピクニック a picnic
 〜に行く go on a picnic, go picnicking
びくびく
ピクルス pickles ……………………[つめる]
ひぐれ 日暮れ (日没) nightfall, sunset; (夕方) evening
ひげ (口ひげ) a mustache; (あごひげ) a beard; (ほおひげ) whiskers, 《米》 sideburns
 〜をそる shave (oneself)

ひげき 悲劇　a tragedy
　〜的な　tragic
ひけつ 否決する　reject, vote down
　..[あん]
ひけつ 秘訣　a [the] secret (to, of), the key (to)
　・the trick ....[のむ]
ひけめ 引け目を感じる　feel inferior (to *someone*), feel small
ひけらかす　show off, display
ひこう 非行　delinquency ....[め²]
　・delinquent behavior ....[ぬく]
　〜に走る　be led into delinquency
　..[ゆうわく]
　〜問題　the delinquency problem
　..[あげる]
　青少年の〜　juvenile delinquency
　..[もんだい]
びこう 尾行する　shadow
ひこうき 飛行機　an airplane, a plane
　〜墜落事故　a plane crash ....[なくす²]
　〜に乗る　board the plane ....[だく]
　〜で行く　go by plane, fly
ひこうし 飛行士　an aviator
ひこうしき 非公式の　informal, unofficial
　〜に　informally, privately
ひこうじょう 飛行場　(小規模の) an airfield; (空港) an airport
ひこく 被告(人)　(一般に) a defendant
　..................................[きたい, とりまく]
　(特に刑事訴訟の) the accused
ひごと 日ごとに　day by day
　・daily ....[ひろまる]
ひごろ 日頃の　everyday, daily
　〜から　always
ひざ (ひざ頭) a knee; (ももの上) a lap
　〜が抜ける　be worn out at the knees ....[ぬける]
ビザ　a visa
　〜を取る　get a visa
ピザ　(a) pizza
ひさい 被災地　the scene of the disaster ....[ほうこく]
ひさし (家の) eaves; (帽子の) a visor
ひざし 日差し　sunlight .....[こころよい]
　・sun ....[やける]
ひさしい 久しい　long

久しく　for a long time
ひさしぶり 久しぶり
　〜だ　it's been a long while [time] since... ....[こんな]
　〜に　for the first time in a long while ....[たずねる²]
　・for the first time in a long time
　..[はなし]
　〜の　the first *something* in a long time
　・after a long absence ....[おもいで]
ひざまずく　kneel down, †fall [go down] on *one's* knees
ひさん 悲惨
　〜な　miserable, tragic
ひじ　an elbow
ひしがた ひし形　a lozenge;《数学用語》a rhombus
ビジネス　business
　〜ホテル　no-frills hotel
　〜マン　a businessman, an office worker
ひしゃく　a dipper, a ladle
びじゅつ 美術　art, the fine arts
　〜界　the art world ....[いち]
　〜館　an art museum, a gallery
　〜的　artistic
　〜展　an art exhibition
　〜品　a work of art ....[ながめる]
ひしょ 秘書　a secretary ....[がまん]
ひしょ 避暑に行く　go for the summer
　〜客　a summer visitor
　〜地　a summer resort ...[じょうけん]
ひじょう 非常
　〜に　exceptionally ....[すぐれる]
　〜のとき　in an emergency [おちつく]
　〜口　an emergency exit
びしょう 微笑　a smile
　〜する　smile, give a smile
ひじょうしき 非常識
びしょぬれ 〜になる　get wet to the skin, be wet through, be drenched to the skin
びじん 美人　a beauty, a beautiful woman, a pretty girl
　・an attractive girl ....[とりまく]
　〜コンテスト　a beauty contest
　..[のぞく¹]

ひじんどうてき 非人道的な inhumane ……[なくす¹]

ビスケット 《英》a biscuit, 《米》a cracker, a cookie

ピストル a pistol; (連発式) a revolver; 《米口語》a gun

ひそかに secretly
- on the sly ……[はな]

ひそめる 声をひそめる lower one's voice ……[こえ]

ひだ a pleat, a fold

ひたい 額 the forehead
〜に汗して by the sweat of one's brow ……[あせ]
〜にしわを寄せる knit one's brow ……[しわ]

ひたす 浸す (水分を含ませる) soak; (つける) dip

ひたすら 〜する do nothing but *do*

ビタミン (a) vitamin ……[ふくむ]
〜剤 vitamin pills

ひたむき 〜な earnest, single-minded
〜に(…に従事する) devote *oneself* to *something*

ひだり 左 the left
〜利きの left-handed ……[のぞく¹]
〜下がり slope down to the left ……[さがる]

ひっかかる 引っ掛かる
(骨がのどに) get stuck ……[ほね]

ひっかく scratch

ひっかける have *something* caught

ひつぎ a coffin
- a casket ……[わかれ]

ひっき 筆記する write down, take notes of
〜試験 a written examination
〜用具 writing materials

ひっきりなし ひっきりなしに (ずっと続いて) continually; (絶え間なく) continuously; (休みなしに) without a break

ビッグバン (宇宙の起源) the Big Bang

びっくり

ひっくりかえす ひっくり返す (倒す) upset; (裏返す) turn inside out

ひっくりかえる ひっくり返る (横倒しになる) be upset; (上下に) turn upside down
- lie upside down ……[めちゃくちゃ]

ひづけ 日付 a date
〜を書く date

びっこ 〜を引いて歩く walk with a limp

ひっこし 引っ越し moving, removal
〜先 one's new address

ひっこす 引っ越す
- move away ……[あいさつ]
引っ越して来る move in …[あいさつ]

ひっこみじあん 引っ込み思案な shy

ひっこむ 引っ込む

ひっこめる 引っ込める

ヒツジ 羊 a sheep; (小羊) a lamb

ひっし 必死

ひっしゅう 必修の required
〜科目 required subject

ひつじゅひん 必需品 necessaries, necessities

びっしょり be soaked with ……[あせ]

ひっせき 筆跡 (a) handwriting

ひっそり 〜した quiet; (人けのない) deserted

ひったくり (人) a purse-snatcher

ぴったり
- perfectly ……[あう¹]
- completely ……[いっち]

ピッチ (速さ) (a) speed; (ペース) a pace

ヒッチハイク hitchhiking

ピッチャー 《野球》a pitcher

ピッチング 《野球》pitching

ピッツバーグ Pittsburgh

ひってき 匹敵する match, equal

ヒット

ひっぱく 逼迫する be on the verge of a crisis ……[けいざい]

ひっぱる 引っ張る

ヒップ hips

ひつよう 必要
(…する)必要はない there's no reason for *someone* to *do* ……[うしろめたい]
〜経費 a necessary expense [おとす]
〜性 the need ……[せつじつ]

ひてい 否定の, 否定的な negative
〜する deny

ビデオ （機械） a video, a videocassette recorder, VCR
〜屋 （レンタル） a video rental shop
〜にとる record, videotape
〜テープ a video tape
ひでり 日照り dry weather
・blistering heat ……………[かれる²]
・drought ……………………[かわく]
〜が続いて under the constant blaze of the sun ………………………[かれる¹]
ひと 人 （男または男女を代表して） a man （複数 men）; （女） a woman （複数 women）; （男女の区別なく） a person （複数 people）; 《文語》 one
（人員） personnel ……………[ふやす]
〜がいい be too easygoing for *one's* own good ……………………[いい]
〜の上に立つ人間 a leader ……[うえ]
ひとあしちがい 一足違いで just miss ………………………………[あし]
ひどい 酷い
〜目にあう have a terrible time ………………………………[あう²]
・be in big trouble ……………[ひどい]
ひといき 一息に at a stretch; （一飲みに） at a gulp
もう〜 a little more work [effort]
〜つく catch *one's* breath ……[おえる]
ひといちばい 人一倍 extraordinarily ………………………………[いよく]
・far more...than the average person ………………………………[おもいやり]
ひとかげ 人影 a man's shadow
・a figure ………………………[みえる]
・a figure ………………………[はるか]
（一人） a soul ……………………[あたり¹]
ひとがら 人柄 personality
・character ……………………[おうよう²]
ひときれ 一切れ a piece, a slice
ひどく severely, heavily, hard
・quite ……………………………[おうぼう]
・terribly, awfully ……………[ぐあい]
・seriously ……………………[けが]
・extremely ……………………[わかる]
びとく 美徳 a virtue
ひとくち 一口 （食べ物の） a mouthful, a bite; （飲み物の） a draft, a sip
〜乗せる let *someone* in on a piece of the action ………………………[のせる]
ひとこと 一言多い say one word too many ……………………………[おおい]
ひとごと 他人事 be other people's [someone else's] affairs, have nothing to do with *one*
ひとごみ 人込み a crowded place ………………………………[よう²]
・a crowd ………………………[わける]
ひところ for a time ………[りゅうこう]
ひとごろし 人殺し （行為） (a) murder; （人） a murderer
ひとさしゆび 人差し指 a forefinger, an index finger
ひとさわがせ 人騒がせなことをする raise a ruckus, cause a commotion
ひとしい 等しい
ひとじち 人質 a hostage ………[しげき]
〜にする take *someone* as a hostage
〜を救出する rescue a hostage ………………………………[きょうこう]
ひどすぎる ひど過ぎる too awful ………………………………[たいてい]
ひとすじ ……一筋だ live only for, devote *oneself* to
ひとそろい ひと揃い （道具の） a set; （衣類の） a suit
ひとつ 一つ one
もう〜 another ………………[たてる²]
〜一つ one by one …………[かぞえる]
〜間違えば one slipup and... ………………………………[ゆだん]
ひとづかい 人使いが荒い push *someone* too hard ……………[あらい¹]
〜の荒い人 an over-demanding person, a slave driver
ひとづて 人づてに聞く hear [pick up] *something* secondhand, hear (*something*) through [by] the grapevine
ひとで 人手 （働き手） a hand; （助力） help
・people, hands ………………[あまる]
〜不足 lack of manpower ……[ぬく]
・a lack of help ………………[ふそく]
ヒトデ a starfish
ひととおり 一とおり（のこと） the basics, the rudiments ………[わかる]

ひとどおり 人通り traffic
～が多い busy, bustling
～が少ない empty, almost deserted
ひとなつっこい 人懐っこい (人・動物が) friendly, amiable; (動物が) love [like] people
ひとなみ 人並みの ordinary ……[なみ]
～に just like everybody else [なみ]
ひとねむり ひと眠りする take a nap ……………………………………[さめる²]
ひとのふり 人の振り見てわが振り直せ You can better yourself by observing others. ………[ふり¹]
ひとのみち 人の道に外れている be immoral ……………………………[たとえ]
ひとはた 一旗揚げる make it big ……………………………………[あげる]
ひとばん 一晩のうちに in a single night ……………………………[うち]
ひとばんじゅう 一晩じゅう all night long ……………………………[なやます]
・till dawn ……………………………[～じゅう]
ひとびと 人々 people
ひとまえ 人前で in front of people ………………………………………[いう]
・in front of others ……………[てれる]
～に出ると in front of people ……………………………………[あがる]
ひとまず (まずは) first; (当座は) for the moment
ひとまわり 一回りする go around
～大きい the next larger size
年齢が～違う be about 12 years apart ………………………………[まわり]
ひとみ 瞳 the pupil (of the eye)
ひとみしり 人見知りの shy
ひとめ 一目で at first sight ……[すき¹]
・at a glance ……[～だけのことがある]
～見る have a look at, glance at
ひとめ 人目を引く attract notice
・draw attention ………………[ひく]
～を避ける avoid being noticed ……………………………………[さける²]
～につかずに without being noticed
～を盗んで in secrecy, by stealth ……………………………………[ぬすむ]
ひとやく 一役買う play a part [role] in
・take part in ……………………[やく¹]
ひとやすみ 一休みする take a (short) rest
・take a break ………………[やすみ]
ひとやま 一山当てる make a killing [pile] ………………………………[やま]
ひとり 一人(の) one, a(n)
一人ひとり one by one, one after another, each
ひどり 日取りを決める arrange the date ……………………………[あわせる]
ひとりぐらし 一人暮らし living by *oneself* ………………………[さびしい]
～をする live alone ……………[きらく]
ひとりごと ひとり言をいう say to *oneself*, speak to *oneself*
・talk to *oneself* ………………[いう]
ひとりたび 一人旅する travel alone ……………………………………[ぼうけん]
ひとりっこ 一人っ子 an only child
ひとりで 一人[独り]で (連れがいないで) alone, by *oneself*; (独力で) *oneself*, by [for] *oneself*
・by *oneself* ……………………[きる²]
・for *oneself* ……………………[うまい]
ひとりでに of *oneself*
ひとりぶたい ひとり舞台 a one-man performance ……………………[ぶたい]
ひとりぼっち 独りぼっちで all alone, by *oneself*
ひとりむすこ〔むすめ〕 一人息子〔娘〕 an [*one's*] only son 〔daughter〕
ひとりよがり 独りよがりの[で] self-righteous, be too full of *oneself*
ひな a chick
ヒナギク a daisy
ひなた 日なた
ひなまつり ひな祭り the Doll [Girl's] Festival
ひなん 非難
～する reproach ………………[こうげき]
～の怒号 a barrage of censure ……………………………………[ゆうゆう]
～の的 the object of criticism [まと]
ひなん 避難 shelter, refuge
～訓練 an evacuation drill

〜訓練を行う hold an evacuation drill ……………[ひじょう]
〜所 a shelter
〜する take shelter [refuge] (from, in)
〜民 refugees
ビニール vinyl, plastic
〜袋 a plastic bag
ひにく 皮肉
・a sarcastic comment ………[おもい²]
ひにひに 日に日に day by day ……………[ぎじゅつ]
ひねくれる
びねつ 微熱 a slight fever …[しんさつ]
ひねる
ひのいり 日の入り the sunset
ひのうちどころ 非の打ちどころがない can't be criticized …………[どの〜]
ひので 日の出 the sunrise
ひのまる 日の丸 the Rising-Sun flag
ひばち 火鉢 a Japanese (charcoal) brazier
ひばな 火花 a spark
ヒバリ a skylark, a lark
ひはん 批評
ひばん 非番である be off (duty)
ひび a crack …………………[つめる]
〜が入る crack, be cracked
ひびき 響き (音) a sound; (反響) an echo
ひびく 響く
ひひょう 批評
びひん 備品 equipment …………[うつ]
ひふ 皮膚 the skin
〜病 a skin disease
〜癌 skin cancer
びふう 微風 a breeze, a gentle wind
ビフテキ (a) beefsteak
びぶん 微分 differential calculus
ひま 暇
・a free moment …………[ぬすむ]
〜さえあれば …………………[むかう]
〜を作る find some time ……[つくる]
ひまご ひ孫 a great-grandchild (複数 great-grandchildren); (男) a great-grandson; (女) a great-granddaughter
ひましに 日増しに day by day, every day
ヒマラヤ 〜山脈 the Himalayas, the Himalaya Mountains
ヒマワリ a sunflower
ひまん 肥満 fatness; (肥満症) obesity
ひみつ 秘密
〜がばれる the secret is disclosed ……………………[びくびく]
〜を漏らす leak the secret [うたがう]
びみょう 微妙
ひめい 悲鳴 a cry, a scream
〜をあげる give a cry
・scream ………………………[あげる]
ひも a string; (太めの) a cord; (平たい) a tape
ひもの 干物 a dried fish
ひやあせ 冷や汗 a cold sweat ….[あせ]
ひやかす 冷やかす
ひゃく 百 a [one] hundred
第100(の) the hundredth (略 100th)
100分の1 a [one] hundredth, one percent
ひゃくまん 百万 a million
〜長者 a millionaire
ひやけ 日焼け (健康的な) suntan; (炎症) sunburn
〜する get tanned; get sunburned [sunburnt]
〜サロン a tanning salon
ヒヤシンス a hyacinth
ひやす 冷やす
ひゃっかじてん 百科事典 an encyclopedia ……………[がくしゅう]
ひゃっかてん 百貨店 《米》a department store, 《英》the stores
ひやひや ……………………[はらはら]
ヒューストン Houston
ひゆてき 比喩的な figurative
・metaphorical ……………[ひょうげん]
ひよう 費用
ヒョウ a leopard, a panther
ひょう 表 (一覧表) a table; (目録) a list
ひょう 票 a vote
〜を読む make a projection of the votes ……………………[よむ]
ひょう 雹 hail; (一粒の) a hailstone
びよう 美容(術) beauty, beauty art;

(手入れ) (a) cosmetic treatment
～院 a beauty parlor, a hairdresser's
～師 a hairdresser, a beautician
・a hair stylist ……………………[うで]
～体操 (shaping-up) exercises
びょう 秒 a second
びょう 鋲 a tack; (画びょう) a thumbtack, 《英》a drawing pin; (鉄板の) a rivet
～でとめる tack (up, on, to)
びょういん 病院 a hospital
～に運ばれる be taken to the hospital ……………………[つつむ]
ひょうか 評価
・appraisal ……………………[しゅかん]
～する evaluate ……………………[こうせい]
ひょうが 氷河 a glacier
～期 the ice age ……………………[いきる]
びょうき 病気
～が重い be seriously [critically, dangerously] ill ……………[あぶない]
～で倒れる fall sick ……………[つごう]
ひょうきん ～な jocular, funny, comical
～者 a joker, a clown
ひょうけいさん 表計算(ソフト)《コンピュータ》a spreadsheet (program), spreadsheet software
びょうけつ 病欠届け a notification for absence due to illness [しょうめい]
ひょうげん 表現
ひょうこう 標高 a [the] height above sea level
ひょうさつ 表札 a nameplate, a doorplate
ひょうざん 氷山 an iceberg
～の一角 only the tip of an iceberg
ひょうし 表紙 a cover ……………[する¹]
ひょうしき 標識 a sign, a marker
びょうしつ 病室 a sickroom; (病院の共同の・大部屋) a ward
びょうしゃ 描写する describe, portray
びょうじゃく 病弱な frail ……[ちから]
・sickly ……………………[くろう]
ひょうじゅん 標準
・average ……………………[ひくい]
～語 standard speech ………[ふきゅう]
ひょうしょう 表彰する commend, award, give *someone* a commendation
～状 a testimonial
ひょうじょう 表情
～が明るくなる *one's* face brightens [lights] up ……………[あかるい]
びょうじょう 病状 condition ……………………[てきする]
びょうしん 病身の sickly, weak
ひょうてん 氷点 the freezing point
びょうどう 平等な equal; (公平な) impartial
～に equally, impartially
・evenly ……………………[りえき]
びょうにん 病人 a sick person; (患者) a patient; (総称) the sick
ひょうはくざい 漂白剤 bleach [おちる]
ひょうばん 評判
・a review ……………………[みじめ]
ひょうほん 標本 a specimen
ひょうめん 表面
びょうよみ 秒読み a countdown
ひょうりゅう 漂流する drift
ひょうろん 評論 a review, a critical essay
～家 a reviewer, a critic
～する review, comment (on), make comments (on)
ひよけ 日よけ a sunshade, a blind
ひよこ a chick; a chicken
ひょっこり ～する just happen to *do*
ひょっとして maybe, possibly, by any chance, happen to *do*
ピョンヤン 平壌 Pyongyang
ビラ (ちらし) a bill, a handbill, a flier; (はり札・ポスター) a poster
～をまく hand [pass] out handbills ……………………[まく¹]
ひらきなおる 開き直る (敵対的な態度を取る) get defensive, assume a defiant attitude, turn on *someone*
ひらく 開く
ひらける 開ける (発展する) develop; (広々とする) open (out)
ひらたい 平たい
ひらてうち 平手打ちを食わす slap *someone* across the face ……[うつ]
ピラミッド a pyramid

ヒラメ　a flatfish, a flounder
・a turbot ……………[くべつ]
ひらめき　a flash
ひらめく　flash
びり　the last, the bottom
ピリオド　《米》a period, 《英》a full stop
ひりひり　〜する　sting ………[しみる]
　〜と痛い　smart ……………[いたい]
ぴりぴり　〜する　(神経が) nervous, touchy, uptight
ひりょう　肥料　(おもに自然物) manure; (おもに化学肥料) fertilizer
　〜をやる　fertilize ………[できる]
　化学〜　chemical fertilizer
ひる　昼　(正午) noon; (昼間) the daytime, day
　〜に　(昼間に) during the day, in the daytime; (正午に) at noon
　〜でも　even in the middle of the afternoon ……………[ぶきみ]
　〜飯　lunch
　〜休み　a noon recess, a noon [lunch] break
　・lunch hour ………[〜まで(に)]
ビル　a building, an office building
ピル　(丸薬) a pill; (経口避妊薬) a (contraceptive) pill
ひるい　比類のない　incomparable
　………………………………[いみ]
ひるね　昼寝　a nap
　〜をする　take a nap
ひるま　昼間　the daytime
　〜は　by day
ビルマ　Burma
　〜人　a Burmese (複数 Burmese)
　〜の　Burmese
ひるむ
　・flinch ……………[なぐる]
ひれ　a fin
ひれい　比例　proportion; (比率) ratio
　〜して　in proportion to
　〜代表制　proportional representation
ひれつ　卑劣な　mean, dirty …[ち]
　・base ……………[みち]
ひろい　広い
ひろう　拾う

ひろう　疲労
　〜困憊する　be exhausted ……[やっと]
ひろうえん　披露宴　a wedding reception ……………[おおげさ]
ビロード　velvet
ひろがる　広がる
ひろげる　広げる
ひろさ　広さ　(幅) width, breadth; (面積) area
ひろば　広場　an open space, a square; (大広場) a plaza
ひろま　広間　a hall; (ホテルなどの) a saloon
ひろまる　広まる
ひろめる　広める　spread; make *something* known
ひろんりてきな　非論理的な　illogical
　………………………………[ことば]
ビワ　枇杷　a loquat
ひん　品
びん　便　(郵便)《米》mail, 《英》post; (飛行機) flight
　航空〜で　by air mail
　鉄道〜で　by rail
　船〜で　by ship
びん　瓶　a bottle; (広口) a jar
　〜詰めにする　bottle
ピン　a pin
　・a bobby pin ……………[とめる¹]
　安全〜　a safety pin
　ネクタイ〜　a tiepin
　ヘア〜　a hairpin
　〜でとめる　pin up, fasten with a pin
ひんい　品位が損なわれる ……[そこなう]
びんかん　敏感
　〜な　be attuned to ……[りゅうこう]
ピンク　pink
ひんけつ　貧血　anemia
　〜を起こす　have an attack of anemia, have a fainting fit, feel faint, have a blackout
ひんこん　貧困　poverty ……[はしる]
ひんしつ　品質　quality ………[てん]
　〜向上 ……………………[しつ]
ひんじゃく　貧弱
ひんしゅ　品種　(動植物の) a breed; (種類) a kind

ひんしゅく ～を買う scandalize, be scandalous
びんしょう 敏しょうな quick
 ～に quickly
びんじょう 便乗する (車に同乗する)《乗せてあげる人を主語にして》give *someone* a ride [lift]; (機会を利用する) use the opportunity (to *do*), jump on the bandwagon
ひんせい 品性の卑しい vulgar ……………………………………[いやしい]
ピンセット (a pair of) tweezers
びんせん 便箋 (とじこみの) a writing pad; (大型の) letter paper; (小型の) notepaper
びんそく 敏速な swift ………[てきせつ]
ピンチ a pinch, a crisis
ピンチヒッター a pinch hitter
ヒント
ピント (写真の) the focus; (話の) the point
 ～を合わせる (写真の) focus
 ～が合って (写真の) in focus
 ～がずれて (写真の) out of focus; (話の) off the point [mark], not to the point
ピンと ～張る stretch *something* taut ……………………………………[はる¹]
ピンとくる
ひんにょう 頻尿である feel the need to urinate frequently
ひんぱん 頻繁な frequent
 ～に frequently, often
ひんぷ 貧富の差 the gap between the rich and the poor ……………[さ]
びんぼう 貧乏
ピンポン ping-pong, table tennis

フ

ふ 府 a prefecture
ぶ 部 (部分) a part; (部門) a department; (クラブ) a club; (本の部数) a copy
ファースト《野球》(一塁) (the) first base; (一塁手) a first baseman
ファーストフード fast food
 ～店 a fast-food restaurant
ぶあいそう 無愛想
 ～な gruff, cranky, unsociable ……………………………………[ちかづく]
 ・brusque, unfriendly ………[ね]
ファイト fight
ファイル
ファインプレー a fine play
ファウル a foul
ファスナー a zipper …………[こわれる]
ファックス a facsimile, a fax
 ～で送る send *something* by facsimile
ファッション fashion
 ～雑誌 a fashion magazine ……[でる]
ファミリー a family
 ～レストラン a family(-style) restaurant
ふあん 不安
 ～を覚える sense an uneasiness ……………………………………[いう]
 ～を持つ feel insecure ……[ばくぜん]
ファン a fan, an admirer
 ～レター a fan letter;《集合的に》fan mail
ふあんてい 不安定な unstable ……………………………………[あんてい]
ふあんない 不案内である be unfamiliar, be a stranger
 ・not know *one's* way around ……………………………………[あんない]
ふい 不意
フィート a foot (複数 feet)
フィギュアスケート figure skating
ふいっち 不一致 (a) disagreement
フィラデルフィア Philadelphia
フィリピン the Philippines, the Philippine Islands
 ～の Philippine
 ～人 a Filipino; (全体) the Filipinos
フィルター a filter
 ～を付ける attach a filter …[つける¹]
 ～つき煙草 a filter-tip cigarette
フィルム a film
フィレンツェ Florence
フィンランド Finland
 ～の, ～語 Finnish
 ～人 a Finn; (全体) the Finns
ふう 封 a seal
 ～をする seal

～を切る cut *something* open, open
ふう 風
ふうか 風化する weather
ふうがわり 風変わりな strange, eccentric, odd
ふうきり 封切り release
　～映画 a newly-released film, a first-run film
ふうきる 封切る release
ふうけい 風景
ふうさ 封鎖する blockade
ふうさい 風采 an appearance
　～の上がらない unimpressive looking ················[あがる]
ふうし 風刺 (a) satire
　～的な satirical
ふうしゃ 風車 a windmill
ふうしゅう 風習 manners and customs
　・a custom ················[ほろびる]
　土地の～ local customs ····[したがう]
ふうしょ 封書 a sealed letter
ふうせん 風船 a balloon
　～を膨らませる blow up a balloon ················[ふくらむ]
ふうそく 風速 wind velocity
ふうぞく 風俗
　・manners ················[へんか]
ブーツ boots
ふうど 風土 (気候) (a) climate; (環境) (an) environment
フード a hood ················[つく²]
ふうとう 封筒 an envelope
ふうひょう 風評 a rumor ····[うむ]
ふうふ 夫婦 a couple; husband [man] and wife
　～げんかは犬も食わない ········[けんか]
ふうぶつ 風物 things; (生活と自然) life and nature
ふうみ 独特の風味 a distinctive flavor ················[ほす]
ブーム
フーリガン a hooligan
ふうりゅう 風流な elegant, tasteful, refined
ふうりょく 風力 wind force; (動力源) wind power
　～発電 wind power generation

ふうりん 風鈴 a wind chime ···[つるす]
プール a (swimming) pool
ふうん 不運
ふえ 笛 (横笛) a flute; (呼び子) a whistle
フェアプレー fair play
ふえいせい 不衛生な insanitary
ブエノスアイレス Buenos Aires
フェリー a ferry(boat)
ふえる 増・殖える
プエルトリコ Puerto Rico
フェロモン pheromone
フェンシング fencing
ぶえんりょ 無遠慮な (無作法な) rude, unreserved
フォーク a fork
フォークソング a folk song
フォークダンス a (folk) dance
フォーマット a format
フォルダ
フォント 《コンピュータ》a font
フカ 鱶 a shark
ふか 孵化した hatched ·······[じんこう²]
ぶか 部下 (総称) one's staff
　・one's workers ················[にがい]
　・one's subordinates ··········[こまかい]
ふかい 不快な (身体的に) uncomfortable; (気分的に) unpleasant, disagreeable
ふかい 深い
　～悲しみ deep sadness ········[うたう]
　～友情 a deep (sense of) friendship ················[ゆうじょう]
　深く愛する really love ········[あい]
　深く味わう appreciate fully ················[あじわう]
ふかいり 深入りする get too engrossed with ················[ひみつ]
ふかくじつ 不確実な uncertain
ふかけつ 不可欠の indispensable, essential
ふかこうりょく 不可抗力の inevitable, uncontrollable
ふかさ 深さ depth
ぶかっこう 不格好
ふかのう 不可能
ふかふか ～の fluffy, soft
ふかまる 深まる deepen

ふかみ 深み (深い所) the depths; (味わい) (a) depth
ふかめる 深める deepen
ふかんぜん 不完全な imperfect
ぶき 武器 (集合的に) arms; (個々の) a weapon
ふきかける 吹きかける (息を) blow on
ふきけす 吹き消す blow out
ふきげん 不機嫌
ふきこぼれる 吹きこぼれる boil over
ふきそく 不規則な irregular
ふきだす 吹き出す (風が) begin to blow; (おかしくて) burst out laughing, burst into laughter
ふきつ 不吉
ふきつける 吹きつける (風が) blow against; (液体を) spray
ふきとばす 吹き飛ばす blow away [off]
ふきとる 拭き取る wipe off [away] ・wipe ……………[くもり]
ぶきみ 不・無気味
ふきゅう 普及
ふきょう 不況 (business) depression, recession
ふきょう 布教する propagate, teach and spread a religion ・preach ……………[あらゆる]
ぶきよう 不器用
ぶきりょう 無器量な plain, homely
ふきん a dishcloth, a (table) napkin, a dishtowel
ふきん 付近
　この～ this neighborhood [れんぞく]
　～の nearby
ふく 服 clothes, (婦人・子ども用の) a dress, (背広) a suit
ふく 吹く
ふく 拭く
ふく～ 副～ assistant, vice
フグ 河豚 a globefish, a blowfish
ふくぎょう 副業 a job on the side
ふくざつ 複雑
ふくさよう 副作用 a side effect
ふくさんぶつ 副産物 a by-product
ふくし 福祉 welfare ……………[へらす]
　・(the) public welfare ……[はかる]
　～行政 welfare policy ……[ち]

～事業 a welfare project …[れいたん]
ふくしき 腹式呼吸 breathing from one's abdomen ……………[こきゅう]
ふくしゃ 複写 (写し) a copy
　～する copy, make a copy (of)
ふくしゅう 復習
ふくしゅう 復讐 (a) revenge
　～する take revenge (on), revenge oneself on
ふくじゅう 服従 obedience
　～する obey, be obedient (to)
ふくすい 腹水 《医学用語》ascites
ふくすう 複数の (2つ以上の) more than one
ふくせい 複製 (a) reproduction, a replica
ふくそう 服装
ふくつ 不屈の unyielding
ふくつう 腹痛 a stomachache, an abdominal pain
ふくびき 福引き a lottery ……[あたる]
ふくむ 含む
ふくめる 含める include
　…を含めて including something
ふくらはぎ a [the] calf
ふくらます blow up, inflate
ふくらみ the swell, a bulge
ふくらむ 膨らむ
ふくれる 膨れる
ふくろ 袋 a bag; (ズックの・布などの大きな) a sack
フクロウ an owl
ふくろこうじ 袋小路 a blind alley ……………[つめる]
ふけ dandruff
ふけいき 不景気
　・an economic slump ……………[まだ]
　・an economic recession ……[へらす]
ふけいざい 不経済な uneconomical; (金のかかる) expensive
ふけつ 不潔
ふける 老ける grow old
ふける 更ける grow [become] late, be advanced, wear on [away]
ふける 耽ける
ふけんこう 不健康な unhealthy, bad for the health
ふけんぜん 不健全な unwholesome

ふこう 不幸
  ・(a) misfortune ……[たね, かなしむ]
  ～中の幸い It could have been worse. ……[さいわい]
ふごうかく 不合格 failure
  ～になる fail (in)
ふこうへい 不公平
  ・unfairness ……[ぶつける]
ふごうり 不合理な irrational [ごうり]
ふさ (毛・糸などの) a tuft; (飾り房) a tassel; (果実の) a bunch
ブザー a buzzer
ふさい 夫妻 husband and wife, a couple
ふさい 負債 a debt ……[かかえる]
  ・liabilities ……[のぼる]
  ～がある be in debt
ふざい 不在 absence
  ～である be out, be away, be absent
ふさがる 塞がる (穴などが) be closed, be shut; (席・部屋などが) be occupied; (用がある) be busy, be engaged
ふさく 不作 a poor crop
  ・a bad harvest ……[ぜんこく]
ふさぐ 塞ぐ
ふざける
  ・clown around ……[たいてい]
ぶさほう 無作法 bad manners
  ～な ill-mannered
  ・rude ……[ちゅうい]
ふさわしい
  ・be suited for ……[～みたい]
プサン 釜山 Pusan
ふさんせい 不賛成である disapprove (of), be against
ふし 節
ふじ 不治の病 an incurable disease
ぶし 武士 a *samurai*, (a) warrior
ぶじ 無事
  ～な safe and sound ……[いる¹]
  ～で safely ……[よく¹]
ふしあわせ 不幸せな unhappy
ふしぎ 不思議
  ～だ it amazes me that...
    ……[おもいつく]
ふしぜん 不自然
ふしだら ～な (異性関係に) loose; (不道徳) immoral
ぶしつけ ～な rude, impolite, forward
ふしまつ 不始末 (a) misconduct
    ……[とく¹, せけん]
  ・carelessness, mismanagement
    ……[めんぼく]
ふじゆう 不自由
  何～なく without experiencing want
    ……[とむ]
  何～なく暮らす ……[おかげ]
  体の～な人たち the handicapped
    ……[けっしん]
ふじゅうぶん 不十分な insufficient
    ……[せつめい]
  ・inadequate ……[せつび]
ぶしょう 不精
ふしょう 負傷する be [get] injured [hurt]
  ～者 the wounded
  ・the injured ……[ただちに]
ぶじょく 侮辱
ふしん 不振 a slump
ふしん 不審
ふじん 夫人 a wife; (敬称) Mrs.
ふじん 婦人 a woman, a lady
ふしんせつ 不親切な unkind
ふせい 不正 an injustice ……[にくむ]
  ・dishonesty ……[ふり¹]
  ～な unjust; wrong; (不正直な) dishonest, foul
  ～事件 a scandal ……[うち]
  ～を働く do wrong (to); (競技で) play foul; (試験で) cheat
  ～乗車をする ride free on the train
    ……[きてい]
ふぜい 風情のある tasteful, charming
ふせいかく 不正確な inaccurate, incorrect
  ～に inaccurately
ふせいこう 不成功 (a) failure
ふせいみゃく 不整脈 《医学用語》 arrhythmia
ふせぐ 防ぐ
ふせっせい 不摂生 ……[もどる]
ふせる 伏せる
ふせんしょう 不戦勝 an unearned win
ぶそう 武装 armaments
  ～する arm *oneself*, be armed

ふそく 不足
 水～ a water shortage ……[くるしむ]
ふぞく 付属する be attached (to), belong (to)
ふぞろい 不ぞろいの irregular, not the same
ふた a lid, a cover; (瓶の) a cap
 ～を閉める put the lid back on
 ……………………………………[ぬける]
ふだ 札 a card; (瓶などの) a label; (荷札) a tag
ブタ 豚 a pig, 《米》a hog; 《集合的に》swine
 ～小屋 a pigsty, a pigpen
ぶたい 舞台
ふたご twins; (そのひとり) a twin
ふたしか 不確かな uncertain, unreliable, not certain, not definite
ふたたび 再び
ブダペスト Budapest
ふたまた 二またになる fork
ふたり 二人 the two ……………[こうへい]
ふたん 負担
ふだん 不断
ふだん 普段
 ～着 everyday clothes ……………[よそ]
ふち 縁 (端) an edge; (茶わん・帽子の) a brim; (眼鏡の) a rim; (川の) a bank
ぶちこわす ぶち壊す ruin, destroy
ふちゅうい 不注意
ふちょう 不調
ぶちょう 部長 a department [division] head [manager, chief]; (自分たちの) the [one's] boss
 ・a department head ……………[かいぎ]
ふつう 不通になる be interrupted, be suspended, be tied up
ふつう 普通
 ～列車 a local (train)
ぶっか 物価 prices ……………[あがる]
 ～が上がる prices go up …[きびしい]
 ～政策 a policy on price control
 ……………………………………[はげしい]
 ～の上昇 an increase in prices
 ……………………………………[よそう]
 ・escalating prices …………[おさえる]

ふっかつ 復活する revive, come back
 ～させる bring back ……………[つよい]
 ～祭 Easter
ぶつかる
ふっき 復帰する return, come back
ふっきゅう 復旧 recovery ……[ひかく]
 ～する (交通機関が) resume normal service
ぶっきょう 仏教 Buddhism
 ～徒 a Buddhist
 ～の Buddhist
ぶっきらぼう ～な blunt, curt
ぶつける
 ・bang …………………[まちがった[て]]
ふつごう 不都合な inconvenient; wrong
ふっこう 復興する 《人を主語にして》restore, reconstruct; 《物を主語にして》be restored, be reconstructed
ぶっしつ 物質
ぶっしょく 物色する (買う前に) shop around; (探す) look for
ぶつぞう 仏像 a Buddhist statue
 ……………………………………[かんせい]
ぶっそう 物騒だ not be safe [ちかごろ]
ぶったい 物体 a body, an object, (a) substance
ぶつだん 仏壇 a family Buddhist altar
ぶっつづけ ぶっ続けに straight (through), without a break, on end
ふっとう 沸騰する boil
フットボール football
ぶつぶつ ～言う murmur, mutter; (文句を) complain
ぶつぶつこうかん 物々交換(する) barter
ぶつり 物理(学) physics
 ～学者 a physicist
 ～的な physical
ふつりあい 不釣り合いな ill-matched, disproportionate
ぶつりゅう 物流 distribution, logistics
ふで 筆 a writing brush; (絵筆) a painting brush
 ～入れ a pencil case
ふてき 不敵な defiant ……[はらだたしい]

ふてきとう 不適当な unsuitable, unfit, improper (for, to *do*)
ふてぎわ 不手際 a mistake, a blunder, blundering
ふてくされる sulk, be sulky
ふでぶしょう 筆不精 be a poor [bad] letter writer, be a poor [bad] correspondent ……………[ぶしょう]

ふと
ふとい 太い
　太く thick …………………[たて]
ふとう 不当な unjust, unfair, unreasonable
ブドウ a grape
　〜園 a vineyard
ふとうこう 不登校である be truant from school, refuse to go to school
ふどうさん 不動産 real estate ……[て]
　〜業者 a real estate agent
ふどうとく 不道徳な immoral, wicked
ふとうめい 不透明な opaque
ふとくい 不得意な be poor at, be weak in, be not good at
ふとくてい 不特定の unspecified
ふところ 懐 (内ポケット) inside pocket
　〜が温かい rich …………[あたたかい]
　〜が寂しい not have much money on *one* ………………[さびしい]
ふとさ 太さ (a) thickness
ふともも 太もも a thigh
ふとる 太る
　・put on weight ………………[〜だけ]
　・gain weight ………………[ひかえめ]
ふとん *futon*; (寝装類) bedding; bed clothes
　掛け〜 a quilt
　敷き〜 a mattress
フナ 鮒 a crucian (carp)
ふなのり 船乗り a sailor, a seaman
ふなよい 船酔いする get seasick
ふなれ 不慣れだ be unaccustomed to, be unfamiliar with, be not used [accustomed] to
ぶなん 無難
ふにおちない 腑に落ちない not sit right with *one*, just can't understand

ふにん 不妊(症)の sterile, barren
ふにん 赴任する (新しい任務に) leave for *one's* new post; (転任する) be transferred
ふね 船 (大型の) a ship; (小型の) a boat; (汽船) a steamer, a steamship
　〜に酔う get seasick …………[はく¹]
プノンペン Phnom Penh
ふはい 腐敗 corruption ……[ほろぼす]
　〜した rotten; (墜落した) corrupt
ふび 不備 (不十分な点) (an) inadequacy; (誤り) a fault
ふひつよう 不必要な unnecessary, needless
ふひょう 不評だ be not well received, be not popular
　〜を買う invite criticism
ふびょうどう 不平等な unequal
ぶひん 部品 a part …………[こうかん¹]
ふぶき 吹雪 a snowstorm
　・a blizzard …………………[えらい]
ふふく 不服
ぶぶん 部分
ふへい 不平
ふへん 不変の (変えることができない) unchangeable; (永遠に不変の) eternal, everlasting
ふへん 普遍(性) universality
　〜的な universal
ふべん 不便
ふべんきょう 不勉強な idle, lazy, non-studying
ふほう 不法な unlawful, illegal, wrong
ふほんい 不本意
ふまじめ 不まじめ
ふまん 不満
　・frustration …………………[つもる]
　〜が爆発する dissatisfaction erupts …………………………[ばくはつ]
　〜をぶつける express *one's* dissatisfaction to …………[いきおい]
　・vent *one's* dissatisfaction to …………………………[ぶつける]
ふまんぞく 不満足な unsatisfactory
ふみきり 踏切 a (railroad) crossing; a level crossing
ふみだい 踏み台 a stool …………[のる]

（目的達成のための）a steppingstone
ふみたおす 踏み倒す （払わない）do not pay
ふみだす 踏み出す step out ……[あし]
ふみとどまる 踏みとどまる （自分を抑える）restrain *oneself*
ふみはずす 踏み外す miss a step
ふみん 不眠症 insomnia
ふむ 踏む
ふめい 不明な unknown
ふめいよ 不名誉 (a) dishonor, (a) shame
　～な dishonorable, shameful
ふめいりょう 不明瞭な （識別のつかない）indistinct; （漠然とした）obscure;
　（不明確な）unclear ……[はっきり]
ふめつ 不滅の immortal
ふもう 不毛の barren; （かいのない）fruitless
ふもと 麓 the foot
ぶもん 部門 a branch, a department, a field
ふやす 増やす
ふゆ 冬 winter
　～休み a winter vacation, 《英》winter holidays
ふゆかい 不愉快
ふよう 不要の （必要がない）unnecessary, needless; （無用の，むだな）useless
　～な物……………………………[つい]
ふよう 扶養する support
　～家族 a dependent
　～控除 deduction for dependents
ぶよう 舞踊 dancing; a dance
ぶようじん 不用心な （人が）careless; （状況が）not safe
フライ 《野球》a fly
フライ 《料理》fried *something*, deep-fried *something*
　～にする fry, deep-fry
プライド ～を持つ be proud of, take pride in
　～が高い have too much pride in *oneself*
プライバシー privacy
フライパン a frying pan
　・a skillet ……………………[かける¹]
ブラウザ 《インターネット》a browser
ブラウス a blouse
プラカード a placard
ぶらさがる ぶら下がる hang (down) (from)
ぶらさげる ぶら下げる （つるす）hang; （下げて持つ）carry
ブラシ a brush
ブラジリア Brasilia
ブラジル Brazil
　～の Brazilian
　～人 a Brazilian; （全体）the Brazilians
プラス
プラスチック(の) plastic
ブラスバンド a brass band
プラチナ platinum
ぶらつく walk about, wander
フラッシュ (a) flash
プラットフォーム a platform
プラネタリウム a planetarium
プラハ Prague
ふらふら
ぶらぶら （目的もなく）aimlessly; （怠けて）idly
　～する hang around ……[せけん]
フラミンゴ a flamingo
プラモデル a plastic model
　……………………………[くみたてる]
ぶらんこ a swing
フランス France
　～の，～語 French
　～人 （男）a Frenchman; （女）a Frenchwoman; （総称）the French
ブランデー brandy
ブランド a brand
　～物 designer goods
ふり 振り
ふり 不利
　・be at a disadvantage ……[どうみても]
～ぶり
フリー ～な （自由な）free
　～サイズ One Size Fits All
フリー ～の （職業）freelance
フリーウェア 《コンピュータ》freeware
フリーエージェント ～制 a free-agent system, free agency

フリーザー　a freezer
フリージア　a freesia
フリーズ
フリースクール　an alternative school
フリーズドライ　〜の　freeze-dried
ブリーフ　(a pair of) briefs
フリーマーケット　a flea market
ふりおとす　振り落とす　throw [shake] off
ぶりかえす　ぶり返す　(病気が) have a relapse
ふりかえる　振り返る
ブリキ　tin plate
　〜缶《米》a can,《英》a tin
　〜屋　a tinsmith
ふりこ　振り子　a pendulum　[しんどう]
ふりこむ　振り込む　(口座に) pay [deposit] *something* to a bank account
ふりだし　振り出しに戻る　go back to square one ……………………[もどる]
プリペイドカード　a prepaid card
ふりまわす　振り回す　swing; (凶器を) brandish
　振り回される　be misled
　………………………[まちがった[て]]
ふりむく　振り向く　turn around, turn *one's* head, look back (at), look behind
ブリュッセル　Brussels
ふりょ　不慮の事故　†an untimely [a sudden] accident ……………[みらい]
ふりょう　不良　(人) a delinquent
　〜品　a defective product ……[だます]
　〜債権　bad loans [debt], unpaid loans [debt]
ぶりょく　武力　military force
フリル　a frill
プリン　(a) (custard) pudding
プリンタ　a printer
プリント　a handout
　・a copy ……………………[わたる]
ふる　振る
　(異性を) reject ……………[みごと]
ふる　降る
…ぶる　pose as, assume the air of
ふるい　古い
　古くから　for a long time　[つたわる]
　古くて新しい問題　an age-old problem ……………………[ふるい]
ふるい　a sieve
　〜にかける　sift; (選ぶ) screen
ふるいおとす　ふるい落とす　screen out
ふるいたつ　奮い立つ　brace *oneself* (up), rise (to the occasion)
フルーツ　fruit
フルート　a flute
ふるえ　震え　a shake
ふるえる　震える
ブルガリア　Bulgaria
　〜の　Bulgarian
　〜人　a Bulgarian; (全体) the Bulgarians
ふるぎ　古着　old clothes, used clothes
ふるさと　故郷　*one's* home, *one's* home town, *one's* native place
　・*one's* old hometown ……[なつかしい]
ふるどうぐ　古道具屋　a secondhand store
ブルドーザー　a bulldozer
ブルドッグ　a bulldog
ふるほん　古本　a secondhand book
　・an old book ……………………[ほる]
　〜屋　(人) a secondhand book seller (店) a used book shop ……[のぞく²]
　・a secondhand [used] bookstore
　………………………[みつかる]
ふるまい　振る舞い　behavior, conduct
ふるまう　振る舞う　behave *oneself*
ぶれい　無礼な　rude, impolite
　〜な態度をとる　be rude to …[わびる]
プレイガイド　a ticket office, a ticket agency, a box office
プレー　(a) play
　・a performance ……………[みせる]
ブレーキ　a brake
　〜をかける　†apply [put on] the brake, brake
フレーム　a frame
プレーヤー　(選手・演奏家) a player; (CDプレーヤー) a (CD) player
ブレザー(コート)　a blazer
プレゼンテーション　〜をする　(make) a presentation
プレゼント　a present
フレックスタイム　〜制　flextime

プレッシャー
プレハブ ～住宅 a prefab(ricated) house
ふれる 触れる
ふろ 風呂 a bath
　～場 a bathroom
　～屋 a public bath
　～おけ a bathtub
　～に入る take [have] a bath
　～を浴びる take a bath ……[あびる]
　～上がりのビール a beer right after taking a bath ……[こたえる]
プロ a professional, a pro
　～の域 a professional level
　………………………[たっする]
ブローチ a brooch ………[つける¹]
ブロードバンド (の) 《インターネット》 broadband
　～で on broadband
ふろく 付録 a supplement; (別冊付録・おまけ) an extra; (巻末付録) an appendix
プログラマー a (computer) programmer
プログラム a program
ふろしき 風呂敷き *furoshiki*, a (Japanese) wrapping cloth
プロダクション promotion agency
　………………………[けいやく]
ブロック a concrete block
ブロッコリー broc(c)oli
フロッピー(ディスク) a floppy disk [disc]
プロデューサー a producer
プロバイダ 《インターネット》 a provider, an Internet service provider (略 ISP)
プロパンガス propane (gas)
プロフィール a profile
プロペラ a propeller
プロポーション (均整) (a) proportion (体型) a figure ………[りそう]
　～がいい have good proportions
　………………………[～として]
プロポーズ a proposal (of marriage), an offer (of marriage)
　～する propose (marriage) to, ask *someone* to marry *one*

ブロマイド a (star's) picture
フロリダ Florida
プロレス professional wrestling
フロン ～ガス 《商標》 Freon gas, chlorofluorocarbon (略 CFC)
フロント (ホテルの) the front desk, the reception desk
　～ガラス 《米》a windshield, 《英》a windscreen
ふわたり 不渡り小切手〔手形〕 a bad check [note], a dishonored check [note], a rubber check [note]
　～を出す write [pass] a rubber check [note], bounce a check [note]
　～になる The check [note] bounced.
ふん (軽べつや不満を表して) Humph!
ふん 分 (時間) a minute
ふん 糞 (動物や鳥の) droppings
ぶん 分 (分け前) a share
　この～では at this rate ……[おそらく]
ぶん 文 (a sentence; (作文) a composition; (文章) writings
ふんいき 雰囲気
　(どこそこに)(…な)雰囲気が漂う an...air pervades *someplace*
　………………………[そうごん]
ふんか 噴火 an eruption
　～する go into eruption
　・erupt ………………………[くりかえす]
　～口 a crater
ぶんか 文科 (人文科学) the humanities
　～系 the humanities course
ぶんか 文化 culture
　～遺産 a cultural treasure …[ほぞん]
　～勲章 an Order of Cultural Merit Award ………………………[もらう]
　～交流 cultural exchange
　～祭 (学校の) an open house, a school festival ………[かつやく]
　・a cultural festival ………[よさん]
　～財 cultural assets
　～的 cultural
ふんがい 憤慨
ぶんかい 分解する take *something* †apart [to pieces]
ぶんがく 文学 literature

〜の　literary
〜作品　a literary work
〜者　a man of letters, a literary man, a writer
〜博士　Doctor of Literature
〜部　the literature department
ぶんかちょう　文化庁　the Agency for Cultural Affairs
ぶんかつ　分割する　divide
〜払い　payment in installments
〜払いで　on an installment plan
ぶんかのひ　文化の日　Culture Day
ふんきゅう　紛糾する　get complicated ……………………………[まとまる]
ぶんぎょう　分業　division of labor
ぶんけん　文献　(a) literature, a book
ぶんこ　文庫　(本) a pocket book [edition], a paperback; (図書館) a library; (蔵書) a collection
ぶんこう　分校　a branch school
ぶんごう　文豪　a great writer ……[また]
ぶんこぼん　文庫本　a paperback
ぶんさん　分散する[させる]　scatter, disperse
ぶんし　分子　(化学) molecule; (分数の) a numerator; (政治上の) an element
ふんしつ　紛失　(a) loss
〜物　a lost [missing] article
〜物取扱窓口　a lost-and-found window
〜する　lose
ぶんしょ　文書　(書類) a document; (記録) a record
ぶんしょう　文章　writing …[ぎこちない]
・a passage ………………………[こせい]
しっかりした〜　a sound composition ……………[しっかり]
ふんすい　噴水　a fountain
ぶんすう　分数　a fraction
〜式　a fractional expression
ぶんせき　分析　an analysis …[こまかい]
〜する　analyze
ふんぜん　憤然と　in indignation [せき]
ふんそう　紛争　a trouble
・a conflict, a dispute ………[かいけつ]
中東〜　the dispute in the Middle East ………………………[はげしい]

ふんそう　扮装する　make *oneself* up as
ぶんたい　文体　a style ………[せんれん]
ふんだん　〜に使う　be lavish in the use of ……………………………[ざいりょう]
ぶんたん　分担　*one's* share, *one's* work assignment
・*one's* work load ……………[かるい]
〜する　share
ぶんだん　文壇　the literary world ………………………………[おしい]
ぶんちょう　文鳥　a Java sparrow
ぶんちん　文鎮　a paperweight
ぶんつう　文通　correspondence
〜する　correspond (with), exchange letters (with)
〜友達　a pen pal, a pen friend
ふんとう　奮闘　a struggle
〜する　struggle (for), make great efforts (in)
ぶんぷ　分布　(a) distribution
〜する　be distributed
ぶんふそうおう　分不相応に暮らす　live beyond *one's* means ………[くらし]
ふんべつ　分別
ぶんぽう　文法　grammar
〜的に　grammatically ……[ただしい]
ぶんぼうぐ　文房具　《集合的に》 stationery; (学用品) school supplies; (事務用品) office supplies
〜店　(人) a stationer; (店) a stationer's, a stationery store
ぶんめい　文明　civilization
〜の　civilized
ぶんや　分野　a field ………[かがやかしい]
ぶんるい　分類する　classify
・categorize ……………………[べつ]
ぶんれつ　分裂　(人々の) (a) division, a split
〜する　divide, split (up), be divided

へ

へ　屁　a fart
〜へ　(方向) for, to, toward; (〜の中へ) into, in; (〜の上へ) on, onto
へい　塀　(石垣) a wall; (木・金属製の) a fence
へいえき　兵役　military service
へいおん　平穏

へいかい 閉会 the closing
 ～式 a [the] closing ceremony
 ～する close (a meeting)
へいがい 弊害 an evil, (a) harm
へいき 平気
 ～で nonchalantly ……………[めうえ]
 ・without giving it a second thought
 ……………………………[こうきょう]
 ～な顔をしている look calm
 ……………………………[ないしん]
へいき 兵器 a weapon, arms
 核～ nuclear weapons
 通常～ conventional weapons
へいきん 平均
 ～以下 below the average ……[いか]
 ～以上 above average ……[いじょう¹]
へいこう 平行
へいこう 閉口
 ～する have had it with …[しつこい]
へいさ 閉鎖する close down
 ～的な closed
へいさしゃかい 閉鎖社会 a closed
 society ………………………[ひかく]
へいじつ 平日 a weekday
へいじょう 平常どおり as usual
へいせい 平静
へいぜん 平然
へいたい 兵隊 (陸軍の) a soldier; (海軍
 の) a sailor; (海兵隊の) a marine;
 (空軍の) an airman, an airwoman
へいてん 閉店する close
へいねつ 平熱 a normal temperature
へいほう 平方メートル a square meter
 ～キロメートル a square kilometer
へいぼん 平凡
 ～な ordinary ………………[つとめ]
へいめん 平面 a plane
へいや 平野 a plain, plains
ベイルート Beirut
へいわ 平和 peace
 ～な peaceful
 ～に peacefully, in peace
 ～のために for peace ………[たつ²]
 ～条約 a peace treaty
ベーコン bacon
ページ a page
ペース
ベースアップ a raise in the wage base

ペースメーカー a pacemaker
ベーリング ～海 the Bering Sea
ベール a veil
へきが 壁画 a mural, a wall painting
へきち へき地 a remote place, an
 inconvenient place
ペキン 北京 Beijing, Peking
ヘクタール a hectare
へこたれる get exhausted [だらしない]
 へこたれない not lose heart
 ……………………………[こんなん]
ぺこぺこ ～する kowtow
ぺこぺこ お腹が～だ be starving, be
 starved
へこむ become hollow, sink, give in,
 be dented, cave in
ベジタリアン a vegetarian
ベスト *one's* best
 ～セラー a best seller
 ～をつくす do *one's* best
へそ a navel
へそくり secret savings
 ～をする save money secretly
へそまがり へそ曲がりな obstinate,
 perverse
へた 不手
 ～である be poor at ……[あいじょう]
 ・be bad at ……………………[あたま]
へだたり 隔たり (a) distance, a
 difference
ペダル a pedal
へちま a loofa(h), a luffa(h)
ぺちゃんこ ～な (平らな) flat,
 flattened; (つぶされた) smashed,
 crushed
べつ 別
べっきょ 別居する live apart
べつじん 別人 a different person
べっそう 別荘 (豪壮な) a villa; (簡素
 な) a cottage
 ・a villa ………………………[とまる²]
 ・a summer house ………[にげる]
ベッド a bed
ペット a pet
ベッドタウン a commuter town
 ・the suburbs ………………[つくる]
ヘッドハント headhunting
 ～する headhunt

ペットボトル a PET bottle (PET= polyethylene terephthalate)
ヘッドホン headphones
べつに 別に ……………………[べつ]
べつべつ 別々の separate
　〜に separately, apart
へつらう
ベテラン
　・a real pro ……………………[みち]
ペテン 〜にかける cheat
　・swindle …………………[ずいぶん]
ベトナム Vietnam
　〜の, 〜語 Vietnamese
　〜人 a Vietnamese (複数同形); (全体) the Vietnamese
へとへと exhausted ………[なさけない]
べとべと 〜な sticky; (汗で) sweaty
　・greasy ……………………[あぶら]
ペナント a pennant
　〜レース a pennant race
ペニシリン penicillin
ベニス (ベネチア) Venice
ベニヤ 〜板 plywood
ベネズエラ Venezuela
ヘビ 蛇 a snake; (特に大形で有毒の) a serpent
へや 部屋 a room
　〜代 the rent ………………[はらう]
へらす 減らす
ぺらぺら 〜だ (流暢だ) be fluent in, speak *something* fluently
ベランダ a veranda(h)
へり (川などの) an edge, a brink; (帽子の) a rim; (布などの) a hem
ペリカン a pelican
へりくだる humble *oneself*
へりくつ へ理屈 quibbling …..[かなう]
　〜ばかり言う ………………[りくつ]
　〜をこねる argue just for the sake of argument ………………[きらい]
ヘリコプター a helicopter
へる 減る
ベル a bell; (玄関の) a door bell [doorbell]
ペルー Peru
　〜の Peruvian
　〜人 a Peruvian; (全体) the Peruvians

ベルギー Belgium
　〜の Belgian
　〜人 a Belgian; (全体) the Belgians
ヘルシンキ Helsinki
ヘルツ (単位) a hertz
ベルト a belt
　〜コンベアー a conveyer belt
ヘルニア hernia; (椎間板ヘルニア) a slipped disk [disc]
ヘルペス herpes
ヘルメット a helmet
ベルリン Berlin
ベルン Bern
ベレー 〜帽 a beret
へん 辺 (図形の) a side
へん 変
　〜な ugly ……………………[うわさ]
　・peculiar ……………………[ふし]
べん 便 (大便) stools
べん 便 (交通の) service
　〜のよい convenient
　〜の悪い inconvenient
ペン a pen
　〜フレンド a pen pal, a pen friend
へんか 変化
べんかい 弁解……………………[いいわけ]
べんき 便器 a toilet (bowl); (男子用) urinal; (病人用) a chamber pot
べんぎ 便宜 (a) convenience
　〜上 for convenience' sake, for the sake of convenience
　〜をはかる offer convenience to
ペンキ paint ……………………[かわく]
　〜を塗る paint
　〜屋 a painter
べんきょう 勉強
ペンギン a penguin
へんくつ 偏屈な crotchety, warped, eccentric, obstinate
へんけん 偏見
べんご 弁護する defend, plead for
へんこう 変更 (a) change
　〜する change, make a change
べんごし 弁護士 a lawyer
　〜の資格を取る pass the bar exam
　………………………………[とる¹]
へんさい 返済する return; (金銭を) pay back, repay

～期限　the date for repayment ……[すぎた]
へんさち　偏差値　deviation value
へんじ　返事
・a response ……[がっかり]
へんしゅうする　編集する　edit, compile
～者　an editor
～長　the editor in chief
・a chief editor ……[さいのう]
～部員　(全体) editorial staff
べんじょ　便所　a toilet, a lavatory, a water closet, a bathroom, a rest room; (男性用) the men's room; (女性用) the ladies' room
べんしょう　弁償
へんしん　返信　an answer, a reply
～用封筒　a return envelope; (住所名前を書いて切手を貼った) a self-addressed, stamped envelope (略 SASE)
～葉書　a reply (postal) card
へんしん　変身する　change ……[わかる]
へんじん　変人　an eccentric person
ベンジン　benzine
ペンス　pence (単数 penny)
へんそう　変装　(a) disguise ……[さとる]
～する　disguise *oneself* (as), be disguised (as)
へんたい　変態　abnormal; (倒錯者) a pervert
ペンダント　a pendant
ベンチ　a bench
ペンチ　(a pair of) pliers
ベンチャー　～企業　(a) venture business
べんとう　弁当　(a) lunch, a box lunch
～箱　a lunch box
～を食べる　have lunch ……[けしき]
～を広げる　open the lunch ……[ひろげる]
へんとうせん　扁桃腺　the tonsils [やく³]
～炎　《医学用語》 tonsillitis
へんぴ　～な　remote, inconvenient
べんぴ　便秘　constipation
～する　be constipated
へんぴん　返品する　return
べんり　便利
～な　handy ……[はいる]

べんろん　弁論　pubic speaking; (討論) a debate; (論争) a discussion, an argument; (弁護) pleading, defense
～する　discuss, debate, argue
～大会　a speech contest [だいひょう]

ホ

ほ　帆　a sail
ほ　歩　a step; (足どり) a pace
ほ　穂　an ear
ほいく　保育　childcare, early childhood education
～園　a day-care, a day-care center
～士　a day-care teacher
ボイコット　～する　boycott
ポイすて　ポイ捨てする　litter
ボイラー　a boiler
ホイル　foil; (アルミホイル) aluminum foil
ぼいん　母音　a vowel
ポインタ　《コンピュータ》 a pointer
ポイント　(要点) the point; (鉄道の) 《米》 a switch, 《英》 points
ほう　方　(方角) a way, a direction
ほう　法　the law
～的な　legal ……[てつづき]
～に触れる　infringe on the law ……[ふれる]
ぼう　棒　a stick, a pole
～高跳び　the pole jump [vault]
～に振る　ruin ……[いっしょう]
・lose ……[ふる¹]
ぼう　某　(ある) (a) certain
ほうあん　法案　a bill ……[たのむ]
ぼういんぼうしょく　暴飲暴食する　overeat and overdrink
ぼうえい　防衛　defense
～する　defend
～問題　a defense problem [さける²]
ぼうえいちょう　防衛庁　the Japan Defense Agency
ぼうえき　貿易　trade, commerce
～会社　a trading company
～収支　trade balance ……[くろ]
～摩擦　trade friction ……[まさつ]
～する　trade (with)
ぼうえんきょう　望遠鏡　a telescope
ほうおう　法王　(ローマ法王) the Pope

ぼうおん 防音の soundproof
ほうか 放火 arson ……………[れんぞく]
・a case of arson ……………[よる¹]
～魔 an arsonist ……………[せけん]
ぼうか 防火 fire-prevention …[せつび]
～シャッター a fireproof shutter
ぼうがい 妨害する interfere with, disturb, obstruct
ほうがく 方角 a direction, a way
ほうがく 法学 law
～博士 Doctor of Laws (略 LL.D.)
～部 the law department
ほうかご 放課後 after school
(…した)ほうがよい should, had better *do*
ぼうかん 傍観する look on
～者 an onlooker
ぼうかん 暴漢 a thug ………[もとめる]
ぼうかん 防寒 protection against the cold
～着 winter clothes ……………[み]
ほうがんなげ 砲丸投げ the shot put
ほうき a broom ……………[はく²]
ほうき 放棄する abandon
戦争～ renunciation of war [うたう]
ぼうぎょ 防御 defense
～する defend
ぼうくん 暴君 a tyrant, a despot
ほうけん 封建的 feudalistic
～時代 the feudal period …..[じだい]
ほうげん 方言 (a) dialect ………[まじる]
～混じりで話す mix in a little dialect when *one* speaks ………[き]
ぼうけん 冒険
～的な risky, dangerous …[あぶない]
～好きな adventurous ……[へいおん]
～物語 an adventure story
……………………………[つうかい]
ほうこう 方向
ぼうこう 暴行 violence, an assault; (強姦) (a) rape
ぼうこう 膀胱 the bladder
～炎 bladder infection,《医学用語》cystitis
ほうこく 報告
～書 a written account ….[かんたん]
ほうさく 豊作 a good [fine] crop
・a large crop ……………[さがる]

ほうし 奉仕 a service
～する serve, devote *oneself* to
ぼうし 防止する prevent
ぼうし 帽子 （ふちなしの) a cap, （ふちのある) a hat
ぼうじゃくぶじん 傍若無人ぶり impudence ……………………[め¹]
ほうしゃせん 放射線 a radiation
ほうしゃのう 放射能 radioactivity
……………………………[あびる]
ほうしゅう 報酬 a reward; (給料) pay
～を与える reward
ほうしん 方針
ぼうず 坊主 a Buddhist monk, a bonze
～頭 a shaven head, a close-cropped head
ぼうすい 防水の waterproof
ほうせき 宝石 a gem, a jewel; (総称)《米》jewelry,《英》jewellery
～鑑定家 a jewelry appraiser
……………………………[とおる]
～商 a jeweler
～箱 a jewel case
ぼうせき 紡績 spinning
ぼうぜん 茫然
ほうそう 包装 packing, wrapping
～紙 packing [wrapping, brown] paper
～する pack, wrap
ほうそう 放送 broadcasting; (1回の) a broadcast
～局 a broadcasting station
～する (放送局が) broadcast, put [send] *something* on the air; (テレビで) telecast, televise
ぼうそうぞく 暴走族 a motorcycle gang ……………………[うなる]
・a hot-rodder …………[ひじょうしき]
ほうそく 法則 a law, a rule
ほうたい 包帯 a bandage ………[まく²]
～を巻く wrap a bandage ….[きつい]
・dress ……………………[にじむ]

～ほうだい ～放題
ほうち 放置する leave *something* around ……………………[えいせい]
ぼうちゅうざい 防虫剤 (an) insect repellent; (衣類の) a mothball

ほうちょう 包丁　a kitchen knife
・a knife …………………………[きれる]
ぼうちょう 膨張する　expand
ぼうちょう 傍聴する　listen to, hear, attend
ほうっておく 放っておく　(人を放任する) let [leave] *someone* alone; (人にかまわない) neglect
・let *someone* be ………………[しぜん]
ほうてい 法廷　a (law) court
ほうどう 報道　news, a report
　～機関　the press
　・the media …………………[くわえる]
　～官《米》the press secretary
　～陣　the press, reporters
　～する　report, inform
ぼうどう 暴動　a riot ………[おさまる²]
ほうとうむすこ 放蕩息子　a wayward son …………………………………[みち]
ほうにん 放任する　let [leave] alone
ぼうねんかい 忘年会　a year-end party …………………………………[よさん]
ぼうはてい 防波堤　a breakwater [さき]
ぼうはん 防犯　crime prevention
　～ベル　a burglar alarm
ほうび 褒美
ほうふ 抱負　(an) ambition, hope, wish
ほうふ 豊富
　～である　have a rich assortment of …………………………………[しなもの]
ぼうふう 暴風　a stormy wind
　～雨　a storm
ぼうふざい 防腐剤　(殺菌剤) (an) antiseptic; (保存剤) (a) preservative
ほうほう 方法
ほうぼう 方々　everywhere, all around
　～から　from all directions
ほうむしょう 法務省　the Ministry of Justice
ほうむる 葬る　bury
ぼうめい 亡命する　defect, take political asylum
　～者　a defector, an exile
ほうめん 方面
ほうもん 訪問
　突然～する　pop in ………[こころよい]

ぼうらく 暴落する　fall sharply, drop
ぼうり 暴利をむさぼる　make excessive [exorbitant] profits …………[りよう]
ほうりだす 放り出す　(物を放り投げる) throw out; (物事をあきらめる) give up, abandon
ほうりつ 法律　a law; (総称的に) (the) law
　～の, ～にかなった　legal
　～家　a lawyer
　～事務所　a law office
　～違反の　illegal, in violation of the law …………………………………[いはん]
　～には触れない　there is no law against *something* …………[たとえ]
ほうりゅう 放流している　be stocked with ……………………………[じんこう²]
ぼうりょく 暴力　violence
　家庭内～　domestic violence, violence toward *one's* family
　～をふるう　use violence
　～に訴える　resort to violence …………………………………[うったえる]
　～で　by force
ボウリング　(球技) bowling
　～場　a bowling alley
ほうる 放・抛る　throw, toss
ホウレンソウ　spinach ………[たば]
ほえる 吠える
ほお 頬　a cheek
ボーイ　(飲食店の) a waiter; (ホテルの) a porter, 《米》a bellboy
ボーイスカウト　(団員) a boy scout; (組織) the Boy Scouts
ボーイフレンド　a (male) friend; (恋人) a boyfriend
ホース　a hose
ポーズ　(姿勢) a pose; (休止) a pause
　～を取る　(姿勢) pose; (休止) make a pause
ほおずり 頬ずりする　press *one's* cheek against
ポータブル　～の　portable
ホーチミン　～市　Ho Chi Minh City
ほおづえ 頬杖をつく　rest *one's* chin in *one's* hand
　～をついて　with *one's* chin in *one's* hand …………………………[ちゃんと]

ボート　a boat
ボーナス　a bonus……………[でる]
　〜が出る[をもらう]　get *one's* bonus
　………………………………[き]
ホーム　(駅の) a platform
ホーム　(家庭) one's home; (野球のホームベース) the home (base, plate)
　老人〜　a retirement home, a senior home
ホームシック　〜にかかる　get homesick
ホームステイ　a homestay
　〜する　stay with
ホームページ
ホームラン　a home run, a homer
　逆転〜　a come-from-behind home run……………………………[しょうぶ]
　逆転サヨナラ〜　a come-from-behind game-ending home run
　……………………………………[かい²]
　満塁〜を打つ　hit a grand slam homer……………………………[だめ]
ホームルーム　a homeroom [home room]
ホームレス　(人) a homeless
ポーランド　Poland
　〜の, 〜語　Polish
　〜人　a Pole; (全体) the Poles
ホール　a hall
ボール　(球) a ball
ボール　(容器) a bowl
ボールがみ　ボール紙　cardboard
ボールペン　a ballpoint pen, a ball pen, a ballpoint
ほおん　保温する　keep *something* warm [hot]
ほか　外・他
ぼかす　(色を) shade; (話を) evade
ほがらか　朗らか
ぼき　簿記　bookkeeping
ほきゅう　補給　a supply
　〜する　supply (with)
ぼきんかつどう　募金活動
　a fund-raising campaign
ほくい　北緯　north latitude
ボクサー　a boxer
ぼくし　牧師　a clergyman, a minister・a pastor………………………[つげる]
ぼくじょう　牧場　a stock farm, a ranch; (牧草地) a pasture, a meadow
ボクシング　boxing
ほくせい　北西　the northwest
　〜の　northwest, northwestern
ぼくそう　牧草　grass
ぼくちく　牧畜　stock farming, cattle breeding
ほくとう　北東　the northeast
　〜の　northeast, northeastern
ほくとしちせい　北斗七星　the Big Dipper
ほくぶ　北部　the north; (米国の) the North
ぼくめつ　撲滅　(望ましくないもの) eradication; (生き物の) (an) extermination
ほくろ　a mole……………………[うえ]
ほけつ　補欠選手　(控え) a reserve; (代理) a substitute (player)
　〜選挙　a special election, a by-election
ポケット　a pocket
ポケベル　a pager, a beeper
ぼける　惚ける　(頭が) become [go, get] senile
　ぼけて　(ピントが) out of focus, blurred
ほけん　保険
　健康〜　health insurance
　火災〜　fire insurance
　自動車〜　automobile insurance
　〜をかける　take out insurance on
　……………………………………[かける¹]
ほけんじょ　保健所　a public health center……………[えいせい, おこなう]
ほご　保護
ぼこう　母校　one's old school, one's alma mater
ほこうしゃ　歩行者　a walker, a foot passenger, a pedestrian
　〜天国　a pedestrian mall
ぼこく　母国　one's native country, one's mother country; one's homeland
　〜語　one's native language, one's mother tongue
ほこり　埃　dust

～っぽい dusty
～を払う dust
・brush the dust (off) ……[はらう]
ほこり 誇り
ほこる 誇る
ほころび ～を縫う restitch the seam
……[ぬう]
ほし 星 a star
ほしい 欲しい
欲しくない not need ……[など]
ほしうらない 星占い (占星術) horoscopy, astrology; (個々の占い) a horoscope
ほしブドウ 干しブドウ raisins
ほしゃく 保釈になる be released on bail
ほしゅう 補習 a supplementary lesson
ほじゅう 補充する supplement; fill up
ほしゅう 募集
～する seek applications from
……[いじょう¹]
ほしゅてき 保守的な conservative
……[きらい]
ほしゅとう 保守党 (英国の) the Conservative Party
ほじょ 補助 assistance; help; support; aid
ほしょう 保証
ほじる dig (up)
(鼻・耳などを) pick ……[はな]
ほす 干す
ポスター a poster
ポスト (郵便ポスト) a mailbox …[だす]
ポスト (地位) a post
・a position ……[あく¹]
ボストン Boston
ホスピス a hospice
ほそい 細い
ほそう 舗装 pavement
～道路 a pavement
ほそく 補足する supplement, add (to)
ほそながい 細長い long and thin; (幅が狭くて) long and narrow
ほぞん 保存
～食料 nonperishable foods
……[そなえる]
ほたてがい 帆立貝 a scallop
ホタル 螢 a firefly

ボタン (服の) a button; (押しボタン) a button
ボタン 牡丹 (花) a peony
ぼち 墓地 a graveyard; (共同の) a cemetery
ほちょうき 補聴器 a hearing aid [みみ]
ほっかい 北海 the North Sea
ほっきょく 北極(点) the North Pole
……[たっする]
～の arctic
～地方 the Arctic regions, the Arctic
～海 the Arctic Ocean [Sea]
～星 the North Star, the polestar
ホック a hook
ホッケー hockey
ほっさ 発作 an attack, a fit ……[さよう]
心臓～を起こす have a heart attack
ぼっしゅう 没収する confiscate, seize
ほっしん 発疹 a rash ……[ひろがる]
ほっそく 発足する be formed, be launched
ほっそり ～とした slender, slim
ほったらかす (仕事を) leave *something* undone [unfinished]; (人を) neglect
ホッチキス a stapler
～でとめる staple
ほっと
ポット a pot; (魔法瓶) a thermos
ぼっとう 没頭
～する throw *oneself* into
……[けんきゅう]
ホットケーキ a pancake
ホットドッグ a hot dog
ポップコーン popcorn
ポップス pop music
ほっぺた a cheek
ボディガード a bodyguard
ボディチェック a body search
ボディビル body building
ポテト a potato
ホテル a hotel
ほど 程
…にも程がある there is a limit to
……[ずうずうしい]
ほどう 歩道 《米》a sidewalk, 《英》a pavement

横断〜 a pedestrian crossing
〜橋 a pedestrian bridge, an overpass

ほどく
・get *something* undone, untie ……………………………………[かたい]

ほとけ 仏 the Buddha

ほどとおい 程遠い be a long way from *something*, nowhere near *something*

ほどほど 〜の、〜で just about right, reasonable, moderate
〜にする not overdo ……[りゅうこう]

ほとんど 殆んど

ぼにゅう 母乳 mother's milk
〜で育てる breast-feed

ほにゅうびん 哺乳瓶 a baby bottle
……………………………………[しょうどく]

ほにゅうるい 哺乳類 a mammal
・the mammal class ………[ぞくする]

ほね 骨

ほねおり 骨折り

ほのお 炎 (ちらちら燃える) flame; (激しく燃え上がる) a blaze

ほのぼの 〜した heartwarming

ほのめかす hint, imply

ホノルル Honolulu

ほはば 歩幅 a stride
〜が広い have a long stride [ひろい]

ポプラ a poplar (tree)

ほほ 頬 a cheek

ほぼ almost, nearly, approximately, just about, practically

ほぼ 保母 a nurse
・a nursery school teacher [ぴったり]

ほほえましい pleasant, heartwarming, make *one* want to smile

ほほえみ a smile

ほほえむ smile

ほまれ 誉れ (物・人) a credit; (名誉) an honor

ほめる 褒める
・say nice things about ………[ある〜]

ぼや a small fire

ぼやく complain, grumble

ほやほや 〜だ (料理が出来たて) be freshly cooked and piping hot; (大学卒業したて) be just fresh out of college; (新婚) be a newly wed, be still in *one's* honeymoon

ほら Look!／There!

ほらあな 洞穴 a cave

ポラロイド a Polaroid (camera)

ボランティア

ほり 堀 a moat; (掘り割り) a canal

ほり 彫りの深い (顔立ちが) well-defined ……………………[ふかい]

ポリエチレン polyethylene

ほりだしもの 掘り出し物 (すばらしい見つけ物) a find; (安い買い物) a bargain

ボリビア Bolivia

ほりゅう 保留

ボリューム volume
〜のある of great volume
〜を上げる turn up the volume
〜を下げる turn down the volume

ほりょ 捕虜 a prisoner, a captive, a prisoner of war (略 POW)
〜収容所 a prison camp

ほる 彫る carve; engrave

ほる 掘る

ボルト (留具) a bolt

ボルト (電気) a volt; voltage

ポルトガル Portugal
〜の、〜語 Portuguese
〜人 a Portuguese (複数同形); (全体) the Portuguese

ポルノ pornography
〜の pornographic

ホルモン a hormone

ほれる 惚れる

ぼろ (ぼろきれ) (a) rag; (ぼろ服) rags, worn-out clothes; (失敗など) a fault

ポロシャツ a polo shirt

ほろびる 滅びる

ほろぼす 滅ぼす

ぼろぼろ 〜の tattered, battered, ragged, worn-out

ほん 本 book
〜屋 (店) a bookstore, a bookshop; (人) a bookseller
〜棚 a bookshelf

ボン Bonn

ぼん 盆 a tray; (大型の) a platter

ほんかく 本格

ほんき 本気
ほんぎょう 本業 *one's* main occupation
ぼんくれ 盆暮れ……………[しゅうかん]
ほんごく 本国 *one's* (own) country, *one's* home
ぽんこつ a piece of junk; (車) an old heap
ほんこん 香港 Hong Kong
ぼんさい 盆栽 a bonsai, a potted dwarf tree
ほんしき 本式の authentic ………[しき]
ほんしつ 本質 essence, the nature
・the substance ……………[かたち]
～的な essential, fundamental
ほんしゃ 本社 (当社) this office; (支社に対して) the head [main] office
・the main office ……………[れんらく]
ほんしょう 本性 *one's* (true) nature [character]
ほんしん 本心
ぼんじん 凡人 an ordinary person
ほんせき 本籍 *one's* legal [permanent] domicile
ほんだい 本題 (the) topic ………[よこ]
～に入る go into *one's* topic …[ぬく]
ぼんち 盆地 a basin
ほんちょうし 本調子ではない be not back to *one's* old [former] self, not in full swing
～に戻る be back to *one's* old [former] self
ほんてん 本店 the head office, the head store
ほんど 本土 the mainland
ポンド a pound (略 lb.〈重量〉; £〈貨幣単位〉)
ほんとう 本当
ほんにん 本人 the person (involved) ……………………………[もしくは]
ほんね 本音
～を吐く confess *one's* real intentions ……………[はく¹]
ボンネット a hood
ほんの
ほんのう 本能 (an) instinct
～的に instinctively, by instinct
ほんば 本場 (産地) the home [center] of production; (発祥地) the birthplace
～の genuine, real
ほんぶ 本部 (組織の指令部) a [the] headquarters; (中心の事務所) a main [head] office
ポンプ a pump
ほんぶん 本分 (a) duty
～を尽くす fulfill *one's* duty
ボンベ a cylinder
ほんみょう 本名 *one's* real name
ほんめい 本命 (最人気馬) the favorite; (最有力者) the top contender
ほんもの 本物 the real thing ……………………………[ちょっと]
～の real
ほんやく 翻訳 (a) translation
～者 a translator
～する translate (into)
・do translation work ………[こづかい]
ぼんやり
・blankly ……………………[そと]
ほんらい 本来 (元来) originally; (生来) by nature
ほんらい 本来の original ………[はしる]
本来…である be supposed to [ある]
ほんりょう 本領を発揮している be in *one's* element ……………………[はっき]
～を発揮できない not do *one* justice ……………………………[はっき]
ほんるい 本塁 《野球》the home (base, plate)
ほんろん 本論 the main body …[なる¹]

マ

ま 間
ま 魔がさす……………………[さす³]
まあ 《感嘆詞》Oh!／Oh, dear!／Oh, my!
マーガリン margarine
マーク a mark
～する mark, pay attention to, be careful with; (人を) keep an eye on
マーケット a market
マージャン mah-jong ………[ことわる]
マーチ a march
まあまあ
まい… 毎… every, each

…まい …枚 （1枚の）a sheet [piece] of
まいあがる （高く）舞い上がる　whirl up
　・soar skyward ……………………[たかい]
マイアミ　Miami
マイク　a microphone, a mike
まいご　迷子　a lost child
　～になる　be [get] lost
マイコン　a microcomputer
まいぞう　埋蔵物　deposits
　石油の～量　petroleum deposits
　………………………………………[すくない]
マイナー　～な　small, small and unknown, minor
マイナス
マイペース　～だ　like doing *one's* (own) thing, go at *one's* own pace
　………………………………………[ペース]
マイホーム　*one's* own house
　～主義者　a family man, a family-oriented person
マイル　a mile
まいる　参る
マイレージ　mileage [milage], miles
まう　舞う
マウス　《コンピュータ》a mouse
マウンテンバイク　a mountain bike
まえ　前
　～から(以前から)　already ……[うわさ]
　～に出る　get out in front [かたまる]
まえあし　前足　(足首から上) a foreleg; (足首から先) a forefoot
まえうり　前売り　(an) advance sale
　～券　an advance ticket
まえがき　前書き　a foreword, a preface
まえがみ　前髪　a forelock; (切りそろえて垂らした前髪) bangs
まえのめり　前のめりに倒れる　fall flat on *one's* face ……………………[たおれる]
まえぶれ　前ぶれ　(予告) notice; (前兆) a sign
まえむき　前向きな[の]　positive
　～の　constructive …………[しせい]
まえもって　前もって　beforehand
　…………………………………………[おく¹]
マカオ　Macao, Macau
まがお　真顔で　with a serious look
まかす　負かす　beat, defeat

まかせる　任せる
まがった　曲がった　bent, curved; (曲がりくねった) winding
まがりかど　曲がり角　a corner
まがりくねった　曲がりくねった winding ……………………………[みち]
まがる　曲がる
マカロニ　macaroni
まき　薪　wood ……………………[もえる]
まきこまれる　巻き込まれる　get caught in ………………………………[こうつう]
　・be involved (in) ……………[やっかい]
　・get *oneself* in ……………[ややこしい]
まきこむ　巻き込む　involve
まきじゃく　巻き尺　a tape measure
まきちらす　撒き散らす　scatter
まきつく　巻きつく　wind around
まきもの　巻物　a scroll
まぎらす　紛らす
まぎらわしい　紛らわしい
まぎわ　間際に(なって)　at the last moment
　…の間際に　just [right] before...
まく　蒔・撒く
まく　巻く
まく　幕
まくあけ　(…の)幕明け　the dawn of
　…………………………………………[じだい]
まくぎれ　幕切れ　an end
マグニチュード　a magnitude
マグマ　magma
まくら　枕　a pillow
まくらぎ　枕木　a railroad tie …[くさる]
まくる　roll up, tuck up; (折り返す) turn up
まぐれ　a fluke, sheer luck
　～だよ　I was just lucky.
マグロ　鮪　a tuna
まけ　負け　a defeat, a loss
まける　負ける
　簡単に～　not stand a chance
　…………………………………………[ほんき]
まげる　曲げる
まご　孫　a grandchild (複数 -children); (男) a grandson; (女) a granddaughter
まごころ　真心　sincerity
　～をこめて　with all *one's* heart

まごつく　get confused, get embarrassed
まこと　真・誠
まことに　誠に
まさか
マザコン　a mama's boy
　～だ　be tied to *one's* mother's apron strings
まさつ　摩擦
まさに　正に
まさる　勝る
まし
マジック　(奇術) magic
マジック(インキ)(太いもの) a (magic) marker; (サインペン) a felt-tip pen;
まじない　a charm
まじめ
　～に　diligently ………[にらむ]
　～人間　a serious person ……[かいしゃ]
まじゅつ　魔術　magic
まじょ　魔女　a witch
まじる　交・混じる
まじわる　交わる
ましん　麻疹　measles
マス　鱒　a trout
ます　増す
まず
ますい　麻酔　anesthesia
まずい
マスク　a mask
マスコット　a mascot
マスコミ　the mass media
まずしい　貧しい
マスター　(喫茶店などの) the owner, the proprietor; (雇われ) the manager
　～する　master, learn
マスト　a mast
ますます
ませた　precocious, be advanced for *one's* age
　～口をきく　talk like a grown-up
まぜる　交・混ぜる
また
まだ
またぐ　step [stride] over, straddle
またせる　待たせる　keep *someone* waiting; (待たせてある) have *someone* waiting for *one*
または
まだら　(はん点) a spot; (動物の) a dapple
まだるっこい　sluggish, tiresome, roundabout
まち　町・街
　～で　on the street ………[なつかしい]
　～じゅう　the whole town ……[きぶん]
まちあいしつ　待合室　a waiting room
まちあわせる
まちうける　待ち受けている　lie ahead for ………………[こんなん]
まぢか　間近　near, close
　～で見る　watch *something* close up ……………………[はくりょく]
まちがい　間違い
　～を指摘する　point out the error ………………………[ゆうき]
まちがいない　間違いない　be assured of ………………[おおきい]
まちがえる　間違える
まちがった[て]　間違った[て]
　・incorrect ………………[けす]
まちくたびれる　待ちくたびれる　get tired of waiting
まちどおしい　待ち遠しい
まちぶせ　待ち伏せする　ambush
まちぼうけ　待ちぼうけを食わせる　stand *someone* up
まちまち　～だ　be different, vary
マツ　松　a pine (tree)
まつ　待つ
まっか　真っ赤(な)　deep red
　・bright red ………………[おこる²]
　・crimson …………………[のぼる]
　～な嘘　a downright lie
マッキンリー　～山　Mt. McKinley
まっくら　真っ暗な　pitch-dark
まっくろ　真っ黒な　pitch-black, jet-black
まつげ　eyelash ………………[こい¹]
マッサージ　massage
まっさお　真っ青な　deep blue; (顔色が) deathly pale, as white as a sheet
まっさかさま　真っ逆さまに　headlong, head over heels

まっさき 真っ先に first and foremost, first of all
まっしぐら ～に at full speed, vigorously
マッシュルーム a mushroom
まっしょうめん 真正面からぶつかる crash head on ……………[ぶつかる]
まっしろ 真っ白な pure-white, snow-white
まっすぐ 真っすぐ
マッターホルン the Matterhorn
まったく 全く
・perfectly ………………[えんりょ]
・absolutely ………………[ただしい]
・entirely ………………[ふゆかい]
マッチ a match
マッチョ ～な男 a macho (guy, man)
まっとう ………………[まとも]
マットレス a mattress
まつばづえ 松葉杖 crutches ……[よう¹]
  ～をつく walk on crutches
まっぴら ～だ No way!／There's no way...
まつり 祭り a festival ………[たたく]
～まで(に)
  (…する)まで by the time... [つくす]
まと 的
  ～を外れる miss the target
  ………………………[はずれる]
まど 窓 a window
  ～ガラス a windowpane
  ～側の席 a window seat ……[うつる³]
まどぐち 窓口 a wicket, a counter
  ………………………[やすみ]
まとまり (統一性) unity; (一貫性) coherence
まとまる
  話が～ agree on ………………[はらう]
まとめ a summary
まとめる
  ・get *something* into shape [おもい²]
まとも
  ～にとる take *something* seriously
  ………………………[ひにく]
マドリッド Madrid
まどわす 惑わす
マナー manners
まないた まな板 a cutting board

まなざし a look ………………[うたがい]
まなつ 真夏(の) midsummer [てらす]
まなぶ 学ぶ
マニア a mania; (人) a maniac, a lover, a fan
まにあう 間に合う
  ・†make it [finish] in time ……[いま]
  その電車に～ make that train
  ………………………[(～と、～に)しても]
まにあわせる 間に合わせる
まにうける 真に受ける take *something* at face value
  ・take *something* seriously ……[うける]
マニキュア (a) manicure
  ・nail polish ………………[そめる]
マニュアル a manual
  ～に従って according to the manual
マニラ Manila
まぬけ 間抜け a fool, a dolt, an idiot
まね 真似 imitation
  ～をする imitate
  ・mimic ………………[ふざける]
マネージャー a manager
マネキン (人形) a mannequin
まねく 招く
まねる 真似る
まばたき a blink, a wink
  ～する blink, wink
まばら ～な sparse
まひ 麻痺
  ～する (体などが) paralyze; (感覚が) be numbed
まぶしい
まぶた an eyelid
まふゆ 真冬(の) midwinter
マフラー (えり巻き) a muffler, a scarf
まほう 魔法 magic, a spell, witchcraft
  ～をかける cast a spell on
  ～瓶 a thermos (bottle)
まぼろし 幻 a vision, an illusion, a phantom
  ～の rare ………………[こころ]
ママ 《小児語》mamma, mama, mom, mummy
まま
ままこ まま子 a stepchild; (息子) a stepson; (娘) a stepdaughter
ままごと ～をする play house, play at

housekeeping
ままはは まま母 a stepmother
まみず 真水 fresh water
マムシ 蝮 *mamushi*, a (pit) viper
まめ 豆 (植物の) a bean; (大豆) a soy bean, a soybean; (エンドウ豆) a pea
まめ (手足にできる) a blister
まめ ～に quite often, frequently
　～だ be quick to do things
まもなく 間もなく
まもる 守る
　(遵守する) abide by ………[～ならない]
まやく 麻薬 a drug
　・a narcotic ………………………[くぐる]
まゆ 眉 an eyebrow
まゆ 繭 a cocoon
まよう 迷う
マヨネーズ mayonnaise
マラソン a marathon (race)
まる 丸 a circle; (球) a globe
まる… 丸… full, whole
　丸一日 the whole day ………[あそぶ]
まるあんき 丸暗記する memorize, learn by rote [heart]
まるい 丸い (円形の) round, circular; (球形の) spherical
　(鉛筆の先が) dull ………………[さき]
　丸く治まる end peacefully
　　………………………………[おさまる²]
まるごと ～の whole, entire
マルセーユ Marseille(s)
まるた 丸太 a log ………………[ころがす]
マルチ ～商法 multi-level marketing
まるで
　(全く) altogether ……………[せいつ]
まるまる (太った) (round and) chubby; (全て残らず) whole, entire, every bit of
まるめこむ 丸め込む induce *someone* to *do*
まるめる 丸める round; (くしゃくしゃにする) crumble up
まれ 稀な rare, uncommon
　～に seldom, rarely
マレーシア Malaysia
　～の Malaysian
　～人 a Malaysian; (全体) the Malaysians
まわしよみ 回し読みする take turns reading *something* ………[じゅんばん]
まわす 回す
　(渡す) pass …………………………[うしろ]
まわり 周・回り
まわりくどい 回りくどい
まわりみち 回り道 a detour
まわる 回る
まん 万 ten thousand
　4万 forty thousand
まんいち 万一 if by some †quirk of fate [chance] ……………………[もし]
　～に備えて for emergencies ……[よび]
　・for a rainy day …………[たくわえる]
　・just in case something comes up
　　………………………………[そなえる]
　～の場合 in case of an emergency
　　…………………………………[ばあい]
まんいん 満員
まんが 漫画 a cartoon; (新聞・雑誌の) comics; (数こま連続した) a comic strip
　(本) a comic book ………………[わらう]
　～家 a cartoonist
まんかい 満開である be in full blossom
まんき 満期になる mature
まんげつ 満月 a full moon
マンゴー a mango
まんじゅう a bun filled with sweetened bean paste
まんじょういっち 満場一致で unanimously
マンション (分譲) a condo(minium); (賃貸) an apartment house, a flat
まんせい 慢性の chronic
まんせき 満席である be completely booked ……………………………[どの～]
　・all seats are filled ……………[せき]
まんぞく 満足
まんちょう 満潮 the high [full] tide
まんてん 満点 full marks
　・a perfect (test) score ………[あがる]
まんなか 真ん中
マンネリ マンネリの stereotyped, routine
　～化する become stereotyped

[routine]
まんねんひつ 万年筆 a fountain pen
まんびき 万引き shoplifting [くるしむ]
　〜する lift ……………[ふらふら]
まんぷく 満腹だ be full
まんべんなく equally, all over
まんまえ 真ん前に right in front of
まんまと completely ……………[かつぐ]
マンモス a mammoth

ミ

み 身
　〜に余る光栄 an undeserved honor
　　………………………………[こうえい]
　〜に覚えのない have no memory of
　　………………………………[おぼえ]
　〜につける learn …………[おうよう]
　・acquire ………………………[ぎじゅつ]
　〜を切るように寒い be bitterly cold
　　………………………………[さむい]
　〜を慎みなさい Watch what you
　　do./Behave yourself. ……[つつしむ]
　〜を包む be dressed in ………[そろう]
　〜を投げる throw oneself into
　　………………………………[なげる]
　〜を滅ぼす be the ruin of …[ふける]
み 実
　〜を結ぶ bear fruit, pay off
　　………………………………[どりょく]
みあい 見合い a marriage interview
　〜結婚 an arranged marriage
みあげる 見上げる look up (at)
みあわせる 見合わせる (中止する)
　cancel, call off; (延期する)
　postpone, put off
ミイラ a mummy
みうしなう 見失う lose sight of, miss
　・lose (sight of) …………[おいかける]
みうち 身内 (親戚) a relative, a family
　〜の family ………………………[けす]
みえ 見栄
みえすいた 見え透いた
　〜うそ a blatant [transparent] lie
　　………………………………[うそ]
みえる 見える
　見えてくる come into view
　　………………………………[そうれい]
みおくる 見送る

みおとす 見落とす overlook, miss
みおとりする 見劣りする （他と比べて）
　do not look as good as
みおぼえ 見覚えがある recognize
　顔に〜がある Someone's face looks
　familiar to one.
みおろす 見おろす look down,
　overlook
みかい 未開の uncivilized,
　undeveloped
みかいけつ 未解決の unsolved,
　unsettled, pending
みかえす 見返す get even with
　someone, show someone what one
　can do
みかく 味覚 (the sense of) taste
みがく 磨く
　センスを〜 refine one's sense
　　………………………………[センス]
みかけ 見かけ one's appearance
　　………………………………[はんだん]
　〜によらず contrary to appearance
　　………………………………[しんぞう]
　・contrary to the way one looks
　　………………………………[ふとい]
みかける 見かける (happen to) see
みかた 味方
みかた 見方 a point of view, a
　viewpoint
みかづき 三日月 a crescent
　〜形の crescent
みかねる 見兼ねる can't bear to
　watch, can't stand by and watch,
　can't stand to see
みがまえる 身構える take a posture
　(of defense)
みがる 身軽な light; (機敏な) agile;
　(束縛されない) footloose
みがわり 身代わり a scapegoat
　（〜の)身代わりに for, in place of
ミカン （日本産の) a tangerine; (オレンジ) an orange
　・a mandarin orange ………[つまる]
みかんせい 未完成の unfinished,
　incomplete
みき 幹 a trunk
みぎ 右 the right
　〜利きの right-handed

みぎうで 右腕 (頼りになる人) *one's* right-hand man
ミキサー a blender
みきり 見切りをつける give up on, go out of, forget (all) about; (手を切る) wash *one's* hands of
みくだす 見下す look down on [upon]
みくびる 見くびる underestimate, make light of
みぐるしい 見苦しい
みけいけん 未経験の inexperienced ………………………………[こころぼそい]
みけん 眉間 the middle of the forehead
　～にしわを寄せる frown ………[しわ]
みごと 見事
　～に splendidly ………[まう]
みこみ 見込み
みこむ 見込む
みごろ 見頃で (最上の状態で) at *one's* best; (満開で) in full bloom
みこん 未婚の single, unmarried
ミサイル a missile
みさき 岬 a cape
みさげた 見下げた despicable ………………………………[いやらしい]
みじかい 短い
ミシシッピー ～川 the Mississippi
みじたく 身支度する dress *oneself*, get dressed
みじめ 惨め
みじゅく 未熟
ミシン a sewing machine
みじんぎり みじん切りにする chop *something* into fine pieces, mince
ミス
　・an error, a flaw ………[おおきい]
　重大な～ a grave blunder ……[せまる]
みず 水 water
　～不足 a water shortage ……[こまる]
　～をまく water ………………[はく²]
　・sprinkle water ………………[まく¹]
　～に流す let bygones be bygones ………………………………[ながす]
　～も漏らさぬ警戒 an airtight cordon ………………………………[もらす]
　～を浴びる splash, bathe ……[あびる]
　(話に)～をさす throw †a wet blanket [cold water] ………[さす³]
みすい 未遂の attempted
　殺人～ attempted murder
みずいらず 水入らずで by themselves, by ourselves
みずいろ 水色 light blue
みずうみ 湖 a lake
みずかき 水かき a web
みずかけろん 水かけ論 a fruitless argument
みずかさ 水かさ (a) water level ………………………………[すすむ]
みすかす 見透かす see (right) through, perceive, read
みずから 自ら *oneself*, personally, voluntarily
　～進んで on *one's* own, by *oneself* ………………………………[すすむ]
みずぎ 水着 a bathing suit; (水泳パンツ) bathing trunks
　～になる change into a bathing suit ………………………………[きぶん]
みすごす 見過ごす let *something* pass ………………………………[こころ]
みずしごと 水仕事 scrubbing and washing ………………………………[あれる]
みずしょうばい 水商売 the alcohol-serving business of nightclubs and bars
みずたまもよう 水玉模様の polka-dot
みずたまり 水たまり a puddle, a pool
ミステリー (なぞ) (a) mystery; (推理小説) a mystery novel
みすてる 見捨てる abandon, desert
　・ignore ………………………[こまる]
みずはけ 水はけ (排水) drainage
　～のよい well drained
　～が悪い ………………………[みぞ]
みずびたし 水浸しになる get flooded
みずぶくれ 水ぶくれ a blister
みずぼうそう 水疱瘡 chicken pox
みすぼらしい
　・shabby ………………………[はずかしい]
みすぼらしく shabbily ………[けいべつ]
みずむし 水虫 athlete's foot
みずわり 水割り whiskey and water ………………………………[こい¹]
みせ 店 a store, a shop; (食堂) a restaurant; (酒場) a bar

みせいねん 未成年者　a minor
　〜である　be underage
みせかけ 見せかけ　appearances, (a) show, (a) (good) front
みせしめ 見せしめ　an example, a warning
みせば 見せ場　(芝居の) the high point (of a play) ……………[まく³]
みせびらかす　show off
みせもの 見せもの　a show
みせる 見せる
みそ 味噌　*miso*, soybean paste soup
　〜汁　*miso* soup, soybean paste soup
みぞ 溝
みぞおち　the solar plexus
みそこなう 見損なう
みぞれ　sleet
　〜が降る　It sleets.
〜みたい
みだし 見出し　(新聞記事の) a headline; (辞書の) an entry, a head word
みだしなみ 身だしなみ　(外見) (an) appearance
みたす 満たす　fill (up); (満足させる) satisfy, meet
みだす 乱す
みだら 〜な　obscene, dirty
　・indecent ………………………[いやらしい]
みだれる 乱れる
　(ダイヤが)乱れている　be thrown off ……………………………[せいじょう]
　乱れた風俗………………………[ふうぞく]
みち 道
　〜を空ける　clear the way …[あける¹]
　〜を渡る　cross the street ……[て]
　学問の〜へ進む　pursue a life of scholarship ………………………[しんり¹]
　我が〜を行く　go *one's* own way [き]
みち 未知の　unknown, strange
みぢか 身近な　close to *one* [ざいりょう]
みちがえる 見違える
みちづれ 道づれ　a fellow traveler
みちばた 道端に　on the side of the road ………………………………[こし]
みちびく 導く　guide, lead
みちる 満ちる
みつ 蜜　honey
みつかる 見つかる

ミックス 〜する　mix up
みつける 見つける
みつご 三つ子　triplets …………[こせい]
みっこく 密告する　inform on [against]
みっせつ 密接な　close, near
みっちり 〜練習する…………[れんしゅう]
ミット 《野球》a mitt
みつど 密度　(a) density
　〜が高い　be of high density
　〜が濃い　(話などの) substantial, full of substance
みっともない
ミツバチ　a honeybee, a bee
みっぺい 密閉する　shut *something* tightly, make *something* airtight
みつめる 見つめる
みつもり 見積り　an estimate
みつもる 見積る　estimate
みつゆ 密輸する　smuggle
みつりん 密林　a jungle, a thick forest
みてい 未定の　undecided
みてくれ　appearances, looks
みとおし 見通し
みとおす 見通す　see through; (予測する) foresee
みとどける 見届ける　see *something* with *one's* own eyes
みとめる 認める
みどり 緑(の)　green
　〜の多い　with a lot of greenery ……………………………………[おおい]
みとりず 見取り図　a sketch …[うつす¹]
みどりのひ みどりの日　Greenery Day
みとれる 見とれる
　見とれて　spellbound, in rapture ……………………………………[かろやか]
みな 皆
みなおす 見直す
　・look over *something* again　[おとす]
　・check *something* over (again) ……………………………………[なおす]
　・reconsider ………………………[ねうち]
みなす 見なす　(AをBと) regard (*A* as *B*), look upon (*A* as *B*)
みなと 港　a harbor; a port
　〜町　a harbor town ………[こくさい]
みなみ 南　the south

～の south, southern
～へ south, to [toward] the south
みなみアフリカ 南アフリカ South Africa
～の South African
～人 a South African; (全体) the South Africans
みなみシナかい 南シナ海 the South China Sea
みなもと 源 (水源) a source [supply] of water; (起源) the origin
みならい 見習い (人) an apprentice, a person learning on the job
みならう 見習う follow *someone's* example ·················[おおいに]
みなり 身なり *one's* appearance
···························[かまう]
みなれる 見慣れる get accustomed to (seeing), grow [get] used to (seeing)
　見慣れた familiar
みにくい 醜い
　ミニスカート a miniskirt, a mini
みぬく 見抜く see through ········[うそ]
みのうえ 身の上話 *one's* personal affairs, the story of *one's* life, all about *oneself*
・*one's* sad story ·················[なく¹]
みのがす 見逃す
・ignore ···························[～として]
・pass up ···························[きかい]
みのしろきん 身代金 a ransom
みのほど 身の程 *one's* place, *one's* limitation
～を知る know *one's* place, know *oneself*
みのりおおい 実り多い fruitful
みのる 実る
みばえ 見栄えがする[よい] look impressive, have a handsome appearance
みはからう 見計らう (頃合いを) choose the time, when the time is right
みはなす 見放す abandon, give up on
みはらし 見晴らし a view
～がよい have a fine view
みはり 見張り watch; (人) a watchman, a guard

～をする keep watch upon
みはる 見張る watch
みぶり 身振り
みぶん 身分
～証明書 an I.D. [identification] card ·····················[はっこう]
～制度 a caste system ········[のこる]
～相応[不相応]の within [beyond] *one's* means
みぼうじん 未亡人 a widow
みほん 見本
みまい 見舞い
みまう 見舞う
・visit *someone* when *he* is sick [ぬう]
みまちがえる 見間違える mistake A for B, mix up, get A mixed up with B; (それとわからない) not recognize
みまもる 見守る gaze (at)
・watch ···························[いき¹]
・keep an eye on ··············[はらはら]
みまわす 見回す look around [round]
みまわり 見回り (巡回) patrol; (人) a patrol; (視察) (an) inspection
みまわる 見回る
みまん 未満
みみ 耳
～に入る get wind of ············[ただ]
～を慣らす train *one's* ears [ならす¹]
～が裂けるような ear-shattering
·······································[さける¹]
　ミミズ an earthworm ···········[ほる]
　ミミズク a horned owl, an eared owl
みみっちい mean, miserly, cheap
みめい 未明に before dawn [daybreak]
みもと 身元 *one's* identity
～の確かな人 a person with a respectable background ····[たしか]
～引き受け人 *one's* sponsor, *one's* guarantor ·····················[ひきうける]
～不明の unidentified
みもの 見もの (もの笑いの種) a sight; (壮観) a spectacle; (呼びもの) a highlight, a feature
みゃく 脈
～を取る take *someone's* pulse
·······································[とる¹]

みやげ 土産 a present; (記念となる品) a souvenir
　～にくれる bring *someone* back *something* ……………[くれる¹]
みやぶる 見破る (正体を) find out; (見抜く) see through
ミャンマー (旧ビルマ) Myanmar
　～人 a Myanmarese; (全体) the Myanmarese
ミュンヘン Munich
みょう 妙
みょうごにち 明後日 the day after tomorrow ……………[つごう]
みょうじ 名字 a family name
みより 身寄り relatives
みらい 未来
ミラノ Milan
ミリグラム a milligram (略 mg)
ミリメートル a millimeter (略 mm)
みりょく 魅力
ミリリットル a milliliter (略 ml)
みる 見・診る
　～のも嫌 hate even the sight of ……………………………[いや]
　～もの聞くもの everything *one* sees and hears ………[あたらしい]
　見ていられない can't stand to watch ……………………[あぶない]
ミルク milk
　～ティー tea with milk
みるみるうちに immediately …[なみだ]
ミレニアム (千年期) the millennium
みれん 未練
みわくてき 魅惑的な fascinating
みわける 見分ける distinguish, tell (the difference)
みわたす 見渡す look around; (～が見える) overlook
みんえい 民営化 privatization
　～化する privatize
みんかん 民間の private, civilian
みんげいひん 民芸品 a folk craft [handicraft]
みんしゅ 民主的 democratic
　～主義 democracy
みんしゅく 民宿 a tourist home, a guesthouse, a family-run inn
みんしゅとう 民主党 The Democratic Party of Japan (略 DPJ)
みんぞく 民族 (国民) a people, a nation, a race
　・a tribe ………………[ほろびる]
　～の ethnic, racial
　～の違い ethnic differences [こえる]
みんな……………………………[みな]
　～で in all …………………[いく～]
みんぽう 民放 commercial broadcasting
みんよう 民謡 a folk song

ム

むいしき 無意識
　～(のうち)に without being aware of ……………………[なかば]
むいている 向いている be fit for
　・have an aptitude for ……[ぎじゅつ]
　・be suited for …………[きちょうめん]
　・be cut out for ……………[みる]
むいみ 無意味な senseless, meaningless
　～である have no meaning ……………………………[ぜんぜん]
むかい 向かいの across, opposite, across the way
　・across from *one* …………[のぞく²]
むがい 無害の harmless
むかいあう 向かい合う (人が) face each other; (建物が) stand opposite to each other
むかいあって 向かい合って across (from) ……………………[すわる]
むかう 向かう
むかえ 迎え ………………[むかえる]
むかえる 迎える
むがく 無学な uneducated, ignorant
むかし 昔
　～から since ancient times ……………………………[つたわる]
むかつく (嘔吐感) feel sick [nauseated]; (むかっとする) get mad, 《原因を主語にして》 make *one* mad, get to *one*
むかって 向かって (～の方へ) toward, for; (さからって) against
むかで a centipede
むかむか ～する (胃・胸が) feel queasy
むかんかく 無感覚な numb; (鈍感)

insensitive
むかんけい 無関係な unrelated to
　〜である have nothing to do with
むかんしん 無関心
むき 向き
むぎ 麦 (大麦) barley; (小麦) wheat; (カラス麦) oats; (ハダカ麦) rye
　〜茶 barley tea
　〜わら straw
むきげん 無期限の indefinite
むきだし むき出しの bare, naked, open
むきめい 無記名の unsigned
むく 剥く
むく 向く
むくい 報い a reward, what *one* has coming
むくち 無口
むくむ swell, become swollen
むくわれる 報われる pay off …[いつか]
　・be rewarded ……………[はたらく]
〜むけ 〜向け for
むけいかく 無計画な poorly planned …………………………………[め¹]
むける 向ける
むげん 無限 infinity
　〜の infinite
むこ 婿 (娘の夫) a son-in-law; (夫) a husband
むごい cruel, merciless
むこう 向こう
むこう 無効
むこうみず 向こう見ずな reckless, rash
むこきゅう 無呼吸症 apnea
むごたらしい 〜光景 a brutal spectacle …………………………………[きょうふ]
むごん 無言の silent
　〜で in silence
むざい 無罪 innocence
　〜の innocent, not guilty
むさくるしい むさ苦しい (おんぼろの) shabby; (乱雑な) messy
むさべつ 無差別の indiscriminate
　〜に indiscriminately, without distinction
むさぼる (利益を) profiteer; (食べる) devour
むざむざ helplessly ……………[さいのう]

むざん 無惨な (悲観的な) tragic
むし 虫 a bug; (昆虫) an insect; (うじ虫など) a worm
　〜に刺される get bit by a bug …………………………………[ふくれる]
　〜が好かない ………………[すく¹]
　〜の息 *one's* breathing is faint …………………………………[いき¹]
　〜の知らせ a premonition, a funny [strange] feeling ……………[しらせ]
むし 無視
むしあつい 蒸し暑い
むしかえす 蒸し返す drag up *something* again ………………[きまる]
むしかく 無資格の unqualified, unlicensed
　〜で without license
むしけん 無試験で without examination
むじつ 無実の innocent ……[かさねる]
むしば 虫歯 a decayed [bad] tooth …………………………………[ぬく]
　〜になる get cavities ………[だから]
　〜を予防する prevent tooth decay …………………………………[よぼう]
むしばむ undermine, eat away
むしぼし 虫干しをする air out …[ほす]
むしめがね 虫眼鏡 a magnifying glass
むじゃき 無邪気
むしゃくしゃ 〜する feel irritated
むじゅん 矛盾
むじょう 無情な heartless, cold, merciless
むじょうけん 無条件の unconditional
むしょく 無職の jobless, unemployed
むしょく 無色透明 colorless and transparent ………………[とうめい]
むしる (草を) weed
　・pluck ……………………………[け]
むしろ
むじん 無人の uninhabited; (乗務員のいない) unmanned, automatic
むしんけい 無神経
むじんぞう 無尽蔵の inexhaustible …………………………………[てんねん]
むす 蒸す
むすう 無数の countless
むずかしい 難しい

- fastidious ……………[このみ]
むすこ 息子 *one's* son
むすび 結びの closing
むすびなおす 結び直す retie ….[なおす]
むすびめ 結び目 a knot ………[とける]
むすぶ 結ぶ
むすめ 娘 *one's* daughter; (若い女) a girl
むせいげん 無制限の unlimited, unrestricted
むせきにん 無責任
むせん 無線の wireless
〜で by radio ……………[つうしん]
むせんまい 無洗米 pre-washed rice
むぞうさ 無造作
〜に casually; (ぞんざいに) carelessly; (苦もなく) easily
むだ 無駄
〜な pointless ……………[さける²]
〜である waste *one's* time ……[あし]
〜ではない not be wasted ….[くろう]
〜にはならない be of some value
………………………………[ながい]
〜に終わる be in vain ………[くしん]
〜に過ごす waste time ……[きちょう]
むだづかい むだ使いをする †throw away [waste] money ….[おもいきり]
 • waste money ……………[けんやく]
むだばなし むだ話をする waste time chatting ………………………[ぬすむ]
むだん 無断で (許可なしに) without leave; (予告なしに) without notice
 • without permission ………[うごかす]
むち 無知 ignorance
〜な ignorant
むち 鞭 a whip
〜打つ whip
むちうち 鞭打ち症 a whiplash, a whiplash injury
むちゃ 無茶
むちゃくちゃ 無茶苦茶な ridiculous, unreasonable, outrageous
むちゅう 夢中
〜である be wrapped up in …[いる¹]
 • be wrapped up *doing* ……………[め¹]
むっと 〜する (機嫌を損ねる) sulk, be offended; (息苦しい) be stifling
むていこう 無抵抗の nonresistant

むてき 無敵の invincible, matchless
むてっぽう 無鉄砲な reckless, rash
むてんか 無添加の additive-free
むとう 無糖の sugar-free
むとうか 無灯火で without a light
………………………………[あぶない]
むとうは 無党派層 unaffiliated voters
むとくてん 無得点の scoreless
………………………………[おさえる]
むとんちゃく 無頓着
むなさわぎ 胸騒ぎがする be [feel] uneasy ……………………[さわぐ]
むなしい 空しい
むね 胸
〜が熱くなる be deeply moved [touched] ……………………[あつい³]
〜にしまっておく keep *something* to *oneself* ……………………[しまう]
むねやけ 胸焼けがする have heartburn
むのう 無能な incompetent, incapable
むひょうじょう 無表情な expressionless, pokerfaced
むふんべつ 無分別な thoughtless, unreasonable, indiscreet
むぼう 無謀な rash, reckless
むぼうび 無防備な defenseless
むほん 謀反 treason
むめい 無名の unknown, obscure
むめんきょ 無免許で without license
むやみ 無暗
むよう 無用 (役に立たない) useless; (必要ない) unnecessary
むら 〜がある be uneven
気分に〜がある be capricious
むら 村 a village
〜人 (ひとり) a villager; (全体) the village
〜の人口 the rural population
………………………………[へる]
〜外れ the outskirts of the village
………………………………[たかい]
むらがる 群がる
むらさき 紫(の) purple; (青味がかった) violet
むり 無理
〜である be out of the question
………………………………[たいかく]
〜に against *someone's* will ….[いや]

~をする　overdo ……………[たおれる]
むりかい　無理解　a lack of understanding ……………[し]
むりょう　無料の　free
むりょく　無力な　powerless, helpless
むれ　群れ
ムンバイ（旧ボンベイ）　Mumbai

メ

め　目
　（視力）one's eyesight ………[わるい]
　~が粗い　coarse, loosely knit, grainy ……………[あらい²]
　~が細かい　fine, fine-toothed ……………[こまかい]
　~が覚めるような赤　a startling shade of red ……………[さめる²]
　~と鼻の先まで　within reach ……………[せまる]
　~の前で　before one's eyes ……[すぐ]
　~を盗んで　without letting on to ……………[ぬすむ]
　~を見張る　gaze on in wonder at, marvel at ……………[きょうい]
め　芽
　~が膨らむ　the buds get bigger ……………[ふくらむ]
めあて　目当て　（目的）a purpose, an aim; （目印）a guide
めい　姪　a niece
めいあん　名案　a good idea
めいえんぎ　名演技　a fine performance ……………[ふんいき]
めいおうせい　冥王星　Pluto
めいが　名画　a famous picture; （映画）a good movie
めいかく　明確な　clear, distinct
めいぎ　名義　（名前）one's name; （所有権）ownership
めいさく　名作　a masterpiece
めいさん　名産　a noted product, a specialty
めいし　名刺　a calling [visiting, name] card
　・a business card ……………[する¹]
めいじ　明治時代　the Meiji Era [とおい]
めいしゃ　目医者　an eye doctor
めいしょ　名所　the sights

~旧跡　famous and historical places ……………[けんぶつ]
めいしん　迷信　(a) superstition
　~深い　superstitious
めいじん　名人　a master, an expert (in)
めいせい　名声　(a) reputation
　・fame ……………[あこがれる]
　・name, fame ……………[きずく]
　~を獲得する　make a name for oneself ……………[たえる¹]
めいそう　瞑想にふける　be lost (deep) in meditation ……………[ふける]
めいちゅう　命中する　hit
　ど真ん中に~する　hit the bull's eye ……………[まと]
めいにち　命日　the anniversary of one's death
めいはく　明白な　clear, obvious
めいぼ　名簿　a (name) list, a directory
　・a register ……………[おとす]
　・a roster, a name list ………[のぞく¹]
　・a roll, a roster, a register　[もらす]
めいめい　銘々
めいよ　名誉
めいる　滅入る　be depressed
めいれい　命令
　~に従う　follow an order ……[ころす]
めいろ　迷路　a maze, a labyrinth
めいわく　迷惑
　~する　be annoyed by　[ひじょうしき]
　~をかける　inconvenience …[かまう]
めうえ　目上
メーカー　a manufacturer ……[こうぞう]
メーター　（計器）a meter; （タクシーの）a taximeter
メーデー　May Day
メートル　a meter (略 m)
メーリングリスト　a mailing list
メール
めかくし　目隠しする　blindfold
めがね　眼鏡　glasses, spectacles
　~屋　（人）an optician; （店）an optician's (shop)
メガバイト　《コンピュータ》a megabyte
メガホン　a megaphone
めがみ　女神　a goddess
メキシコ　Mexico
　~の　Mexican

～人 a Mexican; (全体) the Mexicans
～市 Mexico City
めぐすり 目薬 (洗眼液) eyewash, eye lotion; (点眼液) eyedrops
　～をさす use eyedrops ………[さす³]
めくばせ 目くばせをする signal with *one's* eyes
めぐまれる 恵まれる
　恵まれない underprivileged ………………………………[もよおす]
　恵まれた家庭 a privileged family ………………………………[おおらか]
　恵まれた生活 a good life [せいかつ]
めぐみ 恵み mercy, charity; (神の) a blessing
めぐむ 恵む
めぐりあわせ 巡り合わせ fortune, fate
めくる turn (over)
めげる be discouraged, be (down) in the dumps
めさき 目先の immediate
めざす 目指す aim (at)
　・of *one's* choice ………………[おかげ]
めざましい 目覚ましい
めざましどけい 目覚まし時計 an alarm clock
めざめる 目覚める wake (up); (気づく) awaken
めざわり 目障り an eyesore
めしあがる お召し上がりください Please help yourself. ……[えんりょ]
めした 目下 (年下の人) *one's* junior; (地位が下の人) *one's* subordinate
めしつかい 召し使い a servant
メジャー ～な major, mainstream
めじるし 目印に to mark the place ………………………………[おる]
メス (手術用の) a scalpel
めす 雌 a female, a she
　～の female, she-～
めずらしい 珍しい
　珍しく for a change …………[じかん]
めだつ 目立つ
めたて 目立てをする sharpen ……[は]
めだま 目玉 an eyeball
　～焼き (a) sunny-side up, a fried egg

メダル a medal
めちゃくちゃ
メッカ Mecca
めつき 目つき a look
めっき plating
　金～ gilding
　銀～ plating with silver
　～する plate
めっきり remarkably, significantly, noticeably, visibly
メッセージ a message
めったに 減多に
めでたい
めど 目途・目処
メニュー a menu
めのまえ 目の前で in front of
めまい 目まい dizziness, 《医学用語》vertigo
　～がする feel [get] dizzy
めまぐるしい 目まぐるしい dizzying, hectic, quick, rapid
メモ
　～に書いておく leave a note …[さき]
メモリ
めもり 目盛り a scale
めやす 目安
メルボルン Melbourne
メロディー a melody
メロドラマ a melodrama
　(昼メロ) a soap opera ………[ちんぷ]
メロン a melon
めん 面 a mask
　～と向かう face *someone* ……[むかう]
　～と向かって directly ………[すわる]
めん 綿 cotton
めん 麺 noodles ………………[ゆでる]
めんえき 免疫のある immune (to)
めんかい 面会 an interview
　～時間 visiting hours
　～謝絶 No visitors
　～人 a visitor
　～する see, meet
めんきょ 免許証 a license
　自動車～ a driver's license
めんしき 面識がある be acquainted with
めんじて (…に)免じて out of consideration for, in consideration

めんじょ 免除する exempt *something* from
めんする 面する face
めんぜい 免税店 a duty-free shop
めんせき 面積 area ·················[たかさ]
めんせつ 面接 an interview ······[ふり¹]
　〜試験 an interview; (口頭試問) an oral test
　〜する have an interview (with), interview
めんつ ·······················[めんぼく]
めんどう 面倒
　〜がる not bother ·············[いう]
　〜な問題 a sticky problem [ぶつかる]
　〜見がいい take good care of others ·····························[じょう]
　〜を見る support ············[せきにん]
メンバー a member; (選手などの顔ぶれ) a lineup
　(ゲームの) people to play　[そろえる]
めんぼく 面目

モ

も 喪に服している be in mourning
〜も (また) too, also, as well; (〜もまた〜ない) not either, neither; (AもBも) and, both *A* and *B*; (AもBも〜ない) neither *A* nor *B*; (Aだけでなく Bも) not only *A* but (also) *B*
もう
　・by now ··························[おきる]
　・now ································[かぜ²]
　〜一度 once again ·········[たしかめる]
もうかる 儲かる
もうけ 儲け profits, gains
　・profit margin ·················[うすい]
　〜のある profitable
もうける 設ける (供給する) provide; (設立する) establish, set up; (場・機会などを) prepare, provide
もうける 儲ける make [get] a profit, earn
　・make money ··················[しゅだん]
もうしこむ 申し込む
もうしで 申し出を受ける accept *someone's* offer ················[うける]

もうしぶんない 申し分ない
　・ideal, perfect ·····················[てんき]
もうしわけ 申しわけございません ···[まことに]
もうじん 盲人 a blind person; 《総称》(集合的に) the blind
もうすぐ pretty soon ············[〜よう]
もうすこし もう少し ···············[すこし]
　〜で (危なく) nearly
　・almost ·····························[ちこく]
もうそう 妄想 a delusion
もうちょう 盲腸 the blind gut, the cecum; (虫垂炎) appendicitis
もうてん 盲点 a blind spot
もうひつ 毛筆 a writing brush
もうふ 毛布 a blanket
もうもく 盲目の blind
もうれつ 猛烈
　〜ぶり fiery enthusiasm [ひょうばん]
もうれんしゅう 猛練習する train vigorously ························[きょうぎ]
　・train hard ·····················[れんしゅう]
もうろう 〜と clouded
　〜として be semiconscious, be hazy, be indistinct
もうろく 〜する get [go] senile
もえる 燃える
モーター a motor
モーニングコール a wake-up call
もがく struggle, writhe
もぎしけん 模擬試験 a trial examination
もぎとる wrench
もくげき 目撃する witness
　〜者 an eyewitness
もくざい 木材 《米》 lumber, 《英》 timber
もくじ 目次 (a table of) contents
もくせい 木製の wooden, made of wood
もくせい 木星 Jupiter
もくぞう 木造の wooden, built [made] of wood
もくてき 目的
　・a goal ·····························[だいいち]
　〜地 a destination ··············[こえる]
　〜を達する attain *one's* ends　[おす]
　・attain *one's* goal ···············[なめる]

～を果たす　achieve *one's* goal
　　　　　　　　　　　　　　　　　　　[けいけん]
もくとう　黙とうをささげる　pray in silence, offer a silent prayer
もくひ　黙秘する　refuse to answer, keep silent
～権　the right to refuse to answer
もくひょう　目標
～額　projected goal …………[こえる]
～を定めて　with a fixed goal in mind　…………………………[さだめる]
もくもく　黙々と　silently, in silence; (打ち込む) be absorbed in
もくようび　木曜日　Thursday (略 Th., Thur., Thurs.)
もぐら　a mole
もぐり　(不正に稼ぐ人) a fraud; (無免許の) unlicensed
もぐりこむ　もぐり込む　(腹ばいになって) crawl into; (こっそり) creep into
もぐる　潜る
もくろく　目録　a catalog
もくろみ　(計画) a plan; (目的) an aim
もけい　模型　a model
～飛行機　a model plane …[こわす]
モザイク　(a) mosaic
もし
もじ　文字　a letter; (漢字など) a character
もしかしたら　maybe, perhaps, possibly
もしくは
もじどおり　文字どおりに　literally
もじばけ　文字化け
もしもし
もじもじ　～する　fidget, hesitate
モスクワ　Moscow
もぞう　模造品　an imitation
・a fake ………………………[わかる]
もたもた　～する　dawdle, dally
もたらす　bring
もたれる　lean (against, on, over); (食べ物が) sit heavy
モダン　～な　modern
もち　餅　a rice cake
もちあげる　持ち上げる　hold up
・lift, raise …………………[あげる]
もちあじ　持ち味　special qualities

　　　　　　　　　　　　　　　　　　　[だす]
もちあるく　持ち歩く　carry …[むぞうさ]
もちあわせる　持ち合わせる　have *something* with *one* …………[つごう]
・bring *something* with *one* [ひじょう]
もちいる　用いる
もちかえり　持ち帰り (料理)《米》a takeout,《英》a takeaway
もちこす　持ちこす　carry over
もちこたえる　持ちこたえる　pull through
もちこむ　持ち込む　bring in
もちだす　持ち出す　take *something* out
　　　　　　　　　　　　　　　　　　　[かって]
話を～　bring the matter up …[のる]
もちなおす　持ち直す　(好転する) take a turn for the better, improve
もちにげ　持ち逃げする　run away with
もちぬし　持ち主　the owner
もちば　持ち場　*one's* post, *one's* station
もちはこび　持ち運びできる　portable
もちもの　持ち物　*one's* belongings, *one's* personal effects
もちろん
もつ　持つ
もっか　目下　presently ………[しらべる]
・now ………………………[ゆうせい]
もったいない
もったいぶる　make a big deal (out) of it, keep *someone* in suspense
もっていく　持って行く　take; (持ち去る) take [carry] away
もってくる　持ってくる
・pick up ……………[まちがった[て]]
もっと
モットー　a motto
もっとも　尤も
～だ　I couldn't agree more with
　　　　　　　　　　　　　　　　　　　[こと]
もっとも　最も
もっともらしい
もっぱら　専ら　exclusively
・mainly ……………………[くらい]
モップ　a mop
もつれる　(糸などが) be entangled, be tangled; (事が) become complicated; (足が) trip
もてあそぶ　play with, toy with

もてあます 持て余す　not know what to do with, not know how to deal with
もてなし　(歓迎) reception; (歓待) entertainment
・hospitality ……………[まんぞく]
もてなす
モデム　a modem
もてる　be popular with ……[くやしい]
モデル　a model ……………[ていれ]
もと 元・基
〜のさやに納まる　get back together again ……………[おさまる¹]
もどかしい
もどす 戻す
もとづく 基づく　(根拠を置く) be based on; (起因する) be due to, come from
もとで 元手　(a) capital, funds
もとどおり 元どおりにする　(状態) get *something* back to the way †it was [they were]; (場所) put *something* back to where †it was [they were]
もとめ 求め　request, a demand
もとめる 求める
(…を)求めて　in search of …[ながす]
もともと　originally; (生まれつき) by nature
もどる 戻る
モナコ　Monaco
モニター　(機器・人) a monitor
もの 物　a thing, something
〜を言う　(効果を発揮する) count (for), carry weight
ものおき 物置　a storage room …[くう]
・a storage shed ……………[りよう]
ものおじ 物怖じする　be timid in *doing*, be afraid to *do*, flinch from
ものおと 物音　a sound
・a noise ……………[きこえる]
ものおぼえ 物覚えが悪い　be a poor learner ……………[そば]
ものおもい 物思いに沈む　be lost [deep] in thought ……………[しずむ]
ものかげ 物陰に　in the shadows(s), undercover
〜から　from the shadows …[いき¹]
ものがたり 物語　a story; (寓話) a fable
ものぐさ 〜な　lazy ……………[おっくう]
ものごころ 物心がつく　be old enough to know what's going on around me
〜がついた頃からずっと　(for) as long as I can remember
ものごし 物腰　*one's* manner [おだやか]
ものごと 物事　things, everything
ものさし 物差し　a ruler
ものしり 物知りな　knowledgeable, well-informed
ものずき 物好きな　(好奇心旺盛な) curious; (風変わりな) weird, off-beat, (人) an oddball
ものすごい　terrible, awful
ものすごく　terribly, awfully
〜(した)ものだ　used to *do*, would *do*
ものたりない 物足りない
ものともしない　make nothing of ……………[こんなん]
ものほし 物干しざお　a laundry pole
《米》(綱) a clothesline
〜場　a drying place
ものまね 物真似をする　mimic, imitate, copy
ものもらい　(目の病気) a sty(e)
モノラル 〜の　mono
モノレール　a monorail car
ものわかり 物わかりがいい understanding
ものわすれ 物忘れする　be forgetful
ものわらい 物笑いの種　a laughingstock
ものをいう ものを言う　count ……………[けいけん]
モバイル 〜の　mobile
〜機器　mobile devices
もはん 模範
もふく 喪服姿で　dressed in mourning ……………[ひく]
もほう 模倣　an imitation
〜する　imitate, copy
モミ 樅　a fir (tree)
もみあげ もみ上げ　sideburns
もみけす もみ消す　crush out; (不正など) cover up
もみじ　(カエデ) a maple (leaf); (紅葉)

autumn leaves
もむ 揉む
もめごと もめ事　(a) trouble, a quarrel
もめる　(対立) have a run-in (with), be at odds (with); (口論) have a dispute, quarrel, not reach agreement
もめん 木綿　cotton
モモ 桃　a peach
もも 腿　a thigh
もや　a mist
もやし　a soybean sprout
もやす 燃やす　burn
もよう 模様　a pattern
　・a design ························[した¹]
　(…の)模様である　appear to [のぼる]
もよおし 催し　(会合) a meeting, a party; (余興) an entertainment; (行事) an event
もよおす 催す
もより 最寄りの　the closest
　····································[すみません]
もらいなき もらい泣きする　weep together with *someone* ·······[なく¹]
もらう
もらす 漏らす
モラル　morals
もり 森　a wood, woods, (小さな) a grove; (大きな) a forest
もりあがり 盛り上がり　a surge
　・momentum ··················[ぜんこく]
もりあがる 盛り上がる
もる 漏る
モルタル ~塗りの　mortared
モルディブ　the Maldives
モルモット　a guinea pig
もれる 漏れる
もろい 脆い
モロッコ　Morocco
　~の　Moroccan
　~人　a Moroccan; (全体) the Moroccans
もん 門　a gate
もんがいかん 門外漢　a nonspecialist, a layman ······················[りかい]
もんく 文句　(語句) words, a phrase; (不平) a complaint
　・criticism ·························[み¹]

~をいう　make a complaint
　・complain (of, about) …[いいすぎる]
もんげん 門限　curfew
　~を破る　break curfew ········[おおめ]
モンゴル　Mongolia
　~の　Mongolian
　~語　Mongolian, Mongol
　~人　a Mongolian; (全体) the Mongolians
モンタージュ ~写真　(a) montage
　・a composite photo ········[さんこう]
もんだい 問題
　結婚~　the question of *one's* marriage ·······················[ぶつかる]
モントリオール　Montreal
もんぶかがくしょう 文部科学省　the Ministry of Education, Culture, Sports, Science and Technology
モンブラン　Mont Blanc

ヤ

や 矢　an arrow
やあ　Hello./Hi.; (感動) Oh!/Ah!
やおちょう 八百長　a fix
　~試合　a fixed game
やおや 八百屋　a grocery store; (人) a grocer
やがい 野外の　outdoor
　~で　in the outdoors
やがて
やかましい
やかん　a kettle
　・a teakettle ····················[たつ²]
ヤギ　a goat
　子~　a kid
やきたて 焼き立て　(パンが) fresh-baked; (肉・魚が) freshly broiled
やきにく 焼き肉　roast [grilled, broiled, barbecued] meat
やきまし 焼き増し　an additional print [copy]
やきもき ~する　fret over, be impatient, be nervous
やきもち ~を焼く　get jealous …[やく³]
やきもの 焼き物　(陶磁器) ceramics, china
　(陶器) pottery ··················[せいめい]

やきゅう 野球 baseball
～大会 a baseball tournament
································[つよい]
～部 a baseball team ········[ひっぱる]
やきん 夜勤 a night shift
やく 役
・the post ·····························[いと]
人類の～に立つ serve humanity
································[さいわい]
やく 約
やく 訳 (a) translation
やく 焼く
・brown ······························[あぶら]
体を～ (日光浴する) tan *oneself*
································[ねる]
やくいん 役員 (団体などの) an officer; (会社の) an executive
やくざ a *yakuza*
・a gangster, a hoodlum ········[ふう]
～風の男·····························[ちぢむ]
やくしょ 役所 a government office
································[てつづき]
・public officials ··················[れいたん]
区〔市〕～ a ward [city] office
やくす 訳す
やくそく 約束
～の時間 the time we agreed on
································[まえ]
・the appointed time ·············[よい]
～の時間に遅れる be late for an appointment ············[きちょうめん]
～をすっぽかす stand *someone* up
································[ふむ]
やくにん 役人 a government official, a public officer, a public [civil] servant
やくば 役場 a public office
やくばらい 厄払いをする cast out evil spirits ································[まく¹]
やくひん 薬品 (薬) (a) medicine, a drug; (化学薬品) a chemical
やくめ 役目
やぐら scaffolding ············[くみたてる]
やくわり 役割 a part, a role
～を演じる play a role ······[えいせい]
～を果たす play a part
やけ ～になる get desperate, give in to desperation

～になって in desperation
やけしぬ 焼け死ぬ be burned to death
やけど (火の) a burn; (湯の) a scald
～する get burnt; get scalded
・get a burn ·······················[ひやす]
やけに awfully, terribly
・really ·······························[おとなしい]
やけのこる 焼け残る remain unburned [unburnt]
やける 焼ける
やこう 夜行列車 a night train
～性の nocturnal
やさい 野菜 (a) vegetable; (緑色の・緑色野菜) greens
やさしい 易しい
やさしい 優しい
～面がある have a gentle side
································[きしょう]
優しく gently ·····················[なでる]
優しくする be gentle (with)
································[ちいさい]
やじ booing, heckling, jeering
・a boo ·······························[あびる]
～をとばす boo [jeer] at
やじうま やじ馬 curious onlookers
やしき 屋敷 a mansion, a residence
やしきまち 屋敷街 an affluent residential area [neighborhood]
································[まち]
やしなう 養う
やしゅ 野手 《野球》 a fielder
やじゅう 野獣 a wild animal [beast]
やしょく 夜食 a midnight meal [snack]
やじるし 矢印 an arrow
やしん 野心
やすあがり 安上がりの economical, cheap(er)
やすい 安い
(賃金が) meager ···············[せいかつ]
・low ·······························[くらす]
～給料 a low salary ············[やる]
・meager wages ··················[くらす]
やすい 易い
やすうり 安売り a (bargain) sale
やすっぽい 安っぽい look [seem] cheap
やすみ 休み

～をとる　have the day off　[ためらう]
やすむ　休む
　・take the day off
　(休憩する) take a breather　[ひらたい]
やすもの　安物　cheap
やすやす　～と　easily
やすらか　安らか
やすらぐ　安らぐ
やすり　a file
　～をかける　file
やせい　野生の　wild
　～動物　a wild animal　[げんしょう]
やせがまん　やせ我慢する　put on a good face, pretend *one* doesn't mind *something*
やせる
やそう　野草　wild grasses　[たとえば]
やちん　家賃　a rent　[あがる]
やつ　奴　a guy　[たいだ]
やつあたり　八つ当たりする　take it out on *someone*
やっか　薬科大学　a college of pharmacy
やっかい　厄介
やっき　躍起になって　frantically, emphatically, like mad
やつぎばや　矢継ぎ早に　in rapid succession　[しつもん]
やっきょく　薬局　a pharmacy, 《英》a chemist's, 《米》a drugstore
やっつける　(負かす) beat; (口で) criticize; (手を抜く) do rush jobs
やっていく　get along
やってくる　やって来る　come along
　・show up　[ま]
やってのける　get *something* done　[かるい]
　・carry out　[りっぱ]
やってみる　try　[こわがる]
やってもらう　have *someone* do　[ずるい]
やっと
　・barely　[つく⁴]
　・at last　[はなれる²]
やっぱり　after all　[にらむ]
やつれる　やつれ果てて　haggard　[かげ¹]
やど　宿　(旅館) an inn; (ホテル) a hotel
　・a place to stay　[さっそく]

～代　a hotel bill　[きちょうめん]
～帳　a hotel register　[でたらめ]
やといにん　雇い人　an employee
やといぬし　雇い主　an employer
やとう　野党　an opposition party
　　　　　　　　　　　　　　[ひなん]
　～議員　an opposition party Diet member　[くいさがる]
やとう　雇う
ヤナギ　柳　a willow
やに　(木の) (a) resin; (煙草の) tar, nicotine
やぬし　家主　(男) a landlord; (女) a landlady　[あげる]
やね　屋根　a roof
やねうら　屋根裏部屋　an attic
　　　　　　　　　　　　　　[つかえる]
やはり
やばん　野蛮な　barbarous, savage
　～人　a barbarian, a savage
やぶ　a bush, a thicket
やぶいしゃ　やぶ医者　a quack
やぶへび　～になる　ask for trouble
やぶる　破る
やぶれかぶれ　破れかぶれの　desperate
　～になる　be driven to desperation
　もうこうなったら～だ　I don't give a damn.
やぶれる　破・敗れる
　・split　[こぼれる]
　破れた所　a tear　[ふう]
やぼ　野暮な　(洗練されていない) unrefined; (粗野な) boorish; (間抜けな) stupid
やま　山
　～沿いの　along the mountains
　　　　　　　　　　　　　　[そう]
　～並み　a range of mountains
　　　　　　　　　　　　　　[うつくしい]
　～のように　a mile high　[かさなる]
やまい　病を押して　despite *one's* illness
　　　　　　　　　　　　　　[おす]
やまおく　山奥に[の]　deep in the mountains　[おく²]
やまかん　山勘　a (wild) guess, a hunch
やまくずれ　山崩れ　a landslide
　　　　　　　　　　　　　　[つぶれる]
やましい　feel guilty

やまば 山場 (盛り上がり) the climax, the most interesting part; (決定的な) the crucial moment
 ～に入る reach the critical point ……………………………[はいる]
やまびこ 山びこ an echo
やまみち 山道 a mountain trail ……………………………[けわしい]
やまもり 山盛り a heap
やまやま …したいのはやまやまですが I really want to *do* but..., I'm dying to *do* but...
やまわけ 山分けする divide equally
やみ 闇 darkness; the dark
やみつき 病みつきになる be addicted (to)
 ・get hooked (on) ……………[はんぶん]
やむ 止む
やむをえない やむを得ない
やめさせる (中止させる) stop (from, out of); (解雇する) dismiss (from)
 ・let *someone* go ……………[もんだい]
やめる 止・辞める
やもめ (男) a widower; (女) a widow
ややこしい
やらせ a setup
やられる (殴られる) be beaten up; (負ける) be beat; (被害を受ける) be damaged, be ruined; (だまされる) be taken in
やり 槍 a spear, a lance
やりあう やり合う (口げんか) have a quarrel (with), argue (with)
やりがい やり甲斐がある worthwhile …………………………[せきにん]
やりかけ ～の unfinished, undone
やりかた やり方
 ・a way of handling things …………………………[さんせい]
やりくり
やりこめる やり込める talk down, argue down
やりすごす やり過ごす let *something* pass ……………………………[わき]
やりそこなう やり損なう fail to *do*
やりて やり手 a go-getter, a wheeler-dealer
やりとおす やり通す carry out

 ・see *something* through ………[たび]
やりとげる やり遂げる accomplish, carry out
 ・finish ……………………[なんと]
やりとり an exchange
やりなおす やり直す (もう一度) do *something* over again; (最初から) make a fresh start
やりなげ やり投げ the javelin (throw)
やりにくい difficult, hard; (立場的に) awkward
やりぬく やり抜く finish …………[ぬく]
やる 遣る
やるき やる気 drive ……………[しんぼ]
 ～が出る get motivated ……[いっそう]
 ～がない have no intention of ……………………………[むせきにん]
やれやれ Good grief. ／ Whew.
やわらかい 柔・軟らかい
やわらぐ 和らぐ
やわらげる 和らげる (やわらかくする) soften; (痛みなどを静める) ease
やんちゃ ～な naughty, mischievous

ユ

ゆ 湯 hot water; (風呂) a (hot) bath
ゆいいつ 唯一の the only, the sole
ゆいごん 遺言 a will, *one's* last words
ゆう 結う (髪を) do *one's* hair
ゆうい 優位に立っている be superior to
ゆういぎ 有意義
ゆううつ 憂うつ
ゆうえき 有益
ゆうえつかん 優越感
ゆうえんち 遊園地 an amusement park, a children's playground
ゆうが 優雅
ゆうかい 誘拐 kidnapping, abduction
 ～する kidnap, abduct
 ～犯 a kidnapper
ゆうがい 有害な harmful; injurious
ゆうがた 夕方 (an) evening
ゆうかん 夕刊 an evening paper [edition]
ゆうかん 勇敢
 ～に courageously …………[たたかう]
ゆうき 勇気

〜を持って　courageously ……[もつ]
ゆうき 有機の　organic
　〜栽培された　organic, organically grown
　〜農法　organic farming
　〜野菜〔農産物〕　organic vegetables 〔produce〕
ゆうきゅう 有給休暇　a paid holiday [leave, vacation]
ゆうぐう 優遇する　treat *someone* very well
ゆうげきしゅ 遊撃手　《野球》a shortstop
ゆうげん 有限の　limited, finite
ゆうけんしゃ 有権者　a voter; (集合的に) the electorate
ゆうこう 友好　(a) friendship
　〜的な　friendly
ゆうこう 有効
　〜に　effectively ……………[つかう]
ユーゴスラビア　Yugoslavia
　〜の　Yugoslav, Yugoslavian
　〜人　a Yugoslav; (全体) the Yugoslavs
ユーザー　a user; (コンピュータの共同使用者) a user
ゆうざい 有罪　guilt ……………[てらす]
　〜の　guilty
ゆうし 融資する　finance, provide money for
ゆうしゅう 優秀
　〜な　outstanding ……………[そろう]
　・　 ……………[つづく]
ゆうじゅうふだん 優柔不断
ゆうしょう 優勝
　〜する　win the championship
　　　　　 ……………[ぜんこく]
　〜候補　the leading contender (for the championship) ……………[くう]
　全国大会で〜する　win the national championship ……………[つづける]
ゆうじょう 友情
ゆうしょく 夕食　dinner; (簡単な) supper
ゆうじん 友人　a friend
ゆうずう 融通
ユースホステル　a (youth) hostel
ゆうせい 優勢

ゆうぜい 遊説する　canvass, make an election tour
ゆうせん 優先
ゆうせん 有線放送　closed-circuit [cable] broadcasting
　〜テレビ　cable television
ゆうそう 郵送する　mail, post
　〜料　the postage ……………[そえる]
ユーターン 〜する　make a U-turn
ゆうだい 雄大
ゆうだち 夕立　a shower ……[ようす]
　・a sudden shower ……………[ぬれる]
ゆうどう 誘導する　guide, lead
ゆうとうせい 優等生　an excellent student; (優等賞を受けた) an honor student
ゆうどく 有毒な　poisonous
　〜ガス　a poisonous gas ……[だす]
ユートピア　(a) utopia
ゆうのう 有能
ゆうはん 夕飯が出来た　Dinner's ready.
　　　　　 ……………[できる]
ゆうひ 夕日　the evening [setting] sun
ゆうびん 郵便　mail, 《英》post
　〜局　a post office ……………[きんじょ]
　〜配達人　a mailman, 《英》a postman
　〜番号　the postal code, 《米》the zip code
　〜物　mail
　〜振替　postal transfer ……[もしくは]
　〜料金　postage
　・postal rates ……………[つうじる]
ゆうふく 裕福な　rich
　・wealthy, well-to-do ……[そだつ]
ゆうべ 夕べ　(昨夜) last night; (夕方) an evening
ゆうべん 雄弁　eloquence
　〜な　eloquent
ゆうほう 有望
ゆうめい 有名
　〜な　well-known ……………[いじめる]
ユーモア
ユーモラス 〜な　humorous
ゆうやけ 夕焼け　an evening glow
　・a sunset ……………[まず]
ゆうゆう 悠々
ゆうよ 猶予　(支払いなどの) grace; (執

行猶予) suspension
ゆうり 有利
ゆうりょう 有料の　pay
　〜道路　a toll road
ゆうりょく 有力
ゆうれい 幽霊　a ghost
　〜屋敷　a haunted house
ゆうわく 誘惑
　〜に負ける　give into temptation
　..[まける]
ゆか 床　a floor
ゆかい 愉快
　〜な　jolly, amusing
ゆかげん 湯加減　the temperature of the bath water ....[みる]
ゆがむ 歪む
ゆがんだ 歪んだ　warped ....[わく²]
ゆき 雪　snow
　〜が降る　It snows.
　〜深い　snowy
ゆき 〜行き　(bound) for
ゆきおとこ 雪男　the abominable snowman, yeti ....[おもう、〜そう]
ゆきだるま 雪だるま　a snowman
　〜のように膨れ上がる　snowball
　..[ふくれる]
ゆきづまる 行き詰まる........[いきづまる¹]
ゆきやま 雪山　snowy mountains
ゆく 行く
ゆくえふめい 行方不明の　missing [て]
ゆげ 湯気　steam, vapor
ゆけつ 輸血　(a) blood transfusion
　〜する　give (a) (blood) transfusion
ゆしゅつ 輸出　export
　〜する　export
ゆすぐ rinse
ゆすり extortion, blackmail; (人) an extortioner, a blackmailer
ゆする (恐喝する) extort, blackmail
ゆする 揺する　shake, rock, swing
ゆずる 譲る
ゆそう 輸送　conveyance, transportation
　〜する　convey, transport, carry
ゆたか 豊か
ユダヤ 〜人　a Jew; (全体) the Jews
　〜の　Jewish

　〜教　Judaism
ゆだん 油断
　・negligence ....[ばかり]
ゆっくり
　・leisurely ....[のち]
　〜する　relax ....[なくなる¹]
　〜食事する　enjoy *one's* meal
　..[うるさい]
ゆったり 〜した　(ゆるい) loose; (気持ちが) relaxed
ゆでたまご ゆで卵　a boiled egg
ゆでる
ゆでん 油田　an oil field ....[ほる]
ゆとり
ユニーク 〜な　unique
ユニホーム a uniform
ゆにゅう 輸入　import
　〜規制　restrictions on imports
　..[ゆるめる]
　〜する　import
　〜に頼る　depend on imports
　..[げんりょう]
ゆび 指
ゆびさき 指先　(手の) a fingertip; (足の) the tip of a toe
ゆびわ 指輪　a ring
　〜をする　wear a ring ....[ごうか]
ゆぶね 湯ぶね　a bathtub
ゆみ 弓　a bow; (弓術) archery
ゆめ 夢
ゆらい 由来　(起源) an origin; (来歴) a history
ゆらぐ 揺らぐ　sway, shake
　・crumble ....[もと]
ゆらす 揺らす　shake, rock, swing
ユリ a lily
ゆりかご a cradle
ゆるい 緩い
ゆるす 許す
　・give *someone* permission .....[れい²]
　許しておく　let *someone* go scot-free
　..[うらぎる]
　許せない　won't stand for ....[いう]
　・unforgivable ....[こい³]
ゆるむ 緩む
ゆるめる 緩める
ゆるやか 緩やか
ゆれる 揺れる

・sway ……………………[にぎる]

ヨ

よ 世 (世の中) the world; (時代) the times
　〜も末だ What's this world coming to? ……………………[すえ]
よあけ 夜明け dawn, daybreak
よい 宵 the early evening
よい 良・善・好い
　良きにつけ悪しきにつけ whether it's good or bad ……………………[うわさ]
よい 酔いが回る get drunk [tipsy], feel the effects of †the liquor [a drink]
　・liquor hits *one* ……………………[した²]
　〜をさます sober up ……………………[さます]
よう 酔う
　バスに〜 get [feel] carsick [もよおす]
　船に〜 get seasick ……………………[はく¹]
よう 用
　〜があれば if there's something I can do ……………………[えんりょ]
〜よう
〜(し)よう (勧誘) let's; (意志) will
ようい 用意
ようい 容易に easily
　・readily ……………………[じそんしん]
よういくひ 養育費 the expense of bringing up (a child)
よういん 要因 a factor, (a) cause
ようき 容器 a container
ようき 陽気
ようぎ 容疑 suspicion ……………………[あげる]
　〜者 a suspect ……………………[〜つける]
ようきゅう 要求
　・a request ……………………[くび]
ようけん 用件 business ……………………[まず]
ようご 用語 a term
　特別な〜 a technical term …[ふつう]
ようこそ Welcome (to...).
ようさい 洋裁 dressmaking
ようし 用紙 a blank, a (blank) form; (紙) paper
　解答〜 an answer sheet
　答案〜 an examination paper
　メモ〜 a memo paper [pad]
　申込み〜 an application form

ようし 容姿 *one's* looks; (スタイル) a figure
ようし 養子 an adopted child [son, daughter]
　〜にする adopt
ようじ 用事
ようじ 幼児 an infant; (小さな子) a little child
ようじ 楊枝 a toothpick
ようしき 洋式(の) European style, Western style
ようしき 様式 a mode, (a) style
ようしょ 洋書 Western books and magazines ……………………[せんもん]
ようしょく 養殖 culture, farming
ようじん 用心
ようじん 要人 a VIP ……………………[もよおす]
ようす 様子
　〜を語る describe the scene ……………………[いきいき]
ようすこう 揚子江 the Yangtze River
ようするに 要するに (簡単にいえば) in short, in a word; (結局) after all
ようせい 養成 (a) training
　〜する train
ようせき 容積 (容量) capacity; (体積) volume
ようそ 要素 an element, a factor
〜ようだ ……………………[〜よう]
ようだい 容態・容体 (患者の) a condition
ようち 幼稚
ようちえん 幼稚園 a kindergarten ……………………[でも]
　・a nursery school ……………………[むかえる]
ようちゅう 幼虫 a larva
ようつう 腰痛 a lower-back pain
ようてん 要点 the point
　・an essential point ………[つまむ]
　〜を押さえて to the point [おさえる]
ようと 用途 use; (目的) a purpose
ようは 要は the main point is..., the key is...
ようび 曜日 the day of the week
ようふう 洋風 Western-style
　〜化する westernize ……………………[ふくそう]
ようふく 洋服 clothes; (和服に対して) Western clothes; (一そろいの) a

suit; (女性用) a dress
～だんす a wardrobe ……[ねんいり]
～屋 (人) a tailor, (店) a tailor's (shop); (婦人・子ども服の) a dressmaker
ようぶん 養分 nourishment
ようほう 用法 use, how to use; (言葉の) usage
ようぼう 容貌 looks, an appearance
ようま 洋間 a Western-style room
ようもう 羊毛 wool
～の wool, woolen
ようやく 漸く
ようりょう 要領
～よく concisely ……[のべる]
ヨーグルト yogurt
ヨーロッパ Europe
～の European
～人 a European; (全体) the Europeans
～連合 the European Union
よか 余暇 leisure, one's spare [free] time
・ one's spare time ……[つくる]
ヨガ yoga
よかん 予感
嫌な～ forebodings ……[いや]
よき 予期
よぎ 余儀なくされる be forced to do ……[おぎなう]
よきょう 余興 an entertainment
よぎり 夜霧 a night fog ……[つつむ]
よきん 預金 deposit; (銀行の) a bank account
外貨～(口座) a foreign currency account
～通帳 a bankbook ……[おく²]
～額 a bank account ……[へる]
～する deposit
～を引き出す draw money from the bank
よく 欲
(定期的に) regularly ……[かよう]
～考える think carefully [おちつく]
～言う speak well of ……[いう]
～言えば putting it nicely ……[いう]
よく 欲
よく～ 翌～

よくしつ 浴室 a bathroom
よくできた ～男 a fine example of a man ……[じっさい]
よくなる 良くなる recover ……[かすか]
よくばる 欲張る
よくぼう 欲望 a desire ……[かぎり]
よくよう 抑揚 (an) intonation
よけい 余計
～な unasked-for ……[くち]
～なおせっかい an unnecessary favor ……[おせっかい]
～な一言 an uncalled-for remark ……[もってくる]
よける 避ける
よけん 予見する foresee ……[みらい]
よげん 予言 a prophecy, (a) prediction
～者 a prophet
～する foretell, prophesy, predict
よこ 横
～の horizontal ……[たて]
～向きの顔 profile ……[むき]
～を向く turn one's face ……[むく²]
～になる lie down ……[らく]
よこがお 横顔 a profile
よこぎる 横切る
よこく 予告 a notice
～する give notice (of)
よごす 汚す
よこたえる 横たえる lay (down)
よこたわる 横たわる lie (down)
よこどり 横取りする make off [away] with, swipe
よこみち 横道 a side road
よこめ 横目 a side [sidelong] glance
～で睨みながら keeping an eye on ……[にらむ]
～で見る cast a sidelong glance
よごれ 汚れ a stain, a spot, soil
・ grime ……[もむ]
よごれる 汚れる
よさ 良さ a good point; (長所) a merit
よさん 予算
～の範囲内 within the limits of the budget ……[はんい]
よし (感嘆詞) all right, O.K., OK
よしあし 善し悪しが分かる know right

from wrong; (質の) can judge the quality
　～だ　have its good side and its bad side
よじのぼる　よじ登る　climb (up); (すばやく) scramble up
よしゅう　予習
よじれる　be kinked, be twisted
よす
よせい　余生　the rest of *one's* life ……………………………………[のんびり]
よせる　寄せる
よせん　予戦　a preliminary game ……………………………………[やぶれる]
よそ
　～へ移る　move away ………[たたむ]
よそう　予想
　競馬の～　a hunch about the horse race ……………………………[ぴったり]
よそみ　よそ見する　look the other way, take *one's* eyes off, look away [aside]
よそゆき　よそ行きの　formal
　～の服　*one's* best clothes
よそよそしい　standoffish, cool, cold
　～態度をとる　act distant
よだれ　drool, saliva, slaver
　～を出す　slaver, slobber
よだん　予断　premature conclusions ……………………………………[ゆるす]
よち　余地　room
よちよち　～歩きをする　toddle along ……………………………………[はらはら]
よつかど　四つ角　a crossing, an intersection
よっきゅう　欲求
ヨット　a yacht; a sail boat
よっぱらい　酔っ払い　a drunken man, a drunkard
よっぱらう　酔っぱらう　get drunk
よてい　予定
　(期日) the scheduled time ……[のびる]
　～どおりに　on schedule ………[へた]
　～より早く　ahead of schedule ……………………………………[てつだう]
　～から外す　leave *something* out of [off] the schedule …………[はずす]
よとう　与党　the ruling party　[たのむ]
　・the party in power …………[わたす]
よなか　夜中　midnight
　～に　late at night; (真夜中に) at midnight
　・in the middle of the night　[たのむ]
よなれる　世慣れている　know *one's* way around, be experienced
よにげ　夜逃げする　secretly move out
よのなか　世の中
　～に認められる　achieve general recognition …………………[みとめる]
　～のために　for the good of mankind ……………………………[すてる]
よはく　余白　(欄外) a margin; (埋めるための) a blank
ヨハネスブルグ　Johannesburg
よび　予備
よびかける　呼びかける　call out to *someone*; (協力・参加を募る) appeal for *something*, appeal to *someone* to *do*, invite *someone* to *do*
よびこう　予備校　a preparatory school, a prep school
よびだされる　呼び出される　be summoned ……………………………[きゅう]
よびもの　呼び物　the chief attraction
よびりん　呼びりん　a bell, a doorbell
よぶ　呼ぶ
よふかし　夜更かしする　stay up late at night ……………………………[けんこう]
　・stay up till all hours of the night ……………………………………[くせ]
よふけ　夜ふけに　late at night
よぶん　余分の　extra, excess; (すぐ用のない) spare
よほう　予報
よぼう　予防
　～接種　(protective) inoculation, (a) vaccination
よほど
よみ　読み　(判断) judgment; (予測・計画) projections
　～が深い〔浅い〕　have deep [shallow] insight
よみあさる　読みあさる　read voraciously …………………………[もとめる]
よみかえす　読み返す　read over, read again

よみかた 読み方 (発音) (a) pronunciation; (解釈) an interpretation
よみせ 夜店 a night stall
よみなおす 読み直す reread ……[き]
よみにくい 読みにくい indecipherable ……[みつける]
よみふける 読みふける keep on reading ……[わすれる]
よむ 読む
　読めない illegible ……[にじむ]
よめ 嫁 (息子の) a daughter-in-law; (妻) a wife
　〜と姑の関係 the relationship between a wife and her mother-in-law ……[ふるい]
よやく 予約する reserve, book
　〜席 a reserved seat
よゆう 余裕
より 〜が戻る patch things up ……[もどる]
より
(〜に)より according to ……[ことなる]
よりかかる 寄りかかる lean (against, on, over)
よりそう 寄り添う snuggle [nestle] up to
　寄り添って座る sit beside each other ……[そう]
よりに(も)よって of all things 〔people, days, times, etc.〕
よる 夜 night; (夕方) evening
　〜に at night, in the evening
　〜になって after nightfall …[きえる]
　〜になると at nightfall ……[なる¹]
よる 因る
よる 寄る
ヨルダン Jordan
　〜人 a Jordanian; (全体) the Jordanians
よるとしなみ 寄る年波には勝てない can't fight the advancing years ……[よる²]
〜(に)よれば according to
よれよれ 〜の worn-out, rumpled
　〜になる wear out, rumple
よろいかぶと armor
よろこばしい 喜ばしい delightful, desirable, happy
よろこばす 喜ばす please, delight
よろこび 喜び
よろこぶ 喜ぶ
　・get a kick out of ……[からかう]
　・rejoice (over) ……[こころ]
よろしい
よろしく Please remember me to *someone*./Please give my best regards to *someone*./Please say hello for me to *someone*.
よろめく stagger, totter
よろん 世論 public opinion
　〜調査 a public opinion poll ……[はっぴょう]
　・the polls ……[けいこう]
よわい 弱い
　〜者 an underdog ……[みかた]
よわき 弱気な timid, fainthearted, coward
よわたり 世渡りがうまい know how to get along [on] in the world, be good at getting ahead with people
よわね 弱音を吐く whine ……[はく¹]
よわみ 弱み a weak point, a weakness
　〜を握る have something on *someone* ……[にぎる]
よわむし 弱虫 a weakling; (臆病者) a coward, a chicken
よわよわしい 弱々しい feeble, weak
よわる 弱る
よん 四 four
　4分の1 a [one] fourth
　第4(の) fourth (略 4th)
よんじゅう 四十 forty
　第40(の) the fortieth (略 40th)

ラ

ラーメン Chinese noodles
ライオン a lion; (雌の) a lioness
らいきゃく 来客 a visitor, a guest
らいげつ 来月 next month
らいしゅう 来週 next week
ライスカレー curry and rice, curried rice
ライター a (cigarette) lighter
ライト (明かり) a light
ライト 《野球》(右翼) the right field;

(右翼手) a right fielder
らいねん 来年　next year
ライバル
　〜意識　a sense of rivalry　[はりあう]
らいびょう らい病　leprosy
らいひん 来賓　a guest …………[のべる]
ライフライン　lifelines
ライフル　a rifle
ライン 〜川　the Rhine
ラオス　Laos
　〜の, 〜語　Laotian
　〜人　a Laotian; (全体) the Laotians
らく 楽
らくいん らく印を押す　brand ……[おす]
らくえん 楽園　a paradise
らくがき 落書き　scribbles, graffiti
　・scribbling ……………………[あと²]
　〜する　scribble
らくご 落伍する　drop out
らくさつ 落札する　win a bid
　〜される　be knocked down
らくしょう 楽勝だ　win easily, beat *someone* easily; (容易) be a cinch
らくせい 落成式　an inauguration, a completion ceremony
らくせん 落選　(a) defeat ………[ちから]
　〜する　(選挙で) be defeated in an election, fail to be elected; (展覧会・懸賞募集で) be rejected, not be accepted
　・lose an election ……………[よそう]
ラクダ　a camel
らくだい 落第する　fail a grade
　………………………………[いいきみ]
　・flunk ………………………[ふりょう]
らくたん 落胆
らくちょう 落丁している　be missing
　………………………………[いちぶ]
らくてん 楽天的な　optimistic
　〜家　an optimist
らくのう 酪農　dairy (farming)
ラグビー　rugby
らくらく 楽々と　easily, with ease
ラケット　a racket
〜らしい
　・it appears as if... …………[おさまる¹]
ラジオ　radio; (受信機) a radio (set)
ラジカセ　a radio cassette recorder

〜らしく ……………………[〜らしい]
ラジコン　radio control
ラスト　the last
ラスベガス　Las Vegas
らせん　a spiral
　〜の　spiral
　〜階段　a spiral staircase
らち 〜が明かない　not get anywhere
　………………………………[ちゅうとはんぱ]
らち 拉致　abduction
　〜する　abduct
ラッカー　(a) lacquer
らっかせい 落花生　a peanut
らっかん 楽観
　〜を許さない　can't be optimistic
　…………………………………[ゆるす]
ラック　a rack
ラッコ　a sea otter
ラッシュ　rush
　〜アワー　rush hour …………[つづく]
ラッパのみ ラッパ飲みする　drink *something* straight from the bottle
ラップ　(食品などを包む) plastic wrap
ラップ(ミュージック)　rap music
ラップトップ 《コンピュータ》a laptop (computer)
ラテン　(民族の) Latin
　〜アメリカ　Latin America
　〜語　Latin
　〜音楽　Latin(-American) music
ラバ　a mule
ラベル　a label
られつ 羅列する　enumerate (instances), cite (example after example)
らん 欄　(新聞などの) a column
　〜外　a margin
らん 蘭　an orchid
ランク　(a) rank
らんざつ 乱雑な　disorderly, messy
らんし 乱視　《医学用語》astigmatism
ランチ　(a) lunch
らんとう 乱闘　a scuffle, a confused fight
ランドセル　a (school) satchel
ランニング　running; (軽い) jogging
ランプ　a lamp; (高速道路の) a ramp
らんぼう 乱暴

〜を働く commit an act of violence ……………………………………[はたらく]
らんよう 乱用する abuse, misuse, overuse

リ

リーグ （スポーツの）a league
リーダー （指導者）a leader
リーダー （読み物）a reader
リード
りえき 利益
リオデジャネイロ Rio de Janeiro
りか 理科 science, natural science
〜系 the science course
りかい 理解
りがい 利害 interests
りがくぶ 理学部 the science department ………………………[おく²]
りきし 力士 a *sumo* wrestler [ひいき]
りきせつ 力説する emphasize, stress
りきむ 力む （力を入れる）strain (*oneself*); （興奮する）get worked up
りきりょう 力量 ability, (a) capacity
りく 陸 land
リクエスト (a) request
〜する request
りくぐん 陸軍 the army
りくじょう 陸上競技 track and field
〜競技大会 a track and field meet ……………………………………[まく³]
りくつ 理屈
〜で rationally ……………[わりきる]
りこ 利己
りこう 利口
リコール a recall
〜する recall
りこてき 利己的な egoistic, self-centered
りこん 離婚 divorce ………[てつづき]
・a divorce ………………………[くるしい]
〜する divorce ………………[あんい]
リサイクル recycling
〜する recycle
〜ショップ a secondhand shop, a recycled-goods shop, a thrift shop
リサイタル a recital
りし 利子 interest ……………[つく²]

りじ 理事 a director, a trustee
〜会 a board of directors [trustees]
リス a squirrel
リスト a list
〜アップする list, make a list of
リストラ （再構築）restructuring; （人員削減）a personnel cutback
〜する （再構築）restructure; （人員削減）cutback personnel; （解雇）fire
リスボン Lisbon
リズム rhythm
〜に乗って to the rhythm ……[のる]
りせい 理性
リセット 〜する （タイマーなどを）reset; （コンピュータを）clear, reset
りそう 理想
〜を求める pursue *one's* ideal [やむ]
りちぎ 律儀な sincere, faithful
りちてき 知的な intellectual
りつ 率 a rate
りっきょう 陸橋 an overpass
りっこうほ 立候補する run for ……………………………………[まったく]
りっしんしゅっせ 立身出世する succeed in life
りったい 立体の solid, cubic, three-dimensional
リットル a litter (略 l, lit)
りっぱ 立派
〜な admirable …………………[たいど]
・great ………………………[じっこう]
りっぽう 立方 cube
〜体 a cube
〜メートル a cubic meter
りっぽう 立法 legislation
りてん 利点 an advantage
りとう 離島 an isolated island …[ほね]
リニアモーターカー a linear motor car
りねん 理念 （主義）a principle; （理想）an ideal
リハーサル a rehearsal
〜をする rehearse
リバイバル a revival
リハビリ rehabilitation
リビア Libya
〜の Libyan
〜人 a Libyan; （全体）the Libyans
リフォーム 〜する （建物・服を）

remodel; (古い建物を) renovate
りふじん 理不尽な unreasonable, outrageous
リフト (スキー場の) a ski lift
リボン a ribbon
りまわり 利回り yield
リモコン a remote control
りゃくご 略語 an abbreviation ［いみ］
りゃくす 略す (語などを) abbreviate; (省く) omit
りゆう 理由
　〜をあげる give *someone* a reason ……………………………………［あげる］
りゅう 竜 a dragon
りゅうがく 留学する go abroad for study
　・go to *somewhere* to study ［おもう］
　・study abroad ……………［ないしょ］
りゅうかん 流感 influenza, flu
りゅうこう 流行
　〜遅れになる go out of fashion ……………………………………［かた¹］
　〜語 a trendy word ………［かいわ］
りゅうざん 流産 (a) miscarriage
　〜する have a miscarriage
りゅうせい 流星 a meteor, a shooting star
りゅうせんけい 流線型の streamlined ……………………………………［ていこう］
りゅうちょう 流ちょうな fluent
　〜に fluently
りゅうつう 流通 (商品の) distribution; (通貨の) circulation
　〜している be in circulation
りゅうどう 流動性の fluid; (変わりやすい) changeable
　〜的な (決まっていない) fluid, not be fixed
　〜食 liquid food, a fluid [liquid] diet
りゅうねん 留年する fail [flunk] a year, repeat the year
リューマチ rheumatism ………［まがる］
リュック(サック) a rucksack, a knapsack, a backpack
りよう 利用
りょう 量
りょう 猟 hunting, a hunt; (銃猟) shooting
りょう 漁 fishing
りょう 寮 a dorm ……………［きそく］
　・a dormitory ………………［ばつ］
りょういき 領域 a territory, a field
りょうかい 了解
りょうがえ 両替 (money) exchange
　〜する exchange, change money
りょうきん 料金 a charge, a fee, a rate; (乗り物の) a fare
　大人〜 full fare …………［いじょう¹］
りょうけん 了見 an idea, (an) intention
　〜の狭い narrow-minded
りょうさん 量産する mass-produce
りょうし 猟師 a hunter
りょうし 漁師 a fisherman
りょうじ 領事 a consul
　総〜 a consul general
　〜館 a consulate
りょうしき 良識 good sense, common sense, sound judgment
　〜を疑う question *someone's* judgment ………………………［うたがう］
りょうしゅうしょ 領収書 a receipt
りょうしょう 了承する approve, consent, give *one's* approval to
りょうしん 両親 *one's* parents
りょうしん 良心
りょうせい 良性の benign
りょうど 領土 (a) territory ［ひろげる］
りょうほう 両方 both; (両方とも〜ない) neither
りょうり 料理 (調理) cooking; (料理法) cookery
　(一品の) a dish ……………［ざいりょう］
　手〜 home cooking …………［おとる］
　〜する cook, prepare
　〜の腕前がいい be a good cook ……………………………………［ぶあいそう］
　〜人 a cook
りょうりつ 両立させる cope with both *A* and *B*, have [keep up] both *A* and *B*
りょかん 旅館 a hotel
　・an inn ……………………［たいぐう］
りょけん 旅券 a passport
りょこう 旅行

～中　during the trip ……… [こうどう]
～に行く　go on a trip ……… [いく]
～に出る　go on a trip …… [きゅうか]
りょひ　旅費　travel expenses
　……………………… [こころぼそい]
リラックス　～する[させる]　relax
りりく　離陸　a takeoff
　～する　take off, make a takeoff
リレー　a relay
りれき　履歴　one's personal history
　～書　a personal history [record]
　・one's résumé …………………… [はる²]
りろん　理論
　～派　a theorist ……… [こうどう]
りんかく　輪郭　an outline
りんきおうへん　臨機応変
りんぎょう　林業　forestry
リンク
リング　(ボクシングなどの) a ring
リンゴ　an apple
りんじ　臨時
　～委員会　the provisional committee
　……………………………… [おこなう]
りんじゅう　臨終　the last, one's last, one's death
りんじん　隣人　a neighbor
リンス　(a) (hair) rinse, hair conditioner
リンパ　～腺　a lymph gland [node]
　～腫　《医学用語》lymphoma
りんびょう　淋病　《医学用語》gonorrhea
りんり　倫理　ethics
　～的な　ethical, moral
りんりつ　林立するビル　a forest of buildings ……………………… [ながめ]

ル

るい　塁　a base
るい　類
るいご　類語　a synonym
るいじ　類似　similarity, resemblance
　～している　be similar to
るいじんえん　類人猿　an anthropoid apes
るいすい　類推　analogy
るいせき　累積した　accumulated, cumulative
ルーズ　～な　(不注意な, だらしない) careless, sloppy, lax; (ゆるい) loose
ルーズリーフ　a loose-leaf notebook
ルーツ　(祖先) roots
　(起源) the origin (of) ……… [あいまい]
ルーマニア　Rumania
　～の, ～語　Rumanian
　～人　a Rumanian; (全体) the Rumanians
ルール　a rule
ルクセンブルク　Luxembourg
　～の　Luxembourgian
　～人　a Luxembourger; (全体) the Luxembourgers
るす　留守
　～である　be out …………………… [こい³]
　～中　while one is out ……… [かんじ]
るつぼ　a melting pot, a crucible
ルネッサンス　the Renaissance
ルビー　(a) ruby
ルポ　a report, reportage

レ

れい　礼
れい　例
　～をあげる　give [cite] an example
　……………………………… [あげる]
れい　零　zero
れい　霊　a soul, a spirit
れいか　零下　below zero ……… [み¹]
れいがい　例外　an exception
　～的に　exceptionally; (異常に) unusually
れいぎ　礼儀
　～知らず　not have (good) manners
　……………………………… [こまる]
れいきゅうしゃ　霊柩車　a hearse
れいこく　冷酷
れいさい　零細企業　a small business
れいしょう　冷笑する　sneer
　～的な　cynical
れいじょう　礼状　a thank-you note
　……………………………… [ていねい]
れいすいまさつ　冷水摩擦をする　rub oneself down with a cold wet towel ……………………… [しゅだん]
れいせい　冷静
　～な判断　(a) cool judgment, (a) rational decision ……… [ふせぐ]

れいぞうこ 冷蔵庫　a refrigerator ……………………………[くさる]
　・a fridge ……………………[かためる]
　〜に入れる[入れて保存する]
　　refrigerate ……………………[ほぞん]
れいだい 例題　an exercise
れいたん 冷淡
れいとう 冷凍　freezing
　〜庫　a freezer
　〜食品　frozen food
　〜する　freeze
　〜の　frozen
れいはい 礼拝　worship; (教会の) service
　〜する　worship ……………………[なる²]
　〜堂　a chapel
れいぼう 冷房　(装置) an air conditioner
　(機能) air-conditioning ………[かげん]
レーザー　a laser
レース　(競技) a race
レース　(編物) lace, crochet
　〜編み　lacework
　・crocheting ……………………[つづく]
レーダー　(a) radar
レール　a rail
レーンコート　a raincoat
レオタード　a leotard
れきし 歴史　history
　〜上の　historical, historic
　〜的な　historic
　〜的に　historically
レギュラー　a regular
レクリエーション　recreation
レコード　(記録) a record; (音盤) a record, a disk
レジ　(機械) a (cash) register; (場所) a checkout counter
レシート　a receipt
レシピ　a recipe
レジャー　leisure; (余暇の活動) a leisure activity; (娯楽) (a) recreation
レストラン　a restaurant
レスラー　a wrestler
レスリング　wrestling
レタス　lettuce
れつ 列
　横1〜に　in one row ………[ならべる]
れっきとした　respectable; (反論できない) irrefutable, indisputable
れっしゃ 列車　a train
　〜事故　a train accident ………[れい²]
　〜に遅れる　be late for a train …………………………………[〜よう]
レッスン　a lesson
レッテル　a label
　〜を貼る　(人に) label *someone* (as)
れっとう 列島　an archipelago
　日本〜　the Japanese Archipelago [Islands]
れっとう 劣等
レッドカード　a red card
レバー　(取手) a lever
レバー　(肝臓) (a) liver
レバノン　Lebanon
　〜の　Lebanese
　〜人　a Lebanese; (全体) the Lebanese
レフェリー　a referee
レフト　《野球》(左翼) the left field; (左翼手) a left fielder
レベル
レポーター　a reporter
レポート　a report, 《米》a term paper
レモン　a lemon
　〜ティー　tea with lemon
れんあい 恋愛
れんが　a brick
れんきゅう 連休　holidays (in a row), a long weekend
　三〜　a three-day weekend
れんごう 連合　an association, the united *something*, (an) alliance
　〜した　combined, united, allied
れんこん 蓮根　a lotus root
れんさい 連載　a series, a serial
　〜する　serialize
レンジ　a range
　ガス〜　a gas range; (オーブンも含めた) a gas stove
　電子〜　a microwave oven
れんしゅう 練習
　〜する　(芝居の) rehearse [くりかえす]
レンズ　a lens
れんそう 連想

れんぞく 連続
・be cram-packed with ［いきづまる²］
レンタカー a rent-a-car
レントゲン an X-ray
　〜写真をとる X-ray, take an X-ray
れんぽう 連邦 (a) union, (a) federation, a commonwealth
れんめい 連盟 a league
れんらく 連絡
　〜船 ferry (service) ……………［かよう］
　〜を取る get in touch with ［まいる］
れんりつ 連立政権 a coalition government

ロ

ろ 櫓 a scull
ろう 〜を塗る apply wax ………［みぞ］
　〜人形 a wax figure [doll]
ろうあ 聾唖者 a deaf-mute
ろうか 廊下 (家の) a passage; (玄関の) a hall; (学校・ホテルなどの) a corridor
ろうか 老化 aging; (もうろく) senility
　〜する age
ろうがん 老眼 farsightedness (due to old age),《医学用語》presbyopia
ろうご 老後 one's retirement years
　………………………………………［やすらか］
　〜のために for one's old age
　………………………………………［しっかり］
　〜は when one grows old ［あんらく］
　・when one gets old …………［たよる］
ろうし 労使 management and labor
　………………………………………［かいけつ］
　〜の交渉 negotiations between labor and management
　………………………………………［いきづまる¹］
ろうじん 老人 a senior citizen; (男) an old man, (女) an old woman; (総称・集合的に) old people, the old, the aged
　・elderly people ………………［ひなた］
　〜ホーム a retirement home, a senior home
ろうそ 労組 a labor union …［つよい］
ろうそく a candle ………………［きえる］
ろうでん 漏電 a short circuit
ろうどう 労働 labor, work

　肉体〜 physical work
　精神〜 mental work
　〜者 a laborer, a worker
　〜条件 working conditions
　…………………………………［ちゃくちゃく］
　〜組合 《米》a labor union, 《英》a trade union
ろうどく 朗読する recite ［たどたどしい］
ろうにゃくなんにょ 老若男女の区別なく irrespective of age or sex …［くべつ］
ろうひ 浪費 waste
　〜する waste
ろうりょく 労力 labor, an effort
　・manpower ……………………［せつやく］
ろうれい 老齢にもかかわらず despite one's advanced age
ろうれん 老練な experienced ［たくみ］
ローカル 〜な local
　〜線 a local line ………………［せん］
ロードショー a newly released film, a first-run film, a road show
ロープ a rope
ロープウェー (設備) a ropeway; (乗り物) a cable car
ローマ Rome
　〜の Roman
　〜字 Roman letters
　〜数字 Roman numerals
ローラースケート roller skate
ローン a loan
　住宅〜 a home loan, a mortgage
ろく 六 six
　第6(の) the sixth (略 6th)
　6分の1 a [one] sixth
ろく(な, に)
　〜な satisfying ………………［まずしい］
　〜なことをしない lose all decency
　………………………………………［こじん］
ログアウト 《インターネット》logout
　〜する log out
ログイン
ろくおん 録音 recording
　〜する record
ろくが 録画 a videotape recording
　〜する videotape
ろくがつ 六月 June (略 Jun.)
ろくじゅう 六十 sixty
　第60(の) the sixtieth (略 60th)

ろくでもない　useless, worthless
　　……………………[ろく(な, に)]
ロケ　a location
　〜隊　a location crew　……[ひきあげる]
ロケット　a rocket
ろこつ　露骨
ロサンゼルス　Los Angeles (略 L.A.)
ろし　ろ紙　filter paper
ろじ　路地　an alley
　・a narrow alley　………………[とおる]
ロシア　Russia
　〜の, 〜語　Russian
　〜人　a Russian; (全体) the Russians
ろしゅつ　露出　exposure
　〜する　expose, disclose, bare
ろじょう　路上で　on the street
ろせん　路線　(鉄道) a route, a line; (方針) a line
ロッカー　a locker
ろっかくけい　六角形　a hexagon
　〜の　hexagonal
ロッキー　〜山脈　the Rocky Mountains
ロック　(音楽) rock music, rock'n'roll
ロック　(錠) a lock
　〜する　lock
ロッククライミング　rock-climbing
ロックンロール　rock'n'roll
ろっこつ　ろっ骨　a rib
ろてん　露店　a street stall
ロバ　a donkey
ロビー　a lobby
　〜活動　lobbying, lobby
ロフト　a loft
ロボット　a robot
ロマンチック　〜な　romantic
ろれつ　〜が回らない　cannot speak distinctly, slur (*one's* words)
ろん　論　an argument, an opinion
ロングセラー　a steady seller [かさねる]
ろんじる　論じる　argue, discuss
ろんじん　論陣を張る　take a firm stand
　…………………………………[はる¹]
ろんせつ　論説　an editorial
ろんそう　論争　a dispute, (a) controversy
　〜する　dispute (about, on)
ロンドン　London

ろんぶん　論文　a thesis　………[きわだつ]
　・a paper　………………………[なかみ]
　卒業〜　a graduation thesis
ろんり　論理　a logic
　〜的な　logical
　〜的に　logically

ワ

わ　和　(調和) (a) harmony; (合計) the sum
わ　輪　(円形) a circle; (環) a ring; (車の) a wheel; (ひもなどでつくる) a loop
　〜になる　form a circle　………[まるい]
ワープロ　a word processor; (コンピュータのワープロ機能) a word processing program
わあわあ　〜泣く　cry out at the top of *one's* lungs　………………………[なく¹]
ワイシャツ　a shirt
わいせつ　〜な　dirty, filthy, obscene, indecent
わいろ　賄賂　a bribe　……………[うたがい]
　〜を使う　bribe, offer a bribe
ワイン　(a) wine
わえい　和英辞典　a Japanese-English dictionary
わかい　若い
　〜人たち　the younger generation
　…………………………………[けいこう]
わかい　和解　reconciliation　……[とおす]
　〜する　reach a reconciliation
わかがえる　若返る　rejuvenate
わかさ　若さ　youth
わかす　沸かす
わかて　若手(の)　the younger generation (of)　………………[めだつ]
わがまま
　・selfishness　………………………[がまん]
　〜な　spoiled　………………[あまやかす]
わかめ　若布　*wakame*, soft seaweed
わかもの　若者　a young man; (全体) the young
わかる　分かる・判る
わかれ　別れ
　〜際に　when *someone* leaves [ふきつ]
わかれる　別れる・分かれる
　・break it off with　……[おもいきって]

別れた女房　*one's* ex-wife ‥‥‥[みれん]
わかわかしい　若々しい　look young
わき　脇
わきが　腋臭　underarm odor
わきのした　脇の下　an armpit
わきばら　脇腹　the side, *one's* side
わきまえる
わきみ　脇見をする　look aside, look away from
わきみち　脇道　a side road, a byroad
わきやく　脇役　a supporting role
わく　沸く
わく　枠
わくせい　惑星　a planet
ワクチン　(a) vaccine; (コンピュータのワクチンソフト) vaccine software
わくわく
わけ　訳
わけへだて　分け隔てなく　impartially
わけまえ　分け前　a [*one's*] share
わける　分ける
わゴム　輪ゴム　a rubber band ‥[のびる]
わざ　技　(a) technique, (an) art
・a skill ‥‥‥‥‥‥‥‥‥‥‥[きはく]
〜を磨く　work on *one's* technique
‥‥‥‥‥‥‥‥‥‥‥‥‥‥‥[みがく]
わざと
わさび　a *wasabi*, a Japanese horseradish
わざわい　災い　(a) disaster
・a misfortune ‥‥‥‥‥‥‥[まねく]
わざわざ
わざわざ…する　take the time to *do*
‥‥‥‥‥‥‥‥‥‥‥‥‥[きょうしゅく]
・go to the trouble of *doing* ‥‥[こと]
ワシ　鷲　an eagle
わしき　和式　Japanese style
わしょく　和食　Japanese food ‥[やはり]
ワシントン　(州) Washington; (首都) Washington, D.C.
わずか
わずらう　煩・患う
わずらわしい　煩わしい
わずらわす　煩わす
わすれっぽい　忘れっぽい　forgetful
わすれもの　忘れ物　a thing left behind
わすれる　忘れる
わた　綿　cotton; (植物) a cotton plant

わだい　話題
わだかまり　bad feelings
わたし　私　I; (私の) my; (私を, 私に) me; (私のもの) mine; (私自身) myself
わたしたち　私たち　we; (私たちの) our; (私たちに[を]) us; (私たちのもの) ours; (私たち自身) ourselves
わたす　渡す
わたる　渡る
・cross over to ‥‥‥‥‥‥[のりかえる]
ワックス　wax
〜をかける　wax
ワット　《電気》a watt (略 W, w)
わっと　〜泣き出す　burst into tears
‥‥‥‥‥‥‥‥‥‥‥‥‥‥‥[なく¹]
わな　罠　a trap; (輪なわ) a snare; (姦計) a trap, snares
・a trap ‥‥‥‥‥‥‥‥‥‥[こうみょう]
〜にかかる　get caught in a trap
‥‥‥‥‥‥‥‥‥‥‥‥‥‥‥[かかる²]
ワニ　(アフリカ・アジア産の) a crocodile; (北米産の) an alligator
わび　詫び　an apology
わびしい　侘しい
わびる　詫びる
わふう　和風の　Japanese-style
わめく　yell (out), rant and rave
わやく　和訳　a Japanese translation
〜する　translate *something* into Japanese
わら　藁　(a) straw
わらい　笑い　a laugh, laughter; (ほほえみ) a smile; (歯を見せて) a grin; (くすくす) a chuckle, a giggle
〜をかみ殺す　suppress [swallow] *one's* laughter
・stifle a laugh ‥‥‥‥‥‥‥[おさえる]
わらいごと　笑い事じゃない　It's no laughing matter.
わらいばなし　笑い話　a joke
わらいもの　笑い物になる　be the laughingstock of, be laughed at
わらう　笑う
笑ってしまう　break out laughing
‥‥‥‥‥‥‥‥‥‥‥‥‥‥[ひょうげん]
笑い出す　burst out laughing
‥‥‥‥‥‥‥‥‥‥‥‥‥‥‥[きゅう]

わり 割
わりあい 割合
・ratio …………………………[しき]
わりあて 割り当て (an) assignment, (an) allotment; (輸出入などの) a quota
わりあてる 割り当てる assign, allot; (食糧などを) ration
わりかん 割り勘…………………[さき]
わりきる 割り切る
わりざん 割り算 division
〜をする divide
…(の)わりに for
わりびき 割引
夜間〜 a night discount rate
…………………………………[でんわ]
わりびく 割り引く
わる 割る
わるい 悪い
〜冗談 a bad joke ……………[よす]
〜のは………………………[そして]
わるがしこい 悪賢い cunning, sly
わるぎ 悪気
わるく 悪く言う speak ill of ……[いう]
わるくち (…の)悪口を言う bad-mouth
・insult …………………………[あたま]
・say bad things about, speak ill of
…………………………………[かげ²]
・say awful things about …[きこえる]
・criticize ………………………[ろこつ]
耳を覆いたくなるような〜 such abuses that *one* wants to cover *one's* ears …………………[おおう]
ワルシャワ Warsaw
わるだくみ 悪だくみ a trick, (a) conspiracy
わるぢえ 悪知恵 cunning, craft
ワルツ a waltz
わるふざけ 悪ふざけ a practical joke
わるもの 悪者 a bad [wicked] person
われ 我ながら even if I do say so myself ……………………[〜ながら]
〜を忘れる lose control of *oneself*
…………………………………[ぎゃくじょう]
われめ 割れ目 (ひび) a crack; (裂け目) a split
われる 割れる

わん お碗 a bowl ……………[ふせる]
わん 湾 (大きな) a gulf; (小さな) a bay
東京〜 Tokyo Bay
ペルシャ〜 the Persian Gulf
わんぱく 腕白
ワンピース a (one-piece) dress
ワンマン (独裁者) an autocrat
〜の (独裁者の) autocratic; (1人の) one-man
わんりょく 腕力 physical strength; (暴力) force
〜に訴える resort to force
ワンルームマンション a studio apartment

会話作文 英語表現辞典 (第三版)
Japanese-English Sentence Equivalents
3rd Edition

ISBN 4-255-00255-X C0582

©1982年11月10日	初版第1刷発行
1986年4月25日	新訂版第1刷発行
2004年3月30日	第三版第1刷発行

監修　　　　ドナルド・キーン
　　　　　　Donald Keene

　　　　　　羽鳥博愛 (はとりひろよし)
編集　　　　山田晴子 (やまだはるこ)
　　　　　　伊良部祥子 (いらぶあきこ)

発行者　　　原雅久

発行所　　　朝日出版社
　　　　　　〒101-0065 東京都千代田区西神田3-3-5
　　　　　　電話 03-3263-3321（代表）
　　　　　　振替口座 00140-2-46008

印刷・製本　　凸版印刷株式会社
本文用紙　　　日本大昭和板紙株式会社
表紙クロス　　株式会社ダイヤ商会

本書の一部あるいは全部を無断で複写複製（コピー）することは、法律で認められた場合を除き、著作者および出版社の権利侵害となります。あらかじめ小社あて許諾を求めてください。

造本には十分注意しておりますが、万一、落丁・乱丁などの場合は、お取り替えいたします。

Printed in Japan

函・カバーデザイン　　岡本健＋

生きた言葉には、生きた辞典!!

最新日米口語辞典

E・G・サイデンステッカー+松本道弘=共編　●定価(本体3800円+税)

日常生活の中で使っている口語的な表現の中には、既存の和英辞典ではピッタリの訳が見つからない——。こうした和英辞典への物足りなさを補うべくして生まれたのが本書。頻度の高い日本語見出し約4,000。英語からも検索が可能な便利な索引を完備(対訳米語約13,000)。

アメリカ口語辞典

E・G・サイデンステッカー=監修　●定価(本体3786円+税)

ネイティブと話すとき発音が聴き取れない人、一つ一つの単語は聴き取れても、意味がさっぱりわからない人、そんな人のための口語英熟語辞典。日常会話で頻繁に出てくる口語表現4,000を精選、アメリカ人が実際に話す通りの発音を表示しているので、会話が面白いようにわかってくる。

米英俗語辞典 [新訂版]

藤井章雄=監修　●定価(本体3786円+税)

日常口語から、くだけた表現、卑語・侮蔑語まで総11,000語を収録した、口語英和辞典。会話や、新聞・雑誌・漫画・映画・小説などで使われる、学校では教えてくれなかった生きた英語をマスターしたい人必携。米英のネイティブ・スピーカーが徹底校閲した、豊富な例文を収録。

最新ビジネス英文手紙辞典 [増補新版]

フランシス・J・クディラ=著　●定価(本体5631円+税)

著者が収集した膨大な数のビジネスレターの中から、実際に戦略効果をあげた手紙のみを収録。アプローチのしかた、構成法などの解説で、英語の論理の流れに沿った、説得力のあるビジネス・レターが書ける。手紙辞典の枠を越えた、国際ビジネスを成功に導く優れたビジネス指南書。

朝日出版社　〒101-0065 東京都千代田区西神田3-3-5 TEL 03-3263-3321
FAX 03-5226-9599 http://www.asahipress.com/

すぐ使える完全文例を瞬時にダイレクト検索！
確実な例文をモデルにして英語が正確に書ける！

【CD-ROM版】
asahi press センテンス
SENTENCE

たとえばビジネスで、学校で、家で、こんなとき……

➡ 英語でリポート・Eメール・手紙・ファクスを書くとき。
➡ 英語の試験問題や例文をつくるとき。
➡ 論文や講演用の英文を作成するときなど。

英文が自分でかんたんに書ける、自由に使いこなせる！

お買い上げ後も、文例が限りなく増殖し続ける 無料ダウンロード・サービスが大好評！

ドナルド・キーン／エドワード・G・サイデンステッカー／ジャン・マケーレブ／マーク・ジュエル／F・J・クディラ／羽鳥博愛／藤井章雄／松本道弘／安田一郎／山田晴子／伊良部祥子ほか、信頼のおける豪華執筆陣

● 使用環境
対応OS：日本語対応Windows95（SP1以降）、Windows98、WindowsNT（administrator）、Windows2000、WindowsMe、WindowsXP
CPU：Pentium以上　HDD：空き容量200MB以上　メモリ：32MB以上
モニタ解像度：800×600以上　64000色以上
＊但し搭載OSの最低動作環境以上であること

価格6,000円（税込）
無料サンプルをご希望の方は
小社までお申し込みください
朝日出版社

商品および購入に関するお問い合わせは　☎03-3263-3321
公式サイト　http://www.asahipress.com/sentence

誰でも英語が「訳せる」ようになる！

英和イディオム完全対訳辞典

20,000のイディオム表現を40,000の完全対訳例文で徹底解説！
英語の意味を自然な日本語でつかむ、最新・最大のイディオム辞典！

元NHKラジオ「続・基礎英語」ほか講師　元玉川大学教授
ジャン・マケーレブ＋岩垣守彦＝編著

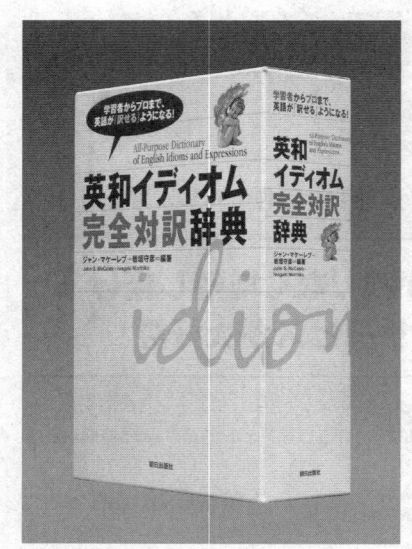

B6判変型／並製カバー函入り
1856ページ／定価(本体4800円+税)

キーワード配列ですぐ引ける
頻出イディオム約20,000表現をキーワードで配列。引きたい表現がすぐ見つかる。

充実した語義でだれでも訳せる
ピッタリで自然な語義をできる限り多く提示。だれでもニュアンスがつかめてすぐ訳せる。

完全対訳例文つきだからよく分かる
収録表現すべてに、使い方がそのまま分かる例文つき。細かいニュアンス、シチュエーションも間違いなくつかめる。

いきいきした面白い例文
すべて書き下ろしの生きた例文は、つい読みふけってしまう面白さ。

最新の意味と使い方が分かる
up to dateな意味の変化も追跡。
例文にも必要に応じてくわしい解説。

ビジネス、会話にも役立つ
よく使う決まり文句、比喩表現、口語・俗語表現、日本人には分かりにくいユーモアや皮肉、よくおどけて使われる古風な表現、諺など、解説とともに徹底収録。

朝日出版社　〒101-0065 東京都千代田区西神田3-3-5　TEL 03-3263-3321
FAX 03-5226-9599　http://www.asahipress.com/